The rough guide to

EASTERN EUROPE
HUNGARY, ROMANIA AND BULGARIA

D0807672

Written

DAN RICHARDSON AND JILL DENTON

With additional research and writing by
Simon Broughton, Charlie Hebbert and Dan L. Andin

Edited by

DAN RICHARDSON
with
Mark Ellingham and Martin Dunford

HARRAP
COLUMBUS
Rough
Guide

CONTENTS

Introduction

HUNGARY

ROMANIA

BULGARIA

Basics 507–525
  Where to go and when (507); Getting there (510); Red tape, visas and *cartes statistiques* (512); Health and insurance (513); Costs, money and banks (513); Information and maps (514); Communications - post, phones and media (515); Police, trouble and sexual harassment (515); Getting around (516); Sleeping (518); Eating and drinking (519); Workcamps and other activities (522); Other things (523); Glossary (524).

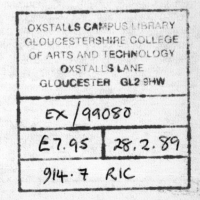

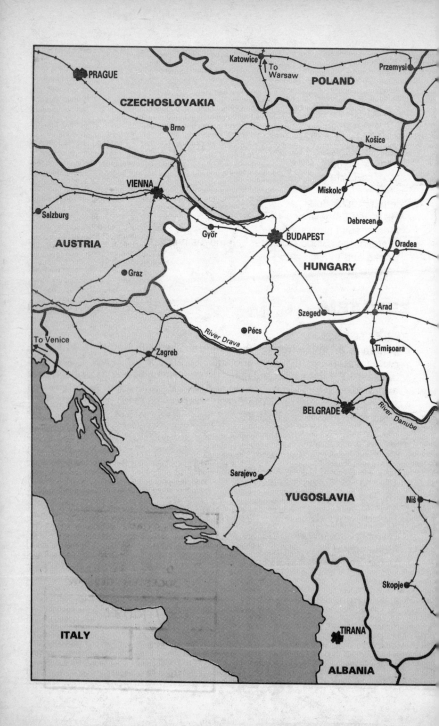

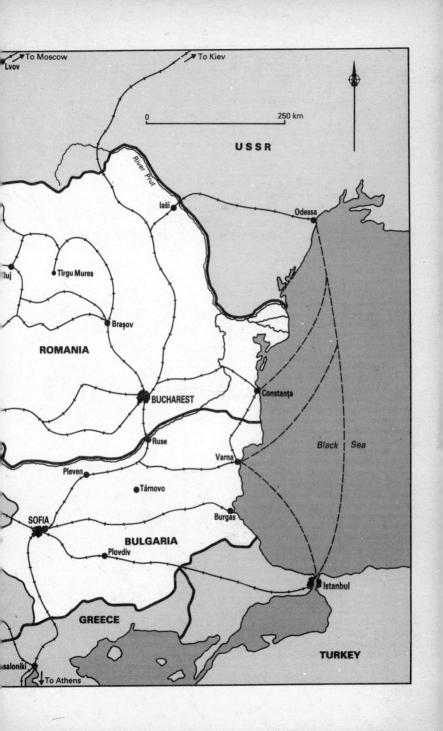

Stumbling along the boundary between
The tolerated and the forbidden
I stand amazed by the world.
Even like this it's beautiful, with these half-words,
In this half-light, with a lock on the door.

— Amy Károlyi

INTRODUCING EASTERN EUROPE: HUNGARY, ROMANIA AND BULGARIA

This book covers the three most accessible nations of **Eastern Europe**, which is arguably less of a geographical region than a political construct. Before the last war, people spoke of 'the Balkans' or 'Central Europe', implicitly excluding the USSR and including Yugoslavia, whereas nowadays we do the opposite with our notion of 'Eastern Europe'. The stereotyped image of a uniform, hard-edged Eastern bloc only remains credible if you never visit the region; on the ground, from inside, the picture looks less like a map than a tapestry or a mosaic. Each nation proclaims its uniqueness, yet has racial, cultural or historical kinships with a neighbour, if not some deep-rooted antagonism as well. Though their Communist regimes were originally imposed by Stalin (who likened the process to 'saddling a cow'), each has gradually developed its own character, evinced most recently by their varying reactions to *glasnost* and *perestroika*.

Hungary has been an Eastern bloc trendsetter since the 1960s, and as this book goes to press the longstanding Party leader, Kádár, has just been ousted by a new generation committed to further reforms – which might conceivably end the Party's monopoly of power. Things are in a state of flux, with market forces and demands for liberalisation coming to the fore, as you're likely to discover in Budapest, the capital. Once the second city of *Mitteleuropa* and still grandiose and cosmopolitan, Budapest is the side of Hungary that's most seductive to visitors, but there's a well established circuit around Lake Balaton, the Danube Bend and the Baroque towns of Transdanubia and the Northern Uplands. Hungarians, though well attuned to the outside world, are acutely conscious of themselves as Magyars, an identity (reinforced by their unique language) that is felt as strongly in Budapest as in the smallest village or provincial town. It's this, along with practical factors like the low costs and a lack of irritating travel-restrictions, that makes the country such a good introduction to Eastern Europe.

There could hardly be a greater contrast than with **Romania**, whose Romance language is virtually the only comfort for visitors to a country afflicted by shortages of everything, and governed by a leader of ruthless and absolute power – to name just two of the Cold War clichés that apply. For all that, it's in many respects the most fascinating of the three nations, with a people whose warmth towards outsiders usually transcends the barriers erected by the state, and a diversity that well rewards an extended stay. The different ethnic groups and spectrum of lifestyles range from the bucolic to the streetwise; the wealth of customs, superstitions, wildlife and scenery are unmatched in Europe; and there are enough castles and morbid fixations to satisfy addicts of the Gothic. Travellers who don't flee the country after a day or so are usually smitten by a bitter-sweet affection for Romania, as well as sadness at the economic and political depths to which this extraordinary country has sunk.

Whereas Romanians and Magyars see themselves as racial islands in a sea of Slavs, the Bulgars feel at home in the Balkan peninsula – which gets its name from the mountain range that divides **Bulgaria**. As monasteries and ruined citadels attest, Bulgaria was a great medieval power before it was swallowed up by the Ottoman empire for five hundred years, and only regained independence after a bitter struggle, helped by Russia. This legacy of gratitude, together with the country's strong pre-war socialist tradition, has given a different twist to the relationship with Communism and the USSR. Bulgars lack the historical Russophobia of other races, though their Russophilia isn't as boundless as their government pretends either. But there's room for the 'Slav elder brother' amidst the folk customs, doomed poet-revolutionaries and other furniture of Bulgaria's national identity.

Some practicalities

As explained in the 'Basics' sections of this book, most travellers require **visas** to visit these countries, with the exception of package tourists to Bulgaria or children listed on their parents' passports. In the normal course of events, applying for visas should be the limit of your dealings with **bureaucracy**; Hungary obliges visitors to register with the police, but in practice the tourist board will do this on your behalf. In Romania, independent travellers are liable to an **obligatory exchange** of $10 per day, but in Hungary and Bulgaria you can change money as and when you choose.

Unless you take a tour, an important factor will be **access from Western Europe**, and in this respect Hungary – linked by flights, trains, coaches and highways to most European capitals (see p.10) – is streets ahead. The availability of cheap aeroplane, railway and international coach tickets in Budapest also makes Hungary the ideal springboard for **travelling around Eastern Europe**, plus a bargain deal if you're **heading for China** (for details of this, see p.86).

On the whole we've indicated comparative rather than actual **costs**, as prices change more often than the upgrading of **accommodation** or **places to eat**, whose rates usually remain *relatively* the same. Since estimated costs appear in the Basics, suffice it to say at this point that Hungary is excellent value for money, Bulgaria pretty reasonable, and Romania rather a rip-off. Whilst not automatically assuming that your budget is very tight, we've suggested various savings in the Basics and in the main body of the text.

Although the cost of flights and accommodation might well be lower on **package tours** (which are covered in detail in the respective country 'Basics' under 'Getting There'), budget travellers are less likely to opt for the few tours **covering several countries**. At the top end of the range, these include the **Danube Cruises** offered by *Swan Hellenic* (☎ 01-831-1515) and *Balkan Holidays* (☎ 01-493-8612), with 14 days flying and sailing between Vienna and Ruse in wealthy, elderly company, starting at around £1,200. More feasibly, *Global* offers air-**coach tours** around the capitals of Austria, Hungary and Yugoslavia (8 days from £329) or Greece, Turkey, Yugoslavia and Bulgaria (15 days from £529). However, for really vivid experiences you can't beat **independent travel** in a region whose potential most Westerners have yet to recognise. Written with such possibilities in mind, this book will hopefully encourage footloose travellers to visit Eastern Europe.

■ HUNGARY

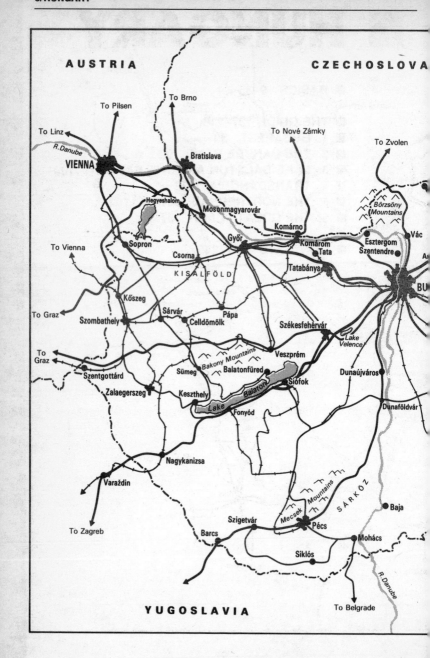

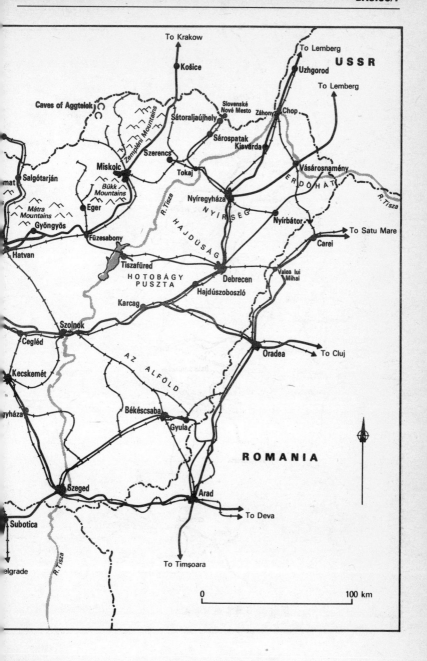

To Krakow

To Lemberg

USSR

Košice

Uzhgorod

To Lemberg

Caves of Aggtelek

Slovenské
Nové Mesto

Záhony

Chop

Sátoraljaújhely

Zempléni Mountains

Sárospatak

Kisvárda

Szerencs

Miskolc

Tokaj

Vásárosnamény

mat

Salgótarján

Bükk
Mountains

Nyíregyháza

ERDŐHÁT

R. Tisza

Eger

R. Tisza

NYÍRSÉG

Mátra
Mountains

Gyöngyös

Nyírbátor

Füzesabony

HAJDÚSÁG

To Satu Mare

Hatvan

Carei

Tiszafüred

HOTOBÁGY
PUSZTA

Debrecen

Valea lui
Mihai

Hajdúszoboszló

Karcag

Szolnok

Cegléd

Oradea

To Cluj

AZ ALFÖLD

Kecskemét

yháza

Békéscsaba

Gyula

ROMANIA

Szeged

Arad

Subotica

To Deva

elgrade

R. Tisza

To Timşoara

0   100 km

HUNGARY
BASICS

HUNGARY: WHERE TO GO AND WHEN

Visitors who refer to **Hungary** as a Balkan country risk getting a lecture on how this small, landlocked nation of 10,000,000 people differs from 'all those Slavs'. Natives are strongly conscious of Hungary (likened by the poet Endre Ady to a ship sailing westwards against the tide of history) and of themselves as Magyars – of a race which transplanted itself from Central Asia into the heart of Europe, and a nation that identifies with 'Western values'. Any contradiction between nationalism and cosmopolitanism is resolved by what the British expatriate Charlie Coutts called the Hungarian 'genius for not taking things to their logical conclusion', and paradoxes are almost the rule in this socialist state where the Communist Party advocates shares and unemployment, and the country most often pilloried in the official media is Romania, a Warsaw Pact ally.

In Hungary you'll encounter few of the clichés of Eastern European travel: no queues for bread or overtly intrusive bureaucracy, nor fear of secret police; and hardly a sign of Marx or Lenin, let alone a personality cult (whoever happens to be the Party leader). **Tourism** is neither straitjacketed or one-way; visitors can travel wherever they please, while plenty of Magyars visit Western Europe despite the expense this entails. Westerners, on the other hand, will find Hungary cheap: the moderately flush can afford a princely lifestyle, and even the impecunious can treat themselves frequently.

Hungary's capital, **Budapest**, inspires a feeling of déja vu. It's not just the vast Gothic Parliament and other monuments of a bygone imperial era that seem familiar, but the latest fashions on the streets, or a poster advertising something that was all the rage back home a year before. In coffee houses, Turkish baths and the fad for Habsburg bric-à-brac, there's a strong whiff of *Mitteleuropa* – that ambient culture which welcomed Beethoven in Budapest and Hungarian-born Liszt in Vienna, currently being revived in a new form by rock stars, film directors, Green activists and millions of tourists, making Budapest the melting pot of East and West.

After Budapest, **Lake Balaton** and the **Danube Bend** vie for popularity. The Balaton, with its string of brash resorts, styles itself as the 'Nation's Playground', enjoying a fortuitious proximity to the Badacsony wine-producing region. The Danube Bend has more to offer in terms of scenery and historic architecture, as do the **northern uplands** and **Transdanubia**. Sopron, Győr and Pécs are rightfully the main attractions in Transdanubia, like the famous wine centres of Tokaj and Eger in the uplands, but for castle-buffs the Zempléni range and the lowlands adjoining Yugoslavia have several treats in store. On the **Great Plain**, which comprises half the country, the cities of Debrecen and Szeged host festivals and serve as the jumping-off points to the archaic Erdőhát region and the mirage-haunted Hortobágy *puszta*, where a folkloric gathering at Nagykálló and the equestrian Bridge Fair are staged to coincide with Hungary's National Day, August 20. See the **chapter introductions** for more details about each region.

Finally, Hungary is an excellent point of departure if you're **heading for China or other parts of Eastern Europe**; railway tickets and MALÉV flights from Budapest to these destinations are probably the cheapest in Europe. Travellers bound for Romania, Poland or the Soviet Union would be well-advised to stock up in Hungary's supermarkets first, and all the visas and reservations for the amazingly cheap train ride from

Budapest to Bejing (Peking) can be made in the Hungarian capital.

When to go
In Budapest the **climate** isn't particularly important, and since the city's major festivals occur in spring and autumn and its comforts, sights and culinary delights can be enjoyed at any time of the year, you don't have to visit between June and September like most tourists do. Elsewhere, however, the snowy wintertime has no attractions, for Hungary's flattish terrain offers poor skiing. May, warm but showery, is the time to see the Danube Bend, Tihany or Sopron before everyone else arrives; June is hotter and drier, with 9 or 10 hours of sunshine most days throughout July, August and September. There's more of a variation in tourism than temperatures across the country: the Great Plain is drier, and the highlands are wetter, during summer, but that's about as far as climatic changes go, whereas some areas get packed out whilst others receive few visitors, even during the high season.

	Average daily temperatures			
	Budapest		Debrecen	
	°F	°C	°F	°C
Jan	29	−2	27	−3
Feb	32	0	31	−1
Mar	42	6	41	5
Apr	53	12	51	10
May	61	16	60	16
Jun	68	20	66	19
Jly	72	22	70	21
Aug	70	21	68	20
Sep	63	17	61	16
Oct	52	11	51	11
Nov	42	6	41	5
Dec	34	1	32	0

GETTING THERE

Besides getting to Hungary, it's important to consider the availability of **visas** (p.13). You can obtain them at Budapest's Airport and Hydrofoil dock or any road-crossing on the Hungarian border, but this may entail an hour's wait, so it's better to fix one up before you go. Visas are not issued at railway crossings, and international buses won't wait for passengers to acquire them at the Hungarian frontier checkpoints.

By Air
Three companies offer reasonably-priced BA or MALÉV (Hungarian Airlines) **return flights from London to Budapest**. All departures are from Heathrow, and travellers are required to stay at least one Saturday night.

Hungarian Air Tours (3 Heddon St, London W1R 7LE/☎ 01-437-9405) offers various deals. In the so-called Money Miser category, there are Weekend flights limited to set periods (eg. Thurs-Sun, Thurs-Tues, Fri-Mon etc), costing £167 during April, May and October, and £209 between June-September; plus 6-30 day returns costing £191 and £209 for the same periods. HAT's Midweek Apex flights (Tuesdays and Wednesdays only) go for £173 and £184, whilst their Apex returns, subject to the same restrictions but valid for up to 3 months, cost £224 irrespective of the season. Complimentary visas are usually included. Similar deals are available from *Danube Travel* (6 Conduit St, London W1R 9TG/☎ 01-493-0263) under different names – ie. Weekend Supersaver, 7-30 day Supersaver and Super Apex – but the fares are identical to HAT's, although Danube Travel also does a one-way Euro Budget flight (£204). Return flights from *Canterbury Travel* (248 Streatfield Rd, Kenton, Harrow, Middlesex HA3 9BY/☎ 01-206-0411) cost £217

(June-September), £197 (Oct) and £179 (Nov – March), but for the extra cost you can leave and return any day of the week. *Slade Thrifties* (15 Vivian Avenue, London NW4 3UT/☎ 202-0111) could also be competitive.

By approaching *MALÉV* (10 Vigo St, London W1/☎ 01-439-0577), Air France, Aeroflot, KLM, Lufthansa or BA directly, you might shave £10-£30 off the above prices, but it's easier to let specialised **agents** do the work. Besides the ever helpful and reliable *STA Travel*, with offices in London (74 Old Brompton Rd, SW7 3LH/☎ 01-581-1022 and 117 Euston Rd, NW1 2SX/☎ 01-388-2261), Bristol (25 Queens Rd, BS8 1QE/☎ 0272-294-399) and Cambridge, you could try *Eastern European Travel* (☎ 01-244-8291), which acts for the Romanian airline TAROM. Alternatively, you might make **savings** by utilising **bargain flights to Vienna or Zagreb**, available from *Intasun, Jetsave, Pegasus* and various 'bucket shops' (see ads in the London magazines *City Limits* and *Time Out*). Returns can cost as little as £90, but of course exclude the expense of travelling to and from Hungary, plus accommodation etc. (See below for addresses of cheap places to stay in both cities, and transport to Hungary from Austria and Yugoslavia).

The cost of direct **flights from other European capitals to Budapest** isn't always proportionate to their proximity to Hungary, but it's certainly worth checking out MALÉV – who fly four times a week **from Dublin** – Air France, KLM, Al Italia, Lufthansa or TAROM in any country. Travellers starting from **Berlin** who are prepared to book months in advance might save money by taking the daily *Interflug* service from East Berlin to Budapest (188 DM/about £62).

MALÉV flies **from the USA** (New York, Boston, Miami, Chicago, San Francisco, Philadelphia, Washington and Atlanta) 7-3 times a week. The cheapest flights are from New York. *Magyar Tours* (☎ 718-816-6828) has twice-weekly return flights to Budapest via Brussels, costing $770 (plus $22 tax) during high season and $695 (plus tax) at other times. *MALÉV* (630 5th Avenue/☎ 757-6480) returns cost more ($899/$799) whatever the season, but their tickets are valid for 6 months. The *Hungaria Travel Bureau* (1603 2nd Avenue, NY/☎ 249-9342) offers return flights for between $799-

$949 (summer) and $699-$849 (winter). MALÉV also flies from Toronto and Montreal in **Canada**, and, indirectly, from Adelaide, Melbourne and Sydney in **Australia**.

Package Holidays

It's worth considering **package deals** if only because the cost of a return flight plus accommodation may sometimes be cheaper than a return flight on its own. British **tour operators** specialising in Hungary include *Hungarian Air Tours* and *Danube Travel* (see above for addresses); *Intra Travel* (5 Cherval Place, London SW7 1EW/☎ 01-225-3266) and *Attila Tours* (Aldermaston St, London W10 6RR/☎ 01-637-5207). *Peltours*, with offices in London (4 Winsley St, W1N 7AR/☎ 01-637-4373) and Manchester (27 Church St, M4 1QA/☎ 061-834-3721) covers all of Eastern Europe, whilst highstreet operators like *Pegasus, Travelscene, Thomson* and *Sovereign* offer Budapest City Breaks, if nothing else.

Unless stated otherwise, the following **prices** refer to a single person sharing a double room, and the 'spread' reflects seasonal variations in cost. Both HAT and Danube Travel use the same 'bands' – ie. January-March (the cheapest period); April-May & October; June-September (the dearest time); and November-December – but other operators reckon things slightly differently, so it's worth comparing their seasonal rates for 'loopholes'. To secure the cheapest accommodation during any of these periods, book as early as possible. All prices include transport to Hungary.

Budapest City Breaks, cover 3 nights stay (extendable by prior arrangement), and the 'Longer Breaks' (starting at £217-£325 for 7 nights) are available from Danube Travel and HAT. Both the latter, plus Pegasus, Sovereign and Thompson, can also arrange **Two Centre Breaks**, combining 3 nights in Budapest with a similar period in Vienna or Prague (£347-£400 from HAT); whilst *Intra Travel* mates Budapest with Istanbul.

Attila Tours offers 2 weeks **self-catering** holidays in chalets or flats in or around Budapest for only £165 during the high season (£30 per extra week), but transport to Hungary is by coach. If you want to fly and see more of Hungary as well, *Danube Travel* runs a number of **coach tours**, lasting 7 (£380-£457) or 12

(£537-£624) nights, inclusive of bed and board and flights. Similar tours, in more youthful company, can also be arranged by *Express* in Hungary – write to their head office (1359 Budapest 62, P.O. Box 567) for details. HAT wraps up flights and car hire within a single **fly/drive** package, the cost of which ranges from £342-£396 for 7 nights (dropping to £210-£261 per head if there's 4 of you), with 4-person bungalows from £39 per night if desired. Danube Travel also does 7-night **Lake Balaton Holidays** (from £148-£270); 14-night **Spa Holidays** (from £691-£772) and 9-day **Riding Tours** (from £692-£711), some of which are duplicated by HAT. For **Danube Cruises**, see p.000.

US package deals are available from two New York operators: *Magyar Tours* (☎ 816-6828) runs 17-day holidays during high season for $1,780, while the *Hungaria Travel Bureau* (1603 2nd Avenue/☎ 249 9342) organises 4-7 day holidays until October 1st for between $250-$500 per person.

By Rail

Those under 26 have three choices: either invest in an **Inter-Rail** pass (£139), which entitles the holder to a month's free travel in most of Europe (50% reductions inside Hungary); or buy a **Transalpino** or **Eurotrain** ticket (valid for 2 months, and stopovers along the way) to Budapest. The Transalpino/Eurotrain fare **from London to Budapest** costs £148 return, £82 one-way, and Eurotrain holders get 25%-30% off railway fares inside Hungary. Most highstreet travel agents sell Transalpino and/or Inter-Rail, and the former's head office in London (71-75 Buckingham Palace Rd, SW1/☎ 01-834-9656) is pretty close to Eurotrain's (52 Grosvener Gdns), opposite Victoria station where the trains for Budapest – connecting with the Oostende-Vienna express – actually depart. If you're 26 or over, **ordinary returns** cost a whopping £224 (£128 o/w), so it's more ecconomical to fly or take the coach.

On the continent, there are two trains **from Paris** (Gare de l'Est) – the midday connection for the *Wiener Waltzer*, and the thoroughly prosaic *Orient Express*. Both take roughly 25hrs to reach Keleti Station in Budapest. **Munich** is the Federal Republic's point of departure (Eurotrain/Transalpino rtns. DM 154/

sngl. DM 77) for Budapest, which can also be reached from **Vienna**'s Südbahnhof (dep.7.45) and Westbahnhof (10.20 & 16.20); an ordinary single to Budapest from either costs about £16. During the summer, trains from **Rome** join the *Maestral Express* which, like the *Adriatica* (connections to Split) stops at Zagreb in **Yugoslavia** en route to Budapest (also accessible by the *Polonia Express* from Belgrade). If you're coming from **the DDR or Czechoslovakia**, the *Balt-Orient Express* (Berlin-Dresden-Prague-Brno-Bratislava) is the one to catch.

By Coach

For over 26s in particular, **Eurolines coaches** (running once a week between 17 June and 2 September) are a viable alternative to trains **from London to Budapest**. Any National Express travel agent can make bookings (☎ 730-0202 in London; 622-4373 in Birmingham; or 541022 in Bristol for details). Coaches depart every Monday morning from Victoria Coach terminal, arriving at Engels tér station 48hrs later. The coaches and drivers are okay, and if you bring ample food the journey can almost be enjoyable. Full returns cost £152 (£95 o/w); the student rate £137 (£85 o/w).

Really hard-up (and hardy) travellers might consider **the Zagreb route** instead. *Olympic* (01-837-9141) is probably the best of many outfits (see ads in the London magazines *LAM*, *City Limts* & *Time Out*) which run coaches to Yugoslavia and Greece, and a single to Zagreb can cost as little as £40. But some firms are real cowboys – our driver kept going for 36hrs on speed, drove 8 times round Salzburg, and only consented to drop us near the centre (rather than on the outskirts) of Zagreb following much argument. After flaking out at the comfortable *Omladinski* youth hostel (17 Petriniska), you can carry on by train to Budapest (£10) or take a bus to Letenye in southwestern Hungary (£5) the next day.

For details of **coaches from elsewhere in Western Europe**, contact *Deutsche Touring Gmbh*, Hauptbahnhof Europabus (2, Arnulfstrasse 3) or *Ungarn und Osteuropapareisen* (Altheimer Eck 1) in **Munich** 2; *Romeatour*, Lista di Spagna 134 in **Venice**; *Heribert Matzer Reisebüro* (Draisgasse 18 and Lendplatz 38) in **Graz**; or one of several companies in

Vienna, such as *Österreichische Bundesbahnen*, at the Wien Mitte bus terminal (Landstrasser Hauptstrasse 1/b) whence services to Budapest – charging about £12 for a single – depart.

By car – driving or hitching

The most direct route to Budapest **from Britain, Holland, West Germany or Austria** is the E5, running via Oostende, Brussels, Aachen, Köln, Frankfurt, Nürnberg, Linz and Vienna between London and the Hungarian capital (a distance of 1,732km). You shouldn't bank on **driving** this in under 36hrs, however, and many motorists could face an insuperable obstacle should West Germany introduce a **ban on cars using leaded petrol** in the near future, as it's currently (and quite rightly) considering. See p.20 regarding licences, insurance and motoring inside Hungary.

Hitching along the same route can take up to 3 days, so you'd be wise to pack waterproofs, a tent, a *good* roadmap and some Deutschmarks and/or food. On all European motorways it's illegal to hitch anywhere but filling stations and motels, and police are generally tough with violators although their attitude to 'law abiding' hitchers can vary – the Austrian *Grenzepolizei* seem almost benevolent. The ideal lift would be a *Hungarocamion* truck going home, but it's realistic to settle for anything heading towards Austria. I found London to Dover the most frustrating stage of the journey, and western Germany to Vienna the most rewarding. To economise on the **Vienna stopover**, stay at the *Student*

Hostel (IX, Säulenpasse 18/☎ 340-335 or 340-336) or the *campsite* on the Linz side of town (Metro U4 to Hütteldorf, then bus #52B). Continuing on to Budapest, start thumbing just before the rd. 10 exit ramp off the Simmeringer Hauptstrasse, more or less accessible by tram #71 from the Schwarzenbergplatz in the centre of Vienna.

Travelling home, like the outward journey, can go either way. On one occasion we hitched from Budapest to Dover in 24hrs; another time I rashly accepted a lift into France and wound up cursing beside a D-road for a day and a half. Outside France, German is the lingua franca of the road: *Wo fahren sie?* means 'Where are you going?' and hitching signs should carry the word *richtung* ('direction').

By Hydrofoil

The frequency of **hydrofoils from Vienna to Budapest** varies with the season (during winter the Danube freezes), though the journey always takes 4½hrs. During low season (30 March to 30 April and 21 September to 24 October) departures occur on Tuesdays, Thursdays and Saturdays only (at 9.30am); but there are daily services between 1 May and 20 September (2.30pm), plus an extra hydrofoil between 1 June and 30 August (8am). Book at least 24hrs in advance at IBUSZ, Kärntnerstrasse 26 (☎ 53-26-86); or the *DDSG boat station*, Praterkai, II. Mexiko Platz 8 (☎ 26-56-36), where the hydrofoils depart; the one way fare costs the equivalent of £25-£30 in Austrian schillings.

RED TAPE AND VISAS

Unless you're a citizen of Austria, Finland, Malta or a socialist country, you'll require a **visa** in your (full, not Visitor's) passport in order to visit Hungary. This can be obtained on arrival at Ferihegy Airport or the Hydrofoil Dock in Budapest, or at any road-crossing on the Hungarian border (*not* on trains), but you'll avoid up to an hour's wait and save a few quid by getting the visa beforehand from a **Hungarian Consulate** abroad. Addresses include:

AUSTRALIA: 79 Hopetown Circuit, Yarralumia a.c.t. 2600 Canberra (☎ 82-32-26); 351/a Edgecliff Rd, Edgecliff

NSW 2027 Sydney (☎ 328-7859).

AUSTRIA: 1, Bank Gasse 4-6, A-1010 Wien (☎ 62-36-21).

BRITAIN: 35b Eaton Place, London SW1 (☎ 01-235-2664/open Monday- Friday 10am-12am).

CANADA: 7 Delaware Avenue, Ottawa K2 P OZ 2 Ontario (☎ 234-83-16).

DENMARK: Strandvej 170, 2920 Charlottenlund, Copenhagen (☎ 451/63-16-88).

W.GERMANY: 5300 Bonn 2 (Plittersdorf) Trumstr. 30 (☎ 37-67-97).

HOLLAND: La Haye Hoheweg 14, Den Haag (☎ 500-405).

NORWAY: Sophus Lies gt. 3 Oslo 2 (☎

47-2/56-46-88).
SWEDEN: Laboratoriegaten 2, 11527
Stockholm (☎ 47-8/61-67-62).
USA: 3910 Shoemaker St N.W. Washington DC 20008 (☎ 362-67-30); 8 East
75th St, New York NY 10021 (☎ 879-
41-26).

Applicants need 2 photos, their passport
and the appropriate fee, which is currently £7 for 30-day tourist visas (£14 or
£32 for double or multiple entry jobs), or
48hr transit visas; all are valid for 3
months. Postal applications (allow 2
weeks) must include the completed form,
your passport, an SAE and a postal
order, not a cheque. In other Eastern
European countries, Hungarian visas are
only purchasable in dollars. Keep the
pink exit visa, since this must be accom-
modation-stamped (see below) and surrendered on leaving the country.
Providing you get there 48hrs before
your visa expires, 30-day **extensions**
can usually be arranged by the local
police (*Rendőrség*); either at the
főkapitányság (in a provincial town), or
the *kerületi* station (covering the city
district that you're staying in). For further
extensions it's necessary to furnish proof
of solvency and deal with **KEOKH**,
whose head office is **in Budapest** at 12,
Népköztársaság útja (open Monday-
Friday 10am-12.30am). Here you'll need
2 photos and a 300Ft stamp, theoretically
available from the photomat and the
IBUSZ desk on the premises, after which
one queues outside the appropriate

room for a final rubber-stamp validation.
The process should be much the same
at KEOKHs in Debrecen, Pécs etc
(addresses in the guide). **Lost passports
and visas** must be reported to the police
(who'll issue a new exit visa); if found,
they'll be forwarded to another KEOKH
office in Budapest (VI, Rudas u.45/
Monday 8am-4pm, Tuesday-Friday
8.30am-12am).

Registration isn't as formidable as it
sounds, for although foreigners are
obliged to notify the police of their place
of residence within 48hrs, in practice it's
not the visitor's concern. The reception
desk at hotels and campsites, or any
tourist office that fixes you up with
private accommodation will automatically
stamp your exit visa and notify the police
on your behalf. Only when staying with
friends, or in lodgings obtained without
official involvement, is it necessary to go
to the police yourself. First get an Alien's
Registration form (*Külföldi Bejelentőlap*)
from any Post Office and have it counter-
signed by your host; then take it to the
district or provincial police station for
stamping. If you're staying in unofficial
lodgings a lot, it's worth buying several
registration forms (2Ft each). Any **gaps**
in the record render one liable to a fine of
100Ft per day; so if you fail to register for
a while it's better to check into a hotel or
campsite for an up-to-date stamp than
go to IBUSZ or the police. Once you've
'closed' the gap there shouldn't be any
problems afterwards.

HEALTH AND INSURANCE

No **inoculations** are required for travel
in Hungary, and standards of public
health are good. Tap **water** is safe to
drink everywhere, while potable springs
(*forrás*) and streams are designated on
maps, and with signs, as *ivóvíz*. The
national health service (*Sz.T.K.*) will provide free emergency treatment in any
hospital or doctor's surgery (although a
charge is made for drugs), so it's not
absolutely necessary to take out **insurance** unless you're a motorist (see
p. 20). If you decide to play safe,
insurance policies issued in the West are
probably better than those obtainable
inside Hungary from the *Állami Biztosító*
(AB) company, whose head office is in
Budapest.

The commonest **minor complaints**
are probably sunburn (*napszúrás* and
insect bites (*rovarcsípés*); sun-tan lotion
can be bought in ABC supermarkets,
while bite-ointment and *Vietnámi balzsam*
(Vietnamese-made 'Tiger Balm' – the
best bug-repellent available) are sold
at **pharmacies**. You'll find these
gyógyszertár or *patika* even in the smallest villages, and staff – who are quite
likely to speak German – have the
authority to issue a wide range of drugs,
including pain-killers. However, pharmaceutical products are mainly of Eastern
bloc origin, so if you require specific
medication, bring a supply with you.
Opening hours are normally Monday-
Friday 9am-6pm, Saturdays 9am-12am/

1pm; signs in the windows give the location (or telephone number) of night chemists.

Provincial tourist offices can direct you to local surgeries (*orvosi rendelő*), while your embassy in Budapest will have the addresses of foreign language-speaking **doctors** and **dentists**, who'll probably be in private (*magán*) practice. Private medicine is much cheaper than in the West, as attested by the thousands of Austrians who come here for treatment. For muscular, skin or gynaecological complaints, doctors often prescribe a soak at one of Hungary's numerous **medicinal baths** (*gyogyfürdő*), whose curative properties are described in an IBUSZ booklet. In case of **emergencies**,

dial **04** for the *Mentők* ambulance service, or catch a taxi to the nearest *Kórház*. Although staff are well trained, municipal **hospitals** often suffer from shortages of equipment and beds, so the quality of public health-care varies from place to place. Westerners are likely to get the best treatment going, or be cold-shouldered; in the event of the latter, it's worth trying to bribe staff as a last resort. To avoid leaving the impression that socialised health-care is invariably faulty, we'd like to mention Budapest's Pető Institute, whose Conductive Therapy for children with spina bifida, multiple sclerosis and cerebal palsy is the best in the world.

COSTS, MONEY AND BANKS

Despite the inflation (and VAT, introduced this year) which obliges many Hungarians to hold two or even three jobs, Westerners should find that travelling **costs** compare favourably with other European countries due to the exchange rate (currently £1=85Ft). Your main expense is likely to be **accommodation**, but with double rooms in 1- or 2-star hotels going for £5-7, and private rooms for less, this shouldn't be too onerous. Although single accommodation is always relatively dearer the difference isn't too serious considering the low costs in other areas. A three course meal with wine can be had for about £5 in most *Étterem*, and even the ritziest **restaurants** charge far less than their equivalents in the West. **Transport** is extremely cheap, with 2-3Ft flat fares in urban areas, a few railway or bus journeys inside Hungary exceeding £6, and many fares well under £1. Eurotrain and Inter-Rail holders get reductions on domestic railway tickets, while by investing in an IUS student card, you can make **savings** on campsite and hostel accommodation (and in restaurants where 'student menus' are provided). By patronising ABCs and self-service restaurants, and hitching, it's possible to live in Hungary even more cheaply.

Hungarian **forints** (Ft) come in notes of 10, 20, 50, 100, 500 and 1,000Ft, with 1, 2, 5, 10 and 20Ft coins; the little *fillér* (100 fillér = 1Ft) coins are practically redundant though still in circulation. Forints can't be exchanged outside the

socialist bloc; and whilst they can be bought at a favourable rate within Austria, importing or exporting banknotes exceeding 100Ft is illegal. There's no restriction on bringing in or taking out convertible currency – although if all your cash is in small dollar bills, declare this on entry (since a zealous customs person might suspect you of smuggling them on the way out).

Providing you produce your passport, **changing money** or travellers' cheques is a painless operation at any IBUSZ or regional tourist office, or the majority of large hotels and campsites; *valuta* desks in *OTP* **banks** take longer over transactions, and work shorter hours (Monday-Friday 8.30am-3.30pm) than the tourist offices. Exchange rates are the same everywhere. Keep the **receipts**, which are required should you wish to extend your visa, pay for international tickets in forints, or re-exchange forints back into hard currency when you leave Hungary. At road checkpoints, 50% of any remaining forints can be re-exchanged up to the value of $50. The advantages of changing money on the illegal **black market** are minimal (15-20% above the official rate), and touts are skilled at cheating, or might even be plainclothes policemen. It's safer to change money with Hungarian acquaintances, who'll find it useful if they're saving for a Western holiday or hi-fi. At Debrecen's Polish Market (to name but one place) there's a fairly organised black market **in other Socialist cur-**

rencies, nicknamed the 'Comecon stock exchange', where one can swop forints or hard currency for Romanian lei, Soviet roubles, DDR Ostmarks or Polish zloty at favourable rates.

Although a modest amount of low-denomination dollar bills or deutschmarks can be useful, it's safest to carry the bulk of your money in **travellers' cheques**. Eurocheques and TCs issued by Australian, British, Dutch, Norwegian, West German and US banks are all accepted; but for speedy refunds in case of loss, American Express (represented here by IBUSZ) is the only reliable brand. Amex, Bank of America, Diners' Club, Carte Blanche and Eurocard **credit cards** can be used to hire cars, buy airline tickets, or pay your bills directly in the smarter hotels and restaurants and in shops catering mainly for tourists. But in everyday Hungarian life, and out in the sticks, they're pretty useless. If you're planning a lengthy stay in Budapest or want to receive money from the West, consider opening an account. Foreigners may hold hard currency **bank accounts** at the OTP *Központi Deviza Fiók* in Budapest (V, Münnich F. u.6), which pay out and give interest in the currency of your choice.

COMMUNICATIONS – POST, PHONES AND MEDIA

Post offices (*pósta*) are usually open 8am-6pm Monday to Friday and until midday on Saturdays, although in Budapest you'll find several offices functioning around the clock. Mail from abroad should be addressesd '*poste restante, posta*' followed by the name of the town; tell your friends to write your surname first, Hungarian-style, and underline it; although even this may not prevent your mail being misfiled, so ask them to check under all your names. To collect, show your passport and ask '*Van posta a részemre?*. A more secure 'drop' is the 24-hour IBUSZ bureau in Budapest (V, Petőfi tér 3), where letters marked 'c/o American Express' are lovingly guarded until collection, and the staff speak English. Letters (*levél*) can be sent to anywhere in the West for 8Ft (5Ft for postcards). It's quicker to buy stamps (*bélyeg*) at tobacconists rather than at post offices, where you'll also find facilities for sending telegrams (*távirat*), which can be dictated by dialling 02.

Local calls (3 minutes for 2Ft/6 minutes after 6pm) present few problems, but otherwise **phones** leave a lot to be desired. Outside Budapest, long distance calls are better handled by the local post office although, in theory, you can call from kiosks by dialling 06, followed by the area code (eg. 1 for Budapest) and then the subscriber's number. Likewise, direct dialling abroad is theoretically possible from kiosks taking 10Ft. coins – by dialling 00, then the country code (44 for Britain) followed by the STD area code (omitting the first 0) – but in practice this may not work . In Budapest it's easier to go through TOURINFORM who charge 30Ft a minute (100Ft minimum), or the international operator (09); in the provinces smart hotels are the best bet, although there's invariably a surcharge which you should enquire about first.

Since few foreigners can understand the Magyar **media**, the tourist board publishes an English/German language paper, the *Daily News*, which combines a cautious selection of world news with tourist information. You'll find it on newsstands alongside the *Morning Star*, while other capitalist organs – *The Times, Herald Tribune, Time, Newsweek* etc. – are sold only in deluxe hotels like Budapest's Intercontinental. If these don't appeal, drop into the British Embassy's library (Monday-Friday 10am-12am, 2pm-4pm) or try the radio. The Hungarians broadcast news in English at 11.00 (weekdays) and 11.57 (Saturdays) between 1 June-1 September, while you can tune into the BBC World Service on the following frequencies:

MHz	24.80	30.77	48.54	49.59
Metres	12.095	9.75	6.18	6.05

Generally, the lower frequencies (MHz) give better results early in the morning and late at night; the higher ones during the middle of the day.

INFORMATION AND MAPS

A large number of photo-packed brochures, maps and special interest leaflets are available free from **IBUSZ**, the Hungarian tourist organisation, and distributed by their agents **abroad**, which include:

BRITAIN: Danube Travel Ltd. 6, Conduit St, London W1 (☎ 01- 493-0263).

W.GERMANY: IBUSZ, 6000 Frankfurt am Main, Baseler Str.46/48 (☎ 252-018) (other branches in München, Köln and Stuttgart).

SWEDEN: 10326 Stockholm, Beridarebanan 1, PO box 16322 (☎ 20-40-40)

USA: 630 Fifth Avenue, Rockefeller Center (suite 520) New York, N.10020 (☎ 582 7412).

The most useful are the large motoring map (which is perfectly adequate for travelling around Hungary), the pamphlet listing the year's festivals and events, and the booklet *Hotel-Camping*, which lists all official accommodation, gives an indication of prices, and tells you where to make reservations. There are also maps designed specifically for campers and cyclists (the latter showing which roads may be used).

In Hungary itself you'll find IBUSZ offices in virtually every town, together with **other tourist agencies** – the addresses of which are detailed in this guide and in the *Hotel-Camping* booklet. Working hours are normally Monday-Saturday 8am-6pm (some main offices until 8pm); 8am-1pm on Sundays. *Volántourist* – an arm of the Volán bus company – specialises in handling travel bookings and tour groups; *Cooptourist* deals with the top end of the market – mainly car and apartment-hire; while the 'Youth Travel' agency *Express* supposedly caters for impoverished under 35s, although their hotels and campsites aren't particularly cheap. All these national organisations can book accommodation and/or tickets, but for guided tours and specific local information you should try the regional tourist offices like *Siótour, Hajdú-tourist, Mecsek-tourist* etc, whose expertise is likely to be greater. In the capital, *Budapest-tourist* handles sightseeing programmes and accommodation, but the TOURINFORM agency is the place for information. For details of **events**, pick up a free copy of the monthly *Programme* magazine from any tourist office.

For reasons of scale, our **town plans** lack the minute details and tram and bus routes that appear on Hungarian *várositérkép*. These cost around 15Ft and are available from local tourist offices or, failing that, from bookshops (*könyvesbolt*), which are also likely to stock **hiking maps**. These *turistatérkép* cover the Mátra, Bükk, Zempléni and other highland regions (costing 30Ft.), and should be purchased in advance, since they may not be available on the spot. The best selections can be found at two **map shops** in Budapest: at Nyár utca 2 (in the VII district) and Bajcsy-Zsilinszky út 34 (in the V district). Both places are outlets for the *Cartographia* company, whose maps of Bucharest and Sofia are far better than anything available in Romania or Bulgaria – which is useful to know if you're planning on visiting either of those countries.

TROUBLE

The Hungarian **police** (*Rendőrség*) have a milder reputation than their counterparts in Bulgaria and Romania; and foreign tourists are handled with kid gloves unless they're suspected of black-marketeering, drug-smuggling or driving under the influence of alcohol. However, the rule on registration (p.14) is taken seriously, and since bored cops ask to inspect passports and visas from time to time, you should make sure that everything's in order. In border regions, it's fairly common to be (politely and briefly) questioned by plainclothes – usually flashily dressed – young secret policemen; but here too, if your stamps are in order the *BKH* shouldn't create any problems. Most policeman have at least a smattering of German, but rarely any other foreign language. If you need the police, dial **07** in **emergencies**, or ask for directions to the district (*kerületi*) or main (*fökápitányság*) police station. Should you be arrested or need legal advice, ask to contact your embassy or consulate (see p.88 for the addresses).

Violent crimes – and theft in general – are rare in Hungary, and most **trouble** can be avoided. Don't sunbathe nude or topless unless everyone else is, photograph 'secret' Russian bases (invariably marked by 'no photography' signs) or deal blatently on the black market, and you've eliminated almost all the likely causes. The exception is **sexual harassment**, which is mainly a problem for women travelling alone, and more likely in certain situations than in others. 'Provocative' clothing (or punkish hairstyles) may encourage unwelcome male attention if you visit rural or working-class *italbolt* (bars), or hitch-hike alone; while the 'black train' (p.190) should be avoided, as should Budapest's VIII district and downtown Miskolc after dark. Mostly, harassment is of the annoying rather than the frightening variety, and it's probably not worth responding with '*ne fogdoss!*' (keep your hands to yourself!) or '*menj a fenébe!*' (go to hell!). The important word to remember is *segítség!* – help! – although it's very unlikely that you'll need it.

GETTING AROUND

Hungarian **public transport** doesn't break any speed records but it reaches practically everywhere in the country, and despite price increases in recent years, Westerners should find costs still absurdly cheap. The problem is in getting *információ*, which is normally displayed in Hungarian only; staff – while generally helpful – aren't likely to speak any foreign language but German (if that). The language section (p.237) contains some pertinent phrases, while the following should be useful for **deciphering timetables**: *érkezö járatok* (or *érkezés*) means 'arrivals', and *induló járatok* (or *indulás*) 'departures'. Trains or buses to (*hova*) a particular destination leave from a platform (*peron*) or coach-stand (*kocsillag*); and timetables also reveal where transport from (*honnan*) a place arrives. Services may run (*közlekedik*) *munkaszüneti napok kivételével naponta köz.* – daily, except on rest days, ie. Sundays and public holidays; *munkanapokon (hetfötol-péntekig) köz.* – weekdays, Monday-Friday; *munkaszüneti napokon köz.* – on rest days; *szabad napon (szombaton) köz.* – on the 'free' day, Saturday; or *09.30-tól 12-ig vasárnap köz.* – on Sunday between 9.30am-12pm. *Atszallás* means 'change'; *at* 'via'; and *kivételével* 'except'.

Trains

Hungarian state railways, **MÁV**, has a highly centralised network. Many cross-country journeys are easier if one travels via Budapest rather than on branch lines where services are slower and less frequent. Domestic **trains** are either *sebesvonat* (stopping only at major centres), *gyorsvonat* (express), or *személyvonat* (halting at every hamlet en route), all of which are slower than their counterparts in most Western countries. Személyvonat are the cheapest of the three, but all fares are so low that the money saved is insignificant compared with the time lost by not travelling on an express. Almost all trains have buffets and 1st and 2nd class (*osztály*) sections; while international services routed through Budapest have **sleeping cars and couchettes** (*hálókocsi* and *kusett*), for which tickets can be bought at MÁV offices, in advance, or sometimes on the train itself. More details are available from the UTASELLÁTÓ company, in Budapest (☎ 140-803), which runs MÁV's catering side.

Tickets (*jegy*) for most domestic services can safely be bought at the station (*pályaudvar* or *vasútállomás*) on the day of departure, but it's possible to book up to 60 days in advance. You can break your journey once between the point of departure and the final destination, but must get your ticket punched within an hour of alighting at the interim station. Most Hungarians purchase singles (*egy útra*), so ask *oda-vissza* if you want a return. **Seat reservations** are obligatory for services marked 'R' on timetables ; one pays a few extra forints for a *helyjegy* when buying the ticket, or can book them at MÁV or Volántourist offices up to two months in advance. For **information** about domestic trains, try ringing 429-

150/227-860 in Budapest. The chunky paperback *Hivatalos Menetrend* or **national timetable** is only worth acquiring from ticket offices (60Ft) if you're prepared to spend some time decoding it.

Tickets for **international trains** – *nemzetközi gyorsvonat* – must be booked in advance and include seat reservations. Hungary is **the cheapest place to buy tickets** if you're planning to travel on to other socialist countries – for example **to China** (see p.86) – and return to the West by way of Hungary. With an IUS card (which even non-students can purchase in *Express* offices for 100Ft), you're entitled to a 30%-50% reduction in the fare; and return tickets (to Bulgaria in particular) generally work out substantially less than the cost of a Hungarian single, plus a single back to Hungary purchased in another socialist state. One can pay for the 'Hungarian stage' of the journey in forints, but the 'international' phase must be paid for in hard currency. The central MÁV ticket office in Budapest (Népköztársaság útja 35) which handles bookings gets crowded during summer; and staff and queueing tourists alike won't thank anybody who tries to pay by cheque or credit card.

Concessions in the form of reduced fares on domestic services are available for groups of 10 or more people (25%), holders of *Inter Rail* tickets (50%), *Eurotrain* card holders (50%) and pensioners with RES cards (33%). Children under 4 travel free if they don't occupy a separate seat. MÁV itself issues various **season tickets**: valid on domestic lines nationwide (but not on the international trains within Hungary); or around the Balaton only; for 1 week or 10 days. You'll need to travel fairly intensively to make savings with a 7 day national *Runaround* (800Ft/-1,200Ft 1st class), and while a week's train travel around the Balaton comes cheap (200Ft), quite a number of the shoreline settlements are easier to reach by bus. For details of season tickets in Budapest, see page 41.

Hungary runs only one **car train**, on the Budapest – Dresden line, which travellers to West Germany via the DDR might find useful, although it doesn't carry caravans or mini-buses. **Bicycles** are freighted free if they accompany Transalpino holders on international trains, while on domestic services they can ride in the guard's van as personal **luggage** for a charge of about 30Ft per

100 kilometres. Most stations have a left-luggage office (*ruhatár*) which charges 3Ft per day for each item deposited – sometimes including 'each item' strapped to your rucksack! Beware of huge queues for baggage at Budapest's main stations (and at some Balaton terminals) during the summer, and keep *all* of the scrappy little receipts, or you'll never get your gear back. A few main stations have automatic luggage lockers, which take two 2Ft coins and your baggage for up to 24 hours. **Lost property** is kept for two months at the station where it was handed in, and thereafter forwarded to the regional MÁV headquarters (except for passports, which are sent to KEOKH immediately).

Buses

The **Volán** ('Wheel') company runs the bulk of Hungary's **buses**, which are called *autóbusz* (*not* 'bus', which means 'fuck' in Hungarian!). It's often easier to travel **between towns** by bus rather than rail, and though the former is more expensive, fares are still cheap (roughly 1Ft per km). Details of useful routes are given in the guide, and at the end of each chapter, but in any case, schedules are clearly displayed in bus terminals (*autóbusz pályaudvar*, sometimes called *autóbusz vasútállomás*) which you'll find in every town. Arrive early to confirm the departure bay (*kocsillag*) and ensure getting a seat. For long distance services, particularly to or from Budapest, it's probably wisest to buy tickets one day (or at least several hours) in advance; **in rural areas** it's more normal to buy one's ticket on the bus. Even the most way-out villages see at least one bus a day, while communities in the vicinity of large towns are well served by public transport. As on trains, children under 4 travel free if they don't occupy a separate seat, and for half-fare up to the age of 10, but otherwise there are no concessions.

Public transport **within towns** is generally excellent. Besides buses, there are usually trolleybuses (*trolibusz*) and trams (*villamos*) running from dawn until around 22.30-23.00 (and night services in Budapest). Express buses (marked 'E', with red signboards) halt only at main stops. **Tickets** for all services are sold in strips by tobacconists and street kiosks, and punched by the passenger on board the vehicle (although in Pécs and a few other towns, one drops a 2Ft coin into a ticket machine on buses). Usually the flat fares are identical in every town and the same 3Ft tickets are valid on both buses and trolleybuses, but tickets issued by one municipality aren't allowed to be used in a different one. In Budapest, one can get various types of **monthly passes**.

In addition, Volán runs **international services** to neighbouring countries and a few points further west. The main depot for these is Engels tér in Budapest (p.62), but some services also run from provincial towns like Siófok, Szombathely, Győr, Miskolc, Salgótarján, Szeged, Baja, Mohács and Debrecen, (detailed under those towns in the guide). It's fractionally cheaper to travel from Budapest to Vienna by bus, but other destinations may cost less by train. Unless you present a receipt showing that your forints were obtained legally, tickets on all international coaches must be purchased in hard currency.

Motoring

Hungary's geographical location means that the country plays an important part in overland communications across Europe, and indeed the E15 (London - Istanbul) highway goes via Budapest. To drive in Hungary you'll require an international **driving licence** and **third party insurance**. Cars registered in EEC countries (except France, Italy, Portugal, Spain, Greece and Turkey) are assumed to be covered by this; drivers from other countries must have a Green Card or purchase insurance at the border. This last only covers for damage to third parties in Hungary, so it's wiser to get a Green Card beforehand. **Accidents** not involving injury should be reported to the Motor Vehicle Insurance Dept. in Budapest (XI, Hamzsabégi út 60; ☎ 669-755), within 24 hours if possible; if someone is injured the police must be notified (dial 07) .

Drinking and driving is totally prohibited, and offenders with in excess of 8 milligrams of alcohol are liable to felony charges. The state requires cars to be roadworthy (steering, brakes and all lights must work); and carry certain **obligatory equipment** – a triangular breakdown sign; spare bulbs for the indicators, head-, rear- and brake-lights; a first aid box ; and a supplementary mud-guard made of a non-rigid material, attached to rear fenders. Passengers

must wear three point safety belts in the front seats, where it's forbidden for children to travel.

Drive on the right. **Speed limits** for vehicles are 60 kph in built-up areas, 80 kph on main roads, and 100 kph on motorways; and at the very least, offenders can expect an on-the-spot fine of 300Ft. **Other rules** worth knowing include the prohibitions against repeatedly switching from lane to lane on highways; overtaking near pedestrian crossings; and sounding the horn in built-up areas unless to avert accidents. At crossroads, vehicles coming from the right have right of way, unless otherwise indicated by signs, and pedestrians have priority over cars turning onto the road. Remember that trams *always* have right of way, and that some traffic islands serve as bus or tram stops. On motorways and secondary roads it's illegal to reverse, make U-turns or stop at islands. **Pedestrian zones** (found in many towns and shaded blue on maps) are indicated by 'All vehicles prohibited' signs – *kivéve célforgalom*.

Roads are generally in good condition, and fall into three categories. Motorways – prefixed by an 'M' – link the Balaton with Budapest, and will doubtless soon do the same for Győr and Miskolc; while first class highways (numbered with a single digit from 1-8) almost all radiate from Budapest like spokes in a wheel; linked by secondary roads which are identified by two or three digits (the first one of which indicates the highway which the road joins – eg. roads 82 and 811 both meet route 8 at some point). Information on nationwide **driving conditions** can be obtained from ÚTINFORM (☎ 227-643); conditions in Budapest are monitored by FÓVINFORM (☎ 171-173). In rural areas, wagons, cyclists, livestock and pedestrians are potential **traffic hazards**, so you should drive slowly – especially at night.

Petrol – *benzin* – isn't rationed in Hungary, and most AFOR filling stations (*benzinkút*) sell 98 octane *extra*; 92 octane *szuper*; and 86 octane *normál*. However, **diesel** is only obtainable with **coupons** (sold at main hotels and IBUSZ agencies; unused coupons aren't refunded). Filling stations usually function from 6am-10pm, except on motorways and in the capital, where many operate around the clock. IBUSZ issues a variety of free and useful **motoring maps**, while

TOURINFORM's *Budapest Guide* contains maps of the capital's one-way systems and ring-roads. By ringing 220-668 or 160-183 you can summon the 'Yellow Angels' **breakdown service**, which is free if the repairs take no longer than 1 hour to complete and your own motoring organisation belongs to the FIA or AIT federations, to which the **Hungarian Automobile Club** – *MAK* – is also affiliated. The MAK's national headquarters is at Rómer Flóris u.4/a in Budapest's II district (open weekdays 8am-2.30pm/alternate Saturdays 8am-12.30pm /☎ 666-404); but their depot for **technical assistance** in the capital is at Boldizsár u.2 in the XI district (☎ 850-722). **Spare parts** for foreign cars are easier to find in Hungary than elsewhere in Eastern Europe, but may still present problems. See under the Budapest 'Listings' and ask the MAK for help.

Hiring a car is quite easy. You can order one from any AVIS or EUROPCAR bureau in the world; and from hotel reception desks or certain travel agencies within Hungary. In Budapest these agencies are FŐTAXI (VII, Kertész u.24/☎ 116-116); Volántourist (IX, Vaskapu u.16 /☎ 334-783); Cooptourist (V, Kossuth tér 13-15/☎ 118-803) and IBUSZ (V, Martinelli tér 8/☎ 186-222). IBUSZ, Volántourist and Cooptourist offices offer the same service in the provinces. Rental costs are reasonable, although there's an additional mileage charge (equivalent to 15 pence per kilometre) which, like petrol and garaging, isn't included in the price of **fly/drive holidays**. Payment for car hire by credit card is fine.

By air and boats

MALÉV doesn't operate any **domestic flights**, since Hungary is such a small country, but many of their **flights abroad** (departing from Ferihegy airport) are good value. If you're heading on to other socialist countries, or to Greece or Turkey, they may prove an attractive alternative to trains – especially for holders of IUS cards, who can sometimes qualify for substantial discounts. MALÉV's central office (Roosevelt tér 2/☎ 186-614) is the place to make enquiries, while bookings are also feasible at desks in the main Budapest hotels, or can be made by telephone (dial 184-333).

The MAHART company organises **passenger boats** in Hungary, which operate on Lake Balaton, between Budapest and Esztergom, on the section of the Danube running through the capital, and on the River Tisza which bisects the Great Plain (although this last service only functions during high season, if at all some years). Details of these can be found in the appropriate chapters. MAHART also operates a daily **hydrofoil service between Vienna and Budapest**. It's a 4½hr journey downriver to Budapest; an hour longer if one travels upriver to Vienna. Tickets to Vienna are sold at the International Boat Station on the Belgrád rakpart (the Pest embankment), where the hydrofoil departs, or at IBUSZ (Tanács kőrút 3/c); in Vienna, tickets are available from IBUSZ (I. Kärntnerstrasse 26) or the Austrian company DDSG (II. Mexiko Platz 8). Prices are subject to regular increase, so the quoted single fare of 600 Austrian schillings (approx. £30) is only an indication of the likely cost.

By bike or hitching

Motorcycling seems to be the favourite means of travel for young West German campers in Hungary, although I'd have thought that they'd find the **speed limits** irksomely low: 80 kph on motorways, 70 on other roads, and 50 kph in built-up areas. Drivers must be over 18, wear a helmet, and have a log book or other registration document, plus an IDP and Green Card **insurance**. Otherwise, rules and conditions are the same as for motorists.

If you bring your own machine **cycling** can be a good way to see the country. Winds are generally light, there's hardly any rain from July until the end of September, and roads are well surfaced and usually free heavy traffic. However, cyclists are forbidden on main roads (with single digit numbers), and on some secondary roads between 'peak hours' – 7am-9.30am, 4pm-6pm. You can obtain a **cycling map** of Hungary from the *Hungarian Camping and Caravaning Club* (VIII, Üllői út 6) in Budapest, which makes the permissable routes clear. The most scenic areas of Hungary are the northern uplands, the Danube Bend and parts of Transdanubia and the Bakony, where you'll find a few stiff climbs and lots of rolling hills. Conversely, the easiest cycling terrain – the Great Plain – is visually the most monotonous. In towns, beware of slippery cobbled streets and sunken tramlines during wet weather. **Hiring bikes** (for the day or week) is possible at some resorts around the Balaton, but unfortunately the machines are heavy and low-slung with limited gears. Your best chance of getting **spares & repairs** is in Budapest, where even parts for 10-speed bikes can some times be found. Ask the Camping & Caravaning Club to recommend suppliers.

It's quite common for young Magyars and East Germans to try **hitch-hiking** or *autostop* to get around, and the practice is only forbidden on motorways. A fair number of drivers seem willing to give lifts, although your prospects at week-ends are pretty dire since the small Trabants and Ladas driven by Hungarians are usually packed with the driver's family. I've not heard of any attacks on **women travelling alone**, but a few positively paranoid precautions helped me feel more secure. Establish the driver's destination before revealing your own; note how the door opens when you get in; never accept lifts from two men; and keep an eye on the roadsigns.

By horse or wagon

Hungarians profess a lingering attach-ment to the horse – their equestrian ally since the time of the great migration and the Magyar conquest – and the horse-herds or *csikós* of the Plain are romantic figures in national literature and folklore. Most native **horses** are mixed-breeds descended from Arab and English thoroughbreds, crossed in recent years with Hanoverian and Holstein stock, and the adjective most commonly used to describe their character is 'mettlesome' or 'spirited'.

Horse-riding tours are organised by *Pegazus Tours* (Károlyi M. u.5) and IBUSZ (Felszabadulás tér 5) in the capital, and come in various forms. IBUSZ's 10 day 'Hungaria Riding Tour' runs each week from mid-April to the end of October, and includes all trans-port, meals and accommodation. You spend 6 days in the saddle, covering 200-250km along one of six or eight different routes across the Balaton Hills, the Danube Bend or the Great Plain, accompanied by a guide. Pegazus's 8-day tours are likewise all inclusive, and offer a variety of routes, but are slightly less expensive than the Hungaria tours. The company also offers a slightly bizarre expedition across the puszta, where tourists drive their own **covered wagons** and navigate themselves. In addition, there are various programmes – not to mention instruction – offered by **riding schools** (*Lovarda*). You'll find these at Üllő-Tornyoslöb, Ady-liget and Alag in the vicinity of Budapest; Taliándorog, Nagyvázsony, Nagyberek, Szentbék-kálla, Szántódpuszta, Siófok and Keszthely around the Balaton; Tata, Szombathely, Sárvár, Radiháza, Nagycenk and Dunakiliti in Transdanubia; Visegrád on the Danube Bend; Szilvásvárad in the northern uplands; and Hortobágy, Bugac-puszta, Tiszafüred, Makó and Szatymaz on the Great Plain. Ask IBUSZ for their *On Horseback* booklet, and check with local tourist offices if you're interested. Although the schools naturally supply saddlery, they can't undertake to provide clothing for riding.

SLEEPING

The cost of tourist **accommodation** here is low by European standards, and finding a room to suit your tastes and budget shouldn't prove difficult. Modest hotels rent double rooms for as little as £8 (singles are rarer and proportionately dearer); private rooms, campsites and the network of hostels are yet cheaper. The only drawback is that the cheapest places tend to fill up during 'high' season (June-September), so if you're heading for a town offering a limited choice of accom-modation it's probably advantageous to make **reservations**. This can be done at short notice through any IBUSZ bureau, nationwide, or through the regional tourist office with responsibility for that area; as listed in the *Hotel-Camping* brochure de-tailing accommodation in each town and village – a useful supplement to this guide, available free from tourist offices.

Hotels (*szálló* in Hungarian, although the English word is widely understood) are graded by stars, descending from princely 5-star establishments down to modest yet comfortable 1-star places, where not all of the rooms have bathrooms (or, rather, showers). A similar system is used to categorise **inns** (*fogadó*) and **pensions** (*penzió* or *panzió*), found in towns and along highways, which cost much the same as their hotel equivalents. A double room should cost between 300-700Ft in a 1-or 2-star hotel; between 600-1,300Ft in a 3* or 4* star establishment, and rarely exceed 2,000Ft even in the smartest places. Incidentally, most **deluxe Budapest hotels** drastically reduce their prices over the winter.

Many visitors prefer to rent **private rooms**, a practice that's encouraged and regulated by the local tourist offices, which term such accommodation *fizetővendégszolgálat* (*Fiz* for short) and can arrange things for a small commission. Going through the tourist office you'll avoid the necessity of **registration with the police** (p.14), which is required should you deal directly with the rentiers, who may advertise *szoba kiadó* ('room for rent'), *Zimmer frei* (the equivalent in German) or even tout for business at railway stations. The drawbacks of private accommodation are that you're supposed to be out of the flat between 11.30am and 5pm (though few landladies insist), and that one may have to rent sight unseen (almost certainly so if you've gone through IBUSZ). Besides the possibility that you may feel an intruder in small family home, in towns it's possible to end up far from the centre in a high-rise flat, although you might strike lucky with a fine old apartment in the Belváros (inner city). Some landladies may provide meals for an additional charge, while the room touts at stations may suggest payment in hard currency and prefer that you don't register. . .both of which are illegal. Single rooms are rare, so solo travellers will have to find someone to share with, or pay the full cost of a double room, which is likely to be between 200-400Ft per night (perhaps 20-50% higher in Budapest or around the Balaton during summer). In western and southern Hungary, some regional tourist offices also offer **farmstead accommodation** in surrounding villages; farm buildings converted into self-catering holiday homes. These come more expensive than private rooms, but if there's a group of you, or you're travelling with children, they could prove to be just the thing.

Hostels divide into *Túristaszálló*, a few of which are located inside castles or former mansions, and, in the highland

areas favoured by hikers, *Túristaház*, which are similar in all but name. Both are graded as 'A' or 'B' depending on the availability of hot water and the number of beds (costing 60 or 40Ft, respectively) per room. There's also the Youth Travel Agency *Express*, which runs a stable of 'hotels for young people' (not noticeably cheaper than other hotels), and, more importantly, can also book beds in vacant **college residences**. These *nyári* – summer – *Túristaszálló* are generally open between July 1 and August 11, but the exact dates (and addresses) vary each year. Some of them (known as *Építőtábor*) are run by KISZ, the Communist Youth League, although in practice there's little difference between the two. Ask at the local Express agency in town (addresses in the guide), where they'll know the locations of hostels and, if pressed, will probably even book you a bed. At the hostel itself you'll need a student card to show (which can be bought at the Express office), while if you're staying more than 48 hours, they'll probably ask you to register with the local police. Beds cost between 40-80Ft (slightly more if there's only 2 or 3 in the room). If you're really skint, it's perhaps worth asking at halls of residence (*diákszálló*) during term time, for students may be willing to let foreigners doss on their floor.

Throughout Hungary, campsites and bungalows come together in complexes where tourists of the world unite. **Bungalows** (*üdülőház*) proliferate around popular resorts and on the larger campsites, and while some are reserved for members of trade unions (SZOT), others can be rented for 100-1,200Ft, depending on their facilities and size (2-4 persons). The 1st class bungalows – with well equipped kitchens, hot water and a sitting room or terrace – are excellent, while the most primitive at have least clean bedding and don't leak. **Campsites** – usually signposted *Kemping* – likewise range across the spectrum from 'deluxe' to 3rd class. The more elaborate places include a restaurant and shops – maybe even a disco – and tend to be overcrowded; 2nd or 3rd class sites often have a nicer ambience, with lots of old trees rather than a manicured lawn ineffectually shaded by saplings, and acres of caravans and trailers. Expect to pay 70Ft in most locations, twice that around jampacked Lake Balaton. Solo campers lose out since fees are calculated on a basic ground rent plus a charge per person and per car or bike (eg. 40Ft + 30Ft + 30Ft) – plus, for non-students, an obligatory *kurtaxe* of 15Ft which is the tourist's contribution to the locals' rates bill. There are **reductions** of 25-30% during 'low' season (before the end of May, and after the beginning of September) when fewer sites are open, and during the high season for members of the FICC (International Camping & Caravaning Club) and for people carrying a student card issued by ISIC or IUS. **Camping wild** is illegal – although many young Hungarians and East Germans do it, particularly in the highland areas where there are 'rain shelters' (*esőház*). In Budapest, a free campsite (closed during daytime) exists in the suburbs.

EATING AND DRINKING

Among the Eastern bloc countries, Hungary's abundance of food is exceptional: material proof of the 'goulash socialism' which amazes visitors from Romania or the USSR. Hungarians are blasé about the range of foodstuffs, but not the spiralling prices; visitors from the West, however, can afford to eat and drink lavishly for (what seems to them to be) remarkably low prices.

For foreigners the archetypal Magyar dish is 'goulash' – historically the basis of **Hungarian cooking** inasmuch as the wagon anticipated the motor car. The ancient Magyars relished cauldrons of *gulyás* (pronounced 'gou-yash') – a soup made of potatoes and whatever meat or fish was available, which was later flavoured with paprika and beefed up into a variety of stews, modified over the centuries by various foreign influences. Hungary's Slav neighbours probably introduced native cooks to yogurt and sour cream (vital ingredients in many dishes); while the influence of the Turks, Austrians and Germans is apparent in the variety of sticky pastries and strudels, plus recipes which include saurkraut or dumplings. Perhaps the main influence was that of France, which revolutionised Hungarian cooking in the Middle Ages and again in the C19 – although nowadays you'd be hard pressed to find anything like *nouvelle cuisine* in a country whose cooking seems designed to thwart Weight-watchers.

Breakfast and snacks

As a nation of early risers, Hungarians like to have a calorific **breakfast** (*reggeli*). Commonly, this includes cheese, eggs or salami together with bread and jam, often accompanied by a shot of *pálinka* to 'clear the palate' or 'aid digestion' in rural areas. By 8am, cafés and snack bars are already functioning, and the rush hour is prime time for the **Tej-bár**. These Milk-Bars serve mugs of hot milk (*meleg tej*) and sugary cocoa (*kakaó*); cheese-filled pastry cones (*sajtos pogácsa*) and rolls (*sajtos-rollo*); dough rings with curds (*túrós táska*), spongy milk-bread with rasins (*mazsolás kalács*) and other dunkable pastries.

Everyone is addicted to **coffee**. At intervals throughout the day, people consume tiny glasses of *káve* – brewed super-strong, served black and sweetened to taste: a brew that can double your heart beat. **Coffee houses** were once the centres of Budapest's cultural and political life; hotbeds of gossip where penurious writers got credit and the clientéle dawdled for hours over the free newspapers. Sadly this is no longer the case, but you'll find plenty of unpretentious *kávéház* serving the beverage – with milk (*tejeskávé*) or whipped cream (*tejszínhabbal*) should you request it. Most coffee houses offer some pastries – although for these, you'll find much more choice in the patisseries (see below) which, of course, also serve coffee themselves. **Tea**-drinkers are a minority here – perhaps because tea with milk (*tejes tea*) is so insipid, although the *tea citrommal* with lemon isn't so bad.

A whole range of places purvey **savoury snacks**, including the *Csemege* or **delicatessens**, which display a tempting spread of salads, open sandwiches, pickles and cold meats, and are really superior take-aways (although in a few, you can eat on the premises). Unfortunately, many delis (like Tej-bár) work using **the 'kassa system'**, whereby customers order and pay at the *kassa* desk in return for a receipt which is then exchanged at the food counter. If your

Hungarian is minimal, this can throw up a few suprises and all kinds of minor misunderstandings. For sit-down nibbles, people patronise **bisztró** which tend to offer a couple of hot dishes besides the inevitable salami rolls; *snackbár*, which are superior versions of the same, with leanings in the direction of being a patisserie; and *büfé*. These last are found in department stores and stations, and are sometimes open around the clock. However their food can be limited to tired sandwiches and greasy sausages filled with rice (called *hurka* and *kolbász*), so it's often better to look elsewhere. **On the streets**, according to season, toothless ancients preside over vats of *kukorica* (corn on the cob) or trays of *gestenye* (roasted chestnuts); while fried fish (*sült hal*) shops are common in towns near rivers or lakes. *Szendvics* and *hamburger* stands are increasingly popular in Budapest and large towns, and a branch of MacDonalds has recently opened in the capital. **Around resorts**, another popular munch is *lángos*: the native, mega-size equivalent of doughnuts; sometimes sold with a sprinkling of salt or a dash of syrup. Fruit, too, is sold on the streets (see the vocabulary below) and **in markets**, where you'll also find various greasy spoons forking out *hurka* and the like. Outdoor markets (*piac*) are colourful affairs which sometimes bizarrely feature rows of poultry sheltered beneath sunshades; in market halls (*vásárcsarnok*), people select their fish fresh from glass tanks, and their mushrooms from a staggering array of *gomba*, which are displayed alongside toxic fungi in a 'mushroom parade' so that shoppers can recognise the difference!

Finally, no list of snacks would be complete without mentioning **bread** (*kenyér*) which, as the old saying has it, is so popular that 'Hungarians will even eat bread with bread'. The mass-produced stuff is bland and white, but private producers have risen to the challenge in recent years, and you can buy rye bread, loaves with poppy and caraway seeds, and other varieties from *házi-kenyér* vans stationed on the city streets.

Main meals

Traditionally, Hungarians take their main meal at **midday**; so the range of dishes offered by restaurants is greatest for lunch (*ebéd*) rather than in the **evenings**, when Westerners expect to find all catering systems go for dinner (*vacsora*). It's important to remember this, and also the annoying fact that many places begin to close down the kitchen at 10pm, so that customers are turned away shortly afterwards – even on Hungary's national holiday, when a capitalist would weep to see the famished masses tramping from place to place being rebuffed by doormen. There are compensations, however: notably the bands of musicians that play in many restaurants during lunchtime and in the evening, whose violin airs and melodic plonkings of the cimbalom are an element of the 'Hungarian scene'.

All eating places display signs signifying their class, or *osztály* (*oszt.*). This categorisation from I-IV is a fair guide to **comparative prices**, but doesn't necessarily reflect the quality of the food served within. I've had some excellent meals in fairly unprepossing III *oszt.* joints, while it's possible that a restaurant's I *oszt.* rating derives from its chi-chi decor rather than the excellence of its cooking. Another sign to watch for is menus in German: places that provide these are likely to prove more expensive than those that don't. Additionally, the law obliges all eating places to provide a minimum of two complete **set menus** (*napi menü*) at moderate prices, while some restaurants also offer a low-priced student menu (*diák menü*) which you might need an IUS/ISIC card to order. It's invariably more expensive to eat **à la carte**, where the choice is bigger, but the difference isn't outrageous. In an average II class restaurant, you can generally eat a three course meal and sink a few glasses of wine for 250-400Ft, while the set menu and a drink will cost about 150-200Ft. Service charges aren't usually included in the bill, and staff rely financially on their customers **tipping** (10% of the total is customary).

Hungarians have a variety of words implying fine distinctions amongst **restaurants** – in theory an *étterem* is a proper restaurant, while a *vendéglő* approximates to the Western notion of a bistro – but in practice the terms are often used interchangably. The sixties saw the advent of *kisvendéglő* – basically smaller versions of bistros – which were originally used as youth hang-outs; nowadays this title may also denote seedy, raucous dives in the vicinity of factories and stations, where single women are likely to attract unwelcome attentions. The old word for an inn, *csárda*, applies to posh places specialising in certain dishes (eg. a 'Fishermen's inn' or *Halászcsárda*), restaurants alongside roads, or with rustic pretentsions, besides the humbler rural establishments that it originally signified. The only certainty is that the cheapest places are the *Önkiszolgáló* restaurants **with self-service**, which function in many towns from 8am-8pm Monday-Saturday. Since you can see the food while ordering it, there's none of the uncertainty inherent in menus or the *kassa* system. The drawbacks of these places are that the decor is grungy, and meals are frequently served lukewarm if you arrive outside peak hours (midday and around 6-7pm).

When they can afford to be, Hungarians are enthusiastic eaters, so as a (presumably rich) Westerner you'll be asked if you want **starters** (*előételek*) – generally a soup or salad. However, nobody will mind if you just have one of the dishes offered as the **main course** (*ételek*) or, alternatively, take a soup and an appetizer and skip the rest. On the same menu you'll normally find **drinks** listed under the heading *italok*. The outlook for vegetarians is pretty bleak unless you're prepared to fend for yourself. Greengrocers (*Zöldség*) and markets sell excellent fruit and veg, but Hungarians are frankly amazed that anyone might forgo meat *willingly* and make smug remarks about all the 'vegetarians' in Romania (where obtaining fresh meat is about as difficult as buying bacon in Libya). Aside from cooked vegetables, virtually the only **meatless dishes** are fried – literally 'mirror' – eggs, *tükörtojás*; soft-boiled eggs (*lágy tojás*); scrambled eggs (*tojásrántotta*) and eggs in mayonaise (*kaszinó tojás*). Even innoccuous vegetable soups may contain some meat stock, and the pervasive use of sour cream in cooking means that Vegans are still more restricted.

Dishes and terms

What follows is by no means a comprehensive list of Hungarian dishes, but by combining names and terms it should be possible to decipher anything that you're likely to see on a menu. Alcoholic and soft drinks are covered separately, as are desserts and pastries, which are best sampled in the ubiquitous *cukrászda*.

Basics, and how to order

bors	pepper
cukor	sugar
ecet	vinegar
egészségedre!	Cheers!
jó étvagyat!	Bon appetit!
kenyér	bread
kifli	croissant
méz	honey
mustár	mustard
rizs	rice
só	salt
vaj	butter
zsemle/ péksütemény	bread rolls

To order, you can say *Kérnék. . .* or *Szeretnék. . .* (I'd like. . .); or *Kaphatok. . .* (Can I have. . .?), which is politer. Using these grammatical constructions, Hungarians add a suffix (*-t, -et, -ot* or *-at*) to the item being requested, so that *vaj* becomes *vajat*, *kávé, kávét*, and so on.

Appetizers (*előételek*), **soups** (*levesek*) **and salads** (*saláták*)

bécsi hering-saláta Viennese-style herring with vinegar

halmajonéz fish with mayonaise

majonézes kukorica sweetcorn with mayonaise

bakony betyárleves 'Outlaw soup' of chicken, beef, noodles and veg, richly spiced

csirke-aprólék leves mixed veg and gibblet soup

csontleves bland bone and noodle consommé

bajai halászlé fish and tomato soup

bableves beans and meat – a meal in itself

burgonyaleves potato, onion and paprika soup

gombaleves mushroom soup

(*kalocsai*) *halászleves* spicy fish soup (with red wine)

gulyásleves meat, vegetable and paprika soup

kunsági pandurleves chicken or pigeon soup seasoned with nutmeg, paprika, ginger and garlic

lencseleves lentil soup

meggyleves delicious chilled sour cherry soup

palócleves mutton, bean and sour cream soup

paradicsomleves tomato soup

szegedi halászlé Szeged-style mixed-fish soup

zöldségleves vegetable soup

alföldi saláta 'Puszta salad' – sliced sausages in a vinaigrette dressing

almás cékla dressed apple and beetroot slices

The names of other **salads** are easy to work out if you refer to the section on vegetables. **Cream** and **sour cream** feature in dishes whose name includes the words *tejszín/krém* and *tejföl*.

Meat (húsételek) **and poultry** (baromfi) **dishes**

alföldi marharostélyos	steak with a rich sauce and stewed veg.
bográcsgulyás	what foreigners mean by 'Goulash'
borjúpörkölt	veal stew seasoned with garlic
csabai szarvascomb	venison stuffed with spicy sausage
cigányrostélyos	'Gypsy-style' steak with brown sauce
csikós tokány	strips of beef braised in bacon, onion rings, sour cream and tomato sauce
csirke	chicken
erdélyi rakott-káposzta	layers of cabbage, rice and minced pork baked in sour cream – a Transylvanian speciality.
fasírozott	meatballs
hortobágyi rostélyos	steak 'Hortobágy style'; braised in stock, with a large dumpling
kacsa	duck
kolbász	spicy sausage
liba	goose
máj	liver
marhahús	beef
nyúl	rabbit
paprikás-csirke	chicken in paprika sauce
rablóhús nyárson	a kebab of pork, veal and bacon
sertésborda	pork chop
sonka	ham
töltött-káposzta	cabbage stuffed with meat and rice, in a tomato sauce
töltött-paprika	peppers stuffed with meat and rice,

	in a tomato sauce
vaddisznó boró-kamártással	wild boar in juniper sauce
virsli	Frankfurter

Terms: *comb* = leg; *félig nyersen* = underdone/rare ; *főve* = boiled; *jól megsütve* = well done (fried); *jól megfőzve* = well done (boiled) *pörkölt* = stewed slowly; *rántott* = in breadcrumbs; *roston sütve* = grilled; *sülve* = roasted; *sült/-sütve* = fried.

Fish dishes (halételek)

csuka tejfölben sütve	fried pike with sour cream
fogas	a local fish of the pike-perch family
fogasszeletek Gundel modra	breaded fillet of *fogas*
kecsege	sterlet
..tejszínes paprikás mártásban	...in a cream and paprika sauce
nyelvhal	sole
paprikás ponty	carp in paprika sauce
pisztráng tejszín mártásban	trout baked in cream
rostélyos töltött ponty	carp stuffed with bread, egg, herbs and fish liver or roe
sült hal	fried fish
tőkehal	cod
tonhal	tuna

In fancier restaurants you may encounter meat or fish dishes served in rich **sauces** (*mártásban*) – a legacy of French culinary influence. They're most likely to be served:

almamártásban . . .in an apple sauce

bormártásban . . .in a wine sauce

gombamártásban . . .in a mushroom sauce

ecetes torma . . .with horse-radish

fehérhagyma mártásban . . .in an onion sauce

fokhagymás mártásban . . .in a garlic sauce

kapormártásban . . .in a dill sauce

meggymártásban . . .in morello cherry sauce

paprikás mártásban . . .in a paprika sauce
tárkonyos mártásban . . .in tarragon sauce
vadasmártásban . . .in brown sauce (made of mushrooms, almonds, herbs and brandy)

Vegetables (zöldség)

bab	beans
borsó	peas
burgonya (krumpli)	potatoes ('spuds')
ecetes uborka	gherkin
fejes saláta	lettuce
fokhagyma	garlic
gomba	mushrooms
hagyma	onions
káposzta	cabbage
kukorica	sweet corn
paprika – édes or *erős*	peppers – sweet or hot
paradicsom	tomatoes
sárgarepa	carrots
spárga	asparagus
uborka	cucumber
zöldbab	green beans

Fruit (gyümölcs) **and cheese** (sajt)

alma	apples
barack	apricots
citrancs	grapefruit
citrom	lemon
dió	walnuts
eper	strawberries
füge	figs
(görög) dinnye	(water) melon
körte	pears
málna	raspberries
mandula	almonds
meggy	morello cherries
mogyoró	hazelnuts
narancs	oranges
őszibarack	peaches
szilva	plums
szőlő	grapes
füsölt sajt	smoked cheese which unwinds like liquorice laces
karaván sajt	tasty smoked cheese
marvány sajt	Stilton-like blue cheese
trappista sajt	rubbery, Edam-type cheese

Cakes and ices

Hungarians are decidedly fond of desserts and pastries, and **patisseries** (*cukrászda*) are almost national institu-tions. *Palacsinta* or **pancakes** are very popular, especially **with fillings**: *almás* (apple); *diós* (walnuts); *kompót* (stewed fruit); *mákos* (poppy seeds); *mandulás* (almonds); or *Gundel*-style (with nut-cream and raisins, flambéd). **Strudels** (*rétes*) are another favourite; made with curds and dill (*kapros túrós rétes*), poppy-seeds (*mákosrétes*) or plums (*szilvás rétes*). On the super-rich side are *dobostorta* (chocolate cream cake topped with caramel), *gesztenyepüré* (chestnut pureé with whipped cream), *kapucineres felfújt* (chocolate soufflé) and *töltött alma* (apple stuffed with vanilla, rasins and cream); while the humble dumpling is transformed into *somlói galuska* – made with vanilla, nuts and chocolate, and served in an orange and rum sauce. If you're still unsatiated, there's **ice cream** (*fagylalt*), the opium of the masses, priced low enough so that anyone can afford a cone. The com-monest flavours are *vanília*, *csokoládé* and *kávé*, but you might encounter cherry, raspberry, lemon or nutty varieties – see the fruit section in the food lists for the Hungarian names. And finally there's *metelt* – a rather unlikely-sounding but actually quite tasty sweet consisting of chopped sweet noodles, served cold with poppy seeds or some other topping.

Alcoholic and soft drinks

Hungary's mild climate and diversity of soils is perfect for **wine** (*bor*), which is perenialy cheap, whether you buy it by the bottle (*üveg*) or the glass (*pohár*). The main wine-growing regions surround Pécs, Eger, Kecskemét, Sopron and Tokaj, and cover large areas of the Balaton and Mátra highlands. Standards are constantly rising as more and more farms try to win the right to label their bottles *minőségi bor* (quality wine), the equivalent of *appelation contrôllée*. During the daytime, imbibers often drink spritzers – a decilitre (*dl.*) measure of wine topped up with water or soda water. **Wine bars** (*borozó*) are ubiquitous and generally far less pretentious than in the West; while true devotees of the grape like to get to the source, and patronise the extensive **wine cellars** (*borpince*) that honeycomb towns like Tokaj and Eger.

Vörös bor or **red wines** can be divided into the light-bodied and the full-bodied types. Examples of the former are *Villányi burgundi*, *Vaskúti kadarka* and *Egri pinot noir*; in the full-bodied category are

Villányi medoc noir, *Tihanyi merlot*, *Soproni kékfrankos* and the famous *Egri bikavér*, or 'Bulls' Blood of Eger'. **White wines** (*fehér bor*) are classified as sweet (*édes*) or dry (*száraz/furmint*). *Olasz rizling* wines tend to be sweet, with the exception of the 'Sand Wines' produced on the sandy soil between the Tisza and the Danube, which are dry. Other sweet whites include *Balatonfüredi szemelt*, *Akali zöldszilváni*, and the richest of the Tokaj wines, *Tokaj aszu*. In the dry category are three wines from the Badacsony vineyards, *kéknyelű*, *szürkebarát* and *zöldszilváni*; *Egri Leányka* from the Gyöngyös region; and two varieties of Tokaj, *furmint* and *szamorodni* (which means 'as it's grown'). Varieties of sparkling wine usually bear the label *Pannonia*.

Hungarians enjoy the ritual of **toasting**, so one of the first words to get your tongue around is *egészségedre* (pronounced 'EGG-aish-shaig-edreh') – cheers! When toasting more than one other person, it's grammatically correct to change this to *egészségünkre* (Cheers to us!).

Spirits are likewise cheap, if you stick to the native brands. The best-known type of *pálinka* – or brandy – is distilled from apricots (*barack*), and is a speciality of the Kecskemét region; but spirits are also produced from peaches (*öszibarack*), pears (*körte*) and other fruits that come to hand. This is particularly true of *szilva* – a lethal spirit produced on cottage stills in rural areas, allegedly using plums – sold privately, and unashamedly from toilets on the infamous 'black train'. Hungarians with money to burn order whisky (*viszki*) to impress – I saw a group inspecting a bottle of J&B with as much reverence as if it was a rare vintage – but most people find its cost prohibitive. Vodka isn't popular, despite the availability of excellent Russian *Stolichnaya* in ABCs. Possibly its reputation has suffered by association with the disgusting, yellowish Vietnamese vodka, bottles of which gather dust on supermarket shelves.

Sör, **beer**, is mostly of the lager-type (*világos*), and there's little to choose between the various local brands (of which *Kőbányai* is the commonest). It's important to ask for *Magyar sört* if you don't want to be served the more expensive imported brands (mainly Austrian, although you might get excellent Czech Pilsen). **Beer halls** (*söröző*) serve draught *világos* in half-litre glasses (*korsó*), and may also stock brown beer – *barna sör*.

Pepsi and Coke are available for those that like familiar **soft drinks**, but there's also a delicious range of Bulgarian bottled fruit juices sold in ABCs under the label *Nektár* (only watch out for the 'sell by' dates). In addition, you can buy bottled *limonádé*, mineral water (*ásvány víz*), soda water (*szóda víz*), and Hungarian *Kóla*.

ENTERTAINMENT

Gypsy and Hungarian folk music

No visitor to Hungary should fail to experience **Gypsy music** or *cigányzene*, which is widely performed in restaurants during the evening, usually by one or two violinists, a bass-player and a guy on the cimbalom – a stringed instrument that's struck with little hammers. *Mulatni* means 'to be possessed by music', and the Gypsies have always venerated the range of sounds and emotions produced by the violin, the playing of which – *bashavav* – traditionally has magical associations. The sense of awe that great violinists used to inspire, and the bohemian life of these musicians, is well captured in Walter Starkie's book *Raggle Taggle* (see p.231). Hungarians are keen to make requests or sing along when the *Primás* (band leader) comes to the table, soliciting tips; and foreigners are also likely to attract his attention, although it's fine to refuse with a *nem, köszönöm*. Nowadays, most musicians are townsmen and graduates of the *Rajkó* music school, rather than wandering, self-taught artists like János Bihari, Czinka Panna and Czermak – a Magyar nobleman turned vagabond – who were legendary figures during the C19. But it's still common for sons to follow their forefathers' profession, as has *Sándor Lakatos*, the most famous violinist performing today.

Confusingly, this archetypally 'Hungarian' music is neither Hungarian nor Gypsy in its origins. The music that

Gypsies perform amongst their own communities (in Szabolcs-Szatmár county, near Szolnok and other towns on the Great Plain) is actually far closer to the music of India and Central Asia – whence the Gypsies originally came; while Bartók himself complained that the Gypsies had transformed – and sometimes deformed – authentic **Hungarian folk music** (*Magyar népzene*), whose ancient roots sprung from the Turkic steppes and the Ural Mountains. The haunting rhythms and pentatonic scale of this 'Old Style' music (to use Bartók's terminology) were subsequently overlaid by 'New Style' European influences – which C20 folk enthusiasts have discarded during the folk revival, centred around **Táncház**. These 'Dance Houses' exist in several towns, and encourage people to build and learn to play archaic instruments; besides providing the site for **dances** which are usually fast and furious – particularly the wild, foot-stamping *csárdás*, or 'tavern dance'. There have also been attempts to revive the traditional wedding and harvest songs, which you might hear in the Palóc region or at Décs, a village in the 'Sárköz' that borders the Danube. A selection of folk records can be found on page 233.

Not only folk, but all kinds of **records**, are available from *zeneműbolt*. Hungarian-made LPs are generally of good quality and cheap compared with Western products, so check the shops out.

Rock and jazz
At resorts the amps blare Western disco rather than Hungarian **rock**, but there's a fair chance of hearing native bands in Budapest and the bigger towns, where posters or discreet stickers advertise rock or punk *zene* at local *klub*s. Since the Illés group braved Party disapproval and opened the door for 'beat' musicians in the early '60s, Hungarian rock has gone through its '70s 'supergroup' phase – epitomised by *Locomotiv GT* (playing a mix of styles from folk-beat to heavy metal); thrown up the Abbaesque *Neoton Family* and the winsome *Kati Kovács*; and spawned a host of new bands during the '80s. Rock's 'official' recognition just anticipated – and possibly depended on – the production of *István a Király*, the smash hit of 1983: a patriotic **rock opera** written by Bródy & Szörényi, Hungary's 'Lennon & McCartney.

Party tolerance didn't extend to *Beatrice* and other early **punk** groups – the most virulent of which, *CPG*, was gaoled – but their **new wave** (and less overtly political) successors have had an easier time of it. *Balaton*, *Europa Kiadó* and *Trabant* have made it on to vinyl at the cost of a little self-censorship, and the Party's 'softer' line is evident in the fact that *URH* (named after the police waveband) can play without being hassled. Groups like *Bizottság* (which moved into music from other arts), flourish in the small world of Budapest's avant garde alongside **'experimental'** or 'Industrial Music' bands such as *KFT* and *Bikini*. Outside Budapest, more **mainstream** tastes prevail. Current fave raves include the poppy *Napoleon Boulevard*; *Dolly Roll*, with its infectious blend of fifties R'n'R and the 'Italian sound'; Robert Szikora's *R-GO*, which draws on Latin American music; the headbangers' mob, *V. Motorock*; and the Country music parodists *Folk Celsius 100*.

It's also possible to catch visiting **foreign acts** at Budapest's *Sportcsarnok*; Tina Turner, the Talking Heads, Elton John, Santana and Queen have all played here.

Jazz musicians like *Aladár Pege* and the *Benkó Dixieland Band* attract large crowds to the annual Debrecen, Székesfehérvár, Nagykanizsa and Zalaegerszeg summer jazz festivals. Periodically, the *Hungarian Supergroup* brings together jazz and rock artists; while jazz musicians like the pianist György Szabados have built bridges towards classical music.

Classical music, opera and dance
Bartók, Kodály and Liszt still enjoy pride of place in the field of **classical music**, but modern composers can be heard at the *Interforum* festival, staged at Keszthely every three years (scheduled for 1990). The 'Budapest Spring' (March) and autumn 'Music Weeks' (late-September to late-October), and the 'Szeged Weeks' (July 20-August 20) are the landmarks of the concert-going year, which also features Haydn's and Beethoven's works (performed in the palatial surroundings of the Esterházy and Brunswick mansions); orchestral concerts at Veszprém, Diósgyőr and Keszthely castles; organ recitals in the main churches of Pécs, Buda, Debrecen, Eger, Miskolc, Szeged and Tihany; and chorales in the Gothic

churches at Köröshegy and Nyírbátor (mainly during the summer).

The reputation of the state **opera** continues to climb, with young singers like Adrienne Csengery winning rapturous acclaim abroad. The Budapest Opera's **ballet** company is classically-orientated, and most of the impetus for **modern dance** comes from the Pécs and Győr companies, choreographed by Imre Eck and Iván Markó. Both have a superb reputation (making it quite difficult to get tickets) and regularly visit the capital, as do foreign companies like the Bolshoi or Mongolian State ballet. Details of performances, and the addresses for making reservations, are published in IBUSZ's booklet 'Music Life in Hungary' and the monthly *Programme* magazine.

Cinema

The latest **Hungarian films** are premiered at the annual Budapest film festival, staged over four days in early February. Performances are dubbed or subtitled for the benefit of foreign critics, and if you can wangle tickets it's a good opportunity to see films that you'll otherwise only be able to understand when they're shown abroad (in the UK, at London's ICA and on C4). His big-budget international productions *Col. Redl* and *Mephisto* have made István Szabó the best-known name abroad; but there are many other talented **directors** whose work is aimed primarily at their own country – and in particular at exposing its flaws – which has made for a lot of harrowing cinema. Subjects tackled by directors include abortion (Pál Zolnay), rape (Judit Elek), incest (Zsolt Kézdi-Kovács), lesbianism (Károly Makk) and Stalinism (Péter Bacsó, Márta Mészáros) – so it's hardly surprising that there's been a swing back towards fantasy, romance and comedy in recent years. **Cinema-going** is very popular, and (often dubbed) foreign films appear regularly at *filmszínház* throughout the country. Tickets are very cheap, albeit hard to acquire at the door if a new Western movie is showing (try reserving through IBUSZ, or buying from touts).

Festivals

The **festival year** kicks off in March with two events. The **Mohács carnival** on March 1 sees processions of ghoulishly-masked revellers re-enacting ancient spring rites and pantomimes reviling the Turks (who won a decisive victory here in 1526); whereas the **Budapest Spring Festival** is devoted to music, drama and dance (from March 14-23). With the onset of fine weather and tourists, the summer months soon get crowded with events. **Historical pageants** are performed in picturesque Szentendre and the ruined castles of Gyula, Visegrád and Esztergom; while at Hortobágy, Apajpuszta, Tamási, Szántódpuszta and Kisbér there are **equestrian shows**. The exact dates of most of these vary from year to year – IBUSZ will know the details – but the Hortobágy *Bridge Fair* always occurs on August 20, and invariably combines amazing displays of horsemanship with a 'rodeo' atmosphere. Like the final day of the **Szeged Weeks** and the **Csűr at Nagykálló**, it coincides with **Constitution Day** – traditionally the name-day of Hungary's patron saint and founder, István – which is celebrated nationwide. All the bigger towns feature **parades**, but the capital and Debrecen trump the lot with their Danube regatta and Flower Carnival. Budapest mounts the most impressive **fireworks** display.

Saint István's relics attract multitudes of worshippers to the great Basilica in Pest but, with a few exceptions, **religious festivals** aren't widely observed in contemporary Hungary. The most obvious exception is Easter, when the churches and cathedrals are crammed – particularly in Esztergom, the seat of Hungarian Catholicism. For reasons of spectacle rather than faith I found the Orthodox (*Görög*) services more appealing. Orthodox believers commemorate their Serbian origins with a *kolo* dance outside the Preobrazhenska Church in Szentendre on August 19.

Sport

The hosting of the 1988 World Ice-Skating Championships in Budapest confirmed Hungary's place on the international sports circuit, and other major **sporting events** are certain to follow. Already, there's an annual *Budapest Marathon* and the *Hungarian Grand Prix*. Full details of these, and national championships in everything from parachuting to canoeing are available from IBUSZ, regional tourist offices and *Programme* magazine. Several pages of the weekly paper *Népsport* are devoted to **football** (*labdarúgás*) and most towns have a *stadion* and a team. These are also organised along 'socialist' lines, with the railway-workers, miners, police and army all fielding their own. Tickets are very cheap, as are facilities at local **sports halls** (*Sportscarnok*).

Windsurfing (*kölcsönző*) and **sailing** (*vitorlázás*) equipment can be hired at the main Balaton boat stations and Lake Velence, while **tennis** (*tenisz*) courts are often attached to the more upmarket hotels in Budapest and the main resorts. Hungary's topography rules out any dramatic or lengthy slopes, but that doesn't stop enthusiasts from **skiing** in the Mátra Mountains and the Buda Hills. For **horse-riding**, see p.22.

OPENING HOURS AND HOLIDAYS, MUSEUMS AND CHURCHES

During the week, most public buildings are open from 8.30am-5pm, but staff at lesser institutions usually take an hour off for lunch (around 12 o'clock). Aside from shops, tourist offices and KEOKH (detailed separately), the most obvious exceptions are museums, which almost always close on Mondays. Otherwise, **opening times** are affected by the shift to and from summer time (p.00), and by **public holidays**, when practically everything shuts down. These are December 25-26, January 1, April 4 (Liberation Day), Easter Monday, May 1, August 20 (Constitution Day) and November 7 (the anniversary of the Bolshevik Revolution).

Museums are generally open Tuesday-Sunday from 10am-6pm or 9am-5pm; and to make up for being shut on Mondays, often stay open until midday or mid-afternoon on Sundays, and have free admission over the weekends. In the case of significant exceptions to this rule, you'll find details in the guide alongside the relevant *múzeum*. Admission charges vary but rarely exceed 30Ft, and IUS/ISIC cards secure large reductions, or free entry in many cases. Hungary has about 600 museums, whose contents range from the crown jewels down to the dullest tat, but almost none of them have captions in any language but Hungarian, although catalogues may be available in German, French or English in the main Budapest and provincial museums. When it comes to surmounting the language-barrier, **Skanzens** are probably the most effective: fascinating ensembles of buildings and domestic objects culled from old settlements around the country, assembled on the outskirts of Szentendre, Nyíregyháza, Zalaegerszeg and Szombathely; or preserved in situ at Öriszentpéter, Hollókő and Csongrád, so as to form 'Village Museums'.

Hungary's few remaining mosques (*djami*) now qualify as museums rather than places of worship, but getting into **churches** (*templom*) may pose problems. The really important ones charge a small fee to see their crypts and treasures, and often prohibit sightseeing during services (*szertartás*, or *Gottdienst* in German). In small towns and villages, however, churches are usually kept locked – opening only for worship in the early morning and/or the evening (between around 6pm-9pm). A small tip is in order if you rouse the verger to unlock the building during the day; he normally lives nearby in a house with a doorbell marked *plébánia csengője*. Visitors are expected to wear 'decorous' dress – ie. no shorts or halter-tops.

WORK AND STUDY

Teaching English is probably the main opportunity for foreigners wanting to work in Hungary, and native English-speaking sixth-formers, students or teachers (up to the age of 45) can apply for jobs at the annual English language summer camp in southern Hungary (3 weeks during July/August). As well as providing Hungarian 15-17 year-olds with a chance to practice the English they've learnt at school, you're expected to organise sports and/or drama and musical activities – so previous experience in these areas is desirable. Board and accommodation is provided but applicants must pay for their own travel to Hungary; applications should be made to the *Youth Exchange Centre*, Seymour

Mews House, Seymour Mews, London W1H 9PE (☎ 01-486-5101) by the end of March. Graduates of the Debrecen summer school (see below) also stand a chance of landing jobs teaching English to employees of MALÉV and other state enterprises involved in international trade. Some foreigners also teach *Angol* privately (without work permits). This can be quite profitable but to find clients advertising in Budapest (with stickers around Felszabadulás tér) and posession of a telephone and a basic knowledge of Hungarian are prerequisites.

Foreigners (aged between 18-30) with previous experience of **workcamps** can apply to join various projects involving agricultural or construction work. Participants rise *early*, work 6-8hrs and spend the afternoons and evenings pursuing various cultural, social and sporting activities, five days a week; the official languages are English and Russian. Board and lodging is provided in student hostels, bungalows or tents, and travel costs to the camp aren't included in the price. In certain camps participants can choose between pocket money (500 Ft) or extra services such as an expenses paid 5/6 days trip to Lake Balaton at the end of camp; in any case, a 5 day trip around Hungary with free board and lodging and travel expenses is the traditional post-camp reward. Camps are normally organised in July and last for 2-3 weeks. UK applicants should contact one of the following, and must attend a preliminary briefing by the Quakers and IVS:

International Voluntary Service, Ceresole House, 53 Regent Rd, Leicester LE1 6YL (☎ Leicester 541862).

Quaker Work Camps, Friends House, Euston Rd, London NW1 2BJ (☎ 01-387-3601).

United Nations Association, Welsh Centre for International Affairs, Temple of Peace, Cathays Park, Cardiff CF1 3AP (☎ Cardiff 28549).

Applicants outside the UK should contact *MIOT*, 1388, Budapest PO Box 72, Kun Béla Rakpart 37-38 (☎ 403-974).

Being keen to make known their cultural acheivements, build bridges across a divided continent and earn foreign exchange, the Hungarians also organise a host of **summer courses**, covering everything from enviromental studies to folk art. Full details are contained in a booklet published each year in the spring, which can be obtained by writing to the Society for the Dissemination of Scientific Knowledge, H-1088 Budapest, VIII Bródy Sándor u. 16. The deadline for most applications is May 1, so it's advisable to write some months in advance. Students are of all ages and come from countries as diverse as Vietnam, Switzerland and Venezuela, so the chance to meet people is as much an attraction as the subjects being studied. These include *photography* (at Vác), *Hungarian language and culture* (Debrecen), *fine arts* (Zebegény, see p.106), *Esperanto* (Gyula), *Baroque recorder music* (Sopron), *jazz* (Tatabánya), *orchestral music* (Pécs and Kecskemét), *music-teaching by the Kodály method* (Esztergom and Kecskemét), folk art (Zalaegerszeg) and *nature studies* (Keszthely). Fees include board and lodging and various excursions and entertainments.

UK citizens applying for the Debrecen language course may be able to get financial help from the **British Council** (Scholarships Department, 10 Spring Gardens, London SW1A 2BN; ☎ 01-930-8466) if they apply before February 26.

OTHER THINGS

ADDRESSES in Budapest begin with the city district in Roman numerals – XII, Hunyadi utca 4 – which is also expressed by the middle two digits of the post code, eg. 1125. In the case of apartment blocks, the floor and flat number are also given: III/21 means flat 21 on the third floor. The most common abbreviation is *u.* for *utca* (street). *Út* or *útja* is an avenue.

BRING... any specific medication or spare parts that you're likely to need. Western magazines like *The Face* are much appreciated in trendy (*divatos*) circles. Passport-sized photos come in handy for season tickets, student cards etc. Imported camera film is quite expensive, and 127 and Polaroid unavailable.

CAMPERS should bring cartouches for Gaz stoves (unavailable here, or anywhere else in the Eastern bloc for that matter). Candles – *gyertya* – are sold in ABCs; buy lots if you're going on to Romania or Bulgaria, since they're hard to find there, or are so badly made that they won't burn.

CIGARETTES are sold in tobacconists (*dohánybolt*), ABCs, bars and restaurants. Marlboro is the most widely-available Western brand, but Hungarian brands are much cheaper, which isn't suprising when you taste them. Rough *Symphonia* are probably the most popular cigarettes. Matches are called *gyufa*. *Tilos a dohányzás* means 'no smoking', and applies to the Metro, all buses, trams and trolleybuses.

CHILDREN (*gyerekek*) qualify for reductions on most forms of public transport (see 'Getting Around'), and 50% off the cost of camping up to the age of 14. Separate visas aren't required for children under 14 who are included on their parent's passport. The best facilities and entertainments for kids are in Budapest and the Balaton resorts. Children are forbidden to ride in the front seat of a car.

CONTRACEPTIVES *Fogamzásgátló* are available from pharmacies in the form of condoms; contraceptive pills (issued on prescription) come from the USSR or East Germany, and have worse side-effects that their Western equivalents.

ELECTRIC POWER 220 volts. Round, 2-pin plugs are used.

GAYLIFE Cruising and known gay-haunts are confined to Budapest, and social pressures ensure that most homosexuals remain closeted. The age of consent is 18 for gays and lesbians, but public displays of affection invite police hassle.

There's no gay movement, and the emergence of one seems highly unlikely.

LAUNDRY Laundrettes (*mosoda*) are rare, while at *Patyolat* you're unlikely to have your washing or dry-cleaned garments back in less than 48 hours. All supermarkets sell washing powder.

NATURISM is officially allowed only on segregated terraces (eg. on Margit Island), in the naturists' haven outside Budapest, and in the garden of 'farmstead accommodation'. However, a fair number of women do get away with going topless around the Balaton and on certain campsites – there's safety in numbers it seems.

SHOPS AND SUPERMARKETS In larger towns, shops are usually open from 9am-7pm (8pm on Thursdays) during the week; on Saturdays until midday or 5pm. On Sundays and holidays, selected restaurants and espressos sell milk, bread and pastries. Supermarkets are called ABC, while most department stores belong to the Centrum chain. Otherwise, shops are named after their speciality: eg. *húsbolt* = a butchers; *italbolt* = an off-licence; *papírírószerbolt* = a stationers (also selling toilet paper!).

SURNAMES When writing names, referring to people or making formal introductions, Hungarians *always* put the surname first. Since this thoroughly confuses foreigners, names of historical personages are rendered conventionally in this book – eg. Lajos Kossuth rather than Kossuth Lajos (Hungarian-style).

TAMPAX Try pharmacies for *tampon* or sanitary towels (*egészségügyi betét*).

TIME 1 hour ahead of GMT; plus 1 hour during summer time (from the end of March to the end of September).

HUNGARIAN TERMS: A GLOSSARY

ABC national chain of supermarkets.

ALFÖLD plain; it usually means the Great Plain (*Nagy Alföld*) rather than the Little Plain (*Kisalföld*) in north-western Hungary.

ÁLLATKERT zoo.

ÁVO (*Államvedelmi Osztály*) the dreaded secret police of the Rákosi era; later renamed the ÁVH and considerably reduced in power.

BARLANG cave; the most impressive stalactite caves are in the Aggteleki karst region.

BELVÁROS inner town or city; most

typically characterised by Baroque architecture.

CALVINIST the Reformed (*Református*) faith, which established itself in Hungary during the C16.

CASTRUM (Latin) a Roman fortification.

CIGÁNY Gypsy (in the Hungarian language); hence *Cigánytelep*, a Gypsy settlement; and *Cigányzene*, Gypsy music.

CSÁRDA inn; nowadays, a restaurant with rustic decor.

CSÁRDÁS traditional, wild dance to violin music.

CSIKÓS *puszta* horse herdsman; a much romantised figure of the C19.

DOMB hill; *Rózsadomb*, 'Rose Hill' in Budapest.

DJAMI or **DZAMI** mosque.

DUNA the River Danube.

ERDÉLY Transylvania; for centuries a part of Hungary, its loss to Romania in 1920 still rankles.

ERDŐ forest, wood.

FALU village;

FALUKUTATÓ 'Village Explorers' who investigated rural life and pressed for reforms in the countryside during the 1930s.

FŐ UTCA mainstreet.

FORRÁS natural spring.

FÜRDŐ public baths, often fed by thermal springs.

GYÓGYFÜRDŐ mineral baths with therapeutic properties.

HAJDÚK cattle-drovers turned outlaws, who later settled near Debrecen in the HAJDÚSÁG region.

HAJÓÁLLOMÁS boat landing stage.

HÁZ house.

HEGY hill or low mountain (pl. HEGYSÉG).

HÍD bridge; *Lánchíd*, the 'Chain Bridge' in Budapest.

HONVÉD Hungarian army.

ISKOLA school.

ITALBOLT 'drink shop', or a village bar.

KÁPOLNA chapel.

KAPU gate.

KASTÉLY fortified manor or small castle.

KERT garden, park.

KÖRÚT boulevard. Some cities have semicircular 'Great' and 'Small' boulevards (**NAGYKÖRÚT** and **KISKÖRÚT**) surrounding their Belváros.

KÖZ alley, lane; also used to define geographical regions, eg. the 'Mud land' (*Sárköz*) bordering the Danube.

KÚT well or fountain.

LÉPCSŐ alley with steps ascending a hillside.

LIGET grove, wood.

LIMES (Latin) fortifications along the Danube, marking the limit of imperial Roman territory.

LOVARDA riding school.

MAGYAR Hungarian (pronounced '*Modyor*'). Also **MAGYARORSZÁG**, Hungary.

MEGÁLLÓ a railway halt or bus stop.

MEGYE county; originally established by István I to extend his authority over the Magyar tribes.

MIRHAB prayer niche in a mosque, indicating the direction of Mecca.

MSzMP (*Magyar Szocialista Munkáspárt*) the Hungarian Communist Party.

MŰEMLÉK historic monument, listed building.

MŰVELŐDESI HÁZ community arts and social centre; literally, a 'Culture House'.

NYILAS or 'Arrow Cross'; Hungarian fascist movement.

OTTOMANS founders of the Turkish empire, which included central Hungary during the C16-C17.

PALOTA palace; *Püspök-palota*, a Bishop's residence.

PÁLYAUDVAR (*pu.*) bus or train station in a town – usually the main one.

PIAC outdoor market.

PINCE cellar; a **BOR-PINCE** contains and serves wine.

PUSZTA another name for the Great Plain, coined when the region was a wilderness.

RAKPART embankment or quay.

ROM ruined building; sometimes set in a garden with stonework finds, a **ROMKERT**

STRAND beach, or any area for sunbathing or swimming.

SZIGET island.

TANÁCS council; also **TANÁCSKÖZTÁRSASÁG**, the 'Republic of Councils' or Soviets, which ruled Hungary in 1919.

TEMETŐ cemetery.

TEMPLOM church.

TÉR square; **TERE** in the possessive case, as in *Hősök tere*, 'Square of the Heroes'.

TEREM hall.

TÓ lake.

TORONY tower.

TÜRBE tomb or mausoleum of a Muslim dignitary.

UTCA (*u.*) road or street.

ÚT Avenue; in the possessive case, **ÚTJA** – eg Vörös *Hadserég útja*, 'Avenue of the Red Army'.

VÁR castle.

VÁROS town; may be divided into an inner Belváros, a lower-lying *Alsóváros* and a modern *Újváros* section. Also **VÁROSKÖZPONT**, the town centre.

VÁSÁRCSARNOK market hall.

VASÚTÁLLOMÁS railway station.

VÖLGY valley; *Hűvösvölgy*, 'Cool Valley'.

ZSIDÓ Jew or Jewish.

ZSINAGÓGA synagogue.

HUNGARY
THE GUIDE

Chapter one
BUDAPEST

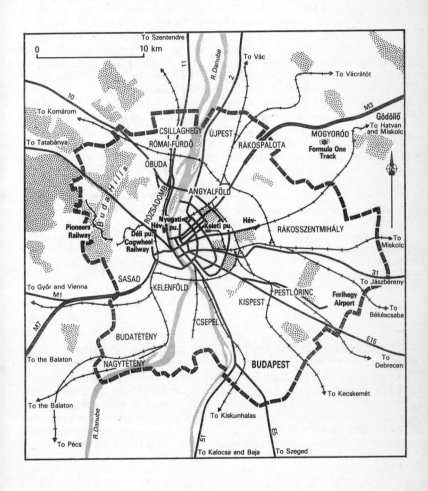

It's difficult to overestimate the importance of **Budapest** to Hungary, and no native of the city would appreciate being accused of doing so. Two million people – over a fifth of Hungary's population – live in the capital, and everything converges here: the roads and railways; flights to Ferihegy (the only civilian airport); opportunities, wealth and political power; industry, commerce and the black economy; state-approved cultural life, and the flourishing 'underground' alternative. Like Paris it has a tradition of revolutions – in 1848, 1918 and 1956; buildings, parks and avenues on a monumental scale; and a reputation for sophistication, hedonism and parochial pride – in short, a city worthy of comparison with other great European capitals.

Surveying the city from the embankments or the bastions of Castle Hill, it's obvious why Budapest was dubbed the 'Pearl of the Danube'. Its grand buildings and many bridges spanning the river look magnificent, especially when floodlit or illuminated by a barrage of fireworks launched from Gellért Hill on Constitution Day. The inner city and the long C19 boulevards suavely combine Western fashions and advertising with totems of Soviet political culture, yet remain distinctively Hungarian in character; for visitors, highlighted by the billboards and signs in the Magyar language, with vowels bristling accents and bizarre series of consonants.

Through a combination of politics and geography Budapest is probably the main point of contact between contemporary East and West; visited by millions of tourists from each side of the post-war European cleavage, who, when added together, actually outnumber the city's inhabitants. Budapest has a surfeit of fine sights, museums and galleries; and while nightlife isn't quite as scintillating as in most west European capitals it's almost always affordable. Restaurants are cheap and abundant and there's a wide variety of entertainments, generally well-publicised by the tourist board and easy to reach using Budapest's excellent public transport system. Since people rise early the city begins closing down at 10pm, so at least you'll be full of beans during the daytime when residents interrupt their labours with frequent breaks in patisseries and *eszpresszó* bars, or a long wallow in one of the capital's famous Turkish baths.

Orientation, transport, rooms and information

Though it's never blue, the River Danube (*Duna*) determines basic **orientation**: Buda occupies the west bank, and Pest the opposite side of the river. More precisely, one can refer to Budapest's 22 districts (*kerület*), designated on maps and street-signs by Roman numerals – eg. V, the Belváros or 'inner city'; I, the Castle district; III, Római-Fürdő etc. – a system also used for addresses, and in the following chapter. In crude terms, the Belváros is the 'city centre' (*centrum*) and the hub of Pest, while Castle Hill is the historic focal point of Buda.

Most **points of arrival** are only a mile or so from the centre, and the outlying ones are well linked by transportation. Coming from the West or Yugoslavia by rail, you're likely to arrive at *Keleti pu.* or *Déli pu.*, two of the city's three main **railway stations** which, like *Nyugati pu.*, are linked by underground Metro to Deák tér in the centre. Arriving at **Ferihegy airport**, simply board the half-hourly shuttle (price 30Ft) to the **Engels tér bus terminal** which adjoins Deák tér. Long-distance coaches from Vienna, Munich, Zagreb, London etc. also arrive here. The **Népstadion** bus terminal is further out but likewise on the Metro; while **hydrofoils** from Vienna dock right alongside the Belváros embankment. Anyone **driving into Budapest** merely follows the *centrum* signs, although you'd be wise to consult a map of the inner city one-way systems beforehand. For **guided tours of the city** see p.82.

Getting around

Running practically non-stop between 4.30am-11pm, the **Metro** is the easiest way of getting around and serves most places you're likely to want to reach. Its three lines intersect at Deák tér, and once you've learned to recognise the signs *bejárat*, *kijárat* and *felé* ('entrance', 'exit' and 'in the direction of'), it's difficult to get lost. There's a flat fare of 2Ft, and one ticket (which must be punched as you enter the station) allows up to one hour's travel on any line. These yellow **tickets** can also be used aboveground, where the same flat fare applies on **trolleybuses** (*trolibusz*), **trams** (*villamos*) and the **HÉV suburban railway** (until the city limits; beyond them, just punch additional tickets). They're available in strips from street vendors, tobacconists and – the worst for queueing – Metro stations; along with blue tickets (3Ft) for use on **buses** (*autóbusz*). **Children** travel free up to the age of six, and for half fare up to the age of ten.

If you're planning to stay awhile a **monthly pass** saves effort if not money; costing 170Ft and requiring a passport photo, passes are available from Metro and railway stations , and valid from the first day of the month to the fifth of the next. They can be used on anything but **night buses**; a skeleton service running from 11pm until dawn, when regular services begin. Red signboards and an 'E' after the route number on bus stops indicates **express buses** which stop less frequently. TOURINFORM and IBUSZ dispense booklets on public transport, and further **information** can be had by calling 178-080.

Taxis are cheap (8Ft basic, 7Ft per kilometre), albeit slightly dearer if privately owned (*magán*). Dial 222-222 or 666-666 for 24 hour service, or 188-888 to order in advance.

Accommodation

During high season it's difficult to get a room in the city's cheaper hotels (see below) without advance booking; so anyone hoping to pay less than £7 a night should consider private accommodation, a bed in a youth hostel or camping.

Private rooms are rented sight unseen, but with a map you can check their distance and accessibility from the centre, both as important as the amenities. The tourist board arranges 'official' private rooms – charging between 300-600Ft and 200-450Ft for a first or second class double; with single rooms ranging from 100-400Ft depending on their rating – so the station touts offering rooms in the region of 700-1,000Ft should be rejected. Note also that payment in hard currency is illegal, though frequently suggested, and is unlikely to save you money. Since anyone lodging 'unofficially' is obliged to register with the local police (*kerületi rendőrség*) within 48hrs, it's probably wiser to get a room **from the tourist office** rather than the private sector. Almost any IBUSZ or Budapest-tourist office will make bookings, though most travellers use the bureaux at the main stations and Ferihegy (open 8am-8pm); the hectic one above the Parisian arcade on Felszabadulás tér; or the **24-hour service** at 3, Petőfi tér on the embankment.

If the tourist offices are willing, use them to enquire about **hotels** on your behalf. Look through the *Hotel-Camping* booklet, which lists addresses, amenities and prices; then check out the ones you feel able to afford. Vacancies are easier to obtain in the morning, so if you're stuck with second-best for the night go hunting for something better the next day. It definitely helps to speak some German if you're calling on your own. On past showing, the following hotels should have double rooms for between £7-12.

Citadella (XI, Gellérthegy/☎ 665-794). Inside the fortress on Gellért Hill; circular corridors and tremendous views. It's essential to reserve the double rooms (550Ft) or beds in the dormitories (60Ft). Overpriced restaurant.

Lidó (III, Nánási u.67/☎ 886-865). No private showers. In the northern suburbs of Buda (bus #134 from Flórián tér to the door, or 10 minutes' walk from Római-Fürdő HÉV stop).

Strand fogadó (III, Pusztakúti út 3/☎ 671-999) A mile or so northwest, near the Csillaghegy HÉV stop and beside the Árpád baths. Sports facilities available.

Sport penzió (II, Szép juhászné út 9). In the Buda Hills near the Ságvárliget halt on the Pioneers' Railway (bus #22 from Moszkva tér).

Unikum penzió (XI, Bod Péter u.13). No singles. Take bus #8/#8A from Felszabadulás tér over to the Buda side; alight at Zolyomi út near the Sashegy (Eagle hill) and start walking.

Trio penzió (XI, Ördögorom u.10/☎ 865-742). Open from May 15 to October 15; no singles. Ten minutes' walk from the end of bus-line #8 in the Sasad district of Buda.

Hotel Saturnus (XIV, Pillangó u.10/☎ 421-789) A few blocks from the Népstadion (Metro line 3) in Pest's eastern suburb.

Depo fogadó (IV, Törökbálint Pf.3/☎ 263-388) Doubles only; in the Újpest district.

For about the same price you can have rooms in the *Express* (XI, Beethoven u.7-9/☎ 753-082) or *Ifjúság* (II, Zivitar u.1-3), two 'young peoples' hotels' run by the **Express Youth Travel Agency**, which has offices at the main stations and at nr.16, Szabadság tér. Express also makes bookings for **youth hostels** operating in college buildings during July-August; dormitory beds cost 40-80Ft and a student card is normally required. Sites change each year, but the Technological University south of Gellért Hill, and XII, Várna u.23, are probably safe bets. Other summer hostels (not run by Express) include: *Csúcshegy* (III, Menedékház u.122/☎ 686-015) and *Strand* (attached to the hotel of the same name).

If there's a group of you it might be worth considering **bungalows**, which can be rented at III, Nánási út 67 and on most **campsites**. The biggest campsites are *Római-Fürdő* (by the HÉV stop of the same name in Buda) and hilly *Hárshegyi* (bus #22 from Moszkva tér); and both sites are packed out during July and August. In the backstreets east of Római-Fürdő there's a smaller private site at Rozgonyi Piroska u.21 (with a few rooms for rent). You could also try your luck at *Feeburg kemping* (XII, Szilassy út 8, near the

Istenhegy halt of the cog-wheel railway) or *Tenisz kemping* (XVI, Csömöri út 222) out in the Rákosszentmihály suburb of Pest. If you're broke there's no point in angering the police by **sleeping rough** in parks or stations, since there's a legal place to doss in Pest's X district. You can reach it by taking Metro 2 to Örs vézer tere and then a bus #61 to the Jászberényi út bridge; but be warned that it's closed during the day, when anything left there is quite likely to be stolen.

Information, maps and contacts

Besides *Hotel-Camping* and the colour booklet on the public transport system, the most useful source of **practical information** is the *Budapest Guide*, detailing restaurants, museums, airlines, shops and services. All three are supplied freely by most tourist offices. In this chapter, see the Listings section for a variety of useful facts. Since IBUSZ bureaus are generally occupied with changing money, booking rooms and hiring cars, they rarely welcome inquirers; and if you want to get help with more esoteric requests or simply speak to someone in your own language, try **TOURINFORM** instead. Located at 17-19 Petőfi utca in the Belváros (open Monday-Saturday 8am-8pm, Sunday 8am-1pm/☎ 179-300), it's staffed by amazingly helpful polyglot women who can answer just about any serious question.

All tourist agencies can supply small free **maps** of the city, but for more precise details invest in the *Budapest Atlasz* – a combined A-Z and Yellow Pages available from bookshops (50Ft). A map showing **one-way systems** appears at the back of the Budapest Guide, while the Atlas crawls with spidery coloured lines denoting **bus and tram routes**.

Details of **what's on** appear in the monthly *Programme* magazine (available from IBUSZ), *Daily News* and other tourist publications; the Hungarian-language weekly *Pesti Műsor* provides fuller details, but you'll need a dictionary and patience to understand it. **'Unofficial' events** like avant garde music and cabaret are publicised through **contacts** or 'private advertising'. Certain clubs like the Young Artists' are frequented by *divatos* (trendy) types who might clue foreigners onto the latest sensation; while the uninitiated rely on **fly-posters** stuck around Felszabadulás tér and downtown subways, which advertise *zene* (music), *punk zene*, *New Wave Klub* and the like, giving details of time and place. Some notices are extremely cryptic – one puzzled a well-informed Hungarian friend for several minutes before he could crack the symbolic cipher and identify the group playing!

BUDA

Seen from the embankments, **BUDA** looks undeniably romantic; its palatial buildings, archaic spires and outsize statues rising from rugged hills. The image conceals mundaner aspects, for Buda isn't all precipices and palaces, but at times, in the right place, it can be appropriate. To experience Castle Hill at its quasi-medieval best, come in the early morning before the crowds arrive.

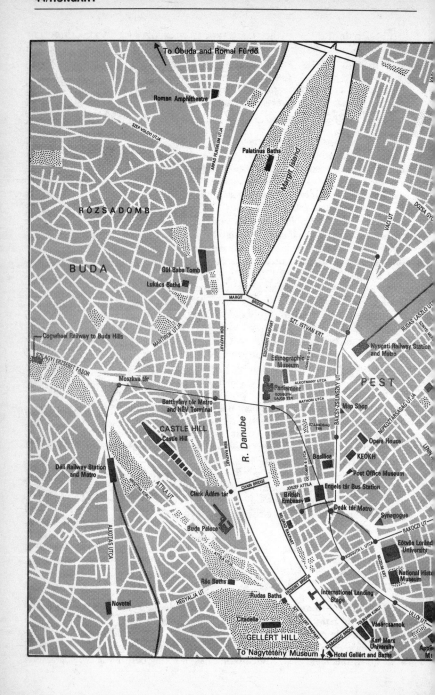

To Óbuda and Romai Fürdő

Roman Amphitheatre

SZEP VOLGYI UTJA

ÁRPÁD FEJEDELEM UTJA

Palatinus Baths

Margit Island

RÓZSADOMB

BUDA

Gül Baba Tomb

Lukács Baths

MARGIT BRIDGE

Cogwheel Railway to Buda Hills

SZILAGYI ERZSEBET FASOR

MARTIROK UTJA

BEM RAKPART

SZECHENYI RAKPART

SZT. ISTVÁN KRT.

RUDAS LASZLO UT

SZENTE UT

Nyugati Railway Station and Metro

Moszkva tér

Ethnographic Museum

Parliament

ALKOTMANY UTCA

KOSSUTH LAJOS TER

BATHORI UTCA

BAJCSY-ZSILINSZKY UT

PEST

Batthyány tér Metro and HÉV Terminal

CASTLE HILL

Castle Hill

SZABADSAG TER

Map Shop

NEPKOZTARSASAG UTJA

Opera House

R. Danube

KEOKH

Déli Railway Station and Metro

BEM RAKPART

OCTBER U

Basilica

Post Office Museum

ATTILA UT

PAULER UTCA

CHAIN BRIDGE

JOZSEF ATTILA

Engels tér Bus Station

Clark Ádám tér

British Embassy

Deák tér Metro

Synagogue

ALKOTAS UTCA

BELGRAD RAKPART

Buda Palace

RAKOCZI UT

ATTILA UT

Eötvös Loránd University

KOSSUTH UTCA

MUZEUM KRT

National History Museum

Rác Baths

HEGYALJA UT

ERZSEBET BRIDGE

International Landing Stage

ULLOI UT

Novotel

Rudas Baths

SZT GELLERT RAKPART

Vásárcsarnok

Citadella

SZABADSAG BRIDGE

TO BURN KORUT

Karl Marx University

Apple M...

GELLÉRT HILL

To Nagytétény Museum

Hotel Gellért and Baths

BUDAPEST

●━━● Metro line and station

THOKOLY UT

HUNGARIA KORUT

NAGY LAJOS KIRALY UT

Funfair

Circus

Zoo

NEPKOZTARSASAG UTJA

HUNGARIA KORUT

Petőfi Csarnok

THOKOLY UT

NAGY LAJOS KIRALY UT

Arts Museum

Millenial Monument

Műcsarnok

Vajdahunyad Castle

East Asia Museum

Városliget

DOZSA GYORGY UT

China Museum

Theatre

HUNGARIA KORUT

THOKOLY UT

KEREPESI UT

ROTTENBILLER UTCA

Keleti Railway Station

KEREPESI UT

+ + + + + +
+ + + + + +
+ + + + + +
+ Kerepesi Cemetery +
+ + + + + +
+ + + + + +
+ + + + + +

JOZSEF KORUT

ák (Hospitals)

KOBANYAI UT

To Népliget and
Ferihegy Airport

HUNGARIA KORUT

KOBANYAI UT

Then you can beat them to the museums; wander off for lunch or a Turkish bath, and return to catch street-life in full flight during the afternoon. Most parts of the Hill lapse back into tranquility around dusk, leaving the views to lingering couples. The outlying Buda Hills – accessible by chair lift and the children's Pioneer Railway – are obviously less-visited during the week; while Gellért Hill, the Rózsadomb and assorted Roman remains can be seen any time the weather's fine, unless you'd rather sunbathe or have a dip in Buda's swimming baths. On the practical front, Buda has a large campsite on its northern outskirts, and two useful railway stations. Trains for the Balaton and Transdanubia depart from Déli station (Metro line 2), while regular HÉV services from Batthyány tér enable one to reach Szentendre (p.94) within an hour.

Castle Hill

CASTLE HILL (*Várhegy*) is Buda's most prominent feature, a plateau one mile long laden with bastions, old mansions and a huge palace, commanding the Watertown. Its grandiosity and strategic utility have long gone hand in hand: Hungarian kings built their palaces here because it was easy to defend; a fact appreciated by the Turks, Habsburgs, Nazis and other occupiers. An oft-battered legacy of bygone Magyar glories, it's been almost wholly reconstructed from the rubble of 1945, when Germans and Russians fought over the hill while Buda's inhabitants hid underground, subsisting on cats and scavenged horseflesh. Since then its decorative aspect has prevailed, and barring a few fortunate diplomats resident on the Hill, the Castle district is no longer involved in politics.

Though it's possible to ride all the way there by bus #16 from Engels tér in Pest, the majority of **approaches** begin from Buda. The most fun is to travel by *sikló*, a kind of miniature railway with C19 carriages which runs from Clark Ádám tér at the western end of the Chain Bridge up to Buda Palace. Approaching on foot, the Chain Bridge, 'kilometre zero' and the Metro stations at Batthyány tér and Moszkva tér (on line 2) are all feasible starting points, although Déli station is rather distant. Batthyány tér is perhaps the best of these: follow Fő utca southwards through the Watertown, and then one of several steep backstreets and stairways (*lepcső*) which lead up to the Fishermen's Bastion, giving access to Trinity Square – the heart of the Castle district.

Trinity Square, the Mátyás Church and the Fishermen's Bastion
By midday **Trinity Square** (*Szentháromság tér*) is crammed with tourists, mime artists and other entrepreneurs; a multilingual spectacle played out against the fantastic backdrop of the Fishermen's Bastion, with the wildly asymetrical **Mátyás Church** (*Mátyás templom*) occupying centre stage and stealing the show. Popularly known after 'good king Matthias' but officially dedicated to Our Lady, the building is neo-Gothic run riot, with its brashly tiled roof and a multitude of toothy spires. Built in the C19, it's a superb recreation of the medieval spirit by *Frigyes Schulek*, grafted onto such portions of the original C13 church as survived the siege of 1686. Prior to that

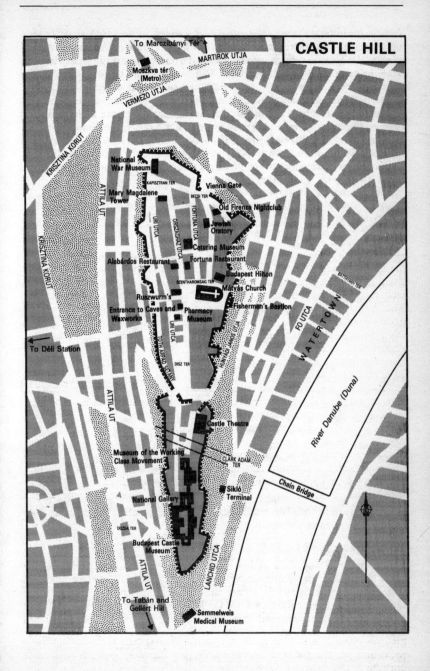

CASTLE HILL

To Marczibányi Tér

MARTIROK UTJA

Moszkva tér
(Metro)

VERMEZO UTJA

KRISZTINA KORUT

ATTILA UT

KRISZTINA KORUT

National
War Museum

KAPISZTRAN TER

Mary Magdalene
Tower

Vienna Gate

BECSI TER

URI UTCA

ORSZAGHAZ UTCA

FORTUNA UTCA

Old Firenza Nightclub

Jewish
Oratory

Catering Museum

Alabardos Restaurant

Fortuna Restaurant

SZENTHAROMSAG TER

Budapest Hilton

Ruszwurm's

Mátyás Church

Entrance to Caves and
Waxworks

Pharmacy
Museum

Fishermen's Bastion

URI UTCA

BATTHYANY TER

FO UTCA

WATERTOWN

To Déli Station

TOTH ARPAD SETANY

HUNTADI JANOS UTCA

DISZ TER

ATTILA UT

River Danube (Duna)

Castle Theatre

Museum of the Working
Class Movement

CLARK ADAM
TER

Chain Bridge

Sikló
Terminal

National Gallery

DOZSA TER

LANCHID UTCA

Budapest Castle
Museum

ATTILA UT

To Tabán and
Gellért Hill

Semmelweis
Medical Museum

date the building was a mosque, the *Büyük Dzjami*, whose Turkish occupants whitewashed over the religious murals – so there's more than a hint of malice in one C19 fresco, which depicts Mátyás's father Hunyadi trouncing the Turks at Belgrade in 1456. It's almost lost amidst the richness of the interior: painted leaves, animals and geometric motifs run up columns and under vaulting, while shafts of light fall through rose windows on to gilded altars and statues with stunning effect. Specific sights include the *Loreto Chapel* beneath the tallest tower, various treasures in the crypt, and the iron-barred tomb of Béla III, who built the first proper palace on the hill. Though the medieval kings were crowned at Székesfehérvár (where Béla's tomb was discovered) a prior appearance at the church in Buda became customary – hence another nickname, the 'Coronation Church'.

In days gone by, the name day of Hungary's patron saint and first monarch Stephen (*István*) was celebrated here with a display of his 'black mummified hand' and other holy relics, accompanied by a heraldic pageant. An equestrian statue of **King Stephen** stands just outside the church, commemorating this ruler who openly embraced Christianity, sought the Pope's recognition and enforced Catholicism on his subjects, thus aligning Hungary with the culture of western Europe; a stern authoritarian who didn't hesitate to put rebels, pagans and apostates to the sword. Much is made of this in the **Son et Lumière performances** staged in the church several evenings a week during July and August (buy tickets from the door in advance), but the 'history of Hungary in lights and music' doesn't fully utilise the building's potential, and the commentary (assuming you attend a show in the right foreign language) sounds rather naff.

The **Fishermen's Bastion** (*Halászbástya*) nearby is an undulating white rampart with gargoyly cloisters and slender turrets, which frames the view of Parliament across the river as its designer intended. Although fishermen from the Watertown district reputedly defended this stretch of the ramparts during the Middle Ages, Schulek's structure is purely decorative in function. By day it's besieged by diverse hustlers: artists crayoning rapidly, countrywomen selling embroidery from Kalocsa (and, occasionally, from Transylvania), and illegal money-changers, skilled at sleight of hand. Like the tourists they're surreally reflected by the copper-glass façade of the *Budapest Hilton*. This incorporates chunks of a C13 monastery and a select clientele which lounges in the courtyard anticipating candle-lit dinners in the *Halászbástya* bar. If you lack the brass to join them, outdoor performances of chamber music (see nearby noticeboards for details) are free.

Streets and caves

Though the Hill's appearance has changed much since building began in the C13, Uri utca, Fortuna utca and Országház utca still follow their medieval courses, with ancient niches, arches and stone-carvings outcropped amongst the Baroque houses of the C18-C19. Diplomats and institutions occupy many of the old, brightly painted dwellings; others have been converted into 'authentic Hungarian restaurants' with vaulted cellars and prices putting them beyond the average Magyar's pocket; and Buda's oldest inn, the *Red Hedgehog* on Hess András tér, has become a private residence. Practically every building displays a *Műemlék* plaque giving details of its history and notable past occupants. András Hess operated Hungary's first printing press on the premises of today's *Fortuna* restaurant, while Beethoven stayed at nr.7 on **Táncsics utca**, next door to the former prison where Lajos Kossuth and the writer Mihály Táncsics were once held for nationalist agitation, from which Táncsics was sprung in 1848 by revolutionaries. The street was predominantly inhabited by Jews during the Middle Ages (when Italians, Germans and French congregated in neighbouring quarters), and at nr.26 the **Jewish Oratory** displays artefacts and gravestones from that era (open from April to October: Tuesday-Friday 10am-2pm/weekends 10am-6pm). A fuller picture of their history emerges at the National Jewish Museum in Pest.

One block away you'll find **Fortuna utca**, named after the medieval inn at nr.4 which now contains the **Museum of Catering**. Here blackened *gulyás* cauldrons and a fearsome array of spits and cleavers mark the slow evolution of Hungarian cookery from *bográcsgulyás* – the communal stew of the Magyar nomads – to the present day. During the Turkish occupation (1541-1686) the Hill's main thoroughfare – now called **Országház utca** (Parliament Street) – was the 'street of the baths', *Hamam Yolu*. The Ottoman chronicler Tselebi noted numerous caravanserai, 34 mosques, 4 *djami*, 3 Dervish monasteries and over 100 tanneries in the Castle district, all of which have long vanished. However, medieval architectural features have survived at nrs.18, 20 & 22, the *Alabárdos* restaurant and nr.9 (which incorporates niches with 'lily-ended' traceries), while at the north end of the street the **Mary Magdalene Tower** still dominates Kapisztrán tér despite being in the throes of restoration. The square adjoins Bécsi Kapu tér and gets its name from a statue of *John Capistranus*, a fiery preacher who exhorted Hunyadi's troops to victory at the siege of Belgrade.

On an equally martial note, gun-toting conscripts guard the National Archives on Bécsi Kapu tér, known as the 'Saturday' (market) square before its devastation in 1686. Given a new and sombre cast in the C18, it was renamed after the chunky **Vienna Gate** (*Bécsi Kapu*), which leads downhill to Moszkva tér. Around the corner on the Tóth Árpád promenade (offering a nice view of Buda's western districts), the soldiers' off-duty comrades can be found rather the worse for booze, lost in contemplation of the sights of the **National War Museum**. Casefuls of rifles and bayonets and a courtyard lumbered with armoured vehicles are the closest this museum comes to the reality of war; upstairs, the brilliantly coloured C19 hussars' uniforms and revolutionary banners merely highlight its 'romantic' image.

Uri utca (Gentlemen's Street) has a plethora of medieval stonework sunk into its buildings, but the main attraction is underground. During the Middle Ages galleries almost 10km long were tunnelled between cavities and fissures in the bedrock and wells were dug, creating a network of **caves beneath the hill** to serve as shelters during wartime. These housed a makeshift hospital during the winter of 1944-45, and could be reached from one of the 'safe houses' sheltering Jews from the Nazis. In recent years a group of ex-students have opened an **underground waxworks** down there, which one enters at nr.9 (Tuesday-Sunday 10am-6pm). The tableaux are incredibly gory and distinctly sub-Tussauds, while the restaurant and bar haven't gelled and attracted the kind of clientele necessary for the place to fufill its potential as a **club** (although this may yet happen – check it out).

For a snack with snob value visitors favour **Ruszwurm's** *cukrászda*, founded a stone's throw west of Trinity Square in 1827. The patisserie's products are delicious and the decor is properly chintzy, but Ruszwurm's is too cramped and frenetic to make you want to linger over a strudel. To the south of Trinity Square the street widens as it approaches the palace, as if to presage grandeur. Named Tárnok utca after the royal treasurers formerly resident here, its C19 inhabitants impressed John Paget with their 'sedateness of air, and not unfrequently a pompous vacancy of expression'. Visitors can marvel at dubious medieval pharmacopoeia and wince at C18 instruments for eviscerating and expurgating, displayed in the **Pharmacy Museum** (once the *Golden Eagle* apothecary); which might once have been applied to revellers who'd over-indulged at the *Arany Hordó*. This restaurant is one of the few buildings on the Hill to have kept its original *sgraffiti* – a bold red and orange checkerboard pattern covering the building's exterior. Tarnok utca ends in Dísz tér, where hussars once paraded (a custom recently revived for Constitution Day), and from here onwards ramparts and gateways buttress the hillside and control access to the palace grounds. On one's left stands the **Castle Theatre** where Beethoven performed in 1808, while straight ahead lies the charred hulk of the old Premier's residence, the last outbuilding of the palace complex still to be restored.

Buda Palace

As befits a former royal residence the lineage of the *Budavári Palota* can be traced back to medieval times, and the rise and fall of various palaces on the Hill is practically symbolic of the fortunes of the Hungarian state. The earliest fortifications and dwellings hastily ordered by Béla III after the C13 Mongol invasion were replaced by ever more luxurious palaces occupied by the Angevin kings, who ruled in more prosperous and stable times. The zenith was attained by the palace of Mátyás Corvinus (1458-90), a Renaissance extravaganza to which European artists and scholars were drawn by the blandishments of Queen Beatrix and the prospect of lavish hospitality. The Turkish occupation – ended by a three month siege – left this in ruins, which the Austrian Habsburgs, Hungary's new rulers, levelled to build a palace of their own. From Maria Theresa's modest beginnings (a mere 203 rooms, which she never saw completed), the **Royal Palace** expanded inexorably throughout the C19; though no monarch ever dwelt here, only the Habsburg viceroy or Palatine. After the collapse of the empire Admiral Miklós Horthy inhabited the building with all the pomp of monarchy until being deposed by a German coup in October 1944, not long before the prolonged siege (lasting until February 1945) which once again resulted in total devastation.

Reconstruction work began in the 1950s and is virtually complete. Grouped around two courtyards, the sombre wings of the Palace contain a clutch of museums and portions of the medieval structures discovered in the course of excavation – too much to see in one day unless you give it an unfairly cursory inspection. In any case frequent bouts on the grand terrace overlooking the river are essential if you want to avoid a bad case of historical overload.

The **Museum of the Working Class Movement** in the northern wing gets into its stride after a slow start on feudalism. The iniquities of capitalist Hungary are vividly portrayed alongside relics of the revolutionary struggle: reconstructed prison cells and evictions; agitprop and Red Guard brassards from 1919. Compare the savage political cartoons of the Horthy era with the bland coverage of the 1956 'counter-revolutionary revolt'. According to the catalogue (available in the foyer), the Uprising was a reaction to the 'bureaucratic, administrative methods' of the Rákosi regime – in plain language, dictatorship and torture – formented by the CIA and 'its mouthpiece Radio Free Europe', which persuaded the insurgents that military aid would be forthcoming when, in fact, the US government had no intention of sending any. Revealing *temporary exhibitions* sometimes turn up on the ground floor. I saw one from Romania entirely devoted to the glorification of Comrade Ceauşescu, and a photographic history of the Czech CP omitting any mention of Dubček, the 'Prague Spring' and the 1968 Warsaw Pact invasion. . .

The **National Gallery** occupying the central and southern wings contains Hungarian art since the Middle Ages. In the main building Gothic stone-carvings, altars and painted panels fill the ground floor, while C19 painting dominates the floor above. **Hungarian painting** really woke up in the 1880s, generating vigorous 'schools' which are well represented here: genre painters; *plein air* painters like Pál Szinyei Merse; the *Barbizon group*; portraitists such as Miklós Barabás; and the dominant school of historical painting led by Lotz, Székely, Madarász and Benczúr. The *Nagybánya Artists' Colony* founded in 1896 opposed all this academic art and made a big impact, securing them an entire floor in the museum alongside *József Rippl-Rónai*, the chief exponent of Hungarian Art Nouveau. The Baroque paintings and ecclesiastical sculptures in the southern wing were mainly confiscated from private collections, and for me at least were less appealing than the **children's section** on the top floor of the main building where, twice a week, some of Hungary's leading artists and performers participate in playgroups and impart their skills.

Outside, beyond the ornate fountain where King Mátyás disports himself amongst his hunting dogs, the treasures and vaults of the **Castle Museum** await visitors on the far side of the Lion Courtyard. Much of it is underground, in the marbled and flagstoned halls of the Renaissance palace (unearthed when rubble was sifted to a depth of 30 metres, and deftly incorporated into the reconstructed C19 buildings). Jewelled robes and banqueting ware, near-lifesize statues of knights and ladies, and carvings from the same rich red marble as used at Visegrád and Esztergom attest to the court's former splendour. In the *Renaissance Room* are relief portraits of Mátyás and Beatrix (whose coat of arms decorates the *Beatrix Courtyard* outside). Upstairs another exhibition – **Two Thousand Years of Budapest** – shows the evolution of Pest, Buda and Óbuda by means of old prints, ceramics and other artefacts. If you want explanations, though, a catalogue is absolutely essential, since captions are in Hungarian only (as is the case in all the Palace museums).

Once terraced with vineyards, the southern end of the Hill supports a maze of paths, ramparts and promenades, guarded by the **Mace Tower** and the

Lihegő Gate leading into the Round Bastion. From 1961 until its closure in 1984, the **Youth Park** (*Ifjúsági Park*) on the hillside overlooking the embankment played a vital role in Hungarian pop culture, since practically every band of note either played here or aspired to do so. (Action has now shifted to the *Petőfi csarnok* in Pest, see p.83). From here you can either backtrack through the Watertown, or head south across what was once the Tabán district towards Gellért Hill, one of the city's landmarks.

Gellért Hill, the Baths and the Watertown district

Tabán, formerly Buda's artisan quarter, has been practically eliminated by urban redevelopment, and barring the Semmelweiss Museum (p.70) there's nothing to detain one here. Between the terraced lawns beyond, flyovers leading to Hegyalja út and the traffic pouring off the Erzsébet Bridge make a formidable obstacle – but press on, for liberation is in sight.

Or almost literally so, because from Tabán or the embankment you can't fail to see the vast Liberation Monument crowning the summit of **GELLÉRT HILL**. A craggy dolomite cliff rearing some 130 metres above the stone-faced quays, the *Gellérthegy* is named after Bishop Ghirardus, who converted pagan Magyars to Christianity at the behest of King Stephen. A statue of **St Gellért** bestrides a waterfall facing the Erzsébet Bridge, marking the spot where he was murdered in 1064 – strapped to a barrow and toppled over the cliff by vengeful heathens following the demise of his royal protector. It's a short walk from Gellért's statue to Buda's oldest Turkish baths and the illustrious *Hotel Gellért* (see below), but I'd advise climbing the hill first, since the view from its summit is magnificent. One can reach the top by bus #27, leaving from Móricz Zs. körtér behind Gellért Hill, although anyone approaching from the embankment or the Castle district will find that walking up saves time, if not effort. The **panoramic view** of Budapest makes it all worthwhile: drawing the eye slowly along the curving river; past bridges and the monumental landmarks on either side of the Danube, beyond which stand the Buda Hills and Pest's suburbs merging hazily with the distant plain.

Every year on August 20, an amazing barrage of **fireworks** is launched from the hilltop **Citadella**; a low fortress built by the Habsburgs to cow Budapest's population with its guns in the aftermath of the 1848-49 revolution. When the 'Compromise' with the Habsburgs was reached in 1867, citizens breached the Citadella's walls to affirm that it no longer posed a threat to them; and nowadays the fort contains nothing more sinister than a few exhibits, a **tourist hostel** and an overpriced restaurant. By entering through the gate marked 'hotel' rather than the one labelled 'Citadella Museum', you can gain free admission to the fortress and get a slightly different perspective on the Liberation Monument, which is too large to be properly appreciated when you stand directly below it.

Poised atop the Citadella, the **Liberation Monument** thrusts over 100ft into the sky; a stark female figure holding aloft the palm of victory with Red Armymen posed belicosely around its base; mandatory viewing for Soviet tour groups which begin arriving here at 7am. The monument officially honours

Soviet soldiers killed liberating Budapest from the Germans and *Nyilas* (Hungarian Nazis), although its history, not to mention the truth of 'liberation' itself, rather differed from the version publicised today. Originally commissioned by Admiral Horthy, a reluctant ally of the Reich, in memory of his own son, the statue was adapted to suit the requirements of Hungary's Soviet liberators by its designer, *Zsigmond Kisfaludi-Strobl*. Much patronised by pre-war high society, he thereafter produced 'Proletarian Art' for new masters and continued to prosper, known derisively as 'Kisfaludi-Strébel' by his compatriots (*strébel* means 'to climb' or 'step from side to side'). Peoples' initial joy at being rid of the Nazis was rapidly dispelled as the Red Army raped and looted its way across Hungary. Once Communist rule became entrenched, mention of the very word rape was forbidden in the media; and a protest delegation of writers received a chilling rebuff from the Party leader, Rákosi. 'What is there to write about? In Hungary there are, say, 3,000 villages. Supposing the Russians violated, say, three women in every village. 9,000 in all. Is that so much? You writers have no idea of the law of large numbers'.

Descending the hillside through the playgrounds of Jubileumi Park, you'll see rough-hewn stone figures seemingly writhing from the massive portal of the **Gellért baths**, adjoining the **Hotel Gellért**. Since bathing details are given on page 71, suffice it to say that the hotel has now been restored to the peak of Art Nouveau perfection attained before 1920, when it was comandeered by Admiral Horthy after his triumphal entry into 'sinful Budapest' riding a white charger. Further to the south, sprawling along the embankment, you'll see the **Technological University** (*Mǔszaki Egyetem*). The halls of residence near the Petőfi Bridge serve as a **tourist hostel** during the summer vacation, while during term time the students' union organises **concerts and discos** in the E-**klub** and R-**klub** (named after the blocks in which they can be found).

Near the Erzsébet bridgehead, puffs of steam and cute little cupolas surmount the *Rudas baths* (*Gyogyfürdő*), an otherwise outwardly undistin-guished building. Since it's for men only, women will have to miss out on Budapest's most atmospheric Turkish baths, the interior of which has hardly changed since it was constructed in 1556 on the orders of Pasha Sokoli Mustapha. Bathers wallow in an octagonal stone pool beneath a vaulted ceiling, idly watching other men or the steam billowing around the shadowy recesses leading away from the pool. On the other side of the Hegyalja út flyover, women have exclusive rights to the **Rác baths**, which were also built during the Turkish occupation but have retained less of the original architecture. More details of both baths appear on page 71.

The Watertown, the Chain Bridge and Batthyány tér

Having visited the abovementioned places, you'll already have seen something of the **WATERTOWN** (*Víziváros*) district, a wedge of streets between Castle Hill and the Danube. Originally a poor quarter housing fishermen, craftsmen and their families, it became depopulated during the C17 save for a few 'Turkified Hungarians selling fruit', as the Mayor of Kassa noted in disgust, and gentrified when it was rebuilt in the C19. Today it's a reclusive neighbourhood of old blocks and mansions meeting at odd angles upon the hillside, reached by alleys which mostly consist of steps (*lépcső*) rising from the main street – Fő utca – below. The southern end of the Watertown is marked by 'Kilometre Zero' (a stone whence all distances from Budapest are measured), while its northern boundary is Batthyány tér (see below).

Just north of Kilometre Zero, the terminal of the *sikló* (p.46), Clark Ádam tér, handles the traffic to and from Budapest's best loved monument, the **Chain Bridge**. Designed by W.T. Clark and built under the direction of **Adam Clark** (a compatriot but no relation), it was opened in 1849 having barely escaped destruction during the revolution which fufilled the worst nightmares of the bridge's real instigator, Count **István Széchenyi** (1791-1860). A horse-fancying Anglophile with a passion for innovation, Széchenyi succeeded in making the nobility pay taxes to finance the building of the *Lánchíd*, overturning the ancient right of tax-exemption and establishing the precedent that the rich were bound to contribute to Hungary's development. Széchenyi died in an asylum having seen revolution and his worst political enemy, Kossuth, triumph; but Adam Clark married a Hungarian woman and settled happily in Budapest. He also built the tunnel under Castle Hill which, Budapesters joked, could be used to store the new bridge when it rained. An apocryphal story has it that the sculptor responsible for creating the bridge's four lions omitted to give them tongues, and then cast himself into the river overcome by shame.

Walking northwards along Fő utca through the Watertown you'll pass an old Capuchin Church (nr.30) featuring Turkish window arches; followed by the spikey polychrome-tiled church on Szilágyi tér. A block or so beyond one enters **Batthyány tér**, a square flanked by venerable old churches, generally busy during daytime with commuters and shoppers. From here one can catch bus #86 up to Flórián tér in Óbuda (see the following section), Metro line 2 to Pest or Déli station, or the suburban **HÉV train** out to Aquincum, Római-Fürdő and Szentendre. The supermarket on Batthyány tér stays open late somedays, while the wine bar next door has a pleasant patio where you can order draught beer until around 5pm. Continuing along Fő utca brings one to the **Király baths** situated near a crossroads; a contemporary of the Rác and Rudas bathhouses, distinguishable by its four copper cupolas shaped like tortoise shells, which admits men and women on alternate days (see p.71).

Fő utca finally ends on **Bem tér**, named after a Polish general who fought for the Hungarians in the 1849 war of independence. As the site of several famous **demonstrations**, its symbolic importance is known to students and police alike. It's here that crowds assembled singing patriotic songs in October 1956, prior to marching over the Danube to Parliament bearing Hungarian flags with the hammer and sickle cut from the centre, the prelude to the Uprising. In 1984 unoffical peace demonstrators joined the state-organised Peace March here, and two years later the police forcibly dispersed marchers protesting against the Nagymaros Dam (p.105) as they attempted to leave the square.

North of Castle Hill: Rózsadomb, Óbuda and some Roman remains

Moszkva tér, northwest of Castle Hill, is where to catch buses to the Buda Hills or Déli station, the Metro to Pest, and lead poisoning if you hang around too long. Aside from the flower-sellers and the *Trombitas-kert* restaurant across the road, there's little incentive to anyway. **Chess** fans gather under the elms to play all comers in **Városmajor Park**, not far from the terminal of the **cogwheel railway** to the Buda Hills (p.57); both of which are situated about 200m west along Szilágyi Erzsébet fasor. This avenue made news in May 1987, just before Budapest hosted the World Jewish Congress, when a **monument to Raoul Wallenberg** was unveiled here. Forsaking a playboy life in neutral Sweden, Wallenberg came to Budapest in 1944 armed with diplomatic immunity and money for bribing officials, determined to save Hungary's Jews from the death camps. Wallenberg and his assistants plucked thousands of Jews from the cattle trains and lodged them in 'safe houses' under Swedish diplomatic protection ('Look, there goes another Swede', Jews joked to each other); maneouvering to buy time until the Russians arrived. Shortly after they did, Wallenberg was arrested as a spy and vanished into the Gulag where his eventual fate remains unknown. A belated token of appreciation, the allegorical statue – representing the struggle against evil – reportedly received Kádár's backing; and was accompanied by a brief article in *Magyar Hirlap* acknowledging that Wallenberg's arrest had been a 'mistake'.

The Rózsadomb and Gül Baba's tomb

To the north of Moszkva tér a colourful **flower market** crams into the alleys behind Retek utca; while if you push up along Ezredes or Lövőház street you'll find Marczibányi tér, where a **craft market** is held on Sunday mornings. It's a good place **for children** too, with play equipment, mime artists and the Magyar equivalent of Punch & Judy shows. Despite the grim factories below Marczibányi tér and the smog-ridden Mártirok útja which dips around the meet the Margit Bridge, you're actually near to the **RÓZSADOMB** (Rose Hill), Budapest's swishest residential district. Few can afford even the smallest of flats here, while a list of the residents would read like a Hungarian *Who's Who*. Famous film directors, government ministers and top *funkcionárusok* live here, including János Kádár, the former leader of the Communist Party. (In the Rákosi era, VIP's homes often had secret exits – a precaution that paid off during the Uprising, when a few ÁVH bosses barely escaped lynching). Resident too is the writer György Konrád, whose flat is a meeting place for underground publishers, Magyar nationalists exiled from Transylvania and peace activists from both sides of divided Europe.

Tucked away in a hillside garden above Mecset u. (off Mártirok útja), the **tomb of Gül Baba** receives pilgrims from across the Muslim world. The small octagonal building is a shrine (*türbe*) to the 'Father of the Roses', an esteemed Dervish who dropped dead during a thanksgiving service in the Mátyás Church – then a mosque – under the eyes of the Sultan. Examples of calligraphy, carpets and Gül Baba's personal effects line the walls of the shrine, which appropriately stands in a rose garden (open from May 1 to October 31/Tuesday-Sunday 10am-6pm).

Óbuda

Slightly further afield, the district of **ÓBUDA** is actually the precursor of Budapest, contrary to the impression given by its old factories and new tower blocks, which hide such ancient ruins as remain. Its Roman founders built a legionary camp and a civilian town, Aquincum, which the Huns later took over and renamed Buda (supposedly in honour of Attila's brother). Under the first Hungarian dynasty, the Árpáds, Buda was an important town; but after the C14 the Castle district eclipsed it, and the original settlement became known as Óbuda (Old Buda). From beside the Margit Bridge you can catch a HÉV train to Aquincum (see below), zip up to the ruins on Flórián tér using bus #60 or #86, or walk northwards along the embankment for 10 minutes to reach the **Komjádi swimming pool**. This trains Hungary's Olympic swimmers and waterpolo players – Komjádi was a famous sportsman and coach – and, until a police raid in March 1986, used to be the main distribution point for underground (*samizdat*) literature. Twice a week in the buffet, Jenő Nagy would sell around 30 titles ranging from *1984* to Konrád's *The Loser*: products of ABC, Hungary's biggest *samizdat* printing house. From the pool one can catch tram #17 to Kolosy tér, whence there are buses (#65/#65A) to the *Pál-völgyi stalactite caves* (see p.57).

Roman remains

Óbuda has several Roman remains although the largest site, Aquincum, is in the Római-Fürdő district. The weed-choked crumbling **amphitheatre** at the junction of Nagyszombat and Korvin utca once covered a greater area than the Colosseum in Rome, and could seat 14-16,000 spectators. Further north along Korvin utca (bus #6/#84) one can see lovely but fragmented hunting murals in the **Camp Museum** at nr.63, which also displays sunken baths, a few sarcophagi and other relics of the legionary camp once sited around Flórián tér. There, graceful columns stand incongrously amidst a grassy plaza near the shopping centre, and large chunks of the old **military baths** and other stone finds are huddled beneath the Szentendrei út flyover. About ten minutes walk away, behind flat nrs.19-21 on Meggyfa utca, three blue canopies shelter the remains of the **Hercules villa**, so-called because of a fine C3 **mosaic floor** under the largest canopy. Depicting Hercules about to puke after excessive boozing in a wine festival, it was originally composed of some 60,000 stones, carefully selected and arranged in Alexandria and then shipped to Aquincum. Another mosiac shows the centaur Nessus abducting Deianeira, who Hercules had to rescue as one of his twelve tasks.

The legionary garrison of 6,000 spawned a settlement of camp-followers to the north which, over time, became a *Municipum* and later a *Colonia*, the provincial capital of Pannonia Inferior. The **ruins of Aquincum** lie a few kilometres north along the Szentendre road; easily visible from Aquincum station on the HÉV railway, and followed by the remains of an aquaduct and another ampitheatre near Római-Fürdő campsite and swimming pool. Enough foundation walls and underground piping survive to give a fair idea of the town's layout, although you'll need to pay a visit to the museum and use a fair degree of imagination to envisage how Aquincum might have looked during its heyday in the C2-C3. A great concourse of people filled the main street, doing business in the Forum and law courts (near the entrance), and steaming in public baths. Herbs and wine were burnt before altars in sanctuaries holy to the goddesses Epona and Fortuna Augusta, while fraternal societies met in the Collegiums and bath-houses further east. The **museum** contains oddments of the imperium – cake moulds, a bronze military diploma, buttons used as admission tickets to the theatre – and statues of gods and goddesses.

Like the Hercules villa and the Camp Museum, Aquincum is open from May 1 to October 31 (Tuesday-Friday 10am-2pm/Saturday & Sunday 10am-6pm).

The Buda Hills

Thirty minutes journey from Moszkva tér, the **BUDA HILLS** provide a welcome respite from summertime heat in the city. While particular hills are often busy with people at the weekend, it's possible to ramble through the woods for hours yet see hardly a soul during the week. Buses #56/#56E run almost to the meadows and small funfair in **Hűvösvölgy**; buses #22/#22E slog up to the Ságvárliget midway between two hills; but the nicest approach is by the **cog-wheel railway** (*fogaskerekű-vasút*). From the terminal west of Moszkva tér (p.55), small trains click up through the **Szabadság-hegy** suburb, traditionally known as 'Schwab Hill' on account of its Swabian merchant founders. The new name – Freedom Hill – obliquely pays tribute to the memory of those who suffered during the Nazi occupation in the local *Hotel Majestic* (nowadays a residential block) when it was a Gestapo torture chamber and Eichmann's headquarters. The cog-wheel line terminates at Széchenyi-hegy, near the beginning of the **Pioneers' Railway**, one of Budapest's strangest sights. It's largely staffed by priggish 14 year-olds in miniature MÁV uniforms; members of the Pioneers, the Communist equivalent of the Scouts. The little trains chug up through the hills towards Hűvösvölgy, stopping along the way. At Normafa there's a modest **ski-run**, while from the summit of János-hegy you can enjoy a **panoramic view** of Budapest and ride the swaying **chair-lift** (*libegő*) back down the hillside. At the bottom, bus #158 returns to Moszkva tér. If you're not planning to see the great caverns at Aggtelek nor their smaller cousins at Lillafüred in northern Hungary, consider paying a visit to the **Pál-völgyi stalactite caves**. Though their full 1,100m extent isn't entirely open to visitors, a goodly portion of the caves can be seen by tour groups, which assemble outside 62, Szépvölgyi út (open April to October/Tuesday-Sunday 10am-6pm). You can get there by bus #65 or #65A from Kolosy tér.

Margit Island and Csepel Island

Located at opposite ends of the city, Budapest's two largest islands are poles apart. **MARGIT ISLAND** is an elegant tongue, green with oak trees and perfumed by flower gardens, where the wealthier folk have traditionally lolled around (before 1945, a stiff admission charge deterred the poor). Nowadays it's a favourite spot for courting couples, offering open-air **dancing** (near the Casino snack bar) and performances of **drama and opera** (on the stage near the water tower) during summer; besides the opportunity to enjoy **nude sunbathing** on the single-sex terraces of the **Palatinus baths**; while rich foreign invalids totter in and out of the luxurious *Grand* and *Thermal* hotels. The island is named after St Margaret who lived from the age of 9 until her death in a C13 convent here, the **ruins** of which can still be seen. It's a nice place to get lost, yet easy to reach from Moszkva tér or Marx tér in Pest (bus #12/#6 or tram #4/#6), although motorists can only approach the island from the north via the Árpád Bridge.

   CSEPEL ISLAND, accessible by HÉV train from Boráros tér, is an entirely different animal: a dusty wedge of land 30 miles long, covered with market gardens, endless high-rise *lakótelep* and the Tököl garrison of the Soviet army. The site of early copper-smelting and Bronze Age graves, Csepel was suddenly transformed by **heavy industry** towards the end of the C19. The militant workers at the huge Manfred Weiss Iron & Metal Works soon earned the island its nickname 'Red Csepel'; and the postwar Communists made this Rákosi's parliamentary constituency. In 1956 it rapidly became one of the strongholds of the Uprising, with factory committees which continued to strike for months after the Russians crushed all military resistance. Subsequent housing-programmes and efforts to improve amenities haven't altered the factory workers' most fundamental grievance, the iniquitous system of 'piecework' (*darabbér*). It's a sensitive subject with the authorities, who gaoled Miklós Haraszti for exposing conditions in the *Red Star* factory in the '70s, and have had to raise prices and production quotas cautiously in an effort to forestall lightning strikes (as happened in 1986/87). Besides permanent residents and the Tököl garrison, Csepel also houses many thousands of **migrant workers** who sleep in *Munkás-szálló* here during the week, returning on the 'black train' at weekends to their families in the countryside. Tourists rarely visit Csepel, and it's one of the few parts of Budapest where single women or obviously-rich foreigners might be at risk on the streets late at night.

PEST

PEST is busier, more populous and vital than Buda: the place where things are decided, made and sold. While Buda grew up around Castle Hill's forts and palaces, the east bank was settled by merchants, artisans and labourers; surrounded by brick-works whose ovens – *Offen* to the original, largely German population – gave the growing town its name, which was later Magyarised to Pest (pronounced 'Pesht'). Much of the architecture and general layout dates from the late C19, giving Pest a homogenous appearance compared to other European capitals. Boulevards, public buildings and apartment houses were executed on a grand scale appropriate to the Habsburg

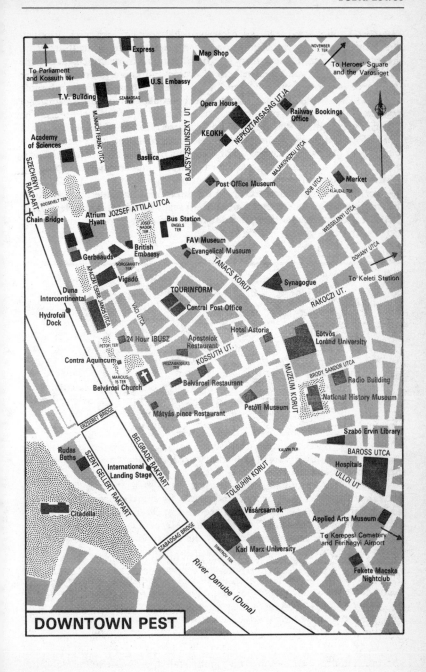

DOWNTOWN PEST

empire's second city, and the capital of Hungary, which celebrated its milleniary anniversary in 1896. Now bullet-scarred and begrimed or in the throes of restoration, these form the backdrop to life in the cosmopolitan *Belváros* (inner city) and the residential quarters; hulking sombrely above the street cafés, pokey courtyards and wine cellars where Pest's inhabitants socialise. There's plenty to see and do here, but the less tangible atmosphere is Pest's most attractive characteristic.

Beginning with the Belváros, the following sections describe fairly distinct areas of Pest, broadly defined by two semi-circular *körút* – the 'Little' (*Kis*) and 'Great' (*Nagy*) Boulevards – and long radial avenues (*út*), which lead to the railway stations and city parks. The Belváros is small enough to explore on foot without much risk of getting lost, but transport and a map (or at least a destination) are required once you go much beyond the Little Boulevard. As the meeting point of 3 Metro lines and several main útjas, Deák tér (p.62) makes a good jumping-off point for such explorations.

The Belváros

Like the walled, medieval town of Pest – and with approximately the same boundaries – the **inner city** BELVÁROS (V district) is very cosmopolitan, consciously adapting to and reflecting foreign influences. For many centuries this owed much to Pest's predominantly German-speaking or Jewish population, consequently arousing the mistrust of provincial Hungarians (the more bigoted of whom refered to the city as 'Judapest'). Charges of 'alien cosmopolitanism' survived the C19 influx of Magyars and the flourescence of Hungarian cultural and artistic life, so that right-wingers denounced the capital as 'sinful' in 1919. Nowadays the area north of Felszabadulás tér positively revels in its international connections; with shops selling French perfume and Japanese cameras; posters proclaiming the arrival of Spielberg films and British rock groups; and streets noisy with the sound of foreign cars and languages.

Around Felszabadulás tér

Accessible by Metro line 3 or buses #7/#7A/#78 from Keleti station, **Felszabadulás tér** is more or less dead centre; its approach from the Erzsébet Bridge flanked by twin Clothild palaces, a last flourish of the empire. Just south of the bridgehead you'll see the deluxe *Mátyás Pince* restaurant, famous for its carp dishes and ensemble led by the Gypsy violinist Sándor Lakatos; while to the northeast stand the *Belvárosi* nightclub and, further along, Budapest's most established if hardly upfront gay bar, the *Egyetem* (see p.83). The latter faces a long gilt and gingerbread concoction, the **Párizsi udvar**: occupied by an ice cream parlour and a big IBUSZ office, but chiefly known for its ornate '**Parisian arcade**' with stained glass ceilings, which gives Budapest's most established if hardly upfront gay bar, the *Egyetem* (see p.83).

From Felszabadulás tér you can head north into the shopping district (see below) or walk up Kossuth utca to meet the Little Boulevard. At the intersection, the **Astoria Metro station** has a lively subway, full of buskers, portrait artists and women selling **handicrafts**. By their conspicuously archaic dress you can usually pick out the women who've come from far away Transylvania; probably from the 'Székely Land' whose ethnic customs and products are currently in vogue amongst Hungarian collectors. The Metro station gets its name from the *Hotel Astoria* on the corner, the site of a **nightclub** frequented by prostitues and their clientele. Opposite you'll see the Soviet Culture House serving the occupying forces, attached to the Soviet Bookshop (torched during the Uprising) and the *Bajkál* restaurant. The Russian cooking there is nothing special, but the **tea-room** upstairs serves a wide range of different brews.

Váci utca and Vörösmarty tér

From the Párizsi udvar, Pest's **shopping district** extends northwards to Vörösmarty Square. *Korso*, the Serbian word for promenade, is the old name for **Váci utca**, the main street where people do just that. Besides having the smartest boutiques and an excellent *foreign language bookshop* (nr.33), Váci utca triumphs architecturally with mock-Gothic fantasies flanking the *Pesti Theatre* (nr.9) where 12 year-old Liszt made his concert début, and a building burdened with mythological structures on the corner of Régiposta utca. Nostalgia buffs should enjoy drinking in the *Apostolok* beside the arcade on Kigyó utca, where the Art Nouveau decor includes murals of 'lost' Hungarian towns in Transylvania; but eating is much cheaper in the stand up delicatessen nearby at nr.6. Running parallel to Váci u., **Petőfi utca** is busier and more chaotic with traffic. **TOURINFORM** (nrs.17-19) is a temporary refuge as well as *the* place to make international calls and get information; while at nr.13 you'll find the poste restante department of the **Central Post Office**.

Assuming that you don't head east towards Deák tér, the flow of the crowd will carry you on to **Vörösmarty tér** which, following extensive repairs, is once again Pest's smartest square. Here, jugglers and singers perform beside the statue of **Mihály Vörösmarty** (1800-50), a poet and translator. Customarily, Vörösmarty's hymn to Magyar identity, the *Szózat* (Appeal), is declaimed by crowds at moments of national crisis; in Romania the beleaguered Hungarian minority are forbidden to sing it, and mark their anniversaries by doing so clandestinely. Europe's first underground actually begins beneath the square: the **Millenary Railway** (Metro line 1) inaugurated in 1896, which runs up the length of Népköztársaság útja to Heroes' Square. Perhaps the best known building on the square is **Gerbeaud's patisserie**, favoured haunt of Budapest's high society since the end of the C19. Its gilded ceilings and china, silverware and starchy service recall la belle époque, while its custom includes Party bosses, film directors, matrons in furs, and chic literati, besides the more transient tourists. The cakes and ices are just as scrumptious but half the price in *Kis-Gerbeaud's*, an annex facing the **British Embassy** on Harmincad utca (attached to which is a public **library**).

Along the embankment

Luxury hotels occupy most of the prime sites along the **Belgrád rakpart** embankment, and of the older buildings only the Vigadó has stood its ground. Starting just north of the Erzsébet Bridge you'll come upon **Március 15. tér**, a square commemorating March 15 when the 1848 revolution began and, more tangibly, the site of a small Roman ruin *Contra-Aquincum*, and the **Belvárosi Church**. Behind its grimy façade hide Renaissance niches, Baroque barrel-vaulting and a *mirhab* from the time of the Turkish occupation, indicating the direction of Mecca. An adjoining square and statue honour **Sándor Petőfi** (1823-49), peasants' son, lyric poet of the *puszta* and revolutionary firebrand. Petőfi's *Nemzeti Dal* (National Song) – the anthem of 1848 – and his romantic death fighting the Russians made him a patriotic icon and a symbol thereafter. Of the many **demonstrations** staged beside the statue, official history records the anti-war protest of 1942, but not demos in the 1970s which opposed conscription and Soviet domination, and compelled the authorities to temporarily suspend the traditional March 15 students' parade. Walk northwards past the **24-hour IBUSZ bureau** (Petőfi tér 3) and you'll soon reach the **Vigadó**: a splendidly romantic concert hall, the name of which translates literally as 'self-amused'. Franz Liszt – whom few foreigners realise was a Hungarian – gave many performances here. From the Vigadó until the Chain Bridge, the *Atrium Hyatt* and *Forum* hotels – both selling **Western newspapers** – hog most of the groundspace. If you're not planning to cross the bridge to Buda or continue northwards to Parliament (p.63), it's possible to cut through József Nádor tér to reach Deák tér and the Little Boulevard.

Deák tér and Engels tér

Two segments of the Little Boulevard and several main avenues meet at **Deák tér**, where the Metro lines also intersect. Though it merges seamlessly with another square, Engels tér, Deák tér can be identified by two landmarks: a huge mansard-roofed edifice flanking its eastern side, and the dome of St Stephen's Basilica arising to the north. Flower sellers and clothes stalls cluster about the Metro entrance between the *NDK Centrum* – displaying photos of Free German Youth and similar DDR propaganda – and the **National Evangelical Museum**. Recognisable by the sombre face of Martin Luther stuck in the window, this contains illuminated Bibles, jewelled crosses and a mass of Magyar captions explaining the history of Protestantism – the *Református* faith – in Hungary. Across the main road beneath the mansard-roofed building (with a great postcard shop on the ground floor), a subway entrance leads to the **Metro Museum** (*FAV múzeum*). With its old ticket offices, wrought iron fixtures, ornately tiled walls and yellow trams it's a place for railway buffs to grow maudlin.

Above ground and back over the tramlines, tourists may find the **Engels tér bus terminal** useful. It's wise to book a few hours in advance on most of the services to the west bank of the Danube Bend and Transdanubia, and a day or so for **destinations abroad**. These include the Tatra Mountains and other spots in Czechoslovakia and Poland; Vienna; Ljubljana and Zagreb in Yugoslavia; Cluj, Oradea and Tîrgu Mureş in Romania (functioning uncertainly); and Venice and Munich (during the summer only). From here you can also catch buses every half hour to **Ferihegy airport** and, if you've got a return ticket, the *Eurolines* coach to London.

The following section begins with the government quarter and the two main avenues running north and northeast from Engels tér; the areas adjoining Deák tér to the southeast and south are covered afterwards (p.66-69).

Between the boulevards

Emulating Baron Haussman in Paris, the architects who redesigned Pest in the late C19 thought big, and were empowered to push their schemes through by imperial decree. Beyond the Belváros enclosed by the Little Boulevard, grand avenues run like canyons for kilometres between blocks of C19 housing or monumental public buildings; giving rise to certain distinctive areas like the government district or the Jewish quarter. Some of these lie just a few minutes' walk from the Belváros; to reach others, around the arc of the enormously long Great Boulevard, buses #12/#12A or trams #4/#6 are useful.

Parliament and Kossuth tér

Immediately north of the Belváros, narrow streets lined with sombre administrative buildings lead towards the **government district** housing the ministries and Party headquarters. Their gloomy progress is interupted halfway along by the verdant expanse of **Szabadság tér** (Liberty Square). While the National Bank (covered with bas reliefs representing honest toil) and Magyar TV occupy the most imposing buildings, foreigners are more likely to enter the **US Embassy** (nr.12) or **Express main office** (nr.16), on the east and north side of the square. I'm inclined to suspect a sly joker in the public works department, since the one street that pursues an undeviating line towards Parliament, bypassing Liberty Square, is named after Ferenc Münnich: a veteran repression specialist responsible for crushing the last vestiges of resistance in 1956. At nr.15 – the office of the *Totó Lottó* state lottery – you can glimpse women sorting heaps of pools coupons.

Continue northwards and Budapest's **Parliament building** (*Országház*) appears suddenly. Variously described as 'eclectic' or 'neo-Gothic' in style, it sprawls for 268m between the embankment and Kossuth tér, dominating the vicinity with a spiky façade embellished by 88 statues of Hungarian rulers. The symetrical wings housing the Assemblies meet beneath a gigantic cupola 96m high topped with a red star, which can accommodate both chambers when they meet in ceremonial conclave to rubber-stamp decisions. Hungarian Parliamentary politics were liveliest during the 'Reform Era' some fifty years before the building's construction (in 1884-1902, according to Imre Steindl's plans), and though the interior is splendid, Parliament's role has been strictly ceremonial during the socialist era. Decisions have been made by the Politburo and Secretariat of the Communist Party (*MSzMP*), whose headquarters stand on Akadémia utca, nearby – though for the past year or so MPs have begun to flex their muscles amidst speculation about a 'greater role for Parliament'. Guided **tours** of the building, starting at Gate XII, are arranged by Budapesttourist (see p.82).

On **Kossuth tér** outside Parliament you'll find an excellent **Ethnographical Museum** (p.69) and two large statues of Lajos Kossuth and Prince Ferenc Rákóczi II, the sanctified heroes of the struggle for Hungarian independence. Inscribed on the plinth of Rákóczi's monument, 'The wounds of the noble Hungarian nation burst open!' refers to anti-Habsburg war of 1703-11, but seems equally appropriate to the events of October 23 1956. Then, thousands of Hungarians filled the square chanting anti-Stalinist slogans at Parliament, and calling for the appearance of Imre Nagy, a popular 'reform' Communist ousted by the Rákosi clique: the prelude for the revolt which erupted later that night. During the brief Uprising Parliament served as the office of Nagy's beleaguered administration; in its aftermath, women protesting against the military repression were shot down on Kossuth tér.

From St Stephen's Basilica to Marx tér
Freshly re-bronzed, the lofty dome of **St Stephen's Basilica** overlooks the edge of the government quarter, a majestic sight when seen above the Coke and *Totó-Lottó* billboards on Engels tér. IBUSZ guides shepherd endless tour groups into the cavernous interior, where lack of light obscures the peeling frescoes and gilding. Two architects, József Hild and Miklós Ybl, died of old age during the prologed construction of the Basilica, and the dome collapsed once before it was finally consecrated in 1905. On August 20, the name day of St Stephen (*Szent István*) – Hungary's first king and patron saint – his mummified hand and other **holy relics** are displayed in the jam-packed building.

Behind the Basilica, **Bajcsy-Zsilinszky út** – named after a Social Democratic MP murdered by local Nazis in 1944 – leads northwards up to Marx tér. Buses run the full length of the út, past an excellent **map shop** at nr.41, while halfway along you can catch trolley #72 to the Városliget (p.68). The site of **Nyugati station** (trains to Szeged, Nyíregyháza and Debrecen), Marx tér is ironically also the location of the glassy, terraced **Skála department store**. Founded as an association of Co-ops in 1973 to provide competition for the state-run *Centrum* chain, Skala exemplifies Hungary's 'market socialism', trading aggressively and issuing bonds (shares) to raise capital. It's similar to a provincial Debenhams but unique in the Eastern bloc.

Up the Avenue of the People's Republic to Heroes' Square
The Avenue of the People's Republic – Népköztársaság útja – is probably Budapest's grandest, longest and most re-named thoroughfare. Opened in 1884, it runs for two and a half kilometres up to Heroes' Square on the edge of the Városliget; a parade of grand buildings laden with gold leaf, stone dryads and colonades. Still known as Andrássy út by older folk, the avenue bore Stalin's name from 1949 until the '56 Uprising. Its shops and pavement cafés retain some of the style that made the avenue so fashionable in the 1890s, when 'Bertie' the Prince of Wales regularly drove down its length in a landau offering flowers to women passing by; the underground Millenary Railway (Metro line 1) beneath it likewise dates from that time.

It's feasible to walk from Engels tér as far as November 7th square, but if you're going any further then take the Metro or bus #1 or #4. En route you'll pass the **Post Office Museum** at nr.3; the **KEOKH** bureau responsible for visa extensions (nr.12); and, on the left, the **Opera House**. Hungary's state opera was founded by **Ferenc Erkel** (1810-93), composer of the national anthem, and occupies a magnificent building designed by Milkós Ybl, recently restored to its original glory. Tickets and bookings are available from the office across the road (or from the bureau on Vörösmarty tér), and opera-goers are apt to patronise the *Művész* (nr.29) and *Negro* patisseries and the *Troika* beer hall nearby. Three blocks beyond the Opera House, the avenue meets the Great Boulevard at **November 7. tér** – an intersection still popularly known by its original name, the *Oktogon*.

The second stretch, up to the Kodály körönd, is equally eclectic in appearance and function. The **MÁV office** at nr.35 sells international train tickets, while nr.69 houses the National **Puppet Theatre** (*Bábszinház*), and nr.70 yet another fin-de-siècle patisserie. Number 60, now the offices of a trading company, was once the most terrifying address in Budapest. Jews and other victims of the *Nyilas* were tortured here; and the specially equipped building was later occupied by the Communist ÁVO, which employed the same gadgets and many of the torturers. Capturing the building in '56, insurgents found no trace of the giant meat-grinder rumoured to have been used to dispose of corpses, but discovered cells capable of being flooded, frozen or filled with steam, and other incriminating evidence left by the ÁVO.

Further up the avenue, the **Kodály körönd** junction is named after the composer *Zoltán Kodály* (p.194) who worked and died at nr.89, flanked by four neo-Renaissance palaces, one of them gorgeously graffitied with gold. Hereafter plane trees run along the út past Ferenc Hopp's **Collection of Eastern Asiatic Art** and mansions and villas, which peter out as one approaches Heroes' Square.

Erected to mark the thousandth anniversary of the Magyar conquest, **Heroes' Square** (*Hősök tere*) is appropriately grand. Its centerpiece is the *Millenary Monument*, portraying Prince Árpád and his chieftains, half encircled by a colonnade displaying statues of Hungary's most illustrious leaders from Stephen I to Kossuth. You'll find two Art Museums, Városliget park and Vajdahunyad Castle in the vicinity (described on page 68), but before going to investigate, spare a thought for the *Stalin statue* that once stood just southeast of the square. As the arch symbol of foreign oppression it was torn down during the Uprising, dragged to Lenin körút, decapitated, doused with petrol and then ignited, so that 'flames came out of the mouth. The headless torso lay there for a week, and a constantly changing crowd surrounded it. . .hammering away to get bits for souvenirs. When the traffic started again, the great bulk was dragged into the nearest sidestreet, and the hammering went on'. The site now serves as a parking lot and an occasional parade ground, where the Politburo reviews banner-toting workers on **May 1** and military hardware on **April 4** (Liberation Day) and **November 7** (the anniversary of the Bolshevik Revolution).

Majakovszkij utca and the old Jewish quarter

The VII district between Népköztársaság útja and Rákóczi avenue is mainly residential, composed of C19 blocks whose bullet-scarred, grimy façades conceal a warren of dwellings, wrought ironwork and leafy courtyards, interspersed with tiny workshops and wine cellars. Vladimir Mayakovsky, the punkish Russian poet who 'trod on the throat of his own song' to serve the Bolshevik cause, gives his name to **Majakovszkij utca** – a street running parallel to Népköz. útja for an inordinate length, unlike the poet's terse, militant verses. Here and in the sidestreets you'll find antique shops, secondhand shops (*bizományi*), and places selling stylish, cheap but slightly flawed (*alkami*) shoes and clothing.

A number of sidestreets heading south lead to Pest's old **Jewish quarter**, a highly atmospheric district fanning out behind the Synagogue on the Little Boulevard. Specific 'sights' here are few, but practically every building around Síp, Rumbach and Kazinczy Street contains a run-down yet beautiful courtyard with stained-glass panels enscribed in Hebrew characters, and sad memorial plaques naming those who perished on the 'Death March' to Hegyeshalom and in the camps of Auschwitz and Bergen-Belsen. Bullet holes in the walls are a grim reminder of the 'autumn that bled' in 1944, when Nazi squads rampaged through the ghetto leaving Jewish corpses piled up in the streets, and Hungarian gentiles walked by, averting their eyes. While the Zionist underground prepared for escape or last-ditch insurrection, the group organised by Wallenberg (p.55) used legalistic maneouvres and bribery to gain time. Unable to prevent many murders by Nyilas gangs – led by Minorite priests and a lady aristocrat – they still managed to forestall the final SS assault on the ghetto, planned as Russian troops were encircling the city.

Budapest's main **Synagogue** is a splendid fusion of neo-Byzantine and Moorish styles, standing at the intersection of Dob utca and Tanács körút beside the Little Boulevard. It incorporates the **National Jewish Museum** (Monday & Thursday 2pm-6pm/Tuesday, Wednesday, Friday & Sunday 10am-1pm/closed on the Sabbath). The first floor contains some beautiful Judaica – torahs, minorahs and embroidered vestments – the treasures of a community resident in Budapest since the C13, which provided much of the impetus for the city's cultural flourescence during the C19. But for most visitors – especially Hungarian-born Jews from America – it's the searing exhibits on the Holocaust that make the greatest impression. Since the war Hungary's 80,000 Jews have underplayed their culture – anti-semitism is by no means extinct here – and the World Jewish Congress held in Budapest in 1987 will probably have a beneficial effect on the community's morale.

Other notable places in the VII district include **Klauzál tér**, the site of two privately-owned restaurants (*Étkezde*) and a small, lively **market**; the **map shop** at Nyár u. 1 just off Rákóczi út and the **Corvin department store**; and two discreet **gay-bars**. The *Emke* lies 100m north of the junction with the Great Boulevard, while the seedier *Diófa* is at nr.38 on Dohány utca, which runs beside the Synagogue back into the Jewish Quarter.

Múzeum körút, Kálvin tér and the city market

South of the Synagogue one can turn east onto Rákóczi út and follow the avenue, lined with shops and cinemas, to Keleti station (bus #7/#7A/#78); or keep going along the Little Boulevard, which begins curving towards the Szabadság Bridge. **Múzeum körút** – the section running as far as Kálvin tér – resembles Népköz. útja in miniature, with its trees, shops and grandiose stone piles. Past the natural sciences faculty of **Eötvös Loránd University**, remains of the **medieval walls** of Pest can be glimpsed in the courtyards of nrs. 17 & 21; and a series of *Antikvárium* selling old books, prints and maps cluster in the vicinity of the National History Museum.

From the steps of the **National Museum**, the poet Petőfi agitated to a crowd of students and apprentices, and first declaimed the *National Song* with its rousing refrain: 'Choose! Now is the time! Shall we be slaves or shall we be free?'. Inside, the museum is divided into two sections – before and after the Magyar conquest – of which the latter is definitely more interesting. All the captions are in Hungarian only, so buying a catalogue for each section is essential. While I was more impressed by the amazing carved pews from Nyírbátor and the tent of the Turkish general, the most prestigious exhibit is undoubtedly the **Coronation Regalia**, reputedly the very crown, orb and sceptre used by Stephen I. Although it's likely they actually belonged to one of his successors, the regalia are nevertheless esteemed as the symbol of Hungarian statehood. Kossuth buried them in Transylvania rather than let them be taken by the Habsburgs in 1849; while in 1945 the regalia was spirited away to America, whence it was later returned by the Carter administration.

Narrow Bródy Sándor utca, running alongside the museum to the north, seems an unlikely place for a revolution to start. Yet one did outside the non-descript **Radio Building** (nr.5), when ÁVO guards fired upon students demanding access to the airwaves: an act which turned hitherto peaceful protests on October 23 1956 into a violent uprising against the secret police and other manifestations of Stalinism. Street-fighting was especially fierce around **Kálvin tér**, the junction of Tolbuhin körút and Üllői út – the roads used by tanks rumbling into Pest from Ferihegy and the Soviet garrison at Tököl on Csepel Island. Given the widespread devastation in other parts of the city it's something of a miracle that the ornate reading room of the **Szabó Ervin Library** survived unscathed on the corner of Baross utca. (There's a club, the *Szélrózsa*, farther along at nr.28).

Take a #182 bus along Üllői út to find the **Museum of Applied Arts**, a grimy but nevertheless flamboyant building designed by Ödön Lechner, who tried to blend Art Nouveau with folk and Turkic motifs to create a unique 'Hungarian style'. A polychrome roof and an octagonal tower rear above the entrance, which is adorned with yolk-coloured tiles bearing intricate designs. The glass-roofed Moorish interior (modelled on the Alhambra in Granada) contains timepieces since the year dot and examples of bookbinding, weaving, furniture and jewellery, including some superb enamelled work from Transylvania. You might also find on display the Tibetan scrolls, pictures and prayer rugs collected by the explorer Sándor Kőrosi Csoma (see p.70). Just beyond Üllői út's junction with the Great Boulevard (Ferenc József körút), **mime artists** perform in the *Színpad Centi* at nr.45, formerly the site of the Killian barracks. Its garrison was the first to join the '56 insurgents, and the building became the headquarters of Col. Pál Maleter, who organised teams of teenage guerillas which sallied forth from the maze of passages surrounding the *Corvin Cinema* to lob Molotov cocktails at Soviet tanks.

Tobuhin körút, which leads from Kálvin tér to the Szabadság Bridge, is notable chiefly for the *Vásárcsarnok*, Budapest's main **market hall** (open Monday 9am-5pm/Tuesday-Thursday & Saturday 6am-6pm/Friday 6am-7pm). A dusty mock-Gothic façade conceals a lofty, wrought iron pillared hall, filled with colourful produce and rich smells. Fish swim in tanks awaiting buyers at the back of the hall, near stalls festooned with strings of crimson and scarlet paprika. In 1984 it was here that Mrs Thatcher endeared herself to the locals by haggling ('I'm a housewife and mother too, you know') and doing a walkabout, a rare phenomenon in the Eastern bloc before the advent of Gorbachev. In the backstreets outside you'll find flower-sellers and cheap workers' cafés; while with a student card it should be possible to gain admission to gigs organised by the **MKKE klub** of the **Karl Marx Economic University** which runs alongside the embankment. These generally take place in one of the subsidiary blocks at the southern end of Ráday utca or, less frequently, in the courtyard of a building on Zsil utca; ask around.

Beyond the Great Boulevard

City Park and the People's Stadium

The **VÁROSLIGET**, Budapest's largest park, starts just back off Heroes' Square. Across the boating lake you'll see **Vajdahunyad Castle** rearing up amongst the trees, an extraordinary sight to behold. Built in 1896 for the Millenary Exhibition, the building is a fusion of architectural styles, incorporating a replica of the Chapel at Ják in western Hungary and two Transylvanian castles. (One of the originals, the Hunyadi Castle in Romania, gives its name to the building). Facing the entrance to the **Agricultural Museum** in the main building – a place to make vegetarians blanch and everybody else yawn – sits the hooded statue of 'Anonymus', who chronicled the times of King Béla III. In the southeastern corner of the park mothballed steam engines filled with excited kids stand outside the **Transport Museum**, where nostalgia buffs will enjoy the antique cars and the earthbound can admire pictures of Bertalan Farkas, Hungary's first man in space courtesy of the Soviet Union. Between here and Vajdahunyad Castle you'll find the **Petőfi Csarnok** where **films, flea markets and discos** are staged at weekends (p.83), while on the opposite side of the park are the **Széchenyi baths** (p.72) and the **zoo, circus** and **funfair** (details given under 'Listings').

Take bus #20 or #30 down Dózsa út, or bus #55 around the first (and once fashionable) part of the Hungária körút, to reach the **NÉPSTADION** district: the city's sports centre. Beside the Metro station (line 2) and the **inter-city bus terminal** serving areas east of the Danube, the *Sportcsarnok* has facilities for skating and most **indoor sports**, for which you can hire equipment (see 'Listings'). The 173,000 seat **People's Stadium** and the smaller *Kisstadion* stand further to the west, brute masses of concrete, while the park with its pantheon of ugly statues is sometimes used for **rock festivals**. Information on **football** matches and other events is available from TOURINFORM or the columns of *Daily News, Programme* and *Pesti Műsor*.

Betting on horses, abhorred by early puritanical Communists, has proved to be ineradicable throughout Eastern Europe. As in the Soviet Union, however, the punters have to be satisfied with horse-trotting races and chicken-feed stakes and prizes, though black market bookies do operate. **Trotting races** (where the horses pull light gigs) are held in the *Ügetőpálya* east of Keleti station on Wednesday (16.30) and Saturday (14.00) – take Metro line 2 or bus #95 westwards along Kerepesi út from the Népstadion.

Mausoleums, lowlife and seeing stars

KEREPESI CEMETERY, best reached by bus#33 or tram#23/#24 from Baross tér, contains the mortal remains of the 'immortals': famous C19 politicians and artists, and figures in the 'Pantheon of the Working Class Movement'. In the well-tended sector of the cemetery you'll find the **mausoleums** of Kossuth, who revolted against the Habsburgs; Batthyány, whom they executed for rebellion; and Deák, who engineered the compromise (*Ausgleich*) between Hungary and the empire. With the aid of a brochure you can also track down the tombs of Lujza Blaha – known as the 'Nightingale of Budapest' for her voice – and László Rajk, a leading Communist executed as an 'imperialist spy' on the orders of Rákosi in 1949. (Rajk was posthumously cleared of charges and ceremonially reburied here in 1956; his son László is now a prominent dissident). Atheistic red stars adorn the graves of Communists in the northern part of the cemetery, while the eastern sector is overgrown and rambling.

The **VIII district** between Kerepesi út and József körút is a maze of battered streets and apartment blocks, and whereas Köztársaság Square's **Erkel Theatre** attracts smartly dressed crowds most evenings, Rákóczi tér adjoining the körút draws seedier types. Around the square and Bérkocsis utca after nightfall, women are likely to be accosted by men who assume that they're prostitutes, for the area is partly a **red light quarter** with regular strip shows in the *Habana* restaurant nearby on the körút. Prostitutes were compelled to undergo 're-education through labour' at Dunaújváros when the hitherto state-licensed brothels were closed in 1950, but gradually drifted back to Budapest during the '60s at the same time as 'amateur' prostitutes (*digozok*) emerged to cater for the influx of Yugoslav and Italian tourists. Today there's a great divide between the 'hard currency' prostitutes earning high fees and frequenting Belváros nightclubs, and the women of the VIII district who cater for Hungarians and may service a man for no more than the price of a bottle of pálinka.

Further to the southeast, out along Üllői út, NÉPLIGET is Budapest's second largest park. It's chiefly notable for the **Planetarium** 100 metres from the Népliget station (Metro line 3): the place to enjoy guided tours around the galaxy and performances of the **Laser Theatre** (for details see p.81).

BUDAPEST'S MUSEUMS AND GALLERIES

Almost invariably, Budapest's museums are open from Tuesday-Sunday, 9am-5pm or 10am-6pm. Admission is free or half price with a student card; no entry charges are made at weekends. Besides the places described in the text (on Castle Hill, Rózsadomb, and Deák tér; the Transport, Applied Arts and Jewish museums; Óbuda's Roman remains), the city's other museums include:

Ethnographical Museum (V, Kossuth tér 12) A diverse collection of Eskimo furs and kayaks, African instruments and barkcloth, totems and wonderfully carved Melenasian masks. Definitely worth a visit.
Museum of Fine Arts (Heroes' Square) Depending on the process of restoration you can see halls containing Egyptian funerary relics, Greek and

Roman ceramics, and paintings and drawings by C13-C20 European masters. Among the latter, big names include Rembrandt, Dürer, Leonardo, Bloc, Chagall, Rodin, Renoir, Picasso and Toulouse-Lautrec.

Museum of Eastern Asiatic Art (Népköztársaság útja 103) Small but fascinating collection of Japanese and Indian silks, puppets, ivory etc. trawled by Ferenc Hopp on his many voyages east.

Tibetan Artefacts Beautiful scrolls, prayer shawls and paintings of Buddhas gathered by **Sándor Körosi Csoma** (1784-1842), who tramped on foot to Tibet, spent many years there and compiled the first Tibetan-English dictionary (also on show). This exhibition changes its venue: try the Applied Arts (IX, Üllői út 33-37), Fine Arts or Ethnographical museums.

China Museum (VI, Gorkij fasor 12) Closed when I enquired. Reputedly contains Chinese ceramics and bronzes; maybe worth a visit.

Kiscelli Museum (III, Kiscelli u.108) Historical paintings of Budapest and a nice selection of pictures by C19 & C20 Hungarian artists.

Post Office Museum (Népköztáraság útja 3) Blunderbusses and thigh-boots testify to mailmen's hard life during the C18. Hungarian stamps galore, an amusing compressed-air mail tube, and push-button displays of *Magyar Pósta* in the telecommunications age.

Stamp Museum (VII, Hársfa u.47) More stamps, strictly for philatelists. (open Wednesday 10am-6pm/Saturday 10am-3pm/Sunday 10am-2pm).

Nagytétény Museum (XXII, Csókási u.9) A long ride on bus #3 from Móricz Zs. körtér to see antique furniture in a rundown stately home.

Semmelweiss Medical Museum (I, Apród u.1-3) Medical instruments through the ages, plus objects belonging to **Ignac Semmelweiss**, known as the 'saviour of mothers' for his discovery of the cause of puerperal fever, a disease hitherto usually fatal for pregnant women.

If you're interested in Hungarian literature and can tolerate unintelligible captions, four **Literature Museums** and memorial rooms (*emlékszobá*) deserve a mention. **Sándor Petőfi** and **Attila József** are reverentially recalled at V, Károlyi u.16 and IX, Gát u.3; while **Endre Ady** – whom many Magyars consider the greatest poet of the three – is commemorated at V, Veres u.4-6. **Nyugat** (*West*), the journal that published the Village Explorers and virtually every writer of note during the '20s and '30s – except for Attila, whom the editor, Mihály Babits, hated – is the subject of another museum (Városmajor u.48) near Moszkva tér. As for the remaining half dozen museums, don't bother.

The main sites for **exhibitions of contemporary Hungarian art** (and foreign artwork on tour) are the *Műcsarnok* on Heroes' Square, the *Vigadó* on the embankment, and the *Studió* (Bajcsy-Zsilinszky út 52). Each year, Budapest's architecture students have their graduation show in the Palace on Castle Hill. **Artwork for sale** is displayed in the *Csók* (V, Váci u.25), *Derkovits* (Lenin körút 63), *Paál* (Rákóczi út 57B), *Csontváry* (V, Vörösmarty tér 1), and *Mednyánszky* (Tanács körút 26) galleries. Most of these places sell **prints and posters**, while the Castle Museum on Várhegy stocks an excellent range of cheap facsimile **engravings** of old Hungarian towns (nice souvenirs), and a shop on the east side of Deák tér specialises in **postcards**.

STEAM BATHS AND SWIMMING POOLS

The best way to immerse yourself in Hungarian history is to wallow away an afternoon in one of Budapest's **thermal baths** (*Gyogyfürdö*). For 2,000 years people have appreciated the relaxing and curative effects of the mineral water from the Buda Hills, currently gushing at a rate of about 70 million litres per day, at temperatures of up to 70°C. The baths at Aquincum (and by implication, the custom of bathing) declined with the Roman empire; but interest perked up after the Knights of St John built a hospice on the site of the present Rudas baths, and Elizabeth – the canonised daughter of Andrew II – cured lepers in the healing springs at the foot of Gellért Hill. The Turks consolidated the habit of bathing, since as Muslims they were obliged to wash five times daily in preparation for prayer.

I felt like an initiate in a ceremony at the *Király Gyogyfürdö*, one of several **Turkish baths** which function in virtually unchanged form: dressed in the ritual apron, ushered through a relentless sequence of hot and icy pools and the hands of a beefy masseuse before dropping onto the bed for the (wisely recommended) 20 minutes of recovery. The heat *is* exhausting, so plan nothing more rigorous than a good meal for the following two hours. A basic *gyogyfürdö* ticket – costing 30-70Ft – covers three hours in the pools, *szauna* and steamrooms (*gözfürdö*), whilst supplementary tickets costing 20-30Ft are available for the tub baths (*kádfürdö*, mud baths (*iszapfürdö*), towels (*törülközö*) and *massasz*. The latter is incredibly vigorous and refreshing and the masseurs and masseuses deserve a tip, for they work long hours on a near constant stream of clients for only 3,000Ft a month. **Specialist treatments** for chronic disorders – cardiac, locomotor, gynaecological and others – are offered by balneological clinics adjoining the baths, but referral to these is undertaken centrally, by *Danubius Travel* (V, Martinelli tér 8/tel:173-652).

The **Rudas Baths** at 9, Döbrentei tér near the Erzsébet Bridge were built by Pasha Mustapha in 1566, and the interior strikingly resembles a chapel. Conspiratorial vaulted cloisters surround a sunken octagonal pool, at the top end of which once sat those *beys* anxious to avoid contamination by lesser mortals who arrived to sluice off the filth of lucre after haggling in the caravanserai which occupied the nearby river bank at that time. The Rudas has an adjoining swimming pool and offers drinking cures for stomach and respiritory complaints; all for *men only* and hence something of a gay venue.

The same springs feed its poor relation, the **Rác Baths** (Hadnagy u.8-10), which squats beneath the Erzsébet Bridge flyover on the edge of the former Tabán district. It was also endowed by Mustapha, and is now reserved for *women only*. The **Király Baths** further to the north (Fő utca 84) is one of the friendliest establishments, open *for men* on Monday, Wednesday and Friday, and *for women* on Tuesday, Thursday and Saturday. Its C19 owners and namesake, the German König family, erected a trim neo-Classical façade which hides the dim warren of domed chambers that date from Mustapha's time.

The **Gellért Baths** – below the hill and adjoining the hotel of the same name – were built in 1913 and have a snob reputation which makes the staff as pompously aloof as the architecture. Perhaps it's a hangover from the 1930s, when debutantes danced upon a glass floor laid over the pool, floodlit from below; or because these days it's full of foreigners paying prices that Hungarians can't afford. If the thermal pool, flanked by carved pillars and lions' heads spouting mineral water, or the mud baths and *outdoor pool with artifical waves* don't appeal, at least take a peak at the feast of majolica tiles and mahogany in the foyer.

The surreal sight of people playing *chess* whilst sitting in the steaming thermal pools was, for me, the most attractive feature of the **Széchenyi Baths** in the Városliget (Állatkerti krt.11). During my visit the place was being restored, and the squat colonades and wilting palms dashed the effect of lofty elegance doubtless envisaged by its founder, the geologist Zsigmondy Vilmos, who discovered the spring in 1895 and is commemorated by a statue near the entrance. The triumph of figuring out the convoluted route to its contemporary, the **Lukács Baths** (II, Frankel Leó u.25-29), is quickly dispelled by the general dinginess and stench of sulphurous waters. Here is the National Institute for Rheumatology and Physiotheraphy and, unofficially, the favourite winter haunt of the capital's gay men. However until restoration is completed, it might leave you scratching at some unwelcome souvenirs.

The **opening hours** of all the above are 6am-7pm, while baths other than the Rác, Rudas and Király have mixed pools and single-sex annexes for saunas, etc. In addition there are numerous **lidos**, notably the *Komjádi Béla* (III, Árpád fejedelem útja 8), the *Csillaghegyi* (III, Pusztakúti u.3), and the *National* on Margit Island. There, you'll also find the *Palatinus*, where **nude sunbathing** is possible on single-sex terraces (a habit that's also spreading to the Csillaghegyi baths, though without official sanction).

EATING AND DRINKING

Hungarians relish – and rarely separate – **eating and drinking**: at their best, keenly sensitive to the nuances of atmosphere, cuisine and conversation; at their worst, gorging as if to efface the memory of subsistence diets or hunger (a fact of life for many people before the '50s). Magyar cooking naturally predominates in Budapest, but the capital has a fair number of places devoted to foreign cuisine, and it's easy to get 'international' dishes and Transatlantic-style fast food. Many restaurants feature **music** (and sometimes dancing) in the evenings, so **bars** are probably better suited for a quiet drink and likely to be cheaper, too.

Prices are always displayed and by Western standards **costs** seem very reasonable indeed. Though your budget might preclude regular meals at the Forum Grill, it's likely to stretch to at least one binge in a top-flight place providing you're otherwise forint-conscious. Soups and salads are invariably cheap, and you'll save money by filling up with a meaty *bográcsgulyás* rather than a succession of snacks and pastries. The following categories – restaurants (for eating), taverns and brasseries (for drinking) and patisseries (for non-alcoholic drinks and the sweeter tooth) – are pretty arbitrary, since all restaurants serve alcohol and all bar-ish places some food, while *eszpresszó* feature both, plus coffee and pastries. Likewise, the order of places listed under each heading only roughly reflects the spectrum of prices within that category.

The *food and drink vocabulary* on pp.26-28 should suffice for **ordering meals**, but if you're unwilling to wrestle with the language it's always possible to try ordering in German or by simply pointing to dishes on the menu (*étlap*) or neighbouring tables.

Restaurants

Second class restaurants generally offer the widest choice of meals around midday, but in deluxe and first class establishments – where reservations and formal dress are required – the range is greatest during the evening. By law all restaurants must provide a set *napi menü* (soup, main course and dessert) priced lower than a combination of these ordered à la carte, and some also offer 'tourist menus' or a rock-bottom 'student menu' for less than 60Ft. As an approximate guide to prices, the following list breaks down into three categories. **Deluxe & first class restaurants** charge between 500-700Ft for a set 3-course meal (including a glass or carafe of wine) and 300-600Ft for one of the richer main dishes chosen à la carte. Second class restaurants form a spectrum of **cheaper possibilities**: set meals can be priced as high as 300Ft (120-300Ft for a main course) or as low as 50-80Ft for the fixed menu (30-100Ft for a substantial single dish). At the lower end of that scale, prices may equal or even undercut **self-service joints**.

DELUXE AND FIRST CLASS RESTAURANTS

Gundel, XIV, Állatkerti krt.2 (☎ 221-002). Named after the famous C19 restauranteur who founded it on the edge of City Park. The Zsolnai room is decorated with brilliant ceramics from Pécs. Open from 12am-4pm and 7pm-midnight.

Fortuna, I, Hess András tér (☎ 161-411). An elegant tavern on Castle Hill, specialising in pork cutlets *Budavári* or *Kedvessy* style, and *Gyulásleves* made with beefsteak. Dancing in the bar.

Bellevue. In the *Hotel Duna*, with a floor show, dancing and a magnificent view of the river. In the same building there's also a deluxe *Csárda* with Hungarian dishes, wines and music, and the elegant 'international-style' *Rendezvous restaurant*. The latter is open for breakfast; all three function from 7pm until midnight.

Forum Grill Barbecues and home-made pasta dishes prepared before one's eyes between 16pm-2am. The *Hotel Forum* also contains the *Silhouette* restaurant, open from noon until 3 pm and between 6pm-11pm.

Étoile, XIII, Pozsonyi út 4 (☎ 122-242). A French restaurant featuring accordian music in the evenings and specialities like trout with roasted almonds and Hunters'-style hare. Open from 12am-3pm, 6pm-midnight, closed on Sundays. The *club* functions from noon until midnight.

Astoria, V, Kossuth u.19 . Famous deluxe Hungarian restaurant; elegant and a touch raffish, since the adjoining *nightclub* is equally well known as a place to find expensive prostitutes.

Nimród, V, Münnich Ferenc u.24. Boar, pheasant and other game specialities, furnished with a 'Hunters' Room', skins, trophys and saddlery.

Kosher cuisine, VII, Dob u.35 (☎ 421-072). Opened since our last visit, hence name unknown. Reservations required. Set lunches 700Ft, main courses 350-400Ft. Open 11.30am-3pm (closed Saturdays).

Berlin, V, Szt. István krt.13 (☎ 316-533). German nosh to the accompaniment of *music by József Radics's folk ensemble*, from noon until midnight. Beer-hall in the cellar (see p.00).

Régi Országház, I, Országház u.17 (☎ 160-225). The 'Old Parliament' in a richly-decorated historic building on Castle Hill. Features private rooms and a wine-cellar, and Gypsy and Schrammel bands. Open daily from 11am-1am.

Százéves, V, Pesti Barnabás u.2 (☎ 183-608). Founded over a century and a half previously, the 'Hundred Years' restaurant displays antique furniture and serves Transylvanian recipies.

Postakocsi, III, Fő tér 2 (☎ 351-159). Hungarian dishes served in an old coaching inn.

Pilvax, V, Pilvax köz 1-3 (☎ 175-604). Notable for lamb dishes, and *József Radics Jr.'s folk ensemble* playing in the evenings. Open from 12am-2am (Monday-Friday), 4am (on Saturdays during the tourist season); closes at midnight out of season (Sundays 4pm).

Mátyás Pince, V, Március 15. tér 7 (☎ 181-693). First class establishment with a slightly cheaper brasserie, both open until 1am. The doyen of Hungarian Gypsy violinists, *Sándor Lakatos*, performs here. House treats include Dorozsma carp and Bridegroom's soup.

Margitkert, II, Margit u.15 (☎ 354-791). A C19 restaurant preserving its original decor, with a garden, near Gül Baba's tomb. The chef (a Maître du mètier) specialises in old Hungarian recipies and meats roasted over charcoal; *music by Lajos Boros's Gypsy band*. Open from noon until midnight.

Vasmacska, III, Laktanya u.3-5 (☎ 887-123). Fish, poultry and beef dishes.

Vadrózsa, II, Pentelei u.12 (☎ 351-118). Fondue dishes and charcoal grills, served in a flower-filled garden. Open 5pm-12pm, closed Mondays.

Ménes Csárda, V, Apáczai Csere u.15 (☎ 170-803). Small and expensive, specialising in pork fillets with various garnishes. Open from 12am-12pm (2am during high season), with *cymbalom music* in the evenings.

CHEAPER POSSIBILITIES

Arany hordó, Tárnok u.16. A borderline case, since a restaurant, brasserie and wine-cellar occupying C16 premises on Castle Hill can hardly be classified as cheap by Hungarian standards, although most tourists should find it affordable. Open daily from 10am-12pm.

Alabárdos, I, Országház u.2 (☎ 160-828). The same applies to this place, which boasts medieval furnishings and a roaring open fire as the centrepiece.

Pest-Buda, I, Fortuna u.3 (☎ 360-768). One of the quieter places on Castle Hill; pricewise, roughly on par with the others. Open daily from 4pm-12pm.

Aranyszarvas, I, Szarvas tér 1. Just south of Castle Hill, its forte is game dishes. *Schrammel music* every evening until closedown at 1am.

Vendéglő a Vörös Postakocsihoz, IX, Ráday u.15 (☎ 176-756). Also at the pricier end of the spectrum, as you'd expect of a mahogany-panelled restaurant with a Maître du mètier. Once the haunt of Gyula Krúdy, a famous writer, epicure and toper, who relished dishes like bone-marrow on toast, bacon stew with egg-barley, and beef and horse-radish soup. (9am-11pm/ Sundays 9am-4pm).

Ezüstsirály, IX, Napfény u.7 (☎ 158-352). Modern restaurant in the centre of the Attila housing estate in Ferencváros, with a palm garden, a brasserie and a qualifed Maître. Prices 30% lower on Sundays and holidays; *music* in the evening; closes at 11pm.

Emke Csárda, VII, Lenin krt.2 (☎ 220-689). Because one pays for the *'folklore' show* (after 9pm), a relatively expensive csárda. Highly colourful decor, with painted furniture, lace, embroideries and flowery murals characteristic of the 'Kalocsa style', and the *Emke Gypsy band*. You'll find cheaper places to enjoy Hungarian food lower down this list.

Hungária, VII, Lenin krt.9-11 (☎ 221-648). Famous pre-war restaurant, damaged during the Uprising. Serves Hungarian and international cuisine. (7am-10pm daily).

Vörös Sárkány, VI, Népköztársaság útja 80 (☎ 318-757). Chinese food, with a mixture of regional dishes (Cantonese, Sechuan etc), some of which don't come off too successfully.

Szofia, V, Kossuth tér 13 (☎ 118-232). An elegant place near Parliament, where Bulgarian wines and dishes are served with more alacrity than you'll find in a Sofia restaurant. Folk music.

Napoletana, V, Petőfi tér. Just along from the 24-hr. IBUSZ. Pizzas, spaghetti and other pasta dishes make this a popular place with tourists.

Capri Pizzeria, I, Krisztina krt. Inside the *Hotel Buda-Penta*; Italian food and Austrian beer. (11am-11pm).

Piccolino Pizzeria In the *Hotel Novotel*; closes at 9pm.

Híd, IX, Ferenc krt.17 (☎ 337-994). Near the Petőfi Bridge. Booths on the ground floor and a swish gallery hung with paintings by Haranghy upstairs. Mainly fried meat dishes; open 9am-11pm.

Gyertya, VI, Bajcsy-Zsilinzsky út 21 (☎ 121-039). Meals until 4am – so it's claimed – and *performances* by guest artists.

Művész, XIII, Vígszínház u.5 (☎ 110-235). Good food, popular with artists from the Vígszínház Theatre.

Royal, VII, Lenin krt.49. Hungarian and French cooking, accompanied by Gypsy music. Good value lunches in the *Hársfa Room*.

Lúdláb, VII, Lenin krt.39. Light *music*, open late (closed Sundays).

Megyeri Csárda, IV, Váci út 102 (☎ 693-964). Popular 2nd class nightspot with a wine cellar, sing songs, *folk dancing and Gypsy music*. Specialises in fish fillets and flambe dishes. Open on weekdays (except Wednesdays) 4pm-12pm, Saturdays 4pm-1am, Sundays 11am-12pm.

Hársfa, II, Vörös Hadsereg útja 132 (☎ 164-002). Garden restaurant offering 'hunters' suppers', accompanied by *Schrammel music* in the evenings. Open 12am-12pm (closed Mondays).

Sipos Halászkert, III, Lajos u.46 (☎ 686-480). Famous 2nd class fish garden-restaurant founded in 1930. Music by *László Oláh's Gypsy band*.

Matrózcsárda, IX, Alsórakpart. Likewise specialises in fish dishes, as well as frogs and snails. Nostalgic music. Summer terrace on the Pest embankment, near the Szabadaság Bridge.

Szeged, XI, Bartók út 1 (☎ 666-503). *Csárda*-style fish restaurant with a tavern and wine cellar. Open daily. 11am-1 am.

Öreghalász, IV, Árpád u.20 (☎ 694-192). Another 2nd class fish restaurant with *Gypsy music* and singing. Open weekdays 10am-12pm, weekends 10am-1pm.

Szerb, V, Nagy u.16 (☎ 111-858). Informal atmosphere and Serbian dishes.

Thököly, XIV, Thököly út 80 (☎ 225-444). Posher type of 2nd class restaurant, featuring *Gypsy music* and a Renaissance-style decor (bookings recommended). Serves better Transylvanian food than you'll get in Transylvania. Near the Romanian embassy; open 11am-1am.

Bajkál, V, Semmelweiss u.1-3. Situated in the Soviet House of Culture near Astoria Metro. Russian cooking – none too inspired – plus regional recipes like *shashlik*. Nice tearoom upstairs.

Karczma Polska-Kis Royal, XII, Márvány u.19 (☎ 151-069). Polish food and drink, served in the garden during summer.

Bukarest, XI, Bartók út.48 (☎ 252-203). Includes a bar, *disco* and brasserie. Romanian and Hungarian food.

Aranyfácán, XII, Szilágyi Erzsébet fasor 33. Traditional dishes from Slovakia and adjoining regions once part of the Kingdom of Hungary.

Kislugas Szilágyi E. fasor 77. Serbian food and a garden.

Ezerjó, XIV, Állatkerti krt.3. Garden restaurant near the Széchenyi baths, with Hungarian food and songs and *Gypsy music*. (10am-12pm).

Borkatakomba, XXII, Nagytétényi út 64. Hungarian restaurant situated in Buda's southwestern suburbs, accessible by bus #3 from Móricz Zs. körtér. Open from 5pm-12pm except on Tuesdays.

Aranykacsa, XIV, Örs vezér tere 2. Open daily, 10.30am-12pm. Poultry dishes and *dance music*.

Csiki, IX, Angyal u.37 (☎ 136-627). A small place with a summer garden in Pest's Ferencváros district, featuring Transylvanian dishes and *Gypsy music* in the evenings. Open from 12am-11pm.

Rózsa, IV, Tito u.20-22 (☎ 695-138). Another Transylvanian restaurant, modestly priced, with light music and a *disco* on Sundays. Open daily, 12am-12pm.

Góbé, VIII, József krt.28. The 'Rascal' specialises in mutton dishes.

Kádár Étkezde, VII, Klauzál u.10. A small privately-owned family restaurant just off Klauzál tér – good for lunch. (Monday-Saturday 11.30am-3.30pm).

SELF-SERVICE JOINTS AND SNACK BARS

Badacsony, VIII, Üllői út 6. Self-service place known for its *Debreceni bogdány* cutlets and macaroni à la Milanese. Open weekdays 7am-9pm, weekends 7am-3pm.

Halló, VII, Majakovszkij u.65. Pork chops stuffed with liver or pork steaks with mushrooms and spuds are house specialities. Self-service from 6.30am-9.30pm.

Torkos, IX, Mester u.12. Modern place where you watch the grills being prepared. Good range of salads.

Ízek utcája, VII, Lenin krt.49. Hamburgers, Hungarian and Mediterranean dishes, and a summer palm garden. 11.30am-8.30pm. The name means 'Street of Tastes'.

Unió, VIII, József krt.6-8. Basic Önkiszolgáló self-service canteen; said to cook a mean *Szegedi* chicken goulash. Open daily between 6.30am-9.30pm.
Central, VII, Tanács krt.7. Big canteen just off Deák tér; very busy at lunch time. A place to sit outside and watch life on the Little Boulevard.
Lotto, VII, Rákóczi út 57. Cheap, basic Önkiszolgáló 200m from Keleti station. The bookshop opposite sells Hungarian hiking maps.
Önkiszolgáló, XII, Alkotás u. 7-9. Over the road and just uphill from Déli station. Open daily, 7am-9pm.

Taverns, brasseries, wine cellars and beer halls

It's difficult to draw the line between **taverns and brasseries** but the city has a fair sprinkling of both, mainly concentrated in Pest. Foodwise the emphasis is on grills, roasts and stews – although snacks are usually available – and busy places are likely to resent visitors who are only interested in drinks. If you're mainly intent on drinking it's better to look for **beer halls** (*söröz*ő), **wine bars or wine cellars** (known as *borozó* or *bor pince*). Unless specified otherwise, most are open from 9 or 10am until 10.30-11pm, so anyone interested in **drinking late** should try the three places around Kolosy tér in the III district (open until 4am); *Zodiac* on Kálvin tér; *Két Bagoly* near the market hall; the *Libella* on Budafoki út near Gellért tér (2am) or the bar in the Technological Institute. As a rule of thumb, the further from Pest's shopping district or Castle Hill, the cheaper the prices. Discovering **really cheap dives** for yourself adds to their appeal, so suffice it to suggest looking behind the Vásárcsarnok, around working class districts like Újpest or Csepel, or in the backstreets of the Jewish quarter.

Pepita Oroszlán, V, Váci u. 40. A quiet place to drink, above a popular but reasonably priced restaurant at the unfashionable end of Váci útja. Open from 11am-11pm.
Trojka, V, Népköztársaság útja 28. Grills and booze on the ground floor and a Russian-style tearoom upstairs.
Halászbástya Reservations, smart clothes and a well-filled wallet are necessary to enjoy this nightspot occupying the lowest cloister of the Fishermen's Bastion, with its spectacular view of the waterfront.
Háry, VIII, Bródy S. u.30A. A fairly upmarket cellar-brasserie with Gypsy music, a wide range of wines and rich food. Open from 4pm-1am.
Apostolok, V, Kígyó u.4-6. A stone's throw from the Párizsi udvar, with an Art Nouveau interior including glass-paintings of faraway towns once part of the Kingdom of Hungary. Also a popular restaurant, so at peak times it may be impossible just to drink here.
Söröző **a két Medvéhez**, IX, Üllői út 45. Located in the vaulted cellar of the one-time Killian barracks, in the same building as the mime theatre (p.84). Hungarian and foreign beers, roast meats, and a set menu during summer. Open 12am-11pm.
Bécsi, V, Eötvös Loránd u.8. Goes for a Viennese ambience (if not quite Viennese prices) as its name suggests. Viennese-style decor, Austrian beers, meat soup, Wienerschnitzel and *gemlütlich*.
Kaltenberger A beer-hall cum miniature brewery on the corner of Üllői út and

Kinizsi utca in the IX district, opened in 1986 as a joint venture by Skála-Coop and the Kaltenberg Brewery.

Söröző a Két Pisztolyhoz, IX, Tompa u.6. Another beer-hall opened 3 years previously; besides the bevy it boasts of grills including flambeed 'Robbers' meat' on a spit.

Bécsi, XIII, Salai u.18. Austrian beers and snacks, just north of Szt. István körút.

Tüköry, V, Rosenberg házaspár u.15. Notable for its *harp music* (Mondays, Tuesdays & Fridays), meals and draught Pilsner. Open Monday-Friday 9am-12pm, closed weekends.

Taverna Borpince, V, Szabadsajtó út 5. Devoted to northern dishes and Eger wines (not just *Egri bikavér*).

Montmarte Brasserie, VI, Népköztársaság útja 47. Baguettes, Kronenburg beer and French music.

The Frigate, V, Molnár utca. Known as the 'English pub', which it doesn't really resemble.

Raabe Diele Bierkeller, V Szt. István krt.13. In the cellar of the *Berlin* restaurant, so prices are relatively high and you're encouraged to partake of a snack, if not stuffed turkey breast with cauliflower or *Berliner Eisbein*. A duet provides Schrammel music in the cellar (open 4.30pm-12pm) while a folk ensemble performs upstairs.

Berlini Suszterinas, VIII, József krt.31A. Beer, hot food and furnishings Berlin-style.

Rondella, V, Régiposta u.4. 'Rustic' decor and a prime downtown location make this popular with tourists – a fact reflected in the prices. There's a range of fine wines to wash down dishes, including house specialities like Serbian *Csája* and Pig's knuckle baked in a loaf of bread.

Kékfrankos, VI, Liszt Ferenc tér 7. Quietly devoted to food and wine from the Sopron region.

Bosodi, V, Honvéd u.18. Located one block east of Parliament, perhaps so as to console MPs from Borsod county with hearty recipes and beer originating from that region.

Krúdy, VIII, Krúdy u.19. Archetypal cellar-bistro with Gypsy music.

Erzsébet, VII, Lenin krt.48. A well-established brasserie on the Great Boulevard, divided into booths.

Lővér étterem, VI, Majakovszkij u.100. Besides its banqueting hall, brasserie and wine-cellar (stocked with products of the Sopron region) the 'Huntsman' also boasts of a bowling alley and accepts tourist coupons.

Bowling Brasserie, XII, Alkotás u.63-67. With four automatic bowling lanes and Austrian beers, a kind of synthesised home from home for Germanic or American business types, or anyone else who cares to enter the *Hotel Novotel*. (Open Monday-Friday 11am-11pm, weekends until midnight).

Krisztina, XII, Krisztina körút 25. For roasts, snacks and draught Wernesgrüner beer.

Wernesgrüner Söröző, II, Bem rakpart 49. Likewise good for snacks and Wernesgrüner beer.

Metropol, VII, Rákóczi út 58.

Numero Uno, IX, Gustav utca 9.

Patisseries, coffee houses, tearooms and ice cream

Daily life in Budapest is punctuated by the consumption of black coffee drunk from little glasses, and for anyone who can afford them, a pastry or ice cream. Together they make a quintessentially Central European interlude, although nowadays less prolonged than before the war, when Budapest's numerous **coffee houses** (*Kávéház*) were social clubs, home and haven for their respective clienteles. Free newspapers were available to the regulars – writers, journalists and lawyers (for whom the cafés were effectively 'offices') or posing revolutionaries – with sympathy drinks or credit to those down on their luck. Today's *cukrászda* or **patisseries** generally have less mystique and more variety; ranging from stand-up places to establishments with Belle Époque decor and smoothly deferential service. Those listed below are the most atmospheric or famous; the majority also serve tea, a beverage best sampled in one of Pest's **tearooms**. Street vendors and many patisseries sell **ice cream** (*fagylalt*), but for the sheer range of flavours and the view of life on Felszabadulás tér one can't beat the *Jégbüfé* occupying one wall of the Párizsi Udvar.

Gerbeaud's The flagship of the fleet, also known as *Vörösmarty's* after its location on Vörösmarty tér. Tourists and wealthy Hungarians favour the elegant salon facing the square, where a coffee and a *torta* will set you back around 60Ft; the same rich pastries cost less in *Kis Gerbaud* around the corner, a less sumptuous annex. Open daily from 9am-9pm.

Atrium Terrace Adjoining the *Atrium Hyatt*. Touristy but undeniably well-situated for breakfast, pastries or ice cream when the weather's fine. (6am-10pm).

Intermezzo Likewise a summer terrace overlooking the Danube, with standards, clientele and prices reflecting its attachment to the *Duna Intercontinental* (9am-11pm).

Bécsi Kávézó A high-quality modern coffee-house within the *Hotel Forum*, equally pricey (10am-9pm).

Hauer cukrászda, VIII, Rákóczi út 49. Performances of the *Mignon Cabaret* on Fridays (from 8.30pm until midnight depending on the duration of impromptu skits); tickets available from Népköztársaság útja 18, or perhaps at the door (☎ 142-002). Otherwise known for its cream and fruit-filled pastries.

Különlegességi, Népköztársaság útja 70 (8am-9pm daily). In the same class as Gerbeaud's (though a mite cheaper), with a more sombrely Edwardian style of decor – plush, with the dark patina of old woodwork.

Művész, Népköztársaság útja 29 (same hours). Likewise posh; patronised by Opera-goers more frequently than by the artistic clientele its name implies.

Angelika, I, Batthyány tér 7. A haunt of poets and writers occupying a former parish church in Buda's Watertown district. Artists from the Radnóti Theatre present *Sarokasztal*, a literary programme, on Tuesday each month from October to May.

Gyöngyszem IX, Tolbuhin körút 15. Notable for its summer garden and piano music in the evenings; located on Kálvin tér (8am-11pm).

Rózsa Eszpresszo A classy joint with samovars, cold Russian hor d'oeuvres (*zakuski*) and a weekly Soviet literary programme to accompany one's tea.

Omnia cukrászda, VIII, Rákóczi út 67. Morello cherry cake and the oddly-named *Lúdláb torta* (goose-foot cake) are specialities. Open from 8am-10pm (Sundays 10am-8pm).

Pálma, VII, Lenin körút 36. In the 1st class category like all the above. Known for its creams in glasses and *parfait* specialities; open from 8am-10pm.

Korona, Dísz tér 16. A popular tourist trap on Castle Hill (10am-9pm daily), lacking in character despite being the venue for literary evenings.

Ruszwurm's, Szentháromság tér 7 (open 10am-8pm). Excellent cakes, served production-line fashion to folks taking a break from sightseeing on Castle Hill, who crowd its diminuitive interior.

Hungária Kávéház, VII, Lenin krt.9-11. Traditionally a meeting place for artists, writers and journalists (open from 7am-10pm).

Astoria Kávéház V, Kossuth u.19. Fairly redolent of the old Pest coffee-houses and furnished in the traditional style.

Híd, IX, Ferenc körút 15. Cosy place next door to the restaurant of the same name, serving cakes prepared on the spot. Open daily 7am-10pm.

Rákóczi, VII, Rákóczi út 40. Dance music and late hours (until 2am); Chestnut purée (*gesztenyepüré*) and a cake called *Eva torta* are both specialities.

Szimfónia, IX, Üllői út 65-67. Features dance music from 6pm-12pm.

Diabetikus cukrászda, XI, József krt.71. Pastries and sweets prepared *for diabetics*. Located on the Great Boulevard (bus #12 or tram #4/#6).

Bajkál Tearoom, V, Semmelweiss u.1-3. Above the Russian restaurant, with a relaxed atmosphere and a range of brews. (7am-11pm).

Trojka, VI, Népköztársaság útja 28. A Russian tearoom above a brasserie, popular with young people.

Tabán teázó, I, Attila út . A teahouse adjoining the *Tabáni Kakas* restaurant.

Te + Én, II, Bem rakpart 30. Cheap and informal, a favourite place for tête à têtes (the name means *You & I*).

ENTERTAINMENTS

Eating out could fairly be classified under **entertainments**, such is the prevalence of music at restaurants, so besides the options covered below, bear in mind the places previously listed. On the more regular front, full details of the **Budapest Spring Festival** (March) and the **Autumn Music Weeks** (from late-September to late-October) are available from TOURINFORM and publicised in *Programme*; drawing the cream of Hungary's artists and top international acts, both are star events in the capital's cultural year. There's only slightly less happening during the summer months, and on **Constitution Day** (August 20) the population lines the embankments to watch a **Danube regatta** and, around 8pm, a fantastic display of **fireworks** (best seen from the Szabadság Bridge, but get there early to secure a place; for other **parades** see p.65). Finally, aspiring Barry Normans should enjoy the 4-day **Budapest Film Festival** which premiers (subtitled or dubbed) Hungarian and foreign pics. The attendent razzmatazz falls short of more profligate displays in Hollywood or Cannes, but the main difference is the weather, for at the beginning of February Budapest is blanketed with snow.

For kids. . .and adults
From the kids' assault-course on Klauzál tér to the imaginative wooden see-saws and swings, based on folk motifs, erected in Margaréta Park in the XII district, there are **children's playgrounds** all over Budapest. Adults could combine a visit to Jubilemi on Gellért Hill with some sightseeing, or extract a series of childish diversions from **the Városliget** with it's mock castle and old trains. Vidám Park **funfair** nearby has a score of cheap rides, although some of them might seem pretty tame to progeny raised on Western Fun Parks. Further along the road are the state **circus** and a **zoo** that's probably best avoided (see Listings). Curiosity about bugs, reptiles and amphibians can be satisfied at the privately-owned **Aquarium/Terrarium** on Párizsi utca in the Belváros; while the **Waxworks** on Castle Hill (p.49) could be just the thing for kids going through a gory phase. The choice of **museums** (p.69) is probably best left to them.

The **Planetarium** near the entrance to the Népliget offers a variety of sensory experiences. Most tourist offices have a leaflet detailing 7-8 programmes at the **Laser Theare** (☎ 344-513/ext.24), ranging from films of classic rock bands to music by Mussorgsky – all accompanied by lasers – not to mention the amusingly tacky, adults-only *Lézerotika*, which avoids serious porn by substituting 'green luminous pencils' whenever 'the photographs and music fail to express the torments of the senses'. Unsuprisingly, the Laser Theatre has pushed astronomical shows into the background, although by prior arrangement (☎ 138-280) groups are treated to the *Theatre of the Sky*, accompanied by a lecture on Magyar folk cosmology in the appropriate language. If you'd rather actually sqint through a telescope, the *Uránia Observatory* (I, Sánc u.3/b; ☎ 869-171) offers the chance to do so between 6pm-10pm on clear nights.

The **Marcibányi tér Fair** on Sundays (9am-2pm) has something for everyone: music, mime and puppet shows, crafts demonstrations and dancing – either inside the Cultural Centre or on the square itself – and there's also a *crèche*. From nearby Moszkva tér (p.55) you can ride the **cogwheel and Pioneers' railway** up into the **Buda Hills**, wander around and then return to the city by **chair-lift** (p.57), while a yet breezier excursion is offered by **riverboat cruises**. IBUSZ organises a 2-hour jaunt (with a stopover for refreshments on Margit Island) for about $5; the boat leaves the Vigadó pier at 10am on Mondays, Wednesdays, Fridays and Sundays, May 1 to October 31. During the same period, there are more frequent small riverboat services – eg. from Boráros tér across to Gellért tér, then over to Petőfi tér, back across to Batthyány tér, and so forth up to Május 9. Park; or from Jászai Mari tér to Margit Island and Római-Fürdő. Tickets, available at the pier, are cheap; but rides are much shorter and there's more waiting involved than on the IBUSZ boats.

If the *Petőfi Csarnok* or *MOM* (see below) aren't putting on something for children, you could take them to a dance club or one of Budapest's two **puppet theatres**. Morning and matinée performances are for kids, whilst the evening's masked grotesqueries or renditions of Bartók's *The Wooden Prince* and *The Miraculous Mandarin* are intended for adults. Tickets and programmes from the *Bábszínház* themselves, located at 69, Nepköz. útja (☎ 215-200), and on

Jókai tér. Thanks to the *Táncház* movement, most local Cultural Centres (*Művelődési Ház*) have **children's dance clubs** on Saturday afternoons or Sunday mornings, which foreigners are welcome to attend – just ask at the nearest centre (addresses listed at the back of the *Budapest Atlasz*).

Guided tours and organised nightlife

Readily available, free brochures detail the various **guided tours** offered by *Budapest-Tourist* (V, Roosevelt tér 5/☎ 173-555) and most branches of IBUSZ. You should book in advance for evening programmes (or the day before for excursions from Budapest, see p.85), but on other tours it's usually okay to pay at the assembly point. Since the Waxworks, the Gellért Baths and Budapest's main landmarks can all be visited at less expense off your own bat, I can't see the attraction of the *Hall of Fame*, *City of Baths* or *Sightseeing by coach* trips; but the one combining a visit to the National Gallery or the Mátyás Church with a *tour of Parliament* is the only way to see the latter's magnificent interior. Tours start at Gate XII at 11am and 2pm unless they've been cancelled because Parliament is in session, which doesn't happen often.

Sadly, the *Hunyadi* no longer hosts cheap Saturday night disco-cruises on the river, having moved into '**Folklore evenings**' ($25 inclusive of a meal and drinks; departures from the Vigadó pier at 7.30pm every evening except Mondays and Wednesdays, from June 15 to September 30). On terra firma, there are two more, fractionally cheaper 'folk evenings' on offer. If the *Goulash Party* and the *Paprika Show* suggest 50 foreigners pigging-out whilst tweely-costumed musicians accompany some ghastly entertainer clasping a giant, imitation paprika to her boosom – well, that's more or less what transpires.

There's a much better programme at the **Folklór Centrum** (XI, Fehérvári út 47/☎ 451-360), where visitors are encouraged to join in the whirling and stamping, which can be fun if you're in the mood. Programmes begin every night at 8.45pm (between mid-May and late September); buy tickets at the door, or beforehand from IBUSZ or Budapest-Tourist ($5). Both organisations can also arrange a visit to *Les Misérables* (or whatever the latest attraction is), or a programme which includes topless showgirls at *Maxims*, dancing at the *Casanova Bar*, and Gypsy music and bean soup somewhere on Castle Hill as a climax. **Budapest by Night** costs around $30, the *Theatre Evening* roughly half that.

Clubs, discos, gigs and Táncház

Most young Hungarians avoid Budapest's best-known **nightclubs** like a plutonium cocktail, dismissing *Maxims* (VII, Akácfa u.3), *Moulin Rouge*, (VI, Nagymező u.17), *Astoria* and the Atrium Hyatt's *Balloon Bar* (open 11am-2am) as 'full of foreigners and hookers'. *Horoszkóp* in the Buda-Penta Hotel (I, Krisztina krt.45/open until 4am), *Pipacs Bar* (V, Aranykéz u.5) and the *Casanova* piano-bar (I, Batthyány tér 4) are staider but equally tourist-orientated, with slow dance music and the odd spot of disco-beat, while its prime location on Castle Hill is enough to ensure the popularity of *Old Firenze* (open until 3am).

Until a few years ago, Magyars looking for a rave-up had to content themselves with student clubs (see below) or the pokey, aeroplane-lounge style *Fekete Macska* (IX, Knézits u.1/open until around 1am), where one needs to make reservations (☎ 250-060), but now there's the **Petőfi Csarnok** in the Városliget. Though the building is pretty unprepossing plenty happens here, mainly on Fridays and at weekends: concerts, cabaret, films and videos (50-80Ft admission); occasional flea markets; but most of all the Saturday night *Starlight Disco* (50Ft), jampacked because young Magyars can afford it. Most of them would find the plate-glass *Margithíd* and the less visible *Víg Matróz* discos (both near the bridge end of Szent István krt) too expensive, but neither lies beyond the means of Westerners, and the tacky *Vénusz* with its Go-Go dancers (behind Római-Fürdő campsite) positively heaves with tourists. All charge between 80-150Ft. (*Vénusz* may admit 'unattached ladies' free) and keep going until 1am-3am, depending on the crowd and the manager's whim.

Student clubs are another locus of activity, although not much happens during the summer vac. Discos, gigs, films etc. are presented under the auspices of KISZ, the Communist Youth, so their offices in the universities are the first place to make enquiries. The *MKKE-klub* is a permanent fixture in the main building of the Economic University on the Pest side of the embankment, but events may also take place in the courtyard of the block on Zsil utca, or at the bottom end of Ráday utca, both farther to the south. Across the river, other clubs are named after different blocks of the Technological University – the no-longer stylish *E-klub* and the newer *R-klub*, for example. Admission to the above should be easy, but you'll need a member to sign you into the *Young Artists' Club* (108, Népköz. útja). A subsidised haunt of the *divatos*, with an excellent buffet, its clientele overlaps with that of other clubs which advertise themselves by small posters on the lamposts around Felszabadulás tér. The *Szélrózsa* (VIII, Baross u.28), *Kassák* (XIV, Uzsoki út 57) or *Vásárhely* (XI, Kruspér u.2-4) clubs may still exist, but transience is part of their appeal and they're liable to official closure (as happened to the *Rakpart klub*); a scan of the lamposts, however, should reveal 3 or 4 going concerns. On Felszabadulás tér itself stands the *Egyetem Bar*, come evenings a focus for **gay life**, which otherwise revolves around the *Emke* and *Diófa* (p.66) and certain baths. The gay scene is miniscule and very discreet, and lesbians constitute a yet smaller, more insecure group.

Cabaret can cover anything from stand-up comics to minimalist mimes, and one can usually find something that's pitched at a foreign audience, or at least doesn't depend on a knowledge of Hungarian. On Friday evenings (8.30pm-10.30pm), Budapest actors and literati perform skits in the *Hauer Cukrászda* (VIII, Rákóczi út 49) to an audience replete with the establishment's rich pastries, whilst at *Mikroszkóp* (VI, Nagymező u.22-24/☎ 313-322) they go in for peckish – as opposed to biting – political satire. Artistic censorship is less a matter of rigid rules than vague ideological moods and internalised taboos, and it's only occasionally that acts overstep the mark, as happened at the *Rakpart*.

New or 'controversial' **bands** usually play the kind of fly-by-night places mentioned above, whereas groups with their foot in the door (see p.30) may be granted **gigs** at the *E-klub* or the *Petőfi Csarnok*. It's only really big names and Western bands that receive proper promotion and a large venue like the

Sportcsarnok or the *Népstadion*, where the Talking Heads, Tina Turner and Queen have appeared (a long-waited Black Sabbath concert was cancelled after the band played Bophuthatswana), but the gravevine carries news of events that don't rate a mention in *Progiamme* or *Pesti Műsor*. However, both will tell you what's on at the **MOM Rock Theatre** (XII, Csörsz u.18/☎ 150-688) – when last heard it was *István a Király*, a kind of Godspell meets Conan the Barbarian.

Finally, there are **Tánchaź** (Dance Houses), which began as a reaction to foreign pop but also the kind of stereotyped **folk music and dance** that was promoted during the 1950s. They aim to revive old Magyar instruments, tunes and dances and get people *involved* in the process – a folkier-than-thou attitude isn't encouraged, and even foreigners will be dragged into whatever's going on. Two places worth trying are the *Téka Tánchaź* on Almássy tér (Friday evenings) and the *Kalamajka Tánchaź* on Molnar utca (Saturdays); TOURINFORM can supply numerous other addresses.

Opera, ballet, classical music and drama

A box at the magnificently plush *Opera Ház* on Népköz. útja costs little over £5, so treat yourself to a grandiose gesture in keeping with the style of the place. Hungarians prefer their **opera** 'old style', with lavish sets and costumes and histrionic performances which they interrupt with ovations after particularly bravura passages. Operas by Mozart, Verdi, Puchini, Wagner and native composers are staged throughout the year, while during the Spring and Autumn festivals 6-8 new productions are premiered. The most recent contemporary Hungarian opera to tour the West earned high praise for its young lead singer, Adrienne Csengery, but little for its composer.

The National Opera is also renowned for its **ballet** company, which fruitfully combines native and Russian choreography. Each year Budapest receives a visit from at least one premier company like the Bolshoi, if not more exotic acts like the Mongolian State Troupe, which appear at the *Erkel Theatre* (VIII, Köztársaság tér/☎ 330-540), commonly also the venue for **modern dance**. Győr's company always sells out when it comes to Budapest, but there shouldn't be much difficulty getting tickets for the **mime** show at the *Színpad Centi* (Üllői út 45).

Opera tickets are sold opposite the Opera House, and at *Philharmonia* (1, Vörösmarty tér), which also handles **bookings** for concerts of **classical music**. Watch out for artists like the violin/cellist Miklós Perényi and the pianists Dezső Ránki and Zoltán Kocsis. The *Vigadó*, where Liszt, Brahms and Dvorak once conducted, is the grandest venue, followed by the *Academy of Music* (VI, Liszt tér 1/☎ 420-179) whose Main Hall presents orchestral and chamber music on a more or less daily basis, whilst the more intimate Chamber Hall is generally used for performances of contemporary works. Smaller concerts may also take place in the Mátyás Church, the Erkel Theatre, the *Pesti Rondella* and the courtyard of the *Budapest Hilton* during summer and the festivals. Moreover, it's only a short train ride from the capital to Martonvásár (p.113), where the *Beethoven Season* takes place.

During the Spring Festival and the summer months there's most likely to be something capable of transcending language-barriers playing at Budapest's theatres – particularly the open-air ones on Margit Island, in Városmajor Park and the courtyard of the *Hilton Hotel*. Programmes are well advertised and seats are usually very cheap.

Spectator sports

The **Hungarian Grand Prix**, first held in 1986, is now an annual event, although at time of writing the exact dates for August '88 have yet to be announced. The **Formula-1** track, 20km northeast of the capital near MOGYORÓD, can be reached by the Hatvan road (M3), or special services provided during the Grand Prix – namely buses from the Árpád Bridge or trains from Keleti pu. to FOT (whence there are buses). Alternatively, board a Gödöllő-bound HÉV train at the terminal near Örs vezér tere (Metro 1) and alight at the 12th stop, SZILASLIGET, which is 1,800m northeast of the racetrack's entrance 'C'. Tickets and programme details from IBUSZ or Budapest Tourist.

Some time during the spring (generally April) the **Budapest Marathon** takes place. The route runs from the Népstadion to Római-Fürdő and the event is thoroughly publicised and televised. Locals seem to get more excited about **football**, exhaustively covered in the pages of *Népsport* and mentioned in the sports section of *Programme*. International matches take place in the Népstadion, league games at smaller stadiums across the city. *Ferencváros* (named after the district of Budapest where their stadium is located) is one of the city's leading clubs; their fans, alas, have a growing reputation for hooliganism.

EXCURSIONS FROM BUDAPEST – AND THE GREAT RAILWAY JOURNEY TO CHINA

Given the range of destinations accessible by bus or train from Budapest's terminals (p.87) or stations (p.89), there are dozens of feasible **excursions from the capital**. You'll find information on getting there from Budapest in the introductions to each of the following chapters, starting with the *Danube Bend*, so detailed here are only those trips **arranged by IBUSZ**. As the $ has recently declined in relation to the DM upon which charges are based, the prices quoted below are probably underestimates.

There a no less than 4 excursions **to the west bank of the Danube Bend**. On Thursdays (May 1 to December 31), a coach leaving Engels tér at 9am takes tourists to Szentendre for a *Nostalgia Program* ($20), including lunch and tea; whilst for the same price you can visit Szentendre and Visegrád by boat, which departs from the Vigadó pier at 8.30am on Wednesdays and Saturdays between May 1 and October 31. The *Danube Bend by coach* ($20) takes in Esztergom as well, with a 9am start from Engels tér on Tuesdays and Fridays (May 1 to October 31) or Saturdays (November 1 to April 31). Another, slightly dearer tour combines Esztergom and Visegrád with both modes of transport and a spot of champagne; the coach leaves at 10am every Saturday between 1 June and August 31.

Second in popularity are day-excursions **to the Balaton**. The basic $30 tour includes sightseeing at Tihany and Badacsony, meals, wine-tasting and a jaunt on the lake; coaches leave Engels tér on Mondays and Thusdays at 8am from May 1 to October 31, and it's wise to book at least 24 hours in advance. A boozier alternative is *Vintage in the Badacsony* ($40), with lunch, a boat ride with champagne, and all the grapes and wine that you can pick or drink (departs Saturdays at 9am from September 1 to October 31). If you don't feel up to the train journey and buying tickets (see p.000), IBUSZ can also arrange outings to the **Beethoven Concerts at Martonvásár** ($7) during July and August. Finally, there are three **folklore/equestrian tours**, to Lajosmizse near Kecskemét ($35); Kalocsa and Solt ($40); and Tök, following a visit to the ruined C13 **Romanesque Church at Zsámbék** ($25).

From Budapest to China by rail
As budget-travellers are discovering, **the cheapest way to China** is the great railway journey from Budapest to Beijing (Peking). *Yorkshire Tours* and *Thomas Cook* can arrange this in the UK for around £600-£800, but by doing your own legwork over a period of a month or so in Budapest a return ticket may be purchased for as little as $150.

The first thing to do in Budapest is visit the IBUSZ office (VII, Tanács krt.17-19/☎ 227-050) responsible for allocating seats on the *Trans-Mongolian Express*. Bookings are heavy during the summer, so ask about cancellations. Your seat reservation will be telexed to Moscow, and you don't actually buy **tickets** until IBUSZ receives a reply (1-2 weeks). It makes sense to travel first class on the 9-day journey, and buy an open return ticket for the *Trans-Manchurian Express*, since a single back to Budapest costs twice as much in Bejing (where some travellers sell their returns for a profit). With an IUS card, first class from Budapest to Beijing costs $70 ($55 2nd class), and the return journey $78 (1st class); without one fares are roughly 30% higher.

Next you must acquire three **visas**, starting at the Chinese Embassy (VI, Benczúr u.17/☎ 224-872), where the process costs $10 and takes one day. Then, with railway ticket and Chinese visa, go to the Soviet Embassy (Népköz. útja 104/☎ 318-985) and apply for one of their visas ($10), which takes 8-10 days. Since they don't retain one's passport, you can simultaneously obtain a Mongolian visa from XII, Istenhegyi út 59/65 (☎ 151-412), which costs the same or $15 for immediate issue. For all this you'll need 6-8 photos – see p.89 for the locations of photomats.

Before leaving Budapest, buy plenty of food and drink for **the journey** to Moscow (2 days), where there's time to wander around before boarding the *Trans-Mongolian Express*. Soviet trains are 'dry' and catering is worse than on British Rail, with the honourable exception of the *provodnitsa* who serve Russian tea from a samovar at any hour. Winning the favour of these formidable ladies may require some effort and a smattering of Russian, but a sympathetic *provodnitsa* will make your journey much smoother. Although the scenery goes on forever in a boring, steppe-ish way, other passengers – hailing from every continent and all over the USSR – can be endlessly diverting. If they're not, take refuge in *The Big Red Train Ride*, Eric Newby's classic account of travel on the *Trans-Siberian Express*. It's possible to trade T-shirts for food, wine or vodka on all these Trans-Union routes, but Soviet customs won't take kindly to the import of a dozen wrapped in plastic, nor obviously saleable quantities of anything else. To help with your arrival in Beijing, and travels thereafter, bring along the *Rough Guide to China*.

LISTINGS

Airlines Mostly in the Belváros. Tickets on MALÉV flights can be reserved at Dorottya u.2, Váci u.1 and Roosevelt tér 5. For foreign agencies, see TOURINFORM's *Budapest Guide*.

Airport Ferihegy, southeast of the city beyond Üllői út. Best reached by the half-hourly coach shuttle from Engels tér (30Ft). For flight information ring 572-122 or 120-000.

Banks Most OTP branches are open Monday-Friday 9am-4pm, but changing money/TCs is easier at almost any tourist office (**24-hr. service** at V, Petőfi tér 3). For information about receiving money transfered from abroad ring 389-133 or enquire at Alagút u.3 in the I district.

Books The *Könyvesbolt* at 32 Váci utca stocks the widest range of foreign novels, plus Hungarian authors in foreign languages and various tourist and coffee-table books. Also try at Váci u.33, Petőfi u.2, Martinelli tér 5 and inside the *Párizsi udvar*. Second-hand bookshops, *Antikvárium*, yield the occasional find, although most foreign books are of German origin. Antikvárium on the corner of Bacsy-Zsilinszky út and Deák tér, and at Váci u.28 & 75, Múzeum körút 15 and Károlyi u.3 are possibilities. You can read books and **Western newspapers** in the **library at the British Embassy**, or buy papers and magazines at the *Atrium-Hyatt*, *Duna Intercontinental* and other top hotels.

Bus terminals The most useful are *Népstadion* (Metro line 2/☎ 187-106) serving areas east of the Danube; and *Engels tér*. The latter is for buses to Transdanubia, the west bank of the Danube Bend, Ferihegy Airport and neighbouring countries (see p.62). *Bulcsú utca terminal* (XIII district/☎ 296-480) covers the Vác region; *Bécsi út* (III/☎ 889-965) the eastern Pilis Hills; and buses from *Széna tér* go to Zsámbék.

Camping and Caravaning Club (IX, Kálvin tér 9/Monday-Friday 8am-4pm/☎ 177-248). Arranges reductions for FICC members, and can advise on equipment.

Car rental *IBUSZ/Avis* V, Martinelli tér 8 (☎ 184-158) and V, Petőfi tér 3 (☎ 185-707); *Főtaxi/HERTZ* VII, Kertész u.24-28 (7am-7pm daily/☎ 221-471); *Volántourist* IX, Vaskapu u.16 (☎ 141-899); Ferihegy Airport (8am-8pm daily); and from most deluxe hotels.

Car repairs *Fiat* models at XII, Boldizsár út; *Ford* & *Mercedes* at XIII, Révész u.1-5 & 11; *Opel* at XX, Láva u.20; *Peugot* & *Renault* at XI, Bicskei út 3; *Volkswagen* at XIII, Szabolcs u.34 and III, Mozaik u.3. For **repair information** try *AFIT* (Váci u.46B/☎ 409-560), for **spare parts** VII, Dózsa Gy. út 36. Ring 260-688 for the Magyar Auto Klub's **breakdown service** (7am-7pm daily) and 327-834 for 24-hour **tow-away**.

Chemists 24-hour service on Felszabadulás tér; other branches open nights are advertised in the windows of day-chemists.

Circus (*Nagycirkusz*) On the north side of the Városliget. Ring 428-300 for details of performances (from Wednesday-Sunday).
Concert bookings from *Philharmonia*, Vörösmarty tér 1 (☎ 176-222). Opera and theatre tickets from Népköztársaság útja 18 (☎ 120-000) opposite the Opera House.
Dry cleaning Flórián tér shopping centre, Párisi u.1, Majakovszkij u.15 and the Skala department store. **Laundries** (*Patyolat*) take a minimum of 24 hours.
Embassies/consulates *Austria* VI, Benczúr u.16 (☎ 229-467); *Bulgaria* Népköztársaság útja 115 (☎ 220-836/824); *Canada* II, Budakeszi út 55 (365-728); *China* VI, Benczúr u.17 (☎ 224-872); *Czechoslovakia* XIV, Népstadion út 24 (☎ 636-600); *Denmark* II, Vérhalom u.12-6 (☎ 152-066); *West Germany* II, Ady u.18 (☎ 150-644); *DDR* XIV, Népstadion út 101-103 (☎ 635-275); *Israel* (represented by the Swedish consulate, see below); *Netherlands* XIV, Abonyi u.31 (☎ 228-432); *Norway* XII, Határőr u.35 (☎ 665-161); *Romania* XIV, Thököly út 72 (☎ 426-941); *Sweden* XIV, Ajtósi sor 27A (☎ 229-800); *UK* V, Harmincad u.6 (☎ 182-888); *USA* V, Szabadság tér 12 (☎ 119-629); *USSR* Népköztársaság útja 104 (☎ 318-985); *Yugoslavia* VI, Dózsa Gy. út 92A (☎ 429-953). For others see the *Budapest Guide*.
Emergencies Ambulance:☎ 04; Police:☎ 07; Fire service:☎ 05.
Funfair (*Vidám park*) Near the Circus on the edge of the Városliget; no Disneyland but plenty of things to ride. (Open April-September 10am-8pm, September-March 10am-7pm daily).
Hospitals The *Városi Kórház*, V, Baross u.69-71 (☎ 690-666); for teeth the *Fogászati Klinikák*, VIII, Mikszath K. tér (☎ 131-639); specialist clinics around *Klinikák* between Baross u. and Üllői út. Embassies can recommend private, foreign language-speaking doctors and dentists.
Insurance *Állami Biztosító* (X, Üllői út 1) for information and policies, claims to XI, Hamzsabégi út 60.
International calls Easiest to make from TOURINFORM (V, Petőfi u.17-19/Monday-Saturday 8am-8pm/Sunday 8am-1pm) or, more expensively, from deluxe hotels. For the international operator dial 09, for information in foreign languages 172-200.
Lost property For items left on public transport, VII, Akácfa u.18 (Monday, Tuesday, Thursday 7am-4pm/Wednesday, Friday 7am-6.30pm/☎ 226-613); otherwise Engels tér 5 (Monday 8am-6pm, Tuesday & Thursday 8am-5pm, Friday 8am-3pm/☎ 174-691). Lost **passports** should be reported to *KEOKH* (VI, Rudas u.45/Monday 8am-4.30pm, Tuesday-Friday 8.30am-12am), and any found will be forwarded for collection there.
Markets (*piac*) Besides the colourful Vásárcsarnok (p.67), you can buy fresh produce at XIII, Élmunkás tér; Klauzál tér; XIV Bosnyák tér, and – popular with countryfolk – near István tér in Újpest. Opening hours are usually Monday 6am-5pm; Tuesday, Wednesday, Thursday & Saturday 6am-6pm; Friday 6am-7pm, but Élmunkás tér and the Fehérvári út market in the XI district also function on Sunday mornings, when the **craft market** occurs on Marczibányi tér in Buda. Budapest's **flea market**, the *Ecseri*, sells everything from bike spares and jackboots to C19 peasant clothing and hand-carved pipes (I even saw an unwanted bust of Stalin!). Bargain hard and avoid being

taken for a West German – they're always overcharged. The Ecseri lies along Nagykörösi út in Pest's XX district – take bus #54 from Boráros tér – and is open Monday-Friday 8am-4pm, 8am-3pm on Saturdays.

Motoring information The *Magyar Auto Klub*, II, Rómer Floris u.4A (☎ 152-040 & 666-040); *Fővinform* for traffic conditions in Budapest (☎ 171-173); *Útinform* (☎ 222-238) for national conditions.

Naturism is slowly catching on in Hungary, and the recently-formed *Naturisták Egyesülete* organises excursions to lakes and pools where the habit can be practised. TOURINFORM can probably supply their address and telephone number. Nude sunbathing is okay on the single-sex terraces of Margit Island's Palatinus baths, and just about acceptable on the fringes of the pool at Csillaghegyi.

Photo-mats at KEOKH, Népköztársaság útja 12, and on the 3rd floor of the Corvin department store on Rákóczi út. The photographer László Ruzsiczky may also do rush jobs for visas: contact him at VIII, József körút 19 (Blaha Lujza Metro stn.) or ring 144-200.

Photographic equipment Váci u.12; Párizsi u.13; Szt. István körút 3; Tanács körút 14, and Rákóczi út 34, all in the Belváros.

Post Offices Main office/*poste restante* V, Petőfi u.13 (Monday-Friday 8am-6pm/Saturday 8am-2pm); 24-hour *póstas* at VI, Lenin körút 105 (Nyugati station) and VIII, Verseny u.1 (Keleti station).

Railway stations (*pályaudvar/pu.*) Keleti, Nyugati and Déli (all accessible by Metro) handle most traffic. *Keleti pu.* is the point of departure for express trains to Miskolc and Békéscsaba; and Austria, East & West Germany, Switzerland, France, Czechoslovakia, Poland, Romania, the USSR, Yugoslavia and Bulgaria abroad. Domestic traffic from *Nyugati pu.* goes to Szeged, Debrecen and Nyíregyháza; international services to Romania, Czechoslovakia and the DDR. *Déli pu.* – serving Transdanubia and the Balaton – is grossly overcrowded in the summer, and has a few trains to Austria and Yugoslavia. The Great Plain west of the Tisza can be reached from *Józsefváros pu.*, south of Kerepesi Cemetery, and the odd train to Romania departs from *Zugló pu.* (bus #7 from Felszabadulás tér). Domestic tickets can be bought on the day of travel from the station, but **international tickets** should be purchased at least 24 hours in advance from *MÁV*, Népköztáraság útja 35 (Monday-Wednesday 9am-5pm/Thursday-Friday 9am-7pm/☎ 228-438), unless you're undertaking the epic train journey **to China** (see above). Expect to queue during the summer. **Suburban HÉV railways** run from Batthyány tér to Szentendre; from Örs vezér tere to Gödöllő; and from Boráros tér to Csepel Island.

Radio Petőfi broadcasts the news in English (11am) and German (10.27am) on weekdays, and on Saturdays at 11.57 & 10.27.

Sports Indoor sports facilities & ice skating in the *Sportcsarnok*, near Népstadion football stadium. Tennis courts for hire at II, Nagykovácsi út (Monday-Friday 8am-2pm). Horse-riding at the Petneházy school (II, Feketefej u./Tuesday-Sunday 9am-7pm) can be arranged by *Pegazus tours*, V, Károlyi u.5 (☎ 171-562). During winter, it's possible to ski at Normafa and Jánoshegy in the Buda Hills. Various types of **equipment** can be hired from II, Török u.2; VI, Jókai tér 7 and VIII, József körút 67.

Supermarkets Generally open Monday-Friday 9am-7pm (Thursday until 8pm), Saturday 9am-1pm. The stores on Flórián tér, Kálvin tér and Blaha L. tér are open on Saturday until 3pm, while the big supermarket on Batthyány tér does business until 5pm (and from 7am-1pm on Sunday).

Zoo (*Állatkert*) Just north of the Városliget (May to September 9am-dusk/closed Wednesdays). Károly Kos's Turkish and Transylvanian style buildings look nice, but aren't fit accommodation for bird nor beast. Animal rights have yet to become an issue in Hungary, and this place surely deserves a visit from the ALF, if nobody else.

FESTIVALS

Winter
The latest Magyar and foreign pictures get a showing at the 4-day *Film Festival* at the **beginning of February**.

Spring
Music, drama and other events during the *Spring Festival* in **March**. Military parades and suchlike to commemorate Liberation Day on **April 4**. Floats, processions and speeches to mark International Workers' Day on **May 1**.

Summer
A Danube Regatta at noon and fireworks around 8pm on **August 20**, *Constitution Day*.

Autumn
From **late-September to late-October**, the Budapest *Music Weeks*. On **November 7**, militaristic displays in honour of the Bolshevik Revolution.

TRAVEL DETAILS

Express trains
Only the fastest services to the main towns are listed here; others appear in the *Travel Details* at the end of each chapter. Some trains are boardable at two Budapest terminals; we've placed them under the station where they wait longest.
From Déli Station to Balatonfüred (*Göcsej* express; 2 hours' journey); Balatonszentgyörgy (*Kanizsa*; 2¾); Dombóvár (*Somogy*; 2); Győr (*Ciklámen*; *Lővér*; 2); Pécs (*Baranya*; *Mecsek*; 3); Siófok (*Kanizsa*; 1¾); Sopron (*Ciklámen*; *Lővér*; 3½); Szombathely (*Bakony-Őrség*; *Savaria*; 3½); Zalaegerszeg (*Göcsej*; 4).
From Keleti Station to Békéscsaba (*Csaba*; *Körös*; 3); Debrecen (*Tokaj*; 3¾); Miskolc (*Borsod*; *Rákóczi*; *Tokaj*; 2).
From Nyugati Station to Debrecen (*Hajdú*; *Szabolcs*; 3); Kecskemét (*Napfény*; *Szeged*; 1¼); Szeged (*Napfény*; *Szeged*; 2¼).

Volán buses
From Bulcsú utca: Regular services to places along the east bank of the Danube Bend.
From Engels tér: Services to all the main towns in Transdanubia, places along the west bank of the Danube Bend, and Ferihegy Airport.
From Népstadion: Services to areas east of the Danube.

International trains
Departure times given below are likely to have changed slightly, but the pattern of services should be much the same.
From Déli Station: *Lehár* (to Vienna; departs around 6.30pm).
From Keleti Station: *Báthori* (Warsaw; 6pm); *Budapest-Moscow* (8.15pm & 11.10pm); *Meridian* (Belgrade; 4.25pm); *Orient Express* (Vienna & Paris 9.20am; Bucharest 9.30pm); *Pannonia* (Bucharest & Sofia 6am; Prague & Berlin 11.30pm); *Polonia* (Belgrade & Sofia; 6.25am); *Saxonia* (Leipzig or Dresden; 11.20pm); *Sofia-Berlin* (Berlin; 5.40pm); *Varsovia* (Warsaw; 7pm); *Wiener-Waltzer* (Vienna & Basel, with connections for Paris or Venice; 4.10pm).

From Nyugati Station: *Amicus* (Prague; 8.15pm); *Balt-Orient* (Prague & Berlin 1pm; Bucharest 6.20pm); *Budapest-Leipzig* (9pm); *Hungaria* (Prague & Berlin; 6.25am); *Mamaia* (Cluj, Braşov & Constanţa 11.30am; Prague 2pm); *Meridian* (Prague & Berlin; 2.10pm); *Metropol* (Prague; 6.50pm); *Trakia* (Cluj, Braşov & Varna 6.15am; Prague, Dresden & Berlin 10.45pm).
From Zugló Station: *Nord-Orient* (Cluj, Braşov & Burgas 8.45am; Warsaw 11.15pm); *Transdanubium* (Timişoara & Burgas 7.50am; Bratislava & Prague 9.45pm).

Volán international coaches
Generally, 1 coach every weekday to each destination; (*) indicates during the summer only.
From Engels tér to Banska Bistrica; Bratislava; Cluj; Demanovska Dolina; Galanta; Graz; Ljubljana; Lusenec; Munich (*); Nitra; Opatija; Oradea; Poreč; Rijeka; Roznava; Samorin; Subotica; Tatranska Lomnica; Tîrgu Mureş; Venice (*); Vienna; Zagreb; Zakopane.

Hydrofoils to Vienna
From the Belgrád rakpart: Between

April 1-26 and September 30-October 25, Mondays, Wednesdays and Fridays at 9am. Between April 29-September 29, daily at 8pm (plus a 1pm service between July 1-September 1). The journey takes 5½hrs.

MALÉV international flights
From Ferihegy Airport to Adelaide (1 each week); Amsterdam (10); Athens (4); Atlanta (5); Barcelona (7); Basle (7); Beijing (7); Belgrade (2); Berlin (33); Bordeaux (10); Boston (7); Brussels (6); Bucharest (5); Chicago (5); Cologne (7); Copenhagen (8); Dresden (8); Dublin (6); Dusseldorf (14); Frankfurt (14); Geneva (7); Genoa (9); Hamburg (7); Hanover (7); Istanbul (6); Leipzig (12); Leningrad (6); Lisbon (7); London (7); Los Angeles (4); Luxembourg (7); Lyon (11); Madrid (6); Manchester (6); Marseille (7); Melbourne (5); Miami (6); Milan (7); Montreal (5); Moscow (37); Munich (14); New York (7); Oslo (9); Paris (11); Philadelphia (3); Prague (12); Rome (8); San Francisco (3); Stuttgart (7); Sydney (6); Toronto (6); Venice (5); Vienna (9); Warsaw (15); Washington (3); Zurich (14).

Chapter two
THE DANUBE BEND

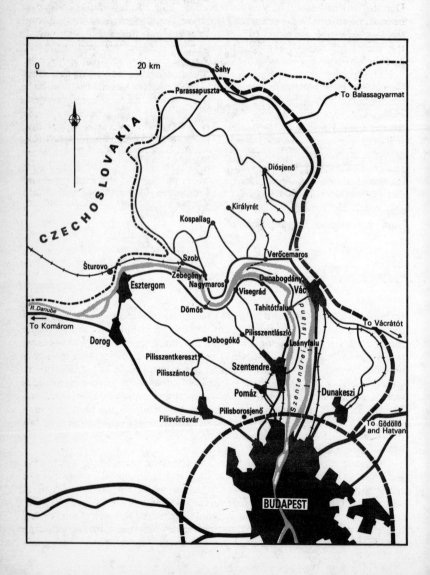

When the capital gets too hot and crowded during the summer, residents and visitors alike head for the *Dunakanyar* or **Danube Bend**. Perhaps the most beautiful landscape in Hungary, this is situated less than 40km from Budapest; having cycled alongside the river from the Black Forest to the Black Sea, Bernard Newman described the stretch between Esztergom and Budapest as 'one of the grandest of the Danube, only outdone by the Kazan Gorge', and few people seeing it are unimpressed. Entering the Carpathian Basin, the River Danube widens hugely, only to be forced by hills and mountains through a narrow, twisting valley – almost a U-turn, the 'Bend' – before dividing around the long strip of Szentendrei Island and flowing into the capital. Not only is the **scenery** spectacular, but the left (west) bank is loaded with **historic towns**, and there's scope for **horse-riding** or **hiking** in the mountains on either side.

Hitherto, the only intrusion on the Danube Bend's tranquility has been people, but over the next few years all this will change. Faced with a cut-back in supplies of energy from the USSR (exacerbated by the Chernobyl disaster), Hungary's economic planners have decided to ,push ahead with the controversial Gabčikovo-Nagymaros Hydro-electric Barrage, a project that will utterly transform **the enviroment** if the fears of *Duna Kör* – an opposition group – are correct. Construction of the dam itself will despoil the lovely scenery at Zebegény and Nagymaros, while the rising water-level may pose the threat of flooding for the low-lying areas of Visegrád and Esztergom and cause a backwash of sewage upriver to Győr in Transdanubia. And if it should ever burst, Szentendre, Vác and Budapest are only just downriver. . .

THE WEST BANK

By building a line of fortified *castrum* to keep the barbarians on the far side of the Danube in the C2-C3, the Romans unwittingly staked out the sites of the future castles of Magyar kings, who had to repulse the Tartars, and the most tourist-ridden places along **the west bank** today. It's better to visit the sights here on days when IBUSZ isn't running **day excursions** (p.85), and Monday would be the ideal time to see the superb-looking baroque town of **Szentendre** were it not for the fact that all the museums are closed then. Thanks to road 11 (and the HÉV train from Batthyány tér), Szentendre is less than an hour's journey from Budapest; and **Visegrád** and **Esztergom** are easily reached **by bus** (services originate from Budapest's Engels tér, and run between the main towns along the west bank).

The nicest, albeit slowest way to travel is **by river**, using boats which leave the Vigadó tér *hajóállomás* around 7.30am and 2pm and take about 5hrs to reach Esztergom. These follow the left channel of the river and call at Szentendre; services stopping at Vác on the east bank (departing around 7am) use the *Váci Duna-ág* route instead. Should you board the wrong one, or feel like a change of scenery, there are regular ferries between towns on opposite sides of the Danube. Esztergom may also be reached **by train** from Budapest's

Nyugati station, or via the less scenic road 10 which passes through Dorog – a mine where slave labour was employed during the Rákosi era. Villages and mountain chalets in **the Pilis range** are accessible by bus from Engels tér (1 each afternoon; 3 daily at weekends), while the southern foothills can be approached by local buses from Pomáz, one stop before Szentendre on the HÉV.

SZENTENDRE

Once clear of the bus station and the HÉV terminal, few visitors are disappointed by **SZENTENDRE** (St Andrew). If you ignore the new housing estates on the outskirts and the *Nosztalgia* and *Folklór* boutiques in the old centre, the town is a charming maze of houses painted in autumnal colours, interwoven with secretive gardens and alleys leading to hilltop churches – a perfect spot for an artists' colony, which it is. Though the Romans and sundry others were here before the Magyar conquest, Szentendre owes much of its character to the Serbian refugees from the Turks, who arrived here in two waves. Their townhouses – now converted into galleries, shops and cafés – form a set piece around the central Marx tér, on one side of which stands the Serbian **Church of the Annunciation** (*Blagoveštenszka templom*), richly adorned within by Mikhail Zivkovic's colourful iconostasis.

A lifetime's work by Hungary's leading ceramicist, **Margit Kovács** (b.1902), is displayed around the corner at Vastagh Gy. u.1. Her themes are legends, dreams, love and motherhood, and the sculptures and reliefs never fail to delight visitors, though sadly her work is little known abroad. Szentendre is stuffed full of **galleries**, with three on Marx tér alone. The *Műhely* (Workshop) exhibits contemporary work – mostly rather tacky; next door is a gallery devoted to the drawings and paintings of **János Kmetty**, while across the square at nr.6 **the Ferenczy family** of artists gets full exposure. Károly, the father, pioneered Impressionism in Hungary, while his children Noemi and Beni branched out into textiles and bronzeware.

Climbing one of the winding *lépcső* above Marx tér will bring you to the hilltop of Templom tér, which offers a **bird's eye view** of Szentendre's steeply-banked rooftops, spires and tiny gardens. Opposite the main Parish Church, another gallery displays the work of **Béla Czóbel**, a contemporary of Kmetty's, who helped to sweep away the dominant neo-Classicism of the 1890s; while the **Serbian Orthodox Cathedral** raises its burgundy spire above the trees in a walled garden nearby. To gain admission and see the iconostasis by Vasilje Ostoic, you must rouse the sexton living in the house marked *plebánia csengője*, who can also open up the strongroom at 5, Engels utca, which contains **ecclesiastical treasures**. I'd recommend saving some sightseeing enthusiasm for the Village Museum (see below), because Szentendre has **more galleries** than most people can absorb. In roughly descending order of interest, there are displays of **folk art** (Rákóczi u.1); outdoor **sculptures** (Ady u.7); work by former and current members of the Artists' Colony (Vörös Hadsereg útja 51 and Vastagh Gy. u.2-5); paintings by Barcsay (Dumsta u.10); and eroded **Roman stonework** at Dunakanyar körút 1 north of the railway station.

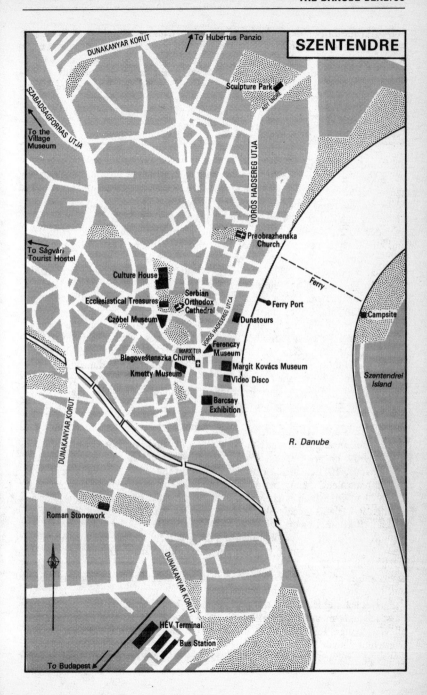

SZENTENDRE

DUNAKANYAR KORUT

To Hubertus Panzio

SZABADSAGFORRAS UTJA

To the Village Museum

Sculpture Park

ADY ENDRE

VÖRÖS HADSEREG UTJA

To Ságvári Tourist Hostel

Preobrazhenska Church

Ferry

Culture House

Ecclesiastical Treasures

Serbian Orthodox Cathedral

Ferry Port

Dunatours

Czóbel Museum

Campsite

VÖRÖS HADSEREG UTCA

MARX TER

Ferenczy Museum

Blagoveštenszka Church

Margit Kovács Museum

Kmetty Museum

Video Disco

Szentendrei Island

Barcsay Exhibition

R. Danube

DUNAKANYAR KORUT

Roman Stonework

N

DUNAKANYAR KORUT

HÉV Terminal

Bus Station

To Budapest

Lunchtimes and weekends during the tourist season bring **musicians and mime artists** out on Marx tér, with more highbrow performances being staged several evenings a week at the Cultural Centre on Engels utca. Each August 19, *Kolo* dancers do their stuff at the **Serbian festival** in the grounds of the Preobrazhenska Church on Vörös Hadsereg útja, while the following evening, Eurovisionesque **pop concerts** generally round off the entertainments on Constitution Day. Otherwise, restaurants with musicians and the **discos** on Pap Island and near Dunatours on the embankment are the main sources of Szentendre's nightlife.

The outdoor Village Museum

By taking a bus from stand 8 at the terminal about 3km out along Szabadságforrás út, you can reach Szentendre's **Village Museum** (*Szabadtéri Néprajzi Múzeum*), open from April 1 to October 31, Tuesday-Sunday 9am-5pm. Though only two 'regional units' are presently complete, the museum is intended to eventually include reconstructed villages from all over Hungary, and already it's a fascinating place. Downhill from the entrance is a composite village from Szabolcs-Szatmár county, culled from isolated settlements in the Erdőhát region (p.211). The brochure on sale at the gate points out the finer distinctions between humble peasant dwellings like the house from Kispalad, and the cottage from Uszka formerly occupied by petty squires, rising amongst the barns and the woven pigstys (which could be erected on the spot). Rural carpenters could execute highly skilled work, as one can see from the circular 'dry mill' and the all-wooden belltower from Nemesborzova. By contrast, the second village 'unit' seems much more regimented, originating from the ethnic German communities of the *Kisalföld* (Little Plain) in Transdanubia. Neatly aligned and whitewashed, the houses are filled with nick-nacks and embroidered samplers bearing homilies such as 'When the Hausfrau is capable, the clocks keep good time'.

Practicalities and Moving on

Accommodation options take in the *Party* and *Danubius* hotels on Ady utca, the slightly cheaper *Coca Cola* (Dunakanyar körút 50) and *Hubertus* (Tyukosdűlő 10) pensions, or private rooms arranged by **Dunatours** at nr.6 on the embankment. Many people end up at the **campsite** on Pap Island just north of town, which is classier but more crowded than the smaller site on Szentendrei Island (accessible by ferry from the northern landing stage). Five and a half kilometres up Lajos-Forrás út, the *Ságvári Endre* tourist hostel – a jumping-off point for walks into the Pilis – can be reached by bus from the terminal; but book your bed in advance, either from Dunatours (☎ 26-10683) or IBUSZ in Budapest, whose office at 55, Lenin körút also makes reservations at the *Kőhegyi* hostel in the hills, which folks without transport will have to get to by hitching.

Ferries leaving from the landing stage near the Dunatours office provide the most leisurely means of **travelling north**. A new road has been constructed to alleviate congestion on road 11 between Szentendre and Visegrád (which runs over the hills via Pilisszentlászló), but most buses still take the embankment route, as follows. Just north of Szentendre, **LEÁNYFALU** is a leafy resort originally popularised by writers like Zsigmond Móricz, where riverboats call and you can take a ferry across to Pocsmegyer on **SZENTENDREI ISLAND** – if only to escape Leanyfalu's tacky riverside campsite. The next settlement has one foot on the mainland – TAHI (with two campsites and a *Fogadó*) – and the other on Szentendrei Island: TÓFALU, where Mihály Pollack, the architect of numerous Hungarian neo-Classical buildings, lived at 474, Pincessor street. As one continues northwards, the land rises and fruit trees and vineyards flourish around DUNABOGDÁNY, just before the Danube Bend heaves into sight. . .

VISEGRÁD

When the hillsides start to plunge and the river twists, keep your eyes fixed on the mountains to the west for a first glimpse of the Castle of **VISEGRÁD** – 'its upper walls stretching to the clouds floating in the sky, and the lower bastions reaching down as far as the river', still almost as it appeared to János Thuroczy in 1488. At that time, courtly life in Visegrád was nearing its apogée, and the palace of Mátyás and Beatrix (described to Pope Sixtus IV as a *'paradiso terrestri'*) was famed throughout Europe, although the involuntary residence here of Vlad the Impaler must have soured the atmosphere somewhat during the previous decade. After the Turkish occupation Visegrád declined to the humble village that it is today, but the basic layout of the Citadel on the hill, joined by ramparts to Soloman's Tower and the Water Bastion below, hasn't altered significantly since the C13, when Béla IV began fortifying the north against a recurrence of the Mongol invasion. The royal palace, however, disappeared, and until János Schulek unearthed one of the vaults in 1934, many doubted that it had ever existed.

Now almost totally excavated, the **ruins of the Palace** are spread over four levels or terraces behind the gate of 27, Fő utca. Originally founded by the Angevin king Charles Robert, the Palace was the setting for the Visegrád Congress of 1335, attended by the monarchs of Central Europe and the Grandmaster of the Teutonic Knights, who failed to agree upon responses to the growing Habsburg threat, but managed to consume staggering quantities of victuals, including 10,000 litres of wine every day. Nothing remains of Charles Robert's Palace, but the *cour d'honneur* built for his successor Louis, which provided the basis for subsequent building by Sigismund and later Mátyás Corvinus, is still to be seen on the second terrace. Its chief features are the pillastered Renaissance loggia and two panels from the *Hercules Fountain*; the upper storey – which was made of wood, heavily carved and gilded – having long ago disappeared.

Mátyás and Beatrix had their suites on the third level, separated by a chapel adorned with mosaics and overhung by a cliff. The most impressive sight was the garden above the bath corridor, where the *Lion Fountain* stood. A perfect copy of the original (carved by Ernő Szakál) bears Mátyás's raven crest and a score of sleepy-looking lions for which the fountain is named, but is no longer connected to gutters and pipes which formerly channeled water down from the Citadel. On some days during June and July (as advertised), the ruins

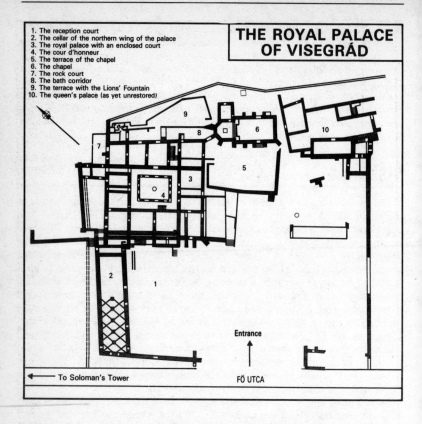

1. The reception court
2. The cellar of the northern wing of the palace
3. The royal palace with an enclosed court
4. The cour d'honneur
5. The terrace of the chapel
6. The chapel
7. The rock court
8. The bath corridor
9. The terrace with the Lions' Fountain
10. The queen's palace (as yet unrestored)

THE ROYAL PALACE OF VISEGRÁD

← To Soloman's Tower

Entrance

FŐ UTCA

provide the setting for **historical pageants** and/or films intended to recreate the splendour of Visegrád's Renaissance heyday.

From the derelict **Water Bastion** (*Vízibástya*) on the embankment, a rampart leads up to **Soloman's Tower** (*Salamán torony*): a mighty hexagonal keep buttressed by concrete slabs, near which lies a ruined Roman *castrum* on Sibrik Hill. Inside, the tower's **Mátyás Museum** houses finds from the excavated palace including the white Anjou Fountain of the Angevins and the red marble 'Visegrád Madonna' carved by Tomaso Fiamberti (the probable maker of the Lion and Hercules Fountains). Visegrád's most dramatic feature is the **Citadel** on the mountain top, which served as a repository for the Hungarian crown jewels until a maid of honour dishonourably stole them (they were later recovered). Only the main gateway and the first hall have been fully restored, but the ruined Citadel is still mightily impressive, commanding a superb view of Nagymaros and the Börzsöny Mountains on the east bank. You can reach it by the 'Calvary' footpath which begins near Nagy L. utca, or by catching a bus (from the Mátyás statue on Salamán-torony u.) which follows the scenic Panorama út. From the parking lot on the summit, one road leads to the luxury *Hotel Silvanus* (...'mit Tennis-platz und disco'), the

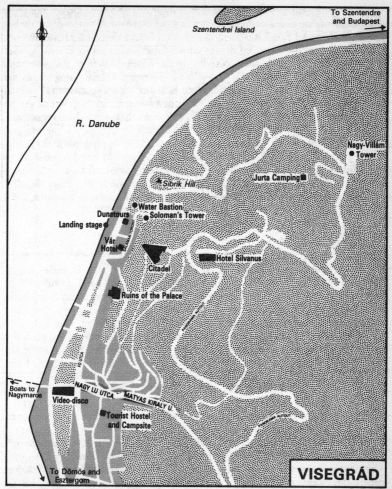

other to the **Nagy-Villám observation tower**, whence views stretch into Czechoslovakia.

Places to stay and things to do
Despite Visegrád's popularity with visitors, finding **accommodation** rarely seems to present problems. Besides the Tourist Hostel (Salamán-torony u.5) there are two moderately-priced hotels – both called *Vár* – near the river; a small campsite with dormitory beds at Széchenyi u.7; and private rooms available from *Dunatours* (Fő utca 3). With transport, another option lies en route to the Nagy-Villám tower: *Jurta camping*, near which stands a restaurant resembling a Mongol stockade.

Dunatours can usually arrange **pony-trekking** in the Pilis range, but most visitors venture no further than the fish **restaurants** and beer-kiosks along the embankment, or the *Kút* beer-garden and the crowded **video-disco** at the junction of road 11 and Rév utca. At nr.30, Fő utca there's a nightclub with mediocre jazz and overpriced drinks which functions as an ice cream parlour during the day. It's forbidden **to swim** on the Visegrád side of the river, and the beach on the opposite bank (accessible by ferry from the landing stage near the disco) has probably disappeared beneath the construction site at Nagymaros by now. However, there's a pool a few kilometres north along the west bank towards **DÖMÖS**, a quiet settlement half-buried in vegetation, with a campsite beside the Danube. Follow one of its tributaries, the Malom, 2-3km upstream from Dömös, and you'll reach a forking path that's the starting point for two **hikes into the Pilis range**. The right-hand route leads to the *Rám precipice* and eventually on to Dobogókő, whilst the left fork brings one to the Vadálló Rocks beneath the towering *Prédikálószék* ('Pulpit Seat') – a 641m crag that only experienced climbers should attempt to scale. Both hikes can be accomplished within a few hours.

ESZTERGOM

ESZTERGOM is beautifully sited in a crook of the Danube facing Czechoslovakia, enclosed by glinting water and soft hills and dominated by the dome of its Basilica, visible from far away. The town once surpassed Buda in importance, being the royal seat until the C13 Mongol invasion demonstrated its vulnerability. Hungary's first king, Stephen, was born and crowned here, and ever since he made it the offical religion this has been the centre of **Hungarian Catholicism**, whose Archbishops frequently wielded temporal as well as spiritual authority until the Communists gaoled the Primate, Cardinal Mindszenty, on trumped-up charges of espionage in 1949. (Freed during the Uprising, Mindszenty seemed bewildered by events and went into exile). Worshippers and sightseers throng Esztergom's immense C19 Basilica and the town enjoys a peaceful prosperity, unpeturbed by the presence of occupying forces. In the shadow of the cathedral the Soviet army has a small garrison beside Béke tér (Peace Square!), and MiL troop-helicopters clatter overhead bound for the huge base on the road to Dorog.

Frowning down on everything is the **Basilica**, the largest in Hungary: 118m long, 40m wide, capped by a dome 71.5m high. Kühneland and Packh supervised the initial construction, but it was József Hild who completed the building in 1856. The interior is on a massive scale, clad in marble, gilding and mosaics, with a collection of saintly relics in the chapel to the right as you enter. Archbishop Tamás Bakócz, who commissioned the red marble chapel (with an an altar by Florentine craftsmen) opposite, had designs on the Papacy, but scuppered his chances when the crusade that he launched turned into the great peasant uprising of 1514. Visitors require a ticket to visit the **crypt** resembling a set from Hammer Horror, with giant stone women flanking the stairway descending to Archbishop Boehm's glass-encased mummy, and gloomy vaults full of prelates' tombs. The **treasury** (*kincstár*) entrance is north of the altar, and having seen its overpowering collection of bejewelled crooks and chalices, it's almost a relief to climb the seemingly

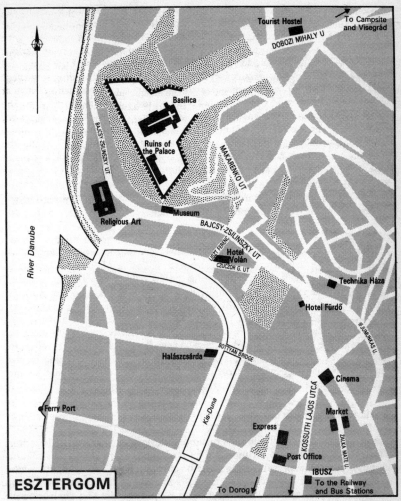

ESZTERGOM

endless stairway to the **belltower** (*harangtorony*) and cupola which, like the treasury, also require admission tickets. Pigeons' droppings and grafitti decorate the bellroom and it's stifling hot inside the **cupola**, but all this is forgotten the moment you step outside and see the magnificent view.

On a crag overlooking the Watertown district, the **ruins of the medieval palace** were once a residence for Béla III, the widowed Queen Beatrix, and sundry Archbishops. According to Djelalzade's boastful account, the Turks 'knocked down idols in the churches and destroyed the symbols of infidelity and error' when they sacked Esztergom in 1543, but left intact the wheel and 'narrow copper tube' which ingeniously piped up water from the Danube. Today, one can visit the remains of a **chapel** with a rose window and interior

Byzantine-style frescoes, Beatrix's suite, and the study of Archbishop Vítez – known as the **Hall of Virtues** after its allegorical murals. The ruined palace is the setting for **historical pageants** between June 25 and July 5.

Religious art gets a showing in the old Primate's Palace (Berényi u.2) down in the Watertown, where you can also view stuff from the Turkish period in the **Museum** at 63, Bajcsy-Zsilinszky út, named after the poet Bálint Balassi who perished sword in hand on the walls of the castle in 1594 during a failed attempt to oust the Turks. Rákóczi tér is the fairly ugly but lively **town centre**, with posters advertising impending discos and parties plastered next door to the cinema. Nearby is a bizarre Moorish-style building on Ifújmunkás utca, and an open-air **market** that takes up the length of Zalka Máté utca. **Nightlife** – such as there is – can be found at the *Halászcsárda* over the Bottyán Bridge, and in the bars and Hotel Fürdő on Bajcsy-Zsilinszky út between the Basilica hill and Rákóczi tér.

In the tradition of *The Baldhead*, Esztergom's C13 inn, the Tourist Hostel offers cheap, sleazy **accommodation** near Béke tér (Dobó u.8), but most visitors prefer the *Hotel Fürdő*, the more expensive *Volán* (József tér 2), or camping at the *Vadvirág* site, 2km from the centre along the Visegrád road. Széchenyi tér has the Post Office, *Express* and *Komtourist* which, like IBUSZ (Kossuth u.24), can arrange private rooms. If you're planning a few days hiking in the Pilis it's worth considering the *Túristaház* at **Vaskapu**, situated about 3km east of town in the hills. Beds are few though, so reservations should be made beforehand at IBUSZ, Lenin körút 55, in Budapest. Halfway towards the **railway station** at the southern end of town you'll find the **bus terminal** on Zalka Máté utca, whence there are fairly regular services to Komárom, the Pilis range and Budapest (via the Bend or Dorog). Travellers in possession of a Czech visa might be allowed **to enter Czechoslovakia** by the hourly ferryboat across to Šturovo, but one can't be certain of this, so the nearest dead cert crossing is Komárom.

THE PILIS RANGE

Sometimes labelled as mountains but more accurately described as hills, the **PILIS RANGE** offers opportunities for **easy hiking** (only a few peaks require climbing experience) and a succession of caves, valleys and splendid views. From Budapest's Engels tér, buses run to Dobogókő (699 m) in the middle of the Pilis, or by using the HÉV train you can alight at Pomáz and catch buses or start walking from there. Alternatively, it's possible to hike up from Dömös to Dobogókő by following the Rám precipice route (p.100), or catch a bus from Szentendre to the village of Pilisszentlászló. Whichever route you take, bring the hiking **map** which shows paths (*turistaút/földút*), caves (*barlang*) and rain shelters (*esőház*) throughout the highlands.

The bus to Dobogókő travels by way of the Kovács Canyon, where an ancient but still functioning lime kiln marks the start of the village of **Pilisszentkereszt**. Though Cistercian monks founded a monastery here during the Middle Ages when the Pilis was a royal hunting ground, almost nothing remains of it nowadays. **Dobogókő**, in the shadow of 756m Pilis-tető, is the only real resort in the highlands, and the *Hotel Nimrod* with its luxury facilities charges accordingly. Fortunately the nearby hostel – a hotel in all but name – is fairly cheap, but it's advisable to book lodgings before you leave Budapest, from *Dunatours*, 17, Bajcsy-Zsilinszky út. The same advice applies to other *Turistaház* (marked *th.* on hiking maps) located in the southern foothills. The *Stromfeld Aurel* is about 1½km north of **Pilisborosjenő** village, while the *Csikovári* lies west of **Pomáz**, where there's also a Gypsy encampment.

THE EAST BANK

The **east bank** is architecturally less well-endowed than its counterpart – **Vác** is the only sizeable town – but, at least until the Hydro-electric barrage is built, the villages of **Nagymaros** and **Zebegény** do much to compensate. Nestled beneath the craggy, wooded **Börzsöny Mountains**, they're the starting points for well-marked trails leading to encounters with the highlands' abundant wildlife. To reach the east bank from Budapest, you can take a train from Nyugati station or a bus from the Bulcsú utca terminal (XIII district) to any point up as far as Szob; but perhaps the nicest way is to travel by boat from Vigadó tér to Vác, or further.

Dunakeszi and Vácrátót might possibly persuade you not to travel straight from Budapest to Vác. **DUNAKESZI**, just outside the capital, is the home of the **Alag Riding School**, patronised by Budapest's diplomatic corps. Less illustrious mortals may also join the cross-country rides (held weekly during September, October and November), providing they have some equestrian experience and book in advance. For details, contact *Pegazus Tours* in Budapest (V, Károlyi u.5/☎ 171-552) or the *Magyar Lóverseny Vállalat* in Dunakeszi (☎ Alag 41-656). The less energetic might prefer to visit the lovely **Botanical Gardens** at **VÁCRÁTÓT**, founded during the C19 by Count Vigyázó, who subsequently bequeathed them to the Hungarian Academy of Sciences. Trains for Vácrátót leave Budapest's Nyugati station around 9.50 and 11.40, with an additonal service running on weekdays only (leaving at 14.25), and continue on to Vác. There are also trains and buses from Vác to Vácrátót, whence another branch line connects with Aszód (departures around 12.30, 14.40 & 17.20), the place to change trains if you're bound for Balassagyarmat in the Cserhát Mountains.

VÁC

The inexorable roll and swell of the Danube swept away the discouraging picture of **VÁC** conjured by my Budapest friends, coloured by the town's once notorious prison, now long-defunct, and IBUSZ (Széchenyi u.14) are currently busy polishing up a more respectable past. Though you're unlikely to spend more than an afternoon here, they can direct visitors to the *Tabán panzió* or arrange private **lodgings**; orientation being fairly simple, since Széchenyi utca runs from the **railway and bus terminals** up to Marcius 15 tér in the centre, whence Bartók u. leads westwards to the **waterfront**.

Barring the concealed entrance in the middle of the tér which leads to a medieval **wine cellar** where you can drink to the accompaniment of Gypsy music, Vác's Belváros is characterised by worthy buildings and relics of ecclesiastical zeal. Hungary's first Institute for the Deaf and Dumb occupies the former Bishop's Palace at nr.6, while patriarchal justice is symbolised on the central gable of the Town Hall (nr.11) by two prostrate females, one bearing the Hungarian emblem, the other the Migazzi coat-of-arms. **Bishop Migazzi** was the moving force behind Vác's C18 revival, an ambitious prelate who also served as Archbishop of Vienna. When Empress Maria Theresa proposed to visit Vác in 1764 he planned theatrical façades to hide the town's dismal housing, but settled for commissioning Isadore Canevale to design an incongruous **Triumphal Arch** on Köztársaság útja, from which Habsburg imperial heads – including Maria Theresa's – grimace a stony welcome.

The arch flanks one windowless face of **Vác Prison**, hung with plaques commemorating Communists killed here during Admiral Horthy's regime, though none bears witness to the political prisoners tortured during the Rákosi era, nor their dramatic mass escape in 1956. Thrown into panic by reports from Budapest where their colleagues were 'hunted down like animals, hung on trees, or just beaten to death by passers-by', the ÁVO gaolers had donned civilian clothing and mounted guns on the rooftop, fermenting rumours amongst the prisoners, whose hopes had been raised by snatches of patriotic songs overheard from the streets outside. A glimpse of Hungarian flags held aloft by crowds – with the Soviet emblem cut from the centre – provided the spark. All thoughts of starvation cells and further torture suddenly vanished; a guard was overpowered, locks were shot off, and the prisoners burst free amidst the bluster of machine-gun fire.

Rather than retrace your steps along Köztársaság útja, dip down behind the prison to the **riverside promenade** – its three sections named after the composer Liszt and the poets Ady and József – which runs the length of town. On Liszt sétány the *Halászkert* serves delicious spicy fish dishes, while beyond lies a flashy indoor swimming pool. From Ady sétány, Rév köz climbs up to the Trinity statue which lends its name to Szentháromság tér. Skip the monastery and church of the Piarists (a Catholic order founded during the C16) to visit the **market** behind them, or turn right for Konstantin square and the museum.

Squat, ugly and impressive only in size, the neo-Classical **Cathedral** dominating the square is more a sign of Migazzi's wordliness than an invitation to celestial heights. Gigantic Corinthian columns topped with crumbling statues guard the entrance to an interior thankfully brightened by Maulbertsch's frescoes – particularly the exuberant *Meeting of Mary and Elizabeth* above the altar. It's worth looking, too, at the exquisitely embroidered chasubles and intricate gold filagree in the **treasury** before crossing over to the gardens surrounding a former palace, which open onto Vak Bottyán tér. From here a short walk along Múzeum u. leads to the **Local History Museum** (Tuesday-Sunday 10am-12am, 1pm-5pm). The pre-Turkish era is reduced to a sorry collection of broken masonry, silver coins from Vác's C14 royal mint, and some lovely, though fragmented, mosaics. Other displays document the development of craft guilds and the 1848 revolution with Hungarian captions, plus which there's weaponry and paintings of C19 markets to look at.

Moving on
From Vác, it's possible to catch a bus or train (5-7 departures daily) northwards through the Börzsöny to Balassagyarmat, enabling one to spend the night in sleepy Diósjenő (p.107). Buses to other **villages in the Börzsöny** follow such roundabout routes that hitching or Shank's pony might be a quicker means of getting there. The more frequent buses and trains travelling **up the east bank** stop at every settlement en route to Szob, whilst riverboats call at Verőcemaros, Nagymaros and Zebegény (see below). Not content with his work in Vác, Migazzi plumped for another baroque church and a summer mansion at **VERŐCEMAROS**, a non-descript village with two cheap hotels – the *Béke Fogadó* and a *panzió* at Árpád u.65 – and a memorial museum in the home of the late ceramicist Géza Gorka. One train stop further north at *VERŐCEMAROS-FELSŐ/KISMAROS*, an **International Youth Camp** run by Express rents bungalows, tent-space and sporting equipment from behind the terminal of the *Kis-vasút*, a **miniature railway** leading up to Királyrét in the Börzsöny (described at the end of this chapter).

NAGYMAROS AND THE DAM

A quietly prosperous village with an air of faded grandeur – it was inhabited by nobles during the time of royal Visegrád – **NAGYMAROS** is about to undergo dramatic changes. Hitherto, horse-drawn carts clopping around the main square and the one record shop's mediocre funk have been the biggest disturbances here outside the tourist season, but state planners have ambitious plans for the village. In 1977 (without consulting the citizens of their People's Republics) the Czech and Hungarian governments signed an agreement to build two Hydro-electric barrages; one at Gabčikovo on the Czech side of the upper Danube, the other at Nagymaros.

Work is underway on the **Dam at Nagymaros**, which is intended to stand 18m high amidst a forest of girders and a control tower, bearing a road and entailing several kilometres of ancilliary works along the river bank. Not merely a localised eyesore either, for the project threatens the whole environment along 250km of the Danube. While a rise in the water level upriver of Nagymaros is likely to cause flooding from Esztergom up to Dunakiliti, and a backwash of sewage against Győr, the consequences downriver could be even worse. Excluding the possibility of a dam burst – which would demolish Vác and Szentendre and seriously damage Budapest – an estimated drop of 5-6 metres and a fall in the river could dry up cropland and the wells that supply 40% of the local population and industries (including the nuclear reactors at Paks, cooled by the Danube).

Opposition to the dam is widespread and continuing in the face of official intransigence. The independent group *Scientists for the Danube* marshals technical arguments for the *Duna Kör* (Danube Circle) to arouse public opinion and use against the government; petitions have circulated; and opposition to the Dam was one of the main planks in the 1985 campaign of László Rajk, a samizdat bookseller whose bid for parliament was blocked by blatant gerrymandering. Despite a change of heart towards demonstrators – who were forcibly dispersed from Budapest's Bem tér in 1986, but actually assisted by the police in May 1988, only days after Grósz (who had previously pledged to 'continue a discussion with dissidents on every level') became Party leader – the dam probably won't be scrapped at this stage.

The dam aside, Nagymaros's claims to attention are muted. The Gothic church by the **railway station** had a facelift in the C18; whitewashed houses straggle up the hillside; and social life centres around the pasrty shops and leafy squares. From the station, duck under the bridge to reach the main road; then turn right for the **campsite** (2km away on the riverbank, with bungalows), or head on up the main backstreet. One kilometre uphill, the path divides at a parking lot – one fork heading south to Hegyes-tető, whence you can enjoy a **panoramic view of the Bend**, the other up **into the Börzsöny**. There, one can sojourn amongst the beech woods at the *Törökmező* hostel: 5km away by footpath (marked with blue signs), or slightly longer if you follow the Panorama-út road. Beds should be booked in advance at IBUSZ in Budapest (Lenin körút 55).

ZEBEGÉNY, SZOB AND CROSSING INTO CZECHOSLOVAKIA

At **ZEBEGÉNY** the Danube turns south before taking the Bend. The scenery here has attracted painters since **István Szőnyi** (1894-1960) first put brush to canvas, and his house at Bartók út 7 is now a **museum** and the venue of an annual summer **International Art School**, offering 2-4 week courses in sculpture, ceramics, enamelling, graphics and painting. If you're interested, write early for a prospectus, since the deadline for applications is May 1. There's no accommodation (take the boat across to Visegrád or Esztergom or use the Nagymaros campsite) unless you're willing to walk for a few hours up to the Törökmező Hostel, which is also accessible from Nagymaros.

Depots, dust and dead-end depression sum up most frontier posts, and **SZOB** is no exception. Tourists rarely come here (and, again, there's no accommodation), but for chance visitors the **Börzsöny Museum** (Hámán u.14) is ready with peasant costumes, carved tombstones, and a piece of the *petrified primeval tree* found at Ipolytarnoc (which is distributed amongst half a dozen provincial museums).

Anyone planning to take a local train across from Szob **into Czechoslovakia** must acquire a visa from the Czech consulate in Budapest beforehand, as must motorists, who are obliged to cross the border farther to the northeast, at **PARASSAPUSZTA** (open 24 hours). Czech border guards have a reputation

for stringent customs searches and turning away 'punk' or 'hippy' travellers –
whether they mellow as the winds of *glasnost* reach Prague remains to be seen.
The road from Szob follows the Ipoly River demarcating the frontier – where
a spotty guard accosted me with, 'Hey baby, passport!' – before joining route
2 at Parassapuszta; **DRÉGELYPALÁNK**, a neighbouring village, is on the
Vác-Diósjenő-Balassagyarmat line (trains roughly every 2 hours).

WALKING IN THE BÖRZSÖNY

The **BÖRZSÖNY RANGE** sees few visitors despite its scattering of hostels
and forest footpaths, and the abundance of rabbits, pheasants and deer,
watched by circling eagles. Though the frontier zone should be avoided, it's
otherwise feasible to camp wild here, but the most of the following sites offer
some kind of accommodation. Would-be walkers should buy Cartographia's
Börzsöny-hegység map, which shows paths and the location of *túristaház*. The
only peak to require any climbing experience is **Mount Csóvanyos**, at 939m
the highest in the Börzsöny, which hikers usually approach from the direction
of **DIÓSJENŐ**. A **campsite** here with chalets lies 1km from the village and
twice that distance from the railway station; both trains and buses for
Diósjenő depart from Vác around 5-7 times daily.

An alternative route into the mountains begins at KISMAROS near
Verőcemaros beside the Danube (p.105), whence narrow-gague trains trundle
more or less hourly up to **Királyrét** between 7.30am-10.30pm. Once
supposedly the hunting ground of Beatrix and Mátyás, this 'Royal Meadow' is
now the site of a forking path; one trail (marked in red) leading 3km to the
Magas-Tax hostel, the other to the 'Big Cold' peak, **Nagy Hideg**.

This latter has excellent views and its own tourist hostel, the starting point
for walks to Mt. Csóványos and two villages. The route marked by blue
squares leads westwards to **NAGYBÖRZSÖNY**, a wealthy town during the
Middle Ages, but ruined by the depletion of its copper, gold and iron mines,
nowadays merely a humble logging village with a *C13 Romanesque church* as
its sole relic of past prosperity, and no accommodation for visitors. The path
with red markings runs south from Nagy Hideg down to **KOSPALLAG**,
another rather dreary village, redeemed only by a cheap hostel with felt-
trimmed boar hides in its restaurant, and a bus service to Vác until 9pm. But
things improve beyond the Vác-Szob junction below the village, where the
path wanders through the beech woods to a lovely open meadow graced with
a solitary tree and the first view of the Danube. Cutting southwest across the
meadow puts you back on the path to the **Törökmező** hostel – a largish place
with tennis courts and a restaurant that's popular with motorists following the
Panorama-út – or you can head west towards Zebegény when the path divides
by the keep-fit outfit in the woods. This leads eventually to a parking lot at the
junction of paths to Hegyes-tető and Nagymaros.

FESTIVALS

Summer

Historical Pageants at VISEGRÁD (throughout **June and July** as advertised) and ESZTERGOM (June 25-July 5). *Kolo* dancing and a celebration of Serbian roots at SZENTENDRE the day before **August 20**, when Constitution Day is marked by folkdancing, jazz, pop, in a televised festival.

TRAVEL DETAILS

Trains

From Budapest to Esztergom (12 daily; 1¼hrs); Szentendre (every ¼-½hr; ¾hr); Váctrátót & Vác (2-3 daily).

From Esztergom to Budapest (9; 1½); Komárom (3; ¾).

From Vác to Diósjenő (½hr) and Balassagyarmat (2hrs), 5-7 daily.

From Vácrátót to Aszód (3; ½).

Buses

From Budapest *Engels tér* to Esztergom (every 1½hrs); Visegrád (hourly); Dobogókő (1 daily; 3 times at weekends). From *Bulcsú tér* to Vác and Szob (hourly).

From Esztergom to Visegrád, Szentendre and Budapest (hourly); Komárom (every 1½hrs).

From Szentendre to Visegrád and Esztergom (hourly, or more frequently).

From Vác to Budapest (hourly); Diósjenő (5-7 daily); Kospallag (every 1½hrs); Szob (every 20-40mins).

From Visegrád to Budapest (hourly); Dömös and Esztergom (every 20-40mins).

Ferries

From Budapest to Esztergom (4-5 daily; 5hrs); Szentendre (3-4; 1); Vác (1-2; 2½); Visegrád (4-5; 3½); Zebegény (3; 4¼).

From Esztergom to Budapest (4; 4); Šturovo (hourly); Szentendre (2-3; 2¾hrs); Vác (1-2; 2).

Chapter three

LAKE BALATON AND THE BAKONY

Few Magyars would subscribe to the old romantic view of **Lake Balaton** as the 'Hungarian sea', but, despite rising prices pushing out natives in favour of Austrians and Germans, it is still very much the 'Nation's Playground'. Holiday resorts line the lake's southern shore, almost wholly given over to the pleasures of guzzling, swimming and sunbathing (no nudism), and with **Siófok** as the prototype, one place is much like another. Nature only reasserts itself at the western end of the lake, where the Zala River flows through the reeds to **Kis-Balaton**, a birdlife reserve. The northern shore is no less crowded, but waterfront development has been limited by reedbanks and cooler, deeper water, so the emphasis here is rather on historic monuments like **Tihany**, the 'Pearl of the Balaton'; the vineyards and scenery of the **Badacsony Hills**; and the town of **Keszthely**, not far from which lies the old **Hévíz** spa.

As prices are much lower there, Hungarians and East Germans opt increasingly for holidays at **Lake Velence**, situated midway between Budapest and Lake Balaton. Summer highlights here include the open-air Beethoven concerts in the grounds of the Brunswick mansion at **Martonvásár**, where the composer used to stay.

If you visit either lake, it would be a shame not to stop off en route to see the colourful belváros and the weird 'Bory Castle' at **Székesfehérvár**; whilst to the north of the Balaton, formerly volcanic hills roll themselves picturesquely up into **the Bakony**. Historically, a **wine**-producing region dotted with small villages and ruined castles, dominated by the towns of **Sümeg** and **Veszprém**, it's now being expoited for its mineral wealth at **Tapolca**, and as a military training-ground deeper in the hills.

APPROACHING THE BALATON

There are various ways of **approaching the Balaton from Budapest,** and much depends on whether you're aiming for the southern or the northern shore. Most **trains** from Budapest's Déli station to Siófok stop at **Lake Velence and Székesfehérvár** en route to the southern shore, which they follow westwards until Balatonszentgyöragy, where the track veers off towards Nagykanizsa; while services to Balatonfüred are routed through Székesfehérvár and continue along the northern shore until the Badacsony Hills, where they make tracks for Tapolca (change there for trains back down to Keszthely).

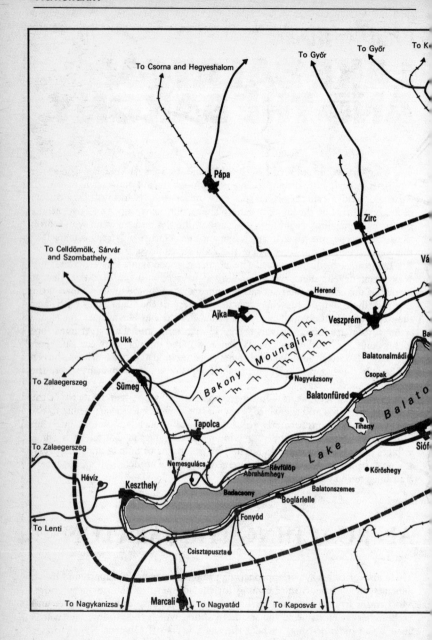

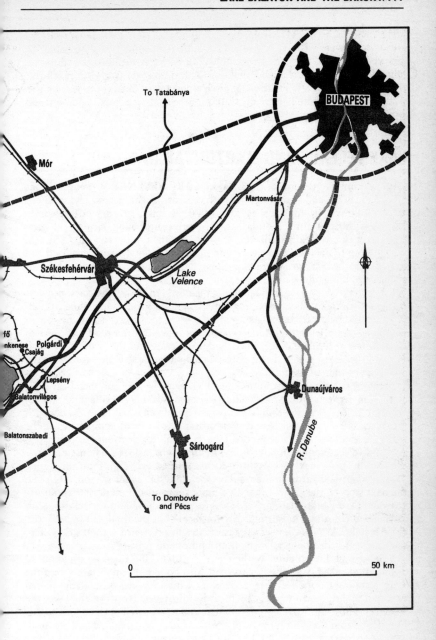

The main **highway** (M7) from the capital bypasses everywhere en route to Siófok, so drivers wishing to keep their options open should take route 70 instead. Using this, one can change on to route 71 (for the northern shore) at Polgárdi or the junction outside Balatonaliga; or stay on course to reach the south side of the lake. It's feasible to **hitch** along any of these routes except the M7, but while there's lots of traffic, there's also a fair ammount of competition from itinerant Magyars and East Germans.

LAKE VELENCE AND MARTONVÁSÁR

Like a diminutive version of the Balaton, **LAKE VELENCE** (*Velencei-tó*) has hills to the north and two shorelines with contrasting characters. The southern shore (followed by the railway and rd.70) is busy, brash, and welcomes visitors with open arms. Holiday homes are mushrooming, closing the gaps between formerly distinct villages; feast-food stalls proliferate (the fried fish, 'straight out of the lake', is a treat); and the shore is slowly being enclosed and turned into *Strandbad* where one must pay for a swim and the dubious privilege of changing rooms.

Reeds make swimming difficult along the northern shore (and the southwest corner of the lake), but provide a superb nesting ground for some 30,000 birds, including a rare egret. As a **nature reserve** the area can only be visited with permission from the *Madárrezervátum* office (on the road just west of Agárd). It's a desolate place, filled with bird cries and the wailing of wind through the reeds, where the occasional reed-cutter or thatched cottage is the only sign of human habitation.

Arriving at Velence train station, head towards the lake and then bear right at the big *Express* office on Fő utca to reach **VELENCE** village and, 2km beyond, the excellent *Panorama* campsite. Open from April 15 to October 15, this hires out canoes, bikes and **windsurfing** (*Kölcsönző*) equipment; as the water is shallow and warm, the lake is ideal for learning to windsurf. Alternative **accommodation** includes *private rooms* (ask at the house opposite the station) or – maybe – a cheap dormitory bed at *KISZ*, the Communist Youth camp, 100 yards up the road on the same side as the station. **AGÁRD**, the next stop on the railway, has two more **campsites**, both noisier and more crowded than Panorama. *Park-camping* is on the shore and very cheap, with kitchens, boats and windsurfing gear for hire – but the road and railway run close behind. At *Nemes Kócsag* campsite, right on Agárd station's doorstep, one can rent little cookers by the hour and obtain private rooms.

Velence **nightlife** is limited to the *Disco Arató* (behind Express) – a bar until 10pm, after which you pay not too much to boogie on until 3am – and the *Lido* restaurant opposite Velence station, which features reasonable priced eats and nightly performances by local headbangers. North of the lake, the **Velencei Hills** are sparsely populated and have well-marked paths for ramblers. From the hilltops most of the views are uninterrupted and pastoral, though at Mészeg-hegy – just east of Palozd village – looms a heap of WW2 hardware and an obelisk commemorating the first battle of the 1848 war of independence. There are fairly regular **buses from Velence** to Székesfehérvár,

Balatonfüred and Siófok in the Balaton region, and to Pusztaszabolcs and Dunaújváros in Transdanubia.

A fifteen minutes' train ride from Velence to **MARTONVÁSÁR** transports you into quite another era. Follow the road opposite the railway station to reach a neo-Gothic castle where Hungary's first nursery school was opened by **Teréz Brunswick**, and **Beethoven** was a frequent guest. Rumours have it that Josephine Brunswick was the 'immortal beloved' to whom Ludwig addressed his love letters, and that the Moonlight and Appassionata sonatas were inspired by his sojourns at Martonvásár. Whatever the truth, a small Beethoven museum contains manuscripts and personal belongings, and on summer evenings **performances of his symphonies** by the State Symphony Orchestra are held on an island in the middle of the park, beneath a great bower of beech and sycamore. Armed with mosquito-repellent and a brace of bottles (there's a bar-buffet in the grounds) you can watch the sun set and hear the soaring music, if necessary catching the last train back to Budapest (around 11.30pm on Saturday). **Tickets** cost between 80-150 Ft – the cheapest ones are fine – and are available on the spot, or in advance from *Philharmonia* at 1, Vörösmarty tér in Budapest.

SZÉKESFEHÉRVÁR

Reputedly the site where Árpád pitched camp and founded his dynasty, **SZÉKESFEHÉRVÁR** was probably the earliest Hungarian town. (The name, meaning 'seat of the white castle', is pronounced 'SAIKesh-fehair-var'). It was later changed to *Alba Regia* by King István, who made it his capital and the centre of his campaign to Christianise the Magyars. The Turkish occupation destroyed Alba Regia, and modern Székesfehérvár owes its character to two events: its C18 resurgence under the Habsburgs, during which the belváros was constructed; and the final German counter-attack in 1945, which ravaged the suburbs but ironically cleared the way for new industries and an encircling girth of *lakótelep*.

From the railway station, follow Lenin út northwards until it becomes Népköztársaság útja, an avenue delineating the longest side of the roughly triangular belváros, which occupies approximately the same area as the great castle once did. The Romkert adjoining Népköz. útja is an obvious first stop, an open air museum containing fragmented medieval masonry, bordered by a stretch of the original town wall. Opposite are King István's tomb and the ruins of the Coronation Church where 38 Magyar rulers were crowned and 18 buried, originally designed by Italian architects to rival St. Mark's in Venice. With its schools, salt-house, markets and mint, well fortified and surrounded by marshes, Alba Regia prospered even after the royal seat was moved to Buda; but fell in 1543 to the Turks, who plundered and them blew up the Church and Basilica.

The **István Király Museum** on Gagarin tér deftly incorporates archaeological finds into a series of rooms comprising a historical record from geological beginnings to the present day, including some nice examples of eastern Celtic pottery. To the west of the Romkert lies **Szabadság tér**, the centre of Székesfehérvár's revival under Maria Theresa; a gracious setting for *Albatour-*

SZÉKESFEHÉRVÁR

To Marx tér
(buses for
Bory Vár)

ENGELS FRIGYES UTCA

Hotel Velence

MARCIUS 15 UTCA

István Király Múseum

ADY ENDRE UTCA

IBUSZ

Fekete Sas Pharmacy Museum

Express

Bishop's Palace

Tourist Hostel

Romkert

SZABADSAG TER

Hotel Alba
Regia

KOSSUTH UT

Albatourist

NÉPKÖZTÁRSASÁG UTJA

PIAC TER

VOROS HADSEREG UTJA

Bus Station

VORÖSMARTY TER

LENIN UT

To the Railway Station

ist (nr.6); a squat Bishop's Palace built with stones from the Basilica, and a severe Franciscan church. Ecclesiastical piles continue north and south of the square: a Baroque Cathedral raises twin spires over Arany J. utca, dwarfing the town's single gothic monument, St. Anna's chapel, while a Rococo church and monastery stand together on Marcius 15. utca, with *IBUSZ* on the corner. Marcius 15. Street is pastel-painted and so perfectly preserved that you almost expect to see crinolined ladies emerging from the ornate C18 *Fekete Sas* pharmacy (now a musuem). Nearby on Bartók tér, a gallery displays the lifetime work of **István Csók** (1865-1961), a painter first associated with the Nagybánya School who fell under the influence of Vuillard and Bonnard in Paris, and returned to Hungary to practice *plein air* painting. He later joined the *MIENK* group's opposition to 'narrative' painting, insisting that art should be 'purely pictorial' and concerned only with the visual experience.

The town's best sight, however, is out in the eastern suburbs, beyond the computer and TV factories which nowadays underpin Székesfehérvár's economy. Accessible by bus from Marx tér, **Bory's Castle** (*Bory Vár*) is a bizarre product of matrimonial obsession; an eclectic structure combining features of Scottish, Romanesque and Gothic architecture, built largely of reinforced concrete (plus other materials that came to hand) by a group of students under the direction of the sculptor Jenő Bory. It is filled with statues and paintings of Ilona Komocsin, Bory's wife and favourite model, whose memory the castle enshrines. Although the overall effect of Ilona's multiple images is slightly morbid, it's a marvellous place to wander around.

Practicalities

The **tourist offices** on Szabadság tér, Ady u. and Rákóczi u. all arrange private rooms (usually in the high-rise zone); cheaper **accommodation** than in the *Albe Regia* or *Velence* hotels, though only a shade below the cost of a double in the *Hotel* (József u.42) or the *Két Góbé* 'Two Rascals' pension at 4, Gugásvölgyi utca. Yet cheaper beds exist – but may be occupied – in the *Török Udvar* hostel at 2, Jókai u., while *Express* (Rákóczi u.4) does its best to fill college dorms during summer.

The *Ősfehérvár* (Táncsics u.1) and *Velence* (Marcius 15. u.) are both upmarket **places to eat and drink**, open until midnight and featuring music in the evenings; locals seemingly prefer the *Kis Kulacs* (at the corner of Lenin and V.H. útja) or *Szabadság* (Vörösmarty tér) restaurants. The *Ezerjó* on Gagarin tér is a nice wine bar. For self-catering or cheap snacks, investigate the **market** just north of the **bus terminal** on Piac tér. Other things you might need to buy can probably be found in the big *Fehérvár* department store, whose once-silvery exterior so impressed a group of visiting Soviet journalists that they concluded that it had to be *pokazuka* – 'for show'. Hopefully you shouldn't have any need of the **pharmacy** on V.H. avenue nor the **hospitals** situated further west, just beyond the junction with Sergélyesi út.

Travelling on from Székesfehérvár

Assuming that you're not boarding the *Kálmán Imre* express for Vienna, the *Favorit* for Leipzig, or a bus to grisly Dunaújváros (p.160), there are basically three routes out of Székesfehérvár. By road 81 or railway, the route **through the Vertes into northern Transdanubia** is generally a scenic one. Trains halt at CSÓKAKŐ (a side road off rd. 81), where a ruined castle surmounting a 600ft hill on the outskirts offers a stunning view of the countryside; while BODAJK to the southwest has a *Fogadó* and an old mansion serving as a tourist hostel. (Reservations here, and subsequently, from *Albatours* in Székesfehérvár).

The starting point for **walking** in the Vértes, MÓR is distinguished by the presence of two formerly aristocratic *kastélys* on its main square, and known for producing **wine**. Vineyards and cellars pervade the community, and you can sample the stuff in the **Wine Museum** opposite the tourist hostel on Ezerjó utca. (There's also a Pension on Kodály street). After KISBÉR, the railway turns north to Komárom, while rd.81 continues until Győr, entering town through its eastern suburbs to encounter a fiendish knot of flyovers.

Heading **towards Veszprém in the Bakony** (p.129) by route 8 or the railway, VÁRPALOTA appears through a haze of lignite smoke. The *November 7* Power Plant's emissions – and those of an aluminium foundry – are quietly falling as acid rain upon the Bakony's forests, the **castle** in the centre of town, and a **Roman wier**, constructed of gigantic stones, which stretches brokenly for almost one kilometre near the suburb (and bathing resort) of Pétfürdő. Rooms are cheap at the *Palota* on Szabadság tér, for surely few wish to stay here, despite the lure of an **C11 circular chapel** with a mushroom-shaped cupola, which graces **ÖSKÜ** 9 km further west by road or railway.

Local trains from Székesfehérvár (but *not* expresses from Budapest) stop at SZABADBATTYÁN **en route to the Balaton**, whence it should be possible to catch buses 5km south to **TÁC**, along route 70. There, signposts direct visitors towards the **Roman ruins of Gorsium**, an Aquincum-style restoration of the town raised by Hadrian to the rank of a city, later abandoned and plundered for building material. If you carry on by route 70 or railway, you'll eventually reach Siófok on the Balaton's southern shore.

LAKE BALATON

With 197km of shoreline to exploit, **LAKE BALATON** is the apple of IBUSZ's eye; a place as geared to the tourist industry as the Nógrád Basin is to coalmining. Since 1945, when private villas and hotels became trade union holiday homes (*üdülőház*), certain **resorts** have become the recognised perks of sections of society – with workers from Kaposvár sugar factory getting their two weeks at Balatonboglár, members of the Writers' Union retreating to a more salubrious place in Szigliget, and Party *funkcionárusok* enjoying the exclusiveness of Balatonvilágos, etc. More footloose and youthful visitors started flocking to the Balaton in the mid '60s, when private life was removed from the Stalinist strait-jacket; while in the '70s, the private house-building and room-letting boom began, fueled by the 'New Economic Mechanism' and an influx of tourists from the West.

Balaton isn't to everyone's taste, but it certainly tries to be. While the southern shore is unabashedly hedonistic (without being 'naughty'), places along the northern shore boast of historic monuments, cultural events and scenic landscape. **Watersports, tennis and riding** can easily be arranged, while most resorts have at least one disco (often inside the classiest hotel) for **nightlife**. The price of hotel **rooms** is equivalent to – if not more than – rates in Budapest; private rooms go for around 200-300Ft per head if you get them through *IBUSZ* or *Siótour*, perhaps marginally less if directly obtained from private landladies (look for *Zimmerfrei* signs). Most Balaton **campsites** operate between May 1 – September 31, but for precise details of opening times pick up a *Camping Hungary* map or a *Hotel-Camping* brochure from any tourist office. During high-season (roughly June-August), auxiliary campsites open to handle the overflow from the main sites near each resort. The Balaton campsites are the most expensive in Hungary – although some sites drop their prices out of season – so the savings incurred by having FICC membership or a student are significant.

Along the southern shore and between Balatonalmádi amd Badacsony on the opposite bank, trains are the easiest way of **getting around**; buses provide the link between Balatonfüred and Tihany, Badacsony and Keszthely, and

Veszprém and Siófok. **Organised tours** are available from *Siótour* (see under Siófok, Balatonfüred and Keszthely), while **ferries** sailing between various points around the lake provide the breeziest, cheapest excursions of all.

THE SOUTHERN SHORE FROM SIÓFOK TO THE 'LITTLE BALATON'

Approaching **the southern shore** from the direction of Budapest by train, you'll catch your first glimpse of the Balaton at BALATONVILÁGOS. One of the lushest, least commercialised resorts, built on wooded cliffs and along the shore, this is reserved for Party officials. Unlike holidaymakers at other resorts, they have something that could properly be called a beach; elsewhere, the *strand* is an expanse of lawn terminating in a concrete embankment with quays and diving boards.

SIÓFOK is the largest port on the southern shore: a plebeian, open-armed place that pioneered the incorporation of video-discos into its traditional nightlife of wine bars and gypsy bands. A string of high-rise hotels – their communal beach is like a sardine can – casts another shadow on Siófok's pre-war reputation as a centre of quiet elegance; of which a token reminder is the Petőfi sétány, the central promenade: leafy, lined with sedate villas and terminated by a rose garden in Dimitrov Park. Fő utca – a stretch of route 70 – is the town's modern axis: full of bustle but unremarkable, save for the *Fogás eszpresszó*'s selection of pastries. From the **bus and train stations** it runs past the Post Office, shops and the meteorological tower on Szabadság tér to **Siótour** (nr. 174); and then to an excellent indoor **market** and an *ABC* on the west bank of the Sió canal.

Emperor Galerius initiated the first canal and locks to regulate the level of the lake in 292, but things were busiest during the Turkish occupation, when a fleet of 10,000 men was stationed here. Before steamboats were introduced (as usual, by Count Széchenyi), crossing the lake could be a hazardous business, as you can imagine from some of the vessels displayed in the **Beszédes József Museum** at 2, Sió utca. Named after a hydraulic engineer, it traces local aquatic history – including the building of the **concrete embankments**, which give the southern shore a sterile appearance but prevent flooding – and outlines future plans for the Balaton.

If this fails to hasten your steps to **the harbour** and a getaway ferry (services to Tihany, Alsóörs, Balatonfüred and Balatonföldvár), excursions and **accommodation** are plentiful. The cheapest hotel, *Touring*, is out on the west road; the Altálános school on Fő tér is a hostel from July 1 to August 20; or there are several campsites on Siófok's outskirts. The 'Golden Beach' (*Aranypart*) is rather a misnomer for the concrete and grass embankment that stretches as far east as **BALATONSZABADI**, and features no less than three campsites. *Kék-Balaton* is nearest Siófok but wedged between the road and railway track, while *Gamasza* (open July-August only) and *Ifjúsági* lie practically on the shore.

Siótour, which can book private rooms and **sports** equipment, also arranges various **excursions and entertainments**. These include coach trips to Székesfehérvár and Gorsium, Veszprém, Herend, Tihany or Hévíz; pleasure cruises with food, music and wine tasting; a 'Hubertus Party' at the Nagyberek farm, and a *Betyár*, or 'Highwayman's' evening in a Bakony csárda; a display of folk dancing at Siófok's cultural centre, and an excursion to Mezőszilas for a horse show and other Puszta-ish tourist rites. In Siófok come evening, bars and discos make a bashful appearance around the waterfront.

BALATONÚJHELY begins west of the Sió canal, but merged with **BALATONSZÉPLAK** in 1949 to form *Ezüstpart Camping* (with free kitchens) and the *Strand* site (offering bicycles for hire by the hour; 200Ft per week). Blink as you pass through **ZAMÁRDI**, the next settlement, and you'll miss it — which isn't a great shame. Red signs lead from the station to **Szamarkő** ('Donkey rock'), thought by archaeologists to have been a sacrificial site of the ancient Magyars, and claimed by some Christians to bear the hoof-print of Christ's donkey; while the **Tájház** displays peasant pottery, tiled ovens and old agriculture equipment. Otherwise Zamárdi offers the standard beach 'n' bars set-up, with *Auto-camping* I & II on the shore road, and *Siótour* at Kossuth u. 12. Neighbouring **SZÁNTOD** has the expensive *Rév camping* (high season only) and a **car-ferry to Tihany** on the northern shore.

BALATONFÖLDVÁR is in a similar vein but on a larger scale. Bathing began here at the turn of the century, and now thousands come to amble from snack bar to snack bar. It's a tedious terrain of carfully laid parks and concrete holiday complexes, though the *Magyar Tenger* campsite down by the *Hotel Neptun* is suprisingly pleasant. A 4km stroll brings one to **KÖRÖSHEGY**, where **chamber-music concerts** are held on summer evenings in a C15 church. Personally I'd recommend only the hills beyond, alive with the choruses of mating deer.

The boundary of **BALATONSZÁRSZÓ** is marked by a cemetery containing the grave of the 'proletarian' poet, **Attila József**, whose anarchic verses have endeared him to Hungarian punks and society at large. Dismissed during his own short lifetime by the literary avant garde — Mihály Babits, editor of the journal *Nyugat*, persistently thwarted Attila's career — the impoverished poet threw himself under a freight train nearby in 1937. The house where he spent his last days is now a memorial museum (József u. 7), while Balatonszárszó also posesses a tourist hostel at Fő utca 3 (May 26 - August 31) and the *Tura* camping site, open during June and July.

BALATONSZEMES, crowned by the ruined ramparts of Bagolyvár Castle, offers a **Post Office Museum**, cheap double rooms in the *Lido Fogadó* (from April to September) and several **campsites**. Of these, *Express* is usually group-booked in advance, so try the *Lido* — expensive but on the beach, *Auto* on Fő utca, or the overcrowded *Vadvirag* development west of town. Three formerly volcanic hills bear the burden of **BALATONBOGLÁR**, a settlement now merged with Balatonlelle. Cemetery Hill (Temetőhegy) hosts art exhibitions during summertime, while Vár-hegy is topped by a spherical **look-out tower**, commanding a sweeping view from Keszthely to Tihany.

BALATONLELLE, nearer to Siófok, has an outdoor theatre in the grounds of a mansion at Kossuth u. 2, the setting for **folk-dancing** performances, and an antiquated smithy at Szabadság u. 52. Its campsite is by the harbour, Siótour operates from Szent István u., and you can hire camping **bikes** on Vasúti sétány. At Balatonboglár are two cheap hotels: *Hullam* at Dózsa Gy. u. 55, and the *Platan* at 56, Hunyadi utca.

FONYÓD grew up between the Sipos and Sándor hills and subsequently spread itself along the lakeside, so the symmetry of its setting is better appreciated from the far shore. Yet another resort with built-up *strand*, bleak modern architecture and various places to placate your stomach, Fonyód's sole relic of antiquity is the overgrown moat of a castle, which during the C16 commanded the swampy countryside around and kept the Turks at bay. Fonyód's low on entertainment value but again, has a cheap hotel – the *Liget* – in the Fonyódliget suburb, 1km east of the town centre. Fonyódbélatelep, another suburb, is the setting for *Napsugár* complex of bungalows, a hotel and campsite.

Between Fonyód and **BALATONFENYVES**, reclaimed swampland now belongs to the **NAGYBEREK** state co-operative farm, where forestation and irrigation work since the '50s has produced less benefits than were expected and simultaneously spoiled the rich breeding ground for fish. **Horseriding** can be arranged nearby at **CSISZTAPUSZTA**, where drilling for oil unexpectedly yielded **warm springs** instead of 'black gold', and the waters – reputedly good for relieving rheumatic diseases and tension – may be reached by **narrow-gauge railway** which begins at Balatonfenyes and runs around the farm. Beyond Fonyód the lake is very shallow and partially banked by reeds, making it the least tamed stretch of the southern shore. You'll see whole tribes of bathers de-camping to the large rafts anchored off-shore, armed with crates of beer and piles of lángos.

BALATONMÁRIAFÜRDŐ and **BALATONKERESZTÚR** are both quiet villages: the former offers the best ice cream I ever ate (at a café by the Balatonmáriafürdő-alsó station), while the latter has a cheap hostel at Ady u. 26, sited in one of the Festetics family's former mansions. There's a reasonably priced hotel, *Kócsag Fogadó*, in **BALATONBERÉNY**, and also arguably the best campsite on this side of the lake. From here, reeds stretch all the way to the Zala River through the **KIS-BALATON** (Little Balaton) **nature reserve**. Hundreds of birds, especially egrets, migrate through or nest on the Kis-Balaton permanently. The reserve can only be visited with prior permission from the Conservation office in Budapest (XII, Költő u. 21) or Veszprém (Tolbuhin u. 31).

From settlements at the far end of the southern shore, there are **buses** (and **trains** from Balatonszentgyörgy) to Keszthely, described on p.124; and **ferries** from Balatonmáriafürdő across to Balatongyörök on the northern shore.

THE NORTHERN SHORE AS FAR AS BALATONFÜRED

To reach Balaton's **northern shore** by road from Budapest, turn off route 70 just ouside Balatonaliga and follow the shoreline around through **BALATONKARATTYA**, a suburb of Balatonkenese distinguished only by the dead trunk of the *Rákóczi fa* – a tree where the honoured freedom fighter (p.182) is said to have tied his horse – and *Piroska* campsite, a pleasant place situated at the bottom of a steep hill. **BALATONKENESE** is larger, with a Baroque church and **peasant houses** along Bajcsy-Zsilinszky, Kossuth and Fő streets; while above the settlement are **caves** dug into the clay banks by refugees from the Turks (hence their name, the Turkish holes), which continued to be inhabited by poor people until the end of the last century.

BALATONFŰZFŐ, site of a large and smelly nitro-chemicals plant, doesn't merit a stop, but beyond Fűzfő bay you reach **BALATONALMÁDI**, the first town on the northern shore. A bathing resort since 1877, it's now modern looking, with only the Chapel of St Job – originally part of Buda Castle – built into its Catholic church (decorated with mosaics by Károly Lotz) to engender historical interest. The *Hotel Aurora* dominates the skyline; *Kék-Balaton* (József A. u. 27), and to a lesser extent the *Tulipán* on Marx tér, are cheaper alternatives. There are also bungalows on József utca, private rooms for rent from IBUSZ at Perőfi u. 21, and a campsite (with another one in the suburb of Vörösberény – whose name derives from the local red, sandy soil). Ferries and trains continue around to **ALSÓÖRS**, formerly a mining village where the red rock was used to make mill-stones. Although it's insufficent reason to linger here, there's an odd remnant of the Ottoman occupation worth a look at 7, Petőfi köz: a Gothic manor house once inhabited by the local Turkish tax collector and distinguished by a turban-topped chimney (a sign of wealth in the days when smoke left most houses through a hole in the roof). Alsóörs has two further campsites, *Kemping* and *Autos strand*, but neighbouring **CSOPAK** is a nicer place to stay. Private rooms here can be booked at Blaha u. 5 in Balatonfüred, although increasingly people are renting them on their own initiative (look for *Zimmer frei* signs). Csopak is famous for its local wines, *Olaszrizling* and *Furmint*.

Seventeenth century chronicles record pilgrims descending on **BALATON-FÜRED** to 'camp in scattered tents' and benefit from the mineral springs here. Nowadays some 30,000 people come every year for treatment in the town's sanatoria. A busy harbour and skyscraper hotels dominate Balatonfüred's approaches, but the centre has a sedate, convalescent atmosphere, typified by the embankment promenade, Rabindranath Tagore sétány, named after the Indian poet who came here in 1926 and planted a tree in gratitude for his cure. Other celebrities followed his example – the origin of the sétány's memorial grove – and some are remembered in the Pantheon beside the Trade Unions' Sanatorium on Gyógy tér (Health Square), onto which the promenade opens. Here you can drink the Kossuth spring's carbonic water at a columned, pagoda-like structure in the centre of the square. Four other springs feed the hospital (which treats around 10,000 people annually), and the adjoining **mineral baths** on the eastern side. Excavated villas suggest that the Romans were the first to use the waters to treat stomach ailments and, when mixed with goats' milk whey, as a cure for lung diseases.

The late-C18 **Horváth House** on the tér's western side was one of Hungary's first public inns, and the development of such institutions merits a brief digression. Inn-keeping developed late in Hungary, and then largely because of the Swabians, for Magyars tended to consider such work beneath them. Petőfi complained that his landlord wouldn't utter a word of welcome until he had been paid, and served food 'as if by the special grace of God'; whilst another C19 traveller reported that his host wore spurs to emphasise his gentlemanly status, and was 'capable of giving his guests a good hammering or throwing them out' if he felt like it.

Much patronised by leading writers and politicians during the Reform era, the Horváth Inn was subsequently transformed into a rest home for uranium miners. It stands at the junction of Blaha Lujza street, named after Hungary's answer to Gracie Fields, for the 'Nightingale of Budapest' spent her summers in a villa at nr. 2 here, and maybe took her tea – as one still can – in the *Kedves cukrászda* (next to the **Balatontourist Nord** office) over the road. The nearby **Jókai** utca is named after the C19 writer whose soujourn here is a testimonial to the spa's efficacy. He came to Balatonfüred at the age of 37, half-expecting to die from a serious lung infection, built the villa which now stands as a **memorial house** so that he could return each year, and lived to the ripe age of 84.

Jókai utca continues over the railway tracks (where it becomes Ady u.) into the original centre of Balatonfüred. Siske út and Vázsonyi út, near a Calvinist church, are dotted with houses in the traditional local folk style; and there's a touch of village atmosphere about the **market**, which takes place just off Arácsi út.

Balatonfüred's cheapest hotels are the *Aranycsillag* (Zsigmond u.1), *Erdei* (Koloska u.45) and *Panoráma* (Kun u.15); all a shade more expensive than private **accommodation** from Balatontourist Nord or IBUSZ (just off Petőfi utca, the main road encircling the centre). The campsite on the eastern outskirts, named after the 27th Reunion of the Federation of Camping & Caravaning Clubs, made me wish that they'd stopped meeting after the twenty-sixth time: encamped and encaravaned victims are bombarded with information about **excursions** through loudspeakers, and harassed restaurant staff may snarl *sprich Deutsch*! at tourists unwise enough to attempt a request in broken Magyar. Buses #1 and #2 run via Jókai utca from the campsite to the **railway station**, while **buses** following Széchenyi utca (route 71) eastwards out of town are usually heading **for Tihany**, which can also be reached **by ferry**. (Other boats sail to Siófok on the southern shore). Heading eastwards, the railway skips Tihany peninsula, going by way of Aszófő (good campsite) and Örvényes; while from Balatonfüred there's also a **bus service to Nagyvázsony** (p.128) in the Bakony.

TIHANY

A rocky peninsula declared Hungary's first national park in 1952, **TIHANY** is historically associated with the Benedictine order, with fishing folk and ferrymen, and with its redoubtable castle (no longer in existence) which withstood 150 years of Turkish hostility. Buses from Balatonfüred follow the road along the peninsula's undeveloped eastern side – no beaches, but plenty of people fishing – past the main harbour ranged beneath the old quarter, and down to *Tihanyi rév*, the tourist complex beside the quay for boats to Balatonföldvár and Szántód. The historic centre of Tihany sits above the harbour where the ferries from Siófok and Balatonfüred pull in; you'll find it by pursuing winding steps up between a screen of trees, like thousands of other people who come to rubberneck around the 'Pearl of the Balaton'. Overcrowded and overpriced it may be, but the lustre hasn't entirely gone.

In days gone by, Tihany's tone was set by the **Benedictine Abbey**, established here at the request of Andrew I to be a beacon of enlightenment for his supposedly benighted subjects, and founded – true to the biblical injunction – upon a rocky promontory overlooking the Balaton. The king's body still lies in the crypt of the **Abbey Church** – the only one of the Árpád line to remain where buried – but the building above it is Baroque, for the original church succumbed to wars and time. Inside are virtuoso woodcarvings by Sebestyén Stulhoff, who lived an worked in the monastery for 25 years after his fiancé died, and is said to have preserved her features in the face of an angel, which kneels to the right of the altar of the Virgin. The frescoes painted a century later by Lodz, Székely and others exemplify the 'narrative' school which dominated Hungarian fine arts before the First World War. Flood-lit during the evenings, the church is a magnificent setting for **organ concerts** held on Tuesdays and Wednesdays, from June to August.

The adjoining monastery now contains a **museum** displaying Balaton landscapes, and an interesting collection of costumes, implements and musical instruments gathered from far-flung communities in the *taiga* beneath the arctic circle and in the Ural mountains – the **Finno-Ugric tribes** from which the Magyars originated. Until linguistic and ethnographic investigations were undertaken by János Sajnovics (1733-85), Antal Reguly and others, it was assumed that Hungarians were descended from the Huns; a theory revived in recent years following the decipherment of inscriptions on the Nagyszentmiklós 'Treasure of Attila' (held in Vienna). In the museum basement are Roman altars, a mosaic pavement and bits from the Paulite Monastery at Nagyvázsony, while for the record, the foundation deed of Tihany is the earliest document to include Hungarian words amongst the Latin – a source for pride, it seems.

Twee adaptation á la Szentendre abounds, from the rip-off restaurant occupying the monastery stables to the Fishermen's Guild Museum down below in a house on Pisky promenade, where **folkloric performances** are staged in the courtyard. Around Perőfi and Csokonai street, **houses** are built of grey basalt tufa, with windows and doors outlined in white and porticoed terraces, including the **tourist office**. Even without a map it's easy to stumble upon *Belső-tó*, one of Tihany peninsula's two **lakes**, for sunlight glinting upon its water is visible from the Abbey Church. From its southern bank, a path runs through vineyards, orchards and lavender fields past the Aranyház **geyser cones** – funnels forced open by hot springs – and down to Tihanyi rév, the tourist-mill. Routes heading eastwards from Belső-tó and Tihanyi rév wind up at **Csúcs Hill** (232 m), where you can enjoy a **panoramic view** of Balaton from an observation tower; while farther inland lies the 'Outer' lake, *Külső-tó*. Drained in 1809, it became a bird sancturary and was permited to refill itself in 1975. Otherwise, what people do is eat and drink (mainly in **Tihanyi rév**) and take to the water, paying for the privilege on the beach at the peninsula's southern tip, although there are various *strand* scattered around the shoreline (and it's not difficult to find a secluded, albeit reedy stretch in between them). Hotels in Tihanyi rév are exorbitant, so the neighbouring campsite, or private rooms (from Petőfi u. 4 in the old town) are the only **accommodation** unless you want to base yourself in one of the shoreline resorts west of the peninsula.

WEST TOWARDS THE BADACSONY

For 30km west of Tihany **the shoreline** is infested with holiday homes and non-descript resorts; perhaps worth stopping if you hit upon a beach or campsite to your taste, but generally nothing special. At ÖRVÉNYES, beyond ASZÓFŐ (good campsite, hard currency only), an **antique watermill** (*mŭemlék malom*) still operates – acclaimed as a conservation triumph by the tourist board, although in the 1950s almost 200 similar mills were demolished on the Party's orders to end private milling, clearing the way for larger, state milling collectives. Its carved bins, loft and workings are interesting, but there's little life before **Killiántelep International Youth Camp**, west of BALATONUDVARI (with its own *v.m.* train halt). During the busy summer months, advance booking (especially of the cheap 2- and 4- bed bungalows) is advisable – and possible through any of the country's *Express* offices – while on the spot, you can hire boats, bicycles and windsurfing boards. **BALATON-AKALI** is known for its *Akali muskotály* white wine, and presumably by a host of Czech nationals, for whom the Vasúti campsite is reserved, while Westerners use the *Strand* – a huge and stony site on the beach east of the station – or the *Holiday* site next door, which has a buffet and more shade.

A fortress-like Miners' rest home guards the road to BALATONSZEPEZD, where *Windsurf* camping lies east of the station, and similar directions apply to the *Napfény* campsite – overpriced and without hot water – in RÉVFÜLÖP, a settlement offering two restaurants, a disco and a ruined C13 sandstone church to break the monotony of holiday villas. Beyond a few private rooms, ÁBRAHÁMHEGY lacks tourist facilities, and for this reason is a good place to stop and bathe.

The Badacsony

Although its coffin-shaped bulk barely qualifies as a mountain, **THE BADACSONY** has four villages prostrated at its feet, whilst behind it dead volcanoes range northwards across the Tapolca Basin. When the land that later became Hungary first surfaced, moulten magma errupted from the seabed, and cooled into a great semi-circle of **basalt columns**, 210m high, which form the Badacsony's southeastern face. *Kökapu*, the Stone Gate, cleaves the northeast side – two natural towers either side of a precipitous drop. The rich volcanic soil of the mountain's lower slopes has supported vineyards since the Age of Migrations, when the Avars buried grape pips with their dead to ensure that the afterlife wouldn't be lacking in wine. Nowadays growers own their plots – small and lovingly-tended as of yore – but being collectivized, must sell two-thirds of their harvest to the state wineries which blend *Badacsonyi Szürkebarát*, *Kéknyelŭ*, *Zöldszilváni* and *Olaszrizling*.

Exploiting these attractions, the tourist industry has developed around the southern tip, where you'll find an **accommodation/information bureau** just behind Badacsony v.m. railway **station**, above the quay. (**Ferries** to and from Révfülöp, Balatonboglárlelle, Fonyód and Szigliget). From there, the trail up Lábdi utca is marked by locals selling wine and careering jeeps taking drunken tourists up to the former Bormúzeum, a large basalt hall now serving as an expensive 'peasant' restaurant festooned with the obligatory strings of paprika and a 'Gypsy' band. Further uphill there's a nicer restaurant in the house once owned by Sándor Kisfaludy, who lauded the Balaton's beauties in verse; his wife Rózsa Szegedy's house is now a local **museum**. Lábdi avenue ends by the **Rose Rock** (*Rózsakő*), of which it's said that if a man and woman sit upon it with their backs to the Balaton and think about each other, they'll be married by the end of the year.

Walking up through the beechwoods to the Kisfaludy look-out tower is a fairly tame, Sunday stroller's route, well trodden as far as the famous **Stone Gate**, where people gape and ooh-aah before returning to the jeeps and wine bars. To escape the crowds, try the 4km **hike to Gulács-hegy**, a perfectly conical hill further north near the Nemesgulács railway halt for trains en route to Tapolca, with the impressive *Szent György Hill* on the other side of the tracks (p.127). Private rooms at the campsite – with a small beach, five minutes' walk westwards from the tourist office – are Badacsony's cheapest **accommodation**, although there's a better campsite at BADACSONYÖRS (the train halt after Ábrahámhegy), which faces the pleasant **Folly arborétum** of pines and cedars from all over the world, viewable with permission from the owners.

After Badacsony the railway veers northwards up to Tapolca in the Bakony (see p.127). While you can switch **trains** there and ride back down to Keszthely, it's easier to continue around the southern shore **by bus**.

AROUND KESZTHELY

Approaching Keszthely along route 71, the small peninsula of **SZIGLIGET** protrudes from beneath the Kamonkő cliffs in a less dramatic fashion than when seen from an incoming ferry. Entwined with a branch road, the Várhegy bears the restored **ruins of a fortress** commissioned by Pannonhalma Monastery in the wake of the Mongol invasion, accessible by a footpath which begins behind the small white church sited on the highest spot in the village. Below the fortress is a lush park, wherein a former castle serves as the holiday resort of the Writers' Union. Non-members may look around the grounds only with permission; the hoi polloi can camp beside the paying-beach at BALATONEDERICS, further west, a place otherwise merely notable as a train halt and the junction for rd.84 to Sümeg (and, farther north, Sárvár, p.149). BALATONGYÖRÖK is still half a village of white-porticied, thatched houses, with a campsite on the beach hiring windsurfing gear, and a grand view from the Szépkilátó (which means, 'beautiful view'). The **panorama** encompasses Szent György Hill, the castles atop Csobánc (p.127) and Szigliget, the Badacsony and – across the lake – the twin peaks of Várhegy in Fonyód. To the west, behind a hill, GYENDESDIÁS has a campsite on Mádach út and a bad beach, while just beyond lie Keszthely's suburbs.

Keszthely
Easily the nicest settlement along the northern shore, **KESZTHELY** is the region's cultural capital, and probably the only resort that doesn't turn comatose when the tourists stop coming. Its Baroque belváros is a legacy of the heady C18-19, when Keszthely was a centre of the Hungarian

enlightenment and independence movements, and like the university, owes much to the patronage of the aristicratic Festetics family. Keszthely's beach is good, there are bars, monuments and museums galore, while the warm waters at Hévíz (a short bus ride away) provide a perfect cure for sightseer's foot.

Arriving at the bus or train station, simply follow Mártirok útja uphill to reach Kossuth utca (rd.71), which cuts across **the centre** of Keszthely from north to south, and the **Balaton Museum** standing on the corner. Exhibits depict the region's zoology, ethnography and archaeology – the latter involving exhibits dating back to the C1AD, when roadbuilding Roman imperialists disrupted the lifestyle of local Celtic tribes. A short distance north of the museum lies Fő tér, the main square, dignified by the presence of a much-remodelled Gothic church once owned by Premonstraten monks, and IBUSZ. From here it's but five minutes' walk from Keszthely's other sights. The daily **market** nearby on Bem u. is particularly good on Wednesdays, when traders bring along painted gourds, embroidery and sheepshins, while a stroll morthwards along Kossuth u. will bring you to the *Festeticspalota*.

Founded in 1745 by Count György, the **Festetics Palace** grew to embrace a library, chapel and archive, and from the C19 onwards attracted the leading lights of Hungarian literature (now recalled by memorial trees) as the country's first public forum for criticism. Guided tours of the palace have as their highlight the **Helikon Library,** a masterpiece of joinery-work and carving by János Kerbl, containing many rare books (chiefly on agriculture and natural science). There's also a vast gilt mirrored ballroom; a fine collection of Chinese vases and ornately tiled ovens, and – for the sentimental – portraits of the family racehorses and dachshunds. Seven generations of aristocratic ease ended in 1945, when the state opened a remand home for boys here; as a museum, the building is now open from 10am-6pm between May and September (9am-5pm October to April).

György's most useful contribution was an agricultural college, or Georgikon; the first of its kind in Europe, and the forerunner of today's **Agártudományi University**, a green and daffodil yellow-painted building sited halfway along Széchenyi utca, which leads off Fő tér. On Bercsényi utca, two blocks west, is the original **Georgikon**, a cluster of white building where the first students lived and worked together, now displaying dairy and viniculture equipment; cartwright's tools, old Ford tractors and suchlike. Visiting hours are 10am-6pm, April to November. On the same street, Bercsényi utca, you'll also find an open-air cinema.

There are **bars** a-plenty around Keszthely's belváros, and in the harbour area – with facilities for tennis, minigolf and football – beyond Helikon Park. Fast-food stands are the norm around **the harbour** (ferries to and from Balatongyörök). More enticing are the *Béke*, where you can dine on a terrace to the accompaniment of violin music, or take-aways from the *Csemege* delicatessen. Both the latter are on Kossuth utca, also the site of *Express* (nr.22) and the place to board a bus to Hévíz.

Hévíz

Six kilometres northwest of Keszthely, the spa of **HÉVÍZ** is founded upon Europe's largest (though by no means huge) thermal lake, the waters of which were used for curative purposes, as well as for tanning leather, throughout medieval times. During the C18 they were subjected to scientific enquiry and salubriously channelled into a bath-house erected by Count György, around which, towards the end of the C19, a grand resort developed. Like Karlsbad and the Baths of Hercules, it enjoyed a brief heyday as the watering-hole of crown princes, Gräffins, magnates and prominent intellectuals.

The terraces and gangways surrounding **the baths** (admission 30 Ft) have a fin de siècle appearance, but the ambience is strictly contemporary. Hundreds of people sup beer or read newpapers whilst bobbing in hired tyres upon the lake's surface. Swimming isn't recommended on account of the slightly radioactive water, 70 million litres of which bubble forth from deep craters daily – supposedly beneficial for people with locomotive and inflamatory disorders, of whom 2,000 at a time can be accommodated in Hévíz's sanatorium. Otherwise, Hévíz seems to be comprised of fodder troughs and overpriced hotels, although there's cheapish accommodation to be had at the *Gyöngyvirág* on Felszabadulás tér, the *Piroska* at 10, Kossuth u., or from any of the tourist offices (main one at Rákózi u.8).

Back in Keszthely, the *Helikon turistaszálló* (Honvéd u.22) provides dormitory **accommodation** and a garden, ten minutes' walk from the railway station: follow the campsite signs to Madách utca, then take the second turn-off to the right. The *Amazon* (Georgikon u.1) is the only cheap hotel, but during summer Express or IBUSZ sometimes offer dormitory beds in the university's colleges. The campsite just south of the railway station is the cheapest option, but squeezed between the tracks and a cement works, so continue 1km soutwards to the beach site (which hires boats, tennis courts and windsurfing boards), or consider the pricey, deluxe *Castrum* site 2 km east of town. Beside booking private rooms, *Zalatour* & *IBUSZ* offer a $10 package, the 'Betyár Party': an evening's fun 'during which tourists are frightened by highwaymen in a csárda of genuine atmosphere', as the blurb runs; wine-drinking, bacon-roasting, and a thigh-slapping floorshow rounded off by dinner.

Moving on, Keszthely's linked by bus with the southern shore and Szombathely and Zala in Transdanubia, besides the regular service to Badacsony. The railway around the lake's curve to Balatonszentgyörgy (change there for Nagykanizsa) is really only a continuation of the mainline down from Tapolca and Sümeg – which provides the easiest means of transport up into the Bakony.

THE BAKONY

The Bakony range cuts a swath across central Transdanubia, as if scooped from the ground to provide space for the lake, and piled as a natural embankment behind the lowlier Balaton hills. Abundant vineyards testify to the richness of the volcanic soil and, more recently, mineheads to the mineral wealth beneath it. With dense woods and narrow ravines, this was the 'Hungarian Sherwood Forest' during the centuries of warfare and turmoil, and also the setting for a dozen castles, the finest examples of which stand at Sümeg and Veszprém, while others – brooding, Gothic ruins – decorate peaks as far afield as Csobánc and Nagyvázsony. Siófok's tourist board organises day trips to Veszprém and the porcelain centre of **Herend**. Or you can get right away from everything **walking** in the Bakony, providing you steer clear of military land.

Tapolca and Sümeg

Behind the Badacsony a succession of **hills** (*hegy*) range northwards toweards the Bakony, offering the chance of **hikes** through woodland up to Szent György-hegy, Csobánc and other heights. Basalt columns looking like petrified dwarves – known locally as 'organ pipes' – ripple the side of **Szent György-hegy**, a hill nearby the *Nemesgulács v.m.* halt along the railway between Badacsony and Tapolca, which can also be reached as an extension of the hike from the Stone Gate to Gulács Hill (p.124). From its summit on a clear day distant Sümeg is in sight, while but a few kilometres east arises **Csobánc-hegy**, its peak crowned by a ruined castle which women once defended against the Turks. Since 1970, when public petitions roused the state to declare these hills a conservation area, reafforestation and orchard-planting have partially alleviated the damage caused by 60 years of ruthless quarrying for basalt, during which one peak, the Holáp, was completely decapitated.

Further north, the town of **TAPOLCA** has become a profitable blot on the landscape with the development of bauxite mining and aluminium processing. This is the subject matter of Tapolca's **Bakony Bauxite Museum**, opened on Miners' Day in 1981, but hardly enthralling stuff. Mining operations have sadly necessitated the damming of the **Tavas Caves** (whence underground springs feed the Mill Lake, *Malom-tó*, in central Tapolca), so that for the next 15 years, only the smallest, least interesting caves can be visited; the entrance is on Kisfaludy u., where there's a tourist hostel at nr.1. Tapolca itself, though the neo-Classical belváros centred around Malom-tó is nice enough, has nothing to keep you. Instead, use the town's **transport links** to move on down to Keszthely or up to Sümeg by train, or catch a bus towards Veszprém, which should call at Nagyvázsony (p.128) along the way.

SÜMEG is a nicer town to visit than Tapolca, and despite its two fine historic monuments, seems far less tourist-oriented and pretentious than Tihany. Possibly the most impressive and certainly the best restored of the many fortresses built around the Balaton region, **Sümeg Castle** is lodged high upon a limestone massif, a unique Cretaceous outcropping amongst the basalt of the Bakony. The citadel to the south, built during the C13, provided the basis for successive fortifications – including the outer wall and gate tower – which kept the Turks out, but succumbed to the Habsburgs in 1713, when the struggle for independence, led by Rákóczi, collapsed. The complex of living quarters and defensive structures was restored between 1959-64, and its history is recalled by exhibits in the oldest tower. It's well worth the climb for the views alone. On the road uphill, Vak Bottyán utca, are a cheap hotel, the *Tourist*, and an old stables mounting a display of saddles, 'jiggling woggles' and suchlike objects.

Much of **the town** dates from the C18, when Sümeg was the seat of the Bishops of Veszprém, whose residence at 10, Szent István tér is now a school, still decorated with stone figures but starting to crumble badly. Like the porticied birthplace of the poet Sándor Kisfaludy (whose belongings are on show inside), and the C17 church commissioned by Bishop Széchenyi, it's outshone by the **Church of the Ascension**, which contains probably the finest **frescoes** ever executed by *Maulbertsch*, the prolific Austrian court painter. With a team of assistants, he was able to cover the whole interior within one and a half years; mainly in Biblical scenes, but also with advertising. Along the rear wall are portraits of his main patron, Bishop Biró, together with local gentry and noblewomen, while on the wall facing the choir are depictions of the building itself and a church in Zala, which Biró also sponsored.

Other **accommodation** is available at the *Kisfaludy* hotel and through the *tourist office*, both on Kossuth street. Most **transport** heads northwards. Travelling up that way by railway, you can switch trains for places in Transdanubia at UKK, BOBA and CELLDÖMÖLK – threee oddly-named but otherwise undistinguished junctions that enable you to reach Zalaegerszeg, Veszprém, and Szombathely or Győr respectively. Rd.84 heads off for Sárvár and Sopron, meeting route 8 (from the Austrian border to Veszprém and Székesfehérvár) near the village of 'John's house', Jánosháza.

Approaching Veszprém

The somnambulant atmosphere of the Balaton gives way along the road **between Balatonfüred and Veszprém**, some 15km away, as low-flying helicopter gunships make their appearance from a base in the hills above SZENTKIRÁLYSZABADJA. One of the many bases belonging to what the government calls the **Soviet Forces Temporarily in Hungary** (see the 'short and the long joke', p.146), this is widely believed to harbour nuclear weapons. Unlike Czechoslovakia and the DDR, Hungary was either never 'asked', or else refused to accept, the basing of SS-20s on its soil; but 'tactical' nuclear missiles and bombs have long been here – a fact that most Hungarians are resigned to. Any resentment is more likely caused by the soldiers themselves, although their behavior rarely matches that of a Soviet tankman in 1986, who responded to bar-room taunts that the USSR-Hungary football match had ben 'fixed' by stealing a tank from his camp outside Veszprém, and returning to bulldoze the *Vendéglő* and its occupants.

A nicer, albeit more roundabout way of **approaching Veszprém** is to go **via Nagyvázsony**, sited along the Tapolca-Veszprém road, and accessible by bus from Balatonfüred). Buses to Nagyvázsony pass the ruined *Zadorvár*, secreted in a wood between Pécsely and Barnag. **NAGYVÁZSONY** itself is a sleepy market town, enlivened annually by a **festival of show-jumping and jousting** (July 25-August 2), and permanently marked by **Kinizsi Castle**. Begun in the C15 by the Veszenyis, this was given by King Mátyás to Pál Kinizsi, a local lad who made good as a commander – being reputedly so strong that he wielded a dead Turk as a bludgeon to slay 100 enemies – and was later buried in the red marble fortress chapel. Fine views and cheap beds may be had here in the *Vár túristaszálló*; for sustenance, the *Kinizsi* restaurant is more prominent, though dearer and less lively than seedier bars along the main street.

Approaches **from the west** run past Herend and Nemesvámos (see below);

the route **from Várpalota** is covered on p.115. Travelling by rail **from Szombathely**, Celldömölk, Boba or **Székesfehérvár**, much of the scenery is marred by industry or trampled underfoot by *Honvéd* conscripts doing their basic training, but the route down **from the north**, following the Cuha Valley, is a picturesque one (see p.131).

Veszprém

Cobbled together by a maze of streets which twist up the interlying valleys, **VESZPRÉM** stands upon hills prone to precipitous halts above the fine panorama of the ancient Bakony forests. While its Chemical Technical University, highrise flats and factories result from the policy of spreading industry and expertise beyond Budapest, the town's perfectly-restored Castle Hill and other historic monuments embody a millenium of ecclesiastical influence. Veszprém's colourful belváros reminded me of Győr or Szentendre, and the town is generally green with parks and orchards.

Entering the town from the west, over Valley Bridge, there's a glimpse of Veszprém's castle en route to **the centre**, where sights and activities cluster about boomerang-shaped Népköztársaság and Bajcsy-Zsilinszky avenues, which join the incoming highways. You can walk there from the **bus terminal** – past the **market** onto Ferenc tér, and then along the pedestrian precinct, Kossuth utca – or take a bus from the **railway station** beyond the northern suburbs, alighting by the big Aruház store just east of Szabadság tér. From this square, graced by Attila's statue, to its triangular neighbour Vörös Hadsereg tér, where the Red Army memorial serves as a begging-spot for Gypsy children, the surrounding architecture is floridly Baroque and Rococo: painted in bright pinks, blues and the shade known as 'Empress Theresa yellow' (which she ordained as the colour-scheme for all public buildings throughout the Habsburg empire). At the top end, the swish plastic *Elefánt bisztró* ensnares tourists seeking the cul-de-sac which leads to the **Firetower**, or *Tűztorony*. Its lower section is medieval and formed part of the castle, while the upper storeys, dome and balcony were added in the C19-C20, together with a mechanical carillon which plays a traditional recruiting tune every hour on the hour.

The **Castle** area (*Várhegy*) occupies a plateau, like its counterpart in Buda, and though containing only one street, its appearance and antecedents are impeccable. True, the *Heroes' Gate* is a bombastic monument of the reactionary '30s; but in the **museum** just behind it, and along Tolbuhin út, both state money and public reverence are lavished upon a romantic past of bejewelled bishops and saintly kings. Here, the Archbishop of Salzburg established a Christian bridgehead amongst the pagan subjects of Prince Géza; here too were crowned Gisella, the wife of Hungary's first king, and her successors, giving Veszprém the title of the 'Queen's town'. **St Michael's Cathedral** on Trinity Square boasts of similar lineage, although the building itself has been razed and resurrected half a dozen times. Its current incarnation (dating from 1907-10) is neo-Romanesque, with only a Gothic crypt to show for its origins. Behind the Cathedral, St György's chapel is a mere fragment beneath a glass dome, but **Gisella's chapel** to the south (likewise open Tuesday-Friday from May to October) contains Byzantine-influenced frescoes, albeit slightly damaged since her residence was demolished in order to build the adjoining U-shaped Bishop's Palace. In the former Franciscan church opposite the Cathedral are exhibited wooden votive statues, chasubles etc, to the sound of mournful, taped Mass; while at the end of the promenade, monuments to István and Gisella overlook the Bakony hills and the graceful Völgy-híd bridge over the Séd Valley. During summer, the Castle district is the setting for open-air **concerts**.

Retrace your steps to Szabadság tér, where commercial life gravitates towards Kossuth utca (Post Office, **Express** and **IBUSZ**) and the market, just as cinemas, theatres and groups of students inhabit the university district extending to the south. A short walk past County Hall brings you out into Lenin tér, flanked by Kálvária Hill and a building housing the **Bakony Museum**. Its best exhibits are the Roman mosaics unearthed in a villa at Balácapuszta, southeast of town, and the artefacts pertaining to the Bakony's highwaymen (*betyár*), but not until I'd seen every domestic implement in the adjoining *Bakony-ház* would the museum's custodian release me.

The **University** is situated on the far side of the park, through which Lenin sétány leads further south to the *Sport bisztró*; a popular place with **students**, serving cheap, filling food. By enquiring here, at Express, or the student hostel (*diákszálló*) opposite the university, you should be able to obtain dormitory beds during June-August; cheaper **accommodation** than in the *Hotel Veszprém* (Budapesti u.6), the *Erdei* motel on Kitten berger u. in the valley, or a private room from IBUSZ (Kossuth u.6). The nearest campsite is at Kárdárta, a village along rd.82 north of town.

Veszprém's *divatos* set frequents the *Marica kávéház*, where a late night café/disco operates on the top floor of the 20-storey building opposite Szabadság tér; another is to be found at the *Vadásztanya kisvendéglő* – on Attila u. out towards Nagyvázsony – where admission and a meal cost a mere 100Ft. Economic meals are also served near the market, while less gluttonous **pursuits** include sports at the complex southwest of the university; viewing films or plays (in the centre); and walking in the Séd Valley. Along the riverbank west of the *Völgy-híd* viaduct (which carries rd.8) is an old watermill; to the south lie the *Erdei Motel*, a **Village Museum** and a ghastly zoo.

Through the Bakony to Szombathely or Győr

Leaving aside the places already covered in this chapter, you have a choice of destinations when it's time to move on. **Westwards towards Szombathely**, both rd.8 and the railway pass through Herend, Hungary's Stoke-on-Trent, while by road it's only 5km to **NEMESVÁMOS**, the site of an old **Bakony inn**, the *Vámosi csárda*. Ignore the odd modern fixture and today's clientele, and it's possible to imagine the csárda's appearance at the end of the C19; servants hurrying from the tap-room with its huge casks into the cellar, where swineherds, wayfarers and *betyár* caroused seated upon sections of tree trunk. Poor though most were, Bakony folk were proud of their masterless lives amongst the oak forests, esteeming the *kondás*, with his herd of pigs, and the highwaymen who robbed rich merchants. These latter called themselves *szegénylegények* – 'poor lads'; of whom the most audacious, Jóska Savanyú, claimed the tavern as his home.

HEREND, 10km further west, is the site of a **porcelain** factory. Established in 1839, its products were to C19 Central Europe what Delft-ware or Miessen china were to more northerly countries. The craftswomen's talents which won international prizes and the acclaim of monarchs are still in evidence – judging by stuff on display in the **factory museum** – and Hungarians are proud of this tradition. One friend told me of a woman 'so rich and snobbish that when she threw tantrums, she only smashed Herend china'! Following Herend, the scenery deteriorates around AFKA, but 6km beyond DEVECSER (where the railway turns northwards towards Celldömölk) there's a great view of the Bakony from a look-out tower near SOMLÓVÁSÁRHELY. In clear weather Mt. Kőris (713m) and even the Austrian Alps may be visible. Sárvár and Szombathely – the most feasible destinations when travelling west – are described on pages 149 & 146.

Alternatively, you can head **northwards towards Győr** by rd.82 or the railway, both of which roughly follow the course of the River Cuha. ZIRC, 23km north of Veszprém, has a Baroque church with Maulbertsch altar paintings on Népköztársaság útja, while 17km to the west by bus, BAKONYBÉL lies at the foot of **Mount Kőris**, the Bakony's highest peak. There's cheap accommodation in Zirc (on Rákóczi tér) and Balinybél (at Fürdő u.59), and opportunities for walking in the surrounding mountains, should you decide to stop. Continuing northwards, the ruined castle on a steep hill at CSESZNEK permits a fine view of the region, and while trains stop some distance away (at *Porva-Csesznek*), the railway journey is itself a scenic one; between cliffs, over bridges and through tunnels, along a line built in 1896. Before reaching Győr, trains stop at **Pannonhalma**, the site of Hungary's greatest Benedictine Monastery (for details of both, see p.140).

Heading down **towards southern Transdanubia** is awkward by public transport from Veszprém. By a three-stage railway journey (changing trains at Lepsény, and then Dombóvár) it should be possible to reach Pécs within 7-8 hours; but it might be quicker to catch a bus from Veszprém to Siófok, whence trains take less time to reach Kaposvár, a short distance from Dombóvár where you switch again for the final leg down to Pécs (p.152).

FESTIVALS

Summer
Chamber music at KÖRÖRSHEGY, organ recitals at TIHANY, Beethoven's symphonies at MARTONVÁSÁR, and open-air concerts in VESZPRÉM's castle district at intervals throughout **June, July and August**. Between July 25-August 2 there's a festival of *show-jumping and jousting* at NAGYVÁZSONY.

TRAVEL DETAILS

Trains
From Budapest to Balatonfüred (13 daily; 2-2½hrs) and Siófok (hourly; 2hrs) call at Székesfehérvár en route (15-20 daily; 1-1½hrs).
From Balatonfenyes to Csisztapuszta (6 daily; ¾hr).
From Balatonfüred to Budapest (hourly; 2-2½hrs).

From Balatonszentgyörgy to Nagykanizsa (10 daily; ¾hr).
From Székesfehérvár to Balatonfüred (hourly; ½-1hr); Komárom (6 daily; 1¼-1¾hrs); Siófok (hourly; ½hr); Szombathely (7 daily; 2½-3¾hrs); Veszprém (10; ¾).
From Tapolca to Celldömölk (5; 1¼); Sümeg (9; 1½); Szombathely (2; 1½).

From Veszprém to Győr (4; 2½); Szombathely (6; 1¼-2¼).

Buses
From Badacsony to Keszthely (hourly, or more frequently).
From Balatonfüred to Nagyvázsony (5-6 daily); Tihany (frequently); Veszprém (roughly every hour).
From Keszthely to Hévíz (every ¼hr); Szombathely (hourly); Zalaegerszeg (hourly).
From Lake Velence to Balatonfüred; Dunaújváros; Pusztaszabolcs; Siófok; Székesfehérvár (all roughly every hour).
From Tapolca to Nagyvázsony; Sümeg; Veszprém (the last two hourly, or more frequently).
From Veszprém to Herend; Nemesvámos; Siófok (all regularly).

International Trains
From Székesfehérvár to Vienna; Leipzig (1 of each daily).

International coaches
One of each per day, except on Sundays.
From Hévíz to Vienna.
From Keszthely to Graz.
From Révfülöp to Vienna.
From Siófok to Bratislava; Semmering; Vienna.

Ferries
Besides the following services (departing every hour or two) there are ferries linking each port with others on the same shore. The crossing takes 10-45 minutes depending on the route.
From Alsóörs to Siófok.
From Badacsony to Balatonboglár; Balatonmáriafürdő; Fonyód.
From Balatonboglár to Révfülöp; Badacsony.
From Balatonmáriafürdő to Badacsony; Balatongyörök.
From Fonyód to Badacsony.
From Siófok to Alsóörs; Balatonfüred; Tihany.
From Szántódrév to Tihany-rév.
From Tihany to Siófok.

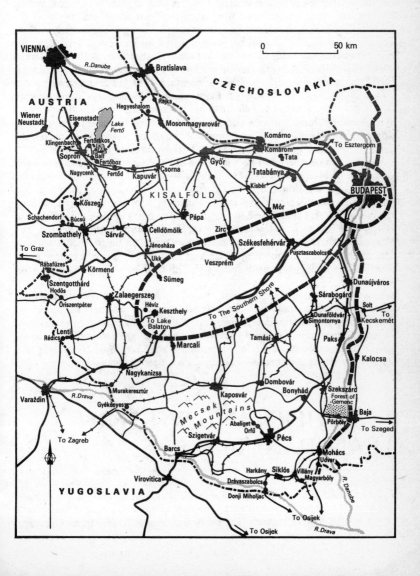

Travelling from Vienna to Budapest it's easy to gain a poor impression of **Transdanubia** – the *Dunántúl* – from the monotonous *Kisalföld* (Little Plain) or the industrial dreck around Tatabánya. What you don't see in passing is lakeside Tata, Győr's antique waterfront, Sopron's cobbled streets, deer in the Forest of Gemenc, or the rolling hills of the Mecsek region.

More than other regions in Hungary, the *Dunántúl* is a patchwork land, an ethnic and social hybrid. Its valleys and hills, forests and mud flats have been a melting pot since Roman times: settled by Magyars, Serbs, Slovaks and Germans; torn asunder and occupied by Turks and Habsburgs; and, within the last 150 years, transformed from a state of near feudalism into what the Party describes as a 'developed Socialist society'. Though **Szombathely** with its Temple of Isis and other ruins has most to show for its Roman origins, all the main **towns** display evidence of this evolution. **Castles** (*vár*) are at the heart of them: survivors of the centuries of warfare that decimated medieval culture, leaving only a few superb churches – for example at **Ják** and **Velemér** – and living evidence in the form of **Pannonhalma Monastery**. Around each weathered vár stands a *belváros*, with rambling streets and squares overlooked by florid Baroque and the odd Gothic or Renaissance pile. **Tata**, **Kőszeg** and **Győr** provide fine examples of the genre; so too does **Sopron**, the most archaic, and **Pécs**, which boasts a Turkish mosque and minaret.

Sopron, Szombathely and Pécs have a wealth of museums and galleries and host some of Hungary's biggest cultural **festivals** during the summer months. Though these are dominated by classical music and drama, there's also a folkloric element, as at the *Busó Carnival* at **Mohács** in March. During summer, concerts are also held in two unique settings – the **Esterházy Palace at Fertőd** and the rock chambers of **Fertőrákos** – both close to Sopron and **Nagycenk**, where you can ride antique **stream trains** on the Széchenyi railway. And finally there's the monthly **market** at Pécs, which is less a tourist event than a celebration of Transdanubia's tradition of combining business with conviviality.

Towns aren't living in the past, however, for their spreading high-rise suburbs (*lakótelep*) testify to the urbanisation of a hitherto rural society, spurred on by industrial development. In **Zalaegerszeg** many of the residents are only a generation removed from the Göcsej peasant farmsteads in the oil town's **Village Museum**, while the booming steel centre of **Dunaújváros** is entirely the product of brute labour and Five Year Plans.

NORTHERN AND WESTERN TRANSDANUBIA

Draw an imaginary line from Budapest to Zalaegerszeg, exclude the Bakony highlands, Szekesfehérvár and Veszprém (see Chapter 3) above it, and what's left is **northern and western Transdanubia**. Approaching from Graz and

Vienna in Austria, it's possible to cross the frontier near **Szombathely**, **Kőszeg** or **Sopron** – the main sites of interest in the west – but most people venture into Transdanubia via the E15 highway or the railway between Vienna and Budapest. The highway, and trains from Budapest's Déli station, pass through **Győr**: the junction for trains going through to Sopron or Szombathely, and linked by road and rail to **Komárom** (a point of entry from Czechoslovakia) and **Tata**. The latter lies just off the E15, and like **Pannonhalma Monastery** between Győr and Veszprém, is worth the detour.

TATABÁNYA AND THE VÉRTES

Following the Budapest-Vienna route, **TATABÁNYA** is inescapable: an ugly mining town surrounded by ravaged countryside. The town's only 'sight' can be glimpsed from a train carriage window, perched on a mountaintop overlooking the grimy sprawl. The giant bronze **Turul statue** was erected to commemorate the thousandth anniversary of the Magyar conquest in 1896, and symbolically clutches the sword of the ancient Magyar tribal chieftain, Árpád, in its talons. Really, the only reason to stay in this drab, polluted town is if you're planning an excursion into the **Vértes**. This modestly-sized range is virtually the only high ground in northern Transdanubia, and some warlord or other took advantage of it by raising **Vitány Castle** (*Vitányvár*), whose ruins lend a sombre cast to a crag some 5 km south of Tatabánya's *felső vasútállomas* railway station (also possible to reach on foot from VÉRTESSOMLÓ, a village accessible by bus from the town). All the **accommodation** is in the new part of town, or *Újváros*: an expensive hotel on Felszabadulás tér; a campsite with bungalows (Tolnai út 1); and private rooms, bookable through the tourist office (Győri út 12).

TATA

A small, sleepy town, **TATA** is interlaced with streams and canals and squeezed between two lakes. Öreg-tó is a delight, surrounded by slender trees and spires and the pillared *Lovarda* riding school. The eastern embankment, Tópart utca, leads past a late night grill/disco, a statue of the 'Tata mermaid', luxuriant gardens and a now-defunct mill to the **Castle** at the northern end of the lake. Once a fortress and then a royal hunting lodge, this was bashed about by the Turks and Habsburgs, notwithstanding its ivy-covered ramparts and moat, which has been dredged by Soviet conscripts (Tata is a small garrison town) and now serves as a fish-farm. In the reconstructed half of the castle, a **museum** displays Roman miniatures, weird ceramics and the spectacular faience-ware of Domokos Kuny, a local craftsman.

Öreg-tó is higher than streets surrounding it to the north, and the water is guided down through lockgates and canals. Previously, almost a score of **mills** (*malom*) were grouped around the lake, and there's the derelict shell of one just east of the castle. Below, and further along Bartók utca, another old mill building (Alkotmány u.2) contains an **Ethnographic museum** devoted to the German communities of the Little Plain. As always the **costumes** are best: the

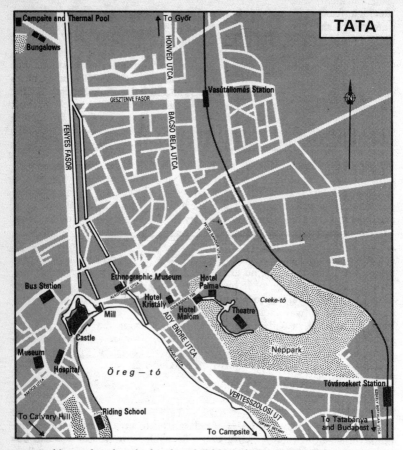

men jackbooted and garbed in braided black and stovepipe hats, the women swathing their layers of petticoats and ruffles with embroidered shawls.

Ady Endre utca, Tata's charmless main street, runs between Öreg-tó and the smaller lake – called just that, **Cseke-tó**. Just north of the 'Miklós' mill (nr. 26, under restoration), Szabadság tér meanders off towards the **park** surrounding Cseke-tó, passing two cheap hotels. Perhaps to compensate for its lack of size and swans, the lake offers opportunities for **fishing**, while there's a swimming pool, theatre and fake ruined church (cobbled together from Roman and Benedictine stonework) in the park. Another area to ramble lies southwest of the castle – the hilly quarter between November 7. tér and Kossuth tér, mostly built in the C18 to the plans of Jakob Fellner. Along the way, at the foot of Rákóczi utca, a **museum** displays lifesize plaster copies of Hercules and Laocoön, Roman statues in the Louvre, and that prize of archaeological piracy, the Elgin marbles. At the top of the hill stands leafy Kossuth tér, behind which back-alleys wend off towards **Calvary Hill** with its bleak crucifixion monument and a blackened observation tower looming above patches of urban wasteland.

Practicalities
Tata has two **railway stations** and two campsites, all located some distance from the town centre. From the main *vasútállomás* in the north of town, buses #1 and #3 run down into the centre, the latter terminating at the **campsite/bungalow** complex on Gesztenye fasor (chesnut avenue) 500m short of the **thermal pool**. Alternatively, you can catch bus #5 from the smaller *Tóvároskert* station to Kossuth tér, or reach the other campsite on the banks of Öreg-tó by following Székely B. u. to its end, turning right and walking to the highway at the finish of Lumumba utca, where you'll see the site signposted over the road.

The **tourist office** stands nearly opposite the 'Miklós' mill and the *Hotel Kristály* – Tata's cheapest – on the main street; the *Malom* on Szabadság tér, and the *Pálma* in Cseke-tó park, are also good value. Rowing boats (*csónakázás*) and pedalloes (*vízibicikli*) can be hired on Öreg-tó. The *Vár-Étterem* on Novermber 7. tér and the grill/disco on Tópart u. are good places to eat. For those with money to burn, there are dearer hotels and bars in the **REMETESÉGPUSZTA** suburb (bus #4) out of town.

From the *Pályaudvar* north of the castle there are 2 or 3 **buses** every day to Komárom, Budapest and Győr (see below), which tend to be quicker but more crowded than **trains** to the same destinations.

GYŐR

Few towns look enticing from a railway siding or a ring road, and GYŐR (pronounced 'Dyur') isn't one of them. The lovely waterfront Belváros, Győr's best feature, is obscured by vistas of smoggy industry, including the giant *Rába* combine, Hungary's biggest truck and tractor plant, and separated from the rest of town by Tanácsköztársaság útja (henceforth T. útja), a grimy wind-tunnel of a road sprouting flyovers at either end. From the **railway and bus stations**, Lenin bridge leads to T. útja and Szabadság tér, site of the grandiose Town Hall – a militant stronghold during the '56 Uprising, when it was the headquarters of Győr-Sopron County's Provisional National Council, headed by Attila Szigeti, which pressed the Nagy government to achieve a rapid withdrawal of Soviet troops.

The Belváros
Lenin út, a pedestrian precinct, thrusts into the old town – throwing off cobbled alleys (*köz*) that lead towards the River Rába. Many streets to the west are narrow and shadowy, with overhanging timbered houses – the stage setting for a conspiracy (and indeed, the Communist Party met secretly at Sárló köz 15, during the 1930s when it was banned). All eventually lead to **Köztársaság tér**, a square overlooking the Rába, largely Baroque though still buttressed by surviving **bastions** of Győr's castle on the opposite side of the square, which house bits of medieval stonework. Beyond it is **Káptalan-domb**

– Chapter Hill – the town's ecclesiastical centre and site of its much restored **Cathedral**. Its star feature is the gilded bust of King Ladislas (who, like István, was also canonised), which contains a fragment of his skull and thus qualifies as a holy relic.

From Káptalan-domb it's only a minute's walk to **the waterfront**, where women flog fish on Duna-kapu tér while their menfolk watch proceedings from the door of the nearest *Italbolt* or wine cellar. Since the Danube grain trade – Győr's economic mainstay in the C19 – stopped, the Rába and Mosoni-Duna embankments have become a favourite spot for anglers and courting couples, but this may change if the Nagymaros-Gabčikovo dam get built. Critics of the scheme (p.105) claim that as the Danube rises, Győr's discharged sewage will float back upriver into the Rába and Mosoni-Duna tributaries, creating an almighty stink. Meanwhile, the Sziget and Révfalu districts **over the river** are worth a brief look.

East of Lenin út lies **Széchenyi tér**, a sun-baked expanse centred on a statue of the Virgin, that is traditionally Győr's main square. Eye-like attic windows regard it from the steep roofs of surrounding, peeling houses, and black-garbed grandmothers attend the Benedictine church under the supercilious gaze of lounging teenagers. The **Patika Museum**, almost next door to the church, functions as a pharmacy (Tuesday, Thursday, Friday 9am-5pm/Wednesday, Saturday 2pm-5pm) whilst attracting sightseers with its beautifully painted ceiling panels and fine cabinet-work.

Diversions, accommodation and practicalities

The brashly tiled *Művelődesi központ*, Győr's **cultural centre** on Széchenyi tér, is home to the town's superb **modern dance** company, under Ivan Márkó. If there's an event on, catch it. More mundane daytime attractions include **boat trips** or **angling** on the river (all arranged by Ciklámen tourist), or a wallow in the **thermal baths** located at the eastern tip of Sziget. Győr's **football** team can be worth a check, too; the stadium, which saw a visit from Manchester United a couple of years back, is in the suburbs near the campsite.

Places to eat include the *Matróz Csárda* and the *Halászcsárda* (specialising in fish dishes) off Rózsa F. utca; the *Vigadó* at Kisfaludy u.2; the self-service *Önkiszolgáló* at Lenin út 13; and the Grill at Kazinczy u.12. Cakes are best value at Lenin út 30; an excellent wine-cellar is the *Vár-borozó* midway along Alkotmámy utca. Other facilities include a **foreign language bookshop** (Kisfaludy u. 7), the **zoo** near the camp-site, the **art gallery** at Lenin út 33, and the **hospitals** and County **police** headquarters – for visa extensions – around Felszabadulás útja, south of the bus terminal. Pay with a 2Ft coin on **buses**.

Accommodation is limited to private rooms from Ciklámen-tourist (Aradi vértanuk út 22, opposite the main supermarket), the expensive *Rába Hotel* overlooking T. útja, and campsite with bungalows, sited just south of the highway. The latter can be reached by bus #8 from the playground on T. útja, opposite Lukács S.utca.

Moving on, the obvious destination to the west is SOPRON (p.141), which is easy to reach by train. If you're heading there, however, it's still worth making a detour to **Pannonhalma Monastery** – described below – which lies along the road and railway to VESZPRÉM (p.129). Lastly, for those **leaving**

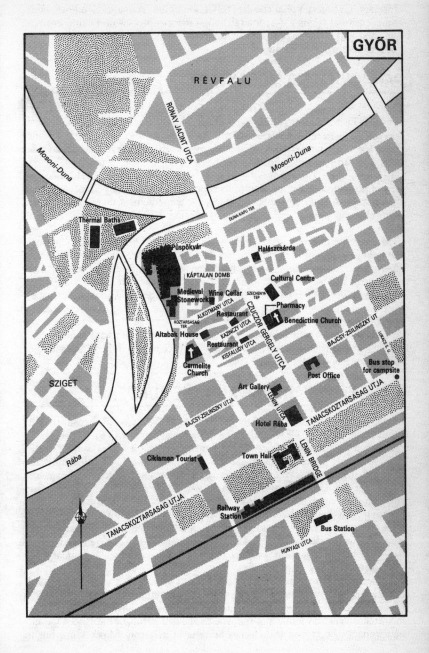

GYŐR

RÉVFALU

RONAY JACINT UTCA

Mosoni-Duna

Mosoni-Duna

DUNA-KAPU TER

Thermal Baths

Püspökvár

Halászcsárda

KÁPTALAN DOMB

Cultural Centre

Medieval Stonework

Wine Cellar

SZECHENYI TEP

Pharmacy

ALKOTMANY UTCA

Restaurant

Benedictine Church

KOZTARSASAG TER

CZUCZOR GERGELY UTCA

KAZINCZY UTCA

BAJCSY-ZSILINSZKY UT

LUKÁCS U.

Altabak House

Restaurant

KISFALUDY UTCA

Carmelite Church

Bus stop for campsite

Art Gallery

LENIN UTCA

Post Office

TANACSKOZTARSASAG UTJA

SZIGET

BAJCSY-ZSILINSZKY UTJA

Hotel Rába

Ciklamen Tourist

Town Hall

LENIN BRIDGE

Rába

TANACSKOZTARSASAG UTJA

Railway Station

Bus Station

HUNYADI UTCA

Hungary, Győr has Volán **coaches** to Galanta and Trnava in Czechoslovakia, and occasional trains to Vienna (although most expresses don't stop between Budapest and Hegyeshalom on the Austrian border). For more details on local border crossings, see below.

PANNONHALMA MONASTERY

Thrusting skywards from the summit of St Martin's Hill, **PANNONHALMA MONASTERY** makes an imposing presence after the low-lying Kisalföld, as was surely intended when **the Benedictine Order**, with the support of Prince Géza, founded an abbey here in 969. Known as the church militant, the Order helped István I to weld the anarchic pagan Magyars into a unified Christian state; rebuffed a Tartar invasion from behind its abbey's fortified walls; and waxed powerful for centuries until its suppression in 1787 by Emperor Joseph II. Reestablished by Joseph's successor, the Benedictines thereafter confined themselves to prayer and pedagogy, founding schools which still function today.

Manifesting different styles and varying degrees of antiquity, the buildings are grouped around several courtyards with C13 cloisters. The **Basilica** is likewise Gothic in origin, with a finely carved portal and marble sepulchres containing the bones of two abbots and a princess. Medieval codices and incunabula are displayed in the 300,000 volume **library**, where you can see a portrait of the legendary King István and, for the linguistically-minded, the first document to include Hungarian words – 55 of them – amongst the customary Latin. During the summer, there are **organ recitals** at Pannonhalma.

Ciklámen tourist (Vár u.1) can arrange private **rooms** if the turistaszálló or camp-site (Fényvesalja u.9) are full.

MOSONMAGYARÓVÁR AND THE BORDER

Guide books normally mention **MOSONMAGYARÓVÁR** because of its small **castle** (now a college) and the twisting River Lajta with its 17 bridges, or the parade of Baroque edifices along Lenin útja; and a veil is usually drawn over the event which briefly made the town notorious, and still haunts the memory of most inhabitants over the age of forty. On 25 October 1956, two days after the Uprising began in Budapest, some 5,000 men, women and children held a peaceful demonstration which the ÁVO fired upon without warning as it approached the town hall, killing more than 100 people. No memorial to the massacre has ever been raised (although the perpetrators were lynched shortly afterwards), and the few tourists that stop here emerge from the local history **museum** with its colourful folk costumes (Lenin út 135) undisturbed by any mention of it.

Mosonmagyaróvár lies close to **the border**, which used to be sealed with deadly efficency until the Uprising; in the chaotic aftermath, roughly 200,000 Hungarians walked, crept or swam across into Austria. Border guards perched in watchtowers and lurking in the woods are still authorised to shoot would-be escapers (the fate of the lesbian heroine in a Károly Makk film), but in practice most Magyars wishing to travel west can now do so legally. Citizens are generally allowed to travel outside the Eastern bloc every three years, if not more frequently for professional reasons; and since emigrants were given the right of return after five years, thousands of those who left in 1956 have opted to come back (retired people especially – an American pension goes a long way in Budapest).

Given cordial relations with Austria (whose citizens don't even need visas to enter Hungary), the state retains an 'iron curtain' partly to limit the export of hard currency, but mainly out of deference to its allies, despite which embarassingly high numbers of Romanians have attempted to use Hungary as an escape route to the West. Lone foreigners travelling around near the border are therefore likely to be accosted by **BKH agents**, who flash a red and white card inscribed *Nincs parancs* ('This is a command') but are otherwise identifiable by their spivvy attire, sunglasses and leather handbags. Providing your passport and stamps are okay, there's no cause to worry.

At any hour of the day or night one can drive across **from Rajka or Hegyeshalom into Czechoslovakia or Austria**. There are infrequent 'local' trains to like-named stations, but these are miles from the checkpoints on the roads (and obviously, strangers wandering around are highly suspect). Leaving Hungary at Hegyeshalom by road, however, the Austrian *Grenzepolizei* are well-mannered and even prepared to tolerate hitch-hikers starting just behind the *zoll*. But their Czech counterparts are notorious for searching, questioning, and sometimes turning back, 'punks' or 'hippies', and even the squeaky clean don't get in without a **Czech visa**. This *can't* be obtained at the border; allow 2 weeks if you apply to the consulate in Budapest.

SOPRON

With its 115 monuments and 240 listed buildings, **SOPRON** can fairly claim to be 'the most historic town in Hungary' despite the drab modern vista that greets visitors outside the railway station. Walk a few hundred metres up Mátyás Király u., however, and you'll see why. North of Széchenyi tér – where the grand buildings start – Lenin körút encircles a horse-shoe shaped Belváros: a treasure trove of antique buildings, most of them refreshingly unmonumental.

The inner town

Templom utca is as nice a street as any to follow into the Belváros, leading to Orsolya tér where the cobbles sink towards a central orb of stone, surrounded by a gothic church and buildings dripping with carved protrusions and renaissance loggias. On the north side of the square above a sturdy vaulted arcade is a standard **Guild museum** (open 9am-5pm; closed Tuesdays). Despite its name, New street, **Új utca** is one of the oldest thoroughfares in the Belváros, a gentle curve lined with arched dwellings painted in red, yellow and pink, with chunky pavements and cobblestones. Until their expulsion from Sopron in 1526 the street was mainly inhabited by Jews and known as Zsidó (Jewish) utca, with two synagogues dating from medieval times: one of them, at nr.22, contains a collection of Judaica.

Up ahead looms the **Firewatch Tower** (*Tűztorony*), the symbol of Sopron,

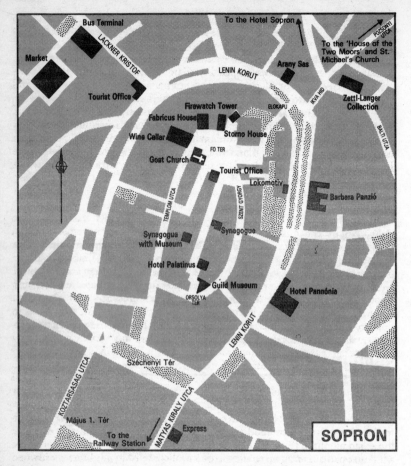

SOPRON

founded on the large rounded stones of a fortress built by the Romans, who established a town – *Scarbantia* – here in the first century. Climbing through the tower's Renaissance and Baroque levels, you emerge beneath its copper belfry to a fantastic view of weathered rooftops, narrow streets and statues. Sadly the sentries – who in times past were expected to play music for the townsfolk while they stood guard – are no longer posted. Fő tér, adjoining the tower, is another parade of Gothic and Baroque drawn up around a Trinity statue crawling with cherubium. King Mátyás and Count Széchenyi once stayed at the Renaissance **Storno house** (nr.8), while the **Fabricus house** (nr.6) contains Roman, Celtic and Avar relics, plus a first-floor 'whispering gallery' which carries the slightest sound from one corner to the other. Another fine example of Gothic is the **Goat Church** on the corner of Templom utca: so-called, supposedly, because its construction was financed by a goatherd whose animals unearthed a heap of gold. When the tér isn't crowded out by tour groups, the church's clanging bells and cooing pigeons make a marvellous soundtrack to the neighbourhood's picturesque decrepitude – an impression that's equally strong on Szent György utca.

Offered the choice of Austrian citizenship in 1921, the townsfolk voted to remain Magyar subjects and erected a 'Gate of Loyalty' at the base of the Firewatch Tower to commemorate this act of patriotism. Walk through it and you'll come out onto Előkapu (outer gate), a short street where the houses are laid out in a 'saw-toothed' pattern and 'errant burghers' and 'gossiping, nagging' wives were once pinioned in stocks for the righteous to pelt with rotten food. Beyond lies **Lenin körút** with its *Arany Sas* pharmacy operating behind a façade of splendid tiles, and the now-defunct *White Horse Inn* where Joseph Haydn stayed when he wasn't enjoying the Esterházy's hospitality out in Fertőd (see p.144).

Outside the Belváros

From the körút, a backstreet leads over the Ikva – a narrow, stinking stream which flooded noxiously in the C19 – to a few other sights. Atmospheric Balfi utca leads in short order to the privately-owned **Zettl-Langer collection** of porcelain, weaponry and faience at nr. 11 (open 10-12 daily), while Pozsonyi utca wends uphill past the 'House of the Two Moors' to the partially-Gothic Church of St Michael, whose gargoyles leer over the Chapel of St Jacob decaying in the graveyard. Roundabouts stand cross-less tombstones of Russians killed during the liberation of Sopron in April 1945. Installed in Sopron where the German front briefly held, the Hungarian Nazi puppet-government carried out a last purge, shooting any Jew or suspected Communist that came to hand, and hostages like the MP Endre Bajcsy-Zsilinszky, at Sopronhidkúti in the hills. After the war, the derranged Ferenc Szalási and other prominent *Nyilas* were tried and hanged, but dozens of underlings were re-employed by the Communist ÁVO, which found their expertise useful.

Sopron's **hills** – the *Bécsi-domb* to the north, and the sub-Alpine *Lőverek* to the southwest – can be good for **walking**. Market gardens partly cover the lower slopes of the Lőverek, before the Hotel Lővér – accessible by bus #1 or #2 – and paths leading up to the top of Károly-magaslat, predictably crowned by a TV mast and a look-out tower. Too late to check the details, I heard of the existence of a **Fool's Castle** (*Taródy-* or *Bolond-vár*) up in the hills near a tree nursery: it's said to be as much fun as Bory's folly in Székesfehérvár (p.114), and Sopron's tourist office can probably give directions.

Other things

Sopron is liveliest and most crowded during the **Festival Weeks** (roughly June 22-July 14) – an occasion for folklore displays, concerts and rock theatre (see the tourist office for details and bookings). *Soproni Kékfrankos* and other local **wines** are sloshed around in the underground *Gyógygödör pinceborozó* on Fő ter, where garrulous ex-partisans mingle with young German tourists; staider foreigners frequent the *Bécsi kapu* near the Hotel Sopron; and serious pálinka boozers the *Magyar Tenger* and seedy buffets around the bus terminal. There's a range of **places to eat,** from the touristy *Gambrinus* on Új

u. to the less pretentious *Deák* on Széchenyi tér, where there's also a self-service *Önkiszolgáló* and a *cukrászda*-cum-bar. The spit-and-sawdust *Finom Fatalok* grill, a *Gulyás* restaurant and a cramped patisserie do business on Lenin Körút, and at nr.90 is the *Lokomotiv* bureau, which organises trips on the **Széchenyi steam train** (see below).

Like IBUSZ on the körút, Ciklámen tourist (8, Ógabona tér) deals in **private rooms**. During June-August, Express at Mátyás u. 7 might be able to find you cheap beds, either in the Jereván high-school or the Forestry college. The *Barbara panzió* (Lenin krt. 53), *Lokomotiv* (Szabadság krt.1) and *Pannonia* (Lenin krt.75) are the least expensive of Sopron's six **hotels**. Lövér **camping** (bus #12 hourly from Május 1. tér) also rents cheap bungalows, which are less likely to be full than the tourist hostels (Ferenczi u.4 & Új u.8) and **bungalows** on Károly hill; reservations should be made at Ciklámen tourist.

There are (mainly afternoon) **trains** to Szombathely, and regular buses to Kőszeg, but it would be a shame not to visit a couple of places much closer to Sopron – accessible by hourly **buses** from the town's terminal and covered in the following section. Should you decide to leave Hungary for **Austria**, there are daily trains from Sopron's *Déli* station to Wiener Neustadt and Ebenfurt; and a 24-hour checkpoint on the road crossing the frontier to Klingenbach in Austria.

THE QUARRY AT FERTŐRÁKOS, THE ESTERHÁZY PALACE AND SZÉCHENYI'S RAILWAY

From stand 7 of Sopron's terminal, buses putter off through the derelict spa of BALF to the village of **FERTŐRÁKOS** which, according to the dictionary, translates as 'Cancerous slough'. Centuries of chalk-mining have produced a monumental **quarry** whose giant chambers and pillars skewed at odd angles form a cyclopean labyrinth like one of the mythical pre-human cities imagined by H.P. Lovecraft. **Concerts** are performed here during the Sopron Festival Weeks, but otherwise there's no reason to linger once you've seen the quarry (open 8am-7pm from May to September/ earlier closing off-season), unless to stay at the **tourist hostel** (141, Fő utca). Sopron's Ciklámen tourist office can book concert tickets and beds.

Twenty-seven kilometres from Sopron (by bus from stand 4), lies a monument of one of pre-war Hungary's most famous dynasties. Originally of the minor nobility, the **Esterházy family** began its rise thanks to Nicolaus (1583-1645), an unashamed opportunist who married two rich widows and sided with the Habsburgs against Transylvania during the struggles of the counter-reformation, thereby being elevated to Count. His son Paul was made a hereditary Duke and published a songbook (tweely entitled *Harmonia Celestis*), and when Nicolaus II inherited 600,000 hectares in 1762, he ordered the construction of a Palace on the swampy ground around Fertőd (then known, unsuprisingly, as Eszterháza).

Nicknamed 'The Ostentatious', Nicolaus intended the **ESTERHÁZY PALACE AT FERTŐD** to rival Versailles and spent 40,000 gulden a year on pomp and entertainments, bragging 'anything that the Kaiser can do, I can do better!'. Squadrons of Hussars pranced around the vast horseshoe courtyard to the music of Haydn – Esterházy's resident maestro – accompanied by cannonades, feasting and fireworks; enjoyed by the parasoled and bejewelled guests, and paid for by the family serfs who got to watch through the ornate wrought iron gates. In 1945 the Esterházys fled and the estate was confiscated, and nowadays tourists in slippers shuffle around the 126-room palace. Highlights of the **guided tour** include the salons decortated in blue and white *Chinoiserie*, panelled, gilded rooms lined with mirrors and the impressive concert hall, with its adjoining roomful of **Haydn memorabilia**.

Concerts still take place here beneath the splendid ceiling fresco of Hermes, which is so contrived that from whichever angle one views it, his chariot seems to be careering towards you across the sky. The moderately-priced **rooms** in the Palace are usually booked in advance (see Ciklámen tourist) but if you argue hard enough, the staff will grudgingly open up the Tourist Hostel in the east wing. For food and drink, try the place opposite the main gate, or the restaurant and supermarket on Fertőd's main street.

It's also possible to stay at the *Gloriette* at FERTŐBOZ, en route to Fertőd, a village where the steam train turns around and returns to **NAGYCENK**, site of the **Széchenyi family mansion** (*kastély*). Less arriviste than the Esterházys, the family is best remembered for István, the prime mover behind the building of Budapest's Chain Bridge (p.54). Though politically conservative, Széchenyi was obsessed with modernising Hungary – especially its communications – and to this end initiated the taming of the River Tisza and the blasting of a road and navigable passage through the Iron Gate of the Danube. A keen Anglophile and a passionate convert to steam-power after riding on the Manchester-Liverpool express, Széchenyi invited Britons to build Hungary's second line of track from Budapest to Vác – designed to carry **steam trains**, not the horse-drawn carriages used on the first railway line to Pozsony. Fittingly, you can ride on one of them today, a 100-year old beauty that chugs along the 3km **Széchenyi Museum Railway** between Nagycenk and Fertőboz. The train – crewed mainly by Young Pioneeers – runs roughly every hour from 9am-5pm, and should you get stranded there's a nearby *Fogadó* and a fairly regular bus service back into town.

KŐSZEG

Skirting lurking dog patrols and watchtowers along the border, buses also make the 50km journey to **KŐSZEG**, south of Sopron. Notwithstanding the summer blitzkrieg of German tourists which briefly arouses avarice and excitement here, Kőszeg is basically a small, quiet town where people are friendly and honest enough to leave fruit for sale (and the takings) standing unguarded in the streets. Buses #1, #1A &#1Y from the **train station**, or a short walk from the **bus terminal**, will take you to Köztásaság tér where three **tourist offices** and two expensive hotels stand ready to do business. The Gothic Church of the Sacred Heart points its diamond-patterned spires aloft, while twin Saints flank the alley to the archway of the **Heroes' Tower** – a product of the nostalgia for bygone glories that gripped Hungary in the 1920s and '30s. This in turn guards **Jurisics tér**, the cobbled main square, surrounded by eye-catching old buildings – a Town Hall embellished with oval portraits of worthies, and a fancifully painted Renaissance façade above the espresszó bar at nr. 7, among them – which put the Pharmacy and Local History **museums** into the shade.

The Turks complained that Kőszeg's **Castle** was 'built at the foot of a mountain difficult to climb; its walls wider than the whole world, its bastions higher than the fish of the Zodiac in heaven, and so strong that it defies description'. Since the castle is actually rather small, with nary a mountain in sight, the hyperbole is probably explained by its heroic defence during the **siege of 1532**, when a tiny garrison under *Miklós Jurisich* defied an army of 100,000, thus foiling the Ottomans' advance on Vienna. Relics of the siege are exhibited in the castle which, come evening, turns into a **disco-bar**.

Private **rooms** are available from IBUSZ and Savaria tourist for a modest sum, while Express tries to inveigle tourists into its overpriced 'Youth Hotel', the *Panorama* on Szabóhegy hill (accessible by bus #2). Though it offers basic dormitory accommodation, the *tourist hostel* in the building facing the castle entrance is a nicer – and the cheapest – place to stay. Kőszeg's restaurants are either attached to hotels or, in the case of workers' cafés, on the approaches to the main square. There's a **beer garden** at the junction of Schneller utca and Várkör – the road surrounding the Belváros.

SZOMBATHELY

SZOMBATHELY ('Saturday market') is western Hungary's largest, liveliest town, and two local jokes cast some light on its modern history. The Austrian who asked his mate, 'Fancy a beer? Right, get your passport', epitomises the hordes that drive across in their Mercedes and BMWs to have their hair and teeth fixed and shop in the country they nickname 'the discount store'; while the 'short and the long joke' refers to Szombathely's large Soviet garrison. 'The short joke is that the Russians are leaving, the long one that they're going one by one'. In truth, most of the conscripts are confined to barracks for the three years that they're posted here; memories of the Russians who fraternised with local people during the first days of the 1956 revolution have led to the rule that only officers can wander around town. Local people may grouse about their 'fraternal allies' and rich Austrians, but they're happy to overcharge them in the markets and tune into fashions and TV emenating from across the border. One suspects that the townsfolk might have reacted similarly during ancient times, when trade and legionaries flowed through here along the Roman Amber road, and foreign idols followed in their wake, notably the Egyptian godess Isis, whose temple still stands here today.

From the **railway station** – the junction for trains to Sopron, Kőszeg, Veszprém and southern Transdanubia – buses #3, #5 & #16Y follow a meandering route to **the Belváros**, itself rather haphazardly laid out and dotted with buildings from the time of Empress Maria Theresa. The **Savaria museum** starts with unearthed mammoth tusks and works through to **Roman times**, represented by a number of baths, columns and reliefs of mythical figures which are less impressive than those in the **Romkert**, situated near the bus terminal.

In the Romkert stands the **Temple of Isis** or *Iseum*, a battered structure built

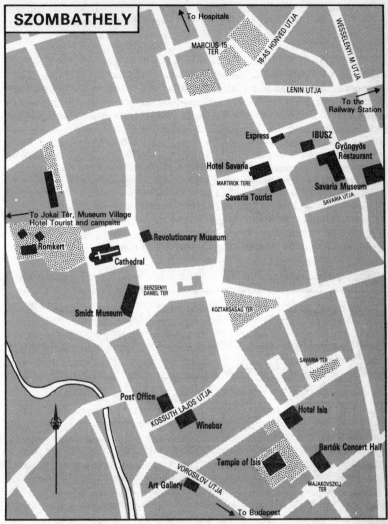

SZOMBATHELY

To Hospitals

MARCIUS 15 TER

18-AS HONVED UTJA

WESSELENYI M UTJA

LENIN UTJA

To the Railway Station

Express

IBUSZ

Gyöngyös Restaurant

Hotel Savaria

MARTIROK TERE

Savaria Museum

SAVARIA UTJA

Savaria Tourist

← To Jokai Tér, Museum Village Hotel Tourist and campsite

Romkert

Revolutionary Museum

Cathedral

BERZSENYI DANIEL TER

KOZTARSASAG TER

Smidt Museum

SAVARIA TER

Post Office

KOSSUTH LAJOS UTJA

Hotel Isis

Winebar

Bartók Concert Hall

VOROSILOV UTJA

Temple of Isis

Art Gallery

MAJAKOVSZKIJ TER

To Budapest

in the late C2. One of the three such temples extant in Europe, it's centred around a sacrificial altar which the rising sun illuminates, and decorated with a pantheon of deities. Reliefs depict Isis riding the dog Sothis, Victoria holding palm-leaves, a glum-looking Fortuna-Abundantia, and Mars-Harpokrates. The custom of daily Isis-worship at sunrise originated in Egypt, where the goddess was believed to be the Pharoah's mother and the Pharoah to be Horus who, in a variant of the myth, was the son of an incestuous union between Isis and her brother Osiris, and avenger of his father's murder by Seth, another brother. Carried to Rome by Greek traders, the cult was supressed by

Tiberius, but then legalised in the C1 when an Iseum was built at Pompeii. Nowadays the temple provides the backdrop for Szombathely's Savaria Festival (see below), and is open to sightseers between 8am-6pm from May to October.

Nearby on Majakovaszkij tér, Szombathely's newest **art gallery** exhibits the work of two proletarian painters. **Gyula Derkovits** (1894-1934) was a member of the **Group of Eight** (*Nyolcak*) of committed socialist artists who 'declared war on the importance of impressions, sensations and moods; on disorder and denial of values, on all those ideologies and styles of art that begin and end with the "I" '. Living amongst the working class – his subject matter – Derkovits strived to rid his art of 'every element of illusion', moved towards Cubism and studied at the Nyergesújfalu Free School during the heady days of the Soviet Republic. The crushing of the 1919 revolution left him desolate, as can be seen from *The Last Supper*, where Christ – with Derkovits's features – sits amidst a group of weary workmen. **István Dési Huber** (1895-1944), regarded as Derkovits's successor, was of working class origin, a goldsmith by trade. He abandoned Naturalism for Cubism to express his Marxist beliefs and together with Derkovits and others in *Nyolcak*, struggled against the dominance of the 'School of Rome' (modelled on Italian fascist art) during the 1930s.

The square is also the site of Szombathely's former Synagogue, a lovely piece of neo-Byzantine architecture similar to the one in Pest, which is now the **Bartók Concert Hall** and music college. Here, as at other Hungarian universities and colleges, entrance is determined by competitive examination, and student grants vary according to parental income and academic performance. The stipends – ranging from 400-1,300Ft a month – barely match the cost of rented private-sector accommodation (at least 1,000Ft a month), so many students live at home and all depend on extra money from their parents.

Like Bory's Castle in Székesfehérvár, the **Smidt museum** (Hollán Ernő u.2) represents the fruits of a life-long obsession, for as a boy, Lajos Smidt scoured battlefields for souvenirs and collected advertisements and newspapers. After qualifying as a doctor he diversified into furniture and pictures, and the destruction of many items during World War Two only spurred him to redouble his efforts during retirement; until finally, he founded this museum. It's quirky enough to warrant a visit, unlike the **Museum of the Revolution** (Alkotmány u. 2): the usual monolingual mass of documents, portraits, flags and exhortations to struggle. Far better – if you're still keen to sightsee – is the outdoor **Village Museum** (*Falumúzeum*), sited just beyond the campsite and accessible by bus #5 from the railway station. Reconstructed here are C18-C19 farmsteads culled from 27 villages in the Örség region, furnished with all the necessities and nick-nacks: an architectural progression from log-cabins to timber-framed wattle and daub dwellings.

Practicalities

Szombathely's **Savaria Festival** features folk ensembles and Hungary's best classical musicians and opera singers, and usually culminates in a performance of Mozart's *The Magic Flute*, with its aria *Isis and Osiris*. The festival takes place during June, and **Savaria tourist** (Mártírok tere 1) or IBUSZ can furnish full details of the programme and book tickets. Like Cooptourist in the vicinity, both agencies rent private **rooms**, while Express can probably arrange dormitory beds (quite likely in the college at Nagykar utca 1-3). These are far cheaper than Szombathely's hotels, of which only the *Tourist-B* (north of Jókai park) charges less than 1,000-2,000Ft for a room, although about the same price as the bungalows for hire at the **campsite** (take bus #5). Pink Floydish music gets an airing in the beer garden in Jókai park – the town's youth hangout, situated south of a swimming pool and boating lake. If you feel like splurging, any of the big hotel restaurants can oblige, while the cheapest **places to eat** are the self-service joint on Mártírok tere and the *Gyöngyös* restaurant on Savaria utca.

Should you decide to leave Hungary at this point, there's a **frontier crossing** at BÚCSÚ, 14km west of town, which takes vehicles heading for Schachendorf in Austria. Despite this proximity, however, the only **international Volán coach service** paradoxically runs to Bratislava in Czechoslovakia. **Local buses** enable one to reach Ják (see below) quite easily, and are usually more frequent than the **trains** to Körmend and Szentgotthárd – two small towns that serve as jumping-off points for excursions to the Örség villages. The main lines leads eastwards through Sárvár to CELLDÖMÖLK and PÁPA (the junctions for Sümeg, Tapolca, the Balaton and Győr), and south through Zalaegerszeg to NAGYKANIZSA – the place to catch trains across southern Transdanubia. On these lines, services are quite frequent.

JÁK, SÁRVÁR, ZALAEGERSZEG AND VILLAGES IN THE ÖRSÉG

JÁK, 14 km southwest of Szombathely, boasts of Hungary's finest **Romanesque church**, which welcomes visitors with benign lions, eleven saints in niches and other splendid stonecarvings about its portal. The entire building with its Gothic frescoes and cloisters is far more impressive than the scaled-down version in Budapest's City Park, but once you've seen it there's nothing else – and no place to stay – in the village. Private **rooms** can be booked (from 11, Rákóczi u.) in **KÖRMEND**, farther to the south, where an old mansion once owned by the Batthyány family provides a bit of colour.

SÁRVÁR ('Mud Castle') was founded in the C12, and enjoyed two centuries of prestige as a centre of Reformation culture under the **Nádasdy family**, whose **palace** – designed by Italian architects – is the town's sight. Buses #1/#1Y run from the train station to the Vár, where halls are adorned with scenes of Ferenc Nádasdy the 'Black Knight' battling the Turks, and Dorffmeister frescoes of Old Testament episodes and allegories of art and science. While Ferenc was at war, his wife Elizabeth Báthori, later known as the 'Blood Countess', amused herself by torturing serving women (p.492); a blot on the Nádasdy escutcheon not mentioned in the **museum** here, which displays such treasures as weren't carted off to Vienna to punish Ferenc for rebellious behavior in 1670. Though there's little cause to stay in Sárvár, *Savaria tourist* on Kossuth tér can rent **rooms** and tell you if the campsite has been finished yet; *Fekete Bec* (Lenin u.25) serves cheap food, and you'll find a hotel about 3km out along the Celldömölk road.

South of Szombathely and moving into Zala County, the road and railway pass through EGERVÁR – a small village with a fortified *Kastély* doubling as a tourist hostel (☎ 6-12) – en route to Zalaegerszeg.

Zalaegerszeg

ZALA, as everybody calls it, is no place to arrive on a rainy Monday: despite the futuristic TV tower featured on all the tourist bumpf, the town's museums are its main interest. Modern Zala with its costly sports palace and drab *lakótelep* depends on oil – the subject of the **Olajipari Museum**. Rigs, models and the like convey an idea of the development of the industry since the 1930s, but for a clue about the workforce and its origins, go next door to the **Village Museum**, a fascinating collection of dwellings from the **Göcsej region** – whence most of Zala's inhabitants originate – complete with mill and orchards. Traditionally, the Göcsej was so poor and squalid that no one would own to being a part of it, and inquirers were always hastily assured that its boundaries began a few miles on, in the next village. Nowadays Göcsej villagers spend their weeks working and sleeping in hostels in Zala, returning home at weekends; some have bought flats in town and are saving up for a holiday home in the hills.

Both museums can be reached by bus #1A from Rákóczi út, close to Szabadság and Marx square, Zala's centre. You'll find oily Göcsej cheese and other local produce in the **market** to the north, and a museum of Göcsej **folk costumes** on the main square adjoining the exhibition of **sculptures by Zsigmond Kisfaludi Strobl** (1884-1975). The son of a sculptor, Zsigmond enjoyed early success with his busts of British Royals, religious figures and a Lady Plunkett. After 1945 he adroitly switched to producing glorified Workers, earning himself medals, further wealth and the nickname 'Step from Side to Side'. See the show and have a laugh.

Though a *Halász-csárda* and a tourist hostel (bus #3/#3Y/#5) can provide sustenance, and IBUSZ on Kovacs tér **rooms** and information, it's tempting to move on a quickly as possible. **Trains** run to Budapest and Pécs, but Keszthely (p.124) and neighbouring areas are better served by **buses** from Kovacs tér.

Villages in the Őrség

To the west of Zala lies a distinctive little region known as **the Őrség**, noted for its dense forest, poor soil and high rainfall. The area was settled by Germans and Serbs during the C11, whose rights to freedom of religion (granted by the Árpáds) were tested during the C17 counter-reformation, when Őrség Protestants began smuggling in Lutheran bibles in wine barrels, and 1,200 of their number were massacred by Catholic mobs during a single night at Csepzeg. Although bellicosity later diminished, sectarian disputes have long occurred over the church in **SZALAFŐ**, which local Protestants triumphantly claimed to be *Református* rather than Catholic when C16 murals depicting the duties of women (!) were uncovered recently. Nearby stands the **Pityerszer** – a group of heavy-timbered peasant dwellings built around a courtyard and connected by covered porches so that the inhabitants

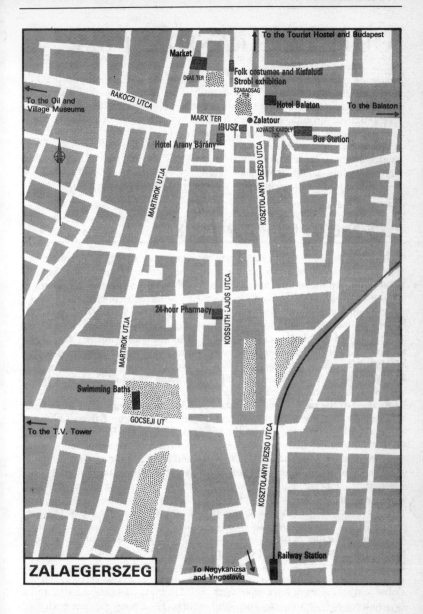

To the Tourist Hostel and Budapest

Market

Folk costumes and Kisfaludi
Strobl exhibition

DEAK TER

RAKOCZI UTCA

SZABADSAG
TER

To the Oil and
Village Museums

Hotel Balaton

To the Balaton

MARX TER

IBUSZ ● Zalatour

KOVACS KAROLY
TER

Hotel Arany Bárány

Bus Station

MARTIROK UTJA

KOSZTOLANYI DEZSO UTCA

24-hour Pharmacy

KOSSUTH LAJOS UTCA

MARTIROK UTJA

Swimming Baths

GOCSEJI UT

To the T.V. Tower

KOSZTOLANYI DEZSO UTCA

ZALAEGERSZEG

Railway Station

To Nagykanizsa
and Yugoslavia

might avoid the perenial rain, and sited on a hilltop to escape flooding. Using
ŐRISZENTPÉTER's campsite or hotel as a base, architecture buffs can
venture out to see the Gothic church at **VELMÉR**, with its medieval frescoes;
while closer at hand is a folksy wooden belltower at **PANKASZ**.

SOUTHERN TRANSDANUBIA

Following one of the roads from Zalaegerszeg, the Balaton or Budapest, I'd advise heading straight for **Pécs**, especially if the monthly market is due. The upper part of southern Transdanubia – **the Völgység**, or valley region – is pretty to drive through, but there's little accommodation here and none of the towns are really worth stopping for. Journeys by rail aren't usually so direct: for from Fonyód and Siófok on the Balaton, the lines head south to Kaposvár (switch trains to reach Dombovár, and then onto the main Budapest-Pécs service); while trains from Balatonszentgyörgy go to NAGYKANIZSA, whence the track approaches Pécs via Barcs and Szigetvár (p.157).

PÉCS AND ITS SURROUNDINGS

If there was ever a uranium minimg town worth visiting, **PÉCS** – pronounced 'Paych' – is it. Tiled rooftops climb the vine-laden slopes of the Mecsek Mountains, pinpricked by church spires, and the mines and mining community of *Újmecsekalja* – nicknamed Uranium City – haven't contaminated Pécs's reputation for cultural and architectural excellence. One of the largest Transdanubian towns and the region's leading educational centre, its population of 150,000 includes a high proportion of students, creating a youthful profile. Besides some fine museums and galleries and a great monthly market, Pécs contains Hungary's best examples of Islamic architecture which, like many of the townsfolk's asiatic features, are a legacy of the long Turkish occupation.

Arriving at the railway station, take bus #30 to reach **the centre**, while from the inter-city bus terminal it's only a few minutes' walk up Bajcsy-Zsilinszky út into **Széchenyi tér**, the hub of the belváros. During the Turkish occupation (1543-1686) this was crowded with 'caravans of camels loaded with merchandise from India and the Yemen', and the Catholic church was torn down and rebuilt as the **Mosque of Gazi Kasim Pasha** – an act symbolic of the occupation, for the Turks came as destroyers but stayed on as builders, merchants and scholars. The building (at the top end of the square) is once again a Christian church, though the ornate windows and the *mirhab* (prayer niche) of the mosque are still plainly visible. Széchenyi tér has its share of museums and galleries (see below), but while you're in the mood for walking, follow Janus Pannonius street eastwards to the **Cathedral**, which looms above Dóm tér. Four-spired, triple-naved and basically neo-Romanesque, it's the outcome of a long line of ecclesiastical structures – each one erected, burned down and raised anew – incorporating an C11 crypt, C14 side chapels, and a lavish decor of blue and gold and floral motifs. The Bishop's Palace enclosing the western side of he square has a humorous C20 addition – a stainless steel knight waving from the balcony.

Behind the palace, a circular stone Barbican tower punctuates a gap in the **old town walls** – once a massive crenellated rampart 5,500 paces long, buttressed by 87 bastions erected after the Mongol invasion – which stretch decrepitly along the northern flank of the belváros. South of the Barbican, smoggy Landler Street runs downhill to meet Rákóczi út, where Pécs' minaret can be glimpsed above neighbouring buildings. Unlike the minaret at Eger, you can enter the C16 **Mosque of Jakovali Hassan**, the best preserved Turkish building in Hungary. Its interior is cool and white, adorned with friezes, carpets and a superbly carved *minbar* – a kind of pulpit on wheels. One block northeast of the minaret, you can see a ruined Turkish bath in front of the *Hotel Minaret* on Sallai utca.

Museums, graves and galleries

For a provincial town, Pécs is loaded with museums and galleries – mostly good ones, and located in the belváros. On Széchenyi square you'll find a gallery full of paintings and sculptures by **contemporary local artists** on the west side, and the **Archaeological Museum** (at nr.12) behind the church. Here, stonecarvings and bronze statues testify to a Roman presence from the C1 onwards, during which the garrison town of *Sophianae* arose to the status of a provincial capital within the vast empire, before the imperial withdrawal in the C5. Káptalan utca, running eastwards from Dom tér, is a hotbed of galleries. Eyeball-throbbing **Op-Art pictures** – a sixties' genre – hang in the birthplace of **Viktor Vásárhely** (b.1908) at nr.3, and the basement provides a temporary home for the **sculptures of Amerigo Tot**, including *Erdély family*: Magyar grave-posts caught in a huge press – a reference to the present plight of the Hungarian minority in Romania.

On the opposite side of the street at nr.2, products of the local **Zsolnay porcelain** factory – which made the tiles covering Budapest's Applied Arts Musuem, among other things – either look magnificent or plunge to the depths of kitsch. Next door are stark Constructivist canvases and drawings exhalting the proletarian struggle; the work of **Béla Uitz** (1887-1972), an associate of the avant garde journal *MA*, and a leading light of the left-wing *Activists* group which took over the Academy during the 1919 Soviet Republic. My favourite gallery, on the southeast corner of Dóm tér, displays the work of **Tivadar Csontváry Kosztka** (1853-1919). Born in the same year as Van Gogh, Csontváry was likewise prone to schizophrenia, largely self-taught, obsessed with following 'the path of the sun', and unappreciated during his lifetime. His fascination with Hebrew lore and the Holy Land was expressed in huge canvases – *Baalbek, Mary's Well at Nazarath* and *Pilgrimage* – and his hallucinatory vision of nature in *Tatra, Storm on the Hortobágy* and *Solitary Cedar*. Don't miss them.

Roman tombs – one of them hopefully decorated with a painting of the gates of paradise – have been unearthed at 8, Geisler utca, and – less impressively – at number 14. On Rákóczi út you can find an **Ethnographic Museum** at nr.15 (closed when I was in town), various stuffed boars and deer at nr.64, and **paintings and sculptures** in the *Modern Magyar Képtár* opposite nr.15. If you've not seen any galleries in Szentendre, this is the place for a quick *tour d'horizon* of C20 Hungarian art.

PÉCS

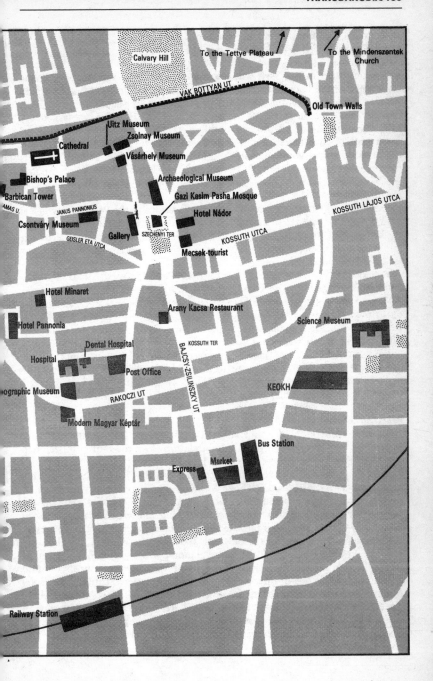

Backstreets, the monthly market and the University

From Kossuth tér, bus #33 climbs up to the **Tettye plateau** overlooking town, where a ruined palace – once used as a Dervish monastery – stands in a park. Branching off Mező u. as it winds around the hillside, various picturesque **backstreets** wend back down into town, passing close to the Mindenszentek Church (where the pastor supplements his income by selling poultry). With luck you'll arrive down on Vak Bottyán u., which runs just below **Calvary Hill**, a sombre garden filled with crumbling statuary overlooking the medieval town wall, bearing traces of glue-sniffers. Last on the antiquity trail, and out of the way unless you're visiting the medical college (see below), exhibits inside the **mausoleum of Idris Baba** explain Turkish death-rites, if you can find the *türbe* amongst the chaos of urban development around the Children's hospital, at Nyár u. 8.

Széchenyi tér's tourist office can furnish directions to the **Pécs Fair**, which is held on the first Sunday of each month (petering out by afternoon), but tends to shift its location periodically. A lively affair with much convivial drinking and hard bargaining over livestock, fresh produce and crafts, it's staged for local people rather than tourists.

Founded in 1367, the fifth in Europe, **Pécs University** had a sickly childhood, hitched up with Pozsony's Arts and Literature faculties during the C19, and now boasts Science (*Tudományi*) and Medical (*Orvostudományi*) departments sited east and west of the belváros ringroad – take bus #M14 or #30 – though for **meeting students**, it might be easier to try the following cafés. Széchenyi tér's slick ice cream parlour is handiest, while *Ifjúság* and *Sophianai* (beside the Park cinema) are near the science faculty, and there's a lively *büfé* behind the ABC closest to the medical college. A youth club, the *Ifjúsági-haz*, halfway down Bajcsy-Zsilinszky út, offers more supervised socialising – and prohibits alcohol – most evenings during the week.

Practical information

Pannónia, *Hunyor*, *Nádor* and *Főnix* are all in the 700Ft-1,300Ft a night range, but you can get cheaper **accommodation** from the tourist office or in hotels further from the centre. The *Agóra Fogadó* (Apáczai Csere János Körtér) is in the southern suburbs, at the end of the #1 bus route; while the *Fenyves* is at 64, Szőlő utca, above Kalinyin utca which bus #33 takes en route to the Tettye plateau. *Mandulás campsite* on Demokrácia út in the foothills of the Mecsek also has a *Fogadó* and bungalows, and can be reached by bus #44 from Széchenyi tér, the site of **Mecsektourist** (nr.9). There, you can book private rooms in the belváros and reserve rooms in neighbouring provincial towns – a good idea if you're planning to stay in Siklós or Szigetvár (see following sections). *Express* (Bajcsy-Zsilinszky út 6) can probably find dormitory beds in one of the colleges during the summer vacation. The *Hotel Minaret* on Sallai u. has recently become a tourist hostel. **Places to eat** include the *Nádor's* restaurant, the *Aranykacsa* and *Rózsakert* off the main square, various buffets and – cheapest of all – above the **market hall** beside the intercity bus terminal. Officals at *KEOKH*, off Rózsa Ferenc utca, handle **visa extensions**.

Őrfű and Abaliget

When Pécs is packed with tourists, the villages of Őrfű and Abaliget offer alternative accommodation – although advance bookings may be necessary – and a scenic retreat from the *dzjamis* and galleries. Regular buses from Pécs' inter-city terminal wind their way northwards along a forested route for about one hour, emerging onto an unexpected plateau set amidst the softly contoured Mecsek Hills. ŐRFŰ, the first settlement, has an old mill (now a museum), a tourist hostel at 6 Petőfi utca and a campsite beside a tiny lake. ABALIGET is slightly larger and boasts a series of **stalactite caves** – the abode of blind crabs and other strange creatures – beside two artificial **lakes**, *Pécsi-tó* and *Hermann Otto-tó*. Snack stands and holiday bungalows abound around them, and there are beds tailored to every pocket at the moderately-priced hotel, *Barlang* tourist hostel, and campsite. Private rooms in both villages may be pre-booked from *Mecsektourist* in Pécs. Should you feel like **walking in the Mecsek Mountains** – large hills, really – a *túristatérképe* is available, detailing paths, escarpments and the like.

SZIGETVÁR

Midway between Pécs and Barcs on the Yugoslav border, rd. 6 and the railway meet at **SZIGETVÁR**, a town of half-remembered heroism. There are plans afoot to build a futuristic cultural centre in the town but, for the moment, the only landmark is the **Castle**, a sun-baked quadrilateral at the end of Vár utca. In 1566, when Szigetvár (Island Castle) was ringed by water and marshes, 2,400 soldiers withstood the onslaught of 100,000 Turks here for more than a month, launching a final, suicidal sally when they could no longer hold the fortress. Enraged by this fierce resistance – which took 20,000 Ottoman lives and halted his seventh attempt to march on Vienna – the Turkish Sultan Süleyman burst a blood vessel and died. Szigetvár's defenders and their commander Miklós Zrinyi were hailed as saviours by Christendom, while the Turks honoured Süleyman with a lovely *djami* in the fortress grounds. Today its minaret has disappeared but the interior – with ornamental grilles and Koranic inscriptions – survives. Richly **coloured miniatures** of Turkish life hang in the adjoining building, together with the inevitable celebration of Hungarian heroism, including copies of the epic poem *Szózat* ('Appeal') penned by Zrinyi's grandson, himself a general. A cry for liberty and a call for endurance, the C17 poem was adapted as a chorale by Kodály early in 1956, and its single performance at the Budapest Academy was a tumultuous occasion. Crowds chanted its refrain, *Ne Bántsd a Magyart!* (Let the Magyars alone!) as a symbolic protest against the Rákosi regime, causing the government members present to walk out.

The castle's casements contain a tourist hostel (often full of army conscripts – Szigetvár is still a garrison town), while the expensive *Oroszlán* **hotel** stands on Zrinyi tér, opposite a Baroque church with Turkish-style windows betraying its origins as a mosque. *Mecsektourist* in the hotel lobby can arrange private **rooms** or beds in the music school (*Zeneiskola*) on Ságvári u. nearby. If you're leaving by bus, there's a barely-distinguishable ruin of a Koran school on Bástya utca, just around the corner from the terminal.

BARCS, 31km southwest by rd. 6 or railway, is a **road crossing into Yugoslavia** (Terezino Polje). There's no call to linger here, but if necessary you'll find a campsite and the cheaper hotel on Nagyhid utca; the costlier hotel and the tourist office on Bajcsy-Zsilinszky útja.

HARKÁNY AND SIKLÓS

An open air **thermal pool** and the chance to wallow in **hot mud** (theraputically rich in sulphur and floride) brings the punters to **HARKÁNY**, one hour's bus journey southwards from Pécs. There's certainly a lure to stopping for the mud and a cheap underwater massage, but aside from the baths (open 8am-4pm, 5pm-11pm/from September to May 9am-5pm) there's not a lot to the place: a few snack stands, three pricey hotels and a campsite with bungalows and a *túristaszálló*. The only bit of life, really, is the **market** near the **bus station**. And the less said about the *Bolgár Hadsereg múzeum* (commemorating the Bulgarian army's contribution to Hungarian liberation) the better.

Thankfully, most buses plough on a further 6km across the dusty plain to **SIKLÓS**, another small town grown up around a castle. The birthplace of the late **George Mikes** (known for his humorous writings in the West), Siklós is sleepier but more appealing than Szigetvár – in short, a nice one horse town. The **fortress**, visible from the bus station, has been continuously inhabited since its construction in the C15, and its rondellas and bastions form an impressive girdle around the C18 mansion at its heart. The main wing contains an expensive hotel and *Mecsektourist*, who'll grudgingly unlock cheaper **rooms** in the tourist hostel across the courtyard if you're persistent or, better, brandish a reservation from Pécs. Fragmented C15 frescoes and a rose-vaulted ceiling ennoble the **chapel**, located (with no sense of incongruity according to medieval values) within whipping distance of a dungeon filled with instruments of torture and rank air.

Locals and tourists make merry in the castle's wine cellar-cum-restaurant most evenings, whilst during the day, action shifts to the *Sport Vendéglő* and dives around Kossuth tér, the site of a cheap *Fogadó*) and a derelict *Djami* undergoing slow restoration. From the terminal nearby, **buses** depart every hour for Harkány and Pécs, and less frequently **for Villány** (to which a few trains also run), whence there are services **to Mohács**. Though there should be the odd bus to DRÁVASZABOLCS, services don't actually travel **across the border** (open 24-hours) to Donji Miholjac in Yugoslavia.

VILLÁNY AND MOHÁCS

Acres of vineyards lap the slopes of Mt. Szarsomlyo, and the appellation **VILLÁNY** appears on bottles of red **wine** sold in *ABC*s across the land. The local wine-making tradition goes back almost 2,000 years but Villány's other noteworthy feature – its **sculpture park** – is of recent vintage. Bronze totems, concrete erections and wooden structures mounted on the hillside testify to the activities of the annual **artists' summer camp**. Officially, there's no accommodation, so you're best returning to Pécs by train, or going on to Mohács by train or bus.

Hot and dusty beside the pounding Danube, the small town of **MOHÁCS** is a synonym for defeat, for as a consequence of a single **battle** here in 1526, Hungary was divided and plagued by warfare for the next 150 years, and the national independence lost then has never since been recovered. The state was tottery before Mohács, however: the treasury empty, advisers bickering and an indecisive boy on the throne. Only after the Turks under Süleyman 'the Magnificent' had taken Belgrade and were nearing the Drava did Louis II muster an army, which headed south without waiting for reinforcements from Transylvania. The armies clashed a few miles south of Mohács on August 29: attacking first, the Magyars broke ranks to loot the fallen and suffered a crushing counter-attack by élite Turkish Janissaries and cavalry, which caused a rout. Amongst the 25,000 Hungarians who perished were Louis – killed in the ditches during flight – and most of Hungary's commanders and high clerics, which left the country unable to organise resistance while the Turks advanced on Buda. **Monuments** to the event rise over the battlefield, Sátorhelyi út, and on Széchenyi tér where a rather ugly Votive Church was erected to mark the 400th anniversary; a commemorative **museum** can be found on the corner of Szerb utca.

Aside from these, the River Danube rolling through town disconcertingly near street level is the only 'sight' for 364 days of the year. The exception manifests itself on March 1, when the streets of Mohács come alive with the annual **Busójárás Carnival**. With its procession of grotesquely masked figures waving flaming torches, the carnival assumes a macabre appearance at night, although people are out to enjoy themselves. Hungarians generally pooh-pooh the carnival as a 'tourist event' – which it is, to some extent – but lots of Yugoslavs from across the border appreciate it as a local version of an old Serbian festival. Originally, it was probably a spring ritual intended to propitiate the gods, but over time participants also began to practice ritualistic abomination of the Turks – hence the hideous masks – to magically draw the sting of reality.

It's the only time of the year when there might be an **accommodation** shortage, so if you're planning to attend the carnival, reserve beds beforehand through *Mecsektourist* (local office on the main street) – either in people's homes, or at one of the two hotels (the *Béke* is the cheaper). The frequency of trains out of town is pretty dire, so travellers generally rely upon **buses** in order to reach BAJA (p.192) on the Plain, or BÁTASZÉK, the junction for **trains** to Pécs, Szekszárd, Pörböly and Baja. There's also a useful Volán coach service from Mohács **across the border** to Osijek, Novi Sad and Slavonski Brod in Yugoslavia (one departure per destination, usually before 10am). The 24-hour checkpoint of UDVAR is 11km to the south of town.

SZEKSZÁRD AND THE FOREST OF GEMENC

Not quite a horse and cart town like Mohács, but certainly no metropolis, **SZEKSZÁRD** is a reasonable place to rest up for a day. The tourist hostel commands a fine view of Szekszárd and the Sió hills, and red **wine** has been produced here since Roman times when a settlement, *Alisca*, stood athwart Pollack utca.

Everything of interest lies along, or just off, the town's main drag, Hunyadi utca. Starting from the bus terminal, you'll soon come to the **Béri Balogh Museum**, housing a rich collection of artefacts from the peasantry and gentry, one block behind which is the *Gemenc Hotel*. Another few minutes' walk brings one to Garay tér, site of the tourist office, several wine bars and a cheaper hotel. Further uphill, porticoed buildings tilt perceptibly around Béla tér and a statue to the plague of 1730, beyond which Munkácsy u. winds up past the supermarket to the tourist hostel, and Babits M. utca wanders off towards the **house of Mihály Babits** (Tuesday-Sunday 9am-6pm). Snug as any writer's residence could be, this is filled with photos and writings related to *Nyugat* (West), an avant-garde literary journal which Babits edited: the launching pad for the Village Explorers' exposés of the rottenness of rural life in interwar Hungary, and for the meteoric careers of Gyula Illyés and Endre Ady.

Tolna tourist (Széchenyi u.38) can give details of coach **excursions to the Forest of Gemenc** (*Gemenci-erdő*), a remnant of the great wilderness of woods, reeds and mudland (*Sárköz*) that once covered the Danube's shifting, flood-prone banks. It remains the habitat of osprey, black storks and deer – the latter being fair game for hard-currency paying hunters in this 'nature reserve'. Without private transport or a package-trip, you'll have to reach the forest via KESELYŰS (bus #7 from Hunyadi utca, or hitch), walking into the reserve from there, or taking one of the rare trains which pass through the *Gemenci Delta* – the richest wildlife site – to PÖRBÖLY. The journey can also be made from Baja, which is linked by rail to Pörböly, where a train leaves for the forest most weekdays at around 7.30am.

Moving on from Szekszárd, the road and railway point definitively **towards Budapest**. The track heads through nowhere in particular, but rd. 6 nudges close to the Danube in places, enabling a **river crossing at DUNAFÖLDVÁR**, and presenting a succession of views which would be better were it not for the towns en route. Buses are fairly regular, but hitching seems poor.

THE DANUBE'S WEST BANK BETWEEN SZEKSZÁRD AND BUDAPEST

Once mud and reeds where boats might run aground, the land west of the Danube has been subjected to technological fixes – the results of which can be seen although the consequences are still uncertain. **PAKS**, a sprawling mass of modern residences, is the site of Hungary's first **nuclear power station**, a Soviet-designed VVER 440 type reactor, which supplies about 16% of the country's electricity. Since the Chernobyl disaster state planners have ordered two more reactors (of the 1,000 megawatt, pressurised water VVER 100 type), but an opinion poll has indicated widespread public unease, and Szeged University's newspaper has called for a referendum on the expansion of Paks. Nuclear waste from Paks is allegedly returned to the USSR, though rumours have it that some may be stored near Bonyhád, southwest of the town.

DUNAÚJVÁROS (Danube New town), further upriver, is a monument to Stalinist economics: created around a vast new steelworks which the Party saw as the lynchpin of its industrialisation strategy. Its construction during the early 1950s was trumpeted as a heroic project, and media coverage of the stakhanovites obscured the exploitation that lay behind *Sztálinváros* (as the town was originally called). In reality, most of the heavy work was performed by peasant women and 'reformed' prostitutes (p.69), who laboured 18 hours a day, slept 100 to a room, fought over the few showers and towels, and got raped by foremen. Ironically, the government now considers Dunaújváros an economic liability like so much of Hungary's heavy industry, and the future of steelworks built with so much cost in suffering looks doubtful.

FESTIVALS

Spring
Grotesquely-masked processions and much merriment at the MOHÁCS *Busójarás* on **March 1**.

Summer
Classical, folk and opera music during SZOMBATHELY's *Savaria Festival* in **June**, hard on the heels of which comes

SOPRON's *Festival Weeks* (roughly June 22 - **July** 14), with symphonic orchestras, folklore ensembles and rock theatre in the city, and smaller concerts in the FERTŐRÁKOS Quarry and the Esterházy Palace at FERTŐD. At some time over the summer, organ recitals at PANNONHALMA and an Artists' Camp at VILLÁNY.

TRAVEL DETAILS

Trains
From Budapest to Győr (6-7 daily; 2-2½hrs); Komárom (5-6; 1½-2); Pécs (3; 3¼); Sopron (5; 2¼); Tata (7; 1¼).
From Dombóvár to Pécs (14; 1-1½).
From Győr to Sopron (5; 1¼); Veszprém (4; 2½).
From Nagycenk to Fertőboz (hourly).
From Nagykanizsa to Balatonszentgyörgy (10; ¾); Pécs (3; 1½-3).
From Pécs to Mohács (5; 2).
From Sopron to Szombathely (7; 1½).
From Szekszárd to Budapest (4; 2½).
From Szombathely to Körmend (7; 1½); Kőszeg (11; ½); Nagykanizsa (5; 1½-2½); Pécs (2; 4); Székesfehérvár (7; 2¼-2¾); Szentgotthárd (7; 2¼).

Buses
From Győr to Pannonhalma (5-6 daily).
From Pécs to Orfü & Abaliget; Harkány; Siklós; Szigetvár (every 1-1½hrs).
From Siklós to Harkány; Pécs (hourly).
From Sopron to Fertőd; Fertőrákos; Kőszeg (every 1-1½hrs).
From Szekszárd to Budapest (4-5 daily); Baja (6-7).

From Szombathely to Ják (5-6); Körmend (hourly).
From Zalaegerszeg to Keszthely (hourly).

International trains
From Pécs to Osijek (2 daily).
From Sopron to Wiener Neustadt; Ebenfurt (daily).

International coaches
One of each, weekdays only.
From Barcs to Zagreb.
From Bükfürdő to Forchtenstein; Krumbach; Oslip; Schwarzenbach; Vienna; Wiener Neustadt.
From Győr to Galanta; Trnava.
From Harkány to Sombor.
From Komló to Osijek.
From Lenti to Ljubljana.
From Letenye to Prague.
From Mohács to Osijek; Novi Sad; Slavonski Brod.
From Szombathely to Bratislava.
From Zalaegerszeg to Murska Sobota.
From Zalakaros to Hartberg.

Chapter five
THE NORTHERN UPLANDS

The **Northern Uplands** of Hungary are generally hilly, mountainous and forested, but otherwise defy easy characterisation. They take in the famous **wine**-producing towns of **Eger** and **Tokaj**, whose appeal goes beyond the local beverage, and a succession of **castles**, either well-preserved as at Sárospatak, or squatting in picturesque decrepitude on crags above the villages of Hollókő, Somoskő, Füzer and Boldogkőváralja. This part of Hungary was the first region to be industrialised, and the idyllic woodlands of the **Bükk and Mátra mountains** lie cheek by jowl with drabbly-utilitarian **Miskolc**, the coal mines of the Borsod Basin, and the despoiled Sajó Valley, themselves less than 50km from the amazing **Aggtelek stalactite caves**. The environment, and peoples' lifestyles, ranges the gamut between two extremes – at one end, bored teenagers sniffing glue outside Miskolc's 'Punk fashion' hairdressing salon; at the other, horse-drawn carts clopping around tiny **Zempléni villages**, where the siesta reigns supreme.

Approaching the uplands
The westerly Cserhát range is adjacent to the Börzsöny Mountains (see Chapter 2), and thus accessible from Vác and Balassagyarmat, but the commonest **approaches** to the uplands are **from Budapest** or the Great Plain. Several times daily, express and slow trains leave the capital's Keleti station, passing through Hatvan and Füzesabony en route to Miskolc and Szerencs – all places to change onto **branch lines** heading further north. Hatvan is the link with the Mátra; trains from Füzesabony run to Eger; Miskolc is the starting point for journeys into the Bükk; while from Szerencs you can reach Tokaj, Sárospatak and many Zempléni villages. Balassagyarmat is accessible by train from Aszód, or bus from Hatvan (whence buses also depart for Hollókő).

Again, trains are the easiest way of approaching **from the Plain**. From Nyíregyháza, frequent services run through Tokaj to Szerencs, before branching off towards Miskolc or Sátoraljaúhely; while Karcag, Tiszafüred and Szolnok are linked by rail to Hatvan and Füzesabony.

THE CSERHÁT REGION

The **Cserhát range**, like its more impressive neighbours, the Mátra and the Börzsöny, was once continuous forest. Farming and railways in the Nógrád and Zagyva valleys have made inroads, however, and today there's little magic about the northern slopes or the monotonous flatlands around the Ipoly River, which marks the border with Czechoslovakia. Such distinction and colour as there is is provided by the indigenous **Palóc ethnic group**, who sport fantastic costumes which have long since become museum-pieces elsewhere: evidence of a backward agricultural economy rather than any consciously 'separatist' feelings.

Balassagyarmat

Since losing its medieval fortress and most of its population to the Turks, **BALASSAGYARMAT** (pronounced 'Bolosho-dyurmot') has declined to a quiet market town. The tourist board are endeavouring to spruce up its few Baroque monuments and promote it as the 'Palóc cultural capital', though few visitors are likely to be impressed by the seedy mainstreet or its Breughel-esque folk.

The **Palóc Ethnographical Museum** (on Palócliget, off Bajcsy-Zsilinszky street) does little to dispel such impressions. The guide propels you at high speed past enticing displays of elaborate **costumes** – Palóc women's lacy head-dresses are very distinctive – and a small collection of modern paintings. For the committed, two rooms are devoted to local writers: **Imre Madách** (1823-64) and Kálmán Mikszáth (1847-1910). Madách began his career as a clerk in the County Hall which still stands on Köztársaság tér, and went on to write *The Tragedy of Man* (1860), commonly held to be Hungary's greatest classical drama. In the 1950s, however, the Party considered that its pessimistic portrayal of human nature dangerously undermined the lofty ideals required of 'Socialist Realist' art, and banned it. (The ban was later lifted, and Madách's drama is now performed each year at the Szeged festival). **Kálmán Mikszáth** won renown with satirical short stories – *St. Peter's Umbrella, The Siege of Besztercze* and *A Strange Marriage* – which exposed the shortcomings of the gentry, his own class. Also featured in the museum, but less prominently, is **Gyula Benczúr**, whose narrative paintings won him a teaching post at the Academy of Fine Arts, but were denounced as 'reactionary art' during the short-lived Hungarian Soviet Republic, when Benczúr was exiled to Balassagyarmat as a punishment. However, he too was posthumously rehabilitated, and now receives due honour in his birthplace, Nyíregyháza.

Private **rooms** can be obtained from *Nográd-tourist* (7, Köztársaság tér), which also makes bookings in Hollókő (see below); or tents pitched at the campsite on Szabadság út near the river. The **bus station** is on the mainstreet.

Szécsény and Hollókő

Buses run eastwards to **SZÉCSÉNY**, a small sleepy town where the monuments are gradually being renovated. When I was here scaffolding hid the details of the **Forgách Castle** that overlooks the town, but down the road to the right you can visit a gruesome **museum** in an outlying tower. Grotesque instruments of torture and engravings demonstrating their use are displayed in the surviving bastion of a C15 fortress which, like so many, was blown up by the Habsburgs during the War of Independence (1703-11). It was here that the Diet elected Ferenc Rákóczi II ruling prince and commander in chief of the Magyar forces, and declared the union of Hungary and Transylvania.

From Szécsény you can catch another bus south to **HOLLÓKŐ** ('Raven rock'), which the tourist board lauds as the 'prettiest village in Hungary'.

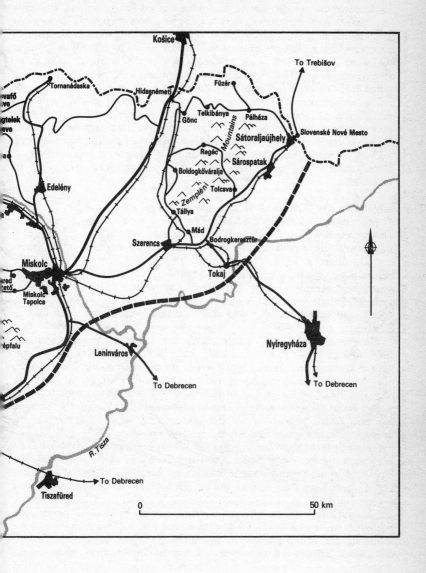

Situated in the shadow of a **ruined C13 fortress** where it was totally rebuilt following a conflagration early this century, Hollókő has become a veritable **museum village** over the last 10 years. Coachloads of camera-clicking tourists amble down the two dirt streets, past whitewashed Palóc dwelling with their broad eaves and exquisitely-carved fences and gables (two of which serve as cheap tourist hostels). It's not difficult to foresee the time when **Palóc costume** is worn strictly for business reasons in Hollókő: men have already dropped it, but some women still wear fringed silk shawls, wrapped into coifs, unselfconsciously. (Traditionally, Palóc costumes were of homespun, and varied from village to village; in Orahalom, for example, the Hollókő-style coif was transformed into a bonnet by the insertion of a stiff cardboard lining). Mass at the restored church – outwardly austere, but decorated inside with vibrant colours and flowers – provides the liveliest entertainment, while the locals' bar is decidedly cheaper and less tacky than the tourist restaurant.

There are usually three buses a day to and from Hatvan, the 'gateway to the Mátra' (p.167), and to Szécsény, from which you can take another bus to Salgótarján.

Salgótarján and the Castles of Somoskő and Salgó

After Szécsény and Hollókő, **SALGÓTARJÁN** whacks you with modernity. This mining town – scarred since the C19 by industrial squalor and poverty – was extensively rebuilt during the 1960s: a tardy response to workers' demonstrations in 1956, when the ÁVO shot dead 85 coalminers. Modern blocks have replaced slums and the downtown is a mass of supermarkets, which the government rightly deemed sufficient to 'shut peoples' mouths with sausage'. However, the old mines are now considered uneconomic, and the state's plan to relocate pits and shed workers caused mass walk-outs in Salgótarján and Tatabánya when it was announced in August 1986.

The town's principal tourist attraction is the **Mining Museum** (*Bányamúzeum*) buried in the inclined shafts of the now-defunct 'József' pit, with an entrance on Ady út, a block behind the market. Cramped and muddy, filled with props, tools and cables, the tunnels lack the dust, danger and noise of a working mine, but the explanatory leaflet still bids visitors good luck. It's vaguer about the government's plans to shut fourteen of Hungary's thirty-six pits and switch production to open-cast mining; which could mean real unemployment in towns like this for the first time since 1949.

From Salgótarján's terminal, buses run 11km northwards to **SOMOSKŐ** on the Czech border, where a five towered **ruined C14 castle** squats on vast blocks of stone, opposite **basalt formations** (*bazaltömlés*) resembling giant organ pipes. Since these lie over the border, tourists can only visit in groups accompanied by a guide from Nógrád-tourist, between April 15 and October 15. No such restrictions apply to the **ruined castle of SALGÓ**, about 3km southwest of Somoskő, which was constructed atop a 625m high basalt cone following the Mongol invasion. Before its ruination during the Turkish occupation, Salgó was once owned by Count István Werbőczy, author of the *Tripartium* law which bound the peasants to 'perpetual serfdom' after the nobles crushed the revolt of 1514.

Accommodation ranges from the pricey *Karancs* hotel, or a private room from *Nográd-tourist* (both on Salgótarján's main square, Tanácsköztársaság tér) to the campsite at the end of the #6 bus route, and Salgo's two tourist hostels. The bus and train stations (separated by the railway tracks) lie just south of the town centre, close to the market and Mining Museum. If you're dependent on public transport, **moving on** from Salgótarján amounts to heading northeast **towards Ózd** or south towards the Mátra region, assuming that you don't take the morning bus **across to Lusenec in Czechoslovakia**. Since the remote Aggtelek caves are the only reason for passing through Ózd, and bus connections are dodgy, **south** seems the obvious direction to take. The railway and numerous buses aim for Hatvan; along the way, ore-buckets and slag hills disappear, and vineyards and fields begin to flourish. Though one can hop off at PÁSZTÓ and hope to find a bus into the mountains from the north, it's wiser to continue on to **HATVAN** where transportation is better. From this old market town Budapest and the Plain are within easy reach, and Volán buses fan out to Gyöngyös, the Mátra settlements, and as far afield as Eger.

GYÖNGYÖS AND THE MÁTRA MOUNTAINS

Hungarians make the most of their highlands, and **the Mátra** – where Mount Kékestető just tops 1,000m – is heavily geared to domestic tourism. Mt. Kékestető is a popular place for winter sports despite the relatively lacklustre resort facilities at Mátraháza and Mátraszentimre, while during summer, families ramble the paths between picnic sites and beer gardens, ignoring the wild boar and deer that live deeper in the thickets of oak and beech. Few of the Mátra settlements have much of interest beyond their amenities, but the mountains and forests are in any case the main attraction.

Gyöngyös

Most visitors approach the Mátra via **GYÖNGYÖS** (pronounced 'Dyurn-dyursh'), the centre of the Gyöngyös-Visonta **wine**-producing area, whence comes white *Muskotály*. It's a pleasant enough town but nothing to write home about. The bus station on Aprilis 4 körút is roughly midway between the two centres of interest, the main square – called just that, Fő tér – and Dimitrov park, with its nearby museum.

Turn left down Kossuth utca – which soon becomes Lenin út – and C19 buildings appear in garish blues and reds together with *IBUSZ* (nr.6), presaging the quaint old dwellings around **Fő tér**. Lively yet shadily tranquil, it's the place to join the Magyars around the wine kiosks opposite the *Hotel Mátra*, before dutifully inspecting the picturesquely decrepit Gothic Church of St Bartholomew on the corner. Heading in the opposite direction from the terminal, Kossuth utca leads past benevolent-looking stone lions fronting Dimitrov park and the museum – both opposite a *Gimnázium* – to the station of the **narrow gauge railway** (*Mátravasút*) to Mátrafüred in the mountains. Trains depart roughly every hour. If you've time to kill, the **Mátra Museum** at nr.40 has a reconstructed mammoth's skeleton and a collection of dazzling butterflies (amongst other dead Mátra wildlife).

The Mátra settlements

The Mátravasút is the fun way to ride to **MÁTRAFÜRED** – and takes no longer than buses. It deposits visitors at the lower end of this sloping, touristy settlement, where the costly *Hotel Avar* ('mit tennis platz') and *Mátra-tourist* (at Vörösmarty u.4) monopolise **accommodation**. Cheaper – and in many ways nicer – is the campsite at **Sás-tó** (sometimes written Sóstó), a lake 3km uphill from Mátrafüred, where buses from Gyöngyös stop off on their way to Mátraháza, the next settlement. It's a friendly place, full of Hungarians boating and fishing amid the usual *lángos* stands, a few hours by footpath from Mátraháza, with **wild boars** reputedly lurking in the forests to the west. At 8pm the restaurant closes and action shifts down to the disco and bars in Mátrafüred.

MÁTRAHÁZA consists mainly of Trade Union hostels, set on an incline with trees, a few bars, and lots of walks around. Accommodation for foreigners is 2km along the road to Parádfürdő, but one can easily do without and make a quick return bus journey to see **Mount Kékestető**, the highest peak in the Mátra. Two **ski-runs** (*sípálya*) descend from the summit, 1,015m high, crowned by a nine-storey telecommunications **tower**, painted red, white and blue and festooned with dish aerials. The view from the tower (open Tuesday-Sunday 9.30am-3pm/4pm in summer) is very impressive.

To the northeast, a group of similarly-named villages gathers around **PARÁD**, where the *Palóc ház* exhibits costumes and artefacts of the villagers' shared ethnic past. From Parád, a promenade flanked by Metro-workers' holiday chalets leads to **PARÁDFÜRDŐ**, a popular **thermal spa**, where people also drink the sulphurous, fizzy water for stomach and digestive complaints. The **Cart Museum** (*Kocsimúzeum*) here is more interesting than it sounds, as carved and brilliantly painted yokes and carts were a Palóc speciality. For the record, the coach – which superseded the cumbersome wagon throughout Europe – was actually invented in a Hungarian village called, one might have guessed it, *Kocs*.

Mention **RECSK**, a village 2km east of Parádfürdő, and most older Hungarians will share recollections of terror. During the late 1940s and early '50s, thousands of the tens of thousands of citizens arrested by the ÁVO were sentenced to labour in the **quarries** a mile to the southwest of Recsk. Half-starved and frequently beaten by their gaolers, prisoners died of exhaustion or in rockfalls, but more usually at night, whilst sleeping in muddy pits open to the sky. Recsk concentration camp was finally closed in 1953, during the brief premiership of Imre Nagy, and unlike notorious prisons such as Vác or Budapest's Gyüjtőfogház, it was never refilled with victims when the hardliners regained control. The 5,500 prisoners freed during the first week of the 1956 Uprising were merely the tail end of a far greater number that passed through Hungarian (and Soviet) gaols during the 'heyday' of the Stalinist era. No monument or plaque commemorates the victims, and nowadays Recsk is merely a stopover for buses heading towards **Eger**, and a halt on the branch line down from Mátramindszent to **Kál-Kápolna**. (The latter is the station before Füzesabony on the main Budapest-Miskolc line).

SIROK, one stop southeast on the same branch line, is worth visiting if you're mad about romantic views. Above the village 1½km northeast of the train halt, a **ruined C13th castle** broods on a mountain top, from which you can admire the mingled peaks of the Mátra, the Bükk and Slovakia. A considerable detour – recommended only to antiquity buffs who own transport or are willing to hitch patiently – takes one to **FELDEBRŐ**, a village with one of the oldest church crypts still extant in Hungary, decorated with **C12 frescos** influenced by Byzantine art. The local **linden leaf wine** (*Debrői hárslevelű*) is good for refreshing weary travellers. Anyone intending to visit Sirok or Feldebrő, or go walking in the mountains, should buy a **large scale tourist map** (*A Mátra túristatérképe*) beforehand.

EGER AND AROUND

Sited in its own sunny valley between the Mátra and the Bükk ranges, **Eger** is famed for its minaret, *Egri Bikavér* wine, and the heroic legend attached to its castle. From town, buses and local trains lead to various villages bordering the Bükk national park, notably Szilvásvárad near the beautiful Szalajka Valley to the north, and Cserépváralja to the south, just below the 'rocking' stones in the Felső-szoros ravine. Thus you can enter the Bükk mountains from the west, or cut straight through on a bus to Miskolc, and re-enter them by train from Lillafüred (see p.173) after you've finished with Eger.

Eger

Sprawling in the sun and ringed by colourful tower blocks, **EGER** seems a fitting place of origin for *Egri Bikavér*, the potent, throat-rasping red wine, marketed as **Bull's Blood** abroad. This brings thousands of visitors to the town, though it's not the only justification: Eger isn't just a hole to get drunk in (even though many do just that).

The **town centre** is the place to begin sightseeing, a melange of boldly painted Baroque edifices interspersed with a cathedral – the second largest in Hungary – and a minaret. Eger's most photographed structure is the **minaret**, the most northerly in Europe, 40 metres high and fourteen sided – which, despite all the kudoes, looks rather pathetic bereft of its mosque – torn down in 1841 during the course of a building boom. The same economic upswing that kibbutzed the mosque financed the construction of **the Cathedral**, József Hild's rehearsal for the even larger Basilica at Esztergom, which stands at the intersection of Kossuth and Széchenyi utcas. It's a huge Neo-Classical pile, with the City of God arising triumphant inside the cupola, while painted evildoers flee the sword and holy water, and a clutter of supplications and testamonial plaques around Saint Rita's shrine show that faith in her miraculous powers hasn't disappeared.

Action-packed statues commemorating Eger's sieges accompany the stately former Minorite Church on **Dobó István tér**, which lies but a short walk over a bridge from the open air **market**. Alternatively, the street running uphill leads past *Cooptourist* and a ruined Turkish bath (under excavation) to the castle – scene of Eger's past triumph and tragedy. Statues, graven plaques, coloured prints and most of all the great *Vár* recall the terrible **sieges** during the Turkish invasion. The first siege of 1552, described in Géza Gárdonyi's

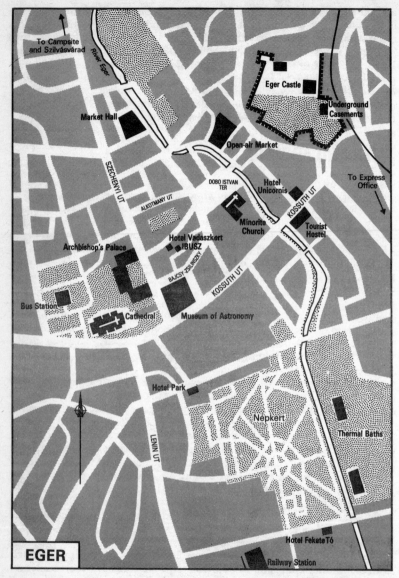

EGER

panegyric novel *Egri csillagok* ('Stars of Eger'), was an unexpected victory for the Hungarians. Esconced in the castle under the command of **István Dobó**, 2,000 soldiers and Eger's **women** (who hurled rocks, hot soup and fat) repulsed a Turkish force six times their number – shattering the impetus of the Ottoman advance until 1596. But in their second attempt the Turks triumphed: Eger's garrison of foreign mercenaries surrendered after a week, and the Ottoman troops sacked the town, leaving only 'blackened walls and buildings razed to the ground' and 'the naked bodies of Christians baking in the sun, in some places four yards high'.

The **Castle** still commands the best view in town, though primed cannon no longer threaten Eger from its ramparts and underground casements. Gárdonyi's grave (inscribed 'Only his body lies here') is enshrined atop the bastion overlooking the main gate, whence a path leads up to the C15 Bishop's Palace and the jumble of medieval foundations aptly signposted as a *Romkert* (garden of ruins). Close by the *Romkert* (once a gothic cathedral, turned into an arsenal by the Turks 'to spite the Christians'), tour groups assemble at the concrete tunnel entrance to the **underground galleries**; a labyrinth of sloping passageways, gun casements, deep cut observation shafts and mysterious chambers, which you can sneak off to explore. Tapestries, faience, Turkish handicrafts and weaponry fill the **museum** upstairs in the Bishop's Palace, while downstairs are two rooms exhibiting painted Palóc furniture, and a **'Hall of Heroes'** (*Hősök terme*), where a lifesize marble István Dobó lies amid a bodyguard of siege heroes, the latter carved in best Stakhanovite style. In the **art gallery** adjoining the Bishop's Palace are some fine Munkácsy's and three romantic Transylvanian landscapes by Antal Ligeti.

Drinking, and more mundane matters

Sights aside, wine drinking is obviously a major part of anyone's stay in Eger. Most foreigners seem to prefer the posher **bars** on Dózsa Gy. tér and Széchenyi utca, but I developed a liking for the spit-and-sawdust *Ráckapu Italbolt* (also on Széchenyi u.), and the cellar in front of the Cathedral, both favoured by locals. Serious drinkers go to the source – the **wine cellars in Szépasszony Valley** (just west of town, bus #3 from Felszabadulás tér to the Hatvan cemetery, then walk), and the huge *Bortakomba* **State Winery** (out along Uttörő utca south of the Népkert, bus #4), and get stuck in. Besides *Bikavér*, Eger's vineyards also produce *Medoc Noir*, a sweet red dessert wine, and *Egri leányka*, which is honey coloured and slightly flavoured with herbs.

Other things on offer include the **horse-riding school** – *lovarda* – in the suburb of Felnémet (Sánu u., bus #10 or #11, but ask at the tourist offices beforehand); the **thermal baths and swimming pool** south of Petőfi tér near the main **park** (Népkert); a **video-disco** at Széchenyi u. 11; and the soporific **Museum of Astronomy** in the tower of the Ho Chi Minh teacher-training college opposite the Cathedral.

The cheapest **places to sleep** are the tourist hostels at Szarvas tér 1 and Kossuth u. 26 (the latter was the 'Buttler house' featured in Kálmán Mikszáth's novel *A Strange Marriage*), followed by the campsite at Rákóczi u. 79 (bus #10 or #11 from nearby the railway station). Private rooms from the **tourist offices** (Bajcsy Zs. u. 9, Széchenyi u. 2 and Hibay u. 22) cost slightly less than the cheaper hotels, the *Unicornis* and the *Egri csillagok*, and two pensions; the *Márka panzió* on Gárdonyi u. above the castle, and the *Kőkút panzió* in Szépasszony Valley. Dormitory beds are usually available from *Express* (Széchenyi u. 28) during the summer.

Though not on the main Budapest-Miskolc line, Eger has **transport** to most places in the vicinity that are worth visiting. Bus #3 runs between the cathedral and the **railway station**, whence trains go to **Füzesabony** – which is on the main line – and to **Putnok** in the north. En route to the latter, trains stop at Bélapátfalva, Szilvásvárad and Nagyvisnyó (see below) – all on the fringes of the Bükk – while at Putnok one may catch buses to **Aggtelek**. Centrally placed behind the cathedral, the Feldszabadulás tér terminal is the place to board **buses** to all the destinations above and – more importantly – **through the Bükk mountains to Miskolc**. Should you prefer to enter the mountains **on foot**, buses also run to Felsőtarkány, Noszvaj, Bükkzsérc and Cserépváralja, where the southern paths and foothills begin (see p.173).

Up to Szilvásvárad and the Szalajka Valley

The road and railway skirt the western foothills of the Bükk as they wiggle northwards towards Putnok, and 12km out from Eger the scenery is promisingly lush around SZARVASKŐ ('Stag rock'), a pretty village with a nearby *Fogadó* and very ruined C14 castle. However, then come quarries and an ugly cement factory at BÉLAPÁTFALVA, where the sole reason to stop is a well-preserved Romanesque **abbey church** founded by French Cistercian monks in 1232, which hides between the main street and hills (open Tuesday-Sunday 9am-4pm).

Eight kilometres farther on, SZILVÁSVÁRAD occupies a dell beside wooded mountains arising to the east. Before 1945 the area was enclosed as the private estate of Count Pallavinici's brood. Expropriated and commercialised, it's now host to a narrow gauge railway, snack and souvenir stands and a lot of blaring radios. Beyond the commercial clutter, small salmon lakes and captive stags, the SZALAJKA VALLEY really begins at *szikla-forrás*, a gushing rock cleft. The **Erdei museum** in the vicinity exhibits weathered huts and tools (including an ingenious water-powered forge) once used by the charcoal-burners and foresters of the Bükk. Higher up, the valley is boxed in by mountains, and paths snake through trees to the triangular Istállóskői cave (*barlang*) and the barefaced **Mount Istállóskő** – which at 959m is the highest in the Bükk range. (The second highest, Bákvány, can be reached by footpath from Istállóskő or from NAGYVISNYÓ, the next settlement after Szilvásvárad).

Szilvásvárad's hotel, tourist hostel, campsite and **Riding museum** are all on, or near, Park utca.

THE BÜKK MOUNTAINS

Beech trees – *bükk* – cover the mountains between Eger and Miskolc, giving the region its name. Unlike most of the northern mountains, **the Bükk** are formed of sedimentary limestone, clay slate and dolomite, riddled with sinkholes and caves which were home for the earliest tribes of *Homo sapiens* who hunted mammoths and reindeer. As civilisation developed elsewhere the Bükk declined in importance – save as a source of timber – until the start of the C19, when Henrik Fazola built a blast furnace in the Garadna Valley, exploiting the iron ore which nowadays feeds the Lenin metallurgical works in Miskolc. While industry continues to shape the grim towns of Miskolc, Ózd and Kazincbarcika, almost 400 square kilometres of the Bükk have been declared a **national park and wildlife refuge**, which can be explored superficially by train and bus, or thoroughly if you're prepared to occasionally leg it.

Exploring the Bükk

Whether you start at Eger or Miskolc is likely to determine your route through the Bükk. **From Eger**, the most direct way is to take a bus, alighting somewhere along the route to Miskolc, or a suburban train to FELSŐ-TARKÁNY – and start walking from there. Paths also lead into the Bükk from Bélapátfalva, Szilvásvárad and Nagyvisnyó (see above), and from villages to the south, accessible by bus from Eger. Arrowheads and other remains were found in the **Subalyuk cave**, a Palaeolithic dwelling 2km from BÜKKZSÉRC and CSERÉPFALU at the start of one footpath, while farther east 'rocking stones' and hollowed out pillars – used by medieval beekeepers and known as 'hive rocks' – line the tufa **Felső-szoros ravine** north of CSERÉPVÁRALJA.

From Miskolc (p.175), trains and buses go to **LILLAFÜRED**, where vacationing Trade Unionists throng the elegant old *Palace Hotel* overlooking Lake Hámori: not a tranquil place, but one with fine views, trains bursting forth from tunnels, and **caves** (*barlang*) in the vicinity. The **Anna-barlang** by the road wending up to the hotel has a long entrance passage and six chambers linked by stairs, formed from limestone tufa, while the **István-barlang**, 1km along the road to Eger, is longer and less convoluted, with a 'cupola hall' of stalactites and various pools and chambers. Two hundred yards beyond the István cave is the wooden **house of Ottó Herman** (1835-1944), where the naturalist and ethnographer spent many years trapping and mounting local wildlife. Stuffed boars, birds and rodents plus an extraordinary collection of giant beetles are the main attraction, but you can also see Ótto's top hat, butterfly nets and a letter from Kossuth. The **Szeleta-barlang** – where prehistoric spearheads were discovered – is tucked away above the road back to Miskolc, and all three caves may only be visited with a guide. Tours start roughly every hour at the entrances (between 9am-5pm/from October 16 to April 15, 9am-4pm).

Filled with shrieking children, **open trains** run from Lillafüred past **Lake Hámori** (opportunities for boating) up to ÚJMASSA in the Garadna Valley, which divides the Bükk plateau. Here **Henrik Fazola**, a Bavarian-born locksmith of Eger, established a blast furnace, while his son Frigyes built a foundry. Today it's a peaceful industrial ruin, surrounded by ferns, giant wild rhubarb and the camps of **charcoal burners**, who live for part of the year in the forests.

From ÓMASSA, further along the valley, it's a few hours walk up a well marked path to **Mount Bálvány**, south of which lies the 'Great Meadow' (*Nagymezõ*) where horses graze. A ski chalet *Síház* and two **more peaks**, Nagy-Csipkés (822m) and Zsérci-Nagy-Dél (875m), can be reached to the east, but more impressive crags lie to the south – Tárkő (950m) and Istállóskő. South of Tárkő the land drops rapidly, and water from the plateau descends through sinkholes, bursting forth in a spring at Vörös-kő ('red rock'). Amongst the Bükk's **flora** are violet blue monkshood which blooms at the end of summer, yellow lady's slipper – an endangered species in Europe – and the Turk's cap lily. Abandoned quarries are the habitat of the **Rock Thrush**, while the non-poisonous 'smooth' snake, various species of dormice and the **Imperial Eagle** (*Aquila heliaca*) tend to keep out of sight. During winter when the plateau is covered with snow, rising stream marks the entrances to

sinkholes which carry the water deep underground to springs (*forrás*) in the foothills.

Practical details and accommodation

If you're planning more than just a ride up the Garadna Valley, a *Bükk hegység* map is essential. Since paths are well marked and settlements are rarely more than 15km apart, it's hard to go far astray **walking**, but a few **preparations** are advisable. Food and supplies should be purchased beforehand, together with insect repellent/bite cream and a canteen. Drinking water (*ivóvíz*) isn't always available, though many of the springs are pure and delicious.

The cheapest **accommodation** is at *Túristaszálló* and *Túristaház*, which should be booked in advance from IBUSZ and other agencies in Eger or Miskolc. The most useful are at Sikfőkúti (near Noszvaj, northeast of Eger); Bánkúti, 1km southeast of Mount Bálvány; and Bükkszentkéreszt, west of Miskolc. **HOLLÓS-TETŐ**, along the bus route between Miskolc and Eger, has a hotel and a campsite, both prone to overcrowding. In addition, there are hotels at Noszvaj and Felsőtarkány, a private accommodation bureau at Losconci u. 21 in Lillafüred, and a campsite – officially reserved for Young Pioneers – between Újmassa and Ómassa. Though it's illegal, some young Hungarians also camp out in the rain shelters – *esőház* – dotted throughout the mountains. Hollós-tető and Bükkszentkereszt can both be reached by walking from BÜKKSZENTLÁSZLÓ, which is accessible by bus #68 from Marx tér in Miskolc.

MISKOLC, TOWNS ALONG THE SAJÓ, AND THE STALACTITE CAVES AT AGGTELEK

Flanking Bükk National Park to the north and east, the polluted Sajó Valley and a clot of mountains ravaged for their ores form a common geographical link between Miskolc, Ózd and Kazincbarcika, the upland's three industrialised giants. **Miskolc** – pronounced 'MISH-koltz' – is a real city; difficult to avoid, since it straddles the road and railway network; and probably worth visiting on account of its monolithic crudeness, the 'Queen's Castle' in the Diósgyőr district, and the 'thrashing' cave-baths in its resort suburb of **Miskolc-Tapolca**. **Ózd** and **Kazincbarcika** are both unadorned, industrialised towns. Ózd is a C19 settlement, parts of which look uncannily like a Rhonda Valley colliery town – in fact some early Hungarian magnates were firm subscribers to the laissez faire 'Manchester School' of economics; while Kazincbarcika is the archetypal Soviet-trained town-planner's design, one of the mega-developments of the 1950s like Dunaújváros (p.160). As such they're hardly

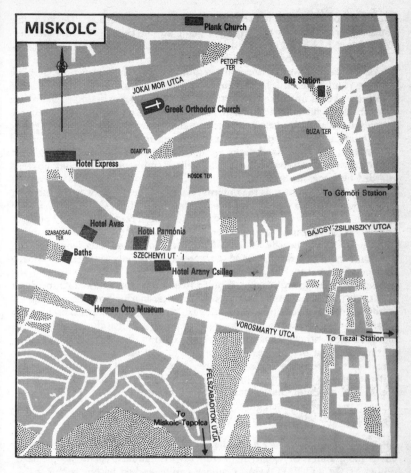

MISKOLC

Plank Church

PETOFI'S TER

JOKAI MOR UTCA

Bus Station

Greek Orthodox Church

BUZA TER

DEAK TER

Hotel Express

HOSOK TER

To Gömöri Station

Hotel Avas

SZABADSAG TER

Hotel Pannónia

BAJCSY-ZSILINSZKY UTCA

Baths

SZECHENYI UT

Hotel Arany Csillag

Herman Otto Museum

VOROSMARTY UTCA

To Tiszai Station

FELSZABADITOK UTJA

To Miskolc-Tapolca

the stuff of tourism, unlike the wonderful **stalactite caves at Aggtelek**, situated right on the Czech border, which can be reached by buses from Putnok (midway between the two towns on the railway), or directly from Ózd itself, and are well worth the journey.

MISKOLC AND MISKOLC-TAPOLCA

MISKOLC (pop. 193,000) is Hungary's second largest city, and initially discouraging. People scurry along arterial roads between endless *lakótelep*, windswept and gritty. Visually, it's only around the centre and Avas Hill that is appealing. On **Széchenyi út**, the main shopping street, Baroque buildings have been repainted in outrageous colours, and people window-shop mournfully on Saturday afternoons (when downtown virtually dies), paying visits to the *cukrászda* and churches. Slightly to the north near Hősök tere, the

Greek Orthodox Church is a real gem, concealed in a garden at 7 Deák tér. Its 16m high *iconostasis* – resembling a giant advent calander – contains the 'Black Mary of Kazan' presented by Tsarina Catherine the Great of Russia, and a cross from Mount Athos brought here by Greek refugees from the Turks. Sunday morning **services** are very impressive. By contrast the spooky wooden **Plank Church** (*Deszkatemplom*) rots away in a graveyard north of Petőfi tér, like an unwanted import from Transylvania.

South of Széchenyi útja an ornate public bathouse on Szabadság tér frames the view of **Avas Hill**, where a picturesque church and wooden belltower cling to the slope, and a maze of paths snake upwards to the observation tower on the summit. The right hand paths are more hazardous – leading through an extraordinary shantytown of tunnels, cellars, minature villas and hovels, guarded by ferocious dogs.

Diósgyőr vár – known as the **Queens' Castle** – hides in the western suburbs (bus #1 or #101); a sturdy four towered pile built in the C13-C14th, blown up in the Rákóczi wars, and recently restored with breeze blocks and poured concrete. From the intact towers there's a fine view of the city hemmed in by hills, and of the nearby Bükk mountains. **Rock and jazz concerts** are sometimes held here during the *Miskolc Summer* (roughly 19 June to 23 July), an annual festival that brings some cheer to the city.

Locals tend to go to Miskolc-Tapolca (see below) for fun, and happenings are sparse in the city. Most mornings the Buza tér **market** provides a splash of colour with its glistening fruit and veg, weather-beaten peasant women wearing layers of aprons, and squawking poultry. **Nightlife** boils down to discos in the penthouse *Tokaj* overlooking Győri út (bus #1/#101/ tram #1) or the Hungaria bar of the *Hotel Avas*, and odd jazz performances in the *jazzpince* on Széchenyi útja. Otherwise, Miskolc youth entertains itself by spraying graffiti, indulging in pills and glue, baying on the **football** terraces of the DVTK stadium and generally being truculent. (This was the only Hungarian city where I felt uneasy after nightfall). The Herman Ótto Museum just below Avas Hill has a great collection of **folk costumes**.

Miskolc-Tapolca and the cave baths

Given the drabness of the city it's hardly surprising that so many people head out to **MISKOLC-TAPOLCA**, a suburb easily reached by bus #2 or #102 from Búza tér. It's crammed with holiday homes, Young Pioneer groups, snack bars and fat cats staying at the *Hotel Juno*, mostly drawn here by the prospect of walking in the woods or the swimming pools and famous **cave baths**. Heavy petting by couples is almost the norm in this series of dimly lit warm water grottos, which culminates in a 'thrashing shower'. Unaware of Westerners' mistrust of most things nuclear, the tourist board guilelessly boasts of its 'mildly radioactive' waters – so be warned.

Transport, accommodation and moving on

Despite the city's size, transport is fairly simple in Miskolc. From the **main railway station**, the *Tiszai pályaudvar*, bus #1 runs past Búza tér, the **bus terminal**, and westwards across town to Diósgyőr and Majális Park. Trams #1 & #2 also depart from the station, and trundle along Széchenyi útja. Buses

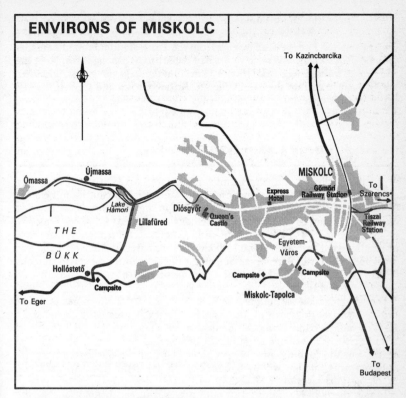

ENVIRONS OF MISKOLC

from Majális Park run to Lillafüred (#5/#105) and deeper into the Bükk, to Ómassa (#5/#115) – see p.173 for more details. **Narrow gauge trains**, leaving from the *Killian Eszák* terminal and others in the west of the city, chug up through Lillafüred and the Garadna Valley, or the more northerly Csanyik Valley.

The **hotel** *Aranycsillag* is a mite cheaper than the *Avas* – also on Széchenyi út – and the *Pannonia* on Kossuth u., but none of them should empty your wallet, and all are probably preferable to private **rooms** from the **tourist offices** at Széchenyi út 3 & 35, which will almost certainly be somewhere amongst the unnumbered *lakótelep*. (Nr. 35 is where to book rooms in the Túristaszálló should you plan to stay in BOLDOGKŐVÁRALJA, see p.181). Express, also on the mainstreet, may be able to arrange **dormitory beds** in *Nyári-Túristaszálló* (summer hostels), either in the University Town *Egyetemváros* – bus #12 from Hősök tere – or on Endre and Élod utcas, which you'll need a large **city map** to find. **Miskolc-Tapolca** has two moderately priced pensions, the *Lidó* and a the *Anna*, and a ghastly campsite like a manicured parking lot near the expensive *Hotel Juno*. If you walk up Koltói utca you'll come to a cheap *Fogadó* (Iglói út 2) which is liable to be full, and – after 2km – another **campsite** preferable to the one near the *Juno*.

Moving on, the **Bükk mountains** are an obvious destination given their proximity, though there are also regular trains to Szerencs, the Zempléni, the Great Plain and Budapest, all leaving from the Tiszai station. From the smaller *Gömöri pályaudvar*, several trains a day depart for Tornanádaska, stopping en route at **Jósvafő-Aggtelek** (about 10 km from the stalactite caves), and there are frequent trains up the Sajó Valley to **Kazincbarcika and Ózd**. If the last prospect isn't appealing, you can always take a morning Volán coach from Búza tér to Rožnava or Košice in **Czechoslovakia**. . . .

KAZINCBARCIKA AND ÓZD

A planner's dream and a resident's nightmare, **KAZINCBARCIKA** was created in the 1950s for the purpose of manufacturing chemicals and energy from the coal deposits of the north, laid out in a grid with endless rows of numbingly identical *lakótelep* ineffectually separated from the smoggy industrial zone by 1½ kilometres of withered grass. Of the three villages that originally stood here, only the **C15th churches** of Barcika and Sajókazinc and the **wooden belfry** of Berente remain, an insufficient motive for staying a night here in the *Hotel Polimer* on Bolyai tér or in a private room (from Tavasz u. 7 and Építők u. 33).

ÓZD, which likewise pollutes the River Sajó, is fractionally more appealing – its southeastern suburb of lace-curtained brick houses with pocket-sized gardens built around a wooded depression reminded me of small towns in Wales. Artisans' dwellings are gradually being replaced by tower blocks in the centre, but the foundry and oxygen plant belch smoke unchecked near the railway tracks, and few will wish to fork out to stay in the *Hotel Kohász* (Ív út 9), or the *Túristaszálló* (V.H. u. 23).

In fact the only reason to go to both places is to get **to Aggtelek** (see the following section), either by bus from **PUTNOK** which lies between Ózd and Kazincbarcika on the railway, or on the three daily buses direct from Ózd to Aggtelek. The latter depart from stand 31 of the terminal, at around 8, 12 and 3 o'clock.

STALACTITE CAVES IN THE AGGTELEKI

Like the Bükk, the Aggteleki range bordering Czechoslovakia displays karstic features, where a mixture of water and carbon dioxide has dissolved gullies, sinkholes and caves in the limestone rock. The **Baradla caves** between the villages of **Aggtelek and Jósvafő**, and the **Béke caves** to the southeast, constitute an amazing subterranean world with stygian lakes and rivers, waterfalls, countless stalactites and 262 species of wildlife. Set in remote countryside that's ideal for walking and cycling, the caves are little visited except by works' outings on national holidays.

The only difficulty is in **getting there**. Accessible by rail from Ózd, Eger, Kazincbarcika and Miskolc, **PUTNOK** is the last outpost of IBUSZ, the post office and banks, and the place to catch **buses** roughly every 1½ hours to Aggtelek and Jósvafő. **Trains** from Miskolc stop off at '*Jósvafő-Aggtelek vá*' en route to Tornanádaska, but the station is actually 10km east of Jósvafő, and with no certainty of catching a rural bus or lift to the cave entrance, it's a poor alternative.

The Caves at Aggtelek and Jósvafő

The main **Baradla cave passage** twists underground for 22km, and can be partially visited on **short tours** (lasting about 1½hrs) that begin whenever enough people have assembled at the *bejárat* entrances at either end, and providing that the guides are willing. The **Aggtelek end** of the passage is more convoluted and rewarding for a 'short tour', and from here one can also sign up for longer **trips to the Domica caves** in Czechoslovakia (no passport is needed).

Trying to describe the variety and profusion of **stalactites and stalagmites** is impossible, and nicknames like *Tortoise, Slaughter House*, and *Diamond Mountain* can only hint at the fantastic rock formations. Glittering with calcite crystals, stained ochre by iron oxides or blackened by smoke, the rocks resemble faces, bodies, fungal growths and grotesque menageries. In the 'Concert Hall' (enquire at the Aggtelek *bejárat* for performance details), boats sway on the River Styx, and the guide activates a light show and tape of Bach's *Toccata in D minor* to create a *Phantom of the Opera* ambience.

Long tours of the Baradla passage begin at the *Vörös-tó* entrance situated in a valley between the two villages, and require some stamina; 5½ hours is a long time to clamber around dank, muddy caves, however beautiful they may be. The same goes for guided tours around the **Béke caves**, which contain a sanatorium – the underground air being judged beneficial to asthmatics; most of these, however, are untamed, even unexplored, and as late as 1973 a new passage was discovered when cavers penetrated a 30m high waterfall. Visitors require boots and warm, waterproof **clothing**, and are issued helmets.

Underground wildlife – bats, rodents and bugs, mostly – keeps out of sight, and is easiest to view in the **Cave Museum** by the Aggtelek entrance, which also has photos and momentoes to gladden a speleologist's heart. Aside from the fortified church with its picturesque cemetery in Jósvafő, and the green lake – used for swimming – outside Aggtelek, both villages are unremarkable. Shops are few and social life centres around the church and *Italbolt* 'drink shop'. Aggtelek has a **campsite**, *Túristaszálló*, and the **hotel** *Cseppkő* – which serves good meals; in Jósvafő the *Hotel Tengerszem* monopolises food and accommodation.

Excursions in the surrounding countryside

The times of the **buses** between Aggtelek and Jósvafő are displayed in both hotels, but you can walk the 8km Cool Valley (Hideg völgy) to reach the Vörös-tó entrance if necessary. Other **walks** in the surrounding hills lead to **more caves** and various peaks marked on the *Aggtelek es Jósvafő környékének* tourist **maps**, which also warns of the **border zone**, where armed guards patrol with dogs. The pretty village of **RAGÁLY** lies on the bus route back to Putnok, but without transport it's difficult to reach **RUDABÁNYA**, where the 10 million year-old jawbone of *Rudapithecus hungaricus* – an ancient primate – is proudly displayed by the iron mine whence it was excavated. **EDELÉNY**, on the branch line to Miskolc, has an C18 *kastély* (mansion).

THE ZEMPLÉNI RANGE

The Zempléni range is the best region in the north – largely unspoiled by industry and tourism, and richly textured by nature and history. Tokaj, the centre of the *Tokaj-Hegyalja* wine-making district, absorbs most tourists, and surprisingly few make it up to Sárospatak, site of the superb Rákóczi castle, or beyond to the little Zempléni villages.

Most people approaching by road or rail usually go through SZERENCS, the junction between Nyíregyháza, Miskolc, Tokaj and the northern Zempléni. A drab town with a reeking chocolate factory and sugar refinery responsible for most of Hungary's output, its only claim to merit is the fortified manor – called a castle – which now serves as a hotel in the park at the far end of Rákóczi út.

TOKAJ

TOKAJ is to Hungary what champagne is to France, and this small town has become a minor Mecca for wine snobs. Perched beside the confluence off the Rivers Bodrog and Tisza, it is a place of sloping cobbled streets and faded ochre dwellings with nesting storks and wine cellars – overlooked by lush vineyards climbing the hillside towards the 'Bald Peak' and the inevitable TV transmission tower. From the railway station it's 10 minutes' walk under the arch and left along Münnich F. utca to the old town centre, just past the bridge (which leads over to the campsite). Here are the first of the wine-cellars (*bor pince*) which pop up along the mainstreet to Kossuth tér, interspersed with fried fish (*sült hal*) shops, and the rainbow-striped *Hotel Tokaj*. Further along are the few architectural 'sights' – the old Town Hall and Rákóczi-Desseweffy mansion and a ruined castle by the river – but inevitably it's wine that attracts most people's attention in Tokaj.

The three main Tokaj wines – *Furmint* (dry), *Aszú* (sweet) and *Hárslevelű* (Linden leaf) – all derive their character from the special soil, the prolonged sunlight, and the wine-making techniques developed here. Heat is trapped by the volcanic loess soil, allowing a delayed harvest in October, when many over-ripe grapes have a sugar content approaching 60%. The juice and paste from these is added by the *puttony* (butt) to 136-litre barrels of ordinary grapes, and the number of butts determines the taste and qualities of the wine: rich and sweet or slightly 'hot', with an oily consistency, ranging in colour from golden yellow to reddish brown.

Though some may find *Aszú* too sweet, Tokaj wine has collected some notable accolades since the late Middle Ages. Beethoven and Schubert dedicated songs to it; Louis XVI declared it 'the wine of kings, the king of wines'; Goethe, Voltaire, Heine and Browning all praised it; and Sherlock Holmes used it to toast the downfall of Von Bork, after troubling Watson to 'open the window, for chloroform vapour does not help the palate'. The Pince Múzeum (Bethlen G. u. 18) complacently displays wine labels from the

Crimea, France and the Rhineland, where attempts to reproduce Tokaj all failed; but the favourite place for pilgrimage is the **Rákóczi cellar** at Kossuth tér 16, where Mrs Borika Vajtho presides over 24 cobwebby chandelier-lit passages containing 20,000 hectolitres of wine. It's as much a takeaway as a place to drink, though, and locals prefer the cheaper *Vendéglős* or the contents of their private cellars.

Other pursuits on offer include rowing, water-skiing and swimming in the Tisza (though the last is officially forbidden). Eating, like the wine, is a serious business. The *Halász Csárda* near the bridgehead specialises in fish dishes and schmaltzy violin music, the places around Kossuth tér are unpretentious, and the *Vendéglő* beyond features **jazz bands and dancing** until 1am some nights. Over the river by the campsite is an open-air bar/disco, patronised by inebriated conscripts and Tokaj's youth. The town's hotel is fairly expensive, and I'd recommend a private **room** or a bungalow from the **tourist office** located on the **campsite**, which is pleasantly shady but plagued by mosquitoes.

VILLAGES, CASTLES AND WALKING IN THE TOKAJ-HEGYALJA

Behind Tokaj's Kossuth tér, a road winds up to the summit of 'Bald Peak' through vineyards, each carefully labelled with its owner's name. From beside the TV tower (which is guarded to prevent photography) views scan the distant Plain and the lush green Tokaj-Hegyalja: the wine-growing region covering the western and southern slopes of the Zempléni. Some of the **Tokaj-Hegyalja villages** are beautifully sited, with the odd historic monument, while higher in the mountains, ruined castles brood on crags awaiting visitors. Most once belonged to the Rákóczi family (see below). One such in **TOLCSVA**, a village better known for its **Linden leaf wine** – *Tolcsvai hárslevelű* – can be reached on the hourly Komlóska bus from Tokaj.

From Szerencs, seven trains a day strain up the Hernád Valley to Hídasnémeti, stopping at a string of settlements. Grape-growing **MÁD** is but a prelude to **TÁLLYA**, the second largest producer after Tokaj, where visitors can see a former Rákóczi mansion and the fount in which Kossuth was baptised. **BOLDOGKŐVÁRALJA**, 2½km from its train halt, is the site of a massive, partially ruined **C13 castle** which now houses a *Túristaszálló*. (Reservations should be made in Miskolc, at Széchenyi út 35). Hikers might enjoy a hard day's **walking** between Regéc and Gönc, on an ill-marked path skirting the 787m high Gergely-Hegy. **GÖNC** is set in splendid countryside and famed for the making of 136-litre **barrels** (called *Gönc*), traditionally used to store Tokaj wine. You can also get there on the Hidasnémeti train, which is just as well as **REGÉC** – the starting point for the walk – lies some 7km from its own train halt of *Korlát-Vizsoly*. Discounting private rooms in TELKIBÁNYA (10 km east of Gönc) and Boldogkővaralja's tourist hostel, there's officially **no accommodation** in this neck of the woods. Walkers should be prepared to camp wild or rely on sympathetic locals, and bring food and a **map** of the *Zempléni hegység*.

SÁROSPATAK

Half an hour's train journey from Szerencs, **SÁROSPATAK** ('muddy stream') basks on the banks of the Bodrog. Walking from the train or bus station through Iskola Park, you'll pass statues of famous alumni – testifying to Sárospatak's once significant role in Hungarian intellectual life which led Magyars given to hyperbole to describe the town as an 'Athens on the Bodrog' – before reaching the Calvinist College on Rákóczi út, the main street leading towards Sárospatak Castle. If resident scholars like Comenius brought Sárospatak prestige, it was the **Rákóczi family**, who really put the town on the map. When Prince György I the 'first' Rákóczi acquired **Sárospatak Castle** in 1616, the family power base was in Transylvania, but subsequently the impetuous György II aroused the wrath of the Turkish Sultan and the clan had to hop it to Habsburg-controlled Hungary. Here the counter reformation was in full swing, and Magyar landlords and peasants reacted against Habsburg confiscations by sporadically ferocious revolts of 'dissenters' (*kuruc*). The original revolt led by Imre Thököly was bloodily crushed in 1685, but rekindled into a full-scale war of independence in 1703. At its head was **Ferenc Rákóczi II** (1676-1735), who after initial hesitations led the Hungarians from victory to victory. But by 1711 the Magyars were exhausted and divided, abandoned by their half-hearted ally Louis XIV of France, and Rákóczi fled into exile as his armies collapsed under the weight of superior Habsburg power.

In the Renaissance wings grouped around a courtyard, the **museum** dotes on the Rákóczi dynasty, even down to a series of watercolours depicting the stages of Ferenc's exile (he died in Tekirdag, in Turkey). Heavy inlaid furniture, jewellery, monstrous stoves and a banqueting hall (complete with piped court music and portraits of tipplers) recreates domestic life *chez* Rákóczi. Among the paintings are life-size depictions of Rákóczi's fearsome irregular cavalry (*század*), and the portrait of Ferenc by Ádám Mányoki that's reproduced on 50Ft banknotes. A romantic C17 loggia, like a prop from *Romeo and Juliet*, joins the residential wings to the C15 keep, known as the **'Red Tower'**. Guided tours take in the dungeons and underground wells, the labyrinth of galleries used by gunners, and a series of impressive halls. The 'Knights' Hall', somehow austere despite its throne and stained glass windows, saw sessions of Parliament during the Independence War, while in the adjoining circular balcony room, anti-Habsburg plots were hatched during the *Kuruc* wars. (Its ceiling is decorated with a stucco rose – hence the expression *sub rosa*, meaning conspiratorial).

Back down Rákóczi út and past the post office, monuments to Sárospatak's cultural eminence face each other on Eötvös J. utca. The Baroque **Comenius College** is colourfully tiled in pink, but outbrazened by the **Művelődesi ház**; a gleaming glass and steel community centre with a bizarre insectile frontage, designed by Imre Mákovecz, who heads a team of Hungary's most avant garde architects. Opposite Iskola Park, the original Calvinist college still functions, and visitors can see the gorgeously ornamented **Great Library** (*Nagykönyvtár*), where Kossuth, Gárdonyi, Zsigmond Móricz and other notables once swotted for their exams.

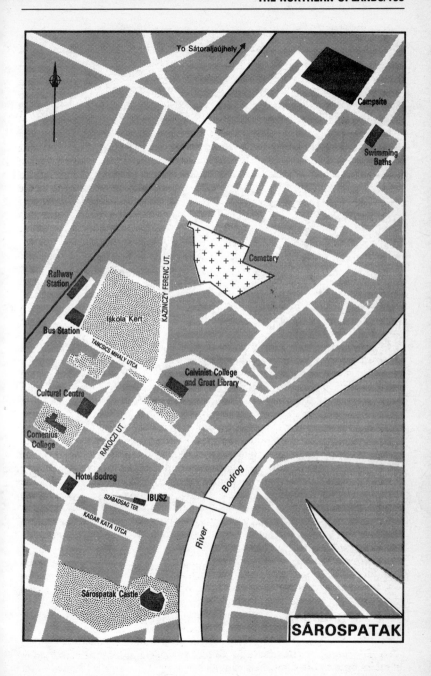

To Sátoraljaújhely

Campsite

Swimming Baths

Cemetery

Railway Station

KAZINCZY FERENC UT.

Iskola Kert

Bus Station

TANCSICS MIHALY UTCA

Calvinist College and Great Library

Cultural Centre

RAKOCZI UT.

Comenius College

Hotel Bodrog

IBUSZ

SZABADSAG TER

KADAR KATA UTCA

Bodrog

River

Sárospatak Castle

SÁROSPATAK

Of the two **hotels**, the *Bodrog*, overlooking Szabadsag tér, is slightly dearer than the *Borostyán* on Kádar u. near the castle, while private **rooms** from IBUSZ/Borsodtourist on Kossuth u., and Miklós Martin at Kazinczy út 28, are cheaper than both. Kazinczy út – a continuation of Rákóczi út beyond the Calvinist College – eventually leads to a **swimming pool** and an expensive but well-equipped **campsite**. The *Megyer kisvendéglő* opposite the Hotel Bodrog and supermarket is the place to eat, drink and meet local students.

SÁTORALJAÚJHELY AND THE RUINED CASTLE OF FÜZÉR

Easier to reach than it is to pronounce – try saying 'SHAR-tor-all-oowee-hay' – **SÁTORALJAÚJHELY** is the last Zempléni town before the border crossing to Slovenskí Nové Mesto in Czechoslovakia. It's a split-level town, perched on the slopes of Mount Magas (509m), surrounded by ravines and thick forests – ideal terrain for partisans who fought against the Czechs in 1919 and the Nazis in 1944 (both times without success, however). A massive wooden church, sinister beyond the dreams of Hammer Horror, rots outside the railway station, while uphill on Várhegy utca are the remains of a castle, and a *Túristaház* and campsite.

Lajos Kossuth (1802-94), leading light of the 1848 revolution and de facto dictator during the subsequent war of independence, began his political career as a lawyer in Sátoraljaújhely, representing the interests of local gentry who were too lazy to do so themselves. His famous oratory was first displayed on the balcony of the Town Hall (Ady tér 5) during the Zempléni chorlera epidemic and riots of 1830, but shortly afterwards Kossuth quit the highlands for Budapest, where he edited the scandal-mongering *Pesti Hirlap* and entered Parliament.

Northwest of town the hills roll in ridges, working up to rocky spines laden with clumps of conifers, and highland valleys containing some of the most unspoilt villages in Hungary. From Sátoraljaújhely, buses bound for Hollóháza pass through **FÜZÉR**, an idyllic village of whitewashed cottages, vines and sunflowers, inhabited by dignified elders and wandering animals. Depending on the time of day, Füzér's social centre shifts from the tiny church to the *Italbolt* and then the bus stop, for the last buses to Hollóháza (20.57) and Sátoraljaújhely (18.53).

Almost directly overhead but screened by trees is **the castle**, one of the many erected in the C13 in case of a re-invasion by the Mongols. From the huge Gothic arches of its ruined chapel one has a magnificent view of blue-green mountains along the border, and the distant Plain, enlivened by flocks of swifts swooping and soaring on the powerful thermals.

Accommodation is available in Füzér's Bodnár Józsefné school, which is signposted, and there's plenty of space for unofficial camping either nearby or outside **PÁLHÁZA**, a village some 12km back along the road to Sátoraljaújhely.

LEAVING HUNGARY FROM THE NORTH

Guardsmen patrolling with alsatians just north of Aggtelek and Nagybörzsöny are an unpleasant sign of **the border with Czechoslovakia**, which was drawn by force majeure in 1918-20, when the Czech Legion wrested highland Slovakia from Hungary. Hitherto, Magyar rule had extended over intermingled Slovak and Hungarian communities stretching from Košice (known to the Magyars as *Kassa*) to Bratislava (formerly *Pozsony*), and the imposition of a new and bitterly resented frontier created economic havoc and severed many families and friends. However, compared to the Magyars of Romania, the Hungarians of Czechoslovakia are well treated (although signs of a Slovak nationalist backlash have recently appeared) and relations between the two countries have steadily improved over the decades.

Therefore, providing you've already obtained a Czech *visa* (apply at home, or at the consulate in Budapest, 14 days in advance) there shouldn't be any great difficulties involved in **getting across**. Motorists can use any of the following 24-hour checkpoints: PARASSAPUSZTA in the Börzsöny; BALAS-SAGYARMAT; SOMOSKŐÚJFALU, north of Salgótarján; TORNYOS-NÉMETI; and a few miles beyond SÁTORALJAÚJHELY. Some of the Slovakian towns beyond can be reached **by Volán coach**; most weekday mornings there are coaches **from Miskolc** to ROŽNAVA and KOŠICE, and **from Salgótarján and Balassagyarmat** to LUSENEC. Since hitch-hiking seems decidedly dodgy, the only alternative to taking a coach is the Sofia-Warsaw *Polonia Express*, which stops briefly at Salgótarján around one in the morning. . .an unappealing prospect.

Finally, it's just conceivable that someone might take advantage of the Volán **bus from Ózd to Uzhgorod in the Soviet Carpathians**. However, one must already be in possession of a Russian *visa* (apply 2 weeks before at the consulate in Budapest), which will only be valid for the date and place of entry specified on your visa-application, so it's hardly a journey for the flexible traveller.

FESTIVALS

Summer
Jazz, rock, classical music etc. during the MISKOLC Summer (roughly **June** **19-July 23**). Concerts in the stalactite caves at AGGTELEK as advertised.

TRAVEL DETAILS

Trains
From Budapest to Miskolc, express (11 daily; 2-2½hrs); Tokaj (1; 2¾); Sártoral-jaújhely (2; 4).
From Éger to Putnok (4; 3).
From Füzesabony to Éger (hourly; 20mins).
From Gyöngyös to Mátrafüred (hourly; 1hr).

From Hatvan to Salgótarján (7 daily; 1½hrs).
From Miskolc to Kazincbarcika (½hr), Putnok (1hr) and Ózd (2hrs), 7 daily; Tornanádaska (8 daily; 2hrs); Nyíregy-háza (8; 2); Sártoraljaújhely (3; 1½); Szerencs (hourly; ½).
From Szerencs to Mád, Tállya, Boldogkőváralja and Gönc (7 daily);

frequent services to Tokaj, Miskolc and Nyíregyháza.

Buses
From Balassagyarmat to Szécsény & Salgótarján (hourly; ½-1hr).
From Eger to Miskolc via the Bükk (6-7 daily; 1½hrs); to Szilvásvárad (hourly; 1hr).
From Füzesabony to Tiszafüred (hourly; ¾hr).
From Gyöngyös to Eger (4-5 daily; 1hr); Mátrafüred (every 20mins; ½hr); Mátraháza (hourly; ½hr).
From Hatvan to Gyöngyös (hourly; ½); Hollókő (3 daily; 1½).
From Hollókő to Szécsény (3 daily; ¾); Hatvan (3; 1½).
From Miskolc to Bükkszentlászló (20 mins; ¾hr); Eger (6-7 daily; 1½); Lillafüred (20mins; ½); Miskolc-Tapolca (10mins; ¼); Ómassa (20mins; ¾).
From Ózd to Aggtelek (3 daily; 1½).
From Putnok to Aggtelek (5-6 daily; ½).
From Sárospatak to Sátoraljaújhely (hourly; 20mins).
From Sártoraljaújhely to Füzér (hourly; ¾).
From Szécsény to Hollókő (3 daily; ¾).

International trains
From Salgótarján to Warsaw (1 daily).

International coaches
All services depart in the morning, weekdays only.
From Balassagyarmat to Lusenec in Czechoslovakia.
From Miskolc to Rožnava or Košice in Czechoslovakia.
From Ózd to Uzhgorod in the USSR.
From Salgótarján to Lusenec.

Chapter six
THE GREAT PLAIN

Covering more than half of Hungary and awesome in its flatness, the **Great Plain**, or *puszta*, can shimmer like the mirages (*délibáb* which occur around Hortobágy), or be as drab as a farmworker's boots. Chance encounters and fleeting details are often more interesting than 'sights' on the Plain, and if vast herds no longer roam freely as in the C19, many villages look virtually unchanged; their whitewashed *tanya* hung with strings of paprika, and long-armed wells and clouds of geese about.

Szeged and **Debrecen** are pleasant cities with large student populations usually eager to befriend foreigners, and annual **festivals** – the Szeged Weeks and Debrecen's Flower Carnival. These coincide with Hungary's national day (August 20), also marked by the folklore Csűr at **Nagykálló**, and the Bridge Fair and Horse Show at **Hortobágy**. The latter is one of two **national parks** (the other is at **Bugac**) where the original grassland and animals of the *puszta* have been preserved. Baja, Kecskemét, Hajdúszoboszló, Nyírbátor and a few other **towns** shine for various reasons, but the real character of the old *puszta* is to be found in the **villages**. Mostly one-street affairs with names prefixed *Nagy-* or *Kis-*, Big or Little, they grow older and poorer the further east one travels. A few adventurous travellers make it to Szabolcs-Szatmár County bordering on Romania and the USSR, where the majority of Hungary's **Gypsies** live, and see the homeland of the thousands of migrant workers who commute each week on the 'black train' to menial jobs and grim hostels in Budapest.

A little about the puszta

The Magyar word *puszta* is practically synonymous with the Great Plain (*az Alföld*), but it's a name that bespeaks of the transformation of this huge lowland. During medieval times **the Plain** was thickly forested, with hundreds of settlements living by agriculture and livestock-rearing, and the mighty **River Tisza**, fed by its tributaries in Transylvania and Maramureş, determined all. Each year it flooded, its hundreds of loops merging into a 'sea of water in which the trees were sunk to their crowns', enriching the soil with volcanic silt from the uplands, and isolating the villages for months on end. But the Turkish invasion of 1526 unleashed a scourge upon the land, 150 years of nearly unceasing warfare. Those peasants as survived fled to the safer *khasse* (tribute paying) towns like Szeged and Debrecen, leaving their villages to fall into ruin, while vast tracts of forest were felled to build military stockades, or burned simply to deny cover to the *Hajdúk* (anti-Turkish partisans). Denuded of vegetation, the land became swampy and pestilent with mosquitoes, and later the abode of solitary swineherds, runaway serfs, outlaws (*betyár*) and

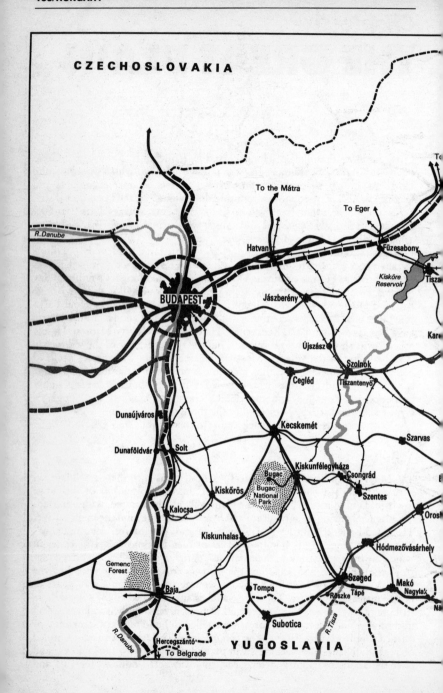

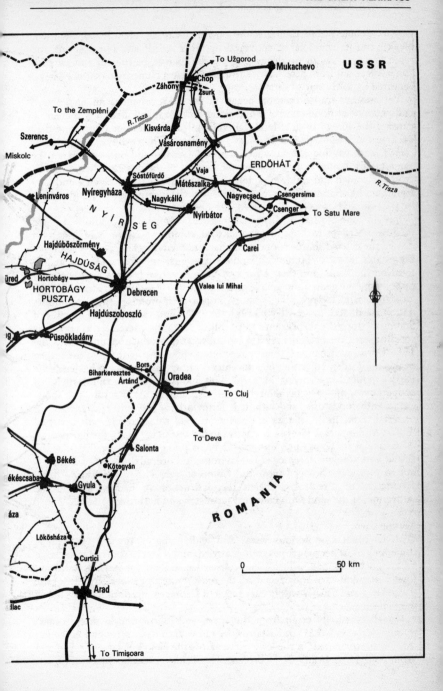

wolves. People began calling it **the puszta**, meaning 'abandoned, deserted, bleak'; and its character is conveyed by other words and phrases with the same root, eg: *pusztít* (to devastate), *pusztul* (perish, be ruined) and *pusztulj innen* (Clear out from here!). Not surprisingly, most Hungarians shunned it, or ventured in solely out of dire necessity.

Yet another transformation began in the C19, when as an unexpected consequence of flood-control work along the Tisza, soil alkalinity increased, causing the spread of **grassland**. Suitable only for pasturage, with time they became the 'Hungarian Wild West'; complete with cowboys, rough-riding *csikós*, and wayside *csárda* where lawmen, Gypsies and outlaws shared the same tables, bound not to fight by the custom of the puszta. It was a man's world – women and children remained in the tanyas close to town – and C19 romantics like Sándor Petőfi rhapsodised it as the incarnation of Magyardom. 'My world and home. . ..the Alföld, the open sea'.

But by the 1920s reality had crushed romance. Irrigation enabled landowners to grow crops on, and enclose, common pasture. Mechanisation denied the evicted share-croppers and herders even the chance of work on the big estates. Most of Hungary's landless peasants, or '**three million beggars**', lived on the Plain, and their efforts to from Agrarian leagues were violently opposed by the gentry and gendarmerie, particularly around *Viharsarok* – the 'Stormy centre', today's Békés County. True to their promises, the Communists **nationalised land** 'for those who till it' in 1949, but, following the dictates of Stalinism, forced the peasants into collective farms thereafter. Treated as socialist serfs, the peasants reverted to subsistence production, and during the 1956 Uprising disbanded 'their' collectives (while vowing to resist the return of the landlords). Since the '60s, **incentives** rather than coercion has been the Party's policy; investment in rural light industry; the encouragement of cooperatives, and a general nod to self-enrichment. As a result, the shops groan with foodstuffs, and although farmworkers may still rise at 3am, in material terms most villages are better off, and some co-ops even boast of 'Forint Millionaires'. However, relative to the rest of the Plain, the northeast – in particular its Gypsy population – remains poor; while some fear that the Alföld as a whole is threatened by enviromental degradation. As in Britain – but to please the Soviet Union and Comecon rather than the EEC – over-production of cereals has meant the destruction of hedgerows and the saturation of the land with chemical fertilisers and herbicides.

Getting there

With its often monotonous vistas and widely spaced towns, the Plain is something most people cross as much as visit, and if you're short of time, large areas can be skipped with a clear conscience. Except for Baja, Kecskemét, Bugac National Park and Szeged, all the most interesting places are east of the River Tisza and usually within easy reach of Debrecen, the unofficial capital of the Plain.

Travellers usually begin **from Budapest**, and follow one of three routes: through Kalocsa (rd.51) or Kiskőrös (by railway) to Baja; through Kecskemét (rd.E5/rail) to Szeged; or the long curve across the Plain by way of Cegléd and Szolnok (E15/rd.4/rail) to Debrecen. The Friday evening '**black train**' to

Debrecen is notorious for drunken passengers (homebrewed *pálinka* is sold in the toilets), gambling, thefts and brawls, so women travellers in particular should avoid using it. Foreigners are likely to be accosted by Gypsies, whom the train's barmen accurately described as 'good company, but then they drink all their wages and want to fight'. There are also trains from Budapest to Békéscsaba in the southeast.

Debrecen can also be reached **from the northern highlands** (by trains from Miskolc, Szerencs and Tokaj), while people crossing the river at Dunaföldvár or Baja **from Transdanubia** are virtually forced towards Kecskemét and Szeged by road – there are no direct trains, but plenty of Volán buses. **Hitching** along the E15 to and from Debrecen seems fairly okay, and might be feasible along other major roads. Between some towns and villages, slow **trains** (*személyvonat*) are the only form of public transport, but at all costs avoid them for the long hauls.

BETWEEN THE DANUBE AND THE TISZA

Approaching from the direction of Budapest, Transdanubia or Yugoslavia, one's first experience of the Plain is of the region **between the Danube and the Tisza**. Here only a few towns are worth a visit, and the old puszta grasslands have shrunk to a remnant, now protected as **Bugac National Park**. To reach Kalocsa or Baja by railway from Budapest it's necessary to switch onto branch lines at Kiskőrös or Kiskunhalas.

SOUTH TO BAJA AND KALOCSA

Road 51 isn't exactly scenic, and the main reason for taking it is BAJA, a nice town on the lower Danube and a river crossing. Along the way is **KALOCSA**, a two street town much promoted by IBUSZ on account of the '**Painting Women**' who once specialised in flowery murals here, and **Kalocsa embroidery**, nowadays made by local women in factories. From the bus station, István Király út leads past *Pusztatourist*, the *Hotel Piros Arany* (nr. 37) and the **Viski Károly Museum** (nr.25) to the Cathedral, whose scruffy façade belies its delicate pink and gold interior. Upstairs in the museum is a terrific collecton of folk costumes from the C19 Hungarian, Swabian (*Sváb*) and Slovak ('*tot*') communities, plus an array of the overstuffed bolsters and quilts which were mandatory for a bride's dowery. ('Why should I spend months sewing them, for some fat pig to muddy with his boots ?' asks a woman in one of Panaït Istrati's *Haidouc* novels).

The passion for floral motifs, evident on the clothes, took full flight in the *tiszta szoba* or 'clean room' of peasant households, where guests were welcomed. Boldly painted flowers border the rooms in the **Folk Art House** (*Népmüvészeti Szövetkezet*) on Tompa utca, signposted near the hospital on Kossuth utca, 300m beyond the Cathedral.

BAJA, 76 km further south, has an almost mediterranean feel, with everyone taking an evening promenade up and down Eötvös utca, and young bloods revving their motorcycles loudly on Béke tér. The shady riverbanks along the Sugovica branch of the Danube, and the **island of Petőfi sziget** (with facilities for fishing, swimming and boating) are really the main attractions: this is basically a place to rest up. The 'sights' were all under restoration when I was here, but neither the Turr István Museum (Roosevelt tér, off the main square), the Greek Orthodox church on Táncsics u. (reputed to have a fine iconostasis), or the ugly Synagogue on Munkácsy utca looked very exciting anyway.

Béke tér, the mellow baroque main square overlooking the river, includes two **tourist offices** and the *Hotel Duna*. The latter is cheap, and hosts **discos** on Wednesday and Sunday, 7-11pm; live music is sometimes also featured in the *Belvárosi cukrászda*, and on Saturdays there are discos in the costlier *Hotel Sugovica* on the island, near the campsite which is the cheapest place to stay (and is overrun by pheasants around dawn).

From the long distance terminal on Marx tér, buses cross the river into southern Transdanubia, cover various points as far east as Szeged, and even strike off for Subotica in Yugoslavia. At time of writing, the 6.50 train to PÖRBÖLY enables one to catch the 7.30 train from there up to the FOREST OF GEMENC, a lovely nature reserve on the west bank of the Danube (p.160).

FURTHER EAST: KECSKEMÉT AND BUGAC NATIONAL PARK

Seventy kilometers southeast of Budapest, en route to Kecskemét or Debrecen, **CEGLÉD** is a sleepy town where the peasants have twice been roused to arms. Both occasions are commemorated in the museum on Rákóczi út (between the railway station and the centre), where a large oil painting in the foyer depicts the gory end of György Dózsa, leader of the 1514 Peasants' Revolt; and proclamations and assorted bric-à-brac recall Lajos Kossuth, who abolished serfdom and fought against the Habsburgs, before fleeing into exile in 1849.

Szabadság tér is glorified by two churches, IBUSZ and the bus terminal, and there's a fairly lively **market** off Kossuth tér, but this is no town to stop for more than an hour or so. If you're pressed, the one hotel is at Rákóczi út 1. Most trains head east towards Debrecen, but some, and numerous buses, go south – passing through NAGYKŐRÖS, which has nothing to reccomend it barring an ornamental garden (*Cifrakert*), to Kecskemét.

Kecskemét

Hungarians associate **KECSKEMÉT** with *barackpálinka* (the local apricot brandy), and Zoltán Kodály, the composer and musicologist born in the building now used as a railway station. From the station or bus terminal, it's a

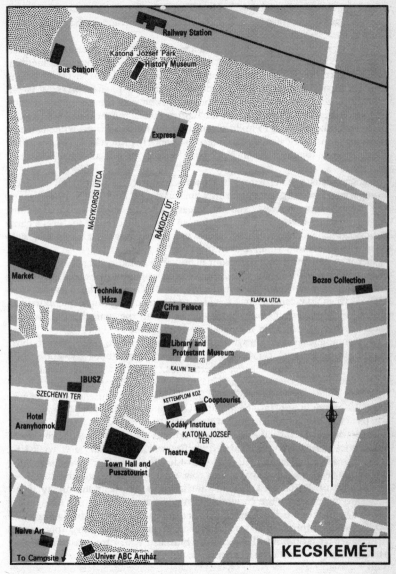

Railway Station

Katona József Park
History Museum

Bus Station

Express

NAGYKŐRŐSI UTCA

RÁKÓCZI ÚT

Market

Bozso Collection

Technika
Háza

Cifra Palace

KLAPKA UTCA

Library and
Protestant Museum

KALVIN TER

IBUSZ

SZECHENYI TER

KETTEMPLOM KOZ   Cooptourist

Hotel
Aranyhomok

Kodály Institute

KATONA JOZSEF
TER

Theatre

Town Hall and
Puszatourist

Naive Art

KECSKEMÉT

To Campsite   Univer ABC Aruház

few minutes walk through the park and down Rákóczi út or Nagykőrösi u. to
the **town centre**, where four handsome squares merge. Kecskemét's chief
charm is its **architecture**: the exuberant Art Nouveau **Cifra palace**, a
gingerbread fantasy sprouting enammeled mushrooms from its roof (now an
art gallery); the white, moorish onion-domed **Technika-háza** (once a
synagogue); the long 'Transylvanian' style **Library** with a central tower and

steeply-pitched roof; and the **Town Hall** with its lavish interiors (by Bertalan Székely) and ornate façade, a deliberate attempt by Ödön Lechner to create a 'Hungarian' style in the 1890s.

On Kéttemplom köz, adjoining the main square, the **Institute of Music Teaching** (*Zenepedagógiai Intézet*) continues to apply the ideas and methods of **Zoltán Kodály** (1882-1967), who believed that 'only actively taking part in music can make you an understander of music – passive listening is not enough'. International students attending the **one year course** are exhorted to approach music teaching through the human voice, 'the most easily accessible instrument for all', and to build on their native folk traditions when teaching children, a task that Kodály considered supremely important: 'No one is too great to write for the little ones' he said, 'in fact one has to strive to be great enough'.

Kecskemét is equally proud of **József Katona** (1791-1830) the 'father' of Hungarian classical drama, who was born and died here and left his name to the **theatre** (unsuprisingly) and the street on which it stands. Its company, directed by the film-maker **Miklós Jancsó**, has a reputation for avant garde productions, and when I was there they were staging *Dr.Faustus*, with Mephistopheles in a Stalin T-shirt.

Other things on the cultural front include the Bozso collection of **paintings** (Klapka u.34, off Rákóczi út), the endearing applique-work and pictures in the **Naive Art Museum** (south of Május 1. tér), and the **Toy Museum** (*Sorakatenus*) at Gáspár A. u. 11, which organises **play groups** for children (all closed on Monday). **The Protestant Museum** (in the main library) and the local **History Museum** (in the park) are pretty dull, though.

Accommodation boils down to three **hotels** – *Szauna*, *Aranyhomok* (both central) and *Szőlőfürt* (on the ring road), all charging about 700-800Ft for a double – plus various cheaper alternatives, namely a **private room** from *Pusztatourist* (in the Town Hall), IBUSZ or *Cooptourist* (Kéttemplom köz 9); **dormitory beds** *Express* (Rákóczi út 32) during July/August; or the **campsite** from 200m down Sport u., beyond the Uszoda **swimming pool** (bus #1 from the terminal, #1 or #11 from Május 1 tér).

Places to eat include the restaurants around the *Aranyhomok*, the cheap self-service *Hirös étterem* (Rákóczi út 3), and the *Tejbár* next to IBUSZ (recommended for breakfast). In the arcade off Kossuth tér, the *Delicatesse cukrászda* serves delicious cakes and ices, while you can find other snacks at the **market** on Budai utca, behind the *Centrum Aruház*. On Sunday nights there are **discos** above the *Univer ABC Aruház* at the corner of Dobó u. and Petőfi u. A limited stock of **English books** can be unearthed at the *Antikvárium* opposite Cooptourist, and it's as well to know that 2 forint coins, not pre-paid tickets, are used on **buses**. Lastly, don't brandish your camera (let alone take **photos**) near the Russian barracks on Izsáki út.

Kiskunfélegyháza and Bugac National Park.

About 6km south of Kecskemét a picturesque **windmill** stands by the road, taken from the courtyard of the Kiskun (Little Cumanian) Museum at Vörös Hadsereg út 9, thus robbing **KISKUNFÉLEGYHÁZA** of one of its two sights. The other is the Town Hall, an ornate Art Nouveau pile which brightens up this otherwise rather drab town; more primitive than Kecskemét and seemingly resentful of the fact. There's a cheapish hotel on Petőfi tér, and a tourist-trap *csárda* opposite the Town Hall, but Kiskunfélegyháza's most useful feature is the bus service to Bugac (about every 1½hrs).

BUGAC NATIONAL PARK begins 3km beyond Bugac village, and buses pass by the entrance before continuing on to Jakabszállás along a new road (unmarked on most maps). From the entrance it's a walk of about 4km along a sandy track to the park's centre; past flower-speckled meadows and lounging *juhász* shepherds, under an immense sky. *Csikós* in traditional white pantaloons bestride this remnant of the *puszta*, cracking whips and stampeding horses for the benefit of geriatric Germans, who are then ferried away in buggies for lunch at the local *csárda*. In the small **Pásztormúzeum** are shepherds' felted cloaks and hand-carved pipes, and a grotesque tobacco pouch formed from a ram's scrotum.

Open Tuesday-Sunday, 10am-5pm, from May 1 to October 31, the Park can also be reached **directly from Kecskemét** by narrow gauge railway (trains depart at 7.55am and 2.30pm) or by **coach tours** organised by Express. Kecskemét's Pusztatourist can book **beds** in the village, or you can make your own deals at nr.37 on Bugac's mainstreet. **Farmstead accommodation** is available from the Lenin Cooperative by prior arrangement at 1, Blaha Lujza tér in Kiskunfélegyháza (☎ 169).

SZEGED

SZEGED straddles the Tisza like a provincial Budapest, 'Great' and 'Small' boulevards encircling its Belváros, as cosmopolitan a place as you'll find on the Plain. Much of its friendly atmosphere is due to students, who throng the downtown area, while the old city's eclectic good looks have been saved by locating the ugly modern housing and industry over the river, in Újszeged.

Though the goddess-worshipping Kőrös culture settled here 4,000-5,000 years ago, and the town flourished after 1225 because of its royal salt monopoly over the mines of Transylvania, Szeged's character really derives from the **great flood** of March 1879, which washed away all but 300 homes and compelled the population to start again from scratch. With aid from foreign cities (after whom sections of the outer boulevard are named) Szeged bounced back, trumpeting its revival with huge buildings and squares where every type of architectural style got a mention. The result generally pleases the eye, although on Széchenyi tér trees obscure practically everything except the tower of City Hall.

The **University**, Szeged's cultural mainspring, is named after the poet **Attila József** (1905-37), whom it sternly expelled for writing:

> *I have no father, I have no mother,*
> *I have no god and I have no country*

during the ultra-conservative reign of Admiral Horthy. The illegitimate son of a washerwoman, a natural anarchist who joined the Communists and was soon dumped, Attila lived in extreme poverty and jumped under a train at Lake Balaton aged 32. Unappreciated in his lifetime, posthumously enshrined by the establishment, he also finds favour today with Budapest's teenage "sewer dwellers" (*csöves*), who approvingly quote 'Culture drops off me, like the clothes off a happy lover'.

Student protests in Szeged inspired the Budapest demonstration which flared into the '56 Uprising, and the radical tradition lives on. Until three members were gaoled for 2 years for 'public incitement to disaffection ', the **CPG punk band** won an enthusiastic following – and outraged local authorities – with songs like *The Schemer* (about Brezhnev); *Rotten Angels*; *Everyone is a Louse* ('where money gives birth to silence/where people are mute'); *SS-20* ('the Soviet bomb is also a bomb'); and *Standing Youth*. There was also much sympathy for the independent **Peace Movement** when it first emerged, especially in the technical colleges, though activities have been subdued since Budapest's *Peace Group for Dialogue* disbanded in 1983 under pressure from the authorities.

Szeged's establishment showpiece is **Dóm tér**, a vast square surrounded by arcades, twisted columns and statues, where the C12/C13 St Demetrius tower and the Greek Orthodox church (containing an elaborate iconostasis) are completely overshadowed by the monstrous brown brick **Votive Church** *. Pledged to build it after the flood, the townsfolk took their time, and the church with its 10,180 pipe organ wasn't finished until 1930, during Admiral Horthy's heyday. Banked alongside are seats awaiting the **Szeged Weeks** (July 20 to August 20), when the square becomes a stage for performances of classical music, rock, and Imre Madách's play *The Tragedy of Man*.

South of Dóm tér, Aradi Vértanúk tere and Április 4. útja meet at the **Heroes' Gate** (*Hősök Kapuja*), which was raised to honour the 'Whites', Horthy's henchmen, who gathered here in 1919, awaiting the defeat of the short-lived Hungarian Soviet Republic by the Romanian army, before they fanned out across the country to murder 5,000-6,000 Jews and 'Reds' in the 'White Terror'. Fascistic stone guardsmen still flank the archway, but Horthy's murals have been erased and the gate's origins aren't publicised.

Alongside the bridge to Újszeged, the **Móra Ferenc Museum** hides a standard mix of art objects and local history (including a dramatic picture of the flood) behind an ageing neo-Classical façade of columns, grim-faced lions and crumbling philosophers. On the promenade to the rear a very **ruined castle** (which housed convicts labouring on the river tow-paths during the C18) now displays stonework finds.

Beyond the inner boulevard, Lenin Körút, Szeged is shabbier, more residential and utilitarian. The *Alsóváros* (**lower town**) still half resembles a village, with rutted streets, rotting ochre dwellings and vegetable plots, centred around the old church on Mátyás Király tér. From here, Háman Kató u. leads to the main **railway station** facing the seedy *Hotel Sárkány* and the *Tóth Vendéglő*, a raucous railwaymen's dive with blind accordionists and drunken singing.

Rókus, another quarter, begins north of Hajnoczy utca where the Synagogue is under repair, and stretches out beyond the Párizsi and Berlini segments of the outer boulevard to **Marx tér**, the **bus terminal** and **marketplace**, full of fried fish stands.

ÚJSZEGED, east of the Tisza, is pretty unappealing, though you might enjoy the **thermal pools** steaming by the riverbank, and the large park with beer-gardens. Only the most dedicated will make the trek to the **botanical gardens** (*Füvészkert*) situated south of Szőregi út, but two alternatives for fresh air freaks are **TÁPÉ**, a fishing village 3km east (bus #73/#73Y from Marx tér), and the **FEHÉR-TÓ NATURE RESERVE**, which is visited by some 250 kinds of migratory **birds** (and tourists, if they're accompanied by a guide from the tourist bureau).

Practicalities

Except for the *Móra* (Bocskai u.3), Szeged's central **hotels** are expensive, and you'd be better off trying the **campsite/motel** on Dorozsmai út, where the Budapest highway begins (buses #78/#75/#75V from Marx tér), or getting a **private room** from *Szeged Tourist* (Victor Hugo u.1) or IBUSZ (Klauzál tér 2) in the city centre. Express (Kigyó u.) can usually book **dormitory beds** in the splendidly-named *Ápathy kollégium* during July/August.

On the food front, Szeged is famed for its local sausage and **fish dishes** like *Halpaprikás*, so there's a wide variety of places to eat out, either in style or dirt cheap. The *Hungária* (Komócsin tér 2) and *Alabárdos* (Oskola u.13) are for those with money to burn, likewise the *Tisza halászcsárda*, a 'Fishermen's inn' on Roosevelt tér; but you can scoff cheap *bográcsgulyás* in the *Tiszavirág Vendéglő* (Kigyó u.1) or the late-night *Búbos étterem* on Mérey utca, near Marx tér. Among the many büfés and beer dens I'd single out the place at Lenin u.56, chiefly for its absolutely whacky Art Deco design, while the *Árjegyzék Tejivó* (Somogyi u.) is the place for breakfast, and the *Virág Cukrászda* (Klauzál tér) dispenses cakes with elegance (and prices) rivalling Gerbeaud's of Budapest. For the decadent, Szeged Tourist can arrange **cocktail cruises on the river**, and the *Szőke Tisza* boat restaurant is moored north of the museum. Besides whatever's on during **the Szeged Weeks** (ask the tourist office for details and tickets), it's fairly easy to get invited to (or gatecrash!) the many **student parties** during term time, and you can usually meet people at the *Film-Téka* on Kigyó utca, where foreign and experimental flicks are screened. **English books** are available from the *Könyvesbolt* (Kárász u.16) – another place for contacts.

Transport is pretty straightforward. Buses #11/#21 and tram #1 loop from the railway station through the town centre to the **Marx tér terminal**, from whence Volán services depart to most towns on the southern Plain, and to Subotica, Dubrovnik and Sarajevo in **Yugoslavia**. There are regular trains to Békéscsaba and Kecskemét, but to reach Debrecen you'll have to change at Szolnok.

CROSSING THE TISZA AT CSONGRÁD OR SZOLNOK

Heading eastwards across the Plain, the **River Tisza** is no longer the great barrier of old, 'three parts water and two parts fish'. 120 river bends, some

---

* A shameful, largely forgotten episode in Szeged's ecclesiastical history involved the mass Witch-trials of 1728-48, organised by the church elders. Under torture, victims confessed to 'stealing the rain and selling it to the Turks' and similar nonsense, until foreign journalists spread the scandal throughout Europe, embarassing Empress Maria Theresa so that she banned further trials. Other trials occured in Békés County and in Debrecen.

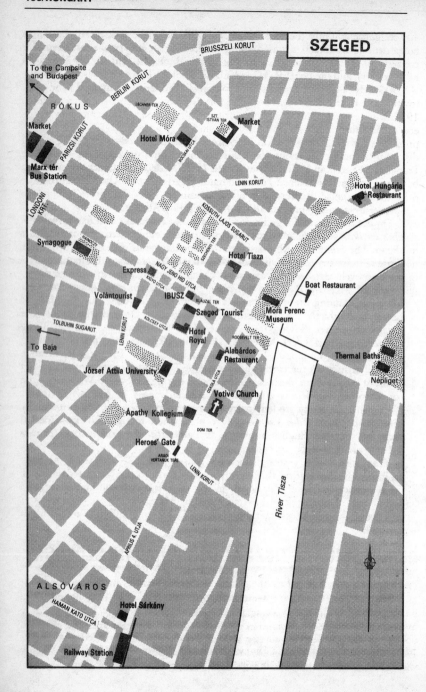

SZEGED

To the Campsite and Budapest

BRUSSZELI KORUT

BERLINI KORUT

PARIZSI KORUT

RÓKUS

LECHNER TER

SZT ISTVAN TER

Market

Market

Hotel Móra

ROOSMAI UTCA

LENIN KORUT

Marx tér
Bus Station

LONDONI KRT

Hotel Hungária
Restaurant

KOSSUTH LAJOS SUGARUT

Synagogue

HAJNOCZY

SZECHENYI TER

Hotel Tisza

NAGY JENO HID UTCA

Express

KIGYO UTCA

Boat Restaurant

Volántourist

IBUSZ

KLAUZAL TER

Szeged Tourist

Móra Ferenc
Museum

KOLCSEY UTCA

TOLBUHIN SUGARUT

LENIN KORUT

Hotel
Royal

ROOSEVELT TER

To Baja

Thermal Baths

Alabárdos
Restaurant

OSKOLA UTCA

József Attila University

Népliget

Votive Church

Apathy Kollegium

DOM TER

Heroes' Gate

ARADI
VERTANUK TERE

LENIN KORUT

River Tisza

APRILIS 4 UTJA

ALSÓVÁROS

HAMAN KATO UTCA

Hotel Sárkány

Railway Station

400 miles in length, were removed during the 19C, and the river has been tamed – one of the many projects initiated by Széchenyi. The two main crossing points by road and rail are Csongrád and Szolnok, and it's tempting to dismiss both towns as no more than that.

SZOLNOK's origins are military – an C11 castle which acquired a township in later life – and its strategic role as a bridgehead was reaffirmed in 1956, when the Russians seized it prior to crushing the Uprising. Now, in the era of *glasnost*, Szolnok's theatre has staged Eastern Europe's first ever production of *Doctor Zhivago*. Old gabled houses, crouching in the Tabán district alongside the Zagyva River, are the main sight, though there's a nice Franciscan church on Költői u. a block back from the Tisza. On the opposite bank are a campsite, hotel and thermal baths. The tourist offices at Kossuth u. 6-8 and Jászkürt u. 1 can arrange private rooms.

For some unknown reason CSONGRÁD has the highest suicide rate in Hungary, and the incidence elsewhere seems to decrease the further the distance from here. One theory is that local funeral rites, where the corpse is publicly displayed, encourage attention-seeking suicides. On a less morbid note, there's a thatched core of peasant houses, a museum and thermal baths in the town centre, and two campsites – one by the Tisza, the other at the mouth of the River Maros. The tourist office and the cheap *Erzsébet* hotel are on Felszabadulás útja.

BEYOND THE TISZA: DEBRECEN AND THE HORTOBÁGY PUSZTA

East of the Tisza the main line from Budapest, the E15 and routes from the northern uplands converge on the Plain's 'capital', Debrecen. Travellers approaching from Füzesabony or Tiszafüred by road or rail will pass near the Hortobágy puszta – Hungary's biggest national park – and the route from Szolnok runs through Hajdúszoboszló; but in most cases, Debrecen is where to start before you visit the Hortobágy or the Hajdúság region.

DEBRECEN

Once upon a time DEBRECEN was the site of Hungary's greatest livestock fair, and foreigners tended to be sniffy about 'this vast town of unsightly buildings' with its thatched cottages and a mainstreet that became 'one liquid mass of mud' when it rained, 'so that officers quartered on one side were obliged to mount their horses and ride across to have dinner on the other'. Nevertheless, everyone recognised that Debrecen (pronounced 'DEB-retzen') was important – economically, and as the chief centre of Hungarian

Calvinism. From the C16 onwards, there wasn't a generation of lawyers, doctors or divines that didn't include graduates from Debrecen's famous Calvinist College (the city is still renowned for its university and teacher-training colleges); while in the crucial years of 1848-49 and 1944-1945, it was here that Hungary's future was debated.

Around the city
Modern Debrecen, Hungary's third largest city, still follows the old mainstreet, now called Vörös Hadsereg útja in honour of the Red Army. From the railway station, tram #1 follows it northwards through the city centre up to the university, and then returns, which makes sightseeing very easy. Along the útja the old County Hall crawls with Art Nouveau statuary, nr. 54 puts up a brave show of domes and turrets, and the *Hotel Aranybika* tries to live up to its faded regency decor, whilst on nearby on Kossuth tér the country's largest bell, the *Rákóczi-harang*, summons people to worship at the old citadel of Calvinist power.

The **Great Church** is an appropriately huge monument to the *Református* faith that swept Hungary during the C16, and with space for 5,000, the building was able to accommodate the Diet of 1849, which declared the country's secession from the Habsburg empire. **Calvinism** took root more strongly in Debrecen than any other town or city, partly because the local Calvinists struck a deal with the Turks, thus ensuring their security, but also because Catholics were forbidden to settle here after 1552. Debrecen's austere Calvinists also waged war on the pagan beliefs that were ingrained amongst the peasantry of the Plain, where village wise men (*táltos*) were generally regarded with benevolence, unlike their female counterparts (*boszorkány*) whom villagers feared.

Until the C18, women accused of **witchcraft** had been able to plead that they were beneficent *táltos* (for example Frau Bártha, who claimed to have learned *táltos* skills from her brother), but as the Calvinists' grip tightened this defence became untenable. Midwives were particularly vulnerable as it was popularly believed that the murder of a relative or newborn child was a pre-requisite for acquiring their 'magical' skills, but women in general suffered from the Calvinists' witch- hunting zeal, which also found scapegoats in herbalists, beggars and vagabonds. **Witch-trials** were finally banned by Maria Theresa in 1768 after the scandalous events in Szeged; and by the C19 the bloody deeds of Debrecen's forefathers were buried beneath platitudes eulogising the 'Calvinist Rome'.

On Kálvin tér, behind the Church, you'll find the **Calvinist College** or *Református Kollégium*. Though venerable in appearance, it's not the original edifice founded in 1538, but the enlarged college built during the C19, where the Provisional National Assembly composed of centre and left-wing parties met under Soviet auspices in late 1944. To the west, on Déri tér, an excellent **museum** depicts women's life and household interiors in the C19, and mounts a dazzling display of shepherds' cloaks (*szűr*), worth a little digression. Traditionally, a herdsman would 'forget' to remove his finest *szűr* from the porch when he left the house of the woman he was courting, and if she welcomed the idea it was taken inside within an hour, indicating that a formal

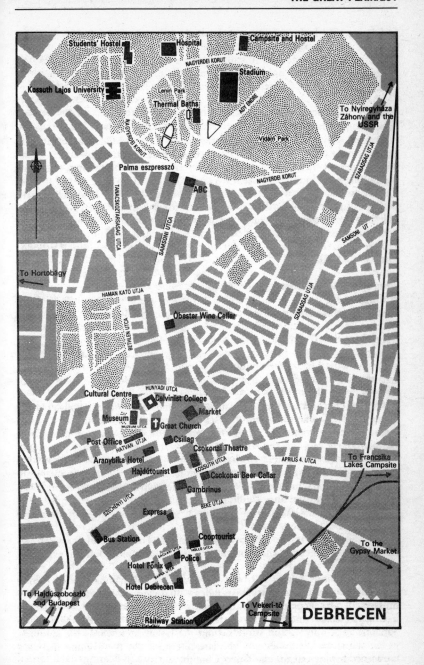

DEBRECEN

proposal could be made. Otherwise the cloak was hung prominently on the veranda – giving rise to the expression *kitették a szűrét* ('his cloak was put out'), meaning to get rid of somebody. Aside from the cloaks, Mihály Munkácsy's dark oil paintings get star billing together with the work of peasant artist László Holló, but my preference was for displays such as 'Mihály Tort's kitchen: birthplace of the Workers' movement'. More artwork, and occasional dramatic performances take place, in the Kölcsey Ferenc **cultural centre** around the corner on Hunyadi utca.

Beyond Kálvin tér Debrecen gets greener, and stylish residences line Péterfia u. and Simonyi út – the approaches to **Lenin Park** and the university. Locals make much of their *barna-víz* (brown water), though the **thermal baths and swimming pool** in the park seem overcrowded and over-built. Better to cross the reedy lake by a wooden footbridge to reach **Kossuth Lajos University**, whose columned bulk is fronted by floodlit fountains, and keep going to find the **Botanical Gardens**. Architecture buffs can hunt down a few more scattered sights like the smaller Calvinist church on V.H. útja, the old houses around the corner on Széchenyi utca, and the neglected multi-domed Greek Orthodox church on Attila tér.

Debrecen's Markets and Flower Carnival.
Though the great bi-monthly Fairs 'held here since time immemorial' no longer galvanise Debrecen, the city's markets are still lively, eye-catching and earthy. The main **fruit and veg market** fills the *Vásárcsarnok* behind the supermarket on Csapó utca (Monday-Saturday 4am-3pm/Sunday 4am-11am). Vendors vie to sell paprika, meats, strange herbs and *feta*-type cheese, tempting would-be customers with proferred morsels. Rich smells fill the air, and the hall resounds with Magyar interrogatives. ('*Hogy a. . .?* is slang for 'how much is the. . .?').

Out behind the *Vásárcsarnok*, ramshackle stalls comprise the **Polish market** (*Lengyel piac*), where desperate Poles hawk tat from the boots of battered Ladas to supplement their meagre foreign exchange. Romanians, identifiable by their Dacia cars marked RO, come here to **trade lei for forints** at a rate of 1:1, which for Westerners works out 3 times better than the official hard currency/lei exchange rate inside Romania. . . though importing lei into Romania is of course strictly forbidden. The **Gypsy market** (*Cigány piac*) happens on Saturday and Wednesday mornings in an industrial quarter of Debrecen. Take a #30 bus from the railway station and alight with the crowd just past the cigarette factory (*Dohánygyár*) – the market is across the road, through a portal, and spread over a wasteland. The 800-odd stalls sell old junk, dubious electrics and timepieces, tools, shoes and clothes; expect to haggle.

Each year on August 20, the **Flower Carnival** trundles north along Tanácsköztársaság útja: thirty floats laden with flowers, bands and operatically dressed soldiers. People hang from windows en route, cheer wildly when the Young Pioneers' band plays tunes from *István a király* ('Stephen the King', a patriotic rock-opera), and surge behind the last float towards the stadium, where the show continues into the late afternoon. In the evening there's a **fireworks** display outside the Great Church.

Eating and Drinking

When the weather's fine, **Lenin park** is the place to go. With the university so close, you're bound to meet young Hungarians (and foreign students during the summer) at the *Pálma eszpresszó* opposite the ABC, the *Levescsárda* beer garden, and the *Új Vigadó* restaurant, which features gypsy music by day and discos into the small hours. The *Óbester Borozó* (wine cellar) on Péterfia u. and the *Csokonai Söröző* (beer cellar) on Kossuth u. are also lively **night spots**.

The *Gambrinus* on V.H. útja – Debrecen's premier restaurant – is the place for gypsy music and jolly sing-songs, but the prices may drive you away to the restaurant on Hatvan utca, less elegant but cheaper. Similarly economic are the stand-up *Csillag étterem* sells produce from the Nádudvár Co-op (on the corner of Csapó utca), and a self-service *Önkiszolgáló*, which incongruously cohabits with a luxurious restaurant on the ground floor of the Hotel *Aranybika*. Debrecen's best ice cream comes from the privately-owned *Ruzicska Károlyné Cukrászda* on Senyei O.I. utca.

Lodgings and other things

The *Főnix* (Barna u.17) is the cheapest of Debrecen's **hotels**, but one can economise still further by booking **private rooms** through IBUSZ or Hajdútourist on the mainstreet, or going for **dormitory accommodation** in the annex behind the university, which is usually less crowded than the **tourist hostel and campsite** past the hospital. A student's card isn't usually necessary to get beds at the university (from July to mid-August) or at other colleges (exact dates and locations vary each year, but the *kollégiums* at Béke útja 2 and Varga u. 2 seem good possibilities). *Express*, V.H. útja 77, can give details and make bookings. Should you stay with someone without going through the tourist office, it's necessary to register with the **police** on the corner of Ságvári utca. Two other **campsites** are **out of town** – at Vekeri-tó to the south (bus #26 from the terminal /rd.47), and by the **Fancika Lakes** to the east (Aprilis 4. utca/rd.48), where there are opportunities for fishing, boating and horseriding.

Money-changing is swiftest in the *Aranybika*'s lobby, where one can make **international calls** (dearer but less hassle than the telephone kiosk in the basement of the university). By posing as a foreign student attending the **Hungarian language summer course** (*Nyári-Egyetem*), it's possible to read **western newspapers**, *Marxism Today* etc. in the university library on the 2nd floor behind the great hall. The **hospital** east of the university reportedly gives preferential treatment to foreigners, but there's no discrimination at the **Pósta** on Hatvan utca: everyone has to wait. Various cinemas and the Csokonai theatre purvey drama, Csapó utca has the best **pharmacy** and watermelons, and the *Könyvhanglemez* on V.H. út stocks an excellent range of English **books**, tourist **maps** and **records**.

Moving on

From Debrecen, the majority of travellers head on to **Hortobágy National Park** or the spa of **Hajdúszoboszló**, and few visit the *Nyírség* region centred around **Nyíregyháza** (which straddles routes to the northern uplands) unless its to see the church or hear the summer concerts at **Nyírbátor**. Further north, the *Nyírség* gives way to **Szabolcs-Szatmár County**, Hungary's most backward province, where a string of ancient villages hug the headwaters of the Tisza, and tourists are rarely seen. There are poor train connections to the **southern Plain**, where Békéscsaba and Gyula are the only towns worth visiting, though you may pass through Karcag and Püspökladány en route to Budapest. See the end of this chapter for details about **crossing into Romania**.

HORTOBÁGY NATIONAL PARK

'Comparable to the sea, boundless and green', the Hortobágy *puszta* once covered most of the central Plain east of the river, a 'glorious steppe. . .. the very brow of God', as Petőfi exclaimed. Great herds of horses and longhorn cattle champed their way from well to waterhole urged on by mounted *csikós*, and racka sheep grazed under the watchful gaze of puli dogs. Earlier still, during the Turkish occupation, Hortobágy's Szendelik hill was alledgedly the setting for a witchcraft duel between Frau Bártha, the *táltos* of Debrecen, and two rivals.

Today the **National Park** commemorates the old puszta with an extensive wildlife reserve and displays of bygone folk culture. State-employed *csikós* handle stallions and lassos outside the much-restored **Great Inn** (*Nagycsárda*), and beasts are strategically placed along the road to the **nine-arched stone bridge** which spans the River Hortobágy. At the **Bridge Fair** on August 20, folklore and equestrian displays fill the stadium, and knives, leatherwork and spitted-cow are sold outside. The international **Horse Show** in June is a more exclusive affair, but you can look at the stabled thoroughbreds anytime.

Wildlife, widely dispersed and hard to encounter, hides in the surrounding 100,000 hectares. Storks, racka sheep and some boars frequent the big fish lake (*halastó*) a few kilometres northwest of the Hortobágy train-halt. If you've no car or bike, slow local **trains** (between Karcag/Debrecen and Tiszafüred, stopping at hamlets across the Hortobágy,) or hitching, are the means to see deer (near Tiszaszőlős), lapwings (east of Kónya) and other birdlife (north of Tiszacsege). Lazier folk can settle for the stuffed creatures in the **Shepherd's Museum**, which also exhibits tremendous cloaks heavy with frogging, inlaid leatherware, carved powder horns and many other objects made by herdsmen whiling away solitary hours on the grassland. When herdsmen met, status was important; horseherds outranked shepherds and cowherds, and all felt superior to the *kondás* (unlike in the Bakony region, where the swineherd was king). Like the ancient Magyars, plainsmen slept under the stars, and only when necessary built crude huts (*kunyhó*) or shared a reed *szárnyék* with their animals.

Mirages – *délibáb* – may occur on dry days. The most likely sites are east of Cserpes village and the Hortobágyi-hálastó, and south of the road between Hortobágy and Elep/Nagyhegyes (near the otter colony). Medieval accounts of cities in the clouds exist, but more commonly travellers would see phantom woods, or 'an extensive lake half enveloped in grey mist' like the one that fooled John Paget.

For those unwilling to share a *szárnyék* the office in the museum can arrange **private rooms**, and two **campsites** operate between May 1 and September 31. Otherwise it's a toss up between the *Fogadó* and the

Nagycsárda, which are both comfortable, fairly dear and liable to be full. Camping wild is not a wise move, so if you're really stuck for accommodation it might be worth travelling up to **TISZAFÜRED**, which links the Plain with the northern uplands. Currently encroaching on the banks of the Kisköre reservoir, Tiszafüred centres on Somogyi B. utca, with the railway station at its western end. The bus terminal, IBUSZ and the main square are to the east. Gáspár Nyúzó's pokey **pottery** (Malom u.12, key from across the road) and the **Kis Pál Museum** (Kun u.6) are the only sights in town, but good **gypsy music** throbs in the dim *Vendéglő* at nr. 8 on the mainstreet. IBUSZ's private **rooms** and the *Vadász Hotel* (Lenin utca 4) aren't expensive, and are preferable to the costlier *Kemény Kastély* on Homokcsárda, or the **campsite** beside a dead tributary of the river, infested by mosquitoes.

THE HAJDÚSÁG

The Hajdúság region, covering an arc of land west of Debrecen, takes its name from the *Hajdúk* communities that settled in eight derelict villages here in the early C17. Originally cattle-drovers and occasional bandits, the Hajdúks' ranks were swollen by runaway serfs and homeless peasants, and they provided a fearsome army for István Bocskai's struggle against the Habsburgs. Bocskai achieved his ambition to be Voivode of Transylvania, whilst the Hajdúk, seen as a threat by Bocskai's allies in the nobility, were pensioned-off with land to avert a peasant uprising. The result was a string of settlements with names prefixed Hajdú-, where the Hajdúk farmed, enjoyed the status of 'nobles' (*natio*) and, if necessary, mustered to fight. The military aspect is still apparent in the layout of **HAJDÚBÖSZÖRMÉNY**, where old houses stand in concentric rings around a walled core – once a fortress – but nowadays the Hajdúság towns hardly differ from others on the Plain, and have acquired a new role as spas.

Hajdúszoboszló and Nádudvár
Driven from Lake Balaton by rising prices, many Hungarians take their holidays in **HAJDÚSZOBOSZLÓ**, where a spa has been operating since 1927. In the vicinity of the **thermal baths** practically everyone is dressed for the pool, and the consumption of beer and *lángos* is staggering. Modern housing and supermarkets along Vörös Hadsereg út/Debreceni út (the mainstreet) nourish the illusion of a hedonistic urban enviroment, but in the backstreets the agricultural past lingers on. Outside the **railway station**, chunky whitewashed cottages – their vegetable gardens fringed with sunflowers – shimmer in the heat. Errant cows, old women and wagon-loads of pigs move slowly in the dazzling sunlight, and a Volán bus runs 2km into the town centre, terminating 100m from the baths.

Hajdúszoboszló gets around 1½ million visitors each year, and the pools can be packed. Surveying the wallowing, guzzling crowds in the steaming brown waters (73°C, good for arthritis and other muscular ills), you might try the old Hajdúk war cry, *Huj, huj, hajrá!*, to clear some space before jumping in yourself. Away from the baths things are more relaxed, with **tennis courts** for hire in the park, and cafés and quaint old buildings around Bocskai and

Hősök squares. Sixty feet of **fortress wall** – part of the C15 defences – lurk behind the inevitable Calvinist church, whilst a comically fierce statue of the Prince guards Bocskai tér and its two hotels.

Around the corner at 12, Bocskai utca, you'll find a **Museum** exhibiting photos of C19 Hajdúk villagers, and assorted military relics – amongst them Bocskai's embroidered silk banner, which is given pride of place alongside the town's charter. Bocskai comes across as a benevolent fellow, although he didn't baulk at betraying a different group of peasants who fought for him – the Székely of Transylvania, butchered during the so-called 'Bloody Carnival' when they outlived their utility. The room across the hall commemorates Hajdúszoboszló's spa, cultural achievements and natural gas extraction plant.

The *Délibáb* is cheaper than the *Gambrinus* nearby, but most folks opt to stay at the *Szabadság fogadó* (V.H. útja 51), on the campsite just beyond the gasometer past the bus terminal, or in private rooms available from IBUSZ (Bocskai tér), Cooptourist or Hajdútourist (both near the baths).

If you're interested in **pottery** it might be worth taking the bus to NÁDUDVÁR, 18km away, where *Lajos Fazekas* carries on a family tradition by producing black, un-fired ceramics at his house and studio on V.H. útja (as always, the mainstreet). Otherwise this sleepy place has two petite churches, a spanking new cultural centre, and **Nádudvár Co-operative farm** sprawled around its outskirts, where foreign students attending Debrecen's summer school are sometimes taken for a glimpse of rural prosperity. In previous years, these visits have often culminated in a riotous *pálinka* binge, with students and workers riding pigs across the moonlit fields!

SZABOLCS-SZATMÁR COUNTY

Northwards beyond Debrecen the Plain rises in gentle ridges – windblown sandhills now anchored by apple groves, orchards and tobacco fields. The *Nyírség*, as it is called, and the land around the headwaters of the Tisza form **Szabolcs-Szatmár County**, the 'Black Country'. Except for Nyíregyháza, centre of the food processing industry, it's overwelmingly agricultural – and densely populated in contrast with the rest of the Plain. Historically isolated by swamps (which kept the Turks away), and by the Treaty of Trianon (1920) which sundered links with Szatmár and the Transylvanian foothills, the region's economy languished, and remains sickly today. Visitors – let alone foreign ones – rarely venture beyond Nyíregyháza and Nyírbátor, and if your interest in rural life is limited you should go no further. **Nyíregháza**'s open-air **Village Museum** shows the old rural enviroment minus people and animals, while a lovely wooden **belltower** of the type mainly confined to **remote villages** near Russia and in Transylvania can be seen at **Nyírbátor**. Beyond the provincial capital the railway forks into the hinterland, *személyvonat* grinding slowly from train halt to hicksville. Other towns muster a few tourist 'attractions' – a riding school, hot baths or castle – but these are hardly sufficent reason to pay a visit. The **experience** of unpredictable travel, insights or encounters with people is far more valuable – and as far as making contact goes, the onus is on you rather than the natives.

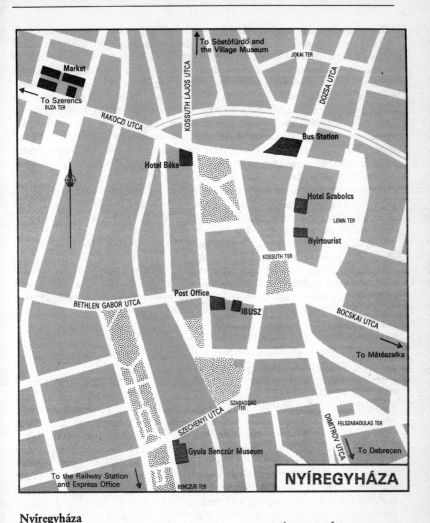

NYÍREGYHÁZA

Nyíregyháza

A sleepy provincial town of 19,000 ten years ago, **NYÍREGYHÁZA** grew into the big apple of Szabolcs as the food processing industry developed here; a cocoon of grey high-rise *lakótelep* enclosing the original core of three squares. Arriving at the chaotic **station** on the southwestern edge of the ring road, you can obtain a street-plan from *Express* (2, Arany utca) outside the terminal before catching bus #8 or #8A into the town centre, or riding to the bathing resort of **Sóstófürdő** at the end of the line in the northern suburbs. The hostels and campsite (open April 15-October 15), and beds in the *KISZ Iskola* on Sóstói út there, are all cheap alternatives to private **rooms** from *Nyírtourist* or the *Hotel Szabolcs* on Dózsa utca in the centre.

The town's only real attraction is the strangely eerie **Village Museum** (*Szabadtéri Néprajzi Múzeum*); located on Berenat utca in the vicinity of Sóstófürdő. With clothes on the washing-line, tables laid and boots by the hearth, the farmsteads could have been abandoned by their occupants only yesterday, leaving mute testimony to their lives in a C19 Black Country village. The size of the barns (*csűr*) and stables (*istálló*) denotes a family's wealth, as does the presence of a Beam Gate onto the street – 'A gate on a hinge, the dog is big, the farmer is great' as the old proverb has it. Other clues to social standing are knick knacks adorning the homes of petty gentry (or 'sandled nobles'); the placing of a bench between two windows – the sign of an Orthodox householder; and the single communal bowl in the poorest dwellings.

Downtown centres on Kossuth tér, where the Catholic church stands tall, whence a shopping precinct runs southwards to pastel-hued Freedom Square (now renamed Lenin tér, much to the locals' disgust) with the hotel and tourist office on Dózsa utca nearby. Benczúr tér, to the west, has a beer garden and the local **museum**; displaying ancient junk, Party relics and the dark formal paintings of **Gyula Benczúr** – denounced as a 'reactionary' artist during the Republic of Councils, but now reinstated as a worthy son of Nyíregyháza. Kossuth tér's *Kis Étterem* offers seedy grandeur, but the cheapest place **to eat** is the *Kolumbia* on Egyház utca. Other places worth noting include IBUSZ and the Post Office on Bethlen utca; the **market** on Búza tér; and Jókai tér's **bus terminal**.

Assuming that you don't take the train north to Tokaj (p.180), the main **routes** into the Szabolcs hinterland lead up to Kisvárda (rail or the T1 highway) or eastwards : through Nyírbátor and Mátészalka, or Vaja and Vásárosnamény, towards the headwaters of the Tisza. Visitors without a car are more or less compelled to travel **by train** – the most reliable form of transport in an area with few buses and hardly any private vehicles on the roads. There are 5 trains every day from Nyíregyháza to Nagykálló, Nyírbátor and Mátészalka, and less frequent services along the branch lines; all of them are slow but punctual. Perhaps the hardest part is trying to leave town, for Nyíregyháza's station has no platforms, and the single indicator board gives cryptic directions like '*Debrecen – 7 balra*'. (Meaning that the train to Debrecen leaves from the left hand side of the seventh track from the main building).

Nagykálló and Nyírbátor

'Go to Nagykálló!' used to be a popular insult east of the Tisza, referring to the large mental asylum in this small town of converging houses painted a flakey ochre; and the sole reason to linger is **NAGYKÁLLÓ**'s annual *Csűr*. Held in a weird 'barn' (hence the name) shaped like a winged Viking's helmet, this workshop-cum-**festival** of Hungarian folk arts normally occurs during the week or so before Constitution Day, culminating on August 20 – Debrecen's tourist office should have details. At other times, happenings are whatever takes place in the local *italbolt* (bars), from which youths are excluded to feel the pall of smalltown life exacerbated by the visions of Budapest sophistication beamed in via their TVs.

Aware of this, the government endeavours to disseminate metropolitan culture, dispatching troupes from leading theatres and ensembles from the State Philharmonic on tours. At **NYÍRBÁTOR** there's a well-established 'season' of **concerts** – mainly choral and chamber music, performed in the Gothic vault of the Calvinist church (from mid-July to September; see tourist offices for details) – preceded by a dramatic recitation of verses by Ady or Petőfi ('It's about the sea,' my companion muttered). The *protokol* of such events is amusing, with unwilling schoolkids firmly seated at the back, town belles wearing the most daring corsage their parents will allow, seeking admiring eyes from gallants in the middle rows, and along the front local worthies and the Party boss.

The **Calvinist church**, where concerts are held, stands upon a hillside overlooking town; an austere structure with a webb-vaulted nave built between 1484-1511 on the orders of **István Báthori**. His tomb at the back is conventional, with a sleeping figure indicating that he died in bed but revealing nothing about the character of this Transylvanian Voivode. A power-mad schemer whom the Transylvanian Saxons (among others) hated, he periodically endowed churches in pious atonement for his well-known bouts of orgiastic cruelty. Most likely these had a hereditary origin, for similar hysterical rages and sadism were also characteristic of 'Crazy' Gábor Báthori, a short-lived Transylvanian ruler, and István's cousin Elizabeth, known to history as the 'Blood Countess'. As Counter-Reformation ordinances required, the church's belfry is separate – and in this case, a splendid C17 example of the type of **wooden belltower** once common in rural Szabolcs, Maramureş and Transylvania. Wide-skirted at its base, the belfry rises 20 metres, with a spire like a wizard's hat sprouting four little towers known as *fiatorony* ('sons of the tower'), which symbolised a civic authority's right to execute criminals. Inside the belltower, which is surfaced with hand-cut shingling, you can climb a crooked stairway amongst ancient joists and beams to the balcony and the huge bells.

On Károlyi utca, on the far side of the mainstreet, are more of Báthori's legacy to Nyírbátor. The **Minorite Church**, paid for by the spoils of war against the Turks (who, perhaps appropriately, gutted it in 1587) has fantastic woodcarvings. The altars (carved by Krucsay's workshop in Eperjes) swarm with figures wearing disquieting expressions. To gain admission, ring at the side door marked *plébánia csengője*, which leads to an exhibition of photos of ancient Szabolcs churches. Next door you'll find a **museum** where various relics with unintelligible captions trace the history of the Báthoris, whose holdings stretched well into Transylvania, but were especially concentrated around **Szatmár**. Though predominantly inhabited by Hungarians, this area was bisected by the diplomats at Versailles, who allotted the provincial capital (nowadays called Satu Mare) and its surroundings to Romania. International relations have been awkward, if not hostile, ever since; which partly explains the small number of border-crossings in these parts.

Private rooms can be arranged at Nyírtourist on Szabadság tér, where the *Kakukk* restaurant offers good cheap **meals** and the occasional video-disco. For fruit and veg, try the **market** at the junction of Váci and Fürst utcas. Men might enjoy the 'old time' barber at 10, Báthori utca.

Gypsy Communities in the northeast

In the Magyar towns and cities, the **Gypsies** one sees are cleaners, flower-sellers, navvies, hustlers or skivvys; housed in *Munkásszálló* hostels, and universally referred to by the vaguely pejorative term *Cigány*. However, Magyar society has always made an exception for Gypsy entertainers, showering esteem and wealth on a few favourites, and the 'Gypsy Music' (*Cigányzene*) associated with Hungary reflects this. To satisfy their audiences, the Gypsy violinists spun together 'Old Style' Magyar folk airs and foreign dances and marching tunes of C17-C18; a mixture that Hungarian purists later deplored, which is equally at variance with the Gypsies' cultural origins. Away from the *gadée*, amongst their own people, they are *Rom*: the descendants of tribes who left India to escape their low caste and wandered across the continent, entering Europe around the C12 (other Rom headed south to Egypt and Arabia). Foreign countries reacted suspiciously to this peaceful invasion, and at different times Rom have been enslaved, banished or subject to forced assimilation.

Their permanent **settlements** are generally on the outskirts of town (eg. Szolnok), or in the the hinterland of the Black Country, and together with urban Gypsies and transient workers, there are somewhere in the region of 250,000-500,000 Gypsies living in Hungary, although nobody knows for sure. Ethno-musicologists occasionally enter these *cigánytelep* to record the Rom's communal singing and stick-dancing, but wild horses wouldn't drag the average Magyar into the Gypsy settlements and foreigners are sternly advised against going near them. Health-care and education have improved slightly since conditions were exposed in Pál Schiffer's shaming documentary film, *Gyuri*, but Gypsies are still light-years from integrating into Hungarian society. The Catholic Church has taken an interest in the matter, providing religious services and primary education in Romany for Gypsies living just outside HODÁSZ, a commune between Nyírbátor and Mátészalka.

Mátészalka and Vaja

A shabby fusion of flaking estates and low yellow houses, **MÁTÉSZALKA** is a place to catch buses and trains to somewhere else; both terminals lie at the western end of Bajcsy-Zsilinszky u., which leads into the town centre where each Sunday the population gravitates in homage to the Catholic church, the Orthodox church, and the steaming **thermal baths**. The *Szatmár* hotel (Hősök út 20) is unwelcoming and expensive, but private **rooms** can be found at Szatmár-tourist (B-Z u. 30) or by asking around. From Mátészalka, infrequent trains run to Csenger, Vásárosnamény and Fehérgyarmat on the borders of the Erdőhát region (see below), and there are fairly regular buses to Vaja 14km away.

VAJA's chief monument is the **castle** – more a fortified manor really – once owned by Ádám Vaj, one of the earliest adherents to Ferenc Rákóczi's campaign against the Habsburgs. Within the thick stone walls, visitors in felt slippers shuffle across the parquet from room to room, gaping at painted furniture and the grand meeting hall, the *Rákóczi-terem*. Officially there's no **accommodation**, but one can return to Nyíregyháza by train, or ride on to Vásárosnamény where there's a hotel and campsite.

The Erdőhát villages. . .

The **Erdőhát** is Hungary's most isolated region, a state imposed by nature and confirmed by history. Meandering and flooding over centuries, the headwaters of the Tisza and its tributaries carved out scores of enclaves beneath the flanks of the Subcarpathians, where dense oak forests provided acorns for pig-rearing and ample timber for building. Though invaders were generally deterred by Ecsedi Swamp and like obstacles, scattered communities maintained contact with one another through their intricate knowledge of local tracks and waterways, which paid no regard to sovereign borders. Today, the chief sign of this link is the similarity in traditional wooden architecture throughout the Erdőhát and parts of Maramureş, for the **borders** have come down like shutters during the C20. Although, as a local rightly put it, 'From here, 20 kilometres – Russia, 20 kilometres – Romania!', there's nowhere to cross into the adjacent Subcarpathian Oblast of the USSR (traditionally known as Ruthenia), and but a single, very dodgy, road-crossing into Romania at Csengersima.

Roads are poor and motorised vehicles are rare in these parts, but if you're interested in traditional rural life, and customs and architecture that have disappeared elsewhere in Hungary, the effort of getting to certain **villages** will seem worthwhile. The first clutch of places can more or less be reached using buses from the small town of **VÁSÁROSNAMÉNY** (hotel on Beregszászi utca, campsite). Across the river in **TÁKOS** there's a wattle and daub Protestant **church** with floral paintings on its gallery, benches and coffered ceiling; outwardly less striking than the C13 wooden-spired **church** in neighbouring **CSARODA**, but inwardly more than a match for the latter's folk-Baroque and faded Byzantine-style decor. Eight kilometres to the north, you'll find a nifty **wooden belfry** in the village of **VÁMOSATYA**.

The restorers have been at work in **TARPA** (to the southeast, easier to reach from Fehérgyarmat), and amongst the wooden cottages stands a large horizontal 'dry' **mill** (*száraz-malom*), beneath an intrcate conical roof known as 'the tent of the roundabout'. MÁND, NEMESBORZOVA, VÁMOSOROSZI and a string of villages bordering the USSR have surendered their best architecture to Szentendre's Village Museum, but **SZATMÁRCSEKE** has retained the 'boat shaped' oaken **gravemarkers** which superficially resemble the heads on Easter Island. To the south of Fehérgyarmat are two small villages with picturesque **churches**: the tiny one at **GYÜGYE** has its panelling decorated with astrological symbols (illuminated in turn by a sunbeam during the course of the year, so the priest says); while **CSENGER**'s is of red and black brick, and dates from the Middle Ages. Be warned that the last train back to Mátészalka leaves Csenger around 3.40pm.

It's theoretically possible **to enter Romania** at two points along the frontier. **CSENGERSIMA**, a few miles from Csenger, has recently been designated a 24-hour road-crossing by the Hungarians. Romanian officials in PETEA aren't quite so keen on this and travellers attempting to cross at ungodly hours risk a lengthy wait in a visa-less limbo until morning. Prolonged customs searches at Petea are another potential hazard, and in 1987 officials closed the length of the frontier with Hungary for several days to demonstrate Romania's displeasure at Magyar protests over the fate of their kinsfolk in

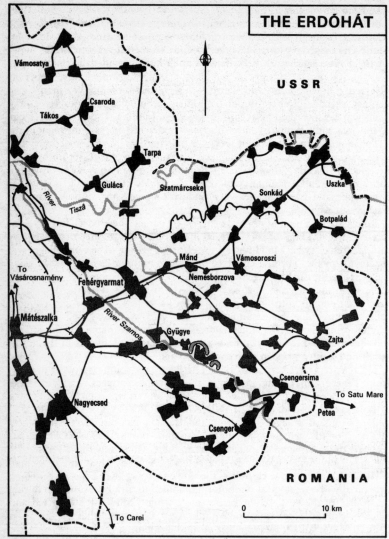

THE ERDÓHÁT

Transylvania. Customs are generally smoother at those checkpoints regularly used by Westerners, which Csengersima isn't. The same applies to travelling **by rail**: passengers on the little-advertised 'local' trains are subjected to more zealous searches and interrogations than on the *Orient Express*. One such 'local' train leaves the small town of **NAGYECSED** every morning around 7.40, and deposits one 3½hrs later at CAREI, where you can buy a ticket for the fast train **to Satu Mare** (p.420) that arrives an hour or so afterwards.

And finally, travellers bound for Transylvania might like to know that

Nagyecsed was the *birthplace of the Blood Countess*, Elizabeth Báthori, whose passions are related on p.492. Originally buried in the village beneath Čachtice Castle where her worst crimes were committed – which understandably caused protests – Elizabeth's body was re-interred within the family vault at Nagyecsed some years later; I don't know if this still remains.

. . .and up to Kisvárda and the Soviet Union.
Northwest of Nyíregyháza, Hungary's 'fraternal socialist ties' with the USSR manifest themselves in the smooth, Soviet-built T1 highway, which – like the railway – is a strategic military link to Uzhgorod. Along the way is **KISVÁRDA**, a backwater **spa** with a riding school and **ruined castle** (the setting for plays during summer). Nyírtourist on Lenin utca has cheap private **accommodation** and details about **horseriding** (the school is on Városmajor utca, just beyond the T1 junction). Couples dance the *disco-csárdás* in the fishless fish restaurant over the road, and Kisvárda's desperadoes gather in the seedy *Sport Falatozó* bar on Vár utca.

ZÁHONY, 23km further north, is the only road/rail crossing **into the Soviet Union**. Soviet visa-applications can take 14 days to process (and specify the time and place to entry to the USSR), so unless you've already acquired one, there's no chance to visit CHOP on the Soviet side, and idle gawping around the checkpoint is discouraged. With a **visa**, you should be able to cross by rail or car (but don't try hitching!), and might also be able to buy a ticket for the daily *Volán* **bus from Debrecen to Mukachevo** (a town with a sizeable ethnic-Hungarian population) in the USSR. Should you arrive in Záhony and get stuck, the *Kemév fogadó* (Zalka u. I) and private rooms (from Szamuely u.22) are both pretty cheap.

THE SOUTHERN PLAIN

Less protected and more sun-baked than the north, the **southern Plain** bore the brunt of the Turkish occupation and suffered frequent droughts, giving rise to such popular anxiety that 'Witches' were burned for 'blowing the clouds away' or 'selling the rain to the Turks', and the region became largely depopulated. Today, little historic architecture remains and many travellers slip through Békés county between Szeged and Debrecen, or simply bypass the southeast altogether.

Püspökladány and Karcag
Along the Budapest-Szolnok-Debrecen route, Karcag and Püspökladány are the junctions for the railway branch lines south. Aside from its station (from which a local train departs mid-afternoon for Valea lui Mihai in Romania), the most striking feature of **PÜSPÖKLADÁNY** is the large number of ageing, blue-overalled *Munkásrendőrség*. It was 'Workers' Militia' such as these who helped the Party break the wave of strikes and passive resistance that the workers resorted to in the months following the suppression of the '56 Uprising – a phase of history nowadays officially known as the 'consolidation of power'.

KARCAG is likewise slightly Orwellian – 'Better work is achieved through Socialism' proclaim the hoardings fronting grubby high-rises – and boasts of the largest rice-hulling mill in Europe (rice is grown around Hortobágy). During my visit, the town's **Folk Art Museum** and Orthodox church (both on Horváth utca) were closed, but the *Kunsági* restaurant at 1, Dózsa út, was keen to serve Cumanian food. The recipies are of dubious authenticity – for the Cumanians, who arrived with the Magyars in 896, died out centuries ago – but tasty. **Rooms** can be arranged by IBUSZ on Lossuth tér or the office at V.H. útja 10, while the *Otthon Hotel* is in the same street. 12km along the road to Kunmadaras, there's a campsite and thermal baths at BEREKFÜRDÖ.

Békéscsaba and Gyula

Travelling between Szeged and Debrecen, **BÉKÉSCSABA** is practically unavoidable and its lack of cheap accommodation surely calculated. Tanácsköztársaság útja, the central shopping precinct, is where to find *Békéstourist* (nr.10), *Express* (nr.29), and an excellent *Halász étterem* with music in the evenings; while the **museum** at Széchenyi út 9, near the canal, exhibits paintings by Mihály Munkácsy and oddments concerning the C18 Slovak settlers, who revived Békéscsaba after a ruinous succession of earthquakes, invasions, fires and plagues. There's more about their lifestyle in the ornate **Slovak Tájház** on Garay utca. Over the canal bridge from the museum is another, albeit unofficial, sight, the *István Malom*. This C19 flour mill, automated at the turn of the century, is crammed with wardrobe-sized shakers, rotating sieves and wooden shutes, objects of pride to the workers who showed me around.

From the Hunyadi tér station, buses head off northeast to BÉKÉS – a boring place with a thermal bath and a half-obliterated castle – or southwest to GYULA, the last town before the Romanian border. Named after a tribal chieftain from the time of Magyar conquest, it became a twin town after the Turkish withdrawal, with Hungarians living in *Magyargyula* and the Romanian and German newcomers in *Németgyula*. In a park on the eastern side of town, a C14 brick **fortress** now lends its thick walls to the **Castle Plays** held here in July and August, the old chapel occupied by a museum and the Powder Tower by a wine bar. Glittering icons fill one wall of the **Greek Orthodox Church** on Groza tér nearby but secular pleasures are pursued in the steamy *Várfürdö* to the south, a complex of twelve **thermal pools** constructed by the townspeople. In the park along Béke sugárút, visitors to the **György Kohán Museum** are greeted by some of the 3,000 works that he bequeathed to his hometown – most notably boldly painted horses, women and houses, lit by flickering hexagonal strip lights. The **Erkel Museum** on Dürer utca makes much of Ferenc Erkel, founder of Hungarian opera, who was born here, and the painter Albrecht Dürer, whose ancestors lived here, but does little to inspire.

The private **campsite** (with a few rooms) at 5, Vár utca is cheaper and nicer than the official campsite/motel southeast of the fortress, while Békéstourist (Kossuth u.16) can arrange **rooms**, and there are **hotels** on the Béke sugárút and south of the Várfürdö. For cheap food, try the *Gulyáscsárda* near the junction of Városház and Kossuth street, and the excellent *cukrászda* at 2, Szent István utca near the bus terminal. Should you need cash, there's a **24 hour currency exchange** at 5, Hétvezér utca. The **railway station** is northwest of the town centre.

CROSSING THE BORDER INTO YUGOSLAVIA OR ROMANIA

From the southern Plain, there are 24-hour checkpoints on the roads **into Yugoslavia** at HERCEGSZÁNTÓ south of BAJA (p.192); TOMPA on the road down from KISKUNHALAS; and RÖSZKE in the vicinity of SZEGED. International express **trains** (the *Puskin, Polonia* and *Meridian*) run from Budapest across the Plain, halt briefly at Kiskunhalas, and then leave Hungary at KELEBIA – near the Tompa road crossing – before carrying on to SUBOTICA and BEOGRAD (Belgrade). It's possible to board these trains at KISKUNHALAS, but probably easier to enter Yugoslavia **by bus**. These *Volán* services depart every morning (except on Sundays) from BAJA, KECSKEMÉT, GYULA and SZEGED, running to SUBOTICA; and from SZEGED to DUBROVNIK.

Travelling **to Romania**, one has the choice between 24-hour checkpoints on the roads beyond NAGYLAK, GYULA, and ÁRTÁND – but no buses across; several international express trains (boardable in Budapest or Szolnok); or a couple of 'local' trains rarely used by tourists. The *Pannonia, Orient, Transdanubium* and *Wiener Waltzer* expresses leave Hungary at LÖKÖSHÁZA (where it's not possible to climb aboard); while the *Balt Orient, Tracia, Mamaia* and *Nord Orient* cross the frontier at BIHARKERESZTES near the Ártánd customs post. Entering Romania at CURTICI or EPISCOPIA BIHOR, you shouldn't have any trouble with customs, purchasing a visa and the obligatory currency exchange (as explained in the Romanian *Basics*). Approaches to the main towns of the region beyond are described in *The Banat* chapter.

As in Szatmár county, there are also a couple of **local trains** that cross the border, used exclusively by natives of the region. The terminals and approximate departure times for these are: BÉKÉSCSABA to CURTICI (6am and 4.20pm); KÖTEGYAN to SALONTA (6.45am and 5pm); NAGYECSED to CAREI (see p.212); and from DEBRECEN (6.47am) and PÜSPÖKLADÁNY (4.14pm) to VALEA LUI MIHAI (arriving two hours later). For some reason, the station in Debrecen refuses to sell tickets to Westerners bound for Valea lui Mihai; and on all these lines there's the potential aggravation of heavy customs. Most passengers are Romanian-born Magyars returning from shopping trips in Hungary, so the guards couldn't care less about holding up the train while they search to ensure that nobody exceeds the permitted 200Ft's worth of food or consumer durables. All sorts of bribery and smuggling is practised – which is understandable once you see the dire lack of most everyday goods inside Romania. For foreigners, the only advantage of these trains is that they enable one to get from eastern Hungary **to northwestern Romania** fairly directly. From VALEA LUI MIHAI or CAREI, you can easily catch a train up to SATU MARE, the hideous portal to Romania's most enchanting region, Maramureş.

FESTIVALS

Summer
Show-jumping at the *International Horse Show* at HORTOBÁGY sometime during **June**. The following month sees the start of *Castle Plays* at GYULA, and a festival of music and drama at SZEGED. The latter runs from **July** 20 until Constitution Day, **August 20**; an occasion for fireworks and an exuberant *Flower Carnival* at DEBRECEN, the HORTOBÁGY *Bridge Fair*, and a musical climax to the weeklong folklore *Csűr* at NAGYKÁLLÓ.

TRAVEL DETAILS

Trains
From Budapest to Debrecen (13 daily; 2½-3½hrs); Kiskőrös (7; 1½); Kiskunhalas (7; 1¾-2¾); Szeged (2; 2¼).
From Cegléd to Szeged (2; 1¾).
From Debrecen to Hortobágy (6; 1); Nyíregyháza (20; ½-¾).
From Füzesabony to Debrecen (6; 2).
From Kecskemét to Bugac (2; 1); Szeged (9; 1¼-2).
From Kiskőrös to Kalocsa (7; 1).
From Kiskunhalas to Baja (7; 1-1½).
From Mátészalka to Csenger (4; 1); Vásárosnamény (5; ½); Záhony (5; 2½).
From Nyíregyháza to Mátészalka (5; 1); Nagykálló (6; ¼); Nyírbátor (5; ¾); Záhony (5; ½).
From Szeged to Békéscsaba (7; 1½-2¼); Keceskemét (7; 1¼).

Buses
From Baja to Szeged (4-5 daily); Szekszárd (6-7).
From Békéscsaba to Békés; Gyula (hourly).
From Debrecen to Hajdúszoboszló (hourly); Nyírbátor (4-5 daily).
From Hajdúszoboszló to Debrecen; Nádudvar (hourly).
From Mátészalka to Vaja (5-6 daily).
From Kalocsa to Baja (hourly).
From Kecskemét to Kiskunfélegyháza (hourly).
From Kiskunfélegyháza to Bugac (every 1½hrs).

International trains
From Békéscsaba to Curtici (2 daily; 1½hrs).
From Debrecen to Chop (1); Moscow (2); Valea lui Mihai (1).
From Kiskunhalas to Belgrade (2).
From Kötegyán to Salonta (2).
From Nagyecsed to Carei (1; 3½).
From Püspökladány to Valea lui Mihai (1; 3).
From Szolnok to Bucharest (7 daily).

International coaches
Weekdays only, usually before 8am.
From Baja to Subotica (1 daily).
From Debrecen to Mukachevo (1).
From Gyula to Subotica (1).
From Kecskemét to Subotica (1).
From Szeged to Dubrovnik (1); Sarajevo (1); Subotica (1).

HUNGARY
CONTEXTS

-MAGYARORSZÁG-

HISTORICAL FRAMEWORK

The region of the Carpathian basin known as Hungary (Magyarország) changed hands many times before the Magyars arrived here at the end of the C9, and its history is marked by migrations, invasions and drastic changes, as Asia and Europe have clashed and blended. Over the centuries borders have shifted considerably, so geographical limits as well as historical epochs are somewhat arbitary. Transylvania, for example, was an integral part of Hungary for hundreds of years, but since the Treaty of Trianon (1920) has been a part of Romania; and is covered as part of that country in this guide.

Beginnings: Prehistory, the Romans and the Age of Migrations

Although recorded history of the area now covered by Hungary begins with the arrival of the Romans, archaeological evidence of **Stone Age** (3,000,000-8,000 BC) humans has been found in the *Istállóskő* and *Pilisszántó* caves in northern Hungary, suggesting that the earliest inhabitants lived by gathering fruit and hunting reindeer and mammoths. The end of the Ice Age created favourable conditions for the development of agriculture and the domestication of animals, which spread up through the Balkans in the Neolithic period, and was characteristic of the **Körös culture** (5,500-3,400 BC); clans herding sheep and goats and worshipping fertility goddesses, living alongside the River Tisza. As humans became more settled and spread into Transdanubia, evidence survives of mounds (*tell*) full of artefacts, seemingly leading towards the rise of the **Lengyel culture** around Lake Balaton.

During the **Bronze Age** (2,000-800 BC), warlike tribes arrived from the Balkans and steppes, introducing cattle and horses. Subsequent migrants brought new technology – the Cimmerians iron, and the Asiatic Scythians (500-250 BC) the potters' wheel and manufactures from Greek traders on the Black Sea coast – while the Celts, who superseded them in the early C3 BC, introduced glassblowing and left mournful sculptures and superb jewellery (most notably the gold treasures of *Szárazd-Regöly*), before being subdued by the Romans.

The **Roman conquest** was initiated by Augustus at the beginning of the Christian era, primarily to create a buffer zone in *Pannonia* between the empire and the barbarians to the east. By the middle of the C1 AD Roman rule extended throughout Transdanubia, from the Sava to the Danube, which was fortified with *castrum* and formed the *limes* – the military frontier. Trade, administration and culture grew up around the garrison towns and spread along the roads constructed to link the imperial heartland with the far-flung colonies in Dacia (Romania) and Dalmatia (Yugoslavia). Archaeological finds at Pécs, Sopron, Szombathely and Buda show that these were originally Roman towns; and examples of Roman aquaducts and baths may still be viewed at *Római-fürdő* and *Aquincum* in the capital, besides the *Temple of Isis* at Szombathely.

During the C4 the Romans began to withdraw from Pannonia, handing over its defence to the Vandals and Jazygians who lived beyond the Danube. In 430 they fell under the invading **Huns**, whose empire reached its zenith and then fragmented with the death of Attila (453). Other warring tribes like the Ostrogoths, Gepidae and Langobards occupied the region for the next 150 years, before they were swept aside by the **Avars**, whose empire survived until the beginning of the C8, when the region once again came up for grabs by any determined invader.

The coming of the Magyars and the foundation of Hungary

The **Magyars**' origins lie in the *Finno-Ugrian* peoples that dwelt in the snowy forests between the Baltic and the middle Urals. In about the C1AD, some of these tribes migrated south across the Bash-kiran steppes and fell under the influence of Turkic and Iranian culture; gradually becoming tent-dwelling nomadic herders who lived on a diet of mares' milk, horse-flesh, fish and berries. Some archae-ologists believe that they mingled with the ancient Bulgars north of the Caspian Sea (in a land known as 'Magna Bulgaria'), before the many fled from the violent Petchenegs (in 750?) and moved west-wards to settle on the far bank of the River Don in the so-called *Etelköz* region, around the year 830. Ties with the Huns and Avars have been postulated – in-cluding a common language - but there's stronger evidence to link the seven original Magyar tribes with three Kavar tribes, known collectively as the *Onogur*, or 'Ten Arrows'.

Overpopulation and Petcheneg attacks forced the Onogur to move westwards in 889, and tradition has it that the seven Magyar chieftains elected **Árpád** as their leader, pledging fealty to his heirs with a blood oath. Accompanied by the small Kun (or Cuman) tribes, the Onogur entered the Carpathian basin and em-barked on **conquest** in 896. Six Magyar tribes settled west of the Danube and in

the upper Tisza region, the seventh took the approaches to Transylvania, while the lower Tisza and the northern fringes of the Plain went to the Kuns and Kavars. For the next 70 years the Magyars remained raiders, striking terror as far afield as Constantinople and Orleans (where people thought them to be Huns), before the Christian powers forced them to desist.

Civilisation developed gradually, after Árpád's great-grandson Prince **Géza** established links with Bavaria and invited Catholic missionaries to Hungary. His son **István** (Stephen) took the decisive step of applying to Pope Sylvester for recognition, and on Christmas Day 1000 István was crowned as a 'Christian King', and began converting his pagan subjects with the help of Bishop Gellért. Royal authority was extended over the non-tribal lands by means of the **Megye** (county) system, and defended by forti-fied *vár*; artisans and priests were im-ported to spread skills and the new religion; and tribal rebellions were ruth-lessly crushed. For trying to unify the tribes and establish order, István was subsequently credited with the **found-ation of Hungary** and canonised after his death in 1038. His mummified hand and the 'Crown of St Stephen' have since been revered as both holy and national relics.

The Middle Ages, Renaissance and decline (C11-1526)

Succession struggles raged for decades following István's demise, and of the sixteen kings who preceded Andrew II (1205-35), only the humane Ladislas I (also canonised), Kálmán 'the booklover' and Béla III (1172-96) contributed any-thing to Hungary's development. Fortu-nately, invasions were few during the C11-C12, and **German and Slovak im-migrants** helped double the population (to about 2 million) by 1200. Parts of **Transylvania** were settled by the Magyars and Székely, perhaps before the second half of the C11, when the 'lands of St Stephen' were extended to

include **Slavonia** (between the Sava and Drava rivers) and the unwillingly 'associ-ated' state of **Croatia**. The growth in royal power caused tribal leaders to rebel in 1222, when Andrew II was forced to recognise the 'noble' status and rights of **the Natio** – landed freemen exempt from taxation – in the *Golden Bull*, a kind of Hungarian Magna Carta.

Andrew's son **Béla IV** was trying to restore royal authority when disaster struck from the east. . .the **Mongol in-vasion** of 1241, which devastated Hungary. Hundreds of towns and villages were sacked; refugees fled to the swamps and forests; crops were burnt or left unharvested, and famine and plague followed. Population losses ranged from 60-100% on the Plain to 20% in Transdanubia, and after the Mongol withdrawal a year later (prompted by the timely death of the Khan), Hungary faced a mammoth task of **reconstruction** – the chief achievement of Béla's reign, to which foreign settlers made a large contribution. Renewed domestic feuding (complicated by foreign intervention and the arrival of Cuman tribes in Hungary) dogged Andrew III's reign; and worsened when he died heirless in 1301 – the **end of the Árpád dynasty**.

Foreign powers advanced their own claimants, and for a while there were three competing kings, all duly crowned. **Charles Robert** of the French Angevin (or Anjou) dynasty eventually triumphed in 1310, when his rivals went home in disgust; and despite colonial skirmishes with Venice, Serbia and Wallachia, Hungary itself enjoyed a period of peace, for the Mongols and other great powers were occupied elsewhere. Gold mines in Transylvania and northern Hungary – the richest in Europe – stabilised state finances and the currency. Charles' son Lajos, **Louis the Great**, reigned (1342-82) during a period of expansion, when the population rose to 3,000,000, and by war and dynastic agrandisement crown territory grew to include Dalmatia, the Banat, Gallicia and (in theory) Poland. Following Louis' demise, leaving three daughters, another foreigner ascended the throne in 1395 – **Sigismund of Luxembourg**, Prince of Bohemia, whom the nobles despised and characterised as the 'Czech swine'. His extravagant follies and campaigns abroad were notorious, and while Sigismund recognised the growing threat of the Turks, he failed to prevent their expansion up through the Balkans.

During the C14, the realm contained 49 boroughs, about 500 market towns and 26,000 villages. Everyone benefited from peace and expanded trade, but the rewards weren't shared evenly, for the Angevin monarchs favoured towns and guilds, and most of all the top stratum of the Natio, on whom they depended for troops (*banderia*) when war threatened. The burden fell upon the **peasantry**, who lacked 'free' status and were compelled to pay *porta* (gate tax) to the state, tithes to the church, and one ninth of their produce to the landlords – plus extra taxes and obligations during times of war, or to finance a new royal palace.

Sigismund died in 1447 leaving one daughter, Elizabeth, just as **the Turks** were poised to invade and the succession struggles seemed inevitable. The Turks might have taken Hungary then, but for a series of stunning defeats inflicted upon them by **János Hunyadi**, a Transylvanian warlord of Vlach (Romanian) origin. The lifting of the siege of Nándorfehérvár (Belgrade) in 1456 checked the Turkish advance and caused rejoicing throughout Christendom – the ringing of church bells at noon was decreed by the Pope to mark this victory – while Hunyadi rose to be *Voivode* or Prince of Transylvania, and later regent for the boy king László. Following Hunyadi's death, László's early demise and much skullduggery, Mihály Szilágyi staged a coup and put his nephew Mátyás, Hunyadi's son, on the throne in 1458 to popular acclaim.

Matthias or **Mátyás Corvinus** is remembered as Hungary's '**Renaissance king**' for his political skills, patronage of the arts and multiple talents (including astrology). His second wife **Beatrix** of Naples lured Humanists and artists from Italy to add lustre to their palaces at Buda and Visegrád (of which some remains survive). Mátyás was an enlightened despot renowned for his fairness: 'King Mátyás is dead, justice is departed', people mourned. By taxing the nobles (against all precedent) he raised a standing force of 30,000 mercenaries, the Black Army, which secured the realm and made Hungary one of the leading powers in Central Europe. When he died in 1490, leaving no legitimate heir, the nobles looked for a king 'whose plaits they could hold in their fists'.

Such a man was Ulászló II, nicknamed 'King Okay', under whom the Black Army and its tax base were whittled away by the Diet (which met to approve royal decrees and taxes), and the nobles increased their exploitation of the peasantry and filched common land. Impelled by poverty, many peasants joined the crusade proclaimed by Cardinal Bakócz in 1514, which soon turned into an **uprising against the landlords**. This was savagely crushed: over 70,000 peasants were killed and their leader, **György Dózsa**, was roasted to death on an iron throne. The nobility passed the 'Werbőczy Code' (1517) binding the peasants to 'perpetual **serfdom**', forbad them to move home, and increased their *robot* (unpaid labour) to 52 days in the year.

Hungary's decline accelerated as corruption and incompetence bankrupted the treasury, forts along the border crumbled, and the revived *banderia* system of mobilisation was makeshift. Ulászlo's son Louis II was only nine when crowned, and by 1520

the Turks under Süleyman 'The Magnificent' had resumed their advance northwards, capturing the run down forts in Serbia. In August 1526 the Turks crossed the Drava and Louis hastened south to confront them at the **battle of Mohács** – a catastrophic defeat for the Magyars, whose army was wiped out together with its monarch, commanders and most of the leading clergy.

The Turkish Conquest and the division of Hungary

After sacking Buda and the south the Turks withdrew in 1526 to muster forces for their real objective, Vienna, the 'Red Apple'. To forestall this, Ferdinand of Habsburg proclaimed himself king and occupied western Hungary, while in Buda the nobility put János Zápolyai on the throne. Following Zápolyai's death in 1541 Ferdinand claimed full soverignty, but the Sultan occupied Buda and central Hungary, and made Zápolyai's young son ruler of Transylvania. Thereafter Transylvania became a semi-autonomous principality, nominally loyal to the Sultan and jealously coveted by the Habsburgs, and in 1568 the tripartite **division of Hungary** was formally recognised. Despite lengthy official truces and localised peace, warfare became a feature of everyday life for the next 150 years, and Hungary was never to recover its previous independence.

Royal Hungary – basically western Transdanubia and the north – served as a 'human moat' against the Turkish forces that threatened to storm Austria and Western Europe, kept at bay by Hungarian sacrifices at Szigetvár, Temesvár, Kőszeg and other fortresses. Although there were constitiutional arrangements to safeguard the privileges of the Natio, real power passed to the Habsburg chancellory and war council, where the liberation of Hungary took second place to the defence and aggrandizement of Austria, and the subjugation of Transylvania.

Turkish-occupied Hungary – *Eyalet-i Budin* – was ruled by a Pasha in Buda, with much of the land either deeded to the Sultan's soldiers and officials, or run directly as a state fief (*khasse*). The peasants were brutally exploited, for many had to pay rent to their absentee Magyar landlords besides the occupying

Turks. Their plight is evident from a letter to a Hungarian lord by the villagers of Batthyán: 'Verily, it is better to be Your Lordship's slaves, bag and baggage, than those of an alien people'. Peasants fled their villages on the Alföld to the safer fields around the expanding 'agro-towns' like Szeged and Debrecen, the nexus of the cattle trade which gradually supplanted agriculture, while neglect and wanton tree-felling transformed the Plain into a swampy wasteland – the *puszta*.

Transylvania's rulers pursued a precarious strategy of co-existence and rebellion; trying to provoke war between the Habsburgs and Turks while increasing their independence from both. The three **Nationes** (Magyars, Saxons and Székely) combined to deny the indigenous Vlachs political power, whilst competing amongst themselves and extending the borders of Transylvania (then much bigger than today). István Bocskai's *Hajdúk* forces secured the Szatmár region; Gábor Bethlen promoted economic and social development; but Prince György Rákóczi II aimed too high and brought the wrath of the Sultan down on Transylvania.

Religion was an additional complicating factor. The Protestant Reformation gained many adherents in Hungary during the C16, and while religious toleration was decreed in Transylvania in 1572, in Royal Hungary the Counter-Reformation gathered force under Habsburg rule. The Turks, ironically, were indifferent to the issue and treated all their Christian subjects (*Rayah*) with equal disdain. After the expulsion of the Turks, Protestant landowners were dispossessed in favour of foreign servants of the crown – one of the causes of subsequent anti-Habsburg struggles.

Hungary under the Habsburgs

A multinational army evicted the Ottomans after heavy fighting between 1683-99, and the Turks relinquished all claims by signing the *Peace of Karlowitz*. Yet for many years peace remained a mirage, for the Habsburgs now bitterly resented the Habsburg's policy and plundering soldiery. The long-running **Kuruc revolt** (1677-85) led by Imre Thököly was but a prelude to the full-scale **War of Independence** of 1703-11, when peasants and nobles banded together under **Ferenc Rákóczi II**, György's grandson, and initially routed the Habsburgs. Ultimately, however, they were defeated by superior Habsburg power and the desertion of their ally, Louis XIV of France, and peace born of utter exaustion came at last to Hungary.

Habsburg rule combined force with paternalism, especially during the reign of Empress **Maria Theresa** (1740-80), who believed the Hungarians 'fundamentally a good people, with whom one can do anything if one takes them the right way'. The policy of *impopulatio* settled thousands of Swabians, Slovaks, Serbs and Romanians in the deserted regions of Hungary, so that in areas like the 'Military Border' along the Sava **Magyars became a minority**; and by the end of the C18 they formed only 35%

of the population of the huge kingdom. For the aristocrats it was a *belle époque*: the Esterházy, Grassalkovich and Batthyány families and their lesser imitators commissioned over 200 palaces, and Baroque town centres and orchestras flourished. Yet the mass of the population were virtually serfs, using medieval methods that impoverished the soil, mired in isolated villages. Cattle, grain and wine – Hungary's main exports – went cheap to Austria, which tried to monopolise industry.

Germanization – in culture and the language of education and administration – was another feature of Habsburg policy. Whereas the richest nobles and most of the urban bourgeoisie plumped for the Habsburgs, the petty gentry and peasantry clung stubbornly to their Magyar identity. The ideals of the Enlightenment found growing support amongst intellectuals, and the revival of the **Magyar language** was inseparable from nationalist politics. **Ferenc Kazinczy**, who refashioned Hungarian as a literary language and translated foreign classics, was associated with the seven Jacobin conspirators executed for plotting treason against the Habsburgs in 1795.

The C19: Reform, revolution and Compromise

Magyar nationalism, espoused by sections of the Natio, became increasingly vocal during the early C19. Hungary's backwardness was a matter for patriotic shame and self-interested concern, especially after peasant riots in the impoverished, cholera-ridden Zempléni, and the publication of *Hitel* ('Credit'), which crushingly indicted the country's semi-feudal economy. However most nobles were determined to preserve their privileges. . .one wrote that 'God himself has differentiated between us, assigning to the peasant labour and need, to the lord, abundance and a merry life'. Moreover national liberation was seen in exclusively Magyar terms – the idea that non-Magyars within a multinational state might wish to assert their own identity was alien and subversive.

The **Reform Era** (roughly 1825-48)

saw many changes. Business, the arts and technology were in ferment, with Jews playing a major role in creating wealth and ideas (although they remained second class citizens). The **Diet** became increasingly defiant in its dealings with Vienna over finances and laws, and parliamentarians like Ferenc Deák, Count Batthyány and Baron Eötvös acted in the shadow of the 'giants' of the time, Széchenyi and Kossuth, who expounded rival programmes for change. Count **István Széchenyi**, Anglophile, author of *Hitel* and a large landowner was a tireless practical innovator; introducing silkworms, steamboats and the Academy, besides an unprecedented tax on the Natio to pay for the construction of his life's monument, the Chain Bridge linking Buda and Pest. His arch rival was **Lajos Kossuth**, smalltown lawyer turned MP and editor of the radical *Pesti Hirlap*, which scandalised and delighted literate citizens. He detested the Habsburgs, revered 'universal liberty' and demanded an end to serfdom and censorship, but Magyar chauvinism was his blindspot. The law of 1840, his greatest pre-revolutionary achievement, inflamed dormant nationalist feelings amongst Croats, Slovaks and Romanians by making Magyar the sole official language. . .an act for which Kossuth's ambitions would later suffer.

The fall of the French monarchy in February precipitated a crisis within the Habsburg empire – which Kossuth exploited to bring about the **1848 revolution** in Hungary. The Emperor yielded to demands for a constitutional monarchy, universal taxation, a widened male franchise and the union of Transylvania with Hungary. In Buda-Pest the nobles took fright and abolished serfdom when the radical poet **Sándor Petőfi** threatened them with thousands of peasants camped out in the suburbs. However anti-Magyar forces assailed the revolution in Croatia and Transylvania, while the Habsburgs regained control in Italy and Czechoslovakia, closing the

noose. The new Emperor Franz Joseph declared that Hungary would be partitioned after its defeat, in reaction to which the Debrecen Diet declared **Hungarian independence**. . .a state crushed by August 1849, when Tsar Nicholas of Russia, the 'Gendarme of Europe' sent his forces to aid the Habsburgs. A reign of terror followed, with mass executions.

Gradually, brute force was replaced by a **policy of compromise**, by which Hungary was economically integrated with Austria and assumed a major shareholding in the Habsburg Empire – now known as the 'Dual Monarchy'. The compromise (*Ausgleich*) of 1867 engineered by Ferenc Deák brought Hungary prosperity and status, but tied the country inextricably to the Empire's fortunes. Simmering nationalist passions would henceforth be focused against Hungary as much as Austria, and diplomatic treaties between Austria and Germany would bind Hungary to the 'Central Powers' in the event of war. In 1896, however, such dangers seemed remote, and people celebrated **Hungary's millenary anniversary** with enthusiasm.

1916-1945

Dragged into the **First World War** by its alliegance to the Central Powers, Hungary faced defeat by the autumn of 1918. The Western or 'Entente' powers decided to dismantle the Habsburg empire in favour of the **'Successor States'** – Romania, Czechoslovakia and Yugoslavia – which would acquire much of their territory at Hungary's expense. In Budapest, the October 30 *'Michaelmas Daisy Revolution'* put the Social Democratic government of Mihály Károlyi in power, which avoided the issue of land reform while trying to negotiate peace with the Entente, and resigned when France backed further demands by the Successor States.

On March 21 the Social Democrats agreed on cooperation with the **Communists**, who proclaimed a **Republic of Councils** (*Tanácsköztársaság*) led by **Béla Kun**, which ruled through local Soviets. Hoping for radical change and believing that 'Russia will save us', many people initially supported it until the enforced nationalisation of land and

capital, and attacks on religion, alienated the majority. The regime collapsed in August before the advance of the Romanian army, which occupied Budapest.

Then came the **White Terror**, as counter-revolutionary gangs spread out from Szeged, killing 'Reds' and Jews, who were made scapegoats for the previous Communist 'Red Terror'. **Admiral Miklós Horthy** appointed himself regent in 'sinful' Budapest and ordered a return to 'traditional values' with a vengeance. Meanwhile at the Paris Conference, Hungary was compelled to sign the **Treaty of Trianon** (July 4 1920), which surrendered two thirds of the country's historic territory, three fifths of its total population, and 3,000,000 Magyars to the Successor States. The bitterest loss was **Transylvania**, whose 103,093 sq.km and 1,700,000 Magyars went to Romania. This had a devastating effect upon Hungarian national feelings – summed up by the popular slogan of the times,

Nem, Nem, soha! (No, No, never!).

In 'rump' Hungary during **the 'twenties and 'thirties**, campaigning for the overturn of the Trianon *diktat* was the 'acceptable' outlet for politics; while workers' unions were tightly controlled and peasants struggled to form associations against the landlords and the gendarmerie, who rigged ballots and gerrymandered as in the old days. Politics were dominated by the *Kormánypárt* or Government Party led by Count Bethlen, which represented the Catholic Church and the landed gentry, and resisted any changes that would threaten their power, despite worsening social and economic conditions. In the countryside lived 'three million beggars' – the **landless peasantry** whose misery concerned the **'Village Explorers'** (*Falukutató*): a movement of the literary intelligentsia consisting of varied political hues, from the populist right to the urban left. With the Social Democrats co-opted by conservatism and the Communist Party-illegal, many workers and disgruntled petit bourgeoisie turned to the **'radical right'** to voice their grievances, which were easily turned against Jews and the 'Trianon Powers'. Resentment against France, Britain and Romania predisposed many Hungarians to admire the way **Nazi Germany** flouted the Versailles Treaty; a sentiment nurtured by Germany's 'penetration' of Hungary by means of credits for **industrialisation**, *Volksdeutsche* communities in Transdanubia and Nazi sympathisers in commerce, the civil service and the officer corps. Politicians like Gyula Gömbös gained votes by passing **anti-semitic laws**, and the country's belated industrial growth was partly due to the acquisition of territory from Czechoslovakia, following Germany's dismemberment of that country. After the annexation (*Anschluss*) of Austria, the Reich's military supremacy in Central Europe made it even harder for Hungary to avoid falling under Germany's hegemony.

With the outbreak of the **Second World War**, the government's pro-Nazi policy initially paid dividends. Romania was compelled to return **northern Transylvania** in July 1940, and Hungary gained additional territory from the invasion of Yugoslavia a year later. Hoping for more, Premier Bárdossy committed Hungary to the Nazi invasion of the USSR in June 1941 – an act that the former Prime Minister Teleki (who had engineered the recovery of Transylvania) condemned as the 'policy of vultures', before shooting himself. The Hungarian 2nd Army perished covering the retreat from Stalingrad, while at home, Germany demanded ever more foodstuffs and forced labour. As Axis fortunes waned Horthy prepared to declare neutrality, but Hitler forestalled him with *Operation Margarethe* in March 1944 – the outright **Nazi occupation of Hungary**.

Under Sztójay's puppet-government, Hungary's **Jews** were forced into ghettos to await their deportation to Auschwitz and Belsen. . .a fate hindered only by the heroism of the underground, a handful of people organised by the Swedish diplomat Raoul Wallenberg, and by the manoeuvring of some Horthyite politicians. Mindful of Romania's successful escape from the Axis in August, Horthy declared a suprise armistice on October 15, just as the Red Army crossed Hungary's eastern border. In response, Germany installed the *Nyilas* or native **Arrow Cross fascists** led by the derranged Ferenc Szálasi, whose gangs roamed Budapest extorting valuables and murdering people on the frozen Danube, while the Nazis systematically plundered the country. They blew up the Danube bridges and compelled the Russians to take Budapest by storm – a siege that reduced much of Buda to ruins. Meanwhile in Debrecen, a 'provisional assembly' of anti-fascist parties met under Soviet auspices and nominated a **provisional government** which took power after the Germans fled Hungary in April 1945.

The Rákosi era

In the November 1945 **elections** the Smallholders' Party won an outright majority, but the Soviet military insisted that the Communists and Social Democrats (with 17% of the vote) remain in government. **Land reform** and limited **nationalisation** were enacted; while the Communists tightened their grip over the Ministry of the Interior (which controlled the police) and elections became increasingly fraudulent. **Mátyás Rákosi**, Stalin's man in Hungary, gradually undermined and fragmented the 'bourgeois' parties with what he called 'salami tactics', and by 1948 – officially called the **'Year of Change'** – the Communists were strong enough to coerce the Social Democrats to join them in a single *Workers' Party*, and neutralise the Smallholders'. Church schools were siezed, Cardinal Mindszenty was gaoled for 'espionage' and the peasants were forced into collective farms. Over 500,000 Hungarians were imprisoned, tortured or shot, either in native concentration camps like the Recsk quarry, or as deportees in the Soviet Union: victims of the **ÁVO** secret police (later renamed the *ÁVH*), which spread terror throughout society.

Soviet culture and the 'personality cults' of Stalin and Rákosi were stiflingly imposed, while Hungarian classics like the *Tragedy of Man* were banned for failing to meet the standards of 'Socialist Realism'. Under the 1949 **Five Year Plan**, heavy industry took absolute priority over agriculture and consumer production. To fill the new factories, peasants streamed into towns and women were dragooned into the labour force. Living standards plummeted, and the whole of society was subject to the laws and dictates of the Party. 'Class conscious' workers and peasants were raised up to

high positions and 'class enemies' were discriminated against, while Party officials (*funkcionáriusok*) enjoyed luxuries unavailable to the populace, who suffered hunger and squalor.

Although the Smallholders' retained nominal positions in government, real power lay with Rákosi's clique, known as the 'Jewish Quartet'. Like elsewhere in Eastern Europe at this time, Hungary saw bitter **feuds within the Communist Party**. In October 1949 the 'Muscovites' purged the more independently-minded 'national' Communists on the pretext of 'Titoism'. The former Interior Minister **László Rajk** was executed; and his friend and successor (and, some say, betrayer), **János Kádár**, was gaoled and tortured with others during a second wave of purges. The Kremlin power struggles following Stalin's death in 1953 led to the replacement of Rákosi by **Imre Nagy**, a less hard-line figure. His **'New Course'**, announced in July, promised a more balanced industrial strategy and eased pressure on the peasants to collectivise, besides curbing the ÁVO terror. But Nagy had few allies within the Party, and Rákosi was soon able to strike back – expelling him from the Party and declaring a **return to Stalinist policies**. However, this brief interlude had encouraged murmerings of resistance.

The 1956 Uprising

The first act of opposition came from the official Writers' Union – the *November Memorandum* objecting to the rule of force. The Party clamped down, but also began to 'rehabilitate' the Rajk-purge victims. During June **1956** the intellectuals' **Petőfi circle** held increasingly outspoken public debates, and **Júlia Rajk** denounced 'the men who have ruined this country, corrupted the Party, liquidated thousands and driven millions to despair'. Moscow responded to the unrest by replacing Rákosi with **Ernő Gerő** – another hardliner – in July; a move which merely stoked public resentment. The mood came to a head in October, when 200,000 people attended Rajk's reburial; Nagy was readmitted to the Party, while **students** in Szeged and Budapest organised to demand greater national independence and freedom.

In Poland, Gomulka's 'reform com-

munists' had just won concessions from the Kremlin, and Budapest students decided to march on October 23 to the General Bem statue, a symbol of Polish-Hungarian solidarity. About 50,000 assembled, patriotic feelings rose, and the procession swelled as it crossed the Danube and approached Parliament. A hesitant speech there by Nagy failed to satisfy them, and students besieged the radio station on Bródy utca, demanding to voice their grievances on the airwaves. Then the ÁVH guards on the building opened fire. News of the shooting spread, triggering a city-wide **uprising** against the ÁVH which the regular police did little to control; while when Soviet tanks intervened, units of the Hungarian army began to side with the insurgents.

Over the next five days fighting spread throughout Hungary, despite Nagy's reinstatement as premier and pleas for order. **Revolutionary councils** sprang up in towns and factories and free newspapers appeared, demanding '*Ruszkik haza*' (Russians go home), free elections, civil liberties, industrial democracy and foreign neutrality. The intellectuals both inside and outside the Party who had led the protests before the 23rd now found themselves left behind by uncontrollable dynamism on the streets. The Party leadership temporised, reshuffled the cabinet and struggled to stay in control, as the 'bourgeois' parties reappeared and the newly liberated Cardinal Mindszenty provided a focus for the resurgent Right.

The negotiated **Soviet withdrawal**, beginning on the 29th, was a delaying tactic. The Russians regrouped in the countryside and brought in fresh troops from the east. On November 1 Nagy announced Hungary's withdrawl from the Warsaw Pact and asked the UN to support **Hungarian neutrality**; while the same night, Kádár and Ferenc Münnich slipped away from Parliament to join the Russians, who were preparing to crush the 'counter revolution'. America downplayed Hungary in the United Nations while the Suez crisis preoccupied world attention, but **Radio Free Europe**, sponsored by the CIA, encouraged the insurgents to expect Western aid. Having surrounded Budapest and other insurgent centres with tanks under cover of a snowstorm, the **Soviet attack** began in force before dawn on November 4.

Armed resistance was crushed within a few days, but the workers occupied their factories and proclaimed a **general strike**, which was maintained for months despite **mass arrests**. Deprived of physical power, the people continued to make symbolic protests like the 'Mothers' March' in December. Inexorably, though, the Party and secret police apparatus reasserted its control. Over 200,000 **refugees** fled to the West, while at home, thousands of insurgents were gaoled or executed, including Nagy and other leading Party 'revisionists', who were shot in 1958 after a secret trial.

Kádár's Hungary. . .

In the aftermath of the Uprising, the new Party leader **János Kádár** was widely despised as a Judas and a Quisling; and gained a reputation for ruthlessness in suppressing the last vestiges of opposition. After the early 1960s, however, his name came to be associated with a different policy – the **gradual reform** of Hungary's social and economic system from a totalitarian regime to one based, at least in part, on **compromise**. Kádár's famous phrase, 'Whoever is not against us is with us' (a reversal of the Stalinist slogan), invited a tacit compact between Party and people. Both had been shaken by the events of '56, and realised that bold changes – as happened in Czechoslovakia in 1967-68 – only invited Soviet intervention according to the Brezhnev doctrine of 'limited sovereignty'.

Having stimulated the economy by cautious reforms in the structure of pricing and management, and overcome opposition within the Politburo, Kádár and Rezsö Nyers announced the **New Economic Mechanism** (NEM) in January 1968. This reduced the extent of centralised planning, and was accompanied by measures to promote 'socialist legality' and make merit, rather than class-background and Party-standing, the criteria for promotion and higher education. While generally welcomed by the populace, the NEM angered 'New Left' supporters of Dubček's 'Socialism with a human face' in Czechoslovakia or the Chinese Cultural Revolution, and, more seriously, conservatives within the Party. With Moscow's backing, they watered-down the NEM and ousted Nyers, its leading advocate, from the Politburo; later expelling Hegedüs and other 'revisionist sociologists' from the Party.

But by 1974 Kádár was able to press forward with reforms. These encouraged consumerism, a limited private sector and even 'forint millionaires' to emerge during **the 1970s**, when Hungary became a byword for **affluence** within the Socialist bloc – the 'happiest barracks in the camp', as the joke had it. Mechanics, carpenters and others with marketable skills moonlighted profitably, as evinced by the boom in private home-building; and workers and unions acquired some say in the management of their enterprises. This so-called **'market socialism'** attracted the favours of Western politicians and bankers, and before *perestroika* the 'Hungarian model' seemed to represent the best hope for reform within Eastern Europe.

In **the 1980s**, however, economic and social problems became increasingly obvious – ranging from 30% inflation, whose effect was felt hardest by the **'new poor'** living on low, fixed incomes, to Hungary's £6,000,000 foreign debt (per capita, the largest in Eastern Europe). Having half-exposed the economy, planners found themselves bound by the logic of market forces, whose rigorous application would entail drastic redundancies and, almost certainly, **unemployment** in towns dominated by the unprofitable mining and steel industries. Although frank analyses of Hungary's economic dilemma started appearing in the media during the mid-'80s, **other issues**, deemed too sensitive, ran up against the limits of state tolerance. These included fears for **the environment** in the wake of Chernobyl and the decision to build a dam at Nagymaros (see p.105); an unofficial **peace movement** that was quickly driven back under-ground; and any discussion of the Party's 'leading role' or Hungary's alliance with the Soviet Union. Discussion of such topics could only be found in *samizdat* (underground) magazines like *Beszelö*, whose publishers were harassed as **dissidents**. Although in 1983 the Party announced that 'independents' could contest elections, it proved unwilling to allow them to enter Parliament, as demonstrated by the official gerrymandering used against László Rajk in 1986.

Yet the need for change was becoming evident even within the Party, where the caution of the 'old guard' – Kádár, Horváth and Gáspár – caused increasing frustration amongst **reformists**, who believed that Hungarians would only accept VAT, income tax and economic austerity if greater liberalisation seemed a realistic prospect. Happily, this coincided with the advent of **Gorbachev**, whose interest in the 'Hungarian model of Socialism' and desire to bring a new generation into power was an open secret.

. . .and the present

At the stormy **May 1988 Party Congress**, Kádár and seven Politburo colleagues were ousted by reformists: **Károly Grósz** (the new Party leader), **Imre Poszgay** (chairman of the *Népfront*) and **Rezsö Nyers**. Their promise that '. . .even the dissidents can be integrated into the political system' is belated recognition of stirrings already manifest in **civil society** (a current buzz-word, meaning everything organised independently of the Party and state). In 1988 three such organisations were founded in Budapest: the Democratic Forum, the Union of Scientific Workers (*TDDS*) and the Young Democrats' Federation (*FIDESZ*). Having served as mere 'transmission belts' for the Party's orders (to quote Lenin), the official SZOT unions and KISZ youth league were losing members even before the formation of TDDS and FIDESZ, whose advent can only encourage yet more **independent unions**. While the Democratic Forum provides a platform for welfare lobbyists, ecologists, pacifists etc, campaigns are also being waged by diverse local groups, many of whom are connected through the **Network for Free Initiatives**.

Given rising demands for **democracy**, no one can predict how much of its power the Party is willing to surrender. It's thought that Poszgay wants a multiparty system but will only countenance gradual steps towards it, and that Grósz is still more cautious; whether the new leadership can satisfy popular expectations is the leading question. The Party may well court support by taking stronger exception to the Ceauşescu regime's treatment of the **Hungarian minority in Transylvania** – an issue that unites public opinion – though here too, domestic politics must be carefully weighed against international ones.

MONUMENTAL CHRONOLOGY

8000BC	Palaeolithic cave-dwellers in the Bükk Mountains.	Remains found at Subalyuk, Szeleta and other caves.
400BC	Celts enter Transdanubia.	Pottery, glassware; gold treasure of Szárazd-Regöly.
C1-4AD	**Romans** occupy Pannonia, founding numerous towns.	Ruins at **Aquincum**, **Gorsium**, **Szombathely**, Pécs etc.
896	Magyar conques. The state and Christianity are established in Hungary by István I during the C11.	Ruins of the Székesfehérvár Basilica; C11 crypts at Pécs and **Tihany** Abbey are virtually all that remain.
C13	Mongol invasion. Castles and new towns are founded during the regin of Béla IV.	**Romanesque churches** at **Ják**, **Lébény**, **Zsámbék**, **Oskü** and **Velemér** stand comparison with **Pannonhalma Monastery**. Ruined *vár* at **Esztergom**, **Füzér**, **Boldogkőváralja** sited on precipitous crags.
C14-15	Zenith of Hungarian power in Europe under the Angevin monarchs and then Mátyás Corvinus.	Remains of **Buda** and **Visegrád** where **Gothic and Renaissance architecture** attained great heights; **Diósgyőr** castle in Miskolc.
1526- -1680s	After defeat at **Mohács**, Hungary is occupied for next 150 years by **Turks** and Habsburgs, and ravaged by warfare.	**Kőszeg**, **Sárospatak**, **Siklós** and other **castles** have remained largely intact; as have a few **Turkish** *türbe*, ex-*djami* and **minarets** at **Pécs** and **Eger**; but most medieval towns were destroyed, although on the Plain, Szeged and Debrecen expanded.
1703-11	Rákóczi War of Independence.	The **wooden belfrys**, pew-carvings and colourful coffered ceilings found at **Nyírbátor**, **Zsurk**, **Csaroda** and other remote churches in eastern Hungary are part-Gothic, and partly the 'folk' equivalent of the **Baroque style**.
C17-18	Under **Habsburg rule**, many towns are wholly rebuilt around new centres; while Buda Palace and other monumental buildings are begun.	This characterised much of C17-C18 architecture, eg. in the *Belváros* districts of **Győr**, **Veszprém**, **Székesfehérvár** etc, and at the **Esterházy Palace** in Fertőd.
1830 -1880s	After the Reform Era and the struggle for independence (1848-49), Hungary accepts the 'Compromise' of 1868. Development of new centres of industry – Miskolc, Salgótarján, Csepel etc.	The **Chain Bridge** presages a spate of construction in Budapest, where large houses are built alongside the new **boulevards**. **Szeged** rebuilt after '79 flood. Rise of **Neo-Classicism** – with Ybl and Hild's huge Basilicas in Eger, Pest and Esztergom – but also

1896	1,000 anniversary of the Magyar conquest.
1918 -1919	Habsburg empire collapses; Hungary briefly becomes a 'Republic of Councils'.
1920s & '30s	Hungary loses two thirds of its territory to neighbouring states. **Regency of Admiral Horthy**.
1944 -45	Nazis occcpy Hungary; heavy fighting with Soviet army.
1948 -56	**'Rákosi era'** characterised by Five Year Plans, police terror, and a propaganda blitz.
1956	**Hungarian Uprising**.
1960s -70s	Emergence of '**Kádárism**' – economic reforms to encourage greater public affluence. During this period, Hungary becomes a byword for '**consumer socialism**' in Eastern Europe.
1980s	Economic problems, made worse by energy shortfall after the Chernobyl disaster.
1988	**Grósz** replaces Kádár as Party leader

Neo-Gothic – the **Fishermen's Bastion** and **Vajdahunyad Castle** (which, like the Metro, was inaugurated in 1896) – plus Lechner's attempts to develop a uniquely '**Hungarian Style**' for the **Applied Arts Museum** and the public buildings in **Kecskemét**. Deliberate evocation of past national glories – the erection of 'Heroes' Gates' in **Szeged**, **Kőszeg** etc.

Budapest and many towns incur massive damage. This is swiftly repaired.

Dunaújváros and other new towns; crash urbanisation and industrialisation; the **Liberation Monument** and other Soviet-style projects exemplify this phase.

Widespread urban damage – Budapest is worst affected.

The **Metro** is completed. **Modernistic** cultural centres at Győr and Sárospatak are notable examples of '60-70's **architecture**; while supermarkets, hotels and resorts around Balaton are more typical of the period. Go ahead for construction of **Nagymaros dam** and more nuclear reactors at **Paks**. Closure of mines and other loss-making industries proposed by the state.

BOOKS AND MUSIC

Books marked * are best not taken to Hungary.

Travel/General accounts
Patrick Leigh Fermor, *A Time of Gifts, Between the Woods and the Water* (Penguin £3.95/£3.95). In 1934 the young Leigh Fermor started walking from Holland to Constantinople, and reached Hungary in the closing chapter of volume one of his adventures. *Between the Woods. . .* is devoted to his travels in Hungary and Romania (with a third volume to come, covering Moldavia and Bulgaria). Lyrical and factually detailed to an amazing degree, they're probably the best travel books on these countries to be found in print.
Gyula Illyés, *People of the Puszta* (Corvina). An unsentimental, sometimes horrifying immersion in the life of the landless peasantry of pre-war Hungary, mainly set in Transdanubia rather than on the Plain. Illyés – one of Hungary's greatest C20 writers – was born into such a background, and the book breathes authenticity. Highly recommended.
John Paget, *Hungary and Transylvania* (Murray 1850; 2 vols). Paget's massive book attempted to explain C19 Hungary to the English middle class, and within its aristocratic limitations, succeeded brilliantly. Occasionally to be found in secondhand-bookshops.
Gyula Antalffy, *A Thousand Years of Travel in Old Hungary* (Corvina). Slightly stodgey in places, but with enough anecdotes and odd details to keep one's attention as it surveys a millenium of Hungary through the eyes of foreign and native travellers.
Walter Starkie, *Raggle-Taggle*. The wanderings of a Dublin professor with a fiddle, who bummed around Budapest and the Plain in search of Gypsy music in the 1920s. First published in 1933 and last issued by Murray in 1964 – a secondhand-bookshop perennial.
Bernard Newman, *The Blue Danube* (Jenkins 1935). The archetypal Englishman abroad during the early '30s, Newman pedalled from the source of the Danube down to Sfintu Gheorghe in the Delta, feeling the pulse of Europe en route. Each country is diagnosed in a single chapter – the Hungarian one is mildly interesting.

History, Politics and Sociology
C.A. McCartney, *Hungary: A Short History* (Edinburgh UP). A basic outline of events from the Magyar conquest to the Rákosi era, in readable if unexciting prose. The bulkier and dryer *October Fifteenth. . .* is restricted to the period 1918-45, which Nagy-Talavera (see below) handles with more flair.
Pál (Paul) Ignotus, *Hungary*. An excellent short history, more colourful than McCartney's, by a former Social Democratic politician who was gaoled and tortured in Vác during the Rákosi era – an experience described in *Political Prisoner** (RKP).
Bill Lomax, *Hungary 1956** (Allison & Busby). Probably the best – and shortest – book on the Uprising, by an acknowledged expert on modern Hungary. Lommax also edited *Eyewitness in Hungary** (Spokesman 1980), an anthology of accounts by foreign communists (most of whom were sympathetic to the Uprising) that vividly depicts the elation, confusion and tragedy of the events in October 1956.
György (George) Konrád, *Antipolitics** (Quartet). Inspiring, witty and humane, described by E.P.Thompson as a 'book of exceptional importance', it contains Konrád's ideas for transforming Hungarian society 'from below' (without directly challenging the Party) and ending the Superpowers' sway over Europe. Essential reading for peace activists and cold war warriors alike, written in an easy style.
Ferenc Kőszegi & E.P. Thompson, *The New Hungarian Peace Movement**. A pamphlet that seems sad in retrospect, despite its optimistic tone; the unofficial 'Peace Group for Dialogue' has been forced to disband since their meeting with Thompson in Konrád's flat, and the publication of this in 1983. **END**, the European Disarmament movement, is the publisher, and their journal prints the latest news of the peace struggle inside Hungary (and worldwide). Other publications obtainable from the *END Hungary Working Group* (11 Goodwin St. London N4 3HQ), which welcomes donations and support.
János Kenedi, *Do It Yourself** (Pluto Press). Building your own home is a herculean task in Hungary today, and Kennedi gives a full account of the

necessary wheeling and dealing, laced with tongue-in-cheek Marxist terminology, showing how fine are the lines between private enterprise, 'socialist construction' and outright cheating.

Miklós Haraszti, *A Worker in a Workers' State** (Penguin). Factual, gritty investigation of 'Piecework' (the book's Hungarian title) in Budapest's Red Star factory, which earned Haraszti a prison term for 'defaming socialism'. He's now active in the *samizdat* (underground publishing) movement.

I. & N. Völgyes, *The Liberated Female*. Despite minor faults, a revealing (if ultimately depressing) survey of women's place in modern Hungary, as contrasted with their status – or rather, lack of it – during feudal and 'liberal' times. Essential reading for anyone interested in understanding Hungarian society – although it doesn't go beyond the 1970s – and a small contribution to the femininist/-socialist debate.

William Shawcross, *Crime and Compromise** (Weidenfeld). An intriguing subject for a biographer: János Kádár, Hungary's longtime Party leader, once reviled as the 'Butcher of Budapest', later fondly known as 'old Jancsi'. Surveying Kádár's life and political career, Shawcross poses the question 'Unprincipled opportunist or principled pragmatist?', but fails to decide either way.

Tamás Aczél, *Revolt of the Mind**. Describes how and why sections of the intelligentsia revolted against Party control. Khrushschev, the Soviet leader, is alleged to have said that the 1956 revolution would never have occurred had a few intellectuals been shot earlier – one of the propositions discussed in *Ten Years After** (Macgibbon & Kee) : a series of eye-witness accounts and essays, published to commemorate the tenth anniversary of the Uprising.

Noel Barber, *Seven Days of Freedom* (Macmillan 1974)*. Vivid but oversimplified account of the Uprising, focused mainly on events in Budapest, by the *Daily Telegraph*'s top reporter. Kádár is unreservedly condemned as a stooge, which is no longer the judgement of most Hungarians or foreign observers.

David Irving, *Uprising** (Hodder). Massively detailed on every aspect of 1956, including events in Győr and the countryside, but marred by crude commie-bashing and the taint of Irving's notorious anti-semitism.

George Mikes, *A Study in Infamy** (Deutsch). Better known in the West for his humorous writings, Mikes exposes the activities of the secret police during the Rákosi period, using captured ÁVO/ÁVH documents which explain their methods for surveillance of the population and using terror as a political weapon.

András Hegedüs, *Socialism and Bureaucracy** and *The Humanisation of Socialism** (Allison & Busby). Two heavyweight critiques of Eastern European socialism from a Marxist perspective. The latter book of essays, by other members of the 'Budapest School', includes two excellent pieces on women in socialist countries by **Maria Márkus** and **Ágnes Heller** (now in exile).

W.F. Robinson, *The Pattern of Reform in Hungary* (Praeger). A thorough, academic report on the 'Kádár model' of socialism in Hungary. All solid stuff, but certainly not bedtime reading.

N.M. Nagy-Talavera, *Greenshirts and Others* (Stanford UP). A well written and researched study of the social dislocations, racism and paranoid nationalism which afflicted Hungary and Romania during the inter-war period, giving rise to native fascist movements and bitter anti-semitism, culminating in the massacre of Hungarian and Romanian Jews. Sadly, anti-semitism is still common in both countries today, although state persecution no longer exists.

John Bierman, *Righteous Gentile* (Allen Lane). The best biography yet of Raoul Wallenberg, the Swedish diplomat whose daring efforts partly frustrated Eichmann's attempt to exterminate the Jews of Hungary during 1944-45.

Art, Ethnography, Cinema and Cooking
Corvina the state publishing house is slowly revealing Hungary's artistic treasures in print, and if *Goldsmith's Work and Craftsmanship in Turkish-Ruled Hungary* are anything to go by, the planned series of books will be excellent

Tekla Dömötör, *Folk Religion and Superstition in Hungary* (Corvina). A superb trove of social history, folk beliefs and customs, recently made available in an English translation.

George Petrie, *History Must Answer to Man* (Corvina). Though you wouldn't guess so from the title, this is an unpretentious and very readable account of Hungarian cinema; surveying its history from the beginnings to the work of directors like Bacsó, Szabó, Jancsó, Makk, Kézdi-Kovács. Could do with an update, though.

George Lang, *The Cuisine of Hungary* (Penguin; £21). A well-written and beautifully illustrated work of coffee-table dimensions, telling you everything you need to know about Hungarian cooking, its history, and how to do it yourself.

Fred Macniol, *Hungarian Cooking* (Penguin). A much cheaper if less glossy alternative to Lang's book. ...unfortunately out of print.

Fiction and Poetry

Hungarian classics in translation *are mostly out of print and difficult to find. I managed to track down*:

Endre Ady, *Explosive Country* (Corvina). Various essays on literature and Hungarian society, by the leading poet of the early C20, whose poems really defy adequate translation from Hungarian.

Mór Jókai, *The Dark Diamonds* (Corvina). A rather padded story of a mining entrepreneur who makes good and moves into C19 Budapest high society, by the Hungarian equivalent of Dickens.

A. Nyerges, *The Poems of Petőfi*; *Ady and Attila József*. Three collections of the work of Hungary's most famous poets, published by the Hungarian Cultural Foundation in Buffalo, New York (1969 & 1973).

Modern authors in translation published in Britain:

György (George) Konrád, *The Caseworker* (Hutchinson); *The City Builder*; *The Loser** (Penguin). In contrast with his optimistic *Antipolitics* (see above), Konrád's novels are overwelmingly bleak – dealing with misery, alienation, escapism, hypocrisy and madness. Despite the subject matter, his powers of insight and rich use of language are seductive and compelling.

József Lengyel, *Prenn Drifting*; *From Beginning to End* and *The Spell*; *The Judge's Chair*; *Acta Sanctorum*; and *Confrontation** (all published by Peter Owen). A dedicated Communist since his youth, Lengyel apparently kept his faith though he was in the Gulag for some years, but later began to display doubts. His colourful semi-autobiographical novels concern morality under

stress, ambition and the question of ends versus means. *The Bridgebuilders* (Corvina) is perhaps the least gripping, although Lengyel reportedly considers it one of his best.

Émigré writers and foreign writers on Hungary include:

Stephen Vizinczey, *In Praise of Older Women* (Penguin 1967). The memoirs of a randy egocentric lad growing up in refugee camps and in Budapest during the Rákosi years. Soft-porn mixed with social comment and supposedly profound insights into the nature of women, which made a splash when first published in the West in 1967.

Sándor Weöres, *Selected Poems* (Penguin). Another exile from '56, Weores is perhaps the best known Hungarian poet writing abroad.

Cecilia Holland, *Rakossy* (Hodder). Shy Austrian princess marries uncouth Magyar baron and goes to live at his castle on the Hungarian marches, where everyone is eventually killed by the Turkish hordes. Stirring stuff.

Hans Habe, *Black Earth** (NEL 1968) The tale of a peasant lad's committment to the Communist underground, and his disillusionment with the Party once it takes power. In some ways similar to Dumitriu's masterpiece *Incognito*, despite the lurid blurb.

Music: Records

The works of Hungary's national composers, **Liszt**, **Bartók** and **Kodály**, would fill a catalogue; and these, together with directors like Dohnányi and the country's finest contemporary soloists and singers, are well represented in record shops abroad. The *Hungarotron* company manufactures good quality LPs covering a wide range of classical music, jazz and native pop music, sold for amazingly low prices in *zeneműbolt* within Hungary.

Folk music (*Népzene*), too, is very popular; and the Hungarians have been assiduously researching and recording their musical heritage since the pioneering work done by Bartók and Kodály. Some of these are produced in excellent boxed sets, including a comprehensive English commentary. Among the many folk **records** the following are recommended:

Magyar népzene 3 (Hungarian folk music). A 4-disc set of field recordings covering the whole range of folk music –

Old and New style songs, instrumental music, and music for occasions – that's probably the best all round introduction. In Britain, the discs are marketed as 'Folk Music of Hungary Vol.1' (Hungartron LPX 18050-53).

Magyar hangszeres népzene (Hungarian Instrumental Folk Music). A very good 3-disc set of field recordings of village and Gypsy bands, including lots of solos. Hungaroton LPX 18045-47.

Muzsikás Traditional pieces and contemporary arrangements by Márta Sebestyén, Hungary's leading Táncház singer. (Hungaroton SLPX 18121).

Márta Sebestyén Highly recommended LP released in Britain by Hannibal (HNBL 1330).

Táncházi muzsika (Music from the Táncház). A double album of the Sebö Ensemble playing Táncház music from various regions of Hungary. Wild and exciting rhythms. (Hungaroton SPLX 18031-32).

Jánosi Égyüttes (Jánosi Ensemble). Another young group, performing 'authentic' versions of some of the folk tunes that Bartók borrowed in his compositions.

A record that makes a bridge between classical and folk music. (Hungaroton SPLX 18103).

Sources

The best all round **bookshops** (*könyvesbolt*) in Hungary are on Váci utca, and in the Párizsi udvar, in the V district of Budapest. In Britain, a fair number of the abovementioned books and records are available from (or can be ordered through) *Collets International Bookshop*, 129 Charing Cross Rd. London W1 (☎ 01-734-0782). For out-of-print books, ask *The Travel Bookshop* (13 Blenheim Crescent, London W11; ☎ 01-229-5260), or try to join – or simply read in – the **library** of the *School of Slavonic and Eastern European Studies*, Mallet St. London WC1. With a reference, non-students can pay a £25 deposit and obtain borrowing rights. In the main hall upstairs are all kinds of **magazines** and journals, including the *Index on Censorship*, *New Hungarian Quarterly*, *New Socialist*, the *END Journal*, and the (CIA-inputed) *Problems of Communism*, which regularly feature articles on Hungary.

LANGUAGE

Hungarian is a unique, complex and subtle tongue, classified as belonging to the Finno-Ugric family of languages, which means that it's totally unlike any other language that .you're likely to know. Its closest (though still distant) relatives are Finnish and the Siberian Chuvash language, although odd grammatical structures and words from Turkish have crept in, together with a some German, English and more recently (a few) Russian neologisms. Consequently, foreigners aren't really expected to speak Hungarian, and natives are used to (but don't honestly appreciate) being addressed in **German**, the *lingua franca* of East European tourism. It's understood by older people – particularly in Transdanubia – and by many students and professional types, besides virtually everyone around the Balaton or in tourist offices. For a brief visit it's probably easier to mug up on some German for your means of communication, but a few basic Magyar phrases can make all the difference. Most Magyars are delighted when a foreigner attempts to speak their language; and a cheery *Jó napot kívánok!* can usually sweeten the surliest shop assistant. People are likeliest to understand **French** or **English** if you mix in educated circles; though I knew a teenager who'd gleaned his entire English vocabulary from Judas Priest records! Despite obligatory basic instruction in schools, people rarely know Russian and use it most unwillingly if they do.

In addition to the following, you'll find a detailed food glossary and a selection of phrases pertaining to transport on pages 26 and 18. *Berlitz Hungarian for Travellers* (£1.95) is the best of the available phrase books and contains a useful basic grammar; while if you're prepared to seriously study the language, *Colloquial Hungarian* (RKP £6.95) is the book. As a supplement, invest in the handy little *Angol - Magyar / Magyar - Angol Kisszótár* dictionaries; available from bookshops in Hungary for 60Ft and, much more expensively, at Collets in London.

Extremely basic Hungarian grammar and pronunciation

Although its rules are fiendishly complicated, it's worth describing a few features of **Hungarian grammar**, albeit imperfectly. Hungarian is an agglutinating language – in other words, its vocabulary is built upon **root-words**, which are modified in various ways to express different ideas and nuances. Instead of prepositions – 'to', 'from', 'in' etc. – Hungarian uses **suffixes**, or tags added to the ends of genderless **nouns**. The change in suffix is largely determined by the noun's context – eg. (the) book = *könyv*; (give me the) book = *könyvet*; (in the) book = *könyvben*; (to the) book = *könyvnek* – but also by complicated rules of vowel harmony (which you're bound to get wrong, so don't worry about them!). Most of the nouns in the vocabulary section below are in the subject form – that is, without suffixes. In Hungarian, **'the'** is *a* (before a word beginning with a consonant) or *az* (preceding a vowel); the word for **'a/an'** is *egy* (which also means 'one'). **Adjectives** precede the noun (*a piros ház* = the red house), adopting suffixes to form the comparative (*jó* = good; *jobb* = better), plus the prefix *leg* to signify the superlative (*legjobb* = the best). **Negatives** are usually formed by placing the word *nem* after the subject, and inverting the word order : *én itt vagyok* = I'm here ; *én nem vagyok itt* = I'm not here. *Ez* (this), *ezek* (these), *az* (that) and *azok* (those) are the **demonstratives**.

Achieving passably good **pronunciation**, rather than grammar, is the first priority. **Stress** almost invariably falls on the first syllable of a word and all letters are spoken, although in sentences, the tendency is to slur words together. Vowel sounds are greatly affected by the bristling **accents** (that actually distinguish separate letters) which, together with the 'double letters' *cs, gy, ly, ny, sz, ty* and *zs*, give the Hungarian **alphabet** its formidable appearance.

A	o	as in hot
Á	a	as in father
B	b	as in best
C	ts	as in bats
CS	ch	as in church
D	d	as in dust
E	e	as in yet

É	ay	as in say
F	f	as in fed
G	g	as in go
GY	di	as in medium, said fairly quickly
H	h	as in hat
I	ee	as in feet
Í	ee	as in see, but longer
J	y	as in yes
K	k	as in sick
L	l	as in leap
LY	y	as in yes
M	m	as in mud
N	n	as in not
NY	ni	as in onion
O	aw	as in saw, but shorter
Ó		aw as in awe, with the tongue high inside the mouth
Ö	ur	as in fur, but without any 'r' sound
Ő	ur	as in fur, as above, but with the lips tightly rounded
P	p	as in sip
Q	qu	as in queue
R	r	pronounced with the tip of the tongue, as in Scotland
S	sh	as in shop
SZ	s	as in so
T	t	as in sit
TY	tti	as in prettier, said quickly
U	u	as in pull
Ú	oo	as in food
Ü	u	as in the German 'unter'
Ű	u	as above, but longer and with the lips tightly rounded
V	v	as in vat
W	w	as in 'Walkman', 'whisky' or 'WC' (vait-say)
Z	z	as in zero
Z	S s	as in measure

Basics

Do you speak English/German/French	*beszél angolul/németül/franciaul?*
yes – OK	*igen – jó*
no/not	*nem*
I (don't) understand	*(nem) értem*
please – excuse me	*kérem – bocsánat*
two beers, please	*két sört, kérek*
thank you (very much)	*köszönöm (szépen)*
you're welcome	*szívesen*
hello/goodbye (informal)	*szia*
goodbye	*viszontlátásra*
see you later	*viszlát*
I wish you. . .(formally)	*. . .kívánok*
good morning/day/	*jó reggelt/napot/*
evening/night	*estét/éjszakát*
how are you?	*hogy vagy?*
how are you? (more formal)	*hogy van?*
could you speak more slowly?	*elmondaná lassabban?*
what do you call this?	*mi a neve ennek?*
please write it down	*kérem, írja ezt le*
today – tomorrow	*ma – holnap*
the day after tomorrow	*holnapután*
the day before	*az előző nap*

yesterday	*tegnap*
in the morning – in the evening	*reggel – este*
at noon - at midnight	*délben – éjfélkor*

Questions and requests

There's a whole range of ways in which to ask questions in Hungarian, the subtleties of which will elude foreigners. Stick to *van. . .?* (is there?/is it?), to which the reply may be *nincs* or *azok nincsenek* (it isn't/there aren't any). Waiters, shop-assistants etc. often rely upon the laconic *tessék?*, meaning anything from 'What do you want?' to 'go ahead' or 'next'. *Kaphatok. . .?* ('Can I have. . .?) is polite, but less widely used than *Szeretnék. . .* ('I'd like. . .) in shops; while in restaurants you can order by saying *'Kérem, hozzon. . .'* ('Please bring me. . .'); *'Kérem, adjon azt'* ('Please give me that') ; *'Egy ilyet kérek'* ('I'll have one of those'); or simply *'. . .kérek* ('. . .please').

I'd like/we'd like	*Szeretnék/szeretnénk*
Where is/are. . .?	*Hol van/vannak. . .?*
Take me to. . .	*Vigyen kérem a. . .*
Hurry up!	*Siessen!*
How much is it?	*Mennyibe kerül?*
per night	*egy éjszakára*
per week	*egy hétre*
a single/double room	*egyágyas/kétágyas szobát*
hot/cold water	*meleg/hideg víz*
a shower	*a zuhany*
It's too expensive	*Ez nagyon drága*
anything cheaper?	*van valami olcsóbbt?*
a student discount?	*van diák kedvezmény?*
Is everything included?	*Ebben minden szerepel?*
I asked for. . .	*Én . . .-t rendeltem*
The bill please	*Kérem a számlát*
we're paying separately	*Külön-külön kívánunk fizetni*
what? – why?	*mi – míért*
when? – who?	*mikor - ki?*

Directions

Where's the campsite/hotel?	*hol van a kemping/szálloda?*
railway (bus) station	*vasút- (autóbusz-) -állomás*
(railway or bus) terminal	*pályaudvar*
(bus or train) stop	*megálló*
Is it near? (far)	*közel (távol) van?*
Which bus goes to the. . .?	*Melyik autóbusz megy a . . . .- ra/re*
a one-way ticket to. . .	*egy útra jegyet . . . .-ra/re*
a return ticket to. . .	*egy oda-vissza jegyet . . .-ra/re*
Do I have to change for. . .?	*át kell szállom . . ..- be?*
towards – on the right/left	*fele – jobbra/balra*
straight ahead	*egyenesen előre*
(over) there – here	*ott - itt*
Where are you going?	*Hova megy?*
Is that on the way to. . .?	*Az a . . . . úton?*
I want to get out at. . .	*le akarok szállni. . .*
please stop here	*ez jó itt*
I'm lost	*eltévedtem*

Reactions and trouble

and – or – nothing	*és – vagy – semmi*
perhaps – very	*talán – nagyon*
good – bad – better	*jó – rossz – jobb*
big – small	*nagy – kicsi*
quick – slow	*gyors – lassú*
now – later	*ekkor – később*

beautiful – ugly	*szép – csúnya*
Take your hands off me!	*fogdoss!*
Help!	*Segitség!*
I'm ill.	*beteg vagyok*

Some signs

entrance – exit	*bejárat – kijárat*
arrival	*érkezés*
departure	*indulás*
open – closed	*nyitva – zárva*
free admission	*szabad belépés*
women's – men's	*női – férfi*
toilet	*mosdók* (or *WC* - 'Vait-say')
shop – market	*. . .bolt – piac*
rooms to let	*szoba kiadó* (or *Zimmer frei*)
hospital	*kórház*
pharmacy	*gyógyszertár*
(local) police	*(kerületi) Rendőrség*
caution/beware	*vigyázat!*
no smoking	*tilos a dohányzás*
no bathing	*tilos a fürdés*

Time

Luckily, the 24-hour clock is used for timetables, but on cinema programmes you may see notations like ¼4, ¾4 etc. These derive from the spoken expression of time which, as in German, makes reference to the hour approaching completion. For example 3.30 is expressed as '*fél négy*' – 'half (on the way to) four'; 3.45 - '*háromnegyed négy*' ('three quarters on the way to four'); 6.15 - '*negyed hét*' ('one quarter towards seven') etc. However, '. . . . o'clock' is . . .*óra* , rather than refering to the hour ahead. Duration is expressed by the suffixes -*től* and *ig* (from. . .to. . .); minutes are *perc* ; to ask the time, say '*Hány óra?*'.

Numbers and dates

1 *egy*	21 *huszonegy*
2 *kettő*	30 *harminc*
3 *három*	40 *negyven*
4 *négy*	50 *ötven*
5 *öt*	60 *hatvan*
6 *hat*	70 *hetven*
7 *hét*	80 *nyolcvan*
8 *nyolc*	90 *kilencven*
9 *kilenc*	100 *száz*
10 *tíz*	101 *százegy*
11 *tizenegy*	150 *százötven*
12 *tizenkettő*	200 *kettőszáz*
13 *tizenhárom*	300 *háromszáz*
14 *tizennégy*	400 *négyszáz*
15 *tizenöt*	500 *ötszáz*
16 *tizenhat*	600 *hatszáz*
17 *tizenhét*	700 *hétszáz*
18 *tizennyolc*	800 *nyolcszáz*
19 *tizenkilenc*	900 *kilencszáz*
20 *húsz*	1000 *egyezer*

half	*fél*
a quarter	*negyed*
a third	*harmad*
a dozen	*egy tucat*
each	*darab*

Sunday	*vasárnap*
Monday	*hétfő*
Tuesday	*kedd*
Wednesday	*szerda*
Thursday	*csütörtök*
Friday	*péntek*
Saturday	*szombat*
on Monday	*hetfőn*
on Tuesday	*kedden* etc.
day	*nap*
week	*hét*
month	*hónap*
year	*év*

ROMANIA

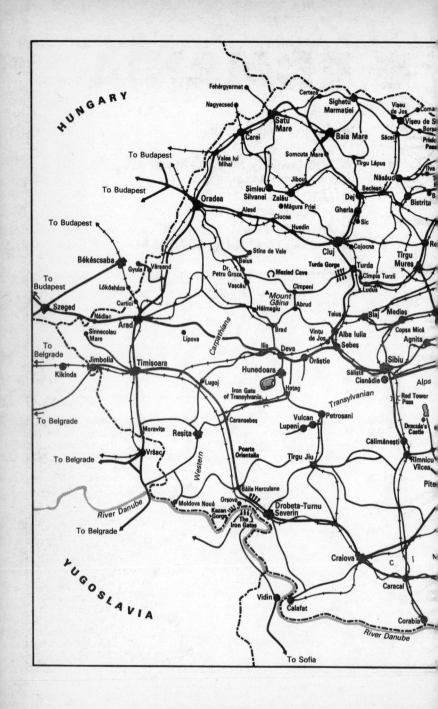

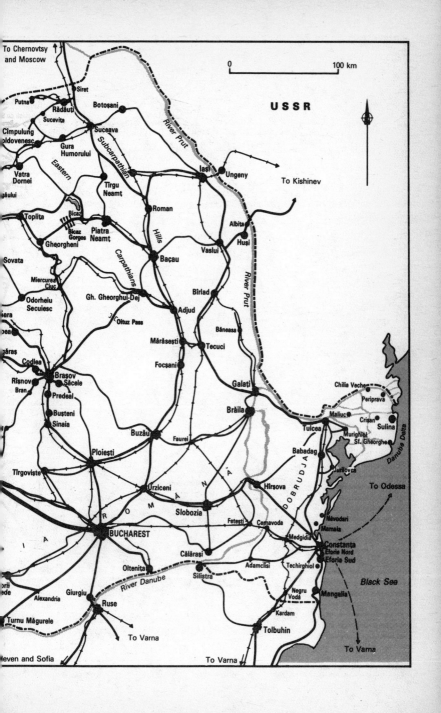

ROMANIA BASICS

ROMANIA: WHERE TO GO AND WHEN

Travel in **Romania** is as rewarding as it is a challenge. The country's mountain scenery and great diversity of wildlife, its cultures and people, and a life that seems at times out of the last century, leave few who visit unaffected. However, unless you visit on a package, it is undeniably the hardest country of the Eastern Bloc to cope with. The current regime of Party leader Nicolae Ceauşescu is rigorous and bureaucratic, and the country verges on bankruptcy: power cuts are frequent; food is scarce; and buses scarcely function. Coming to Romania on a **package** – to the Black Sea or on one of the (more worthwhile) 'Dracula Tours' – you will be effectively shielded from such realities. Shielded, too, from many of the costs imposed by state bureaucracy. Package tourists are given visas for the duration of their visit and exempted from the obligatory exchange of $10 (US) a day which 'independent' travellers must undergo for the duration of their stay. Travelling **independently**, by necessity, involves balancing your inclinations with your budget – and some frustrating moments. However, it would be a shame to let such factors deter at least a brief exploration. Much of Romania's charm lies in the less-visited, more 'primitive' regions, and it's the experience of getting there that really gives you an insight into the country. Rather than expect an easy ride, try to accept whatever happens as an adventure – encounters with Gypsies, wild bears, oafish secret policemen and assorted odd characters are really far more interesting than anything purveyed by the tourist board.

Romanians (the largest ethnic group) trace their ancestery back to the Romans, and it's not unfair to say that 'Latin' traits prevail. **People** are generally warm, spontaneous, anarchic, and appreciative of style and life's pleasures – sadly, in contrast to the austerity with which they're saddled. In addition to ethnic Romanians, there are communities from half a dozen other races and cultures. Transylvanian Germans (Saxons) reside around the fortified towns and churches built to guard the mountain passes during the Middle Ages; so do some two million Magyars, many of whom pursue an archaic lifestyle long since vanished in Hungary; and along the coast and in the Delta there's a mixture of Ukranians, Serbs, Bulgars, Gypsies, Turks and Tartars.

In spite of increasingly heavy-handed 'modernisation', few countries can offer such a wealth of distinctive folk **music, festivals and customs**, all still going strong in remoter areas like the Apuseni Mountains, Maramureş and northern Moldavia, or the Hungarian-influenced Csángó and Székelyföld regions. Romania's diversity is also expressed in **architecture**, with forbidding castles, log houses in Maramureş and Oltenia, Delta villages built of reeds, not to mention churches and monasteries painted with imaginatively nasty visions of Judgement Day. As distinct from the lowlands (apt to be disfigured by hideous and polluting industry), the mountainous **scenery** is usually a treat to behold. There are bears, stags and eagles in the wild Carpathians, while during spring and autumn in particular, 300 species of birds from the world over migrate through the waterlogged Danube Delta. You'll get an idea of each region's character from the **chapter introductions**; the main festivals are listed at the end of each chapter.

When to come

The **climate** is pretty crucial in deciding **where to go and when**, since life is literally at risk during **winter** unless you come securely booked on a **skiing** holiday, or equipped as if for a short walk in the Himalayas. Even in the capital, Bucharest, you can be pushed to find hotel rooms whose heating functions for more than an hour or two a night.

Conditions, though, obviously improve with **spring**, bringing rain and wildflowers to the mountains, the softest of blue skies over Bucharest, and prompting the great **migration** of birds from the Delta. By May the lowlands are warming up and you might find strong sunshine on **the coast** before the hordes arrive in June.

Summer or early autumn is the perfect time to investigate **Transylvania's festivals** and hiking trails, and see the **Painted Monasteries of Bucovina**, and towards the end of **autumn** the birds return to the Delta.

Average daily temperatures							
	The Banat		Bucharest		the coast		the mountains
	°F	°C	°F	°C	°F	°C	°F	°C
Jan	28	−2	26	−3	31	−1	33	1
Feb	33	1	30	−1	34	1	34	1
Mar	42	5	40	4	39	3	42	6
Apr	52	11	52	11	55	13	51	11
May	61	16	62	17	66	19	61	16
Jun	67	20	69	21	75	24	67	19
Jul	67	20	69	21	79	26	70	21
Aug	65	18	67	20	79	26	70	21
Sep	64	18	65	18	72	22	64	18
Oct	53	12	54	12	62	17	55	13
Nov	43	6	42	5	51	11	45	7
Dec	35	1	34	1	43	6	36	2

NB *These are average temperatures – they can rise or fall 10°F (5°C) at midday or nightfall. Spring is short and changeable; brief showers are common in the Carpathians during summer, whereas the Banat and Wallachian lowlands are prone to drought. In wintertime strong, icy winds sweep down from Russia and snow blankets most of Romania.*

GETTING THERE

Deciding how to get to Romania is in large part a question of choosing between a package and 'independent' travel. If Romania is your sole destination, packages are certainly worth considering. At all events, take note of the comments in the introduction and the details on bureaucracy and compulsory exchange on p.219.

By Air

Currently, the cheapest **scheduled returns from London to Bucharest** are offered by *Friendly Travel* (PO Box 50, Rickmansworth, Herts WD3 5DX; ☎ 092-78-2577) and *Romanian Holidays* (54 Pembroke Rd, London W8 6NX; ☎ 01-602-7094). These run at about £180 rtn; departures are from Heathrow or Gatwick on Wednesdays, Saturdays and Sundays. Both companies also do scheduled flights from London **to Constanţa** between May 4-September 24, departing from Gatwick and Manchester on Saturdays. Friendly Travel charges £140 and £150, depending on which airport one uses; Romanian Holidays £180 irrespective of this.

TAROM (Romanian Airlines), Air France and other airlines usually charge more for **APEX returns**, but just occasionally they'll offer a bargain deal. Rather than ring around yourself, it's easier to let **agents** such as *STA Travel* (74 Old Brompton Rd. London SW7 3LH; ☎ 01-581-1022) or *Eastern European Travel* (☎ 01-837-2811) do the work for you.

It's possible that vacancies on charter **flights from Ireland** might be available from *Balkantours* in Belfast and Dublin (see 'Packages', below).

From the USA, several New York operators can arrange flights. *EPS* (☎ 563-0780) returns cost $719 during the summer, $550 during the winter (plus tax), whilst TAROM (☎ 687-6013) itself charges $996 ($842 off season). *Literal Travel* (☎ 535-7446) can also be worth a call.

By Rail

For under 26s, the cheapest way **from London to Romania** is an *Inter-Rail* ticket (£139), allowing the holder one month's free travel on most European railways, including Romania's. The alternatives to this are a *Eurotrain* or *Trans-alpino* ticket, both valid for 2 months, which allow you to travel – and stopover – along a predetermined route. A single to Bucharest costs £187, and a return ticket £357, so there's a big incentive to go for Inter-Rail instead. Travellers aged 26 or over would do better flying, since the ordinary fares are a whopping £216 (o/w) and £420 (rtn). Trains depart from Victoria, connecting with the *Orient Express* in Paris.

The situation is little better elsewhere in Western Europe – a Eurotrain ticket **from Munich** to Bucharest costs 174 DM (348 DM rtn) – but prices drop dramatically once you're inside the Eastern bloc. It's best to start **from Budapest**, whence no fewer than 8 services run to Romania, although neither the *Nord-Orient*, *Mamaia* or *Tracia Express* call at Bucharest. The *Balt-Orient* and *Orient Express* arrive there before or shortly after dark, stopping at Sighişoara and Braşov en route, like the *Pannonia Express*, whereas the *Wiener Waltzer* is unique in travelling via Sibiu, and the *Transdanubium* only halts at Arad and Timişoara before entering Yugoslavia. Tickets are amazingly cheap – Budapest-Bucharest return costs less than $40 – and yet cheaper if you've got an IUS card to present at the MÁV bookings office at 35, Népköztársaság útja. Since

the journey takes around 24 hours it's definitely worth paying a few dollars more for a sleeper. Romania can also be reached by train **from Yugoslavia or Bulgaria**, East **Berlin**, **Prague**, **Warsaw** or **Moscow**. You'll find some advice on which services to take in the chapters covering the Banat and Transylvania.

By coach, or Danube cruiser

Because of the many Greek students studying in Romania, there's a **coach service between Athens and Bucharest** running 3-4 times a week during the summer and less frequently at other times of the year. You can probably get tickets in Athens from most of the student/youth operators (around Filellinon street, especially), or seats can be booked in the UK through *Romanian Holidays* (see above), who charge £25 for a single and £45 for a return. The journey takes 24 hours and is routed through Sofia; get a Bulgarian transit visa before you leave home, since we're dubious about assurances that they're issued at the border.

Worsening diplomatic relations between Hungary and Romania could well have affected Volán **coaches from Budapest to Oradea** in the Banat and **Cluj and Tîrgu Mureş** in Transylvania, so you'll have to ask at the Engels tér bus terminal in the Hungarian capital for up to date information. If services are still running they're probably as cheap, or cheaper, than the train, but likelier to bear the brunt of rigorous searches and other demonstrations of official Romanian displeasure whenever the Magyars say something rude about Ceauşescu.

Various **Danube cruise-ships** visit Drobeta-Turnu Severin and other ports along the Romanian stretch of the river, but considering the cost of such cruises (see p.4) they're more of once-in-a-life-time's experience than a feasible means of getting there.

By road – driving or hitching

Travelling from Western Europe, one follows the route to Budapest (see p.13), and then the E15 down to the Borş frontier-crossing near Oradea. This shouldn't pose any problem if you're **driving** (but see p.256) as the road is well surfaced all the way through Transylvania. We haven't heard of anybody **hitching** to Romania and it doesn't sound like a good idea.

Package holidays

The main advantages of **package deals** are the cheaper flights, assured lodgings and meals, and exemption from obligatory exchange. . .against which you have to set the drawbacks, which are less related to economics than matters of personal taste. If you dislike being organised and screened from Romanian realities, it's still worth considering 'Two Centre' and 'Carpathian Holidays' (see below) **as a springboard for independent travel**, particularly during May and late September, when such deals are cheapest. Staying at Poiana Braşov, you could easily make sallies to other parts of Transylvania (if not further afield) using the railways, a CFR timetable and this guide. You'll have to offically exchange some money to pay for odd nights in different hotels, but all other expenses can be covered by a judicious currency swop on the black market. The alternative is to take a *Freewheeler* (£213-£233) which exempts one from the obligatory exchange but includes £33 worth of accommodation vouchers rather than a hotel. Freewheelers are only available from *Peltours* (4 Winsley St, London W1N 7AR/☎ 01-637-4373). All **prices** quoted here reflect the low- and high-season 'peaks', and unless stated otherwise they're for one person sharing a double room, on full board.

At least six UK tour operators offer **holidays at Mamaia on the coast**. *Balkan Holidays* (19 Conduit St, London W1R 9TD/☎ 01-493-8612) manages to undercut the rest with 7 (£169-£245) and 14 (£199-£289) nights at half board, but if you want full meals and a superior hotel, try either *Sunquest* for a week (£179-£207) and *Page & Moy* (136-140 London Rd, Leicester LE2 1EN/☎ 0533-552521) – otherwise known as *TV Times Travel* – for a fortnight (£219-£279). It's hard to see the attraction of Mamaia **combined with Golden Sands in Bulgaria**, but Balkan and Sunquest both offer this package, the latter more cheaply (£239-£339). Fourteen-night **Two Centre Holidays**, equally divided between Mamaia and Sinaia or Poiana Braşov, seem more appealing, and Page

& Moy's deal (£269-£299) – which includes a visit to Bucharest and Bran Castle – is definitely the best. Alpine freaks and would-be independent travellers might go for 7-night **Carpathian Holidays** at Sinaia or Poiana-Braşov (£222-£271), or a fortnight at both (£294-£351), these deals being available from Romanian Holidays in the UK and Balkantours in Ireland (see below).

For those with an urge to see something more than the beach, several companies offer 2-week **Dracula Tours**, with visits to Bucharest, Snagov, Tîrgu Mureş, Braşov .and Bran Castle, followed or preceded by a week at Mamaia. Sunquest's tour is cheapest (£283-£321), but Balkan Holidays also includes Sibiu on their itinerary, which is well worth the extra dosh (£289-£339). Peltours can arrange an exhorbitant 'drive yourself' version of this starting at £688, but as with their **fly/drive** package (also offered by Friendly Travel) it costs much less to hire a car inside Romania than to fix things up in the UK. Currently, the only British operators to run **skiing holidays** at Poiana-Braşov are *Intasun, Enterprise* and *Inghams*, and whether you want 7 nights (£145-£182), a fortnight (£211-£245) or the obligatory ski pack (£71), the latter company is much the cheapest. More **specialised tours** (eg. to the Delta or the Moldavian Monasteries) can be arranged by Page & Moy, Friendly Travel, Romanian Holidays or Peltours on request; but all of them are pretty expensive.

Anyone **coming from Ireland** can travel courtesy of *Balkantours*, with offices in Belfast (10 Lombard St, BT1 1RB/☎ 246795) and Dublin (5/6 South Great Georges St, 2/☎ 794415). Booking in Belfast, you'll pay £197-£240 or £229-£295 for 7 or 14 nights at Mamaia; £335-£390 for Two Centres; £299-£345 for a Dracula Tour; and £239-£305 for Mamaia and Golden Sands. Dublin prices (in Irish Punts) are £220-£268 or £256-£330; £375-£436; £335-£386; and £267-£342, respectively. Balkantours also does 1-week skiing holidays at Sinaia (£185-£219) or Poiana-Braşov (£209-£245) and a ski pack for £60.

RED TAPE, VISAS AND CUSTOMS

Passports and visas

You'll need a (full, *not* visitor's) passport to

enter Romania, plus a visa unless you're a citizen of Austria, Cyprus, Denmark, Finland, Iceland, Norway, Portugal, San Marino, Sweden or Turkey. **Visas** are granted gratis to package tourists, but everyone else must pay for them (at border checkpoints, aboard international trains, and at Bucharest or Constanţa airports) if they haven't already obtained one from a Romanian consulate abroad:

BRITAIN: 4, Palace Green, London W8 4QD (Monday-Friday 10am- 12am).
HOLLAND: Catsheuvelstr. 55/4, Den Haag.
W.GERMANY: Köln-Bayenthal, Oberlander Ufer 68.
USA: Washington DC, 1601 23rd Street, N.W.

The price of visas is pegged to the US$, but in the UK they currently cost £20 whether you get a tourist visa (valid for 3 months from date of issue) or a transit job. The latter, valid for 72 hours stay, is only issued to travellers in possession of a visa for a neighbouring country. Applicants can normally obtain a visa at the Romanian consulate within 48 hours (for same-day service there's a £4 surcharge); whilst for postal applications, enclose your passport and an SAE and allow up to 2 weeks. Cheques and postal orders aren't accepted, so payment must be in cash. No photos are required.

However, no visa is valid until it's been endorsed, which is where obligatory exchange comes in.

Obligatory exchange

Package tourists' visas are valid for the exact duration of their holiday; but the visas of independent travellers have to be endorsed before entry to Romania is permitted. At the frontier you'll be asked how long you wish to stay, and required to change **$10 (US) per day** (or the equivalent in TCs or other hard currencies) on the spot, the exchange being calculated at the miserable, official rate. Only package tourists, children under 14 and holders of pre-paid accommodation vouchers are exempted from **obligatory exchange**, and the minimum amount ($30) also applies to transit visa-holders. You *must* keep the **receipt** (*bordereu de schimb*), without which it's impossible to pay for accommodation using lei, and you might be forced to exchange yet more cash when leaving the country.

In theory, **refunds** are possible should you leave ahead of schedule and still have the receipt; but in practice customs

are highly reluctant to part with valuta, and often try to fob you off with COMTOURIST vouchers or promises that they'll 'keep the money until you return to Romania'. **Overstaying** isn't an offence providing you exchange $10 for each 'missing' day at the border when you leave (in which case, you'll be stuck with lei that can't be exported), or obtain a **visa extension** from the seedy, unmarked office in Bucharest on the first floor of 27, Str. Nicolae Iorga (9.30am-1pm Monday, Wednesday & Friday; 5.30pm-10pm Tuesday; 9.30am-2pm & 5.30pm-8pm Thursday; 9.30am-1pm Saturday). For the latter, first change the appropriate sum into lei at ONT, and take the receipt to the CEC bank on Piaţa Amzei, where you pay about 120 lei for an 'endorsement'. Then take both papers around the corner to Str. Iorga, where the visa is finally ammended. Some travellers try forging a new date to avoid changing extra money, but we'd advise against this.

Customs

Romanian **customs** generally don't search Westerners' luggage very thoroughly, but they've got some byzantine **import regulations**. Books about Romania, phrase-books, dictionaries and detailed maps of the country are sometimes confiscated, so these should be buried at the bottom of your bags; Scotch, Kent cigarettes and coffee are commonly used to bribe officials, but open displays may merely invite official cupidity. More seriously, importing bibles is a criminal offence. Aside from this, customs are mainly concerned with preventing one selling things on the black market (p.254), so they levy a 'deposit' on certain items, which isn't refunded if the object – or the customs receipt – goes missing. Video equipment, radios with built-in recorders, Walkmans and the fancier types of calculator are all liable; but not ordinary cameras (with up to 10 rolls of film), radios, cassette-recorders or 'simple' calculators. Besides the usual quotas of booze and cigarettes, you can import clothing and medication (including contraceptives) for personal use without paying a deposit. The import or export of lei is forbidden, but you can bring in 'foodstuffs in quantities strictly limited to the duration of transport' – in other words, enough food to last for your sojourn in Romania.

When **leaving Romania**, *never* carry

out the addresses of Romanian friends – memorise them instead. Discovery could mean an unpleasant interrogation for you (women are particularly at risk) and worse for them.

HEALTH AND INSURANCE

Inoculations aren't required but a typhoid booster is a wise precaution if you're planning to stay in remote areas where cooking is sometimes none too hygenic. Diarrhorea can be a problem, so stock up with Diocalm before you leave, besides any specific medication – and tampax – if required, since these are hard to find in Romania.

There's no reciprocal health agreement between Romania and countries outside the Eastern bloc, though emergency treatment (excluding drugs) is free. It's advisable to take out **travel insurance**, too. With insurance cover, you'll still have to pay for treatment, but can reclaim the money later if you keep the receipts. Many schemes include theft insurance (about £15 for a month's cover); unfortunately, though, the Miliția often refuse to issue insurance reports, so reclaiming the cost of lost property might prove to be impossible.

In case of minor complaints, go to a **farmacie**, where the staff are often highly trained and have the authority to prescribe drugs, and – in the big towns at least – are likely to understand French, German or English. By law, one pharmacy in town must be open 24 hours, or at least display in the window an emergency number. In Bucharest, the British and American embassies can supply the address of an English-speaking doctor or dentist, and there's a special clinic for treating foreigners. **In emergencies** dial **061** or ask someone to contact the local *stația de salvare* or *prim ajutor* – the casualty and first aid stations – which might or might not have ambulances. Provincial capitals have fairly well-equipped *Spitalul Județean*, but **hospitals** in smaller towns can be dire, and most places suffer from overworked and underpaid staff and a shortage of drugs. Foreigners are likely to receive preferential treatment, but Romanians frequently find it necessary to bribe the doctors and nurses to ensure that they're well cared for, which rather makes a mockery of the vaunted 'free medical care'.

Dogs should be avoided (there's a slight risk of rabies), but tap **water** is safe to drink practically everywhere. When in doubt about drinking from streams etc, ask if the water is *apă dulce*.

COSTS, MONEY AND BANKS

Package tours offer many advantages: flights and lodgings are much cheaper than when purchased individually; there's no obligatory exchange; and there aren't the various problems that beset independent travellers. A 'Dracula Tour' could enable you to see as much of Romania as you would travelling independently, in less time and more comfort, for little extra cost.

Despite Romania's abysmally low standard of living, independent travellers will find **costs** quite high because of the inflated value of the lei. The tourist board reckons most things in US dollars, and all lodgings, flights, car rental and ONT excursions must be paid for in hard currency or in lei purchased at the official exchange rate. However, meals, bus and rail tickets and other items can be paid for in lei without having to show exchange receipts, which creates a loophole that the daring – or foolhardy – can exploit to substantially cut these costs (see below).

Accommodation is likely to be your main expense, since the 'cheapest' hotels charge $30-$40 for a single room, $40-$60 for a double (some hoteliers permit two people to share a single). And in first class or deluxe places the sky's the limit. For budget travellers, the alternatives are student hostels (charging between $7-$12 a head), cabanas ($5-$8 per bed), or camping (around $5 per person; slightly less with a student card). Unfortunately, such accommodation is often situated out of town, and can be awkward to reach by public transport. The cost of **eating out** varies considerably, but you can get a meal with a glass of wine or beer for between $6-$10 providing you avoid restaurants in first class or deluxe hotels, imported drinks (especially whisky) or such delicacies as caviar or sturgeon – and providing that there's a restaurant to be found. Public **transport** is cheap, even at the official exchange-rate – it costs less than $30 to take an express train from one side of Romania to the other – but car hire involves various charges on top of the $15 a day basic rate, and petrol can only be bought with special coupons (minimum quantity 20 litres/4 gallons = $17).

Travelling independently, a few **savings and reductions** are possible. Romania participates in the *RIT* (Rail Inclusive Tour) scheme, by which accommodation and transport come 'free'; while of wider benefit is the country's acceptance of *Inter-Rail* tickets, whose holders can ride for nothing on the national railways. *ISIC* and *IUS* **student cards** theoretically entitle you to a 30% reduction when buying international rail and airplane tickets inside Romania, and a reduction of up to 50% on the price of camping, besides free or reduced admission to museums; but in practice the relevant officials may say nay, and there's little you can do about it. For *child reductions*, see page 269.

Other ways of cutting costs are strictly illegal, and boil down to currency smuggling and/or some kind of trading on the **black market**. Within Romania, dollars, pounds and deutschmarks (in that order of preference, trailed by other 'hard' currencies) fetch roughly 4-5 times their official value in lei; and all kinds of Western or Hungarian products can be sold for lei which, calculated at the official rate, represents hefty sums in hard currency. Alternatively, you can buy lei in Hungary (Debrecen's Polish market is one place) or get Magyar friends to do it for you in the banks: both the official and unofficial rates of exchange from forints to lei give the purchaser more Romanian currency than would result from a legal exchange of dollars for lei inside Romania itself. The money is then smuggled into Romania.

With both scams, the aim is to acquire 'cheap' lei to increase one's purchasing power, so as to offset the loss incurred due to the official exchange rate. The 'official' lei is used to pay for accommodation – when the exchange receipt has to be shown – and the 'cheap' lei finances other spending. Obviously, both schemes are fairly risky and we'd advise anyone considering the idea to read the *warnings* on page 254, and then think twice.

Money

The **lei** (singular *leu*), Romania's currency, comes in notes of 1, 3, 5, 10, 25, 50 and 100 lei, with coins of 1 and 3 lei; plus fiddly little 5, 10, 15 and 25 *bani* coins (100 bani=1 leu). As explained under 'Red Tape', independent travellers are obliged to change $10 per day on arrival in Romania, **at the official exchange rate**, which fluctuates at around $1 = 12 lei, £1 = 16 lei. Exchanging money involves less hassle if you do so at ONT offices; queueing and wodges of documents are the norm in **banks** (*banca*), and anyway, their hours (8am-3.30pm Monday-Friday) are shorter than ONT's. Save the exchange **receipts** (*borderou de schimb*) that you are given, since without them you'll be unable to pay for accommodation or international tickets using lei, and have no chance of obtaining a hard currency refund when leaving Romania.

When travelling, it's safest to carry the bulk of your money in **Travellers' cheques**, but also wise to take a stash of dollar bills, preferably in small denominations. Banks and ONT accept all major brands of TCs, but the only brand that guarantees a speedy refund in the case of loss is *American Express*, whose Romanian 'agent' is the main ONT office in Bucharest. Hotels, airlines and the posher sorts of shops and restaurants will usually accept **credit cards** to settle bills – Diners Club, Amex, Master Card, Access, Carte Blanche, Eurocard, Visa, Avis, Hertz, Inter-rent and Europcar (the last four for car rental) – but elsewhere, plastic money has little utility.

COMMUNICATIONS – POST, PHONES AND MEDIA

Post offices in towns are open daily from 7am-8.30pm (Sundays 8am-12am),

and, like the yellow-painted post boxes, are marked *Poşta*. It's easier to buy stamps (*timbru*) and envelopes (*plic*) at tobacconists, bookshops or hotels than queue for them in post offices. When sending letters to Romania, address them *Poşta centrala, poşte restante* for collection at the main post office in town. At the *biroul poşte restante*, show your passport and ask '*Aveţi vreo scrisoare pentru mine?*'; then pay a small fee to claim your mail. Tell your friends – and bear in mind yourself – that mail entering and leaving Romania may be scrutinised by the secret police.

If the electricity is flowing, it's feasible to make local **telephone calls** using public booths (taking 1 and 3 lei coins; the rate is 3 minutes per 1 leu); but long distance calls are best made from the post office, where you state the number you want, or dial it yourself from the kiosk. In theory, you can call abroad using the IDD system; dial the country code, and then the STD (area) code, omitting the initial 0, followed by the subscriber's number. In reality, you're more likely to get through via the operator (071 for international calls), or by phoning from a 'deluxe' hotel. Using hotel facilities inevitably means a service charge, which can be high, so ask the price beforehand. In Bucharest's main post office the telegram service functions overnight (8pm-7am). Assume that *all* phone calls are tapped.

The **Romanian media** is directed from the *Casa Şcinteii*, and even if you can't understand the language, it's hard to miss *Tovarişul* Nicolae Ceauşescu's name and picture, which feature prominently in every edition of every newspaper. Television is less depressingly uniform, but even in the midst of the national equivalent of 'Tomorrow's World', I heard obeisances to the Leader. For foreign consumption, *Romania Today* appears each week, and an even duller magazine, *Lumea*, monthly; both lie around ONT offices, along with the tourist mag *Holidays in Romania*, which occasionally features interesting articles.

In the classier hotels, Western **newspapers** may be available; sold furtively in the case of capitalist organs like *The Times* or *Herald Tribune*, or openly, as with the *Morning Star* and *L'Humanite*. Foreigners can visit the US or British embassies in Bucharest, both of which contain reading rooms and small libraries. Reportedly, the German-language *Karpathischer Rundschau* (printed for the Saxons of Transylvania) can also be worth reading.

For news, many Romanians tune into foreign **radio**; notably the Romanian-language broadcasts of the BBC, and the World Service. The following chart gives the frequencies (MHz) and wavelengths (Metres) of the BBC World Service; reception quality varies greatly; generally, lower frequencies give better results early in the morning, and late at night, higher ones in the middle of the day.

MHz	15.07	12.09	9.41	6.18
Metres	19.91	24.80	31.88	48.54

TROUBLE AND SECURITY

For visitors, Romania is perhaps the safest country in Europe. Despite the high incidence of **petty theft** (popularly attributed to Gypsies), robbery with violence is practically unheard of, and a few commonsense precautions should minimise the risk that your possessions might be stolen.

If your **passport** goes missing while in Bucharest, telephone your consulate immediately; anywhere else, contact the police, who'll issue a temporary visa. It's almost impossible to replace **Travellers' cheques** here, so these should be guarded fanatically. The other catastrophe to avoid is losing an object previously 'registered' at customs (p.248): the police won't believe that you haven't sold it; and thus you'll forfeit the deposit as well as the item. Don't bother reporting other, minor losses, since this merely invites time-consuming bureaucratic hassle.

Foreigners are sometimes stopped and asked to produce **identification** (which should be carried at all times). Barring mishaps, however, this should be the extent of your **dealings with the police** (*Miliţia*). **Trouble** is unlikely unless you break the law or infringe the grey area of 'state security' (see below). Firstly, it's obviously safer *not* to become involved with the **black market**, which is such a major feature of Romanian life that it merits a section unto itself (see p.254). **Photography** is permitted everywhere except in areas designated by a sign (showing a crossed-out camera); while **nudism** and topless bathing are forbidden except on a few single-sex beaches (although offenders are more likely to be cautioned than punished). I've yet to hear of anyone getting into trouble for **camping wild** in rural areas, though it's not allowed in nature reserves and forests, and litterbugs face a £25 fine. **Sleeping rough** in towns will attract the Miliția's ire unless you do so in a railway station and claim to be waiting for a train departing in the small hours. Should you be arrested, identify yourself, be polite and stay cool; try to avoid making a statement unless the officer speaks your language fluently; and demand to contact your consulate.

Unfortunately, Romania is a country where the State Security Police – the **Securitate** – play a major role; infiltrating every level of society with informers, many of whom are blackmailed into doing their distasteful jobs. Though verification is obviously impossible, it's been claimed that between 1 and 3 people in ten report to the Securitate at least once during their adult lives. In practice this means that almost anyone could be a police informant. The Securitate don't normally concern themselves with tourists, but you should bear their existence in mind, particularly since the 1974 *State Security Act* obliges Romanian citizens to report all contacts with foreigners, and prohibits them from disclosing 'state secrets' (an infinitely elastic category). In practice, of course, Romanians rarely report chance encounters, and the state tolerates conversations on innocuous subjects like football, cars and family life. But should someone regularly approach tourists, maintain contacts or have sexual relationships with them, then the Securitate take a dim view, especially in the case of known 'anti-socialists' or those who have foreigners to stay (which is illegal).

I wouldn't discourage anyone from forming **friendships with local people**, but if you do it's well to practice a few **precautions**. The most obvious are: memorise, don't write down addresses; dress inconspicuously and don't talk in communal hallways when you go visiting; and behave discreetly in public. It's easy to exaggerate the risks of involvement with people, but it would be foolish to deny their existence. For foreigners who fall afoul of the Securitate, immediate deportation is normal (and a lucky escape!); whereas Romanians are liable to be fined, beaten up, sacked, expelled from college, or imprisoned.

INFORMATION AND MAPS

Romania's **national tourist office** – the **ONT**, sometimes known as *Carpaţi* – produces a range of maps, brochures and special interest booklets (on spas and folklore, for example), distributed in the appropriate languages through their offices **abroad**, including:

BRITAIN: 29, Thurloe Place, London SW7 2HP (☎ 01-584-8090).

NETHERLANDS: Weteringschans 165 Amsterdam C - 1017 X.D. (☎ 020/23 90 44).

DENMARK: 55-A Vesterbrogade, Copenhagen C (☎ 01-246219).

SWEDEN: 33, Vasahuset Gamla Brogatan, 11120 Stockholm (☎ 08/ 210253-63).

USA: 573, Third Avenue, New York N.Y.10016 (☎ 212-697-6971).

In Romania itself you'll find ONT offices in virtually every town and also regional tourist offices (**OJT**s). ONT is likelier to have better linguists who can (hopefully) make arrangements as well as handle questions, while the OJT people are usually better on specific local **information**; hours are usually 7.30am-3.30pm Monday-Friday, 8.30am-1.30pm on Saturdays.

A number of maps appear in the guide section, but it's always worth asking either office, or hotel receptions, for **town plans** – *plan oraşului* – including those of other places (since these may not be obtainable when you get there). These detail everything from monuments to filling stations, and even the Romanian-language **maps** (most commonly all that's available) aren't usually difficult to figure out. Among commercially available maps, *Cartographia*'s map of Bucharest is useful; and the same Hungarian firm (in partnership with *Falk-Verlag* abroad) also produces a fairly good 1:1,000,000 map **of Romania** and Bulgaria (available in the West, but cheaper in Hungary, see p.17). Also available in Britain is an excellent *Lascelles 1:800,000 scale* map of Romania (£3.95 from *Collets*, or by post from 47 York Road, Brentford, Middlesex TW8 OQP, plus p&p).

ONT's freebie maps are adequate **for motoring**, and offices can also usually supply *Popasuri turistice* (showing campsites) and *Cabane turistice* (giving the location of cabanas), which are essential **for hiking**. Hikers are strongly advised to pick up the booklet *Invitation to the Romanian Carpathians* abroad, since the Romanian-language version *Invitaţie în Carpaţi* is the only one available inside the country. Maps in this booklet show trail markings, chalets, peaks etc, and the most popular walks are briefly described. Individual mountain ranges and a few counties (*judeţ*) are covered in greater detail by maps in the *Hartă Turistică* series, as likely to be found in bookshops as in tourist offices. ONT's *Delta Dunării* map indicates the likeliest places to see **wildlife**, besides the maze of channels and lakes in the Danube Delta.

SUPPLY AND DEMAND

Just as the Middle East has *baksheesh* and Mexico has *la mordida*, Romania has **ciubuc**, a little word signifying all kinds of inducement and illicit exchange. As anyone familiar with the country knows, bribery and corruption are rife in Romania, oiling the creaking machinery of everyday life. Bribes are the means to secure scarce foodstuffs in the shops, proper medical attention, petrol, luxuries, educational opportunities, promotions. . . the list is practically endless. Nor is money always involved; frequently, what happens is a reciprocal exchange of favours. Romanians refer to *pile* or 'files', meaning people who can smooth over rough edges and expedite matters. Naturally enough this ties in with the **black market**, to which almost all citizens resort regularly. This has less to do with supplying what would be illegal in most countries than with meeting the shortcomings of the economy.

As a visitor, there's really no need for you to become involved with such things, and the safest policy is simply *don't*. Securitate agent provocateurs sometimes offer tourists large sums for their camera, watch or dollars, and a polite but firm refusal gives them no grounds for an arrest. Having said that, however, it would be naive to pretend that there aren't temptations. Some foreigners recoup their losses on obligatory exchange, and the high cost of hotel rooms, by selling their dollars, pounds or deutschmarks for 4 or 5 times the official exchange rate; while items like Kent cigarettes, Scotch and coffee beans (available for hard currency in the COMTOURIST shops) can be sold on the black market for a substantial profit. Almost anything made in the West (or Hungary) has value – ranging from obvious commodities like jeans, fancy T-shirts, rock music tapes and Walkman sets down to humble disposable lighters, cosmetics and even bars of soap. Since they're practically illegal in Romania, contraceptives are also highly valued, although personally I'd rather give them away than take money from people denied such a basic essential.

It's for you to form your own judgement on the morality and risks of such dealings, and whether to use the following advice. Firstly it seems better to 'pay' for meals, services or whatever by giving presents (which isn't technically illegal) rather than a cash bribe; restaurant staff, garage hands or other state employees may propose such a deal. Secondly, 'genuine' black marketeers will be highly wary of the Securitate, so if you invite anyone proposing a deal to discuss it in your hotel room, the only people likely to agree will be police spies, who naturally don't fear that the receptionist might report them.

GETTING AROUND

By train

As Romania's energy crisis reduces the number of cars and buses on the roads, **trains** have increasingly become the best – if not the only – means for people to get around. Consequently, trains are usually crowded, making seat reservations virtually a necessity, and the passengers' body heat sometimes manages to warm the unheated carriages. Many routes are extremely scenic – particularly in Transylvania – and as railway journeys are good occasions to strike up conversation with Romanians, visitors should try to ignore any discomforts and enter into the spirit of things. The 11,000km network run by **CFR** (*Căile Ferate Romane*) covers most of the country, and should enable travellers with patience to reach the majority of places in this book. Details of routes and times are given in the text, and summarised at the end of each chapter.

Perusing a station (*Gara*) timetable, check out the **types of train** (*felul trenului*) doing the journey you plan to undertake. *Rapid* services, halting only at major towns, are the most expensive type, whilst *Accelerat* are slightly cheaper and slower, with more frequent stops. Fares are pretty reasonable all round, though – it costs just over 200 lei for 1,000 km in first class. The excruciatingly slow *Personal* and *Cursa* trains should be avoided as a rule, unless you're heading for a particular *halta* along the route. Each service has a number prefixed by a letter denoting its type – *R, A, P* or *C*.

Generally, trains conform more or less to their **timetables**, which are displayed in stations and CFR offices (see below). The vital terms are *sosire* (*sos.*) and *plecare* (*pl.*), arrival and departure; *de la. . .* (from) and *pînă la. . .* (to); the train's duration in the station (*oprire*); and the platform or track (*linia de Garare*). Also watch for *annulat* (cancelled); and services that only run – *circulă* – during certain months (eg. *intre 9.V şi 8.IX* – between May 9 and September 8), or not at all – *numai* – on particular days (indicated thus: 1 = Monday, 2 = Tuesday, etc). If you're planning to do a lot of travelling by rail, invest in the national CFR timetable, the *Mersul Trenurilor de Călători*, which is fairly easy to figure out.

All long distance trains have **sleeping cars** (*vagon de dormit*) and **couchettes** (*cuşete*), for which a surcharge of about 40 lei is levied. **Advance bookings** for rapid and accelerat services are recommended, and on most such trains it's required to have a **seat reservation**. Rather than queue at the station, book tickets at the local **Agenţia CFR** at least 24 hours in advance (allow 7 days for services to the coast during summer). Addresses are detailed in the guide, and most offices function from 8am-8pm Monday-Saturday, Sunday 8am-1pm. **Tickets** (*bilete*) usually come in three pieces, indicating the service (*nr. trenului*), your carriage (*vagonul*) and reserved seat (*rezervare de loc*). Return tickets (*bilet dus întors*) are rarely issued except for international services. Should you fall victim to **doublebooking**, Romanian friends advise me that a bribe to the ticket collector can work wonders.

By bus

Petrol shortages have all but crippled intercity and rural **bus services** (run by regional ITAs), and only cylinders of methane gas keep buses running in the towns. The timetables one sees at urban *Autogară* terminals are mere wishful thinking, for the reality consists of scrums for irregular departures and long queues for last minute sales of tickets. In the countryside, knowing when and where to wait for the day's bus is a local art form, and on Sundays many regions have no public transport at all. Buses mentioned in the text may now run at different times, or not at all; you'll have to ask around. The same applies in towns, where bus stops (*staţie autobuz*) mysteriously change their location, and the schedules fluctuate wildly. There too you'll find **trams and trolleybuses** (*tramvai* and *troleibuz*), which at least stick to their routes. **Tickets** for urban buses, trolleybuses and trams cost 1.75, 1.50 and 1 leu each, flat rate, and are normally sold in bunches by tobacconists and ITA street kiosks. Punch them yourself aboard the vehicle, if you can get to the machine through the crush.

Motoring

Given the state of public transport, it makes sense to travel by car – *assuming* that there is **fuel** currently available. National stocks, especially in winter, can run perilously low: in January 1988, private cars were banned from the roads for a while, ostensibly as a safety measure during heavy snow but also perhaps to save reserves. During the spring and summer, though, you should find petrol available, at least in the cities and along main routes (see below).

Regulations are fairly standard. A national driving **licence** suffices (though not in most neighbouring countries), and if you don't have Green Card **insurance**, a month's cover can be purchased at the border, or from ADAS agencies (100 lei). Foreign motorists belonging to organisations affiliated to the **ACR** (Romanian Automobile Club) receive free or cut-price technical **assistance**; and you can get motoring information from their head office in Bucharest at 27, Str. Beloiannis (☎ 59-50-80). For breakdown services ring 027 or 123456 in the capital, 12345 elsewhere in the country. Details of car repair depots (called Auto-Service, Dacia-Service, Automechanica etc.) and provincial ACR offices are given in the guide. The mainstay of Romanian motoring, the Dacia 1300, is based on the Renault 12, so **spare parts** for Renault and Peugeot models are easiest to come by. For other models, seek the advice of ACR or ONT in Bucharest and see under *Listings*.

Romanians queue for days at *PECO* stations to get their meagre ration of **petrol**. Foreigners can obtain *benzin* with special **coupons**, sold for hard currency at border checkpoints, ONT desks or COMTOURIST shops, which entitle them to jump the queues. Most coupons are for 4-star Super petrol, and the minimum quantity (20 litres/4 gallons) costs around $17. Unfortunately, garages frequently only stock Regular and may refuse to accept the more expensive Super coupons, so the golden rule is, fill up whenever you can. In theory, unused coupons can be refunded when you leave the country.

Most **fly/drive** deals are a rip-off, since the rental charge is three times what one is charged inside Romania. There, the basic **car hire** rate of $15-20 per day (depending on which make of Dacia you're offered), is topped up by a mileage charge (25 cents per km) assessed at a minimum rate of 150 km per day, plus $3.30 a day for insurance (non-refund-

able) unless you prefer forking out $120 deposit. In theory you can pay using credit cards, but in practice this isn't always the case. One also has to sign an inventory of the car's contents (check that it matches), and masses of documents. Always lock up and put windscreen wipers in the glove compartment when not in use, since thefts of car parts are commonplace.

Highways (*Drum National*/DN) are fairly well maintained, but the quality of **roads** declines as you move from *Drum Modernizat* onto *Drum Nemodernizat*, which can be little more than tracks. In rural areas the danger isn't so much other motorised **traffic** as the risk of hitting wagons, people and various animals that have yet to accept the impact of the motor age. In the case of **accidents** you're legally obliged to await the arrival of the Miliția; **drinking and driving** is absolutely prohibited and severely punished. The most important **rules** are *drive on the right and overtake on the left side*, while **speed limits** depend on your vehicle's cylinder capacity:

Type of car	Speed limit in kilometres per hour	
	in built-up areas	on the open road
over 1800 cc.	60	90
1100-1800 cc.	60	80
under 1100 cc. jeep-type,	60	70
spark ignition jeep-type,	60	70
diesel	60	60

Romania would be a fine country for **motorcycling**, except that the speed limit for bikes is ludicrously low: 40 kph in built up areas and only 50 kph on the open road. Helmets are compulsory and you're advised to bring vital spares and a tool kit.

Hitching and cycling

Hitch-hiking (*autostop*) is legal on all Romanian roads with the exception of the *Autostradă*. Cars are relatively scarce on the roads, and it's accepted practice to pay for lifts. Advertising an inducement – such as a packet of *Kent* – can increase your chances of snagging a driver, who you should then ask: *cît costa pînă la. . .?* ('How much to. . .?'). Other useful phrases include *Doresc sa cobor* *la. . .* ('I want to get off at. . .'); *Opriţi la. . .* ('Stop at. . .'); and *Opriţi aici* ('Stop here').

Cycling, given the mountainous terrain and the poor state of rural roads, you'll need to be fit and are strongly advised to carry a spare tyre.

Flights

TAROM's **domestic services** depart most days from Bucharest's Băneasa airport, to Iaşi, Piatra Neamţ, Suceava, Bistriţa, Baia Mare, Satu Mare, Oradea, Cluj, Tîrgu Mureş, Sibiu, Arad, Timişoara, Caransebeş, Ploieşti, Constanţa and Tulcea. During summer, there are also flights to most of these places from Constanţa. Fares are roughly 30%-100% higher than the cost of the equivalent railway ticket, but with a student card you can sometimes get reductions. To pay in lei you'll need an exchange receipt to prove that the money was acquired legally. Bookings should be made – preferably 36 hours in advance – at TAROM offices, the addresses of which appear in the guide section.

By boat

NAVROM, the national shipping agency, maintains a small fleet of **passenger boats** which operate along the arms of the Delta, between Constanţa and Mangalia, and on the Danube between Turnu Severin and Ostrov; besides the plusher *Olteniţa* and *Carpaţi*, which are reserved for package tourists on the Danube cruise from Vienna to Cernavoda. Schedules vary from service to service, and in any case are subject to frequent alterations, so that anyone interested in making a journey by riverboat should first consult NAVROM. The main offices are in Bucharest (Blvd. Golescu, near the Gara de Nord; ☎ 167454), Mamaia (Bucureşti B Hotel; ☎ 31251) and Tulcea (on the pier). Smaller motorboats may also carry passengers along the Cernavoda-Agigia and Dîmboviţa-Danube canals, and across Lake Bicaz in Moldavia. As always, buying tickets necessitates queuing and getting into a scrum with other would-be passengers; tickets are normally sold an hour or less before departure.

SLEEPING

Accommodation rarely comes cheap in Romania, and the tourist board tends to point visitors towards the most expensive on offer, forcing one to plead poverty before they'll divulge the location of more modestly-priced establishments. If you pay in lei it has to be at the official exchange rate, since doing so requires you to show the exchange receipt (*borderou de schimb*), which is ammended and stamped by the receptionist when you register. When travelling independently, it's safer – if not always necessary – to make **reservations** ahead of you, since cheap hotels, cabanas, and cabins on campsites, can get crowded during summer, especially on the coast. Beds can be booked through ONT, whose responsibilities are nationwide, or at the county tourist offices (OJTs), which handle accommodation within their own baliwick: both charge a fee of $1 for this service.

Hotels are graded as 'deluxe', first or second class, but given the frequency of power and water cuts, it's hardly worth paying extra for features such as a TV ($3) or a private bathroom. If available, single rooms cost about 30% more than the price of one bed in a double room, and pennypinching couples are sometimes permitted to share a single. Sleeping in their parents' room, children pay 50% of the 'third person' tariff up to the age of 6 (70% between the age of 7-12).

The following estimates refer to the cost of a bed in a double room (assuming you're sharing), and are given in dollars since the tourist board often quotes prices in this way. In the cheapest 2nd class hotel, a bed should cost between $16-$20 – probably nearer to the latter than the former; while having a private shower (*cu duş*) adds another $10 to the bill. In slightly ritzier 2nd class places, or the cheapest 1st class hotels, the price of a bed climbs to between $20-$30; while in most 1st class establishments and anything graded deluxe, beds start at $40 and after that the sky's the limit. In 2nd class hotels the charge normally includes breakfast (usually taken in a restaurant or café nearby). On the coast, breakfast is only included for residents in deluxe hotels. Hotel bars and restaurants may double as the town's nightclub (featuring dancing at the weekends), while in the foyer you can usually buy Kent or Marlboro cigarettes, whisky and ground coffee for hard currency. **Motels** have similar facilities and prices as first class hotels, but since they're situated along the main highways (between Oradea and Cluj, Bucharest and Piteşti, etc) or beyond urban ring roads, they're not much use unless you have private transport, or want to try hitching.

In towns with a sizeable student population, the vacant college rooms – **caminul de studenti** – may be rented out between July 1-August 31. The Youth Travel Agency **BTT** is responsible for bookings, but prefers groups to individuals. Before you leave Bucharest contact BTT head office (7-15, Str. Mendeleev; ☎ 14-42-00) about the possibility of booking beds in colleges around the country. We've listed regional BTT offices where known, and when you're in the towns it's worth checking them out personally. Even if the agency won't help, they should at least know which colleges are being used, and by going there and begging you might secure a bed. Having an IUS student card is probably essential. Going rates seem to be around $7.25 for a bed in a shared room, $12 for a single, although prices are open to negotiation if it's not an official transaction. Most Romanian universities have contingents of Arab, African and Asian students, many of whom remain in halls of residence over vacation, and they're sometimes willing to argue with – or smuggle you past – the porter, to let you doss in their rooms.

In the countryside, particularly in the mountainous areas favoured by hikers, there are well over 100 **cabanas**; ranging from chic alpine villas with dozens of bedrooms to fairly primitive chalets with bunk beds, a rudimentary bar and cold running water. Some cabanas (mainly in the Bucegi range) can be easily reached by cable car from a railway halt; others are situated a few miles from towns; but the majority are fairly isolated, only accessible by mountain road or footpaths. Their locations are shown rather vaguely on an ONT map, *Cabane Turistice*, and more precisely on hiking maps. Mountain cabanas are supposedly forbidden to turn hikers away, but I'd advise playing it safe by booking in advance, through ONT or the local OJT office. Beds cost $5-$8, slightly more if in a private room or in one of the plusher cabanas. The

hikers' chalets are generally friendly places where you can pick up information about trails and the weather.

Likewise, Romania has well over 100 **campsites**, situated all over the country. One pays around 30 lei ($2.50) for tent space, and 30 lei per head, unless you possess an IUS student card, which normally secures a 30-50% reduction. Third class campsites are hardly more than a field with a tap and a loo, but second and first class sites often have **cabins** for rent (about $8 per head), hot showers and even a restaurant. However, the water shortage seems to hit campsites especially hard, while along the coast overcrowding is a major disadvantage. In the mountains, certain areas may be designated as a *loc de campare* where it's permitted to pitch camp, but in fact there's few regions where one can't get away with **camping wild**. Providing you don't light fires in forests nor litter nor transgress nature reserves, officialdom turns a blind eye to campers, or – at the worst – may tell you to move along or levy an on the spot fine (maximum £25). If you get discovered late in the day, it may be plausible to argue that you were feeling sick, saw nightfall approaching, and felt compelled to pitch camp. . .

If you're travelling around a lot, it's a good idea to use **trains as accommodation**. On the long overnight journeys by rapid or accelerat train, it costs about 40 lei to book a comfortable couchette (*cuşete*). Save the cost of a hotel and arrive refreshed the following morning. Couchettes (and the costlier sleeping cars, *vagon de dormit*) should be booked 4-7 days beforehand using the CFR agency, which has branches in all towns, or centrally, through ONT. Trains can also provide an alibi should you be forced to **sleep rough** in a town. Whole families spend the night in station waiting rooms, where it's feasible to doss without fear of arrest (tell the Miliţia you're waiting for an early departure should they pay a visit). Beware, however, of theft, which is common.

Lastly, **staying with Romanians is illegal** for foreigners unless they're close relatives of their host. Private accommodation ceased to be available in the early 70s, with limited **exceptions** such as the odd room in a fisherman's cottage, which may still be rented from ONT in Tulcea. In rural areas or in anonymous cities, people might offer to put you up out of friendship or the desire for money, and should you accept, follow any **precautions** they might specify. (Like dressing inconspicuously, not talking in the communal hallways, or sneaking out at the crack of dawn). If apprehended, the foreigner is liable to instant deportation, but the Romanian faces the possibility of a huge fine or worse.

EATING AND DRINKING

It's a cruel irony and an indictment of Ceauşescu's policies that **food** has become a precious commodtity in what used to be the breadbasket of Eastern Europe. Whereas in the old days, the rich feasted on everything from wild boar to caviar while the peasantry subsisted on *mămăligă* (corn mush), nowadays the only people not driven to the black market are package-tourists – fed huge meals to obscure Romanian realities – and the Party élite, who have their own supply network. The resentment this causes can be imagined, and food shortages were a major factor in the Braşov riots.

Visitors can either opt for the security of a package tour, confine themselves to eating in tourist restaurants (which receive priority allocations of food), or come prepared for Romanian austerity – combining the last two should get you by. Winter is dire everywhere, but in large towns and agricultural areas the availability and variety of food improves as the months progress, so that one can eat relatively well during the summer. Nevertheless, anyone planning to spend time here should bring as much concentrated, non-perishable food as possible – and be prepared guard it against theft.

Staying in a hotel, you'll normally be guaranteed **breakfast** (*micul dejun*) on the premises or in a nearby café, the cost of which is usually included in the charge for accommodation. Typically it's a light meal, featuring rolls and butter (*chifle şi unt*) and an *omleta* – or long, unappealing-looking skinless sausages (*patricieni*) – washed down with a large white coffee (*cafea mare cu lapte*) or a cup of tea (*o ceaşcă de ceai*). Should you rise late, or not fancy the above, then hit the streets looking for **snacks** – known as *gustări*, which is also the Romanian word for hors d'oeuvres. The most common are flaky pastries (*pateuri*) filled with cheese (*cu brînză*) or meat (*cu carne*), often dispensed through hatches in the walls of bakeries; brioches (*cozonac*), a speciality in Moldavia; sandwiches (*sandvici* or *tartină*); and a variety of spicy grilled sausages and meatballs called *mititei* and *chiftele* which, like *patricieni*, are normally sold by street vendors.

For **sit down meals** it's best to go upmarket if you can afford to, since the choice and quality of dishes in restaurants is way above the grisly stuff dished out in the drab, self-service *Autoservire* canteens (open 7am-10pm) which the Leader intends to make the mainstay of Romanian catering by 1990. If your budget is tight, it's preferable to look out for *Lacto-Vegetarian* restaurants (most towns have one) rather than the Autoservire; they tend to be less crowded and offer better food. Whatever place you settle on, always enquire *Care feluri le serviţi astazi, vă rog?* (What's there to eat?) or *Ce îhmi recomandaţi?* (What do you recommend?) before taking the menu – *la listă* – too seriously, for it's sometimes the case that the only thing going is the set menu (*un meniu fix pentru prînz*).

However, at smarter **restaurants** and places with an olde-worlde decor, known as **Han**, there's a fair likelihood of finding **traditional Romanian dishes**, which can be delicious. The best known is *samarle* – bitter cabbage stuffed with rice, meat and herbs, usually served (or sometimes baked) with sour cream; also made with vine leaves – *sărmăluţe in foi de viţă* – or with corn – *sarmale cu pasat*, as is done in Maramureş. Stews (*tocane*) and other dishes often feature a sclerotic combination of meat and dairy products. 'Shepherd's Delight' (*muşchi ciobanesc*) is pork stuffed with ham, covered in cheese and served with mayonaise, cucumber and herbs; while *muşchi poiana* is beef stuffed with mushrooms, bacon, pepper and paprika, served in a vegetable purée and tomato sauce. Also watch out for **regional specialities** (*specialităţile regiunii*). Moldavia is known for its rissoles – *pîrjoale*, but also for more elaborate dishes such as *rasol Moldovenesc cu hrean* (boiled pork, chicken or beef, with a sour cream and horseradish sauce) and *pui Cîmpulungean* (chicken stuffed with smoked bacon, sausage, garlic and vegetables). Because of the Turkish past, one also finds *musaka* and varieties of *pilaf;* while the German and Hungarian minorites have contributed such dishes as smoked pork with saurkraut and Transylvanian hot-pot.

Vegetarians in ordinary restaurants could try asking for *ghiveci* (mixed fried veg); *ardei umpluţi* (stuffed peppers); eggs with a spicy filling (*ouă umplute picante*) or mushroom stuffing (*ouă umplute cu ciuperci*); poached eggs (*ouă românești*) or vegetables and salads

(see below). When in doubt, stipulate something . . .*fără carne, vă rog* (Without meat), or enquire *este cu carne?* (Does it contain meat?).

Establishments called *Cofetărie* serve **coffee** and cakes, and sometimes ice cream. Ground coffee is practically unobtainable except on the black market (where it sells for about 600 lei a kilo), so Romanians indulge their taste for the beverage in Cofetarie, usually drinking it black and sweet in the Turkish fashion (*cafea neagră*); ask for it *cu lapte* or *fără zahăr* if you prefer it with milk or without sugar. **Cakes and desserts** are sticky and very sweet, as throughout the Balkans. Romanians enjoy pancakes

---

BASICS

Bread	pîine
Butter	unt
Cheese	brînză
Do you have. . .?	Aveţi. . .?
Eggs	ouă
(hard/soft boiled)	tare/moale
I/we would like. . .	Aşl am vrea. . .
A glass	un pahar
Milk	lapte
Oil	ulei
Pepper	piper
Rice	orez
Salt	sare
Sugar	zahăr
Vinegar	oţet
Yoghurt	iaurt

Soups (supe) with sour cream (ciorbe)

Ciorbă de cartofi	Potato soup
Ciorbă de fasole	Dried or green bean soup
Ciorbă de miel	Lamb broth
Ciorbă perişoare	Soup with meatballs
Ciorbă de peşte	Fish soup
Ciorbă ţăranească	Broth with meat and mixed veg
Supă de carne	Consommé
Supă de găină	Chicken soup
Supă de găluşti	Dumpling soup
Supă de roşii	Tomato soup
Supă de zarzavat	Vegetable soup
Supă de taitei	Noodle soup

Salads (salată)

Salată de cartofi cu ceapa	Potato and onion salad
Salată de fasole verde	Green bean salad
Salată de icre de crap	Carp roe salad
Salată de roşii şi castraveţi	Tomato and cucumber salad
Salată de sfeclă roşie	Beetroot salad
Salată verde	Lettuce salad

Meat (carne) and poultry (pasăre)

Babic (Ghiudem)	smoked (goat's meat) sausage
Berbec/Oaie	mutton
Biftec	steak
Chiftele	fried meatballs
Curcan	turkey
Găină	hen
Ghiveci cu carne	meat and vegetable Hotpot
Gîscă	goose
Miel	lamb
(Pastrama de) porc	(salted and smoked) pork
Porc	pork
Prăjit	liver
Pui	chicken
Raţă (pe varză)	duck (with saurkraut)
Rinichii	kidneys
Salam	salami
Şniţel pane	Wiener schnitzel
Sunca	ham
Tocană de carne/ de purcel	meat/pork stew
Vacă	beef
Varză acră cu costiţe afumate	saurkraut with smoked pork chops

TERMS: *Anghemaht de. . . . . .*in a white sauce; *. . .cu mujdei de usturoi . . .*in a garlic sauce; *friptură de. . ./fripţi* fried or roast; *..la grătar* grilled; *pulpă de. . .la tavă* roast leg of. *. . .*

(*clătite*) and pies (*plăcintă* with various fillings; Turkish-influenced *baclava* and *cataif cu frisca* (crisp pastry soaked in syrup, filled with whipped cream); and the traditional *dulceaţă*, or glass of jam.

As an aperitif, and to finish their meals, people like **to drink** *ţuică*, a tasty, powerful brandy made of plums, taken neat. In rural areas, homemade **spirits** can be fearsome stuff, often twice distilled to yield *rachia*, best diluted with water, and much rougher than grape brandy or *rachiu*, called *coniac* by urban sophisticates. They're all alarmingly cheap and served in large measures, like rum (*rom*) but unlike whisky, which retails for around £5 a glass (or $10 a bottle in

COMTOURIST shops). Most **beer** (*bere*) is like lager – Azuga is probably the least odious brand – but one occasionally finds *bere blondă* (light ale) and *bere neagră* (brown ale). They're usually sold by the bottle (*sticlă*), so requests for *una sticlă* are assumed to be for beer.

Romania's best **wine** – *Grasca* and *Feteasca* from the Cotnari vineyards of Moldavia – is exported or reserved for the ruling class, but most restaurants should be able to conjure up a bottle of Murfatlar Riesling, Muscat, Pinot Noir or Chardonnay; *Segarcea* or *Dealu Mare* cabernet; *Sadova* rosé; or Moldavian *Pinot Gris* and *Aligote*. Wine is rarely sold by the glass, but it does no harm to ask

---

Fish (*peşte*) **and seafood**

Cegă	sterlet
Chiftele de peşte	fish-cakes
Crap	carp
Icre Negre	caviar
Midii	mussels
Nisetru	sturgeon
Păstrăv	trout
Scrumbii	herring
Şalău	pike-perch
Ton	tuna

TERMS: *la grătar/prăjit* grilled; *rasol* poached; *cu maioneză* boiled with a mayonaise sauce.

Vegetables (*legume*)

Ardei (gras/iute)	(green/chilli) pepper
Cartofi	potatoes
Ceapă (verde)	(spring) onion
Ciuperci	mushrooms
Conopida	cauliflower
Dovleci (cu floare)	marrows (courgettes)
Fasole (albă grasă/ verde)	(broad/string) beans
Lăptucă	lettuce
Mazăre verde	peas
Morcovi	carrots
Roşii	tomatoes
Sfeclă roşie	beetroot
Spanac	spinach
Usturoi	garlic
Varză	cabbage
Vinete	aubergines

TERMS: *Ghiveci* mixed fried veg, sometimes eaten cold; *fierţi* boiled; *piureu de...* mashed; *prăjiţi* chipped; *umpluţi* stuffed.

Fruit (*fructe*)

Caise	apricots
Căpşuni	strawberries
Cireşi	cherries
Mere	apples
Pepene galben	melon
Pepene verde	watermelon
Pere	pears
Piersici	peaches
Prune (uscate)	plums (prunes)
Smeură	raspberries
Struguri	grapes

Desserts and sweets (*dulciuri*)

Baclava	baclava
Bomboane	sweets
Cataif cu frişcă	pastry soaked in syrup, topped with whipped cream
Clătite cu rom	pancake with rum
Cozonac	brioche
Dulceaţă	jam (served in a glass)
Ecler	éclair
Gogosi	a kind of doughnut
Halva	halva
Îngheţată	ice cream
Mascotă	chocolate cake
Miere	honey
Mir in foietaj	baked, stuffed apple
Papanasi	cream doughnut
Pasca	Easter cake
Plăcintă cu brînză	cheese pie
Plăcintă cu mere	apple pie
Plačintă cu vişine	cherry pie
Rahat	Turkish delight
Rulada rarau	a kind of Moldavian Swiss Roll

Serviti vinul la pahar? With the exception of mineral water (*apă minerală*), **soft drinks** are uninviting: fruit juices (*suc de fructe*) are thick with sediment, and only severe dehydration justifies a resort to *sirop*.

Shopping for food is a dispiriting task, since milk, fresh meat, butter, cheese and yoghurt attract massive queues whenever they appear in shops, while sugar, cooking oil (and occasionally even bread) are rationed. Although foreigners with proof of identity are entitled to buy these provisions in supermarkets, this ruling is frequently ignored in village *alimentare* on the grounds that some for you means none for a local person (which is fair enough, but still frustrating). Eggs are normally obtainable in supermarkets, which also stock dried and canned foodstuffs (pasta, sardines etc). The outlook for fruit and veg is better, particularly in **markets** (*piaţa*).

Most towns also have a **Gospodină** selling pre-cooked meals, originally established as an aid for working mothers but equally useful to independent travellers. *Kent* cigarettes, coffee or Western toiletries can be bartered for food in rural areas, and travellers with enough self confidence and a command of Romanian might also consider **bribery**. *Ciubuc* is commonplace in shops, for everyone knows that staff hide things beneath the counter for sale after the item is officially *s-a terminat*.

MUSIC, FESTIVALS AND FOLKLORE

Music

If your musical horizons are limited to **rock** then Romania has little to offer but recycled Western disco-fodder; regarded by the state with suspicion, but also as a lesser evil than the development of an autonomous Romanian 'youth culture', so that only the blandest 'pop' groups receive any encouragement (or rather, aren't stomped upon). **Jazz** music is deemed acceptable – indeed, there's periodically a jazz festival in Sibiu – but it's **classical music** and indigenous folk music that are strongest. Since *George Enescu* (1881-1955) virtually created the genre, classical music has been lavishly funded by the state, and such culture has far less elitist connotations than in the West. Most large towns have a philharmonic orchestra and/or an opera house, and tickets (available through the local *agenţia teatrală*) are very cheap – deliberately so, to encourage a working class audience.

But it's Romania's amazing **folk music** that really stands in a class of it's own; a flourishing field with ancient roots and an incredible diversity of styles, that's probably richer here than anywhere else in Europe. Ballads, work songs, and music for dancing, weddings, funerals and other occasions has been improvised (though until recently, rarely written down) and passed from generation to generation, evolving yet retaining a continuity. Forms like the *doina* – a soulful kind of 'blues' singing – have spread throughout the country but are still associated with their place of origin; Maramureş for the doina; the alpine regions for shepherd's music performed on pan pipes (*nai*) and longhorns (*bucium*); the Saxon communities for choral singing; strongly Hungarian areas for 'old style', semi-asiatic rhythms; and so on. As ever, it's the Gypsies who dominate amateur music of all kinds and switch effortlessly from style to style, although it's increasingly rare to find the wandering Gypsy musicians who used to comprise the *Lautari* tribe.

Polished and sanitised folk music can be found in Bucharest nightclubs and in some Hans, but for the authentic stuff one has to go into the countryside where, as a general rule, the more remote the village the better the likelihood of hearing something special. Areas like the Iza Valley in Maramureş, the Hungarian villages of Transylvania, the Apuseni Mountains and the hinterlands of the Dobrudja, Bucovina and Wallachia all repay exploration, and weekends and market days seem to be the most propitious times. However to be assured of encountering folk music, it's best to attend one of the many festivals, which range from small, essentially local, affairs to jamborees that attract visitors from far and wide. You'll find a selection of **recordings** listed on page 498.

Festivals

Romanian **festivals** can be categorised

under various headings: having originated from the Orthodox religion, with its 'Twelve Great Feasts' and hosts of lesser festivals; as occasions marking events such as marriage, birth and death; to commemorate phases in the agricultural and pastoral lifestyle; and as secular anniversaries (ie May Day and Liberation Day). While the last two are national holidays, and never change their **dates**, many festivals take place on a particular day (eg. the first Sunday of June), the date of which varies from year to year. This is especially true of the Orthodox festivals, three of which are dated in relation to Easter, a 'moveable feast' which in the Orthodox religion is still reckoned according to the 'Old Style' or *Julian calendar*, rather than the Gregorian calendar used in the West (and in Romania for secular purposes). In 1989, Orthodoxy's Easter Sunday will fall on April 30 – a month later than in the West – so you'll have to take this into account; in 1990 both Western and Orthodox Easter Sunday falls on April 15th. Festivals specific to particular regions are also listed in the relevant **chapter introductions** – what follows is an 'overview'.

Christmas and New Year celebrations are spread over the period 24 December-7 January, and preparations often begin as early as December 6 (St Nicholas' Day) when pigs are slaughtered for the forthcoming feasts. Groups of young men and boys meet to prepare the festival costumes and masks, and to rehearse the *colinde* – allegorical songs wishing good health and prosperity for the coming year, which they sing outside each household on Christmas Eve (*Ajun*), when the faithful exchange thin pastries called *turte* (symbolising Christ's swaddling clothes).

In Moldavia and Bucovina, processions follow the *Capra* (Goat), a costumed dancer whose mask has a moveable lower jaw which he clacks in time with the music (to represent the death pangs of the old year). The week-long masked carnival in the Maramureş town of **Sighet** likewise has pagan origins, although it has been considerably modernised. On New Year's Eve throughout the countryside, groups of *plugăraşi* pull a plough festooned with green leaves from house to house, cutting a symbolic furrow in each yard while a doina calling for good health and fecundity is recited, accompanied by carolling in Transylvania, for example at **Arpaş** and **Şercaia** in Braşov county). In **Tudora** and the villages around Suceava, New Year's greetings are delivered by the *buhai*, an instrument shaped like a bottomless barrel which, when drawn with horse hair, imitates the bellowing of a bull. This may be accompanied by a mime play of people masked as goats, little horses (*căiuţi*) and bears (*urşi*), sometimes with flute music. At dawn on New Year's Day the 'little ploughmen' take over, sowing in the furrows ploughed the day before; and although the official holiday ends on January 2, villagers may keep celebrating through to Epiphany (the 6th), when horse races are staged in areas like **the Wallachian plain** and the Dobrudja.

In southern Romania, there's a traditional belief (still held by a minority) that groups of village mimes and dancers could work magic if all the rites were correctly observed; and selected young men were initiated into the **ritual of Căluş**. This took place in secret (the word means 'gag' as well as 'little horse'), and was performed by a *vătaf* who had inherited the knowledge of *descîntece* (magic charms) and the dance steps from his predecessor. On Whit Sunday (Pentecost), these *Căluşari* began their ritual dance from house to house, accompanied by a flag-bearer and a 'Mute' (*Mut*, who traditionally wore a red phallus beneath his robe and muttered sexual invocations), thus ensuring that each household was blessed with children and a bountiful harvest; and, if need be, exorcising anyone possessed with the *Rusalii* – spirits of departed friends and family, who entered the bodies of villagers who violated any of the taboos during the 'week of Rusalii' immediately following Whitsun.

Căluş rites are still enacted in some Oltenian villages, and the Căluşari now hold an annual celebration of their dancing and musical prowess at **Deva** during the second week of January – a colourful festival called the *Căluşarul Transilvanean*, which doesn't have any particular magical significance, but is nevertheless impressive. Sometime in May (the exact date varies) there's a similar two day event at **Slatina** which, being closer to Căluş country, attracts a higher percentage of believers. The 30th of the month is *Three Hierarchs' Day*, celebrated with great pomp in Iaşi's Trei Ierarhi Church, which is dedicated to the saintly trio.

Transylvania's Saxons seem to have abandoned the practice of their hardier forebears, who considered the third day of **February** a propitious date for weddings; and nowadays, autumn seems to be the boom time for Saxon marriages (p.356). **Rimetea**'s village fair traditionally occurs on the 22nd. A review of Gorj county's folk ensembles and miners' brass bands – the *Izvoare fermecate* or 'Enchanted Water Springs' – held on the third Sunday of the month at **Tirgu Jiu** (winter conditions permitting). Though few Romanians are nowadays so devout, or well nourished enough to observe the traditional Lent fast, which begins seven weeks before Easter on a day falling in **March**, some rural folk still bake twisted loaves – *colaci* – on the 9th, *Forty Saints's Day*, and take them to the village church to be blessed and distributed as alms. On one weekend during the month (it's decided at fairly short notice, but OJT Arad should know the day) there's an early spring festival at **Hălmagiu**, called the *Kiss Fair*, which provides the opportunity for villagers from the Apuseni and Banat regions to socialise and trade crafts.

With the onset of spring in **April and May**, agricultural work begins in earnest; roughly coinciding with Easter, the holiest festival of the Orthodox year. Urbanisation and collectivisation have both affected the nature of **Spring festivals**, so that **Reşiţa**'s *Alaiul primaverii* features firemen and engineers as well as folklore ensembles within its parade of floats (throughout the first week in April). Village festivals have tended to conglomerate. Thus, instead of a dozen smallish fêtes, one now finds a single, large event drawing participants and visitors from across the region – for example the *Florile Oltului* (Flowers of the Olt) at **Avrig** on the second Sunday of April, attended by contingents from dozens of communities around Sibiu, many of whom come wearing the rich velvet and paste-jewellery finery of traditional Saxon costume. Similarly, the *Girl Fair* at **Gurghiu** is an occasion for villagers from the Gurghiul, Beica and Mureş valleys to make merry on the second Sunday in May. For pomp and crowds on a larger scale, it's better to go for **Braşov**'s *Pageant of the Juni* (p.334), held on the first Sunday of May unless this clashes with May 1.

Commemorated and broadcast nation-wide, **Workers' Solidarity Day** (May 1-2) is a travesty of the anniversary's original meaning. Delegations from factories and institutes parade under obligation, marshalled by Party activists; uniformed Youth march like the military; and over the crowds and dais rise red banners displaying the words, achievements or radiantly illuminated visage of the Wise Leader.

Happily, some May festivals have stayed truer to their origins, like the Székely equivalent of the *Festival of the Plough* at **Băile Jigodin**, near Miercurea Ciuc, on the third Sunday of the month. Once common practice, the ritual garlanding of the plough nowadays rarely occurs in rural Romania. But the age-old **pastoral rites and feasts** marking the sorting, milking and departure of the flocks are still widespread throughout Maramureş and the Apuseni Mountains during late April or early May, depending on local tradition and climatic factors. The best known *Sîmbra oilor* occur at the pass beyond **Certeze** (p.426), and on the ridge of **Măgura Priei** (p.376), on the first Sunday; but lingering snows can delay the spring *Tînjua* festival until mid May, so that in remoter parts of **Maramureş**, small pastoral feasts can still be happening at the beginning of July.

Easter (*Paşte*) generally falls in April – or late in March/early May (see **dates**, above). From *Floriile*, Palm Sunday, through the 'Week of Sufferings' (*Săptămîna patimilor*, during which, it's believed, souls will ascend directly to heaven), the devout attend Orthodox ceremonies, culminating in the resurrection celebrated at midnight on Easter Sunday. The cry 'Christ has risen', to which all reply 'Yes, truly he has risen', resounds through the candle-lit churches which, on this night if none other, are full to overflowing with worshippers. With the exception of **Pentecost** or Whitsun, fifty days after Easter Sunday, subsequent Orthodox festivals are nowadays less widely observed. So, too, sadly, are the ancient Wallachian customs that allowed women to drink wine together and amuse themselves by insulting their menfolk (sanctioned on the third Tuesday following Easter!); while on the third Thursday, Gypsy children dressed in leaves used to dance *Paparude* to invoke rains on the parched fields, being given coins and doused with water as they proceeded from house to house. As mentioned earlier, the Whitsun rite of *Căluş* used to be staged in villages everywhere (and during May can still be seen at Slatina); but nowadays, perhaps the most genuine event is the *pilgrimage to Csikszereda* (**Miercurea Ciuc** in the Székely Land). Since this isn't an Orthodox festival, Whitsun's date is determined according to the Western Christian calendar (falling on May 15 in 1989; June 4 in 1990).

The *Cherry Fair* at **Brîncovenești** on the first Sunday of **June** anticipates other harvest festivals later in the month, and the round of great **Summer fairs** known as *Tîrg* or *Nedeias*. In the days before all-weather roads, these events provided the people of remote highland villages with an annual opportunity to acquire news from the outside world, and arrange deals and marriages. On the second Sunday of June, folk from some thirty Banat settlements attend the *Nedeia of Tăaşele* at **Avram Iancuc**; and another commune with the same name lies but a few miles from **Mount Găina**, where the famous *Girl Fair* occurs on the Sunday before July 20. **Fundata**'s *Nedeia of the Mountains* on the last Sunday of June is the traditional gathering for people of the Brașov, Argeş and Dîmbovița regions; while the Wallachian highlands have their own equivalent in the great **Polovragi** Fair (on *July* 15 or 20).

Other summer festivals perpetuate Romania's old customs and folklore: the light-hearted *Buying Back of the Wives* at **Hodac**; and the funereal declamation of *bochet* during the *The King of the Fir Trees* (p.345) at **Tiha Bîrgăului** in the heart of fictional Dracula country (on the second and third Sundays of June). The diversity of folk costumes and music within a particular area can be appreciated at events like **Şomcuta Mare**'s pastoral *Stejarul*, or the larger *From the Rarău Mountain* at **Ilişesti**, held respectively on the first and second Sundays of July. *Drăgaica*, the pagan pre-harvest celebration in the fields on Midsummer Day, is only practised in a few districts in Wallachia today.

August is probably the best month for **music**, with four major festivals. During the first week at **Călimănești** in Wallachia, the *Songs of the Olt* draws musicians and folklore ensembles from all over Oltenia, and coincides with a big *pottery fair*. On the second Sunday, people from Maramureş, Transylvania and Moldavia meet for the great *Hora* near the **Prislop Pass** to socialise, feast and perform Round Dances in their finest costumes; while on the same day, to the south across the mountains, the *Festival of the Ceahlău Mountain* is held at **Durău** near the shores of Lake Bicaz. The music of pan pipes and the bands of Gorj county characterise another festival, *At Tismana in a Garden*, staged near **Tîrgu Jiu** on the 15th, where one can also find a large range of handicrafts (for which bartering, rather than paying in lei, may secure better bargains).

And finally, August 23 is **Liberation Day**, commemorated by a national holiday and whatever bands or floats a town or village can come up with. For its picnic on the hill above the station and the cacophonous but bluesy town band performing in the medieval town centre, I'd recommend the celebrations at Sighişoara; but wherever you are, something's bound to happen.

Reaping preoccupies many villages during **September**, giving rise to **harvest festivals**, although the custom is gradually declining. The timing of these varies with the crop, and from year to year, but one can usually rely upon *At the Vintage* at **Odobeşti** in the eastern Carpathians being held on the last Sunday. Earlier in the month, on the first Sunday, you can hear the pan-pipers of the northwest perform the *Rhapsody of the Trişcaşi* at **Leşu**, in Bistriţa-Năsăud county. Many of the musicians are shepherds, who also play alpine long-horns and bagpipes, and compete with each other at *The Vrancea Shepherd's Long Pipe*, a festival held at **Odobeşti** on the third Sunday of **November**.

Folklore

Past generations of travellers have always been struck by the wealth of **myths and folklore** in Romania; and it's hardly surprising that the fictional Dracula resided here, in the wild Carpathian mountains where belief in ghosts and vampires (*strigoi*, see p. 493) still exists, if not as commonly as romantics might like to imagine. Today, few rural folk fear the 'witches' nights' – April 23 and November 29 – nor the cannibal *Mama Pădurci*, the legendary Mother of the Forest; but other traditional beliefs and attitudes are ingrained, or just submerged beneath modernity. Meanwhile, given the rigidly controlled media, **rumours** have become the main means of spreading truth, which inevitably mixes with distorted information and sheer fantasy, giving rise to a host of bizarre stories that the student of Romanian affairs, Steven Sampson, has likened to modern-day folklore. If you're interested in traditional folklore, Maramureş is undoubtedly the place where it persists most strongly. Obviously, however, not understanding Romanian is a barrier to comprehension; and I'd recommend reading *Rumanian Bird and Beast Stories* and *Children's*

Stories from Romanian Legends and Fairy Tales (both by Moses Gaster), or one of the C19 classics like Emily Gerard's *The Land Beyond the Forest* (all out of print, but sometimes available from second hand bookshops). Andrew MacKenzie's *Dracula Country* is also rewarding. 'Socialist folklore' one either hears when travelling around and talking to local people, or doesn't, depending on the circumstances. Steven Sampson's article 'Rumours in Socialist Romania' (*Survey*; Winter 1984) quotes a good many juicy examples of the genre.

SCENERY, WILDLIFE AND OUTDOOR ACTIVITIES

Although two thirds of Romania is either plains or hills and plateaux, the country's geography is dominated by mountains, which almost enclose the 'Carpathian redoubt' of Transylvania, and merge with lesser ranges bordering Moldavia and Maramureş. In such areas the **scenery** is usually beautiful, with pastoral valleys nestled between foothills ascending to wild crags or precipitous gorges. Much of it has escaped the ravages of hasty industrialisation visible in lower-lying regions, and some areas like the Harghita mountains and the ranges north of Bistriţa and Maramureş are still essentially wildernesses, inhabited by bears and wolves and birds of prey. The Danube Delta is a totally different environment, unique for its topography – of which only one tenth is dry land – and as a **wildlife** habitat which attracts some 300 species of birds during the spring and autumn migrations. Both regions offer opportunities to pursue **outdoor activities** – hiking, skiing, caving or even shooting rapids in the mountains; and the experience of navigating a canoe through the reedy Delta when it's overflowing with varied birdlife.

Hiking, caving and winter sports in the mountains
The Carpathians – a continuation of the Alps – are the most sinuous chain of mountains in Europe; and in Romania they form a natural barrier between Transylvania and the old *Regat* provinces, interrupted by a few narrow passes or wide depressions which have played a significant part in the country's history. While the Mureş Valley opens Transylvania to Hungary and the west,

the region's northwestern quarter is a fastness – the Apuseni Mountains, whose Dacian inhabitants escaped conquest by the Romans. The mountains of eastern Transylvania merge with the Sub-Carpathians of Moldavia, their valleys inhabited by descendants of the Székely and the Csángó 'Wanderers' who trekked eastwards centuries ago; while the great southern wall of the Transylvanian Alps is still traversed by **passes** whose names bespeak of past battles – the Red Tower and the Iron Gate.

Though few of Romania's Carpathian peaks are higher than 8,000 feet, and the majority are between 3,000-6,000ft, lack of altitude is more than compensated for by the variety of geological formations and rockscapes. There are mighty **gorges** (*cheile*) at Turda and Bicaz, and spectacular valleys cut by the Olt and Prahova rivers, to mention but a few. Bizarrely eroded **rock formations** characterise the Padiş Plateau; Mount Ceahlău, and karstic depressions like the 'Valley of Hell', while the Bucegi range is famous for the 'Babele Sphinx', and the sheer walls of the massif overhanging Buşteni in the Prahova Valley. Several large **caves** (*peşteri*) in the mountains are regularly visited by the public on account of their magnificent **stalactites** (at Chişcău, Meziad, Scărişoara and Horezu for example), but most are known only to Romania's dedicated band of pot-holers. Perhaps the most popular sites are the regions with alpine **lakes** – in particular the Făgăraş and Retezat ranges.

Dozens of hiking **trails** – signposted with red triangles, blue stripes or other markings – are shown on *Hartă Turistica* maps and in ONT's useful brochure *Invitaţie în Carpaţi* . A few walks are detailed and others are mentioned in this guide. Many individual ranges are minutely covered by booklets in the 'Our Mountains' series – unfortunately, however, published in Romanian (*Munţi Nostri*) and German (*Unsere Berge Reihe*) only, and sporadically available from bookshops rather than tourist offices. The Bucegi massif is perfect for **short hikes** within a limited time; for it offers dramatic crags, caves and waterfalls within a few hour's walk of the cable cabin, which ascends from the valley an hour's train ride from Braşov or the capital. Roundabouts, trails descend towards Bran Castle, karst depressions and the ridge of Piatra Craiului, beyond which stretches the Făgăraş range with its scores of lakes. This, like the Padiş Plateau, is well suited for **weekend walkers**, while the Retezat and Parîng mountains to the southwest offer the chance of **longer hikes** crossing several ranges.

In previous years several British tour operators organised all-inclusive **walking holidays** in the Carpathians, namely: *Ramblers Holidays Ltd.* (13 Longcroft House, Fretherne Rd. Welwyn Garden City, Hertfordshire AL8 6PQ); *Countrywide Holidays Association* (Birch Heys, Cromwell Range, Manchester M14 6HU; ☎ 061-225-1000); *Holiday Fellowship Ltd.* (142-144 Great North Way, London NW4 1EG; ☎ 01-203-0433); and the *International Explorers' Club* (2 Mount Close, Woking, Surrey GU22 OP2). Though none are scheduled for 1988, such trips might be available in the future. **Independent hikers** should bring camping gear and **food**, since unless you book (through ONT or the regional OJT), **accommodation** in mountain Cabanas can't be guaranteed, and some chalets don't serve meals. These Cabanas (marked on hiking maps) are convivial places where one can learn much about the mountains; but many Romanians simply pitch camp by rivers, and providing it's not in a nature reserve, you can do the same.

Some **important terms** are: *potecă/traseu* = path/route; *nerecomandabil iarna* = unsafe during the winter; *refugiu (salvamont)* = refuge (with first aid); *şa* = ridge; *stînca* = rock; *colţ* = cliff; *aven* = hollow; *poiana* = glade; *izvor* = spring; *cascada* = waterfall; *telecabina* = cabin lift; *teleschi* = ski lift; *telescaun* = chair lift; and *cale ferată îngustă* – a narrow gauge railway.

The science and practice of **caving** owes much to a Romanian, *Emil Racoviţa*, who founded the world's first speleological institute at Cluj University, near the karstic zones of the Apuseni Mountains. Although the last major discovery was the Bears' Cave in 1975, the nether regions of many 'known' caves are still being explored by Romanian enthusiasts, and constantly yield fresh surprises. Interested groups or individuals should write to to the Racoviţa Institute about participation and the details of prospective caves, several months in advance. Stating your experience, and an offer to contribute gear and a share of the costs, should increase your chances of acceptance. It's likely that the institute can also put foreigners in touch with canoeing freaks devoted to **shooting the rapids**: a dangerous sport practised on rivers like the Vaser in Maramureş, which descend steeply from their highland sources (or from caves in the karst zones). Bring all your own **equipment**, since there's little chance of renting any, and the stuff in shops is expensive, given the official exchange rate.

Skiing is a popular sport in the mountains from November or December through until March, or even April, depending on conditions at the nine **resorts**. Foreign tour operators favour Sinaia and Poiana Braşov for their superior slopes and facilities, but by going through ONT or turning up on the spot you should also be able to attend the **ski instruction** at Borşa in Maramureş (for beginners; December-March), Semenic in southwestern Transylvania (November-March) or Durău/Ceahlău on the edge of Moldavia. The majority of pistes are rated 'medium' or 'easy' (red or blue according to the colour coding), but each of the major resorts has at least one difficult (black) run, and the Costila-Caraiman descent above Buşteni is positively hazardous. Details of the slopes, chair-lifts and snowcover at each resort is contained in the *Invitation to the Carpathians* booklet. Ski **equipment** for hire at the resorts is slightly antiquated compared to the latest western models – though otherwise serviceable; package tourists, however, get priority, so independent skiers should if possible bring their own gear.

Wildlife and the Danube Delta

Many of Romania's scores of nature reserves are in the Făgăraş, Retezat, Bucegi and Piatra Craiului mountains where, as in remoter parts of the country, the woods covering the mountainsides are inhabited by chamois, deer, Carpathian stags, brown bears and wild boar, to name only a few **animals**. In the reserves they've become accustomed to human interlopers; but in remote, sparsely populated regions like the Harghita and Maramureş mountains, wild animals are just that. During winter there are sometimes wolf hunts, for hungry *lupu* occasionally attack livestock or even solitary walkers in the forests – though it should be stressed, the chances of encountering a wolf are very small! Bears – most numerous around Bistriţa – are rarely aggressive unless in defence of their cubs. While the imperious stags whose mating cries resound through the Vaser Valley during autumn permit people to observe their ritual conflicts from a distance.

Eagles, grouse and nightingales can be spotted in the mountains, but the best place for seeing **birdlife** is without a doubt **the Danube Delta**. Millions of birds winter here, or stop over during the spring and autumn migrations to northern Europe, the Mediterranean, China, Siberia and parts of Africa – a unique concentration of different species, including the Delta's own resident pelicans (slowly losing the fight against local fishermen). For the well-heeled, ONT can arrange boat tours down the main Sulina channel of the Delta, and their Tulcea or Crişan offices may sometimes be wheedled into renting small boats, which are the only means to penetrate the backwaters, where most of the birds nest amongst the floating reed islands (*plaur*) and the luxuriant vegetation covering the mud banks, or *grind*. Canoes or kayaks are best for exploration, since boats with outboard motors scare the wildlife and get clogged by vegetation.

Bring your own boat, suncream, mosquito repellent and a compass for navigation (since the reeds exceed head height), and you can make any number of fantastic journeys **by kayak through the Delta** using ONT's *Delta Dunării* map. Without a boat, you'll have to find a fisherman with one and ask, *Pot să inchiriez o barcă?*; if he's interested you can negotiate about *la costa ora/ziua* (the cost per hour/day), bearing in mind that he'll probably act as rower and guide, not wishing to entrust his boat to a foreign landlubber. Doing it this way lessens your freedom of movement and is likely to be fairly time consuming – all business in the Delta seems to be oiled by libations of vodka. . .

CHURCHES, MONASTERIES, CASTLES AND MUSEUMS

Romania's abundance of **churches** testifies to its history of religious faith – and competing faiths. During Transylvania's feudal period these became aligned with the stratification of society into *Nationes*, so that the rights of 'four religions' and 'three Nations' – but not those of Orthodoxy and its Romanian adherents – were recognised; an order stigmatised as the 'Seven Deadly Sins of Transylvania'. In Moldavia and Wallachia Orthodoxy's monopoly on faith was total, and supported by the boyars and princes; but the clergy and the Patriarchate consisted of Byzantine (and later Phanariot) Greeks more often than Romanians, and performed the liturgy and rites in incomprehensible Slavonic rather than the native tongue, as late as the C19th.

The effects of this, and the frequency of invasions, at least partly accounts for the extraordinary diversity of styles. Churches range from the inspired *biserici de lemn* **built of wood** in Maramureş villages to the Gothic *Hallekirche* and austere structures **with fortifications** raised by the Saxons around Braşov and Sibiu. Having absorbed Byzantine architecture in Moldavia and Wallachia, masons and architects ran riot with colour and mouldings (as at Curtea de Argeş) before producing wonderful **ornamental stone façades** – most notably at Iaşi's Three Hierarchs' Church, and in Wallachia, where the **'Brîncoveanu style'** with its porticoes and stonecarving derived from native woodwork motifs flourished.

The **frescoes** so characteristic of medieval Orthodox churches achieved nightmarish sophistication (judging by those still extant at Poienile Izei) at the hands of unknown artists, and were boldly executed **on the exterior walls** of Sucevița, Voroneț and other 'Painted Monasteries' in northern Moldavia, which are nowadays recognised as some of Romania's greatest artistic treasures. The Orthodox church maintains dozens of **Monasteries** with financial assistance from the state, the most famous being Snagov, where Dracula is buried.

On Sunday mornings and during the great festivals like Easter, Orthodox **services** – *liturghia* – are impressive rites (which non-believers may discreetly observe). The sonorous chanting of the hidden choir and the incantations amidst the candles and censer's smoke create a wholly different atmosphere to that in Protestant services – although there too (in Sibiu and Săliște for example), the **choral singing** may be fantastic.

Romania's most spectacular **castles** are located in Transylvania, where you'll

also find towns such as Sibiu and Sighişoara, built around an inner ring of fortifications, or *cetate*. Bran and Hunedoara are both superb Gothic/Renaissance castles, while at Arad, Alba Iulia and Oradea stand three colossal Habsburg fortresses laid out in the convoluted style of the Swiss military architect Vauban. Castles, like **museums** (*muzeu*) great and small, are normally open from 9am-5pm or 10am-6pm daily, except on Mondays and national holidays. For visitors, many museums soon pall because of the lack of information in any language but Romanian, but the **village museums** are interesting even without the benefit of captions; containing peasant houses filled with artefacts, huge oil presses, watermills and other structures rescued from the agrarian past, laid out as if in a real community. Student reductions are only granted to groups of ten or more, but in any case, museum **admission charges** are rarely higher than 5 lei.

OTHER THINGS

ADDRESSES are written as Str. Eroilor 24, III/36 in the case of apartment buildings; ie. Street (*stradă*) of Heroes, the third floor of number 24, flat 36. Some blocks have apartments back to back, in which case the entrance (*scara*) is also given, eg. *scara B*. Outlying suburbs of Bucharest have a sector number, while in some towns, districts are known as *cartierul*, and by name, like the Schei quarter of Braşov. Streets, boulevards (*bulevardul*), avenues (*calea* or *şoseaua*) and squares (*piaţa*) are commonly named after national heroes like Stephen the Great – *Ştefan cel Mare* – or Michael the Brave – *Mihai Viteazul* – or the date of an important event such as August 23, when the fascist Antonescu regime was overthrown in 1944.

BRING... everything that you think is necessary, having read the sections on eating and drinking and the black market. The list is potentially endless, but should include: candles and a collapsable container for use during power and water cuts; film; tampax, contraceptives, batteries, razor blades and prescribed medication, if required; a supply of concentrated food and your favourite tit-bits, for emergencies and morale boosting; plus books to read. Campers should

bring stoves powered by gas (and the cartouches, which aren't available here) or solid fuel of the 'survival' type, since petrol is hard to get.

CHILDREN under 14 years of age are exempt from obligatory exchange and, depending on their age, qualify for various reductions. Railway transport is free for under fives, and reduced by 50% for under tens. On TAROM flights, children under 2 pay only 10%, and up to the age of 12, 50%, providing they share a seat with an adult. In hotels, children under 10 may share an adult's bed for free, or pay 50% of the adult cost for an extra bed in the room. In big coastal resorts and at Poiana Braşov there are kindergartens, with foreign language speaking staff, for the benefit of holidaymakers; while most stations and some trains have a specially heated room for mothers with babies (*camera mama şi copilul*). For travellers with children, the big problems are the power and water cuts, and the unavailability of nappies and baby food. Mamaia and the main ski resorts offer the best entertainments for kids, but most large towns have a puppet theatre (*Teatrul de Păpuşi*).

CIGARETTES The only Western brands (available from hotels and COMTOURIST for hard currency) are Marlboro and Kent. Mysteriously, the latter has great status on the black market, although its uses as an 'alternative currency' have been over-rated. Romanian cigarettes are generally unappealing; the cheapest *Carpați* are of rough black tobacco; *Snagov* are milder and slightly more expensive; while the deluxe brand, *Cișmigiu*, aren't worth the extra cost. Native brands are usually filtered (*cu filtru*), and matches are called *chibrit*.

CONSULATES AND EMBASSIES are all in Bucharest (see the city Listings), and Romania has diplomatic relations with almost every country except South Africa. Most diplomatic buildings have a policeman at the gate who'll demand to see your passport before permitting entry. If you've lost this, ring beforehand (and immediately, even outside working hours). In the the case of Britain and the US, they'll repatriate if absolutely necessary. Most embassies and consulates stock their national newspapers, while the US, French and British have reading rooms.

CONTRACEPTIVES have been virtually outlawed, as have abortions, in order to force up the birth rate, and it's hard to think of anything from the West that can make a bigger difference to the lives of Romanian women and men. Tourists may only import contraceptives for 'personal use', though claims that one uses large ammounts are obviously difficult for customs officers to dispute!

ELECTRIC POWER is frequently cut off for several hours during the day, but nominally delivers 220 volts at 50 cycles.

FEMINISM Romanian women carry a double burden of work and child-care in an economy that's steadily disintegrating; and – since the prohibition of contraception and abortion, and the introduction of compulsory pregnancy screening – are being forced by the state to choose between childbirth or celibacy (lesbianism is hardly an option). Given the state's intolerance of any opposition, widespread bitterness has yet to give rise to any feminist movement, and seems unlikely to in the future. What does exist is a kind of underground solidarity; a fair number of women in positions of low- and middling-authority; and a *National Women's Organisation* that preaches the primacy of motherhood, whose figurehead is, predictably, Elena Ceaușescu.

FISHING permits can be arranged through OJTs in provincial towns; the Danube Delta is an angler's paradise; and other bodies of water like Lake Ceahlău and Lacu Roșu in the mountains between Moldavia and Transylvania are also rewarding.

FOOTBALL is popular and most large towns have a stadium (*stadion*). Teams are organised around professions as well as regionally, so fans come to cheer *Bucharest Steau* (the army), who made it to the European Cup semi-final in 1988 – and have the remarkable Gheorghe Hadji, currently being sought by Inter Milan, who have offered to build a Fiat plant in Romania for his transfer! – or hiss teams like *Dinamo* (the police). Most terms – like match, goal etc. – have been borrowed from English. Tickets for matches are very cheap.

GAY ATTITUDES The Romanian government doesn't merely discriminate against gays, but pursues a policy of outright **persecution**; and any gay foreigner knowing that isn't going to come *here* for their holiday. Before 1945, attitudes to homosexuality were fairly tolerant, at least in Bucharest, but since coming to power the current regime has been relentlessly homophobic. In the Party's eyes, homosexuality not only 'sabotages' the 'duty' of all Romanians to breed children, but is also equated with dissidence, Western decadence and connivance with foreign powers. Sexual relations between consenting adults of the same sex are illegal; offenders are gaoled or forced to submit 'voluntarily' to 'treatment' including electric shocks, drugs or even castration; unless they take up the 'option' of becoming an informer for the Securitate, a bait for other victims.

HOSPITAL EMERGENCIES Dial **061** and see the advice on page 250.

LAUNDRIES Launderettes don't seem to exist, and for travellers it's a choice between washing yourself or paying a hotel to do it. It's often difficult to find washing powder in supermarkets.

LEFT LUGGAGE offices – *bagaje de mînă* – exist in most railway stations, where you'll also find left luggage lockers, which should be avoided since the locks are likely to jam. Always allow plenty of time to reclaim your baggage.

SEXUAL HARASSMENT Whether because of ingrained courtesy or fear of the consequences of hassling foreigners, it's rare for Romanian men to subject women tourists to sexual harassment. Most foreign women come in tour groups which are practically secluded from the populace – except on the coast where everyone mingles, though even there, machismo acknowledges its limitations. Because independent **women travellers** are a rare thing, they're likely to be accorded some respect (if not excessive solicitude) – but also viewed with some amazement, particularly in rural areas. Romanian women themselves hitch-hike – but always in pairs, so there's obviously a certain amount of caution justified. Within earshot of other people, you should be able to scare away any local pest by shouting, *lasaţi-ma in pace!* (Leave me alone!) or merely mentioning the *Miliţia*.

SHOPS are generally open from 9am or 10 am to 6pm or 8pm on weekdays, but may close for several hours during the middle of the day. Supermarkets (*magazin universal*) are open daily from 8am-8pm, 8.30am-1pm on Sundays.

SPAS Many of the *Bai* dotted throughout the mountains and along the coast are open year round and function as health resorts – *Staţiune balneoclimaterica* – offering specialist treatments. For mineral and thermal baths, Sovata, Băile Herculane and Băile Felix offer the best facilities, while you can plaster yourself with theraputic black mud at Eforie Nord, or wallow in Lake Techirghiol's sapropelic sludge. Romania has also patented several products described as 'highly effective': *Gerovital H3* and *Aslavital*, invented by Dr. Ana Aslan for geriatric treatment; *Pell-Amar*; *Boicil Forte* herb extract and *Ulcosilvanil*, all of which ONT is keen sell to the afflicted wealthy. You can obtain a booklet on spas from ONT abroad, and detailed info from the main office in Bucharest, which also makes bookings for treatment.

SWIMMING POOLS (*ştrand*) are a feature of most large towns.

TAMPONS are unobtainable, so bring all that you'll need.

TIME is normally 2 hours ahead of GMT, while during Romanian Summer Time (from the last Sunday of March to the last Sunday of September) clocks go forward one hour.

WORK for foreigners in Romania seems out of the question unless you land a job at the *Bucharest International Fair* in October as a company rep or translator. A list of exhibitors should be available in advance from the Fairs and Exhibitions Co, 1, Piaţa Şcinteii (☎ 177593), since the closing date for registrations is some time in April.

ROMANIAN TERMS: A GLOSSARY

ALIMENTARĂ food shop.

ARDEAL 'forested land', the Romanian name for Transylvania.

BAI bath, spa; also the old word for 'mine'.

BISERICA church; **BISERICI DE LEMN**, the wooden churches of Maramureş.

BIVOL buffalo, introduced from India by the Gypsies; **BIVOLARI** are buffalo-drovers.

BOYAR or **BOIER** feudal lord.

BUCIUM alpine horn used by shepherds (**BUCIUME** pl.)

BULEVARD (*B-dul* or *Blvd.*) boulevard.

CALEA main street; Calea Victoriei, 'Street of Victory'.

CĂLUŞ traditional Whitsun fertility rite performed by **CĂLUŞARI** in rural Wallachia and southwestern Transylvania.

CAPRA masked 'Goat dance' to celebrate the New Year.

CASA house.

CETATE fortress or citadel; sometimes applied to rock formations, like the 'Citadels of Ponor' (*Cetaţile Ponorului*).

CHEI gorge; the most famous is the *Cheile Bicazului* near Bicaz. Also **GÎT**, 'neck'.

CÎMPULUNG meadow or long field, for which settlements like Cîmpulung Moldovenesc are named.

CSÁNGO areas of Moldavia settled by Hungarian 'Wanderers' from Transylvania.

DACIANS earliest recorded inhabitants of Romania, subjugated and colonised by the Romans during C1-C4. According to the Daco-Romanian Continuity Theory, the two races mingled to form the ancestors of the Romanian people.

DEAL hill; for example *Dealul Metropoliei*, 'Hill of the Patriachate'.

DOINA traditional, usually plaintive Romanian folk song; a form that's believed to have originated in

Maramureş.

DRUM road; **DRUM NATIONAL** highway; **DRUM BUN** bon voyage.

ERDÉLY the Magyar name for Transylvania.

GRADINĂ garden.

GRIND raised area of accumulated silt in the Danube Delta.

GURA mouth; hence *Gura Humorlui*, village at 'the mouth of the Humor' river.

HORA traditional village Round dance.

HOSPODAR feudal prince of Moldavia (from the Slav *Gospodar* = lord)

ICONOSTASIS decorated screen in an Orthodox church containing tiers of icons that separates sanctuary from nave and priest from congregation during Eucharist.

JUDEŢ county.

LAC lake; *Lacu Roşu*, 'Red Lake'.

LEGION or **IRON GUARD** Romanian fascist movement, 1927-44.

LIPOVANI ethnic group living by fishing and gardening in the Danube Delta, descended from Russian 'Old Believers'.

LITTORAL the coast.

MAGYARS Hungarians, roughly 2 million of whom live in Romania, mainly in Transylvania.

MĂNĂSTERIA monastery.

MOARA watermill.

NAI pan-pipes.

NAOS or sanctuary; the innermost part of an Orthodox church, lying below the central cupola and in front of the iconostasis.

NARTHEX entrance hall of an Orthodox church, often decorated with frescoes.

NATIONS or **NATIONES** historically, the privileged groups in Transylvania. In 1437, the Magyar aristocracy, Saxon burghers and free Székely established the *frateram unionem* of Nations following the Bobîlna serf uprising.

NEDEIA village fair or festival characteristic of the mountain regions.

PADURE a wood.

PAS a mountain pass, eg. *Pasul Bran*.

P.C.R. *Partiudul Communist Roman* – the national Communist Party (or *RCP*).

PEŞTERA cave. Romania has many spectacular stalactite grottos, like *Peştera Vintului*, 'Cave of the Wind'.

PHANARIOTS Greek administrators, and later rulers of Moldavia and Wallachia

during the centuries of Ottoman hegemony.

PIATRA stone or crag.

PIAŢA square; also a market.

PLAJA beach.

PLAUR floating reed islands, characteristic of the Delta.

POD bridge.

POIANA glade.

POPĂ Orthodox priest.

POTECA path.

RĂSCOALA peasant rebellion; usually refers to the great uprising of 1907.

REGAT or 'Old Kingdom', as Moldavia and Wallachia were known after they united in 1859.

RIU river.

ROM Gypsies, who arrived in Romania during the middle ages. In Romanian, Gypsies are called **ŢIGANI**.

SAT village.

SAXONS name given to Germans who settled in Transylvania from the C12 onwards, concentrated around seven towns.

SECURITATE state security police.

SIEBENBURGEN Saxon name for Transylvania (literally, 'seven towns').

ŞOSEAUA (*Şos.*) long tree-lined avenue.

ŞTÎNA sheepfold.

STRADĂ (*Str.*) street; *Stradă Eroilor* 'Street of the Heroes'.

SWABIANS name given to Germans who settled on the Banat after the end of the Ottoman occupation.

SZÉKELY Hungarian-speaking ethnic group inhabiting parts of eastern Transylvania known as the **SZÉKELYFÖLD** in their language.

ŢARA land, country (Romanian); Gypsy encampment.

TÎRG fair or festival; hence Tîrgu Jiu – 'Jiu Fair' – and other market towns.

TOVARIŞ comrade; honorific term for Party members.

VALE valley; *Valea Iadului* 'Valley of Hell'.

VĂTAF leader of Căluşari dancers (Romanian); tribal chieftain (Gypsy).

VIRFU (*Vf.*) peak, mount; *Virfu Omu*, Mount Omu.

VLACHS (or *Wallachs*; *Oláh* in Hungarian) foreign names for the Romanians of Wallachia, Moldavia and Transylvania before the C19.

VOIVODE prince of Transylvania or Wallachia; the title is **VODĂ** in Romanian, **VAJDA** in Hungarian.

ROMANIA
THE GUIDE

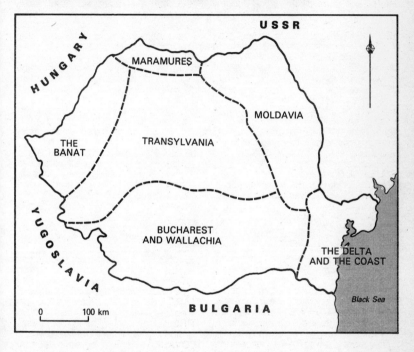

Chapter seven

BUCHAREST AND WALLACHIA

The pearl lies at the bottom of the sea whilst the corpse floats on the surface
Old Romanian proverb

Like Romania itself, **Bucharest**'s charms and deficencies inspire an extreme reaction. An architectural jumble of Empire-style, concrete and disguised shantytown, it is softened by abundant greenery and warm, rich sunlight, and inhabited by roughly one million Romanians, whose natural urges towards spontanaeity and *joie de vivre* are pitted against a creaking urban infrastructure and an oppressive bureaucracy. There's much for visitors to see here, but *doing* things frequently presents problems, for more than most capitals Bucharest is an insider's city. Good food and drink, opportunities for fun or profit, gossip and political rumours – all lie just below the threadbare surface, available to those with friends to open doors or, as Romanians say, *pile* ('files', to smooth over rough edges).

With a fair chunk of its population less than one generation removed from the soil, Bucharest still grows from the land between the Carpathian wall and the Danube, the region formerly known as **Wallachia**. Here lie the old capitals of Cîmpulung, Curtea de Argeş and Tîrgovişte, and a string of monasteries, mostly raised at the behest of 'progressive' despots otherwise famed for their handling of incessant invasions or rebellions. The basis for each regeneration was always the peasantry, who preserved the thread of native culture, wherein Orthodoxy, magic, music and a deep reverence for land were entwined. Industrialisation has wrought huge changes around Ploieşti, Piteşti, Craiova and the Jiu Valley, but life largely continues to follow the ancient pastoral or agricultural cycle in the highlands and on the Bărăgan Plain, where old rites such as *Ariet* and *Căluş* are still practised.

BUCHAREST (*BUCUREŞTI*)

BUCHAREST has a lingering reputation as the 'Paris of the East' – dating from before the last war – but anyone who takes this literally will be disappointed. Though there is an *Arc de Triumpf*, everyday life in the 'City of Joy' is stricken by shortages, and nightlife centres on a few downtown hotels and restaurants where spindly-legged champagne buckets filled with beer

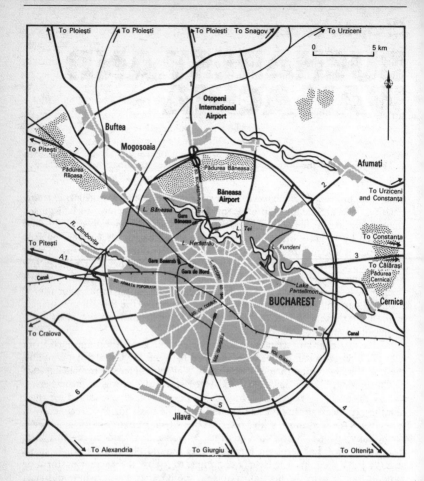

bottles symbolise the waning of *la vie Parisienne*. Romania's economy is coming apart at the seams, and it shows in the capital. Power cuts plunge Bucharest into semi-darkness, rendering the rutted streets more perilous; water mains are turned off for hours on end; heating levels are reduced each winter. ('Don't open the window or passers-by will catch cold' runs one mordant joke). Womens' regular ordeal of shopping for scarce foodstuffs culminates in a frenzy of bottling and preserving come autumn, for everyone knows that fresh produce will virtually disappear during the winter, when snowdrifts grip the city and the temperature can fall to minus 20° C. (George Schultz cancelled a state visit to Bucharest when his hosts hinted that heated accommodation might not be available).

Yet people keep their savoir faire and city **life** revives with warmer weather, blooming like an outlandish orchid alongside the brimming baskets of Gypsy flower-sellers. Residents experience it as a whirl of encounters, string-pulling and mutual back-scratching, rife with rumours and scandal, where private pleasures are all the more treasured for having been wrested from adversity. Foreign visitors who aren't cocooned in the lap of a tour group usually find the city bewildering, if not horrendously frustrating – but Bucharest is truly worth getting to know.

Recorded as a nameless 'citadel on the Dîmbovița' in 1368, and by name in an edict from the time of Vlad the Impaler, Bucharest – like Rome – has a legendary founder; in this case Bucur, a shepherd who supposedly built a settlement amidst the Vlăsia forest. Wallachia's princes (voivodes, or *vodă* in Romanian) alternated between Tîrgoviște and Bucharest as the site of their capital, before the latter finally secured its claim in 1659. Foreign visitors considered it a hick town then, and for a long time afterwards, but Bucharest loomed as a paradise in the minds of the peasantry (*bucurie* means 'pleasure' or 'joy').

Bucharest's charm – at least for the present – lies in its patchwork of different quarters, green with lime and horse chestnut trees. Much of this, however, is inexorably being demolished on Ceaușescu's orders to create a concrete Civic Centre worthy of the 'capital of the New Socialist Man' (as the Party press puts it). The area south of the Calea Victoriei has already gone, with the demolition of around 9,300 houses, many of them dating from the C18, and of some fifteen churches – the Cathedral included. For the old atmosphere, you now need to wander towards the northern stretches of the Calea Victoriei and between Cișmigiu Gardens and the Gara de Nord, where discreet bourgeois households slowly give ground to the proletarians and the Gypsies, vine-smothered façades merge with crumbling cherubs and dingy *alimentară*, and life retains a village-like slowness and intimacy, seemingly untroubled by the police spy on each block.

Arriving and finding lodgings

Your means of travel and the time of day can greatly affect your **arrival in Bucharest**, as public transport, roads and streetlighting leave much to be desired. Getting there in your own vehicle **by road** from Giurgiu (the point of entry from Bulgaria) or Transylvania is much the easiest way, although drivers should beware of cyclists and wandering animals on the 'highways' at night. Approaching from Transylvania you'll pass both airports and Băneasa campsite before encountering the Șos. Kiseleff, which points towards the centre. The approach from Giurgiu is less inspiring, with a long run through high-rise suburbs until Bulevard Cantemir finally reaches the Piața Universitații.

Depending on petrol shortages, passengers on international flights arriving at **Otopeni Airport** face insignificant or lengthy waits for TAROM coaches or taxis to carry them 20km into the centre, usually a spot near the Intercontinental Hotel. (ONT also arranges transfer by car for $18). Internal flights land at **Băneasa Airport**, just outside which one can catch trolleybus #81 or #82 into the centre, or bus #149 to Băneasa campsite (bus #348 on Sundays), until around 11.30pm.

But most travellers arrive **by train**, and generally after dark when Bucharest is doubly bewildering. All international and most domestic services terminate at the **Gara de Nord**; and you're unlikely to arrive at the **Gara Basarab** (northwest of the main station) or **Gara Băneasa** (north of the Casa Şcinteii). A busy, squalid hive with queues for everything, the Gara de Nord's most useful feature is not the hopeless ONT bureau (open Monday-Friday 7.30am-9.30pm/weekends until 2.30pm), but the signboard nearby, which lists hotel addresses and telephone numbers.

Unfortunately, only category II **hotels** are remotely affordable, and even these don't come cheap. The easiest to reach from the station are the *Bucegi* on the corner of Str. Witing (☎ 495-120), opposite a costlier establishment, and three places on the Calea Griviţei. *Dunarea* (nr.140) comes first on the corner, followed by *Griviţa* (nr.130) and then the *Oltenia* – the cheapest of the three. A shabby and vaguely mysterious warren with English-speaking receptionists, it's pretty similar to other hotels in the $20-$30 a night range. Being further from the station, the *Opera* (37, Str. Brezoianu), *Cişmigiu* (18, B-dul Gheorghiu-Dej; ☎ 147-410), and *Muntenia* (21, Str. Academiei; ☎ 146-010) are awkward to find after dark; if hotels on the Calea Griviţei are full, start with the *Marna* around the corner on Str. Buzeşti, which has probably re-opened by now.

The main alternative is **Băneasa campsite** – with tent-space and chalets to rent – situated out towards Otopeni Airport. To get there, take trolleybus #81 from the Gara de Nord (or #82 from the Piaţa Victoriei) as far as Băneasa Airport, and then wait for a bus #149 to the campsite (bus #348 on Sundays): #148 buses from the airport pass the campsite turn-off. The one kilometre-long avenue is unlit at night. **Dormitory beds** in student hostels (*caminul di studenti*) are a more uncertain possibility, since the booking agency, BTT (7-15, Str. Mendeleev; Monday-Friday 8am-5pm; ☎ 14-42-00), only seems willing to accommodate groups. You could try your luck, though, at either the *N. Bălcescu Agronomical Institute* near the Casa Şcinteii (trolleybus #81/#82) or the *Institutul Politehnic* (south of the Grozăveşti Metro station). Arab, African and Asian students staying at college over vacation when the hostels function (July 1-August 31) are probably the people to ask for assistance. Foreign students' cars can be recognised by special number plates (prefixed 5-B), while their owners tend to congregate on the Piaţa Universitaţii and patronise the self-service restaurant beneath the Intercontinental.

Finally, if a Romanian should offer to put you up, remember that **staying in private lodgings** is illegal. Should you accept, follow any precautions that your host might specify; eg dressing inconspicuously, not talking on the stairs, or leaving at the crack of dawn. After all it's they – not you – who'll suffer if the police get to hear of it.

Getting about

Bucharest's main **tourist office** at 7, General Magheru Blvd. keeps the same hours as the branch in the station, and is equally disinclined to part with much **information** (although they'll change money, rent cars and arrange 'programmes' with alacrity). Staff are generally politer and a mite more informative in the Athénée Palace (or some of the lesser hotels), but the tendency is for visitors not flashing the old valuta to be fobbed off with a poor city plan, and sold a labyrinthine *ghidul de transport* map if they're really persistent. Most of the practical information you're likely to require can be found under 'Listings' (p.297), and an ONT pamphlet, *Bucharest, Services, Programmes, Excursions*, contains some other useful snippets. ONT's free **maps of Bucharest** will serve at a pinch, but it's worth acquiring the superior effort printed by *Falk/Cartographia* beforehand, if possible; it's available in Hungary, or from good map shops in the West, but not inside Romania. This shows bus, tram and trolleybus routes fairly accurately (barring dislocations caused by construction work), although the Metro diagram is out of date.

Still expanding, the **Metro** is half *în explotare* (with trains running from 5am until 11.30pm; 1 leu flat fare), and half *în constructie* or *în proiectare*, which accounts for the excavations throughout the capital. The first line, M1, built to serve the working-class suburbs, runs east-west; and until the completion of M2 (running north-south through the centre) and the link-up between the Gara de Nord and Piaţa Victoriei Metro stations, visitors aren't likely to find the system much use for sightseeing purposes.

In fact, without a car, you must walk a lot – no great hardship in this city of green, picturesque backwaters – or join battle with **public transport above ground** which, to put it mildly, is in a mess. Buses powered by rooftop cylinders of *gaz methan* (because of the energy crisis) wallow across potholes, which afflict all but the downtown thoroughfares; trams seem set to rattle themselves to pieces, and trolleybuses frequently slip their cables and stall. But the real problem is overcrowding. Boarding normally requires scrum-tactics, and 'full up' means precisely that (at least during daytime, when doors are closed; at night, people hang from the open doorways). Once crammed inside, however, Romanians are remarkably restrained, even good-natured about their situation. Solidarity amongst long-suffering users also mitigates the problem of ever-changing bus stops and timetables – especially late at night, when rumours of the imminent arrival of vehicles, and where they might be boarded, are constant. There are flat fares on all **trolleybuses** (*trolibuz*; 1.50), **buses** (*autobuz*; 1.75) and **trams** (*tramvai*; 1 leu), which hit the streets around dawn and fade out by 11.30pm or midnight. As in Hungary and Bulgaria, passengers cancel their own **tickets**, which are sold singly or in bunches from street kiosks. With the types valid for two rides, you punch each end of the ticket in turn.

Your hotel receptionist can phone (03) for a cab if you don't fancy walking to the Gara de Nord or the Intercontinental, the favourite loitering spots for **taxis**. Because of the petrol shortage cabbies rarely cruise, and may be forced off the road (or at least obliged to refuse longer journeys) by late evening. The offical rates are reasonable, though: 5 lei to begin, 6 lei per kilometre thereafter.

THE CITY

'A savage hotch-potch' was Ferdinand Lasalle's verdict on Bucharest between the wars, with its nightlife and boulevards in emulation of Paris; its slums and beggars; aristocratic mansions and crumbling Orthodox churches. The extremes of wealth and poverty have been mitigated, but otherwise the city

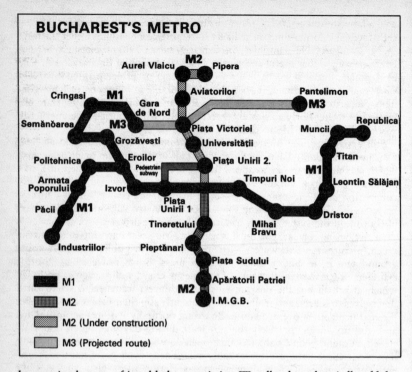

BUCHAREST'S METRO

- ▬ M1
- ▦ M2
- ▨ M2 (Under construction)
- ▧ M3 (Projected route)

has retained many of its old characteristics. Woodlands and a girdle of **lakes** freshen its northern outskirts, beyond a triumphal arch and a tree-lined chausée extending from Bucharest's main thoroughfare, the **Calea Victoriei**. As in the past it's the artery of city life, the principal strand in a webb of *bulevardul* and backstreets woven around Bucharest's diverse quarters. By custom, citizens **promenade** a mile or so of the Calea around noon and in the early evening, while throughout the day people nip across it between their homes and workplaces, markets and cafés in the surrounding neighbourhoods, or simply to catch an hour's snooze in **Cişmigiu Gardens**. Motorists may only drive southwards down the Calea, and all northbound **traffic** restricted to the Ipatescu-Magheru-Bălcescu boulevard route, also used by buses (#134/#300) and trolleybuses (#82/#83) travelling in both directions. The majority of **sights** in the inner city are within walking distance of the Calea Victoriei, so the itineraries that follow are pretty arbitrary. In any case, Bucharest is the kind of place that's best sampled somewhat randomly.

Along the Calea Victoriei

During the C19 the thoroughfares of Bucharest were surfaced with timber baulks – and known as 'bridges'. Many boyars (nobles) built their residences along the Mogoşoaia Bridge, the forerunner of the **Calea Victoriei** (Street of

Victory). Nearing the city centre begun the 'huddles of low, open-fronted shops where Lyons silk and Shiraz carpets were piled in the half-darkness beside Siberian furs, English guns and Meissen porcelain'. After the street was paved, to stroll became de rigueur, and travellers recounted that 'to drive down the Calea Victoriei between twelve and one o'clock will prove you a provincial or a stranger'. Visitors and local bourgeoisie alike revelled in the 'women's hats agog with pertness and invention', the Gypsy flower-sellers and establishments like the 'miraculous shop of Dragomir Niculescu, where one drinks țuică and eats minute caviar sandwiches and rich, hot little pastries filled with mushrooms'. Nor was the grim side of the 'City of Lights' ever far away, for starving groups of unemployed, lupus-disfigured beggars and dispossessed peasants vainly seeking justice in the capital waited in the side streets.

Today, the caviar shops have disappeared and beggars have been shifted to the Gara de Nord, but the Calea is still a place of vivid contrasts. At its **northern end** near the Piaţa Victoriei, it seems verdant and sleepy with touches of ancien régime elegance, like the clamshell-shaped glass porch of the **Museum of Music** (nr.141). Two more museums, exhibiting **ceramics and glassware** and other **art objects** (likewise described on p.293) occupy former boyar's mansions at nrs. 107 and 111, marking a change of character in the Calea. Beyond them the street becomes an eclectic jumble of old apartment blocks, glass and steel façades, and shops selling cakes and *pulloverul* – the setting for the promenade – while to the east and west lie Str. Amzei and Piaţa Pintilie, two areas with busy markets. On the right-hand side of the Calea stands the pretty *Biserica Alba*, or White Church, adorned with Tattarescu frescoes.

If the neatly-suited *Securitate* agents patrolling the lower end of the Calea start whispering nervously into their radios, prompting Militiamen to hustle people and cars off the road, then get ready for the presidential cavalcade of armoured, curtained limosines that charges down towards Party headquarters on the **Piaţa Gheorghiu-Dej**. As a friend once remarked, this large square (previously called the Piaţa Republicii) seems to be 'waiting for a coup', and, indeed, the piaţa was created during the 1930s on Carol II's orders to ensure a field of fire around his Palace for precisely that eventuality.

The **Athénée Palace Hotel** on the corner has been a notorious hotbed of espionage since the 1930s, when foreign correspondents filed pieces on the liveried staff and 'demi-mondaines who sat professionally in the lobby', all working for Carol's police chief, and for 'the Gestapo or British Intelligence as a sideline'. Symbolic of that fevered, corrupt era, Bucharest's élite partied through the night here while police were shooting strikers in the Red Griviţa district only a mile away. The German officers who filled the Athénée after Carol's abdication marvelled how native politicans combined venality with the most dignified bearing, and were seduced by 'liquid-eyed daughters of princely houses who made them go to bed with them before they had a chance to check up on their Aryan grandmothers'. During the early 50s the establishment was extensively refurbished as a hotel and an 'intelligence factory', with bugged rooms, tapped phones, and everyone from chamber-maids to the prostitutes and 'arty types' who sit discussing politics over a glass

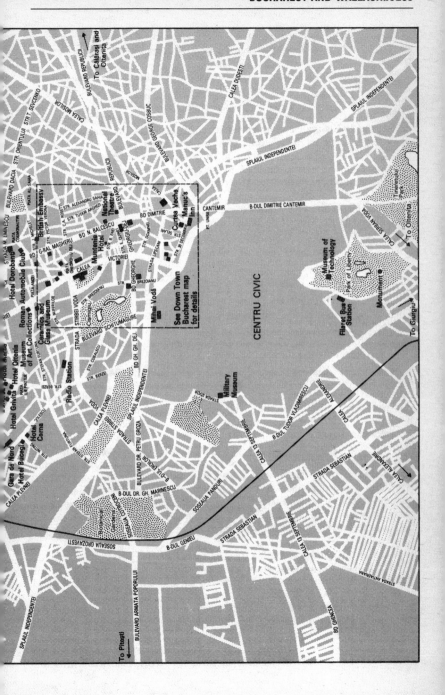

of *ţuică* in the lobby reporting to the secret police. By all means investigate its tawdrily plush interior or the expensive **nightclub** with its sub-*Folies Bergeres* troupe – but watch your step.

Nearby stands the Classical-style **Romanian Athenaeum**, erected in 1888, beneath whose dome – decorated with lyres – the *George Enescu Philharmonic Orchestra* gives **concerts** in a hall that's rampantly fin de siècle.

The **former Royal Palace** on the western side of the square was also built during the 1930s, replacing the original 'single-storeyed dwelling with a sort of sentry-box at its door' and 'pigs wallowing in mud', which Carol's grandfather – Carol I – had reluctantly occupied in 1866. Born Karl Hohenzollern, he was persuaded to accept the Romanian throne by the Prussian chancellor, who urged, 'Go on, it will give you interesting memories of your youth'. A stern workaholic unlike his grandson, he later bitterly remarked 'Only the very young consider their youth the best years of their life'. The northern wing of the palace now contains the **National Art Museum** (entrance on Str. Ştirbei Vodă, which leads to Cişmigiu Gardens), described on p.293. The **Central Committee building** diagonally opposite the Palace is cordened off, but you can imagine the scene in 1968, when Ceauşescu publicly defied the USSR from one of the balconies. His denunciation of the attack on Czechoslovakia, coupled with assertions that Romania would resist invasion, stirred the crowd to wild approbation and chants of *Ceau-şes-cu, Ceau-şes-cu*. Then, when passions had cooled shortly afterwards, Romanians admired their president's nimble retreat from the brink of catastrophe. For a brief moment, the hearts of the Leader and his people had thudded as one.

To the south of the Palace, the **Creţulescu Church** fronts a tangle of streets wending off towards Cişmigiu Gardens. A venerable C18 building with mock arches, elaborate carvings over the entrance, bricks laid in saw-toothed patterns around the towers, and other features of the 'Brîncoveanu' style, it was paid for by the boyar Iordache Creţulescu and his wife Safta, Prince Brîncoveanu's daughter. Her name reminded me of the *Stafia* – ghosts once believed necessary to ensure that large edifices remained intact. Romanian builders would measure the height of a person or animal with a piece of string and then incorporate this within the walls; superstition had it that the 'victim' would then die, and its ghost be drawn into the structure, whence it would repel any misfortune. For all that, the church is quite battered and little remains of its frescoes by Tattarescu. Under the arcade facing the church are a good bookshop and an *anticvariat* (secondhand bookshop), while on the corner of the next street, Matei Millo, stands the main **Post Office** (see Listings for details).

The Calea continues southwards past the *Berlin Restaurant* and the Tăndărică Theatre, behind which the **Pasagiul Victoriei** – a good place for **snacks** – sneaks through to the **Enei Church** one block further east. Shops and cinemas cluster about the junction with Bucharest's main east-west boulevard (see below); while nearby, an alleyway slips off to the courtyard of the picturesque **Doamnei Church** – haunted by devout grandmothers and their pampered felines. Yet further south, the Calea crosses **Stradă Lipscani**, a narrow street which between the wars served as Bucharest's equivalent of Petticoat Lane. It remains an area of little shops, interspersed with cafés (including the *Terass Rhapsodia* at nr.53) and slightly labyrinthine, with passageways like the **Hanul cu tei** (a fairly slick bazaar in the courtyard of a C19 inn) and the **Consignaţia**: a warehouse-full of junk, **secondhand goods and antiques** where one can browse for hours. Commercial hustle is more subdued than in the old days, however, and offers of illegal money-changing should be firmly refused – the people making them are almost certainly agent provocateurs.

Nearing the river, the **National History Museum** looms up at nr.15; the place to see some fine treasures, and two halls full of kitsch tat spawned by the cult of personality that surrounds the Leader and his wife Elena, including the less valuable of *Ceauşescu's 60th birthday presents*, given by communes, towns and institutions. 'The Beer Cart' (*Carul cu Bere*), around the corner on Str. Stavropoleos, is a better stop, with its ornate façade and vaulting; serving spicy grilled *mititei* famed throughout Bucharest, it rivals Manuc's Inn as the premier hangout. Further along the road stands the small **Stavropoleos Church**, built between 1724-30, with gorgeous, almost arabesque, mouldings and patterns decorating its façade, and a columned portico carved with delicate tracery.

At this point you can backtrack and follow the Calea to its end, the Splaiul Independenţei, or wander off into the surrounding neighbourhoods. Some of Bucharest's oldest churches and foulest slums were formerly close at hand to the south, but the whole area is now in the throes of re-development (see p.291). To the west lies a fairly nondescript quarter, with only the **Airline and Railway Tickets Bureau** on Str. Brezoianu worth mentioning before one reaches the B-dul Gheorghiu-Dej. But to the north, east and southeast of the Calea's end, things are more promising. . .

Dracula's Palace, Manuc's Inn, the Piaţa Unirii, and northwards to the University

Just east of the Calea, a maze of streets and pleasantly decrepit houses surrounds the historical centre of Bucharest, where Prince Vlad the Impaler – otherwise known as Dracula – built a citadel in the C15. Severely damaged during Dracula's attempt to regain the throne in 1467 (crowned with success, although the Impaler was murdered a few months later), the building succumbed to earthquakes and fire and was subsequently auctioned off as wasteland. Thus the remains of the **Curtea Veche** (Old Court) are pretty modest: a few rooms, arches and shattered columns, and a cellar containing a **museum** where the skulls of boyars whom Dracula had decapitated and hung from the town gates are lovingly displayed (open Tuesday-Sunday 9am-5pm). Adjoining the complex is a church raised by Mircea the Shepherd, with the horizontal bands of brick facing and rows of small niches beneath the cornice typical of C16 Wallachian church architecture.

A few doors along from the antiquarian bookshop opposite the Curtea Veche, an austere white building with barred windows conceals Bucharest's most famous establishment, **Manuc's Inn**. Within *Hanul Manuc*'s walls, elegant wooden verandas made by craftsmen from Maramureş surround a

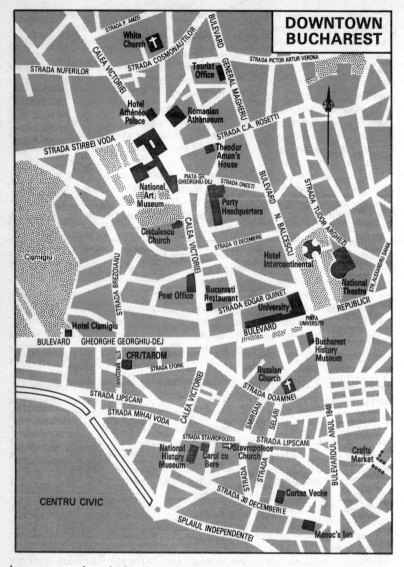

DOWNTOWN BUCHAREST

large courtyard, packed with profusely gesticulating bon viveurs. Originally a caravanserai founded by a wealthy Armenian, Manuc-bey, the building contains a restaurant and a *cramă* or wine cellar (open until 12pm and 11pm, respectively), and admits sightseers between 9am-11am and 5pm-11pm.

The inn's southern wall forms one side of the **Piaţa Unirii**, or Square of Union; the site of a large **market** where all kinds of Romanians congregate, including the capital's Gypsy flower-sellers and hawkers. The market hall selling fish, meat and dairy produce (open 6am-8pm/Sundays 6am-12pm) is the worst for queuing; buying fruit and vegetables from the stalls outside (which also trade on Sunday afternoons) is a less frustrating business. Piaţa Unirii is something of a cog in the **transport** system, with several bus and trolleybus lines groaning northwards *to the University*; tram #12's rattling off *towards the Park of Liberty*; and two *Metro stations*, linked by a pedestrian subway. Once line 2 is complete you'll be able to travel from Piaţa Unirii 2 up to the University or Piaţa Victoriei; but at time of writing the line only extends southwards; Tineretului Park (p.292) is one stop away. Piaţa Unirii 1 stands on the east-west Metro line; but some of the trains heading in the direction of Eroilor continue on up to the Gara de Nord (which will ultimately be linked by line 3 to form a circular system).

During my first visit to Bucharest, the southern edge of the square was delineated by a corrugated iron fence, behind which lay a vast building-site – the projected Civic Centre (see p.291) – extending south of the River Dîmboviţa. It seemed a good enough reason for heading northwards up along the **Bulevard Anul 1848**, whose name comemmorates Wallachia's first and only liberal revolution. On the right-hand side you'll pass Str. Decebal, leading off to a small **crafts market** (mainly wickerwork). Nearing the top end of the boulevard, the Hotel Intercontinental – towering above the Piaţa Universitaţii – comes into view.

The **Piaţa Universitaţii** is a nexus for city life and traffic, notwithstanding the disruptions caused by several nearby building sites. Just to the east rises the new **National Theatre**, resembling an Islamicised re-working of the Colosseum, a pet project of Elena Ceauşescu's. According to one joke, all the socialist countries responded to her appeals for donations except Hungary. With the loss of Transylvania to Romania after the First World War in mind, the Magyars replied: 'We've already given you the land'. Only rich or important foreigners can afford to stay in the **Hotel Intercontinental** (and be spied upon), but in a commendable display of egalitarianism there's a cheap **self-service restaurant** beneath the hotel (open 7am-10pm; avoid the lunchtime crush). The circular **coffee bar** beneath the piaţa is another popular place, particularly with foreign students (7am-9pm/10am-8pm on Sundays); in the same subway you'll find a place doing shoe-repairs. Opposite the Intercontinental on the western side of the boulevard, there's an interesting amalgam of two architectural styles. Le Corbusier seems to have inspired the design of the concrete apartment blocks, while the School of Architecture facing them bears the hallmarks of the neo-Brîncoveanu style – ornate pillars, prominent and richly carved eaves, and a multitude of arches.

Further to the west, **Bucharest University** occupies the first block on the Bulevard Republicii; its forecourt thronged with students and snack-stands, whilst statues of illustrious pedagogues and statesmen gaze blindly at the crowds. Established in 1859 after the union of Wallachia and Moldavia, the University equipped the sons of bourgeois families to become lawyers and men of letters up until the Communists took over. Technical skills and education for women were subsequently given top priority, and while students suffer worse material hardships than most other Romanians, their training and enthusiasm are impressive.

The small, bulbous domes of the **Russian Church** appear through a gap in the cupola-ed buildings lining the southern side of the boulevard. Faced with yellow brick, art nouveau green tiling, and pixie-faced nymphs, the church has a small interior, with frescoes so blackened with age and smoke that only the saintly haloes glow like golden horseshoes surrounding the Christ figure, who floats above a beaten gold iconostasis. 'Kitsch' describes most of the icons, particularly the cut-out Jesus with a light-bulb halo.

The long boulevard that runs **between University Square and the Piaţa Romană** serves as Bucharest's main artery for north-south traffic and public transport, and halfway along, changes its name from General Magheru to N. Bălcescu. At 7, B-dul Magheru there's the main **tourist office**; further north near the Piaţa Romana you'll find two offices of the **Romanian Automobile Club** (*ACR*). With a bit of hassle (p.249), **visa extensions** can be obtained at 27, Str. Nicolae Iorga, leading off the square; while any Brits with the misfortune to lose their passport should make tracks down another backstreet, Jules Michelet, to the **British Embassy** at nr.24. The embassy has a small **library** (see Listings), and even the three-day old Murdoch newspapers come as a relief after the Romanian media. Str. Amzei, which also leads off the piaţa, runs westwards past Bucharest's main **flower market** to the Calea Victoriei, whilst the Calea Griviţei (p.289) begins over the road.

Between Bulevard Gheorghiu-Dej and the Gara de Nord

Bulevard Gheorghe Gheorghiu-Dej bears a lot of traffic and the name of Romania's first Communist leader, who died of throat cancer shortly after returning from a holiday in the USSR. Suspecting that his predecessor was secretly irradiated by the KGB, Ceauşescu took fright when he developed throat pains following a visit to Moscow. Eminent specialists were secretly brought to Bucharest, until finally 'an old, very conservative West German doctor' said bluntly 'Sir, you talk too much and too loudly, and your vocal cords are terribly irritated'. (Or so Ion Pacepa, head of Romania's intelligence service until he defected to the US in 1978, says). That tit-bit aside, the boulevard is mainly notable for its **shops, restaurants and cinemas**, attracting shoppers with no great expectations and kids keen to watch the latest American import or an epic relating the mythical deeds of their ancient forebears, the Dacians. Crossing the boulevard, Str. Brezoianu leads southwards to the **CFR & TAROM bookings office** and runs northwards alongside the edge of Bucharest's oldest park, *Gradină Cişmigiu*.

Cişmigiu Gardens originally belonged to a Turkish water inspector, and fittingly contains a serpentine lake upon which glide small **rowing boats**, hired by courting couples seeking solitude amongst the fronds of weeping willow trailing in the water. (Boats from 9am-8pm; 7 lei per hour plus deposit.) Pelicans and swans and open-air **concerts** performed by the Ciprian Porumbescu Conservatory enliven the park, a favourite place for workers to snatch a snooze beneath the trees despite prohibitory *interzis* notices. Cişmigiu is a meeting place for different classes, though social status isn't as obvious as in the 1930s, when Olivia Manning espied the bourgeoisie in their Parisian-style suits and dresses and immigrants from the countryside wearing colourful homespun garb (to be discarded in favour of urban fashions as soon as their fortunes permitted).

The **Opera Română** lies further west along the boulevard opposite Piaţa V. Babeş; from here, buses (#126/#274) and trolleybuses (#90) trundle down the avenue – named after Dr. Petru Groza – to Bucharest's **Botanical Gardens**. In the southern sector of this large parkland stands the **Pioneers' Palace**, originally built for the headstrong Princess Marie, who needed a place to get away from her father-in-law, the first King Carol. If you can charm your way inside, the Palace is well worth seeing; lavishly equipped to cater for the capital's Young Pioneers (the Communist equivalent of the Scouts).

My favourite part of Bucharest is the rambling residential area **between Cişmigiu and the Gara de Nord**, with its urban-village character. Devout women genuflect passing tiny street-corner churches while neighbours gossip outside the dimly-lit neighbourhood workshops, respectfully greeting Orthodox *popăs* sauntering by. Ivy and flowering-creepers cloak the houses – all outwardly rundown, but often concealing parquet-floored apartments with elegant antique furniture and other relics of the pre-war bourgeois lifestyle. Traffic is surprisingly sparse, even on the main Calea Griviţei, and after nightfall – almost a black-out since there's virtually no street-lighting – it's not unusual for horse-drawn carts to rattle over the cobblestones around the shuttered **market** stalls on Piaţa Ilie Pintilie.

The **Calea Griviţei** – formerly the Tîrgovişte road – is over three miles long; a ragged street along which Walter Starkie (author of *Raggle Taggle*, see p.495) tramped in the heat, making 'many attempts to discover a humble hotel' (me too). Approaching the **Gara de Nord**, the Calea gets poorer and shabbier; tin shacks screening squalid drinking dens; pavements collapsing into potholes; and interminable construction work compelling pedestrians to squeeze past melon stalls and begging Gypsy waifs clustered about the station. 'I imagined it as a miniature city of the Arabian Nights,' recalled Starkie of his arrival in Bucharest, but on leaving the station 'only saw dirt and squalor everywhere', and after a few days spent in spendthrift society on the Calea Victoriei, had to move to the slums south of the river. The Gara de Nord **Metro** station will ultimately be linked to the centre by lines 2 and 3.

Calea Griviţei extends far beyond the station, past the **Railway Museum** (p.294), the **Gara Bassarab** and the Grant Bridge, into the sprawling **Griviţa-Roşie suburb**. Solidly working class and socialist (hence 'Red Griviţa'), it was the site of violent clashes between troops and striking railway-workers in February 1933; while in 1944 the district was bombed flat by British and American planes whose crews mistook it for the oil-town of Ploieşti. The suburb was rebuilt after the war as a model housing development, and although railway-workers have suffered like other sections of the proletariat during the waning of the Years of Light, they're relatively affluent by Romanian standards.

The Arc de Triumpf, Lake Herăstrău and other things in the northern suburbs

Until their disappearance during the 1940s, the **Skopţi** coachmen used to be one of the curiosities – or grotesqueries – of Bucharest. Members of a dissident sect founded in Russia during the C17, they interpreted literally the words of Christ in the Gospel according to St Matthew concerning eunuchs, and ritually castrated themselves in the belief that 'the generative organs are the seat of all iniquities'. (This was done after two years of normal married life – a period necessary to ensure the conception of future Skopţi.) Driving *droshkys* pulled by black Orloff horses, the coachmen wore thick caftans sprouting two cords, which passengers tugged to indicate when the driver should turn left or right.

The Skopţi used to seek fares on the **Şoseaua Kiseleff**, a long avenue lined with lime trees, which extends northwards from the Piaţa Victoriei. Modelled on the Parisian chausées, it's a manifestation of the wave of Francophilia that swept Romania's educated classes during the C19, and has a triumphal arch halfway along to rub the comparison home. Places along the chausée's initial length include the Swedish and Soviet embassies (the latter deploying a barrage of propaganda against the US ambassador's residence across the road) and the elegant *Doina* restaurant designed by Ion Mincu, favoured by the Party élite. Of the three museums here, the **Village Museum** (*Muzeul Satului*) adjoining Lake Herăstrău is undoubtedly the most interesting; a wonderful ensemble of spiky wooden churches and peasant dwellings, including a bizarre subterranean house. Eighty-two thousand butterflies and the skeleton of a *Deinotherium gigantissimum* are possibly good reasons for visiting the **Natural History Museum** at nr.1, but the **Museum of Party History** at nr.3 induced yawns even amongst the visiting Chinese delegation that I saw (whose members, presumably, were used to that kind of thing). More details of all three museums appear on p.294.

Ignored by hooting traffic, the **Arc de Triumpf** in the middle of the Şos. Kiseleff was originally a jerry-built structure raised to commemorate Romania's ill-fated intervention on the side of the Anglo-French Entente during the First World War. Between 1935-36 it was more fittingly rebuilt in stone along the lines of the Arc de Triomphe in Paris. Beyond it to the west lie the Tineretului (Youth) **sports complex** and the N. Bălcescu Agronomical Institute; to the east, trees screen the Village Museum and Parcul Herăstrău.

Lake Herăstrău is the largest of a dozen lakes which form a continuous line across the northern suburbs, and its verdant surroundings are beautiful. **Rowing** boats and **windsurfing** equipment can be hired on the shore, and curving bridges lead to a small and fragrant Island of Roses. The park contains an open-air theatre and three **restaurants** – *Moriţa*, *Pescăruş* and *Parcului* – with summer terraces. The residential area adjacent to the park (parts of which are fenced off) is one of Bucharest's most exclusive, inhabited by technocrats, favoured artists and other members of the privileged *nomenclatura*. Imagine the Leader's surprise and chagrin when Silviu Brucan, an ex-ambassador and former editor of *Şchintea*, issued a statement from his Herăstrău residence to the Western press to the effect that the anti-Ceauşescu riots in Braşov constituted a 'watershed' in the regime's existence.

By contrast, only hackneyed propaganda emanates from the 'Spark House' or **Casa Şcinteii** overlooking the Şoseaua's junction with Băneasa highway. This vast white wedding-cake in the 'Stalin style' is the fountainhead of official culture, occupied by the editorial staff of the Party daily, *Şcinteia*, and state committees supervising the publication of Romania's newspapers and scores of brochures every day, many of them printed on the premises. A huge, commanding statue of Lenin stands outside the Spark House, while to the west you'll see the obtrusive Exposition Pavilion. Although the **Pavilion Expoziţei** was built for Bucharest's annual International Trade Fair (in October), it's normally used to hold rallies, and festooned with bunting and billboards hailing the Leader. These presumably struck him as rather ephemeral tributes, for in 1986 he ordered the erection of a Triumphal Arch at the entrance, stating *The Golden Epoch – the Epoch of Nicolae Ceauşescu.* The Romanian media has been equally enthusiastic, proclaiming his reign to be the 'Years of Light'.

Further out along the Şos. Băneasa (or 'Nixon boulevard', as it was dubbed during Tricky Dicky's visit) stand the **Popular Arts Museum**, housed in a semi-fortified villa once owned by Dr. Minovici, and the **Feudal Arts Museum** occupied by Minovici's collection of foreign antiques (details on p.293). Beyond, the highway passes Party villas and the Securitate barracks; a filling station where motorists queue day and night for *benzin*; Băneasa Airport; Băneasa campsite and out of Bucharest. . .heading for Transylvania.

The Dîmboviţa and the Centru Civic

Dîmboviţa apă dulce,
Cine o bea nu se mai duce

There's an old saying that whoever drinks the 'sweet waters' of the **River Dîmboviţa** will never wish to be parted from Bucharest, to which one C19 traveller retorted that anyone who did 'would be incapable of leaving the city for ever afterwards'. The river – always prone to flooding – has been canalized during the last century, and there's currently an ambitious project underway to restore pure mountain water to the canal, with the effluent being carried underground. A parallel undertaking aims to link the Dîmboviţa with the Danube by means of a canal, so that Bucharest may become a port. ONT promises that when work is complete, the canal will also be used for **pleasure cruises**.

But that's not the half of it, because since 1984 acres of Bucharest – including thousands of houses and dozens of historic monuments – have been demolished to create a downtown worthy of 'the first socialist capital for the new socialist man': **the Centru Civic**. Work is still in progress, but the Centru Civic is intended to consist eventually of scores of tower blocks lining a six-lane, quarter mile-long **Victory of Socialism Boulevard**. At the lower end, a great circle of 50 fountains awaits sufficient water-pressure so that they may play, while at the opposite end ministries, Party organs and high functionaries' apartments are to be relocated within the vast **House of the Republic**. 'This Acropolis of ours' is really Ceauşescu's apotheosis, for it's an open secret that he's given orders for the construction of his own mausoleum within the Centru Civic. Meanwhile he is proving a demanding patron, allowing little more than a technical role to the architects employed. One of the first of the new structures was a block of flats, sited near the House of the Republic. They survived only a matter of days, being judged by Elena Ceauşescu too close to the palace, whose gardens they overlooked.

The Demolisher's vandalism has, however, been impartial – the slummy old **Cahea Rahovei** district, C18 and C19 mansions of the **Uranus quarter**, and Bucharest's 300 year-old **Church of the Patriarchate** on Dealul Mitropoliei Hill have all been razed or scheduled for imminent demolition (the Patriarchate is to be replaced by a pedestrian underpass). You'll have to see for yourself the eventual outcome, and what follows is basically an obituary. The old and new Spirea **churches**, St Antim's and the Bucur Church have gone, and in the process of moving the church of **Mihai Vodă Monastery** 279m on rails, the medieval cloisters and ancillary buildings were destroyed. Since the whole area was still a building site when we last saw it, we'd appreciate hearing from anybody who manages to fill in the blank area on the map in this book, and can furnish a proper description of the Centru Civic.

If services have resumed, buses, trolleybuses or trams heading southwards down the boulevard should continue along Calea Şerban Vodă, which runs between two parks. **Tineretului Park**, dedicated to 'Youth', contains a **fairground**, a lake and the old **Şerban Vodă Cemetery** which adjoins the junction of highways to Olteniţa and Giurgiu. The **Park of Liberty** (*Parcul Libertăţii*) features a 'Giants' Grotto' by one of the lakes, but also serves a didactic purpose as the site of both the **Monument to the Heroes of the Struggle for the Freedom of the People and of the Motherland, for Socialism** – wow! – and the **Museum of Technology** (reviewed below).

BUCHAREST'S MUSEUMS

Bucharest has more than twenty museums and memorial houses, but at any one time, several will be closed; the following selection is roughly in order of interest. Unless stated otherwise, **opening hours** are 9am-5pm or 10am-6pm, Tuesday-Sunday, although the *casa* may refuse to sell admission tickets during the hour before closing time. No student reductions except for groups of ten or more persons.

The Village Museum (28-30, Şos. Kiseleff), Established in 1936, this fascinating ensemble of nearly 300 peasant houses and other structures from every region of Romania, shows the extreme diversity of folk architecture. My favourites included the oaken houses from Maramureş with their beam-gates, 'rope motif' carvings and shingled roofing (also featured on the amazing Dragomireşti Church and the cruder effort from Turea in Cluj county); gateways carved with suns, moons, the Tree of Life, Adam and Eve, animals and hunting scenes; heavily thatched dwellings from Sălciua de Jos; dug-out homes from Drăghiceni (with vegetables growing on the roof) and Castranova; and the windmills from Tulcea in the Delta. Mud-brick dwellings from the fertile plains ironically appear poorer than the homes of peasants in the less fertile highlands (where timber and stone abound); while the importance of livestock to the Székely people of Harghita county can be seen by the barns, which are taller than their houses.

The National Art Museum (1, Str. Ştirbei Vodă). Beginning with a splendid Transylvanian diptych and larger than lifesize murals from Curtea de Argeş, the National's collection works through halls of embroidered boyars' garments and iconostases to the exhibition of paintings upstairs. Nicolae Grigorescu (1838-1907) gets star billing for his dark portraits and bolder, more impressionistic landscapes, but keep your eyes peeled for the fine portraits by Gheorghe Tattarescu (1820-94), Constantin Rosenthal's revolutionary table-auxs (similar to the work of Delacroix), and Theodor Aman's *Bulgarians Massacring the Turks*. Twentieth century work seems rather more derivative, though Corneliu Baba's grim scenes of peasant life transcend imitation. The top floor features collections of oriental carpets, Chinese and Dutch porcelain, French furniture and tapestries, and minor works by Rembrandt, Cranach, the Breughels, Renoir etc.

The Ceramics and Glass Museum (107, Calea Victoriei). Small and varied enough not to induce museum-itis, most of the rooms are furnished with splendid mirrors, carpets, chandeliers and tiled stoves. Aside from products of the pre-Christian era, the best Romanian work generally hails from Cluj or Bistriţa (whose factories were also responsible for the vases decorated with Ceauşescu's image). Upstairs you'll find C18-C19 Turkish and Iranian tiles, European, Japanese and Chinese porcelain, and lovely Art Deco pieces, including a Tiffany lamp.

The National History Museum (15, Calea Victoriei). This contains a fine collection of prehistoric Goddess figures from Vadastra and Cucuteni, and the Neolithic 'Hamangia Thinker', besides Celtic and Dacian jewellery, Roman statues and armour, and clothing and manuscripts from the medieval period. The rest of the museum traces the struggle of the principalities towards independence and union (a process in which women took no part, judging by the exhibits), culminating in the establishment of a socialist state. The culmination is two rooms entitled 'Proofs of the love, high esteem and appreciation that President N. Ceauşescu and Comrade E. Ceauşescu enjoy', including Nicolae's 60th birthday presents.

The Museum of Popular Art and the **Feudal Arts Museum** (both off Şos. Băneasa). A pair of villas built to hold the collection of Dr. Minovici, a successful engineer. The large, dark rooms of the Popular Art Museum contain woven blankets, Transylvanian blue pottery, spinning wheels, musical instruments, furniture and beautiful peasant garments. The other building is a bizarre fusion of Tudor, Italian Renaissance and fortress-architecture, filled with hunting trophies and weapons, Flemish tapestries, Florentine furniture, and German and Swiss stained glass windows. Minovici and his wife still live upstairs, though the museum was made over to the state in 1945.

The Museum of Art Collections (111, Calea Victoriei). Occupying the old Ghica Palace, an assortment of paintings, furniture and other antiques donated to (or confiscated by) the state. Contemporary art and films may also get a showing here – check the posters outside.

The Bucharest History Museum (2, B-dul Anul 1848). The city's evolution traced by means of old documents, photographs and prints; if they look familiar, it's because copies also hang in the Curtea Veche. The neo-Gothic building was once a boyar's residence, the Şuţu Palace.

The Railway Museum (193, Calea Griviţei). A display that examines the history of Romanian transport from the cart to the diesel train, with emphasis on the role of the railway-workers during the period 1912-45, when they were a force for socialist militancy. The country's first steam train, built at Reşiţa in 1873, stands in the museum courtyard.

The Museum of Technology (Parcul Libertăţii). This is an oddball museum, formed to assert the dramatic growth of technology in Romania, and several 'firsts' by Romanian inventors that the outside world has yet to recognise, to whit: the aerodynamic motor car (A. Persu, 1920), the metal-bodied aeroplane (A. Vlaicu, 1912) and the jet-propelled aircraft (H. Coanda, 1910). It's probably unfair, but I can't resist a Soviet joke: Q. Is Comrade Nyetev the greatest inventor of all time? A. In principle, yes. He invented the radio, television, the jet engine and the tape recorder. But Comrade Potalov was an even greater inventor. Q. Why? Did he invent more things? A. No, he invented Comrade Nyetev.

The National History Museum (1, Şos. Kiseleff). Named after Grigore Antipa, the founder of Romanian icthyology, includes a 15-foot high skeleton of a dinosaur discovered in Moldavia, and 82,000 butterflies and moths amongst its collection of 300,000 items.

The Military Museum (137, Str. Izvor). Weaponry, banners, and uniforms galore, although Romania has rarely gone for martial adventures. Since 1958 it has been the only Warsaw Pact country without Soviet troops on its soil, and Ceauşescu has called vociferously for disarmament, announcing peace proposals and cuts in the defence budget. The country retains, however, a considerable arms industry, exporting to the Third World.

The Party History Museum (3, Şos. Kiseleff; entrance around the corner on Str. Monetăriel). Photos and documents relating the Communist Party's struggle, culminating in the usual paeans to the Leader and boasts of unreal economic achievements. The building itself is an impressive neo-Brîncoveanu pile.

The Museum of Music (141, Calea Victoriei). This was shut when I called, but probably has some interesting musical instruments. Judging by the look of its exterior, the building is probably nice inside, too.

Memorial houses. Anyone with a particular interest in Romanian art might like to visit a few houses once occupied by famous artists, where their work and personal effects can be seen. These include the former residences of **Theodor Aman** (8, Str. Rosetti), **Gheorghe Tattarescu** (7, Str. Domnita

Anastasia), **Corneliu Medrea** (13, Str. Gen. Budişteanu) and **Frederic Storck &**
Cecilia Cuţescu-Storck (16, Str. V. Alecsandri).

EATING OUT AND ENTERTAINMENTS

In an American spoof on the film genre, Party officials evict Dracula from his
castle to convert it into a workers' holiday resort. 'You can't do this,' Dracula
scowls, 'Without me this country will be as exciting as Bucharest on a Monday
night'. An unjustified slight, perhaps, but only on the country, for on any night
of the week **Bucharest's nightlife** is hardly scintillating. Between the wars the
'City of Lights' was famed for its bacchanals, gourmet cuisine and Gypsy
music, available to any citizen with the readies; but nowadays the emphasis is
on 'serious' culture, and while the average person has more lei in their pocket,
the treats in life – not to mention many necessities – are in short supply.

Public catering receives priority over shops during food distribution, so
buying your own food is hardly an option. Markets (see Listings) sell a fair
variety of fruit and veg depending on the season, but for **snacks and cheap**
meals look for holes in the walls (literally) that dispense freshly baked *pateuri*
cu brînză, or check out the *Pasagiul Victoriei* running between the Calea and
the Enei Church, Piaţa Universitaţii (with a Lacto-Vegetarian place at nr.12),
Piaţa Romană and along the Bulevard Gheorghiu-Dej. *Autoservis* restaurants
(weekdays 6am-8pm/Sundays 8am-6pm) serve cheap dishes, but the quality
and the surroundings aren't much cop. The 'best' – and hence the most
crowded – are the *Intercontinental* and *Dorobanţi*, beneath their respective
hotels. *Express Lido* near the ONT, *Gastronom* (35-37, Str. 13 Decembrie),
Rapid (40, B-dul Anul 1848) and the *Simplon* (nr.31) and *Caraiman* (nr.116)
on Calea Victoriei are mediocre; while the places inside and outside the Gara
de Nord are downright grisly.

Patisseries – *cofetărie* – are remarkable less for their syrupy confectionary
than for the fact that they serve **coffee**, which is virtually unobtainable in the
shops (although ground coffee and Nescafé can be purchased in
COMTOURISTs). *Athénée Palace* is noted for its ice cream and, like the
Bucureşti (nr.34), commands a fine view of the Calea. *Universitaţii* and the
café beneath University Square naturally attract students, while *Opereta*
scoops the evening theatre-crowd. *Casata* at 26, B-dul Magheru has a nice
summer terrace.

Terraces overlooking streetlife or lush foliage are also a feature of many
restaurants. The *Cina* beside the Athenaeum is a lazy oasis on the Calea, while
Terass Lipscani and *Terass Rhapsodia* survey the hustle on Lipscani and Şelari
streets. For a greener ambience, try *Monte Carlo* in Cişmigiu Gardens or one
of the establishments in Herăstrău Park – *Pescăruş* (for fish dishes), *Parcul* or
Moriţa. The cuisine tends towards salads and grills (or 'international' fare in
restaurants attached to deluxe hotels), but several places are **devoted to**
Romanian cooking. The three most famous – pricey but not exorbitantly so –
occupy historic premises: *Hanul Manuc* (p.285), the neo-Gothic *Carul cu Bere*
(5, Str. Stavropoleols) and the elegant *Doina* on the Şos. Kiseleff. Lunchtimes
and evenings are the times to hear Gypsy musicians or doina singers, the best

of whom can move diners to open-mouthed amazement by their shrieks and laments.

Other places inclining towards traditional entertainments and food include *Bucur* (2, Str. Poenaru Bordea), *Rhapsodia* and *Cramă Domneasca* (both on Str. Şelari), plus two spots in the green belt on Bucharest's outskirts. *Parcul Privightorilor* is in the Băneasa forest, while the 'Two Cocks' – *La Doi Cocosi* – at 6, Şos. Străuleşti can be reached by riding bus #177 from Piaţa Romană to the end of the line in the direction of Mogoşoaia.

A few restaurants serve **foreign cuisine** under the supervision of foreign chefs. *Nan Jing* (in the Hotel Minerva, 2, Str. Lt. Lemnea) owes its origins to the diplomatic honeymoon between Romania and the Peoples' Republic of China during the 1960s; while trade reps and tourists missing the *Heimat* invariably gravitate to the *Berlin* (4, Str. C. Mille), which also features a knees-up bierkeller. Bucharest's Hungarian restaurant, *Budapest*, decorated with murals of the Magyar capital, was the subject of incredible rumours in 1983. The original story had it that a customer was taken sick (or died) after unwittingly eating human liver filched from the city morgue; later versions held that the whole scandal had been invented and spread by Securitate agents, in an effort to disrupt this 'hotbed of Magyar chauvinism'. (Both stories seem equally far-fetched, but illustrate the extent to which rumours flourish in Romania). There's also an unmarked den selling *Kosher food* (18, Str. Popa Soare) – foreigners are supposed to show their passports to gain admission, God knows why.

A fair number of the above places feature **live acts** in the evenings; usually a quartet of Gypsies, or amplified youths playing last years pop hits. The folk dancers and singers in *Rhapsodia Romană* (at 2, Str. Şelari) are polished by comparison, and the show (daily between June 1 - September 30, 6-7.30pm) is the high-spot of ONT's *Romanian Evening*, which includes a meal and drinks for $13. For $16, ONT can arrange 4hrs at one of Bucharest's **nightclubs** on Mondays or Thursdays, with a limited amount of free booze and glitzy floorshow that strains itself to be 'naughty'. It might or might not be cheaper to skip the tour and pay 40-60 lei at the door of the *Athénée Palace*, *Intercontinental* or *Melody* (2, Str. Pictor Verona), depending on your **drinking** habits. Anything imported from the West will be ruinously expensive (£5 for a glass of whisky at the official rate), but vodka and *ţuică* (plum brandy) are good value for money. The bar at 116, Calea Victoriei, known to regulars as the *Spanish Salon*, is a good little hangout. Throughout our time in Bucharest, the beer generally ran out by 9pm, which is why canny drinkers stockpile bottles in the ice-buckets beside their tables.

Finding **discos** and rock bands largely depends on pot luck or contacts. Bucharest's *Students' Club* (61, Calea Plevnei behind the Opera) is one place to make enquiries; another is the *Architects' Club* (2-4, Str. Academei) which often features drama, foreign films and **jazz**. (To gain admission, ask at the nearby Institute of Architecture first). On summer evenings there's a bit of a 'scene' around the **funfair** in Tineretului Park.

Bucharest's cultural forte is really **classical music and drama,** and several internationally-acclaimed musicians cut their teeth with the *George Enescu Philharmonic Orchestra*, a flagship berthed in the Romanian Athenaeum under the direction of Ion Voicu. Concerts are also held at the *Opera Romană* (70, B-dul Gheorghiu-Dej), the *Radio Studio* (62-64, Str. Nuferilor) and the *Opereta* (Piaţa Natiunilor Unite); and outdoors in Cişmigiu and Tineretului Park during summertime. Most stage productions lose a lot if you don't understand Romanian, but performances at the following might just surmount linguistic barriers: the *Tăndărică Puppet Theatre* (nr.50) and two *music halls* (nrs.33-35 & 174) on the Calea; the *Comedy Theatre* (2, Str. Mandineşti) and the *State Jewish Theatre* (15, Str. I. Barasch).

Information on these should be available from your hotel reception desk or ONT, which can be prevailed upon to make **bookings**. Including the reservation fee, tickets cost between $1-$11.

LISTINGS

Airlines Bookings for TAROM internal flights (leaving Băneasa Airport) are handled at 11, Str. Mendelev (☎ 594-185); the upstairs office at 10, Str. Brezoianu (Monday-Saturday 7am-7pm/Sunday 7am-1pm; ☎ 163-346) deals with international flights. Most foreign airlines have their offices on Magheru/Bălcescu Blvd. or Str. Batiştei; addresses in ONT's pamphlet on Bucharest.

Boats along the Danube When the Dîmboviţa canal is finished it should be possible to sail from Bucharest down to the Danube, where a fairly irregular riverboat service operates between the major towns. For details of prices and schedules, contact ONT or the shipping office *NAVROM* (☎ 167-454), located on B-dul Dincu Golescu near the Gara de Nord.

Books and newspapers *Dacia* (45, Calea Victoriei) and *M. Sadoveanu* (6, B-dul Magheru) stock Romanian novels and poetry and books on native art and ethnography in English, French and German. They might also possess the invaluable *Mic Dicţionars* in those languages. Curious volumes, old prints and the occasional find might justify checking out the secondhand *anticvariat* bookshops at 14, B-dul Anul 1848, and facing the Curtea Veche and the Creţulescu and Enei churches. The *library in the British Embassy* (24, Str. Jules Michelet; Monday-Thursday 10am-1pm, 2pm-5pm/Friday 10am-1pm) has books galore and Western newspapers.

Bus terminals Bucharest has three *Autogară*, all nightmarish: *Filaret* (Piaţa Gării Filaret; ☎ 410-692) and *Rahova* (164, Alexandrei highway; ☎ 804-795) are in the south of the city, *Băneasa* (Str. Ionescu de la Brad; ☎ 795-645) to the north. Our advice is to forget 'em and go by train instead.

Car rental See ONT at 7, B-dul Magheru or in the deluxe hotels.

Car repairs and spares Try the *Dacia-Service* depots on Str. Fagotului near the Gara de Nord, and at 450, Şos. Pantelimon (☎ 275-345); the *Automechanica* centres at 35, B-dul Aerogarii (☎ 331-621), 464, Şos. Colentina (☎ 876-440) and 234, Calea Floreasca (☎ 334-352); or *Ciclop* at 3, Str. Bodnăraş (☎ 312-630) and 6-8, B-dul Magheru. *Piese Auto* claims to have spare parts for Fiat (212, Calea Griviţei; ☎ 654-880) and Renault (124, B-dul Dimitrov; ☎ 350-091), but items for other makes are fairly unlikely. A 'tip' in whisky, hard-currency or Kent cigarettes might expedite repair jobs.

24-hour Chemists 18-20, B-dul Magheru (☎ 146-116) and 345, B-dul 1 Mai; others as currently posted.

Cinemas Bulevard Magheru has the *Patria* (nr.12), *Scala* (nr.2) and *Studio* (nr.29); Bulevard Gheorghiu-Dej the *Capitol* (nr.16), and B-dul Anul 1848 the *Luceafărul* at number six. Imported or avant garde films often get first showing at the *Young Architects' Club* (2-4, Str. Academei).

Circus 15, Aleea Circului (☎ 110-120), accessible by tram #4 or bus from the Piaţa Victoriei.

Contraceptives Only available on prescription and highly valued on the black market.

Department stores *Unirea* (Piaţa Unirii); *Victoria* (17, Calea Victoriei); *Cocor* (33, B-dul Anul 1848); *Bucur-Obor* (2, Şos. Colentina); *Romata* (60-68, Calea Victoriei) and *Tineretului* (10, Calea Dorobanţi).

Embassies and Consulates *Austria* 7, Str. Dumbrava Roşie; *Belgium* 32, B-dul Dacia; *Bulgaria* 5, Aleea Modrogan; *Denmark* 20, Aleea Modrogan; *Federal Republic of Germany* 12, Aleea Modrogan; *Great Britain* 24, Str. Jules Michelet (Monday-Thursday 9am-12am, 2pm-5pm/Friday 9am-12am; ☎ 11-16-35); *Hungary* 65, Str. Alexandru Sahia (Monday, Tuesday, Thursday & Friday 9.30am-11.30am); *Netherlands* 18, Aleea Zoe; *Sweden* 13, Şos. Kiseleff; *USA* 7-9, Str. Tudor Arghezi (☎ 12-40-40); *USSR* 8, Şos. Kiseleff. You'll need to show your passport at the gate to gain admission.

Emergencies Ambulance 061; Police 055; Fire Service 081.

Football Fans usually root for the army team *Bucharest Steau*, or the railway-workers' team *Locomotiv-Rapid*.

Hospitals The *Clinica Batiştei* (28, Str. Arghezi; ☎ 497-030) behind the Intercontinental and the *Spitalul Clinic Municipal* (169, Splaiul Independenţei) are both used to dealing with foreigners, but for emergency treatment you should go to the *Spitalul Clinic de Urgenta* (8, Calea Floreasca). Your embassy can recommend doctors speaking foreign languages. **Dentistry** at 19, Calea Plevnei (☎ 155-217).

Markets Fresh produce is sold on the piaţas Unirii, Amzei and Pintilie; I recently heard of a big new market opened to coincide with Gorbachev's state visit – where is it? There's a colourful flower-market on the Piaţa Amzei, while at the junction of Str. Decebal and Calea Mosilor they sell basketwork.

Motoring information is dispensed by *Touring ACR* at 2, Str. S. Cihoschi (7am-8pm; ☎ 129-420) and its parent organisation the *Auto Clubul Roman* (*ACR*) at 27, Str. N. Beloiannis (☎ 595-080), both off the Piaţa Romană. The latter sells petrol coupons and provides an insurance and breakdown service for members of foreign affiliates.

Petrol stations Queues at the *PECO* stand on Str. Arghezi near the Intercontinental are normally shorter than outside the 24-hour filling station by the Gara de Nord and out along the Ploieşti, Piteşti, Giurgiu, Constanţa and Călăraşi highways. Foreigners with petrol coupons are entitled to jump queues.

Photos *Foto-Urgent* (17, Str. 13 Decembrie and 8, B-dul Gheorghiu-Dej) can do passport-photos in 4hrs while Cişmigiu Gardens is the place for souvenir snaps. With hard currency one can buy imported film and photographic equipment for inflated prices at COMTOURIST shops and the top hotels.

Post Offices Poste restante operates from the main office at 10, Str. Matei Millo (7am-12pm daily; ☎ 167-554); other *poştas* can be found at 90, Calea Plevnei, 43, B-dul Magheru, and on the Piaţa Gaŕii. It's better to arrange international calls from the larger hotels.

Railway tickets On no account try to buy them at the station; the queues are bad enough at *Agenţie CFR* (10, Str. Brezoianu and 139, Calea Griviţei; open Monday-Saturday 7am-8pm/Sunday 7am-1pm), where you should book seats at least 24 and preferably 48 hours in advance, being sure to get a seat reservation. Tickets to destinations abroad must be purchased in hard currency, or in lei covered by an exchange receipt.

Records *Muzica*, 41, Calea Victoriei.

Shoe repairs *Listragerie* in the Piaţa Universitaţii subway.

Sports facilities at the *23 August Centre*, 43, B-dul Muncii; *Republica*, 12, Str. Maior Ene; *Progresul*, 42, Str. Dr. Staicovici; *Floreasca*, 2, Str. Aviator Popa Marin (both have tennis courts); and *Tineretului*, off the Şos. Kiseleff. *Alpin* (24, B-dul Balcescu) sells Romanian-made sporting equipment.

Stamp collecting *Philatelia*, 25, Str. 13 Decembrie.

Swimming pools can be found alongside Lake Floreasca and Lake Băneasa, and at 1, Aleea Strandului.

Zoo Str. Vadul Moldovei in the Băneasa forest.

EXCURSIONS, AND MOVING ON FROM THE CAPITAL

For visitors with ample funds and limited time, ONT can readily arrange **excursions from the capital**, ranging from day-trips by coach or car to week-long journeys around Romania, including accommodation and flights. These eliminate the hassle of getting to places independently but rather sanitise the experience, which in some cases may fall short of the image advertised (read the small print before parting with your dollars).

SNAGOV, 40km north of Bucharest, is a popular destination; a beautiful **lake** with *watersports* facilities, a *campsite* and a reserve for water plants, surrounding an island occupied by a **monastery**. Crowds of Bucharesters pack the trains leaving Băneasa station (around 6.35am, 3.50pm & 8.50pm) and the Gara de Nord (7.50am), so you might well consider ONT's coach trips a preferable alternative, especially the 5-hour excursion ($15), which includes a visit to Căldăruşani Monastery. At Snagov, launches motor over to the island, where monks have become resigned to visitors seeking the **tomb of Dracula**, sited in front of the church altar. Though lacking identifying inscriptions, it's likely that this is the burial place of the Impaler. Vlad's murder is believed to have occurred in the forests near Snagov; the monks would have been predisposed to take the body, since both Dracula and his father had patronised the monastery; and finally there's the forensic evidence. The richly dressed corpse exhumed in 1935 had been decapitated; a fate known to have overtaken Dracula, whose bonce was supposedly dispatched wrapped and perfumed as a gift to the Sultan.

CĂLDĂRUŞANI MONASTERY can't be reached by public transport from Bucharest, which didn't stop the world press from mobbing it when tennis stars Mariana Simionescu and Bjorn Borg were married here in 1980 (a match subsequently annulled). The church where the wedding took place is smaller but otherwise similar to the one at Curtea de Argeş, and was previously noted for its school of icon-painting, established in 1787. Among the many **icons** displayed are eight by Grigorescu, who started painting at the age of eight and studied here between 1854-56. With wheels one can also reach **CERNICA MONASTERY**, situated near a lakeside village southeast of the city (off road 3), which was founded in the C17. ONT's Cernica Monastery excursion costs $15, but half of the time is actually spent visiting museums in the capital. The lovely Brîncoveanu palace at **MOGOŞOAIA** (10km northwest of Bucharest by DN1) is off the excursions list until earthquake damage has been repaired, but the atmospheric gardens are still open. Here lies the grave of Elizabeth Asquith, daughter of the British statesman, whose epitaph reads: 'My soul has regained the freedom of the night'.

Between June 16-September 30, ONT organises **longer itineraries**, including weekends at Sinaia, Predeal and the seaside for between $25-$50; 2-day excursions to Maramureş ($100), the old Wallachian capitals ($55), the monasteries of Bucovina ($90), Tulcea in the Delta ($85) and the Prahova and Olt valleys ($70); and jaunts around the country lasting 3, 5 or 7 days. The 3-day tour ($98) takes in Curtea de Argeş, Cozia Monastery, Sibiu, Braşov and Sinaia; 5-day excursions ($150) add Răşinari, Bran Castle, Sibiel, Tîrgu Mureş, Sighişoara and Sovata to this list; while the week-long itinerary also includes Cluj, Alba Iulia, Bistriţa, and several of the Moldavian monasteries ($210).

Before **travelling on from Bucharest**, motorists should fill their tanks and anyone wishing to travel by rail or air is advised to book a seat at least 36 hours in advance. (For the addresses of ticket offices and petrol stations, see above). TAROM **flights** from Băneasa Airport are the speediest way to reach many places (listed under *Travel Details* at the end of the chapter) and cost between 30%-100% more than the equivalent rail journey. Anyone paying for aeroplane tickets in lei must produce a receipt certifying that the money was exchanged legally; this regulation also applies to railway tickets for destinations outside Romania, but *not* to domestic routes.

Trains are crowded, unheated and battered, and for journeys of over 100km, travel by anything but an *accelerat* or *rapid* service is pretty horrendous. However, most overnight services have good couchettes, which for a surcharge of about 40 lei leave travellers refreshed, and with money saved by not paying for a hotel room. These also exist on all *international services*, which are listed after domestic routes in the Travel Details.

Hitch-hiking is apt to be slow, and it's common practice to pay for lifts (standing beside the road waving a packet of Kent cigarettes seems an effective way to snag drivers). Bucharest's highway exits can be reached as follows: Braşov/Transylvania (tram #81/#82 to Băneasa Airport); Constanţa/the Coast (tram #89 from Piaţa Universitaţii, then tram #14); Buzău/Moldavia (bus #109 from B-dul Republicii to Şos. Colentina). Hitching to Giurgiu, and then over **into Bulgaria**, is inadvisable, as neither country's Militia likes people doing it. Better to fix yourself up with a lift going all the way...Băneasa campsite is the best place for this. (See below for details of trains to Bulgaria and the frontier town of Giurgiu).

Leaving Bucharest bound for Transylvania, Moldavia or the Black Sea Coast and Delta (Chapter 12), your route is likely to cross some part of **Wallachia**, a region described in the remainder of this chapter. Romania's busiest railway line and highway (DN1) run northwards to Ploieşti (p.304) and up the Prahova Valley **into Transylvania**, while regular *rapids* head eastwards towards Constanţa and Mangalia on **the Coast**, passing through Slobozia (see below) and Medgidia, the place to change trains for Tulcea in **the Danube Delta**. (Drivers, follow DN2A for Constanţa, and turn off onto rd.22A near Hîrşova in order to reach Tulcea.) The long haul up **to Moldavia** by road (DN2) is nothing on the railway journey. The fastest trains to Suceava take between 5½-6½hrs. Given the lack of direct services to Iaşi, one usually has to ride as far north as Mărăşeşti, Roman or Paşcani, and switch onto branch-lines leading towards the Moldavian capital. More details of trains and routes to particular regions can be found in the appropriate **chapter introductions**.

TRAVELLING FROM BUCHAREST TO BULGARIA

Most days there are four **trains from Bucharest to Bulgaria**: the *Dunav* (7am), *Sofia* (10.45am) and *Pannonia* (9.30pm), which aim for Sofia; and the *Varna* (leaving at around 2.45am), whose destination is the city of that name on the Bulgarian coast. Tickets must be purchased in hard currency, and railway passengers – like people **travelling by road** – must obtain Bulgarian **visas** beforehand, since these can't be obtained at the border. There's really no reason to stop at **GIURGIU** beside the Danube, but should you need to the *Hotel Victoria* and the tourist office share premises on Str. Gării about a hundred yards southeast of the railway station, while you'll find a campsite on the Danube meadow (*Lunca Dunării*). Cars and trains cross the river by the **Friendship Bridge** inaugurated in 1954, on the far side of which lies the pleasant Bulgarian town of RUSE, described on p.591.

BETWEEN BUCHAREST AND THE COAST

East of Bucharest the lowlands are sun-baked and dusty, and few foreigners stop there en route to the Delta or the Coast. One who did was Peter O'Conner, who went to **SLOBOZIA** in search of authentic **Gypsy music** and found a town where 'old women squatted by shop windows, selling sunflower seeds by the tumblerful, and carts rattled by, their shaky structures piled high with pigs, foals and humans'. Venturing out from his room in a local household (this was a few years before a law was passed forbidding foreigners to stay in private lodgings), he found that the 'cafés were open and gave out a powerful stink of beer, silage and ţuică'. Unfortunately, 'the Gypsies looked like everyone else in Slobozia, except that they were invariably dark-featured', and 'they did not consider themselves Gypsies' – hence the audible lack of ţigani music. There's a fair chance of hearing Gypsy music during April if Slobozia once again hosts the **festival** called *Floare de pe Bărăgan* – although this doesn't happen every year. **Accommodation** in town boils down to the *Hotel Muntenia* on B-dul Chimiei (dbl.$38/sngl.$28) or *Privighetoara*, respectively north and east of the railway station, but the tourist office in the former can advise about buses to the neighbouring holiday resorts of AMARA and LAKE FUNDATA, both of which have cheaper lodgings in the form of bungalows.

WALLACHIA

Centuries before the name Romania appeared on maps of Europe, foreign merchants and rulers knew vaguely of **WALLACHIA** – the land of the Vlachs or Wallachs – which served as a distant outpost of Christendom before being conquered by the Turks and largely forgotten about until the C19. Occasional travellers reported on the region's backwardness and the corruption of its ruling boyars. But few predicted its sudden union with Moldavia in 1859 – the first step in the creation of modern Romania – just as in 1600, none had expected Wallachia's Michael the Brave (*Mihai Viteazul*) to storm forth and overcome Moldavia and Transylvania, briefly uniting the three principalities under a single crown. Historically subject to forces beyond their control, Wallachia's peasantry adapted and endured whoever their master; believing that 'Great is God, but clever also is the Devil' and counting themselves lucky when ruled by an efficent tyrant such as the Impaler, who could bring the boyars to heel and repulse the marauding Ottomans.

From the ruins of **Tirgovişte** and **Poienari** (**Dracula's Castle** to the Episcopal Church at **Curtea de Argeş**, Wallachia's voivodes and clerics have left their monuments across the highland regions (*Muntenia*) and the extensive plain known after its chief river as *Oltenia*. But of course, this isn't all Dracula Country. Geographically, Wallachia includes the sun-baked **Dobrudja**, and its inhabitants range from ethnic-Bulgars and shepherds to miners under martial law in the **Jiu Valley**. Unless in search of **Gypsies and their music** in places like **Slobozia**, most visitors bypass **the south**, and rightly so; but travelling around the rest of Wallachia or entering it from Transylvania, you can't avoid the big industrialised centres of **Piteşti**, **Ploieşti** and **Craiova**. Their railways are virtually the only public transport to the above mentioned places, and enable one to reach several **festivals**. During the third week in February, musicians gather for the *Izvoare fermecate* at **Tirgu Jiu** (the town is also the location of three monumental **sculptures by Brancuşi**, who was born nearby); while **Polvragi** to the east is the setting for a big fair between July 15-20. Another fair, devoted to pottery, coincides with the *Songs of the Olt* festival at **Calimăneşti** during the first week in August; and at **Tismana**, pan-pipers congregate on the 15th of that month.

Approaches to Wallachia
The easiest **approaches to Wallachia** are from Bucharest or Transylvania, although it's not difficult to move inland from the Coast, nor cross the Danube at the Iron Gates **from Yugoslavia**, or by ferry from Vidin or over the Friendship Bridge from Ruse if you're coming **from Bulgaria**. Breaches in the

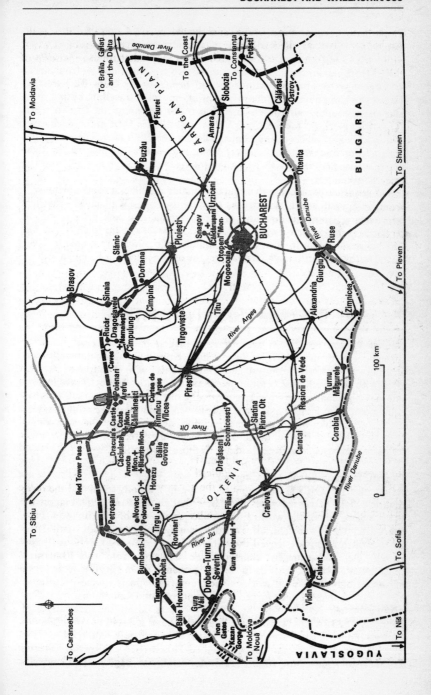

Carpathians permit access **from Transylvania** by road or rail, using Băile Herculane, Petroşani, the Red Tower Pass or Braşov as starting-points; while with your own transport it's also possible to take other roads – across the Făgăraş range to Poienari, or down from Rişnov to Cîmpulung, or from Sinaia to Tîrgovişte (see below). Motorists can head directly **from Bucharest** to Tîrgovişte, Cîmpulung and the monasteries, but folks travelling by rail must take more roundabout routes: changing trains at Ploieşti or Titu to reach Tîrgovişte; at Piteşti for the Argeş Valley; or at Piatra Olt (on the Bucharest-Craiova line) for places near Rîmnicu Vîlcea in the Olt Valley. There are daily flights from Bucharest to Craiova, while hitch-hikers wishing to try their perseverance may reach DN7 (the Piteşti road) by trolleybus #84 from the Piaţa Universitaţii.

The **sequence of places in this chapter** roughly describes a route northwards from Bucharest, which then tracks westwards across Wallachia. Travellers approaching from the direction of Transylvania can pick up the trail at Drobeta-Turnu Severin and the Iron Gates (p.317); the Jiu (p.314), the Olt (p.311) or the Argeş (p.306) valley; Cîmpulung (p.306); Tîrgovişte (p.308); or the following section, which describes the region below the Prahova Valley.

PLOIEŞTI, DOFTANA PRISON AND PITEŞTI

Neither Ploieşti nor Piteşti are attractive places, but both serve as useful springboards for more enticing destinations. Ploieşti lies along the main road and railway between Bucharest and Transylvania; with a couple of sites of interest to the north, just before one enters the Prahova Valley. Travellers by rail may also change here for Tîrgovişte, the old Wallachian capital, roughly equidistant from Ploieşti and Piteşti (departures from the *Sud* station every 1-2hrs). Piteşti is likewise an important junction, situated astride the main routes from Bucharest to Cîmpulung and the Argeş Valley (see below), so both the following sections constitute 'bridges' to those destinations.

Ploieşti, Doftana Prison and Cîmpina
As one nears **PLOIEŞTI** (pronounced 'Ploy-esht'), an oily smell and the eerie nightime flare of vented gases proclaims that this is Romania's biggest **oil** town, where one of the world's first refineries was established in 1856. Fifty years later there were ten, all owned by foreign oil companies, until 1916 when British agents destroyed the oilfield to deny it to the Germans (Royal Dutch Shell subsequently claimed huge damages from the Romanian government, which paid them under pressure from British financiers). Unsurprisingly, native oil-workers took umbrage and led local protests in 1919 and, thanks to links forged by the underground Communist Party, co-ordinated their actions with the railway-workers during the great strike of February 1933. While British firms like Vickers and ICI sold out profitably to Hitler's industrialists before the war, it was the townsfolk who paid for it in 1944, when allied aircraft carpet-bombed Ploieşti (see exhibits in Oil and Local History **museums**; 10, Str. Teatrului & 10, Str. Bagdascar). Hence the

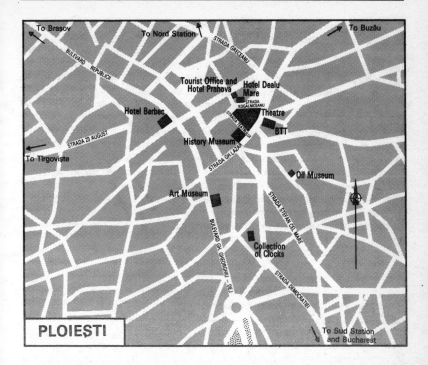

PLOIEȘTI

town's almost total concrete uniformity, with the welcome exception of the *Princely Church* on Str. Bassarab, and the engagingly varied **collection of clocks** at 1, Str. 6 Martie. Apparently, Ploiești's **theatre** company is the best in Romania, which might just tempt you to linger, but a likelier reason for staying is the chance of visiting Doftana Prison the following morning. Of Prahova's **hotels**, the *Dealu Mare* (2, Str. Kogălniceanu) is cheaper than the *Berbec* (2, Str. Doftanei) or *Prahova* (11, Str. Dobrogeanu-Gherea), whilst during June-August, *BTT* (6, Str. Poștei; ☎ 4-61-72) might have rooms for rent in town – an economical alternative to the **campsite** 49km out along the Bucharest highway.

An unlikely yet compelling tourist attraction, **DOFTANA PRISON** was a place of torture and confinement for participants in the 1907 peasant rising and a whole generation of Communist militants. Its worst section was the *H-block*, 'completely dark, humid and without any furniture', where Gheorghiu-Dej and other Communist leaders were held (including Ilie Pintilie, who died when an earthquake demolished part of the prison). Today it serves as a **museum**, displaying instruments of torture, police files, and miniature Marxist tracts which the prisoners studied in secret. Flying a huge red flag visible from the nearby village of Telega, Doftana may be reached by bus or narrow-gauge railway from **CÎMPINA**, 4km away. This oil town's only other tourist attractions are both at the end of Str. 23 August on Cîmpina's northern outskirts. The **Nicolae Grigorescu Museum** commemorates Romania's most prolific C19 painter (1838-1907), whose talents gained him an apprenticeship at Căldăruşani Monastery at the age of 12; while **Hasdeu Castle** is an odd cruciform structure with battlements and buttresses, built for a linguist with the splendidly Rococo name of Bogdan Petriceico Hasdeu.

Continuing northwards from Cîmpina takes one **into the Prahova Valley** with its magnificent scenery, as described in the opening pages of the chapter on Transylvania.

Piteşti: en route for Cîmpulung or the Argeş Valley

Piteşti may be reached by road from Ploieşti, via Tîrgovişte (p.308), but chances are that you'll start **from Bucharest.** The E15A *autostradă* bypasses everything en route except for Kilometre 80, a motel-caravan site located that far from the capital, but DN7 and the railway follow a more interesting route, past Gaesti, beyond which the plain yields to the Subcarpathian hills, covered in orchards and vineyards. None of the various trains running between Bucharest and Craiova via Piteşti halt at the roadside commune of TOPOLOVENI (which has a womens' crafts co-operative), but all of them pause at Titu (see below) and GOLEŞTI, whence **trains to Cîmpulung** depart every 3-4hrs.

PITEŞTI is now dominated by the woodworking and petrochemical industries, but is actually liveliest on Fridays and Saturdays, when it fulfils its traditional role as a market town for the countryfolk of the Argeş Valley. Its sights are limited to the **Naive Art Collection** in a passage off Str. Victoriei; an **exhibition of Eco-systems** in the Country Museum (44, Str. Horia); and **Trivale Hermitage** which stands in Trivale Park together with a statue of the 'Master Builder' Manole. But you might wish to stay the night before pushing on up the Argeş Valley. Besides the *Muntenia* (sngl.$32/dbl.$40) and *Argeş* hotels on the central Piaţa Muntenia, there might also be seasonal **accommodation** known to BTT (1, Str. Justiţiei; ☎ 2-26-71) or the **tourist office** on the main square, which can reserve chalets in the Trivale Park, southwest of the centre. From Piteşti's station or the CFR bureau at 13, Str. Doamna Balasa, you can buy tickets for the **journey to Curtea de Argeş** (2-3hrs; 7 trains daily); turn to p.309 for a description of the town.

CÎMPULUNG AND TÎRGOVIŞTE

Though the Piteşti road and the line from Goleşti pass through a roe-deer reserve, the **Cilceasa Forest**, en route to Cîmpulung, **the approach from Transylvania** offers more excitement for motorists. Descending from the Giuvala Pass in a series of hairpin bends, DN73 encounters the 'Bridge of the Dîmboviţa', a spectacular limestone gorge carved by the river and its tributary, which vanish into the yet narrower Gimbav Gorges further to the south. Just north of Dîmbovicioara village, the *Brusturet* chalet lies within 2hrs walk of the Piatra Craiului range; while beyond the gorges you'll find a campsite near RUCAR. The traditional wooden houses with verandas that make Rucar so attractive appear in force at DRAGOSLAVELE, the next village, which also features an C18 wooden church. Sixteen kilometres before Cîmpulung the road forks at NAMAEŞTI, the site of a rock church complete with cells hewn from the sandstone mountain by monks during the C16.

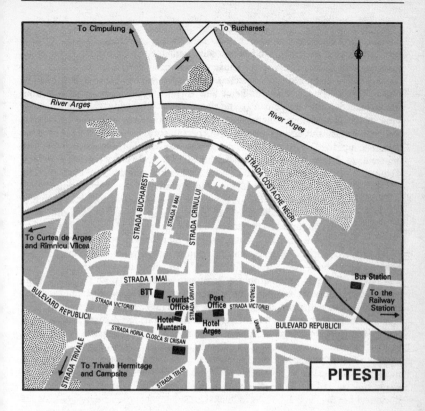

To Cîmpulung
To Bucharest
River Argeş
River Argeş
STRADA COSACHE NEGRI
To Curtea de Argeş
and Rîmnicu Vîlcea
STRADA BUCHAREŞTI
STRADA 4 MAI
STRADA CRINULUI
Bus Station
STRADA 1 MAI
To the
Railway
Station
BTT
BULEVARD REPUBLICII
STRADA VICTORIEI
Tourist
Office
STRADA GRIVITA
Post
Office
STRADA VICTORIEI
STRADA
Hotel
Muntenia
Hotel
Argeş
UNIRII
BULEVARD REPUBLICII
STRADA HORIA, CLOSCA SI CRISAN
To Trivale Hermitage
and Campsite
STRADA TRIVALE
STRADA TELOR

PITEŞTI

After such a journey **CÎMPULUNG** comes as something of an anti-climax, overshadowed by mountains to the north and south, and begrimed by industries. But the town's pedigree is impeccable, going back to pre-Roman times and including a stint as Wallachia's first capital after the voivodate was forged in the C13. Cîmpulung's main sight is the **Negru Vodă Monastery**, attributed to the legendary Voivode Negru and subsequently rebuilt and enlarged by his successors following several earthquakes. Like the old Baraţiei Church (nr.116) and the historical and fine arts departments of Cîmpulung's **Museum** (118 & 119), it can be found on Negru Vodă street, together with the **tourist office** (nr.146). The *Cross of the Oath* at the junction of Negru Vodă Street and the main square is inscribed with the privileges and duties of the townsfolk as laid down by Voivode Duca in 1674; and philologists might also appreciate the fact that Cîmpulung means 'long field', as in the Count de Longo Campo, whose tombstone lies within the Baraţiei Church. If you can't afford **rooms** at the *Muscelul* on Negru Vodă (sngl.$30/dbl.$40), there should be buses from the terminal on Str. 16 Februarie out to the *Voina Chalet* beyond the village of Lereşti north of town – make bookings at the tourist office (☎ 1-24-00).

Tîrgovişte

TÎRGOVIŞTE, 64km to the south, is considerably larger, with 80,000 inhabitants and factories producing equipment for the oil industry. As usual, **getting there** by road is easy for those with wheels (DN71 from Bucharest or Sinaia; DN72 from Ploieşti or Piteşti), but almost impossible to accomplish by bus. If you don't fancy shelling out $18 to join *ONT's day-excursion from Bucharest*, the alternative is a roundabout journey by railway. The route via Ploieşti has already been mentioned above. The other option is to travel as if towards Piteşti, but change onto a northbound train (9 daily) at TITU for the 1hr ride up to Tîrgovişte. Arriving at the **railway station**, board any bus heading up Bulevard Castanilor and Str. 30 Decembrie to reach the centre. Tîrgovişte's *Turist* and *Dîmboviţa* hotels on either side of the Parcul Central charge $38 for doubles and $28 for single **rooms**, so it's worth enquiring at *BTT* (Str. Prieteniei Bloc H1; ☎ 3-42-24) about dormitory beds before resigning yourself to their prices. The campsite with chalets is 8km out along the Cîmpulung road, and in the absence of buses from the terminal at 34, Str. 1 Decembrie, you'll probably have to hitch there unless you have a car.

By following Str. 30 Decemrie until its junction with Str. Bălcescu and then turning left, you'll come upon the **ruined Princely Court**, Tîrgovişte's main attraction. A mass of crumbling ramparts and rooms with a few well-preserved sections, it was once the royal seat of Wallachia, whence more than forty voivodes exercised their rule between 1415-1659. The brevity of their reigns was largely due to the intrigues of the boyars, and plots and Princely Court (*Curtea Domnească*) figured large in the life of **Dracula** (see p.490),

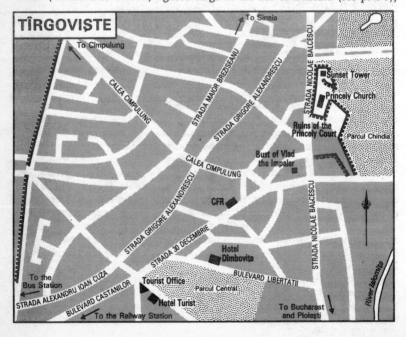

whose bust can be seen as one nears the ruins. His early years were spent here together with the other children of Vlad Dracul, until young Vlad and his brother Radu (later known as 'The Handsome' for his homosexuality) were sent to Anatolia as hostages. Following the murder of his father and his eldest brother, Mircea, who was buried alive by the boyars, Vlad returned to be enthroned here in 1456, and waited for three years before taking **his revenge**. Invited to feast at court with their families, the boyars were half-drunk when guards suddenly grabbed them and impaled them forthwith upon stakes around town, sparing only the fittest who were marched off to labour on Dracula's castle at Poienari. A veritable **museum of Dracula's life and times** occupies the *Turnul Chindiei* or **Sunset Tower**, whilst nearby stands the C16 **Princely Church** where Dracula's successors used to attend mass, sitting upstairs in a special section screened from the congregation.

Three kilometres northeast of town upon a hill rises the graceful bulk of **Dealu Monastery**. With its towers above the pronaos and cornice arcades separated by cable moulding, this set the pattern for much of Wallachian church architecture until the advent of the Brîncoveanu style. Within, beneath a marble slab topped by a bronze crown, lies *the head of Michael the Brave* – severed from his shoulders within a year of Michael's conquest of Transylvania and Moldavia, which put paid to the unification of Romania for another 350 years. The inscription reads: 'To him who first united our homeland, eternal glory'.

CURTEA DE ARGEŞ AND DRACULA'S RUINED CASTLE AT POIENĂRI

The Dracula trail continues with the small town of **CURTEA DE ARGEŞ**, which lies some 36km northwest of Piteşti, whence it's accessible by road or railway. Chronologically the second capital of Wallachia (after Cîmpulung and before Tîrgovişte), the 'Court of Argeş' now comprises a set of **ruins** within a wall made of boulders taken from the river, together with a **Princely Church** decorated with frescoes painted in 1384. Though not his original capital, the complex was raised by Radu Negru, the founder of Wallachia, otherwise known as Basarab I (whence Bessarabia, the land between the rivers Prut and Dneistr, later ruled by his descendants).

A more impressive monument is sited not far away on Bulevard Republicii, the **Episcopal Church** (or Monastery) of Curtea de Argeş. It resembles the creation of an inspired confectioner given carte blanche; a boxy structure enlivened by whorls, rosettes and fancy trimmings, rising into two twisted and two octagonal belfries, each festooned with little spheroids and the three-armed cross of Orthodoxy. Though its colours are less dramatic, the building's form invites comparison with St Basil's – the whacky church on Moscow's Red Square – and the architects of both experienced a similar reward. While the Russian Tsar blinded his Italian architect so that he might never surpass St Basil's with other work, **Manole** the 'Master Builder' of Curtea de Argeş is said to have been marooned on his creation's rooftop when Vlad Dracul ordered the scaffolding removed. In Manole's case it may have been crude justice, however, for the legend holds that he had previously immured his wife within the walls to stop them crumbling (see the belief in *stafia*, p.284). Stranded on the roof, he attempted to escape with the aid of wings made from roofing shingles – only to crash to the earth, whereupon a spring gushed forth immediately: the origin of **Manole's Well**, which visitors to the monastery can drink from to this day.

The *Hotel Posada* (27, Blvd. R.S.R.) has the only **rooms** in town, while the terminal at 23, Str. 1 Mai is the sole source for **buses** to neighbouring villages. You'll need a good map to plot the way to SĂLĂTRUCU, whose village **fair** – the *Nedeia Topologului* – is held on June 1; and most people opt for the relatively straightforward route **up the Argeş Valley** (hitching is feasible). Growing steadily more barren as it rises, the valley beyond CORBIENI (*Dumbrava campsite*) once witnessed a pitiful procession of boyars – the survivors of Dracula's massacre in Tîrgovişte. Vlad had already given orders for lime kilns and brick ovens to be constructed at AREFU – nowadays a long, ramshackle village just off the valley road – and other nearby settlements, and when the exhausted nobles arrived, they were set to work building Dracula's Castle.

Situated on a crag 1,200ft above Arefu, **DRACULA'S CASTLE AT POIENARI** can only be reached by climbing 1,400 steps, which surely exacerbated the mortality rate amongst the slave labourers, just as today, they prove a powerful disincentive to visitors. Struggle to the top and you'll find that the citadel is surprisingly small – one third collapsed down the mountainside in 1888. It is entered by a narrow wooden bridge, with the remains of two towers within. The prism-shaped one was the old keep, Vlad's residential quarters, whence – according to one legend – the Impaler's wife flung herself from the window, declaring that she 'would rather have her body rot and be eaten by the fish of the Argeş' than be captured by the Turks, who were then besieging the castle with cherry-wood cannons. Historians doubt the veracity of the story, but legend has it that Vlad himself escaped over the mountains on horseback (fooling his pursuers by shoeing his mount backwards, or affixing horseshoes that left the impression of cow-prints, according to some versions). Stories of the Impaler still persist in villages like Arefu and CĂPĂŢINENII PAMINTENI over the river, which contains a statue of him.

Poienari is only a few kilometres south of **Lake Vidra in the Făgăraş Mountains**, where you'll find the *Casa Argeşeana* chalet just inside the gorges, and two others on the southeastern and northwestern shores of the lake. However, unless you've the means and intention to drive on to Făgăraş in Transylvania (p.348), Poienari is something of a dead end. Though Curtea de Argeş is only 37km from RÎMNICU VÎLCEA, connecting buses are highly uncertain, and without private transport or a willingness to hitch, you'll have to make a major detour by railway to reach this town – the gateway to places of interest in the upper Olt Valley.

THE OLT VALLEY

From its headwaters behind the Făgăraş range, the River Olt turns southwards at the Red Tower Pass below Sibiu, carving a stupendous gorge for 50km through the Carpathians and down into Wallachia. The **Olt Valley** can thus be approached by road or rail from the north – where it's most spectacular – or by road from Piteşti, Curtea de Argeş or Tîrgu Jiu (the latter route being the longest but most scenic). But the scarcity of public transport may dictate that you travel by railway instead, using northbound services from PIATRA OLT on the Piteşti-Craiova line (6 daily). Taking this approach, you'll pass vineyards covering the slopes around DRĂGĂŞANI, where the grape harvest in October is used to produce light, dry **wine**. Further north there's a motel/caravan site at the junction with the Piteşti road, shortly beyond which lies Rîmnicu Vîlcea.

RÎMNICU VÎLCEA sprawls across successive terraces above the River Olt, as if recovering from a surfeit of *ţuică*, the locally-made plum brandy. From the railway station it's a fairly short walk along Str. Cerna to the park adjoining Piaţa Mircea cel Bratin, near which you'll find *BTT* (nr.4; ☎ 1-87-20), the **tourist office** and the *Hotel Alutus* (sngl.$30/dbl.$40). It's difficult to think of reasons for staying here when there are more interesting places (and cheaper **lodgings**) along the Horezu road (p.312) and farther up the valley, but if that's where you're heading it's worth reserving accommodation there in advance, checking out the dates of the Călimăneşti festival, and picking up a map of the region.

Heading northwards, personal trains stop at BUJORENI – the site of Vîlcea county's **Village Museum**, which includes a few subterranean houses of the type once common throughout Oltenia – before CĂLIMĂNEŞTI, where the *Songs of the Olt* folklore festival and a **pottery fair** usually take place during the first week in August. *Caciulata spa* marks the entrance to **the Olt defile**, a deep, sinuously twisting gorge of great beauty, which is the site of several monasteries. While the main road runs along the Olt's west bank, the railway (and a lesser road as far as Gara Turnu) follow the other side of the defile, which the railway sometimes escapes through tunnels. Just beyond Căciulata, a hotel and motel/caravan site have sprouted in the vicinity of a ruined *castrum* (once part of the Roman Dacia's eastern frontier defences, the *Limes Alutanus*); while over on the east bank stands a monastery.

The church in **COZIA MONASTERY** marks the advent of Byzantine architecture in Wallachia during the C14, featuring alternating bands of brick and stone, and the fluted, false pillars that decorate Byzantine-influenced churches from Armenia to the Adriatic. Just as the monasteries in Moldavia are generally attributed to Stephen, so in Wallachia, Radu Negru usually gets the credit. But Cozia's completion was owed to the patronage of Dracula's grandfather, Mircea the Old, who accepted Turkish suzerainty after the Crusaders' defeat at Nicopolis and now lies within the monastery. The church portico was added by Prince Constantin Brîncoveanu, whose name has entered Romania's architectural lexicon to describe a style drawing upon folk-motifs to create monumental structures – although in this case, it's not a particularly striking example. From the belvedere nearby, containing specimens of religious art, there's a fine view over the Olt Valley and the mountains.

About 2km north, near the *Gara Turnu* halt, **Turnul Monastery** is based around rock cells hewn by hermits from Cozia at the end of the C16, who inhabited them for 72 years. From here it's a 5-6hr walk up a trail marked by red stripes to the *Cabana Cozia* chalet, situated in the vicinity of the highest peaks on the Cozia Massif. Sheltered from northeasterly winds by the Făgăraş, this has the mildest climate of all Romania's ranges, allowing oak, walnut and wild roses to grow at altitudes of up to 4,200 feet.

Down in the valley, the railway enters a tunnel between *Lotrişor Motel* (opposite a train halt) and LOTRU, a small village named after a nearby tributary, before stopping just beyond at **Cornetu Hermitage**. Here, the use of diverse materials to decorate exterior surfaces includes glazed ceramics, tiles and studs. From CORNETU onwards the valley gradually broadens until CÎINENI, forming a depression formerly known as *Lovişte* or 'Hunting Country'. Thereafter it narrows again, and local trains halt briefly at RÎU VADULUI and VALEA MĂRULUI (campsite and tourist chalet, respectively), as if reluctant to approach the Red Tower Pass. Its current name *Turnu Roşu* and its former Hungarian title, *Vöröstorony*, both derive from the ruined fortress commanding the entrance to the defile: the site of many battles between Wallachian, Transylvanian, Habsburg, Turkish and German forces over past 500 years. But as the ruins of a Roman fort, *Caput Stenarum* prove, its embattled history is even longer, for the pass is one of the few natural breaches in the Carpathians. Beyond the pass lies Transylvania, where travellers should change trains at Podu Olt station if they want to reach Sibiu (p.350).

MONASTERIES AND CAVES ALONG THE HOREZU ROAD

Rather than pursuing the Olt into Transylvania you might prefer to follow DN67 westwards from Rîmnicu Vîlcea, cutting across beneath the Căpăţineni range towards Tîrgu Jiu (p.314). Buses from Rîmnicu Vîlcea should reach as far as OCNELE MARI and BĂILE GOROVA (two mineral spas with campsites), not to mention **Gorova Monastery** just before the băile, where the *Pravila de Gorova*, a legal codex, rolled off the presses in 1640. Beyond this, however, bus services are far less reliable, and while the prospects for hitching seem fair, many of the 'sights' are off the main road. **Bistriţa Monastery**, which the boyars of Craiova endowed during the C15, lies about 10km up the minor road which leaves DN67 at COŞTEŞTI, while **Arnota Monastery** stands on a hill a further 3km from Bistriţa. By financing the construction of Arnota during the C17, voivode Matei Basarab guaranteed himself a tasteful burial place within the monastery church's pronaos, surrounded by fragmentary murals of his bride and chattels.

Back on DN67, it's only a few kilometres from Coşteşti to **HOREZU**, a small town set amidst orchards, sweet chestnut trees and wild liliac – the abode of numerous owls (*huhurezi*), hence Horezu's name (given as 'Hurez' on some maps). Though wooden furniture and wrought-iron objects are also produced here, Horezu is best known for its **pottery**, especially the plates, which by tradition are given as keepsakes during the wakes held in the weeks following a funeral. Most of them are made by Victor Vicsoreanu, a third-generation craftsmen, whose pottery is on the town's outskirts. Some years, the town holds a pottery **fair** (*Cocoşul de Hureazu*) during June – OJT should have up to date information. Tourists can stay at the motel, or on the campsite with chalets.

But the real attraction lies a couple of miles to the northeast of town, near the little village of Romanii de Jos. The largest and finest of Wallachia's Brîncoveanu-style complexes, **Hurez Monastery** is centred around the '*Great Church*' built in the 1690s, which one enters via a porchway with ten pillars and doors of carved pear-wood. The colours of the interior frescoes (which include portraits of Brîncoveanu and his family) have been tarnished by the smoke from fires lit by Turkish slaves who encamped here, but those in the *Nuns' Rectory* show their original hues. A few gory punishments can be discerned from the damaged Last Judgement on the church exterior, although they're not a patch on the Painted Monasteries of Bucovina nor the nightmarish murals at Poienile Izei in Maramureş. The monastic complex also includes *Dionisie's Fire-tower*, a structure with finely-carved columns and a stone balustrade, and – set apart – the small *St Stephen's Hermitage*.

Five kilometres south of Horezu along road 65C, **MĂDĂREŞTI** is the site of two **fortified manors** of stone and brick with their lower floors raised above the ground, which helped the Greceanu and Duca families survive marauding Turks during the C18-C19, and probably their own peasants during the 1907 *răscoala*. The main road forks just west of Horezu: DN67 continuing via Bumbeşti-Piţic and Bengeşti towards Tîrgu Jiu, while a minor road makes a **scenic detour** further to the north, taking in Polovragi and the various caves and sites below.

POLOVRAGI is dominated by the Căpăţîii Mountains, which overlook the high tableland where a great Wallachian **Fair** is held. An occasion for highlanders to dress up, dance and forge deals in the old fashion, the *Nedeia* usually occurs on July 20 – but check with ONT beforehand to be sure. From the commune, a forestry road runs northwards into the mile-long Olteţu Gorges, providing access to the Polovragi cave and monastery. Lurking behind the eastern rockface at the mouth of the gorge, the **Polovragi Cave** was once believed to be the abode of Zamolxis, the Dacian's chief deity. Now fully illuminated and open for guided tours (9am-5pm daily), it was first explored by the French nauralist Lancelot in 1860, who marvelled at the cave's 'Candlesticks gallery'. Near the end of the gorge you'll find **Polovragi Monastery**, a relatively small establishment founded in the C16, in a mixture of pre- and post-Brîncoveanu styles.

Three kilometres from the neighbouring commune of BAIA DE FIER, you'll find another beautiful stalactite grotto in the smaller **Galbenul Gorges** (9am-5pm daily). Although only two passages out of the **Women's Cave's** 10km of convolutions have been illuminated, sightseers get their money's worth. About halfway in are multi-coloured stone columns resembling petrified wood, while in the lower passage the skeletons of 183 cave bears were discovered;

probably the victims of *Homo primigenius*, 150,000-100,000 years ago. The *Peştera Muierii* gets its name from the human skeletons – mainly those of women and children – found on the upper levels of the cave, and gives it to a nearby *chalet* at the start of the footpath up to the **Rînca tourist complex** in the Parîng Mountains, about 15km away. There's a *motel* beyond the next settlement, NOVACI; while 25km further west, where the road meets the railway near BUMBEŞTI-JIU, you'll find *Castru Roman campsite*. Being accessible by rail from Tîrgu Jiu or Petrosani, this could serve as a base camp for anyone planning to check out the Jiu Valley.

THE JIU VALLEY

Forewarned about **the Jiu Valley**, foreigners often decide to ignore it completely, though for almost all Romanians it's crucially important even if they never go there. From Petroşani (p.381), Vulcan and Lupeni down to Rovinari, the valley's brown-coal **mines** support the sagging energy sector on which all other industries depend. With a few exceptions it's a bleak landscape, made grimmer by slag heaps, pylons and the mining towns themselves, where austerity has become the norm. Ceauşescu was forced to intercede personally after near-violent confrontations between workers and the pit bosses in August 1977, when the Jiu miners went on strike for higher wages and better living conditions. Faced with the need for more coal as oil production steadily declines, Energy Ministers (who rarely hold their job for two winters) have raised the output quotas consistently; resorting to draconian discipline as financial incentives have failed. In October 1985 the mines were, in effect, placed under **martial law** (supervised by Ilie Ceauşescu, deputy Minister of Defence), so that workers' pay could be docked 50% if quotas weren't achieved, and the miners became liable to charges of 'desertion' should they miss a week's work. Students and members of the Young Communist League are exhorted by the media to volunteer for the mines; rumours have it that many 'volunteers' have been forced there, and that outspoken Magyar youths from Transylvania are particularly likely to be drafted into the work brigades.

Having said all this, **TÎRGU JIU** still holds a few attractions for visitors: namely the town's **Festival of Enchanted Water Springs** (*Izvoare fermecate*), normally staged during the third week of February; and four **monumental sculptures by Constantin Brancuşi**. Arguably one of the greatest sculptors of the C20, Brancuşi (1876-1957) donated several pieces to the town of his boyhood. The most noticeable is the *Endless Column*, a totem-pole of rhomboidal blocks that 'clambers skyward in imitation of that well-known peasant motif, the Pillar of Heaven', whose rippling form adorns many a veranda (*pripsa*) on old wooden houses throughout Gorj county. You'll find the other sculptures along the Calea Eroilor, which runs from the Endless Column to the park beside the banks of the Jiu River. Thirty stone chairs line the *Avenue of Seats* behind the *Gate of the Kiss* at the entrance to the park, wherein stands the *Table of Silence* surrounded by twelve stools (representing the continuity of the months and the traditional number of seats at a funeral feast).

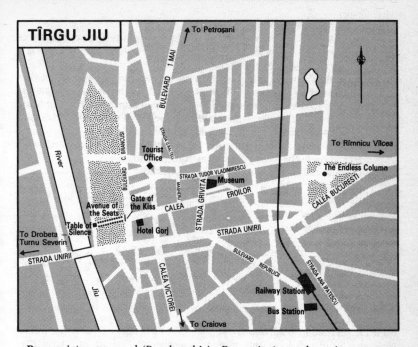

Brancuşi (pronounced 'Brankoosh' in Romanian) was born in a peasant cottage that still remains at **HOBIŢA**, some 28km west of Tîrgu Jiu; to which town he came at the age of nine to work as an errand-boy, and later learnt the techniques of the local wood-carvers, who chiselled sinuous designs on rafters, verandas and well-heads in the region. Forty years later, having established his artistic reputation in Paris, Brancuşi travelled to New York taking *The Bird* – strikingly strong and simple like all his sculptures. When US Customs classified it as 'a piece of metal' and levied import duty Brancuşi appealed against the decision, thereby starting a critical furore which made him a household name in America. He began the Tîrgu Jiu sculptures as a monument to his native land (envisaging 12 of them), but died before completing the project, and now lies in Montparnasse Cemetery in Paris. (Tourist bungalows in Hobiţa).

If Tîrgu Jiu's *BTT* (27, Str. General Tell; ☎ 929/1-24-56) can't arrange dormitory beds, the *Hotel Gorjul* on Calea Eroilor (dbl.$38/sngl.$28) is the only place to stay in town, and one has to travel some distance for other **accommodation**. DRĂGOENI campsite lies 10km east of Tîrgu Jiu (road 67), whilst slow trains heading up the Jiu Valley to Petroşani call at BUMBEŞTI (campsite nearby), LAINICI (campsite/chalet) and LIVEZENI (where some services turn off for Lupeni), in the vicinity of which stands the *Motel Gambrinus*. Reservations should be available from the **tourist office** at 17, B-dul Vladimirescu. **Railway bookings** can be obtained from Bloc 2, Str. Unirii, whilst **buses** from the terminal at 13, Str. Libertăţii might provide the means to reach Tismana.

Tismana and the Cerna Valley road
Since few foreigners are around for *Izvoare fermecate* in February, **TISMANA**
definitely deserves a mention. Less than 40km west of Tîrgu Jiu (route 67D),
it's a complete contrast to the mining areas, harking back to Gorj county's
traditional pastoral ways, which still persist beyond the reach of all-weather
roads. The **Tismana Monastery**, 5km to the north, is the oldest in Romania,
founded in the 1370s and surrounded by a high wall during the reign of Matei
Bassarab; and served as a meeting place for rebels during the 1821 rising led
by Tudor Vladimirescu (born at Vladimir off the road between Tîrgu Jiu and
Drăgăşani). Tismana is the setting for an annual **festival of music and crafts**
(August 15), where the most popular instrument is the *nai* or shepherd's pan-
pipes. Though prices in lei aren't particularly cheap (at least at the official
rate), the festival, titled *At Tismana in a Garden*, can be a good place to
bargain for wooden utensils and sculptures and embroidered clothing and
Oltenian rugs.

Buses rarely venture beyond Tismana, but motorists can continue along
road 67D **towards the Cerna Valley** and visit several interesting places en
route. Just before the logging town of BAIA DE ARAMĂ, a turn-off leads
5km northwards to **PADEŞ-CĂLUGĂRENI**, where menfolk still favour **folk
costume**. Piped with braid, their narrow white homespun trousers and
voluminous cloaks resemble the uniforms worn by Vladimirescu's soldiers in
1821. There's a beautiful **chalk cave** burrowed into the limestone massif
behind **CLOŞANI** village, 10km farther north, whilst if you turn southwest
off the main road instead, one can see the **'Giant's Bridge'**. Twenty-five metres
wide and 50 metres long, this was formed when the ceiling of a large cave
collapsed. Other picturesque **karstic formations** abound in the vicinity of
PONOARELE, a village 7km from the main road. The Cerna Valley and Băile
Herculane at its lower end are described on p.385.

Moving on from Tîrgu Jiu
The main lines of communication run northwards up the valley **into
southwestern Transylvania** (see p.317), and down **to Drobeta-Turnu Severin
on the Danube**. DN67, the shortest route to the Danube, is usually full of
dump-trucks and bulldozers and badly surfaced, while going by train, you'll
have to travel down to FILIAŞI to join the Turnu Severin-Craiova railway.
This takes one past the monastery near GURA MOTRULUI (p.320) – but
only 'slow' trains stop there.

TURNU SEVERIN, THE IRON GATES AND THE KAZAN GORGE

Passengers aboard cruise ships en route between Vienna and the Black Sea
approach Drobeta-Turnu Severin as nature intended – by the **River Danube**,
which narrows beyond Moldova Nouă and thrusts itself through the Kazan
Gorge towards Orşova, to be tamed and harnessed by the dam at the Iron
Gates. Motorists can see something of this magnificent panorama driving
down from Băile Herculane in Transylvania (the railway journey is less

scenic); but if you're coming from Tîrgu Jiu or Filaşi, the Subcapathians will have to serve as an hors d'oeuvres, since the real feast of landscapes starts after Turnu Severin.

Drobeta-Turnu Severin

Nicknamed the 'town of roses' for its beautiful parks, **DROBETA-TURNU SEVERIN**'s modern appearance belies its origins as *Drobeta*, a Dacian settlement more than two millenia ago. Its Roman conquerors left more enduring landmarks, however, notably the **ruins of Trajan's Bridge**, which Apollodor of Damascus built to span the Danube at the order of the emperor in 103-105 AD. The two stone towers marking its northern extremity can be seen near the ruins of a Roman baths, and the more extensive remains of a **medieval citadel**, a stone's throw from the excellent **Museum of the Iron Gates** (*Portile de Fier*) at the end of Strada Independenţei. The *aquarium* of various species from the Danube is its chief attraction, although the ethnographic and archaeological departments aren't to be sneered at. Alas, however, the history section doesn't mention the arrival of Karl Hohenzollern in town, an amusing story.

Selected to be the future King Carol I, Hohenzollern feared kidnapping by foreign powers and thus travelled incognito by Danube steamer, masquerading as the valet of the Romanian politician Ion Brătianu, with a passage booked to Odessa on the Black Sea. At Turnu Severin, Karl first set foot on Romanian soil, a 'sagging jetty', whereupon the skipper yelled, 'Get back on board – it's another 800 kilometres to Odessa!'. Instead, Brătianu knelt in the mud to kiss his 'valet's' hand as a *droshky* hansom cab materialised, and they heard the captain exclaim, 'My God, that must be the Prince of Hohenzollern'.

Cheapish dormitory **beds** in town might be bookable through *BTT* (25, Str. Crişan; ☎ 2-09-11), but otherwise it's a toss-up between the *Hotel Traian* on the corner of Brîncoveanu and Smirdan street, or the costlier *Parc* (sngl.\$40/dbl.\$53) at 2, B-dul Republicii. If the tourist office (last recorded at 41, Str. Decebal) is still playing hide and seek, the *Parc* is where to seek **information about riverboat services**. The last reports I had were discouraging, with only 4 boats a week downriver **to Ostrov** (departing at 4pm on Tuesday, Thursday, Saturday and Sunday, arriving at 6.45pm), but with luck there might again be services out **to Şimian Island** (site of Eugene of Savoy's fortress and other buildings from the submerged Island of Ada Kaleh), or even boats travelling upriver **to Moldova Nouă**. Repairs on the road through the gorge should by now be complete, but the current state of the bus service between Turnu Severin and Moldova Nouă is unpredictable, although it's probably worth asking at the terminal at the end of Str. Topolniţei. The **railway** (bookings at 43, Str. Decebal) runs via Gura Văii to Orşova, and then up to Băile Herculane in southwestern Transylvania.

The Iron Gates and the Kazan Gorge

Eight kilometres upriver at *Gura Văii*, the **largest hydro-electric dam in Europe** (excluding the USSR) harnesses the Danube's flow through **THE IRON GATES** which separate Romania and Yugoslavia. Conceived in 1956, the project was undertaken as a joint venture – each country built a turbine-

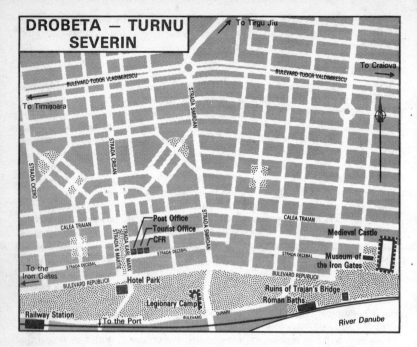

DROBETA – TURNU
SEVERIN

To Tirgu Jiu

To Craiova

BULEVARD TUDOR VLADIMIRESCU

BULEVARD TUDOR VALDIMIRESCU

STRADA SMIRDAN

To Timişoara

STRADA CRISAN

STRADA CICERO

CALEA TRAIAN

CALEA TRAIAN

STRADA KARL MARX

STRADA 6 MARTIE

Post Office

Tourist Office

CFR

STRADA SMIRDAN

STRADA DECEBAL

Medieval Castle

STRADA DECEBAL

Museum of
the Iron Gates

To the
Iron Gates

STRADA DECEBAL

BULEVARD REPUBLICII

BULEVARD REPUBLICII

Hotel Park

Ruins of Trajan's Bridge
Roman Baths

Legionary Camp

BULEVARD DUNARII

Railway Station

To the Port

River Danube

generator plant and a navigational lock-system on their respective banks, linked by a slipway dam and an international road crossing; a task that took from 1960 until 1971. Romantics have deplored the environmental results, for the dam 'has turned 130 miles of the Danube into a vast pond which has swollen and blurred the course of the river beyond recognition', turning 'beetling crags into mild hills'. The river is no longer turbulent, and its rising waters have submerged to places worthy of a footnote in history: old Orşova and the island of Ada Kaleh.

Before 1918, Orşova was the frontier-crossing into Magyar-ruled Transylvania, and it was nearby that Kossuth buried the Crown of St Stephen on his way into exile after the failure of the 1848-49 Hungarian revolution. Legend has it that the Argonauts discovered the olive tree on **Ada Kaleh**, which was famous at the beginning of this century for its Muslim community, complete with mosques, bazaars and fortresses (its Turkish name meant 'Island Citadel'). The Turkish presence here at so late a date arose from a diplomatic oversight, for at the conference where the Ottoman's withdrawal from the region was ratified, everyone forgot about Ada Kaleh, which thereby officially remained Turkish territory until much later. Before Ada Kaleh's submersion, Eugene of Savoy's citadel and the mosque were removed and reconstructed on Şimian Island, 7km downriver from Turnu Severin. Leigh Fermor laments that 'these creditable efforts to atone for the giant spoilation have stripped the last shred of mystery from those haunted waters'.

Though the river is over a kilometre wide and the surrounding mountains are quite modest, foreigners usually imagine the Iron Gates as a narrow, lofty gorge – as did the hare-brained British saboteurs who planned to dynamite it and block Hitler's oil supplies in 1940. Rather, the Iron Gates' formidable reputation arose from its navigational hazards – eddies, whirlpools and rocks – which restricted safe passage to the 200 days of the year when the river was in spate, and necessitated that boats had a shallow draught and took aboard a pilot at Moldova. The blasting of a channel in 1896 (and nowadays the dam) obviated these terrors, but nothing can detract from the awesomeness of the *Cazanele Dunării* or **KAZAN GORGE** (beyond new ORŞOVA, a boring town), which is everything that one imagines the Iron Gates to be. Here, almost sheer cliffs fall 2,000 feet into the river which 'twists and turns, ever seeking an easier egress from this enchanting belt of mountains', their 'sides covered with great forests, broken only by great streaks of grey rock thrusting through the greenery'.

Sheer it might be, but the gorge hasn't always been impassable. On the Yugoslav side near the dam complex, the *Tabula Traiana* marks the completion of the Roman road, which has disappeared since its engineers bored holes for jutting beams upon which they laid planks (roofed to discourage Dacian ambushes) rather than attempt to cut a path through the rock. The first proper road was created in the C19 on the initiative of Count Széchenyi, but had barely been finished when the Treaty of Trianon transferred it to Romania, whereupon it was deliberately neglected until its submersion by the rising waters.

If work on the new road has been completed, you should be able to drive through the gorge up to **MOLDOVA NOUĂ** (hotel on Str. Bălcescu), 4km north of its port, MOLDOVA VECHE (tourist office). Within sight of the port the river divides around an island near the isolated **rock of Babakai** where, according to legend, the Turkish governor of Moldova marooned one of his seven wives, Zuleika, who had eloped with a Hungarian noble but been recaptured. Admonished to 'Repent of thy sin!' (*Ba-ba-kai*) and left to die, Zuleika was rescued by her lover who later had the joy of taunting the mortally wounded governor with the news that she was alive, and had become a Christian. Another legend refers to the caves near the ruined fortress of **Golumbac** on the Yugoslav bank of the river, where St George is said to have slain the dragon. Thereafter, its carcass has fed the swarms of bugs that infest Golumbac, 'by popular tradition the nursery for all the mosquitoes and other noxious insects of the region'.

Crossing the frontier by road **into Yugoslavia** is easiest at the Iron Gates, but can also be accomplished at NAIDAS (though without a car, getting there is difficult). **Ferries across to Vidin in Bulgaria** (p.586) depart roughly every one and a half hours until 6.30pm from **CALAFAT**, which can be reached by road 56A from Turnu Severin, or by railway from Craiova (see below). You'll find Calafat's hotel and tourist office at 3, Str. 30 Decembrie if needed; the bus terminal is on Str. Stere. If you're staying within Romania, heading towards Craiova or up to Băile Herculane (p.385) seem the likeliest options once you've finished with this neck of the woods.

TOWARDS CRAIOVA, AND ACROSS SOUTHERN WALLACHIA TO THE DOBRUDJA

In many respects **southern Wallachia** is a tedious, uninviting terrain, for while the Subcarpathians provide varied scenery and harbour picturesque villages, below them stretch miles of plain – dusty or muddy according to season – with the odd state farm lost amidst fields of corn or sunflowers. En route **from Turnu Severin to Craiova**, DN9 passes through GURA MOTRULUI at the junction of the Jiu and Motru rivers, where a **fortified monastery** is sited two miles south of the road. Founded by the Brîncoveanu clan around 1500, the monastery surrounds a three-towered church and is guarded by a mighty belfry which doubles as a gateway. Local *personal* and *cursa* trains stop here, but not express services to Craiova.

Every locomotive on the tracks in Romania originally emerged from the workshops of **CRAIOVA**, a sprawling place surrounded by derricks testifying to the discovery of oil beneath this, Wallachia's oldest industrial town. Craiova's sole tourist attractions are the former governatorial *Ban's House*, now occupied by an **Ethnographic Museum** (14, Str. Bassarab), and two **art collections** on the Calea Unirii, but you might choose to stay in order to travel on to Bulgaria the following morning. Guests at the *Jiul* and *Minerva* are charged $53 for double **rooms** ($40 for a single), which seems a powerful reason to pester *BTT* (8, Str. Olteţ; ☎ 1-73-96) about the possibility of vacant college beds, particularly since both **campsites** are miles out along DN6 either side of town and inaccessible by public transport. CFR in the Complex Unirea on Piaţa Unirii can book seats on the 8.18am, 2pm or 4.10pm train **down to Calafat**, enabling you to get there before the last of the **ferries across to Vidin in Bulgaria** which leave every 1-1½hrs until around 6.30pm. Ferry-tickets can be purchased when you get there and the charge for vehicles is quite modest, but you must already have a *Bulgarian visa*.

There are two railway lines **between Craiova and Bucharest**. The one taking the southerly route across the plain goes by way of CARACAL, ROŞIORI DE VEDE and VIDELE, and the journey to Bucharest takes about 3½hrs by express train, or roughly double that if you travel by *cursa* like the weather-beaten local peasants do. There's nothing in particular to see along this route, but should you fancy a spot of **camping near the Danube**, there are sites at CORABIA and near TURNU MAGURELE. Both places are accessible by branch lines, but note that between Calafat and Giurgiu on the Danube there are **no crossings into Bulgaria**. (Some of the Romanians who've attempted to escape by swimming across to Yugoslavia have been swept downstream and repatriated from Bulgaria.)

Despite its rich soil, the southern plain has traditionally been one of Romania's poorest areas, for the boyars (and worse still, their estate managers) squeezed the peasants mercilessly. Land hunger grew as the peasant population, taxes and rural unemployment increased – building up to the explosive **1907 uprising** (*răscoala*). Detonated near Vaslui in Moldavia, where Jews believed to prey upon peasants were the first targets, the uprising spontaneously raged southwards into Wallachia. Panic-stricken boyars flooded into Bucharest, demanding vengeance for the burning of their property – and the army obliged, quelling the ill-armed peasantry with cannon fire, and then executing 'ringleaders' by the thousand. Though there's a **Museum of the Uprising** at 54, Str. Dunării in Roşiori de Vede, Telorman county, the English translation of Liviu Rebreanu's novel *Uprising* is a more gripping exposition of the subject.

The alternative **route to Bucharest via Piteşti** runs further to the north, and its final phase has already been described (in reverse sequence of places) earlier in this chapter. Bucharest can be reached in 4½hrs by express train, and since the track avoids everywhere worth mentioning (except Piatra Olt, the railway junction for Rîmnicu Vîlcea, p.311), there's no point in taking a slower service. The journey by DN65 (Euro-route 94) is more interesting, inasmuch as at kilometre 72, a minor road turns off and passes a chalet/campsite awaiting pilgrims to **SCORNICEŞTI**, the **birthplace of Nicolae Ceauşescu**. Born into a family of ten children on 26 January, 1918 – 'a holy day whose echo is still resounding through the nation' (in the words of the Party press) – he was apprenticed as a slipper-maker before joining the illegal Communist Party. Life as a Communist activist during the monarchist and fascist periods was perilous, but probably less nerve-wracking than during the early years of Communist rule, when purges and executions savaged the ranks of the *stabii* – the Party hierarchy through which Ceauşescu was steadily climbing.

Following Gheorghiu-Dej's demise, he became RCP General Secretary in 1965 and began promoting himself as a champion of Romanian nationalism. Today, Ceauşescu monopolises power like no other Eastern European ruler – he's currently President, Prime Minister, Commander-in-chief of the Armed Forces and Chairman of the Supreme Council of Economic Development, besides being Party leader. In the mould of ex-president Marcos of the Philippines, his chief confidante and lieutenant is his wife, **Elena**, while well over a dozen members of the Ceauşescu family hold important positions. Their son **Nicu**, head of the Union of Communist Youth, is generally believed to be the heir-apparent despite his notorious alcoholism, although **Ilie**, the deputy Minister of Defence, has displayed more competence and could be a contender following the Leader's demise. Paeans to the 'historic couple whose existence merges with the country's destiny' are virtually ubiquitous in Romania, and Scorniceşti – understandably – is no exception.

FESTIVALS

Winter
The bands and folk-ensembles of Gorj county bring a little colour to TÎRGU JIU during the *Festival of Enchanted Water Springs* in the **third week of February**.

Spring
SLOBOZIA might host the *Flowers of the Bărăgan* festival sometime in **April**.

Summer
SĂLĂTRUCU's fête on **June 1** warms up the highlanders for the big Pottery Fair (*Cocoşul de Hureazu*) at HOREZU later that month. Another lively fair is held at POLOVRAGI, sometime between **July 15-20**. In **August**, CĂLIMĂNEŞTI hosts the *Songs of the Olt* during the **first week**, whilst pan-pipers and peasants gather at TISMANA on the **15**.

TRAVEL DETAILS

Trains

From Bucharest to Braşov (14 daily; 2¾-3¾hrs); Cluj (1; 7); Constanţa (7; 3-5¼); Craiova, via Caracal (5; 3); Iaşi (4; 5¾-7); Piteşti (8; 1½-3); Ploieşti (16; ¾-1½); Snagov (4; 1¼); Suceava (6-7; 5½-6½).

From Craiova to Bucharest, via Caracal (7; 3½) or Piteşti (2; 4½-7); Calafat (4; 2¼); Drobeta-Turnu Severin (6; 2-3); Filiaşi (13; ½-1); Gura Motrului (4; 1); Piatra Olt (7; 1¼); Piteşti (3; 2¼-3½).

From Drobeta-Turnu Severin to Băile Herculane (4; ¾-1¼); Caransebeş (5; 2-2¾); Craiova (4; 2); Orşova (6; ½-¾); Timişoara (4; 3-5).

From Goleşti to Cîmpulung (5; 1¾).

From Piatra Olt to Lotru (3; 2¼-3½); Podu Olt (4; 2½-4¾); Rîmnicu Vîlcea (6; 2½); Turnu Monastery (3; 3¼).

From Piteşti to Bucharest (8; 2-2¾); Curtea de Argeş (5; 3); Goleşti (9; ¼); Titu (8; 1).

From Ploieşti to Braşov (16; 2-3); Bucharest (14; ¾-1½); Tîrgovişte (5; ¾).

From Tîrgovişte to Ploieşti Sud (6; ¾); Titu (5; 1).

From Tîrgu Jiu to Filiaşi (6; 1-1½); Simeria (4; 2¼-4); Subcetate (4; 2¾-4¾).

From Titu to Tîrgovişte (9; 1)

TAROM domestic flights

From Bucharest, Băneasa Airport to Arad; Bacău; Baia Mare; Caransebeş; Cluj; Constanţa; Craiova; Galaţi; Iaşi; Oradea; Satu Mare; Sibiu; Suceava; Timişoara; Tîrgu Mureş; Tulcea (1-2 daily).

From Craiova to Bucharest (1-2 daily).

International trains

From Bucharest to Athens (2 daily; 31hrs); Belgrade (1; 11½); Budapest (4; 13-14); Dresden (2; 29½); Kiev (3; 24¾); Moscow (3; 34½); Paris (3; 40); Prague (2; 24); Rome (1; 44); Ruse (3; 2½); Sofia (3; 11); Varna (1; 8½); Vienna (2; 20); Warsaw (2; 28½).

From Giurgiu Nord to Athens (1; 30); Budapest (3; 15½); Burgas (1; 8½); Kiev (2; 26); Moscow (2; 38); Prague (2; 26); Ruse (6; 1¾); Sofia (4; 8½).

TAROM international flights

From Bucharest, Otopeni Airport to Amsterdam (2 each week); Athens (3); Belgrade (2); Beijing (2); Berlin (10); Brussels (2); Budapest (8); Copenhagen (3); Frankfurt (9); Istanbul (4); London (3); Los Angeles (1); Moscow (6); Munich (4); New York (5); Oslo (3); Paris (5); Prague (4); Rome (3); Seattle (1); Sofia (2); Stokholm (3); Toronto (2); Vienna (7); Warsaw (4).

Ferries

From Calafat to Vidin in BULGARIA, every 1½hrs until 6.30pm.

From Drobeta-Turnu Severin to Ostrov; 1 on Tuesdays, Thursdays, Saturdays and Sundays (2¼hrs).

Chapter eight
TRANSYLVANIA

Thanks to Bram Stoker and Hollywood, **Transylvania** (Latin for 'beyond the forest': *Transilvania* or *Ardeal* in Romanian) is famed abroad as the homeland of Dracula: a mountainous place where storms lash medieval hamlets, while wolves – or werewolves – howl from the surrounding woods. Happily, the fictitious image is accurate – up to a point. **The scenery** is dramatic as hell in the Prahova Valley, the gorges of Todra and Bicaz and from the high passes. There are spooky gothic citadels, around Braşov, and at Sibiu, Sighişoara, Bran and elsewhere. And one Vlad, born in Sighişoara did later style himself **Dracula**, and earn his grim nickname 'The Impaler'*.

But the Dracula image is just one element of Transylvania, whose 99,837 square kilometres take in ice-caps, caves, alpine meadows, dense forests sheltering bears and wild boars, and lowland valleys where *bivol* (buffalo) cool off in the rivers. **The population** is an ethnic jigsaw of Romanians, Magyars, Germans, Gypsies and others, formed over centuries of migration and colonisation. Since the Treaty of Trianon (1920) which placed Transylvania firmly within the Romanian state, the balance of power among the ethnic groups has shifted sharply in favour of the Romanian majority. Transylvania's history is still often disputed along nationalist lines, and popular feelings concerning the region run high inside Hungary and Romania.

Most people in Hungary view *Erdély* (their name for Transylvania) as a land 'stolen' by the Romanians, where some two million Magyars face what the writer Gyula Illyés calls 'ethnocide', causing 8,000 of them to flee across the border in three months of 1988 alone. All Romanians assert the opposite: that Transylvania has always been rightfully theirs and that, for centuries, it was the Magyars who practised discrimination. Meanwhile Transylvania's Germans are quitting their 800 year-old settlements for a new life in the West, whilst the Gypsies (*Ţigani*) still go their own way, untramelled by Five Year Plans or the *epoca Ceauşescu*. The result is an intoxicating brew of different characters, customs and places that is best taken slowly.

Places and events
The **Carpathian mountains** are never far away in Transylvania, and for anyone fond of walking amidst rugged nature this must be one of the most beautiful, least exploited regions in Europe. **Hikes** to stunning places in the Făgăraş, Apuseni and Retezat ranges can last several days, but it's perfectly feasible to make briefer yet equally dramatic forays into the Bucegi mountains, or to one of Transylvania's many spectacular gorges.

* See p.490 for a discussion of the Dracula myth.

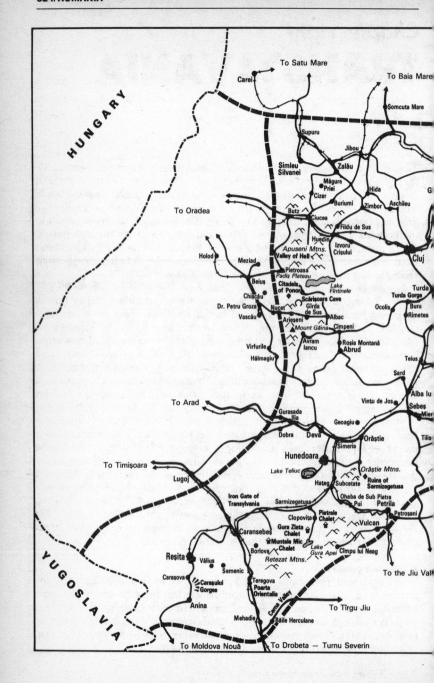

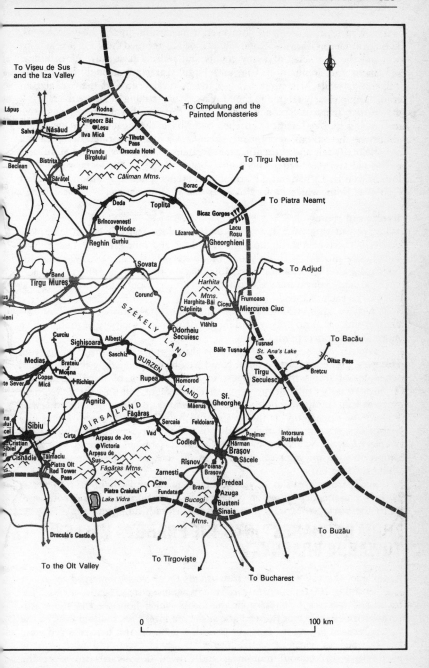

To Vişeu de Sus
and the Iza Valley

To Cîmpulung and the
Painted Monasteries

Lăpuş

Rodna

Şingeorz Băi

Leşu

Ilva Mică

Salva

Năsăud

Tihuţa Pass

Dracula Hotel

Prundu
Bîrgăului

To Tîrgu Neamţ

Bistriţa

Beclean

Sărăţel

Căliman Mtns.

Sieu

Borac

To Piatra Neamţ

Deda

Toplița

Bicaz Gorges

Brîncoveneşti

Hodac

Lăzarea

Lacu
Roşu

Reghin Gurhiu

Gheorghieni

Sovata

To Adjud

Band

Harhita

Tîrgu Mureş

Corund

Mtns.

Frumoasa

Harghita-Băi

Ciceu

Miercurea Ciuc

Căplinita

SZÉKELY

Curciu

Vláhița

Sighişoara

Albeşti

Odorheiu
Secuiesc

To Bacău

Medias

Saschiz

BURZEN

Băile Tuşnad

Tusnad

St. Ana's Lake

Oituz Pass

Brateiu

LAND

Moşna

Copsa
Mică

Richişu

Rupea

Homorod

Tîrgu
Secuiesc

Bretcu

te Sever

LAND

Agnita

Sf.
Gheorghe

Măerus

BÎRSALAND

Făgăraş

Sercaia

Feldoiara

Sibiu

Cirta

Arpaşu de Jos

Vad

Prejmer

Intorsura
Buzăului

Cristian

Victoria

Codlea

Hărman

Braşov

Cisnădie

Tălmaciu

Arpaşu de
Sus

Rîşnov

Poiana-
Braşov

Săcele

Piatra Olt
Red Tower
Pass

Făgăraş Mtns.

Zarnești

Predeal

Piatra Craiului

Cave

Bran

Azuga

Lake Vidra

Fundata

Bucegi

Buşteni

Dracula's Castle

Sinaia

Mtns.

To Buzău

To the Olt Valley

To Tîrgovişte

To Bucharest

0

100 km

If you're pushed for time, however, concentrate on the **historic towns**. Though modernisation and Romanianisation have eroded the sharp distinctions of yore, the character of many towns still reflects past patterns of ethnic settlement and domination. **Cluj** and **Tîrgu Mureş** are strongly Hungarian-influenced, while Miercurea Ciuc is the cultural centre of the Székely, an ethnic group closely related to the Mayars. Most striking of all are the *stuhls* – the former seats of Saxon power – with their medieval streets, defensive towers and spooky fortified churches. **Sighişoara**, the most picturesque, could almost be the Saxons' monument: their *kultur* has evaporated here, leaving only their citadels and churches, as it threatens to do in **Braşov** and **Sibiu**, and in the old German settlements roundabouts. While in the vicinity you'd be foolish to miss Cisnădioara, Hărman and Prejmer, not to mention '**Dracula's Castle**' at **Bran**, which looks almost as one would imagine.

Events and routes

When considering your itinerary bear in mind the **festivals** which take place across Transylvania throughout the year. May and June offer the most choice, but during months with only one or two events there's usually something happening over the mountains in Moldavia, the Banat or Maramureş. To help with planning **your route** we've listed festivals just before the *Travel Details* at the end of each chapter.

Travellers approaching Transylvania **from Bucharest** can follow this chapter through until Braşov, and then opt for one of a variety of routes which more or less converge on Cluj.

Obviously, the sequence of places is different when you're coming **from Hungary**, and your starting point could well be determined by the routes and schedules of trains from Budapest to Bucharest. All of them barring the *Transdanubium* call at Braşov while there's daylight, but only the *Balt-Orient* stops at Cluj (in the wee hours). The *Pannonia* skips Alba Iulia but otherwise follows the same route as the *Orient* and Balt-Orient, through Mediaş and Sighişioara (during daylight) to Brasov. The only service to Sibiu is the *Weiner-Waltzer*, which zooms past the Făgăraş range. Wherever you start, simply turn to the appropriate place in this chapter, or see Travel Details about moving on.

Coming **from Yugoslavia**, you can pick up the trail at the Iron Gates or Băile Herculane, depending on whether you enter Romania at the Iron Gates or by the *Bucureşti* express (from Zagreb, Belgrade and Ljubljana).

FROM BUCHAREST INTO THE PRAHOVA VALLEY TOWARDS BRAŞOV

Aeons ago, the site where Bucharest stands today was submerged by a vast sea, extending 100 miles northwards to lap against a small island of crystaline rock. The remains of Cretaceous life-forms which flourished in the warm waters formed reefs that trapped grit as the sea-level rose, holding it when the waters receded during the Neozoic period. The mountains that emerged were later shaped by glaciers which formed fantastic caves and other karstic phenomena; carved out moraines; and flowed downwards to create the

Prahova Valley. Nowadays the Prahova and its twin river the Ialomiţa slip almost unnoticed across the flatlands between Bucharest and Ploieşti, but the Prahova becomes a force to be reckoned with higher up, beyond Cîmpina. From Sinaia to Predeal the river froths white beneath gigantic **mountains** which overhang Buşteni with 2,000ft of sheer escarpment, receding in grandiose slopes covered with fir, beech and rowan trees. Even if you don't stop off to climb one of the peaks in the Bucegi range (or ride up by ski-lift), from a scenic standpoint the valley's upper reaches are unforgettable.

Getting there is comparatively simple, for the first proper road (constructed in 1846) has been upgraded into the well-surfaced DN1, and although bus services from Bucharest have effectively ceased, the railway runs straight up the valley after clearing Ploieşti. (A description of Ploieşti and Cîmpina appears on p.304). The journey from Bucharest to Braşov takes about 2¾hrs on the *Wiener-Waltzer* (overnight), *Orient Express, Decebal* and *Transilvania rapid* services, which only stop at Ploieşti, Sinaia and Predeal en route. From either of the last two, you can catch a slow *personal* train to Busteni or Azuga. (N.B. The 9am train from Bucharest also stops at *Dîrste campsite* just outside Braşov).

Sinaia

Named after the monastery founded here by the boyar Cantacuzino in 1695, **SINAIA** has been dubbed the 'Pearl of the Carpathians' for its magnificent mountain scenery, while the presence here of Peleş Castle – once a royal, now a preşedential residence – has led one writer to liken it to a Balmoral in the Balkans. Originally the preserve of a few hermits and shepherds, and later an exclusive aristocratic resort, it's nowadays full of workers on health cures, and holidaymakers keen to climb the Bucegi (or ski while the snow lasts, until April) . Many of the timber-framed villas look starkly impressive, while from the park opposite the station it's a short walk to the House of Culture (formerly a casino), whence Str. Mănăstirii leads up to **Sinaia Monastery**. An ensemble of petite churches and courtyards named in honour of the monastery on Mount Sinai (which Cantacuzino once visited), it superceded an earlier hermitage endowed by a pious Haiduc. To the north lies a **park** landscaped in English fashion, containing a Swiss style belvedere known as **Foişor,** while in the vicinity you'll see Peleş Castle.

Outwardly resembling a German *schloss,* **Peleş Castle** was founded in the late C19 by Romania's imported Hohenzollern monarch, Carol I, and largely decorated by his eccentric wife Carmen Sylva, the 'Romanian Sappho', who once decreed that court life at Sinaia be conducted in folk costume. Peleş contains over 160 rooms – some decorated in ebony, mother of pearl, walnut or leather – all alien to the traditional styles of Romanian art; 'yet another expression of the former royal family's disdain for the people whom they exploited', as a 1960s guide book notes didactically. It was here in 1923 that Prince Carol (later crowned Carol II) first encountered Magda Lupescu, a Jewess from Iaşi who remained his mistress for forty years and became the power behind the throne to the outrage of Romanian society, which tended towards anti-semitism. Following the monarchy's demise in 1946 Peleş was opened to the public, until the Ceauşescus appropriated it as a 'state palace'.

Still, the **Bucegi Mountains** are Sinaia's real attraction. From the terminal near the Hotel Montana, a cable cabin (Tuesday-Sunday 9am-5pm) whisks visitors aloft to **Cota 1400**, halfway up the mountainside and the site of a hotel and (much cheaper) chalet, the *Popasul Alpin cabana*. Another cable cabin rises to **Cota 200**, while a ski lift ascends to **Cota 1500** where you'll find the *Valea cu Brazi* chalet and a chair lift (Wednesday-Monday 9am-5pm) to **Cota 1950**, near the *Miorița cabana* and the start of the taxing 'Papagul' ski run back down to Cota 1400. Skiing equipment can be rented at the Montana Hotel. Below and southwards of Cota 1950, a crag gives its name to the *Virful cu dor cabana*, and from there it's 2½-3½hrs walk down the Dorului Valley to the beautiful **tarns of La Lacuri**, following a path marked with yellow crosses and red stripes (which returns by way of Mount Virfu). Another beautiful, easy walk is from Mount Furnica – north of the Miorița chalet – to the *Piatra Arsa cabana* behind Mount Jepi Mari. There, blue triangles indicate the route downwards to Bușteni via **La Scari**, a spectacular stairway hewn into rock, while paths and a road wend northwards over the Bucegi plateau. (Drivers can reach the Bucegi's interior via a road turning off into the Izvorașu Valley just south of Sinaia.)

Mountain walks around Bușteni and Predeal

Romanian-language **maps** of the *Munții Bucegi* are invaluable for anybody serious about **walking in the mountains**, and shouldn't be hard to understand if you refer to the vocabulary on p.267. Hotels in all the Prahova Valley settlements are expensive, but you're rarely far from a cheap mountain cabana which – so I was told – aren't allowed to turn hikers away. (If you're really stuck, the map also locates *Refugiu* and sheepfolds, or *stînă*). Some **cabanas** are pretty primitive and may lack water, but their inhabitants are a friendly crowd and there's usually a bar.

As in any mountain range favoured by shepherds and climbers, there's a wealth of nostrums for predicting the **weather**. Cloudless mornings with a southerly wind, an early mist which evaporates without forming clouds, morning winds which disperse or flatten clouds over the valleys and the Mălăiești depression all auger well; as do bluish or orange-coloured skies above the Gîrbova Mountains at sunrise, dewy evenings or a dewy morning after a clear night. Morning mist which forms layers of cloud racing in opposite directions, strong winds from Mt. Postăvru and Magura Codlei, the closing of flowers and the sight of birds and insects taking shelter all presage rain, which can be ferocious on the peaks.

Snow covers Mount Omu for 219 days of the year, but retreats during April elsewhere, leaving the meadows to **wildflowers**. First come crocuses, snowdrops, sweet violets and ladies' gloves, followed by forget-me-nots, grapeferns and marigolds, with violets, primroses, bellflowers, edelweiss and camomiles flourishing higher up, alongside junipers and rhododendrons. The forests shelter woodcocks, hazel grouse and nightingales from the circling golden eagles, while **other wildlife** includes the Carpathian stag (around the Bran region), lynx, foxes, rodents and wild boars. The latter, like wolves and bears, are only a potential threat to humans during the winter, or if their litters seem endangered.

BUŞTENI is the place to begin, a small town overshadowed by the sheer Caraiman (2,384m) and Coştila (2,498m) peaks, separated by the dark, perpetually snowy Albă Valley. From Buşteni's 1 Septembrie paper-mill, a path marked with red dots leads past a **zoo** to the **Urlătoarea waterfall** (2hrs), while a footpath and a **cable cabin** ascend Jepi Valley to the *Caraiman* and *Babele* cabanas. Babele offers a panoramic view, and is only 10-20 minutes' walk from an impressive skull-like rock formation, the **Babele Sphinx** (continue along a path marked by yellow stripes to reach Mt. Omu in about 4hrs); or you can ride the funicular on to the *Peştera* cabana. Just north of here is the **Ialomiţa Cave**, a complex of grottos, the largest of which is over 100m in length, and an unmarked path leading up through the Horoaba Valley past waterfalls, the 'Gorge of the Bear' and two natural tunnels. Alternatively, from Peştera you can follow a blue-striped path to *Piatra Arsa* cabana (see above) or head southwards to *Padina* chalet and a camping spot near **Lake Bolboci**, with more caves in the vicinity (all accessible by road from the south).

Though completely cloudless days are rare in the viciniy of **Mount Omu**, from the Bucegi's highest peak (2,505m) it's possible to see the Bîrsa Land, the ridge of Piatra Craiului, and the Făgăraş range beyond: a mountain vista of unparalleled splendour. From the *Omul* cabana, closed during winter, a path marked with blue stripes descends a glacial valley past eroded rock 'chimneys' to the *Mălăieşti* chalet (2-3hrs). Two other **paths** lead downwards **towards Bran**. Both take 6-7hrs, the route indicated by yellow triangles being easier going, while the path marked with red crosses passes near the 'Devil's Mill' Waterfall – *Cascada Moara Dracului* – a fitting approach to 'Dracula's Castle' in the village below (described in the section following Braşov).

The Gîrbova or **Baiului Mountains** flanking the Prahova to the east are the site of numerous **ski runs** in the vicinity of **PREDEAL**. A chair-lift (9am-5pm) from the Hotel Clăbucet-Sosire ascends to Clăbucet-Plecare where the *pistes* begin. Most of them are graded as 'average', although the 'Sub Teleferic' is classified as difficult, and the run southwards towards the Gîrbova chalet as 'easy'. Once again hotels are expensive but there are cabanas around: *Gîrbova* and *Susai* within a few kilometres walk of Clăbucet-Plecare, and others northwest of Predeal, in the foothills of the Bucegi massif. The latter include *Cerby* (with a camping place nearby), *Piriu Rece* and *Poiana Secuilor* – all within walking distance of the Hotel Trei Brazi – and *Diham*, higher up and further south with a slalom run in the vicinity. Centres at 134, Gh. Dej Blvd, the Orizont and Cioplea hotels and at the chair-lift station, rent out **equipment**; and the *Cioplea* and *Căprioara* contain **discos**.

Around Predeal the valley is wide, for the River Timiş flows into the Prahova, but thereafter the highway and railway enter the geologically younger Timiş Valley and the mountains close in again. Just before the Braşov depression, DN1A turns off towards **SĂCELE**, a township created by the amalgamation of seven villages. Formerly their inhabitants were largely shepherds who spent many months in the mountains, and included many Csángó Hungarians who migrated southwards from the eastern Carpathians, often working as cabbies in Bucharest during the 1930s. Săcele's **Museum of the Seven Villages** hardly merits a visit, but you might like to attend the local **festival** held on the Sunday before July 20.

BRAŞOV

With an eye for trade and invasion routes, the medieval Saxons sited their largest settlements within a day's journey from Transylvania's mountain passes. BRAŞOV, which they called *Kronstadt*, grew prosperous and fortified as a result, and for many centuries the Saxons constituted an élite whose economic power long outlasted its feudal privileges. Understandably, perhaps, post-war governments have wanted 'their own' skilled working class, and to this end brought thousands of Moldavian villagers to Braşov, where they were trained to work in the new factories and given modern housing during the 1960s. Everything was hunky-dory until the economy began collapsing in the 1980s.

As a result, there are two parts to Braşov (pop. 200,000): the quasi-Gothic bit coiled beneath Mt. Tîmpa and Mt. Postǎvru, which looks great; and the surrounding sprawl of flats and factories, which doesn't. **Old Braşov** – whose Schei quarter, Black Church and medieval ramparts provide a backdrop for the colourful *Pageant of the Juni* – is worth at least a day's sightseeing; and the proximity of the Alpine resort of **Poiana Braşov** and 'Dracula's Castle' at Bran has previously made the city 'a must'.

However, after the **events** of November 15 1987, any endorsement of Braşov has to be cautious. Signs of the riot during which the Party headquarters was sacked and a Militia officer was reportedly killed have been effaced, and the 10,000 workers involved have returned to mark time at the *Red Star and Tractorul* factories where their grievances – over back-pay and the prospect of mass redundancies – originated; but Securitate investigations – if not arrests – are doubtless continuing. 'Order' has been restored, but local pride in the rebellion is barely covered by the 'security' blanket, so future visitors will almost certainly be watched by the police, and possibly approached by Romanians wanting to tell all.

Arriving

Motorists driving up from Bucharest pass the *Dîrste* campsite on the outskirts of town, and enter Braşov's industrial areas gradually; arriving **by train** you're confronted with their concrete drabbness immediately. The best thing to do is to get straight out. Trolleybus #4 lurches down to central park, where you'll find the OJT and ONT **tourist offices** at 27, B-dul Gheoghiu-Dej, and in the lobby of the exorbitant *Hotel Carpaţi*, a few doors down (open 7.30am-3.30pm/ Sundays in the Carpaţi only). If prodded, either office might enquire about vacancies at the *Cristian* and *Postǎvrul* **cabanas** out in Poiana-Braşov (the only cheap beds to be had in that mountainous resort) or ring up **hotels** around town. Of these, the most moderately-priced are the *Carpaţi-Sport* (Str. Maiakovski, around the corner from the Carpaţi); the *Postǎvrul* on Str. Republicii; and – nearer to the railway station – the *Turist* at 32, Str. Karl Marx. There are two **campsites**. *Zimbrul* is along the road to Poiana-Braşov (bus #20 from the central park), while *Dîrste* – with 2-person chalets for 170 lei – is about 7km from Braşov's centre, near the Bucharest highway. To reach Dîrste, take bus #17 from the Parc Central as far as it goes out along the Calea Bucureştilor. When the bus turns off, walk parallel to the motorway for another 1km, cross under the railway and over the river and you'll find the campsite. (It can also be reached from the railway station by catching bus #8 to the huge *Autocamion* factory, where #17s stop outside the gates).

Around Town
One legend has it that when the Pied Piper enticed the children from Hamelin, they vanished underground and emerged in Transylvania near the site of Braşov's main square, now called the **Piaţa 23 August**. As if on parade, sturdy buildings line the square; their red rooftiles tilted rakishly, presenting their shopfronts to the C15 *Rathaus* or council house – which raises aloft its belltower in salute, despite having been relegated to the role of **History Museum** (Tuesday-Sunday 10am-5pm). As can be guessed from the exhibits, Braşov used to be dominated by Saxon guilds whose main hangout was the **Merchants' Hall**, built in the 'Transylvanian Renaissance' style of the C16, which now contains craft shops, a wine-cellar and the 'Carpathian Stag' (*Cerbul Carpatin*) restaurant. Within sight of its terrace is the town's most famous landmark, **the Black Church**, which stabs upwards like a series of poniards. An endearingly monstrous hall church which took almost a century (1385-1477) to complete, the *Biserica Neagră* is so-called for its soot-blackened walls – the result of a great fire that swept Braşov in 1689. Inside, by contrast, the church is startlingly white, with oriental carpets hung in isolated splashes of colour along the walls of the nave. **Organ recitals** on the 4,000 pipe instrument are held on Wednesdays, 6pm-6.30pm; the church admits sightseers Monday-Friday, 9.30am-6pm.

When Turkish expansion became an evident threat in the C15, the inhabitants began to fortify Braşov, assigning the defence of each bastion or rampart to a particular guild. A length of **fortress wall** runs along the foot of Mount Tîmpa, beneath a maze of paths and a cable-car running up to the summit (see below). Of the original seven **bastions** the best preserved is that of the Weavers, on Str.Coşbuc, which now contains the **Museum of the Bîrsa Land Fortifications** (Tuesday-Sunday 10am-6pm). Inside are models, pictures and weaponry recalling the bad old days when the surrounding region – then known as the Bîrsa and Burzen Lands – was repeatedly attacked by Tartars, Turks and, on a couple of occasions, by Dracula. Catherine's Gate (which bears the coat of arms of the citadel), the Blacksmiths' Bastion – *Bastionul Fierarilor* – and the Black and the White Towers on Warthe Hill all managed to remain despite these onslaughts, but the inhabitants didn't always fare so fortunately. During the heyday of Saxon rule the Romanian-speaking population was compelled to live beyond the citadel walls, in the southern **Schei district**, and many doubtless fell victim to Dracula when he attacked Braşov in 1458-60, burning the suburbs and impaling hundreds of captives along the heights of St Jacob's Hill to terrorise the townsfolk. Referring to allegations that Vlad dined off a holy icon surrounded by his suffering victims, his biographer Stoicescu writes that 'being on campaign . . . the terrible Prince may not have had the time to take his meals otherwise'.

Once, Romanians living in the narrow streets of *Scheiul* could only enter the centre at certain times, and had to pay a toll at the gate for the privilege of victualling their haughty neighbours. These restrictions were only waived on

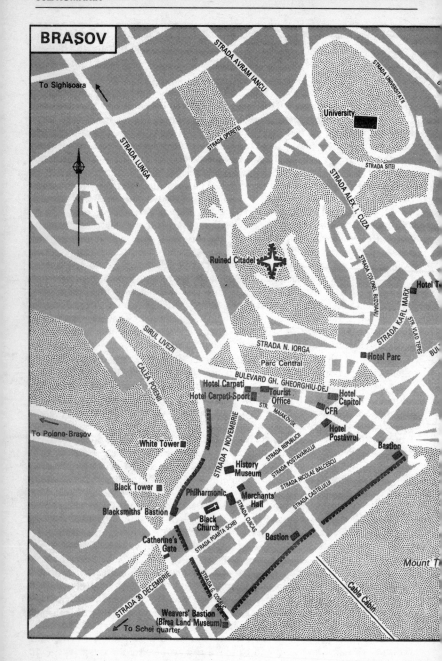

BRAŞOV

STRADA AVRAM IANCU

To Sighişoara

STRADA UNIVERSITĂŢII

University

STRADA OPERETEI

STRADA LUNGA

STRADA SITEI

STRADA ALEX. I. CUZA

Ruined Citadel

STRADA COLONEL BUZDIANU

STRADA KARL MARX

Hotel Te

Hotel Parc

SIRUL LIVEZII

STRADA N. IORGA

STR. VLAD ŢEPEŞ

Parc Central

CALEA POENI

BULEVARD GH. GHEORGHIU-DEJ

Hotel Carpaţi

Hotel Carpaţi-Sport

Tourist Office

Hotel Capitol

STR. MAIAKOVSKI

CFR

To Poiana-Braşov

Hotel Poştăvrul

White Tower

STRADA 7 NOVEMBRIE

Bastion

STRADA REPUBLICII

STRADA POŞTĂVARULUI

History Museum

Black Tower

STRADA NICOLAE BĂLCESCU

Philharmonic

Merchants' Hall

STRADA CASTELULUI

Blacksmiths' Bastion

STRADA CUCAS

Black Church

STRADA POARTA SCHEI

Catherine's Gate

Bastion

Mount T

STRADA 30 DECEMBRIE

STRADA G. COŞBUC

Cable Cabin

Weavers' Bastion
(Bîrsa Land Museum)

To Schei quarter

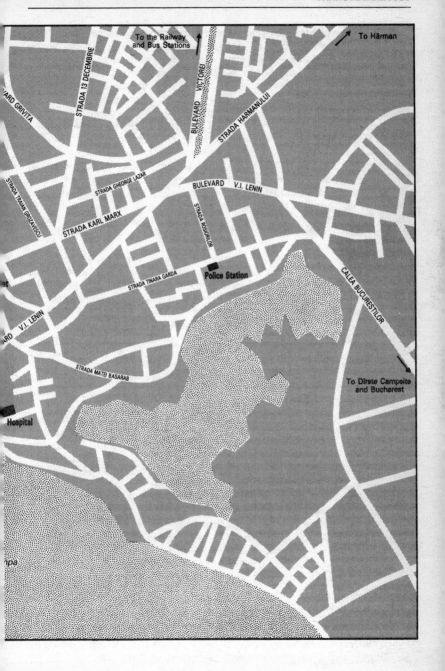

To the Railway
and Bus Stations

To Härman

STRADA 13 DECEMBRIE

BULEVARD VICTOREI

STRADA HARMANULUI

VARD GRIVITA

STRADA GHEORGE LAZAR

BULEVARD V.I. LENIN

STRADA TRAIAN GROZAVESCU

STRADA KARL MARX

STRADA KOSORILOR

Police Station

STRADA TINARA GARDA

CALEA BUCURESTILOR

st

V.I. LENIN

STRADA MATEI BASARAB

To Dirste Campsite
and Bucharest

Hospital

npa

the first Sunday of May each year – hence the origin of the **Pageant of the Juni** (*Sărbătoarea junilor*) which, as its name derived from the Latin for 'young men' suggests, is a festival allowing the town's young men to show off. Costumed and accompanied by brass bands, they ride through town in groups named for famous regiments – the *Dorobanţi*, or the *Roşiori* (whose honourary colonel was once Queen Marie, causing Hemingway to sneer that 'corsets and lipstick' were part of the regimental uniform) – while the married chaps, or 'Old Juni', bring up the rear. The parade assembles in the morning on the **Piaţa Unirii** which, together with the C16 **Church of St. Nicholas**, forms the historic heart of Scheiul. It then marches to the main square, back into Scheiul's backstreets, and then climbs a narrow valley to the **Gorges of Pietrele lui Solomon**. There, spectators settle down to eat and drink and watch the Round Dances, or *Horas*, which for the participants are really a kind of endurance test. Some of the elaborate Juni costumes are 150 years old, while one of the Roşiori wears a shirt sewn with 44,000 spangles that weighs 9 kilos – the product of four months work by women, whose efforts underlie the whole Juni shindig.

Normally, the hub of Braşov's social life is the **Str. Republicii**, where people stroll around noon and in the early evening, between work and intermissions in coffee houses (*cofetărie*), or a lengthy session with beer and sausages on the terrace of the *Cerbul Carpatin*. Walking down this street, you'll pass the theatre bookings bureau (nr.4); a cheap stand-up buffet; the **24-hour pharmacy** (nr.27); the *Hotel Postăvrul*, which has a good restaurant; and at nr.53, the **CFR** office (open 8am-8pm/Sunday 7am-12am). At its lowest point, Str. Republicii joins the **Bulevard Gheorghiu-Dej**, a union giving rise to an **Art Museum** (with a good selection of Grigorescu, Aman and Tattarescu canvases) and a crowded, down-at-the-heel department store. Across the road from the latter, there's a small fruit & veg **market** and the stop to board trolleybus #4 for the station.

Northwards of Bulevard Gheorghiu-Dej and the Parc Central stand the **Post Office** (Str. Iorga) and a lowish hill crowned by the overgrown **ruins of a citadel**. Nearby is the beginning of Str. Lungă – Long Street – which, sure enough, stretches interminably until the Gothic **Church of St.Bartholomew**, when it becomes DN13 – the road to Tîrgu Mureş. Braşov's **University** lies some distance from the centre, and to **meet students** you might try the cafés around Piaţa 23 August or the *Casa de Studenţilor* at 29, B-dul Gheorghiu-Dej (bring your passport, and student card if you have one). **Nightlife** is basically whatever happens in the restaurants attached to the hotels – gypsy music, singing or disco depending on pot luck – in Braşov as in the rest of Romania. **Concerts** (mostly of classical music) are cheap, and generally sold out at the *Gh. Dima Philharmonic* on Str. Ciucaş. So if you're interested in them, or in the **Puppet Theatre** on the same street, make bookings beforehand at 4, Str. Republicii.

Mount Tîmpa and Poiana-Braşov

Forested heights half-surround old Braşov, the closest at hand being **Mount Tîmpa** (967m), accessible by cable-car or by various paths which wind up to the summit. At the top you can enjoy a superb view of the old town and, by walking to the other side of the ridge, the neighbouring valley. The *Panoramic* restaurant is open daily from 9am-10pm.

The Alpine resort of **POIANA-BRAŞOV**, 10km from town (bus #20 from central park), is spectacularly dominated by Mount Postăvru, where one can go **skiing** between December and March on easy runs (*Intim* & *Drum Roşu*) or steep ones such as *Lupului* or *Sub-Telereric*. Skiing lessons are organised by the **tourist office** in the *Hotel Sport*, who also supply guides for **mountaineering** all the year round. Skiing **equipment** can be hired at the *Ciucaş* and *Teleferic* hotels or at the Sport, where they also rent out climbing gear. All Poiana-Braşov's hotels are dear, so *Zimbrul campsite* or the two cabanas are the only cheapish **places to stay**. Both *chalets*, on the high slopes of Mt. Cristianu (1,960m), can be reached by gondola or cable car, but beds should be reserved beforehand at the tourist office here or in town. What the hotels *are* useful for is their services: **massages & sauna** at the Alpin, Teleferic and Soimul; **tennis** courts and equipment from the Poiana; and **kindergartens** at the Teleferic and Bradul (9am-5pm; overnight at the Ciucaş). The resort's **restaurants** (10am-12pm) go in for 'folk' architecture and cuisine, as you'd expect with names like *Şura Dacilor* (Dacians' Shed), *Vînatorul* (Hunter) and *Coliba Haiducilor* (Outlaws' Hut); while an orchestra and dancing are included at the *Capra Neagră*, open until 1am. The Teleferic's **disco** runs from 10pm-4am, electricity supplies permitting.

Travelling on from Braşov

Braşov is one of Romania's most important railway junctions, and from here long hauls run up to Baia Mare (see the Maramureş Chapter) by way of Băile Tuşnad, Miercurea Ciuc and Gheorghieni – the 'Székely Land' described on p.341. **Trains** following this route pass through *Hărman* and *Prejmer* (see below) and DEDA, the place to change trains **for Tîrgu Mureş.**

However, the most useful lines are those which run northwest **to Sighişoara** and then on **to Cluj**; and westwards alongside the Făgăraş Mountains **to Sibiu.** Details of Sighişoara (p.338) and the Făgăraş route (p.348) appear later in this chapter. Another useful – though minor – line heads southwest to Zărneşti, by way of Rîşnov whence there are **buses to Bran Castle** (see following section). It's also worth asking about direct buses from Braşov's *Autogară*, outside the railway station.

Motorists planning excursions should tank up at a *PECO* station (along Str. Lungă or the Făgăraş & Bucharest highways), and consult the *Romanian Automobile Club* (2, Str. Coresi) if planning to visit anywhere off the beaten track.

AROUND BRAŞOV: 'DRACULA'S CASTLE', HĂRMAN AND PREJMER

Bran is situated only 28km from Braşov, in the beautiful Bîrsa depression, but getting there by public transport requires some perseverance. Assuming you don't opt for one of ONT's **organised** excursions, start by catching the early morning train (currently departing at 8.32am) for **RÎŞNOV**. A ruined C14

peasant citadel crowns one of the fir-covered hills that surround the town, but whether you'll have time to climb up to view it depends on when the daily bus leaves Rîsnov for Bran. The 'bus terminal' is the muddy lumberyard beside the railway station, and when I was here the bus departed as soon as it was full, well before the advertised time of 1pm.

The small town of **BRAN** commands the pass of the same name. Formerly the main way into Wallachia until the opening up of the Predeal Pass, a castle was built here in 1377 to safeguard this vital route. What's now billed as **'DRACULA'S CASTLE'** has only tenuous associations with Vlad the Impaler – it's likely he attacked it during one of his raids on the Bîrsa Land – but the hyperbole is forgivable as Bran really looks like a vampire count's residence. Perched on a rocky massif, it rises in tiers of towers and ramparts from amongst the woods, against a glorious mountain background. The scariest experience is climbing the steep, dark stairway just inside, though since an American tourist dropped dead of a heart attack, the staff have stopped hiding in chests (not coffins, alas), which they used to swing open menacingly.

A warren of 'spiral stairs, ghostly nooks and secret chambers' overhangs the courtyard; filled with elaborately carved four-poster beds, throne-like chairs and portraits of grim-faced boyars and voivodes. Despite its medieval aspect, most of the interior actually dates from a conversion job early this century, the work of a 'crazed old architect' hired by Edinburgh-born **Queen Marie of Romania**. A grandaughter of Queen Victoria married to Prince Ferdinand in 1892, she soon rebelled against the confines of court life in Bucharest – riding unattended through the streets, pelting citizens with roses during the carnival, and appointing herself a colonel of the Red Hussars (*Roşiori*). Marie's popularity soared after she organised cholera camps in the Balkan war and appeared at the Paris peace conference in 1919 to announce that 'Romania needs a face, and I have come to show mine', and Ferdinand (who felt that 'some spring was broken' within him), indulged her passion for collecting castles. Marie called Bran a 'pugnacious little fortress', but whether because of her spirit pervading the rooms or the profusion of flowers in the yard, it seemed to me a welcoming abode, at odds with its foreboding exterior. In the grounds are some old peasant buildings and an **Ethnographic Museum** displaying folk costumes, many of them from Marie's (regular) wardrobe.

Across the road, beyond a tiny park and river, the *Castelul Bran cabana* offers double **rooms** for about 70 lei and a long and varied menu. However the kitchen only produces sausages in the mornings, and chicken – *pui* a full half-carcase – thereafter; so if you want a fancier meal or room, go to the costlier hotel on the Braşov side of town. But they do serve large cheap brandies.

Hikes, scenery and the 'Nedeia of the Mountains'

Mountains dominate Bran: skyscraping peaks and escarpments arising from wooded slopes and defiles, striped with crazily angled alpine meadows which ascend beyond one's sight. To the east is the almost sheer back of the Bucegi range, while to the west, gentler slopes run up to Piatra Craiului, a narrow ridge at the eastern extremity of the Făgăraş Mountains. From Bran it takes about 8hrs to climb the path **to Mount Omu in the Bucegi**, where there's a cabana. The Piatra Craiului is easier to reach from ZARNEŞTI (accessible by train from Rişnov and Braşov, or a 3km side road from Bran); a fairly mundane place, but only 2-3hrs walk from the *Plaiu Foii* chalet, following the Bîrsa Mare River, or slightly longer to the *Curmătura* cabana. From either place it's but a few hours' trek to **the Piatra Craiului Massif** – a karstic limestone and chalk ridge, 9km long, formerly known by the Hungarians as *Király-kö* ('Royal Rock'). There are **caves** along its eastern face, Carpathian bears, lynx, chamois and other **wildlife** hiding out here, and a rare pink flower growing on the northeastern side.

On the last Sunday of June each year, a big **peasant festival** – the *Nedeia of the Mountains* – takes place at **FUNDATA**, attracting people from three counties. The underlying purpose of the festival is to transact business: exchanges of handicrafts and livestock, and marriages. Fundata itself is one of the highest villages in Romania, situated about 14km from Bran – wait for the odd bus or hitch – at the top of the spectacular **Giuvala Pass** (1,240m). On the far side of this, the road hairpins down to the karstic Podul Dîmboviţei depression, and ultimately to Cîmpulung (p.306).

East of Braşov: Hărman and Prejmer

A short train ride north-eastwards from Braşov are two communes, Hărman and Prejmer, with remarkable **fortress-churches**. Though the Magyars occasionally fortified their places of worship and the Moldavians raised walls about their monasteries, it was the Transylvanian Germans who perfected this style of architecture in the C15. Visiting the Burzen Land around Braşov on the eve of the Second World War, Elizabeth Kyle found churches in the Saxon villages prepared for siege as in the times of Sultan Süleyman and Vlad the Impaler.

HĂRMAN (formerly known as *Honigberg*) still looks much as she described it; situated 'in a wide and lovely valley, its houses arranged in tidy squares off the main street which sweeps up towards the grim fortress that closes the vista'. Inside the fortified outer walls, wooden staircases lead to the rows of 'Meal Rooms' (*Speisesaal*), where each family stored a loaf from every baking plus other supplies. Here, Kyle encountered a Saxon fraulein wearing the high, brimless *borten* connoting maidenhood, who 'flung open the door, and immediately a mingled stench of ancient cheeses, mouldering ham and damp flour rushed out to meet us. From the roof rows of hams were suspended on hooks. Those nearest us looked comparatively fresh, but the highest ones were green with age.' Having been informed that 'some of those hams have been hanging there 200 years', Kyle enquired why. 'Because, *Gott sei Dank*, they were not required', came the answer, 'There was no siege'.

At **PREJMER** (pronounced 'Prezh-mur'), two miles off the main road, a five-towered wall 40ft high, lined with 4 tiers of Meal Rooms, surrounds the C13 church. The entrance tower is itself protected by another fortified enclosure – the *Town Hall Courtyard* – added during the C16-C17, to which the Saxons appended an arcaded corridor or *Bakers' Courtyard* as a Baroque flourish in less perilous times. The land around Hărman was the first to be collectivised in the Braşov region(in 1950), and today Prejmer is the centre of a large agricultural cooperative, with a trout farm and textile factory.

Braşov's tourist offices organise **excursions** to both places, but on the railway you can travel further – up to **Băile Tuşnad**, set in a beautiful defile, and on to **Miercurea Ciuc**, a place of pilgrimage in the 'Székely Land' – a journey described (in reverse sequence) on p.343. Roads 11 and 10 fork up and down over the Carpathians into Moldavia, to Bacău and Buzău respectively, but public transport is effectively non-existent beyond the railheads in each valley – *Breţcu* (from Sf. Gheorghe) and *Întorsura Buzăului*.

BETWEEN BRAŞOV AND SIGHIŞOARA

Formerly known by Saxons as **the Burzen Land**, the Tîrnave plateau between Braşov and Sighişoara is dotted with the remnants of citadels and fortified churches. Though road DN13 and the railway diverge in places due to the narrowness of gorges cut by the Olt, it's fairly easy to reach at least some of the settlements en route. *Personal* trains stop at **FELDOIARA**, where the Teutonic Knights built a citadel – now in ruins – before their expulsion from Transylvania, and halt near the riverside villages of **ROTBAV** and **MĂERUŞ**, both of which have fortified churches. Beyond them the road crosses one of the wooded summits of the Perşani Mountians, rejoining the river where it emerges from a defile at Hoghiz. **RUPEA**, a small town on the railway, is dominated by a basalt hill crowned by the remains of three peasant citadels; from the hill gush springs of sulphurous, salty water. Just off the main road are **CAŢA** (near a train halt), **DRĂUŞENI** and **HOMOROD**, all with fortified churches, of which Homorod's is the largest and strongest; and **SASCHIZ** ('Saxons'), where a hilltop citadel looks down on the village's fortified church. Entering the Tîrnava Mare Valley you'll pass **ALBEŞTI**, where the poet Petőfi was killed (p.342), followed in short order by my favourite Transylvanian town, Sighişoara.

SIGHIŞOARA

A forbidding silhouette of battlements and needle spires looms over SIGHIŞOARA as the sun descends behind the hills of the Tîrnava Mare Valley, and it seems fitting that this was the birthplace of Vlad Ţepeş 'The Impaler' – the man known to posterity as Dracula. Visually archaic even by Romanian standards, Sighişoara makes the perfect introduction to Transylvania: especially as the *Pannonia*, *Orient* and *Balt-Orient* express trains stop here during daylight, enabling travellers to break the long journey between Budapest and Bucharest. Arriving at the station it's best to seek **accommodation** first. The *Hotel Steaua* (12, Str. Gheorghiu-Dej) has doubles for 288 and 388 lei; *Hula Danes* – 4km along the Mediaş road – offers bungalows and tent space; but I'd recommend the campsite and chalets on the hilltop overlooking the station. An underpass leads to Str. Primăverii on the opposite side of the tracks where you can find the footpath to the summit.

The Citadel dominates the town from a rocky massif whose slopes support a jumble of ancient, leaning houses, their windows sited to cover the steps leading up from Piaţa 23 August to the main gateway. Above rises the mighty **Clock Tower** where, at the stroke of midnight, a new wooden figure emerges

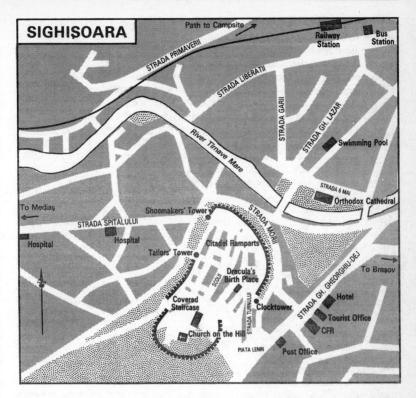

SIGHIŞOARA

from the belfry to mark the change of day. (Tuesday the day of Mars is represented by a soldier; Friday by Venus, to whom a cherub profers a mirror; and so on.) The tower was founded in the C14 when Sighişoara became a free town controlled by craft guilds – each of which had to finance the construction of a bastion and defend it during wartime – and rebuilt after earthquakes and fire in the 1670s. Originally a Roman garrison town known as *Castrum sex* (Fort Six), Sighişoara waxed rich on the proceeds of trade with Moldavia and Wallachia, as the tower's **museum** (Tuesday-Sunday 9am-3pm) attests. Judging by their moneybags, strongboxes and regalia, the burghers were a cautious, haughty bunch – and mainly Magyar or German to boot. Romanians – or Vlachs as they were then called – became inferior citizens in Transylvanian towns following edicts passed in 1540. These excluded Vlachs from public office and forbad them to live in townhouses with chimneys, or windows overlooking the streets, and also prohibited them from wearing furs, embroidered dress, shoes or boots.

In a two-storey house (nr.6) within the shadow of the Clock Tower in 1431, or thereabouts, a woman whose name is lost to posterity gave birth to a child christened Vlad, who in later life earned the title of 'The Impaler'. Abroad, he's better known as **Dracula**, which can be translated as 'Son of the Devil', or more accurately as 'Son of the Dragon' – referring to his father, **Vlad Dracul**, whom Sigismund of Hungary made a knight of the Order of the Dragon for his prowess against the Turks. When Vlad Jr. was born, Vlad Dracul was merely the guard commander of the mountain passes into Wallachia; but in 1436 he secured the princely throne and moved his family to the court at Tîrgovişte. Young Vlad's privileged childhood there ended eight years later, when he and his brother Radu were sent to Anatolia as hostages for Vlad Dracul's good behavior. There, they lived in daily fear of the silken cord with which the Ottoman's strangled dignitaries; Radu sleeping his way into the favours of the Sultan whilst Vlad observed the Turks' use of terror, which he would later turn against them as the Impaler. Nowadays, Vlad's birthplace contains a restaurant, and a small **museum** commemorating his life and times.

Churches are monuments to social identity in Sighişoara, as in many old Transylvanian towns. The Germans – whose importance here is past – have theirs opposite the Clock Tower, and on the hill's summit, closest to *Gott*. The former building has a stark, whitewashed interior hung with colourful carpets as in the Black Church at Braşov, and an altar like a wooden carpet-beater. The **Church on the Hill**, *Bergkirche*, is approached by an impressive **covered wooden stairway** with 175 steps and 29 landings, which ascends steeply from the far end of Str. Şcolii. Ivy-grown and massively buttressed, the Bergkirche has a roomy interior that seems austere despite the blue and canary yellow-painted vaulting (a colour-scheme 'greatly approved of by the Saxons, because it brightens everything up'). Some lovely stone tombs lodged near the entrance are a harbinger of the **German cemetery**, a melancholy, weed-choked mass of graves spilling over the hilltop beside the ruined citadel walls. Tending the church (open 12am-1pm) are an old couple who inhabit the former Ropemakers' Tower together with their pigs and poultry. Nine of the fourteen original **towers** survive, the most impressive being the hexagonal *Turnul Cizmanilor* (Shoemakers' Tower) and the *Turnul Croitorilor* or western gateway formerly defended by the Tailors' Guild.

The **lower town** is less picturesque than the citadel, but there's a nice ambience around the shabby centre – consisting of Piaţa Lenin and Str. Gheorghiu-Dej – where townsfolk gather to consume grilled sausages, *ţuică* and watery beer, conversing in Romanian, Magyar and antiquated German. The number of hang-outs is so small that it's easy to track down sporadic jazz-sax performances or impromptu singing and dancing, while any Western film – I saw the worst California pap – draws record crowds to the open-air cinema behind the main street: as much a place to get sloshed and flirt as to oggle the unattainable delights of capitalism. On **national holidays**, especially August 23, a bluesy brass band performs on the citadel's Piaţa Cetaţii, and people stream up to Dealul Gării – the hill above the railway station – with bottles and hoarded food. Gypsies arrive by cart, their hats crowned with flowers, to *bashavav*, tell fortunes and steal; and it was here that I was regaled with stories of knife-fights between the local Romanian 'Mafia' and the *Ţigani* over black market operations.

Leaving the centre, follow one of the main bridges over the Tîrnave Mare River to find the Romanian **Orthodox Cathedral** in the northern district. Its gleaming white, multifaceted façade is in striking contrast to the dark interior, where blue and orange hues dominate the small panels of the iconostasis. Close by are a pool, an antique locomotive which travelled the Sibiu-Sighişoara line between 1896-1965, and two streets leading towards the **railway and bus stations.**

Moving on: some possibilities

Enquiries at the decrepit *Autogară* seem so unrewarding that I'd advise travellers to forget about leaving Sighişoara **by bus.** Though Tîrgu Mureş is only 53km north by road DN13, many locals **hitch** rather than rely on the creaking services. En route is a fortified church at MĂGHERUS. Without private transport, travellers usually rely on **trains.** Fortunately there are frequent, albeit slow and overcrowded services along the Cluj-Blaj-Braşov-Bucharest line, with *personal* trains stopping at Aţel, Brateiu and Mediaş before COPŞA MICĂ, the place to switch trains **for Sibiu:** a route described on page 350. More challenging are the routes heading **into the eastern Carpathians,** an area formerly known as the Székely Land, which eventually lead back around **to Tîrgu Mureş** or on into Moldavia.

FROM SIGHIŞOARA INTO THE EASTERN CARPATHIANS

In the ethnic patchwork of Transylvania, the eastern Carpathians are traditionally the habitat of **the Székely*,** a people closely related to the Magyars who speak a distinctive Hungarian dialect and cherish a special historic identity. For a long time it was believed that they were the descendants of Attila's Huns – who entered the Carpathian basin in the C5, 500 years before the Magyar Conquest – but nowadays this romantic origin is considered suspect. Most modern historians and ethnographers believe that the Székely either attached themselves to the Magyars during the latter's long migration from the banks of the Don, or are simply the descendants of early Hungarians who pushed ever further into Transylvania, having been assigned the task of guarding the frontiers by King László in the C12. Whatever the truth of their origins, the Székely feel closely akin to the Magyars who, in turn, regard them as somehow embodying the finest aspects of the ancient Magyar race.

For visitors, the chief attractions of the region are likely to be the **Székely culture** and the scenery. Religion plays an important part in Székely life, as evinced by the fervour displayed at the **Whitsun festival at Miercurea Ciuc** – by a dramatic pilgrimage until this was prohibited – and the existence of Székely mystics. Traditional Székely architecture (such as carved gateways and blue-painted houses) can be seen at **Corund** where there's a **pottery market** in early August, and in smaller villages throughout the *Székelyföld* ('Székely

---

*Pronounced 'Saik-ehyy', derived from the Hungarian word *szék*, meaning 'seat' or settlement. Some writers refer to them as 'Szeklers' or 'Zeklers'.

Land' in Hungarian). **The landscape** gets increasingly dramatic as one moves through the Harghita Mountains, culminating in the Tuşnad defile and St Ana's Lake to the south, and Lacu Roşu and the Bicaz Gorges just before the borders of Moldavia.

Two basic **routes** are described in the section below – one leading through Corund and Sovata to Tîrgu Mureş, the other passing through Miercurea Ciceu and Gheorgheni, whence one can double back by rail to Tîrgu Mureş, or travel on past Lacu Roşu through the Bicaz Gorges into Moldavia.

Eastwards to Odorheiu Secuiesc and up to Corund and Sovata

For both routes the initial destination is the same – the town of Odorheiu Secuiesc, which is accessible by hitching or train from Sighişoara. Along the way is **ALBEŞTI**, where a small museum commemorates the life of the Hungarian poet **Sándor Petőfi**, who was killed nearby in battle against the Russians in 1849. As foreseen in one of his own ultra-romantic poems, Petőfi's body was never found; most likely it was trampled beyond all recognition by the Cossacks' horses. At the end of the railway line you'll find **ODORHEIU SECUIESC**, the centre of the Székelyföld, still known to many residents by its tongue-twisting Magyar name, *Székelyudvarhely*. The pretty town centre and the medieval **citadel** (Str. Horia) are the chief sights here, unless you should happen to arrive during the **Seiche festival**, which normally occurs on the first Sunday in June. Both the tourist office and the *Tîrnava Hotel* can be found on Piaţa 23 August, the main square. From Odorheiu Secuiesc, one can hope to struggle aboard a bus (terminal on Str. Tîrgului) or start hitching towards Miercurea Cuic (see the second route, described below), or do likewise but in a northerly direction. This takes you past the **baths and campsite** at BĂILE SEICHE, 3km out along the north road.

CORUND, 25km north of town, is famed for its green and brown figure **pottery**, although the stuff sold by locals along the road is blue pottery imported from the DDR. To find the real thing it's better to look for workshops in the backstreets (where there are some traditional red and green carved Székely gateways), or turn up for the big **market**, a colourful event attracting many peasants from the surrounding countryside, held around August 10-11 every year. There's supposed to be a **ruined medieval castle** on the summit of 1,062m high Firtoş Hill nearby; I didn't make it to check.

For a complete change of atmosphere, push on to **SOVATA**, a kind of Clacton in the Carpathians. Like Ocna Sibiului, it's a **bathing resort** based around a series of lakes that occupy old salt workings. A layer of fresh water on the surface of the lakes acts as an insulator so that the lower, salt water stays at a temperature of 30°C-40°C all the year round. Sovata has several hotels, but the cabana on Cireşul Hill and the campsite out east along Str. Vulturului are the cheapest **accommodation**. There are beautiful forests nearby, and a single train departs each day for TÎRGU MUREŞ (currently at 2.40pm; see p.345 for a description of the regional capital).

Miercurea Ciuc and beyond

Heading eastwards from Odorheiu Secuiesc might require some hitching since buses are so infrequent and crowded, but the prospects for this seem good.

Four kilometers from town near BRADEŞTI, a badly-surfaced road turns off towards the isolated *Harghita Mădăraş cabana* in the mountains, while further along DN13A are low-lying **BĂILE HOMOROD**, with hot springs and a cabana used by Scouts and vacationing Trade Unionists, and CĂPÎLNIŢA and VLĂHIŢA, two villages at a higher altitude with campsites (Vlăhiţa's is more developed). About 13km beyond Vlăhiţa, a turn-off to the north runs up to another resort, **HARGHITA BĂI**, which has a hotel and chalet (possibly accessible by workers' bus). Amongst the varied wildlife of the beautiful **Harghita Mountains** roundabouts, there are quite a few **bears**. I met a traveller who related hearing a roaring sound coming from a nearby village, where he found a crowd surrounding the pit normally used for disposing of animal carcasses, into which a bear had fallen. Eventually a log was lowered into the pit, up which the bear scrambled, swiping at its benefactors before lumbering off into the forest.

Assuming that you stick to DN13A and don't succumb to bears or bear-pits, you'll eventually arrive at the capital of Harghita county, **MIERCUREA CIUC**. Extensively rebuilt in concrete from the centre outwards (just sparing the **Mikó Citadel** on Str. Gh. Doja beyond the *Bradul* and *Harghita* hotels), the town's principal attractions are two events. On the third Sunday of May, there's usually a **Spring Festival** at Băile Jigodin just south of town, which provides an opportunity for the Székely to dress up in traditional costumes and make merry; whilst Whit Sunday is the time of the hallowed Székely **pilgrimage to Csíkszereda** (as Hungarian-speakers call Miercurea Ciuc). To witness this, follow Str. Coşbuc northwards until you reach the *Liceum*, then turn right and continue on for 2km to find the cloistered Catholic church run by Franciscans which is the focus for the pilgrimage. Though overnight camping and the traditional procession outside the church were banned in 1947, pilgrims garbed in black still fill the yard and church interior, singing hymns and queueing up to touch the wooden Madonna in the sanctuary. At the back are two stones – relics of ancient pagan worship – brought down from the nearby hilltop, to which people flock to sing psalms and venerate an old chapel.

From the hilltop you'll see **Székely villages** dotted across the plain – whitewashed or with the 'old blue farmsteads' that a native, far from home, declares his yearning for in a traditional Székely ballad. Hungarians sometimes describe the Székely mind as *csavaros* (literally 'propelling', but in the sense of 'penetrating'), and admiringly ascribe to them a canniness encapsulated in the expression *góbé* – meaning 'Székely rascals'. Conversely, some jokes mock their mentality, like the one about the Székely farmer driving home from the fields, who stops off at the pub. Emerging somewhat befuddled an hour later, he finds that his horse has gone and thinks, 'Hmm, either I'm Székely Zoltán and someone's stolen my nag, or I'm not and I've just found somebody's cart'. The Székely retained a nomadic, clan-based society for longer than their Magyar kindred, and were granted a large measure of autonomy and recognised as one of the three 'Nations' of Transylvania during the Middle Ages: privileges that the Habsburgs attempted to abolish, culminating in the massacre at Madéfalva (1764), which prompted many Székely to flee to Moldavia and Bucovina, where they founded new villages with names such as 'God Help Us' and 'God Receive Us'.

Travelling on from Miercurea Ciuc

Though it's worth enquiring about buses at Miercurea Ciuc's *Autogară* outside the station in the western part of town, **trains** provide a more reliable means of moving on. Services **heading south** towards Prejmer, Hărman and Brașov almost invariably stop at **BĂILE TUȘNAD** en route: a bathing resort set amidst larch and fir woods, with three hotels and a couple of bungalow-campsites. Nearby, the Olt has carved the beautiful **Tușnad defile**, just beyond which a road leads eastwards to Lacu Sf. Ana or **St Ana's Lake**. Occupying a volcanic crater on Mount Ciumatu (3hrs walk from the Tușnad spa), this was the site of a nationalist demonstration by 6,000 Magyars during the 1970s, which the local Securitate kept a secret from their superiors. Ceaușescu reportedly learned of it only because his son Nicu heard the story from a hitch-hiker whom he picked up whilst driving his red Jag, and was furious with the Securitate. For descriptions of Prejmer, Hărman and Brașov, see p.337 and p.330 of this chapter.

Nine kilometres **northeast of Miercurea Ciuc** lies **FRUMOASA**, one of the Csángó communes described in the chapter on Moldavia, which you can probably reach by bus or hitching. Other Csángó settlements in the Trotuș Valley may also be reached by train from CICEU, one stop north along the line that runs from Miercurea up to Gheorgheni. The largest one, **GHIMEȘ-FĂGET**, has a **fair** on January 20-21.

Heading north by rail without changing at Ciceu, the next main stop is **GHEORGHENI**, where arriving trains are met by buses to spare passengers the half hour's walk into the town centre. This, Piața Liberății, has 'Zopf' style buildings, redolent of the town's era under Austro-Hungarian rule (when it was called *Gyergyoszentmiklós*). The town's **tourist office** should be able to confirm the precise dates of the Gurghiu festival and the Artists' summer camp at Lazar Castle (see below).

Lacu Roșu and the Mureș Valley

The 'Red Lake' or **Lacu Roșu** lies in a small depression 25km east of Gheorgheni. It was formed in 1838 when a landslide dammed the River Bicaz, and the tips of a few pines still protrude from the water, which is rich in trout. Surrounded by lovely scenery and blessed by a yearly average of 1,800 hours of sunshine, this is an ideal place to relax for anyone planning to cross the Carpathians **into Moldavia** through the wild BICAZ GORGES (p.398). There are bungalows, villas and a campsite, although nobody seems to mind if you just pitch camp anywhere. Unfortunately, there are only three buses a day to the lake from Gheorgheni, and the last one departs around 9am, passing another campsite 4km from town beside road 12C.

If you're not heading on into Moldavia it's best to follow the Mureș Valley **towards Tîrgu Mureș** – a semi-circular route via DN15 or the railway. 6km north of Gheorgheni, the commune of **LĂZAREA** is notable for **Lazar Castle**, situated just below the one time Franciscan Monastery whose white tower is visible from the railway station. The castle's fine Renaissance hall and frescoed façade are being gradually restored by artists who hold a **summer camp** here each year, staying in the monastery cloister and leaving their work to adorn the nearby **sculpture park**. Trains continue on to **TOPLIȚA**, a bathing resort

26km west of **BORSEC**, a similar establishment with a campsite that's rather overcrowded and run down. To the north of the Mureş Valley rise the wild, unpopulated **Căliman Mountains**: a paradise for hunters, where one can walk for days without meeting a soul. In the narrow, rugged defile between Topliţa and Deda, retreating German soldiers made a vain attempt to ambush the advancing Red Army in 1944.

The only noteworthy fact about **DEDA** is that it's the place to change **trains for Tîrgu Mureş**; six daily slow trains travelling in that direction provide the means to reach the commune of **BRÎNCOVENEŞTI**. Founded on the site of a castrum with a five-towered **castle** dating from the C14 which Sava Armaşul, a lieutenant of Michael the Brave, once owned, Brîncoveneşti celebrates its most important harvest with the **Cherry Fair**. Villagers wear their finest costumes for the *Culesul cireşelor*, which normally takes place on the first Sunday of June. **REGHIN**, the first proper town beyond, is ringed by factories which have dispelled seasonal unemployment (traditionally the bane of rural life) but done nothing for the town's appearance; and the only incentive to stop here is a couple of old churches and the possibility of **buses** to surrounding villages from the terminal on Str. Gării. The objects of the exercise are two villages some 20km east of town: Gurghiu and Hodac.

Splendid folk costumes and decorous coquetry are the order of the day during the **Girl Fair** or *Tîrgul de fete* at **GURGHIU** on the second Sunday of May; whilst the economic underpinnings of matrimony are reaffirmed during the **'Buying back of the Wives'** at **HODAC** (6km down the road, then follow a turn-off northwards for 1km) on the second Sunday in June. To guard against a wasted journey, it's best to enquire at the tourist office in Reghin (1, Str. Mihai Viteazul), Gheorgheni or Tîrgu Mureş in case the dates of these festivals change. The nearest accommodation is in Tîrgu Mureş, but there's no reason why you can't camp wild near the villages.

TÎRGU MUREŞ

'A stupid militarist town', said Andrei Mira of **TÎRGU MUREŞ**'s pre-war incarnation, referring to the military academy here (now a pharmaceutical college), and to the waves of chauvinistic nationalism sadly prevalent throughout Transylvanian history. It's an inaccurate characterisation of Tîrgu Mureş today, but indicative of the roots of ethnic conflict that underlie several buildings and institutions in this attractivly modernised town on the banks of the Mureş.

Downtown, grandiose buildings awash with cupolas and fancy tiling dominate the length of **Piaţa Trandafirilor**, which bears a passing resemblance to Prague's Wenseslas Square. Flanking the Soviet war memorial at its lower end are two fantastic piles constructed in 1912, typical of the late imperial era when a self-consciously 'Hungarian' style of architecture (exemplified by Ödön Lechner's work in Kecskemét) reflected Budapest's policy of Magyarizing Transylvania within the framework of the Dual Monarchy. Beneath a huge tower mighty as a Saturn V rocket, the rooftops of the former Town Hall (now housing regional Party headquarters) blaze with almost psychedelic, polychromatic tiling. Its twin, the **Palace of Culture**, looms and glints nearby,

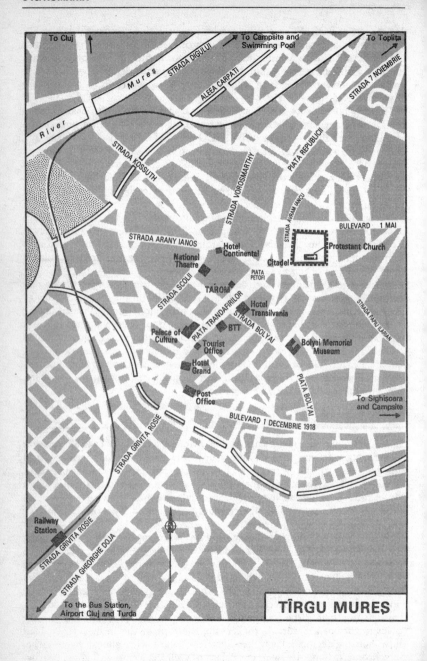

To Cluj

To Campsite and Swimming Pool

To Toplița

M u r e s

STRADA DIGULUI

ALEEA CARPATI

STRADA 7 NOIEMBRIE

River

STRADA KOSSUTH

STRADA VOROSMARTHY

PIATA REPUBLICII

STRADA AVRAM IANCU

BULEVARD 1 MAI

STRADA ARANY IANOS

Hotel Continental

Protestant Church

National Theatre

Citadel

PIATA PETOFI

STRADA SCOLII

TAROM

STRADA PAPU ILARIAN

Hotel Transilvania

PIATA TRANDAFIRILOR

STRADA BOLYAI

BTT

Palace of Culture

Bolyai Memorial Museum

Tourist Office

Hotel Grand

PIATA BOLYAI

Post Office

To Sighișoara and Campsite

BULEVARD 1 DECEMBRIE 1918

STRADA GRIVITA ROSIE

Railway Station

STRADA GRIVITA ROSIE

STRADA GHEORGHE DOJA

To the Bus Station, Airport Cluj and Turda

TÎRGU MUREŞ

and both were recently and sumptuously restored. Inside the Palace you'll find a grandly frescoed hall; a strikingly purple theatre; a **Hall of Mirrors** with stained glass windows illustrating songs and myths (guide tapes available in French & German); lotus-shaped chairs reserved for wedding ceremonies; a library and the **County Museum**. The latter's Ethnographic section is colourful, while the historical exhibits emphasise the town's links with Moldavia, Michael the Brave and anti-Habsburg fighters such as Avram Iancu. Amongst the portraits, look out for the careworn face of György Dózsa (**Gheorghe Doja** in Romanian), a local Székler mercenary in the crusade launched by Archbishop Bákocz, who thrust himself to the forefront when the peasants' crusade became a radical anti-feudal uprising in 1514. After the rebellion's suppression, the aristocrats led by János Zápolyai arranged a particularly ghastly execution for Dózsa and his followers at Timişoara (p.443).

Beginning with the Post Office at the bottom of Piaţa Eroilor Sovietici, you'll find almost every place of use or interest along the main drag. On the right hand side are the *Grand* and *Transilvania* hotels, with bars and restaurants where T-shirted travellers aren't welcomed; the **tourist office** and **BTT**; and the *Mureşul* restaurant whose smoky upstairs bar is the place to hang out almost by default. The opposite side of the piaţa boasts of the 'Toldalagy House' (nr.11), and hosts TAROM, a 24-hour pharmacy, and a line of cafés surrounding the best-stocked supermarket I've encountered in Romania. Approaching the square's upper end, architectural bombast rides again. Just as the Magyars built grand administrative structures to emphasise their control over *Marosvásárhely* (the town's Hungarian name), so the large **Orthodox Cathedral** in a neo-Byzantine style was the Romanians' riposte after 1918 – in Cornforth and Lindsay's words, 'shouldering aside the more modest Baroque church of the Hungarian Catholics that faces it from the side'.

Further up and just off to the right is Piaţa Petőfi, where the old 'Teleki House' confronts the walls of the Tîrgu Mureş **Citadel**. Near the square, a small gate permits entry into a secluded C15 Protestant Church, but the larger gateway farther uphill is *verboten*: the Romanian army still occupy most of the fortress and don't appreciate sightseers. Talking of visitors dropping in, a bizarre rumour had it that Romania's ex-King Michael landed by helicopter in Tîrgu Mureş sometime in the 1970s. I'm sure it never happened, though a royal family does still pretend in exile.

Despite its longstanding role as a garrison town, Tîrgu Mureş takes pride in its cultural traditions, though here too, ethnic grievances bubble beneath the surface. While native Hungarians like **Farkas Bolyai** and his son János – founders of non-Euclidean geometry – receive due credit in a museum at 17, Str. Bolyai, contemporary Magyar culture here is being steadily undermined. Since the abolition of the 'Hungarian Autonomous Region' in 1968, the town's Magyar-language theatre has been merged with the **National Theatre** (Piaţa Teatrului) under a Romanian director; primary and secondary education in Hungarian have been virtually eliminated; and unauthorised expressions of ethnic culture – such as giving children non-Romanian names – invite administrative reprisals.

Practicalities

Most trains approaching from the direction of Deda halt briefly at *Tîrgu Mureş Nord* before pulling into the main station, and if you're planning to camp (by far the cheapest option) that's where to get off. *Strand* **camping** is near an expensive swimming pool between the canal and the Mureş; accessible on foot from T.M. Nord; by bus #4/#14 from the centre; *'Estival Cars'* from Piaţa Petőfi (hourly, Monday-Saturday 10am-7pm, Sunday 12am-8pm); or bus #14 from the **main station**. Another campsite, *Stejeris*, lies alongside the Sighişoara road, Str. Corunca. Both **hotels** on the main square charge $40 for a single and $53 for a double, whilst the *Continental* on Piaţa Teatrului whacks on a few dollars for good measure. However, there are **places to eat** to accommodate anyone's pocket on Piaţa Trandafirilor, and *BTT* might just rustle up **dormitory beds** during summer vacation (roughly, late June-end of August). Cars can be repaired and filled with **petrol** at the top end of Str. Gh. Doja, while *ACR* should help with **motoring information**, and *CFR* with **railway bookings** (both on Piaţa Teatrului).

The autogară on Str. Gh. Doja doesn't offer much hope of **buses** to Cluj, and even the tourist office acknowledged that **hitching** was more feasible (take buses #2/#14/#17 to their terminal beside a huge chemical plant, and pray you get a lift before asphixiation occurs). **Trains** are more reliable, but awkwardly timed and routed. Currently, a train runs to Sovata in the early morning and mid-evening, but there are more frequent services towards Războieni (change for Cîmpia Turzii/CLUJ) and Deda (on the Braşov-SATU MARE line).

THE FĂGĂRAŞ MOUNTAINS BETWEEN BRAŞOV AND SIBIU

Beyond the Petroşani Mountains northwest of Braşov, DN1 and the railway follow the River Olt across the Transylvanian plateau towards Sibiu, parting company at Turnu Roşu (Podu Olt station), where the river turns southwards, descending into Wallachia through the Red Tower Pass. For much of the journey, a fringe of ice-caps along the southern horizon delineates the **Făgăraş Mountains**, whence snow-melt and water from the lakes that locals call the 'eyes of the sea' feeds the Olt's tributaries. Seen at a distance, the Făgăraş range is less impressive than the Bucegi or Harghita, and walking amongst them is really the only way to experience the beauty of these mountains. Composed mainly of crystalline schists with occasional limestone outcrops, a series of pyramid-shaped peaks linked by narrow ridges harbours more than 70 lakes at heights of 5,900-7,500 feet. Up to 6,000 feet the mountainsides are covered with forests sheltering deer, Carpathian bears, chamois and other wildlife, while above this line, snow can lie heavily until the end of May.

Most footpaths are well marked and fairly simple to follow with a *Munţii Făgăraşului* map or (better still for German speakers) an *Unsere Berge Reihe (nr.32)*, which can usually be bought in Braşov, Făgăraş or Sibiu. If you're planning any **hikes**, reserve Cabana beds through OJT and go well provisioned with food.

Almost invariably, the starting point is one of the settlements along the valley, where *cursa* and *personal* (but not fast) trains disgorge peasants returning from shopping trips, and groups of climbers. From **ARPAŞU de Jos/de Sus** and VICTORIA (south of the UCEA halt), paths marked with triangles lead past the *Arpaş* and *Turnuri* chalets up to *Pidragu* Cabana (2,136m) in about 10-11hrs. The following day you can walk eastwards or westwards to Romania's highest peaks, **Moldoveanu** (2,544m) and **Negoiu** (2,535m); head on to Lake Bîlea, returning to Arpaşu via the Bîlea Waterfall and chalet; or contemplate some **longer hikes**. From Podragu it's 9-10hrs over the mountains down to *Gumpăna* chalet at the northern end of 16km-long **Lake Vidra**; while on the lake's southeastern shore are two more cabanas and the beginning of a D-road down through the gorges into Wallachia, where you'll find the **ruins of Dracula's Castle** perched high above the valley just beyond Căpăţîneni (p.310). Alternatively you can head eastwards – following the red-striped path – past the small lakes near Mt. Dara and on into the Piatra Craiului range (p.337).

But there's more to the Făgăraş region than just mountains. A predominantly Romanian population with a leavening of Saxons gave rise to characteristic local art forms, such as the **icons on glass** still painted at ARPAŞU, and found in the C15 church at **VAD** (4km by minor road from Şercaia, at the Braşov end of the valley). About the same distance from Vad, a clearing in the *Dumbrava Vadului* oak forest is carpeted with **daffodils** each summer – a beautiful sight. Villagers still dress up in embroidered costumes for **New Year celebrations** – particularly at **ŞERCAIA, ARPAŞ, PORUMBACU DE JOS** and **PORUMBACU DE SUS** – and gather en masse together with Saxon dancers from Tilişca for the **Flowers of the Olt festival** (*Florile Oltului*) at **AVRIG** on the second Sunday of April.

Other sights include the ruins of Transylvania's first monastery, established at CÎRŢA in 1202, and the town of Făgăraş itself. Between 1366-1460, **FĂGĂRAŞ** and the surrounding region (or Duchy of Amlaş) were under Wallachian rule, and the sturdy **fortress** distinguishing the town centre was raised on the ashes of an earlier citadel, sacked by Dracula in revenge for the loss of his fiefdom during the course of a murderous rampage from the Red Tower Pass towards the Bîrsa Land. Despite the town's partial modernisation, the old custom of **ritual insults** still prevails. On a certain day at the beginning of summer, townsfolk who bear grudges or grievances assemble on the hilltop overlooking town, and shout insults at their opponents; the aim being to vent their spleen, and hopefully become reconciled thereafter. The town's **tourist office** is on Piaţa Republicii, and its **hotel** on Mihai Viteazul Square, whilst **buses** from the terminal on Str. Sibiu might enable you to reach neighbouring communes.

Beyond Avrig the road forks: one branch leading on past Veş **to Sibiu**; the other veering off to TĂLMACIU, the junction with DN7/E15 which descends through Turnu Roşu (Red Tower) Pass **into Wallachia**. Travelling by rail, switch trains at PODU OLT for Wallachia; services in the direction of PIATRA OLT pass several of the Monasteries in the Olt Valley (see p.311).

FROM SIGHIŞOARA TO SIBIU

An alternative approach to Sibiu is to follow the Tîrnave Mare River westwards from Sighişoara. From DN14 or a train window, you'll see buffaloes pulling wagons or wallowing, watched by their drovers; and glimpse the spires of **fortified churches in villages** situated off the main road. With a car or bike it's possible to reach **BIERTAN**, **RICHIŞU** and **MOŞNA** to the south and **CURCIU** to the north (all by minor roads); local personal trains (about every 2hrs) enable you to stop at **BRATIEU**, where there's an especially fine church and a **festival**, *Pe Mureş şi pe Tîrnave*, which occurs some time during June.

The only proper town en route is **MEDIAŞ**, which despite the tanneries and chemical works feeding off the Tîrnava Valley's methane deposits, gets more prepossessing the further one ventures from the railway and bus stations on Str. Unirii. Follow Str. Pomperilor to find the town centre, Piaţa Republicii, characterised by its subdued café life, queues for watermelons, and the **Evangelical Church** with a 250ft belltower slightly askew. The C14-C15 church is surrounded by store rooms and high ramparts with towers (one of which served as a gaol for Dracula in 1467), and is a citadel in all but name. Originally an Iron Age and then a Roman settlement, Mediaş – or *Medgyes* – was a predominantly Hungarian town for many centuries, walled and with gate towers (one still remains halfway down Str. Lenin). After 1918 it began to develop an industrial and Romanian character, stemming from the construction here of Transylvania's first gas pipeline, and the severance of the region from Hungary at the end of the First World War; an inkling of which can be gleaned from the museum at 46, Str. Vitorului (parallel to Str. Lenin). Near the central square you'll find **ONT** (1, Str. Roth) and the **hotel** (4, Str. Rozmarinului), together with a *Lacto-Vegetarian* restaurant opposite the *Progresu* cinema. I was told that camping wild in the surrounding hills is okay, and that some picturesque villages lie along the road to **AGNITA**, an old Saxon settlement (*Agnethelm*) with a grimly-towered church. With patience, you should find buses heading towards Agnita at the *autogară* beside the train station.

Otherwise it's on to sooty **COPŞA MICĂ**, the centre of the lamp-black industry since 1936, and probably Romania's most polluted town. Hopefully you shouldn't have to endure its noxiousness for too long whilst waiting for one of the six daily **trains to Sibiu**, most of which stop at the bathing resort of OCNA SIBIULUI (p.356) en route.

SIBIU

'I rubbed my eyes in amazement', wrote Walter Starkie of **SIBIU** in 1929. 'The town where I found myself did not seem to be in Transylvania, for it had no Romanian or Hungarian characteristics: the narrow streets and old gabled houses made me think of Nuremberg'. Nowadays the illusion is harder to sustain, belied by burgeoning high-rise suburbs, Ceauşescu banners and food queues, but the town is still startling. Sibiu's older quarters could serve to illustrate the Brothers Grimm, while many people speak German, pray in Evangelical, not Orthodox churches, sing their *leider* seriously, and cherish links with faraway Germany.

Hermannstadt

Not a few residents still call Sibiu *Hermannstadt*, the name given by the Transylvanian **Saxons** to their chief city. Like Braşov and other towns, it was founded by Germans whom the Hungarian King Géza II invited to colonise strategic regions of Transylvania in 1143. The first settlers were mainly from Flanders and the Rhineland, but with subsequent waves of emigration, the appellation *Sachseh* stuck. *Siebenbürgen*, the German name for Transylvania, derives from the original 'seven towns' raised by the Saxons, of which Hermannstadt became the most powerful. Clannish, hard working and thrifty, its inhabitants prospered and came to dominate trade in Transylvania and Wallachia, forming exclusive guilds under royal charter and exploiting the 'dimmer-witted and carefree'. (A separate colonisation of the Bîrsa Land by the Teutonic Knights in 1211 ended with their expulsion for trying to establish a state within a state).

Rich and privileged under the feudal system, the Saxons were envied by others and knew it. Their literature and proverbs are marked by admonitions to beware of outsiders – for example:

> Trust yourself to only one –
> 'Tis not wise to trust to none;
> Better, though, to have no friend
> Than on many to depend.

and

> When I have both gold and wine,
> Many men are brothers mine;
> when the money it is done,
> and the wine has ceased to run
> Then the brothers, too, are gone.

– whilst a plethora of **fortifications** testifies to their historical caution. Mindful of the destruction of their first citadel by the Tartars in 1241, the townsfolk surrounded themselves with walls and forty towers during the C15; built of brick since firearms were then transforming siege warfare, they were so mighty as to withstand the Turks, who dubbed Sibiu the 'Red Town' for the colour of its walls and the blood shed attempting to breach them. Behind these *Cetăţii* the Saxons linked their buildings and streets with tunnels and gateways, and set heavily-grated windows to cover the stairways and corners where intruders might be ambushed. Alas for the Saxons, their citadels were no protection against the tide of history, which steadily eroded their influence after the C18, and put them in a devilish position during the Second World War. Although many bitterly resented Hitler's award of northern Transylvania to Hungary in 1940 (Saxons stoned a *Gaulieter*'s car in Braşov), others relished their new status as *Volksdeutsche* and embraced Nazism (not least one Artur Phelps, who became an SS General and Himmler's brother-in-law). Thousands of them were conscripted into – or volunteered for – the Waffen-SS; in particular the *Prinz Eugen* division, whose atrocities in Yugoslavia inevitably brought odium upon the entire German community after the war.

Sibiu today

Notwithstanding the vestigial fortifications and guilt, Sibiu doesn't seem a grim town. Many of the houses are painted sky blue, red, apricot or pea green, and cafés and restaurants do roaring trade along the length of the promenade. To reach **the centre** from the main railway and bus terminals, cross Piața Gării – where a small chapel with a stone crucifix attracts lots of worshippers – and follow Str. Gen. Magheru until you hit the **Piața Republicii**. This is the 'Great Square', traditionally the hub of public life, surrounded by the renovated premises of C16-C17 merchants, whose acumen and thrift were proverbial. How galled the Saxons must have been by the visit of Prince István Báthori, who obliged them to 'provide brandy and sulphur' for treating his dogs' paws, and wine 'at a price fixed by the Prince himself'. One can imagine sullen mutterings within the **Councillers' Tower** (*Turnul Sfatului*), which forms a phalanx together with a Catholic church, partially blocking access to the 'Little Square' behind them. You can cut through a gate-tower nearby the Turnul Sfatului (which contains Sibiu's history museum), or walk around the corner past the Baroque Brukenthal palace (see below) into the Piața Griviței.

Here the **Evangelical Cathedral** – a massive *hallekirche* raised during the C14-C15 – dominates its neighbours; confirming – together with the town's Theological Institute – Sibiu's pre-eminence as a centre of the Lutheran faith, to which about 150,000 Transylvanian Germans belong. According to their bishop, Albert Klein, devotion runs deep amongst the Saxons, especially in the villages. The day before Communion, neighbours meet to reconcile their quarrels and forgive one another, and those who neither seek nor grant forgiveness are excluded from the rite. The cathedral's superb choir is best heard on Sundays. Its crypt contains the *tomb of Mihnea the Bad*, Dracula's son and voivode of Wallachia for one year only, who was stabbed to death outside after attending Mass in 1510 (when the building was a Catholic place of worship).

Nearby the church, an alley sneaks off to join the **Passage of Stairs** (*Pasajul scărilor*) behind the hill, which descends into the lower town overshadowed by arches and the medieval citadel wall. Piața 6 Martie – the Little Square's northern extension – bumps up against the old Town Hall at nr. 31, where an adjoining gate-tower leads through into **Str. Iancu**, a street pock-marked with medieval windows, doorways and turrets. Just to the east – within bristling distance of the former Furriers and Skinners' Guildhouse (nr.21) – Str. Karl Marx runs down through a kind of miniature urban canyon spanned by an elegant wrought-iron *Podul de Fier*. Affectionately nicknamed the 'Municipal', it's also known as the **'Liars' Bridge'** because of a legend that no one can tell a lie whilst standing upon it without the structure collapsing; Ceaușescu gave a speech from the bridge during a visit to Sibiu. Down in the rambling **lower town** are the octagonal-based **Tanners' Tower** (Str. Pulberăriei), a surviving tower from the now-demolished Ocna Gate (Piața Engels), and a busy food market on Piața Cibin beside the river.

Sibiu's **promenade** occurs between Piața Republicii and the Piața Unirii,

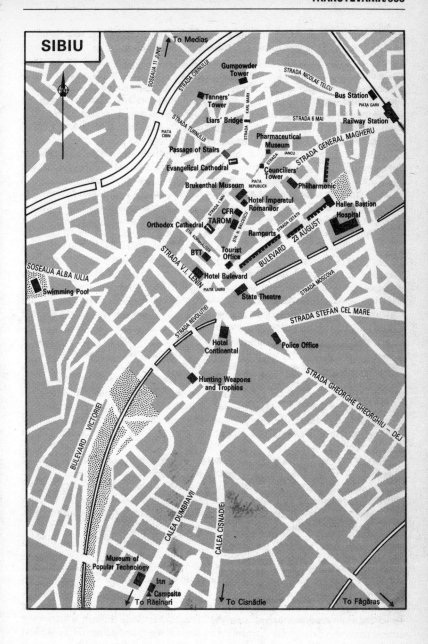

SIBIU

To Medias

SOSEAUA 11 IUNIE

STRADA CIBINULUI

STRADA NICOLAE TELCU

Gumpowder
Tower

Tanners'
Tower

Bus Station

PIAŢA GARII

STRADA TURNULUI

Liars' Bridge

STRADA 6 MAI

Railway Station

PIAŢA
CIBIN

STRADA KARL MARX

Pharmaceutical
Museum

IANCU

STRADA GENERAL MAGHERU

Passage of Stairs

Evangelical Cathedral

Councillers
Tower

Brukenthal Museum

STRADA
REPUBLICII

PIAŢA
REPUBLICII

Philharmonic

Hotel Imperatul
Romanilor

STRADA 1 MAI

CFR

Haller Bastion

TAROM

STR. N. BALCESCU

Hospital

Orthodox Cathedral

STRADA CETATII

STR. KOMNHAUSER

Ramparts

23 AUGUST

BTT

Tourist
Office

BULEVARD

STRADA V.I. LENIN

Hotel Bulevard

PIAŢA UNIRII

STRADA MOSCOVA

SOSEAUA ALBA IULIA

State Theatre

Swimming Pool

STRADA STEFAN CEL MARE

STRADA REVOLUTIEI

Hotel
Continental

Police Office

BULEVARD VICTORIEI

Hunting Weapons
and Trophies

STRADA GHEORGHE GHEORGHIU - DEJ

CALEA DUMBRAVII

CALEA CISNADIE

Museum of
Popular Technology

Inn

Campsite

To Răsinari

To Cisnădie

To Făgăras

mainly along **Str. Bălcescu**; the place to find shops, snacks, the **tourist office** (nr . 53), **TAROM** (nr.10) and **CFR** (nr.6). On the corner is Sibiu's oldest hotel, the *Împăratul Romanilor* (Roman Emperor), still bearing a faded resemblance to the grand establishment once patronised by the likes of Liszt, Strauss and Eminescu. By then the town had out-lived its militaristic architecture – exemplified by the unguarded **ramparts** and bastions along the length of Str. Cetăţii to the southeast, where three mighty **towers** were once manned by contingents of the Carpenters', Potters' and Crossbow-makers' guilds, and by the Haller Bastion to the northwest.

With the encouragement of **Samuel Brukenthal**, the imperial governor between 1777-87, Sibiu developed as a centre of intellectual life, which during the C19 provided a haven for Romanians bent on raising their own people's cultural horizons. **Gheorghe Lazar** and others opened a Romanian *Liceul* (still functioning today); Ioan Slavici and George Coşbuc edited the campaigning *Tribuna* (at 1, Str. Bălceşcu); and on the premises of 20, Str. 1 Mai, the first congress of **ASTRA** – an organisation for the propagation of Romanian culture in Transylvania – was held in October 1861 (attended by the wittering young poet Titu Heredlea, in Rebreanu's novel *Ion*). In the same street you can't fail to miss the **Orthodox Cathedral**, an early C20 copy of the Ayia Sofia, embellished with all manner of neo-Byzantine flourishes and frescoes. Here too, the **choir** is fantastic, and it's worth visiting both the Evangelical and Orthodox churches during Sunday morning services to compare the different liturgical and choral styles (but do so discreetly).

The chance to get inside the Councillers' Tower is probably sufficient reason to visit Sibiu's **History Museum**, while the **Brukenthal Museum** – partly assembled by the governor and housed in his former palace – stands on its own merits. Besides the best of local silverware, pottery and furniture, and various pictures by European masters, there's a wonderful, evocative collection of works by **Transylvanian painters**; mainly genre and romantic depictions of peasant life, the nobility in their crumbling castles, and wild Transylvanian landscapes, by Franz Neuhauser, Friederich Meiss, Antal Ligeti, Wellmann, Smigelschi and others. Both places are open Tuesday-Sunday 10am-6pm, as are the **Pharmaceutical Museum** (26, Piaţa 6 Martie) and the exhibition of **Hunting Weapons and Trophies**, which musters stuffed animals and a fearsome armoury at 4, Str. Şcoala de Înot, three blocks beyond the Piaţa Unirii. Yet further afield lie the *Mercenaries' Bastion* on Str. Al. Sahia, and the open-air **Museum of Popular Technology** near the **Zoological Gardens** in the Dumbrava forest just southwest of town.

Practicalities

Shops, supermarkets and **places to eat** cluster along Str. Bălcescu and around the Piaţa Unirii, with most wining and dining occuring in the *Împăratul Romanilor*, *Bulevard* and *Continental* hotels (the latter, on Calea Dumbravei, also contains an *autoservis* joint). **Rooms** at the Roman Emperor and the Bulevard aren't particularly cheap ($40 sngl./$53 dbl.), though fractionally less expensive in the Continental, so it's worth hassling **BTT** (4, Str. Kornhauser) for **dormitory beds** if you don't fancy the **campsite** or the **inn** along the road running through the Dumbrava forest (accessible by buses marked *Pădurea Dumbrava*, leaving from the station). Alternatively, it's possible to stay in nearby villages, either courtesy of ONT (for around $15 per head) or by camping out in the vicinity of Cisnădioara (see the following section).

Plays in German are sometimes performed at the State Theatre (2, B-dul 23 August) and there are regular **concerts** of classical music at 2, Str. Filarmonicii. You'll find **books** at *Anticvariat* at 41, Str. Bălceşcu and the shop on the corner of Str. Telefoanelor: the latter stocks a fair amount on Saxon architecture and folk-culture (mostly in German), dictionaries, and maps and books on the Făgăraş Mountains – useful if you're heading that way. **Sports facilities** are clustered around the open-air *Ştrand* at the end of Şos. Alba Iulia, past a **petrol** station and *Autoservice* car-repair yard. Other useful places include; *ACR* in block 13, Str. Gheorghe-Dej; a **24-hour pharmacy** beside the tourist office; the **post office** on Str. 1 Mai; a **hospital** (☎ 06 for emergencies) on B-dul 23 August; and the **police** at 4, Str. Armata Roşie.

IN THE NEIGHBOURHOOD OF SIBIU

With patience and the aid of buses from the terminal on Piaţa Gării, you can see something of the **old Saxon settlements** around Sibiu. Many of the original villages that grew up alongside Hermannstadt now have sizeable Romanian populations (in some cases outnumbering the Germans), but all have fortified churches and rows of houses presenting a solid wall to the street – hallmarks of their Saxon origins. 'They have existed for 700 years, a mere handful, surrounded by races that have nothing in common with them, and yet they have not lost those customs that attach them to their fatherland', observed Starkie in the twenties. It's still true of Saxon communities today – for example Cisnădioara, where the sight and feel of the place suggested Bavaria 200 years ago, and I was invited to go bear hunting during the winter.

Once an hour from Sibiu's autogară, a bus lurches off towards CISNĂDIE, 10km away, groaning under the weight of passengers and rooftop cylinders of *gaz methan*. Assuming they accomplish the journey, you'll find that Cisnădie's modern outskirts quickly give way to the old 'Red Town' – a convergence of streets around the **church** whose walls are lined with the medieval equivalent of bomb shelters, where the community sought refuge during times of danger and stored a percentage of their harvest. If requested politely, one of the pastor's daughters will guide you up through the massive C13 **tower**; a succession of lofty vaults linked by creaking ladders and narrow stairways, culminating in the belfry. From here the view of Cisnădie's angular courtyards and red rooftops is superb, while overhead rise the four turrets – medieval symbols of civic importance – whose construction so irked Sibiu's burghers that they obliged the locals to sign a bond declaring themselves 'but humble villagers' and promising to treat their haughty neighbours with 'all due honour, fear and friendship'. Just visible in the distance is the conical rock crowned by a church that overlooks Cisnădioara.

In Cisnădie – *Heltau* in German – people still weave white frieze cloth on household looms, and lay down copious supplies of homemade ham, *schnapps* and *wurst* in their cellars. **Saxon weddings** last three days, and begin with the groom and his friends driving by cart to the bride's house, where they fix pine trees around the gateway and sing songs. Feasting and drinking then continues into the small hours, resuming the following day after the marriage ceremony; traditionally, February 3 and November 25 are auspicious dates. According to Charles Boner in the C19, the Saxons considered marriage – and divorce – essentially a commercial transaction, believing that 'it is not the youth who marries maiden, but acre marries acre, one vineyard the other vineyard, and a herd of oxen the other herd' (or, in the words of a Romanian proverb: 'Vineyard and land will marry the horror'!). When I was in Cisnădie the Germans seemed more concerned about **emigration**; apparently one family a week was quitting Transylvania for the ancient *Heimat*, having carefully taught their children the type of German spoken in the Federal Republic, so different to their own antiquated dialect.

Officially there's no tourist **accommodation** in Cisnădie, and if you're planning to camp out it's better to do so at **CISNĂDIOARA**. From Cisnădie's centre it's roughly 5km's walk past flats and the funfair on the outskirts of town, out along the valley road towards the striking 200ft-high rock that looms over *Michaelsburg* (to use Cisnădioara's German name). The C12-C13 church on its summit frequently withstood the Tartars, villagers defending it by hurling down rocks which had previously been carried into the citadel by aspiring husbands. The custom was that no young man could marry until he had carried a heavy rock from the riverbed up a steep track, for the villagers were 'anxious to prevent the weaklings from marrying lest they spoil the hardy race'. Follow the river down through the village and you'll pass a few shops (selling little) and rows of neat, unmistakably German houses. Should you be invited inside, you're likely to be offered schnapps in the parlour – furnished with heavy cabinets and sepia photographs. In return for **hospitality** people will always appreciate some sugar or cooking-oil to supplement their rations (which foreigners can buy, on production of their passport, at Sibiu supermarkets). The riverside meadow on the far side of Michaelsburg is a nice place to camp – cowbells and a herd moving past awakened me in the mornings – though villagers warned of light-fingered *ţigani* wandering over the hills from their camp near Răşinari.

Going by hearsay and old photos, there are also Saxons and doughty fortress-churches in **AGNITA** (2 trains daily from Sibiu), **SURA MARE** and **SURA MICĂ** (*Gross-Schuren* and *Klein-Schuren* in German). The last two are accessible by bus, and services to Sura Mică usually continue on to **OCNA SIBIULUI** (also a halt on the Sibiu-Copşa Mică railway line), a bathing resort with fizzy, salty water recommended for gynaecological and locomotive disorders, which bubbles up from the lakes that have formed in abandoned salt-workings.

Păltiniş, Hikes in the Cibin Mountains and places along the way to Sebeş
RĂŞINARI, along the bus route to Păltiniş, contains a couple of fine churches and an ethnographic museum plus a house once occupied by the poet Octacian Goga, but is more noteworthy for the large Gypsy encampment (*ţara*) on its outskirts, and the commune's annual 'Pastoral Album' folklore

festival, held on the third Sunday of April. From Răşinari's outskirts, a track petering out into a path (mark: red stripes) leads over the mountains to Păltiniş in 6-7hrs. Halfway along, near Mt. Tomnaticu, it meets another path (blue triangles) leading to the *Şanta* mountain chalet, a few kilometres west of the larger hotel-chalet complex at **PĂLTINIŞ**. From Păltiniş (4,760ft) it's only 3-4hrs walk through the **Cibin Gorges** – *Cheile Cibinului* – past Lake Cibin to the *Fîntînele* Cabana, following the red dots. In the morning you can push on to Sibiel (see below).

Alternatively, there's the possibility of **longer hikes** (1-2 days) from Păltiniş into the mountains east of Petroşani. One route, marked with red triangles, leads to the *Gîtu Berbecului* cabana in 2½hrs, and thence to Dobrun. There, the left-hand fork descends to the Lotru Gorge, while the main path – marked with blue stripes – leads southwest towards Lake Vidra. The other route, indicated by red stripes, follows a mountain ridge to the *Cînaia refuge* (5½-6hrs) and then continues to the *Obîrsia Lotrului* Cabana, the gateway to several lakes situated further south in the mountains to the east of Petroşani.

Travellers not bound for the mountains will most likely head **towards Sebeş**, along road 1/7 or by railway. *Personal* and *cursa* services (around five daily) halt a short distance from several settlements en route which deserve a mention. The first is **CRISTIAN**, where a double wall protects a C14 church with massive towers; followed by **SIBIEL** where, according to Andrew MacKenzie, some villagers still believe in **witchcraft**. Traditionally – and understandably in a community established by Mărgineni shepherds – witches and ghosts were more feared for their attacks on livestock than on people. While blowing horns to prevent *strigoi* from stealing their ewes' milk on St George's Day, villagers also credit witches with occasional good deeds, such as magically shutting the jaws of wolves intent on ravaging their flocks. In Sibiel you'll find lovely **glass paintings** amongst the collection of peasant art, and the start of a footpath which leads uphill past a ruined citadel to the *Fîntînele* chalet (route marked with blue dots). From there you can **hike through the Cibin Gorges to Păltinis**.

SALIŞTE, originally another Mărgineni settlement, is famous for its peasant **choir**, which sings in the community centre here, and for its Co-op producing carpets and embroidered costumes. The latter are displayed in the Ethnographic Museum and worn during Salişte's 'Meeting of the Youth' **festival** (December 24-31). They're more likely to appear during the course of everyday life at **TILIŞCA**, an older, more eye-catching settlement tracing its origins back to a Dacian settlement on nearby Cătinas Hill (where there's an unremarkable ruined fort). The road and railway continue on through **MIERCUREA SIBIULUI**, a commune whose name derives from the word *miercuri*, Wednesday, the traditional market day. In the centre is a small, well-preserved C13 church, fortified like other Saxon buildings during the C15, when the Germans called this settlement *Reussmarkt*. The railway also halts 5km further on at **BĂILE MIERCUREA**, a modest spa resort with a tourist chalet.

Moving on, you're likely to hit SEBEŞ (p.360) followed by VINŢU DE JOS, and some decisions have to be made. The mainline and DN7 follow the Mureş Valley **towards Arad**, but one can change trains at SIMERIA for **Hunedoara, the Dacian citadels and southwestern Transylvania** (p.380). Alternatively, trains from Vințu de Jos head up through **Alba Iulia** (see following section) to TEIUȘ, the place to switch trains yet again for CÎMPIA TURZII (branch line to the **Turda Gorge**, p.372) and northbound services **towards Cluj**.

BLAJ, ALBA IULIA AND SEBEȘ

Though it's no reason to get off the train at **BLAJ** (between Sighișoara and Cluj), this small town was once the ark of Romanian nationalism in Transylvania. In 1738 Blaj became the headquarters of the **Uniate Church***, whose newly-elected bishop, **Ioan Inocențiu Mici**, proved to be a tireless campaigner for the rights of Transylvania's Romanians. When Hungary revolted against the Habsburgs in 1848, Magyar demands to re-incorporate Transylvania within the 'lands of Saint Stephen' provoked a Romanian response at Blaj. Following an earlier demonstration called by Avram Iancu, 40,000 Romanians – mostly serfs – gathered on the '**Field of Liberty**' on May 15: proclaiming their equality; demanding political representation lest they were steamrollered into a union with Hungary; chanting 'No decision about us, without us' (*nimic despre noi fără noi*). Nowadays, visible reminders of that struggle are limited to the **Museum** (2, Str. Armata Roșie), Liberty Field's **statues** and the **Cathedral** – with a splendid iconostasis – raised by Micu, but the Romanians' eventual triumph is grandly enshrined at Alba Iulia.

Alba Iuila

Unlike Blaj, the 'sights' of **ALBA IULIA** are worth the effort of changing trains (at Teiuș from the direction of Sighișoara or Cluj, or Vințu de Jos if you're approaching from Arad or Sibiu). The town itself is dominated by one of them: a huge **Citadel** – in effect the upper town – laid out in the shape of a star. The plateau on which it stands has been fortified since Roman times, but previous efforts must have paled before this monster. Between 1715-38, 20,000 serfs under the direction of an Italian architect built the Vauban-style fortress, which was named *Karlsburg* in honour of the reigning Habsburg monarch. Imperial levies on the countryside did much to embitter the Romanian peasants, who in the **1784 rising** led by **Horia, Cloșca and Crișan**, turned on their (mainly Hungarian) landlords. After the uprising was crushed, Horia and Cloșca were broken on the wheel before the Citadel gates, were a statue now stands on 'Horia's field'. Above the Citadel's richly-carved Baroque gateway is Horia's death-cell (Crișan cheated the excecutioner by suicide); while within its walls, splendid buildings jostle to impress.

---

*In 1699, the synod of the Orthodox Church in Wallachia, Moldavia and Transylvania accepted the authority and protection of the Vatican, hoping to elevate the status of their church (particularly in Transylvania, where it was under attack by the Hungarian Calvinist church). Thus was born the **Uniate Church** (or 'Catholics of the Eastern Rite'). However the new Church failed to carry with it most Orthodox believers, and became a fairly marginal sect when Romania's Orthodox Church gained autonomy in the 1920s. The Communists regarded the Uniate clergy and believers as 'agents of imperialism', and forcibly merged them with the Orthodox Church. Uniates remain a harassed minority, with no status under the 1948 and subsequent constitutions, which recognise the existence of 14 other denominations (or 'cults').

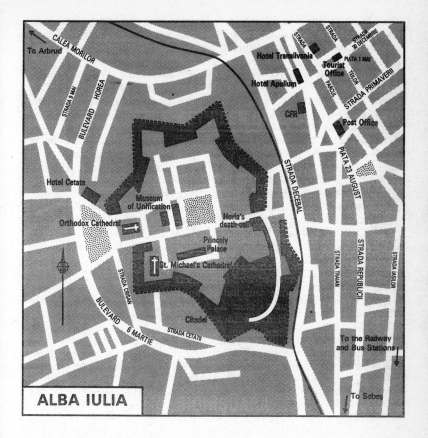

ALBA IULIA

Just off to the right, the **Museum of Unification** embodies the credo that Romania's history has been a long search for national unity, for in its ornate marble halls on December 1 1918, Romanian delegates proclaimed Transylvania's union with the *Regat* as the Austro-Hungarian Empire commenced its death throes. Here too, exhibits glorify the Wallachian prince **Michael the Brave** (1593-1601) who briefly united Wallachia, Transylvania and Moldavia under his crown in 1600. (An act subsequently viewed as the first manifestation of Romanian nationalism, although Michael recognised the Three Nations rather than siding with the oppressed Romanian peasantry of Transylvania.) In a fit of pique, the Magyars later demolished his Coronation Church, so unsurprisingly, the Romanians built a vast new **Orthodox Cathedral** in 1921 (where King Ferdinand and Queen Marie were crowned the year after) filled with neo-Byzantine frescoes including portraits of Michael and his wife Stanca in the pronaos.

The Catholic **St Michael's Cathedral** on the opposite side of Str. Mihai Viteazu testifies to the Hungarian connection, for István I made *Gyulafehérvár* (the Magyar name for Alba Iulia) a bishopric to consolidate his hold on Transylvania; and this C13 Romanesque structure – loaded with the accretions of later styles – contains the **tomb of Hunyadi**, the greatest of Transylvania's warlords (see p.378). The **Bishop's Palace** facing the entrance to St Michael's is flanked to the north by a bastion still partially occupied by the Romanian army, whilst to the west stands the former **Prince's Palace** where the Transylvanian Diets met during the C16-C17. On the plateau southwest of the Citadel are the remains of the Roman fortress of *Apulum*, once the strongest on Dacia.

The **lower town** contains everything of practical importance, including Alba Iulia's three **hotels**. The *Cetate* (41, Blvd. Horea) is marginally more expensive than the *Transilvania* and *Apullum* on Piaţa 1 Mai ($38 dbl./$28 sngl.), whilst **BTT** (1, Str. 30 Decembrie) might be able to arrange dormitory beds. Alba Iulia's **tourist office** (22, Piaţa 1 Mai) should know whether it's feasibile to catch a bus from the terminal on Str. Iaşilor out to the **campsite** along DN1 (the Sebeş road). **Trains to neighbouring towns** are all routed through VINŢU DE JOS, whence the main line heads eastwards to Sebeş (see below) and Sibiu; and westwards via Orăştie, Simeria (change trains for Hunedorara, p.378), and Deva on to Arad.

Sebeş

Despite its proximity to the '**Wine country**' between Alba Iulia and Aiud, where white *Fetească* is produced at Şard, Ighiu and other **villages** for storage in the huge vaults tunneled by serfs beneath Telna, the town of **SEBEŞ** grew up on the proceeds of the leather-working industry, trading mainly with Wallachia. In 1438 the townsfolks' biggest client, Vlad the Impaler, arrived under the walls of *Mühlbach* (as the Saxon population called it) together with the Turkish army, demanding that the town be surrendered. A number of inhabitants refused, barricading themselves in one of the towers of the (now ruined) **Citadel**, which the Turks burned and stormed. The only survivor, a student aged sixteen, was then sold as a slave at Adrianople, but escaped twenty years later to write *Of the Religion, Manners and Infamies of the Turks* – a bestselling exposé of the bogeymen of C15 Europe – signing himself the 'Nameless One of Sebeş'. The **Student's Tower** is thus one of the sights of Sebeş, together with a large **Evangelical Church** in a mixture of styles, and the C15 **House of the Voivodes** – now housing a museum – where Ioan Zapolya (János Zápolyai) died in 1540. Together, they offer little incentive to linger, but should you wish **to stay** overnight, there's a *hotel* on Str. 9 Mai, a *motel* on the highway on the east side of town, and a *campsite* at BĂILE MIERCUREA (16km out along DN1).

CLUJ (CLUJ-NAPOCA)

With its cupolas, Baroque outcroppings and weathered fin de siècle backstreets, downtown **CLUJ** looks like the Hungarian provincial capital that, in a sense, it once was. In Hungary and (more circumspectly) within Transylvania itself, many people still regret the passing of *Kolozsvár*, fondly recalled as a city that embodied the Magyar belle époque, with a café-society and reputation for letters surpassing that of other cities in the Balkans. Most Romanians think otherwise: for them, Kolozsvár was the 'city of the Hungarian landlords' until its restoration to the national patrimony in 1920, and consider the addition of *Napoca* to its name, by Ceauşescu's decree in 1974, just recognition that their Dacian forbears settled here 1,850 years ago, long before the Magyars entered Transylvania.

Modern Cluj has much industry and over 300,000 inhabitants, but the city has retained something of the langour and raffish undercurrents that characterised it in the olden days – not to mention cultural fixtures like its opera and university. Compared to other large Romanian towns, restaurants and bars seem livelier, and the contents of *alimentarie* more varied. Hotel dance floors jive, while café life has a certain zaniness – possibly attributable to Cluj's student population of 24,000 (including foreigners). If **trains from Hungary** didn't arrive during the small hours, this would be an ideal place to begin one's travels in Transylvania, but as it is, the city's comforts will be irresistible should you come here **from Moldavia** (the railway journey involves changing trains at Ilva Mică), particularly after roughing it in the sticks of Bucovina.

The town

Arriving in Cluj, take a trolleybus (#2/#3/#4) from the railway station, or follow one of the arterial stradăs and caleas leading into **the centre**, where the spacious **Piaţa Libertaţii** allows people to socialise and do business whilst rubbing shoulders with monumental architecture. The square's centrepiece is **St Michael's Church** – a vast statement in stone nowadays surely emptier than envisaged by the building's founders in the mid-C14, when Catholicism and the Magyar nobility ruled unchallenged over Cluj. Dwarfing the congregation in the nave, mighty pillars curve into vaulting like the roof of a forest, austerely bare of all but chiselled Magyar and Latin inscriptions.

St Michael's 'Gothic' phase of construction ended three years before the death of **Mátyás Corvinus**, whose formidable 'Black Army' kept the Kingdom of Hungary safe from lawlessness and foreign invasion for much of his reign (1458-90). A popular lament that 'justice departed' with his death, and the defeat at Mohács 36 years later, highlight his political and military achievements. But Mátyás reputation equally derives from his Renaissance attributes, for which his wife **Beatrix of Naples** should share the credit. By introducing him to the Renaissance culture of Italy, selecting foreign architects and craftsmen, and humanists like Bonfini to chronicle events and utterances, Beatrix was a catalyst during Hungary's own C15 Renaissance; and personally commissioned many volumes in the *Biblioteca Corvina*. Although his father's stronghold was at Hunedoara (where the great castle stands to this day), Mátyás was actually born here, in a small mansion up a sidestreet leading off the square (6, Str. Matei Corvin). Outside the church an imposing **equestrian statue** of the king accepts the battle standards laid in homage by four dignitaries, with the crescent banner of the Turks trampled.

Around the square you'll find various unpretentious shops and restaurants; the *CFR* **railway bookings** office (8am-8pm/Sunday 8am-1pm) on the corner

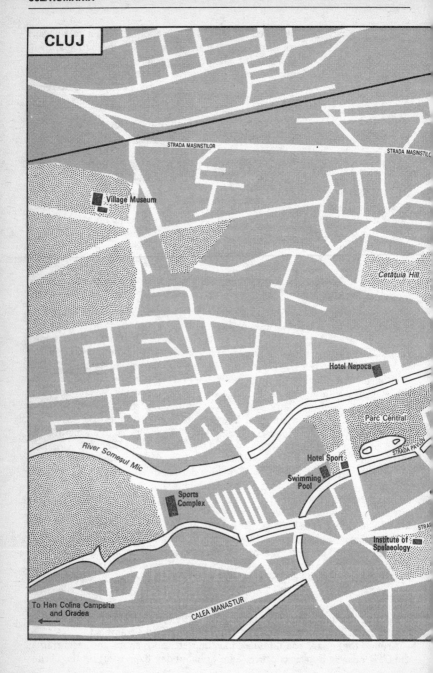

CLUJ

STRADA MASINSTILOR

STRADA MASINSTILC

Village Museum

Cetăţuia Hill

Hotel Napoca

Parc Central

STRADA PAL...

River Someşul Mic

Hotel Sport

Swimming
Pool

Sports
Complex

Institute of
Spelaeology

STRAD...

To Han Colina Campsite
and Oradea

CALEA MANASTUR

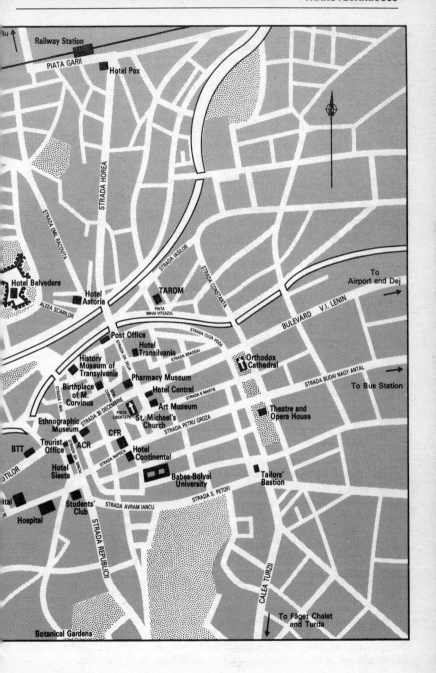

Railway Station

PIATA GARII

Hotel Pax

STRADA HOREA

STRADA EMIL RACOVITA

ALEEA SCARILOR

Hotel Belvedere

Hotel Astoria

TAROM

PIATA MIHAI VITEAZUL

STRADA IASILOR

STRADA CONSTANTA

To Airport and Dej

BULEVARD V.I. LENIN

STRADA CUZA VODA

Post Office

Hotel Transilvania

STRADA BRASSAI

History Museum of Transylvania

STRADA GH. DOJA

Pharmacy Museum

Birthplace of M. Corvinus

Hotel Central

STRADA 6 MARTIE

Orthodox Cathedral

STRADA BUDAI NAGY ANTAL

To Bus Station

STRADA 1 MAI

CORVIN

Art Museum

Ethnographic Museum

STRADA 30 DECEMBRIE

PIATA LIBERTATII

St. Michael's Church

STRADA PETRU GROZA

Theatre and Opera House

BTT

Tourist Office

ACR

CFR

Hotel Siesta

STRADA GH. SINCAI

STRADA NAPOCA

Hotel Continental

Babes-Bolyai University

Tailors' Bastion

...TILOR

Students' Club

STRADA AVRAM IANCU

STRADA S. PETOFI

Hospital

STRADA REPUBLICII

CALEA TURZII

To Faget Chalet and Turda

Botanical Gardens

opposite the *Hotel Continental*; and, facing this, the university **bookshop** where it's worth looking for dictionaries and books on Romanian ethnography and arts. The **Pharmacy Museum** on the corner of Str. Gheorghe Doja displays ancient prescriptions on the premises of Cluj's first apothecary, the *Hintz House*, in a setting Dr. Jekyll might have enjoyed; while you can't miss the *Hotel Central*, otherwise known as the *Melody* (presumably because of the dancing there).

Practically next door to the latter stands the **Art Museum**, whose collection embraces icons, weaponry, carpets, a superbly carved C16 altar from Jimbov, and paintings by Transylvanian artists. Many of the items were expropriated from the Magyar aristocracy; in particular the *Bánffy family*, whose mansion this building once was. Since this élite made foreign travellers welcome, there are many written accounts of them. Some appear as benevolent or even progressive; others as bigoted exploiters, like the elderly countess who complained to Ethel Pantazzi in 1920 that Romanian peasants no longer knelt in the mud so as to permit her to walk across their backs to the church door, as in the 'good old days' when Transylvania was the jewel in St Stephen's Crown.

The university quarter begins one block beyond the Continental, with Str. Napoca leading to the **Students' Club** and the old library on Piaţa Păcii, while Str. Universităţii heads soutwards to **Babeş-Bolyai University**. Since its foundation in 1872 the University has produced scholars of the calibre of Edmund Bordeaux Székely (translator of the *Dead Sea Scrolls*), but also served as an instrument of cultural oppression. Long denied an education in their own language before 1918, the Romanians promptly proscribed teaching in Hungarian once they gained the upper hand; only to hurriedly evacuate students and staff when Hitler gave northern Transylvania back to Hungary in 1940, correctly anticipating Horthy's counter-chauvinism.

After the liberation, separate universities were created to provide an **education** in the mother-tongue of both ethnic groups (Hungarians form about two-fifths of Cluj's population), and for a while it seemed that inequality was a thing of the past. However, in 1959 the authorities decreed a shotgun merger (prompting several professors to commit suicide), with the predictable result that provision for higher education in Hungarian declined rapidly. This, and a similar running down of Hungarian-language primary and secondary schooling, have convinced many Magyars that the state is bent on 'de-culturising' them.

Notwithstanding this, the university gets a lot of work done: producing staff for the **hospitals** on Str. Clinicor; agronomists, some of whom tend the impressive **Botanical Gardens** at the end of Str. Republicii; humanities and science graduates; and supporting the world's oldest **Speleological Institute**, founded by Emil Racoviţă (1868-1947), which pot-holers are advised to contact should they wish to go caving in the Apuseni Mountains. Along the same street as the university building stands a group of statues representing the **School of Transylvania** whose philological and historical researches provided ammunition for the Romanian intelligentsia's resistance to Magyarization during the C19. At the far end of Str.Kogălniceanu, the restored **Tailors' Bastion** is an outcrop of the more decrepit **remains of a C15 citadel**, which surrounds the *Belvedere Hotel* on Cetăţuia Hill north of the river.

Walk northwards from the bastion and you'll find yourself on an elongated square bisected by Str. Budai Nagy Antal (leading to the **bus terminal,** about 1½km east). In the southern half stands the neat yellow and white **Romanian National Theatre and Opera,** while the square's northern end is embellished with a huge and startling **Orthodox Cathedral** that could have fallen through a time warp in Justinian's Constantinople. It was in fact founded during the 1920s, like many other grandiose structures raised to celebrate the Romanians' triumph in Transylvania, and the neo-Byzantine façade of stonework conceals a concrete structure. Inside, the building subtends beneath its cupola, and the frescoes — though religious in content — bear the ugly heavy-handedness characteristic of the 1950s, when Leonte Rautu dictated 'Socialist Realism' to the arts.

Continue north — across Bulevard Lenin, up Cuza street, and over the bridge — to reach the Piaţa Mihai Viteazul. *TAROM* (nr.11) and a fruit & veg market operate here on weekdays and Saturdays; while on Thursdays the square is taken over by the '**village market**', attended by peasants from the Apuseni highlands and the Transylvanian Heath who sell craftwork, and Poles who turn up in their Ladas to run the **black market.** In the side-streets leading towards the Little Someş River, you'll also come across the *Republica* cinema and *Auto-Moto,* useful for **car parts.** Further east, Stradă Gh. Doja leads back towards the town centre, while on its far side are the **Post Office** (nr.33), the *Hotel Astoria* (just north of the river), and a side-street leading off onto Piaţa Muzeului.

Museums and the 'Continuity Theory'
Unsurprisingly, Piaţa Muzeului is called after a museum; namely the **History Museum of Transylvania** just around the corner at 2, Str. Isac, that's open from 9am-5pm, Tuesday-Sunday. On the first floor, strange skulls and mammoth tusks are succeeded by arrow and spearheads charting progress from the Neolithic and Bronze Ages to the rise of the **Dacian civilisation** (which reached its peak between the C2 BC and the C1 AD), whose highland citadel, Sarmizegetusa, is reconstructed in models and pictures. The *Dacii* were subdued by the Roman legions, and the two races subsequently intermingled to form the ancestors of today's Romanians — or so the official version of Romanian history goes.

According to this **Daco-Roman Continuity Theory** and the maps in hall 2 upstairs, the Daco-Roman civilisation thrived in Transylvania (where it was divided into three voivodates) until the Magyars began their incursions towards the end of the C10, and gradually wrested control of the region from the 'Vlachs' (as Anonymus, the chronicler of King Béla, calls them in his *Gesta Hungarorum*). Thus was planted the seed of one of Europe's most enduring disputes, which scholars and propagandists in Bucharest and Budapest pursue to this day. The Vlach and Magyar peasants might combine against their landlords in uprisings (in 1514 and 1784) and men of Vlach birth like Iancu de Hunedoara might occasionally climb to the heights of Hungarian society, but considered overall, Transylvania is a land where first one ethnic group, then another, has pursued progress at the expense of its rivals. Down in the ground floor lapidaium across the courtyard, there's something symbolic about the long corridor that runs through a succession of stone portals, each one carved with the names or emblems of defunct noble houses, including one with a figure of a god ferociously devouring its own child.

West of the main square, out along Str. 30 Decembrie, Cluj's **Ethnographic Museum** at nr.21 contains what is probably Romania's finest collection of **carpets and folk-costumes**. Here, you can appreciate the different styles of weaving – from the dark herringbone patterns of the Pădureni region to the bold yellow, black and red stripes typical of Maramureş – and the even greater variety of clothing and headgear. While blouses and leggings might be predominantly black or white, women's apron-skirts and the waistcoats worn by both sexes for 'Sunday best' and special occasions are brilliantly coloured. Peacock feathers serve as fans or plumes, and the love of complicated designs spills over onto distaffs, cups and other wooden objects, not to mention the Goat-mask sewn with multi-coloured tassels (worn during *Capra* festival, see p.410), or even the humble stalks of corn tied into elaborate stars and crosses for harvest celebrations.

Three neat wooden churches and other specimens of rural architecture have been assembled at the open-air **Village Museum**, and a visit there will help to put the costumes in perspective, if not give you a hankering to see something of Apuseni communities (known as the *Moţi* people) and one of their festivals, like the 'Girl Fair' described on p.373.

Eating, sleeping and other things

Cluj has plenty of **places to eat and drink**, and Str. 6 Martie (where the painter Carol de Popp Szathmary once lived at nr. 17) is as good a spot as any to begin. The *Gradina de Vara Boema* beer garden (nr.34) features grills, and often a singer in the evenings; whilst nearer the main square you'll find a restaurant specialising in mushroom (*ciuperci*) dishes and the *Polar* café-bar. The main square itself has a Lacto-Vegetarian set-up (nr.12), the *Someşul* restaurant (nr.30), the *Ursus* brasserie, and bars and restaurants in the Melody and Continental hotels (often with dancing and bands). Just nearby on Str. Napoca there's the popular *Bar Zis* (opposite another vegetarian café, seemingly never open), and further along, a student hangout, *Tineretului*. Traditional Romanian dishes and music justify higher prices at the *Transilvania* (13, Str. 30 Decembrie) and the *Hubertus* – which specialises in game – on Lenin Bulevard. There are two similarly upmarket establishments in the Parcul Central, just west of the town centre, and a women's restaurant, *Intim*, at 2, Str. Corvin.

Students have their 'House of Culture' on Piaţa Păcii (IUS card required to gain admission), and another club at 34, Str. Observatorului. Neither place serves alcoholic drinks though both feature **films and discos** at irregular intervals. It's usually only the richer – usually Arab or African – students that can afford to patronise the *Napoca* or other bars attached to the first class hotels.

Pax, opposite the railway station, is the cheapest and sleaziest of Cluj's **hotels**, which otherwise lie nearer to the centre. The *Astoria* (3, Str. Horea), *Transilvania* (20, Str. Doja) and *Central* (or *Melody*) have beds for just under $20 a night; whilst Cluj's first class hotels charge between $32-$44 for a single, and $42-$57 for a double room. If you can afford their prices, it's really a toss-up between hotels in the centre (*Continental, Siesta*) or those in greener parts of town, like the *Belvedere* on Cetăţuia Hill or the *Sport* and *Napoca* further to the southwest. BTT (18, Calea Moţilor) can possibly arrange **cheaper lodgings** in college dormitories during summer vacation, or there's a range of **places outside town**. The Făget Hills to the southeast can be reached by bus #10 or #46 (from behind the Romanian Theatre), and you should ask passengers where to alight for the *Cabana Făget Pădure* or the *campsite* there. Alternatively, there's the *Han Colina* campsite a few miles out along DN1, accessible by trolleybus #1, #25, #26 or #35 (from halfway down Str. 30 Decembrie), a mile before which, a side-road heads southwards to another tourist chalet, *Făget Izvor*.

To avoid disappointment, check first with the **tourist office** on Str. Şincai (8am-1pm, 2pm-7pm/Sunday 9am-12am), and make **reservations** if necessary. This particularly applies should you be planning excursions into the mountains, where *cabanas* are virtually the only form of accommodation; while a chat with the folks at **ACR** (27, Str. 30 Decembrie) might be wise for travellers intending to motor through the Apuseni highlands. In any case, fill up with **petrol** before you go: there are filling stations on all the main roads out of town.

Moving on
The remaining sections of this chapter cover the **Apuseni Mountains** (including the route to Oradea); the **Dacian citadels** and **Hunedoara**, whence it's natural to carry on into **southwestern Transylvania**; and lastly, a couple of routes through **northern Transylvania** into **Moldavia or Maramureş**. Details of how to get there appear at the beginning of each section, so what follows is a summary of the other options.

Including $10 charge for a car to the Airport (west of town), flying **to Bucharest** costs about 30% more than the journey by express train; IUS cardholders generally get a 30% discount on flights, but payment must be in hard currency or lei covered by an exchange receipt (the same applies to international railway tickets). Most people catch the *Rapid Transilvania* to Bucharest (7½hrs; arrives 10.30pm) which, like all trains bound for the capital, goes by way of Blaj, Sighişoara, Braşov and Ploieşti. The southbound *Mamaia Express*, leaving around 9pm, is the only direct train **to Constanţa** on the coast (12½hrs), while the northbound service bound for Budapest and Prague (dep. 6.30am) is one of four lines serving **destinations abroad**. The *Nord Orient* runs to Budapest and Warsaw (4.30pm), or Burgas in Bulgaria (5.20pm); *Tracia* to Varna (3.20pm), or Budapest, Prague and Dresden (2.15pm); and the *Balt Orient* to Budapest, Prague and Berlin (5.40am). Seats on all express trains should be booked 24-36 hours in advance through CFR.

THE APUSENI MOUNTAINS: MUSIC, FESTIVALS AND CAVES

As many a musicologist has testified, the region surrounding Cluj – particularly the Transylvanian Heath and the Apuseni Mountains – harbours some of the richest, most varied **folk music** in Europe. Not just folkloric ensembles at festivals (though there are these too), but villages and small towns whose inhabitants have been making music together for generations; where almost every street has its band, and people that don't play an instrument will happily sing, dance or interject dramatically. Depending on where and who its performers are, the music can parade ancient roots in the Urals or the Turkic steppes; repeat the riff of a recruitment tune from the Rákóczi wars; mimic some soulfully overblown *doina* from Bucharest's nightclubs in the 30s, and more besides.

Music usually occurs spontaneously in villages, houses and sleazy smalltown bars, so finding the best – or anything at all – depends on local tip-offs, luck and your own efforts. It's sometimes easy to spot musicians since so many of them are Gypsies – occasionally descended from the wandering *Lăutari* tribe – and thus noticeably darker than other people. Weekends seem the best time to investigate **Cojocna** and communes such as **Sic**, **Rimetea** and **Izvoru Crişului**, all within relatively easy reach of Cluj; if you don't mind venturing off the beaten track a little, there are rich pickings to be had at spring and summer **festivals**. Moreover, the scenery of the **Apuseni Mountains** is generally magnificent, and the region abounds in **caves** – particularly on the **Padiş Plateau** – with impressive defiles like the **Turda Gorge** thrown in for good measure.

With a car, one could probably see the main attractions within a week, including a day's hiking or a visit to a festival; but even making maximum use of the railway, such buses as run, and hitching, car-less travellers will require more time or selectivity. If you've only 1 or 2 days to spare, limit yourself to a single area – perhaps around Turda or the Padiş Plateau – or a particular festival; the rite of 'Measurement' in May occurs relatively near Cluj, whereas others, like the *Nedeia of Tăcaşele* in June, are easier to reach from the Banat. The following **itineraries** are loosely structured around the railway network, so if buses or lifts are better than anticipated, you can hop from one to another more freely. Travellers unwilling to camp out are strongly advised to book **lodgings** in advance through OJT, whose large map of the *Munţii Apuseni* is superior to the one in this book. As always when venturing into remoter parts, bring **food** in expectation of of local shortages – one can easily stock up in Oradea or Cluj.

Music at Sic and Cojocna

One of the best places for music in this neck of Transylvania is the commune of SIC; otherwise known to its Magyar residents as *Szék* ('Seat'). Northeast of Cluj, it spreads over several hills, with a number of churches and municipal buildings testifying to its former importance as a centre of salt mining. Szék is one of the principal villages of the Transylvanian Heath – or *Mezőseg*, as the Hungarians call this region – and although Romanians nowadays predominate here, there's a high proportion of Magyars and some Saxons and Gypsies; their dwellings neatly thatched and painted blue as if to defy the incredibly muddy streets.

It's said that every street in Szék has its own band: typically three **musicians** on violin, *kontra* and bass, sometimes with another violinist for a fuller sound.

The violin plays the melody whilst the *kontra* – often merely three-stringed – provides a chordal accompaniment in tandem with the bass, which probably also has three strings, although perhaps only one is played. During the weekend **markets**, Gypsies inspire the villages to wild **dances** with a steam of rough-edged music overlaying a pulsating bass rhythm. As the musicologist László Lajtha recognised in 1940, the Hungarians of Szék and other Transylvanian villages have preserved a taste for sounds evolved from the music of the ancient Magyars who wandered beside the Urals, without the 'Western' accretions aquired by folk music in Hungary itself. Although one can't be purist, since Sic's musicians also weave in Romanian *horas* and Gypsy riffs brought from India and Central Asia, some consider Szék a kind of repository of Hungarian folk culture. Certainly, the Magyars here wear **costumes** the like of which have long disappeared into museums in Hungary: the men narrow-brimmed, tall straw hats and blue waistcoats; the women leather waistcoats and black headscarves embroidered with flowers, blouses and full red pleated skirts.

Thanks to a crowd of Széki villagers so attired, you don't have to ask from which bay of Cluj's *autogară* **buses to Sic** depart. (*When* they leave is a different matter – services are irregular and overcrowded as per usual.) When you arrive, check the times of buses back to Cluj, since there's no tourist accommodation and the police are hot on visitors staying in villager's homes (though it might be possible to camp out of sight in the vicinity). The nearest authorised lodgings are in GHERLA, about 20km away, which the bus passes through en route between Cluj and Sic; this town of 20,000 with a tourist chalet on Str. Izvorului is also linked by **railway** to Cluj and Salva (5-6 trains daily in both directions).

COJOCNA, east of Cluj, looks and feels different from Szék, being a spa-town of fairly recent origin. Music here is less upfront and more a hybrid of Romanian tunes and Gypsy styling. According to Peter O'Conner's amusing account of his sojourn there in 1970, Cojocna was founded by a single extended family, the Stoicas, which, liking the company of its own members and suffering no adverse consequences, happily interbred and multiplied for generations. (Appropriately, O'Conner's hostess bedded him to her husband's delight!) There's really no need to stay at the hotel attached to the spa, since Cojocna is only a short *personal* or *cursa* ride **from Cluj** (trains towards Cîmpia Turzii and Copşa Mică).

South into the mountains around Turda

With so many caves, rockscapes and picturesque villages, and the number of festivals throughout the year, one would have to spend months in the **Apuseni Mountains** to experience even half the region's attractions. Although roads and modernisation in general have affected the traditional, largely pastoral, lifestyle of the inhabitants, the Ţara Moţilor (or 'Land of the Tufted Ones' as the Romans called it) is still a world apart.

It makes sense to begin with **TURDA**, 31km south of Cluj, whence there are buses to a grand gorge, and slow trains heading up the Arieş Valley. Unfortunately the bus service from Cluj to Turda is abysmal, and to make the journey by rail requires changing at CÎMPIA TURZII – which also applies to

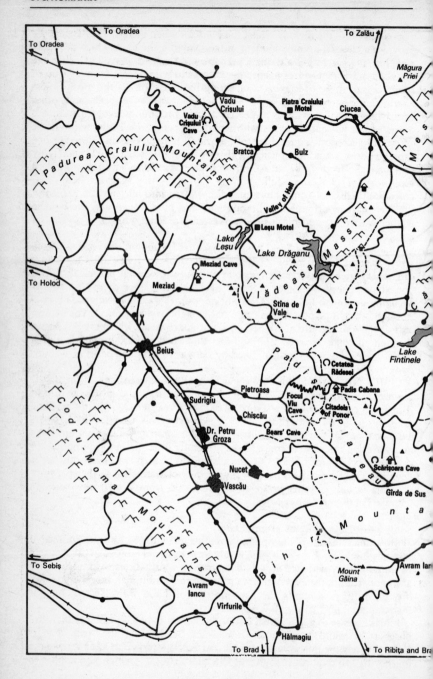

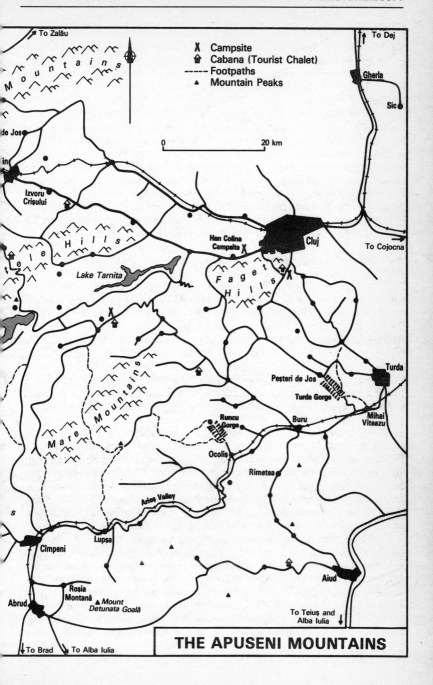

THE APUSENI MOUNTAINS

travellers approaching from the direction of Blaj, Deda or Deva – so hitch-hiking could well prove the quickest way of **getting there**. Modern Turda with its 58,000 inhabitants produces chemicals and building materials. It is not a pretty place, and only around the main square do you find evidence of the time it was one of the wealthiest towns in the country, 'with stately stone houses and beautiful streets'.

The Gothic/Renaissance pile just off the Piaţa Republicii which now contains a historical **museum** hosted meetings of the Transylvanian Diet between the C16–C18, and witnessed the promulgation of the **Edict of Turda** in 1568. This recognised the equality of four faiths in Transylvania at a time when religious wars were all the rage in Europe, but merely 'tolerated' Orthodoxy, the religion of the Vlachs; contributing to the systematic discrimination along ethnic and religious lines that wags would later dub the 'Seven Deadly Sins of Transylvania'.

Turda's **campsite** (north of town near the baths on a plateau) undercuts the hotel on Piaţa Republicii, but there's little reason to stay at either. Rather, ask the tourist office (nr.34) about buses to the gorge and reserve **beds** at the chalet there. Schedules might have changed since my visit, when **buses** left around 11am and 2pm, but services should still depart from the terminal on Str. Lazăr. Let the driver know that you're heading for the *Cheile Turzii* and he'll tell you when to alight at the village of MIHAI VITEAZU, whence it's 5–6km by a fairly obvious footpath to the **TURDA GORGE**. This begins with a valley where you'll find a hotel, campsite and chalets, and then rapidly narrows to a rough path passing between high rock walls for some 3km until it emerges at Peşteri de Jos, near which are several caves that were once inhabited by outlaws.

Travelling **from Turda up the Arieş Valley** towards Abrud is frustrating if you're relying on the trains – they take 6½hrs to complete the 93km journey, and there are only three services running each way. (Departures from Turda at 3.30am, 11.25am and 8pm, when I last checked). Riding up on the morning train and returning by the afternoon service allows time to visit several interesting places. 8km south of the BURU halt (tourist chalet), **RIMETEA** is a pleasant village whose largely Hungarian population still favours traditional dress (particularly for the local fête on February 22); while the third stop after Buru, OCOLIŞ, is just 2km from the **Runcu Gorge**. Another three stops later one can leave the train and walk to the Romanian village of SĂLCIUA DE JOS. Here, people wearing local folk dress complement the traditional architecture during village **festivals** (April 4 and October 20).

CÎMPENI, 5hrs ride up the valley, is the old capital of the *Ţara Moţilor* and a feasible base camp, with a hotel at 22, Str. Moţilor. With luck, though, you won't need to stay; buses run from the terminal (19, B-dul 23 August) in the direction of **GÎRDA DE SUS**, 40km to the northwest. A pretty commune with old houses, a wooden church and villagers wearing traditional dress, as in Arieşeni down the road (p.437), Gîrda de Sus is also the starting point for several excellent hikes. The most popular trail, designated by blue stripes, begins near the local **campsite**; leading through the Ordîncuşa gorges, past a mill, and into a forest whence it emerges to meet the karstic Scărişoara region (4hrs walk). From the tourist chalet there, it's a day's hiking to the Padiş

Plateau (see below), but only 20 minutes' walk to the **Scărişorara Ice Cave** along the path marked by red spots. Located near a glacier, this grotto with its intricate stalactites of ice is usually open every day from 9am-6pm.

Another subterranean curiosity lies a few miles from **ROŞIA MONTANĂ**, the penultimate stop on the railway. Evidence suggests that Transylvania was a major source of gold for the ancient world, and certainly the Romans used slaves to mine the neighbouring mountains, for 25 wax tablets recording details of the operation have been found. These can be seen during the course of a guided tour, the highlight of which is shuffling along a 400-metre section of the winding, ancient galleries, romantically dubbed the **Citadels of Gold**. Since the morning train from Turda doesn't arrive until after closing time (around 5pm), would-be visitors should be prepared to pitch camp here, or stay at the railway terminus, **ABRUD**. Abrud's hotel is on Piaţa 9 Mai near the bus terminal, where it's worth asking about services to **BUCIUM** ('Alpine Horn'), 13km away. Bucium is the commune for some thirty small villages and mining settlements such as Bucium-Şasa, whence it's an hour's climb to two basalt crags in the Detunata Mountains, designated as a monument of nature. Quite a few people here wear **folk costumes** which combine typical features of highland, pastoral clothing with embellishments peculiar to the mining communities. As in parts of Poland, the miners also have a ceremonial 'uniform' – although the full rig is hardly everyday attire.

On one day of the year, at least, traditional garments are donned in households across the Apuseni Mountains. The **'Girl Fair' at Mount Găina** is the region's largest festival. It's called a *Tîrgul de fete* because such events traditionally allowed young men and women from different communities to meet and – their parents willing – pursue matrimony; for with villages largely isolated and most males away in the highlands with their flocks for a third of the year, circumstances were normally unfavourable. Naturally, would-be-weds made – and still make – every effort to enhance their appeal, wearing their finest attire and (in the case of families with daughters) displaying linens, pottery and other items of dowry – even to the extent of carting along hired furniture. Nowadays, of course, many of the thousands who attend are here for the music and spectacle rather than for marriage, but the event is still a high point in the region's calendar.

The fair takes place on the Sunday before July 20 on a high mountain roughly 7km from the commune of **AVRAM IANCU**. Without a car, you'll probably have some difficulty in **getting there** (it's also necessary to camp out). Preferably, travel up the previous evening, stay overnight, and then rise early to look for a bus or lifts **from Cîmpeni** (see above) to Avram Iancu, 25km away. Alternatively, catch an early train down from Roşia Montană, or ride up the valley on the overnight service **from Turda**, which arrives in Cîmpeni around 9am. (See p.438 for suggestions on approaching Mount Găina **from the southwest**). The road from town to Avram Iancu passes through ALBAC, the birthplace of Vasile Nicola-Ursu: better known as **Horea** (or Horia), the main leader of the 1784 peasant uprising.

Hikes around the Padiş Plateau

From a tourist's standpoint, one of the focal points in the Apuseni region has to be the **Padiş Plateau** (*Plateul Padiş*), which involves a slight detour off the route between Cluj and Oradea. For speleologists and hikers, it's a paradise of dramatic peaks and gullies, so riddled with stalactite caves and subterranean rivers that the region has been nicknamed the 'Lost World' or the 'Underground Waterhouse'. There are numerous **approaches** open to motorists, but if you don't have a car the surest way is probably to hike from Gîrda de Sus. Marked by blue stripes, the trail runs via the Scărişoara chalet, whence it's 7-8hrs to the 'crossroads' of the plateau, the **Cabana Padiş**. Though officially the property of Bihor county's OJT (based in Oradea), beds here can usually be booked through Cluj or Turda's OJTs too. Reservations are advisable since the chalet is also used by folks who've completed day-long hikes over the mountains from the caves at Meziad and Chişcău (see p.436), or the ski resort of Stîna de Vale.

Of the various **trails** starting from the Padiş chalet, one of the most popular leads **to the underground Cetatea Rădesei** complex. Follow the route marked by red stripes until the Vărăşoaia clearing, where you should find another path (red spots) which leads off down towards the 'Citadel' itself. The underground part of the hike seems spooky but is quite safe (except during winter), and upon emerging near a brook, you have a choice of routes heading back towards the chalet via the Someşul Cald gorges (7-8hrs round trip). Another trail from the chalet, designated by blue dots, takes one southwards **towards the Citadels of Ponor**, a series of karstic springs and hollows. En route to the *Cetaţile Ponorului*, you'll see the Ponor Spring emerge and then be sucked back underground through a series of whirlpools; the area is like a sieve, with sink-holes and a wild watercourse that rushes into a cave. If you return directly to Cabana Padiş the round-trip should take about 6hrs (follow the blue dots back through the wood); but it's tempting to take a longer route back via the **Focu Viu Cave**. From the third hollow of the Ponor Citadel to the cave, this trail is designated by yellow dots, whilst the homeward leg is marked by red stripes.

Other hikes essentially follow mountain roads – westwards **to Pietroasa** (see p.437), or northwestwards **to Stîna de Vale** (marked by blue crosses or red stripes, respectively). The latter route begins at the Vărăşoaia clearing, but instead of heading towards the Rădesei Citadel, you ascend to a ridge and then make a long climb to the Cumpănăţelu saddle overlooking the Someş River. Later, one passes three more peaks before leaving the main ridge and descending through a forest to the ski resort (see below). Unlike most trails, this 6hr walk is considered safe for experienced hikers during the winter.

Detours off the route between Cluj and Oradea

Another batch of interesting places can be found **between Cluj and Oradea**: some railway halts and/or along the highway, others located amidst the mountains rising to the north and south. Anyone relying upon **trains** has to make a basic choice between *rapid/accelerats* services, which save time by limiting stops to Aleşd and Huedin, or the slow *personal/cursas* which open up vistas of exploration by halting at every village and hamlet en route. You'll find coverage of the 'western' half of this route in the Banat chapter; the following relates the first leg of the journey from Cluj.

Trains take a more northerly route to Huedin than the highway, so it's only the latter that passes through **IZVORU CRIŞULUI**. It's not uncommon to see local people selling **pottery** or embroidery by the roadside – particularly to Hungarian tourists on 'pilgrimages' to wellsprings of Magyar folk culture like the villages of the Transylvanian Heath. The 'pilgrims' (generally members of Budapest's intelligentsia) inspire mixed feelings amongst residents, who may welcome their money and moral support, but realise that this can equally encourage heavier 'Romanianisation' by the state. (Some believe that this was the reason why Izvoru Crişului's old wooden church was demolished by the authorities). The village's original name, *Kórósfő*, reflected its once exclusively-Hungarian character; its **festival** on the last Sunday of August most likely began as the local celebration of St Stephen's Day, though public demonstrations of affinity to Hungary are nowadays discouraged. It's easy to spend time here, since there's a bungalow/campsite 3km to the east beside the springs of the Criş (just off the highway), and the *Leghia* chalet in a meadow a similar distance to the north (3-4km walk from the Leghia P.O. railway *halta*).

HUEDIN is a small town where 'Horea often stopped on his way to Vienna with the demands of the oppressed peasants' (one can imagine inn-keepers saying 'Ah, *domnul* Horea! And how goes the petition?'). Its only 'sight' is a C16 Evangelical Church of such bulk that the adjoining wooden guard-tower seems a superfluous precaution, built in the days when Huedin was known as *Bánffyhunyad* after the local Magyar count. The chief reason to stop here is the chance of **buses** from the terminal on Piaţa Republicii to settlements in the neighbouring valleys, where traditional Romanian customs, architecture and crafts have so far escaped decimation by the C20. Log homesteads and a host of objects show that **woodcarving** skills haven't disappeared amongst the Romanians of **CĂLĂELE**, 15km south of Huedin and 5km farther down the same minor road, the Magyars of **CALATA** have yet to discard home-made **folk costumes** for mass-produced attire.

In the valleys to the **north of Huedin** there are half a dozen villages with striking **wooden churches** – examples of the Gothic-inspired *biserici de lemn* which once reared above peasant settlements from the Tisza to the Carpathians. The nearest one to Huedin figuratively dominates **FILDU DE SUS**, a small commune linked by 10kms of track to Fildu de Jos on the Zalău road. The others are probably beyond the range of buses from town, but quite easy to reach by car. **ZIMBOR**'s church, erected during the C16, is the oldest; and by the C17-C18 (when most of the remaining churches were built), peasant craftsmen had got around to adding flourishes like carved wooden gates on the church at **SÎNMIHAIU ALMAŞULUI**. From this commune, a minor road heads off towards Jibou, past **HIDA** (4km away) and **RACÎŞ** (another 6km), whose respective churches are distinguished by carved columns and old murals.

By timing things right, you could also attend local **festivals** like the one in a daffodil glade near Racîş (on the Sunday between June 1-15), or the *Mailişul* at **POARTA SĂLAJUILI**, a village 10km along the Zalău road with a late-C17 wooden church. Two more events are accessible by road, and then track, from the small town of **CIUCEA**, where Endre Ady and the Romanian poet Octavian Goga both formerly resided in a mansion (Goga's tomb and a small wooden church lie within its grounds). A minor road (and just possibly the odd bus) run northwards to **BUCIUMI**, an old Romanian settlement noted for its local costumes and choral and flute music (festival on August 15). Rising to the west are the Meseş (or Mezes) mountains – rugged highlands whose pastures support a scattering of communities.

Like pastoral folk in Bulgaria, Spain and Greece, the inhabitants entrust their sheep and goats to shepherds, who spend summer in the high pastures protecting the flock from wolves whilst making cheeses for the community's winter sustenance. In Romania, this has given rise to *Măşul lapteliu* or the '**Measurement of the Milk**' – a custom observed by folks from PRIA and other small villages on the slopes of **Măgura Priei**, the highest ridge in the Meseş range. At dawn on the first Sunday in May, villagers take the flocks up to a glade where the 'measurement' takes place. Women milk the she-goats – better than men, it's believed – and then shepherds milk the ewes, whose yield is measured to determine the quota of cheese that each owner will receive at the summer's end when the flocks return. Playful body searches ensure that nobody tops up their 'sample' with water, and the ritual is accompanied by much feasting and dancing.

To attend the festival, you'll probably have to camp the previous night near Pria, which lies just off the road between Ciucea and Lake Crasna, beyond Cizer. As the crow flies, the glade is less than 20km from Ciucea; but the paths approaching it (including trails across the mountains from Buciumi) meander considerably. In this region of the Apuseni, the only tourist **accommodation** consists of two bungalow/chalet/campsites: one 6km south of the highway before Ciucea, with its own railway halt, Valea Drăganului; the other in a birchwood 7km southwest of Zalău. Motorists are most likely to find them useful, and have the option of making **longer detours** to places north of Zalău (see p.386).

Another tempting detour begins relatively closer to Oradea, where a road leaves the highway near BULZ and heads southwards **through the Valley of Hell to Stîna de Vale**. Buses are unlikely to venture along this poorly-surfaced route, so travellers who alight at the *Bulz* or *Stîna de Vale* rail halts will have to hitch-hike or walk the 40 kilometres. This shouldn't be too much of a hardship, with the wild karst and a motel midway up the valley. At the end lies **STÎNA DE VALE** (3,610ft), a modest alpine resort with three slopes appropriate for beginners and **skiing** courses to match (6 days for $30), both operational between November and April, more or less. At other times of the year, the 'Sheepfold in the Valley' rents its hotel rooms, chalets and campsite out to the **hiking** fraternity. From here it's 5-6hrs walk *to the Padiş chalet* (see p.374), taking a path marked by red stripes which runs via the Poieni peak, the Cumpănăţelu saddle and the Vărăşoaia clearing (whence a separate trail runs to the Cetatea Rădesei, as related on p.374). Experienced walkers might prefer the more challenging trail *to Meziad* (6-8hrs; marked by blue triangles). With many twists and bends, this follows the ridge between the Iadului and Meziad valleys, surmounting the Piatra Tisei crag before descending to meet the tourist chalet below (the *Bears' Cave* there is described on p.437).

Should you eschew the Valley of Hell and continue westwards **towards Oradea**, turn to p.431 and 'backtrack' through the Banat chapter to find details of the route.

THE DACIAN CITADELS, HUNEDOARA AND DEVA

As monuments to ancient civilisations go, the **Dacian citadels** in the mountains between Timişoara and Sibiu are less impressive than the treasures and tombs of their contemporaries, the Thracians of Bulgaria. However, this part of Transylvania does have two striking medieval structures: the ruined fortress on the 'Hill of the Djinn' overlooking **Deva**, and the huge, practically undamaged Gothic/Renaissance castle of the Corvin family at **Hunedoara**. Deva lies along DN7 and the main line linking Sibiu with Timişoara while Hunedoara is accessible by railway from Simeria, but so off the beaten track are the Dacian citadels that **getting there** can be awkward without private transport. Coming **from Cluj**, motorists simply turn onto DN7 at Sebeş (p.360), but the journey **by rail** requires several changes. First, take any Braşov-bound train stopping at TEIUŞ, where you ride another train a couple to stops to VINŢU DE JOS. This lies along the main line running through Orăştie to Simeria and Deva, which serve as springboads to reach places of interest raised above the Plain of Bread (*Cîmpul Pînii*) watered by the Mureş River.

The Dacian Citadels
The jumping-off point for the Dacian citadels is the nondescript town of **ORĂŞTIE** (hotel and tourist office on Str. Bălcescu; campsite a kilometre or so west along the highway), where you'll hopefully find buses at the terminal on Piaţa Griviţa Roşie heading 18km south to the village of COSTEŞTI. Thick limestone walls and other vestiges of what some believe to have been the residence of King Burebista cling to Cetăţuia Hill, 3km from the village, whilst 4km to the south a four-towered citadel commands Blidaru Hill.

But the largest of the **Dacian citadels** lies deeper in the mountains, accessible by 8km of bad road leading from the hamlet of GRĂDIŞTEA DE MUNTE. Covering an area of 3.5 hectares 4,000ft above sea level, the ruins require imagination to conjure up what was once the Dacian capital from the weathered walls and stumps of pillars. Archaeological evidence suggests that **SARMIZEGETUSA** was divided into two distinct quarters: the citadel, used as a refuge by people from the surrounding residential areas during times of war; and the remains of four sanctuaries, believed to have served a religious purpose. These latter were originally upheld by andesite blocks and piles or wooden columns, the number and arrangement of which constituted a kind of calendar (a calendar carved into stone has also been discovered). Grădeştii Mountain was considered sacred by the Dacians, who called it *Kogaion*, and within the sanctuaries they performed ritual sacrifices to Zamolxis, Gebeleizis and Bendis – the deities of the Earth, Heavens and Hunting. Shrewd imperialists, the Romans appropriated the shrines and re-dedicated them to Diana and other figures in their pantheon; rebuilding Sarmizegetusa after capturing it in 106, and stationing a detachment of the IV Legion here.

Hunedoara
SIMERIA, further west along the highway, is worth mentioning only as a **railway junction** where one can board trains heading southwards down the main line towards Petroşani (change at *Subcetate* for Haţeg and Caransebeş,

see p.382), or services along the branch line to Hunedoara (9 daily). Motorists intending to follow either of these routes should take DN66 or road 68B (to the west of town), respectively.

HUNEDOARA could be dismissed as a smoggy, ugly iron and steel town were it not also the site of the greatest fortress in Romania, **Corvin Castle**. To quote Leigh Fermor, its appearance is 'so fantastic and theatrical that, at first glance, it looks totally unreal'. The castle is moated to a depth of 100 feet and approached by a narrow bridge upheld by 'precariously tall stone piers', terminating beneath a mighty barbican 'supporting a vertiginous roof' bristling with spikes, overlooked by multitudes of towers, 'some square and some round and all of them frilled with machicolations'. Founded during the C14 and greatly enlarged over the next 200 years, it was extensively (and tastefully) restored between 1965-1970. Within, the castle is an extravaganza of galleries, spiral stairways and Gothic vaulting, with an impregnable donjon and a Knights' Hall with rose-coloured marble pillars, now occupied by two museums.

The historical museum relates the achievements of **Iancu de Hunedoara**, the warlord known as János Hunyadi in Hungary, where a scaled-down replica of the castle (called *Vajdahunyad* by the Magyars) adorns Budapest's largest park. Whatever the truth of the story that Hunyadi was the illegitimate son of King Sigismund (who gave the castle to his nominal father, Voicu, a Romanian noble), the 'White Knight' rose largely by his own efforts – winning victory after victory against the Turks, whom Hunyadi devastatingly routed beneath the walls of Belgrade. Appointed Voivode of Transylvania, Hunyadi subsequently became regent of Hungary and a kingmaker (responsible for the overthrow of Vlad Dracul and the coronation of Dracula, see p.490), whilst his own son Mátyás Corvinus won even greater fame.

Once you've seen the castle there's no reason to remain in Hunedoara unless you require **accommodation** at the *Hotel Rusca* on Piaţa Victoriei or the campsite with cabins on the shore of Lake Teliuc (14km southwest of Hunedoara; buses from Piaţa Gării). The **tourist office** (16, B-dul Dacia; ☎ 1-36-06) can make reservations at the latter, and hikers' chalets in the Retezat Mountains should be you be heading that way. Approaches to – and walks through – the mountains are detailed on pp.381-385.

Deva

Hunedoara county's capital, **DEVA**, is a slightly smaller and considerably more salubrious town, gathered around a **citadel**. Raised during the C13 and transformed into one of Transylvania's strongest fortifications on Hunyadi's orders, the citadel crowns a hill in the shape of a truncated cone – supposedly the result of a stupendous battle between the djinns (spirits) of the Retezat mountains and the plain, hence the fort's old nickname, the 'citadel of the Djinn'. Although the mason charged with building it reputedly immured his wife, like Manole at Curtea de Argeş, in order to guarantee his creation's indestructability, a great explosion blew the citadel apart in 1849, leaving only the ramparts and barracks that one sees today. An exhausting climb rewards with views over the Mureş valley – which enters a narrow defile between the Metaliferi and Poiana Ruscă mountains near Deva.

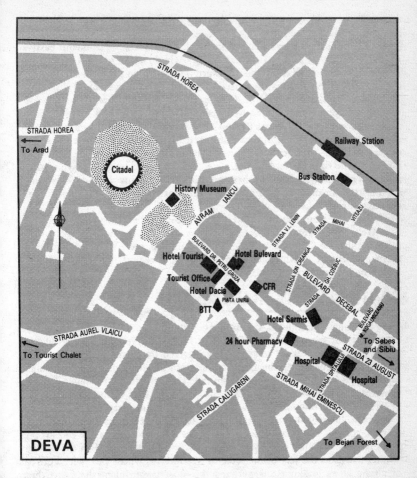

DEVA

The park beneath the hill contains a statue of Decebalus, the last king of the Dacians, and a **museum** exhibiting archaeological finds in the Orăştie Mountains, occupying the residential Magna Curia Castle once owned by Voivode Gábor Bethlen. En route there from the railway station, you'll pass the *Bulevard* and *Turist* hotels on the main drag, near the **tourist office** and the *Hotel Dacia* coexisting on the Piaţa Unirii together with a statue of Dr. **Petru Groza**. A delegate at the Assembly of Alba Iulia in 1918, Groza was an important politician before and after the Second World War. With the Communist Party banned or subject to severe harassment, it was he who led the legal opposition during the fascist era, founding the agrarian party known as the Ploughmen's Front in 1933, which had its headquarters in Deva. Elected Prime Minister of the coalition government in 1944, Groza tried to moderate the nationalism of the Communist leader Gheorghiu-Dej; his eventual dismissal was viewed as a harbinger of the regime's crack-down on Romania's Magyar minority.

Roundabout the second week of January, Deva hosts the colourful **Festival of the Căluşari** (*Căluşerul transilvănean*) which, alas, few foreigners see. Ensembles from Wallachia and southern Transylvania perform the intricate dances and rituals originally devised to ensure good harvests and dispell the *Rusalii*. In Romanian folklore, these spirits of departed friends or relations would take possession of the living should they violate any of the taboos associated with the 'Week of Rusalii' following Whitsun; for which the only cure was exorcism by a group of *Căluşari* led by a *vătaf* who knew the secrets of magic charms or *descîntece*. The rite was also intended to promote fertility, and in the old days the male dancers were accompanied by a Mute who wore a huge red phallus beneath his robes and muttered lewd invocations. Nowadays such antics are discouraged, and the Mute carries a more innocuous wand covered in rabbit-fur.

The journey **from Deva to Arad** is quite straightforward whether one drives or travels by railway (trains every hour or so), and the latter stages of this route are described in reverse order in the Banat chapter. What follows below is an account of southwestern Transylvania, a region that's accessible by DN66 or by trains originating from Simeria.

SOUTHWESTERN TRANSYLVANIA

Over the course of millenia, the stone age tribes that once huddled around the caves and hot springs of the Carpathian foothills developed into a cohesive society, whose evolution was crucially affected by events in **the southwest**. Rather than penetrating the Dacians' heartland by way of the Timiş Valley, the Romans fought their way up from the Danube through the narrow passes subsequently known as *Poarta Orientalia* and the Iron Gate (*Poarta de Fier*) of Transylvania to found a new capital, **Roman Sarmizegetusa**. During the C19, the Austro-Hungarian empire exploited a felicitous combination of thermal springs and classical legend to make **Băile Herculane** one of Europe's poshest spas; with its chintzy promenades, a different world to the smoggy mining towns at the feet of the **Retezat Mountains**, whose peaks feed dozens of alpine lakes, making this perhaps the most beautiful of the Carpathian ranges. It's deservedly popular with hikers, while further to the west, **winter sports** are catching on in the **Semenic** range, where **Reşiţa's** tourist office organises visits to several deep **caves**.

Heading south from Simeria, there are two **routes** around the mountains, offering some access to the interior should you wish to take advantage of it. Anyone bent on **hiking** should weigh the pros and cons of the different approaches described below, and reserve cabana beds through OJT in Deva, Hunedoara, Haţeg or Petroşani; but otherwise, transport will probably be the main consideration. All southbound **trains** from Simeria aim for Petroşani and the lower reaches of the Jiu Valley (see p.314); so travellers intending to reach Haţeg or Caransebeş should change at Subcetate, and be prepared to walk through the Iron Gate if there aren't any **buses**. During summer, there may also be buses from Haţeg and/or Sarmizegetusa up to the Gura Zlata chalet, and from Ohaba de Sub Piatră up to Cîrnic – OJT should know the schedules.

Routes into the Retezat Mountains

Besides the approach from Sarmizegetusa, it's possible to make your way **into the mountains** by footpaths and/or roads starting from communes along the railway line between Subcetate and Petroşani, or the mining towns at the top of the Jiu Valley. The only trains to halt at the former are *personale* and *cursas*; if you want to reach Vulcan or Lupeni by rail, it's necessary to change on to the branch line at Livezeni. You could do worse than start **from Ohaba de Sub Piatrăa**, whence it's 5½hrs walk up **to the Pietrele chalet**, with a good road and the chance of buses as far as Cîrnic during the summer. This trail can get quite crowded, however, so some hikers prefer to start **from Piu** (campsite) and trek for 6½hrs up a very steep, 23 kilometre-long mountain road **to the Baleia chalet**. (See below for walks beyond these chalets).

Other people opt to get there **from the mining towns** – grim places surrounded by bleak mountains. Unless you're interested in the history of the coalfields (first exploited during the C18), which is related in a *museum* on Str. Bălcescu, the only reason to visit **PETROŞANI** is to reserve cabana beds through OJT (27, Str. Republicii; ☎ 4-17-33), if you haven't already done so. There's accommodation a few kilometres to the north and south of town (*Peştera Bolii* chalet is cheaper than the motel), but it makes sense to push on to VULCAN or LUPENI (chalets 2-3hrs walk away). From here, there should be buses heading up the valley **to Cîmpu lui Neag** (tourist chalet and motel), whence one can walk into the mountains.

Of the numerous **trails from Cîmpu lui Neag**, two of the most popular lead **to the Buta chalet**. Red crosses mark the quickest route (5½-6½hrs), which runs through a forest of Douglas firs and up to the La Fete sheepfold, offering great views of the 'karst cathedrals' en route. Red triangles designate the longer trail (10-12hrs) to the chalet, which goes via the weirdly-formed Sococu Jiului gorge, and the plateau of Piatra lui Iorgovan where chamois may sometimes be seen. At various points along the initial stretch, there are (not always signposted) paths heading southwards, **to Tismana** (roughly 6hrs) and down **towards Băile Herculane** (allow 2 days). Descriptions of these places appear on p.316 and p.385.

The best hikes take one **across the mountains** past serried peaks and alpine lakes. Starting from cabana Baleia, red triangles designate a taxing but wonderfully scenic route **to the Gura Zlata chalet** (7-8hrs). However, more hikers reach Gura Zlata **from Sarmizegetusa or Clopotiva**, catching buses or walking up the Rîul Mare valley road (5½-6hrs). It's wise to reserve beds here through OJT in Haţeg or Hunedoara, since the chalet is also used by hikers pursuing other routes. Red triangles and spots and yellow and blue stripes mark successive phases of the trail **between Gura Zlata and the Pietrele chalet**, going by way of Lake Zănoaga, Lake Tăul Portii and the Bucurei Saddle. This hike should take 9-10hrs, but the trail is only considered safe for experienced climbers during the summer. The Gura Zlata road continues 12km south to the 'Mouth of the Water', **Lake Gura Apei**, from whose western extremity well-equipped hikers can follow a trail across the mountains **to the Muntele Mic chalet** in the vicinity of Caransebeş (allow 2 days). Should you have entered the mountains from the south, there are two trails leading on **from the Buta chalet**. Red stripes, and then blue crosses, designate a switchback path **to Cabana Pietrele** (7½hrs) leading past Lake Bucura and the *Genţiana* hikers'

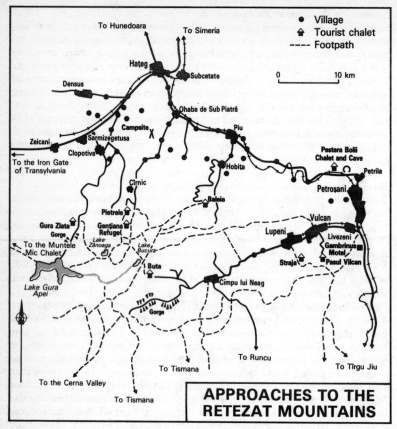

APPROACHES TO THE RETEZAT MOUNTAINS

refuge; whilst red crosses mark the trail **to the Baleia chalet**, going by way of the Bărbat springs and the Ciumfu Waterfall (9hrs; forbidden during winter).

Haţeg and the ruins at Sarmizegetusa

The tourist office on Piaţa Unirii in **HAŢEG** (☎ 7-04-52) might be able to help with buses to, and reservations at, the Gura Zlata chalet; and motorists may find the motel to the north of town on DN66 useful; but otherwise there's no reason to stop here if you're **heading southwest**. People travelling down **from Simeria by rail** should change at SUBCETATE, timing their arrival to catch the afternoon train for Sarmizegetusa (departing around 4.30pm), since this is probably more reliable than buses from Haţeg.

Heading across the Haţeg depression, one retraces the route taken by Trajan's legions when, having forced the Iron Gate, they marched northwards to subdue the Dacian citadels in the Orăştie Mountains. Within a few years they had founded towns, most notably *Colonia Ulpia Traiana*, to which the name of the old Dacian capital, **SARMIZEGETUSA**, was later appended.

Today, the commune has a **campsite** and serves as a starting point for the Gura Zlata path (see above); but its fame still derives from the nearby **Roman ruins**. The excavated portions are less extensive than the original town, which probably covered an area of 32 hectares and contained a citadel measuring some 2,000 feet long by 1,750 feet wide. Visitors can see the remains of the *Forum*, the *Palace of the Augustales* where priests were trained, and the elliptical brick and stone *Amphitheatre* where gladiatorial combats and theatrical spectacles were staged. The *museum* exhibits artefacts and stonework finds, and appears not to mention the hypothesis that most of the 'Roman' colonists believed to have interbred with the Dacians to create the ancestors of today's Romanians were actually rather of Greek or Semitic origin (an argument advanced by critics of the 'Continuity Theory').

From the Iron Gate of Transylvania to Caransebeş

Trains from Subcetate terminate at Sarmizegetusa, but even if you have no luck with buses or hitching it's only about 6km to **ZEICANI** at the entrance to the **Iron Gate of Transylvania**. A narrow pass 2,293 feet above sea level, the *Poarta de Fier a Transilvanei* is named after the **battles** fought here. A monumental mace erected near Zeicani commemorates the defeat of 80,000 Turks by 15,000 Transylvanians under the command of Hunyadi in 1442; while it was further up the pass that the Dacians had their fateful clash with the Romans. As recorded by military scribes in 106, *Tapae* was a disaster for the Dacians: their forces were crushed, and their ruler Decebalus committed suicide rather than be ignominiously paraded through the streets of Rome.

The pass itself is 10-11km long, and while DN68 cruises right through, railway services aren't resumed until BOUŢARI on the far side of the Iron Gate, a feldspar-mining village with a local *fair* on October 15. If you miss the through-**trains to Caransebeş** leaving at around 11.15am and 4.50pm, there are other services running as far Oţelu Roşu, whence there are connections. A few **places en route** deserve a mention: namely MARGA with its fortified homesteads (2km south of Marga train halt); ZĂVOI, whence a minor road runs 20km south to the health resort of POIANA MĂRULUI (hotel); and GLÎMBOCA, a commune whose frescoed Greek-Orthodox church has been called 'the Voroneţ of the Banat' (*folklore event* on September 8).

CARANSEBEŞ lies beneath the mountains at the confluence of the Timiş and the Sebeş stream, around which Gypsy *Zlatari* used to pan for gold. Leigh Fermor encountered a group of them 'busy dipping wooden pans into the current. . .kneading and sifting the mud and the gravel, wringing and searching shaggy wet sheepskins which had been cunningly placed under their flimsy sluices; all of them peering down, rapt as kestrels'. Having served as the Banat's judicial centre during the Middle Ages, and commanding communications between Timişoara and Orşova on the Danube by virtue of its location, Caransebeş inevitably became a Habsburg garrison town – hence the outcrops of belle époque amongst the pre-fabricated structures of the socialist era. You'll also see two lions flanking a memorial to locally-born General Ion Dragolina, who died at the head of his troops in the Jiu Valley in 1916.

Having booked beds through OJT (1, Piaţa Republicii) and found the bus terminal on Splaiul Sebeşului, there should be nothing to stop you riding

12km out to **BORLOVA**. This commune is noted for its embroideries and peasant weddings, and holds a *Măsurişul laptelui* **festival** roundabout April 23, but visitors tend to pass through en route to the **MUNTELE MIC**. The 'Little Mountain' **resort** can be reached by bus, and then a cable-cabin ride; and thanks to heavy snowfall, is used for **skiing** from late autumn until late spring. Basing oneself at the hotel or the cheaper villas and chalets, it's easy to walk to the Muntele Mic (1hr) or other peaks further afield; while for more dedicated **hikers** there's a trail heading eastwards towards Lake Gura Apei – just follow the red stripes, but be prepared for an expedition lasting 1-2 days (a tent's essential, and this route is forbidden during winter).

Most **trains from Caransebeş** run westwards to Timişoara on the Banat, or down to Orşova and Turnu Severin on the Danube (p.316); but there are also five services a day **to Reşiţa**. There, travellers should alight at the *Sud* terminal in the centre rather than the *Nord* station unless they're keen to see the old locomotives parked near the latter (see below).

Reşiţa and the Semenic range

People have been beating iron into shape around **REŞIŢA** since Dacian times, so it's hardly surprising that this was one of the first towns in the country to industrialise. The metallurgical works here can trace its history back to 1771, and erected a funnel-shaped monument to mark its bicentenary (though the 'eternal flame' within has been extinguished for reasons of fuel economy); whilst visitors entering town via the Timişoara road (B-dul Lenin) will pass a **collection of locomotives**, which Reşiţa has been manufacturing since 1873. Local steelworkers have a long tradition of militancy (see the museum at 103, Str. Văliugului), and contingents from the steelyard take pride of place in the *Alaiul Primăverii* **spring parade**. Besides this event (normally held during the first week in April), the town also hosts the **Bîrzava Song Festival** some time in August. The *Bistriţa* (2, Str. Marx) and *Semenic* (2, B-dul Lenin) hotels charge $38 for a double and $28 for single **rooms**, so if you're considering attending either event, it's cheaper to stay outside town at Semenic or Crivaia (reservations from OJT on Piaţa 1 Decembrie just south of the *Reşiţa-Sud* station).

Walk southwards from OJT and eastwards along Str. Libertăţii) to find the *autogară* on Str. 6 Martie, whence there are fairly regular buses out to VĂLIUG, the starting point for excursions into the **Semenic Mountains**. From here, one road leads 3km to **CRIVAIA** (hotel, bungalows, campsite), whilst another leads to the terminal of the cable-chair that carries visitors up to **SEMENIC** in 30 minutes. Pistes at Semenic are graded from 'difficult' to 'very easy', and normally fit for **skiing** from November until April. Although the massif is lower and less rugged than others in the Carpathians, it still offers the chance of good **hiking**. One of the most popular treks is from Semenic to the Comarnic Cave, and on to the **Caraşului Gorges** (10-11hrs; blue stripe markings). Situated just before the eastern entrance to the gorges, the **Comarnic Cave** is the Banat's largest grotto, with a spectacular array of rock 'veils', calcite crystals and 'cave pearls' distributed around its 400 metres of galleries on two levels (guided tours). The gorges themselves are extremely wild and muddy (good boots required) and harbour several more caves, of which *Popovăţ* – likewise open for tours – is the most impressive. If you don't fancy hiking there from Semenic or Crivaia, the gorges can also be entered near **CARAŞOVA**, a village accessible by bus from Caransebeş.

Băile Herculane and the Cerna Valley

Heading south by road or railway, you'll pass through the **Poarta Orientalia** or 'Eastern Gate' of Transylvania a few miles beyond the Roman *castrum* near TEREGOVA (accessible by an unmarked trail from Semenic; 5½-6½hrs). All trains halt briefly at the Băile Herculane stop, 5km from the spa of the same name at the bottom of the Cerna Valley (buses and taxis).

BĂILE HERCULANE gets its name from the Roman legend that Hercules cured the wounds inflicted by the Hydra by bathing here, and the nine springs with their varied mineral content and tempertature (38°C-60°C) are used to treat a wide range of neurological, gynaecological, muscular and metabolic disorders. During the C19, royal patronage made this one of Europe's most fashionable watering-holes, and even after the demise of the Austro-Hungarian empire 'colour and vivacity stamped its denizens and the crowded tables', giving the **spa** 'the comic and engaging charm of an operetta'. Nowadays, several ugly modern hotels have arisen amongst the 'terracotta balustrades, palmetto-palms' and 'fin-de-siècle stucco' and the resort hasn't escaped the country's slide towards austerity.

Besides wallowing in the **Apollo Baths**, Băile Herculane's chief attraction is its surroundings – statuesque peaks clothed in lush vegetation and riddled with caves. You can bath for free in the **Seven Hot Springs** about 35 minutes' walk upstream just beyond the Cerna Rapids, while another 2hrs hiking will bring you to the white **Gisella's Cross** whence there are magnificent views. From there, an unmarked path leads to a spectacular 1,000ft precipice with boulders strewn about the forest of black pines (30 minutes' walk). Other paths provide access to the vaporous **Steam Cave** on Ciorci Hill (1½hrs) and the **Outlaws' Cave** where stone age tribes once sheltered (30mins), or the **Mt. Domogled nature reserve** with its rare trees and flowers and more than 1,300 varieties of butterfly (4hrs). History buffs might enjoy the Roman votive stones and other artefacts in the **museum**, which occupies the former Casino where Leigh Fermor's evening 'spun itself into a golden haze'. Hotel **accommodation** is on the costly side, but there are reasonably-priced bungalows to be had on the campsite near the resort.

The middle and upper reaches of the **Cerna Valley** are still much as Leigh Fermor described them: 'a wilderness of green moss and grey creepers with ivy-clad water-mills rotting along the banks and streams tumbling through the shadows', illuminated by 'shafts of lemon-coloured light' striking the 'vapour coiling along the stream-bed and into the branches' like 'a world emerging from primordial chaos'. Amongst the butterflies and birds that proliferate here you might see rollers, which the Romanians call *Dumbravăveancă*, 'one who loves oak-woods'. It's roughly 40km from Băile Herculane to the watershed of the Cerna, whence there's a **path into the Retezat Mountains** which joins the trail between Cîmpu lui Neag and the Piatra lui Iorgovan plateau (red stripes; allow 1-2 days; see p.381); but well before this, the road turns off **towards Tismana** (places along the way are detailed on p.316).

Moving on
With a good road and frequent trains heading southwards, the obvious destinations are ORŞOVA and DROBETA-TURNU SEVERIN on the Danube, near the Iron Gates and the 24-hour road **crossing into Yugoslavia**. Most European citizens can painlessly acquire the requistite **visas** at the border, but Americans, Canadians, Australians and New Zealanders are supposed to obtain them beforehand from a Yugoslav embassy or consulate (although by paying extra and pleading, you might be able to wrangle one despite the rules). If you're heading that way, the *Rough Guide to Yugoslavia* will prove useful.

NORTHERN TRANSYLVANIA AND THE ROUTES TO MARAMUREŞ AND MOLDAVIA

Northern Transylvania is a handy label for the swath of ranges extending from the Apuseni Mountains to the Eastern Carpathians – an area divided into two counties, Salaj and Bistriţa-Năsăud. None of the towns here are as interesting as places like Cluj or Braşov, but there are numerous picturesque villages and small festivals that might well justify the effort required to get there. Broadly speaking, the sections below are arranged with the idea of travelling from Cluj to Maramureş, or eastwards over the Carpathians into Moldavia. The emphasis is on rail routes since the longer the distance to be covered the smaller the likelihood of buses; but travellers with private transport can be considerably more flexible.

Approaches to Maramureş
The quickest way of getting to Maramureş from Cluj is to follow DN1C northwards past ŞOMCUTA MARE up to Baia Mare, or catch a train to Dej and then change onto the Baia Mare-bound *Rapid Maramureş*, which leaves around 3.20pm and does the journey in 2hrs. Motorists passing through might be able to attend Şomcuta Mare's *festival* in July; while CĂŞEIU, just north of Dej, is the place to turn off onto the poorly-surfaced *Tîrgu Lăpuş route*. (For more about both, see p.420).

Places along the road between Cluj and Zalău have already been mentioned on p.374, and the point to stress about the **Zalău route** is that it's roundabout, especially travelling by rail. To spend any time at villages or festivals en route, one has to be prepared to start early, stop somewhere, then catch a later train on or camp out at the end of the day. To begin, catch an early service from Cluj up to JIBOU, and then the 10.50am Carei-train as far as GURUSLĂU if you want to witness the colourful *pageant* commemorating Michael the Brave's victory over Sigismund Báthori (1601), held on the first Sunday in August. Alternatively, ride on to Şărmăşag and hope for a bus or walk 4km down the Şimleu Silvaniei road to SIGHETU SILVANIEI, where another village *fair* takes place on the second Sunday of July beneath Michael's Oak. DERŞIDA, two stops beyond Şărmăşag, has a fine C18 *wooden church*, and by following a minor road for 8km through Bobota you'll find a similar edifice in the village of ZALNOC. There's another wooden church at CORUND,

8km southeast of the Supuru railway halt, which has its own fête on January 14-15. After ACÎȘ the road continues northwards to SATU MARE (44km), but the railway veers westwards through TĂȘNAD (hotel) to CAREI, where it's possible to board through trains to Satu and Baia Mare in Maramureș.

The third option is **to approach Maramureș from the southeast**. Services from Cluj to Ilva Mică (see below) call at SALVA, whence there are two trains daily (3.20pm & 7.20pm) up to Săcel and Vișeu de Jos near the Iza Valley, which terminate at Sigetu Marmației 3½hrs later. Should you miss the connection and need to stay overnight, there's a *campsite* with chalets just near **BECLEAN PE SOMEȘ**, a small town at the junction of DN17 and DN17D, a few stops before Salva on the Ilva Mică line. Motorists should turn north there to reach Salva, and more or less follow the railway thereafter.

This last route coincides at several points with the journey from Cluj to Moldavia, so motorists or travellers willing to rely upon local trains could feasibly combine elements of the two itineraries.

Travelling from Cluj to Moldavia
As far as driving **from Cluj to Moldavia** goes, you simply pick up DN17 at Dej, and then follow it eastwards through Bistrița and the Bîrgău Valley as described shortly. The railway journey to Moldavia involves a more northerly route, and the first step is to take any service from Cluj to ILVA MICĂ, timing your arrival to catch the 9am, 1pm, 3.20pm or 6.25pm Suceava-bound trains. Using these one can reach VATRA DORNEI or several of the Painted Monasteries, as related in the chapter on Moldavia; but it's also worth considering **detours** to some of the following places.

Beautifully embroidered vests and blouses similar to those displayed in the museum (25, Str. Republicii) are actually worn by some residents of NĂSĂUD, a small town several stops *before* Ilva Mică, along the Bistrița road. If you're into literary pilgrimages, the birthplace of **Liviu Rebreanu** (1855-1944) – whose novels *Ion, Uprising* and *The Forest of the Hanged* give a panoramic view of Romanian society before the First World War – can be found in a village, now named after its most eminent son, 3km south of town. A small branch line running from Ilva Mică up to Rodna Veche beneath the Rodna Mountains (3 trains daily) provides access to the shabby **SÎNGEORZ-BĂI** spa, and terminates a couple of miles before the object of the exercise, ȘANȚ. This attractive village of wooden houses with open verandas and shingled roofs is noted for its wedding celebrations (usually at weekends) and the kind of **winter customs** practised at Tudora in Moldavia.

Your visit is more likely to coincide with the **festival** at LEȘU, which is usually held on the first Sunday of September (but check with OJT first). The *Rhapsody of the Trișcași* brings together pipers from the counties of Vîlcea and Maramureș, so it's a great opportunity to hear *nai* music. With the exception of the 3.20pm, all Suceava-bound services stop at the Leșu halt roughly 8 minutes after leaving Ilva Mică.

Bistrița
Although the real Vlad Țepeș merely travelled through, rather than resided, in this part of Transylvania, it was here in the Bistrița that Bram Stoker sited the

castle of Dracula, Vlad's fictional namesake. Stoker never visited Romania though he read widely in the British Museum Library in London. He adopted the foreign appellation 'Borgo' for the narrow Bîrgău valley, but accurately described the hills covered with orchards that surround the town of Bistriţa, where Jonathan Harker received the first hints that something was amiss. The journey to Bistriţa by road is quite straightforward, but **getting there** by rail involves changing at *Sărăţel*, just south of Beclean on the Satu Mare-Deda-Braşov line (trains depart around 11am, 12am, 2.30pm, 5.30pm, 6.50pm & 7pm).

Digs have revealed human settlements in Neolithic times, but the first mention of **BISTRIŢA** roughly coincided with the arrival of Saxon settlers, who made this one of their 'seven towns'. Its medieval prosperity owed much to trade with Moldavia, under whose authority the town was placed during the mid-C16. On Str. Dornei you'll find a stone-framed Renaissance silversmith's house now occupied by the **History Museum** with its collection of Thracian bronze-ware, Celtic artefacts and products of the Saxon guilds (nr.5). The **Şugălete** buildings on Piaţa Centrală – formerly occupied by merchants – give a partial impression of how the town must have looked then. Like Braşov and Sibiu, Bistriţa used to be heavily fortified, but successive fires during the C19 have spared only vestiges of the citadel around Piaţa Unirii and four neighbouring streets, plus the **Coopers' Tower** (*Turnul Dogarilor*) in the Parc Municipal. Nowadays, Bistriţa's appearance is predominantly modern, and for evidence of its folk traditions you have to investigate the **Ethnographic**

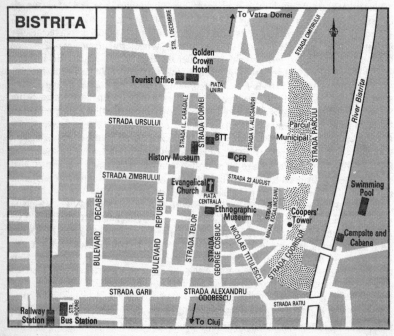

Museum or, better still, the neighbouring Bîrgău Valley.

Exploiting the Dracula connection, Bistriţa's **hotel** sells bear salami and blood-red alcoholic 'Elixir Dracula', and bears the name of the 'Golden Crown' (*Coroana de aur*) after the inn where Harker was warned not to travel on St George's Day: 'Do you not know that tonight, when the clock strikes midnight, all the evil things in the world will have full sway?'. At $28 for a single and $38 for a double, its rooms are 'cheap' by Romanian standards; but *Codrişor campsite* (with bungalows for rent) takes a smaller bite from one's pocket. The **tourist office** can arrange excursions to, and reservations at, the Dracula Hotel (see below), and you might also ask them to confirm the dates of festivals at Leşu and the Bîrgăului villages.

The Bîrgău Valley and the Tihiuţa Pass

If buses aren't forthcoming at the terminal, the train that leaves Bistriţa around 8.20am will get you about one third of the way **towards Vatra Dornei in Moldavia**, although there's still another 60km or so from Prundu Bîrgăului, not to mention the 4,000ft Tituţa Pass, to be crossed. Since lifts may be few and wolves have occasionally attacked solitary humans after dark at the pass, car-less travellers should think twice before attempting the final stretch; drivers, too, should bear in mind the possibility that snow might block the road at its highest point.

However, there's nothing to stop you exploring the **Bîrgău Valley**, where 'the scenery is awe-inspiring, with towering mountains, massive rock faces and occasional forests of fir trees', as MacKenzie writes. Nowadays, one no longer sees women leading pony-trains of flax and wool from Vatra Dornei through the valley to the Saxons' fulling mills, but the ceramics, woodcarvings and folk dress displayed in LIVEZELE's museum are part of everyday life in other villages farther up the valley – for example **JOSENII BÎRGĂULUI**, where black pottery is manufactured and old fulling mills and cottages remain in use. **PRUNDU BÎRGĂULUI** is one of the few places where Saxon **wedding customs** (p.356) are still observed during February, with the participants wearing **traditional dress**. Unusually, men wear more flamboyant garb than the womenfolk during weddings and the *Ţăinari* **Raftsmen's Festival** on March 28-29. Unmarried chaps crown their satorial ensemble – which includes sheepskin jackets sporting rows of coloured tassels – with a small hat buried beneath a plume of peacock feathers. On St George's Day (April 23), it's customary for young men to light bonfires over which the unmarried girls jump; only one attempt is permitted, success portending marriage within the year, whilst failure is taken to mean another year of maidenhood.

If you leave the train at Prundu Bîrgăului it's less than a kilometre's walk to **TIHA BÎRGĂULUI**, which some years (check with OJT first) hosts an interesting event on the third Sunday of June. Traditionally, the peasantry viewed death as 'a long journey into another world not much different from real life', requiring an accounting of one's deeds in this world as a prelude to new experiences in the next. This was the duty of the deceased's relatives and friends, who took comfort from the message of renewal in the *Great Song*, *Dawn* and the *Fir Tree* (the latter's evergreen nature being a symbol that particularly appealed to Romanians, whose empathy with forests runs deep).

The **festival of Regele Brazilor** ('King of the Fir Trees') provides an opportunity to hear these songs, and the part stereotyped, part improvised lamentations known as *bochet*; accompanied by various manouevres with fir-branches associated with old Romanian **funerary rites**.

Steadily climbing as it heads eastwards, DN17 passes the village of Piatra Fîntînele and the **Dracula Hotel**, which outwardly resembles a forbidding castle, erected more or less where Stoker located Dracula's castle at the 'Borgo Pass'. Just beyond lies the **Tihuţa Pass**, often blocked by heavy snowfalls between late October or early November and mid-May. The surrounding ranges harbour more **bears** than any other part of Romania, not to mention Carpathian stags, boars, deer and **wolves**, whose gleaming eyes and terrifying howls are by no means uncommon after night falls on the Tituţa Pass. From here one has a marvellous view of the green 'crests' or *obcinele* of Bucovina, while the road descends past the picturesque village of Poiana Stampei **down to Vatra Dornei** (see Moldavia).

FESTIVALS

Winter
Colourful events at ŞANŢ (in the Rodna Mountains), ILIA, DOBRA (both east of Deva) and SĂLIŞTE (near Sibiu) in **late December**, sometimes merging into the **New Year**'s *Pluguşorul* rites (practised in many villages), with festivities continuing through until **January 1-2** at AŞCHILEU (northwest of Cluj), ARPAŞ and ŞERCAIA (both east of Braşov). During the **second week** of **January** scores of *Căluşari* assemble at DEVA, whilst CORUND hosts a festival for the folk of Zalău county on the **14-15**. *Saxon weddings* might occur in villages around SIBIU, BISTRIŢA, BRAŞOV on **February 3**, and the Hungarians of RIMETEA have a fête on the **22**.

Spring
Festivities kick off with the *Raftsmen's Festival* at PRUNDU BÎRGĂULUI on **March 28-29**, followed by a local fair at SĂLCIUA DE JOS on the **4** of **April**. Then come two major events – the Spring Parade through REŞIŢA during the **first week**, and the *Flowers of the Olt* folklore festival at AVRIG (near Sibiu) on the **first Sunday**. On the **23**, *St George's Day*, villagers blow horns to repel *strigoi*, Saxon maidens jump bonfires at Prundu Bîrgăului, and BORLOVA near Caran-sebeş puts its sheep through the 'Rite of Measurement'. A similar *Măsurisul* occurs on the ridge of MĂGURA PRIEI in the Apuseni Mountains on the **first Sunday** in **May**, at the same time as BRAŞOV

hosts the *Pageant of the Juni*. The onset of spring work on the land occasions Székely and Romanian ceremonies at BĂILE JIGODIN (outside Miercurea Ciuc) on the **third Sunday**, and sometime during the second half of the month there's a festival for peasants of the upper Mureş region at GURGHIU.

Summer
BRÎNCOVENEŞTI's *Cherry Fair* on the **first Sunday** of **June** coincides with a Székely folklore festival at ODORHEIU SECUIESC. There's a nice local fair at RACIŞ sometime between the **1-15**, the curious *Buying back of the Wives* festival at HODAC on the **second Sunday**, and a chance to hear folk songs and laments (*Bocet*) during the *Regele brazilor* at TIHA BÎRGĂULUI (between Bistriţa and Moldavia) on the **third Sunday**. BRATIEU's *Pe Mureşul şi Tîrnave* (exact date uncertain) and the *Nedeia of the Mountains* at FUNDATA on the **last Sunday** anticipate other highland fairs in **July** – on the **second Sunday** (at SIGHETU SILVANEI) and the **Sunday before the 20th** (at SĂCELE, and the famous *Girl Fair* at MOUNT GĂINA). In **August** there's a historical pageant at GURUSLĂU on the **first Sunday**, and a pottery fair at CORUND roundabout the **10-11**. The date of REŞIŢA's *Bîrzava Song Festival* varies, but the choral fête at BUCIUMI on the **15** and IZVORU CRIŞULUI's Magyar fair on the **last Sunday** are regular fixtures.

Autumn
Pan-pipers from all over assemble at LEŞU (near Tiha Bîrgăului) for the *Rhapsody of the Trişcaşi* on the **first Sunday** of **September**, whilst the feldspar-miners of BOUŢARI host a colourful fair on the **15**. On **October 20** there's another fête at SĂLCIUA DE JOS.

TRAVEL DETAILS

Trains

From Beclean pe Someş to Baia Mare (2 daily; 3-4hrs); Cluj (6; 1½-2); Deda (1; 1¼); Dej (11; ½); Sărăţel (6; ½).

From Bistriţa to Bistriţa Bîrgăului (3; 1½); Luduş (2; 3¼); Prundu Bîrgăului (3; 1¼); Sărăţel (8; ¼).

From Blaj to Cluj (4; 2-3¼); Copşa Mică (12; ¼-¾); Sighişoara (7; 1-1½); Teiuş (12; ¼-1½).

From Braşov to Baia Mare (2; 8½); Băile Tuşnad (5; 1-1½); Bucharest (5; 2¾); Ciceu (4; 1¾-2½); Cluj (5; 4¾); Deda (4; 4-7¼); Făgăraş (6; 1-1½); Hărman (8; ¼); Miercurea Ciuc (4; 1½-2); Prejmer (5; ½); Rîşnov (6; ½); Sibiu (4; 1¾-3½).

From Bucharest to Braşov (14; 2¾-3¾); Buşteni (5; 2-2¾); Cluj (1; 7); Sinaia (13; 1¾-2¼).

From Caransebeş to Băile Herculane (6; 1¼-1¾); Drobeta-Turnu Severin (4; 2); Lugoj (9; ½-¾); Orşova (4; 1¾); Reşiţa (5; 1½); Timişoara (8; 1-2).

From Ciceu to Adjud (1; 2¾); Braşov (5; 2½); Deda (4; 2); Ghimeş (4; ¾-1¼); Miercurea Ciuc (8; 10mins); Mihăileni (3; 7mins).

From Cîmpia Turzii to Cluj (11; ¾-1); Teiuş (10; ¾).

From Cluj to Braşov (5; 4¾-7½); Bucharest (1; 7½); Cojocna (6; ½); Constanţa (1; 12½); Dej (9; ¾-2¼); Huedin (7; 1-1¾); Ilva Mică (4; 2¼-3¾); Oradea (9; 2½-4); Salva (6; 1¾-2¾); Sighişoara (5; 3-4½).

From Copşa Mică to Blaj (10; ½-¾); Cluj (5; 2¼-4¾); Sighişoara (9; ¾-1); Sibiu (8; 1-1¾); Teiuş (6; ¾-2¼).

From Deda to Beclean pe Someş (1; 1½); Braşov (2; 5¼); Brîncoveneşti (5; ¼); Reghin (6; ½-¾); Tîrgu Mureş (6; 1-1½).

From Dej to Baia Mare (4; 2-3); Beclean pe Someş (11; ½); Cluj (9; ¾-1); Ilva Mică (5; 1¼-2); Jibou (5; 1-2); Năsăud (5; 1-1¼); Salva (5; 1¼).

From Făgăraş to Braşov (6; 1½); Podu Olt (4; 1¾); Sibiu (5; 1¼-2).

From Jibou to Baia Mare (5; 1-1¼); Carei (3; 1¾-2¾); Sărmăşag (4; 1¼); Zalău (7; ½).

From Podu Olt to Lotru (7; 1½); Rîmnicu Vîlcea (6; 1½-2½); Sibiu (15; ½-¾); Turnu Monastery (4; 1½).

From Sărăţel to Beclean pe Someş (5; ½); Bistriţa (6; ¼); Deda (3; 1).

From Sibiu to Agnita (2; 3); Copşa Mică (6; 1-1¾); Podu Olt (14; ½-¾); Sălişte (5; ½); Sibiel (5; ½); Simeria (3; 1½-2½); Tilişca (5; ¾); Vinţu de Jos (6; 1½-2).

From Sighişoara to Braşov (10; 1¾-3); Cluj (6; 3¼); Copşa Mică (10; ¾-1); Feldioara (3; 2¼); Odorheiu Secuiesc (2; 1¼); Rupea (5; 1¼).

From Simeria to Alba Iulia (12; ¾-1½); Arad (6; 2¼-3¼); Deva (17; ¼); Hunedoara (6; ¼-½); Petroşani (5; 1¾-2¾); Sibiu (3; 2½); Subcetate (7; ½-1); Teiuş (11; 1½-2); Vinţu de Jos (10; 1-1¾).

From Subcetate to Haţeg (2; ¼); Petroşani (6; 1-1¾); Sarmizegetusa (2; 1); Simeria (7; ½); Tîrgu Jiu (2; 2¼-3¼).

From Tîrgu Mureş to Deda (7; 1-1¼); Luduş (6; ¾-1); Reghin (7; ¾); Sovata (2; 3½).

From Turda to Abrud (3; 6½); Buru (3; 1); Lupşa (3; 4½); Ocoliş (3; 1½); Roşia Montană (3; 6¼).

From Vinţu de Jos to Alba Iulia (12; 10mins); Simeria (14; ¾-1½); Sibiu (5; 1½-2); Teiuş (14; ¾).

From Zalău to Jibou (7; ½-¾).

Flights

From Cluj, Sibiu and Tîrgu Mureş to Bucharest (1-2 daily) and Constanţa (during the summer only).

International trains

From Braşov to Berlin (2 daily; 32¾hrs); Budapest (7; 11¾); Burgas (1; 14¾); Dresden (3; 29); Paris (2; 37); Prague (4; 24); Varna (1; 13½); Vienna (2; 15¾); Warsaw (1; 28½).

From Cluj to Berlin (1; 24); Budapest (4; 7¼); Burgas (1; 18¾); Dresden (2; 23¼); Prague (3; 18); Varna (1; 18); Warsaw (1; 22).

From Sibiu to Budapest (1; 10½); Paris (1; 34½); Vienna (1; 14½).

From Caransebeş to Belgrade (1; 4¾); Paris (1; 25).

Chapter nine
MOLDAVIA

> 'Give me, O God, the Moldavian's wisdom last.'
> – Romanian proverb.

The 'wisdom' of **Moldavia** is not easy to define. The region, more than all others in the country, has experienced a succession of invasions, tumult, oppression and corruption. Its people, traditionally, were meditative and philosophical, as revealed by two of their own proverbs: 'Water flows but the stones remain', and 'a sword won't cut a lowered head'. Instead of searching for military power, they burned lamps before the icons of a glorious past – embodied in the hero-figure of Stephen the Great –. and awaited their resurrection. It seemed to begin in the C19, with a flowering of art, liberal politics and land reform, but the wheel kept turning – through a bloody uprising and its suppression, fascist and communist terror – until the present, stagnant eighties, when icon-burnishing is as fashionable as ever.

For travellers, Moldavia is generally more interesting the farther north one goes, and the difficulty of some journeys by public transport can, perversely, add to the attraction of your final destination. This is particularly true of the jewels in the Moldavian crown, the **Painted Monasteries of southern Bucovina**. Secluded in valleys near the Soviet border, their splendid medieval fantasies of redemption and damnation blaze in polychromatic splendour at the misty, fir-clad hills. All are more or less accessible from the regional capital of the north, **Suceava**, but anyone who prefers not to battle with trains and buses can see them on a 2-day *ONT tour* for $89 ($79 if you start from the coast), including flights, transport and accommodation. Farther south, there's another cluster of monasteries around **Tîrgu Neamţ**, while its namesake **Piatra Neamţ** isn't far from Mount Ceahlău and the **Bicaz Gorges** – some of the most impressive scenery in the eastern Subcarpathians. Through gaps in this range, it's possible to travel between Transylvania and Moldavia, and a couple of valleys are inhabited by the descendants of people who did just that – the so-called **Csángó communities**, which have their own distinctive music, culture and language.

Moldavia's cultural capital is **Iaşi**, a friendly if over-monumental university town near the River Prut, where the C19 renaissance began. It's a nice place to visit almost any time of the year, but when planning your route, take account of **Moldavian festivals**. The *Peony Festival* at Băneasa on the second Sunday of May is probably easiest to reach by train from Bîrlad or Galaţi (p.458), but the others are just off the main routes. At Odobeşti, a short ride by branch line or bus from Focşani, they celebrate their *wine harvest* with a bash on the last Sunday of September; while the Vrancea shepherds compete here with

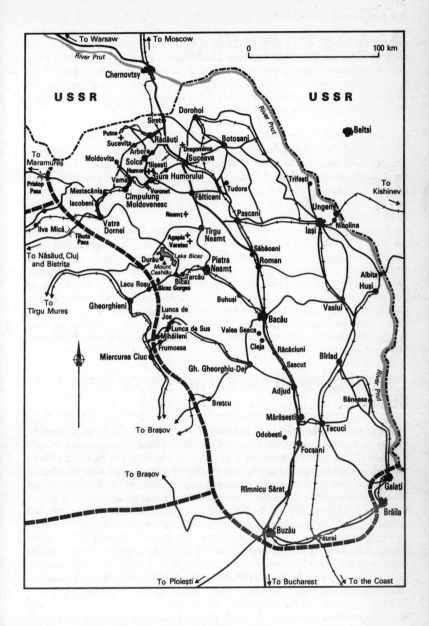

bagpipes, *nai* and alpine horns on the third Sunday of November. A week after commemorating Navy Day, Durău on the shores of Lake Bicaz pulls the crowds in for the *Ceahlău Feast*, on the second Sunday of August. Ilişeşti near Suceava is the site of a folklore jamboree, *From the Rurău Mountain*, on the second Sunday of July; while Botoşani and Tudora (among other places) go in for some fascinating winter customs. Finally, from Vatra Dornei in northwestern Moldavia, one can nip over the mountains during June, August or September to attend various festivals in Transylvania and Maramureş (see the appropriate chapter introductions).

Access

TAROM's daily flights from Bucharest (and Constanţa during the summer) provide the quickest means of **getting to Iaşi and Suceava**, albeit more expensively than by rail. Like DN2, the main line runs northwards up through Moldavia to Suceava: a journey of 5½-6½hrs on the *Rapid Carpaţi* or one of the midday *accelerate* (or the overnight *Varna Express*, which leaves Bucharest around 4am). All services stop briefly at Adjud – change there for the Csángó regions – and at Bacău, the junction for trains to Piatra Neamţ and Lake Bicaz. Of the four direct services to Iaşi, the overnight ones get you there in the morning, while the afternoon services from Bucharest arrive in Iaşi at an ungodly hour. Alternatively, one can follow the Suceava line as far as Roman or Paşcani before switching onto the Iaşi-bound branch lines (although beware – not all trains stop at the latter). From Mărăşeşti there's a branch line to Tecuci, whence several trains run to Iaşi, which is also accessible from Bîrlad (the railway connection to Galaţi). For motorists, the route from Bucharest to Iaşi is quite simple: just follow DN2 northwards until Săbăoani, and then take road 28.

THE SUBCARPATHIANS BETWEEN BUCHAREST AND SUCEAVA

The first leg of the journey **from Bucharest to Moldavia** cuts across a corner of the monotonous Romanian Plain or *Cîmpia Română* (trains are routed through Ploieşti), and it's not until Buzău that you'll see the outlying hills of the Subcarpathians. In the unlikely event that motorists need accommodation en route, there's an inn with bungalows and a campsite at SINEŞTI, 31km from Bucharest. BUZĂU, a long-established market town claimed at different times by Moldavia and Wallachia, really only merits attention on the last Sunday in June, when it hosts a **festival** derived from the **rite of Drăgaica**. Once widespread in rural Romania, this Midsummer's Day custom required young girls wearing crowns and hoods to go singing and dancing into the fields to verify the readiness of the wheat for harvesting. Otherwise, Buzău's attractions are solely architectural: the Episcopal Palace on Aleea Episcopiei, including monks' cells where scribes toiled at the expense of Prince Brîncoveanu; and the imposing Communal Palace on the corner of the main square and the Focşani road, Stradă Unirii, next door to *OJT*. If *BTT* (Bloc 2, Str. Vladimirescu) can't arrange **rooms**, there are two hotels not far from the square. *Buzău* stands at the top of Bulevard Bălcescu (way down the other end is the County Museum), while *Pietroasa*, renting singles for $30 and doubles for $40, lies in the direction of the railway station.

Continuing northwards, you'll soon hit **FOCŞANI**, with a campsite on the Bacău road and a hotel and tourist office on Piaţa Unirii, whence you can make a detour into the wine-growing region just west of town. There, the commune of **ODOBEŞTI** produces the yellow wine that's Ceauşescu's favourite tipple (Elena's is French champagne), and celebrates its grape harvest with a **festival**. This normally occurs on the last Sunday of September; while the musically-inclined shepherds of Vrancea county gather to entertain each other with performances on alpine horns and pan-pipes on the third Sunday of November. Be warned, however, that Odobeşti has no tourist accommodation, and buses and trains linking it with Focşani are fairly unreliable.

MĂRĂŞEŞTI, the next town, is where to change trains for Tecuci and connections to Iaşi. In 1917 this railway junction was bitterly contested by the Germans advancing towards Iaşi, and the Romanians, who were determined to preserve the last unoccupied region of their country, and ultimately successful. Assuming you don't aim for IAŞI (p.399) at this point, there's a choice between continuing northwards to Suceava or making a few **detours** – the subject of the following sections, which describe **the Csángó** regions and **monasteries and gorges** in the eastern Subcarpathians.

The Csángó regions

Csángó means 'wanderer' in Hungarian: an appellation given by the Székely to those of them – primarily religious dissenters – who fled over the Carpathians from Transylvania during the C15, to be joined by war refugees in the C18-C19. Once there were some forty **Csángó villages** in Moldavia, a few as far afield as the River Dneistr, but today their community has contracted into a hard core, numbering perhaps 40,000-60,000 people in all, living alongside the rivers between Adjud and Bacău, and in the Ghimeş district at the upper end of the Trotuş Valley. Their absorption into the new (and predominantly Romanian) industrial towns is probably inevitable in the long term, despite the fierce conservatism of most rural Csángós, who farm and raise sheep outside the collectives, wear a distinctive folk costume, speak a Magyar dialect amongst themselves, and remain fervently religious – none of which pleases the authorities.

Mutual suspicions and long memories of the armed uprising of the Gyimesi-Csángós in 1934 means that the state is sensitive about this area, which poses **problems** for visitors. Not only is there no tourist accommodation, but tales abound of travellers being turned back by police road-blocks (although the tourist board assures us that this is nonsense). Police keep a close watch for foreigners (particulary Hungarians) staying in Csángó households, and should you decide to spend any time here, come prepared to pitch camp somewhere out of sight, with ample food supplies.

The starting point for the Ghimeş (Gyimesi) Csángós is **ADJUD** on the Bucharest-Suceava line, whence about seven trains a day plough up past the ugly chemical town of GH. GHEORGHIU-DEJ to Ghimeş at the top of the

Trotuş Valley. **GHIMEŞ**, or Ghimeş-Făget, is the largest of four Csángó settlements in the valley, and the only one that's directly accessible by rail (using the Adjud-Ciceu line). It's also the venue for a **Winter Fair**, held every year on January 20-21. However, **FRUMOASA** ('Beautiful') can quite feasibly be reached **from eastern Transylvania**, since it's only 9km by road from Miercurea Ciuc (p.343), and 2km walk from the village of Mihăileni, one stop before CICEU, the railway junction between Adjud and Miercurea Ciuc. With luck, there should also be the odd bus or at least hitchable traffic along the valley, enabling one to see **LUNCA DE JOS** and **LUNCA DE SUS** too.

A separate, and rather less isolated Csángó community lives farther north in several villages a few miles west of the road and railway **between Adjud and Bacău**. **SASCUT, RĂCĂCIUNI** and **VALEA SEACA** are all stops for slow trains, whilst the minor road between the last two villages runs past **CLEJA** and **FUNDU RĂCĂCIUNI**. Hanging around here is somewhat easier, since there's a motel on the main road near Răcăciuni.

Bacău and Piatra Neamţ

The industrial town of **BACĂU** has little to recommend it to visitors except for its accommodation and transport facilities – the latter providing the means to reach other, more interesting places. Should you wish **to stay** here overnight, all four hotels are in the centre: *Moldova* and *Central* on Str. N. Bălcescu; *Bistriţa* at 3, Str. Luminii; and *Decebal* at 2, Str. 6 Martie. Otherwise, there's no point in leaving the railway station (linked to the centre by Str. Griviţa Rosie), whence there are regular services northwards to Suceava, and six or seven **trains** up the branch line to Piatra Neamţ, most of which continue on to Bicaz (see below).

Running alongside DN15, the branch line passes through the fertile Cracău basin to meet **PIATRA NEAMŢ** where the River Bistriţa emerges from the mountains. Despite its ironworks and paper mill powered by the Bicaz Hydro-electric dam, Piatra Neamţ is one of Romania's oldest settlements, occupied more than 3,000 years ago by folks since classified by their pottery shards as the 'spherical amphora culture', and later by the Dacians, whose citadel, *Petrodava*, has been excavated on Bîtca Doamnei hill just outside town. Assuming that you don't ride on to Bicaz (see below), it's a relatively short distance from the station up Bulevard Republicii into the centre, to find **rooms** at the *Hotel Bulevard* (incorporating *OJT*, nr.38) or the *Hotel Central* (nr.26); *BTT* are at nr.29 on the same street. Unusually, the **campsite** isn't on the road outside town, but on the south bank of the Bistriţa, some distance west of the train station. Downtown Piatra Neamţ is a fusion of two squares, Ştefan cel Mare and Libertăţii, and it's here that you'll find the *Hotel Ceahlău*, the **Fine Arts Museum** and a couple of historic buildings. The C15 **Church of St John** is one of the earliest examples of Moldavian ecclesiastical architecture, buttressed and niched, with a cable moulding and ceramic discs decorating its exterior. Nearby stands an impressive **Bell-tower** and the fragmentary remains of the old Princely residence. Travellers hoping to reach Tîrgu Neamţ and the monasteries off route 15C (p.398) by bus should make enquiries at the terminal at 1, Str. Bistriţei.

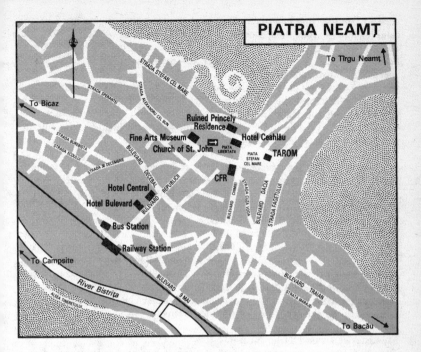

Lake Bicaz, Mount Ceahlau and the Bicaz Gorges

Passing the village of Tarcău with its old wooden houses, road and railway run to the small town of **BICAZ**, just north of which rises its raison d'être, the hydro-electric **dam** or *baraj* built in 1960 (tourist chalet nearby). Over 120 metres high and 435 metres long, this holds back the storage lake of IZVORU MUNTELUI (otherwise known as **Lake Bicaz**), with a **campsite** on its eastern shore (6km by road from the barrage). With mountains all around, the view is superb, particularly to the west where **Mount Ceahlău** arises from its foothills, half-encircled by the lake. This can be reached by boat from the Bicaz landing stage, or by footpaths (mark: red stripes and blue crosses) leading from *Izvoru Muntelui cabana* around the mountain's sheer escarpments and up to the *Dochia* chalet in the heart of the massif. Ceahlău's peaks have weathered into fantastic rock formations – Dorobantul, Toaca and Panaghia – whose shapes inspired Eminescu's poem *The Ghosts*, and various legends. It's said that the daughter of Decebalus was transformed by the gods into the Dochia peak; whilst the mountain was once considered to be the abode of Zamolxis, the Dacian god. One can also approach the massif from the direction of Durău, whence it's 4-5hrs walk to the Dochia chalet along a path running by way of the **Duruitoarea Falls** (mark: red crosses), or 2hrs trek to the Fîntînele chalet by another trail (red stripes).

During the winter, **skiing** replaces walking as the chief activity around the **DURĂU** resort, which features a small **hermitage** adorned with naturalistic paintings by Nicolae Tonitza, who used local backgrounds for his biblical scenes. Durău's hotel (with a disco and sauna) rents singles for $30 and doubles for $40, but there's cheaper **accommodation** to be had in villas and bungalows. On the second Sunday in August, a week after Navy Day, Durău hosts the **Ceahlău Feast**, which attracts peasants wearing embroidered sheepskin waistcoats besides more casually dressed holidaymakers. Fuel supplies permitting, a variety of **boats** cruise between the landing stages around the lake (near the dam, Piriul Mare below Durău, etc), which is rich in fish, including the Rainbow trout whose natural habitat is the mountain streams. Other **wildlife** in the vicinity of the mountain includes black nanny goats, mountain-cocks, wild bears and boars, and the majestic Carpathian Stag.

Though the bus service seems to have collapsed, it should be possible to hitch-hike the 25km from Bicaz to the famous gorges of the same name – a route which takes you through the village of BICAZ ARDELEAN, with its cute wooden houses and a local festival on the first Sunday of April. Just beyond one enters the **BICAZ GORGES** (*Cheile Bicazului*), whose limestone walls rise vertically to a height of 200-300 metres above the river, pressing so close around the 'Neck of Hell' (*Gîtul Iadului*) that the road is hewn directly into the rockface. The *Cheile Bicazului* Cabana is fairly near the road, whilst another hiking chalet, *Piatra Singuratica* ('Lonely Rock'), is located on a crag in the Hasmasului Mountains. Besides being incredibly scenic, the gorge also serves as the main **route into Transylvania**, with LACU ROŞU and the town of Gheorgheni on the other side of the mountains (p.344).

Monasteries around Tîrgu Neamţ

Travellers without private transport are definitely at a disadvantage when it comes to **moving on from Lake Bicaz**, since buses through the gorge into Transylvania, or northwards to Vatra Dornei (p.415), are practically non-existent, and services seem equally dismal along route 15B, which runs from the northern end of the lake towards Tîrgu Neamţ. It's probably easier to reach this town by hitch-hiking from Piatra Neamţ (whence there might even be a few buses), and since Tîrgu Neamţ is relatively close to the following monasteries, it could well be the best point of departure.

En route **between Piatra Neamţ and Tîrgu Neamţ**, you can reach two monasteries by turning west off road 15C. About 4km south of Tîrgu Neamţ, the first turn-off leads to AGAPIA, 3km from the highway: a village of shingle-roofed cottages with verandas, fretwork and tall gates in the traditional style, picturesquely situated in the Moldavian foothills. Follow the Topolniţa upstream for another 5km past a tourist inn and you'll come to **AGAPIA MONASTERY**, consisting of two complexes: one on the hillside (*din Deal*), the other in the valley (*din Vale*). The main church, founded by Basil the Wolf's brother, has been extensively remodelled over the centuries, and during the C19, was decorated inside with murals and icons by Nicolae Grigorescu. Its treasures are now exhibited in the two-storeyed row of cells. **VARATEC MONASTERY** can be reached by following a path from Agapia through the woods (1½hrs), or from the main road, and dates from the C18. Smaller than Agapia, it likewise contains a museum displaying icons, carpets and embroideries, and serves as the burial place for the poetess Veronica Micle.

TÎRGU NEAMŢ is gradually expanding to fill a depression beneath the Carpathian foothills, having originally developed around the **Neamţ Citadel** on the northern side of the valley. Founded by Petru Muşat and strengthened by Stephen the following century, this quadrangular fortress defied the Turks until the Phanariot Prince Cantacuzino demolished it at the order of the Sultan, but once again saw service during the war between Moldavia and Poland at the end of the C17. The motel here (48, Str. Cetăţii) is an alternative to the *Hotel Plaiesu* in town, located at 181, Str. Kogălniceanu (the tourist office is near the other end of the street). 5km west of the citadel along road 15B is the old village of VÎNATORI-NEAMŢ whose inhabitants were once responsible for manning the fortress; the site of a C19 *wooden church* and a tourist halt with bungalows (accessible by bus from the terminal on Str. Alexandrescu).

Another 7km to the west, a turn-off leads northwards to a clearing in the foothills where you'll find **NEAMŢ MONASTERY**, once famed for its printing press and school of miniaturists. The main church was built by Stephen on the site of Alexander the Good's C14 wooden hermitage, and pioneered many features of Moldavian church architecture. A gracefully curved roof supports a slender octagonal tower in its saddle, crowning the building with its buttresses and niches and enamelled discs suggestive of a diadem. Roundabout are chapels, monks' cells and other churches dating from the C19, and an onion-domed pavilion intended for *aghiasmatar*, the 'blessing of the water'. A similar rite used to be performed on Epiphany beside the River Dîmboviţa in Bucharest, attended by the King, Patriarch and other high dignitaries. According to Edith Nepean, a wooden cross was cast into the icy river, whereupon 'peasants wearing white embroidered garments' dived in to retrieve it before the Patriarch officially blessed the waters, which the faithful then took home in bottles 'to be used in times of critical illness'.

The next two sections of this chapter describe the old capitals of Moldavia, Iaşi and Suceava. Motorists can easily reach either from Tîrgu Neamţ, but if you're relying upon trains, it's first necessary to hitch or find a bus to **PAŞCANI** (hotel: 7, Str. Gradiniţei). From there, you'll find regular trains eastwards to **Iaşi** and northwards to **Suceava** (p.406).

IAŞI

Statues of bygone pedagogues and statesmen stand watch over every square and boulevard in the leafy centre of **IAŞI**, the cultural capital of Moldavia, whose orchestra, theatre and university rival those of Bucharest, which was merely a rude market town when Iaşi became a princely seat in 1565. It was from Iaşi (then known as *Jassy*) that the feeble successors of Stephen the Great and Petru Rareş oversaw Moldavia's decline into a Turkish satellite – notorious for its corrupt *hospodars* and thieving Greek administrators – while in the C19, conversely, Iaşi was at the forefront of Romania's renaissance. Nicolae Iorga, Ion Creangă, Mihail Kogălniceanu and other local men of letters achieved national stature, and it was Iaşi's elected prince, Alexandru Cuza, who clinched the unification of Moldavia and Wallachia in 1859. With such traditions as these, Iaşi's history and architecture can virtually be reduced to a roll-call of the 'sons of educated men' whose deeds and riches fill numerous museums and beautiful churches, while in their former homes – now memorials – women still dust their domestic clutter.

Around Piaţa Unirii and Ştefan cel Mare

Appropriately, many of Iaşi's disparate elements come together around the Square of Union, **Piaţa Unirii**, where *CFR* and TAROM serve travellers behind the bronze statue of Cuza which must have dominated the square before the *Hotel Unirea* was raised. The hotel's lobby, restaurant and 13th-floor terraced café are all **student hangouts**, like the restaurant in the *Hotel Traian* on the western side of the square – a reflection on the dearth of alternative night spots, particularly as both places close at 10pm. Near the **tourist office** (nr.12) a pedestrian way lined with cafés and shops leads through the square to the Independence monument: a statuesque woman striding forth with banner aloft, sculpted by Gabriela and Gheorghe Adoc in 1980. To the left of it, basketwork is sold alongside food and clothing in a lively **market**; behind which is tree-lined Str. Lăpuşneanu, with beer-bars and restaurants.

At number 14, next to a cinema, stands the **Museum of Union**; personal effects and mementoes from the C19 reformist and nationalist movements, which fill the empire-style palace once occupied by **Alexandru Ioan Cuza**. A coffee set – each piece adorned with an imperial N – symbolises Napoleon III's diplomatic support for the act of unification in 1859, while his declaration that 'the interest of France is everywhere where there is a just and civilising cause to promote' was shrewdly calculated to promote Francophilia. In the new *Regat* Cuza founded universities at Iaşi and Bucharest, introduced compulsory schooling for both sexes, and secularised monastic property, which then accounted for one fifth of Moldavia. Another reform – freeing the serfs of tithes and *robot* without giving them the means to repay the 'gift' of land (which soon passed into the hands of bankers and speculators) – so enraged landowners and military circles that in 1866 they staged a coup against him. Bursting into his bedroom, armed officers found Cuza making love to the daughter-in-law of the King of Serbia, and when pressed to sign a decree of abdication, he protested, 'But I haven't a pen'. 'We have thought of that', one said, producing ink and a pen; whereupon Cuza arose from bed complaining of the lack of a table. 'I will offer myself', said a colonel, presenting his back to forestall further procrastination. . .and so Cuza signed, and went into exile.

Most of the sights of Iaşi can be found on the streets radiating from the Piaţa Unirii. Behind the Independence monument and the hospital on the corner, Str. Bălcescu climbs steeply up to Ţicău, the town's oldest and prettiest residential quarter, dotted with the former homes of famous citizens (about whom, see below). Alternatively, you can follow Str. Dimitrov towards Golia Monastery and the main market; walk northeastwards to the Piaţa Tineretului, or proceed past the splendid churches **along Stradă Ştefan cel Mare**. As the former capital and Orthodox Patriarchate of Moldavia, Iaşi is loaded with churches. The **Metropolitan Church**, built in 1833, is vast and

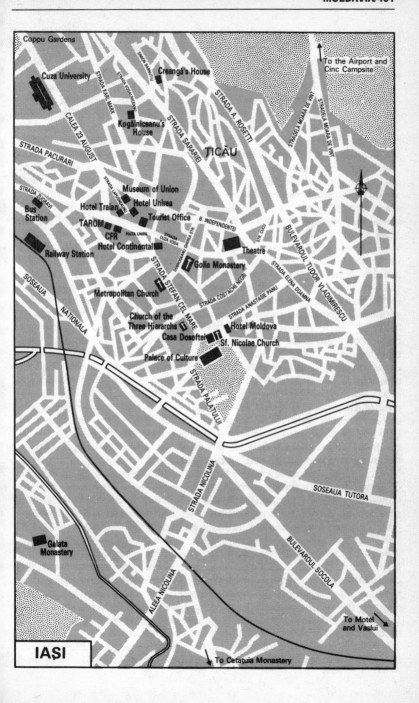

Coppu Gardens

Cuza University

Creanga's House

To the Airport and
Cinc Campsite

STRADA SIMION BARNUTIU

STRADA KARL MARX

STRADA COSANICEANU

STRADA A. ROSETTI

STRADELA MOARA DE VINT

STRADA MOARA DE VINT

Kogălniceanu's
House

STRADA SARARIE

TICĂU

CALEA 23 AUGUST

STRADA PACURARI

STRADA ZUGRAVI

STRADA LAPUSNEANU

Museum of Union

Bus
Station

Hotel Traian

Hotel Unirea

Tourist Office

B. INDEPENDENTEI

STR. DICU

TAROM

CFR

PIATA UNIRII

Hotel Continental

STRADA CUZA VODA

STRADA GHEBCA STR.

DAROGOARISA STR.

Theatre

BULEVARDUL TUDOR VLADIMIRESCU

Railway Station

Golia Monastery

STRADA STEFAN CEL MARE

SOSEAUA

Metropolitan Church

STRADA COSTACHE NEGRI

STRADA ANASTASIE PANU

STRADA ELENA DOAMNA

NATIONALA

Church of the
Three Hierarchs

Hotel Moldova

Casa Dosoftei

Sf. Nicolae Church

Palace of Culture

STRADA PALATULUI

STRADA NICOLINA

SOSEAUA TUTORA

Galata
Monastery

ALEEA NICOLINA

BULEVARDUL SOCOLA

To Motel
and Vaslui

IAŞI

To Cetatuia Monastery

grand, decorated with frescoes by Tattarescu, and very busy. I saw masses of people scurry in for a quick genuflection and dispensation – visits apparently squeezed in between work and hurrying off to queue for food – and the marble floors and huge colonades dwarfed them.

A more meditative atmosphere prevails within the **Church of the Three Hierarchs** – *Trei Ierarhi* – where sunlight falling through the tall rear windows illuminates the gilded walls and frescoes, as if beamed from the eye of God painted above each vault and arcade. Built in 1638 with a tribolate plan and octagonal towers mounted above the naos and pronaos in the typical Moldavian style, Trei Ierarhi's exterior masonry is an intricate mass of meanders, chevrons and flowers. Basil the Wolf (Vasile Lupu), its patron, once had the outside walls gilded, desiring this to surpass all other monasteries in beauty. The printing press established here in 1641 preserved chronicles by Ureche and Costin, and Moldavian scholarship and literature generally received a boost in the early C18 during the reign of the enlightened Dimitrie Cantemir.

However, after Cantemir's death Moldavia fell under the control of the **Phanariots**: Greeks – originally from the Phanaros quarter of Constantinople – who administered it on behalf of the Turkish empire, and later usurped the thrones of both principalities from the Romanian boyars. Their policy of using Iaşi's presses to spread Greek as the language of Orthodox worship had the unintended result of displacing the ossified **Old Slavonic** tongue from this position, clearing the way for clerics and intellectuals to agitate for the use of their own language, Romanian. When Trei Ierarhi was restored by a Frenchman in 1882, the original press and a Turkish caravanserai that had attached itself were demolished; although the Gothic hall of the monastery (now housing a small museum) was spared for posterity. The **Theatre** in the park on the opposite side of the street bears the name of its first director, **Vasile Alecsandri** (1821-90) who, owing to a lack of plays in Romanian, had to write much of its initial repertory. He followed farces like *Boyars and Upstarts* with historical dramas, poems, travel sketches and collections of folk ballads – and if you're interested, theatre and **concert tickets** can be obtained from the *Agenţia teatrală* at 17, Str. Lăpuşneanu.

Iaşi's largest, most impressive building is the black and white **Palace of Culture** – the architectural equivalent of a symphony by Beethoven, erected on the site of the former Princely Palace in 1907. The vaulted *Sala Voievozilor* on the first floor contains dozens of portraits of Moldavia's rulers: a study in decline given their increasing rapacity and corruption. Between 1711-1821 there were thirty-six changes of *hospodar*, while the boyars adopted Turkish dress (hence the expression 'to acquire a boyarage' – *a kaftani*), competing to win the favour of the Phanariots, who alone could recommend their promotion to the Sultan. During the 1930s, Romanians drew comparisons between the Phanariots and **Magda Lupescu**, who grew up in Iaşi and later became the mistress of Carol II. Widely hated for amassing a fortune by shady speculations like the king himself, Lupescu and Carol eventually fled abroad in a train stuffed with loot, hotly pursued by the fascist Iron Guard. However, there seems to be no mention of her in the *Museum of Moldavian History*, one of several museums in the building, described on p.404.

Outside the Palace, an equestrian statue of Stephen the Great looks set to gallop down the main street bearing his name, while around the back is Iaşi's **open-air pool**. On the eastern side of the square stands the small, pillared 'Arcade House' or *Casa Dosoftei*, dating from the C17 and named after the scholar Dosoftei. His statue, pen in hand, sits close to Iaşi's oldest monument, the **Sf. Nicolae Church** (1492), with a severe but svelt brick façade inlaid with glass and mosaics, standing beside the *Hotel Moldova*.

The Ţicău quarter and the University

Trolleybus #6 or tram #8 or #4 run to the Tudor Vladimirescu **student halls of residence** and Science faculty. Alternatively, walk or take trolleybus #6 back towards the centre, following Str. Dimitrov past the main **market** (open until 10pm except on Sundays); Str. Cucu, the turn-off for the **campsite** (bus 15); and Golia Monastery. Situated near the end of Str. Cuza Voda, **Golia Monastery** is less striking for its C16 church than the massively thick walls surrounding it, and the 90ft-high tower, whence there's a superb view of Iaşi and the countryside roundabouts.

The **Ţicău district** is Iaşi's nicest, most rambling quarter, and in this salubrious area at number 15 on the street that now bears his name lived **Mihail Kogălniceanu**. Banned from lecturing after lambasting 'oppression by an ignorant aristocracy', Kogălniceanu had to flee to Bucovina in 1848, but returned to help secure the election of Ioan Cuza, and as Foreign Minister sent Romanian troops to the siege of Plevna (p.600). You can look around his *casa memorială*, but the cute cottage or *bojdeuca* of **Ion Creangă** is more entertaining. Situated down a steep passage from Str. Barnutiu, it's full of first editions and prints of Creangă's work, including stills from films made of them. Trained as a priest and then as a teacher, defrocked and then suspended, Creangă wrote *Recollections of Childhood* and fairy tales like *The Giants of Irunica* with a quirky sense of humour, using a rich regional vocabulary that endeared him to Romanians during and after his lifetime (1837-89).

Northeastwards of the Piaţa Unirii, statues of illustrious leaders stand as role models on the Square of Youth – Piaţa Tineretului: site of the Eminescu Library, a busy **Youth House** and self-service restaurant near the market, and the place to board trams #8 and #4, which rattle up Calea 23 August towards **Cuza University**. Founded in 1860, this is now an umbrella for 26 faculties and 8 research institutes of the Romanian Academy; attended by students struggling to live on 700 lei a month, of which 670 is deducted for board and lodging. With 30 lei left to cover textbooks, bread, cigarettes and coffee (when obtainable), Romanian students have little chance to enjoy what passes for nightlife in the downtown hotels, and resent their foreign colleagues with access to the almighty dollar. Despite this, and the risk of hassle from the Securitate, I found the students here keen to make friends with visitors; and the solo traveller might well be offered a clandestine bed in one of Iaşi's many dormitories. Beyond the University lie the lovely **Copou Gardens** (open Tuesday-Sunday 9am-8pm; 3 lei admission) where the poet Eminescu used to sit under the limes; take tram #4 or #8 to the Soviet war memorial, and keep right to find the entrance.

Regrettably, Moldavia has a long tradition of anti-semitism, and during the 1920s and 30s, the 'League of National Christian Defence', organised by a prominent professor, virtually closed the University to Jews, who then comprised a third to a half of Iaşi's population. The League's most ardent student member, **Corneliu Codreanu**, later founded the notorious Legion of Archangel St Michael, better known as the **Iron Guard**, which murdered Jews and politicans whom it deemed insufficiently nationalistic. Wearing green shirts and bags of Romanian soil around their necks, the *Legionari* rode from village to village, digging wells and chasing away baliffs to the approbation of the peasantry, who were enthralled by Codreanu's speeches and self-proclaimed messianism. Together with the Nazis, the Guard exterminated many of Romania's Jews during the war. In recent decades, whilst Ceauşescu has never promoted anti-semitism, the burning of a Synagogue at Buhuşi in 1987 suggests that hatred of the eternal scapegoats is having a resurgence. Nationalist resentment concerning the 'lost provinces' of Bessarabia and Bucovina – annexed by the USSR in 1940 – also remains; and during the 60s, the police went so far as to tolerate a demonstration on the banks of the Prut – the *riul blestemat* or 'accursed river' which demarcates the Soviet border.

Museums, monasteries and Mihai Eminescu

Iaşi has over a dozen museums and memorial houses to edify the town's population of more than 200,000, and the sheer weight of exhibits – let alone the monolingual captions – will exhaust any visitor. From the descriptions below you should be able to pick out the ones that appeal; the first four are all in the Palace of Culture, and opening hours are normally 9am-5pm, Tuesday-Sunday.

The **Ethnographic Museum**, occupying two floors at the rear of the building, displays colourful woven skirts, embroidered sheepskins, six-foot long Moldavian alpine horns, hollow trunks once used as beehives and grain stores, and oil-presses the size of trees. On the upper floor you'll find patterned blankets and rugs in an incredible spectrum of hues, obtained from roots and berries. The **Museum of Moldavian History** covers just that – though if you can't understand the captions, guesswork is unavoidable. Exhibits include savage caricatures of Petru Groza, the Agrarian leader, and Ilie Pintilie, the Communist militant, drawn in 1924 when the CP was outlawed; and photos – almost the credentials – of Nicolae and Elena Ceauşescu, organising an anti-fascist demonstration in 1939. Beginning with copies of Greek and Egyptian reliefs held in foreign cities, the **Art Museum** moves on through motley Europeans like Murillo, Poussin and Tinteretto, to paintings of C19 Iaşi, notably a superb market scene by Starski. Amongst the Romanian 'moderns' are work by Grigorescu; Petrascu's *Interior with a Woman sewing*, Pallady's *Nude on a Yellow background* and other products of the post-1919 Colourist School; orientalist fantasies by Theodor Aman; and Ştefan Luchian's blending of Symbolism and folk traditions. Finally, the **Polytechnica** devotes one section to the power industry (symbollically closed during my visit), and another to an appealing **collection of symphoniums**. Just attach yourself to a tour group for a demonstration of these instruments of Swiss, German and French manufacture; together with a showing of '*Popper's Bianca*' – an ingenious contraption anticipating the motion-picture show.

The **Museum of Old Romanian Literature** has probably reopened by now in the Casa Dosoftei outside the Palace, but during my visit it was closed like the **Museum of Natural History** (16, B-dul Independenţei). The **Theatre Museum** on Str. Alecsandri behind the main square displays a mixture of thespian and folkloric items, including horse-headed masks worn by the *caiuţii* (p.410), and posters, costumes and other memorabilia of the *Theatre Français* founded by Elena and Gheorghe Asachi, and the first stage performance in the Romanian language, in 1838.

For a change of atmosphere, visit **Cetăţuia Monastery** to the south of town (bus #28 and then a steep climb). Within its fortified walls the monks claim to be self-suffcient (although women come in to cook for them), and the monastery church's twin towers aim skywards like a piece of field-artillery in some undeclared Orthodox jihad. Cetăţuia was founded in 1672, and a museum exhibits its accumulation of beautifully embroidered vestments, old icons and precious chalices. Another, older monastery, **Galata**, is situated on a hill to the southwest of town.

Finally, any survey of Iaşi's cultural horizons has to light upon the figure of **Mihai Eminescu** (1850-89), born near Botoşani in northern Moldavia, and a librarian and member of the literary circle *Junimea* for several years after 1874. *Luceafărul* – a 96 stanza ballad of love and the Evening Star – is acclaimed as his masterpiece (and defies adequate translation), but Romanians also revere his shorter lyrics. Recounting the tale of the lost provinces, Russian perfidy or Magyar chauvinism, people are wont to soulfully recite Eminescu's protest at the abject state of their country –

> From the banks of the Dniestr to those of the Tisza every Romanian cries out that he can hardly breathe because of so many foreigners. . .
> If any shall cherish the stranger may the dogs eat his heart; may the weeds destroy his house; may his kin perish in shame

– before offering you another glass of *ţuică*.

Practicalities

Trams #1 and #9, which run from the **railway station** to the Palace of Culture via the Piaţa Unirii, make it easy to get around, although for the student halls of residence you'll need to take a trolleybus #6. Along the route of the latter, Str. Cucu (near the main market) is where to switch onto bus #15 for **Ciric campsite** in the forest of the same name. The chalets there are the cheapest **accommodation** in town unless you can wrangle unofficial lodgings in halls of residence, or a *caminul de studenti* from BTT (30, Str. Engels). Iaşi's hotels are all on the steep side, but it's worth comparing prices at the *Continental* (4, Str. Cuza Vodă) and *Moldova* (Str. Anastasie Panu) with those at the *Traian* (sngl.\$36/dbl.\$47) and *Unirea* (sngl.\$32/dbl.\$42) on Union Square, since rates seem to vary according to receptionists' whims.

The Traian's *Salonul Alb* has a spiffing decor, while the *Mioriţa* (open 7am-10pm) opposite the Continental is one of the livelier **places to eat** on the main square, and there are plenty of other restaurants, cafés and bars on backstreets like Str. Lăpuşneanu. Eminescu himself used to patronise the *Bolta Rece*

Crama (10, Str. Rece), whilst if you're interested in trying the classic Romanian dish, sarmale, the *Trei Sarmale* (75, Blvd. Socola) has the works.

Iaşi's main **Auto-service** depot (☎ 3-28-91) comes just before the restaurant, while further out along Blvd. Socola (the Vaslui road) you'll find a filling station at nr.95 and a motel at kilometre 12. For technical advice, contact *ACR* at 11, Str. Alecsandri (☎ 1-23-45) or 13-15, Bloc L, Bulevard 30 Decembrie. Services to neighbouring villages from the **bus terminal** (42, Str. Zugravi) are a hit and miss affair; but getting railway or airline tickets from *CFR* or TAROM on the main square is a fairly straightforward process. TAROM can tell you whether there's still a coach service to the **airport** on the Trifeşti road some miles from town, or telephone 4-29-53 for information.

Despite its proximity to the border, it's impossible to enter the Soviet Union by road or rail starting from Iaşi. A couple of trains do cross over from NICOLINA to UNGENY (sometimes spelt 'Ungheni'), but you can't actually board them at the Moldavian capital. The nearest road crossing is at ALBITA, where there's campsite, 64km to the southeast of Iaşi (DN28). For more details, see the final section of this chapter.

SUCEAVA, DRAGOMIRNA MONASTERY, RĂDĂUŢI AND FESTIVITIES AT TUDORA AND ILIŞEŞTI

Confronted with the wood-pulp and oxygen factories sprawling across the river, it's difficult to envisage SUCEAVA as an old princely capital, although various ruins testify that the town once fufilled this role. Suceava's heyday more or less coincided with the reign of **Stephen the Great** or *Ştefan cel Mare* (1457-1504), who warred ceaselessly against Moldavia's invaders – principally the Turks, then advancing confidently after capturing Constantinople – and won all but two of the thirty-six battles he fought. This record prompted Pope Sixtus IV to dub Stephen the 'Athlete of Christ' – a rare tribute to a non-Catholic, which wasn't extended to Stephen's cousin Dracula, who massacred 45,000 of the infidel during one year alone. (Rumour has it that Stephen is one of Ceauşescu's great heroes; Napoleon is another). It's said that after each victory, the *hospodar* ordered the foundation of a new church or monastery, whence came the brilliant flowering of Moldavian religious art during the C16. All this is more or less the theme of Suceava's main **museum** (33, Str. Ştefan cel Mare), whose exhibits include a reconstruction of Stephen knighting two soldiers, but not the falcons which, legend has it, watched from the heights and warned him of approaching foes.

The tradition of endowing religious buildings was maintained by Stephen's successors, Bogdan the One-Eyed and Petru Rareş (1527-46), although both were conspicuous failures on the field of battle. The confusingly named **St George's Church of the Monastery of St John** has badly corroded exterior murals (those in the sanctuary, including a portrait of Bogdan with two eyes, are better preserved), yet defiantly thrusts up its coloured roofs and spire a short distance from the main square, **Piaţa 23 August**. The Church of St Dimitriu at the beginning of Str. Ştefan cel Mare is more derelict, but not so far gone as the ruins of the one-time Princely Court or *Curţii Domneşti*, around the corner from the main square. The restored Princely Inn once used by visiting hospodars after the capital was shifted to Iaşi, which stands not far away at 5, Str. Ciprian Porumbescu, now contains a fine collection of **folk art and costumes**.

At the stop near the main square, you can board bus #29 or #30, which travel out towards the **Zamca complex** on a plateau overlooking town from the west. Gothic and Oriental motifs used to decorate the building can be picked out, and the surrounding walls have retained their trapezoid formation. Suceava's **ruined Princely Citadel** occupies another, higher plateau on the eastern outskirts of town, about 10 minutes walk from Blvd. Ipatescu. Huge walls and a moat are all that remain of the *cetatea* raised by Petru Muşat (1374-91), which is hardly surprising since the fortress was thrice assailed by Turks and given the coup de grace by an earthquake during the late C17.

Suceava's **market** one block behind the Curţii Domneşti is full of peasant vendors, many of whom wear embroidered sheepskins or sombre homespun, but otherwise the town's ambience is pretty much industrial. *CFR*, *TAROM*, the Post Office and **OJT** are all on Str. Bălcescu adjoining the main square, where a *BTT* office has apparently opened shop in Bloc 10 since it was last recorded around the corner on Str. Mestesugarilor, and before then at 18, Str. Frimu. Suceava has four first-class **hotels** – *Arcasul* (4-6, Str. Mihai Viteazul), *Balada* (3, Str. Lenin), *Bucovina* and *Suceava* (both on Blvd. Ipatescu), charging $40 for a single and $52 for a double; the second-class *Parc* (6, Ipatescu Blvd.) and *Casa Tineretului* (5, Str. Lenin); and a **campsite with chalets** going for 100 lei. This lies down a lane turning off Str. Pintilie at the Dacia-Service depot (identifiable by its blue and white tower), two stops by bus from *Suceava Nord*, the most useful of the town's **railway stations** (linked to the centre by bus #1 and #9). The other two are likewise in the suburbs: *Suceava-Vest*, which mainly handles freight, and *Gara Suceava* (otherwise known as *Gara Burdujen*), which can be reached by bus #26 or #16. Hotel restaurants are probably the best **places to eat**, although you'll find various cheap cafés and a *gospodina* along Ştefan cel Mare, leading to the shopping centre where I tried in vain to buy sugar, cooking oil and meat.

Assuming that you don't make use of the **airport** (8km east towards Salcea), there are various options for **moving on**. OJT can rent cars and attach visitors to *guided tours of the monasteries* for hefty sums, but for the benefit of independent travellers they're only willing to cough up a map of the Suceava region. **Buses** from the chaotic *Autogară* (2, Str. Alecsandri) are just about feasible as a means of reaching Dragomirna Monastery or Ilişeşti (see below and p.409), but otherwise **trains** are more reliable. There are regular services along the Gura Humorlui-Vama-Cîmpulung-Vatra Dornei-Ilva Mică line, which enable one to reach several monasteries (or change trains for Cluj or Sighetu Marmaţiei at Ilva Mică). Also, two trains a day from Gara Suceava, and more from the Suceava Nord, run up through Rădăuţi to Putna (as described shortly).

Dragomirna Monastery
Four kilometres from the commune of Mitocu Dragomirnei north of Suceava, **DRAGOMIRNA MONASTERY** stands walled – and was once moated – like

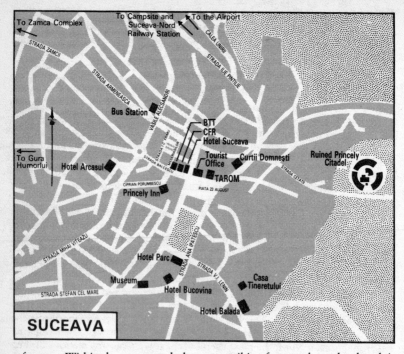

SUCEAVA

a fortress. Within the compound, the most striking feature about the church is its proportions – long, narrow and high like a submarine's conning tower, with the spire serving as a periscope. Dragomirna's slender lines are accentuated by the sweeping, overhanging roof and the paucity of decoration on the building's façade, in contrast to its elaborately carved tower. Whilst the floral and geometric carvings resemble those on Iaşi's Trei Ierarhi Church and the iconostasis came from Socola Monastery, the **frescoes** and treasures in the **museum** are Dragomirna's own. Most impressive are the *Lord's Ascension* covering the vault of the sanctuary, and the seven illuminated manuscripts which (together with nineteen others in Romania and abroad) are the only surviving products of the school of illuminators started by Dragomirna's C17 founder, Metropolitan **Anastasie Crimca**. Given this, Dragomirna's fortific-ations (added by Prince Barnovschi) don't seem an excessive precaution – particularly when one considers that wooden village churches were sometimes actually mounted upon wheels so that they could be towed away whenever Moldavia was invaded. The frequency of such invasions gave rise to the expression *Nu dau Turcii nici Tartarii* (Neither the Turks nor Tartars are coming) – meaning 'There's no hurry'. Not far from the monastery you'll find a **campsite**.

Rădăuţi

The chief reason to visit **RĂDĂUŢI** is its Friday **market**, easily found if you follow the crowd. Kitchen utensils, herbs and spices, cloth and garish scarves comprise the bulk of its merchandise (although wooden handicrafts are also sold), and the attraction is less the market than the people – mainly peasants, wearing white woollen pantaloons (*iţari*) or the traditional wrap-around skirts (*catriniţă*), topped by a *pieptar*, the fur-lined leather or sheepskin waistcoat worn since medieval times. One of the oldest settlements in Moldavia, Rădăuţi became its first capital when the principality was established by Voivode Bogdan I (1359-65), which accounts for the presence of the **Bogdana Church** here. Though it was Moldavia's Patriarchal seat before the Metropolitan moved to Suceava, the church is a simple building, lacking any frills. Within the dark interior, it's just possible to make out *Bogdan's tomb* and the C15 frescoes, which display Byzantine stylistic influences. Rădăuţi's other sight is the **Museum of Bucovinian Folk Technology** (63, Piaţa Republicii), which displays oil presses, fulling mills, agricultural implements and traditional dress from the Bucovina region.

Both hotels (on Str. Ştefan cel Mare) are pretty basic, and to be honest, there's really no reason to stay here. Once you're ready to move on, it's easy to reach Putna Monastery (p.411) by rail, and probably possible to catch buses from the Piaţa Republicii terminal to Suceviţa (p.411) or Arbore (p.415).

Festivities at Ilişeşti and Tudora

Every year on the second Sunday of July, the commune of **ILIŞEŞTI** hosts a **folklore festival** called 'From the Rarău Mountain' (*De sub montale Rarău*). Since ensembles from three counties – Maramureş, Neamţ and Bacău – participate, the festival provides an excellent opportunity to appreciate the diversity of Romanian folk music and dance. It's a chance to enjoy horas and shepherds' dances, fiddles, flutes and alpine horns, and a wealth of traditional costumes which, sadly, are less and less worn in the country as a whole, although the habit lingers in regions like Maramureş and Moldavia.

If the bus service from Suceava has collapsed and you don't fancy hitching 25km from town along DN17, most of the journey can be accomplished by rail. En route between Suceava and Gura Humorlui (p.413), trains stop at Stroieşti and Păltinoasa, respectively 7km northeast and 9km southwest of Ilişeşti. For the duration of the festival, Ilişeşti's **campsite** and **motel** are likely to be full; but at other times the only 'attraction' is the birthplace of the composer **Ciprian Porumbescu** (1853-83), located 5km to the south of the commune (which appears on some maps as 'Ciprian Porumbescu'). Porumbescu himself is chiefly remembered for composing the national anthem, *Tricolorul*.

Due to its timing and the isolated location, few visitors attend the **Christmas and New Year festivities** at **TUDORA**, a large commune with several satellite villages, situated well off the main road between Suceava and Paşcani, which makes it difficult to reach without private transport. However, since the festivals here (and in other remote villages) continue a tradition that was once widespread, a short digression on winter customs might be appreciated by those unable to attend.

As elsewhere in Romania, preparations for Christmas become obvious on St Nicolas's Day (December 6), when people butcher pigs for the feast beside the roads – not a sight for the squeamish. In Tudora and other villages, women then get to work baking pies and the special pastries called *turte*, symbolising Christ's swaddling clothes, whilst males rehearse the allegorical songs and dances. On Christmas Eve (*Ajun*), boys go from house to house singing *colinde*, which combine felicitations with risqué innuendoes (much to the listeners' delight), accompanied by an instrument called the *buhai*, whose sound mimics the bellowing of a bull. After days of feasting and dancing, the climax comes on New Year's Eve day, when the *Capra* or Goat is unleashed. Garbed in black and red, wearing a goat's head mask with a moveable jaw which he clacks to the music of drums and flutes, the Capra dancer whips another figure, chained and costumed as a bear (*urşi*), through the streets. Symbolising the forces of nature, the Bear dances until he drops, only reviving when other dancers – dressed as lancers, fiendishly-masked Turks or 'little horses' (*caiuţii*) – appear. Then a brass band starts playing and the villagers begin downing *ţuicăs* and dancing, setting the pattern for a binge that will last through the night.

THE MONASTERIES OF SOUTHERN BUCOVINA

When the Habsburgs annexed northern Moldavia in 1774, they coined the name *Bucovina* – 'beech-covered land' – to describe their new acquisition. It's a region divided by imposing hills or 'crests' (*obcinie*) branching off from the Carpathians, and also by history – for the Russians occupied northern Bucovina in 1940 and still hold it, while **Southern Bucovina** is what remains. Beyond the smoke-stacks of Suceava, the valleys are misty and green, with meadows half-flooded by rivers spilled down from rocky shoulders heaving up beneath a cloak of beech and fir – the setting for Romania's most beautiful monasteries. Founded by boyars or hospodars through whatever mixture of pride, prudence or humility during the C15-C16, they were endowed with estates and serfs, and at the lords' behest, propagandised the illiterate faithful. Metropolitan Roşca is credited with the final synthesis – **Painted Monasteries** whose outer walls vividly portrayed the rewards and terrors of the afterlife which awaited those on earth. Most visitors today see **Voroneţ**, **Suceviţa**, **Humor** and **Moldoviţa** in a different light – as billboards or time capsules from the late medieval world, and brilliant artistic achievements.

As with the Maramureş villages, **getting there** can be awkward without private transport, but if you're willing to hitch, ride slow *cursa* trains or claw your way onto buses, none of the monasteries should be inaccessible. **Accommodation** presents less difficulties since there are just enough hotels and campsites to make camping wild generally unnecessary – but **food** (or rather the lack of it) can be a real problem. Stock up beforehand in Suceava or you might end up as I did, making a 'hearty meal on a piece of bread and garlic' like the peasants observed by Baron Camplehausen in 1808.

Putna

From Suceava or Rădăuţi it's easy to reach **PUTNA** by train, and to my mind, this is the place to begin. After a slow ride past meandering rivers which the peasants used to punt down on *pule*, it's difficult not to feel impatient – nor gratified when you finally arrive. Mountains and dark firs rise all around the

village – a wonderful jigsaw of wooden houses with carved gables and gateways, shingled roofs and delicate lattices. Above the railway station and timber yard, gaggles of geese and the odd cow roam the muddy alleys straggling up to the mainstreet which runs towards the monastery. Along the way you'll pass a hotel, an old church (worth investigating) and a campsite with chalets, whose bar-restaurant serves as Putna's nightspot.

PUTNA MONASTERY was the first of forty religious edifices founded by Stephen, and legend has it that he fired an arrow from a nearby summit in 1466, and where it landed 'marked the place for to be an altar'. Stephen then bade his companions to shoot, and 'where the arrow of the children's chieftain fell, there he made the gate, whereas where the arrow of a page fell, there he made the belfry'. Putna's walls are plainly designed for defence, but once through the main gate (adorned with the emblem of royal Moldavia – a buffalo's head, sun, moon and star) tranquility reigns within. The monastery church is of plain white stone with a raised cable motif, overhung by the steeply pitched, sweeping roof characteristic of all the monasteries; while the nave and narthex are equally austere. A graceful arch, inscriptions and a hanging votive lamp are all that distinguish the *tomb of Stephen the Great*; and the tombs of his wife, Maria, and successors Bogdan and Petru Rareş are even simpler.

Putna is still a working monastery (partly supported by the state since it lost the right to tithes from twenty-four villages), and the **monks** live in a row of cells along one side of the courtyard. Uphill and slightly east of the monastery, there's a curious hollowed-out rock with a door and window, allegedly once the **cell of a hermit**, Danill. Reportedly, it's possible to **hike from Putna to Suceviţa Monastery**, although snow on the high ground during April prevented me from doing so. Apparently, you follow the Putnişoara Struiinoasa up to its source, then head southeast and follow the Barcheza River down to Suceviţa – about 20km in all. There are no villages en route, only forests and hills, and perhaps the odd bear.

Suceviţa Monastery

By contrast to Putna, **SUCEVIŢA** is the last, largest and perhaps grandest of the monastic complexes, owing nothing to Stephen or his descendants, but rather a monument to the Movilă family of boyars. It was founded by Iremia and his brother Simion (who succeeded him as hospodar), and by Elisibeta – Iremia's widow – who poisoned Simion so that her own sons might inherit the throne. Their first foundation was a village church (now surrounded by a graveyard), followed by the monastery church in 1584, and its enclosing walls, belfry and towers in stages thereafter.

Painted both inside and outside, Suceviţa's **frescoes** are spectacular. *The Ladder of St John from Sinai* covering the exterior of the north-facing wall ascends to the roof, flights of angels assisting the righteous up to paradise (*rai*) while sinners fall through the rungs into the arms of demons, who drag them down to perdition. A multitude of angels, saints, prophets and martyrs in the Suceviţa colours of red and green decorate the apse (the eastern end, curved around the sanctuary, incorporating niches). The outside of the southern wall portrays the Virgin Mary beneath a red veil, a bizarre frieze of philosophers –

including Plato, carrying a coffin of bones upon his head – and a representation of the *Tree of Jesse*. This last literally depicts the prophecy in Isiah, which holds that the messiah will come from 'the stem of Jesse'. Thus a tree springs from the loins of Jesse with Christ's ancestors in its branches, culminating in the Virgin and Saviour.

The monastery church follows the usual Orthodox configuration of three chambers: the sanctuary or naos, containing the altar and iconostasis at its eastern end; the main nave; and lastly the narthex, just inside the porch. Typically, a *Last Judgement* covers the wall beneath the porch, while the narthex displays episodes from the lives of the saints and martyrs – or, to be more accurate, their deaths. Here you'll see saints being burnt, boiled, dismembered or decapitated with gay abandon. Fishes, rams, suns and other Zodiacal symbols occur frequently, whilst in the nave, frescoes tend to depict the Virgin, a particular saint, or events in the Old Testament. Smoke from votive candles invariably blackens frescoes in the sanctuary, which generally portray the life of Christ, the saint to whom the church is dedicated (on the west wall) and, more often than not, the church's patron. At Suceviţa, for example, you'll see a picture of Elisabeta leading her children along the southern wall – without much luck, incidentally, for her ambitions came to nought and she died in a Sultan's harem 'by God's will', as a chronicler noted sanctimoniously.

There's a magnificent view from the hill behind the monastery, and it's easy to locate the **campsite and motel** near the complex. In fact the only difficulty is **getting there**, for without a car you'll have to hitch from Moldoviţa or hope to catch one of the two or three daily buses from Rădăuţi (no services on Sundays).

Moldoviţa Monastery

In Suceviţa I was told that buses to **MOLDOVIŢA** ran depending on whether the driver had to feed his pigs or not, but happily it's also possible **to get there by rail**. The place to start is VAMA, midway along the line between Cîmpulung Moldovenesc and Gura Humorlui (p.413), which is also accessible from Suceava. Currently, trains leave Vama around 7.20am, 3.40pm and 11.15pm for the return trip up to Moldoviţa village. Confusingly, however, the monastery is actually closer to VATRA MOLDOVIŢEI (one stop before), where there's a **campsite**. From either place you can see the tower of **MOLDOVIŢA MONASTERY** over the rooftops. It's a smaller complex than Suceviţa but equally well defended, for the monasteries had, in addition to their religious and cultural roles, a quasi-military function. Moldoviţa was founded in 1532 by Stephen's illegitimate son, Petru Rareş, during whose reign the Turks finally achieved domination over Moldavia, though initially they merely extracted tribute through the hospodar.

The **frescoes** on the south wall make an oblique reference to the Turkish advance, which became inexorable after the *Siege of Constantinople*. Its namesake, dating from the C16, is a splendid piece of historical revisionism (by no means a rare practice in Romania), depicting the Christians routing the infidel with arrows and cannons and the help of miraculous icons being paraded around the ramparts – in fact, a complete reversal of the outcome of the siege in 1453. On the same wall are also a *Hymn to the Virin* and the *Tree of Jesse*, with scenes beautifully entwined amongst lush foliage painted upon a rich blue background (obtained by using lapis lazuli as pigment). In the open porch there's a fine *Last Judgement* showing a crowd of boyars growing agitated as a black demon drags one of their number by his beard towards the fires below. Within the church, saints and martyrs are decapitated en masse around the nave and narthex, whilst the sanctuary features a bit of blatant self-advertisement – a picture of Petru Rareş holding Moldoviţa Monastery. Monks' cells can be found along the southern wall of the complex, and on the north side stands the former *clisarniţa* or guest house for visiting notables, which now exhibits icons and furniture.

The Monasteries at Voroneţ and Humor

Two of the finest Painted Monasteries lie a few kilometres either side of **GURA HUMORLUI**, a small logging town 'at the mouth of the Humor', accessible by train from Cîmpulung or Suceava. A few places to eat are strung out along the main street which ends in Piaţa Republicii, where you'll find *OJT* and *CFR* (Monday-Friday 8am-3pm; Saturday 8am-12.30am); the turn-off beside the church nearby leads eventually to Humor Monastery. First, however, ask for directions to *Hanul Ariş* hotel across the river, which isn't hard to find once you've reached the dendrological park and the iron suspension bridge beyond it. Though **rooms** here aren't particularly cheap (195 lei for a single), there's a good restaurant; and if you baulk at the price it's possible to camp beside the river (it's forbidden to do so in the forest). The *Autogară* near the station is the place to enquire about **buses to Voroneţ and Humor**; the timetable implies almost hourly services, though in my experience there was only one bus a day to each monastery. Since Humor is farther away, the bus there (leaving at 12.45am) is the one to take if you don't want to rush back after catching the 10.50am service to Voroneţ, which is 1½hrs easy stroll by road from town, or 4hrs by *footpath* (starting from the hotel).

Ion Neculce's chronicle records that Stephen founded **VORONEŢ MONASTERY** in 1488 to fufill a pledge to the hermit Danill, who had previously assured the despondent hospodar that, should he undertake a campaign against the Turks, he would be successful. The Turks were duly forced back across the Danube, and Voroneţ was erected within a few months. Chronologically it comes between Putna and Neamţ (p.398), while the superb frescoes were added about 1547-50 at the behest of Metropolitan Roşca. At Voroneţ, the open porch has been replaced by a closed esonarthex and the church is entered via a door in the southern wall, thus creating an unbroken surface along the western wall for the muralists to work with.

This they covered with a magnificent **Last Judgement**, probably the finest single composition amongst all the Painted Monasteries. Fish-tailed bulls, unicorns, lions and other Zodiacal symbols form a frieze underneath the eaves, beneath which Christ sits in majesty flanked by the blessed elect. Below Christ's feet (licked by a tongue of flame from the Fire of Gehenna) is a chair symbolising the 'Toll Gates of the Air' – *vămile văzduhului* – where the newly deceased are judged and have prayers for their souls counted. On either side are those in limbo, the Turks and Tartars (recognisable by their turbans and tall hats) marked out for perdition as Moldavia's enemies. Beneath them devils and angels despatch sinners into the flames where a half-obliterated, scaly thing writhes; whilst two angels sound the last trump on *buciume*, Moldavian alpine horns. In response, graves open and wild animals come bearing the limbs they have devoured – all except the deer, a symbol of innocence in Romanian folklore. On the opposite side of a flaming river, prophets and the righteous await admission to the Mother of God in a garden.

Weather has damaged the frescoes along the north-facing wall, but one can still distinguish Adam and Eve, the first childbirth, the discovery of fire and the invention of ploughing and writing. The southern wall is covered by three compositions: comic-strip scenes from the lives of St Nicholas and St John on the buttress; a Tree of Jesse (again using lapis lazuli for the background); and a register of saints and philosophers where, as usual, Plato is depicted with a coffin load of bones. Inside, the esonarthex is painted all over with gory martyrdoms and saints performing miracles. It's possible to identify St Elijah riding behind two red horses in his 'cart of fire', probably intent on zapping devils with his God-given powers (according to native folklore, the deity promptly had second thoughts and restricted Elijah's activities to his Name-day). There's also a picture of Stephen and his family, the former carrying the monastery to symbolise its debt to him.

As suggested by a photograph of Ceauşescu showing Voroneţ to 'lofty foreign guests – the Shahinshah of Iran and Empress Farah' – this is perhaps the most visited of the monasteries. The nearest accommodation is in Gura Humorlui, but it should be possible to camp wild in the vicinity.

In a separate valley about 8km from Gura Humorlui, the village of MĂNĂSTERIA HUMOR straggles towards its namesake, **HUMOR MONASTERY**. Unlike the other complexes, Humor is protected by a wooden stockade rather than a stone rampart, and lacks the customary spire over the naos, indicating that it was founded by boyars instead of by a hospodar – namely, Teodor and Anastasia Bubuiog, who are buried here. The prevailing hues at Humor are reddish brown (from oriental madder pigment), but rich blues and greens also appear. The *Last Judgement* on the western wall is similar to that at Voroneţ, with one significant difference: the Devil is portrayed as a woman (although when I saw it, this patch of fresco was too damaged to be identified anyway). Such misogyny had its counterpart in the peasant conception of hell (*iad*) – said to be a place upheld by seven old women who during their lifetimes had surpassed Satan in wickedness. Since the women are mortal, the legend goes, *Dracul* must constantly search the world for replacements. . .and never fails to find them.

The Tree of Jesse along the northern wall has been virtually destroyed by erosion, but restorers are busy touching up the polychromatic *Hymn to the Virgin* on the south front. Composed like a comic strip, this depicts her miraculous intervention at the siege of Constantinople – not the one in 1453, but the siege by the Persians in 626, although the enemy has been changed into Turks to make a propaganda point. Morale may have been stiffened, but neither murals nor the fortified tower added by Basil the Wolf could protect Humor from marauding Turks during the C17, and a century later the monastery was declared derelict.

Arbore

ARBORE is the smallest of the Painted Monasteries, and the hardest to reach without private transport. You might try hitching on from Humor via Solca, or from Rădăuţi by way of the village of Cliţ. The monastery church was founded in 1503 by one of Stephen's generals, Luca Arbore, who's buried in the dark interior, while such frescoes as have remained on the outside walls – depicting saintly lives and Old Testament scenes – are dominated by green shades, probably obtained from chromium oxide. In the courtyard are two heavy, hollowed-out stone slabs thought to have been used by the painters for mixing colours. As a glance at most Romanian buildings makes plain, the secret of the frescoes' durability has been lost, but chemical analysis suggests that the walls were rendered with charcoal and lamp-black, and covered with paint admixed with animal size, lime, egg, gall, vinegar, honey and turpentine.

CÎMPULUNG MOLDOVENESC AND VATRA DORNEI

Cîmpulung Moldovenesc and Vatra Dornei aren't particularly interesting in themselves, but their location on the Suceava-Ilva Mică line makes them useful way-stations en route between northern Moldavia and Transylvania or Maramureş – especially if you're planning to attend the great *Hora at Prislop* in August (p.429), or other festivals on the western side of the Carpathians during June and September (see below).

A logging town of 20,000 souls with some old wooden houses lending it an alpine flavour, **CÎMPULUNG MOLDOVENESC** ('Moldavian settlement in the long field') is handily sited along the railway from Suceava, near Vama junction (with its branch line to Moldoviţa) and on the road to the Prislop Pass into Maramureş. The **Wood Art Museum** (10, Str. 7 Noiembrie) shows the manifold local uses of timber, whilst at 3, Str. Popovici you'll find Ion Ţugui's life-long **Collection of Spoons** – over 4,500 of 'em in all shapes and sizes. There's a variety of **accommodation**. Cîmpulung's *Hotel Zimbrul* (1, Str. 23 August) charges $38 for a double, $28 for a single, but if you baulk at the price there's the cheaper *Carpaţii* 4, Str. 7 Noiembrie; a **campsite** on the Vatra Moldoviţei road; and a cabana, *Deia*, 3km from town in the woods beneath Tomnatec hill. From the terminal on Str. 11 Iunie, there should be buses south to **Mount Rarău** (motel), on the slopes of which are three **nature reserves**. *Pietrele Doamnei*, 30 minutes' walk to the north, consists of tower-shaped limestone rocks arising from boulders and scree; whilst the *Pădurea Slătioara* is an old forest of larches and spruce-firs covering an area of 600 hectares.

There's more accommodation further southwest along the road to Vatra Dornei, where the majority of trains halt briefly at Mestecăniş, the site of a cabana and campsite. **VATRA DORNEI** itself has three **hotels** (on Str. 7 Noiembrie and Str. Republicii – the latter is where to find the tourist office), and a **campsite** 1km west of town near a small **spa** (*bai*). The town's location at the junction of roads to Lake Bicaz (p.397) and Bistriţa (p.387) makes it a feasible springboard for attending two **Transylvanian festivals**, which might be possible to reach by bus from the terminal on Str. Oborului. The journey to one involves crossing over the 4,000 feet high **Tihuţa Pass**, just beyond which lies the village of TIHA BÎRGAULUI, where the '*King of the Fir Trees*' (p.389) is held on the third Sunday of June. On the first Sunday of September, another festival, the '*Rhapsody of the Trişcaşi*', occurs at LEŞU, within walking distance of the Ilvei Leşu railway halt, one stop before **ILVA MICĂ**. From there, fairly regular services run on to **SALVA**, where one can change again for **trains to Cluj** (p.360).

Crossing into Soviet Moldavia

Beyond the 'accursed' River Prut which demarcates Romania's eastern frontier stretch the fertile plains and rolling hills of **Soviet Moldavia**, 'one of the fifteen sovereign republics forming the USSR'. As official guide-books blandly acknowledge, 65% of the population is 'Moldavian' – a polite way of saying (or rather, obscuring) that the majority of inhabitants are culturally and ethnically Romanian. The Soviet annexation of the region in 1940 was a reassertion of traditional Tsarist claims on *Bessarabia* (as the land between the Prut and Dniestr rivers was once known), and was followed by mass deportations to Kazakhstan in Central Asia, where post-war censuses disclosed thousands of Moldavians resident. To be fair, conditions in Soviet Moldavia are nowadays less onerous than in Romania, but as recent reports suggest, the Moldavians still yearn to express their own culture. Disaffection isn't confined to those of Romanian origin either, for ethnic German, Jewish and Gypsy minorities also reside here, not to mention large numbers of Ukranians.

Considering the length of the frontier and traditional cultural affinities, there are very few places **to cross the border**. International **trains** do so at NICOLINA, just east of Iaşi, into Soviet UNGENY; and at VICŞANI, northwest of Suceava, to VADU SIRET on the other side; but neither the *Romania* nor *Danubius* expresses stop at Iaşi before Nicolina, and to board them you'll need to do so at Ploieşti Sud or Bucharest (their point of departure, around 8pm and 10pm). By contrast, all four services crossing at Vicşani halt briefly at Suceava Nord where they can be boarded: the *Carpaţi* and *Varna* expresses, which whizz through the USSR towards Warsaw; and the *Marea Neagră* and *Sofia*, stopping at Chernovtsy in Soviet Moldavia en route to Kievsk station in Moscow. **By road**, there are 24-hour checkpoints at ALBIŢA, where there's a campsite (take route 28 from Iaşi or road 24B from Huşi), and at SIRET, northeast of Rădăuţi in the Suceava region. Entering the Soviet Union at any point, trains are delayed for 2hrs while wide, Russian-gauge bogies are fitted to the wagons, and for foreign passengers and motorists alike, there are stringent **visa and travel regulations**. Visas – obtainable from any Soviet consulate abroad (allow 2 weeks) – specify a certain place and time of entry, which must be adhered to; accommodation has to be pre-booked, and one's itinerary approved in advance. Unsurprisingly, this deters independent travellers, and practically all visitors to the USSR come on a package tour arranged by *Intourist* (who have branches in most capitals abroad).

Such **tours of Soviet Moldavia** normally focus on KISHINEV, a modernised city hosting the *Mertsishor Festival* of traditional dance and music every year

(March 1-10); and include the option of motorboat rides down the Dniestr to BENDERY, the site of an impressive fortress; or a trip to BELTSI, a town famed for its brandies. If you're interested enough to sign up for one, I'd advise reading Henry Baerlein's *Bessarabia and Beyond* which, despite its turgid prose, depicts the inhabitants and settlements of the region during the 1930s in affectionate detail.

FESTIVALS

Winter
Colinde, dancing, and the full panoply of 'Bears', 'Little Horsemen' etc. at TUDORA, ILIŞEŞTI and other communes in the Suceava region over **Christmas and New Year**. A large and predominantly Csángó winter fair occurs at GHIMEŞ on **January 20-21**.

Spring
To mark the onset of work, or nature blooming, a time for small village fêtes, for example at BICAZ ARDEALAN near Lake Bicaz on the **first Sunday of April**; or the *Peony Festival* in a flower-strewn clearing near BĂNEASA on the **second Sunday of May**.

Summer
A belated performance of the *Drăgacia* spring rite at BUZĂU on the **last Sunday of June**. In **July**, a folklore extravaganza involving three counties at ILIŞEŞTI on the **second Sunday**. Lake Bicaz, and DURĂU in particular, hosts a Navy Day regatta of sorts, and the more rumbustuous *Ceahlău Feast* on the **first and second Sundays in August**, whilst ODOBEŞTI celebrates its wine harvest on the **last Sunday of September**.

Autumn
Vrancea shepherds get together for a blow on their pan-pipes at ODOBEŞTI on the **third Sunday in November**.

TRAVEL DETAILS

Trains
From Adjud to Ghimeş (6 daily; 2¼-1¼hrs); Mihăileni (2; 3½).
From Bacău to Bicaz (6; 1½-2¼); Piatra Neamţ (7; 1-1¼); Suceava (6-7; 1¼).
From Bîrlad to Galaţi (5; 3).
From Bucharest to Buzău (1½hrs), Adjud (3), Bacău (3¾), Roman (4), Paşcani (4½) and Suceava (5½-6½); 6-7 times daily; to Iaşi 4 times daily (5¾-7hrs).
From Mărăşeşti to Tecuci (7; ¼); Galaţi (6; 3½).
From Paşcani to Iaşi (7; 1¼-1½).
From Suceava to Cîmpulung Moldovenesc (4; 2); Ilva Mică (2; 4); Putna (5; 2); Rădăuţi (5; ¾); Vama (6; 1½); Vatra Dornei (4; 3¼).
From Tecuci to Bîrlad (7; ¾-1); Iaşi (5; 3-3¾).
From Vama to Moldoviţa (3; ¾).

Buses
Poor and unpredictable everywhere, but some possibility of services:
From Gura Humorlui to Humor Monastery; Voroneţ.
From Piatra Neamţ to Tîrgu Neamţ.
From Rădăuţi to Arbore; Suceviţa.
From Suceava to Dragomirna; Ilişeşti; Moldoviţa; Rădăuţi.

Flights
One of each, daily.
From Bucharest to Iaşi; Suceava.
From Iaşi to Bucharest.
From Suceava to Bucharest; Constanţa (summer only).

International trains
From Suceava Nord to Kiev (12½hrs) and Moscow (27hrs), or Warsaw (23hrs), twice daily; to Varna (2 daily; 10hrs); Sofia (1; 17).

Chapter ten
MARAMUREŞ

Romania has been likened to a country with one foot in the communist future and the other in the Middle Ages – a fairly accurate characterisation of its northwestern counties, Satu Mare and **Maramureş**. Within 80km of heavily industrialised Baia Mare, thickly forested mountains and a dearth of transport maintain a score of villages in a state of almost medieval isolation, amidst a landscape of rounded hills with clumps of oak and beech and scattered sheep. One C19 traveller compared it to an arcadian vision of England pervaded with 'a feeling of remoteness', and since Maramureş – unlike other regions – was never conquered by the Romans, some features of life are believed to have changed little since Dacian times.

This is certainly true of many **villages**. The majority of buildings are made of wood by craftsmen whose skill is renowned (Maramureş carpenters were brought to Bucharest to rebuild Manuc's Inn), and the inhabitants produce virtually everything that they wear, use and eat – and if not, do without. Nowhere else in Europe do **folk costumes** persist so strongly, the women weaving boldly-striped *catriniţă* skirts, cloth for the water-powered fulling mills (*piuă*), and embroidering intricate designs on the wide-sleeved cotton blouses worn by both sexes – most conspicuously on Sundays and during markets and **festivals**, when the villages blaze with colourful attire. Just as people wear the rawhide *opinchi* footwear of the C12 or archaic felt boots bound with thongs, so villagers have retained their traditional religion – a mixture of pagan beliefs and Christianity – their myths and codes of behaviour. Large families, personal integrity and skilled work are all esteemed; the church and community exerts powerful sanctions against transgressors; and I was warned that local men are wont to react to perceived slights on their honour by drawing knives (which are eschewed at the table in some villages, being reserved for butchering animals, whittling wood, and fighting). This might explain why **doinas** (the Romanian equivalent of the blues) originated here.

Above all, perhaps, there's the marvellous **woodwork** of Maramureş – grudgingly acknowledged by John Paget as the 'only occupation in which the Wallack shows any peculiar talent'. Carvings decorate the eaves, doorways and windows of houses lining each village main street; every household subsisting with its livestock and barns within a compound fenced with timber, brush or lattice-work; entered via a gateway (*poarta*), the size of which indicates the family's prosperity. Many are elaborately carved with the 'tree of life', astrological symbols, human figures and animals, and I saw gateways erected as recently as the 1970s. The most elaborate structures are the *biserici*

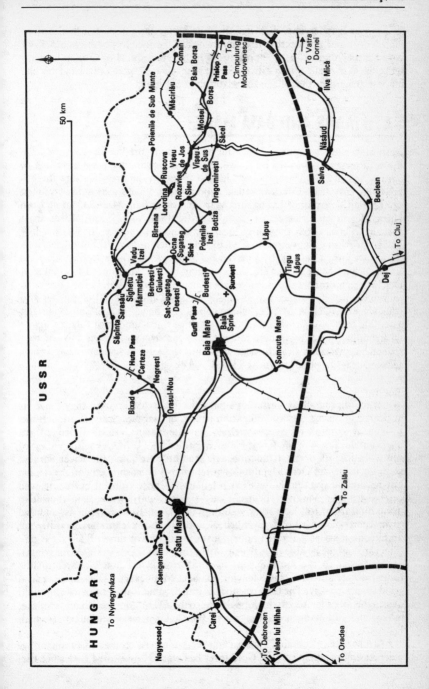

de lemn or **wooden churches**, mainly built during the C18 when this form of Gothic-inspired architecture reached its height. Founded upon huge blocks of wood rather than stone, they rear up into fairytale spires or crouch beneath humpbacked roofs like fugitives from Transylvania, generally sited on the highest ground in the village to escape seasonal mud.

SATU MARE AND BAIA MARE

Maramureş can be approached from Moldavia via the Prislop Pass, or from the southeast as described on p.386, but most visitors begin by travelling to Satu Mare or Baia Mare, the two largest towns in the area. **Getting there** is relatively easy **from Oradea**, with a good road and five trains a day (running up through Valea lui Mihai to Satu Mare and on to Baia Mare). Coming **from Hungary** you can drive across from CSENGERSIMA to PETEA (15km from Satu Mare), or catch the daily 'local' train from Debrecen to VALEA LUI MIHAI, or from Nagyecsed to CAREI, and switch onto northbound services. Both towns are accessible **by air from Bucharest**, whilst there are various ways to reach Baia Mare **from Cluj**. Approaching by rail, you'll need to change at Dej, where motorists should take DN1C heading north unless they prefer to follow the poorly-surfaced road through Tîrgu Lăpuş. DN1C is quicker and runs via ŞOMCUTA MARE, where choirs and bands of the Chioar district assemble for the *Stejarul* **festival** on the first or third Sunday of July (campsite with bungalows 6km farther on in Finteş forest), but reports have it that several fine **wooden churches** can be found in Dobricu Lăpuşuli, Lăpuş and Libotin near the small town of **TÎRGU LĂPUŞ**.

The towns

When the diplomats at Versailles signed the Treaty of Trianon they drew an arbitary line across the old Hungarian county of Szabolcs-Szatmár and left the provincial capital of *Szatmárnémeti* in Romanian hands, shorn of its traditional links with the Great Plain. Renamed **SATU MARE** ('Big Village'), the town lost its original function as a trading post along the River Someş, shipping salt from Ocna Dejului downstream to Vásárosmanény on the Tisza, but retained a sizeable Hungarian population whose cultural needs are still catered for by a Magyar Theatre. Satu Mare's **County Museum** includes the usual mixture of folk costumes, paintings and Daco-Roman remains, and the town centre has Catholic, Evangelical and Orthodox churches in different architectural styles – though none constitute any great draw. BTT (7, B-dul Eliberării) might be able to rustle up dormitory beds if you can't afford **rooms** at the *Someş* or the more expensive *Aurora* or *Dacia* hotels nearer to the **tourist office**, but with **trains** leaving for Baia Mare every 2-3hrs one needs a good reason to stay. The only one that comes to mind is the notion of stopping overnight in order to catch the 8.10am to LIVADA (on the Bixad line, see p.426) the following morning, where **fairs** take place on January 14 and February 11.

BAIA MARE is Romania's largest non-ferrous metals centre and, predictably, a depressing concrete sprawl. Gold fever has waxed and waned here since the

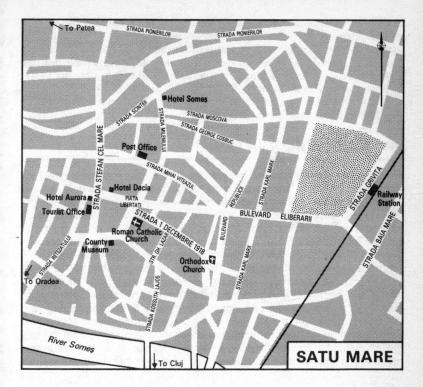

On the map: To Petea, STRADA PIONIERILOR, STRADA PIONIERILOR, Hotel Someş, STRADA SONTEI, STRADA MILENIULUI, STRADA MOSCOVA, STRADA GEORGE COSBUC, Post Office, STRADA MIHAI VITEAZUL, STRADA STEFAN CEL MARE, Hotel Dacia, PIATA LIBERTATI, Hotel Aurora, Tourist Office, STRADA RETEZATULUI, County Museum, Roman Catholic Church, STR GH LAZAR, STRADA 1 DECEMBRIE 1918, Orthodox Church, STRADA KOSSUTH LAJOS, To Oradea, River Someş, To Cluj, REPUBLICII, STRADA KARL MARX, BULEVARD, BULEVARD ELIBERARII, STRADA KARL MARX, STRADA GRIVITA, STRADA BAIA MARE, Railway Station, **SATU MARE**

C14 when *Nagybánya* (the town's Hungarian name, also meaning 'Big Mine') replaced the depleted Börzsöny as the Magyar monarchs' chief source of bullion. Mining and coining are both heavily represented in the **County Museum**, which incorporates the medieval mint, or *Bastionul Monetăiei*. Baia Mare's main tourist attraction lies farther north, at the foot of Florilor Hill: a **Village Museum** with over a hundred examples of peasant houses, watermills and other buildings from the Lăpuş, Codru and Chioar regions. Many of them are extremely eye-catching and slightly kooky, and if you haven't time to visit the Iza Valley, this museum is the next best thing.

Aside from the public **Observatory** (16, Str. Coşbuc), the town's other sights cluster around the main Piaţa Libertăţii. The thick-walled C15 house of Iancu de Hunedoara stands on the square itself (nr.20), whereas **Stephen's Tower** can be found together with a Baroque **cathedral** (whose medieval precursor once incorporated the 150ft-high tower) on the neighbouring Piaţa Cetăţii. The nearby **Fine Arts Museum** exhibits C18-C19 paintings on wood and glass, and a number of canvases by artists of the **Nagybánya School**, which transformed Hungarian art at the beginning of this century. Most of their work is now in Budapest, however, and the stuff here is attributed to the 'Baia Mare School' – a sly piece of Romanian revisionism.

The *Carpaţi*, *Bucureşti* and *Minerul* **hotels** are pretty dear ($28 sngl/$38 dbl), and there's no certainty that **BTT** (29, Str. 17 Octombrie) can arrange cheaper lodgings (the campsite is 19km out along the Satu Mare road). The main reason for staying here is to prepare for expeditions into the countryside (see below), for which you'll need a good map of the region, available from the **tourist office** on Bulevard Culturii. If you can't afford to hire a car from OJT, at least reserve accommodation in the hinterland and find out all you can about local **buses**. Services for Sighet usually, but not invariably, depart from the main terminal near the railway station.

THE MARAMUREŞ VILLAGES

From Baia Mare onwards the going gets uncertain: many of the villages are well off the main roads, and even those along the road to Sighetu Marmaţiei (Sighet for short) are awkward to reach without private **transport**. The costliest but most flexible option is to rent a car from OJT; otherwise you'll have to rely upon infrequent and overcrowded buses or on hitching. Private cars are scarce on the roads so be prepared for intermittent lifts or short rides between villages in the back of wagons or vans (a good way to meet local people, incidentally). Given patience it should be possible to see some excellent wooden churches – at Deseşti, Bîrsana, Bogdan Vodă etc – in this way. There are hotels in Borşa and Sighet, but otherwise come prepared to camp wild, with plenty of food supplies. If you get really stuck in a village, ask the priest (*popă*) for advice, but never force yourself upon anyone for **accommodation** and try to repay any hospitality with gifts. What follows doesn't pretend to be an exhaustive coverage of the region, for the whole area has yet to be opened up to visitors and its relative isolation only adds to its charm.

Places on and off the Sighet road
10km out along the Sighet road, just beyond the small town of BAIA SPRIE (noted for its autumn *Chestnut Carnival*), one can detour off the main road to reach some classic Maramureş villages. At ŞURDEŞTI – pronounced 'Shure-desht' – a magnificent **wooden church** rises from a hill above a stream. Its wooden tower, clad in thousands of oak shingles, is over 150ft high, three times the length of the church itself (built in 1737), which someone from the painted house near the stream will unlock for visitors. PLOPIŞ a few kilometres farther on has a similar – though slightly smaller and not quite so old – church, which likewise features four corner 'turrets' on its spire, a feature of many wooden churches in Maramureş and the Erdőhát region of Hungary – evidence that communities around the headwaters of the Tisza enjoyed close links before the frontiers were redrawn in 1918 and during the 1940s. If you keep driving northwards along the minor road, it eventually leads over the **Neteda Pass** (1,039m) and down *to Budeşti* (see p.424).

Continuing from Baia Sprie, the main road crosses the 1,109 metre-high **Gutîi Pass** (motel) before descending into another valley, past splendidly carved houses and gateways. The wooden church at DESEŞTI is hidden amongst some trees above the road to the left, and when I arrived the bells were tolling for a funeral. According to the verger, the bells are rung regularly

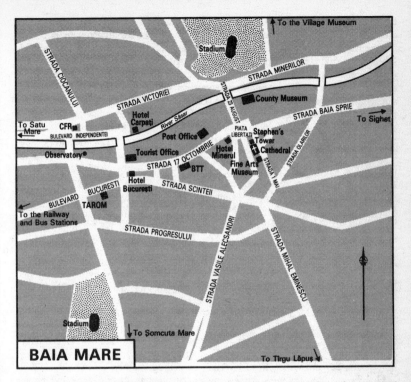

BAIA MARE

over the 2-3 days that the deceased lies at home awaiting burial, a period during which neighbours pay their respects and receive knot-shaped rolls or round buns bearing the inscription *IC XC NI KA* (for 'Jesus Christ is victorious') which is stamped in the dough by special seals called *pecetar*. Though the top of the spire has been clad in sheet metal, the Deseşti church is a fine example of the 'double roof' style which enabled the builders to construct windows high up inside the nave to increase the illumination.

It's dark inside nonetheless, and even with candles your eyes must adjust before you can see the marvellous **wall paintings**. Probably executed when the church was built in 1770, they seem more primitive yet less stylised than the frescoes in the Moldavian monasteries which were painted some 200 years earlier. Boldly coloured in red, yellow and white, the figures of saints and martyrs are contrasted with shady-looking groups of Turks, Jews and Franks; presumably so that the villagers could recognise the latter and revile them. The frescoes also include folk-style geometric and floral motifs, while the inscriptions are in the Cyrillic alphabet (since old Slavonic remained the liturgical language of Romanian Orthodoxy until the C19), but many of the paintings are flaking and peeling and may soon be lost unless something is done – perhaps by UNESCO, which assisted in the preservation of the Moldavian monasteries.

The next church is in the village of **SAT-ŞUGATAG**, sited beside the road.

Built in 1642, as solidly as a ship, it's accompanied by a graveyard containing a number of beautiful stout wooden crosses, and some picturesque cottages. To the right, a minor road leads off to Călineşti, Sirbi and Budeşti (see below), whilst the main route continues northwards to **GIULEŞTI**, which has a **watermill** (*moară*) of the sort otherwise seldom seen outside an ethnographic museum. Its two mill wheels are driven by water sluiced off a fast-flowing stream, the drive shafts running into a building where the miller can control the wheel with a kind of tension brake. The two millstones grind wheat and corn (though the latter was in short supply during my visit) and by tradition the miller takes one cupful of maize for each hopper-load that he grinds. Everthing is made of wood, down to the little channels siphoning off water to lubricate the spindles of the wheels, and the mill house doubles as a dying works, the wheel turning a spindle driving levers which cause wooden mallets to thoroughly stomp the cloth. Dyes are obtained by women from apple rind or onion (for varying hues of yellow), a plant called dyer's madder, and marjoram (which if picked on St Foca's day, July 23, is believed to give the deepest red).

At the next commune, **BERBEŞTI**, a carved wooden crucifix stands beside the road adorned with four mourning figures and symbols of the sun and moon. Similar wayside crosses can be found in Moldavia, sometimes inscribed *Doamne, apără-mă de dracul* (Lord, protect me from the devil), for traditionally travel was considered a hazardous undertaking. Tuesday was an unlucky day on which no journeys were made nor important work begun, and it was believed that after sundown ghosts and vampires (*strigoi*) roamed, seeking victims. From Berbeşti, the main road continues to VADU IZEI (leading to the Iza Valley covered on p.426-430, and Moldavia), a few kilometres beyond which lies SIGHET, described shortly.

However, travellers with wheels might consider **another detour**, taking the minor road that turns off to the right at Berbeşti. This leads upstream to several picturesque villages, which can also be approached from the south, crossing the Neteda Pass (p.422), or from the east, using the road between Sat-Şugatag, Ocna Şugatag and Călineşti. At **CORNEŞTI**, nearest to Berbeşi, there's another **watermill**, which was serving as a laundry when I arrived. Women were beating clothes with carved wooden laundry bats beside the river, and having accepted their invitation to drink ţuică with them, I soon became the subject of several impromptu songs and verses, for music and rhyme are living arts in Maramureş, derived from village life rather than some distant recording studio. Although few can learn the technique, there's a distinctive local form called **songs** 'with knots', in which the voice is modulated using the throat while the singer doesn't breathe for lengthy periods, an art made famous by the chanteuse Anuţa Tita. Certain instruments are also peculiar to Maramureş, for example the *zongora*, a guitar tuned after a violin, and the *dobra*, a kind of drum. Continuing southwards one comes to three villages with **wooden churches**, spaced 5-10km apart. At **CĂLINEŞTI** there's a side road to Ocna-Şugatag and Sat-Şugatag, but it's worth pushing on to see the fine church at **SIBRI**, if not the last one before the Neteda Pass in **BUDEŞTI**.

Sighetu Marmației and the 'Merry Cemetery' of Săpînța

SIGHET (as it's generally known) stands but a few kilometres from the Soviet border and has the air of a frontier town, though in fact there's nowhere to cross nearby. When the territory to the north was called Ruthenia, the easternmost province of Czechoslovakia, Sighet was a famous smuggling town. In the 1930s, Sacherevell Sitwell pondered what would become of its large Jewish population – lamenting their refusal to assimilate or modernise themselves, but little dreaming that in 1944 the Hungarian gendarmerie would round them up for forced labour and extermination. Nowadays a peaceful modern town with 40,000 inhabitants, Sighet is dignified by two fairly imposing central squares. You'll find the **tourist office** on the westerly one, Piața Libertății, more or less opposite the *Tisa* **hotel**; and from either place you should be able to get directions to the *Hotel Marmația* in the park at the foot of Solovan Hill. Sighet's **Ethnographic Museum** (2, Str. Lenin) exhibits pottery, woodcarvings, masks and wall rugs (*scoarte* – from the Latin for 'bark'), and has an open-air section – or **Village Museum** – situated on Dobăieș Hill on the town's eastern outskirts. Here you can see dozens of houses, farm buildings and churches collected from the Iza Valley – an essential sight if you're intending to give the real thing a miss. Sighet is famed for its **winter carnival** where many of the participants wear extraordinary costumes and masks, but few foreigners are around to witness the event at the end of December.

From the terminal at 1, Str. Republicii, there should be **buses** to Săpînța, if not to villages along the Iza Valley (see below). **Trains** from Sighet travel non-stop through a slice of Soviet Moldavia before they re-enter Romania and track the Vișeu Valley down to *Vișeu de Jos* – a less spectacular route than along the Iza but still scenic, particularly around the village of Petrova. From Vișeu de Jos there are trains to Borșa and up the Vaser Valley (see p.429), but most services continue southwards towards SALVA, the junction for **trains to Cluj**. This route is described in more detail on p.360.

Alternatively, hope for a bus or a lift to **SĂPÎNȚA**, about 16km northwest of Sightet. This charming village has achieved a star on every tourist map, largely thanks to the work of Stan Ion Pătraș, with the posthumous collaboration of folk now reposing in the **'Merry Cemetery'**. The *Cimitrul vesel* features beautifully worked, colourfully painted headboards carved with portraits of the deceased or scenes from their lives (chosen by the relatives), and inscribed with witty limericks (composed by Pătraș as he saw fit). Two examples give their flavour. . . .

> Why, since Pișta bade farewell,
> we've been resting mighty well;
> Our estates we gave on lease,
> and we idled and lived in peace.
> (A rich widow's epitaph)

> My lot was to die a bride
> 'cause of an engine I died.
> Near the village Sarasău
> a cruel driver laid me low.
> (A woman killed by a train on her wedding day)

Some are terse – 'who sought money to amass, could not escape Death, alas!' – while a surprising number bespeak of violent deaths, like the villager killed by a 'bloody Hungarian' during the last war, or a mother's final message to her son: 'Grigă, may you pardoned be, even though you did stab me'. Pătraş himself died in 1977 – his memorial house near the church contains a Săpînţaesque portrait of the Great Leader – but left two apprentices, Turda Toader and Vasile Stan, to continue the funerary masterwork.

Between Satu Mare and Săpînţa

Beyond the village of the Merry Cemetery the road turns southwards towards Satu Mare, passing splendid scenery and several places of interest en route. On the first Sunday in May, shepherds assemble at the **Huta Pass** (640m) for the **festival of Sîmbra oilor**, where barren ewes are separated from the milchy ones and the milk is 'measured'. Whether this process – known as *Ruptul Sterpelor* – occurs in May or early July (as it does in other areas), the participants dress for the occasion in waist-length sheepskin *cojoc*, covered in embroidery and tassels, or fluffy woollen overcoats called *guba*, and heartily consume fiery Maramureş brandy and sweet whey cheese.

Most of the shepherds come from communes beyond the **campsite with bungalows** on the other side of the pass: namely, HUTA-CERTEZE and CERTEZE itself. In both villages, you'll see people wearing traditional Oaş **folk costumes**, also widely worn during the **festival** (September 1) at NEGREŞTI, sometimes called Negreşti-Oaş on account of it being the largest settlement roundabouts. From here, a side road runs northwards to the small spa of BIXAD, linked by a branch line to Satu Mare. Using the 4 daily trains, one can reach LIVADA (2 stops before or beyond ORAŞUL NOU, depending on whether you're coming from Satu Mare or Bixad), but the only reason for doing so is to catch the local **fairs** on 14 January and 11 February.

THE IZA VALLEY BETWEEN VADU IZEI AND MOLDAVIA

Some of the loveliest villages and wooden churches in Maramureş are situated in the **Iza Valley**, which extends for roughly 60km until the Prislop Pass leading into Moldavia. The odd bus from Sighet might venture in this direction, but it's probably better to start hitching from town, or from **VADU IZEI** at the start of the valley road. Although there's no tourist accommodation and practically no shops along the valley until Borşa, you could also hike it in a couple of days. Locally, Vadu Izei is well known as the workplace of Gheorghe Borodi, who carves the monumental **gateways** which Maramureş families erect as status symbols.

The church at **BÎRSANA** (15km from Vadu Izei) is small and neat and perfectly positioned atop a hillock in the middle of the village. As is traditional in village Orthodox churches, the congregation are segregated according to sex: women pray in the narthex, just inside the porch, while men do their devotions in the nave. The narthex is adorned with saints and processional images, while the nave is painted with Old and New Testament scenes, each in its own decorative medallion (some are best viewed from the balcony). Being a hinterland region, Maramureş remained vulnerable to attacks by nomadic tribes until the C18, and the wooden church at **ROZAVLEA** (12km on) was built of fir beams in 1717, just after the last Tartar invasion. Its magnificent 'double' roof was recently restored and looks a little new, but will doubtless weather nicely with time. Nearby is a free-standing wooden belltower, while 2km farther along the valley there's another fine church at **ŞIEU**.

From Şieu it's possible to make a detour southwestwards to the village of **POIENILE IZEI** if you don't mind slogging about 10km up an execrable track over the hills. The Popă was away performing the last rites on somebody when I arrived, but anyone in the cottage at the bottom will unlock the church for visitors. Inside, the church is filled with **nightmarish paintings**, its walls red with the fires of Hell, wherein dozens of sinners have their vulnerable white bodies tortured by demons (*draci*) with goat-like heads and clawed feet. A woman is being pressed with a hot iron, a man is hung from a butcher's hook by his tongue, while others are furrowed by sharp ploughs or casually sawn in two. Beneath it all processions of sinners are driven into the mouth of Hell – an enormous bird's head with fiery nostrils.

The pictures constitute **an illustrated rule book** too terrifying to disobey, whose message is still understood by the villagers, for they explained the significance of each punishment to me. A huge pair of bellows up the bum is the reward for farting in church, while the woman being ironed had burnt the priest's robes while pressing them. Violations of traditional morality governing women bring torments in the afterlife: adultresses are courted by loathsome demons and a woman who aborted children is forced to eat them. These Hell scenes presumably formed the nasty part of a huge *Day of Judgement* in the narthex, which has half disappeared. Opposite are paintings of gardens and distant city-scapes in a sort of Gothic *Book of Hours*-style, seemingly executed at a later date. Murals in the nave are badly damaged and soot-blackened, but from the balcony one can recognise Adam and Eve, the Fall, and episodes from the lives of Christ and John the Baptist.

From Poienile Izei you can return to Şieu taking a triangular route via **BOTIZA**, where there's another church; around 20km in all. Back in the Iza Valley and about 5km farther along, another turn-off (known as Gura Ieudului) leads upriver to the village of **IEUD**, 3km away. Some say that the village's name is derived from *e ud* – 'it's wet' – and there's a rhyming ditty that goes, 'For the sake of my sweetheart of Ieud, I pass through water and don't get wet'. Lanes fenced with lattices run between the houses, clustered within their courtyards, and during summer the air is pervaded by the scent of lady's-mantle, a plant mixed with elder and wormwood to make 'face water', which also used to be plunged into baths to invigorate weak children.

Around fifty of Ieud's women are **'heroine mothers'**, having borne fourteen children each, and nigh on half the population of 5,000 is of school age. It was Ieud artisans, supervised by the master carpenter Ion Ţiplea (nicknamed 'the rich' for his talent), who restored Manuc's Inn in Bucharest some years ago, and the tradition of woodworking has been maintained since the building of the **Church on the Hill** here in 1364. The oldest church in Maramureş, with a terraced roof and tiny windows, it serves as the repository for the *Ieud Codex* (kept in the garret, to which one climbs by a stairway carved from a single piece of wood), the earliest known document in the Romanian language. Ieud's other church was built in 1699 and – unusually – lacks a porch.

BOGDAN VODĂ – one of the valley's main communes – stands beside the road leading to Moldavia, and has longstanding ties with that region. The local voivode, Bogdan, left from here to march over the mountains and found the Moldavian state in 1359, while the influence of Stephen and other rulers seems to have imparted a semi-Byzantine style to the frescoes inside Bogdan Vodă's church. The building materials used in 1772 were typical of Maramureş, however: thick fir beams rather than the stone used at Putna and other Moldavian monasteries. From the commune a road leads northwards, via Bocicoel, *to Vişeu de Jos* in the neighbouring valley (see p.429), while the main road continues on through DRAGOMIREŞTI to SĂLIŞTEA DE SUS. The church here, built in 1680, has a large porch with its own belfry, as if to toll the imminent end of *biserici de lemn* in the Iza Valley. 10km on you'll find the last one in SĂCEL, the home of a well known potter, Tănase Cocean. Săcel lies along the Sighet-Vişeu de Jos-Salva railway line, on which one can reach many of the places described below.

Around the Vişeu Valley, Borşa and the Rodna Mountains

11km beyond Săcel, the Iza Valley road enters the Vişeu Valley at MOISEI, a large village beneath the foothills of the Rodna massif, whose peaks can be snowy while fruit is ripening in the orchards surrounding the settlement. Though its present existence is bucolic, within living memory Moisei suffered a tragedy that's become a symbol of atrocity and martyred innocence in Romania, akin to the village of Lidice in Czechoslovakia. In October 1944, retreating Hungarian troops machine-gunned twenty-nine villagers and set Moisei ablaze – a massacre commemorated by a circle of twelve stone figures with faces modelled upon those of two of the victims and of the masks that are worn during festivals in Maramureş.

Such **atrocities** were common during the 1930s-40s, when racial supremacists gained the upper hand in both Hungary and Romania. Besides the Jews whom both governments persecuted savagely, Horthyite troops massacred Romanians at Ip, Trăsnea, Şimleul Silvanei and other villages in the area of Transylvania controlled by Hungary between August 1940-October 1945; while terrorist groups organised by the National Peasant Party attacked Hungarian villages such as Aiţa Seaca in the aftermath of the Soviet-Romanian 'liberation'. Today, Moisei's peaceful existence is symbolised by its womenfolk – spinning wool as they walk down the lane, or working in the fields with their babies nearby, hung in cradles from trees.

As a tributary of the River Tisza the Iza is less important than the Vişeu, a river fed by numerous sources in the wooded highlands above the Vişeu Valley, surrounded by mountains that merge with the 'crests' of Bucovina. Buses along the road from Sighet are uncertain, but trains departing around 8am and 3.30pm stop at picturesque **villages** like PETROVA and LEORDINA (just beyond which, near Ruscova, a track leads 20km upriver to POIENILE DE SUB MUNTE, which is said to be even better). The morning and the two evening **trains** from Sighet turn southwards at **VIŞEU DE JOS**, passing through Săcel en route to Salva (see below); while the 3.30pm train, and services leaving Vişeu de Jos at 7am and 9pm, follow a branch line through Vişeu de Sus and Moisei to the alpine resort of Borşa.

From **VIŞEU DE SUS**, a larger settlement than its namesake, earlybirds can catch the 7am **log train**: a vintage steam loco that carries lumberjacks (*butinarii*) up to their camps in the steep **Vaser Valley**, and at 3pm begins the journey back down from Coman. **Bears** and **deer** drink from the river, unperturbed by the trains and loggers, while in the forests ascending the mountainsides live **stags** (whose courtship enlivens the month of autumn), elusive and rare **lynxes**, and also **wolves**, a dozen or so of whom are shot each winter when the packs become too ravenous. The Vaser River, rich in trout and umber, descends rapidly through the 50km long valley, and its whirling waters have begun to attract **kayaking** enthusiasts to logging settlements like MĂCIRLĂU, whence there's a very rugged trail over the Jupania range of the Marmureş Mountains to Baia Borşa.

9km east of Moisei the branch line ends at the town of **BORŞA** (*Hotel Iezer* on Str. Victoriei). The road continues on past the Baia Borşa mining settlement towards the Prislop Pass, about 12km away. Roughly 2km before the pass you'll find the **Staţiunea Borşa ski resort** with a chalet, villas and the *Cascada Hotel*. The **hiking** fraternity are catered for by the *Puzdra* chalet – about 2-3hrs trek from the hamlet of Poiana Borşa, following the route marked by blue triangles, which leads further south into the mountains. With a map, you can hike **across the Rodna massif** and down towards Năsăud and the Bîrgău Valley in a couple of days, camping wild en route, and attend the **festivals** at Tiha Bîrgăului or Leşu if you're around during June or September (see p.416).

Another major festival takes place near the *inn* at the **Prislop Pass** (1,146m) linking Maramureş with Moldavia. Held on the second Sunday in August every year, the great **Hora at Prislop** attracts thousands of participants and spectators. The Round dances or *Horas* (performed in villages throughout the Balkans under various names, and with local differences) are less integral to rural society than they once were, but still have the power to draw onlookers into the rhythmically stepping, swaying and stamping circles. It used to be that Horas also served as a sanction in village society: local miscreants seeking to enter the circles were shamed when the dancing immediately ceased, and only resumed when they withdrew.

On the far side of the pass **into Moldavia**, the road eventually reaches Cîmpulung Moldovenesc, from which you can reach Suceava and several of the Painted Monasteries by railway. For those **travelling between Maramureş and Transylvania**, there's a 10am service from Vişeu de Jos down to **SALVA**; a busy junction on the line from Cluj to Năsăud, which ends up at ILVA MICĂ (connections with Vatra Dornei and other places in Moldavia). **En route to Salva**, the train halts briefly at Săcel and – four stops later – at TELCIU, whence there's a minor road leading up to the **Izvoru Rece cave** and other grottoes in the vicinity of Mount Varatec. From Salva itself, one can use the railway **to reach Cluj** (p.360), **Deda and the Székely Land** (change at Beclean) or **Bistriţa** (via the branch line from Sărăţel, between Beclean and Deva). Likewise, taking services in the opposite direction, trains from Salva (departing at around 3.20pm and 7.10pm) enable travellers **to approach Maramureş from the southeast.**

FESTIVALS

Winter
Colinde, masked processions etc. throughout rural Maramureş over **Christmas and New Year**, with a big *Winter Carnival* at SIGHET towards the end of December. On **January 14** and **February 11**, LIVADA hosts a fête.

Spring
As the snows retreat the pastoral cycle begins anew, giving rise to *Sîmbras* throughout Maramureş in late April or early May — some small affairs, others involving several villages, notably at the HUTA PASS on the **first Sunday in May**.

Summer
The *Stejarul* at ŞOMCUTA MARE on the **first or third Sunday** in **July** and the *Hora* at PRISLOP on the **second Sunday in August** are both large, colourful festivals. Moldavians also participate in the latter, whilst the former — like the event at NEGREŞTI on **September 1** — is mainly for Oaş folk.

Autumn
Harvest festivals everywhere, but their exact timing varies according to the locality, crop and weather that year. One event to ask about is the *Chestnut Carnival* at BAIA SPRIE.

TRAVEL DETAILS

Trains
From Baia Mare to Beclean pe Someş (2 daily; 2½hrs); Cluj (1; 3); Dej (4; 2¼-3¾); Jibou (7; 1-1¼); Satu Mare (6; 1-1½).
From Salva to Cluj (2; 2-3); Dej (4; ¾-1); Ilva Mică (7; ½); Sighet (2; 3½); Vişeu de Jos (2; 1½).
From Satu Mare to Baia Mare (5; 1-1½); Negreşti (4; 2½).
From Sighet to Salva (3; 2½-3¼); Vişeu de Jos (4; 2).
From Vişeu de Jos to Borşa (4; ¾); Sighet (4; ½-1½); Vişeu de Sus (4; ¼).

Flights
From Baia and Satu Mare to Bucharest (and Constanţa during the summer only); one of each daily.

International trains
Actually, 'local' trains used by folk with relatives, or shopping to do, in Hungary; consequently regarded with some suspicion when leaving Romania.
From Carei to Nagyecsed (1; 1).
From Valea lui Mihai to Debrecen (2; ¾).

Chapter eleven

THE BANAT

The **Banat***, or western marches of Romania, has much in common with Hungary's Great Plain and Yugoslavia's Vojvodina region, sharing similar scenery, great rivers and chunks of history, with an intermingling of different ethnic groups so variegated that 'a chameleon placed on a coloured population-map of the Banat would explode'. Since the frontier was to be settled according to the principle of 'national self-determination' at Versailles in 1918-20, delegates from each country arrived at the conference bearing reams of demographic maps and statistics to support their claims – claims which were totally irreconcilable, needless to say. During the socialist era, policies towards ethnic minorities have been generous in Hungary and Yugoslavia, and comparatively fair in Romania until the 1960s – but since then, an increasingly hard line has caused a haemorhaging of the population, particularly of ethnic Magyars.

From a visitor's standpoint, **Arad**, **Oradea** and **Timişoara** overshadow the rest of the Banat – partly on their own merits, but also because each town dominates a route between Transylvania and Hungary or Yugoslavia, as well as providing access to most other places of interest in the region. When you're tired of such sights and café life as the towns have to offer, flick through the routes described below which radiate from Arad and Oradea to the western ranges of the Apuseni Mountains, for **stalactite caves** or village **festivals**; or simply choose the quickest way to reach whatever destination you might have in mind – Belgrade, Debrecen, Szeged, Cluj, Sibiu and other major sites are only a few hours away. You'll find the details of roads, trains and border crossings under the relevant towns.

ORADEA AND ITS SURROUNDINGS

Oradea – the capital of Bihor county – is situated a mere 16km from BORŞ, the 24hr checkpoint on road DN1 (Euroroute E15) that **approaches** from ÁRTÁND in Hungary; and a similar distance from EPISCOPIA BIHOR, where international trains are delayed for an hour of customs and visa palaver after clearing BIHARKERESZTES (where Magyar officialdom takes half as long). By rail, it's 5-6hrs journey **from Budapest** on the *Tracia*, *Mamaia* or *Nord-Orient* express (which may also be boarded at Szolnok or Puspökladány) – all of which arrive in Oradea between midday and the late afternoon,

---

*Historically and pedantically, the term Banat (*Bánság* in Hungarian) refers only to the region between the Timiş and the Mureş, but it has come to be applied also to the *Crişana* – the area bounded by the rivers Crişul Alb and Crişul Repede.

enabling you to get orientated and find a room before nightfall. Driving from Budapest, simply follow the E15 though Szolnok and Puspökladány across the plain towards the frontier, while approaching **from Debrecen**, take rd.47 via Berettyöujfalu to reach ÁRTÁND. **From within Romania**, Oradea is directly accessible by road or rail from Arad and Satu Mare, and from Cluj (see p.360 and below); by flying or a 7½hrs train journey from Bucharest; or from Deva by following DN76 northwestwards through the Apuseni Mountains (a route that isn't feasible by rail).

Oradea

A city of 200,000 people on the banks of the Crişu Repede, **ORADEA** occupies the site of *Bihara* – the capital of a Vlach voivodate whose duke, Menumorut, resisted Hungarian claims on the region during the C10 – and bears the stamp of subsequent rulers. Founded around a monastery, the medieval town of Nagyvárad (as the Magyars called it) prospered during the reign of Mátyás Corvinus, who was raised at the Bishop's court here; later acquiring a mammoth Vauban-style Citadel and the wealth of stately neo-Classical and Baroque piles which constitute Oradea's most characteristic feature.

Heading westwards from the railway station, you'll come upon two of them alongside Str. Stadionului. Countless serfs toiled to finance the construction of Romania's largest Baroque Catholic **Cathedral**, with its huge organ (see posters for details of concerts) and variegated marble facings; and their labour was doubtless also exploited to build the vast U-shaped Bishop's Palace, with its 100 rooms and 365 windows modelled on the Belvedere Palace in Vienna. Presumably because such extravagance appeared unseemly in a more secular age, the latter now serves as the **Museum of the Crişana** region, exhibiting ethnographic and historical material, *engravings by Albrecht Dürer* (whose father was born in a village near Oradea), and a collection of 13,000 eggs (open Tuesday-Sunday 10am-6pm). In the leafy nearby park stand three giant **Californian Redwoods** and an C18 **wooden church**.

Shops, cinemas and a 24hr pharmacy (nr.7) line the main Calea leading down to **Piaţa Republicii**, along with *CFR*, TAROM (nr.2), the State Theatre and one of Oradea's tourist offices (nr.4). Buildings around the square, and the Piaţa Victoriei over the river, were obviously designed to maximise the appearance of **the waterfront**. The old City Hall with its tower is a monumental restatement of well-worn classical themes to which the architects added a fun touch: a mechanism within the clock that chimes each hour with notes from the March of **Avram Iancu**. Given that the Austro-Hungarians were still in control when the building was raised in 1902-03, it seems odd that they chose to commemorate Iancu – a Romanian revolutionary whose agitation inspired the protest on the 'Field of Liberty' at Blaj in 1848, and who then took to the hills with a guerilla band, harassing Magyar troops and landlords and urging the serfs to revolt.

Facing City Hall on the Piaţa Victoriei stands an ornate secession-style edifice with the splendid name of the **Vulturul Negru** or 'Black Eagle'. Running through this is a passageway with a stained glass roof, connecting three neighbouring streets. Part of the complex is occupied by a hotel that

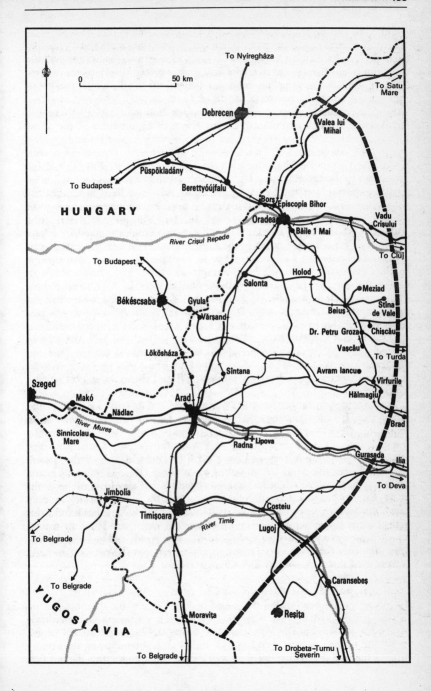

could have sprung from the pages of a Graham Greene thriller – an ill-lit labyrinth of rooms and corridors inhabited by brooding staff and a secretive clientele. To the south, Oradea's main Orthodox church marks the stylistic transition from Baroque to neo-Classical, but is better known as the '**Moon Church**' after the large sphere mounted beneath its clock, which rotates to indicate the lunar phases over a period of 28 days.

Beyond Parcul 23 August rises the imposing bulk of Oradea's **Citadel**, a Renaissance stronghold enlarged during the C18 by disciples of the Swiss military architect Vauban. Pentagonal in shape, with bastions guarding each corner, the citadel used to be additionally protected by a moat filled with warm water from the Peţa, which never froze. Of less interest to the average visitor are two **memorial houses** in the northern half of town. One (in Traian Park) commemorates the Magyar poet **Endre Ady** who lived in Oradea for four years and – unusually for his era – opposed Hungarian chauvinism towards the Romanians; the other (at 16, Str. Vulcan) remembers **Josif Vulcan**, in whose literary magazine, *Familia*, Mihai Eminescu made his début.

Oradea's main **tourist office** in the *Hotel Dacia* (1, Aleea Ştrandului) can arrange **excursions** to Băile Felix, Stîna de Vale, the Bears' Cave and various folklore events in the Apuseni Mountains (see below and p.368), although most of them can be reached without the services of OJT. The town's **Philharmonic Orchestra** (10, Piaţa 23 August) is well regarded, while children might enjoy performances at the **Puppet Theatre** (9, Str. Alecsandri) – tickets for both available from the bureau at 9, Calea Republicii. Places **to eat** include the *Dacia* and *Transilvania* hotels; *Oradea* (1, Str. Vulcan); the *Crşma Bihoreană* – specialising in regional dishes – at 2, Str. Grigorescu; and the *Ciuperca* with its outdoor terrace on Viilor Hill. The bar in the Hotel Astoria is the smart place to go **drinking**, while you'll find the main **market** on Str. Kogălniceanu.

Accommodation ranges from $42 for a single and $54 for a double in the *Hotel Dacia*, down through the *Astoria* (1, Str. Teatrului), *Transilvania* (opposite), *Crişul Repede* (6, Piaţa Libertăţii) and *Parc* (5, Calea Republicii) to the cheapest of Oradea's hotels, the *Vulturul Negru*. Otherwise, the alternatives are a dormitory bed from BTT (9, Str. Vulcan), or the *chalet-campsite* beside the river, 19km east of town along DN1. Though it doesn't seem very likely, there might just be **buses** heading that way from the terminal at 81, Str. Războieni. If you're planning to visit the Vadu Crişului cave or break the journey towards Cluj, reserve rooms at the local cabana from the main tourist office before **leaving Oradea**. CFR can book seats on **trains**, which depart every 1½hrs for Cluj, Satu Mare or Arad; and at around 9am, 5pm and 7pm for Budapest. Tickets for Budapest must be paid for in hard currency, or in lei covered by an exchange receipt.

Local spas, and places on and off the Cluj road

Bihor county has been called the 'Land of Hot Waters' for its profusion of thermal springs, two of which have been exploited to create **spas** in the vicinity of Oradea. **BĂILE FELIX** (8km southwest along DN76; take tram #4 or #5 to the end of the line, and then bus #14; or a Vaşcău-bound train, see below) offers a thermal pool surrounded by mock-rustic buildings, and a plethora of

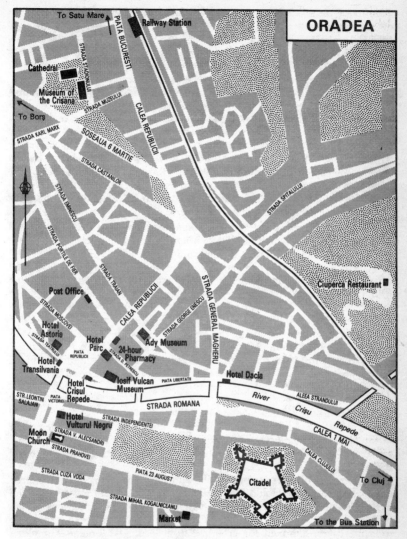

expensive modern hotels – plus **mud-baths**, either in sapropelic fossil mud or the local peat bog, both of which have therpeutic properties. Similar salubrious gunge may be enjoyed at **BĂILE 1 MAI** (nearer to Oradea, but about 3km off DN76), the site of a chalet-campsite complex and the source of the Peța – a mildly radioactive brook in whose warm waters the **thermal lotus** has survived since the Tertiary Period, a plant that's otherwise found only in the Nile Delta.

The journey **towards Cluj** doesn't require any stops or changing unless you want to see the **stalactite caves in the Crişul Repede Gorges**. If so, turn south off the highway at ALEŞD and follow a minor road eastwards through Măgeşti, or take a slow train – not an *accelerat* or *rapid* – as far as the PEŞTERA halt, two stops beyond the 'Ford on the Criş', **VADU CRIŞULUI**. Nearby lies a cabana and the entrance to the **Vadu Crişului cave**, the subject of one-hour tours (between 9am-6pm every day). Alternatively, you can reach the cave by walking 2km through a gorge from Vadu Crişului, a commune traditionally known for producing unglazed red and white **pottery**. At the cave entrance or the Cabana nearby, make enquiries before embarking on the path (marked by blue triangles) which leads off to the **Cave of the Wind**. Exploring the *Peştera Vintului*'s 32km of passages on four levels (entered through the 'ground floor') has taken years; limiting access to experienced cavers accompanied by members of Cluj University's Racoviţa Institute of Speleology (p.364), and in a manner calculated not to harm the trogdolyte fauna; but it seems likely that part of the cave will be opened to the public in the near future. OJT or local people should be able to say.

Shortly beyond the *Motel Piatra Craiului*, the highway converges with the tracks near the railway halt for BULZ, whence drivers can turn off and follow a road up **through the Valley of Hell to Stîna de Vale**. The valley's hellish karsts and blasted heaths compensate for the frequently diabolical road; but since buses rarely venture along it, those without private transport will have to hitch or walk the 45km to the ski resort of Stîna de Vale (p.376). Throughout the Apuseni Mountains, pastoralism still determines many people's lifestyle, and some of its habits and rituals go back a millenia or more. During early May, travellers might like attend the *Measurement of the Milk* held in a glade at MĂGURA PRIEI in the Mezes Mountains on the first Sunday (as described on p.376). Again, public transport is non-existent, and roads to the mountain are abysmal; but if you're interested in going, CIUCEA is the point to turn off the Cluj road.

Approaches to the Apuseni Mountains

Places, festivals and hiking in the **Apuseni Mountains** are generally described in the chapter on Transylvania; and what follows is a quick run down of attractions along the mountains' **western approaches**, starting from Oradea or Băile Felix.

The first stage of the route entails following DN76 or taking one of the three daily trains along the Holod/Vascău line to **BEIUŞ**, a small town where the Banat's first girls' school was opened in 1896. The town's irregular **bus service to Meziad and Chişcău** is the only public transport to these impressive stalactite caves; although for around $20 a head, OJT organises minibus excursions. It's impossible to predict the frequency of buses, but hopefully it shouldn't be necessary to kill much time in the town's **Ethnographical Museum** on Str. 23 August (actually, the folk art and ceramics are worth seeing), let alone spend a night in the solitary **hotel** (2, Str. Păcii). Try pumping the **tourist office** (20, Piaţa 23 August) for information before tackling the the problem by its horns at the bus terminal (16, Str. 6 Martie).

10km to the northeast of Beiuş, the village of **MEZIAD** is named after the **cave** a further 3km away, or vice versa. Guides shepherd parties around the cave, commentating in Romanian on the stalactites and other features of this warren with a total length of 4¾km; the hour-long tours occur whenever the custodian feels like it between 9am-6pm every day. Starting from the **cabana** nearby, it's possible to make an exciting 68hr **hike to Stîna de Vale** , crossing the ridge between the Meziad and Iad valleys, with splendid scenery and a wealth of varied vegetation and karstic curiosities along the way. The trail – marked at intervals by blue triangles – requires some hiking expertise, and ONT stress that it should never be attempted during bad weather. There's a slim possibility of buses from Beiuş to Stîna de Vale, but hitching prospects are probably better.

The bus service from Beiuş to **CHIŞCĂU** is also fairly unpredictable but at least everyone understands that you're aiming for the **Bears' Cave**. Accidentally discovered by local quarry-workers in 1975, this was found to contain dozens of Neolithic ursine skeletons – hence the name, *Peştera Ursilor*. The frequency and duration of guided tours is similar to that at Meziad, and experience is not to be missed. The rock formations – shaped like castles, wraiths or beasts, and textured as if to simulate mushrooms, diamonds, porcelain or enamel – have an echo of their virgin state in the sound of water shattering reflections in subterranean pools.

Access to Chişcău is via a road leading off the route to **PIETROASA**, a picturesque commune on the upper reaches of the Crişul Pietros. Water-powered saw-mills rasp and oldsters wearing traditional Bihor garb empty slops from the *pripsas* of their sturdy houses, while on the first Sunday in August, villagers troop to a site 8km away for the **festival** of *Bulciugul de Valea Aleu*. It's faintly possible that buses might run to Pietroasa and/or Chişcău from **SUDRIGIU**, a large commune on the railway line midway between Beiuş and Dr. Petru Groza; but the probability that buses might continue beyond Pietroasa along the forest road up **to the Padiş Plateau** near the 'Citadels of Ponor' (p.374) seems practically zero. The hiking trail follows the road for about 5km (mark: blue crosses) and then diverges; the path to the Focul Viu Cave is designated by yellow triangles, while blue crosses signify the route to the Padiş Cave.

Motorists also have the option of taking another, equally scenic, route to the plateau along **the road to Gîrda de Sus** and the Scarişoara Ice Cave (p.373). Some way south of Sudrigiu, the commune of **RIENI** might tempt you with its C18 **wooden church** and watermill, but the best part of the journey comes once you turn off DN76 beyond the small industrial town of DR. PETRU GROZA (whence, again, there might be buses) and drive eastwards. The village of **BĂIŢA** just past Nucet has several caves nearby and holds a lively **fair** on the last Sunday in September; while on the far side of the Vîrtop Pass lies **ARIEŞENI**, with its traditional dwellings and wooden church. There's a campsite there, and at Gîrda de Sus a further 8km down the road, from which it's 2-3hrs walk to the Scarişoara Ice Cave and chalet.

The branch line from Oradea terminates at VASCĂU, but route 76 continues through the mountains until it joins the Arad road near the village of **VÎRFURILE** – a distance of 31km. At CRIŞTIORU DE JOS en route, a crummy track leaves DN76 and winds up 30km to the southeast at the village of Avram Iancu below **Mount Găina**, where the famous *Girl Fair* occurs every year on the Sunday before July 20 – an event described on p.373, together with perhaps the best way to get there. Approaching from the west and relying upon public transport, the outlook is fairly bleak; but there is, however, a faint possibility of buses – or at least, hitchable traffic – from the commune of RIBIŢA. This last is a stop along the Arad-Brad line, as are HĂLMAGIU where the *Kiss Fair* is held in March, and Vîrfurile whence there's a minor road to another commune called AVRAM IANCU – this one the venue for the *Nedeia of Tăcaşele* in June. For more details of both **festivals**, see the section following Arad.

ARAD AND AROUND

Approaching Arad from Hungary, motorists on the road from Szeged enter Romania at NĂDLAC, 40km away, or at VARŞAND (on the road from Gyula), situated midway between Arad and Oradea; while travelling by rail, you'll cross over from Lökösháza to CURTICII. The *Pannonia* and *Transdanubium* **from Budapest** reach Arad around midday, whereas the *Orient* and *Wiener-Waltzer* pull in about 3.30am and 10pm – not the best times to arrive. You can board any of the above expresses at Szolnok, while 'local' trains **from Békéscsaba** (departing around 6am and 4.30pm) also run to Curticii (on these, customs checks are much tougher than on the international services). It's a straight-forward journey of ll7km by DN79 (motel en route) or railway **from Oradea** to Arad, and getting there **from Deva** – see below – or Timişoara is equally simple.

Arad

ARAD's chief sight is either an eyesore or an attraction depending on your taste in architecture: a huge **Citadel** commanding a loop of River Mureş, facing the sprawling town on the west bank. Shaped like a six-pointed star with its ramparts and bastions obliquely sited to provide interlocking fields of fire, the Citadel represented the 'state of the art' of fortification when it was constructed in 1762-83 in the style of Sebastian Vauban, designer of the even huger fortress of Petrovaradin at Novi Sad in Yugoslavia a century earlier. Like Petrovaradin, it proved something of a white elephant from its inception, since the Turks against whom it was ostensibly raised had already been pushed out of the Carpathian basin in 1718; but its three levels of underground casements provided the Habsburgs with a ready-made prison following the suppression of the 1848 revolution.

Previously, the Habsburgs had deliberately settled Swabians, Serbs and Romanians in the devastated, depopulated area known as the *Partium*, and excluded Magyars from this strategic region so as to facilitate its assimilation into their empire. But despite this, Arad's population rose up against Habsburg domination several times in 1848-49. The revolt was finally crushed with the help of Tsarist Russia (the 'Gendarme of Europe'), and the Habsburgs made an example of the ringleaders by executing thirteen Hungarian generals outside the fortress walls – an event commemorated by a monument nearby.

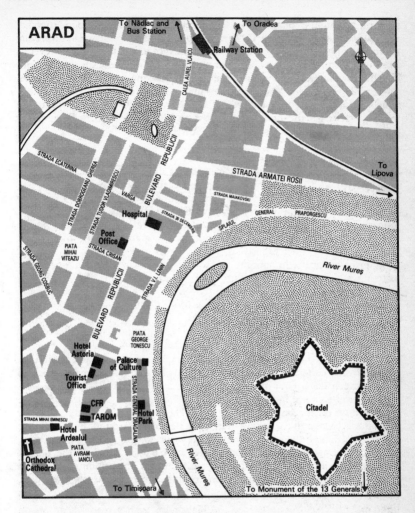

The execution features prominently in the **Museum** housed within the eclectic **Palace of Culture** on George Enescu Square, which also contains Arad's **Philharmonic Orchestra**. Town life centres around the **Bulevard Republicii** west of the big administrative complex. Here you'll find a 24hr pharmacy (nr.80) and the hospital; the *Astoria* and *Zarandul* **restaurants** (with a disco and regional cuisine, respectively); the post office and the regional **tourist bureau** (nr.72). The latter is almost next door to the *Hotel Astoria* which, like the *Parc* (1, Str. Dragalina), charges $53 for a double and $40 for a single room. The *Hotel Ardealul* (nr.98) is fractionally cheaper and incorporates a large hall where Liszt, Brahms and Pablo Casals have performed in their time, but if you want reasonably priced **accommodation** it's necessary to enquire at BTT (16, Piaţa Avram Iancu) or camp. *Subcetate campsite* (with bungalows) is situated 7km west of town along the Nălac road, but a new campsite may be opening in the park near the Generals' Monument. The **bus terminal** lies just west of the **railway station** on Calea Avram Iancu, while CFR and TAROM occupy the same premises on the corner of Stradă Unirii. Should you require **car repairs**, check with ACR (8, Str. Unirii) before making tracks for the *Autoservice* depot at 284, Calea Armata Roşie (24hr **petrol** stations on Str. Marx and Calea Aurel Vlaicu).

Local festivals in communes beyond Arad

SÎNNICOLAU MARE deserves a mention as the birthplace of **Béla Bartók** (1881-1945), although the memorial house hardly justifies visiting the town. In 1906, Bartók joined his fellow Hungarian Zoltán Kodály in a quest to collect and record the unwritten peasant music of Hungary and Transylvania; journeying into remote areas like Ghimeş and the Sárköz, where they had to surmount peoples's mistrust of their 'monster' – a gramophone with a cutting stylus. Years of meticulously organised work laid the foundations of subsequent musical ethnography in Hungary – which has maintained their exacting standards – while both men found inspiration for their own compositions, which after years of rejection caused a musical renaissance in Hungary. *Nagyszentmilkós* (Sînnicolau Mare's Hungarian name) is also remembered for the fabulous hoard of C5 goldwork unearthed nearby – known as the 'treasure of Attila' or the 'Nagyszentmilkós treasure', and kept since its discovery in Vienna's Kunsthistoriches museum.

Starting from Arad, it's possible to reach a number of communes noted for their **festivals**; either by road (if you have private transport), or by judicious use of branch lines. First off, there's the commune of SÎNTANA, 7km west of the Arad-Oradea highway, which hosts a festival called *Sărbătoarea Iorgovanului* on the last Sunday of May. This can be reached by using the Arad-Brad branch line, taking the train departing around 8am (50mins journey). Although the festival is an occasion for dancing, music and dressing up in traditional costumes, it originated as a parish fair, like the one at PÎNCOTA on February 1 (another 25mins by train). The commune of BÎRSA (where the train stops about an hour after Pîncota) has its own fête, *Săbătoarea Druştelor*, on the first Sunday in April. Around midday the train stops at Vîrfurile.

As mentioned above, a minor road from VÎRFURILE runs northwards for 6km to the small village of AVRAM IANCU, where people from thirty mountain villages gather for the *Nedeia of Tăcaşele* on the second Sunday of June. Besides being an occasion for trade and socialising, this large **fair** provides a chance for musicians to play together, and the *Nedeia* is an excellent time to hear *cetera* (fiddles), *nai* (pan-pipes) and alpine horns (*buciume*). The connection between new life and stirring lust probably underlies a good many spring festivals, and it's one that the delightfully-named 'Kiss Fair' (*Tîrgul sărutului*) at HĂLMAGIU acknowledges. Traditionally, the event has allowed young men and women to cast around for a spouse while their elders discuss crops and the fecundity of livestock – an occasion for decorous flirtation, extravagant promises and dressing up in one's smartest attire. You can easily reach the commune, two stops beyond Vîfurile on the line to Brad; the exact date of the festival – held some time during March – varies, although Arad's tourist office should know what's happening.

Unfortunately, all the above communes lack tourist accommodation, so that one has to return to Arad (check the times of the last train back) or carry on to BRAD where the *Hotel Crişul Alb* can be found at 10, Str. Minerilor. For an account of the neighbouring **Apuseni Mountains**, see the chapter on Transylvania.

Between Arad and Deva

While walking the 154km **between Arad and Deva** in the 30s, Patrick Leigh Fermor stayed with Magyar aristocrats whose dusty mansions and diminished bands of retainers spoke eloquently of the decline in their fortunes since the Trianon Treaty. Nowadays, these châteaux are museums and the journey can be accomplished by DN7 or by railway – although if you're using the latter, be warned that only *cursa* trains make halts along the way before Ilia. **GHIOROC**, one such halt, is basically a pit-stop with a chalet 500m away, whence walkers make the 3hrs hike to the *Căsoia Cabana* in the Zărand Mountains. At **LIPOVA** – a small town accessible by bus from the Radna train halt – Leigh Fermor played skittles with a monk from the Franciscan Abbey until 'we were both in a muck-sweat when the bell for Vespers put an end to play'. 3km to the south of Lipova is a spa with villas and bungalows for rent.

A short distance beyond Lipova you'll see the **ruined Şoimoş Citadel** built to guard the Mureş defile between the Zărand and Ruscăi mountains. As Leigh Fermor described, the river loops away for a mile or two, then meanders back, 'the clouds of willows and aspens that mark its windings interspersed with poplars tapering in spindles or expanding like butterfly nets'. In the narrowest part of the gorge lies **SĂVÎRŞIN**, which celebrates its communal existence with **fairs** on January 30 and November 27. The woods to the north of this railway-halt are rich in small game, which once provided meat for guests at the former Nádasdy family château secluded in the forest. Leigh Fermor's host at **CĂPÎLNAŞ** (7km to the south) was a count with abtruse genealogical interests, who deprecated his *kastély* as 'only C19 and perhaps a bit showy'. Another 5km west along the Căpîlnaş road lies the commune of **BIRCHIŞ**, where a fair number of people still wear **folk costume**.

Slow trains make a couple more halts before Ilia, notably at **ZAM** and Gurasada. The former juxtaposes an C18 **Castle** with the *Parc* bungalow-site, and has a local **fair** on November 30. **GURASADA** combines the incongruous with the faintly sinister. A bamboo plantation has somehow established an unlikely niche, not far from the commune's C13 Greek Orthodox Church, whose **murals** depicting women sinning and then suffering suggest a sadistically misogynistic bent to the characters of the C18 artists, Nicolae of Piteşti and Ion of Deva.

At **ILIA**, the chance of seeing the ruined castle once owned by Gábor Bethlen, or attending one of the parish **fairs** held every year (January 7 & March 25), might just tempt you to linger, although there are strong reasons to keep going. From here, DN7 and the majority of trains continue eastwards towards **Deva, Simeria, Orăştie and Sibiu**, a route more or less described in reverse order in the penultimate and ante-penultimate sections of the chapter on Transylvania. Alternatively, you can head southwest across the Zărand range **towards Lugoj**, using DN68A or the branch line (3 fast and 3 slow trains daily). For details of this route, see the section following Timişoara.

TIMIŞOARA AND BEYOND

Approaching Timişoara from within Romania there's the choice of well-surfaced roads from the other Banat towns; direct *rapids* and *accelerats* from Arad, Bucharest, Craiova, Orşova, and Caransebeş; and slower services from Lugoj (change trains at Ilia if you're coming from Deva or Sibiu). Motorists can accomplish the 105km journey **from Belgrade** within a couple of hours, using the E94 which enters Romania at MORAVIŢA, 58km south of town (open 24hrs); but travellers relying on trains aren't so fortunate. Most people opt for the daily *Bucureşti Express* despite its arrival in Timişoara nigh on midnight, since the alternative is to catch a train from Belgrade to *Kikinda*, and then the 10am or 4pm 'local' train across the frontier at JIMBOLIA, arriving in town some 3hrs later. Coming **from Hungary**, the *Transdanubium* from Budapest arrives in town around 3pm (like other services, at the *Nord* station to the west of Timişoara's centre), while the nearest road crossing is at NĂDLAC, acutally much closer to Arad.

The town
The town now called **TIMIŞOARA** originally grew up around a Magyar fortress, *Castrum Temesiensis*, at the marshy confluence of the Timiş and Bega, and from the C14 onwards functioned as the capital of the Banat – hence the old name for that region, the *Banat of Temesvár*. As a stronghold it played a crucial role during the 1514 uprising and Hunyadi's campaigns against the Turks, who subsequently conquered the town, whence they ruled the surrounding *pashalik* until 1716. The Habsburgs who ejected them proved to be relatively benign masters over the next 200 years, the period when *Temeschwar* (as it was then called) acquired many of its current features.

A prime example is the **Bega Canal** flanked by a procession of stately **parks** (of which Timişoara has more than any other town in Romania). Dug to drain the surrounding marshes and permit the shipment of Banat grain to the Danube, the canal has outlasted both requirements but continues to lend neighbouring parts of town a pleasant ambience. More recently, it was along the embankments that citizens, singing *Romania Awake!*, staged a sympathy demonstration following the anti-Ceauşescu riot in Braşov. Approaching via the Calea Aradului, or from the *Nord* station along Bulevard Republicii (past several hotels; the *Parc* is cheapest), the town's architectural assets don't become evident until one enters **the centre**, with its carefully planned streets and piaţas. During the late C19, the municipality rode a wave of progress, being one of the first towns in the world to have horse-drawn trams (1864), and the first in Europe to install electric streetlighting (1884), followed shortly afterwards by railway and telegraph lines to Vienna.

On Piaţa Huniade you'll find the **Museum of the Banat** occupying the castle

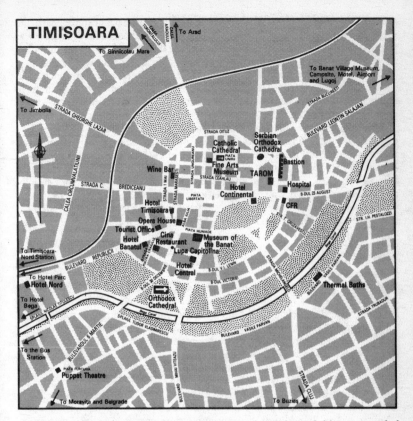

once inhabited by the Hungarian monarch Charles Robert and later extended by Hunyadi. Warlords and rebels figure prominently in the large historical section, as do the local Workers' Association (the first organisation in the country affiliated to the Communist International) and the great strike of 1920 in support of the Banat's union with Romania; but the museum (open Tuesday–Sunday 11am–6pm) also exhibits nearly 21,000 stuffed birds and mounted butterflies. One can imagine lepidopterists working under the eye of some *Herr Direktor* given to attending the plush **Opera House** like most of Timişoara's bourgeoisie, if not to discourse on the significance of the **Lupa capitolina** – a replica of the statue of Romulus and Remus given by the city of Rome, which stands halfway down B-dul 30 Decembrie.

The central Piaţa Libertăţii boasts as fine a Baroque Town Hall as any proud municipality could wish for, but the edifice is modest compared to the huge **Dicasterial Palace** at one end of Str. Ceahlău. A complex of 450 rooms built for the Habsburg bureaucracy of the C19, its sheer bulk was redolent of the state's power, never more savagely displayed than during the **execution of György Dózsa**. The peasant uprising that swept across Hungary and Transylvania in 1514 terrified the nobility, and it was some months before they rallied behind János Zápolyai and defeated the peasants beneath the walls of Timişoara. Their leader, a former mercenary of Székely origin, was put to death on the main square, where an iron throne and crown for the 'King of the Serfs' were both fired to red-heat. Then, Dózsa was seated and 'crowned' before his body was torn asunder by pincers; parts of the charred corpse being force-fed to his followers (who had been starved and were compelled to watch before their own executions), while others were hung above the gates of Oradea, Alba Iulia and Buda as a warning.

One block north of the palace, Piaţa Unirii's **Museum of Fine Arts** displaying work by minor Italian, German and Flemish masters is overshadowed by the monumental Roman-Catholic and Serbian-Orthodox **Cathedrals**. Built between 1736-73, the former is a fine example of Austrian Baroque, designed by von Erlach of Vienna. The latter is roughly contemporaneous and equally impressive in its own way. An ecclesiastical poor relation before 1918, the Romanian Orthodox church initially settled for a cathedral humbly sited far from the centre on Piaţa Furtună. After Trianon this no longer seemed appropriate, so from 1936-46 work proceeded on a new cathedral, located between the main square and the river, which blends neo-Byzantine and Moldavian architectural elements and exhibits a collection of C18 Banat **icons** in its basement.

In 1868 the municipality purchased the redundant citadel (previously redesigned after Vauban in the manner of Arad's and Oradea's) from the Habsburgs, and demolished all but one section, loosely known as the **Bastion**, to the east of Piaţa Unirii. The entrance at 2, Str. Hector admits one to the portion converted into a patisserie and beer and wine bar, whilst further to the north (4, Str. Popa Şapcă), another section is occupied by an **Ethnographic Museum**. Varied folk costumes and coloured charts illustrate the region's ethnic diversity effectively, but in an anodyne fashion – for example, there's no mention of the thousands of Serbs exiled to the Dobrudja when the Party turned hostile towards Tito's Yugoslavia, which radically altered the Banat's ethnic make-up. In addition, the museum has an **open-air section** just outside town, where old Banat homesteads and workshops have been reassembled in the **Pădurea Verde** or Green Forest. The forest is a popular recreation spot, full of pheasants.

Diversions and practicalities

Timişoara offers the cultural experiences deemed essential for any self-respecting C19 municipality: an Opera House and three theatres – two of them staging **plays** in German (2, Str. Mărăşeşti) or Hungarian (2, Str. Albla Iulia); **puppet shows** for the kids; and, at 2, B-dul Victoriei, regular **concerts** by the Banat Philharmonic. For informal entertainment, folks that can afford it frequent **patisseries** such as *Violeta* (B-dul 30 Decembrie), *Trandafirul* (5, Str. Eminescu), *Flora* on the Vladimirescu promenade, or the place in the *Bastionul*, which conveniently adjoins a couple of **bars**. Another wine bar, *Timişoara 700*, might occasionally have live music during the evenings; but **dancing** is more likely to take place in **restaurants** like the *Cina* (4, Str. Piatra Craiului) or the ones in the hotels Continental, Timişoara and Central.

There's little difference in price between the various first-class **hotels**, which charge around $55 for a double and $42 for single rooms; although the *Nord* (17, Str. 13 Decembrie) and *Banatul* (5, B-dul Republicii) are nearer to the main station whilst the *Timişoara* (1, Str. Mărăşeşti), *Central* (6, Str. Leanu) and *Continental* (2, B-dul 23 August) are more central. The *Parc* (11, B-dul Republicii) and *Bega* (12, Splaiul Titulescu) are both slightly cheaper, but for significant savings you'll have to prise **dormitory beds** out of *BTT* (26, B-dul 23 August; ☎ 3-31-48) or settle for the **campsite** with bungalows out in the Pădurea Verde.

With services so unpredictable, it can be difficult to reach the latter by bus, and it's advisable to ask the **tourist office** about routings and schedules before trying to do so. The regional and national tourist agencies are both represented at 6 B-dul Republicii, as is the international department of *CFR*, whose domestic **railway bookings** office can be found at 2, B-dul 23 August. See *TAROM*, opposite, regarding flights to Bucharest from Timişoara's **airport** (east of town; transfers by car for $15). Aches that can't be cured by a soak in the **thermal baths** might succumb to something from the **24hr pharmacy** (11, B-dul 23 August) or treatment at the *Policlinic* **hospital** nearby. For **car repairs**, consult *ACR* (94 Calea Dorobanţilor; ☎ 1-23-45) and *Autoservice*, both out along the Lugoj road.

Connections abroad, and with Caransebeş and Deva

Most days there are several departures from Timişoara's *Nord* station for **destinations abroad**; tickets being sold for hard currency at CFR's bureau for *Trafic internaţional* (6, Blvd. Republicii). Predictably, the state grabs this last chance to gouge all the *valuta* it can get, and even with an IUS card (usually good for 30% reductions), it's expensive to buy a railway ticket from Romania to anywhere further afield than, say, Budapest. However, the *Bucureşti Express* (leaving town at around 7am) normally gets one to **Belgrade** in time to book seats on connections through to **Italy** (Venice, Padova, Milan Rome, Naples), Lausanne in **Switzerland**, **France** (Dijon, Paris) or **Greece** (Athens & Thessaloníki); and Yugoslav railways charge substantially less than their Romanian counterparts. The *Transdanubium Express* is useful going both ways: departing about 4.30pm bound for **Budapest** and **Prague**, and at around 3pm for **Burgas** on the Bulgarian coast. Only afficianadoes of slow, uncomfortable carriages will opt for one of the 3 daily 'local' trains across to KIKINDA, whence one may catch equally legthargic Yugoslavian rolling stock to Belgrade.

Heading east from Timişoara the most obvious destinations are Deva or Caransebeş in Transylvania. Eastbound trains run **to Caransebeşes**, and travellers have to veer northwards towards Ilia before they can get **to Deva**. The place to do this is **LUGOJ**, the birthplace of the opera singer Traian Grozăvescu: a quiet town with a Baroque hall-church and an C18 coaching inn on its Piaţa 23 August. Lugoj also has some Thracian relics from the tumulus of Susani in its museum (2, Str. Bălcescu), and two hotels on Str. Gheorghiu-Dej, should you be tempted to linger.

DN68A and the branch line follow slightly different routes **between Lugoj and Ilia**, and one has to ride by *cursa* rather than an *accelerat* service (3 of each daily) should you aim to visit any of the places along the way. COŞTEIU, 7km north of Lugoj, has a bathing place by the river and chalets and tentspace at the *Parc* site; the nice atmosphere there earns the village of FĂGET a mention. Farther along the road to Ilia, there's another campsite, *Dumbrava*, near the railway halt for LĂPUGIU DE JOS, a village with an C18 wooden church.

FESTIVALS

Winter
Local fêtes at ILIA and SĂVÎRŞIN on **January 7 and 30**. A larger parish fair at PÎNCOTA on **February 1**.

Spring
The *Kiss Fair* occurs at HĂLMAGIU sometime during **March**, and a smaller festival at ILIA on the **25**. The *Sărbatorea Druştelor* at BÎRSA on the **first Sunday in April**.

Summer
SÎNTANA has its own *Sărbătoarea Iorgovanului* on the **last Sunday in May**. There's a great opportunity to hear music at the *Nedeia of Tăcaşele* at AVRAM IANCU (near Vîrfurile) on the **second Sunday in June**. A shepherds' do, the *Bulciugul de Valea Aleu*, in the valley of the same name 8km from PIETROASA on the **last Sunday in August**, with a smaller village fête at BRĂIŢA on the **last Sunday in September**.

Autumn
Village fairs at SĂVÎRŞIN and ZAM on the **27** and **30** of **November**.

TRAVEL DETAILS

Trains
From Arad to Bîrsa (3 daily; 2hrs); Brad (2; 5); Cluj (1; 4¾); Deva (7; 2-3½); Hălmagiu (2; 4); Ilia (4; 2¾); Oradea (4; 2-2¾); Pîncota (5; ¾-1¼); Sîntana (5; 1); Timişoara (7; 1-1¼); Vîrfurile (2; 3¾).
From Ilia to Lugoj (5; 1½-2¼).
From Oradea to Arad (3; 2-2½); Beiuş (3; 2¼); Ciucea (5; 1½-3¼); Cluj (8; 2¾-4); Dr. Petru Groza (3; 2¾); Satu Mare (5; 2-3).
From Timişoara to Bucharest (2; 8); Caransebeş (7; 1¼-2¼); Lugoj (8; ½-1).

Buses
Probably a spavined service **from Beiuş** to Meziad and Chişcău, if not other communes farther into the mountains.

Flights
From Arad, Oradea and Timişoara to Bucharest; 1 daily.

International trains
From Arad to Basel (1; 13¾); Budapest (3; 3); Paris (2; 22-24); Sofia (1; 21); Vienna (2; 9).
From Curtici to Békéscsaba (2; ¾).
From Oradea to Budapest (3; 5-6); Burgas (1; 22); Dresden (1; 20); Gyula (2; 4¼); Prague (2; 14); Warsaw (1; 20).
From Timişoara to Athens (1; 7¾); Belgrade (1; 3¼); Budapest (1; 5); Burgas (1; 18) Paris (1; 23); Prague (1; 16).

Chapter twelve
THE DELTA AND THE COAST

In theory, Romania's Black Sea *littoral* and the Danube Delta have a lot going for them, and should be on any traveller's hit-list. The coast is blessed with abundant sunshine, warm water and sandy beaches, and a string of Roman remains plus the odd mosque run between the main resorts. Nature is the main attraction of the *Delta Dunării*, a vast area of reeds and shifting land which provides a unique habitat for over 300 species of birds (many of them found nowhere else in Europe) and a host of other creatures. But in practice things aren't quite so rosy. . .

Much of **the Coast** has been ravaged by industry or tourism, or both, and it can get so overcrowded between June-September that the only way to avoid endless hassles over transport, rooms and meals is to book a package holiday (best done abroad, see p.248), leaving you free to enjoy the beach at **Mamaia**, **Neptun**, **Venus** or one of the other resorts. Somehow, there's more of an atmosphere about the city of **Constanţa**, which boasts lots of sights in the old quarter around the seaport, originally established by the ancient Greeks.

Although the **Delta wildlife** is as rich as one could ask for, it mostly chooses to nest away from the main arms (*braţul*) of the river – in particular, the one flowing from the Delta capital of **Tulcea** down to **Crişan**, where ONT tour groups are taken. To really appreciate the diversity of birdlife, you'll need to bring a canoe or pay one of the fishermen to row you into the backwaters and lakes; negotiations can be time consuming, so if you're seriously bent on bird-watching, be prepared to spend at least a week here.

Approaches to both the Delta and the coast are fairly simple. Package tourists fly directly into Constanţa, which, like Tulcea, can also be reached by TAROM flights from Bucharest. **From Hungary** (Budapest's Nyugati pu.), it's about 22hrs on the *Mamaia Express* to Constanţa and Mangalia. **From Bulgaria** by train is quicker, though on 'local' services there's usually a lengthy wait at NEGRU VODĂ - the first station inside Romania – before the connection to Medgidia, where you switch trains yet again for Constanţa or Tulcea. Entering Romania by road at VAMA VECHE is straightforward enough except for hitch-hikers, who'll need a lift to whisk them past potentially hostile border guards on either side. However, most travellers approach **from Bucharest**, either **by road** or rail. Motorists shouldn't have any problems following DN2A (see p.301 for places along the way) towards Constanţa, where it joins the coastal road, or turning off onto rd.22A near HIRŞOVA for Tulcea. **Trains** to Constanţa and Mangalia – including *Rapid* services – are fairly frequent, but grossly overcrowded. Book well in advance (the return journey too, if possible), and change at Medgidia if there's no direct service to Babadag and Tulcea.

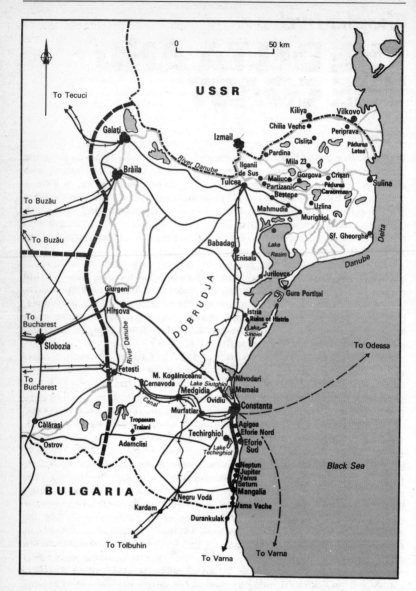

THE DANUBE DELTA

Every year the river dumps another 70 million tonnes of alluvium into the **DANUBE DELTA** (*Delta Dunării*), Europe's youngest, most restless landscape.

Near the regional capital, Tulcea, the river splits into three branches (named Chilia, Sulina and Sf. Gheorghe after their respective ports), dividing the Delta into large areas of reeds and marsh, around 3,000 square kilometres in all, of which only 9% remains permanently above the water. These are the **grind** – tongues of accumulated silt supporting oak trees, willows and poplars twined round with climbing plants – as distinct from the **plaur**, or floating reed islands, which amount to some 700 square kilometres. Over time the distinction is a fine one, for 'they move imperceptibly on the sluggish streams set up by the spring and autumn floods, splitting or merging and sometimes vanishing, to leave a stretch of wind-swept water behind', making any detailed map of the Delta outdated as soon as it's drawn. Although fishing communities have lived here for centuries, it's an inhospitable environment for humans: 'in winter hungry wolves howl amid the reeds, and in summer water-buffaloes bathe in the open stretches, only showing their muzzles above water, for the area is infested with great horse-flies whose trunks, sharp as thorns, can pierce the garments of men and hides of beasts'.

Yet it's a paradise for wildlife, particularly **birds**, which migrate here from as far afield as China, India and Mongolia during the spring and autumn. Besides herons, glossy ibises, cormorants, golden eagles, avocets, sheldrakes and other *Mediterranean types*, the Delta is visited by reed buntings, sea swallows, fishing eagles, sea eagles and various *European songbirds*; singing swans, plovers, polar grebes, cranes and half-snipes *from Siberia*; Saker falcons *from Mongolia*; egrets, mute swans, cormorants and mandarin ducks *from China*; and its remoter lakes support Europe's largest *pelican colonies*. Otters, mink, muskrat, foxes, boars, wolves, polecats and other **animals** live upon the abundant small game and **fish**; although the bulk of the latter goes to the fishermen, for whom the caviar-bearing sturgeon that spawn in these waters are the most valuable catch. According to their rarity, different species recieve the designation *peste tot în Deltă* (common everywhere); *parţial* (mainly in certain areas); or *izolat* (only on reservations) on maps of the Delta.

The following outline is rather sketchy on **transport and accommodation**, since the Delta is even more unpredictable in these matters than other parts of Romania. Beds in hotels, bungalows and private homes can theoretically be reserved through OJT in Constanţa or Tulcea, although their staff, and the parent ONT in Bucharest, is more concerned with booking people onto organised **tours**. The 2-day trip from Constanţa – including a visit to Tulcea, a hydro-bus ride to Crişan, lodgings at the hotel there, and a short exploration of the backwaters by fisherman's canoe – seems reasonable value for $48; but time actually spent on the water accounts for very little of the so-called Delta tour organised by ONT from Bucharest ($85). As a rule of thumb, wildlife gets more varied and abundant the greater the distance from the main 'arms' of the river, so dedicated enthusiasts should either bring their own dinghy or canoe and embark on **expeditions**, or be prepared for slow and arduous negotiations. Though OJT claims that it can arrange the hire of rowing boats with a boatman at Maliuc, Crişan, Sf. Gheorghe or Murighiol ($1 per person per hour; $1.60 for an outboard motor), it's actually quite likely that you'll have to rely upon your own efforts.

Patience, an iron gut and an adamantine head count for more than trotting out the few relevant Romanian phrases (p.500) in **negotiations with local fishermen**. Invariably, these involve partaking of **vodka** – which is effectively a medium of exchange amongst the Lipovani fishing-folk, whose prodigious consumption is legendary. Normally, a single glass circulates incessantly; each drinker knocking back the contents before replenishing it and passing it on. Apropos of which a joke: three Lipovani arrive at a bar. The long-bearded elder, respectfully addressed as *stareţ*, orders three litre bottles of vodka, which they swiftly drain; another round follows, and then the youngest man slides beneath the table; '*Dva botilki*' ('Two bottles'), bawls the *stareţ*, 'No more for him, he's our driver!'.

TULCEA

TULCEA has probably been tagged as the 'Gateway to the Delta' ever since ancient Greek traders established a port here; duly recorded by Herodotus, and later by Ovid, who used the town's Roman name, *Aegyssus*. Its maritime significance was fairly small until the closing stages of the period of Ottoman domination (1420-1878), when other powers suddenly perceived it as commercially and strategically important; then Tulcea underwent a cycle of rapid development and calamitous slumps, like other sectors of Romania's young capitalist economy. Nowadays, the port is too shallow for modern large-capacity freighters, but it's still the means by which passenger vessels enter, and tonnes of dead fish leave, the Delta.

The **waterfront** includes a promenade with a carousel and restaurants, which counterpoint the oily-smelling harbour where frenzied scrums develop around the *NAVROM* office and piers. Should you arrive at the **station** on the western edge of town, simply turn left outside, and walk past *CFR* along the mainstreet – running parallel to the harbour – towards the centre. With the exception of the Delta Museum, the only place of interest to the south of the main street is the **market** – good for buying snacks and expeditionary provender – which faces the *TAROM* office at the end of the row of shops backing on to the waterfront. On Str. Isaccea you'll find the **tourist office** and the *Hotel Delta*, which charges $30 for a single and $40 for double **rooms**. Moving into the *Egreta* on Str. Păcii will only save you $3, but cabins and tent-space can be rented at *Lake Ciuperca* just west of town (buses from the railway station or the terminal on Str. Gării), and **BTT** (Bloc 1, Str. Babadag) might be able to arrange dormitory beds. If necessary, it's feasible to sleep in the park outside the station.

Bear left shortly after the Delta Hotel and you'll come to Tulcea's **Art Museum** (open Tuesday-Sunday 10am-6pm). Its fine collection of paintings and contemporary sculpture includes Impressionistic female nudes by Pallady; Iosif Iser's and Theodor Aman's fanciful 'Turkish' scenes; and Delta landscapes by Sirbu and Stavrov. Igolesco's *Balchik* was painted at a time when Romania ruled the southern Dobrudja – a bone of contention with Bulgaria, which finally regained the area in 1940, followed by a relatively humane transfer of ethnic minorities and their assets. The varied groups inhabiting the Tulcea region are the subject of an **Ethnographic Museum** (4,

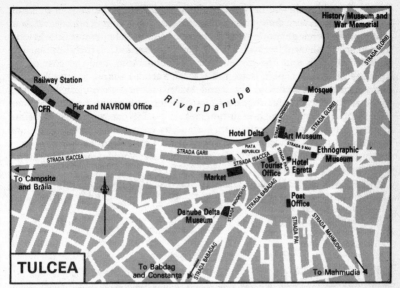

River Danube

History Museum and War Memorial

Railway Station

CFR

Pier and NAVROM Office

STRADA GLORIEI

Mosque

Hotel Delta

Art Museum

STRADA 9 MAI

Ethnographic Museum

PIATA REPUBLICII

STRADA GARII

STRADA ISACCEA

Tourist Office

Hotel Egreta

STRADA ISACCEA

Market

STRADA N NOIEMBRIE

To Campsite and Brăila

STRADA PROGRESULUI

STRADA BABADAG

Post Office

STRADA PAL

STRADA MAHMUDIE

Danube Delta Museum

TULCEA

To Babdag and Constanța

STRADA BABADAG

To Mahmudia

Str. 9 Mai); descendants of the Ottomans who ruled the Dobrudja before 1878 now form small **Turkish communities** living peaceably in Murighiol, Techirghiol and Constanța. The dereliction of the **Azizie Mosque** on Str. 14 Noiembrie suggests that few Turks live in Tulcea itself.

Strada Gloriei runs through a pretty area of small white houses in gardens to end at the Parcul Monumentului, where you'll find the vestiges of Aegyssus, an obelisk to the dead of the 1877-78 war, and the **History Museum**. Numismatists should enjoy the Roman, Greek, Byzantine and medieval coins (Moldavian ones struck with the dubious claim that the hospodars ruled the Black Sea), but most visitors are more impressed with the **Danube Delta Museum** (Tuesday-Sunday 9am-5pm; 32, Str. Progresului). Equipped with multi-lingual guides and captions, it explains all about the Delta as an eco-system, and houses an excellent **aquarium** of fish from the region.

Before leaving Tulcea. . .
Assuming that you're bound for the Delta, it's wise to make a few **preparations** before leaving Tulcea. The tourist office (2, Str. Isaccea) might deign to reserve accommodation for you at Maliuc, Crişan, Ilganii de Sus, Mila 23, Sf. Gheorghe, Sulina, Murighiol, or Gura Portiței on the spit of land opposite Jurilovca; and at least supply a **map** of the Delta, if not some information on hiring boats, the state of tracks across the *grind*, or the latest wildlife sightings. Buy essentials like bread, canned food, fruit and cheese in the market; candles, a container for drinking water, and plenty of stuff to repel stinging *tînțari* (available from pharmacies) are also vital **supplies**.

Predictably, there's a certain amount of hassle involved in **leaving by river**. Queues and confusion sum up the experience of trying to buy **tickets** from *NAVROM*'s office on the pier (open Monday-Saturday 8am-8pm/Sunday

8am-3pm), since they're only sold half an hour before the boat in question sails. Find out beforehand when and from which pier your service leaves, and then double-check once you have the ticket. NAVROM operates two services along each main 'arm' (*braţul*) of Delta, and upriver to Galaţi and Brăila. The *Rapid* hydrofoils run roughly every 1-2hrs until 4pm, and the cost of the longest journey, to Galaţi, is around 100 lei. Fares to Sulina, Sfîntu Gheorghe and Periprava (respectively, 1½, 2 and 4½hrs journey) are roughly half this if you take the slower, less frequent *Classic* ferries. Lumbering vessels crammed with people and piled high with dinghies, rods, and camping gear, these are greeted at every jetty-stop along their route by crowds of kids selling melons and fish – a mad-cap scene. Merely riding one is an encounter with the weird mystique of the Delta, and with a bit of luck you'll learn some useful information on board, too.

Buses leave Tulcea yet more crowded and irregularly, and the only reason to use them is to reach settlements along the road **to Murighiol**, or Jirilovca on the shores of Lake Razim.

The **following sections** cover each arm of the Delta in turn, and then the Lake Razim region.

INTO THE DELTA. . .

Passenger boats ply the main 'arms' of the Delta, but the myriad lakes and backwaters where most of the wildlife hides are difficult to reach without the aid of local fishermen. The most characteristic are those hailing from a hereditary sect known as the **Lipovani** – easy to recognise by their long beards and on-shore garb of tall hats and black cloaks. The Lipovani originally came to the Delta from Russia, where their opposition to the reform of Orthodox ritual incurred the wrath of Peter the Great. It was an era of diaspora for 'Old Believers' (*Raskolniki*) and schismatics; and Romania provided a haven for Lipovani, the self-mutilating Skopţi (p.289), and the equally strange but less masochistic *Molokhi*, who imbibed vast quantities of milk in the belief that this guaranteed ascension to heaven. Adapting to their watery environment, the Lipovani became skilled fishermen and gardeners, speaking a 'sort of Russian' amongst themselves but equally fluent in Romanian like the region's other ethnic minorites. (Interestingly, Romanian also served as the common language for Danube boat people until early this century.) Since you're likely to rely upon Lipovani boatmen to guide you through the confusing side channels (*gîria*), be prepared for their drinking habits (see above), and the abhorrence that fundamentalists have for the 'Devil's weed', tobacco.

From Tulcea to Periprava

The **Chilia arm of the river** (*Braţul Chilia*) and its auxiliaries carry 62% of the Danube's water for 103 kilometres to Periprava, itself some distance from the sea, but very little tourist traffic, perhaps because it also demarcates the Soviet border. For travellers, there are two major drawbacks to this route: the total lack of tourist accommodation, and the poor prospects of finding smaller boats heading into the interior.

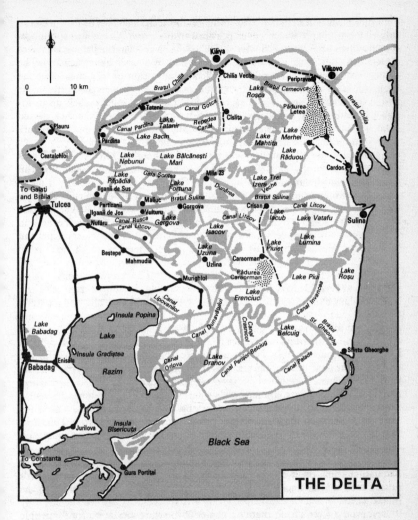

THE DELTA

The raison d'être of small settlements like CEATALCHIOI is basically the gathering of **reeds**, which are used to build Delta houses and as a raw material by diverse industries. The cutting, which merely stimulates the reeds to grow up to 8ft in two months, can only be done by hand; a task that thousands of prisoners performed during the Stalinist era. Priests, ex-*Legionari*, former captains of industry, and purged *Securisti* suffered beatings, starvation rations and leaky barracks – and died like mosquitoes multiply. Other plants succumb to the reeds, which 'stifle them at the root' and sow the top-soil with their rhizomes, but the reeds provide a warm, windfree shelter for countless small birds, rodents and amphibians.

Larger birds and mammals generally inhabit secluded lakes or the forests of ash, oak and maple which cover portions of the *grind*. **Geese** and **spoonbills** may fly to an island in the 'Soviet sector' of the river from the fishing village of PARDINA, but most visitors are constrained by – and strongly advised to respect – the frontier. There's no particular indication of this, these days, at least, but in 1849 Felicia Skene found it demarcated by 'a wretched little hut at stated intervals', before which stood 'a miserable-looking Cossack up to his knees in water, with his spear erect, which he duly elevated when we passed him'. (These luckless Tsarist minions usually succumbed to malaria before their six months stint of solitary guard duty ended.)

In the days when Bessarabia was part of Romania*, CHILIA VECHE was merely a suburb of Chilia (Soviet KILIYA) across the river. Today you can travel only southwards, to the hamlet of CÎŞLIŢA, 8km away. The track is unusable at many times of the year, and for much of its length runs through an old forest frequented by **foxes** and **wild boar**. LAKE ROŞCA – roughly 10km to the south of the Cerneocva tributary between Chilia Veche and Periprava – harbours geese, **sea egrets**, **storks** and Europe's largest **pelican colony**; but the likelihood of being able to get there by small boat from PERIPRAVA seems small. However, you can walk southwards into the **PĂDURA LETEA** – a protected oak forest that's a haven for falcons, eagles, wildcats and owls, a few miles inland of Periprava. Periprava itself is nearly 30km from the sea, and communications with Sulina practically non-existent.

Downriver to Sulina

Constant dredging of its deepwater channel enables large sea-going freighters to make the journey from Tulcea to the coast via the *braţul Sulina*, and the additional tourist traffic makes this the busiest and least serene of the Danube's branches. However, it has the advantages of a tourist infrastructure and several settlements where there's a fair chance of hiring boats to visit a range of diverse wildlife habitats, and on balance the **Sulina arm of the river** probably offers the most rewarding prospects. The journey from Tulcea to Sulina takes 1½hrs by hydrofoil or 3hrs by *Classic* ferry, but anyone with sense will disembark before reaching that dismal sea-port. Travellers who come equipped to explore the Delta **by kayak** face turbulence from the wakes of passing ships on the main waterway, but beyond Iglani de Sus one can escape into calmer backwaters – broken by the odd rapid – leading to the inland lakes.

Beyond the river's fork, there's a chalet with **accommodation** for 40 people at ILGANII DE SUS, opposite the fishing village of PARTIZANI. From there, it might be possible to rent boats to visit two lakes further to the north, Meşterul and Lunga. **MALIUC** on the left bank of the river at mile 27 is a larger commune, with a research station and **Museum of the Reed Industry** and – more importantly – a **campsite** and **hotel**, the *Salcia* (single rooms $20,

---

*'Finland is Finnish, Poland is Polish, Bessarabia is Romanian. . .this is purely and simply a theft', wrote Friedrich Engels of Tsarist Russia's occupation of Bessarabia in 1890. There's a joke about a Russian and a Romanian border guard who meet while patrolling, and simultaneously chance upon a chest of gold. 'We'll divide it like brothers', says the Russian. 'No', retorts the Romanian, 'Fifty-fifty!'.

doubles $34). Fishermen here might be prevailed upon to row you to the **mute swans** nesting on LAKE FURTUNA, going by way of several verdant **backwaters** (*gîria*) like the Păpădia or 'Dandelion' channel, which leaves the main river shortly after Ilganii de Sus.

The reeds roundabouts provide a home for prolific-breeding great crested **greebs**; solitary and less successful red-necked greebs; bearded **reedlings**, which nest in piles of cut reeds; and **herons** and little **egrets**, which favour nests in the overhanging willow trees. **Canoeists** can follow the Şontea channel into the original Dunărea Veche branch of the river, leading to Mila 23 (see below), if they relish the challenge offered by powerful currents, submerged roots and aquatic plants (*rizac*), and a series of small rapids. GORGOVA, 8km downriver on the south bank, is another fishing village whence trips might be arranged. LAKE GORGOVA nearby is rich in carp and sheat fish, and frequented by eastern **flossy ibises**.

CRIŞAN is the main tourist centre along the Sulina waterway: a fishing settlement following the shoreline for 7km, with its administrative centre a couple of kilometres to the north at MILA 23 on the 'old' branch of the Danube. Mila 23 is a large village of reed cottages (rebuilt after a flood in the 1960s) with a *Cherhana* for storing the fishermen's catch. While the men fish, women work the gardens that supply vegetables, plums, pears, grapes and quinces, and tend the poultry, pigs and beehives. **Golden oriels** (which nest in pear trees) and bladder-frogs are the commonest forms of wildlife around here, for the **pelicans** have been driven further north to Lake Merhei. Though disliked by the fishermen for reducing their catch, pelicans are sociable birds and great travellers – flying up to 100km a day in groups – but also possessive. A pair of adults will feed their young for two months until they can fly, and promptly 'beak' any strange chick that wanders into the nest.

Passenger boats stop near the **hotel** *Lebăda* (sngl.$27/dbl.$37) and a **campsite** with bungalows but no running water, midway between the two; and should you wish to it's quite feasible to camp wild somewhere. During my stay the wind howled through the reedy wilderness and demolished my tent several times, but at least it dispersed the mosquitoes (*ţînţari*). They're a real pest during sultry weather, despite the spraying of their breeding grounds which was initiated in the 1950s. Mila 23 is the starting point for **excursions** to most of the surrounding **lakes**, while from Crişan it should be possible to walk 10km inland to the **Pădurea Caraorman forest**. Amongst the varied **wildlife** here are owls, eagles, falcons, wildcats, boars and wolves.

Ever since – if not before – it was recorded by a Greek scribe in 950, SULINA has depended on shipping. Genoese vessels used to call here during the C14, while throughout the period of Ottoman hegemony it was less a trading port than a nest of pirates who preyed upon shipping in the Black Sea. Later, Sulina became the headquarters of the International Danube Commission established by the big powers after the First World War. But world recession and larger vessels emptied the port within a decade, so that by 1940 John Lehmann found 'a hopeless, sinking feeling' in a place where 'people get stranded. . .feel themselves abandoned by civilization, take to drink, and waste into a half-animal existence'. The state has tried to revive Sulina as a freeport, though economics remain opposed: expensive annual dredging is required to enable even small- and medium-capacity ships to enter, while large-capacity freighters can now bypass the Delta altogether by taking the Danube-Black Sea Canal. Unless you like shabby bars and decaying waterfronts there's really nothing to draw. The *Hotel Farul* is used to guests **staying** through no wish of their own.

From Tulcea towards Sfîntu Gheorghe

The Delta's oldest, most winding arm is the least used by freighters and fishing boats, but carries a fair amount of tourist traffic; and unlike other parts of the Delta, some settlements can also be reached from Tulcea by road (irregular buses). A fisherman at **VICTORIA** might be willing to row you into the water-lilly smothered *Litcov Canal* but it's by no means certain, so it's worth mentioning the five BEŞTEPE hills, whence there's a **panoramic view** of the Delta – its 'limitless fields of green enfolding a thousand hidden recesses, surging with life', to quote Ethel Pantazzi. Ferries call at **MAHMUDHIA**, which has a motel and vestiges of a Roman-Byzantine citadel nearby. It's preferable, however, to take the road to **MURIGHIOL**. Besides cheaper lodgings on the *Pelican* campsite with chalets (a hotel is planned), Murighiol has natural attractions – namely **blackwinged stilts**, **avocets** and **red crested pochards** nesting around the salt lakes nearby. From here, it should be possible to hire a boat and travel through the backwaters to **UZLINA**, which is otherwise accessible by ferry. The Isac and Uzlina lakes to the north of the fishing village are a protected **pelican colony**, but villagers have permission to take visitors there.

    SFÎNTU GHEORGHE (St George), 64km downriver, lives by fishing. The most prized catch is sturgeon, a 'creature like a dogfish crossed with a mackerel, measuring ten feet from tip to tail', whose eggs are exported as black **caviar**. Nowadays, the conditions under which *icre negre* is extracted and packed are hopefully more hygenic than in the old days, when the roe was 'cleaned' by immersing it in brine and sluicing the lot through hair sieves whilst the fishermen chewed upon the embryo-sac (*pajus*), but I couldn't verify this personally. Although private rooms can reportedly be rented in the commune, NAVROM in Tulcea persistently refused to sell me a ticket to Sf. Gheorghe on the grounds that I had no accommodation there! It's said that from here one can make boat trips into the Ivancea Canal, or out to the **SACALIN ISLANDS** at the river's mouth; the latter are inhabited by **gossanders, red-necked geese, goldeneyes** etc. Should anyone make it down this far, a report on the area would be appreciated for the next edition.

Around Lake Razim, and down towards Constanţa

Birdlife buffs should also consider **LAKE RAZIM**, whose waters are separated from the Black Sea by two long, tongue-like grinds. From the village of SARINSAUF, 11km southwest of Murighiol, a fisherman will probably take you out to **INSULA POPINA**, a nesting-ground for two types of **shelduck**. Lake Razim's western shoreline is invaded by over a million red-breasted and white-fronted **geese**, which arrive from arctic Russia (November/December) and then nest here, or around Lake Sinoie further to the south, until the reeds freeze.

From Tulcea, DN22 and the railway head southwards through the eroded Palaeozoic foothills of the Măcin range to **BABADAG**, a town of 9,000 people. Turkish artwork displayed in the former **Mosque of Ali Ghazi** (14, Str. Geamiei), and the *Doi Iepuraşi* bungalow/caravan site (4km south of town along DN22) are Babadag's most notable features, since buses to Enisala or Jurilovca are pretty uncertain. A quiet place with reed cottages, **ENISALA** lies 8km from Babadag and about 1km from the **ruined Heracleia citadel** which overlooks Lake Razim. Built by Genoese merchants during the C13 on the site of an earlier Byzantine fortress, it was ceded to Mircea the Old so that he might call himself 'Prince reigning as far as the Great Sea', and now lies abandoned – the **wading birds** frequenting the shoreline and Gradiştea Island aren't interested.

JURILOVCA further down the coast merits more attention, even if you can't afford **rooms** at the *Hotel Albatros*. Trawling the rich fishing grounds of Lake Goloviţa, 'syndicates' bring their catch to Jurilovca's big *cherhana* for weighing. Sturgeon is the most valuable of the 31 species of fish harvested, but **carp** accounts for the bulk of the catch. They move up into the shallows to spawn when the water temperature reaches 14°C, and the Chinese variety introduced during Romania's honeymoon with the People's Republic in the 1960s has since surplanted the indigenous species by virtue of its greater voracity and fertility. (Alas for the fish's credibility amongst English-speaking people, Romanians call it *crap*!). Romanians, **Lipovani** (served by two Lipovani-Orthodox churches, one of them wooden) and a few Muslim Turks and Tartars co-exist quite happily here; for unlike Transylvania, the Delta has never been noted for ethnic rivaly and apartheid.

Vestiges of a C2-C6 Greek citadel on Cape Doloşman face Bisericuţa Island with its medieval ruins (including that of a church, hence the name), while from Jurilovca motorboats take people out to **Gura Portiţei**. A **chalet/campsite** with a restaurant, sited on a spit of land between Lake Razim and the sea, it's the starting point for excursions to the **Periteasca-Leahova nature reserve**, largely frequented by sea-birds.

Heading southwards, **towards the Coast**, you'll pass two more places that deserve a mention. Though it's not worth leaving the train at BAIA DOBROGEA, the nearest station, **HAMANGIA** was the site of a **Middle Neolithic culture** known for its sculptures of fertility goddesses (often marked with chevrons or whorls) and the 'Hamangia Thinker', an untypically male figure that's now the prize prehistoric exhibit in Bucharest's National History Museum. 8km from the **ISTRIA** halt, there's a more substantial reminder of the past in the form of the **ruined Greek city of Histria** with its shattered temples to diverse deities and 13ft-thick walls. The ruins cover a fairly small area despite the fact that this was the most important of the Greek settlements along the coast during the C5-C6; for within a few hundred years, alluvial deposits and sand smothered the port and put paid to the town. In the vicinity of the ruins you'll find a **campsite** with chalets; while another lies farther south along the road to NĂVODARI (p.467).

GALAŢI AND BRĂILA

From Tulcea there are also **boats upriver to Galaţi and Brăila**, although when I last heard, the service had been cut to one ferry and one hydrofoil a day (dep. 12am & 5pm/4 & 1½hrs journey, respectively). Both towns exemplify the thrust of Romania's economic progress, having been transformed from grain ports to centres of heavy industry within a few decades; and if high-rises, smoke-stacks and dusty roads don't appeal, just use their transport facilities **to reach other places** instead. There are one or two direct services to **Bucharest**, while FĂUREI farther down the line is the junction for services towards **the coast**, and trains up to **Iaşi in Moldavia**. From Galaţi, you can also join the Iaşi line by taking a train to Bîrlad: en route there's a halt in the vicinity of **BĂNEASA** village, near which a wood provides the setting for the **Peony festival** on the second Sunday of May.

Galaţi

Situated between the confluences of the Siret, Prut and Danube rivers, GALAŢI became Moldavia's chief port after the Turks captured Chilia and Cetatea Albă in 1484, and developed busy shipyards during the C19, when two remarkable men lived here. Alexandru Cuza was a Galaţi magistrate when he was unexpectedly elected Prince of Moldavia (see p.482); while on a 'quiet street overlooking Lake Brateş' lived a British officer who impressed neighbours with his 'religious mania, curious economies and shabby attire', later immortalised as 'Gordon of Khartoum' for his courageous folly.

Badly damaged in 1944, Galaţi was largely rebuilt and swelled to its present size (pop. 240,000) during the 1960s, when Romania's largest **iron and steel combine** was constructed here. East Germany and Czechoslovakia were hostile, wishing to keep Romania a 'breadbasket' and a captive market for their industries, but Gheorghiu-Dej and Ceauşescu deemed an iron and steelworks the prerequisite for Romania's emergence as a fully industrialised nation. The Galaţi *combinat* and other big plants are thus symbolic and concrete assertions of national independence – but also highlight **Romania's economic dilemma**. Steelworks, car factories and forays into everything from nuclear energy to biotechnology have been financed by $12,000m loans from Western banks and countries, but the products have sold badly, so the reduction of the debt (to roughly $6 billion by 1987) has only been achieved by exporting food and yet more food. . .leaving precious little for the country's workers, which hardly encourages productivity. Moreover, even to produce the steel that it can't sell abroad, Galaţi must import iron ore – virtually the only mineral resource lacking in Romania.

The **practicalities** can be briefly summarised. Arriving at the *gara fluvială* port, catch any bus heading northwest to the Bulevard Republicii, where you'll find the *Dunareă* and *Galaţi* **hotels** (nr.35 & 12). The former is the least expensive (sngl.$28/dbl.$38), while the latter charges about $5 less than the yet costlier *Hotel Turist* on the start of Coşbuc Blvd. (sngl.$39/dbl.$53). Cheaper beds might be available from *BTT*, formerly located at 100, Str. Dunării, but now reportedly operating at 11, B-dul Republicii (☎ 1-55-62); while the *Tirighina* **campsite** lies about 4km out along the Brăla road (look for buses at the terminal on Str. Ipatescu, near the railway station).

Brăila

Laid out in concentric streets radiating from the port esplanade with its concrete warehouses and steps of Dobrudjan granite, **BRĂILA** doesn't look as old as it really is. According to the *Libro de conoscimiento* it was Wallachia's principal harbour by 1350, and after spending three centuries under Turkish occupation, once again began shipping the harvest of the Bărăgan Plain to the rest of Europe, creating huge fortunes for a few landlords who built elegant residences and places of enjoyment here.

Until Skopje attained the distinction during the C20, there were reckoned to be more **Gypsies** in Brăila than any other town in Europe. Most of them were in domestic service (generally as slaves before Wallachia abolished Gypsy slavery in 1855) or lived by entertaining the *gadjé*. The celebrated **Barleaza** was called the 'gold violinist', because when he placed his instrument down after playing it, no listener ever insulted him by dropping in a silver coin. Eventually, a drunken boyar ordered him to accept coppers at gunpoint; Barleaza refused, so the boyar shot him dead. Other Gypsy musicians reverentially dissected Barleaza's violin, splinters of which are probably embedded in violins played to this day.

Unlike in Galaţi, you can comfortably walk from the **boat station** into the centre – just follow Str. Impăratul Traian westwards for a couple of blocks, and there's the main Piaţa Lenin. Prices at the three neighbouring **hotels** seem to fluctuate, so it's worth comparing the *Traian* (sng.$36/dbl.$47) with the *Delta* (56, Str. Republicii) and the other hotel just around the corner from *BTT* – another potential source for rooms. Brăila's Historical and Ethnographic **museums**, and the towerless Sf. Arhangheli Church (originally a mosque), also lie on, or just off, the main square; the **tourist office** can be found next door to the *Hotel Delta* on Str. Republicii. Most buses heading up the Str, Victoriei run to the **railway station** (a little north of which is the bus terminal); and by asking around the quay you should be able to find small boats **across the river to Corotişca**, a bungalow/campsite on the shore of Insula Mare a Brălei – an island covered with willows and reeds. Another **campsite** is situated near LACUL SĂRAT (Salt Lake), about 8km southwest of town.

THE COAST

The Romanian *littoral* holds the promise of pale beaches, dazzling water and an average of 10-12 hours of sunshine every day between May and October. That's more or less what it delivers, but whether you enjoy yourself there will more likely depend upon other factors, like your role in the logistical nightmare created by 1½ millon people flocking to **the COAST**. The demand for rooms and food outstrips supplies at most **resorts**, and experiences on railways, campsites or buses can easily snowball into a bad case of stress. Curiously, that doesn't seem to be the case with **Constanţa**, a relaxed seaport-cum-riviera-town, dotted with Turkish, Byzantine and Roman remains and the justly proud possessor of a superb Archaeological Museum.

To get the best out of resorts like **Mamaia, Neptun, Venus, Saturn** or **Mangalia**, there's really no alternative to **package tours** – you'll find the main operators listed on p.248. Despite significant differences between packages (like which resort or hotel, and whether all meals are included), they all basically guarantee a room and something to eat, and minimise extraneous hassles so that you're free to spend hard currency on extras like hiring powerboats or watching cabaret shows. The cost of bed 'n' board (not to mention the air fare) in such deals works out far less than one would pay should you try to do the whole thing independently, so the argument for taking a package tour seems unassailable. Besides tours run by Western operators, there's the option of holidays at the **International Youth Camp** run by *BTT*. Package tourists from socialist countries and Romanians on union-financed holidays get billeted in bungalows or less comfortable hotels; while **footloose travellers** of every nationality make do with whatever accommodation or food remains, unless they can afford to buy into the smartest hotels and restaurants. Should you make friends, practically all the resorts would be tolerable from this standpoint with the exception of **Năvodari**, which is irredeemably horrible. Romanians looking for somewhere as yet 'undeveloped' still have **Doi Mai**, just a few miles from the Bulgarian border.

From September 1 until June 30, hotels charge **out of season** rates (on campsites, from September 16 till June 14), which generally means a 10%-30% reduction on the high season prices quoted in the text. See p.467 for **hire charges** for surf boards, tennis courts etc, which don't fluctuate seasonally.

THE DOBRUDJA AND THE DANUBE-BLACK SEA CANAL

The overland approaches to Constanţa cross one part or another of **the Dobrudja**, long known as a 'scrub country of grey goat pasture, limestone outcrops, the stalks of dead trees and the cracked earth of dry ponds' (Gardiner). It's difficult to think of any reason for stopping here, but the changes wrought over the last forty years certainly merit some explanation. Driving across the river at GIURGENI (DN2A) you'll see orchards and fields planted on what used to be pestilential marshland surrounding the confluence of the Danube and the Ialomiţa, but this transformation is nothing compared to the great works farther to the south, starting at Cernavoda.

After Chernobyl, it seems cruelly apt that **CERNAVODA** was chosen as the site of Romania's first **nuclear power station** – the name ominously translates as 'Black Water'. Unlike its allies, Romania has chosen a Canadian rather than a Soviet-designed reactor, although the Romanians are actually building it themselves. Ceauşescu has been personally involved, for having inspected a similar reactor during his visit to Canada in 1985, he returned home and immediately criticised managers for using too much concrete at Cernavoda. The resulting confusion caused the programme to stall for six months, and now the 660-megawatt reactor, intended to supply 16-20% of the country's energy needs, is not expected to be operational before 1991.

Cernavoda is also the western entrance to the **Danube-Black Sea Canal**, which could make Romania's fortune in the C21 if the planners' assumptions are correct. Opened to shipping in 1984, the canal enables vessels to travel a mere 60km from Agigea just outside Constanţa to Cernavoda on the Danube, rather than make the 400km journey via the Delta which, in any case, is impassable for larger freighters. Savings in fuel, time etc. are obvious, but realising a profit after the huge investment depends on a Danubian economic renaissance which, in turn, hangs on the completion of the Nürnberg-Regensburg Canal. Charlemagne's vision of a continuous 2,000 mile-long waterway linking Rotterdam with the Black Sea is only 48km from fulfillment, but soaring costs and environmental protests within Bavaria have stalled the final stage of the project for the last ten years.

Work on the Danube-Black Sea Canal started as long ago as 1949, when the Party launched this 'hero project', and writers like Petru Dumitriu (who made his name with a book on the canal, *Dustless Highway*) waxed lyrical about the transformation of humble peasants into class-conscious proletarians through the camaraderie of the construction site. But as Dumitriu acknowledged after his defection in 1960, the '*Canalul Mortii*' claimed the lives of over 100,000 workers, the bulk of whom were actually there under duress. *Securisti* protegés of the purged Ana Pauker, and people of 'putrid social origin' could be found amongst the forced labourers, but 'peasants were the most numerous – kulaks or labourers who had not delivered their quota of corn or milk, or had beaten-up the secretary of the local Party-cell, or had stolen a corn-cob from the collective farm'. After untold suffering and the realisation that the chosen route – through the 84m-deep Canara Hills towards Năvodari – was plain crazy, the project was abandoned in 1953. When work was resumed in 1973, a new route was selected and the canal was successfully pushed eastwards to join the sea.

According to ONT, it's now possible to travel **by motorboat from Cernavoda to Agigia**, or vice versa, within a couple of hours, which would seem to offer anyone that's interested a good look at this awesomely ugly feat of engineering (that's how it appeared from the train, anyway). If not, quite a few trains stop at the only places that you might otherwise contemplate visiting – the BASARABI or MURFATLAR vineyards (p.471), and the town of MEDGIDIA. As far as the latter goes, it's sole significance derives from the two daily **trains to Kardam in Bulgaria**, leaving around 7am and 8.40am.

CONSTANŢA

Many people first encounter the coast at **CONSTANŢA**: a busy riviera town and Romania's principal seaport, with other claims to fame besides. Its ancient precursor *Tomis* was in legend – and quite possibly in fact – founded by survivors of a battle with the Argonauts, following the capture of the Golden Fleece. Centuries later the great Latin poet Ovid resided here until his death in AD 17, albeit in exile and always bemoaning his fate. Since then, all kinds of people have settled or paid a visit – countless sailors (including the *Potemkin* mutineers), Turks and Gypsies, Tsar Nicholas and Richard Nixon. The whole business has left the population a legacy of Graeco-Roman remains, mixed bloodlines and Turkish mosques, besides a liking for what *Pravda*'s war correspondent deplored in 1944 as 'jazz bands. . .tinsel vulgarity and commercialism'. All of which blend well with the city's crisp modern boulevards, swept and watered daily by Gypsy women wearing flashy jewellery and bright headscarves.

Around town

Should you fly in, it's 30 minutes journey by ONT Littoral coach from *M. Kogălniceanu Airport* into the centre, which people arriving at the *Gara* can reach by trolleybus #41/#43. Passengers on the *Dierna* dock at the *portul turistic* just beneath the spit of land occupied by Constanţa's old quarter, to the south of which extend the docks and shipyard. Exploring the area between the two waterfronts, its central square is unavoidable. A statue of **Ovid** gazes mournfully down on its beholders, as well might the celebrated Publius Ovidius Naso have done when he was exiled from Rome by Emperor Augustus (probably for intriguing at court and writing *The Art of Making Love*) in 8 AD. Marooned in backwater Tomis where he found the natives uncouth and the winters appalling, Ovid spent his last years unsuccessfully petitioning emperors for his return, and composing his melancholy *Tristia*:

> Rain cannot pit it, sunlight fails in burning
> This snow. One drift succeeds another here.
> The northwind hardens it, makes it eternal;
> It spreads in drifts through all the bitter year.

Behind his back, Constanţa's **Archaeological Museum** has an excellent collection (open Tuesday-Sunday 9am-8pm); especially of statues of deities, displayed in the hall just left of the entrance. A menhir of a Hamangia-culture Earth Goddess, complete with battle-axes, occupies the first room, while in the lower section you'll find Fortuna and Pontos, the protectors of Tomis; an Aedicula carved with the chillingly lovely Nemesis twins, goddesses of Revenge and Universal Equilibrium; and other statues, including the mysterious **Glykon Serpent**. Though considered to have been carved during the C2 like the others, the Glykon statue is unique and extraordinary: about the size of a squatting toddler, with an antelope's head, human hair and ears, and a gracefully coiled serpentine body ending in a lion's tail. The exhibits upstairs are more numerous if less remarkable, and even without a guide-book (on sale downstairs) it's easy to recognise Nicolae Ceauşescu, the Dobrudja regional Party Secretary in 1946 and now the subject of two whole rooms on the top floor.

Around the corner from the museum, on the edge of Ovidiu Square, a modern structure encloses a fine **Roman mosaic**, 600 metres square. It was discovered sixteen feet below street level in 1959, and may have once graced a C3-C4 commercial building, although it could equally have adorned the upper hall of the Roman *thermae*, whose outer walls, their archways sealed, can be seen from B-dul Marinarilor. From the square, it's probably more tempting to make a beeline for the **Mahmudiye Mosque** one block to the south, whose 160ft-high minaret is a feature of the skyline and offers a great view of the town and harbour (open 9.30am-5.30pm for visitors). Built of concrete in

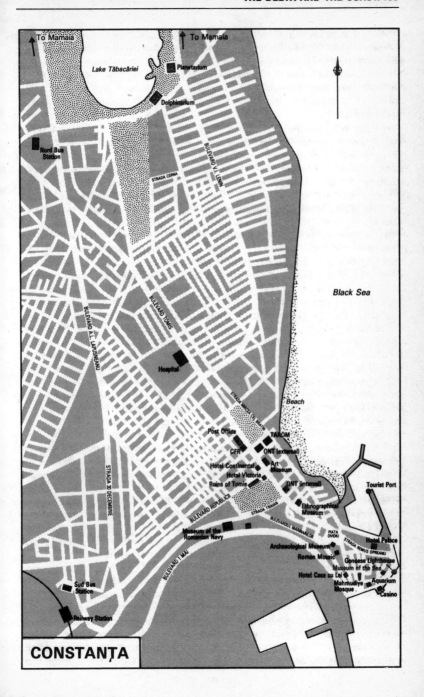

To Mamaia To Mamaia

Lake Tăbacăriei

Planetarium

Dolphinarium

Nord Bus
Station

STRADA CERNA

BULEVARD V.I. LENIN

Black Sea

BULEVARD TOMIS

BULEVARD A.L. LAPUSNEANU

Hospital

STRADA 30 DECEMBRIE

STRADA KARACA CI BACIN

Beach

Post Office

TAROM

CFR

ONT (external)

Hotel Continental

Art
Museum

Hotel Victoria

Ruins of Tomis

ONT (internal)

Tourist Port

Ethnographica
Museum

BULEVARD REPUBLICII

STRADA TRAIAN

BULEVARDUL MARINARILOR

Museum of the
Romanian Navy

PIATA
OVIDIU

Hotel Palace

BULEVARD 1 MAI

Archaeological Museum

STRADA REMUS OPREANU

Roman Mosaic

Genoese Lighthouse

Museum of the Sea

Sud Bus
Station

Hotel Casa cu Lei

Aquarium

Mahmudiye
Mosque

Casino

Railway Station

CONSTANŢA

1910 and pebble-dashed, it's the seat of the Mufti, the spiritual head of Romania's 55,000 Muslims (Turks and Tartars by origin), who live in the Dobrudja, along the coast and in the Delta. Further south along Str. Muzeelor are the fancy **Orthodox Cathedral** of SS. Peter and Paul, one of Ion Mincu's finest designs, built between 1883-85, and at the street's end, the **Ion Jalea collection of sculptures** bequeathed by a local artist (open Tuesday-Sunday 11am-4pm).

Having reached **the waterfront**, you can't mistake the former **Casino** (nowadays a restaurant) on a jutting promenade. Originally erected as pavilion for Romania's eccentric queen, Carmen Sylva, during the royal family's visit to Constanţa in 1914, it was the venue for a gala performance of mystical allegories by little girls, which 'collapsed in a tangle of scenery and broken limbs' before the eyes of the Russian Imperial family, who had arrived on their yacht *Standart* with vague intentions of marrying a daughter to Prince Carol.

Alas, Princess Marie bickered with the Tsarina, and remarked that 'Nicky is Tsar of all the Russias – and my cousin – but nothing can make him look like anything but a cook'; whilst the townsfolk 'groaned at the ugly sunburned daughters of the Tsar and complained they looked no better than peasant children, and sulky ones at that'. Despite a *Te Deum* in the Cathedral and an amicable spitting contest 'between the Tsarevitch and his Romanian cousins, with grape-pips for ammunition and a lemonade jug for a target', the Russians sailed away less than a day later to a farewell display by Prince Bibesu, 'pilot of the one-man, one-aircraft Romanian air force'. They were not to return in force until September 1944, in the form of the Red Navy, whom the townsfolk welcomed with 'hearty cringing', as *Pravda*'s man in Constanţa reported.

The **Aquarium** opposite the Casino contains 4,500 species of aquatic life from the Dobrudjan lakes, the Delta and the Black Sea in its tanks; whilst a little to the north, flora and historical material relating to region are exhibited in the **Museum of the Sea** (15, Str. Remus Opreanu). Near the latter one can see the so-called **Genoese Lighthouse**, erected in 1860 in memory of the C13-C14 mariners who tried to revive the port. (Some remains of the ancient port are visible between Gates 2 and 3 of the modern one). In a quiet sidestreet off Str. Titulescu, you'll also find the appealing **'House with Lions'** (so named after the statues flanking its doorway), filled with suites of rooms decorated in Romanian, Venetian and Spanish styles, which especially curious travellers could possibly inspect under the pretext of considering renting a room at the *Hotel Casa cu Lei*.

Just north of Piaţa Ovidiu, the *Muzeul de Arta Populara* (32, B-dul Tomis) mounts a fine display of colourful **Dobrudjan rugs and folk costumes**, while the **Art Museum** (82, B-dul Tomis) has the usual sampling of Aman and Grigorescu, with a room set aside for painters of the Dobrudjan landscape, like Iosif Iser, Ştefan Dumitrescu and Francisc Şirato. Personally, I was more intrigued by how worshippers formerly gained access to the derelict mosque whose small **minaret** surmounts a tangle of dingy coffee houses and fish joints at the top end of Str. Traian (with a basement disco-bar in the vicinity). From here, a short cut through the park brings one to the **Bulevard Republicii**, which links the old quarter with modern Constanţa. One corner is dominated by the *Hotel Continental*, but the humbler (and cheaper) *Victoria* opposite has history on its side, for practically adjoining it are ancient walls, serried amphorae and other **ruins of Tomis**. Tomis was founded by Greeks from Miletus in the C6 BC as a subsidiary to Histria, which it later superseded before being incorporated within the Roman empire as 'Pontus Sinister' at the beginning of the Christian era. The most prominent remains are those of the defensive wall created in the C3-C4 – which failed to repel the rampaging Avars a century later – and the Butchers' Tower, raised in the C6 by Byzantine colonists who revived Tomis and renamed it to honour Constantine.

South of the archaeological park, Str. Traian executes a graceful curve overlooking the commercial *portul maritim*, and provides an appropriate setting for the **Museum of the Romanian Navy** at nr.53. The title is slightly misleading, since the museum includes models of Greek triremes that sailed before the name 'Romania' existed, and photographs recording the unexpected visit of the battleship *Potemkin*, whose mutinous sailors disembarked at Constanţa and scattered in July 1905. Moreover, extensive material on the wartime exploits of the Red Navy is surely a red herring to obscure the role of Romania's own navy during the last war – which was to support the occupation of Odessa and aid the Nazi fleet. A little way east of the museum, however, you'll find a restaurant with a nice summer garden, the *Terasa Colonadelor*.

Visitors with children or a low tolerance of museums often head straight for the **beach**, extending beneath a terraced cliff beyond the breakwater separating it from the *portul turistic*. Another popular spot is the park surrounding **Lake Tăbăcăriei**, reached by boarding any trolleybus heading northwards up B-dul Alexandru Lapuşneanu. A miniature train carries children around the lake, stopping at the Romanian Holiday Village (*Satul Românesc de vacanţă*) on the northern shore, and the *Tăbăcărie Wharf* on the south bank, not far from which stand a **planetarium** and a more than usually depressing **dolphinarium** (both open 9am-7pm). **Luna Park**, north of the lake, features various rides and games, including **bowling**, and there is an **ice-skating** rink on the edge of the Pioneers' Park, also the site of Constanţa's football stadium. Children might enjoy the **shows** at the *Fantasio* (11, B-dul Republicii) and *Puppet* **theatres** (l6, Str. A.Caratzali), for which reservations can be made at the *Agenţia Teatrală*, 97 Tomis Blvd.

Rooms, restaurants and practicalities

The cheapest **hotels** in town are the *Victoria* on B-dul Republicii, and the *Constanţa* above the main **tourist office** at 46, B-dul Tomis (8am-6pm/Sunday 9am-1pm), where it should be possible to obtain single **rooms** for $10-$12, and doubles for around $15-$20. The *Continental* and *Intim* (9, Str. Titulescu) charge $36 and $47 for the same, whilst prices at the *Casa cu Lei* and *Pelican* (on Piaţa Ovidiu) are nearly on par with rates at the *Palace* on Str. Operanu ($39 sngl/$53 dbl). BTT (20-24, Blvd. Tomis; ☎ 1-66-24) might be able to arrange dormitory beds during summer, along with holidays at the International Youth Camp in Costineşi, but otherwise, the slack gets taken up by **campsites** – the closest ones are on the outskirts of Mamaia and Eforie Nord (see below). If you're hoping for a bungalow there, or a room in any of the other resorts, ask ONT to make **reservations**.

Most hotels have **restaurants** on the premises, but it's more fun to eat out. Popular places include the *Cazino* in the Casino; *Zorile* and *Balcan* on Str. Ştefan cel Mare; Piaţa Ovidiu's *Victoria*; the above-mentioned *Terasa Colonadelor*; and the *Furnica* on Tomis Boulevard. Near the latter, there's also a cheap but dismal self-service place – the *Pescăruş* at nr.56. In the backstreets of the old town – particularly around the derelict mosque – one can stumble upon various seedy yet appealing **bars**.

Other **useful addresses** include the **post office** (nr.79) opposite the **24hr pharmacy** on Tomis Blvd, where one can also find the *Librăaria Noastră* **bookshop**, and the *Romanian Automobile Club* (nr.26). **Car** repairs are handled by *ACR Service* and *Dacia Service* (☎ 3-10-80 & 3-18-65; open 7.30am-5.30pm) on the Blvd. Aurel Vlaicu, where there's also a petrol station open 24hrs (other pumps alongside all the highways leaving town). The *Gara* has a 24-hr luggage office, but if it's **railway tickets** you want, the place to go is *CFR*. Formerly halfway along Marinarilor Blvd, the office has reportedly moved to 4, Canarache Street near the post office. *TAROM* (15, Str. Ştefan cel Mare) sells **flights** to Bucharest and neighbouring countries (during summer, there are also flights to most of Romania's provincial airports). The **airport** itself (☎ 1-52-76) is located about 25km northwest of town along the DN2A; depending on fuel supplies, TAROM or the tourist board might lay on coaches, but otherwise you'll have to find a taxi or fork out $17 for a chauffeur-driven car (arranged by ONT).

Excursions and moving on

The tourist office is keen to sign visitors up for **excursions**, some of which are worth considering. Given the relative inaccessibility of Adamclissi (p.471), $10 is a fairly reasonable charge for a 4hr trip to the *Tropaeum Traiani* ($3 extra gets lunch on the coast); while on the same principal, ONT's 2-day *Delta Tour* – taking in some of the backwaters near Crişan – seems good value for $48. Besides these, there are 4-, 6- and 8-hr *tours of the coast* (well, some of it, anyway) for $7, $9 and $17 (the latter includes dinner and a folklore show); *cruises on the Danube-Black Sea Canal* by day or night ($12/$21); trips out to *Ovid's Island* (see below); and three different *excursions to Murfatlar* (p.471). ONT's *evenings out* encompass 4-5 hrs at a restaurant in Eforie Nord, Neptun or Mamaia, with a floorshow, food and drink (but not necessarily transport) for between $11-$17.

ONT's sister office at nr.69 fixes **trips abroad** which, as you'd expect, are rather dearer. If you're rich and feel like a change of environment, one can spend a day in *Istanbul* ($124), *Athens* ($160) or *Cairo* ($205) and help fill TAROM's seats; while $30 buys you a day's visit to Balchik, Druzhba, Golden Sands and Varna in *Bulgaria*, travelling by coach.

Trains to other parts of Romania get incredibly crowded during the summer, and if you can't get a reserved seat (preferably 3-4 days in advance) the only alternative is to fight your way on, hunker down somewhere, and hope for the best. However, there are fairly frequent and tolerably crowded **buses along the coast**, divided below into two sections – north and south of town. Generally speaking, services from the *Autogară Sud* cover areas to the south of Constanţa, while buses from the *Autogară Nord* run to places north of town; but by catching a trolleybus #41 one can get directly from the town's railway station to **Mamaia**.

MAMAIA, LAKE SIUTGHIOL AND NĂVODARI

MAMAIA, 6km north of Constanţa, is Romania's best known coastal resort; and the majority of package tourists who go through UK operators wind up here. The beach of fine, almost white sand, fringed with olive trees, is Mamaia's greatest asset, while its gentle gradient and the absence of currents and strong tides makes it particularly safe for children. Legend has it that the gods created the beach to reunite a kidnapped princess with her daughter, who was abandoned on the sea shore wailing 'Mamaia, Mamaia!' (Mummy!); but the name could equally be derived from *Mamakioi*, meaning 'village of butter' in Turkish.

Since they're ranged along a narrow spit of land between the Black Sea and Lake Siutghiol, most of Mamaia's 55 hotels are within 150 yards of the beach. Approaching from Constanţa, the 13-storey *Parc Hotel* marks the beginning of **the resort**, with an amusements park and bowling ground located on the west side of the main drag, which curves around to follow the lake shoreline. Taking this route, you'll pass in succession the *Select* restaurant/disco; tennis courts, basketball and volleyball pitches; the *Hotel Perla* (with a disco); and then the area used for **watersports**. Unless your package deal includes hire-charges, sporting activities and equipment must be paid in hard currency at the following $-equivalent rates, standard along the coast: waterskiing ($18 p/h); yachting ($9.50 p/h); surf boards ($30 p/h, 5hrs for $11). Fifty minutes on a **tennis** court costs $2 (10 sessions for $15.50), and $1.50 gets you the use of a racquet and two balls for one hour. However, there's a sting in the tail, for all these are *charges per head* rather than group rates (nasty!).

Farther north beyond the breakwater you'll find the *Miorita* restaurant and disco and, just to the east, a kindergarten (free of charge for people on package holidays). Motorists are restricted to the lakeside road, leaving the seafront promenade to pedestrians and flower beds, while between the two are lawns and diverse emporia clustered around the **hotels**. Such rooms as haven't been booked by travel operators are allocated to visitors by the main **tourist office** (in the *Bucureşti B* hotel; ☎ 3-11-52 or 3-11-79) on a 'take it or leave it' basis. To give an example of prices, places like the *Junona*, *Unirea*, *Perla* and *Doina* charge $32 for doubles and $26 for singles, while *Caraiman I & II*, *Select*, *Apollo* and a dozen or so others rent the same for $29 and $23. Below this come the *Paloma*, *Favorit* and other **villas** (dbl.$24/sngl.$19), and then 2-person **bungalows** on **campsites** ($17). *Turist*, the nearest campsite, is just beyond the mini-hotels at the northern end of the resort; whence it's about 5km up the road to the equally crowded *Hanul Piraţilor*.

There are scores of **places to eat and drink**, no less than 31 of them decked out as 'traditional' bars or restaurants and concentrated in the Romanian Holiday Village (*Satul Româñnesc de Vacanţă*). Tourist **cliques** tend to form around certain hotels – for example, Brits on Balkan Holidays at the *Junona-Jupiter*, *Venus* and *Majestic*, and the Club Mediteranée crowd at *Thallassa*, their own exclusive complex. There's a fairly stiff admission charge to the glitzy cabaret – transmuted 50s Las Vegas routines – on offer most nights at the *Melody* and *Orient* **nightclubs**; or you can pay $17 for 4hrs show and snacks à la carte. Remember that Western drinks – especially whisky – are expensive; so if you insist on Johnny Walker (or whatever), smuggle in a bottle purchased at one of the **hard currency shops**, which exist in most hotels. The *Orient* and *Hanul Piraţilor* entertain diners with 'folklore' displays, while the *Miorița*, *Select* and *Delta* restaurants have nightly **discos**, as does the *Perla Hotel*.

While the International Tourist Agency near the lakefront can book you on **excursions** abroad, the main office arranges trips to Adamclissi (p.471) or motorboat rides out to **Ovids's Island** at the northern end of **LAKE SIUTGHIOL** – the latter jaunt costs $8.50, and includes a meal at the rustic-style *Insula Ovidiu* on the island. Inspired by her presence on Ovid's Island, Carmen Sylva 'declaimed poetry to ships at sea through a speaking trumpet', for the freshwater lake lies surprisingly close to the sea. Also known by the easier name of *Lacul Mamaia*, the lake was formed when a river's outlet became silted-up, and for many centuries it was a watering hole for herds of sheep and cows brought down from the Carpathians – hence the origin of *Siutghiol*, 'Lake of Milk' in Turkish.

It's inadvisable to travel much further northwards, since **NĂVODARI** looms on the horizon. The beach here must have been lovely once, but with characteristic concern for the environment, a gigantic, reeking superphosphates factory has been constructed nearby, its pipelines running through the campsite which, unbelievably, has been designated a children's resort. All round, this was probably the most depressing place that I ever saw in Romania. However, beyond Năvodari a minor road heads northwards past LAKE NUNTAŞI (*campsite*) **towards Histria**, whose Greek ruins are described on page 457.

SOUTH OF CONSTANŢA: FROM AGIGEA TO VAMA VECHE

On Constanţa's southern outskirts, excavators and cranes are completing the new AGIGEA port complex (named after the village that originally stood here) where the Danube meets the coast. Beyond this, the array of **resorts** extending to Mangalia is another facet of Romania's progress over the last twenty years – modern complexes created where scrubland or flyblown villages existed before. Except for the fact that most are situated along a clifftop overlooking the beach, they resemble their prototype, Mamaia, though some models are classier, others more tawdry. From Constanţa you can reach those along the line to Mangalia by railway or, if you don't mind riding the equivalent of mobile steambaths, by travelling on short-hop local buses (hitching along DN39 is possible, but unrewarding). Leaving aside the hassle of buying a ticket and actually boarding the vessel, the daily *Dierna* sailing down to Mangalia is probably the best form of travel.

The older resorts around Lake Techirghiol
From Constanţa's *Sud* terminal, trolleybus 11 runs 10km southwards to **EFORIE NORD** before skirting the lake and terminating at Techirghiol. Founded in 1899 and originally named after Carmen Sylva, Eforie Nord clambers along a cliff-top 50-60 feet above its beach, which is steadily growing as sand accumulates around the concrete groynes built for that purpose. Though the beach is an obvious asset, the resort is best known for its **therpeutic black mud** scooped from the shores of **Lake Techirghiol**, whose mineral-saturated waters (96.663 grams of magnesium and soduim chloride, sulphates, bromides, iron oxide per litre) got the lake its name, derived from *tekir*, Turkish for 'salt' or 'bitter'. Therpeutic **baths** by the lake (south of the railway station) specialise in treating rheumatic and gynaecological disorders and the after-effects of polio; while on the single-sex **nudist beaches** people plaster themselves with mud, wait until it cracks, and then jostle good humouredly underneath the showers.

The resort itself is basically two streets running parallel to the cliff-top Vladimirescu esplanade, with some thirty lacklustre restaurants (*Nunta Zamfirei* puts on a folklore show) and dozens of hotels and villas. An overworked tourist office (13, B-dul Republicii; ☎ 4-13-51) allocates **rooms**, the availability of which is unpredictable. Prices range from $26-$53 per head for a double in the *Hotel Europa*, or a luxury villa-suite, down through a swathe of middling-cost hotels and villas (dbl.$29-$42/sngl.$23-33) to the ones where beds, if available, go for $9-$12. Without reservations, there's little chance of renting a bungalow at *Şincai* or *Meduza* ($7-$9 per head), and luckless travellers will have to pitch a tent alongside the hundreds of others in these overcrowded, seedy campsites.

Although there's nowhere to stay, it's tempting to flee across the lake to **TECHIRGHIOL**, where a *jamis* serves three hundred Muslim families (Turks and Tatars by origin) amongst the commune's population. **EFORIE SUD**, founded in 1899, largely resembles its northern neighbour, albeit slightly more circumscribed by the lakeside (where trains halt) and the sea. Sports grounds, pools, twelve restaurants, a disco and bars hardly soak up the guests at Eforie Sud's twenty-five hotels, and there's a predictable wait before anyone can allocate **rooms** (bureau in the Lilacul villa; ☎ 4-12-31). Prices range from $25-$30 for a double ($20-$24 sngl.) at 2nd class hotels like the *Flamingo*, *Riviera* or *Ancora*, to $19-$23 for a double and $15-$20 for a single room at a score of lesser hotels (*Orizont, Dumbrava, Turist* etc), with the last resort of staying in bungalows or squalidly camping at the big *Cosmos* site.

Bigger resorts further down the coast
Originally a fishing village, **CONSTINEŞTI** is now the site of Romania's principal **International Youth camp**, replete with minihotels, a campsite, sports facilities, discos and a fine sandy beach sheltered by Cape Tuzla. Unfortunately, the only people allowed to stay here are those on tours organised by *BTT*, so contact head office in Bucharest or BTT in Constanţa beforehand if you're interested.

NEPTUN, a few kilometres down the coast, is one of the better resorts, purpose built in 1960 between the Comorova forest and the sea, thus ensuring a lush setting for the artifical lakes and dispersed villas (Comrade Ceauşescu's is somewhere in the vicinity). Shopping centres, discos, sports facilities and hotels here are a cut above the Romanian average, which is also the case in Neptun's satellite resort, **OLIMP**. Most **rooms** are assigned to package tourists, however, so anyone hoping to get something through the tourist office in Neptun's *Hotel Decebal* could well be disappointed. Lodgings in both resorts fall into three categories: deluxe hotels where breakfast is included in the charge (dbl.$70/sngl.$53); middle-ranking ones (dbl.$28-$30/sngl.$17-$24); and finally bungalows in holiday villages ($16 dbl. only). Four **restaurants** are particularly popular: *Calul Bălan* (folkloric show), *Popasul Căprioarelor*, the *Insula* specialising in fish dishes on an island, and *Neptun*.

Just down the road, **JUPITER** also rubs shoulders with the forest and a gently sloping beach with fine sand. Jupiter is centred around an artifical lake, called Tismana like the 538-bed hotel overlooking it (dbl.$28/sngl.$22), and night-life focuses on the *Paradis* bar/disco or the *Zodiac* holiday village. It's cheaper **to stay** at one of the hotels named after flowers (*Camelia* etc) or try to get a bungalow on either the *Zodiac I & II* or *Lilacul* campsites. There's a similar choice of lodgings a few miles down the coast in **VENUS**, which has several man-made semi-circular beaches, a disco and two main bars (*Calipso* and *Auto-Night-Club*). The number of the accommodation bureau is 3-16-74.

Imagine Mayan architects called upon to design Palm Beach and you'll get some idea of the pyramidical complexes that are **AURORA**'s most striking feature. Small and elegantly designed compared to the other resorts, Aurora has ten hotels named after jewels, all charging $44 for a double, twice that for a suite, and $35 for singles. The **Comorova forest** behind Aurora extends as far south as **SATURN**, a high-rise resort with various grades of hotels, a campsite and two holiday villages, *Dunărea* and *Delta*. You can hire horses and go **riding** in search of the roe-deer, grouse and pheasants inhabiting the forest; play tennis, minigolf or bowls; or dine to music at the *Balada*, *Prahova* or *Mercur* **restaurants**. As in Venus, CFR shares premises with the post office, and there's a number to ring if you're in search of accommodation (☎ 5-19-83).

Mangalia, Doi Mai and crossing the border at Vama Veche

When the forest comes to an end the modern suburbs of **MANGALIA** take over, and the cliff descends in a series of broad terraces to the beach and harbour, where the *Dierna* docks behind the long breakwater. Like Constanţa, Mangalia's appearance of modernity belies its ancient origin, for the Greeks founded *Callatis* during the C6 BC, when population pressure impelled them to colonise many points along the Black Sea. Leaving the station, strike southeast towards the *plaja* and you'll come upon the **ruins of Callatis** in Stadionului Park, near a small **Archaeological Museum** with sarcophagi and the vestiges of a Christian basilica in the vicinity. Further south on Str. Mircea cel Bătrîn stands the C16 **Sultan Esmahan Mosque**, built in a Moorish style and surrounded by a Muslim graveyard. The **medicinal baths** on the town's outskirts utilise radioactive, sulphorous hot springs beside **Lake Mangalia** to treat various muscular and neurological afflictions. On the southern shore you can visit the **Limanu Cave**, a speleological reserve once quarried by the Romans.

Reasonably priced **rooms** can be had at most of Mangalia's hotels (*Zenit*, *Astra* and *Orion* are the cheapest), but you might prefer to seek lodgings in the more laid back village of **DOI MAI**. Check with the tourist office in the Hotel Mangalia before going in search of a bus from Str. Libertăţii, since the status of foreigners in the 'Second of May' is ambiguous. Unmarked on most tourist maps, the commune is an unofficial home from home for artists, intellectuals and Bucharest trendies, who camp here or avail themselves of Doi Mai's private landladies. Depending on their mood, the local police may frown upon or turn a blind eye to foreigners staying.

From Doi Mai, it's only a few miles further south until **VAMA VECHE** on the border (open 24hrs). It's inadvisable to try hitching across **into Bulgaria**, and on no account can *visas* be obtained at the border. For a description of places beyond the Bulgarian customs post of DURANKULAK, turn to p.688 and start backtracking through the text.

INLAND: MURFATLAR, ADAMCLISSI AND OSTROV ON THE DANUBE

The last section of this chapter covers a few remaining sights situated **inland**, which motorists might enjoy checking out before taking DN38 down to Negru Vodă and crossing over **into Bulgaria**. Travellers without private **transport** shouldn't have any difficulty getting from Constanţa to Basarabi, but Adamclissi is impossible to reach by bus or train. However, ONT do organise day **excursions** to the ruins, lasting 4hrs ($10) or stretching to include lunch on the coast ($13).

Excursions to Murfatlar and crossing into Bulgaria

Most Medgidia-bound trains, and irregular cruise boats on the Danube-Black Sea Canal, stop near BASARABI, an old wine-producing centre better known as **MURFATLAR**. Constanţa ONT organises three separate *excursions* to Murfatlar, of which the shortest and best value for money is the 4hr **wine** tasting tour ($12). Participants can sample wines from the Pinot, Chardonnay, Cabernet-Sauvignon, Muscat and Merlot vineyards that cover the surrounding chalky hills, and receive a bottle of Murfatlar wine as a present after visiting the **museum** with its old presses, reliefs of Dionysos and withered vines. Dug into the hills near Murfatlar you'll find the so-called **Rupestral Complex**, including six small churches and a few rooms linked by passageways. Discovered in 1957, the complex was created during the C9-C11, judging by the Greek and Slavonic inscriptions and pictures of humans and animals inscribed on its rock walls.

Though the Vama Veche crossing is more suitable if you're driving down to Varna, it's also possible **to enter Bulgaria** from NEGRU VODĂ at the end of DN38 (open 24hrs), or **by rail** should you catch the 7am or 8.40am train departing from Medgidia. This chugs over to KARDAM in Bulgaria, where you hopefully shouldn't have to wait long for a train to the neighbouring town of Tolbuhin (see p.596). All travellers must already be in possession of a Bulgarian *visa* before they reach the border.

The Tropaeum Traiani, Ostrov and the Dobrudja's Gypsies
If you're interested in ancient monuments you might consider travelling about 50km further west along DN3 to visit the remains near **ADAMCLISI**. Just north of the road and the commune of Adamclissi rises an arresting structure that, seen from afar, looks like a giant marble sink-plunger, but is in fact a reconstruction of the **Tropaeum Traiani**. The original was erected in AD 109 to glorify Trajan's conquest of the Dacians (whose leader, Decebalus, prefered suicide to capture and ignominy in Rome), and every facet reflects unabashed militarism, not least the dedication to Mars Ultor. The trophy-statue – an armoured, faceless warrior – gazes from a height of 100ft above the plateau; surmounting a hexagonal plinth rising from a truncated conical base, 106ft in diameter. Carved around the side of the base are 49 bas-reliefs or metopes (originally, there were 54), portraying the Roman campaign in a cyclical fashion. Each of the six groups of metopes is comprised of a marching scene, a battle, and a tableaux representing victory over the enemy, a sequence then repeated with different details; an identical arrangement underlies scenes XXXVI-XLII of Trajan's Column in Rome, which was also created to mark the emperor's triumph over the Dacians. Around the statue are **other ruins** of buildings once inhabited by the legionary garrison or serving religious or funerary purposes. Unfortunately, there's no tourist accommodation in the vicinity.

For **rooms** you have to go another 60km west along DN3 to the small town of **OSTROV** on the Danube, which has a *campsite* with chalets near the jetty whence ferries sail across to CĂLĂRAŞI on the north bank – but no checkpoint enabling travellers to drive over the border to the Bulgarian town of ŞILISTRA.

Traditionally, one group of people have never let borders and checkpoints dictate their travels – the **Gypsies**. The Dobrudja and the banks of the Danube have been their stamping ground since at least the C14; and even today one sees families encamped around burlap tents and wagons in the countryside; wandering tinsmiths of the Khalderash tribe; and, occasionally, a troupe of fiddlers accompanied by a performing bear. In the towns it's the Gypsy womenfolk that are unmistakable, dressed in swirling scarves and multi-coloured skirts, flashing gold earrings and teeth, and besting even the Romanians with their expressive gestures and fierce volubility. Sixty years ago, Konrad Bercovici witnessed a whole tribe of Gypsy *Bivolari* (buffalo-herders) stampede their beasts into a small army of Romanian cavalry, before fording the river into Bulgaria unscathed; even today, Gypsies brag about members of their race outwitting the *gadjé* authorities. One tale tells of a Gypsy so impatient to go abroad that he left Romania at the border with Yugoslavia, visited thirteen European countries and returned home without once acquiring a visa.

TRAVEL DETAILS

Trains
From Bucharest to Constanţa (7 daily; 3-5¼hrs); Mangalia (4; 4¾-6); Medgidia (7; 2½-3¾).

From Constanţa to Braşov (1; 7); Bucharest (10; 2¾-3½); Medgidia (20; ½-¾).

From Galaţi to Bîrlad (6; 3); Bucharest (2; 4).

From Medgidia to Babadag (4; 1¼-2); Bucharest (10; 3-4); Constanţa (17; ½-1); Istria (4; 1¼); Mangalia (6; 2½-3½); Negru Vodă (6; 1-½) Suceava (1; 8): Tulcea (4; 2¼-2¾).

Hydrofoils and ferries

Cruises between Constanţa and Mangalia during the summer, as advertised.

Hydrofoils from Tulcea to Galaţi (1 daily; 1½hrs); Periprava (4½); Sf. Gheorge (2); Sulina (1½); the last three every 1-2hrs until 4pm.

Classic ferries from Tulcea to Galaţi (1 daily; 4hrs); Periprava (5-6; 9); Sf. Gheorge (5-6; 4); Sulina (5-6; 3).

Flights

From Constanţa to Bucharest (1-2 daily); Arad; Bacău; Cluj; Iaşi; Oradea; Satu Mare; Sibiu; Suceava; Tîrgu Mureş (1 daily during the summer).

International trains

From Constanţa to Budapest (1 daily; 22hrs); Prague (1; 29).

From Medgidia to Budapest (1; 20); Dresden (1; 39); Kiev (1; 24); Moscow (1; 36); Prague (1; 31); Varna (1; 6).

ROMANIA
CONTEXTS

ROMÂNIA

HISTORICAL FRAMEWORK

Although inhabited since prehistoric times, Romania only achieved statehood during the C19, and one third of its present territory – Transylvania – was acquired as recently as 1920. Hence, much of Romania's history is that of its disparate parts – the Dobrudja, the Banat, Bessarabia, Maramureş and, most of all, the principalities of Moldavia, Wallachia and Transylvania. For the sake of brevity, the following historical framework has been greatly simplified.

Origins: Greeks, Dacians and Romans (4,000BC-271AD)

Despite the discovery of bones, weapons and implements within Carpathian caves, very little is known about the nomadic hunter-gatherers of the early **Stone Age**. With the recession of the glaciers, humans seem to have established their first settlements on the Dobrudja; where the excavation of a Neolithic village at Habaşeşti and the discovery of numerous statues suggest that the tribes – known to archaeologists as the **'Hamangia Culture'** – probably had a matriarchal society, worshipping fertility goddesses and the great Earth Mother.

During the C7-C6BC, **Greek traders** established ports along the Black Sea coast, the ruins of which can still be seen at *Histria*, Constanţa (*Tomis*), Mangalia (*Callatis*) and other sites. Commerce flourished between the Black Sea and Aegean ports, but the interior remained basically unknown to the Greeks until 514BC, when Darius of the Persians attempted to expel the Scythians from their new settlements along the Danube. The chronicler Herodotus reported that of the numerous and disunited tribes of Thracians (see p.643) – akin to the Illyrians of Albania – who inhabited the mountains on both sides of the river, the 'bravest and most righteous' were those subsequently known as the 'Getae-Dacians'.

Over the centuries these related tribes gradually coalesced and were brought under centralised authority, so that by the C1BC a single leader, Burebista, ruled the **Dacians**, who occupied the territory of modern day Romania, if not a larger area. Agriculture – and a pastoral lifestyle in the highlands – provided the basis for the Dacian society, at the apex of which was the religious and political capital, Sarmizegetusa, located in the Orăştie Mountains. Digs have revealed Dacian settlements as far afield as Maramureş and Mount Ceahlău, and the sheer size of the kingdom contributed to its fragmentation after Burebista's demise.

Before Decebalus (87-106AD) managed to reunite the kingdom, the lower reaches of the Danube had already been conquered by the **Romans**, who began expanding northwards. The Dacians resisted, but were defeated during the course of two campaigns (in 101-2 and 105-6) organised by the Emperor Trajan. Although the Apuseni Mountains and Maramureş were never subdued, most regions fell under Roman hegemony, maintained by the building of roads linking the garrison posts and trading towns. Besides the capital, *Ulpa Traiana*, important Roman towns included *Apulum* (Alba Iulia), *Napoca*, (Cluj) and *Porolissum* (near Gherla). For the **colonisation of Dacia**, settlers were brought from imperial territories as far afield as Greece and Spain and – on the evidence of shrines to Isis and Mithris – from Egypt and Persia. Later, the adoption of Christianity as the official religion led to its acceptance in Dacia, at least superficially; and in Hadrian's time the region was divided into two provinces to make its administration easier. With increasing incursions by nomadic tribes in the C3, however, the defence of Dacia became too costly, and in 271 Emperor Aurelian ordered the withdrawal of Roman legions and administrators from the region.

The Dark Ages, the Continuity Theory and the occupation of Transylvania

Hard on the heels of the Romans came the Goths, who seem not to have settled, followed by other nomadic peoples such as the Huns (C5), Avars (C6), Slavs (C6-C7) and Bulgars (en route to Bulgaria) during the **Age of Migrations**. The low-lying regions were greatly exposed to these invasions, whereas high mountains protected the region that would later be called Transylvania. Excavations there have yielded coins bearing Roman inscriptions ranging from the time of Aurelian until the beginning of the C5, suggesting that the settlements continued to trade with the empire despite the Roman withdrawal – one of the arguments used to butress the 'Continuity Theory'.

First propounded by Dimitri Cantemir, and elaborated later in the C18, the **Daco-Roman Continuity Theory** holds that the Romanian people were descended from the Roman settlers and the indigenous Dacians, who interbred and formed a hybrid culture. Since the poorer colonists (as opposed to rich ones, officials and troops) were likely to have remained following the imperial withdrawal, this process of formation continued for longer than the relatively brief period of Roman occupation (about 160 years) would suggest, and thus had a lasting impact on the culture of the population. Documentary evidence for this is practically non-existent, but Romanian philologists point to numerous words in their language which appear to be derived from Latin; in particular,

terms refering to pastoral activities (the mainstay of the Dacian lifestyle) and Christian worship.

The theory would be of academic interest only, were it not entwined with the centuries-old dispute between the Magyars and Romanians over **the occupation of Transylvania**. By claiming this racial and cultural continuity, and their uninterrupted residence within the Carpathian redoubt, Romanians assert their original, rightful ownership of Transylvania, and dismiss their rivals as usurpers. Conversely, the Magyars claim that their occupation of the 'land beyond the forest' (between the late C9-C13) met little resistance, and that the indigenous people were of Slavonic stock, ruled by chieftains who owed their loyalty to the Bulgars (whose state extended northwards into the Carpathians during its heyday in the C8-C9). According to Magyar historians, 'Vlachs' (Romanians) are first mentioned in Transylvania during the C13, when groups of these nomadic pastoralists crossed the Carpathians, having wandered over the course of centuries from their original 'homeland' in Macedonia and Illyria (where ethnic Vlach communities still migrate with their flocks from winter to summer pasturing). This, together with other evidence (such as the Slavonic rather than Latin derivation of the names of places and rivers), undermines the Romanian claim to prior occupation. . .or so Hungarian scholars argue.

The Medieval Principalities

Transylvania

Whatever the indigenous population's identity, István I and subsequent Árpád monarchs gradually extended **Hungarian rule over Transylvania**, using foreigners to bolster their own settlements around the Mureş and Someş rivers, which allowed the region's mineral wealth to be shipped west despite the swamps extending across the Great Plain. Besides subduing local 'Cumans, Bulgars and Vlachs' (according to King Béla's chron-

icler Anonymous), the colonists had to withstand frequent invasions by nomadic warriors like the Mongols (or Tartars), who devastated much of Eastern Europe in 1241. While the Teutonic Knights invited to colonise the Bîrsa Land were evicted in 1225 for defying Andrew II, other groups of Germans – subsequently known as **Saxons** – settled around and developed powerful market towns like *Hermannstadt* (Sibiu) and *Kronstadt* (Braşov), which were granted self-government on the basis of 'seats' (*sedes* or *stuhle*). Another ethnic group, the **Székely** (p.341), acted as the vanguard of colonisation; moving during the C13 from their settlements in the Bihor region to the eastern marches, where they too were allowed relative autonomy.

Unlike the Székely who originally held land in common and enjoyed 'noble' status, the Hungarians in Transylvania were either classed as plebs liable to all manner of dues and taxes, or as members of the tax-exempt nobility (*Natio*). This group dominated **the feudal system**, being represented alongside the Saxon and Székely 'seats' on the Diet which advised the principality's military and civil leader, the *Voivode*, who acted for the Hungarian king. During the Árpád dynasty, Diets included *knezes* drawn from the Romanian-speaking **Vlachs** who, even then, may have constituted the majority of Transylvania's population. From the mid-C14 onwards, however, Vlachs faced increasing discrimination; being gradually excluded from areas inhabited by Saxons or Magyars, and barred from public office. Besides the mistrust sown by Bogdan Vodă's rebellion in Maramureş (see below), **religion** played an important part in this process. Whereas most Vlachs were Orthodox (barring a few apostate nobles), the other communities adhered to to the Catholic church, which sought to undermine Orthodoxy throughout the Balkans. Over time, these divisions of class, race and religion coalesced into a kind of medieval apartheid system, which was to bedevil Transylvania's inhabitants for centuries to come.

Wallachia and the Dobrudja

On the far side of the Carpathians, fully fledged principalities emerged somewhat later. Chronicles attribute the foundation of **Wallachia** to Negru Vodă, who made Cîmpulung its first capital in 1290; but some confusion exists as to whether they refer to his C14 successor **Radu Negru**, who consolidated princely power and likewise belonged to the Basarab dynasty. The shift in Wallachia's capitals over the centuries – from Cîmpulung in the highlands down to Curtea de Argeş, Tîrgovişte and then Bucharest on the plain – expressed a cautious emergence from the safety of the mountains. Oppression, anarchy and piety were commonplace: the tithes and *robot* squeezed

from the enserfed masses allowed the landowing **boyars** to pursue their favourite occupations – endowing Orthodox churches and engineering coups against the ruling voivodes. In centuries to come, the average duration of their reigns dropped to less than three years.

Important trade routes linking Poland with the Black Sea passed through Wallachia, but commerce was entirely in the hands of Germans, Poles, Greeks and Jews. Though lavishly endowed, Wallachia's **Orthodox church** was subordinated to the Bulgarian and Byzantine patriachates, writing its scriptures and conducting its rituals in Old Slavonic rather than the vernacular tongue. This was partly a legacy of Bulgar rule during the C8-C9, but also reflected the policy of Wallachia's rulers, who tended to look south across the Danube for allies against the powerful Hungarian kingdom. These allies themselves faced a dangerous threat – the expansionist Ottoman Turks, who inflicted decisive defeats on Bulgaria and Serbia in 1371 and 1389. Being preoccupied with digesting these gains, the Ottomans accepted a huge payment from **Mircea the Old** (1386-1418) in return for ceasing their rampage through Wallachia in 1391. Appeals to Sigismund of Hungary and the Pope led to the dispatch of a crusading army, which through its own folly was crushed at Nicopolis in 1396 (p.590). This, and subsequent Christian defeats left the Turks entrenched along the lower Danube; whence they finally compelled Mircea to acknowledge Ottoman suzerainty in 1417. By surrendering the fertile **Dobrudja** region and paying tribute, outright occupation was avoided and Wallachia's ruling class retained their positions; but henceforth both rulers and ruled were confronted with the alternatives of submission or resistance to an overwelming force.

Moldavia and Bessarabia

From Maramureş, where attempts to enforce Hungarian rule provoked resistance amongst the indigenous population, communities followed the rebel leader **Bogdan Vodă** over the Carpathians in 1359. Their settlements around the headwaters of the Moldova were the cradle of a new principality, **Moldavia**, which emerged in the 1360s; but the process of occupying the hills and steppes beyond the Carpathians began centuries earlier, more or less spontaneously. Groups of Romanian-speaking pastoralists and farmers gradually crossed the River Prut, moving on to the Dniestr where they encountered Ukranians who called them 'Volokhi'. Feudalism and the *hospodars*' writ lagged behind them, and the Moldavian capital was only shifted eastwards from Rădăuţi to Suceava, and then southwards to Iaşi when safety permitted. **Alexandre the Good** (1400-32) may have gained his honorific by ousting Turks from the eastern marches, though it could well

have been bestowed by the Basarabs whom he made feudal lords of the region subsequently known as **Bessarabia**; or retrospectively by Moldavia's peasantry who suffered during the prolonged, violent anarchy that followed Alexandre's death. Besides Tartar invasions and rebellious boyars, Moldavia faced the threat of ambitious neighbouring powers – the kingdoms of Hungary and Poland on the western and northern borders, and the growing menace of the Turks to the south.

Ottomans, Nationes and Phanariots

From the mid C14 onwards, the fate of the Balkan countries was greatly affected by the Ottoman empire, which spread inexorably northwards. With the final subjugation of Bulgaria in the 1390s – and Serbia's shattering defeat at Kosovo – Wallachia, Moldavia and Transylvania became Christendom's front line of **resistance against the Turks**. Throughout the C15, the principalities' history is overshadowed by this struggle and the names of their military leaders. The Transylvanian voivode **János Hunyadi** (Iancu de Hunedoara) led multi-national armies to victory at Belgrade and Niš, rising to become regent of Hungary, which for a time previously had been allied to the Polish crown. Conflicting Polish and Hungarian ambitions periodically caused **fighting between the principalities**, whose rulers engaged in duplicitous manoeuverings as often as they collaborated; while the Sultans' willingness to accept tribute led to sporadic truces secured by appeasement. The Ottomans were dislodged from southern Bessarabia by **Stephen the Great** and temporarily checked by the fortresses of Chilia and Cetatea Alba, but their resurgence under Bajazet II presaged the demise of Moldavian independence, as was apparent to Stephen by the end of his embattled reign (1457-1504). Due to Wallachia's greater vulnerablity, its rulers generally prefered to pay off the Turks rather than resist them; **Vlad Ţepeş** (The Impaler) being a notable exception.

In **Transylvania**, the least exposed region, the **Bobîlna peasant uprising** of 1437 rocked the feudal order. To safeguard their privileges, the Magyar nobility

concluded a pact known as the **Union of Three Nations** with the Saxon and Székely leaders, whereby each each party or *Natione* agreed to recognise and defend the rights of the others. As a consequence, the Vlachs were relegated to the position of 'those who do not possess the right of citizenship. . .but are merely tolerated by grace', and a spate of decrees followed, effectively prohibiting them from holding public office or residing in the Saxon and Magyar towns. This medieval version of apartheid was augumented during the C16, when Transylvania became a stronghold of the religious reformation. While the Nationes averted sectarian strife by decreeing equal rights for the Calvinist, Lutheran, Catholic and Unitarian faiths to which their members subscribed, both the Edict of Turda (1568) and the Diet of 1571 merely 'tolerated' the existence of Orthodoxy, the **religion** of the Vlach population. The gradual enserfment of numbers of Székely added to the pent-up bitterness, which exploded in another peasant uprising in 1514. This was savagely repressed by the nobles, who imposed yet more onerous conditions of **serfdom** with a new feudal code, the *Tripartium*, in 1517.

The Hungarian defeat at Mohács (1526) and the Turkish occupation of Buda (1541) exacerbated the **isolation of the principalities**. Voivode **János Zápolyai**, who rallied the nobles to crush the 1514 uprising, managed to counterbalance Ottomans against Habsburgs, and thus maintain a precarious autonomy for Transylvania; but rulers like **Petru Rareş** in Moldavia could only hold their thrones (as he did between 1527-38 and 1541-56) by acts of breathtaking duplicity. Yet (to quote Professor Seton-Watson), Petru's 'shifty and unstable improvisations stood out as real statecraft in contrast to the utter degeneration of his successors', such as 'The Locust', Aron the Tyrant, Basil the Wolf and Ion the Cruel (who eventually displeased the Turks and was torn apart by camels).

Understandably, Romanian history has scant regard for such figures, and prefers to highlight the achievements of **Michael the Brave** (Mihai Vitezul, or Mihai Bravul). Crowned ruler of Wallachia by the boyars in 1593, his triumphs against the Turks were followed by the overthrow of Andrew Báthori in Transylvania (1599) and a lightning campaign across the Carpathians in 1600, which secured Michael the Moldavian throne. This short-lived **union of the principalities** under one crown – which immediately fragmented following his demise in 1601 – has been subsequently presented as a triumph of Romanian nationalism; and evidence suggests that the Vlachs in Transylvania welcomed Michael as a liberator. However, although he improved the status of the Vlach nobles and the Orthodox church in Transylvania, his policy reflected class interests rather than popular ones; the Nationes kept their privileges, and the serfs laboured on.

Between 1606-57 Transylvania attained genuine independence from the Habsburgs and Ottomans, although the region was rarely at peace. **István Bocskai** pushed its border westwards (and, incidentally, enabled the *Hajdúk* to establish their settlements around Debrecen); while his successor '**Crazy**'

Gábor Báthori pursued a vendetta against the Saxon towns until overthrown by **Gábor Bethlen**, whose encouragement of economic development and resistance to the tide of counter-Reformation made his reign (1613-29) a golden age by comparison with others.

From the 1630s onwards, **Moldavia and Wallachia** avoided direct occupation as Turkish *pashaliks* by accepting Ottoman 'advisers'. These Greek families – the Ghicas, Cantacuzenes, Rosettis, Ducas and others – originated from the Phanar district of Constantinople, and hence collectively became known as the **Phanariots**. In Moldavia, they encouraged the Orthodox church to abandon Old Slavonic as the **language** of the scriptures and ritual, in favour of Greek; but this policy had the unintended result of stimulating a move towards the Romanian language, using books printed at Gorova and Trei Ierarhi. This presaged a minor cultural renaissance – particularly in the field of architecture – during a period of relative stability provided by the reigns of **Constantine Brîncoveanu** and **Dimitri Cantemir**, before their overthrow in 1714 and 1717. Thereafter the Turks dispensed with native rulers, and began appointing **Phanariot princes** instead. These were purely concerned with plundering the principalities to pay the huge bribes necessary to remain in good standing at court, and enrich themselves before the axe fell. Their rapaciousness and more than seventy coronations in Moldavia and Wallachia between 1711-1821 beggared both regions, and gave rise to the proverb that 'madmen rejoice when the rulers change'.

The struggle for unification

Between 1682-99, the alliance of Christian powers known as the 'Holy League' succeeded in driving the Turks out of Hungary, Croatia, Slavonia and Transylvania, which the Ottomans renounced claims upon by signing the Peace of Karlowitz. Thereafter, the **decline of Ottoman power** in the Balkans was exceeding gradual, but nonetheless real; and while nationalist movements struggled to free their countries during the C19, the main European powers became increasingly preoccupied with **the 'Eastern question'** – which of them

would inherit the Ottomans' influence? Foreign interests were generally entangled with local ones, so that the principalities' internal conflicts between the old nobility, the bourgeoisie and the peasantry could have repercussions on an international level, and vice versa.

This first became apparent in **Transylvania**, where Habsburg recognition of the privileged 'three Nations and four religions' – as established by the *Leopoldine Diploma* (1691) – was followed by attempts to undermine this status quo, principally directed against the

Hungarian nobility. As Catholics and imperialists, the Habsburg monarchy persuaded the Orthodox clergy in Transylvania to accept Papal authority, and promised that Vlachs who joined the new **Uniate Church** (see p.358) would be granted equality with the Nationes. Although the Diet's opposition ensured the retraction of this promise in 1701, Bishop Ion Micu and the intellectuals of the 'Transylvanian School' (*Şcoala Ardealana*) agitated for equal rights and articulated the Vlachs' growing consciousness of being **Romanians**. By far the largest ethnic group, they now began to assert their 'original claim' on Transylvania and solidarity with their kinsfolk across the Carpathians. Attempts to challenge the feudal order by violence culminated in the great 1784-5 **peasant rebellion** led by Horea, Crişan and Cloşca; the defeat of which only stimulated efforts to attain liberation by constitutional means – such as the famous *Supplex Libellus Valachorum* petition submitted to the Emperor in 1791, which was predictably rejected by the Transylvanian Diet.

The gradual development of liberal and nationalist movements in **Moldavia and Wallachia** stemmed from a variety of causes. The ideals of the Romantic movement and the French Revolution gained hold amongst the intelligentsia and many young boyars; while the success of Serbian and Greek independence movements and the emergence of capitalist structures in the principalities signified that Turkish dominance and feudalism were in decline. A rebellion in support of the Greek independence struggle organised by the Phanariot Alexandre Ypsilanti attracted little following within Moldavia, but the example inspired a major uprising against Phanariot rule in Wallachia, led by **Tudor Vladimirescu** (1821). Although defeated, this uprising persuaded the Turks that it was high time for **the end of Phanariot rule**, and the restoration of power to native boyars.

Fired by ambition, Panslavist ideals, and fear of Habsburg encroachment (manifest in 1774, when Austria annexed the region henceforth known as **Bucovina**), Tsarist **Russia** presented itself as the guardian of the Ottomans' Christian subjects in 1779, and played an increasing role in Balkan politics during the C19. A series of Russo-Turkish wars during which Moldavia and Bessarabia were occupied by foreign armies led to the Treaty of Adrianople (1829), by which Moldavia and Wallachia became Russian protectorates. The Tsarist governor General **Kiseleff** was in no sense a revolutionary, but introduced liberal reforms and assemblies in both principalities under the terms of the **Règlement organique**, which remained in force after the Russians withdrew in 1834, having selected two rulers. Of these, **Michael Sturdza** was the more despotic but also the most energetic; levying heavy taxes to construct roads, dikes, hospitals and schools in Moldavia.

Given the boyar's dominance of the assemblies, economic development took precedence over the political and social reforms demanded by sections of the liberal bourgeoisie, particularly the growing number of Romanians who had studied in France. The **democratic movement** which emerged in both principalities – led by **Nicolae Golescu**, **Ion Brătianu**, **Nicolae Bălcescu**, **Mihail Kogălniceanu** and others – campaigned against the *Règlement* and for the unification of Moldavia and Wallachia, which was anticipated by the removal of customs barriers between the two in 1846. These movements briefly came to power during the **revolutions of 1848**, which heightened nationalist consciousness in the principalities and amongst the Romanians of Transylvania (see below).

Russian occupation (1848-51) and Habsburg opposition at the Paris Congress (1856) thwarted the nationalist cause until 1859, when both assemblies were persuaded to elect a single ruler, **Alexandru Ioan Cuza**, thereby circumventing the restrictions imposed to prevent the **unification of Moldavia and Wallachia**. French support enabled the *United Principalities* (renamed *Rumania* in 1862) to weather Habsburg hostility, and the government embarked on a series of reforms, the most important of which were the **abolition of serfdom** and the expropriation of the huge monastic estates. Although the peasants were still bound to pay for the land 'given' to them (and, as a result, fell into greater debt than before), these measures enraged the landowning classes and other conservative elements, who forced Cuza's abdication in 1866. They decided that henceforth 'the dynasty shall remain apart' – ie. without native ties – and selected a foreign candidate for the throne, Prince Karl (later King Carol I), the first of Rumania's **Hohenzollern monarchs**.

During the C19, events **in Transylvania** followed a different course. There, popular support for the **1848 revolution** split along nationalist lines. Whereas the peasants universally welcomed the abolition of serfdom, the Romanian population opposed the Diet's unification of Transylvania with Hungary, which Magyars of all classes greeted with enthusiasm, while the Saxons were luke-warm on both issues. Following protest meetings at Blaj, **Avram Iancu** formed Romanian guerilla bands to oppose the Hungarians; and belated attempts by Kossuth and Bălcescu to compromise on the issue of Romanian rights came too late to create a united front against the Tsarist armies which invaded Transylvania on behalf of the Habsburgs. As in Hungary, the Habsburgs introduced martial law and widespread repression in the aftermath of the revolution.

As a result of the *Ausgleich* establishing the Dual Monarchy (1867), the Transylvanian Diet was abolished and the region was united with Hungary under the direct control of Budapest. The government of **Kálman Tisza** (1875-90) and subsequent administrations pursued a policy of **'Magyarisation'** in Transylvania, on the grounds that 'Hungary's interests demanded adoption of the most extreme chauvinism' (in the words of Dezsö Bánffy, the PM during the late 1890s). Hungarian was made the official language and a barrage of laws relating to education and the press were passed in an effort to undermine Romanian culture. The cultural association *ASTRA* (founded in 1861) acted in defence of this until the establishment of the **Romanian National Party** in 1881, which maintained close links with kindred parties across the Carpàthians.

There, the last vestiges of Ottoman control were abolished by the Berlin treaty (1878) ending the Russo-Turkish war, which restored the **Dobrudja** to Rumania. By this treaty Rumania also acquired territory to the south of the Danube, which was one of the many bones of contention underlying the **Balkan Wars** (1911-13) embroiling Rumania, Bulgaria, Serbia, Macedonia and Greece. The influence of **foreign capitalism** increased enormously around the turn of the century, as Rumania's mineral wealth – particularly its **oil** – inspired competition amongst the great powers. While liberal and conservative politicians engaged in ritualistic parliamentary squabbles, however, nothing was done about the worsening impoverishment of the peasantry and the conditions of the industrial working class. Peasant grievances exploded in 1907 during the **răscoala** – a nationwide uprising which was savagely crushed and then followed by a series of limited, ineffectual agrarian reforms.

Rumania stayed neutral during the **First World War** until 1916, when it joined the Triple Entente and attacked the Austro-Hungarian forces in Transylvania (which was allied to the Central Powers). After brief advances the tide turned against Rumania, as first Bucharest and then Iaşi were captured, and the country was forced to sign an onerous peace treaty in May 1918. By October, however, the collapse of the Central Powers on the western front reversed this situation entirely. The Austro-Hungarian empire rapidly fragmented as its subject races established their own states with the support of the Entente and President Wilson. In **Transylvania**, the Romanian assembly of Alba Iulia declared the region's **union with Rumania** to scenes of wild acclaim, and in the face of furious Hungarian opposition. This union was subsequently upheld by the Entente powers and the **Treaty of Trianon** in 1920.

'Greater Romania' (1921-44)

The country's enlarged territory was signified by the adoption of the name **Greater Romania**, but hardly improved the lives of the mass of the population. The expropriation of Hungarian estates in Transylvania applied not only to the nobility, but to Magyar smallholders; and the many of the peasants who expected to benefit from the agrarian reform of 1921 were rapidly disillusioned when speculators and boyars appropriated much of the **land** by financial manipulation. Despite its parliamentary majority after 1928, the **National Peasant Party** led by **Iuliu Maniu** pursued conservative policies, constrained by falling demand for Romanian exports following the world **economic crisis** of 1929, vested interests and entrenched corruption. Foreign companies exploited Romania's assets with the help of native politicians and compradors, while the government crushed workers' protests led by the illegal **Communist Party** – such as the **1933 strike** of railway and oil workers – by using the army, which was also employed against Csángó Hungarians' revolt the following year.

Political repression and corruption worsened during the reign of **Carol II**, who was crowned in 1930. The speculations of the palace *camarilla* and Carol's influential Jewish mistress **Magda Lupescu** were a public scandal which fueled the anti-semitism rife in Romanian society. From 1927 onwards, the enactment of discriminatory laws was the milder face of **anti-semitism**; far worse were murderous attacks by the *Legion of St. Michael*, a fascist movement later known as the **Iron Guard**. The Guard's terrorism was also directed against the government, and provided the excuse for Carol to ban all political parties in 1938, after ordering the execution of the Legionary leader **Codreanu**.

During the late 1930s, **Nazi Germany's influence** grew through economic penetration, the Iron Guard, *Volkdeutsche* sentiments amongst the Saxons, and the Reich's burgeoning military power; which was feebly opposed by France and Britain. Secret protocols in the Ribbentrop-Molotov pact and the defeat of France allowed the Soviet Union to present an ultimatum demanding control of **Bessarabia and northern Bucovina** in June 1940; while on August 30, Hitler decided to meet **Hungarian claims on Transylvania** halfway, and 'advised' that Romania surrender the northern part of the region to Hungary. Carol was obliged to abdicate and flee, while his heir Michael ceded dictatorial powers to **Marshal Antonescu**, who styled himself *Conducator*, or Führer.

Romania entered the **Second World War** by joining the Nazi invasion of Russia in June 1941, with the objective of regaining Bessarabia and northern Bucovina. In Romania and the Hungarian-controlled area of Transylvania, Jews were rounded up and used as slave labour before their deportation to extermination camps in central Europe; both governments giving enthusiastic support to the **Holocaust**. By 1943, however, the USSR was rolling-up Antonescu's *Transdniestrian Republic* (Bessarbia, plus land beyond the Dniestr, which Romania had annexed for good measure), and using POWs to form a 'Free Romanian Legion'. Back home, opposition to the war mounted as the Russians drew nearer, and on **August 23 1944** a military coup overthrew the Antonescu regime just as Soviet troops crossed the border – a date henceforth commemorated as **Liberation** Day.

The People's Republic (1944-65)

While the Romanian army subordinated itself to Soviet command, and fought alongside the Red Army and the POW legion to push the Nazis out of Transylvania, Hungary and Czechoslovakia, the struggle to determine the state of **post war Romania** was already underway. The government formed under the premiership of Dr. **Petru Groza** in March 1945 included right-wing politicians as a sop to conservative opinion and the Western powers (which maintained observers in Bucharest), but the key posts were occupied by Communists, whose influence ultimately derived from the presence of the Red Army. The **land reform** of 1945 benefited millions of peasants at the expense of the Saxons and Swabians of Transylvania and the Banat, who had become the biggest landowners since the dispossession of the Magyars; while **women** were enfranchised for the first time in 1946, their votes contributing to the election of another ostensibly 'balanced' government.

Like Groza's first administration, this included leading capitalists and former Guardists, whom the **Communists** initially wooed, since their first aim was to eliminate the left and centre parties. The leadership of the **National Peasant Party** (itself hardly less tarnished than the right, having organised anti-Hungarian atrocities in Transylvania) played into their hands by secretly meeting US officials, enabling the Communists to dispose of them on espionage charges in 1947. At the end of the year King Michael abdicated and Romania was declared a **People's Republic**.

The **nationalisation** of industries, banks and utilities (June 1948) placed the main economic levers in Communist hands. Thereafter the bourgeoisie were assailed on all fronts, and the Party openly declared its intention to reshape society by applying **Stalinist policies**. While vital sectors of the proletariat were favoured to secure their loyalty, 80,000 arrests were necessary to overcome peasant resistance to **collectivisation**, which began in March 1949. **Police terror** was used against real or potential opponents, and formed the ultimate weapon in the Party's policy of **religious persecution**. This was primarily directed against the 'renegade' Uniate Church, which was 'liquidated' in 1949, and the churches of the ethnic minorities. Victims were incarcerated in prisons like Jilava and Piteşti, or conscripted for reed-cutting in the Delta or work on the **Danube-Black Sea Canal**, a 'hero project' which claimed over 100,000 lives before the '*Canalul Mortii*' was abandoned in 1953.

The purging of 192,000 members and powerful 'Muscovites' like **Teohari Gregorescu**, **Vasile Luca** and **Ana Pauker** in 1950-52 resulted from bitter **conflicts within the Party**, and heralded the ascendancy of the 'nationalist' faction led by **Gheorghe Gheorghiu-Dej**. These Communists resented the exploitative terms of Soviet-Romanian trade, and

doubted the wisdom of blindly applying Soviet policies to the economy, which had failed to meet the targets set by the 1951-55 Plan. The **'New Course'** announced in 1953 laid more stress on balanced economic development, and achieved its planned target of 13% annual growth; while the Party leadership became increasingly assertive of Romania's right to be a developed industrial nation, which contradicted the role of 'breadbasket' assigned to the country by the Eastern bloc organisation **Comecon**.

The Party's refusal to sever contacts with China after the Sino-Soviet split, and increasing disagreements with Comecon during the early 1960s, reflected the **Romanian nationalism** which had first become evident on the domestic front a decade earlier. By arresting the leadership of the left-wing Hungarian People's Alliance and establishing an 'Autonomous Hungarian Region' in the Székely Land, Gheorghiu-Dej simultaneously decapitated the Magyar political organisation in Transylvania while erecting a façade of minority rights which allowed him to state that the 'nationality question' had been resolved in 1952. Ever since then, the Party has endeavoured to create a 'unitary' state whose population accepts the RCP as the best guarantor of 'national interests' – crudely defined as the freedom to pursue economic and foreign policies at variance with those laid down by Moscow, the Warsaw Pact or Comecon. Formulated during the mid-'50s and early '60s, when the first moves towards attaining them were made, these goals have been relentlessly pursued by Nicolae Ceauşescu, who became Party leader following the **death of Gheorghiu-Dej**.

'Years of Light': the Ceauşescu era

In Romania today, the period since 1965 is officially known as the *epoca* of **Nicolae Ceauşescu**, whose impact on the country has been undeniable. His **foreign policy** has gained Romania the reputation of being the 'maverick' or 'independent' state in the Eastern bloc, which maintained links with **Albania**, **China** and **Israel** after the USSR and its satellites severed relations; refused to join the Warsaw Pact's attack on **Czechoslovakia**

in 1968; criticised the invasion of **Afghanistan**; and symbolically defied the Soviet boycott by sending its national team to the Los Angeles Olympics. Other well-publicised acts have included calls for the removal of **nuclear weapons** from Europe and the announcement of a unilateral 5% cut in Romanian **military spending**.

The sincerity of many of these actions has recently been questioned following revelations of a concerted campaign of **disinformation** designed to conceal espionage and arms sales abroad, and win Western support for the country's **industrialisation** programme. This absorbed 30% of the GNP throughout the 1970s, but the expected rewards have failed to materialise, whilst shortages of energy and Ceauşescu's insistence that food be exported to repay Western loans has exacerbated already **declining living standards** during the 1980s.

Ceauşescu's image in the West has also been tarnished by reports of growing **human rights** violations. Censorship, the 'Typewriter law' (requiring that every machine be registered with the police) and the persecution of ethnic minorities have attracted most attention. But it's his policy of trying to force up the birth-rate by effectively outlawing contraception and abortion, lowering the marriageable age to 15, and ordering that **women** be screened for pregnancy by the 'Baby Police' that's had the most widespread effects. The underlying reasons for demands that every couple should produce four children as a 'lofty patriotic duty' are probably fears that a diminishing workforce might jeopardise economic growth, and anxiety about the higher birth-rate of the country's million or more Gypsies.

Gypsies' status as the 'untouchables' of Romanian society excites no comment, but other **ethnic minorities** have champions abroad, mainly in Hungary and West Germany. Although Romania's ethnic minorities are ostensibly protected by the Constitution (Articles 17 and 21) and other laws, evidence suggests that in reality the Party is committed to their '**Romanianisation**'. Minority-language education and literature has been severely restricted, and their history and cultural artefacts have been rewritten, expropriated or destroyed; whilst on a more personal level, communication with friends and relatives abroad is curtailed, and families are pressured to give their children Romanian names. Official chauvinism has chiefly been directed against the 1½-2 million **Magyars**

(including the Székely and Csángós), causing a notable worsening of diplomtic **relations with Hungary**; nowadays, neither government does much to conceal their mutual animosity. Ceauşescu can live with this, but West German demands that Romania's 200,000 ethnic **Germans** (Swabians and Saxons) be granted the right of unrestricted **emigration** threatens to end the practice of selling exit permits for 8,000 DM per head, which has previously earned the regime roughly £250,000,000 a year.

In November 1987 there were totally unexpected **anti-Ceauşescu riots** in Braşov, followed by non-violent sympathy demonstrations in Timişoara and Iaşi. **Silviu Brucan**, a former Party eminence, then issued a statement to the Western press warning that 'the cup of privation is now full and the workers no longer accept that they can be treated like obedient servants'. Ceauşescu's response was to rush food and Securitate to the cities, but at the subsequent RCP Congress he rejected any change in economic or social policies and gave notice of a purge within the Party.

Almost everyone agrees that **the future** looks bleak, with further austerity on the cards and only the token sacking or reshuffling of ministers to provide scapegoats for the utter failure of the Leader's grand strategems. His policy of allocating vital posts to relatives and preventing anyone else from developing a power base seems likely to stave off the possibility of a coup unless the bulwark of the regime, the Securitate, engineers it. Ceauşescu has made plain his opposition to *glasnost*, and few Romanians see any possibilty of change until their President dies (his ill-health is rumoured), in which case it's expected that surviving members of the brood will attempt to remain in control. Aside from a rebellion by the Securitate, the only force that seems capable of overthrowing the nastiest regime in Eastern Europe is the Soviet Union – a prospect which arouses both alarm and hope.

MONUMENTAL CHRONOLOGY

pre-4000 BC	Tribes roam the valleys and plains.	Remains of bones and weapons found at Băile Herculane.
4000BC	Earliest settlements on the Dobrudja.	Habaşeşti Neolithic village; 'Hamangia Culture' carvings include **goddess figures** and the **'Hamangia Thinker'**.
3000BC	Copper-working in Transylvania.	Axes, adzes etc. exhibited in Cluj History Museum.
C7-C6BC	Coast colonised by Greek trading ports (ruled by Roman and Byzantine empires from C1 AD onwards).	Walls dating from foundation of **Histria** (675BC), **Tomis** and **Callatis** (C6BC) overlaid with **Roman and Byzantine** remains, including a fine mosaic floor at Constanţa.
C3-C1AD	**Dacians** inhabit area of present day Romania; ruled by Burebista in C1Bc, and Decebalus (87-106AD).	**Goldwork** (C3BC). Excavations of many earthworks, citadels and sanctuaries, including **Sarmizegetusa**, the Dacian capital in the Orăştie Mtns.
101-271	**Roman conquest** of Dacia (completed 106) produces a fusion of cultures: the **Daco-Romans**, held to be the ancestors of the Romanian people.	**Trajan's Bridge** at Turnu-Severin, forts and the ruins of **Ulpa Traiana** show the Roman line of advance. The **Tropaeum Traiani** at Adamclissi commemorates the Roman victory.
271-C9	Goths, Huns, Avars and Bulgars carve successive empires here; Slavs begin to settle from 567 onwards	Inscriptions, coins and burial remains either support the **Theory of Daco-Romananian continuity**, or don't; the debates continue.
896-C13	**Magyars** gradually wrest control of Transylvania from native voivodes; **Saxons** settle there after 1143; and in 1224 **Székely** migrate into eastern Transylvania.	Indigenous structures – the **Bihara Citadel** near Oradea, the **Rupestral Complex** (C9-11) at Basarabi – and those of the newcomers: eg. **Cîrţa Monastery**, the 'Passage of Stairs' in Sibiu, and parts of some **walled towns**.
C13	Radu Negru founds the Bassarab dynasty and the principality of **Wallachia** south of the Carpathians, Tartars invade Transylvania in 1241 and 1284, giving impetus to the building of walls and citadels.	**Negru Vodă Monastery** founded in 1215 at Cîmpulung, the first Wallachian capital, together with many churches (walled during the C15). The one at **Cisnădioara** (c, 1200) at **St. Michael's Cathedral** in Alba Iulia are examples of C13 **Romnesque architecture**.
C14	East of the Carpathians, Bogdan Vodă founds the principality of **Moldavia** (1364) with Rădăuţi as its capital.	**Citadels** of **Făgăraş** and **Rîşnov** (rebuilt C15). The Court at **Curtea de Argeş** (c. 1370) precedes **Cozia Church** which marks the advent of **Byzantine architecture** in Wallachia, Styles in the north are divergent – eg, the wooden **Church on the Hill** at Ieud (c.1364) and Rădăuţi's **Bogdana**

Church, Braşov's **Black Church**, the first phase of St Michael's in Cluj, and **Bran Castle** (1377) exemplify Transylvanian **Gothic architecture**.

C15   **Turkish expansion** is checked by Hunyadi in Transylvania, Vlad Ţepeş in Wallachia and Stephen the Great (1457-1504) in Moldavia. After the 1437 Bobîlna peasant uprising the Magyar nobility, Saxons and Székely form the **Union of Three Nations** to defend their privileges.

Bistriţa Monastery founded in Moldavia (1407), **Hărman**, **Prejmer** and other **fortified churches**, the **castles at Lazar, Poienari and Hunedoara** and the strengthening of the **walls around Sighişoara, Cluj and Sibiu** are all monuments to a period of violence and insecurity. Stephen founds the **monasteries** of **Voroneţ** (1488), **Neamţ** (1497) and **Putna** (1504) in Moldavia.

C16   **Peasant uprising** of 1514, Following the Ottoman and Habsburg partition of Hungary, Transylvania struggles to stay independent, while Moldavia and Wallachia acknowledge Ottoman suzerainty.

Monasteries of **Arbore**, **Humor**, **Moldoviţa** and **Suceviţa** are built; later, their walls and those of Voroneţ are painted with magnificent **frescoes**. The **Episcopal Church** at Curtea de Argeş (1517) rises above the limitations of Byzantine architecture in Wallachia; while Sibiu's Councillers' Tower and the **Sighişoara citadel** are typical of C16 Saxon buildings in Transylvania.

C17   In 1600, **Michael the Brave** briefly unites Moldavia, Wallachia and Transylvania, Moldavia and Wallachia have a respite from misrule during the reigns of Vasile Lupu (1633-52) and Constantin Brîncoveanu (1688-1714) but later succumb to the **Phanariots**; while Transylvania has its 'Golden Age' under Gábor Bethlen (1613-29).

Between the construction of Dragomirna and Cetăţuia monasteries, **Moldavian church architecture** reaches its apogee with the building of Iaşi's **Trei Ierarhi** (1639) covered in intricate stone-carvings. In Wallachia, the monasteries of Arnota, Gorova and Polovragi precede **Hurez Monastery** (1691-93), the largest, most impressive example of **Brîncoveanu-style architecture**, which also characteries Sinaia Monastery (1695).

C18   The **Ottomans withdraw** in 1718. Serbs and Swabians settle on the Banat. In 1784 a peasant uprising occurs in Transylvania. The Romanians' petition for political equality is rejected in 1791.

Despite the Creţelescu Church in the Brîncoveanu style, the C18 is more notable for the construction of splendid **wooden churches in Maramures** – at **Rozleava**, **Bogdan Vodă** and **Şurdeşti** – and many **Baroque churches, palaces and cathedrals**, eg. in Oradea, Cluj, Sibiu and Timişoara. Huge **Vauban-style citadels** are raised at Arad, Alba Iulia and Oradea.

C19	Magyars revolt against Habsburg rule and declare the union of Transylvania with Hungary despite Romanian opposition (1848-49). In 1859 **Moldavia and Wallachia unite** to form Romania, while after 1868 the Hungarians pursue a policy of '**Magyarisation**' in Transylvania.	In Bucharest, the construction of the Şos. Kiseleff and the Calea Victoriei reflects **French influence**; Manuc's Inn, the Şuţu Palace and many new buildings are founded in the capital and after 1859 universities are established at Iasi and Bucharest. Sibiu's *Podul de Fier*, the Brukenthal Museum, electric streetlighting in Timişoara, the building of railways and a channel through the Iron Gates are all aspects of **modernisation** affecting Transylvania. Monumental buildings in Iaşi, Tîrgu Mureş etc. embody the era's assertive nationalism.
1907	**Peasant uprising** in Romania.	Ploieşti oilfields developed by foreign capital. The Mosque at Constanşa is the first **ferro-concrete** structure (1910).
1918	**Union of Transylvania with Romania**; confirmed by the Trianon Treaty (1920) despite Magyar opposition.	**Monumental Orthodox Cathedrals** constructed in Alba Iulia, Tîrgu Mureş, Timişoara, Cluj etc. to celebrate the status of 'Greater Romania' in the 1920s. In the '30s, the Royal Palace and the **Arc de Triumpf** are built in the capital.
1944	Romania liberated from Nazis.	Damage caused by Allied bombs is rapidly repaired and **high-rise blocks** are built to meet the housing shortage (eg. in Ploieşti and Bucharest).
1949	Establishment of **Communist Party** rule.	Romania's **industrialisation** and the style of architecture are strongly **Soviet-influenced** – eg. the *Casa Şcinteii* and the first, abortive attempt to dig the Danube-Black Sea Canal using slave labour. The **Friendship Bridge** (completed in 1954) and the **Iron Gates dam** (1971) are both joint ventures with neighbouring socialist countries; while the Galaţi steel mill and the coastal **tourist complexes** have a Western-input. The **Danube-Black Sea Canal** is opened in 1984. Currently, major construction projects include the **Metro extension** and the *Centru Civic* in the capital; the Dîmboviţa canal; and the creation of Romania's first **nuclear power station** at Cernavoda on the Danube.
1965	**Ceauşescu** becomes leader following the death of Gheorghiu-Dej, and pursues a nationalist economic policy contrary to the wishes of Comecon, which is reluctant to help. This persuades Ceauşescu to seek credit and technical assistance from the West.	
1977	Earthquake in Bucharest.	

DRACULA, THE 'BLOOD COUNTESS', VAMPIRES AND WEREWOLVES

Truth, legends and fiction swirl about the figure of **Dracula** like a cloak, and perceptions of him differ sharply. Inside Romania today, schoolbooks and historians extol him as a patriot and a champion of order in lawless times; while the outside world knows Dracula as the vampire count of a thousand cinematic fantasies derived from Bram Stoker's novel published in 1898 – a spoof-figure or a ghoul. The disparity in images is easily explained, for while **vampires** feature in native folklore (about which, more below), Romanians make no associations between them and the historical figure of Dracula, a Wallachian prince known in his homeland as *Vlad Țepeș* – or **Vlad the Impaler**. During his lifetime (1431?-1476) Vlad achieved renown beyond Wallachia's borders as a successful fighter against the Turks and a ruthless ruler; his reputation for cruelty spread throughout Europe by the newly-invented printing presses (whose pamphlets were the bestsellers of the C15) and the word of his political enemies – notably the Saxons of Transylvania. Yet at this time, Vlad was not known as a vampire, although some charged that he was in league with the Devil.

During the C18, numerous well-publicised incidents of vampirism sparked a 'vampire craze' in Europe, while in 1871 Sheridan Le Fanu wrote a short story, *Carmilla*, which featured a female vampire. These fired the imagination of Bram Stoker, who unearthed the figure of Vlad Țepeș during his researches in the British Museum library (or may have learned of him from the Hungarian traveller Armenius Vambéry), and delved deep into Romanian folklore. Stoker's fictional Dracula also owed something to another historical personage – **Elizabeth Báthori**, the **'Blood Countess'**, born almost a century after Vlad's death – and was possibly influenced by the ghastly 'Jack the Ripper' murders which happened a decade before Stoker began his book, part of which he wrote whilst living near Whitechapel.

The life and times of Vlad Țepeș – the historical Dracula
'*He was not very tall, but very stocky and strong, with a cold and terrible appearance, a strong and aquiline nose, swollen nostrils, a thin reddish face in which very long eyelashes framed large wide-open green eyes; the bushy black eyebrows made them appear threatening. His face and chin were shaven, but for a moustache. The swollen temples increased the bulk of his head. A bull's neck connected his head to his body from which black curly locks hung on his wide-shouldered person*'.

Such was the Papal legate's impression of Vlad Țepeș – then in his thirties and a prisoner at the court of Visegrád in Hungary. He had been born in Sighișoara and raised at Tîrgoviște after his father, Vlad Dracul, became Voivode of Wallachia in 1436. Young Vlad's privileged **childhood** effectively ended in 1444, when he and his brother Radu were sent by their father as hostages to Anatolia, to curry favour with the Turkish Sultan. By this move, Vlad Dracul incurred the emnity of János Hunyadi, prince of Transylvania, who arranged for Dracul to be murdered in 1447; and Vlad and Radu were released by the Turks to be pawns in the struggle between their expanding empire, Hunyadi and the new ruler of Wallachia. The experience of five years of Turkish captivity and years of exile in Moldavia and Transylvania shaped Vlad's personality irrevocably, and educated him in guile and terrorism.

Seeking a vassal, Hunyadi helped Vlad to become **ruler of Wallachia** in 1456; but promptly died, leaving him dangerously exposed. 'Bowing even Our head and the heads of Our subjects' to the Hungarian king, and signing a defence pact and free trade agreement with the Saxons of Brașov, Vlad quickly decided that it was also prudent to pay an annual tribute of 10,000 gold ducats to the Sultan whilst he consolidated his power in Wallachia. For generations there, the boyar families had defied and frequently deposed their own rulers, including Vlad's father and his elder brother Mircea, whom they buried alive; now, Vlad's policy towards the Turks and boyars followed the old Romanian proverb *Saruta mana pe care n'o poti musca* – 'Kiss the hand you cannot bite'.

His method of law enforcement was

simple: practically all crimes and individuals offending him were punished by death; and Vlad's customary means of execution was **impaling people**. Victims were bound spreadeagled whilst a stake was hammered up their rectum, and then raised aloft and left to die in agony, for all to see. The size of the stake was determined by the victim's rank — high dignitaries rated ones as big as telegraph poles. To test his subjects' honesty, Vlad disguised himself and moved amongst them; left coins in shops and over-compensated merchants who had been robbed; and slew all that failed the test. Foreigners reported the demise of theft, and Dracula symbolically placed a golden cup beside a lonely fountain where 'whoever would like to drink water' could use it and 'no one dared to take it away'. On Easter day in 1459, Vlad eliminated the potentially rebellious boyars en masse by inviting them and their families to dine at his palace; guards then entered and seized them, impaling many forthwith whilst the remainder were marched off to labour at Poienari. In a similar vein, he invited Wallachia's disabled, unemployed and workshy to feast with him at Tîrgovişte, and asked if they wished to be free of life's sufferings. Receiving an affirmative reply Dracula had them all burnt, justifying his action as a measure to ensure that 'there be no poor people in my country but all rich people, and so that none ever be concerned with poverty or disability'.

All this was but a ramp for **Dracula's ambition** to be the acknowledged ruler of a mighty power, which caused much **feuding with the Saxons** of Braşov, Sibiu and the Bîrsa land. It began in 1457, when he accused them of supporting claimants to his throne, and decided to end the Saxon merchants' practice of trading freely throughout Wallachia. When they persisted, Dracula led his army through the Red Tower Pass to burn Saxon villages, and had any of their people found inside Wallachia impaled. In 1460, Vlad annihilated the forces of his rival, Dan III, who invaded with the support of Braşov; and on this occasion dined in a garden amongst the impaled bodies of his enemies, using a holy icon as a dish, according to the *Chronicon Mellicense*. A month later he attacked the Bîrsa land, and impaled hundreds of townsfolk on Sprenghi Hill within sight of Braşov's defenders before marching off to ravage the Făgăraş region.

At the same time, Vlad plotted to turn **against the Turks** and form alliances with his cousin Stephen in Moldavia, and the Hungarian monarchy. Having defaulted on payments of tribute for two years, and nailed the turbans of two emissaries to their heads when they refused to doff them, Dracula declared war by raiding Turkish garrisons from Vidin to Giurgiu. He boasted of having killed 23,883, 'apart from those who were burnt inside houses, or whose heads were not brought to Our officials'. A massive army led by Sultan Mehmet II crossed the Danube into Wallachia in June 1462, but found itself advancing through countryside denuded of inhabitants, food and water, 'with the sun burning so that the armour of the *ghazzis* could well be used to cook kebabs'. On the night of the 17th Dracula's army raided the Turkish camp inflicting heavy casualties, and a few days later the demoralised invaders approached Tîrgovişte only to recoil in horror. En route to the capital Vlad had prepared a forest of stakes 1km by 3km wide, upon which 20,000 Turkish and Bulgarian captives were impaled. Shattered by their losses and these terror tactics, the Turks retreated home in disorder.

Dracula's downfall has been attributed to the Saxons, who used every opportunity to support his enemies and defame him throughout Europe. Most likely they forged the implausible 'treason note' (in which Vlad puportedly offered to help the Sultan capture Transylvania) — the pretext for Mátyás Corvinus to order Dracula's arrest in November 1462. Until 1475, he was a 'guest' at Visegrád, where Mátyás would introduce him to Turkish ambassadors to discomfort them, while Wallachia's throne was occupied by Dracula's pliable brother **Radu 'The Handsome'**, who had once served as the Sultan's catamite. Released by Mátyás to continue the anti-Turkish struggle, Vlad resided for a year in Sibiu (where the townsfolk deemed it politic to allow him hospitality) and regained his throne in 1476. His triumph was short-lived, however, for Radu offered the boyars an alternative to 'rule by the stake' and the chance to placate the Turks, which they seized gratefully. In circumstances that remain unclear (some say that a servant was bribed to slay him), Vlad was betrayed by the boyars and killed. His head disappeared – reputedly sent to the Sultan as a present – while the Impaler's decapitated body was buried inside the church at Snagov Monastery, where it remains to this day. **His tomb** bears no inscription, and was originally sited just inside the door, as if to denigrate him. The lack of any fresco portraits of the Impaler in medieval churches suggests that for many years afterwards, attempts were made to erase **the memory of Dracula in Romania**; although in the Ceauşescu epoch, Vlad has been rehabilitated as a wise lawgiver and a fighter for national independence. In 1985, the writer Adrian Panescu denounced Stoker's novel and the Dracula films as 'only one page in a vast output of political pornography directed against us by our enemies', an attack 'on the very idea of being a Romanian'. Vlad's cruelties are minimised or forgiven , and apologists argue that impalement was widely practised by the Turks (as Vlad would have seen in his youth), and by Stephen of Moldavia, besides being prescribed in the old Wallachian *Vlastares* penal code.

The 'Blood Countess' of Čachtice

If Vlad won renown and had his deeds posthumously justified on the grounds of political exigency, the same cannot be said of the **Countess Elizabeth Báthori**, whose crimes were plainly motivated by personal sadism alone. Due to her sex (then considered to be incapable of such deeds) and rank, records of her belated trial for mass murder were hidden, and mention of her very name subsequently prohibited by royal command. She was born in 1560, the offspring of two branches of the noble Báthori family, whose constant intermarriage may have accounted for her periodic fainting spells and fits of uncontrollable rage. (Other Báthoris, such as Prince 'Crazy' Gábor, were similarly afflicted). As a child she was intelligent and well educated, being fluent in Latin, Hungarian and German at a time when many nobles, including the ruling prince of Transylvania, were barely literate. Brought up in the family castle at Ecsed (today Nagyecsed, a humble town near the Hungarian-Romanian border), she absorbed from her relatives the notion that peasants were little more than cattle – to be harshly punished for any act of insubordination.

As was customary in the C16, her marriage was arranged for dynastic reasons, and an illegitimate pregnancy hushed up. Betrothed in 1571 – the same year that her cousin István became Prince of Transylvania – she was married at fifteen to twenty-one year-old Ferenc Nádasdy. Over the next decade Ferenc was usually away fighting Turks, earning his reputation as the 'Black Knight', and Elizabeth grew bored at their home in Sárvár Castle (p. 149). There she began to torture serving women, an 'entertainment' that gradually became obsessional. With the assistance of her maids Dorothea Szentes and Anna Darvulia (with whom she had a lesbian relationship), Elizabeth cudgelled and stuck pins into servants to 'discipline' them; forced them to lie naked in the snowy courtyard and then doused them with cold water until they froze to death. On his return Ferenc baulked at this (although he, too, enjoyed brutalising servants), and it wasn't until after his demise in 1604 that Elizabeth started torturing and murdering without restraint. Her victims were invariably women or girls, and – most importantly – were only peasants.

Killing peasants could be done with impunity. Poor women could always be enticed into service at Castle Beckov and Castle Čachtice – Elizabeth's residences after she quit Sárvár, both then located within the borders of Transylvania – and, should word of their deaths leak out, the authorities would hardly believe the accusations of the victims' parents against the Countess Báthori. With the assistance of Szentes, Darvulia, her son's former wet-nurse Helena Jo and one man, the dwarflike Fizcko, Elizabeth allowed her sadistic fantasies full rein. On occasion she bit chunks of flesh from servants' breasts and necks – probably the origin of the legend that she bathed in blood to keep her own skin white and translucent.

In this fashion Elizabeth murdered over six hundred women, and could probably have continued doing so undetected, had not Darvulia died. Griefstricken, she formed an attachment to a local widow, Erzsi Majorova, who encouraged the Countess to seek aristocratic girls for her victims. Inquiries by *their* parents could not be so easily ignored by the authorities who, in any case, by now had their own motives for investigating '*Die Blutgräfin*'. Ferenc Nádasdy had loaned the Habsburg crown

17,000 gulden, which Elizabeth had persistently – and vainly – demanded back. Should she be found guilty of serious crimes this debt would be forfited. Others also had the knives out – notably Paul, Elizabeth's son, who had grown up apart from her at Sárvár, and the Palatine, Count Thurzo, both of whom were anxious to prevent the confiscation of the Báthori estates and gathered evidence against her throughout 1610.

On December 29 Thurzo's men raided Čachtice manor, and on entry almost tripped over the corpse of a servant whom Elizabeth had just bludgeoned for stealing a pear. Thurzo imprisoned the 'damned woman' in her own castle immediately, and a few days later her accomplices were tried in camera at Bytca, implicating themselves after torture, though she was secretly imprisoned in Čachtice so that (in Thurzo's words) 'the families which have won such high honours on the battlefield shall not be disgraced...by the murky shadow of this bestial female'. Due to his cover-up the scandal was mainly confined to court circles, although when Elizabeth died in 1614 the locals protested at her burial in Čachtice cemetery. She was later re-buried at Nagyesced in the precincts of the family vault.

Vampires and Werewolves

Horrible though their deeds were, neither Vlad the Impaler nor Countess Báthori were accused of vampirism during their lifetimes, but only during the early C18, when a 'vampire craze' swept across Europe. Centuries before then, however, **vampires** were an integral part of folklore in Eastern and Southeastern Europe: known as *vámpír* in Hungary, *upir* in Poland and Russia, and *strigoi* in Moldavia and Wallachia. Details of their habits and characteristics vary from place to place, but in their essentials are fairly similar. A vampire is an undead corpse, animated by its spirit and with a body that fails to decay, no matter how long in the grave. Although vampirism can be contagious – as described below – a vampire is usually created when a person dies and the soul is unable to enter heaven or hell. The reason may be that the person has died in a 'state of sin' – by suicide, for example, or without receiving the last rites (in the case of heretics) – or because the soul has been prevented from leaving the body. Hang-ing was a form of death dreaded by Romanians, who believed that tying the neck 'forces the soul down outward'; while the Orthodox custom of shrouding mirrors in the home of the deceased was intended to prevent the spirit from being 'trapped' by seeing its reflection. People might occasionally be born as vampires, and bear stigmata such as a dark-coloured spot on the head or a rudi-mentary tail.

Once created, a vampire is almost immortal, and becomes a menace to the living. **In Romanian folklore**, vampires frequently return to their former homes at night, where they must be propitiated with offerings of food and drink, and excluded by smearing garlic around the doors and windows. Should a new-born baby lie within, it must be guarded until it is christened, lest a vampire sneak in and transform it into another vampire. Two nights of the year are especially perilous: April 23, St George's Day (when, as Jonathan Harker was warned in *Dracula*, 'all the evil things in the world will have full sway') and November 29, the eve of St Andrew's Day. On the latter night, vampires rise with their coffins on their heads, lurk about their former homes, and then gather to fight each other with hempen whips at crossroads. Such places were considered to be unlucky, being infested by spirits called *Iele* or 'Man's enemies'. **In Gypsy folklore**, vampires (*Mulé*) also live at the exact moment of midday, when the sun casts no shadow. Gypsies must cease travel-ling, for at that instant *Mulé* control the roads, trees and everything else. Inter-estingly, Gypsies only fear their own *Mulé* – the ghosts and vampires of *gadjé* (non-Gypsies) are of no account.

The greatest danger was presented by **vampire epidemics**. Though in horror films and *Dracula*, vampires must bite their victims and suck blood to cause contagion, in Eastern European folklore the vampire's look or touch can suffice. A classic account refers to the Austro-Hungarian village of Haidam in the 1720s. There, before witnesses, a man dead ten years returned as a vampire to his son's cottage, touched him on the shoulder and then departed. The man died the next morning. Alarmed by this report and others relating how long-dead villagers were returning to suck their children's blood, the local military commander ordered several graves to be exhumed, within which were found corpses showing no signs of decay. All were incinerated to ashes – one of the classic methods of exterminating vampires. Another epidemic occurred in the village of Meduegna near Belgrade, between 1730-55. A soldier claimed to have been attacked by a vampire whilst in Greece (where vampire legends also abound), and died upon his return home. Thereafter many villagers swore to have seen him at night, and ten weeks later those who had, or had dreamt about him, complained of inexplicable weakness. The body was exhumed, was found to have blood in its mouth, and had a stake driven through its heart. Despite this precaution there was an outbreak of vampirism a few years later, and of the fourteen corpses examined by a medical commission, twelve were found to be 'unmistakably in the vampire condition' (ie. undecayed). Only **recently**, in 1988, outside Niš in southern Yugoslavia, a thirteen year-old girl was killed by her family, who believed her to be a vampire.

Sceptics may dismiss vampires and vampirism entirely, but some of the related phenomena have rational or scientific **explanations**. The 'return of the dead' can be explained by premature burial, which happened frequently in the past. (It's estimated that in Britain at the beginning of this century, one case took place each week. As recently as 1975, doctors dissecting a corpse for a kidney transplant discovered that the body was still breathing!). Nor is the drinking of blood confined to legendary, supernatural creatures. Aside from the Maasai tribe of Kenya – whose diet contains cattle blood mixed with milk – numerous examples can be found in the annals of criminology and psychopathology. During the Russian civil war a 'White'

baron, Von Sternberg-Ungern, believed himself the reincarnation of Ghenghis Khan and drunk the blood of Bolsheviks. In Sumatra in 1969, a barber was charged with sucking the blood of two babies; in 1980 an American 'shot his grandmother twice and sucked the blood out of the bullet holes because he believed a vampire told him that was what he had to do'; and so on, ad nauseam.

Psychologists label such behaviour 'extreme oral aggression', especially when it's accompanied by savage biting (as in the case of Countess Báthori): the hallmark of another creature of legend, the Werewolf. **Werewolves** also occur in Romanian folklore (known as *Pricolici*), and legends of their activities were once widespread throughout Europe. Most people no longer believe that humans can turn into wolves, although medical science recognises the condition of *Lycanthropy* (the firm conviction that one *is* a wolf); the rare disease *erythropoietic porphyria*, which causes reddish teeth, skin lesions and makes the sufferer shun sunlight; and *hirsutism*, whereby the afflicted person grows so much body and facial hair that they resemble Lon Chaney in *The Wolfman*. R.T. McNally, author of books on Dracula, vampirism and werewolves, suggests that 'someone afflicted with porphyria, half-crazed by the accompanying nervous disorders made worse by other people's reactions, would seek the relative safety and tranquility of a nice dark cave deep in the woods. On occasion, starved by lack of small game, he might even kill an unwary child or peasant. Certainly the disappearance of any local villagers would be attributed to such a person. This could be some of the 'reality' behind the werewolf legends of folklore'.

BOOKS AND MUSIC

*Books marked * should on no account be taken to Romania.*

Travel/general accounts

Andrew MacKenzie *Romanian Journey* (Hale £13.95). The most recent travel book on Romania. Its dollops of history, architectural description and bland travelese wouldn't be so bad if MacKenzie didn't also whitewash the Ceauşescu regime, of which his strongest criticism is that there's 'nothing soft' about it. Since it doesn't purport to describe contemporary Romania, and assembles all kinds of interesting folklore and facts about Vlad the Impaler, his *Dracula Country* is a more admirable book (Hale 1977).

Patrick Leigh Fermor *Between the Woods and the Water* (Penguin £3.95). Transylvania provides the setting for the second volume in this unfolding, retrospective trilogy, based on Leigh Fermor's diaries for 1933-34, when he walked from Holland to Constantinople. His precocious zest for history and cultural diversity rose to the challenge of Transylvania's striking contrasts and obscurely turbulent past; the richness of his jewelled prose and the deluge of details are impressive, if not overwhelmingly so.

Henry Baerlein *Romanian Scene* and *Romanian Oasis* (Frederick Muller; 1945 and 1948). Editor of two fine anthologies of travellers' tales in which most of the authors below are featured, Baerlein also wrote three turgid accounts of his own travels throughout the '30s: *Bessarabia and Beyond* (Methuen 1935), *And Then to Transylvania* (Shaylor 1931) and *In Old Romania* (Hutchinson 1940).

Hector Bolitho *Romania Under King Carol* (Eyre & Spottiswoode 1939). Reporting Romania's slide towards fascism from the Calea Victoriei, with ţuică glass and caviar close at hand, Bolitho set the style for the Bucharest 'Bright Lights' school of writing – gossipy, smug and cynical by turns.

R.G. Waldeck *Athénée Palace Bucharest* (Constable 1943). Subtitled 'Hitler's New Order Comes to Romania', this captures the unease, corruption and hedonism of Bucharest before the outbreak of war. The machinations of Carol, the Iron Guard and Antonescu get a look in, but Waldeck's account is more an evocation of the times than a political study.

Sacherevell & Edith Sitwell *Romanian Journey* (Batsford 1938). Motoring around, the Sitwells were both politely appalled, and vaguely charmed, by Romania; but most of all seem to have been relieved that their gastronomic fortunes didn't suffer unduly. Nice colour plates in the early editions.

Walter Starkie *Raggle Taggle* (Murray 1964). After his exploits in Hungary, Starkie tramped down through Transylvania to Bucharest, where his encounters with Gypsies and lowlife are recounted in a florid but quite amusing style. A secondhand-bookshop regular.

Peter O'Conner *Walking Good: Travels to Music in Hungary and Romania* (Weidenfeld 1971). Another Irish fiddler in search of Gypsy music, forty years after Starkie. O'Conner's quest took him to Slobozia, Cojocna and Făgăraş, where he stayed with local people a few years before this became illegal. Entertaining.

Bernard Newman *Blue Danube* (Jenkins 1935). Aside from a memorable encounter with some Gypsies near Orşova and a description of the Kazan Gorge, the Romanian chapters of Newman's cycling epic contain little of interest.

Emily Gerard *The Land Beyond the Forest* (2 vols. Blackwood 1888). One of the classic C19 accounts of Transylvania, written by an an expatriate Scotswoman. Massive and rambling, but highly informative on folk customs, superstitions, proverbs and the like.

Teresa Stratilesco *From Carpathians to Pindus* (Unwin 1906). Covers the same ground as Gerard, with an equally sharp eye for quirky details. Suitably cut, edited and combined, both women's books would make an excellent volume in the *20th Century Travellers* series. As things stand though, you'll have to root around dusty bookshelves to find either work.

John Paget *Hungary and Transylvania* (2 vols. Murray 1850). An earlier but likewise prolix description of Transylvania – in this case written by an English agriculturist who wed a Magyar baroness and managed her estates around Cluj.

Charles Boner *Transylvania: Its Products and its People* (Longmans 1865). Another long-winded but useful source, particularly informative about the Saxon and

Magyar communities.

Maude Parkinson *Twenty Years in Romania* (Unwin 1921). Having gone there to teach, Parkinson grew to love the country and wrote this amusing testimonial, partly to raise Romanian prestige abroad during the disasterous years of the First World War.

Ethel Greening Pantazzi *Romania in Light and Shadow* (Unwin 1921). A similar book, by a Canadian woman who married a Romanian naval officer.

J. Lindsay & M. Cornforth *Rumanian Summer* (Weishart 1953). Aside from exposing the iniquities of pre-communist Romania, this euology to Gheorghiu-Dej's 'Popular Democracy' is as blind as the Webbs' famous book on Russia (which was also written during a period of police terror). The authors enthused around the Danube-Black Sea Canal but failed to spot the slave labourers on this 'hero project' of the era.

Leslie Gardiner *Curtain Calls* (Travel Book Club 1977). A more critical, but never unsympathetic picture of Romania, Albania and Bulgaria emerges in this lighthearted account of Gardiner's visits during the '60s and early '70s. Worth reading just for the Albanian pieces, although the Romanian chapters contain lots of funny anecdotes about the pre-war monarchy, and a description of steamy Valcov in the Delta, where Gardiner made an unauthorised landing.

D.W. Hall *Romanian Furrow* (Harrap 1939). Discounting a few folk verses and some nice photos, this account of rural life hardly deserved King Carol's description of it as the 'best book' about the Romanian peasantry in the 1930s.

Queen Marie of Romania *My Country* (Hodder 1916), *The Country that I Love* (Duckworth 1925) and *The Story of My Life* (Cassell 1935) are all gushingly twee, and fail to convey the forceful character of this Edinburgh lass who won the hearts of Romania's people (see below). Many of the photos are lovely, however, and the books do have a certain period charm.

History and Politics

R.W. Seton-Watson *A History of the Roumanians* (Cambridge UP 1933). Although it ends in 1920, practically ignores social history and eschews atmospherics, and even the author admits his despair at the welter of dynastic details, it's still the standard English work on Romanian history – mainly because nobody has provided an alternative. Seton-Watson's *Roumania and the Great War* (1915) and *The Rise of Nationality in the Balkans* (1917) somewhat influenced British policy in favour of the Successor States, and for this reason his writings attracted great hostility in Hungary after Trianon.

S. Fischer-Galaţi *Twentieth Century Rumania* (Columbia UP 1977). An easy read with good illustratons, this complements Hale's book (see below) by providing more background, and is basically sympathetic to the changes that have happened since 1949.

Ion Pacepa, *Red Horizons** (WH Heinemann £12.95) A lurid, rambling 'exposé' of the Ceauşescu regime, written by its former intelligence chief (who defected in 1978), describing disinformation and espionage abroad; corruption and perversions amongst the élite, and much else. Pacepa was deeply involved but reveals little about himself; I got the impression of a Himmler who jumped ship. Lots of slurs on Arafat, Qadaffi and others, too – the hand of the CIA is evident on every page.

A. Cretzianu *Captive Romania** (Praeger 1956). As the title suggests, a totally hostile examination of how the Communist Party came to power and used it, written by various political exiles. As such it can can be skimmed as an antidote to *Rumanian Summer* (see above), or vice versa.

Julian Hale *Ceauşescu's Romania* (Harrap 1971). Readable and informative, albeit dated. Hale's judgements on the system now seem overly optimistic given the waning of Romania's fortunes and the waxing of Ceauşescu's megalomania since this was written.

Ion Ratiu *Contemporary Romania** (1975). A generally negative portrayal of the system by an émigré who now heads a small opposition group based in London and Paris, which publishes a newspaper, *Free Romanian**.

Richard Wurmbrand *In God's Underground** (Allen 1968). The memoirs of a Lutheran priest who spent many years incarcarated at Jilava, Craiova, Piteşti and other notorious prisons.

Andrew MacKenzie *The History of Transylvania* (Unified Printers 1983; £1). MacKenzie takes the Romanian side in all the contentious issues of Transylvanian history, so this can safely ride in the rucksack. Informative, but biased and stodgy.

C. Bodea & V. Cândea *Transylvania in the History of the Romanians* (Columbia UP 1982). More detailed, but even more biased and turgid than MacKenzie's booklet.

C. Michael-Titus *Romania Under Pressure*, *Europe in Romania* and *The Magyar File* take up the cudgels on Romania's behalf, mainly on human rights, where Titus refutes evidence of discrimination against the Hungarian minority (see below). The latter is published by Panopticum Press (1984) while copies of the other reports might be available from the author (write to 44, Howard Road, Upminster, Essex).

George Schöpflin *The Hungarians of Rumania** (Minority Rights Group; £1.20). This careful presentation of the evidence on discrimination against the Magyars is worth reading while you're in the UK (where it's available from Collets International Bookshop or the MRG, 36 Craven St. London WCN 5NG). Various **other books on Transylvania** which dispute the official Romanian version of history and minority-rights in considerably stronger terms include *Witness to Cultural Genocide** (available from PO Box 1671, Grand Central Station, New York 10017, which contains various samizdat articles from Transylvania; and *Transylvania and the Theory of the Daco-Roman-Romanian Continuity** (PO Box 3869, Rochester, New York 14610), a historical rebuttal of Romanian claims on the region.

Hannah Pakula *The Last Romantic* (Weidenfeld 1985). A colourful biography of Queen Marie, but at £14.95 only the most infatuated will buy it.

Terence Elsberry *Marie of Romania* (Cassell 1973). Much the same stuff, but slightly cheaper.

On folklore and Dracula

Romanian books on folklore and ethnography (of coffee-table dimensions) are cheaper to buy and easier to find in Romania. The illustrations are often great, but many of the books have garbled or tweely touristic English text. I particularly liked Ion Milcea's *Sweet Bucovina* and Malița & Banateanu's *From the Thesaurus of Traditional Popular Custom* (both published by Editura Sport-Turism). Dracula buffs might like to contact the **British Dracula Association**,

headed by Rob & Linda Leake (36 Elliston House, 100, Wellington Rd, London SE18 6QF; ☎ 01-317-9007). Nicolae Stoicescu's *Vlad Țepeș, Prince of Wallachia* (Bucharest 1978) is the standard Romanian **biography of the Impaler**, whom Stoicescu practically attempts to sanctify. Otherwise, the following books on folklore and Dracula are in print or lurk around antiquarian bookshops, abroad:

Moses Gaster *Rumanian Bird and Beast Stories* (1915) and *Children's Stories from Romanian Legends and Fairy Tales* (1923) are both difficult to find, but worth the effort if you're curious about such things.

Gail Kligman *Căluș: Symbolic Transformation in Romanian Ritual* (Chicago UP 1977). An interesting anthropological investigation of the Whitsun *Căluș* rite, which still lingers in parts of southern Romania.

Bram Stoker *Dracula* (1898). The Gothic horror original that spawned several inferior sequels and a thousand movie spin-offs. From a fairly promising start with undertones of fetishism and menace in Dracula's Transylvanian castle, the tale degenerates into rambling pathos thereafter.

Radu Florescu & Raymond McNally *In Search of Dracula* (1973) and *Dracula, a Biography* (Hale 1974) are founts of knowledge about the Impaler; while McNally's *The Blood Countess of Transylvania* divulges the perverted deeds of Elizabeth Báthori. You'll find potted biographies of these enduringly fascinating characters on pp. 490-494 of this guide – our debt to McNally is substantial.

Daniel Farson *The Man who wrote Dracula, a biography of Bram Stoker* (1975) completes the picture by relating the life of the fictional Dracula's creator.

Fiction and poetry

Only a small number of ROMANIAN NOVELISTS have been translated into English (although most have been published in France), so what follows is by no means the sum total of Romanian literature. . .

Liviu Rebreanu *Uprising* (1964), *Ion* (1965) and *The Forest of the Hanged* (all published by Peter Owen) comprise a panoramic picture of Romanian social life from the late C19 to the First World War. *Uprising* (which deals with the 1907 peasant rebellion) shocked Romanian readers with its violent descriptions when it first appeared in 1933.

Petru Dumitriu *The Family Jewels* (Collins 1961); *The Prodigals*; *Incognito** (Sphere 1964). A literary prodigy lauded by the Party for his book *Dustless Highway*, Dumitriu fled Romania in 1960 and subsequently published two tales of dynastic ambition, followed by his masterpiece of moral and psychological exploration, set against the backdrop of the war and the Communist takeover, *Incognito*.

ROMANIAN POETS are better represented, for some reason. Forest Books publish *Gates of the Moment* (1984), a collection of poems by **Ion Stoica**; while Bloodaxe is gradually making available the work of **Martin Stoicescu**, **Paul Goma*** and other writers. In Bucharest, you can sometimes find an anthology of C20 poets, *Like Diamonds in Coal Asleep* (Minerva 1985).

In the case of FOREIGN NOVELISTS, the screening of *Fortunes of War* has made **Olivia Manning**'s epic story of thoroughly exasperating characters – initially set in Bucharest – widely known in Britain (although many viewers might not realise that filming actually took place in Dubrovnik). Rendered in exquisite prose, the atmosphere of wartime Bucharest seems strikingly apposite today; but as an extended study of human relationships I found the *Balkan Trilogy* (Penguin £5.95) weakly constructed and eventually wearisome. **Saul Bellow**'s *The Dean's December** (Penguin £2.25) is leaner and more challenging, contrasting the repression and poverty of contemporary Romania with the hypocrisy and decadence of American society.

Music: records

In recent years, Romania's best-known musical export has been Gheorghe Zamfir, who piped away in the background to *Picnic At Hanging Rock* (EPC 81780). Inside Romania, it's fairly easy to buy **recordings** of *popularni* music – ranging from sanitised pop to powerful singers like Maria Tanase. Sadly, though, *Electrecord*'s recordings of traditional folk music are not often available. You might

be able to order them from Artexim, the Foreign Trade Company (1, Piaţa Şcinteii, Bucharest).

In London, Collets Bookshop stocks many of the following (mainly foreign-made) discs:

Romanian Songs and Dances A good all round selection, including doinas, Capra dances, songs and instrumental music. The recordings come from the Romanian Ethnological Institute but the disc is American (Folkways FE 4387).

Roumanie – La Vraie Tradition de Transylvanie Vocal, pastoral and instrumental music from Transylvania; an excellent disc, although the sleeve notes are skimpy (Harmonia Mundi Ocora 558596).

Reflections of Romania: Village and Urban Folk Traditions Doinas, colinde, dance tunes and the music of nai and buciume (Nonesuch Explorer Series 72092).

Roumanie – Musiques de Mariage de Maramureş The accompanying dance music and ritual songs for weddings in Maramureş, inexplicably lacking the *Bride's Farewell* song (Harmonia Mundi Ocora 558506).

Les Flutes Roumaines In two discs; volume 2 is devoted to nai music (Arion 30/T/095).

Roumanie: polyphonie vocale des Aroumains Songs from the Dobrudja region (Le Chant du Monde LUX 74803).

Bucharest by Night: songs by Maria Tanase The doyenne of the doina croons for bon viveurs; the Balkan equivalent of nightclub music in Humphrey Bogart films (MFS 439).

Rapsodia Romina Barbu Lautaru's orchestra performing horas (Monitor MFS 377).

Moldavian Folk Dances and **Moldavian Love Songs** (MF 314 and 328).

Sources

Addresses of the best Romanian **bookshops** in Bucharest, Cluj and Sibiu appear in the guide. In Britain, the best sources are London's *Collets International Bookshop*, *The Travel Bookshop*, and the *School of Slavonic and Eastern European Studies* – you'll find details of all three on p.234.

LANGUAGE

The apocryphal story of the Wallachian yokel visiting Italy who thought that Italians spoke his own tongue, 'but badly', underscores that **Romanian** is basically a Romance language with a grammar similar to Latin. This familial resemblance makes it easy for anyone who speaks French, Italian or (to a lesser extent) Spanish to recognise words and phrases in Romanian, even though its vocabulary also contains words of Dacian, Slavonic, Greek and Turkish origin. Romanians are usually prepared to grapple with **Italian** or **French** in order to converse with outsiders, and in the big towns and around the coastal resorts some people speak one or two foreign languages fluently. **German** is widely understood – if not spoken – in the areas of Transylvania and the Banat traditionally inhabited by Saxons and Swabians; and many educated Romanians (eg. engineers) have learned the language for professional reasons, although the tendency amongst students nowadays is increasingly towards **English**. Foreigners who can muster any **Hungarian** phrases will find them appreciated in the Magyar enclaves of Transylvania and Moldavia, but their use elsewhere invites hassle rather than sympathy, which is even more the case with **Russian** – a language that's greeted with derision by almost everyone except the Lipovani communities of the Delta.

Phrase books and courses

Unfortunately, the best *Romanian Phrasebook*, by G. Vorvoreanu and J. Norman (Penguin 1973), is out of print; although Collets International Bookshop, London WC1, stocks both Mihai Miroiu's highly formal *English-Romanian Conversation Book* (£2.50) and invaluable pocket-sized *Mic Dicţionar* (£2.95), which are hard to buy inside Romania. If you're serious about **learning the language through books**, Collets also stocks *Teach Yourself Romanian* (Hodder £4.50), *Colloquial Romanian* (RKP £6.95) and Irina Panov's 2 volume Romanian-English-Romanian dictionary (£9.35 each). The School of Slavonic and East European Studies, Mallet St. London WC1, occasionally run evening classes in Romanian, and can supply information about summer language **courses** in Romania organised by Bucharest University.

Basic grammar and pronunciation

Romanian **nouns** have three genders – masculine, feminine and neuter. **Adjectives** (usually placed after the word they describe) and pronouns always 'agree' with the gender of the noun. *Mai* and *cel mai* are generally used to make comparatives and superlatives: eg. *ieftin* (cheap); *mai ieftin* (cheaper), *cel mai ieftin* (the cheapest). In Romanian **'a'** comes before the noun and is *un* for masculine and neuter words, *o* for feminine ones; the word for **'the'** is added to the end of the noun: *-a* for feminine words, *-l* or *-le* for masculine or neuter ones. The plural forms of nouns are slightly more complicated, but tend to end in *-i*.

    Pronunciation is likewise fairly straightforward. Words are usually, but not always, stressed on the syllable before last, and all letters are pronounced. However, certain letters change their sounds when combined with other ones, as the following rough guide to pronunciation shows. When speaking, Romanians tend to slur words together.

A	'o' sound as in 'd*o*ne'
Ă	'er' sound as in 'moth*er*'; the combinations **AU** and **ĂU** resemble the sounds in 'h*ow*' and 'g*o*'.
B	as in 'b*u*d'.
C	as in 'country'; except when it precedes certain letters, ie. **CE** as in 'ch*es*t'; **CI** as in 'cheek'; **CHE** as in 'kept'; and **CHI** as in 'keep'.
D	as in 'd*u*st'.
E	as in 'ten'; but **at the start of a word** it's pronounced as in 'year'; while the combined **EI** sounds like 'bay' or 'ray'.
F	as in 'fox'.
G	as in 'gust'; except for the dipthongs **GE** = 'gesture'; **GI** = 'jeans'; **GHE** = 'guest'; and **GHI** = 'gear'.

H	as in 'hand'.
I	'ee' sound as in 'feet'; except for the vowel combinations **IU** as in 'you'; **IA** as in 'yap'; and **IE** as in 'yesterday'.
Î	is pronounced midway between the o in 'lesson' and the o in 'sort'.
J	's' sound as in 'pleasure'.
K	only occurs in imported words like 'kilometre'.
L	as in 'love'.
M	as in 'must'.
N	as in 'noise'.
O	as in 'soft'; except for **OI**, as in 'boy', and **OA** as in 'quark'.
P	as in 'put'.
R	is always rolled.
S	as in 'soft'.
Ş	as in 'shop'.
T	as in 'tall'.
Ţ	as in 'bits'.
U	'oo' sound as in 'book' or 'good'; but **UA** is pronounced as in 'quark'.
V	as in 'vow'.
Z	as in 'zero'.
W	occurs in such foreign words as 'whisky', 'western' etc.

Basics and greetings

Do you speak English?	*Vorbiţi englezeste?*
I don't understand	*Nu înţeleg*
Please speak slowly	*Vă rog să vorbiţi mai rar*
Please write it down	*Scrieţi, vă rog*
Say that again, please	*Vreţi să repetaţi, vă rog*
Yes, no, and	*da, nu, şi*
I, we, you	*Eu, noi, dumneata (Tu is informal)*
Hello	*Salut*
Good morning	*Bună dimineaţa*
Good day	*Bună ziua*
Good evening	*Bună seara*
Good night	*Noapte bună*
How are you?	*Ce mai faceţi?*
What's your name?	*Cum vă numiţi?*
Cheers!	*Nuroc!*
Good, that's fine	*Bun, minunat (De acord = it's agreed)*
Please, thank you	*Vă rog, mulţumesc*
Sorry, excuse me	*Regret, permiteţi-mi*
Goodbye	*La revedere (or ciao)*
Bon voyage	*Drum bun (literally, 'Good road')*
Leave me alone!	*Lăsaţi-ma în pace!*

Directions and accommodation

Where is..?/where are..?	*Unde este..?/unde sînt..?*
The nearest. . .	*. . .cel mai apropiat*
a (cheap) hotel	*un hotel (ieftin)*
campsite	*loc de campare*
toilet	*toaleta, WC*
Is it far?	*Este departe?*
What bus must I take?	*Ce autobuz trebuie sa iau?*
Is there a footpath to..?	*Exista vreo poteca spre..?*
Right, left, straight on	*Dreapta, stînga, dreapt înainte*
North, south, east, west	*Nord, sud, est, vest*
Have you a room?	*Aveţi o camera?*
with, without	*cu, fără*
twin beds	*două paturi*
a double bed	*un pat dublu*
for one person	*pentru o persoană*

shower, bathroom	duş, baie
There's no water	Nu curge apa
How much per night?	Cît costa pentru o noapte
Including breakfast?	Micul dejun este inclus în pret?
Have you nothing cheaper?	Nu aveţi altceva mai ieftin?
Can you suggest another (cheaper) hotel?	Puteţi să-mi recomandaţi un alt hotel (un hotel mai ieftin)?

In addition to the following, see the **specialist vocabularies** for eating and drinking (p.259), transport (p.255) and hiking (p.267).

Requests and buying

I want/should like. . .	Aş vrea. . .
I don't want. . .	Nu vreau. . .
How much?	Cît costă?
Is there. . .?	Există. . .?
Have you/do you sell..?	Aveţi..?
Where can I buy..?	Unde pot să cumpăr..?
It's too expensive	Este prea scump
Waiter, waitress	Chelner, Chelneriţa
What do you recommend?	Ce îmi recomandaţi?
There's no more. . .	S-a terminat. . .
two glasses (bottles) of beer, please	două pahare (sticle) de bere, vă rog
Same again, please	Incă un rînd, vă rog
What's that?	Ce este aceasta?
Is it any good?	Merita?
Bill, receipt	Nota, chitanţa
When will it be ready?	Cînd este gata?
At once, we're in a hurry	Imediat, ne grăbim
How much do I get for a pound/dollar?	Care este cursul lirei/dolarului?
Will you refund my money?	Vă rog sa-mi daţi banii înapoi?
Any letters for me?	Aveţi vreo scrisoare pentru mine?

Getting around

Does this bus go..?	Autobuzul acesta merge..?
to the railway station	. . .la gară
to the coach terminal	. . .la autogară
to the beach	. . .la plajă
into the centre	. . .în centru
Does it stop at..?	Opreşte la..?
Has the last bus gone?	A trecut ultimul autobuz?
I want to go to. . .	Vreau să merg la. . .
Stop here (at. . .)	Opriţi aici (la. . .)
Is it a good road?	Este bun drumul?
It isn't far	Nu este departe
Crossroads, bridge	Intersecţie, pod
When does the train leave?	Le ce ora pleacă trenul?
Which platform does the train to. . .leave from?	De la ce peron pleacă trenul către..?
Two seats on the train (tomorrow) to. . .	Două locuri pentru (mîine) la trenul către. . .
I want to reserve a sleeper (couchette)	Vreau sa rezerv loc de vagonul de dormit (cu cuşete)
I want to change my reservation to. . .	Aş vrea să rezerv un alt loc pentru. . .
Is this the train for..?	Acesta este trenul de..?
Where do I change?	Unde schimb trenul?

Is there a boat from here to. . .?	Există curse de vapor de aici la..?
When does the next boat leave?	Cînd pleacă vaporul urmator?
Can I hire a (rowing) boat?	Pot să închiriez o barcă (cu vişie)?
How much do you charge by the hour/for the day?	Cît costa ora/ziua?

Signs

Arrival, departure	Sosire, plecare
Entrance, exit	Intrare, ieşire
Vacant, occupied	Liber, ocupat
No vacancies	Nu mai sînt locuri
Open, closed	Deschis, inchis
Admission free	Intrare gratuită
Ladies' (Gents') WC	WC femei (bărbaţi)
Waiting room	Sală de asteptare
Operating, cancelled	Circulă, anulat
No smoking	Fumatul oprit (Nefumatori)
No entry, danger	Intrare interzisa, pericol

Time and dates

What's the time?	Ce oră este?
It's early/late	Este devreme/tîrziu
(this) morning	(azi) dimineaţa
day, afternoon	zi, după masă
midday, midnight	prinzului, miezul nopţii
evening, night	seara, noapte
today, yesterday	azi, ieri
(day after) tomorrow	(poi) mîine
soon, never	curînd, niciodată

Monday	Luni
Tuesday	Marţi
Wedensday	Miercuri
Thursday	Joi
Friday	Vineri
Saturday	Sîmbătă
Sunday	Duminică

January	Ianuarie
February	Februarie
March	Martie
April	Aprilie
May	Mai
June	Iunie
July	Iulie
August	August
September	Septembrie
October	Octombrie
November	Noiembrie
December	Decembrie
New Year	Anul Nou
Easter	Paşte

Numbers

1 unu, una	17 şaptsprezece
2 doi, doua	18 optsprezece
3 trei	19 nouăsprezece
4 patru	20 douăzece

5 cinci
6 şase
7 şapte
8 opt
9 nouă
10 zece
11 unsprezece
12 doisprezece
13 treisprezece
14 paisprezece
15 cincisprezece
16 şaisprezece

21 douăzeci şi unu/una
30 treizeci
40 patruzeci
50 cincizeci
60 şaizeci
70 şaptzeci
80 optzeci
90 nouăzeci
100 o sută
500 cinci zece
1000 o mie

1 kilo
½
⅓
¼
¾

un kilo
jumătate
o treime
sfert
trei sferturi

■ BULGARIA

BULGARIA

BASICS

BULGARIA: WHERE TO GO AND WHEN

If Westerners have an image of **Bulgaria**, it tends to be coloured either by commodities – the Black Sea resorts, ski centres and wine – or by the murky intrigues of Balkan politics, exemplified by the infamous tales of poison umbrellas and plots to kill the Pope. In the Eastern Bloc, too, there are distinct pre-conceptions – of Bulgaria's conformism and its role as the USSR's most loyal satellite. Bulgarians, understandably, resent both views. From their standpoint, the nation has come a long way since it threw off the 500 year-old yoke of the Ottoman empire in the 1870s, and made great strides towards prosperity and security during the socialist era. They feel that foreigners should take a look before they judge – and welcome them in the spirit of the old proverb: 'I receive you according to your dress, but see you off according to your mind'. And in fairness, it should be emphasised that the Russian links, both cultural and historical, long pre-date the Warsaw Pact era; it was Russian aid that freed Bulgaria from the Turks.

In recent years, **tourism** has become a year-round business, with the first holidaymakers hitting the **Black Sea resorts** as the last person quits the slopes at Borovets and other **skiing centres**. Their growing popularity is largely due to shrewd promotion and pricing by tour operators, who offer cheap holidays (see p.511) to both destinations. Neither experience, however, is particularly Bulgarian, and you'll get more sense of the country and people outside the confines of a tour. **Independent travel** here is not common and attitudes shaped by a conservative tradition as well as by Western packages can be frustrating. But there are relatively few restrictions; the costs are low; and for the committed there is much to take in.

The main attractions are the mountainous **scenery** – offering great hiking, especially in the **Rila and Pirin Mountains** of the southwest – and the web of towns with craft traditions where you'll find the wonderfully romantic architecture of the National Revival era. Foremost among these are **Koprivshtitsa** in the Sredna Gora range, where the heroic April Rising started; **Plovdiv**, the second largest city; and **Veliko Târnovo**, the old medieval capital, round which are clustered several smaller examples of the genre. The **monasteries** can be startling, too. The finest, **Rila**, is on every tourist's itinerary, but less well-known establishments like **Rozhen** – in the 'sandstone sea' surrounding the picturesque town of **Melnik** – are equally well worth seeing. The capital, **Sofia**, is disappointing by comparison: a showcase city with little spontaneity for all its fine sights.

Climate presents few problems. Winter snow is as reliable in the mountain resorts, as is warmth, through from late May to September, on the coast – and almost everywhere else. If you're looking to travel, there's no reason to restrict yourself to the summer. Romanian-style winter freezes are rare, and spring can be a delight, with the orchards and market gardens in full bloom. Unlike Romania, **festivals** are not a major feature. However, Sofia boasts an impressive *jazzfest* in the second week of November, which follows hard on the heels of the anniversary of the Bolshevik revolution – celebrated here (like Mayday) in grand old style.

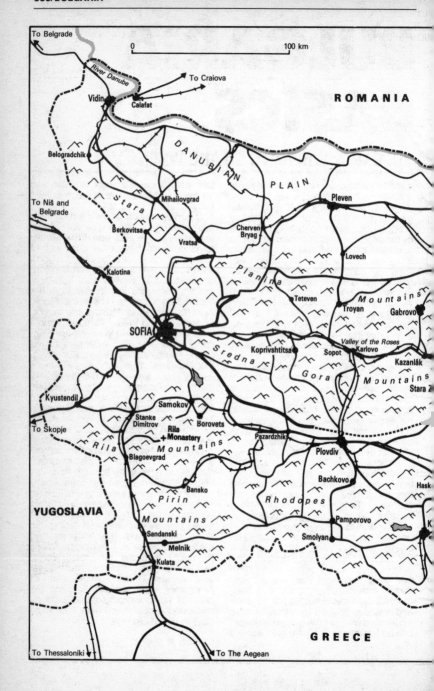

Average daily temperatures

	Borovets		Plovdiv		Varna	
	°F	°C	°F	°C	°F	°C
Jan	30	−1	33	1	36	3
Feb	33	1	34	3	43	6
Mar	41	5	44	7	43	6
Apr	48	9	54	12	54	12
May	59	15	62	17	62	17
Jun	65	19	73	23	70	22
Jly	71	22	74	23	75	24
Aug	74	23	76	24	74	23
Sep	61	16	65	19	68	20
Oct	54	12	55	13	60	16
Nov	42	6	45	8	49	10
Dec	33	0	36	3	39	4

GETTING THERE

Bulgaria, like Romania, is geared towards package tourism, rather than independent travel. It doesn't pose the same level of problems – transport and accommodation are generally straightforward enough to arrange – but undoubtedly the **package deals** on offer make visits simpler (if duller) and invariably cheaper. It's worth considering a package for expense alone; if you're happy with a two week stay they can sometimes be worthwhile just for the flight and first/last night's acccommodation. Flying to **Budapest** is also an option: onward travel (see 'By Rail') is relatively good value.

Flights

The cheapest **flight-only** deals from Britain are inevitably **London-Sofia**. *Canterbury Travel* (248 Streatfield Rd, Kenton, Harrow, HA3 9BY; ☎ 01-206-0411), currently offer returns for £225, departing Monday, Wednesday and Saturday from Heathrow. You're obliged to spend at least one Saturday night, and no longer than 30 days, in Bulgaria. Similar return flights are also sporadically available from the tour operator *Sunquest* (9-15 Aldine Street, London W12 8AW; ☎ 01-749-9933). Although you're unlikely to get a visa for that long, there are also APEX returns (which must be bought one month beforehand) valid for up to 90 days; *Air France* and the Bulgarian airline *BALKAN* (322, Regent Street, London WC1; ☎ 01-637-7637) charge around £270 for these.

Listed under 'Package tours' (see below), *Balkan-tours* can also be worth approaching for flights. They sometimes **discount fares** to Sofia, Burgas or Varna **from Glasgow, Belfast or Dublin**. They are, though, of course primarily concerned with package holidays.

There are no flights from Australia or Canada, and only indirect ones **from the USA**, where *KLM* and *JAT* fly from New York to Sofia via Amsterdam or Belgrade. Return flights cost around $700-$800 depending on the time of year; tickets can be booked through the Bulgarian Tourist Office in New York (161 East 86th Street; ☎ 722 1110).

By rail

Anyone **under 26** has two obvious choices: either invest in an **Inter-Rail** pass (£139), which entitles you to a month's free travel on European railways as far as Bulgaria (but *not* inside the country); or buy a **Transalpino/Eurotrain** ticket **from London to Sofia**, which is valid for 2 months and permits stopovers along the way. Transalpino tickets cost £99 one-way, £197 return if you travel via Dieppe and Paris, or £102 (£175 return) for the slightly quicker route via Oostende. You can't use Transalpino beyond Sofia, but 2-month 'Runaround' tickets – enabling one to travel along a predetermined route, for example from Sofia or Ruse to Turkey – are available from British Rail (see p.517). Either way, it makes sense to get a return rather than a single, since international tickets are very dear if purchased in Bulgaria.

Standard train tickets, if you're 26 or over, are about 25% more expensive than Transalpino/Eurotrain; London-Sofia is presently £241 return, or £220 one-way.

Travel **within Eastern Europe**, however, is better value and you can reach Bulgaria economically **from Hungary, Romania or Yugoslavia**. Current fares are around £20 from Budapest or Belgrade to Sofia, or from Bucharest to Ruse.

By car – driving or hitching

Driving is not the most relaxed way of getting to Bulgaria, and unless you take it easy you'll need a couple of days to recover when you arrive. The most direct route is **through Yugoslavia**, following the E5 from Belgrade down to Kalotina on the Bulgarian border. You can choose between several routes to Belgrade – for example, across the Austrian Alps and then along the E94, or going **via Hungary** using the E5 (see p.13). Driving via **Romania** is more demanding (see 'Romania Basics') and not recommended just as an approach route.

I've yet to hear of anyone **hitching** to Bulgaria, and the road down through Yugoslavia is notoriously awful for lifts. However, hitching **from Turkey** is quite feasible providing someone is willing to take you across the border, and it might also be possible to hitch up from **Greece**, entering Bulgaria at Kulata in the southwest.

Package tours

The main advantage of **package deals** are the cheap flights – often less than the cost of an ordinary 'flight-only' fare. For independent travel, the obvious drawback is lack of flexibility. You are usually tied down to a 2-week stay, and generally deposited at a beach or ski resort: neither very typical of the country. However, there is scope for using packages as a **springboard for independent travel**, and one tour, the 7-night 'Freewheeler', available from *Peltours* (4, Winsley Street, London W1N 7AR; ☎ 01-637-4373 and 27-29, Church Street, Manchester M4 1QA; ☎ 061-834-3721), is actually designed for this. Costing from £214-£232, it includes vouchers which can be used in part-payment for accommodation anywhere in Bulgaria.

Most packages, though, are to one – sometimes two – centres. They are offered by almost all the major companies – like *Phoenix*, *Intasun*, *Sunquest* or *Global*, whose brochures can be obtained at any highstreet travel agent – and from a few smaller **tour operators** which specialise in Bulgaria. *Balkan Holidays* (19, Conduit St, London W1R 9TD; ☎ 01-493-8612) lead the field **in Britain**, while *Balkantours*, with offices in Belfast (9-10, Lombard St, BT1 1RB; ☎ 246795) and Dublin (5-6 South Great Georges Street; ☎ 794415) are pre-eminent in **Ireland**. All these operators offer a range of accommodation, and the **prices** quoted below refer to the cheapest option. Package deals cost more during the 'peak' seasons, which are January-February in the ski resorts, and from mid-June until early September everywhere else – hence the 'spread' of prices, which are for an adult sharing a double room on half board unless stated otherwise.

Inghams (☎ 01-785-7777) currently offers the best value **skiing holidays**: six days on the slopes at Borovets for £137-£177 (£245-£255 for 12 days), with tuition, equipment-hire and lift passes for an extra £66. However, the market is very competititive, so it's well worth checking out *Ski Falcon* (☎ 01-229-9484), *Global* (☎ 01-637-333), *Skiscope* (☎ 0444-459921), *Enterprise* (☎ 01-439-7611) or *Balkan Holidays*, some of whom also offer skiing at Pamporovo, or Aleko-Vitosha just outside Sofia, and departures from Glasgow, Manchester, Birmingham or Newcastle. Skiing holidays are available from *Balkantours* in Ireland from around £180.

There's a wide range of **holidays on the coast**, with new operators joining the market every year (although, thankfully, *Club 18-30* have pulled out). If several of you are going for a week, *Global* does the cheapest holiday villas at Sozopol (£127-£192), Nesebâr (£126-£192) and Dyuni (£139-£229), while *Balkan Holidays* and *Phoenix* do the best deals at Zora (£157-£239) or Elenite (£165-£249) – though bear in mind that these prices are for 3-5 people sharing, not couples. The latter would do better to take Balkan Holidays' offer of a hotel at Sunny Beach (£137-£255), Albena (£156-£255) or Golden Sands (£137-£225), or Druzhba if you fancy a luxurious hotel (£163-£259). Broadly speaking, these operators also do the cheapest 2-week holidays on the coast.

Various 2-week **two centre holidays** combine Golden Sands and Sunny Beach (£187-£325), or one of them with Mamaia in Romania (£229-£297), or Kumburgaz (£195-£213) or Istanbul (£304-£383) in Turkey, and of these, *Sunquest*'s are the cheapest. Alternatively, a coastal resort is paired with Pamporovo (£229-£349) or Borovets (£225-£385) in the mountains, and here Sunquest and Balkan Holidays are neck and neck. If you want to see more of the country, you can combine the seaside with a week **touring Bulgaria by coach**. These 'Discover Bulgaria' tours usually take in Nesebâr, Sliven, Plovdiv, Rila Monastery, Sofia, Koprivshtitsa, Veliko Târnovo and Madara, and either begin or end with a week on the beach. Prices start from around £269-£425, with full board while on tour; operators include Sunquest, Balkantours, *Contiki* (☎ 01-290-6777), *Cosmos Coach Tours* (☎ 01-464-3400), *Swan Hellenic* (☎ 01-247-0421), *Trafalgar Tours* (☎ 01-828-4388) and Balkan Holidays, who also do a 2-week 'Best of Bulgaria' tour (£295-£371) with an 'Istanbul extension' for £40-£60.

Balkan Holidays can also arrange **mountain holidays** at Borovets and Pamporovo (£285-£415 for 2 weeks), 'Wine and Dine' tours with a different itinerary to the coach trips and better food (£279-£435), two **fly/drive** deals (£235-£375), and, on request, **specialist tours**. These are on the dear side, like the 9-day 'Frescoes and Icons' package from *Inter-Church Travel* (45, Berkley Street, London W1A 1EB; ☎ 01-734-0942).

There's less choice of **packages available in the USA**, where the Bulgarian Tourist Office (161 East 86th Street, New York; ☎ 722 1110) is the sole agent. Since variations on the theme of summer holidays cost between $1,000-$2,500 per head for 9-19 days, you could probably save at least $100 by arranging to join a tour in Britain.

RED TAPE: VISAS AND *CARTES STATISTIQUES*

A full (not Visitor's) passport is needed to enter Bulgaria, and unless you go on a package tour it's necessary to have a **visa**. This can only be obtained from Bulgarian consulates or embassies abroad, but under no circumstances at the border. Tourist visas (£20), valid for 3 months, entitle you to 30 days stay; transit visas are good for 30 hours stay and cost £20 or £40 depending on whether they're valid for single or double entry. We'd advise travellers to get a tourist visa either way, since Bulgarian customs sometimes view transit ones as an implied slight on their country, and have been known to pester holders to change large sums into leva as the price for gaining entry. Applying in person to a consulate, you should receive a tourist visa in 7 working days, and a transit visa immediately; postal applications (enclose your passport, a note specifying the type of visa required, and an SAE) take a week or so longer. Payment must be in cash or by postal order, and one photograph is required.
Bulgarian consulats abroad include:
AUSTRALIA: 1/4 Carlotta Rd, Double Bay, Sydney, N.S.W. 2028/☎ 36-75-81.
BRITAIN: 188 Queen's Gate, London SW7 5HL/☎ 01-584-9400 (Monday-Friday 9.30am-12.30am).
CANADA: 100 Abelaide Street West, Suite 1410, Toronto/☎ 363-7307.
DENMARK: A.N. Hansens allee 5, 2900 Hellerup, Copenhagen/☎ (01) 62-11-20.
HOLLAND: 9 Duinroosweg, Den Haag 2597 KJ/☎ 55-30-51.
IRELAND: 22 Burlington Rd, Dublin 4/ ☎ (01) 68-40-10.
NORWAY: Tidermandst Gate 11, Oslo 2/☎ 56-29-85.
SWEDEN: Stockholm 11431, Karlavagan 29/☎ 20-90-38.
W.GERMANY: Frankfurt: Eckenheimer Landstr. 101/☎ 59-80-39. Hamburg: Benedictstr. 5/☎ 48-61-69. München: Wintrichring 85/☎ 17-40-56.
USA: New York: 1028, 11 East 84th Street/☎ 737-47-90. Washington DC: 20 008, 1621 22nd Street NW 667-3870/☎ (202) 387-7969.
Visa **extensions** are hardly ever granted, so before visiting the *Bureau for*

Registering Foreign Guests on Pl. Narodno Sâbranie you should seek advice from your embassy in Sofia. Alternatively, you could make a trip into neighbouring Yugoslavia and get a new visa from the Bulgarian consulate in Belgrade (Ul. Birchaninova 26; ☎ 646-243).

The **carte statistique** issued to all independent travellers on arrival must be date-stamped at reception whenever you check into and out of a hotel or campsite (where staff sometimes keep the *carte* meantime). Considering the fuss they make about stamps, it's ridiculous how small this vital document is − mine rapidly became an illegible mess of imprints after a week, to the ill-natured

consternation of more than one receptionist.

Unless you visit Melnik or the southern Rhodopes you're unlikely to encounter граничен зоне signs warning of the **border zone**, to enter which one needs a special permit. Where you need one to visit certain sites, we've mentioned this in the text. Aside from the permanent *granitsen zone*, localities are occasionally and temporarily declared off-limits because something 'secret' is happening there. It is always wise to approach the local tourist office first: a 'no' from Balkantourist will be altogether politer than a refusal from the police, to whom even the enquiry might seem suspicious.

HEALTH AND INSURANCE

Inoculations aren't required for travel in Bulgaria, but if you're heading on to Turkey jabs for cholera and typhoid are advisable. The most common complaints are diarrhoea and sunburn, so stock up on *Diocalm* before you leave home, and don't expose yourself rashly to the sun while in Bulgaria. It seems safe to drink tap **water** everywhere.

Minor complaints can be solved at **Apketa** (see the guide for addresses of 24hr pharmacies), but if you require a doctor (*lekar*) or dentist (*zâbolekar*) head for the nearest **Polyclinic**, whose staff might well speak English or German. Urgent cases go to **hospitals** (*bolnitsa*) courtesy of the *bârza pomosht* or ambulance service (☎ 150 in most towns) and emergency treatment is free of charge although you must pay for **medicines**. In Sofia there's a pharmacy selling Western drugs for hard currency at the *Tsentr po*

Higiena, and a special clinic for foreigners in the *Mladost 1* suburb (1, Ul. Evgeni Pavlovski/☎ 75-361).

On production of a passport, British citizens and nationals of other countries with which Bulgaria has a reciprocal health agreement receive all treatment free of charge, so it's not essential to carry **insurance**. However, taking out a policy before you leave home (available from travel agents or insurance brokers for about £15 a month) will normally give you cover for theft, or damage to your gear, so it's probably still worthwhile. To claim compensation back home you'll need receipts for any medicines purchased, or in the case of theft, an official police report. If local police are unwilling to issue one, be persistent and invoke the name of your embassy (*posolstvo*) or Balkantourist.

COSTS, MONEY AND BANKS

Bulgaria's national currency − the **leva** − is arbitarily over-valued, though, unlike Romania, not so much that **costs** seem unreasonable. Your main expense will probably be hotel **accommodation**, which is generally priced at the same rate per person whether one occupies a single or a double room. Second class hotels, where breakfast is often included in the tariff, charge between 25-40 leva (roughly £11-£18) per head; and if this seems too steep there's always the

option of chalets, which can be rented for as little as 10 leva (just under £5). When available, private rooms vary from the ridiculously cheap (£1-£3 per head) to the moderately priced (£10 per person in Sofia); whilst campsites rarely cost more than £1 or £2 per night. All forms of public **transport** are cheap, with flat fares of 6 stotinki (2 pence) in most towns, and inexpensive rates on intercity buses and trains (international services are another matter, see p.517). Providing you avoid deluxe hotel restaurants, **eating** should likewise prove to be a economical business, especially if you stick to standard local fare like cheese, kebabs, salad and fruit. **Drinking** Bulgarian wine or spirits, too, will hit your liver harder than your wallet.

The cost of car hire and some accommodation may drop as much as 30% **out of season** (October to March on the Coast; April to December at ski resorts; most cities during the spring and winter months). IUS **student cards** (available from *Orbita* offices) entitle the holder to small discounts on campsites and museum admission charges, and 30% reductions on the price of international railway tickets and internal and external BALKAN flights. There are some *child reductions*.

All the above prices are reckoned according to the special 'bonus' **exchange rate** available only **at Balkantourist offices**, rather than the 'normal' rate offered by **banks** (which is 80% lower). Both rates are fairly stable – at the bonus rate, £1=2.3 leva and $1=1.8 leva – and 1% commission is always charged. (Turkish lire cannot be exchanged for Bulgarian currency). The bonus rate exists to reduce the incentive for changing money on **the black market**, where $1 can fetch 3-4 leva (with a similar mark-up for pounds, Deutschmarks and French francs). Such illegal exchanges are widespread, and under-cover cops pose less of a problem than rip-offs. Besides sleights-of-hand, dealers may cheat tourists by selling them Yugoslav or Greek money, or 50 leva banknotes (withdrawn after the Bulgarian Mafia began counterfeiting them). Changing money legally, be sure to get – and keep – the exchange **receipts** (*bordereau*), since these must be produced whenever you pay for accommodation in **leva**. Bulgarian currency comes in 1, 2, 5, 10 and 20 leva notes, and 1 and 2 leva coins; subdivided into *stotinki* (100 stotinki = 1 lev). It's forbidden to import or export leva, and any surplus can be re-exchanged for hard currency at the frontier before leaving Bulgaria if you have the receipts.

Though a stash of small-denomination dollar bills is useful, the bulk of your money is safest in the form of **Travellers' Cheques**. Balkantourist will cash any of the better-known brands, but their head office in Sofia will only replace lost American Express cheques, and even then with reluctance. Amex, Diners Club, Bankamericard-Visa, Access, Eurocard, Mastercard and Carte Blanche **credit cards** can be used for car rental and to pay at hotels, restaurants and shops in the main towns and resorts, but aren't much use in the sticks. You can get **cash advances** in leva to the value of $100 with Eurocard, Access and Mastercard, or the equivalent of $200 with a Diners Club card.

INFORMATION AND MAPS

Free leaflets and brochures covering various places, events and activities are available from the **Bulgarian Tourist Organisation**'s offices **abroad**:
BRITAIN: 18 Princes Street, London W1R 7RE (☎ 01-499-6988).
DENMARK: 6 Vester Farimagsgade, 1606 Copenhagen V (☎ 01/12-35- 10).
HOLLAND: 43 Leidsestraat, 1017 Amsterdam (☎ 020/24-84-31).
SWEDEN: 30 Kungsgatan, III 35 Stockholm (☎ 11-51-91).
USA: 161 East 86th Street, New York, N.Y.10028 (☎ 212/722- 1110).
W.GERMANY: 1-3 Stefanstrasse, 6 000 Frankfurt/Main I (☎ 069/29- 52-84-6).
Most of the publications are designed to whet your appetite rather than impart practical information, but the motoring and camping maps and the *Tourist Calendar* are worth taking to Bulgaria.

Inside Bulgaria you'll find that information – like hotels and most tourist services – comes under the aegis of the unpredictable **Balkantourist**. While Balkantourist's **Comprehensive Service Bureaux** (in the main resorts and towns; open 24hrs on road-crossings into Bulgaria) can book rooms and furnish information nationwide, their **provincial offices** (8.30am-5.30pm) are often useless at anything beyond exchanging money. Much depends on the woman behind the desk, and finding a common language. Though staff in Sofia and the main coastal and ski resorts generally speak English, their colleagues elsewhere are likelier to understand German,

French or Russian. Addresses of most Balkantourist offices appear in the guide.

Although *Falk/Cartographia* **maps** of Romania and Bulgaria (available abroad) have yet to be updated to take account of new roads, they'll probably suffice **for motorists**; but if you can read the Cyrillic alphabet (p.715) there's more information to be gleaned from the Bulgarian-made *Pâtna Karta* map or the *Pâtno-Turisticheski Atlas*, both sold in bookshops. Balkantourist's *Camp-sites Bulgaria* lists the odd non-existent site,

which is rather disconcerting **for campers**, but their plan **of Sofia** is quite reasonable – if not as good as Cartographia's map of the city (available only in Hungary). The *Bulgarian Tourist Union* (BTS) produces **hiking maps** covering the Rila, Pirin and Balkan ranges in some detail, but all legends are in Cyrillic only. Aside from the places mapped in this book, **town plans** are conspicuous by their absence, unless you count the crude efforts at the back of the *Pâtno-Turisticheski Atlas*.

COMMUNICATIONS – POST, PHONES AND MEDIA

Street kiosks sell envelopes (*plika*) but stamps (*marki*) are only sold at **Post Offices**, which are usually open 8.30-17.30 Monday to Saturday in large towns. The main *Poshta* will have a **poste restante** desk where mail can be claimed by showing your passport (ask *Ima li pisma za mene?*), and letters should be addressed писма до пойскване централна поща, followed by the name of the town. However, letters from Western Europe take around a week to get here and Bulgar postal officers are apt to misfile or return mail to the sender if it's not claimed immediately, so don't hold high hopes for poste restante communications. To get stuff home in less than a fortnight (3 weeks to the US) it has to go by airmail (*vâzdushna*) or express (*bârza*) post.

Most hotels will place **international phone calls**, but it's cheaper to do so at a Post Office; queue at the relevant desk, state the number you want and either take the call or dial it from a booth. In the cities and resorts you might find International call boxes taking 1 or 2 leva coins, but it's commoner to pay at the desk. To dial direct, first use the international code and then the STD (area) code ommitting the initial 0. Some international codes: *Britain* 0044; *Denmark*

0045; *Holland* 0031; *West Germany* 0049. **Domestic calls** seem dogged with problems, so amass a hoard of 2-stotinki pieces before trying your luck with public telephones.

Outside of the British Embassy and the American Library in Sofia, the only English-language **newspapers** around are *Sofia News* or the *Morning Star* (though *The Times* and other capitalist papers are sometimes available in Varna). For obvious reasons, few foreigners read the Bulgarian press, which broadly resembles its Soviet counterpart before glasnost, ranging from the turgid *Rabotichesko Delo* (Workers' Deeds) to the livelier, occasionally daring weekly, *Mladost* (Youth). Two monthly **magazines** appear in English, French and German: *Discover Bulgaria* is glossy and tourism-orientated; *Bulgaria* more concerned with 'social questions' and promoting national achievements. Bulgarian **television** and Varna **radio** broadcast a tourist programme during the summer, but for news you'd be better off tuning to the BBC World Service on:

| **MHz** | 15.07 | 12.09 | 9.41 | 6.18 |
| **Metres** | 19.91 | 24.80 | 31.88 | 48.54 |

Lower frequencies give better results early in the morning and late at night, higher ones in the middle of the day.

POLICE, TROUBLE AND SEXUAL HARASSMENT

Most tourists have little or no contact with the Bulgarian **Militia** милиция beyond an occasional request to show one's **passport**, which should therefore be carried at all times. The only bad stories we've heard relate to motorists in transit

between Yugoslavia and Turkey, whom traffic cops sometimes book for spurious speeding or safety violations, and travellers idiotic enough to start fights or abuse the police. Be polite, observe a few rules and there shouldn't be any **trouble**.

Anyone **photographing** airports, railways, bridges or anything obviously military risks losing their camera and at least an hour of liberty, and even the landscape is potentially taboo in **border zones** (*granitsen zone*) which are, in any case, off-limits unless you have a special pass. The risk of being caught changing money on the **black market** seems pretty small, but a heavy fine or deportation awaits those who are. Though **topless bathing** and nudism are prohibited everywhere, the authorities turn a blind eye to them on certain beaches. Camping wild and sleeping rough are both illegal, and **unaccounted nights** (ie gaps in the record on your *carte statistique*) are theoretically punishable by a 200 leva fine – although arguing that you've been travelling on overnight trains is an acceptable excuse. However, no mercy is shown to anyone caught **drinking and driving** or in possession of **drugs**, for whom years in gaol are very likely.

If you do find yourself in trouble, wait until you can explain matters to someone in English (misunderstandings in a foreign language can make things worse), if at all possible, and then request that your consulate be notified. **Consulates** may be helpful in some respects, but never lend cash to nationals who've run out or been robbed. You'll find the addresses in Sofia Listings.

Women travelling alone can expect to encounter stares, comments and sometimes worse from macho types, and discos on the coast are pretty much seen as 'cattle-markets', but a firm response should be enough to cope with most situations. If not, holler *Pomosht!* (Help!) or *Militsia*. Remember that local **attitudes** are invariably conservative, particularly in rural areas and above all amongst ethnic Turks (where the notion of woman as a chattel and beast of burden dies hard). Punk hairstyles or 'unusual' attire often arouse strong feelings, and it was a young Bulgarian woman who yelled at me 'Take those socks off!', deeply offended by their flourescent pinkness.

GETTING AROUND

By rail
Bulgarian State Railways БДЖ BDZh) can get you to most towns mentioned in this book and trains are punctual – if very slow by Western standards. Express **services** (*Ekspres vlak*) are restricted to trunk routes, but on everything except the humblest branch lines you'll find socalled Rapid (*bârz vlak*) trains. Use these rather than the snail-like *pâtnicheski* services unless you're planning to alight at some particularly insignificant halt. Long distance/overnight trains have a wagon with reasonably-priced **couchettes** (*kushet*) and/or **sleepers** (*spalen vagon*). For these, and on all expresses and many rapids, you need seat **reservations** (*zapazeni mesta*) as well as *bileti*, or **tickets**. Be sure to ask for them, since ticket clerks seem to delight in the prospect of unwitting travellers riding in the aisles! In large towns, it's usually easier to obtain tickets and reservations from **railway bookings offices** (BDZh) rather than the station; and wise – if not always essential – to book a day in advance. Advance bookings are required for international tickets, which are handled by a separate organisation, the *Rila Agency*. (Addresses for both in text).

It's rare to see **timetables** in anything but Cyrillic, so to make things easier we've included a list of town names in that script at the end of each chapter. On timetables, the three types of services are indicated by the abbreviations Е, Б and П; and express services are usually lettered in red. Confusingly, 'Departures' can be rendered as Тръгва (abbreviated to Тр.,) *or* Заминаване; and 'Arrivals' as Пристита (Пр) or Пристигане. Most railway stations sell a paperback national timetable (Пътеводител бдж), with international services printed in the Roman alphabet. Trains running on a particular day only are indicated by a numeral in a circle: eg. 1 = Monday, 2 = Tuesday, etc. Commonly, a single sign halfway down the platform is all that identifies **stations** (*gara*). You won't see this until the train starts up if you're sitting at the back, so the wise traveller will sit up front. Most stations have **left-luggage offices** (*garderob*); in the large ones it may be necessary to complete a form before stowing your gear.

Transalpino is only good as far as Sofia, and **Inter-Rail** has no validity at all.

However, British Rail and other foreign railways can issue **2-month tickets** which allow unlimited stopovers at places along a predetermined route: eg. Ruse-Pleven-Sofia-Plovdiv-Kapitan Andreevo for £24. You'd pay about the same for a series of 'ordinary' tickets inside Bulgaria, but considerably more if you're **heading on to Turkey**, since Rila charges 76 leva (around £40 at the 'non-bonus' exchange rate) for a ticket on the *Istanbul Express*. The Bulgars discourage the hoary dodge of paying to ride only as far as the border by refusing to sell tickets to Svilengrad (although guards may be bribeable; see p.658). Once the train is inside Turkey, buying a ticket to Istanbul (for the equivalent of £5) is quite straightforward. We've had reports that the Rila Agency in Sofia sometimes refuses to make seat reservations on the *Istanbul Express*, despite selling the ticket.

Bulgaria overcharges for all **international tickets** – the fare from Sofia to Budapest is twice what the Hungarians charge for a ticket from Budapest to Sofia (allowing for different exchange rates) – so it's always worth buying a return ticket outside Bulgaria if you're planning to travel back along the same route. International tickets purchased here must be paid for in leva exchanged at the 'non-bonus' rate, backed by a receipt; so you have to check the fare before exchanging the requisite sum at a Balkantourist office or bank, and then go back to the Rila bureau to buy the ticket and seat reservation (remember to include this in your calculations). Travellers with an *IUS* card (available from Orbita) are entitled to **reductions** of 30%.

By bus

Practically everywhere is accessible by bus (*avtobus*), though in remoter areas there may only be 2 or 3 services a day. We've suggested towns from which particular villages or sites can be reached, but haven't attempted to list the full range of services between major centres, from which there are buses to places up to 150km away. Generally, you must buy a ticket at least an hour in advance when **travelling between towns**, but on some routes they're only sold when the bus arrives, in which case people queue outside the shuttered ticket hatch. *Tova li e gisheto za bileti za. . .?* means 'Is this where I get tickets to. . .?' (remember that a shaken head means 'yes' and a nod

'no'). On **rural routes**, tickets are often sold by the driver rather than at the terminal (*Avtogara*). If you're aiming for a campsite or monastery along a bus route, ask the driver for the *spirkata za kamping* (or *manastir*), or call *Tuka!* ('Stop!') as it heaves into sight.

On **urban transport** there's a flat fare of 6 stotinki on all routes, so it's sensible to buy a bunch of 10 tickets (from street kiosks) whenever you arrive somewhere, which must then be punched on board the bus. Fare-dodgers risk a 200 leva spot-fine. Strictly speaking, tickets issued by one municipality aren't valid on another's buses, but most inspectors will be mollified if you plead ignorance of this. Routes are usually displayed at each bus stop (*spirka*) together with the times of first and last services. The same applies to trolleybuses (*troleibus*) in Plovdiv and Sofia, and trams (*tramvai*), which are unique to the capital.

Everyone obeys the no-smoking regulation except the drivers!

Driving and hitching

A current UK or other foreign **driving licence** is acceptable in Bulgaria (though not in most neighbouring countries), but third party **insurance** plus a 'Green' or 'Blue' card – the latter can be bought at the frontier – are obligatory. It's not necessary to take out CASCO insurance, although this Bulgarian policy claims to pay up when you're in the country (whereas Western ones do so back home). *Bulstrad*, the national insurance company, has offices in Ruse, Varna and Burgas, and its headquarters in Sofia (5, Ul. Dunav; ☎ 85-191). Entering Bulgaria, your vehicle will be registered with a special **'visa tag'** which must be presented on leaving the country – a rule intended to prevent foreigners from flogging their cars here.

86-, 93- and 96-octane **petrol** can only be obtained in exchange for **coupons**, available for hard currency at border crossings, motels, large hotels, or from the Shipka Travel Agency. These are non-refundable, and also cover the purchase of lubricants. You'll find filling stations (*benzinostantsiya*) on the main roads leaving most towns, and spaced 30-40km apart along the highways, as shown on town plans and Cyrillic-script road atlases (*Pâtno Atlas*) and **motoring maps** (*Pâtna Karta*) available from bookshops. Names signposted along the highways appear in both alphabets, and although the system of transliteration is slightly different from the one used in this book, they're recognisably similar. Other **signs** are basically identical to those employed in the West.

Roads are inconsistently numbered (some highways carry 2 or 3 designations), but as a general rule trunk routes – marked in red on maps – are reasonably surfaced, whereas minor roads – indicated in yellow – are gravelly, bumpy or both. **Traffic** is pretty light everywhere and drives on the right; at crossroads, vehicles approaching from that direction have right of way. Right turns and moving on are forbidden when the traffic light is red. In urban areas buses have the right of way and parking is restricted to specified spots. **Speed limits** in built-up areas (60 kph), on the open road (80 kph) and highways (120 kph) are reduced to 50 kph, 70 kph or 100 kph for minibuses or cars with caravans or trailers.

Mountainous Bulgaria has lots of hairpin bends, and in rural areas it's important to watch out for donkeys, farm animals and carts. Motorists are legally obliged to report **accidents** and, in case of injury, render assistance where appropriate whilst awaiting the Militia. Spot-**fines** for trival offences are common practice, and policemen have been known to abuse this by demanding payment in dollars and pocketing the cash. Requests for a receipt might put a stop to this, or make things worse. In case of arrest, insist on being allowed to contact your embassy (see Sofia 'Listings' for addresses). **Drinking and driving** is absolutely prohibited (there's no acceptable limit), and the Bulgarians justifiably punish offenders with a heavy fine or imprisonment.

Car hire is arranged by Balkantourist, who reckon payment in US$ and charge each passenger separately (so if there's a group of you, only one should rent the car). Expect to pay $15 per day for a cronky Lada and upwards of $20 for a Western car ($90-$140 per week), plus 15-30 cents per kilometre. Insurance, driving licences and petrol coupons as described above.

I found **hitching** fair to good in most parts of Bulgaria, and never had any problems with the police. It's advisable to carry a sign in Cyrillic if you're heading for somewhere distant, while a clue to drivers' movements may be gained from their number plates, the first letter(s) of which indicate their home town (eg. П = Plovdiv; С = Sofia; Бл = Blagoevgrad, etc). Given the low price of buses and trains, the main reason for hitching is to reach somewhere inaccessible or badly served by public transport.

By air

Daily *BALKAN* **flights** are the quickest way to travel between Sofia and the Danubian and Black Sea ports, and given the length of the railway journey a flight to Varna or Burgas is certainly worth considering. Fares are very reasonable – from Sofia to Varna costs 26 leva – and at BALKAN offices (listed in the guide) you're not always asked to show an exchange receipt when paying in leva. Book the day before (since most flights leave around 7-8 am) if not 2 or 3 days in advance for services to the coast. Tickets may also be obtained through Balkantourist Comprehensive Service Bureaux, though here one must pay in hard currency.

SLEEPING

Visitors from capitalist countries (*kap. strana*) are officially limited to **accommodation** run or arranged by Balkantourist, which tends to rule out really cheap hotels and hostels, and a number of campsites. However, the ruling isn't always adhered to, so we've deailed the full range of possibilities below (and in the text) in case you fancy trying your luck. Anyone planning to spend all their time on the coast should consider **package tours**, which include accommodation at a much lower price than if you pay on the spot.

Travelling independently, you must obtain a date stamp on your **carte statistique** (see p.513), which policemen may inspect hoping to discover 'unaccounted' nights (punishable, in theory at least, by a 200 leva fine). Travellers **paying in leva** are usually required to show an exchange receipt from which the rent is 'deducted' – a measure intended to stop one using leva acquired on the black market. If you're given two receipts for an exchange, both can be used alternately to make your 'official leva' last longer. It's seldom necessary to make **advance bookings** through the local Balkantourist office (or Comprehensive Service Bureaux, nationwide).

A few Balkantourist **hotels** хотел charge as little as 12 leva per head, but the average 2- or 3-star establishments rent doubles for between 30-50 leva, and in ritzier hotels upwards of 60 leva is commonplace. Hotel rooms in the big costal resorts are allocated through the tourist office, which often tries to push the dearest place, so insist on being told about everything that's available. If there's a group of you, it might be cheaper to rent a **villa** in one of the **holiday villages** there. **Motels** along the main highways cost about the same as 2- or 3-star hotels. Westerners are hardly ever allowed to stay at cheaper, scruffier **non-Balkantourist places** (which pretend to be full if one asks), and one the rare occasions that they are, **unmarried couples** must book separate rooms in conformity with Bulgarian law (this rule also applies to the 'Youth' Hotel in Lovech).

In Sofia, Ruse, Varna, Nesebâr etc, Balkantourist can arrange **private rooms** for between 2-15 leva per head during the holiday season. The quality of *chastna kvartira* varies enormously (it's rarely possible to inspect the place first), but as a rule anywhere outside the centre of town will be in a tower-block. Although it's illegal **to stay unofficially** in someone's home, people are much less paranoid than in Romania, and my hosts often scoffed at the notion of police hassles. Professionals, who tout at Sofia station, will probably be the wariest and most unreliable hosts; but a sincere invitation is always worth considering. Most towns of interest have a **campsite**, *Kamping*, on the outskirts. The majority have 2-person **chalets** (10-15 leva per night), though to get one on the busy coastal campsites you'll need to make a reservation through Balkantourist. Three campsites on the Balkantourist camping map actually come under the control of

local monasteries; *Preobrazhenski* and *Rilski Manastir* admit Westerners but *Bachkovo* won't. Until a few years ago Westerners were also allowed to rent **monastic cells** at Rila, Troyan and Bachkovo, but nowadays this is restricted to Eastern Europeans.

Between July 15 and September 15, travellers with IUS cards might consider **Orbita accommodation** in Sofia, Pleven, Târnovo, Burgas, Varna and other towns (addresses in the text). Depending on where you are, this can mean **rooms** in a special block (if they're not already booked by Youth groups), or **dormitory beds** in some vacant college. Expect to pay $4 in Sofia and 12 leva elsewhere.

Two further types of accommodation are mainly found in the mountains or small towns. Dirt cheap, very basic **hostels** (*Turisticheska spalya*) run by the Bulgarian Tourist Union lurk in the backstreets of places like Tryavna and Melnik, and sometimes admit Westerners on the quiet, but you should never count on this. In highland areas favoured by hikers there are scores of **hizhas** хижа or alpine chalets, some primitive, others comfy hotels in all but name. Balkantourist is gradually laying claim to the ones around Borovets, but most *hizhas* come under the aegis of the Tourist Union. In practice, this means that Westerners lacking authorisation from the **Pirin Travel Agency** in Sofia (30, Blvd. Stamboliiski; ☎ 87-06-87) might be turned away; in practice, staff in the remoter chalets are unlikely to be bothered. Contact the Pirin agency before you leave for the mountains if you want proper authorisation, which may only be granted to those who sign up for hiking tours.

Lastly, **wild camping** and **sleeping rough** are both illegal and punishable with a fine if you get caught in the act; tentative suggestions are indicated in the guide, but all things considered it's probably not worth taking the risk unless you have to.

EATING AND DRINKING

Bulgaria is stuffed full of vegetable plots and orchards ('Bulgar' used to be a synonym for 'market gardener' in several Balkan countries), and fresh fruit and vegetables are half the secret of **Bulgarian food**. The other half lies in the

techniques – slow roasting or stewing in earthenware dishes – and a single, vital ingredient, yoghurt, which could almost be the national dish. Traditionally, food was eaten in the fields or pastures, or consumed on returning home – which meant subsisting on bread, cheese, vegetables and fruit throughout the day until an evening meal of stew or grilled meat. Nowadays, people eat rather less frugally: a quick kebab or a syrupy pastry fill out the day, and industrial workers enjoy hearty lunches in socialised canteens.

Unfortunately, the canteen-ethos has rubbed-off on many **restaurants** (*restorant*; ресторант), and to escape surly service or lukewarm dishes it's usually best to go upmarket, or look for humble 'family' places, patronised almost exclusively by Bulgarians. Restaurants in deluxe hotels tend either to serve 'international' food, foreign cuisine (Japanese at Sofia's *Vitosha-New Otani*, for example) or regional specialities, which are quite a lot cheaper in 'inns'. Whether these **Han** (хан) or **Hanche** (ханче) are recently-built 'folk' restaurants or – better still – ensconced within some sumptuously-appointed mansion dating from the National Revival period, the cooking should be a cut above that of most ordinary restaurants'. Tavernas, or **Mehanas** (механа), are less predictable: although their grills and salads can be excellent, some places are just for drink-ing wine or spirits in. The same applies to **Skara-Bira joints**, a lower form of culinary life serving little more than beer and kebabs – which are, in rural areas at least, a male preserve. In towns, you'll also find **self-service** (*Autoservis*) restaurants; invariably cheap, but often with reason. Refreshingly, most larger towns also have a **vegetarian restaurant** (вегитариянский ресторант) – often a good option for meat-eaters, too.

With the exception of deluxe hotel restaurants, none of these should **cost** the earth, and providing you avoid imported drinks or restaurants featuring a floorshow, the bill should be very modest indeed. Cheaper still if you **buy some of your own food** in supermarkets – *Gastronom* (гастроном) or *Magazin* (магазин) – and markets – *Hali* (хали).

Snacks and dishes

Foremost among **snacks** are *kebapcheta*, little wads of grilled mincemeat served with a chunk of bread, or variations on the theme like *Shishche* (shish kebab) or *kebap* (spicier, with a rich sauce) – all sold at street stands, *Mexanas* and *Skara-Biras*. Another favourite is the ubiquitous *Banitsa*, basically a flaky-

Basics

Imate li...?	Do you have...?
Molya, donesete mi/ni...	Please bring me/us....
Listata	the menu
Hlyab	bread
Maslo	butter
Med	honey
Mlyako	milk
Kifli	rolls
Kiselo Mlyako	yoghurt
Piper	pepper
Solt	salt
dve bira	two beers
Nazdrave!	Cheers!
Smetka, molya	the bill, please

Appetizers, soups (supi) and salads (salati)

Kyopolou	aubergine, pepper and tomato salad
Lyutenitsa	piquant sauce of red peppers and herbs
Postna supa	vegetable soup
Ruska salata	Russian salad
Shopska salata	Shoppe salad,

	topped with grated cheese
Supa s meso	consommé
Tarator	yoghurt and cucumber soup

Meat (meso)

Agneshko s kartofi	lamb and potato stew
Gyuvech	stir-fried veg, baked with meat
Imam Bayaldu	stuffed aubergines
Kebap	braised, spiced meat in rich sauce
Kebapcheta	grilled, spicy sausage-shaped meatballs
Kyufteta	meatballs
Musaka	moussaka
Ovheshko s pryasno zele	mutton and cabbage
Pile	chicken
Salam	salami
Shishcheta	lamb or pork shish-kebab
Slanina	bacon

pastry (or pancake) envelope with a filling – usually cheese or curds and raisins, less often meat, spinach and eggs, or fruit. In a similar vein are the **bread and buns**, which can vary a lot: if freshly-baked, small *pitka* loaves, larger *purlenka*, or glazed buns made of chickpea flour (*simitli*) can be delicious. Bulgarians consider their **yoghurt** (*kiselo mlyako*) the world's finest, and hardly miss a day without consuming a glass (eaten with a tall spoon or drunk, according to consistency).

Yoghurt also occurs as an ingredient in *tarator*, a cold cucumber soup-cum-salad. More conventional **salads**, include a ubiquitous cucumber, red pepper, onion and tomato mix topped with grated white cheese – *Shopska salad* – which accompanies any main meal almost automatically. Aside from salads, **vegetarian dishes** include fried courgettes (*pârzheni tikvichki*) and peppers (*pârzheni chushki*), purée of aubergines (*kyopolu*) or potatoes (*pyure ot kartofi*), eggs fried on spinach (*pârzheni yaitsa s pyure ot spanak*) or scrambled with peppers and tomatoes into aptly-named *mish-mash*, and finally *gyuvech-zarzabat* the vegetarian version of a quintes-

sentially Bulgarian dish.

Gyuvech literally means 'earthenware dish', and a range of **traditional Bulgarian dishes** are baked and served in such receptacles. The best guyvechs are rich in peppers, aubergines, and beans, to which are added either meat or meat stock, stewed for as long as possible (Bulgarian lamb and beef are on the tough side and steaks, *biftec*, are not recommended). *Sarmi* – stuffed cabbage or vineleaves – is tasty and filling, and if you don't mind waiting for the dish to be prepared, ask for *Imam Bayaldu*, aubergine stuffed with all manner of vegetables, meat and herbs – a Turkish dish, whose name translates as 'the priest burst' (from overeating). Stews are tasty and filling, although offal-haters should be careful about ordering them in the Rhodopes, where *pluck* (tripe rouleau) is another recipe best not ordered lightly. Finally, along the coast and around the highland lakes and reservoirs there's fish – most often fried or grilled, but sometimes in a soup or stew.

Sweets
Bulgarian pancakes can be sweet as often as savoury. *Banitsa saralia* (with

Svinsko (*s kiselo zele*	pork (and saurkraut)

TERMS: *divech* = game; *pârzheni* = fried; *pechno* = roast; *ptitsi* = poultry; *zadusheno* = braised

Fish (riba)

Byala riba	pike perch
Chiga	sterlet
Esetra	sturgeon
Kalkan	turbot
Kefal	grey mullet
Palamud	tuna
Pâstârva	trout
Popche	bull-head
Skumriya	mackeral
Som	sheat fish
Sharan	carp

Vegetables (plodove)

Chesân	garlic
Chushki	peppers
Domati	tomatoes
Grah	peas
Karfiol	cauliflower
Kartofi	potatoes
Krastavitsa	cucumber
Morkovi	carrots
Praz	leeks
(Presen) luk	(spring) onions
Sini domati	aubergines
Spanak	spinach
Tikvichki	courgettes
Zelen fasul	runner beans

Fruit (zelenchutsi) **and cheese** (sirene)

Chereshi	cherries
Dinya	watermelon
Grozde	grapes
Kaisii	apricots
Krushi	pears
Limon	lemon
Malini	raspberries
Praskovi	peaches
Slivi	plums
Vishni	morello cherries
Yabâlki	apples
Yagodi	strawberries
Sirene	salty, feta-type cheese
Pusheno sirene	smoked cheese
Kashkaval	Edam-type cheese

walnuts and syrup) and *banitsa mlyaka* (cooked with milk) are both delicious. They're sometimes sold on the street, like brioches (*kozunak*) and pastry sticks (*solenski*), and always to be found in **patisseries** or *Sladkarnitsa* (сладкарница), alongside *baklava* and *revane* (nut-filled flaky pastry) and the gooey rich *kadif* – all of Turkish origin – plus various cakes (*torta*) with butter-cream (*maselna*), fruit (*frukti*) or chocolate (*shokoladova*) filling. Rice pudding (*mlyako s orez*), creme caramel (*krem-karamel*), Turkish Delight (*lokum*) and *halva* are also firm favourites. More importantly, perhaps, patisseries serve **coffee** (*kafe*) – which is otherwise virtually impossible to buy outside of the hard currency CORECOMs – and often runs out by midday even in *Sladkarnitsa*. If you don't specify, it comes milky (*kafe s mlyako*) or black (*shvarts*) and sweet, sometimes with a sediment of grounds, Turkish-style (*tursko*). **Tea** (normally green) is sold in supermarkets, but hardly ever in patisseries; when it does appear, it's usually insipid tea-bag stuff.

Drinks

From having an insular **wine** industry before the Second World War, Bulgaria has muscled its way into the forefront of the world's export market. Tried and tested grapes like Cabernet Sauvignon and Merlot have been planted in different regions (eg. Pomorie, Haskovo, Asenovgrad or Suhindol), under whose name they're marketed abroad. Inside Bulgaria there's a greater variety and more differentiation between the various blended wines, all of which cost less than £1.50 a bottle in supermarkets and mehanas. Amongst the **reds** are full-bodied *Cabarnet*, heavier, mellower *Melnik* and *Gâmza*, rich, dark *Mavrud*, and the smooth, strawberry-flavoured *Haskovski Merlot*. Sweet *Pamid*, first grown by the Thracians and verging on rosé, is blended with Mavrud to produce *Trakiya*, or with Melnik wine to make *Pirin*, while *Madara* is obtained from concentrated Gâmza and Dimyat grapes (a similar mix is used for the more acidic *Târnovo*). *Asenovgradski Mavrud* and the red Muscatel *Slavyanska* are both dessert wines. The sweeter **whites** are preferable to *Dimyat* unless you like your wine very dry; *Karlovski Misket* (Muscatel) and *Tamyanka* are widely available, the golden-coloured *Euxinovgrad* much harder to find.

Native **spirits** are highly potent and cost very little; drunk diluted with water in the case of *mastika* and *rakiya* (like ouzo and raki in Greece), or downed in one, Balkan-style, in the form of plum brandy, *silva* (brandy is also made from apricots, apples etc. – see the names of fruit to figure them out). *Pliska* cognac and excellent Russian *Stolichnaya* vodka are only slightly dearer, and to blow a significant amount you have to order Western imports – whisky is particularly expensive, but Austrian or German **beer** isn't cheap. Unfortunately, bottled Bulgarian *bira* is pretty unexciting, and only a few places serve it from a cask.

The situation improves with **soft drinks** insofar that there's a range of delicious bottled fruit juices (*Nektar* or *fructovi suk*) which, in the case of apple, also come in carbonated form (*Yablitsa*). There's no halfway-decent equivalent of Coke or Pepsi, though the Bulgarians for one don't seem to mind, having their own special beverage, *Bozo*. Made of millet and invented in Albania, the kindest thing to say about Bozo is that it's an acquired taste.

WORKCAMPS AND OTHER ACTIVITIES

Every August more than 100 volunteers from 35 countries participate in 3-week **workcamps in Bulgaria**, which combine project work with discussions on peace, detente and East-West relations, alongside various social events. Recent projects have included restoration work on the ruins at Veliko Târnovo, and agricultural work around Plovdiv. Volunteers should be between 18-30 years of age, have previous workcamp experience, and an interest in East-West contacts; speaking Russian or German is an advantage. The work involves a 5-day week (8hrs daily) but board, lodging and work clothes are all supplied, plus a limited travel allowance. Would-be participants must attend a preliminary orientation meeting organised by IVS and the Quakers. Applications in the UK (enclosing an SAE) should be made by the end of May to one of the following:

International Voluntary Service, Ceresole House, 53 Regent Rd, Leicester

LE1 6YL (☎ Leicester 541862).

Quaker Work Camps, Friends House, Euston Rd, London NW1 2BJ (☎ 01-387-3601).

United Nations Association, Welsh Centre for International Affairs, Temple of Peace, Cathays Park, Cardiff CF1 3AP (☎ Cardiff 28549).

Applications from outside the UK should be made directly to the *National Committee for Voluntary Brigades*, 11, Blvd. Stamboliiski, 1040 Sofia, Bulgaria.

Other possible **activity holidays**, all organised by Balkantourist, include **craft courses and workshops** at Kotel, Koprivshtitsa and Troyan – to name but a few; **hiking** and **horseriding** in the Sredna Gora, Pirin and Rila ranges; and **folkdancing** at Burgas and Blagoevgrad.

Festivals, as such, are less authentic and more organised than in Romania, but four events stand out nonetheless. **Gabrobvo's Bienial Festival of Humour and Satire** takes place in mid-May (see p.618); **Kazanlâk's Festival of the Roses** in early June (see p.631); and if it's not yet time for the great **Koprivshtitsa Folklore Festival** (held every five years – next in 1991), there's a similar, international event at **Burgas**, annually, in the second half of August.

For dates and details of **other festivals**, see the listings at the end of each chapter.

OTHER THINGS

ADDRESSES are normally written in the Cyrillic alphabet, like everything else in Bulgaria. In the text, they're transcribed into Roman script according to system on p.715. Main streets and squares are named after the same historical figures or dates – Levski, Botev, Dimitrov, May 1, September 9 – everywhere, whilst the most common abbreviations are *ul.* for 'street' (*ulitsa*), *pl.* for 'square' (*ploshtad*) and *bul.* for *bulevard*. Addresses in the high-rise suburbs include the *bloc* (*bl.*) number, a letter denoting the entrance (*vhod*), Roman numerals signifying the floor (*etazh*), and finally the number of the apartment itself.

BODY LANGUAGE Although head-wobbling means **yes** and nodding **no** according to local custom, natives sometimes shake or nod their head in the 'normal' way when talking with foreigners. Bulgarians are tolerant of misunderstandings over gestures, but it must be disconcerting for them to have a chat with someone who constantly nods 'no, no'. Anyone **waving** at you is probably signalling 'come here' or 'step inside', not 'goodbye'.

BRING. . . camera film, camping gas cartouches, razor blades, tampax and contraceptives, which are either unavailable or difficult to procure. Coffee is rarely sold in shops and tea is of the 'green' variety, so it's wise to bring both if you're planning on self-catering.

CHILDREN Many package deals offer child reductions, and the main Black Sea resorts are well-equipped for kids. Bring baby food and nappies.

CIGARETTES There's good Bulgar tobacco in *Marlboro*, sold in CORECOM shops, and in *Foeniks* cigarettes (*tsigari*), but other native brands (*Rodopi*, *Styurdesa* etc) have only the merit of being cheap. Matches are called *kibrit*.

ELECTRICITY 220 volts; continental 2-pin plugs.

EMBASSIES (*Posolstvo*) and consulates are all in Sofia; see the listings for addresses.

GAY LIFE The mere idea of homosexuality raises hackles in Bulgaria, where 'odd' clothing and hairstyles also invite trouble from the police. Little surprise, then, that gays are invisible.

LAUNDRY Laundrettes (*prelnya* or *gladene*), let alone *himichesko chistene* (dry cleaners), are exceedingly rare. At the larger hotels, it's sometimes possible to have cleaning done on the premises.

LEFT LUGGAGE Most large stations have 24-hour *garderob*.

NATURISM is forbidden on beaches (and everywhere else), but Germans lead the way in nude sunbathing just around the dunes from the 'official' beaches along the coast.

PUBLIC HOLIDAYS All shops, offices and banks, and many museums, are closed nationwide on January 1; May 1, 2 & 24; September 9-10 (Liberation Day) and November 7 (Anniversary of the Bolshevik Revolution).

SHOPPING HOURS Big city shops and supermarkets are generally open from 8.30am (or earlier) through until 6pm (or later, in the case of neighbourhood supermarkets). In rural areas and small towns, a kind of unofficial siesta may prevail between 12am-3pm.

SKIING Several UK operators offer excellent value skiing holidays at the main resorts of Pamporovo (p.667) and Borovets (p.561), as detailed on page 511, while Aleko-Vitosha near the capital, and Bansko and Malyovitsa in the mountains of the southwest, are up and coming resorts.

TIME One hour ahead of GMT and BST; Bulgarian Summer Time lasts from April 1 to September 31.

WATER (*voda*) is safe to drink everywhere, but supplies may be restricted to set periods (*regim na vodata*) during the summer.

BULGARIAN TERMS: A GLOSSARY

ALAFRANGA Term for the combination of native woodwork and textiles with Western fashions in C19 interior design (from *à la française*); or painted niches and walls in National Revival-style houses.

BANYA Public bath; Narechenski Bani, the 'Baths of Narechen'.

BASHIBAZOUKS Murderous bands of Pomaks (see below) and Turks, employed to punish rebellions against Ottoman rule.

B.K.P. Bulgarian Communist Party.

CARAVANSARAI Hostelry for merchants; in Bulgarian, *Han* or *Hanche*.

CHARDAK Balcony or porch.

CHARSHIYA (or **PAZAR**) A bazaar or street of workshops, once a typical feature of Bulgarian towns.

CHERKVA Church.

CHERNO MORE Black Sea.

CHETA Unit of resistance fighters (originally applied to the Bulgarian Legion of the 1860s).

CHORBADZHII Village headmen (literally, 'Meat eaters') or rich landowners; also perjorative term for those who collaborated during the Ottoman occupation.

D.S. State Security police (*Dârzhavna Signurnost*).

DUPKA Hole or den (*Mechata Dupka*, the Bear's Den) – another word for 'cave'.

DZHAMIYA A mosque (also spelt **DJAMI**, **DZHAMIJA** etc).

EZERO A lake (**YAZOVIR** is a dam).

GORA Forest, hill or mountain (eg *Sredna Gora*, 'Central Range').

GRAD City or town. The oldest quarter is often known as the *Stari Grad*.

GRADINA Garden.

HAIDUK (plural *Haiduti*) Outlaws, whom many Bulgarians esteemed as enemies of the Turks, and the Ottomans considered bandits.

HALI Market hall.

I.M.R.O. Macedonian separatist organisation, predominantly terroristic in later life (1893-1934).

IZVOR A spring.

JANISSARIES An élite military corps raised from foreigners whom the Turks abducted during childhood (under the hated *devsirme* system), and indoctrinated with fanatical loyalty to the Sultan.

KHAN (or **HAN**) Supreme ruler of the Bulgar tribes and, later, the first Bulgarian state; the title is of Central Asian origin.

KONAK The headquarters of an Ottoman *chiflik* or region; including the governor's residence, a garrison and a prison.

KREPOST Fortress (in Turkish, **HISAR**).

KÂSHTA House.

MANASTIR Monastery.

MINDER Couches or seats built into a room.

MOST Bridge.

NATIONAL REVIVAL-STYLE Architecture developed during the C18-C19, characterised by the use of oriels and decorative features such as carved wooden ceilings, stylised murals and niches. Best seen in Târnovo, Tryavna and Plovdiv.

NOS Cape.

PAMETNIK Monument or memorial.

PÂT Road.

PESHTERA Cave (see also *Dupka*).

PLOSHTAD (*Pl.*) Square.

POMAKS Bulgarians who converted to Islam during the Turkish occupation, or their descendants; mainly resident in the Rhodopes.

POP An Orthodox priest.

PROHOD Mountain pass.

PROLOM Gorge or defile.

PÂT Road.

RAYAH (or **RAYA**) 'The Herd', as the Ottomans called and treated the non-Muslim subjects of their empire.

REKA River.
SELO Village.
SHOSE Avenue or highway (from the French Chaussée).
SOFRA Low table with a circular top of copper or brass.

SVETA (*Sv.*) Saint; blessed or holy.
THRACIANS Inhabitants of Bulgaria during the pre-Christian era.
ULITSA (*Ul.*) Street.
VRÂH Summit or peak.

BULGARIA
THE GUIDE

ROMANIA

YUGOSLAVIA

THE BALKAN RANGE,
VALLEY OF THE ROSES
AND SREDNA GORA

THE
COAST

Black Sea

SOFIA AND THE
SOUTHWEST

THE RHODOPES AND THE
PLAIN OF THRACE

TURKEY

GREECE

0   100 km

Chapter thirteen
SOFIA AND THE SOUTHWEST

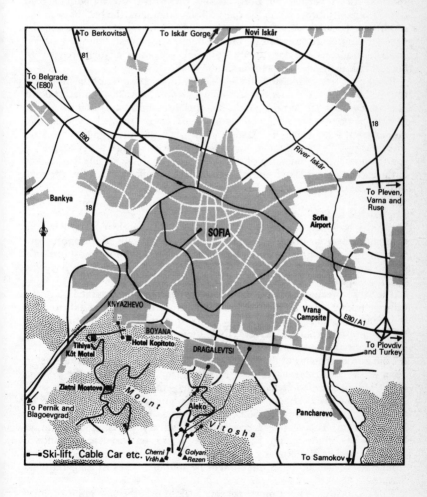

Sofia is not an exciting capital. Its parks, diverse churches and museums are diverting enough for a couple of day's wandering, and the heights overlooking the city a relief from the bland uniformity of the streets below. But the life of the place seems lacking – too ordered and conventional – and it's not long before, like the locals, you feel the urge for something a little more rural and anarchic.

This, fortunately, is close at hand. Sofians, at the slightest opportunity, head for the hills. Close to the city, there is **hiking** around Mount Vitosha or **winter sports** at Aleko. Further out, **Borovets** and **Malyovitsa**, too, are both devoted to such pursuits, practised in the rugged Rila mountains, the backbone of the southwest. Formerly noted for their bandits and hermits, the **Rila**, and the neighbouring **Pirin mountains**, contain Bulgaria's highest, stormiest peaks; swathed in forests and dotted with alpine lakes awaiting anyone prepared to hike or risk their car's suspension on the backroads.

Bansko – a nest of old stone houses – is the most attractive of the mountain towns; but in terms of its historical importance, **Samokov** claims pride of place as a great crafts' centre and the first socialist municipality in the Balkans. It was Samokov artisans who adorned the most revered of Bulgarian monasteries, **Rila**, which, like **Zemen** and **Rozhen**, enjoys magnificent natural surroundings. Beyond Zemen, trains follow a scenic route to **Kyustendil**, a spa-town retaining something of its C19 Turkish character; while Rozhen lies at the end of a great hike from wine-producing **Melnik**, which skims the edge of the 'sandstone sea' on the Greek border.

Approaches to Sofia and the southwest

The order in which you see Sofia and places in the southwest will likely be determined by your original point of departure and means of transportation. Coming by rail or air from abroad (or from the coast), you'll almost certainly see Sofia first; coming from Greece or southern Yugoslavia, you have the option of starting with the southwest proper.

The most direct approach by land is **from Yugoslavia**, using the E80 or the railway linking Belgrade and Niš with Sofia. Motorists should be able to drive the 300km capital-to-capital in a few hours, subject to minimal formalities at the 24-hour checkpoint of KALOTINA. By train, it's 8½hrs (5hrs from Niš) by international express, with a prolonged customs inspection at DRAGOMAN, the old border crossing of the Ottoman empire. The *Istanbul* express arrives in Sofia at the most reasonable hour (7.30pm), much better than the *Polonia* (10.30pm) or *Istanbul-Hellas* (after midnight) – though you can, if you wish, break the journey at Dragoman where there's a motel; there's also a hotel on the highway 18km west of Sofia, plus a hotel and campsite in Slivnitsa. Driving from Yugoslav Macedonia, you can try to enter Bulgaria at GYUSHEVO on the road to Kyustendil (see p.559) or, with less assurance of success, at the border crossing west of Petrich (p.576). There are no railways from Macedonia, although there might be sporadic buses to Bulgaria from Skopje.

Open non-stop, with a motel nearby, KULATA is the sole point of entry **from Greece**. For motorists it's simply a matter of following the E79 northwards to Sofia, unless they want to turn off at Novo Delchevo to see

Melnik (p.573) or at Kocherinovo for Rila Monastery (p.566). International trains stop at Sandanski and Blagoevgrad en route to Sofia, and if you're prepared it's possible to alight during the 1 minute halt at Kocherinovo (about 2hrs after clearing the frontier) and go directly to Rila Monastery. The overnight service from Thessaloníki stops there around 6.20am, and the morning train (leaving Athens the previous night) in the mid-afternoon, reaching Sofia by early evening.

Coming **from Romania** you're likely to enter Bulgaria at RUSE, a pleasant town on the banks of the Danube (p.591). Breaking your journey there is a good idea, since trains from Bucharest (or the *Bulgaria* from Ploieşti) take 11-12hrs to reach Sofia; Pleven (p.599), halfway towards the capital, is a less attractive stopover. International trains arrive at Sofia in the morning (*Pannonia* & *Bulgaria*), mid-evening (*Danubius*) or around 10pm (the *Sofia* express): all services go by way of Gorna Oryahovitsa, where you can change for Veliko Târnovo instead. There is a second possible approach, by ferry from Calafat to VIDIN (p.586). From here it's just under 200km by road E79 to the capital, but takes 5hrs by express train, so here too an overnight stop might be in order.

Travelling **from Turkey**, you cross the region described in Chapter 15, where PLOVDIV alone is ample reason to interrupt one's journey. Aside from the scenic attractions on the way, it's 14hrs from Istanbul to Sofia by the *Istanbul Express* (or the off-season *Istanbul-Hellas*), which arrives in the evening. Motorists can rely upon the well-surfaced E80 all the way, but travelling by road can have its drawbacks. Besides the possibility of having your car dismantled in the search for heroin at the KAPITAN ANDREEVO border crossing, I've heard of motorists being harassed by police should they have breakdowns or stray off the highway. The risks of both are much higher for Turkish nationals, but Westerners fitting the Militia's conception of 'hippies' could also suffer. Customs checks on the trains at SVILENGRAD (p.660) are equally thorough, and to minimise the risk of hassle it's best not to be associated with Turkish passengers. The motel at Kapitan Andreevo and the hotel in Svilengrad are both expensive, so if you want cheaper accommodation, carry on until Harmanli or Haskovo.

The highways **from the coast** need no explanation, while information on Sofia-bound flights and trains appears at the end of Chapter 16. **Approaches from the northeast** are laid out in the Chapter 14. Travellers with private transport or a willingness to chance their luck with buses might also consider **routes through the mountains** to towns like Samokov or Razlog in the highlands of the southwest.

SOFIA

According to its motto, **SOFIA** 'grows but does not age' (*raste no ne stare*): a tribute to the mushrooming suburbs occupied by one tenth of Bulgaria's population, and a cryptic reference to its ancient origins. The modern city resembles a kind of Communist Geneva, with fresh wreathes laid before its monuments and a police force that one could imagine clubbing litterbugs or jaywalkers. Under the People's Republic the downtown streets and parks are pristine, with a gargantuan **Largo** and **National Palace of Culture** symbolising a post-war era that's nothing if not proud. As recently as 1910, foreigners sneered at this capital whose trams struck Arthur Symons as a 'mockery in this city of dust and rags', and the Bulgars have preserved much to remind them of the milestones along their tortuous road to progress.

As various **Byzantine ruins** attest, Sofia was once a walled city which reached its zenith under Emperor Constantine (306-337), originally descended from a town called *Serdica* after the Thracian tribe which founded it some 3,000 years ago. The Bulgars didn't arrive on the scene until the C9, and with the notable exception of the C13 **Boyana Church** their cultural monuments largely disappeared during the Turkish occupation (1381-1878), of which the sole legacy visible today is a couple of defunct **mosques**. Sofia's finest architecture post-dates Bulgaria's liberation: handsome public buildings and parks, and the magnificent **Aleksandâr Nevski Cathedral**. The socialist era, too, has its shrines – most notably the ghoulish **Mausoleum of Georgi Dimitrov** on 9 September Square.

If all this suggests that Sofia's dead from the waist down – well, it's partly true. *Skromnost* or 'modesty of habits' has traditionally been a virtue in Bulgaria, and the Party – which fulminates against drinking, 'decadent' pop music and jeans – rarely tolerates wild or autonomous behaviour. *Shops* (Sofian cockneys) and students might indulge in bacchanals behind closed doors, but accessible **nightlife** boils down to folklore shows, the odd disco and a few bars, plus lots of drama and 'serious' music, especially during the **Sofia Music Weeks** (roughly, May 24-June 20). However, the range of diversions may yet expand as Sofia develops as an international centre, particularly if, as is hoped, the **winter sports** complex of **Aleko** is chosen as the venue for the 1992 Winter Olympics.

Arriving, information and transport

It makes sense to time your **arrival** to catch Balkantourist or Orbita, which can arrange private rooms or hostel beds. After closing hours these options are out, and unless your budget runs to a hotel room it's best to make straight for one of the campsites, which offer chalets as well as tentspace and can be economically reached by taxi even after the buses have stopped running. Most trains arrive at **Central Station** (*Tsentralna Gara*): a concrete barn with the weirdest way of numbering its platforms, and a totally unhelpful tourist bureau (open until 8pm) in its underground forecourt. Five minutes ride along Blvd. Dimitrov (tram #1 or #7) is Lenin Square and central Sofia, within walking distance of several hotels and the main tourist office. Alternatively, take a #213 bus from the station to the big CORECOM store on the Plovdiv highway, from which bus #5 runs to Vrana campsite. Buses #284 (express) and #84, running every 10-20mins, connect **Sofia Airport** with the Orlov

Most (p.537), from where you can walk into the city centre or catch bus #5 to Vrana camping; the last buses leave the airport at 10pm and 12pm. Arriving at one of Sofia's **other railway stations**, catch tram #3 from *Gara Poduyane*, the nearby *Sever* bus terminal, or *Gara Zaharna Fabrika* to reach Balkantourist; or tram #1 from *Gara Sofia-Sever* to the downtown area. Approaches **by road** are well signposted; coming from the direction of Pernik, Samokov or Plovdiv you'll pass a campsite (see below) en route to the city.

Information, maps and transport

The station Balkantourist kiosk doesn't have much time for casual enquirers, and it's better to try the tourist offices at 37, Knyaz Dondukov, beneath the NDK centre (☎ 59-70-95), or on Lenin Square, or even reception desks in the grander hotels, if you want **information**. Depending on their mood, these offices can also supply various **maps** of the capital, though none of them are as good as Cartographia's map of Sofia, which is only available outside Bulgaria.

Public transport is dirt cheap and reasonably efficent, with a metro due to open some time in the future. Currently, folks get around on buses (*avtobus*), trolleybuses (*troleibus*) and, slowest of all, on trams (*tramvai*). Most buses run from 4am until 11pm-12pm; trams and trolleybuses stop running about an hour after the buses. Triple-digit route numbers indicate express buses, which stop less frequently and are useful for travelling across town in a hurry. There's a flat fare of 6 stotinki on all urban routes; tickets (*bileti*) are sold from street kiosks and must be punched on board the vehicle (there are spot-fines for fare-dodgers). Though few foreigners find it worthwhile to buy one, you can also purchase monthly season tickets, valid for a single route or the whole city transport system. **Taxis** charge 20 stotinki per kilometre until 10pm, after which the rate is 30 stotinki per kilometre until 5am; with a surcharge of 60 stotinki (1 lev at night) you order by telephone (☎ 142).

Somewhere to stay

Westerners can't stay at the cheapest, non-Balkantourist hotels, though staff at the *Iskâr*, *Sredna Gora*, *Lyulin*, *Preslav* and *Zdravets* say that they're full up rather than admit this. Budget-travellers are more or less limited to renting a chalet or camping on the outskirts, or a dormitory bed in the suburbs. The cheapest accommodation in the centre is a private room, bookable through Balkantourist.

Motels, private rooms and dormitory beds

Motorists might consider one of the **motels** on Sofia's outskirts, which charge between 20-30 leva per head. *Iztok* is 500m past the junction with the outer ring road, and like *Gorublyane*, lies just off the Plovdiv highway; while *Boyana* (☎ 56-30-35) is located in the city district of the same name; and the cheapest motel, *Tihyat Kât*, stands on the road leading to Zlatni Mostove on Mount Vitosha.

For 20 leva per head (and an obligatory exchange equivalent to 10 leva 'for breakfast'), you can rent centrally-located **private rooms** from *Balkantourist*,

To Vidin

BULEVARD GEORGI DIMITROV

Tsentralna Gara

To Belgrade

BULEVARD SLIVNITSA

BULEVARD SLIVNITSA

LEON BRIGG

Dimitrov Memorial House

ULITSA TSAR SIMEON

ULITSA OPALCHENSKA

BULEVARD HRISTO BOTEV

Open-air Market

ULITSA GEORGI SAVA RAKOVSKI

ULITSA GEORGI DIMITROV

BULEVARD GEORGI DIMITROV

BULEVARD VOLGOGRAD

Banya Bashi Mosque

Hotel Iskâr

ULITSA EXZARH IOSIF

Synagogue

Turkish Baths

Hotel Preslav

Hotel Lyulin

DONDUKOV

Hali

Vietnamese Restaurant

TsUM

Lenin Statue

PLOSHTAD LENIN

Balkantourist

KNYAZ

Party House

Natural History Museum

Vasil Levsi Monumen

PLOSHTAD AL. NEVSKI

Alek Nevs

BULEVARD ALEKSANDAR STAMBOLIISKI

Hotel Balkan

THE LARGO

PLOSHTAD 9 SEPTEMVRI

Russian Church

St. Nedelya Church

National History Museum

US Embassy

Dimitrov Mausoleum

City Garden

Museum of the Revolutionary Movement

PLOSHTAD NARODNI SABRAN

Museum of Revolutionary Vigilence

ULITSA ALABIN

BALKAN (internal)

National Theatre

BALKAN (external)

Hotel Slavyanska-Besed

Rila Ticket Agency

ULITSA

Ivan Vazov Museum

IVAN VAZOV

Hotel Rodina

VITOSHA BULEVARD

ULITSA VASIL

KOLAROV

Central Post Office

ULITSA GENERAL GURKO

BULEVARD HRISTO BOTEV

ULITSA GRAF IGNATIEV

BULEVARD MARSHAL

BULEVARD PATRIARH EVTIMII

British Embassy

1300 Years Monument

BULEVARD BALGARIA

National Palace of Culture

To Tihiya Kât and Zlatni Mostove

Yuzhen Park

Hotel Hemus

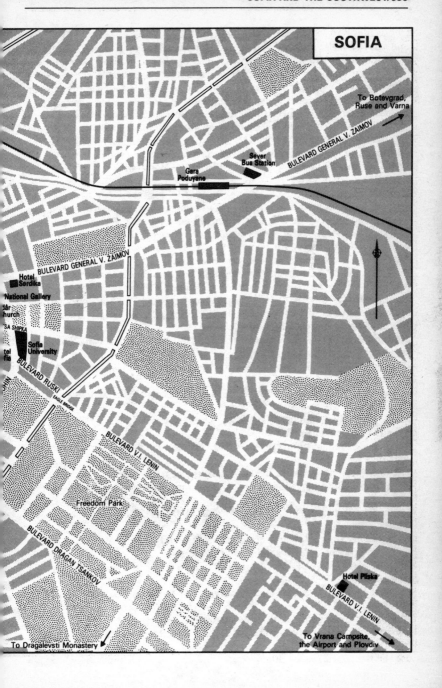

SOFIA

To Botevgrad, Ruse and Varna

Sever Bus Station

BULEVARD GENERAL V. ZAIMOV

Gara Poduyane

BULEVARD GENERAL V. ZAIMOV

Hotel Serdika

National Gallery

18r hurch

'SA SHIPKA

tel fia

Sofia University

BULEVARD RUSKI

EAGLE BRIDGE

BULEVARD V.I. LENIN

Freedom Park

BULEVARD DRAGAN TSANKOV

Hotel Pliska

BULEVARD V.I. LENIN

To Dragalevsti Monastery

To Vrana Campsite, the Airport and Plovdiv

whose office at 37, Knyaz Dondukov (☎ 88-44-30) is open until 10.30pm every day. They're more reliable than the **unofficial lodgings** which Bulgarians sometimes offer to foreigners arriving at Central Station. The going rate for these seems to be around 10 leva per head or a negotiable sum in hard currency; bear in mind that accepting means foregoing a date-stamp on your *carte statistique*, which is illegal and might cause problems later. Between July 15 and September 15, there's also the possibility of **dormitory beds** arranged by *Orbita*, the Youth Travel Bureau, at 45a, Stamboliiski Blvd. (Monday-Saturday 9am-5pm; ☎ 87-95-52). The staff aren't exactly helpful, but the deal seems to be that folks with an IUS card can get a bed for $4 in the *Hristo Botev Studentski Komplex* (bus #280 from the University).

Hotels

Rates at Balkantourist **hotels** reflect the grading system (2-5 stars); you'll pay between 20-30 leva at a 2-star place, 40-60 leva at a 3-star hotel (with breakfast included), and anything upwards of 150 leva in deluxe establishments, which stand half empty for want of guests. The following hotels are ranged roughly in order of cost, the cheapest ones first.

Kopitoto (☎ 57-12-56) In the foothills of Mount Vitosha above the Knyazhevo district; accessible by tram #5 from the centre, and then bus #62.

Shtastlivetsa (☎ 66-50-24) Higher up the mountainside, and likely to become more expensive as Aleko is developed. Take tram #2 from Graf Ignatiev to the Hladinka stop, and then bus #66.

Moreni (☎ 65-49-83) Like the nearby *Shtastlivetsa*, also accessible by chair-lift (from Dragalevtsi suburb).

Prostor (☎ 65-48-81) Another Mount Vitosha hotel, full of package-skiiers during winter.

Slavia (2, Ul. Sofiiski Geroi/☎ 52-55-51). Out along Deveti Septemvri Blvd; tram #5 from Ul. Alabin in the centre.

Pliska (87, Blvd. Lenin/☎ 72-37-21). Unprepossessing, but easily reached from the Eagle Bridge.

Serdika (2, Blvd. Zaimov/☎ 44-34-11). Located by the Levski Monument, near the centre.

Bulgaria (4, Blvd. Ruski/☎ 87-19-77). In the heart of Sofia.

Hemus (31, Blvd. Traikov/☎ 66-14-15); tram #6 or #9 from the NDK Centre.

Slavyanska Besseda (127, Ul. Rakovski/☎ 88-04-41). On a busy downtown street.

Grand Hotel Sofia (Pl. Narodno Sâbranie/☎ 87-88-21) Just off Blvd. Ruski; a few single rooms and a nightclub on the premises.

Moskva Park (25, Ul. Nezabravka/☎ 7-12-61). At the southern edge of Freedom Park.

Novotel Evropa (☎ 3-12-61). A snooty, costly block on Blvd. Dimitrov near the station.

Rodina (4, Pl. Ruski). Another businessmen's preserve.

Balkan-Sheraton Newly-refurbished Stalinist pile (formerly the *Hotel Balkan*) overlooking the Largo, built around St George's Rotunda. Non-residents can use the bar, open until 4.30am.

Vitosha-New Otani (100, Ul. Ivanov/☎ 62-41-51). Sofia's most palatial tower-block, with Panoramic and Japanese restaurants, a bowling alley, etc. In 1980, the Pope's would-be assassin, Mehmet Ali Agca, stayed in room 911 under the name of 'Yogander Singh'.

Campsites
Sofia's Militia take a very dim view of anyone **sleeping rough**, and raid the Central Station around midnight. If you're forced to sleep there, be polite to the brutes and claim that you're waiting for a train out in the small hours. All of Sofia's offical **campsites** also rent out **chalets**. Sleeping two, these go for around 11 leva per night (28 leva with private shower), while campers are charged just under 2 leva per head, and 2 leva for ground-space. The best site is *Vrana Camping* (☎ 78-12-13), which is accessible by bus #5 from the Orlov Most or the CORECOM store on the Plovdiv highway (see above for transport from the airport or central station). *Cherniya Kos* (☎ 57-11-29) lies 11km out towards Pernik on the Deveti Septemvri highway – take tram #5 to the end of the line, then bus #59 or #58. *Lebed* (☎ 77-30-45) beside Lake Pancharevo is chalets-only, and can be reached by bus #1, #2 or #3 (bound for Samokov), which leave the Geo Milev quarter (the terminal for trams #4 & #10). There's yet another campsite with chalets in the suburban watering-hole of BANKYA – the last train leaves Sofia's *Gara Zaharna Fabrika* at 11.45pm.

THE CITY

The heart of Sofia fits compactly between two rivers, the Perlovets and Vladaya, whose weak trickle and modest width didn't deter architects from designing two fancy bridges during the 1890s, and it's these which most people still cross when **approaching the centre**. Both bridges are within a mile of practically all the sites, and it's feasible to walk almost everywhere in the centre. For the benefit of the many visitors that approach Sofia from the southeast, arrive by air, or stay at Vrana campsite, the following section begins with the Orlov Bridge, which serves as the starting point for explorations. Should you approach by road from Kalotina or Vidin, or arrive at the station, drive or catch a tram (#1 or #7) down Blvd. Georgi Dimitrov, which crosses the **Lion Bridge** (*Lavov Most*) and runs directly into the centre. Once you reach the Banya Bashi Mosque, alight and start walking: the Largo and Dimitrov's Mausoleum are close by, while most other places can be reached on foot within 15 minutes.

The Eagle Bridge to Aleksandâr Nevski Church

Crowned with four ferocious-looking statues and set amidst weeping willows, the **Eagle Bridge** (*Orlov Most*) marks the spot where liberated prisoners of war were greeted by their victorious Russian allies and compatriots in 1878. Popular regard for the 'Slav elder brother' stems from Russian support for Bulgarian liberation in the C19, and has little or no parallel in most other parts of Eastern Europe. Whereas the Red Army's arrival in 1944-45 inspired anxiety amongst Poles, Hungarians and Romanians, most Bulgarians were predisposed to welcome them, as shown by the tableaux in front of the towering **Monument to the Soviet Army** near the Eagle Bridge. Its centerpiece is a Red Army soldier flanked by a worker and a peasant woman with a child, the archetypal symbol of Bulgaro-Soviet friendship (*druzhba*); elsewhere in Bulgaria you'll see posters proclaiming the need for World Peace, depicting a child and a Soviet soldier embracing. **Freedom Park**, to the southeast of the monument, is described on page 546.

From the bridge it's a short ride (tram #4) or a brief stroll up Blvd. Ruski to **Sofia University**. Named after *Klement Ohridski* (Clement of Ochrid), a pupil of Cyril and Methodius, it was founded a decade after Sofia became Bulgaria's capital, and has since become the country's most prestigious university. The number of students trained each year in different fields is determined by the needs of the economy as perceived by state planners; and competition for the university's 6,000 places is intense. Besides its own nationals, Bulgaria educates citizens from both oil-rich and dirt-poor countries; students from the latter are famously dedicated (I met a Vietnamese man separated from his wife for 5 years while they pursued their respective specialities in Bulgaria and the Soviet Union), but there's an undercurrent of resentment towards the Arabs, who are perceived as flashing dollars around what pass for fleshpots in Sofia. By comparison with their Western counterparts, Bulgarian students seem disciplined and (at least outwardly) respectful of authority, and given the recent strictures against smoking cigarettes and drinking, the annual **Students' Day Carnival** (December 8) is rarely riotous.

At the intersection with Blvd. Volgograd, a few hundred yards north of the university, stands the weathered stone **Vasil Levski Monument,** marking the spot where the 'Apostle of Freedom' (p.627) was hung by the Turks in 1873. It's a mournful sight, and I'd advise you to visit the park across the road from the university instead, where a glint of gold betrays the proximity of the Aleksandâr Nevski cathedral.

Arguably the finest piece of architecture in the Balkans and certainly Sofia's crowning glory, the **Aleksandâr Nevski Memorial Church** honours the 200,000 Russian casualties of the 1877-78 War of Liberation, particularly the defenders of the Shipka Pass. Financed by public subscription and built between 1882-1924, it's a magnificent structure, bulging with domes and semi-domes and glittering with 18lbs of gold leaf donated by the Soviet Union in 1960. Within the cavernous interior, a white-bearded God glowers down from the main cupola, an angelic sunburst covers the central vault, and as a parting shot Vasnetsov's *Day of Judgement* looms above the exit. Expressive frescoes lacking the stiffness of Byzantine portraiture depict episodes from the life of Christ in rich tones, and the grandeur of the iconostasis is enhanced by twin thrones with columns of onyx and alabaster.

Orthodox congregations stand or kneel during services, and traditionally the 'weakest go to the wall' (the origin of this phrase) to lean or sit on benches. The church's capacity is 5,000 souls, which is insufficent to accommodate all the would-be worshippers during Easter week and other holy times in the Orthodox calendar, but ample for daily **services** (9.30am-11.30am). At such times sightseers are forbidden, although unobtrusive ones might gain admission to appreciate the spectacle, rich with incense, candlelight and sonorous chanting. The crypt (entrance outside, open Wednesday-Monday 10.30am-7pm) contains a superb **collection of icons**.

Secular art was practically non-existent in Bulgaria before the C19, so it's perhaps understandable that fledgling artists were greatly influenced by foreign movements, as can be seen from the paintings in the **National Art Gallery** on the northeastern corner of Aleksandâr Nevski Square, which used to be exhibitied in the cramped premises of the former royal palace until a few years back.

Heading west across Aleksandâr Nevski Square (in Roman times, the necropolis of Serdica), you'll pass two recumbent lions flanking the Tomb of the Unknown Soldier, set beside the wall of the brown brick **Church of St Sofia** (*Sveta Sofia*). Raised during the C6 in the reign of Justinian, it stands on the site of two earlier churches and follows the classic Byzantine plan of a regular cross with a dome at the intersection (though with rounded Romanesque arches supporting the vaulting). Sofia means 'wisdom', and the name of the Saint was adopted by the city towards the end of the C14. The church crypt is said to be impressive, but was closed for restoration when I last looked. Around the back an engraved boulder marks the **grave of Ivan Vazov** (p.629), who requested that he be buried amidst the daily life of his people; you'll notice his statue, seated book in hand, in a park nearby.

Rather than heading directly for 9 September Square, cut down past the stolidly florid Bulgarian Academy of Sciences or the building housing the National Assembly (*Narodno Sâbranie*) on to the **Bulevard Ruski**, an attractive thoroughfare surfaced with yellow stone and partially lined with wild chestnut trees. The Monument to the Liberators, on a plaza backed by cafés, the *Hotel Sofia* and BALKAN airlines, is probably unique outside the Soviet Union, giving pride of place to a statue of the 'Tsar Liberator' Aleksandr II. Further west along the boulevard are the **Museum of the Revolutionary Movement** (p.549), the **House of the People's Army** (formerly the Military Club where the *Zveno* hatched several conspiracies), and the small but striking 'Russian Church'.

The **Russian Church** (open Tuesday-Sunday 7.30am-7.30pm; Sundays 7.30am-4.30pm) is an unmistakeable, zany firecracker of a building with an exuberant bright yellow, tiled exterior, five gilded domes and an emerald spire, concealing a dark, candlewax-scented interior. Officially dedicated to St Nicholas the Blessed, the church was built in 1913 at the behest of a Tsarist diplomat, Semontovski-Kurilo, who feared for his soul to worship in Bulgarian churches, which he believed to be schismatic. Across the road stand the *V. Yugo* foreign-language bookshop and the *Hotel Bulgaria*, while beyond the **Natural Science Museum** at nr.1 (p.548) the boulevard joins 9 September Square.

9 September Square and the Largo

If the Bulgarian Communist Party (BKP) had a soul it would probably hover over **9 September Square** – *Ploshtad Deveti Septemvri* – where major anniversaries are celebrated with **parades**. On September 9 (the Victory of the Socialist Revolution in Bulgaria) and May 1 (International Labour Day) these emphasise economic achievements and the component groups of Bulgarian society, with lots of floats, gymnastics and contingents from factories and schools; while the anniversary of the Bolshevik Revolution (November 7) features soldiers goosestepping and armoured vehicles grinding across the plaza in emulation of mightier parades in Moscow. Militia cordens keep the uninvited at a distance (events are televised nationwide), and the regimented proceedings – known as 'spontaneous demonstrations of the people' during the Stalinist era – are a tiresome obligation for many participants. 'We have seen so many of these demonstrations which humiliate human dignity, where normal people are expected to applaud some paltry mediocrity who has proclaimed himself a demi-god and condescendingly waves to them from the heights of his police inviolability', wrote Georgi Markov before his murder.

On such occasions, attention is focused upon the Politburo line-up atop the austere white mausoleum from which Party leaders take the salute. Inside lies the body of **Georgi Dimitrov**, the first leader of the People's Republic of Bulgaria. Born into a humble background in 1882, Dimtrov was a teenage apprentice printer when he converted to Communism, and, with characteristic nerve, he doctored the speeches of reactionary MPs before they went to press – the prelude to a lifelong militant career. He organised Party cells, unions, strikes and propaganda inside Bulgaria and later abroad, and for a time was the secretary of the *Comintern* or Communist International. In 1933 he was arrested by the Nazis and charged with instigating the Reichstag fire; withstood months of maltreatment by the Gestapo and defended himself so vigorously as to be acquitted after a show trial which became an international cause célèbre, afterwards taking refuge in the Soviet Union, surviving Stalin's purges and returning in triumph to guide Bulgaria through the immediate post-war years.

Following his death in July 1949 while on a visit to Moscow, **Dimitrov's Mausoleum** was erected in 6 days and nights, in time for the body's return. Closed most of the time, it's guarded by sentries wearing red-braided tunics and plumed hats who goosestep the changing of the guard every hour on the hour – but on Wednesdays, Fridays and Saturdays between 2pm-5pm it's open to the public, who, having deposited their hand luggage (next to the concert bookings office on the corner of Blvd. Ruski) and queued, file through antiseptic corridors into the dim, guarded vault where Dimitrov's corpse is displayed. Shrouding conceals all but its face and hands, which are spectrally lit but appear to have been well preserved by the techniques of Professor Zaborsky, the Soviet expert who also embalmed Lenin (1924) and Stalin (1953). To the east of the exit lies the grave of *Vasil Kolarov*, Dimitrov's predecessor as Party leader. Both men, and *Dimitâr Blagoev*, the 'father' of Bulgarian Marxism, whose statue stands nearby, are the subjects of memorial museums elsewhere in the capital (see p.549).

Opposite the mausoleum stands the former royal palace, which was once so delapidated that a ceiling came down upon the head of Tsar 'Foxy' Ferdinand, who had just taken up residence. Before this the building was the *Konak* where Vasil Levski was tortured prior to his execution. The relocation of the

National Gallery from the palace to Aleksandâr Nevski Square necessitated the closure of the **Ethnographic Museum**, but by now this has probably re-opened.

Since the last war the seat of power has shifted westwards across the square, to the massive buildings grouped around **the Largo**. Flanked on three sides by severely monumental buildings, this elongated plaza was built on the ruins of central Sofia, pulverised by British and American bombers in the autumn of 1944. Of the complex, which occupies several blocks, the **Party House** is the most arresting structure: a white, colonaded supertanker flaunting the red star from its masthead. Besides housing sporadic Party congresses, the building accommodates the office of the Central Committee (*Tsentralen Komitet*), and features in the following joke. A Bulgarian cycles up to the building and leans his bike against it, whereupon a policeman shouts: 'Hey! You can't leave that there, a high Soviet delegation is due to arrive any minute'. 'That's okay,' replies the cyclist, 'I'll chain it up'.

Militiamen outside shoo pedestrians down into the subway: either to prevent jaywalking across the Largo, or to promote encounters with the **ruins of Serdica**. The underpass gives onto the brick stumps of walls (originally 8-12m high) from the C5-C6 Byzantine fortifications, a section of original pavement and eventually, the Eastern Gate of the city. Most of the ruins here, and in other parts of Sofia, post-date the devastating C5 Hun invasion; the majority are fragments of the new walls and buildings that were raised during the reign of the Byzantine emperor Justinian (527-565).

Just south of the Largo, the *Hotel Sheraton* (formerly the *Hotel Balkan*) casts its sombre wings around a courtyard containing the C4 **Rotunda of St George's Church**. This brick building has been under restoration for years (like the early medieval frescoes reported to adorn its cupola), so the courtyard – with a public entrance on Blvd. Stamboliiski – may still be officially closed – though pedestrians often inch their way through the chaos of mud and scaffolding to avoid street repairs outside. On the northern side of the Largo an equally large structure houses the Council of Ministers, Bulgaria's supreme executive body, and Sofia's main department store, the **TsUM** (pronounced 'Tsoom', the initials stand for 'Central Universal Store') – alongside which runs an arcade where photographers and flower sellers solicit custom and public taps gush noisily. Another underpass gives access to a sunken plaza laid out with café tables, whose gesticulating patrons and bright awnings contrast with the weathered brick and stone **Church of St Petka Samardzhiiska** girded with concrete platforms, its tiled rooftop poking above street level. It's barely recognisable as a church and was built deliberately so by the Saddlers' Guild in an effort not to irritate the Turkish conquerors. Today it seems to shrink before the gaze of Lenin, whose rough-hewn statue dominates Lenin Square.

Around Lenin Square

Barring the commanding figure of Vladimir Ilyich, **Lenin Square** (*Ploshtad Lenin*) isn't much more than a junction spruced up with dwarf-greenery, with a big **Balkantourist office** behind the statue. With St Nedelya's Church marking its southern boundary, the square elongates northwards to join **Dimitrov Boulevard**, the main thoroughfare and the 'most horrible street in Europe' for Arthur Symons when he was here in 1903, a 'kind of mongrel East' existing 'between two civilisations. . .a rag-heap for the refuse of both'. Though it has been considerably cleaned up since then you can see what he was getting at, if only in the vaguely oriental mixture of buildings which line the street.

Of these, the **Banya Bashi Mosque** is the most eye-catching: a 'Sultan style' edifice with one large dome and a single minaret, built in 1576 by Hadzhi Mimar Sonah, who also designed the great mosque at Edirne in Turkey for Selim 'the Sot'. During our visits the mosque was closed for restoration (seemingly proceeding at a snail's pace), and even if it has reopened you're still unlikely to see anyone worshipping there. In 1960, Bernard Newman noted 'scarcely enough Turks in Sofia to make up a congregation', while in the present climate any remaining Muslims are bound to keep a low profile.

As the name 'Banya' suggests, the mosque stands in proximity to Sofia's **Mineral Baths**; occupying a stylish but tatty neo-Renaissance pile decorated with ceramics, which overlooks the rear of the park. Inside, marble pillars support a domed roof with small skylights beaming shafts of light down onto the steaming bath, from which overweight Bulgars lumber to flop down in alcoves around the pool. Outside, people lounge on benches gossiping and spitting sunflower seeds or fragments of *kebabcheta*, or come with jugs to collect the mineral water, which is efficacious for various ailments.

The market hall or **Hali** facing the mosque is elaborately carved and crowned by a clock tower, and you expect to find a thriving bazaar within. It is, however, an anticlimax, with drab stands and limited stocks, which are only redeemed by the lively outdoor market a block or two away, past the **Sofia Synagogue**. This, a fanciful structure seemingly upheld by its dome, which might have been conceived by some Jewish or Moorish Leonardo with a premonition of airships, was actually built in 1910 according to the designs of Grunanger, and is the main centre of Bulgaria's small Jewish community. Notwithstanding Bulgaria's historical tolerance of Jews (mostly maintained during the wartime alliance with the Reich), large numbers emigrated to Palestine in the late 1940s – which accounts for the discreet 'Israel Contact Office' around the back of the Synagogue.

Continuing westwards along Ul. Ekzarh Iosif, you'll pass unpretentious shops and cheap restaurants which ultimately merge with the **fruit and vegetable market** on Georgi Kirkov Street: an intensely crowded affair that quietens down around the far line of stalls, of which one end sells flowers while the other displays heaps of raw wool, which pong of sheep and serve the robust women vendors as cushions. The backstreets north and west of the market comprise one of Sofia's **older quarters**, with rutted cobblestones and low houses built around courtyards: a far cry from the modern housing estates, and in the long term probably destined for demolition.

Ulitsa Iskâr, just east of the Hali, is where to board trams #3, #4 or #10, which maneouvre through the backstreets and rattle their way on to **Knyaz Dondukov**, a long avenue running behind the high ground occupied by St Sofia and the Aleksandâr Nevski Church. Bereft of monuments and sights, it's worth mentioning as the location of the **Youth Theatre** (nr.36), the **Balkantourist bureau** which arranges excursions and accommodation (nr.37/7am-10.30pm daily) and, further up the avenue, the *Dunav* **self-service vegetarian restaurant** (nr.80 Monday, Tuesday, Friday, Saturday 11am-3pm/Wednesday & Thursday 4pm-9.30pm).

Cut down Ul. Rakovski past the neo-Classical **Opera House** and you'll see (indeed, it's impossible to miss) the statue of **Aleksandâr Stamboliiski** outside the theatre, moustaches bristling and chest braced. A fiery orator, Stamboliiski led the Agrarian Party's campaign to assert 'peasant power' over the bourgeoisie and state bureaucracy, turning the established order upside down during the brief period of Agrarian government (1919-23) and propounding a 'Green Alliance' of peasant parties throughout the Balkans. Stamboliiski's renunciation of Bulgarian claims on Macedonia – the cause of two wars with Serbia – united conservative factions with the fanatical IMRO, who staged a coup in June 1923. Peasants were murdered by the thousand, and the IMRO amputated Stamboliiski's hand (which had signed the treaty of Niš with Serbia) before killing him.

Bearing his name, **Stamboliiski Boulevard** cuts across Lenin Square just south of the Hotel Balkan-Sheraton, behind which you'll find the *Astoria* nightclub (nr.3) and the **US Embassy** – where window-displays attract such crowds that the police are often forced to corden off the embassy and its adjacent reading room (for details of opening hours, see p.552). The boulevard ends at the City Garden (p.545) just to the east, while around the corner of the hotel stands a sombre nine-domed building, formerly the **Buyuk Djami** or 'Big Mosque', dating from 1494. Until recently it was possible to gain entry here since the building housed the National Archaeological Museum; but since the exhibits were transfered to the new History Museum on Vitosha Blvd (see below), it's been closed to the public. The other section of Stamboliiski Blvd. – running west from Lenin Square – is much longer, less scenic, and more practical. Along its length you'll find a bookshop with a rare supply of **maps** (nr.17), a dairy-shop at nr.25, offering the best choice of **cheese** in Sofia, the offices of Eastern European travel agencies and ten **foreign airlines** and the Youth Travel Bureau, **Orbita**.

The **Church of St Nedelya**, near Lenin Square, stands upon the former site of Serdica's *praetorium* and chief crossroads, the current building having been constructed after the liberation as the successor to a line of churches that has stood here since medieval times, when aristocratic families built private chapels and endowed the monastic schools which formed the nucleus of the Varosh quarter. During the Ottoman period it was known as the Church of the Blessed King – *Sveti Kral* – on account of the remains of the Serbian monarch, Stefan Urosh, kept here; while in 1925 it almost claimed another king, when bombs exploded amongst high dignitaries attending a funeral mass, killing 123 people but failing to harm their intended victims, Tsar Boris and his Cabinet. The Communists – whose attempted revolution had been crushed in 1923 – were naturally blamed but denied all responsibility. Dimitrov later laid claim to the attack, which is nowadays ascribed to 'ultra leftists'.

The following section describes Blvd. Vitosha and Yuzhen Park, lying directly to the south of St Nedelya's. To the east of this lies one of the busiest quarters of the inner city, and Freedom Park beyond the river; covered in the subsequent section.

Down Vitosha Boulevard to the National Palace of Culture

The silhouette of Mount Vitosha surmounting the rooftops is the first thing you see on **Vitosha Boulevard**. Its foothills are hazy beyond the boulevard's trolleybus wires and exhaust-fumes, the vanishing point of parallel lines of greyish buildings, many of which date from the 1950s when the thoroughfare was called Stalin Blvd. At street level, shaded by low trees, pedestrians window-shop or negotiate the barriers screening excavations for the Sofia Metro; if construction work has finished by now, traffic should be flowing along the boulevard unhindered. Among the useful addresses here are the *Koprivshtitsa* tavern (nr.3) and, further along, a small **Orbita** bureau, a **late night supermarket** (on the corner of Ul. Albabin) and the *Café Brazilia*, but the main attraction has to be Sofia's premier museum.

The **National History Museum** occupies the former Palace of Justice on the western side of the boulevard (open 10.30am-6.30pm/Friday 2pm-6.30pm/-closed Mondays), a superbly arranged museum only marred by the lack of catalogues and captions in foreign languages. This may have been remedied by now, but if it hasn't the museum is still worth seeing. On the ground floor, pride of place is given to the magnificent **gold treasures** of Vâlchitrân and Panagyurishte, soon to be joined by the silver treasure of Rogozen which, like various objects in halls 5-8, show the achievements of Thracian civilisation (p.643) during the pre-Christian era. Less is known of earlier (6500-3500 BC) cultures, although the contents of halls 1-4 – including stone **goddess figures** inscribed with rams, birds, chevrons, labyrinths and other motifs associated with Great Earth Mother, found around Varna – suggests that their religion and society were matriarchal. Bas reliefs, ceramics, silverware and frescoes (halls 10-11) give some idea of the artistic heights attained during the medieval era, when Pliska, Preslav and Veliko Târnovo enjoyed their heyday as capitals; although these pale before the superb collection of **ecclesiastical art** (jewellery, frescoes and icons) displayed in halls 12-14 upstairs. Centuries of Ottoman rule are ignored in favour of the National Revival of the C18-C19, when progressive Bulgarians struggled for education, civic reforms and, ultimately, independence, giving rise to revolutionaries like Levski and Botev, whose banners and proclamations are prominently featured. The upper floor also exhibits a wonderful and varied collection of C19 **folk costumes** (hall 22) and **carpets** (in the corridor); plus two beautiful and very cosy-looking **rooms from Bansko and Tretebanya**, furnished in the National Revival style.

Balkantourist maps omit the **Museum of Revolutionary Vigilance**, occupying a nondescript building guarded by Sofia's strictest curators (2, Ul. Lavele), and you will probably (like me) be refused entry. I suspect that the museum contains evidence of Imperialist plots against the Socialist countries and testimonals to worthy bodies like the Cheka and *Dârzhavna Sigurnost*, with an underlying message that would rather spoil the effect of all the Peace posters flaunted along public highways.

If the trams (#1/#7/#9) are running, ride one down the boulevard until Patriarh Evtimii: a busy avenue on the edge of the park-like Baba Nedelya Square, which serves as the setting for two structures symbolising Bulgaria's achievements. The **1,300 Years Monument** is boldly (some might say hideously) modernist: huge wrench-shaped blocks emerging from a pit which represents centuries of servitude, garnished with anguished-looking figures (one of whom has Zhivkov's features, it's rumoured) and bearing Levski's maxim: 'We are in time and time is in us' ('We transform it and it transforms us' he continued, to clarify the message). At the top end of the park, the gleaming **NDK** or **National Palace of Culture** (*Naroden Dvorets na Kulturata*) rears up like a Dalek spaceship come to earth. Covering an area of 17,000 sq. metres, the complex contains a press centre, some overpriced shops, a disco and an unusually-efficent **tourist bureau** in its subterranean arcade. As a tribute to her cultural work, the building now bears the name of *Lyudmila Zhivkova*, the current Party leader's daughter, who died in her thirties of a brain tumor. But the most telling aspect of the NDK was its colossal cost, and with this in mind, Sofians have invented a sarcastic pun on its initials, which can also stand for 'another hole in the belt' – although some citizens are well-heeled enough to patronise the swish **Magoura ice cream parlour** on the eastern side of the square, a trendy hangout.

From the northern edge of the square you can walk up Ul. Angel Kânchev to reach the busy downtown area around Graf Ignatiev (see below); or take any of the trams heading eastwards along Patriarh Evitimii as far as the Friendship Bridge, which leads into Freedom Park.

The City Garden to Freedom Park

Sofia's southeastern quarter is probably the liveliest part of the inner city, its City Garden and pavement cafés providing the focus for social life during the day, its theatres and restaurants during the evening. Free of rubbish, hustlers, punks or sex shows, the area is more decorous than its counterpart in any Western capital and quite safe at night; it can be approached from more or less any angle, and the best way to appreciate the area is to just walk in and wander as you will.

Sofia's **City Garden**, with its manicured flowerbeds and shady paths, invariably attracts courting couples and office workers taking their lunch break. Several fountains splash opposite the **Ivan Vazov National Theatre**: a handsome neo-Classical building decked out in red, white and gold, with Gobelin tapestries and Panagyurishte hangings inside, which provides a welcome contrast to the other, sombrely ministerial, buildings along Vasil Levski Street. At the southern end of this, one comes upon Ul. General Gurko, where you'll find the **Puppet Theatre** (nr.14), the **City Art Gallery** (on the edge of the park) and the *Rila Ticket Agency*, which stands opposite the **Central Post Office**.

Ulitsa G.S. Rakovski is one of Sofia's longest streets, extending north and south from the Blvd. Ruski, although from a visitor's standpoint only the latter section really merits attention, with a scattering of **patisseries** (*sladkarnitsa*), **restaurants** and **theatres** (see p.550 & p.551). Further down it joins **Graf Ignatiev**, a meandering thoroughfare lined with shops, named after the Russian count who persuaded Tsar Aleksandr to support Bulgarian liberation (and appears in some of the *Flashman* books as a devious scoundrel). In the small garden beside the intersection with Ul. Tsar Shishman stands the **St Sedmochislenitsi Church**, built on the site of the so-called 'Black Mosque' where the Turks imprisoned Bulgarians during the struggle for liberation.

Beyond Slaveykov Square, Graf Ignatiev leads towards the *Most na Druzhba* or **Friendship Bridge**, one of the approaches to **Freedom Park** (*Park na Svobodata*). Here, young Bulgarians have interpreted freedom to mean sartorial liberty: promenading up and down just inside the park wearing T-shirts emblazoned with pictures of Kiss or the Dead Kennedys, and occasionally flaunting CND badges. Whether the adopted foreign styles have survived the Party's latest injunctions, I don't know; but this is likely to remain the place in the capital to encounter 'youth culture'. The park itself is the oldest and largest in Sofia, partially influenced by St James's in London, with a rich variety of flowers and trees. At weekends the roar of massed supporters emanates from two huge **football stadiums**, the northern one of which, named after Vasil Levski, also houses the **Museum of Physical Education and Sport**. The smaller *Druzhba Stadion*, nearest the Friendship Bridge, is devoted to basketball, handball and volleyball (ice hockey and skating during the winter), and around the *Narodna Armiya Stadion* are outdoor **tennis** courts. There's a big **swimming** pool just before Blvd. Yavorov, to the east of which rises the monument to the Anti-fascist fighters, otherwise known as the **Common Grave**.

Mount Vitosha: the Boyana Church, Dragalevtsi Monastery and winter sports at Aleko

A wooded mass of granite 12 miles long by 11 miles wide, **MOUNT VITOSHA** is very much a part of the capital, and the source of its pure water and fresh breezes. Sofians come here for picnics, solitude, the magnificent views or to ski, and the ascent of its highest peak, Cherni Vrâh, has become a traditional test of stamina for the capital's Young Pioneers. If you're seeking absolute tranquility it's best to come on a weekday, or at least get some distance from the chair-lift terminals. Most people approach Mount Vitosha by way of one of the villages (really suburbs) at its foothills: Knyazhevo, Boyana, Dragalevtsi or Simeonovo.

To reach the first two, take a tram #15 or #13 from the centre, and change to bus #61 or #62 at the Deveti Septemvri stop, halfway out along the highway of the same name. These take the Velikya Prelom ring-road, skirting the walled *Rezidentsiya Boyana* where Zhivkov and other high functionaries have their villas, before reaching **BOYANA**. There, follow Ul. Belite Brezi uphill and you'll come to a small garden surrounding the **Boyana Church** (open Monday-Friday 8.45am-5pm), home to a recently restored set of **medieval frescoes**. Largely executed in 1259, these, with their realism and rejection of the hieratic Byzantine style, anticipate the work of Giotto, which heralded the beginning of the Italian Renaissance – and are famous as such. As well as Biblical themes the unknown artist drew on contemporary life for inspiration: clothing the saints in medieval Bulgarian dress and setting garlic, radishes and bread – the peasants' staples – upon the table in the *Last Supper*. Perhaps the finest portraits are those of Boyana's patrons, Dessislava and Sebastocrator Kaloyan (depicted holding the church in the customary fashion), and the haloed figures of the King and Queen, Asen and Irina, whose authority Kaloyan recognised despite his control of the Sofia region.

Bus #61 continues on to **KNYAZHEVO**, from where there's a cabin-lift up to the *Hotel Kopitoto*, while bus #62 ascends through the forests past the *Tihya Kât* motel to *Zlatni Mostove*, a restaurant just to the east of the so-called **Stone River**. Beneath the large boulders running down the mountainside (the moraine of an ancient glacier) burbles a rivulet which one attracted gold-panners – hence the name, which means 'Golden Bridges'. Signposts by the restaurant indicate the paths leading to Trades Union chalets like *Bor* and *Rodina*, a mile or so beyond which is the winter sports complex of Aleko (see below).

Another route to the mountain runs via **DRAGALEVTSI** village, which you can reach by taking tram #2 from Graf Ignatiev or Patriarh Evtimii to the Hladinka stop on Cherni Vrâh Blvd, and then bus #66. Climbing the road beyond the village the bus passes three old mills now serving as the *Vodenicharski* taverna (p.550), near which begins a chair-lift to the *Shtastlivetsa Hotel*. Situated in a beech wood 2-3km further on, **Dragalevtsi Monastery** (Monday-Friday 9am-5pm) is the Patriachal residence, with a C14 church – the only part of the original monastery that remains – and cells around its leafy courtyard which often sheltered the revolutionary, Vasil Levski, during the C19.

Some 20 minutes later bus #66 arrives at **ALEKO**, an expanding **winter sports centre** which has a range of pistes to suit all grades of skiers and operates from November through until late-spring. At the end of March/-beginning of April there's a competition for the **Aleko Cup**, with slalom and giant slalom races open to both sexes; qualifying heats for the European Cup may also take place here at the beginning of March. Tuition at the national **Ski School** is of a high standard but organised primarily for package tourists (p.511), who also have first claim on skiing equipment, which is rented from the *Prostor* and *Shtaslivetsa*. In the vicinity of these hotels are the chair lifts up to the Stena crag or Maluk and Golyan Rezen. Vitosha's loftiest 'Black Peak', **Cherni Vrâh** (7,513ft), is accessible by a trail from the Rezen heights, or by ski-drag. **Nightlife** centres around the restaurants, discos and bars of the two main hotels (the Prostor also has a pool and sauna), and there's a **carnival** arranged for skiers on Balkan Holidays. Finally, lovers of long and vertiginous rides should enjoy the **cable-car** linking Aleko and the suburb of SIMEONOVO (bus #98 from Dragalevtsi).

MUSEUMS AND GALLERIES

The lack of foreign-language captions and catalogues is the main problem with Sofia's museums and galleries. If you're lucky, there might be a tour-group doing the rounds with a guide giving commentary in a language that you can understand; otherwise, until the situation is remedied, the exhibits have to speak for themselves. A fair proportion of places seem likely to be shut pending repairs or relocation, and to a casual observer the 'revolutionary' museums are all remarkably similar. Unless stated otherwise, all the following charge an admission fee (usually under 1 leva) – though it's normally waived for anyone with a student card.

National History Museum (2, Vitosha Blvd; 10.30am-6.30pm; Friday 2pm-6.30pm; closed Mondays). The best museum in Sofia, if not in all Bulgaria; for a description of its contents see p.544.

Archaeological Museum (Buyuk Mosque) Despite having lost its finest treasures to the National History Museum, this long-established collection will probably open its doors again at some future date.

Dimitrov Museum (86, Ul. Opâlchenska; 10am-6pm daily; admission free). The residence of the Dimitrov family from 1888-1923. The ground floor – where his parents lived until 1906 – is small and folksy, featuring the loom on which Dimitrov's mother, 'Granny' Parashkeva, used to weave. Dimitrov and his wife, Lyuba Ivosevits, also a revolutionary, lived upstairs. Their library of 3,000 volumes, Georgi's pipe and slippers, and other personal effects are displayed; while Dimitrov's political career is the subject of a memorial hall adjoining the house.

City Art Gallery (1, Ul. General Gurko; 6am-3.30pm daily). On the edge of the City Garden, this exhibits contemporary paintings, drawings and sculpture by Bulgarian (and sometimes foreign) artists.

Permanent Art Gallery (133, Ul. Rakovski; 10am-6pm daily). Contemporary artworks and crafts for sale.

Applied Arts Gallery (117, Ul. Rakovski; Monday-Saturday 10am-6pm). Another commercial gallery, with the emphasis on ceramics, sculpture and textiles.

Graphic Art Gallery (62, Ul. General Gurko). Possibly the best of Sofia's galleries, if only because Bulgarian graphic art is generally far superior to contemporary paintings.

National Gallery (Pl. Aleksandâr Nevski; Wednesday-Sunday 9am-12am, 2pm-6pm; Mondays 9am-12.30am). The first section, displaying C19 portraits by Zahari Zograf, Georgi Donchev, Hristo Tsokev etc, is the most appealing. Subsequent halls contain works of 'Socialist realism' tackling themes such as heroism in war and a man's love for his tractor; attempts to do so in 'modernist' styles are, with a few notable exceptions, disappointing. Classical and modern paintings by foreign artists may also be on display.

Ethnographic Museum (9th September Square; 9am-12am, 1pm-6pm; Monday 9am-2.30pm; closed Tuesdays). Now possibly defunct, since the best items in its collection have been transfered to the National History Museum on Vitosha Blvd, but worth checking out anyway – it's in the former royal palace opposite Dimitrov's Mausoleum.

Natural Science Museum (1, Blvd. Ruski; Tuesday-Thursday 9am-12am, 1pm-6pm). While mainly concerned with Bulgarian fauna and flora, the museum includes an insect collection of 500,000 different species, stuffed birds and reptiles from all over the world, and dinosaur skeletons.

Military History Museum (23, Skobelev Blvd; Monday-Friday 9am-12am,

2pm-6pm; Sundays 1pm-7pm). Bulgaria has fought few wars abroad; banners flaunt the slogan 'Liberty or Death' rather than the names of foreign battles. The prolonged 'people's war' against Turkish domination during the C19 and the partisan campaigns of WW2 have made military service a hallowed obligation. All Bulgarian teenagers – with the exception of Turks, Gypsies and other 'unreliables' – receive military training; one can see 12 year-olds with Kalashnikovs standing ceremonial guard on major war memorials.

Museum of Bulgaro-Soviet Friendship (4, Gottwald Blvd; 10am-6pm daily; Sundays 9am-3pm). A hagiographic exhibition of Comradely *druzhba*, unmarred by any evidence of disagreements, such as reputedly occurred between Zhivkov and Gorbachev during the latter's visit to Sofia in October 1985. The sort of place schoolchildren are obliged to visit.

Museum of the Revolutionary Movement (14, Blvd. Ruski; Tuesday-Sunday 12am-7pm; Fridays 8am-1pm). Tells a dramatic story, unfortunately unintelligle to anyone who doesn't understand Bulgarian. Mainly given over to weaponry and photographs commemorating the partisan struggle. Admission free.

Museum of Revolutionary Vigilance (5, Ul. Lavele; Tuesday-Sunday 8am-6pm). Something of an enigma (see p.544). A report on its contents from anyone who manages to gain admission will be appreciated for the next edition.

Museum of Physical Education and Sport (Vasil Levski stadium; Tuesday-Sunday 10am-6pm). Devoted to Bulgarian sports and sportspersons of the C20.

Other Memorial Houses include those once inhabited by *Aleksandâr Stamboliiski* (22, Ul. Souhodolska); the writers *Ivan Vazov* (10, Ul. Vazov) and *Petko and Pencho Slaveykov* (138, Ul. Rakovski); the revolutionary poet *Hristo Smirnenski* (116, Ul. Shekerdzhiiski); the founding father of Bulgarian Marxism, *Dimitâr Blagoev* (34, Ul. Kossuth); and his disciple *Vasil Kolarov* (5, Ul. Asen Zlatarov). All contain personal effects, original furnishings and samples of the great men's works. Opening hours vary, but most are closed on Saturdays or Mondays.

RESTAURANTS AND CAFÉS

Sofia would be lucky to get one star if Egon Ronay graded cities according to gastronomic merit, and the offerings of its restaurants are generally inferior to those of Plovdiv's. Hotel **restaurants** concentrate on grills and salads, pitched midway between Bulgarian and international tastes, although the *Vitosha-New Otani* aspires to higher things with its Japanese and 19th-floor Panoramic restaurants. Prices are fairly reasonable if you stay out of deluxe hotels and avoid imported drinks; most places are open for lunch (11.30am-3pm) and in the evenings (from 6pm-11pm). The *Botevgradska Sreshta* (1, Ul. Positano; 11.30am-2.30pm, 4.30pm-11.30pm) and *Gambrinus* (80, Ul. Tsar Simeon; same hours) are restaurants proper, but otherwise essentially similar.

In the foothills of Mount Vitosha are several places devoted to **Bulgarian specialities**, with a 'folk' decor. *Boyansko Hanche* (11am-11pm daily) in the Boyana district is a custom-built 'inn' with a folklore show in the evenings, while in neighbouring Dragalevtsi village three renovated mills contain the *Vodenicharski Mehani* (☎ 66-50-88), serving traditional millers' nosh, such as *Kachamak* (fried maize dough and meat). You can sample tripe soup, *Kachamak* with cheese and various snacks invented by the Shops – Sofian cockneys, originally from the surrounding villages – at the *Shumako* (8am-12pm), on the road to the Simeonovo district, and the *Gorublyansko Hanche* (11am-11pm), 10km out along the Plovdiv highway. **Tavernas** (*mehana*) also serve grills and salads, though the accent is on drinking. Two centrally-located, and thus rather touristy places are the *Koprivshtitsa* (3, Vitosha Blvd; 9am-11.30pm) and the *Strandzhata* (19, Pl. Lenin; 9am-12pm).

Alternatively, you can follow 'Moscow Rules' and go for places with **foreign cuisine**; none of them would pass muster in their respective homelands, but at least the menu is slightly more varied. *Krim* (2, Ul. Dobrudja; ☎ 87-01-31) has Russian food and a summer garden, the *Budapest* (145, Ul. Rakovski; 12am-3pm, 7pm-11pm) features a Hungarian-style band, the *Berlin* (2, Blvd. Zaimov) and *Warshava* (15, Blvd. Zaimov) offer German and Polish cooking, while the *Havana* (27, Blvd. Vitosha) and *Vietnam* on Blvd. Botev promise, if not actually deliver, authentic Cuban and Vietnamese dishes. The *Japanese Restaurant* in the Vitosha-New Otani is the farthest upmarket, and a meal with *sake* will set you back a small fortune.

Ordinary Bulgarians tend to frequent the kind of **cheaper dives** one finds along Ul. Exzarh Iosif and around the open-air market; most of which are **self service** and real greasy spoons. However, there's a decent, unpretentious restaurant beyond the Balkantourist office on Knyaz Dondukov and, more or less opposite it, the dirt-cheap *Dunav* (Monday, Tuesday, Friday & Saturday 11am-3pm, Wednesday & Thursday 4pm-9pm), which serves **vegetarian food**.

Ground **coffee** is sold by news vendors and tobacconists on the streets rather than in shops or supermarkets, and you'll be lucky to find a cup of the stuff anywhere after midday. Likely places to look include the *Bålgaria* (in the hotel on Blvd. Ruski) and the Balkantourist snack bars on Lenin Square and around the NDK Centre, plus the following **cafés** and **patisseries**: *Brazilia* (24, Vitosha Blvd.), *Columbia* (4, Ul. Levski), *Roza* (4, Ul. Sofiiska Komuna) and three places on Ul. Rakovski – the *Opera*, *Prague* and *Havana*. The *Magura*, at the junction of Pl. Baba Nedelya and Vitosha Boulevard, serves the best **ice cream** in the city.

BARS, NIGHTCLUBS AND LIVE MUSIC

Bars and nightclubs are few and far between in Sofia, and it's hard to resist the conclusion that the authorities would rather have citizens conserve their energies for 'deeds and deeds alone' (to quote Party leader Todor Zhivkov). Few natives can afford the prices anyway, which are roughly on par with those in Britain, or higher still if one orders imported beer or spirits. All the big Balkantourist hotels feature bars with a vaguely 'international' ambience, most of which are open until midnight or the wee hours. The *Orient* (2, Stamboliiski Blvd) and the *Sofia* (inside the hotel of the same name on Narodno Sâbranie Square) both feature **floorshows**, and like the *Astoria* (3,

Stamboliiski Blvd) and *Hemus* (31, Traikov Blvd.) are open from 10pm-4am. So-called **folklore shows** with dancers wearing costumes and fixed smiles occur most evenings at the *Vodenicharski* taverna (uphill from Dragalevtsi), *Boyansko Hanche* (near the Boyana Church), and the restaurant on Vrana campsite, where the performance ends with the troupe walking barefoot across a bed of glowing coals.

Bulgaria's annual **Jazz Festival** takes place in the second week of November, probably at Sofia's *Universiade* sports hall (2, Ul. Shipchenski Prohod/☎ 72-21-48), where **rock concerts** are also sometimes held (ask at 7a, Ul. Aksakov for information). **Discos** are few in number and short on style. Those in the NDK Centre and Bâlgaria Blvd. underpasses attract a mixed clientèle, while the one in the *Hotel Prostor* caters for the aprés-ski crowd, and the *Durvenitsa* for students. The latter, located behind Block 10 of the Hristo Botev Students' Complex (bus #80, #280 or #94 from the University), functions from 7pm-11pm daily, charges 2.50 leva admission, and doesn't serve alcohol. Of course, Bulgarian youth isn't always as sober or conformist as the state would desire, and **unofficial events** and wild parties do occur – but discreetly, so that only savvy locals can provide an entrée. If you fancy trying your luck, Freedom Park or the University are probably the best places for **making contacts.**

Performances at the **Puppet Theatre** (14, Ul. Gurko/☎ 88-54-16) and the **Circus** (on the corner of Positano street and Blvd. Hristo Botev/☎ 88-00-00) seem to be the choicest entertainments **for children,** who might also enjoy the cable-cabin rides up Mount Vitosha (see above), or the **bowling alley** in the New-Otani Hotel (100, Ul. Anton Ivanov).

Sofia's real forté is **drama, ballet and classical music.** Plays are naturally performed in Bulgarian, so not knowing the language is a distinct drawback, but productions at *Satirical Theatre* (26, Ul. S. Karadya), the *Youth Theatre* (36, Knyaz Dondukov), the modern *Drama Theatre* (23a, Ul. Zaimov) and the *Sulza i Smyah* (5, Ul. Slavyanska) are likliest to be most rewarding should you decide to have a go. Opera and ballet (at the Opera House adjoining Aleksandâr Nevski Square) and operetta (at 4, Blvd. Volgograd) are less dependent on language, which shouldn't be any barrier to enjoying symphonies or concertos at the *Bâlgaria* (1, Ul. Benkovski) or *Slaveykov* (Slaveykov Square) concert halls, or the *NDK*. Famous foreign soloists and ensembles appear during the annual **Sofia Music Weeks** (around May 24-June 20); while the **Music Evenings** in the first week of December are primarily a showcase for native talent. **Tickets and information** can be obtained from the NDK tourist bureau or the Concert Bookings office at 1, Blvd. Ruski; performances normally start at 7pm.

OUT FROM THE CITY

Balkantourist organises **day-excursions** by minibus or coach to Pleven and Plovdiv (see the following chapter), Rila Monastery and Borovets (described in this chapter, p.566 & p.564), and the museum-village of Koprivshtitsa (p.635). Since Rila and Koprivshtitsa are both awkward to reach by public transport, it's worth considering signing up for these trips, especially if your time is short, but the others are relatively accessible to independent travellers. Zemen Monastery, Samokov and other places to the south of Sofia are covered later in the chapter; below are a few alternative possibilities.

Less than 20km **north of Sofia**, the River Iskâr has carved a stupendous defile through the Balkan Mountains, whence minor roads or small railway halts lead to several **stalactite caves** and **monasteries**. These are easily reached by car, but getting there by rail involves paying some attention to train schedules – see p.582 for more details. Another place to the north of Sofia which you might find interesting is the restored **Partisan hideout** near the village of **KUBRATOVO**. Between January and November 1944, this sheltered members of *Chavdar Partisan Brigade* which, together with the Shoppe Partisan Detachment, entered Sofia to consolidate the military coup that preceded Liberation Day. Ex-members of the Brigade have the same status in Bulgaria that veterans of the Long March enjoy in China, and many hold important posts – not least the unit's former commander, Todor Zhivkov, who now leads the country. Kubratovo can be reached by bus from the Orlandovtsi district in the north of Sofia.

A mere 17km **west of Sofia** (regular trains from the Zaharna Fabrika station), **BANKYA** has the manicured parks, twee statues and aimless pedestrians that one associates with spa resorts. If you fancy a good wallow in salubrious mineral water this could be the place; otherwise, aside from a campsite, various hotels and snack bars, Bankya has nothing to recommend it.

LISTINGS

Airlines Most foreign airlines have their offices on Blvd. Stamboliiski or Blvd. Ruski. For BALKAN's international services ring 88-11-80/88-54-06, or enquire at 12, Narodno Sâbranie Square or 19, Ul. Lege (☎ 88-49-89). Tickets for **internal flights** are available for hard currency or leva backed by an exchange receipt at the NDK tourist centre; or may be purchased for leva at 10, Ul. Sofiiska Komuna (☎ 88-44-36/88-13-94) *without* having to produce receipts.

Airport Ring 45-11-13 for information on domestic flights, 72-24-14 for international services. The airport is situated 10km east of the city and accessible by #84 or #284 (express) bus, boardable at the Orlov Most. The last express bus leaves the airport at 10pm, the last regular bus at midnight. Driving to the airport, follow the Lenin highway and then turn off along the Iskârsko Shose. The taxi fare is around 10 leva.

American Centre 1, Stamboliiski Blvd, adjacent to the US Embassy. Contains a library, a video and a range of Western newspapers. Open more frequently than the advertised time – Wednesday 8am-1pm – suggests.

Barbers/hairdressers 1, Knyaz Dondukov and 7, Slaveykov Square.

Books Very few books in English (though more in German) at the *V. Yugo* foreign-language bookshop, opposite the Russian Church on Ruski Blvd, or the *Antikvarium* at 18, Graf Ignatiev.

Bulgarian Hikers' Union Contact the *Pirin Travel Agency* branch of the Union (30, Blvd. Stamboliiski/☎ 87-06-87) **for information** on potholing, hiking and caves; or to reserve **beds** in the cheap chalets (*hizha*) and hostels (*turisticheska* *spalya*) in Bulgaria's highland regions, which otherwise normally refuse to admit Westerners. If you fix something up with the Union, get it in writing with a rubber stamp.

Bus Stations General information is best obtained from the *Transport Service Centre* in the NDK building (☎ 59-70-95), or by dialling 59-71-83. The *Sever* terminal on Pirdop Square (near the Poduyane station/tram #2 from the Levski monument) handles services to points north and east of Sofia (☎ 45-30-14). Buses to Rila Monastery and Pernik leave from *Ouchna Kucha*, halfway along Deveti Septemvri Blvd. (tram #5 from the centre), but other destinations in the southwest are covered by the *Yug* terminal on Blvd. Bâlgaro-Sâvetska Druzhba (beyond Freedom Park/☎ 72-00-63). Western regions are served by the *Zapad* station on Vâzrazhdane Square (☎ 87-41-06). *International services* – to Niš and Skopje in Yugoslavia – may still operate from 23, Blvd. Hristo Mihailov (☎ 52-50-04), but don't count on it.

Car rental From Sofia airport (☎ 72-01-57), the *Vitosha-New Otani Hotel* (☎ 62-41-51), or the *Grand Hotel Sofia* (☎ 88-06-48).

Car repairs Advice at the *Union of Bulgarian Motorists*, 6, Ul. Sveta Sofia (☎ 883-856); dial 146 for their **breakdown service**. Repairs might be possible at the *Iztok* service centre (17km along the Plovdiv highway) or at *Bozhour* (18km out on the Kalotina road). **Spare parts** for Peugeot, Renault, Opel, Ford, Volvo and Mercedes cars can be purchased for hard currency from the CORECOM shop on the Zaharna Fabrika housing estate.

Central Post Office on Ul. General Gurko (7am-9pm daily); telegraph and international telephone service open 24 hours.

24-hour Chemists at 29, Ul. Alabin (☎ 87-90-29); 159, Ul. Rakovski (☎ 87-92-06); 102, Blvd. Zaimov (☎ 44-18-67) or 123, Blvd. Hristo Botev (☎ 83-56-51). These may have changed, but current information can be obtained by dialling 178. Medicines manufactured in the West are available for hard currency at the International Pharmacy in the *Tsentr po Higiena*, open Monday-Friday 7.30am-1pm, 2pm-4.30pm (trolleybus #4 or #7 from the University).

Circus At the intersection of Ul. Positano and Blvd. Hristo Botev (☎ 88-00-00): see below for bookings.

Concert Tickets Bookings at 1, Blvd. Ruski (Monday-Friday 8am-12am, 3pm-7pm), or in the NDK centre. Information on theatres and concerts can be obtained by telephoning 171, but don't bank on getting a foreign-language speaker.

Embassies/consulates *Denmark*, 10, Blvd. Ruski (☎ 88-04-55); *Federal Republic of Germany*, 7, Ul. Barbusse (☎ 72-03-82); *Holland*, 19a, Ul. Denkoglou (☎ 87-41-86); *Hungary*, 57, Ul. Sesti Septemvri (☎ 66-20-21); *Romania*, 10, Ul. Polyanov (☎ 44-35-81); *UK*, 65, Blvd. Tolbuhin (☎ 88-53-61/open Monday-Thursday 9am-12am, 2pm-3.30pm, Friday 9am-12am); *USA*, 1, Stamboliiski Blvd. (☎ 88-48-01/open Monday-Fri 8.30am-1pm). Australians, Canadians and New Zealanders have no representation in Sofia but the British Embassy might help out; Denmark will do the same for other Scandinavian nationals.

Emergencies Medical treatment for foreigners at 1, Ul. Evgeni Pavolvski in the Mladost I housing estate (bus #75 from the Eagle Bridge/☎ 75-361). Dial 150 for an *ambulance* and 160 for the *Militia*.

Feminism There's no autonomous feminist movement in Bulgaria, but should you be interested in meeting the Party officials responsible for women's issues, pay a visit to the *Committee of Democratic Women in Bulgaria* (82, Vitosha Blvd.).

Legal advice See your embassy first, and then perhaps the Union of Bulgarian Lawyers (31, Ul. Alabin; ☎ 87-77-82).

Maps Road atlases and hiking maps from 19, Ul. Levski and 17, Blvd. Stamboliiski; supplies are erratic, so it's worth trying other bookshops.

Markets The main fruit & vegetable market is on Ul. Georgi Kirkov, west of the Synagogue; there's a smaller one on Ul. Hristo Smirnenski.

Motoring insurance Should you be covered by Bulgarian insurance and need to renew your policy, or make a claim, do so at *Bulstrad*, 5, Ul. Dunav (☎ 851-191).

Opticians 14, Vitosha Blvd. and 7, Ul. Graf Ignatiev.

Peace The *National Peace Committee* – a state organisation – has its headquarters on Knyaz Dondukov a few doors down from the Balkantourist bureau.

Petrol coupons From Balkantourist offices or the *Shipka Travel Agency*, 6, Ul. Sveta Sofia (☎ 87-88-01).

Philately Increase your stamp collection with purchases at 14, Vitosha Blvd. or 1, Ul. Stefan Karadzha, or converse with fellow stamp buffs at the Union of Bulgarian Philatelists (5, Ul. Traikov/☎ 65-30-79).

Photographs Passport photos in 24 hours from 96, Ul. Rakovski (weekdays 8am-7pm/Saturday 9am-2pm). The photographer speaks French and German.

Photographic supplies 125, Dimitrov Blvd. (Western makes of film for hard currency); 3, Blvd. Stamboliiski; on the 4th floor of the TsUM.

Radio Sofia Summer broadcasts in English from 9.30am-10pm (on 19m) and from 9.30pm-10pm (25m).

Railway stations/tickets Most services leave from the *Tsentralna Gara* (☎ 31-31-11) at the end of Dimitrov Blvd. Tickets for Lom, Vidin, Ruse and Varna are sold on the ground floor; all others in the basement. The system of platform numbering is incredibly confusing, so allow plenty of time to catch your train. To beat the queues, make **advance bookings** at 1, Slaveykov Square (☎ 86-57-42) or 23, Blvd. Dimitrov (☎ 87-02-22), unless you want a sleeper (79, Blvd. Dimitrov/☎ 83-34-16). **International services** are handled by the *Rila Bureau* (5, Ul. General Gurko/☎ 87-07-77/Monday-Saturday 8am-11.30am, 12am-7pm), and you're required to pay with leva exchanged at the 'non-tourist' rate. Check the fare at the Rila Bureau, change the requisite sum in hard currency at a Balkantourist office and then bring the leva and the receipt back to buy your ticket. Fares to foreign countries are grossly inflated, and you'll save 30-50% by having an IUS student card. To make things more confusing, sleeping cars on international services must be booked through the *Bureau Wagon Lits* (10, Ul. Legue/☎ 87-34-52).

Records LPs of Bulgarian folk and classical music available from *Balkanton* shops – 29, Dimitrov Blvd; 7, Slaveykov Square; 53, Ul. Graf Ignatiev – and from *Maestro Atanassov*, 8, Blvd. Ruski.

Shops & Supermarkets Aside from the TsUM and the Hali, most of the food shops are on Blvd. Stamboliiski or Blvd. Vitosha. The big stores are generally open from 8am until 8pm-9pm. For souvenirs and imported goods try the arcade in the NDK centre.

Sport The *Vitosha-New Otani*'s pool, sauna, gym, bowling alley and tennis courts are open to non-residents (100, Anton Ivanov Blvd.), but facilities are generally cheaper at the *Universade* (2, Ul. Shipchenski Prohod) and *Slivnitsa* (186, Slivnitsa Blvd.) Sports Halls. Liberty Park has tennis courts (☎ 65-31-69 for reservations) plus a swimming pool and two stadiums – Druzhba and Vasil Levski – with lavish facilities. For skiing on Mount Vitosha see p.547.

Visa extensions Granted only in case of dire emergencies, and the *Bureau for Registering Foreign Guests* (on Narodno Sâbranie Square) is a madhouse.

THE SOUTHWEST

With barely a pause Mount Vitosha gives way to the mountains of **THE SOUTHWEST**, which the Thracians considered sacred to the Thunder God, Petrun, and the IMRO once planted with opium poppies. Enclosing fertile valleys, the Rila and Pirin ranges lend grandeur to the landscape and harbour monasteries and ski resorts which constitute the region's chief attraction, not to mention offering opportunities for some superb walks. If you're planning to go **hiking**, I'd strongly recommend that you first see the *Pirin Agency* in Sofia (30, Blvd. Stamboliiski; ☎ 87-06-87) about reserving beds in the *hizhas* dotted around the mountains.

Pernik and Radomir are the easiest, and may well be the first places you reach; so too the Zemen Monastery and Kyustendil. But these are really sideshows. If you're pushed for time it's better to head straight for the main attractions like Rila Monastery, Melnik and the walk to Rozhen Monastery. To be honest, the towns along the main route down the Struma Valley haven't much to hold you on the way.

PERNIK AND RADOMIR

Although both have played a significant role in Bulgarian history neither Pernik nor Radomir are attractive towns in any sense, and if you can avoid them, so much the better. Motorists on the E79 can escape with a brush of Pernik's eastern outskirts. However, travellers **heading south** by rail will – at least briefly – find themselves in both towns, since the line from Sofia passes through Pernik and divides at Radomir en route to Kyustendil (see below) or Stanke Dimitrov (p.565). Happily, though, you can minimise contact; you don't need to get off at Pernik and at Radomir you shouldn't have to wait more than an hour or so for the right connection.

The remains of a fortress on Krakra Pernishki hill and the derivation of its

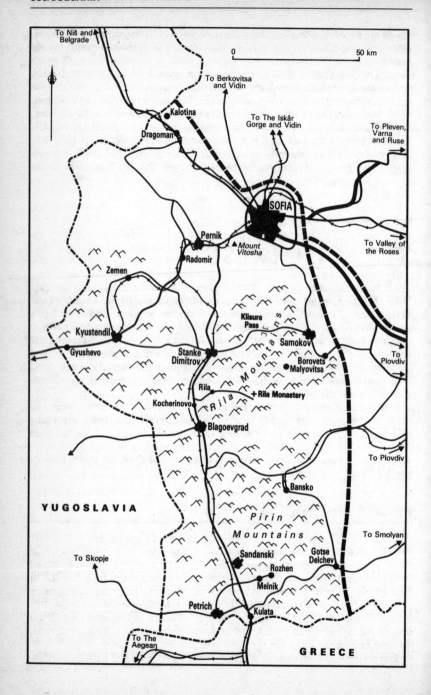

name – from the Slav god Petrun – are the sole traces of antiquity in **PERNIK**. After 1891 this hitherto agricultural village became Bulgaria's largest centre of coal mining – an industry that still employs 90% of the workforce, although nowadays Pernik also produces power and cement. From the beginning, rampant exploitation forced the **miners** to organise a union, which was grudgingly recognised in 1905 following a 35-day strike led by Dimitrov. Pernik, an almost entirely working-class town, was also one of the strongholds of the Communist-led **1923 uprising**, and suffered the worst police repression as a consequence. During the early '50s, some of those responsible were sent to forced labour in the mines, and urban living conditions were vastly improved; today, miners receive wages almost 70% higher than other industrial workers, enjoy early retirement, subsidised holidays and other benefits.

For all its modern amenities, Pernik's sole attraction is an ancient one: the **Festival of the Kukeri**, a re-enactment of the old *kukeri* and *survakari* rites, which were originally intended to ward off evil spirits and promote fertility. About 3,500 dancers participate, wearing terrifying or grotesque masks, yelling and chanting. The festival supposedly takes place every five years some time during the second half of January; the scheduling of the next event, however, remains a mystery.

On the slopes of 'Bare Mountain' in a valley to the southwest, **RADOMIR** has developed in conjunction with Pernik, on whose coal and power its industries depend. The Machine-Building Works here – nicknamed 'Goliath' – specialises in the production of heavy cranes, blast furnaces and open-cast mining gear. Historically, the town is famous as the site of the short-lived **Radomir Republic**, proclaimed by soldiers back from the front in 1918, who began marching on Sofia to punish those responsible for Bulgaria's entry into the First World War. Prevented from doing so by German troops, they so alarmed the government that it released the Agrarian leader Stamboliiski to avert a revolution. The village of KOVACHEVTSI, five or six miles from Radomir, was the birthplace of Georgi Dimitrov.

ZEMEN MONASTERY AND KYUSTENDIL

Zemen Monastery, some lovely wild countryside and the old Turkish spa-town of Kyustendil can be reached from Sofia in 1-2 hours, either by taking the highway to IZVOR, and then following minor roads, or – far better – by taking one of the trains to Kyustendil, which leave the capital around 8am, 9am, 12.30am and 6pm, and Radomir about fifty minutes later. These actually stop near the monastery, and pass through an imposing gorge en route to Kyustendil. Since it's hard to find cheap accommodation there, you might consider making this a day excursion from the capital.

Lacking high walls, tiers of cells and decorative façades, **ZEMEN MONASTERY** (*Zemenski Manastir*) seems humble by comparison with Rila, and its small C12 cruciform *Church of St. Ivan the Theologian* outwardly conforms to this impression of modesty. Inside, however, are some of Bulgaria's finest surviving **medieval frescoes**, sensitively restored between 1970-74. The frescoes – produced by anonymous artists during the 1350s for boyar Konstantin Deyan – are examples of the *Macedonian School* of painting, which was somewhat cruder and less formalised than the predominant style of Târnovo. Against a background of cool blues and greys, the saints with their golden halos and finery are depicted in hierarchies (including Deyan and his wife Doya); while the narrative scenes are mainly rendered in ochreous hues, with dark blues and reds employed to highlight the gravity of episodes like the treason of Judas and the judgement of Pilate.

To the southwest of Zemen, the River Struma has carved a rugged 12 mile-long defile between two massifs, known as the **Zemenski Prolom**. Various **rock formations** – dubbed the Cart Rails, the Dovecote, etc. by locals – are visible from the carriage window when the trains aren't plunging through a series of tunnels to escape the precipitous gorge. On inaccessible bone-dry crags you can also see the ruins of ancient forts, believed to have once defended the long-vanished town of Zemlen against incursions by the Byzantine empire. The gorge ends near the village of Râzhdavitsa, beyond which lies the broad **Kyustendil plain** – which locals proudly describe as the 'largest orchard in Bulgaria'. Fragrant in spring, the plain is richly coloured during autumn by the red apples, yellow pears and lustrous grapes which hang profusely in the **orchards** and vineyards.

Kyustendil

Bisected by the Bansko River, the town of **KYUSTENDIL**, with its fertile plain and thermal springs, has attracted conquerors since Thracian times. The Romans developed this into the 'town of baths', and the Turks who settled here in large numbers after the C14 constructed the *hamams* and mosques that gave Kyustendil the oriental character remarked upon by C19 visitors. Kyustendil has been considerably modernised since then, but it remains a spa-town, with some of its former atmosphere lingering in the old backstreets around the centre and to the south of Blvd. Lenin.

From the railway station catch a bus or follow the path shaded with lime trees south along Dimitrov avenue into **the centre**. On the central Ploshtad Velbâzhd opposite the post office, Kyustendil's premier hotel, the *Pautalia*, might have a decent town plan, or there's a **tourist office** at 37, D. Kalyashki Street which leads east off the square towards the municipal gardens, a popular hangout bounded on one side by the Regional Council building, an edifice in the traditional Kyustendil style. Nearby stands one of Kyustendil's ubiquitous **baths**. Fronted by a fountain with three kitsch statues of babies, and open from 5.30am-8.30pm, Sundays and Wednesdays 5.30am-1pm, it charges 50 stotinki to bathe in its hot (74°C), sulphate-rich waters – waters which are used in several union-run sanatoria for the treatment of gynaecological and nervous disorders, including the heavy metal poisoning that is an occupational hazard for certain miners.

A few blocks northwards another **bathhouse** (open 7am-5pm) admits men on Tuesdays and Thursdays and women on other days. Nearby there's an **art gallery** (*Kartinnata Galeriya*) largely dedicated to **Vladimir Dimitrov** (1882-1960), a successful modern painter who earned his title 'the Master' (*Maistora*) by treating standard uplifting themes in a vigorous if rather uniform style. The neighbouring cartoons by **Stoyan Venev** are more controversial, inasmuch as they suggest that Bulgarian men once treated women as pack animals or worse, rather than repeating the usual stereotype of freedom-loving Bulgars united in *druzhba*.

A few minutes walk south of the municipal gardens you hit the main Blvd. Lenin, along which are scattered several old churches and a tumbledown, overgrown **mosque** with unusual brickwork. There's a **market** to the east of this on Ul. Pârvi Mai, and if you head southwards it's not far to the large park covering **Hisarlâk hill**. In its eastern sector you can see the **ruins** of what was originally an extensive Roman settlement around the *Asclepion*, the sacred baths where Emperor Trajan cured his skin complaint and renamed the town *Ulpia Pautalia* to mark the occasion. Intermingled are the remains of a medieval fortress once occupied by the boyar Deyan. The Ottomans, who surplanted his rule over the region during the mid C14, designated their new acquisition 'Konstantin's land' – *Kostandinili* in Turkish – which eventually gave rise to the name of the town, Kyustendil.

Accommodation is something of a problem. The *Pautalia* is the only hotel you're really allowed to stay at, and it's expensive. However, there is an alternative, and if you've got prior permission you can sleep at *Osogovo* or *Trite Buki*, two hikers' chalets situated about 4 hours walk from town en route to Mt. Ruen – at 7,389 feet the highest point around. A picnic on the Osogovo massif is one of the **excursions** organised by Balkantourist, who also offer day trips to Rila, Melnik, Rozhen, Sofia or Skopje across the border in Yugoslavia. The Hotel Pautalia is also the centre of Kyustendil's **nightlife**, such as there is, with a taverna (open 5pm-12pm) featuring a floorshow and musicians; a café with a jukebox (closing at 11pm) and a restaurant (open until midnight).

Assuming you don't drive 22km or catch a train to GYUSHEVO, the Bulgarian checkpoint where the road crosses **into Yugoslavia**, it's fairly certain you'll end up heading **towards Stanke Dimitrov**, a place that's easy to reach by bus or hitching (by rail one must backtrack and change at Radomir). Just beyond Nevestino (9 miles from Kyustendil), the road crosses a famous old **bridge over the Struma**, the *Kadin Most*. Supported by five arches, the 330ft-long bridge was constructed in 1463-70 to guarantee the Ottoman lines of communication and convey caravans en route between the Danube and Salonika, although **local legends** advance different explanations. According to one story, the Turkish Vizier Isak Pasha took pity on a maiden separated from her betrothed by the river, and had it built as a wedding present – hence its original name, the Bride's Bridge. Another tale has it that the builder, Manuil, suggested to his brothers that they appease the river god by offering one of their wives as a sacrifice, the victim being whichever woman arrived first with her husband's lunch. Manuil's wife turned up and was promptly immurred, weeping and begging that they leave holes so that she might see daylight and continue to suckle her child.

THE RILA MOUNTAINS: SAMOKOV, THE SKI RESORTS AND RILA MONASTERY

Motorists can visit **Samokov**, **Borovets** and **Malyovitsa** during a day's outing from Sofia, but to appreciate them – and for anyone reliant on public transport – it's more realistic to allow at least two days. Reasonably-priced accommodation is scarce here (though you might strike lucky with unofficial lodgings or beds in hizhas), so it's worth considering the chalet-complex on Lake Iskâr, 10km north of Samokov, as a possible base camp. Anyone planning to visit Rila Monastery afterwards should bear in mind that it's almost easier to *walk* across the mountains than get there by bus from Malyovitsa or Samokov.

Happily, the journey **from Sofia to Samokov** isn't difficult: simply catch a tram (#4/#10) to the capital's Geo Milev quarter, and then one of the buses (#1/#2/#3) which regularly make the 62km journey south, following the Iskâr River past **Lake Pancharevo**, a centre for watersports. Entering the defile between the Lozhen and Plana massifs, you should be able to glimpse the ruined fortress of **Urvich**, where Tsar Shishman allegedly withstood the Turks for seven years, and on the opposite bank, deep in the forest, **Zheleznitsa Monastery**. Beyond the defile lies the massive **Iskâr Dam** and **Lake Iskâr** – an artificially created body of water 9 miles long, sometimes known as the 'Sea of Sofia'. It might be wise to leave the bus and rent a chalet here at the Storks' Nest (*Shturkelovo Gnezdo*) before proceeding the last 10km up onto the highland plateau of Samokov.

Samokov

Though it lacks the cachet of antiquity, **SAMOKOV** has a tradition of skilled work, artistic achievement and popular socialism second to none in Bulgaria. Founded as a mining community in the C14, it soon became one of the busiest manufacturing towns in the Turkish empire – hence its name, which means something like 'automatic forge'. All kinds of crafts guilds flourished here, particularly weavers and tailors, who turned flax (still a major product) into uniforms for the Ottoman army. During the C17 (in fact right up to the end of Turkish rule) Samokov's stature eclipsed that of Sofia and Kyustendil – a prestige which was raised even higher by the artistry of its woodworkers and painters, who decorated Bulgaria's finest monasteries.

There's plenty of evidence of Samokov's past in and around the town **centre** and off to the east of Ul. Boris Hadzhisotirov. Rising from the main square like an outrageous bloom stands a large *cheshma* trickling water: a legacy of the Turks, who considered fountains inseparable from civilised living. Of Samokov's once-numerous *dzhyami* only the **Bairakli Mosque** remains, preserved as a monument to the skills of local builders rather than as Muslim place of worship (it now contains a museum). Commissioned by the pasha in 1840, the mosque's design betrays Bulgarian influences: its roof-line mimics the shape of the *kobilitsa* (a yoke used for carrying buckets); while the interior decoration relies upon plant motifs rather than arabesques, with a magnificent sun set beneath the dome – a piece of Orthodox iconography.

Near the main square, a **museum** traces Samokov's evolution up to the present day. Though a school and library were founded during the era of industrial prosperity, greater strides were made after the slump, during the period of the **Samokov Commune**. Within months of their election the socialist-dominated council inspected factory conditions, supplied workers' quarters with sewers and electricity, granted books and clothing, and levied a progressive income tax. It flew a red flag from the town hall until ordered to desist by the Interior Minister, and claimed rent for a palace built on municipal land, which so infuriated Ferdinand that he had a new road built to bypass Samokov en route to Borovets. Having increased its vote during the 1912 election, the commune was overthrown by the police and conservatives; but returned to haunt them in 1919, and again during the 1923 uprising. As Dimitrov himself said, the commune was the 'first practical attempt of the working people to govern themselves in the name of their own interests, against the blood-suckers, chorbadzhii and capitalists'.

Copperware and wrought-ironwork embodied the fusion of art and industry during the town's commercial heyday, but the greatest fame accrued to the **Samokov School of woodcarvers**. Collectively, this refers to local craftsmen (some of whom studied on Mount Athos in the late C18), in particular to a group formed in the early C19, primarily to make the iconostasis for Rila Monastery. Although executed in 1793, the iconostasis of Samokov's **Metropolitan Church** (*Sveta Bogoroditsa*) is characteristic of their work, covered with intricate figures linked by plant-like traceries, interspersed with rosettes – which sometimes took the form of a six-petalled narcissus. Barring the odd angel, Samokov woodcarvers generally eschewed human figures (unlike the School of Debâr), prefering to represent eagles, sparrow-hawks, dragons, falcons and, above all, plants. A large iconostasis could require several years work, and most craftsmen probably undertook less ambitious commissions, such as fitting couches (*minder*) and panelled ceilings in the homes of wealthy citizens. These still exist in a few **old houses** among the backstreets between Ul. Blagoev and Ul. Hadzhisotirov, which are known after the names of their onetime owners: Marikin, Ksenofontov, Obrazopissov and Kokoshov.

Painting also flourished here, for Mount Athos-trained local artist, **Hristo Dimitrov**, took on many pupils. Of these, **Zahari Zograf** became the most famous, producing numerous religious and secular frescoes during the first third of the C19 – at Rila, Preobrazhenski, Bachkovo and Troyan monasteries. Frescoes by other, later artists decorate the **Belyova Church**, which lies 4km from Samokov (turn left off the Borovets road).

Samokov lacks tourist **accommodation**, so it's a toss-up between the chalets by Lake Iskâr (see above) or BELCHINSKI BANI's *Belchanitsa* hostel, 15km from Samokov and reachable by bus. Failing that, you could try your luck at Borovets or Malyovitsa. There are frequent **buses** to Borovets, 10km south of town, and buses to Malyovitsa leave Samokov's terminal at around 11.30am, 1.40pm & 4.10pm.

Travellers hoping to make the 40km journey from **Samokov to Stanke Dimitrov** by bus will probably have an easier time if they reserve seats and board at the terminal rather than use the local buses which run sporadically between villages. Some services go by way of **SAPAREVA BANYA**, Bulgaria's most ferocious **mineral baths**. The hottest spring is fed by a super-heated geyser (102 °C), which gushes 550 gallons of sulphurous water every minute.

Borovets: winter sports and hiking
Roundabout the turn of the century, Prince Ferdinand of Bulgaria ordered

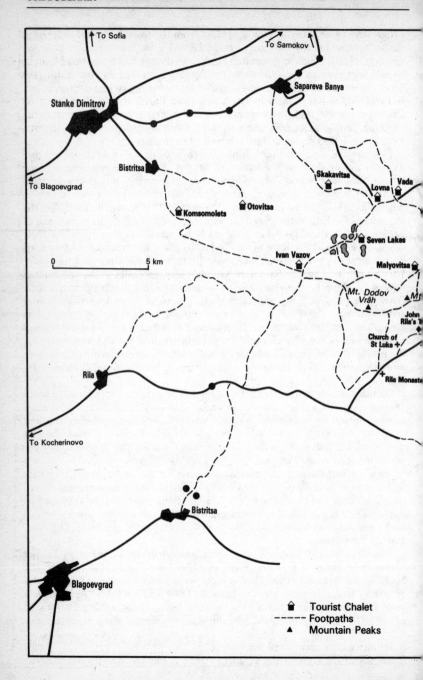

To Sofia

To Samokov

Sapareva Banya

Stanke Dimitrov

Bistritsa

To Blagoevgrad

Skakavitsa

Lovna

Vada

Komsomolets

Otovitsa

Seven Lakes

0   5 km

Ivan Vazov

Malyovitsa

Mt. Dodov
Vrâh

Mt

John
Rila's

Church of
St Luke

Rila

Rila Monaste

To Kocherinovo

Bistritsa

Blagoevgrad

🛖 Tourist Chalet
- - - - Footpaths
▲ Mountain Peaks

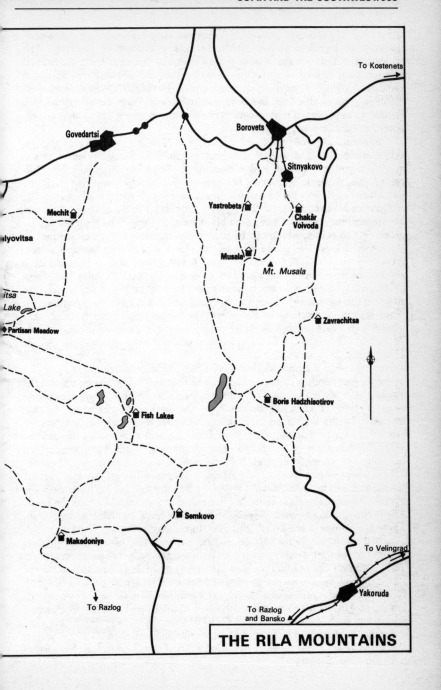

To Kostenets

Govedartsi

Borovets

Sitnyakovo

Mechit

Yastrebets

Chakăr
Voivoda

alyovitsa

Musala

Mt. Musala

itsa
Lake

Zavrachitsa

Partisan Meadow

Boris Hadzhisotirov

Fish Lakes

Semkovo

Makedoniya

To Velingrad

Yakoruda

To Razlog

To Razlog
and Bansko

THE RILA MOUNTAINS

himself three villas and a hunting lodge amongst the aromatic pinewoods covering the northern slopes of Mt. Musala, a mile above sea level. The Mamrikoff family – after whom a verb meaning 'to steal from an exalted position' was coined – and other wealthy folk did likewise, founding an exclusive colony, Tchamkoria, from which **BOROVETS** has developed. Effectively nationalised for the benefit of union and Party members in 1949, Borovets has become a major **winter sports resort** in recent years, increasingly geared towards package tourism.

Competitively-priced **package holidays** (p.511) ensure that you get lodgings, skiing equipment and a high standard of tuition – though none of this is assured if you just turn up in Borovets. Also, since most companies offer lift-passes and 'ski packs' (covering equipment rental) for a lower cost than you pay on the spot, you might as well take a package in the first place.

From mid-November until late April the fountains in the centre of Borovets are frozen into icy cones and snow blankets everything. The resort is wholly given over to **skiing**, which can be practised as late as May, or even June, on the upper slopes. Off to the west of the Hotel Rila are the nursery slopes, served by 10 drag lifts (operating from 9am-4.45pm) and overlooked by a steep slope down from *Sitnyakovo*, once one of Ferdinand's villas (accessible by chair lift; same hrs). Experienced skiers favour the pistes on the western ridge of the mountain, which can be reached by a 3-mile long gondola lift (9am-4.30pm) running up to *Yastrebets*, the former royal hunting lodge (now a hotel with a café nearby). Another chair lift serves the two ski jumps (55m & 75m long). There are also buses to the start of three *cross-country runs* (3, 5 & 10km long), 2km away.

Finding cheap **accommodation** can be very difficult, particularly since one of the biggest hotels was gutted by fire. The *Rila* and *Edelweiss* hotels and the *Yagoda* and *Malina* cottage colonies are likely to be booked solid, and the original climbers' chalets – *Borovets* (by the Sitnyakovo chair-lift), *Chakâr Voivoda* (30mins walk from Sitnyakovo) and *Yastrebets* – are being upgraded into hotels for package tourists, though getting a bed there isn't impossible. With the exception of the *Iglika* complex owned by the Pirin Agency, all bookings can be made through Balkantourist.

Chuchiliga (open 8am-11pm) offers the best value of all the various **restaurants** and tavernas, while *Chaina* – with jolly folklore performances – is liveliest. **Discos** take place on its 2nd floor, and in the snack bar near the Hotel Rila (11pm-2am; admission 5 leva), and the Rila has a nightclub and a casino. There are **saunas** in the Polish and Finnish holiday villages.

Balkantourist organises various excursions, including **hikes from Borovets** during the summer months, which least guarantee beds if these are required. The *Yastrebets* chalet (3hrs walk or 20mins by gondola from Borovets) is the starting point for the ascent of **Mount Musala**, the highest peak in Bulgaria (2,295m), which takes about 2½hrs; get a weather forecast before you set off. From Mt. Musala it's 6hrs trek southwards to the *Boris Hadzhisotirov* chalet, where one path leads down to YAKORUDA on the railway line **to Bansko**; the other trail runs **to the Fish Lakes** (5hrs). From here, having stayed overnight at the *Ribni Ezera* chalet, hikers usually push on to **Rila Monastery** next morning (5-6hrs).

Malyovitsa and beyond

Beyond Govedartsi to the southwest of Samokov, a branch road snakes up to **MALYOVITSA**, 1,750m above sea level, another ski resort with all mod cons, and pistes, a slalom track and nursery slopes on the neighbouring peak from which its name derives. However, Malyovitsa doesn't really compare with Borovets as a **skiing** centre, but it's a good starting point for **walks in the mountains**, particularly the trek to Rila Monastery. Climbers' huts and the trails themselves are marked on *BTS* maps of the Rila Mountains, which should be available from the *Hotel Malyovitsa*. The ascent to the *Malyovitsa* chalet above the resort constitutes the first leg of several hikes, for from here it's 4-5hrs walk to the beautiful **Seven Lakes** (*Sedemte ezera* cabin), or 6hrs to the *Ivan Vazov* lodge, depending on which trail you follow after the Ourdin Lakes. Blasted crags surround another lake, *Strashnoto ezero*, which lies to the east of the Malyovitsa cabin. Refuges there, and to the north of the Dry Lake (*Suhoto ezero*), serve as way-stations along the route to the chalet beside the **Fish Lakes**: 9hrs hike in all. But the most popular trail leads south to **Mount Malyovitsa** and **Rila Monastery**. Climbing the 2,799m mountain takes about 3hrs; an easier ascent than by the steeper southern face. After, follow the path westwards along the ridge before taking the trail branching left, which leads to the monastery in the thickly wooded valley below (a further 3-4hrs).

Around Stanke Dimitrov

It's tempting to dismiss **STANKE DIMITROV** as a stepping-stone to other, more attractive destinations. It has a good hotel, the *Rila*, pleasantly situated on the landscaped Drenski Rid hill, but otherwise nothing to recommend it except for its **transport facilities** – this is the railway junction between Sofia and places further south and the terminal for buses to Samokov and villages in the foothills of the Rila Mountains, from where hikes can be made. Stanke Dimitrov's other main claim to fame is its **tobacco** industry: every year some 8 million kilos of the stuff pass through the town's warehouses and processing plants, the river is tinted a nicotine yellow, and you can see huge quantities of the weed growing, or spread out to dry, throughout the surrounding countryside. As the industry developed in the early C20, the tobacco workers founded a union – the Commune of Dupnitsa – with the help of *Stanke Dimitrov-Marek* (1899-44), a local Communist now commemorated by a granite monument in the centre of the town which bears his name.

The Samokov road offers several **routes into the Rila Mountains**, but hiking trails begin just a few miles southeast of town at the village of BISTRITSA (accessible from Stanke Dimitrov by bus). From there, the shortest most southerly trail leads to the *Konsomolets* chalet, while the right hand route brings one to the *Otovitsa* hut, and it's about 7hrs walk, following the central path, up to another lodge, *Ivan Vazov*. This is well-placed for various **hikes** – for example to Mount Damga (1½hrs), the Seven Lakes (2½hrs), or Mount Malyovitsa (6½hrs). The average altitude is well over 5,000 feet, so be sure to ask about weather conditions and travel properly equipped.

Travellers **heading south** might consider a stopover at BOBOSHEVO, a village situated 2 miles west of the railway line, where trains halt briefly.

Cherry orchards abound here, while during autumn the vines overhanging the streets are heavy with grapes destined for Boboshevo's extensive wine cellars. The Monastery of Sv. Dimitâr here contains some C15 frescoes, while paintings by Stanislav Dospevski can be seen in the Church of the Virgin. Seven and a half miles from the Boboshevo turn off, the main road encounters KOCHERINOVO, the start of the road to Rila Monastery.

Rila Monastery

As the best known of Bulgaria's monasteries — justly famed for both its architecture and its mountainous setting — Rila receives a stream of visitors, most of whom now arrive by coach or car rather than on foot or by mule, as did pilgrims in the old days. Without a car, there are basically three ways of **getting there from Sofia**. Balkantourist day-excursions cost about 24 leva per head, or there are 5-6 daily buses to Rila Monastery from the Ouchna Koucha terminal out along 9 Septemvri Blvd. (tram #5 from the centre of Sofia), or you can travel most of the way by train. The Petrich-bound service leaving Sofia at 7.30am halts briefly at KOCHERINOVO, being met by a minibus which conveys you up through the town of Kocherinovo and surrounding communes to the village of RILA. Here there's a wait of about 40 minutes before the bus to the monastery departs around 12.10am. (For those returning from Rila by public transport, it's advisable get here early if you want a seat on the 11.15am bus to Sofia). It's also possible to hike over the mountains to the monastery from Malyovitsa or the Ivan Vazov chalet (see above).

The single road leading to the **RILA MONASTERY** runs above the foaming River Rilska, fed by innumerable springs from the surrounding mountains covered with pines and beech, to which damp mist adheres, beneath peaks flecked with snow. Even today there's a palpable sense of isolation, and it's easy to see why **John of Rila** (*Ivan Rilski*) chose this valley to escape the savagery of feudal life and the laxity of the established monasteries at the end of the C9. To disciples drawn to his hermit's cell, John preached that 'he who would be chief among you must be as he that doth serve'; and while monasticism was condemned as escapism and selfishness by Presbyter Cosmas — the scourge of the Bogomils (see p.704) — after John's death in 946, the hermitage became an important spiritual centre. The monastery, established in 1335, forged links with others in Serbia, and played a major role in Bulgarian Christianity throughout the Middle Ages.

Founded 2½ miles from the original hermitage, the monastery was plundered during the C18, and repairs had hardly begun when the whole structure burned down in 1833. Its resurrection was presented as a religious and patriotic duty: urged on by Neofit Rilski, public donations poured in and master craftsmen such as Alexii Rilets and Pavel Milenko gave their services for free. Work continued in stages throughout the C19, while the east wing was built as recently as 1961 to display the treasures of the monastery, which UNESCO has recognised as part of the World Cultural Heritage. Like the old monastery it's ringed by mighty walls, giving it the outward appearance of a fortress. Once through the west gate, however, this impression is negated by the harmonious beauty of the interior, which even the milling crowds don't seriously mar. Graceful arches surrounding the flagstoned courtyard support tiers of monastic cells, and stairways ascend to top floor balconies which – viewed from below – resemble the outstretched petals of flowers. Bold red stripes and black and white check patterns enliven the façade, contrasting with the sombre mountains behind, and creating a visual harmony between the cloisters and the church within.

The **monastery church** has undulating lines, combining red and black designs with arches and a diversity of cupolas. Richly coloured *frescoes* shelter beneath the porch and within the interior – a mixture of scenes from rural life and the usual Orthodox iconography, executed by muralists from Razlog, Bansko and Samokov, including Zograf. The *iconostasis* is particularly splendid, almost 10m wide and covered by a mass of intricate carvings and gold leaf – one of the finest achievements of the Samokov woodcarvers. Beside the church arises **Hyrelo's Tower**, the sole remaining building from the C14, which should be open to visitors if restoration work on the top-floor *chapel* has been completed. Its founder – a local boyar – apocryphally took refuge as a monk here and was supposedly strangled in the tower, hence the inscription upon it: 'Thy wife sobs and grieves, weeping bitterly, consumed by sorrow'.

Huge cauldrons once used to feed pilgrims occupy the old **kitchen** on the ground floor of the north wing, where the soot-encrusted ceiling has the shape and texture of a gigantic termites' nest. Things are more salubrious on the floors above, where the spartan refectory and some of the panelled guest rooms (named after the towns which endowed them) are open for inspection. The **ethnographic collection** is most notable for its carpets and silverware, while beneath the modern east wing there's a wealth of objects in the **treasury**. These include icons and medieval Gospels, Rila's charter from Tsar Ivan Shishman, written on leather and sealed with gold in 1378, the door of the original monastery church, and a miniature *cross* made by the monk Raphael during the 1970s. Composed of 140 Biblical tableaux containing more than 1,500 human figures (each the size of a grain of rice), this took 12 years for Raphael to carve with a needle, and cost him his eyesight. The lustrous *Pomme d'Or*, awarded to Rila by the International Federation of Writers and Journalists on Tourism in 1980 is prominently displayed near the entrance upstairs. Both museums are open from 8am-5pm.

Sadly, it's no longer possible for visitors to repose in Rila's cells (as did George Sava before the war, when he performed a stomach operation on a monk in the sacristy), and the only **rooms** on offer are those in the *Hotel Rilets*, just west of the monastery. Predictably, the hotel restaurant and beer hall serve dearer **food** than the bakery (run by monks) and the *skara-bira* den situated opposite the east gate. Follow the road east for a mile or so, past the hiking trails to the left (see below), and you'll see a track crossing the river, which leads to *Bor* **camping**. A field with loos and a reception kiosk (rarely open), it's primitive and unsupervised, with campers lighting fires amidst the rugged scenery. Since the road east soon peters out, most travellers (unless they're intending some hiking) return to Kocherinovo (**buses** depart from the monastery entrance every hour or two).

If you are into a spot of walking, the shortest trail begins by the roadside about 2km beyond the monastery, and leads up to the **Church of St Luke** (*Sveti Luka*), near **John of Rila's tomb** and the **'Miracle Hole'**, where he spent his last 20 years. According to Sava, pilgrims were required to enter the hole before proceeding to the monastery, and the conscience-smitten were regularly unable to do so. These people were judged as sinners and were forced to go home to repent for a year before coming back to Rila. Guided through the mountains by the rougish Vasil, Sava also saw secluded valleys planted with poppies – the source of the **opium** which partially funded the IMRO struggle.

Hiking in the Rila Mountains
Immediately north of Rila Monastery, two **hiking** trails (which later diverge at Dodov Vrâh) lead to the *Ivan Vazov* hut – about 6hrs hard slog. From the right-hand path a trail branches off **towards Mount Malyovitsa**, which can also be approached from the Dry Lake (if you camp overnight there) or by bus from the direction of Samokov. Paths to the **Dry Lake** (*Suhoto ezero*) begin at the Partisan Meadow east of the monastery, and the walk takes about 5 hours. To the southeast of Rila, the **Fish Lakes** (*Ribni ezera*) are another feasible destination, with a mountain chalet nearby. You can reach them by following the road to its end, and then hiking up alongside the Rilska to its source in the mountains, or by a trail bearing southeast about halfway along the road, which crosses the ridge and passes some smaller lakes en route. Both walks take roughly 6hrs. Due **south of Rila** is another chalet, *Makedonia*, accessible by several paths originating from the minor road which forks off a few miles west of the monastery. From the chalet it's a day's hike west down to Bistritsa, from where buses run to Blagoevgrad, or a few hours' walk eastwards to the *Semkovo* hut.

   This can also be reached from the Fish Lakes, and may serve as a way-station for walkers making **longer hikes** (2-3 days) towards the Pirin and Rhodope Mountains adjoining the Rila range. *Semkovo* lies on the way to Belitsa and Yakoruda, two villages linked by bus and rail to Razlog, Bansko and Velingrad; the *Boris Hadzhisotirov* hut situated east of the Fish Lakes serves hikers bound for Mt. Musala and Borovets, or those pursuing a more easterly path down to Yakoruda. For any of these hikes food supplies and a map of the Rila Mountains are essential, and it's prudent to pack a tent in case the chalets are full or refuse to admit capitalist interlopers.

FROM BLAGOEVGRAD TO SANDANSKI

Continuing further south towards Melnik or Greece, you're bound to pass Blagoevgrad and Sandanski, the main towns in the Struma Valley. Neither place is much to get worked-up about, but should you feel like taking a break, there could be worse stopovers.

   A few miles beyond the *Riltsi Motel* a slip-road leads from the highway into **BLAGOEVGRAD**, running past concrete flats, factories and the railway station in the southern half of town. From there it's approximately one mile to **the centre**, where a rose garden and the end of Blvd. Nikola Vaptsarov separates the bus terminal from *Balkantourist* and the *Hotel Alben Mak*. Doubles and singles or a camp-bed in the office – their final offer – cost about 40, 20 and 12 leva here. The cheaper *Hotel Bor* (past the park and post office

5 minutes' walk away) isn't licensed for Westerners, but by acting 'stranded' you might be offered unofficial **lodgings** at someone's house for around $5-$10.

Performances by Blagoevgrad's **Folklore Ensemble** (at the theatre on the main square), the annual **Women's Peace Rally** or the **Young Photographers' Festival** held in March every even-numbered year might coincide with your visit. But if they don't, follow Nikola Kalapchiev street eastwards from the centre towards the River Bistritsa, where the town's older quarter provides some incentive to linger. Several pseudo-national revival-style buildings and a brightly-painted C19 church adorn the far bank, where the stump of a bridge now serves as a monument to Macedonia, while further downriver lies the slummy but picturesque remains of the former '**Turkish quarter**'. Previously, *Gorna Dzhumaiya* ('mountain market') was an important crafts' town, predominantly inhabited by Turks from the C16 until their mass flight in 1912, after which Bulgar peasants and displaced Macedonians moved in. Since 1950, when it was renamed in honour of the founding father of Bulgarian Marxism, Dimitâr Blagoev, Blagoevgrad has switched to producing textiles and loudspeakers – and, above all, tobacco.

You'll see fields of the stuff during the 50km journey south to SIMITLI, a small thermal spa, just beyond which a branch road heads off towards Bansko (p.570). Reserve seats on the 4.50pm bus from Blagoevgrad to Bansko, or chance your luck with services from Simitli (every couple of hours). From Blageoevgrad there are also buses up to BISTRITSA village, whence it's about 8hrs walk eastwards to the *Makedoniya* chalet in the Pirin Mountains (for walks, see p.571). The route southwards from Simitli is a scenic one, whether you follow the road through the Kresna gorge or take the train, which forges its way through 13 tunnels before halting at the station 1km west of Sandanski.

A modernised town producing cigarettes and hot-house vegetables, **SANDANSKI** is believed to have been the birthplace of **Spartacus**, who led the great slave-revolt against the Roman empire in the first century BC. This originated in Sicily, where Spartacus – like others of Thracian Medi tribe – had been deported to labour on the island's *latifunda* following the Roman conquest of Thrace. You can see the Spartacus monument from the highway, and most people come for the **Sandanski Hydro**, the largest health-complex in the Balkans – with hot mineral baths, 4-star lodgings and diverse treatments (including massage and electro-acupuncture) the high-tech equivalent of the Roman establishment later known to the Slavs as *Sveti Vrach*, or 'Blessed Doctor'. Sveti Vrach languished during the Middle Ages, since the early Bulgars hardly swore by baths, but was revived as a provincial *chiflik* under Turkish rule, rivalling Melnik as a market town during the C19, when a great fair was held here every Monday. A few Roman and Byzantine ruins and a local **History Museum** can be found around Georgi Dimitrov, the main drag through the centre (accessible by bus from the station); while every June there's a **festival of sculpture**.

Balkantourist at nr.28 on the main street (☎ 20-98) should have details of this, and can also reserve beds in the *Yane Sandanski* and *Begovitsa* chalets if you fancy making **excursions into the Pirin range**, but most travellers keep going south: Sandanski is the last reliable spot for boarding **trains to Greece** (daily at 3.20pm & 11.30pm), and the only place to catch **buses to Melnik** (3-4 departures daily).

BANSKO AND THE PIRIN RANGE

Bansko – the nicest of the small Pirin mountain-towns – can be reached by train from Septemvri or Velingrad (see p.664), or by buses from Blagoevgrad or Simitli, which follow the valley down to the Graddevska River which divides the Rila and Pirin ranges. Cultivatable land is so scarce that there's only one village between Simitli and the next town, RAZLOG, 36km away on the other side of the 1,140m-high Predel Pass. From here it's a short bus ride on to Bansko.

Bansko. . .

Winter lasts for almost half the year in **BANSKO**, a town of 12,000 people nestled amongst greenery in the shadow of ice-capped Mount Vihren, the highest peak in the Pirin range. In recent years Bansko has shrewdly promoted itself as a winter sports resort, but its attractions aren't limited to skiing. The atmosphere here is mellow yet invigorating, and the community – which has a woman mayor – is tightly knit and proud of its achievements. Founded by exiled clans in the C15, Bansko has lived by trade and hard graft – growing tobacco at an altitude of 1,000m above sea level – and has the lowest divorce rate in Bulgaria. This might be a result of sobriety, for Bansko's women had all the pubs shut down from 1946 to 1947, but most locals attribute it to their clanishness, and believe that divorces would be still rarer were it not for the presence of 2,000 'outsiders'.

Unlike many Bulgarian towns, Bansko's largely modernised centre exists easily with the older quarters, a maze of cobbled lanes where the timber-framed stone houses hide behind walls with stout double doors, as if built for siege. During the centuries of Ottoman rule Christian households were required to provide 'hospitality' to travellers bearing the Sultan's *firman*, and worse still, were preyed upon by the rapacious Bashibazouks. Although the monasteries preserved religious arts and Orthodoxy, and Bulgars nursed memories of resistance with their songs of haiduks and King Marko, the history of Bulgaria before the conquest was almost submerged by 1762, when Bansko-born **Paissi of Hilendar** (1722-73) completed his seminal *Slav-Bulgarian History*. Began after 1745, when Paissi became a monk at the monastery on Mount Athos, it both exalted past glories and the task of national revival. Circulated in manuscript form for decades before its publication, Paissi's history inspired generations of Bulgarian nationalists.

Another patriot associated with the town is **Neofit Rilski** (1793-1881), who advanced Bulgarian education and Orthodoxy in the face of Turkish restrictions and Greek influence, and led the campaign to restore Rila Monastery and build Bansko's **Church of the Holy Trinity**. To accomplish this required a bribe to the governor and the official witness to the 'discovery' of an icon on the site (which qualified it as 'holy ground' suitable for a Christian place of worship). Then a wall was raised to conceal the townsfolks' enlargement of the church beyond the dimensions set by Turkish clerks, for which the mayor of Bansko was gaoled for five years in Thessaloníki. Some years later a belfry was added, whose bells must have rung during the frequent wars, uprisings and massacres which afflicted Bansko between 1878-1925. Local artisans also carved iconostases for the Trinity Church and the older **Church of the Virgin** on the other side of town, although Bansko's reputation for such work was overshadowed by the fame of Samokov's woodworkers and icon-painters.

A third famous Banskoite is the poet **Nikola Vaptsarov** (1909-42), whose house is now a **museum**. An engineer by training, he shared the Futurists' enthusiasm for the machine age and joined the wartime resistance in the courage of his Communist convictions. Vaptsarov's final poem was composed in a Sofia prison as he awaited execution:

> The fight is hard and pitiless
> The fight is epic, as they say:
> I fell. Another takes my place —
> Why single out a name!
>
> After the firing squad — the worms.
> Thus does the simple logic go.
> But in the storm we'll be with you
> My people, for we loved you so.

As for **practicalities**, you'll find restaurants and the post office on or just off Georgi Dimitrov, the main drag. The *bus terminal* adjoins this just east of the centre, while the *railway station* can be reached by following Blvd. Lenin northwards. Although there's a much cheaper *hostel* in the backstreets south of Blvd. Dimitrov, you'll probably have to settle for **beds** in the *Hotel Pirin* on the edge of the park. The **tourist bureau** there should be able to supply a map of Bansko and make bookings at the ski school. **Skiing** is practised just outside town from December through until March: facilities include one 1,500m ski run with chair lifts and two 300m practice slopes with ski-tows. Instructors speak various foreign languages (although Bansko has yet to become a centre of package tourism), and there's a range of equipment for hire.

...and further into the Pirin range

Both Bansko and Dobrinishte (6km east by bus or rail) serve as starting points for excursions into the **Pirin Mountains**, Bulgaria's wildest range. The heart of the massif consists of 45 peaks (*vrâh*) over 8,500 feet tall, snow-capped for much of the year and subject to such powerful winds and violent storms that the Thracians were convinced that this was the abode of the Thunder God, Petrun. Pure water tarns and short-lived wild-flowers abound in the highland valleys, and the slopes are a botanists delight, with clumps of Scots, Corsican, Macedonian and white pine. The highest peaks and most of the lakes are in the northern Pirin, which is criss-crossed with hiking trails between *hizha* — simple hostels with rooms, bunk-beds (and perhaps food and drink). If you're considering **hiking**, the first requirement is a map published by the *BTS* — clear enough although the text is in Bulgarian only, and available from Bansko's tourist office, where it's also important to make enquiries about staying in *hizha* – and reserve beds in advance, if possible. Besides this, stout boots, warm clothing, a sleeping bag and food are essential. You can camp at designated spots (not within nature reserves), but only during the summer; inexperienced hikers should avoid high peaks and snowy ground, and, ideally, join a group familiar with the mountains.

Beginning **from Bansko**, take the minor road heading directly south, which forks after 6km. The right-hand, better surfaced, fork leads to the *Bunderitsa* hut 8km away, and on past the **Baikushev Fir** – a mighty tree 1,200 years old – to the larger *Vihren* chalet, 2km on. From here on the scenery is magnificent, whether you make the 2½hrs walk northwards to **Mount Vihren** (2,914m), Bulgaria's second highest peak, or trek for 6hrs in the opposite direction via Lake Tevetno to the *Begovitsa* chalet or the larger *Yane Sandanski* – which serves meals and attracts weekend hikers from Sandanski, 18km to the southwest. A third trail from the Vihren chalet runs eastwards, past two lakes and **Mount Todorin** (2,746m) to the *Demyanitsa* cabin 4½hrs away, which awaits folks who've conquered the 11km ascent by way of the left-hand fork of the road leaving Bansko. Heading south from *Demyanitsa*, the second turn off to the east leads to the **Balyavishki Lakes**, while the main trail brings you to Lake Tevetno in 3hrs. If the weather's good and there's time to spare, consider pushing on from there to reach the *Pirin* or *Begovitsa* chalets (3-4hrs), or head north from Balyavishki Ezero to the *Bezbog* hut.

You can, alternatively, start **from Dobrinishte**, from where it's 11km by mountain road (petering out into a track) to the *Gotse Delchev* chalet, and a further 2½hrs walk to the *Bezbog* cabin (meaning 'Godless' in Russian) – whence you can hike to most of the places mentioned above. Few foreigners go further south into the Pirin range, although there are sporadic buses down the Mesta valley to the small town of **GOTSE DELCHEV**, a sleepy place engaged in tobacco-growing, near which stands the **remains of Nicopolis ad Nestrum**, a staging-point on the Roman road from Constantinople to the Adriatic. From town a minor road runs through the mountains to KULATA on the Greek border.

The town itself is rather less remarkable than its namesake, the revolutionary **Gotse Delchev** (1872-1903). Inspired by Levski and Botev's example, he dedicated himself to the achievement of a free Macedonia, laboriously organising a network of underground cells for the IMRO (p.577), while publicly leading the life of a penurious teacher. Delchev hoped for the establishment of utopian socialism within an autonomous Macedonia – anathema to the right-wing *Verkhovitsi* who urged a terrorist campaign and sought the region's fusion with Bulgaria. Killed in a skirmish with Turkish troops, he never witnessed the failure of the long-awited uprising nor the IMRO's decline into sectarian butchery.

Since Macedonia was liberated from Turkish rule to be divided by neighbouring states (the Balkan Wars of 1912-13), the governments ruling them have generally been down on the **Macedonians**. A cold war tension prevailed for decades after the 1916-18 war, when frontiers were again re-drawn in blood; and IMRO bombings and Yugoslav retaliation served to justify state repression of Macedonian culture (even speaking the language was a crime in royalist Yugoslavia). Talks between Tito and Dimitrov in the late 1940s – aimed at resolving the 'Macedonian question' by forming a federation of south-Slav republics – collapsed, and as Yugoslav-Soviet hostility worsened there were renewed witch-hunts for saboteurs, and sabre-rattling on both sides of the border – something which only abated in the late 1950s.

Governments in Yugoslavia and Bulgaria have since pursued almost opposite policies towards their Macedonian minorities. Some political autonomy and a high degree of cultural expression has been institutionalised by the creation of a Macedonian national republic in Yugoslavia, whereas in Bulgaria the Macedonians have assimilated without a murmur. Whereas 187,000 people (63% of the Pirin region's population) declared themselves Macedonian in 1956, less than 9,000 did so in the next census nine years later. The wholesale adoption of Bulgar ethnicity that may not have been exactly voluntary. It's been alleged that when citizens' identity cards were reissued in the early '60s, the majority of new ID documents stated Bulgar ethnicity, while all the old ones (recording Macedonian status) became invalid. Since ownership of a valid *EGN* is essential for normal life here, this 'administrative' measure has been a powerful tool of coercion.

MELNIK AND THE WALK TO ROZHEN MONASTERY

Three buses daily run **from Sandanski to Melnik**, past tobacco fields hugging the roadside above the fertile bed of the Struma Valley, between hills that become arid and rocky, swelling into desolate mountains which stretch towards Greece and Yugoslavia. Off the highway, roads deteriorate and villages seem like triumphs of tenacity, clinging to hilltops burrowed with bunkers, or crouched around waterholes. Except for the highway strip and the road and mountain path leading to Melnik and Rozhen, this territory is a *Granitsen zone*, closed to non-residents lacking a special pass and delineated by signs in Polish and German for the benefit of foreigners.

Approaching **MELNIK** you'll catch glimpses of the wall of mountains which allowed the townsfolk to thumb their noses at Byzantium in the C11. The town itself hides until the last moment, encircled by hard-edged crags, scree slopes and rounded sandstone cones. Its straggling square is lined with tavernas, whitewashed stone houses on timber props festooned with flowers and vines overhang cobbled alleys and narrow courtyards, through which even tourist crocodiles don't manage to upset the local drinkers' equanimity. Visually, Melnik is stunning – marred only by the Balkantourist hotel on the hillside – but socially and economically it's fast becoming its own monument, a living fossil. In 1880 Melnik had 20,000 inhabitants, 75 churches and a thriving market on the *Charshiya*, the main street whence camels and horses departed twice weekly, laden with wine for foreign lands. The economy waned towards the end of the C19 and the Balkan War of 1913 burned the town to the ground and sundered its trade routes. Nowadays there are only 570 inhabitants, and the town survives on wine-making – the traditional standby – and tourism.

Melnik's backstreets invite aimless wandering and guarantee a succession of eye-catching details, like chimney pots in 10 different styles. In a lovely **church** (situated below the hotel, more or less opposite the post office), the C19 iconostasis is painted in a bold, almost naive style, the lowest row of panels depicting the Fall, while scaly fishes – a traditional motif – flank the crucifix topping the altar screen. There are turbaned Turkish gravestones in the crypt museum and medieval frescoes inside the nave. Melnik's oldest ruin – known as the Byzantine or **Bolyar House** – is sited above the hotel, and was clearly built (between the C10-C14) with defence in mind. It was probably the residence of Melnik's C13 overlord, Alexei Slav, who invited rich Greeks – then persecuted in Plovdiv – to settle here, thereby ensuring investment in the town in the form of businesses, churches and residences. Rebuilt during the National Revival in the C19, these houses are now Melnik's most impressive buildings, and none more so than the Kordopulov mansion on the outskirts of town.

Follow the track up from the river gully and you'll see the stone-walled **Kordupulov House** protruding from the hillside, its 24 windows surveying every approach. Above the ground floor, now a *mehana*, the spacious rooms are intimate, the reception room a superb fusion of Turkish and Bulgarian crafts, with painted panelling, rows of cushioned *minder* lining three walls, an intricate lattice-work ceiling and a multitude of stained glass windows. It's also worth noting the Kordopulov's secret room, built as a refuge for the family in case of emergencies. The **Pashov House**, another venerable relic (located just below the main square), contains the **Town Museum** (8am-12am, 1pm-6pm Monday-Wednesday). The creaking stairways and elegant rooms are more arresting than most of the exhibits – though photos and engravings of old Melnik manage to leap the language barrier. For me, the highpoint is the top floor room decked out with the accoutrements of Melnik's haut-bourgeoisie at the turn of the century – lace gloves, plush armchairs with antimacassars, the frock coats and ballgowns all redolent of the *Forsythe Saga*, although the icons and samovar do strike a Bulgarian note.

Wine, food and accommodation
Full-bodied red **Melnik wine** is justly famed throughout Bulgaria, and once enjoyed an international reputation through the wine trade organised by the merchants of Dubrovnik, which enriched Alexei Slav and continued under Ottoman rule when Melnik was a tribute-paying *kaza* town (the Turks weren't fundamentalists when fine wine and healthy profits were involved). Nowadays it provides a modest livelihood – restaurants and tavernas slosh it around and locals are keen to flog tourists their homebrew – but the wine sold here isn't much cheaper than in a Sofia supermarket, and can be more expensive. The vineyards laden with small, dark grapes (of the variety known as Melnik Broad Vine) are ritually pruned and sprinkled with wine on February 14 to ensure a bumper crop – an event known as **Vinegrowers' Day** (*Trifon Zarezan*) – while the harvest time is decided a week beforehand, and may occur as late as the middle of October if the summer has been particularly dry and sunny. The grapes are allowed to cool in basements before being pressed and left to ferment in the chilly cellars that riddle the hills around – every family has at least one, and casks of wine for the consumption of 'insiders only', which is better than the stuff sold to visitors. Melnik is also a fine place to drink *Mastika* (similar to Greek ouzo), which packs a delayed-

action punch. If none of this is to your taste, you'll find draught beer (and cheap grilled snacks) at the *Skara-bira* joint down near the bus stop.

Of the half-dozen **places to eat**, my favourite was the mehana just beyond the bridge at the top end of the square; pretty standard fare, but the staff are friendly and the place buzzes until closedown at 11pm. Decadence-seekers can rent the 'Turkish suite' upstairs for 25 leva a night (illicitly, I think), a palatial and reasonably cheap alternative to the antiseptic *Hotel Melnik* on the hillside. You should be able to get a private room by asking around, or at the **accommodation** bureau near the bus stop. Otherwise there are cheap dormitory beds in the *Turisticheska spalya* perched above the river gully (look for the signs beyond the mehana), or – throwing registration stamps to the wind – you can camp out in the caves further up the valley, at the start of the route to Rozhen Monastery.

Walking to Rozhen Monastery

Although the bus from Sandanski continues on to Rozhen, turning off the Pirin road (see below) at Kurlanovo to reach the village, it's more fun to walk over the mountains to the monastery. The 6½km footpath ascends the river gully – follow the right hand fork after about 1½km – and up into the hills, offering great views of the valleys around Melnik. Scrambling up a mountain ridge is the only hard part of the journey, and the scenery repays any effort. Miles of rippling sandstone mountains ranged behind the mushroom-like slabs of hard rock poised upon eroded columns of softer sandstone make up a surreal landscape reminiscent of *Dune*. In Robert Littell's novel *The October Circle*, it's here that the blind Witch of Melnik resides, foretelling the townsfolks' destiny for lumps of sugar in lieu of silver coins – a scenario that seems quite possible in the eerily unreal surroundings. Suddenly, the descent onto a grassy plateau reveals the monastery.

ROZHEN MONASTERY (*Rozhenski manastir*) is small and – outwardly at least – austere, having survived looting and burning many times since its foundation in the C12, on the site of an earlier monastery. Rozhen is dedicated to the 'Mother of God's Nativity' and its name derives from the ancient form of the word *roden*, meaning 'born'. The irregular courtyard is unadorned, and only at the far end, where cell is stacked upon cell, does the woodwork display the finesse found at Rila. The cells themselves contain rugs and cushions whose vivid colours counterpoint the simplicity of the furnishings, although the leading clerics once enjoyed silver coffee sets and book-holders inlaid with mother of pearl. In the bakery the oven and walls consist of the same mud and straw bricks, giving the entire room the texture of a very coarse wholemeal loaf. The Church of the Birth of the Holy Virgin's single cloister shelters a battered *Judgement Day*, where sinners meet a gory end (prodded by toasting forks and suchlike), while inside the tarnished murals – now under restoration – are eclipsed by a magnificent iconostasis. Flowers, birds, fishes and flounces swirl about the richly coloured icons, and the whole screen – unusually wide in proportion to its height – is a triumph of the woodcarver's art.

Beyond the monastery is a larger C19 church, with crudely 'marbled' columns, cumbersome fittings and a brash iconostasis. The track descends to **ROZHEN VILLAGE** in the valley; conspicuously poorer than Melnik, with houses like overgrown chicken-coops, a shop, a mehana and little else. The villagers can be amazingly friendly and might invite you to join the dancing (which is similar to that in northern Greece) if they're having a bash; try the local **strawberries**, which are delicious.

THE BORDERLANDS AND PETRICH

Given *granitsen zone* restrictions and the limitations of public transport, relatively few travellers contemplate **heading south** from Melnik unless to cross into Greece or Yugoslavia. Most foreign motorists and truckers (who seem unwilling to pick up hitchers) follow the E79 straight down to **KULATA**: the 24-hour checkpoint whence they cross the border **into Greece** and hove on to Thessaloníki. If you're heading for Greece it's better to board the two **international** trains at Sandanski (around 3.30pm and 11.30pm), since Bulgar security men may hassle travellers attempting to do so during the brief stopovers at Kulata, which can be reached by domestic trains from Sandanski (7 daily) and has a motel should you get stranded overnight. An equal number of trains from Sandanski veer west at Gen. Togorov, and wind up in Petrich, situated halfway along the route **to Yugoslavia** (motorists should turn off the E79 at NOVO DELCHEVO), though the border crossing – 22km west of town – sees little tourist traffic, and it's important to check beforehand that it's actually open.

PETRICH contains few reminders of the past, having been reconstructed at the foot of Mt. Belasitsa on the site of the old town destroyed during the First World War, but the town harbours a respect for ancient traditions. There's been a succession of **oracles** here over the years, most recently a woman named Vanga, who at the age of six witnessed an angel who offered her the choice between sight and clairvoyance, and went blind after she chose the latter. Her subsequent prophecies gained a wide following (including Politburo members), and a vision of Varna engulfed by water was vindicated when it was discovered that the city stood upon an underground lake, following which additional high-rise buildings were prohibited.

Many of the townsfolk are fairly recent migrants from the surrounding villages, which perch upon volcanic cones overlooking the fertile **Strumeshnitsa Valley**. Thanks to its excellent climate the valley produces Bulgaria's earliest crops of cherries, melons and grapes, and the experimental orchards planted in 1951 now yield superb **peaches** in vast quantities. Tourist amenities boil down to the **hotel** in the centre and the **mineral baths** 10km from town, and if you're not interested in peach growing, there's little to see but a few ruins.

Remains of Thracian *Petra* dot the slopes of the Kozuh Mountains (near the baths), and in a park 15km west of town near the border stands a **ruined fortress** accompanied by a monument to perhaps the most infamous event in Bulgarian history. After being defeated in battle at Strumitsa in 1014, 14,000 Bulgarian prisoners were blinded on the orders of the Byzantine emperor **Basil the Bulgar-slayer**, except one man in every hundred to guide the victims back to Tsar Samuel in Ohrid, who died of apoplexy at the horrible sight.

The IMRO
Nowadays there's no reminder of the years between 1923-34, when Petrich

was the 'murder capital' of Bulgaria - rife with so many gunmen that price of an assassination dropped to £4. The warring factions then controlling the region descended from the most legendary of Balkan revolutionary movements, the **IMRO**. The **Internal Macedonian Revolutionary Organisation** was founded in Salonika in 1893 by two schoolmasters, Damian Gruev and Hristo Tatarchev, to liberate Macedonia from Ottoman rule by means of a mass insurrection. To prepare for this, the later leader, Gotse Delchev, and his supporters painstakingly constructed an underground 'shadow' administration complete with schools, elected committees, taxation and a postal service, besides arming *komitadzhi* to wage guerilla war in the hills.

Following Delchev's death, the Sofia-based *Verkhovitsi* (Supremists) persuaded the IMRO to launch the Macedonian uprising prematurely, in August 1903. Despite three months heroic resistance this was defeated by the Turks, who took savage revenge on the populace. Regrouped around Petrich and Kyustendil, the surviving IMRO members became increasingly dominated by Supremists, who aimed to incorporate Macedonia within a greater Bulgaria. The Turks were driven from the region in 1912 by Greece and Serbia, which promptly quarrelled with Bulgaria over the division of the spoils and partitioned Macedonia amongst themselves. Macedonian nationalism became fratricidal as the Supremists battled the 'Federalists', who pursued the original goal of an autonomous Macedonia, federally allied with its Balkan neighbours. Mussolini secretly supported the latter to undermine Yugoslavia, while Bulgarian conservatives used the IMRO to crush the 1923 uprising and overthrow the Agrarian government. Finally, the IMRO's terrorist activities exceeded the tolerance of its right-wing backers, and in 1934 'bloody' Tsankov sent in troops to end the organisation's power over southwestern Bulgaria.

FESTIVALS

Winter
Musical evenings during the **first week**, and a *Student's Carnival* on **8 December** in SOFIA. Every 5 years PERNIK hosts a festival of Mummers during the **second half of January**. *Vinegrowers' Day* is celebrated at MELNIK on **February 14**.

Spring
Every even-numbered year, a Young Photographer's festival at BLAGOEV-GRAD sometime in **March**. At the end of the month, or early in **April**, skiers compete for the *Aleko Cup* on MOUNT VITOSHA. A huge parade in SOFIA on **1 May**, with a Rowing Regatta on Lake Iskãr near PANCHAREVO around **3-4 May**.

Summer
Between **May 24-June 20** or thereabouts, the SOFIA *Music Weeks*. Sometime during June, SANDANSKI hosts a *Festival of Sculpture*.

Autumn
MELNIK's *Youth Festival of Poetry* every even-numbered year during the **second half of October**. Following the militaristic parade in honour of the Bolshevik Revolution on **7 November**, SOFIA holds a *Jazz Festival* during the **second week**.

TRAVEL DETAILS

Trains
From Blagoevgrad to Kocherinovo (8 daily; ¼hr); Sandanski (8; 1-2¼); Sofia (8; 2½-3½); Stanke Dimitrov (9; ¾).

From Kyustendil to Gyushevo (3; 1¼); Pernik (9; 1½-2); Radomir (8; 1¼-1½); Sofia (7; 1¼-3); Zemen (10; ½-1).

From Sandanski to Blagoevgrad (8; 1-2¼); Kulata (7; 1½); Petrich (7; ¾); Sofia (7; 3½-4¾); Stanke Dimitrov (7; ¾).

From Sofia to Bankya (every ½hr; ½); Blagoevgrad (5 daily; 2½-3½); Kocherinovo (6; 2¼-3¼); Kyustendil (4; 2); Pernik (every ½hr; ¾); Sandanski (5 daily; 3-5); Stanke Dimitrov (7; 2-2¾); Zemen (5; 1½-1¾). For trains **to other parts of Bulgaria** see the *Travel Details* at the end of each chapter.

From Stanke Dimitrov to Blagoevgrad (9; ½-¾); Kocherinovo (8; ¼-½); Kulata (7; 2-3¾); Sofia (9; 2-2¾).

Buses
From Blagoevgrad to Bansko (1 daily); Simitli (every 2hrs).
From Rila Monastery to Kocherinovo (every 1-2hrs).
From Samokov to Borovets (every ½hr); Malyovitsa (3 daily); Sofia (every ½hr); Stanke Dimitrov (5-6 daily).
From Sandanski to Melnik (3-4 daily).
From Sofia to Samokov (every ½hr).
From Stanke Dimitrov to Bistritsa (5-6 daily); Samokov (5-6 daily).

International trains
From Sofia to Athens (1 daily; 19hrs); Belgrade (2; 7-7½); Bratislava (3; 20-30½); Bucharest (4; 9¼-10); Budapest (3; 14-25¾); Dresden (3; 35-42); Istanbul (1; 15); Kiev (3; 33½-35¼); Moscow (3; 45-47); Munich (1; 33); Prague (3; 27-36¾); Suceava (1; 16); Thessaloníki (2; 8½-11); Vienna (1; 16¼); Warsaw (2; 32-44).

BALKAN domestic flights
From Sofia to Burgas (1-2 daily; ¾hr); Gorna Oryahovitsa (2; ¾); Kârdzhali (4 weekly; 1hr); Ruse (2 daily; ¾); Silistra (2; 1); Târgovishte (4-5; ¾); Varna (4-5; 1); Vidin (1-2; ½).

BALKAN international flights
From Sofia to Amsterdam (2 each week); Athens (1-3); Barcelona (1); Belgrade (3-4); Berlin (4); Bratislava (2); Brussels (2); Bucharest (7); Budapest (10); Frankfurt (7); Istanbul (4); Kiev (4); Leningrad (4); London (3); Moscow (7); Munich (4); Paris (4); Prague (9); Rome (3); Vienna (10); Warsaw (7).

Bansko	Банско
Blagoevgrad	Благоевгад
Borovets	Боровец
Boyana	Бояна
Dragalevtsi	Драгалевци
Dragoman	Драгоман
Dobrinishte	Добринище
Gotse Delchev	Гоце Делчев
Kalotina	Калотина
Knyazhevo	Княажево
Kyustendil	Кюстендил
Malyovitsa	Мальовица
Melnik	Мелник
Pernik	Перник
Petrich	Петрич
Radomir	Радомир
Rila	Рила
Rozhen	Рожен
Samokov	Самоков
Sandanski	Сандански
Sapareva Banya	Сапарева Баня
Sofia	София
Stanke Dimitrov	Станке Димитров
Zemen	Земен

Chapter fourteen

THE BALKAN RANGE, VALLEY OF ROSES AND SREDNA GORA

The great **Balkan range** cuts right across the country: a forbidding swathe of mountains in which the Bulgar nation-state was forged. It was here, at **Pliska** (and later **Preslav**), that the Khans established and ruled over a feudal realm – the 'First Kingdom'. Here too, after a period of Byzantine control, that the boyars proclaimed the 'Second Kingdom', and created a new and magnificent capital at **Veliko Tarnovo**. This remains one of Bulgaria's most visually impressive cities and is a rewarding place to stop and stay, poised for exploration of a string of medieval **monasteries**, founded alongside the capital in the C12-14, and a yet more brilliant ensemble of craftworking towns, established in the C19 National Revival.

In the **Sredna Gora** and **Valley of the Roses**, the past reflects more recent struggles. The Sredna Gora mountain villages were at the centre of the 1876 April rising against the Turks – the first shot was fired at at Koprivshtitsa – whilst the valley was birthplace of several of its most illustrious figures. The war and final liberation, wrested with the aid of Russian weapons, is commemorated by a dozen museums in **Pleven** and by a vast monument overlooking the **Shipka Pass**. This latter, perhaps the most spectacular pass across the Balkans, is a route worthwhile for itself. But it also links two places known for their offbeat festivals – **Gabrovo** and **Kazanlâk** – which bring colour to what are otherwise drab towns. Gabrovo's biennial *Festival of Humour and Satire*, is certainly unique, capitalising on the townsfolks' traditional reputation as the 'skinflints of Bulgaria'. There are other, mainly arts-related **festivals**, usually biennially or yearly, at **Vidin**, **Sliven**, **Ruse** and **Svishtov** – see p.640 for more details.

Given the mountainous topography and the vagaries of the road and railway network, **routes** through this part of Bulgaria are many and complex. The mountains that form the backbone of the Balkan range are best reached from Ruse or Pleven in the north, or from the Valley of the Roses to the south; the Sredna Gora, in the extreme south of the region, is, again, reachable from

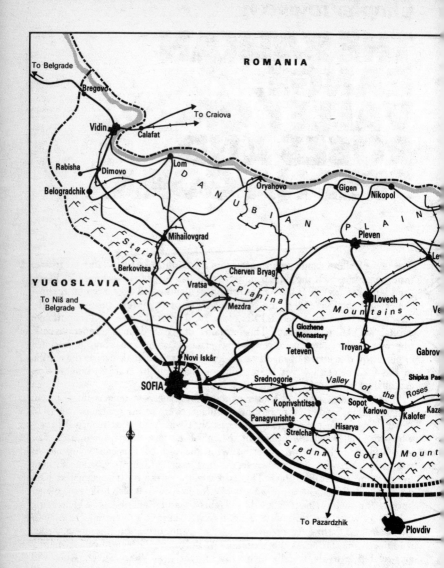

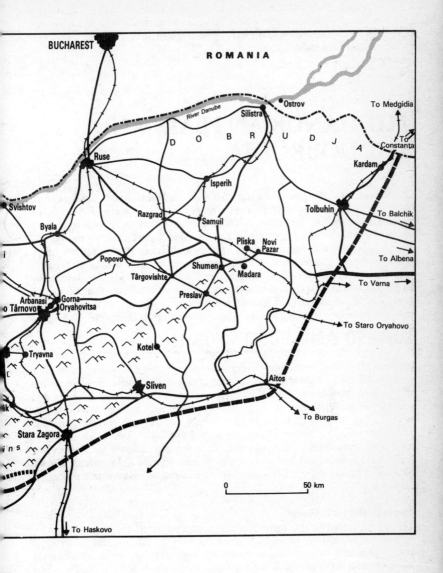

the Valley of the Roses or the Plain of Thrace (see Chapter 15). To the north, an alternative, though on the whole less inspiring, route runs through the **Danubian Plain** – a journey that's best by boat – and on towards the coast, via the hot, dusty **Dobrudja** region.

THE DANUBIAN PLAIN AND THE DOBRUDJA

The **Danubian Plain** (*Dunavska Ravnina*) and the **Dobrudja** are not Bulgaria's most interesting areas, though if you're heading on up into Romania, or making a beeline for Varna, on the coast, there are positive threads to pick up along the way. Coming up from Sofia, the **Iskâr Gorge** through the Balkan Range is mightily impressive, as are the **Belogradchik Rocks**, further north towards the old citadel town of **Vidin**. From here you can take the (only) ferry into Romania, or, staying in Bulgaria, make the trip down the Danube by hydrofoil to **Ruse**, an agreeable and laid-back town which hosts a prestigious festival of classical music in March. Heading more directly to Varna, you go through **Pleven**, interesting for its military history if nothing else.

SOFIA TO VIDIN: ROUTES NORTH

It's possible to fly from Sofia to Vidin in 30 minutes for a very reasonable cost, so there has to be a good reason for taking one of the overland **routes across the Balkan Mountains**. Happily, there are several: the E79 (199km) and express trains (5hrs) both pass through the magnificently rugged **Iskâr Gorge** where caves and monasteries in the vicinity compensate for the generally lacklustre appeal of the towns en route; and the other routes can muster at least one remarkable sight, whether it's the old quarter of **Berkovitsa**, prehistoric paintings at **Rabisha**, or the weirdly-formed **Belogradchik Rocks**. And, of course, there's revolutionary **Mihailovgrad**, where the routes all converge.

Through the Iskâr Gorge

The Iskâr Gorge is the most scenically impressive of the three routes to Mihailovgrad, and the only one you can travel by rail. Be careful, however, if you're planning to stop off, to board the right train in Sofia: it's only the Varna-bound services which tend to stop at the small halts along the gorge (from where you can make excursions) or the two daily slow trains to Vidin. There's also no tourist **accommodation** in the gorge, so you have to choose between a fleeting visit (perhaps staying the night at Mezdra) or come equipped to camp out (illegally) in the vicinity.

From just beyond the town of NOVI ISKÂR, the **ISKÂR GORGE** burrows north into the Balkan massif, gradually becoming narrower and deeper, the road and railway competing for space above the river. Strewn with boulders and gouged by gullies, it's archetypal partisan country. There's a monument near BATULIYA village commemorating the 24 who clashed with gendarmerie in May 1944, and a train halt called *Tompsân* after Major Frank Thompson (E.P. Thompson's brother) who fought and died with them. (His uniform is exhibited in Sofia's Museum of the Revolution). From the GARA LAKATNIK halt, overlooked by sheer crags, a minor road runs south to **LAKATNIK** 8km away, the site of two **caves** known as *dupka* or 'dens', around which (depending on numbers) guides conduct short tours. *Temnata Dupka* is the larger of the two, extending for nearly 3km over four levels and including several lakes fed by a subterranean river. This part of the Balkan range also harbours two **monasteries**: *Sedemte Prestola* (named after its seven altars), 10km south by minor road from ELISEYNA village, and the more accessible *Cherepeski* near the CHEREPISH halt, midway between the villages of Zverino and Lyutivbrod. Both were founded during the Second Kingdom, but Cherepish – with icons by Father Vitan of Tryavna and frescoes by the Macedonian, Iliev – has more to show for it. Not far away is a grotto known as **Shishman's Cave** after the Tsar whose forces battled with the Turks here before the latter sacked Cherepish Monastery – which was rebuilt in 1600 and again during the C19. The Iskâr Gorge ends with a final geological flourish nicknamed *Ritlite* or the **'Cart Rails'**: three parallel ribs of fissured rock up to 650 feet high which you'll see to the west of LYUTIVBROD, a few miles before the road and railway enter Mezdra (see below).

Botevgrad, Mezdra and Vratsa

This route is for drivers or hitch-hikers and follows the E79 over the Vitinya Pass, though much of the traffic is heading for Pleven and Varna and turns off before long, bypassing the former coastal road junction, **BOTEVGRAD** – nowadays useful for hotels (the *Botevgrad* and *Sinyo Nebe*) and as a terminal for fairly regular **buses to Pravets, Yablanitsa and Teteven** (p.597), and less frequent long distance services. **MEZDRA**, also, is a useful transport hub, and junction of the Sofia-Vidin and Sofia-Pleven-Varna railway lines (with a hotel should you miss your connection).

Heading across the plain towards Vratsa, you'll pass Mount Okolchitsa with a monument indicating where Hristo Botev was killed on June 2 1876 after days of running battles between his *cheta* and the Turks. Botev is also remembered by a monument bearing his epitaph for Hadzhi Dimitâr, which stands on **VRATSA**'s main square 500m from the Vratsa Gorge. Nowadays the cultural capital of the region – with an art gallery, theatre and philharmonic orchestra – Vratsa began as a medieval fortress called *Vratitsa* ('Small Door'), but lost its military significance sometime after the construction of two **fortified towers** (*Meschii*) during the C17. One of them displays a good portion of the local history museum's collection, but the prized silver death mask, found in the tomb of a princess with other **Thracian treasure** and dating from the C4 BC, is exhibited in a separate building just west of Georgi Dimitrov, the town's main street.

However, the main reason **to stay** at one of the hotels near the museum is to visit the **Ledenika Cave**. The cave, 17km southwest of town and accessible by bus, gets its name from the icicles which form here during the winter – *lednik* means glacier – and its largest chamber has aptly been dubbed the 'Great Temple'; of the 23 species inhabiting the cave, 10 are purely troglodyte. Another geological curiosity can be seen from the minor road heading north from town: a rock tunnel about 25m wide, 20m high and 100m long, which locals call **God's Bridge** (*Bozhiya Most*).

There's a regular bus service from Vratsa **on to Mihailovgrad**, which the railway avoids in favour of BOYCHINOVTSI, the junction for the branch line to Mihailovgrad and Berkovitsa. Since Mihailovgrad is no great shakes anyway, you might prefer to miss it out altogether and ride on to ORESHETS or DIMOVO, the jumping-off points for excursions to **Belogradchik** and the **Magura Cave** (see below).

Via the Petrohan Pass and Berkovitsa

There's no direct bus service from Sofia (nor trains before Berkovitsa), so travellers without private transport will need to hitch if they're to take this route. Leaving Sofia by Blvd. Stanke Dimitrov, follow road 81 northwards for about 65km to reach the **Petrohan Pass**, 4,744 feet above sea level. Deer, rabbits and roe-deer reportedly abound here, and *Petrohan campsite* (with chalets) provides an alternative to the *Hotel Mramor* 20km down the road in Berkovitsa.

Surrounded by orchards, raspberry plantations, rest homes and hills, **BERKOVITSA** is a strange mixture: one part given over to its climatic station facing Mt. Kom, where Bulgaria's wrestlers and weight-lifters train, the other to an old maze of narrow streets, high walls and anonymous-looking doorways. Many folks visit Berkovitsa simply for the local **strawberry wine** (*yagodovo vino*), which is difficult to buy elsewhere in Bulgaria but can be purchased at the big marble food store on the main street, or sampled at the State Winery – easily found by following your nose or groups of people looking excited. Other wines, made from raspberries (*malinovo vino*), blackcurrents, and grape-and-blackcurrent, are also produced here, but don't imbibe unless you plan to stay the night, since Bulgarian law sensibly prohibits you from driving with *any* alcohol in the bloodstream.

Aside from wine, the mild climate and the lovely view from Mt. Kom (should you make the climb), Berkovitsa's charm lies chiefly in its old quarter. Here stands the **Ivan Vazov Museum**, occupying the house where Bulgaria's 'national writer' spent two years, having come here to die of tuberculosis but, spurred on by the climate and peaceable environment, instead recovered, going on to write *Under the Yoke* and die at a ripe old age. Extolling Vazov's literary and patriotic endeavours (p.629), the museum omits to mention the story (related to Leslie Gardiner by his guide) that local admirers who 'knew his tastes so well' would 'catch a young Turkish girl and tie her up in a sack' and throw her over Vazov's wall 'as a token of their esteem' twice a week.

From Berkovitsa there are numerous daily trains and regular buses to Mihailovgrad, 24km away. By the roadside leaving town you'll see the **Gramada**, a pile of stones accumulated over the years as local people threw down a rock here – accompanied by a muttered curse – to vent their resentment of Berkovitsa's chorbadzhii and Turks, which was immortalised by a poem by Vazov.

Mihailovgrad

Bulgarian towns with a revolutionary tradition tend to look drably modern or prettily archaic, and **MIHAILOVGRAD** – largely rebuilt in concrete – belongs to the former category. The town's present name and many of the monuments here commemorate the September **1923 Uprising**, when local workers led by Hristo Mihailov rose against the right-wing Tsankov regime which had overthrown the Agrarian government three months earlier. Widely supported in provincial industrial towns and to a lesser extent in the countryside, the uprising was crushed by the forces of the state, who massacred 30,000 Bulgarians within a couple of weeks. The poet Geo Milev spoke out against the massacre in his poem, *September*, for which he was murdered by Tsankov's police. . .

> Uprooted from villages
> Peasants are followed by troops
> In grim convoy
> To be shot.

A locomotive and a cannon from the time stand just outside the railway station (near the bus terminal), and on the main town square a monument bears three flames, symbolising the town's struggles in 1688, 1923 and 1944. Photographs and memorabilia connected with the rising are exhibited in Mihailov's former **house** (he was killed fighting in Sofia in 1944) and in the town's **museum**; and there are the remains of some Roman temples and a necropolis around the Kaleto fortress, in a park beside the river. Otherwise, though, the town is of most use as a stopover. There are two **hotels**: the *Ogosta* and cheaper *Zhitomir*, which also houses the tourist bureau.

The Belogradchik Rocks and the Magura Cave at Rabisha

BELOGRADCHIK, or 'small white town', gives its name to Bulgaria's most spectacular rock formations, which cover a wide area just outside the town. **Getting there** by road is easy – a minor road branches off the E79 just north of Mihailovgrad – but by public transport it's more complicated. Most of the trains running between Boychinovtsi and Vidin make brief stops at DIMOVO and/or ORESHETS, of which the former is the best base: there are regular buses from there and it's also the starting point for excursions to the Magura Cave.

Covering an area of ninety square kilometres, the limestone **Belogradchik Rocks** impressed Adolphe Blanqui as 'an undreamt landscape' rising to heights of 650 feet in shades of scarlet, buff and grey, with shapes suggestive of 'animals, ships or houses', 'Egyptian obelisks' and 'enormous stalagmites'. Entwined about the rocks is a **fortress** (open 8am–10pm/noon–2pm) begun in Roman times, continued by the Bulgars during the C7–C8, and completed by the Turks a millenium later. Hundreds of Bulgarian insurgents were decapitated here as they sought to escape through a low door after capturing the citadel in 1850.

Beyond the second portal you'll recognise the *Rock of the Dog* which overhangs the third gate, the uppermost part of the fortress, while to the right is another formation known as the *Elephant*. From the terrace there's a panoramic view of the Danubian Plain, the *Head of Haiduk Velko* and the *Pine-tree* (so-called because of the conifer growing from its summit, whence a young Pioneer fell to his death after raising a flag). Two other rock formations are associated with misogynistic **legends**: the *Nun* who was supposedly turned to stone for becoming pregnant by a knight, and the *Schoolgirl* who was likewise afflicted after she was deserted by her husband. Both fables suggest that not all Bulgars conformed to what is now recalled as the 'innately moral traditional way of life', although C19 travellers were often told that 'our women are so chaste that they only sleep in bloomers' unlike – the implication was obvious – heavily swaddled Turkish womenfolk.

You can, if you wish, stay in Belogradchik – there's a **campsite** five minutes' walk south of the station and two **hotels** nearby. There might be the odd bus from Belogradchik or Vidin to the Magura Cave at **RABISHA**, but for regular services the place to start is Dimovo, from where it's about 12km to the cave. The **Magura Cave** (daily 7.30am-7.30pm) was occupied by hunters as early as 2,700 years BC, traces of whom are now displayed in a small museum. It's best known, though, for its **rock paintings** executed in bat-droppings, which depict a giraffe, hunting scenes and a fertility rite, though some of the other chambers – with names like the Hall of the Poplar and the Hall of the Fallen Pine – are just as interesting. Guided tours last about 1½hrs, and from the hill there's a fine view of the Belogradchik Rocks to the southeast. There's also a **campsite** and **restaurant** in the vicinity.

VIDIN

'One of those marvellous cities of eastern fairy-tale which, secure behind their fortress walls, decorated with spires and cupolas and minarets piled one upon another in a fantastic medley of creeds, ages and styles'. So **VIDIN** was described by Lovett Edwards in the days when the dock for the Calafat ferry was located in the centre of town. Nowadays, though, however you get here, the initial reality at least is much more prosaic. The bus, train and hydrofoil terminals are located a few minutes' walk south of the modern centre, a fair distance from the great riverside fortifications, and first views of the town leave a lot to be desired.

Around the main square, dominated by the Party headquarters (Vidin's tallest building), you'll find several cafés, the *Hotel Bononia* and the **Stambul Gate**, a stocky portal (*kapiya*) in the Turkish style. Beyond lies what was formerly the fortified town, nowadays quietly residential and totally lacking the forbidding atmosphere reported by visitors during the reign of **Osman Pazvantoglu** (1792-1807). Energetic, despotic and fond of inventing tortures, Pazvantoglu pillaged as far afield as Sofia in defiance of the Sultan, strengthening Vidin's fortifications with the assistance of French engineers sent by Napoleon, who envisaged him as a potential lever for toppling the Ottoman empire. Along with some thirty other mosques, the one containing Osman's green marble sarçophagus has disappeared, but on the edge of the park a single **Mosque** named after him remains. Like the small *kitabhane* (religious library) nearby, it was shuttered and derelict when I was here, whether as a prelude to restoration or demolition I couldn't discover. To the west of this are two small **churches** partly sunken into the ground: *Sveta Panteleymon*, dating from the C12, and *Sveta Petka*, built around 500 years later. Continuing northwards you'll probably stumble upon three more buildings from the despot's time: the **Old Post Office** (*Starata Poshta*), the cross-shaped **Barracks** (*Krastatata Kazarma*), and the **Konak** which adjoins the park beside the river. Though mysteriously closed when I came looking, the last two supposedly contain Vidin's **Historical** and **Ethnographic museums**.

Stone **ramparts** run alongside the shoreline for over a kilometre, largely overgrown and deserted, and curving inland towards the north to protect the **Fortress of Baba Vida** or 'Grandmother Vida'. The Celts who founded *Dunonia* in the C3 BC were probably the first to build fortifications here, and it was these which the Romans inherited and renamed *Bononia*. The existing fortress (summer daily 8am-12am, 1pm-7pm; winter 8am-12am, 2pm-6pm) is essentially medieval, dating from the end of the C13, around about the time that Louis of Hungary claimed sovereignty over Vidin. In the C14 it was the power-base of Mihail Shishman, whom the boyars elected Tsar rather than see Vidin secede from Bulgaria, and after 1371 the capital of an independent kingdom ruled by **Ivan Stratsimir**, which resisted the Turks until 1398. Forced to acknowledge Ottoman supremacy, Vidin expelled the Turks as soon as the Crusaders reached the lower Danube, only to be recaptured by Sultan Bajazet's army after the debacle at Nicopolis. Vidin's defences were continuously improved under Turkish and later Habsburg occupation: huge walls and empty moats extend well to the west of the citadel, and crumbling Turkish gates stand surrealistically amid the modern housing estates.

Practical details

There's an irregular outdoor **peasant market** on a patch of wasteland on Vidin's northern outskirts, which you can reach by following Blvd. Dimitrov past fortifications still occupied by the Bulgarian army, and then your nose. The local treat is *Gâmza*, a full-bodied red **wine** that's been justly likened to Bordeaux. Most **places to eat** or hang out are on or just off the main square, where the Hotel Bononia's **tourist office** should be able to supply details of what's on. **Historical pageants** are staged in the citadel during the summer of odd-numbered years, and on alternate years an international **Car Rally** brings excitement to the roads around town. The charge for double **rooms** in the *Hotel Rovno*, on T. Petrov Street, or the more central *Bononia* includes breakfast, but if you baulk at paying 31 leva there are cheap chalets for hire at *Nora Pazanti campsite*. This lies in a park on the western edge of town – take a bus out along Blvd. Lenin and alight just before the level-crossing.

Travellers **entering or leaving Bulgaria** at Vidin usually do so by **ferry** (*feribot*), using the grandiously-named international dock located a mile or so north of town (connected by sporadic bus or taxi). The ferry crossed the Danube to Calafat in Romania roughly every hour from 7am-7.30pm when I was last here, but since then the service has reportedly been extended to run around the clock; for up-to-date details contact *OJT* in Calafat (3, Str. 30 Decembrie; ☎ 1-13-03) or Balkantourist, either in Vidin or at the border-post itself (☎ 2-58-51) – open 24hrs and able to change money, sell petrol coupons and book accommodation anywhere in Bulgaria. Besides this crossing into Romania, there are also two places where one may enter or leave Bulgaria by road: BREGOVO and VRÂSHKA CHUKA (respectively 29km northwest and 45km west of Vidin) on the Yugoslav border. Both checkpoints are open 24hrs but the reception facilities on the Bulgarian side of the border are inferior to those at the Vidin landing-stage, and the likelihood of buses or taxis to Vidin is slimmer.

The BALKAN office (6, Ul. Rovnenska) can book seats on the one or two daily flights to the capital, but there's no BDZh bureau so you have to buy tickets for trains at the railway station. Luckily for travellers aiming to reach Belogradchik or the Magura Cave (see above), the five daily express services to Sofia all stop at DIMOVO en route; if you're riding on as far as the capital (5hrs) it's wise to reserve a seat. The schedule for ferries to Calafat (charging passengers 2 leva per head and 11 leva for vehicles) is displayed in the Hotel Bononia's lobby, as is the timetable for hydrofoils downriver to Ruse.

DOWN THE DANUBE: VIDIN TO RUSE

Unless you're keen to emulate Bernard Newman's bicycle ride along the banks of the Danube it's better to travel the 370-odd kilometres between Vidin and Ruse by hydrofoil than take the poorly-surfaced road which skirts inland for much of the way. There are three *Meteor* services in each direction daily: an express stopping at Lom, Kozlodui, Oryahovo, Nikopol and Svishtov, and two 'slow' services, which also halt at smaller places on the way. Express services (leaving Vidin at 7am and Ruse at 6am) take 5½-5¾hrs, the slow boats (departing from Vidin and Ruse at 8am and 1.30pm) 6¼hrs. The main problem with travelling by express hydrofoil is that tickets are only sold an hour before departure, which means getting up to queue unpleasantly early. Whichever you choose, bring some food and drink to supplement the inadequacies of the hydrofoil buffet.

The strategic significance of the Danube, which runs about 3,000 kilometres from the Black Forest to the Black Sea, was first grasped by the Romans, who travelled downriver to conquer Dacia and Thrace, and fortified the banks of the so-called 'dustless-highway'. Until well into the C20 the river's lower reaches were deemed to be of vital strategic importance, and the conflicts waged over them read like a roll-call of imperialist powers. As neighbours sharing the river, Bulgaria and Romania were generally either rivals or reduced to the status of hapless bystanders until after the last war, when both governments undertook to build the Friendship Bridge providing the first overland link – and symbolising the end of emnity – between the two countries. Maps demarcate the border with a line that wriggles amongst the scores of islands in the river, but topography confirms the saying that 'when God made the Danube he scooped mud out of the channel and dumped it all on the Bulgarian side'. Whereas the Bulgarian shoreline is buttressed by steep bluffs and table-top plateaus, the opposite bank is low-lying and riven by shallow lakes called *baltas*, which merge with marshes, and eventually the Romanian plain. Both river and *baltas* are extremely rich in fish, while the willows, lime-trees and poplars along the north shore are inhabited by herons, cranes, storks and wild ducks.

Thirty or so kilometres **downriver from Vidin,** the village of ARCHAR was once the site of *Ratiaris* – the capital of Upper Thrace, from where the Emperor Trajan consolidated Roman rule over *Dacia Ripenisis* – though there's little enough to see now. Beyond DOBRI DOL, the road runs behind a wooded cliff several hundred feet high which continues in an unbroken line for about 20km like – as Bernard Newman had it – a 'table mountain flattened out and indefinitely extended', nowadays better surfaced than in the thirties, when Newman described it as 'alternatively bad and very bad'. The first stop for express hydrofoils is **LOM,** once woundingly characterised as 'a little place spread over a large area', surrounded by fields of watermelons – its chief export. Slightly closer to Sofia by rail, Lom has traditionally rivalled Vidin as the capital's Danube port, and the local **museum** boasts that Lom was founded upon a Roman settlement, *Almus,* and in 1857 provided the venue for Bulgaria's first ever theatrical preformance – a melodrama, *The Misfortunes of Genevieve.* Across the river, stagnant *baltas* along the Romanian shoreline provide a breeding-ground for mosquitoes, which are likely to plague anyone who pitches tent or rents a chalet at Lom's *Chaika campsite.*

The next place of any size is **KOZLODUI,** where a monument near the small harbour commemorates the **'landing of 1876'.** On hearing of the April Rising, Hristo Botev assembled 200 volunteers from the Bulgarian émigré community in Romania, who boarded the Austrian steamer *Radetsky* disguised as market-gardeners, hijacked the vessel and disembarked at Kozlodui under the banner 'Liberty or Death'. Alas, by this time the Turks had already crushed the main uprising, and on learning of Botev's partisans, harried them through the mountains until their death near Vratsa. Kozlodui is also notable as the site of Bulgaria's first **nuclear power station,** finished in 1974 and currently being expanded. 40km downriver, **ORYAHOVO** slopes up the hillside overlooking a port used for the export of grain and grapes. In 1396, the Bulgarians holding Oryahovo's fortress, *Rachowa,* surrendered willingly to the Crusaders rather than fight for the Turks, but the French pillaged and burned the town anyway, later claiming that the place was taken by force because their soldiers had already climbed the walls. Oryahovo is nowadays useful as a rail junction: **trains** leave here daily at around 6.30am, 10.30am and 5.30pm for CHERVEN BRYAG on the Sofia-Pleven-Varna line.

At the confluence of the Iskâr and the Danube beyond BAIKAL (a halt for slow-boats), the **ruins of a Roman town** can be found about a mile north of GIGEN village. Excavations have uncovered ramparts, foundation walls, drains and large paving-slabs that give a fair idea of the layout of ancient *Oescus,* though the most impressive find – an ornate mosaic depicting a scene from Menander's comedy *The Achaeans* – has been transfered to Pleven's History Museum. Like other Danubian settlements, Oescus was razed by the Huns in the C5, rebuilt during the reign of Justinian and then destroyed again by the Avars, so it's hardly surprising that nothing remains of the great bridge over Danube built for the Emperor Constantine. Reportedly 3,800ft long and mysteriously abandoned after less than forty years, it was designed by Apollodor of Damascus, the architect of Trajan's Bridge at Drobeta-Turnu Severin.

NIKOPOL, further downstream, is chiefly known for its ruined fortress glowering from a crag. Founded in 629 by Emperor Heraclius I, *Nicopolis* ('City of Victory') was considered impregnable until its capture by the Turks in 1393, and the threat of Sultan Bajazet's next move frightened the Christian powers into organising a crusade to retake the lower Danube. Feasting and pillaging their way south, the Crusaders treated the campaign as a sport, bringing 'wines and festive provisions' instead of siege weapons. Unable to storm Nicopolis's 26 mighty towers, they instituted a blockade and began squabbling amongst themselves (the French, in particular, resented that Sigismund of Hungary had been chosen by the Pope as supreme commander). Pigheadedness and disunity proved fatal on November 25 1396, when Bajazet's army appeared on the neighbouring plateau. Against Sigismund's orders the French cavalry charged uphill after fleeing irregulars, only to be impaled on hidden stakes and then butchered by the Turkish cavalry, while the Wallachians fled. The Crusaders' defeat was shattering, and no further attempts were made to check Turkish expansion until the battle of Varna fifty years later, by which time the Ottomans were entrenched in the Balkans.

Between Nikopol and Svishtov the hydrofoils pass a cluster of green islands whose name is only whispered in Bulgaria – **Belene**, the site of an infamous labour camp. Established in 1947 (together with a smaller women's camp which was later closed), Belene still holds both political prisoners and dangerous criminals – the latter being favoured by the guards, who apparently permit them to tyrannise the 'politicals' according to Stalinist practice. During the early 1950s when the purges were at their height, hundreds of Bulgarians perished here through a combination of malnutrition, overwork and brutality. Prisoners directed to woodcutting on neighbouring Burzina Island had to chop 1,120 cubic metres per day before receiving their rations, and inmates who violated camp rules (by scavanging for food, or addressing a guard as *drugaryu*, for example) were used for target-practice or marooned on rafts to freeze or suffer clouds of mosquitoes. According to our informant (a prisoner in the 1970s), conditions improved somewhat during the 1960s following a limited amnesty, but Belene remained a savage place. . .and the labour camp functions to this day.

Without prior knowledge of Belene, it's easy to step off the hydrofoil and feel good about **SVISHTOV**, the last port-of-call before Ruse. Coyly encircled by the Danube and surrounding hills, this long-established port and crafts town features a couple of defunct mosques, two sunken C17 churches, and a **museum** in the former house of **Aleko Konstantinov**. As a satirist, Konstantinov is remembered for creating *Bai Ganyu*: an itinerant peddler of rose-oil and rugs who remains one of the best loved characters in Bulgarian fiction. The museum's prize exhibit is Konstantinov's heart, pierced by the stab-wound which killed him in 1897 at the age of 34, while the historical section dwells on Svishtov's military significance – as the easiest place to cross the Danube it witnessed the arrival of the Russian liberators in 1877, and the invasion of Romania by German and Bulgarian forces in 1916. Svishtov hosts a prestigious **festival of Choral Music** every 2 years (scheduled for 1988), and has a *hotel* on the main square; while the 3 daily **trains** to ORESH make connections with services to Levski on the Pleven-Varna line.

RUSE

RUSE, Bernard Newman decided, 'belongs to Europe and not to the Balkans', an observation which seems fair enough when you compare the modest contentment and prosperity of life here with the bitterness, austerity and corruption in neighbouring Romania. Yet Ruse's history has often overlapped with that of Giurgiu, across the water: the Romans captured and fortified both during the C2, and Vlad the Impaler kidnapped thousands of the inhabitants of Ruse to re-populate Wallachia. During the Ottoman period, Giurgiu also provided employment for Bulgar market-gardeners and a haven for émigré revolutionaries, though in recent years its chemical factory – emitting chlorine gas which sometimes blows across the river – has been the chief bane of life in Ruse.

Any bus heading up Blvd. Dimitrov will get you from the station into **the centre**, which lies about 8 minutes' walk along Ul. Blagoev from the hydrofoil dock. Ruse's **promenade** down Blvd. 9 Septemvri is one of the liveliest in Bulgaria, and the pavement cafés – where it's always possible to get a cup of coffee – compare favourably with Sofia's. It's unfortunate that relatively few tourists are around for the **Music Weeks** in March, which attract some of the best classical ensembles, soloists and conductors in Europe, but then again, it gives the Bulgarians a chance to hear them. Opera, a symphonic orchestra and a theatre can be enjoyed at other times, however, and if they're not your scene there's always café-life (centred around the boulevard, Pl. Lenin and Pl. 9 Septemvri) or the sights.

Sited on a sterile plaza, the **Pantheon** is a grossly overstated building: a kind of high-tech Mayan temple surmounted by half a giant ping-pong ball covered in gold. Its cool vault (Tuesday-Sunday 9am-noon/3pm-6.30pm) has four sepulchral effigies keeping watch over an eternal flame while hushed crocodiles of schoolkids proceed from grave to grave of partisan and national Revival heroes, among whom are Stefan Karadzha (whom the Turks hanged in 1868) and no less than eight members of the same family – the five sons and two daughters of **Baba Tonka**. Her former home beside the Stamboliiski embankment, now a museum (Wednesday-Sunday 9am-noon/3pm-6pm), was used as a safe-house and arms dump by the revolutionary underground, and 'Granny' Tonka smuggled rifles through swamps, led Ruse's women in an armed assault on the prison, raised her children as fervent patriots and preserved Karadzha's skull as a *memento mori*.

Tonka's house also displays photos and prints of Ruse in the days when it was known as *Ruschuk*: a predominantly Turkish town whose fortress (of which the sole remainder is the **Kyuntoukapu Gate** 300m west of the railway station) formed part of the 'quadrilateral' protecting the Ottoman empire's northern flank. Schools, hospitals and Bulgaria's first railway line – linking Ruse and Varna – were created during the enlightened governorship of Midhad Pasha (1864-77), and for some years after the liberation, Ruse had more inhabitants, consulates, factories, hotels and banks than Sofia did. A **Russophile Memorial House** at the corner of Kârdzhiev and Tsar Kaloryan Street commemorates the pro-Russian officers hanged in 1887 for plotting a coup against the Stambolov dictatorship, but this was unaccountably closed during my last visit.

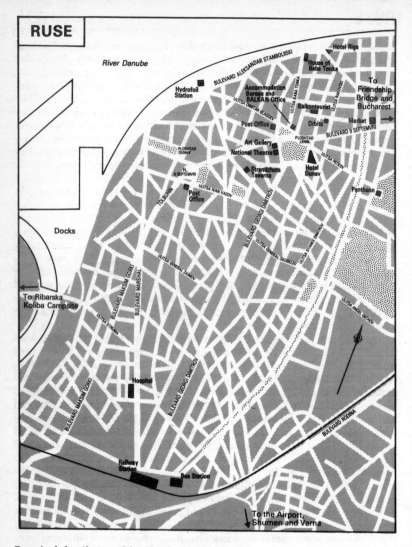

Practical details – and border formalities

If you can't afford to stay at the *Hotel Riga*, the *Dunav* lets doubles for 24 leva, while private rooms (5 leva per head) and student accommodation (2 leva) can be obtained through the bureaux next to the BALKAN office on Lenin Square, and on Ul. Rakovski, respectively. You could also rent a chalet or camp at *Ribarska Koliba*, 6km west of town, which can be reached by boarding a #6 or #16 bus on Blvd. Maksim Gorki just beyond the Marshal Tolbuhin intersection. With the river so close, the campsite is mosquito-infested, but just nearby you can savour a good **meal** in the bug-free

Fisherman's Hut restaurant. Like the *Strandzhata* (Ul. I. Dimitrov), the hotel-restaurants and the *Leventa* (out along the Razgrad road), it's a popular and fairly upmarket place to eat. If money's tight, the *Pirin*, on the corner of Gen. Zaimov and Marshal Tolbuhin, and a *self-service joint* opposite the market, serve really cheap meals but in grotty surroundings.

If you're **entering Bulgaria** by way of Ruse you'll first cross the 3km-long **Friendship Bridge** (*Most na Druzhbata*) spanning the Danube on the outskirts of Ruse and Giurgiu, an ugly yet technically-impressive structure built by both countries with Soviet assistance between 1952-54. Providing you already have a visa, there shouldn't be any hassles **entering Bulgaria**: motorists can change money, buy petrol coupons or book rooms at the 24-hour Balkantourist office beside the Bulgarian bridgehead. After undergoing customs checks on the train in Ruse's railway station, passengers are released onto the 'international platform', where a surlier bureau should consent to exchange valuta into leva.

Travellers **leaving Bulgaria** by rail have a choice of trains and destinations (tickets and seat reservations from the *Rila Agency*, 39, Ul. Blagoev; ☎ 2-28-45). The *Sofia Express* – departing at around 4.30pm – is the best service **for Bucharest** as other trains arrive there after nightfall or leave Ruse at an inconvenient hour, but be warned that one-third of the 3hr journey is spent waiting in GIURGIU (see p.301). As for other routes on, the *Pannonia*, leaving Ruse around 5.45am, makes tracks for **Budapest** and **Dresden**, calling at Bucharest, Bratislava and **Prague** en route, and the *Bulgaria* (dep. 4.30am), *Sofia*, *Dunav* (7.40pm) and *Varna* (12.25am) make even longer hauls to **Moscow** or **Warsaw**.

Alternatively, Ruse can be the starting point for journeys deeper into Bulgaria. There are direct trains or flights on **to Sofia**, and direct trains **to Varna**, though both bypass most places of interest on the way; travellers heading **south into the Balkan range** will probably have to change trains at Gorna Oryahovitsa. There are also three daily **hydrofoils along the Danube** to Vidin, leaving at 6am, 8am and 1.30pm (the first departure is the express) and one downriver to Popina, near Silistra, which departs at 7.20am daily. Tickets are only sold shortly before the service's departure from the *Rechna Gara* (Hydrofoil Dock); the ticket office is open from 5.30am-8pm.

Around Ruse

Silistra, Lake Srebârna and the Thracian tomb at Sveshtari (p.595) are feasible destinations for day **excursions from Ruse** if you've got a car or the money to sign up for a Balkantourist trip (see the tourist office for details), but if you're relying on public transport an overnight stay is probably inescapable. However, three more sites – much closer to Ruse – might merit your attention. **Lipnik Park**, 12km away near the commune of NIKOLOVO, is a half-tamed forest where the townsfolk go for picnics and strolls at the weekends, reachable by bus from Ruse's terminal, or by driving out of town along Angel Gechov Street.

More interestingly, the gorges of the Rusenski Lom to the south of town hold two sets of **medieval Bulgarian ruins**, both more or less accessible by public transport. To visit the so-called **Rock Monastery of Ivanovo**, 18km away, you must first reach IVANOVO village, which you can do by one of three Byala-bound trains daily. Once here, ask a resident '*Kâde tserkvata?*'

and they should direct you towards 'the Church' among the rocks on the left bank of the Rusenski Lom – one of several hewn into the craggy gorge whose caves provided a shelter for stone age tribes, and hermits in medieval times. A royal donation enabled Yoakim of Târnovo to establish a large monastery dedicated to the Archangel Michael on the other bank of the river during the C13, of which some cave-buildings remain. Further on, another church, the so-called 'Buried Church', features a damaged mural of Tsar Asen presenting a model of it to the Archangel, and a depiction of Michael's miracles on the ceiling. Nearby is another, more derelict rock church decorated with a scene of St Peter of Alexandra's vision. Along the same bank are the Lord's Valley Chapel (with portraits of its patron saints, Vlassius, Spiridon and Modestus) and the aptly-named 'Demolished Church', all containing murals, variously faded by time or faint from over-sensitive restoration.

Several miles further south, a fork in the gorge provides a niche for the **ruins of Cherven**, clinging to the rocks like Tsarevets at Târnovo. Formerly known as the 'City of Churches' or 'City of Bishops', Cherven was founded during the C6-C7 when recurrent barbarian invasions compelled the inhabitants of Prista (Ruse) to seek a more defensible site inland. It was then devastated so thoroughly by the Turks that it was abandoned. It's probably easiest to reach the ruins from the nearby village of CHERVEN, which is visited by the odd bus from town and lies at the end of a 7km long turning off the Dve Mogli road.

THE DOBRUDJA

The Bulgarian **Dobrudja** is a relatively unknown part of the country. Tucked away in the far northeastern corner, most travellers simply pass through when either entering or leaving Bulgaria, barely bothering to stop on the way to more obvious attractions further inland or on the coast. And certainly it's not one of the country's more immediately attractive regions. Much of it is dully flat and heat-hazed, there are few centres of size and, although the Bulgarians have done their best to irrigate the area (unlike the Romanians, across the border), it's a parched and rather inhospitable land. **Silistra** and the nearby **Srebârna birdlife reserve** are notable highlights, though the Thracian tomb at **Sveshtari**, near Isperih to the south, is the area's most remarkable draw. There are also any number of stop offs worth making – **Razgrad**, **Tolbuhin** among them – if you're heading towards the coast.

Silistra and the Srebârna nature reserve

The port of **SILISTRA** about 130km downriver can be reached by bus (4-5 daily) or hydrofoil (followed by a bus from POPINA if the vessel terminates there, as some do). With the exception of its aluminium-plated **Theatre** (heir to a long theatrical tradition), the modernised part of town isn't very interesting, but Silistra does have a couple of antiquities and two live attractions up its sleeve.

Balkantourist are in the **hotel** *Zlatna Dobrudja*, on the corner of Otets Paisii and Ulista Dimitrov, the main street. It's worth contacting them before you do anything, since you'll need directions (or, better still, a town plan) to find

Silistra's **Roman tomb**, a modestly sized and vaulted structure that's chiefly known for its paintings. The tomb dates from the twilight phase of imperial rule over *Durostorum*, the XI Legion's garrison, and the paintings were probably executed in the late-C3 or early-C4, during the reign of Theodosius I. Facing the low entrance are portraits of the interred couple, flanked by male and female retainers bringing them sumptuous objects as indication of their wealth and status, painted on the side walls. The ceiling is decorated with octagons and circles containing bird-figures, hunting scenes or plant motifs, while the owners' portrait is surmounted by the image of two peacocks and a bronze vase. Other finds associated with Durostorum, plus an **Ethnographic Collection**, are exhibited within the semi-circular bastion on the hill to the south of town. Together with some outlying walls, it's all that remains of the **Medzhidi Tabiya fortress**, another leg of the defensive 'quadrilateral' built by the Turks, which was embattled during several Russo-Turkish wars.

Unless you're driving, it's not a bad idea to sink a glass of the local **apricot spirit** (*kaissieva rakiya*) before visiting the **Lake Srebârna nature reserve** – something which must be arranged through Balkantourist. Tour groups are allowed within a safe distance of the lake (located 17km west of town between the road and the Danube) and from a tower with viewing equipment can observe what the C19 Magyar naturalist Felix Kaniz called 'the Eldorado of **wading birds**'. Besides the 90 species breeding there, Lake Srebârna is also frequented by around 80 migratory species, particularly during the autumn when there's a fair likelihood of being able to see **pelicans**.

Despite their proximity, Silistra and Romanian OSTROV (p.472) only intermittently function as a **border-crossing**, mainly for the benefit of locals with relatives on the other side. Tourists risk being turned away or, much worse, getting stranded in limbo when one lot of militiamen permit emigration while the other refuses them entry (on the Romanian side baksheesh in hard currency might resolve difficulties). Otherwise, the main alternative to returning to Ruse is **heading south**, by train via SAMUIL, the railway junction for *Novi Pazar* (p.625), and ISPERIH.

The Thracian tomb at Sveshtari

The **Thracian tomb** found beneath a mound near the village of **SVESHTARI** in 1982 is quite as remarkable as the one at Kazanlâk (p.631). A corridor lined with well-cut slabs leads to three chambers united by a semi-cylindrical vault: the central one is occupied by two stone couches on which once lay a Thracian king and his wife (five horses were buried in the antechamber to ensure them a ride in the afterlife). Adorning the chamber is a frieze showing obvious Hellenistic influences, with Doric semi-columns interspersed by ten stone caryatids. However, their sturdy upraised arms and full skirts suggest that they represent aspects of the Thracian Mother Goddess, mistress of fertility and of plants, this world and the afterlife. Archaeologist Maria Chichikova believes that the tomb was part of a necropolis associated with a large town belonging to **the Getae**, who inhabited both banks of the lower Danube during the first millenia BC, and constituted the 'link' between the Thracians of Bulgaria and the Dacians of Romania. The Getae were the first to be subjugated by the Romans, and it's hoped that examination of the detritus found in the tomb – which was looted after it was sealed during the first half of the C3 BC – will provide new evidence of their civilisation.

One way of getting there is to sign up for the minibus trip organised by Balkantourist in Ruse or Razgrad, but since schedules are vague and prices vary according to demand, it's preferable to travel independently. There are regular buses from Ruse or Razgrad to the town of ISPERIH, from where you can easily catch a local bus 6km northwest to Sveshtari itself. However, do ask Balkantourist about opening times, which weren't at all reliable when I made enquiries (daily 9am-5pm, closed Mondays, seems most likely). You can also reach Isperih by taking one of the 12.30pm Samuil-bound train from Silistra, or the 9am train from Samuil if you're coming from Varna or Shumen. Bear in mind, though, that neither Isperih nor Sveshtari has any tourist accommodation.

Tolbuhin – and crossing the border

Thirty seven kilometres from the Romanian border, **TOLBUHIN** has reaffirmed its status as capital of the Dobrudja by developing diverse industries over the last forty years. Its centre is resolutely modern, with stark concrete piles and plazas, and the main attraction is a rather antiseptic part of the C19 artisans' quarter, known as the **'Old Dobrich' complex** (*Stariat Dobrich*). Visitors can see demonstrations of traditional crafts in some twenty workshops – pottery, blacksmithing, woodcarving, bookbinding, jewellery – while it's planned to have a bazaar ready by 1992, plus a National Revival-style home for the **Dobrudja Song and dance Ensemble**. Details of performances by the ensemble and Tolbuhin's renowned **Chamber Orchestra** and **Children's Choir** are available from Balkantourist, 3, Ul. Dimitrov. Should you need to **stay**, the *Moskva* and *Dobrudja* hotels are both cheaper than the main *Balgaria*, but it's more tempting to catch one of the regular trains **to Varna**, or buses **to Balchik** – for details of which see p.640.

Due perhaps to the once sensitive nature of the frontier here, there's only one place to cross the border into the Romanian Dobrudja, and no buses run from KARDAM (5km from the frontier) to Romanian Negru Vodă (p.471). Motorists can simply drive across, but if you're trying to leave Bulgaria by train it's necessary to choose between three services: the *Trakia* or *Varna Express*, which leaves Tolbuhin's *Sever* station at 8.30pm and 10.30pm, winding up in Romanian BUZĂU 7hrs later, or the northbound local train which departs from Tolbuhin's other station at around 10.15pm and arrives in KARDAM in time to connect with the slow train to NEGRU VODĂ – from where there are connnections on to Medgidia. The latter route is the cheaper, but you might have trouble persuading the Tolbuhin BDZh (1a, Ul. Marx) to sell you a ticket.

Along the road to Varna

If you're in no hurry to reach Varna, it's worth considering a few stopovers **between Ruse and Shumen**. However, the hitching can be pretty dreadful, and since trains bypass everything of interest on the way, you'd be well advised to take the bus. Through-buses cover the 116km in just under 2 hours, and depart roughly every 1½hrs – though you might prefer to catch one of the more frequent services to Razgrad and do a little sightseeing before continuing.

RAZGRAD sprawls messily around the banks of the Beli Lom, but you can spot its chief sight while cruising down Lenin Blvd. towards the bus terminal at the southern end of town. Bulgaria's largest mosque, the **Ibrahim Pasha Mosque**, commands immediate attention, its imposing bulk gracefully tapering into a minaret as a lasting tribute to the skills of its Albanian and Bulgarian builders – and to the Turkish governor Ibrahim, who commissioned it in 1614. Inside, murals and elaborate Arabic calligraphy are said to decorate the interior, though sadly it was closed for restoration when I was last here and looked like being so for some time.

As for the rest of Razgrad, you can see that it once had character, though since the iron-domed white stone mausoleum was raised on the main square to commemorate Razgrad's liberation in March 1879, the artisans' stalls and narrow lanes that characterised the town during Ottoman times have gradually succumbed to mass-produced wares and urban-planning. In 1953, workers building an antibiotics factory unearthed the ruins of the Roman town of *Abritus*, just southeast of town – although as ruins go, they're not very exciting. Part of the walls that once surrounded Abritus (originally standing 12-15m high) can be seen above the steep western bank of the Beli Lom; while near the site of the town's eastern gate stand the foundation walls and columns of 23 rooms grouped around a courtyard, believed to have been the mansion of a landowner.

For directions to the ruins and the variable opening times of the **museum** there, call in at **Balkantourist** (29, Lenin Blvd), whose staff can also book rooms at the main *Hotel Razgrad* or the cheaper *Abritus* (33, Beli Lom Blvd). The main reason **to stay** is to join one of the Balkantourist excursions to Sveshtari, although this is easy enough to reach by bus, changing at Isperih. Failing that, simply push on to Shumen, also reachable by bus. . .

SOFIA TO PLEVEN

The foothills of the Balkans northeast of Sofia hold a handful of attractions that might tempt you off the highway to Ruse or Varna, not least a couple of caves and monasteries, and Bulgaria's equivalent of Milton Keynes. Visiting the sights involves several minor detours by road, which shouldn't pose too many problems for travellers on foot, since there's lots of traffic (for hitching) and a network of local **buses** – better than the train which avoids most sights. By quitting the train at Mezdra (p.583) you can catch local buses on to Pravets or Yablanitsa (and from the latter to Teteven and the various caves).

Pravets and the Etropole Monastery
Though construction work was still underway when I last saw it, the gorge-defying A2 highway should by now be carrying traffic on traffic towards **PRAVETS**. Previously an unremarkable village, this is now a centre for computer technology, with a landscaped cultural complex and the best-stocked supermarkets in Bulgaria – not to mention a new *Motel-Campsite* beside an artifical lake on its outskirts, with tennis courts, a variety bar,

boating and waterskiing facilities. You might wonder what lies behind this, and it all becomes clear when you know that Pravets is the birthplace of **Todor Zhivkov**, the Bulgarian leader, whose modest childhood home is now a **museum**. Born into a peasant family in 1911, Zhivkov joined the Young Communists in 1928 while a print worker and became Mayor of Sofia after wartime service with the Chavdar Partisan Brigade. In 1954, within three years of joining the Politburo, he secured the post of First Secretary or Party leader with the approval of Moscow, and elbowed aside the old Stalinist, Anton Yugov, to claim the premiership in 1962. By his own admission 'a good judge of character', Zhivkov has always adapted to changes of leadership and policy in the Kremlin, only recently launching economic and administrative reforms in emulation of Gorbachev's *perestroika*. Rumours have it – and Zhivkov has hinted – that he intends to step down soon, but the shrewd septuagenarian will doubtless remain influential even after he retires.

If you've time to kill, **ETROPOLE**, a 13km detour from Pravets, deserves a passing mention for its small **Monastery**, whose monks copied and distributed Bulgarian literature during the Turkish occupation. It's located 4km east of the town, which has a 3-star *hotel*. Several buses from Pravets, and from Etropole itself, continue onwards, crossing the **Zlatishka Pass** (1365m) en route to Srednogorie (p.629).

Caves, and the parting of the highways. . .

Assuming that you stick with the main highway, the next place of any significance is **YABLANITSA**, the 'town of apples', which also produces Bulgaria's finest *halva* and acts as the lynchpin of the regional bus network. Reaching out to neighbouring towns and villages, and further afield to Pleven, Lovech and Târnovo, these **buses** should enable you to reach most of the region's points of interest.

Behind the village of BRESTITSA on the E771 highway, a backroad runs southwards for about a mile to the **Sueva Dupka Cave**. Open daily from 9am-5pm for guided tours, the 205 metre-long cave consists of five halls dripping with water and stalactites. On the Yablanitsa side of the same massif (6km northeast of town), there's another subterranean shaft known as the **'Bottomless Beehive'** (*Bezdanniya Pchelin*). Anyone interested in exploring this should contact the potholing section of the Bulgarian Hiking Union in Sofia beforehand, since it's over 400 feet deep and off-limits to casual visitors. The main chamber, 100 by 130 feet, has a profusion of stalactites and stalagmites, which are also reportedly much in evidence at *Haidushka Pest* and *Temna Dupka* – a couple of **other caves** further to the northwest near the villages of KAMENO POLE and KARLUKOVO.

Karstic limestone formations lurk underground throughout the region, and the river running beneath the **junction of the Pleven and Varna highways** emerges as the *Glavna Panega* spring near ZLATNA PANEGA on the Pleven road (bear right just before the village), where it forms two lakes whose waters remain at an even temperature (10-12.5°C) whatever the season. The Roman legend of the fair but afflicted Panega, who was cured by bathing here, seems to have been the model for apocryphal stories relating to other spas – the 'Virgin's Pass' near Kostenets, for example. Another river, the Vit, is favoured by Bulgarian anglers, and runs alongside *Bâlgarski campsite*, which has a restaurant and chalets and lies roughly 5km east of Brestnitsa, where the E771 meets the Teteven road. The bus stop opposite is the place to pick up the Teteven bus, every 45 minutes or so.

Teteven and around

Entering the Vit Valley, the Teteven road passes a turn-off to the left running up to the village of GRADEZHNITSA, where locals will direct you to the **Gradezhnitsa Cave**. Almost half a mile deep in all, this contains underground lakes and a small river, with karst formations bearing names like *Petrified Curtains* and *Fairyland*. Ten kilometres up the valley, the road hits GLOZHENE, a drab industrialised hamlet that is the nearest settlement to **Glozhene Monastery**, perched high above and practically invisible from the valley. Most vehicles baulk at the track, which is incredibly rough and steep, although it can be climbed within a couple of hours.

Surrounded by imposing mountains further up the valley, **TETEVEN** once inspired Ivan Vazov to declare that if he had not come here, 'I should regard myself as a stranger to my native land. . . nowhere have I found a place so enchanting as this'. Vazov's endorsement seems rather too fulsome for modern Teteven, but the town is certainly appealing in a laid-back way. People seem willing to stop and chat over a handful of fruit at the drop of a rucksack, and the old houses rising behind Georgi Dimitrov Street are bright with flowers and grapevines. Among them you can easily spot the ugly *Hotel Teteven*, which contains the **tourist office** and a **disco** and rents double **rooms** for 40 leva. Just uphill from the hotel there's a decent little *mehana*.

Buses from Teteven's terminal run to most towns in the Balkan mountains, and to Sofia, but the nearest destination is RIBARITSA at the end of the valley. Ribaritsa's campsite and chalets are exclusively for Bulgarians, but if they don't mind staying elsewhere, Westerners can hang around the little resort. Two and a half miles away near the village of KOSTINA, there's a monument to **Georgi Benkovski**, the Koprivshtitsa-born revolutionary killed here in May 1876.

The last stage of **the route to Pleven** is pretty straightforward, and after passing through **CHERVEN BRYAG** (the junction for trains to Oryahovo on the Danube), the railway follows the same course as the E83 highway. Trains don't stop there, but motorists can visit **Lavrov Park** near the village of GORNI DUBNIK en route. On October 24 1877, during the War of Liberation, the Russians flung themselves upon the Turkish redoubt blocking the road to Plevna that stood here, inspired by the suicidal heroism of General Lavrov, their commander. There's now a small museum near the park entrance exhibiting the kind of plans beloved of wargamers, and a statue of a Bulgarian and Soviet soldier entitled 'Eternal Friendship'. On the opposite side of the road, an ossuary contains the bones of Lavrov and his men.

PLEVEN

PLEVEN isn't particularly appealing unless you're keen on war memorials and military history, since most of the parks and old buildings that mitigate its concrete sterility contain monuments or museums to **the siege of Plevna** – probably the most decisive campaign of the War of Liberation. When the Russians crossed the Danube at Svishtov in 1877, their flank was threatened by the Turkish force entrenched at Plevna (the town's former name), which resisted three assaults that cost the Russians thousands of casualties. In response to Grand Duke Nicholas's pleas, Romanian reinforcements came with King Carol, who personally led his troops into battle (the last European sovereign to do so) crying 'This is the music that pleases me!'. Russia's top generals, Skobelev and Totleben, then arrived to organise a professional blockade, weakening the defenders by starvation and blasting each redoubt with artillery before the attackers made repeated bayonet charges, finally compelling the Turks to surrender on December 10. Over 40,000 Russians and Romanians and uncounted numbers of Turks and civilians died, but as a consequence of Plevna's fall and its shattering affect on Ottoman morale, northern Bulgaria was swiftly liberated.

Around town

Arriving at the bus or train station, take any bus heading down Blvd. Lenin to reach 9th September Square in **the centre**, where fountains splash near the Russo-Byzantine style **Mausoleum**, which contains a fine iconostasis by Ivan of Tryavna. This commemorates only the Russian soldiers (one of whom, Vereshchagin, painted the murals entitled *Before the Attack* and *Prayer for the Dead*), although the number of Romanian names on the lists commemorating the dead makes it clear who saw the worst of the fighting. Not far away, adjoining a park, stands the **Museum of Liberation**, occupying the house where the Turkish commander, Osman Pasha, formally surrendered to Tsar Aleksandr II. Here you'll see weaponry, mementoes and plans lovingly detailing each phase of the battle, which is the subject of a huge **panoramic painting** (measuring 115 by 15 metres) housed in a purpose-built museum in **Skobelev Park**. The park is laid out on a hill overlooking Pleven's southwestern outskirts, where the third stage of the battle was fought around the **Isa Aga Redoubt**, which has been restored and crowned with an obelisk to the 405 troops who died capturing it. Skobelev's bust stands near the park entrance, and secreted within the greenery roundabouts are numerous cannons.

The **Regional History Museum** within the former barracks on the main street (nr.104) predictably contains more exhibits relating to the siege, but also part of the magnificent *gold treasure of Vâlchâtrin*, and a mosaic depicting a scene from Meander's comedy *The Achaeans*, removed from the Roman ruins at Gigen. Partly sunk beneath street level, the **Church of St Nicholas** is less remarkable for its simple form than for the *collection of icons* within (68 of them, with the Zograf brothers and Stanislav Dospevski represented as usual). The opposite is true of Pleven's **Art Gallery**, which occupies the old town baths – an elegant building with a red and white striped façade that could be mistaken for a church.

In the unlikely event that you're here during November you can witness the **Katya Popova International Festival**, which is mainly devoted to literary recitals (culminating in the award of a poet laureate prize), but also featuring plays at the Georgi Kirkov Theatre and symphonic concerts. Details of events are available from the **Balkantourist** offices at 3, Ul. Buckstone (☎ 2-41-19) and 3, Ul. San Stefano (☎ 2-91-23), which should hopefully be able to supply a map of town. As far as **rooms** go, the choice is between the costly *Hotel Pleven* (2, Republika Square) and the slightly cheaper *Rostov na Don* (2, Ul. Slavi Alexiev), which charges about the same as the *Kailuka* in the park of the same name (see below). Dormitory beds are supposedly available from *Orbita*, but the address that I was given (2, Ul. Zamenhoff) turned out to be that of the **railway & airline tickets** bureau. However, you can pitch a tent or rent a chalet at *Kailuka campsite*, just south of town along the Lovech road and reachable by bus.

Kailuka Park

Leaving Pleven by Ul. San Stefano, it's 2km to **Kailuka Park**, laid out around the lush and rocky Tuchenitsa defile, and connected by regular bus. There are swimming baths, watersports facilities, an open-air theatre and the vestiges of a Thracian settlement taken over by the Romans, who called it *Storgosia*. There's also a 2-star hotel, the *Kailuka*, and the *Peshtera restaurant* in a cave at the foot of the limestone cliff – and below the baths a monument to the Jews who perished here in 1944 when the camp in which they were imprisoned burned down. (Although anti-semitism has never been prevalent in Bulgaria, the government gaoled the Salonikan Jews during the latter stages of the war to appease its Nazi allies). Three kilometres upriver, a bronze statue of the General surmounts the **Totleben Rampart** which separates two reservoirs: the walls of the smaller one of these were founded upon the remains of a dam erected during the siege to cut off the water that powered Pleven's mills.

Moving on

From Pleven it's possible to head south across the Balkans via Lovech (p.626), or reach many of the smaller towns along the Danube (p.589) by bus, although most travellers use the **trains** which run between Sofia and Varna (or Sofia and Ruse) every half hour or so. Depending on the service and your ultimate destination, you might have to change at LEVSKI (for Svishtov or Lovech, though the latter can be reached directly by bus) or GORNA ORYAHOVITSA (for Târnovo and Gabrovo or Ruse).

THE BALKAN RANGE

With stern and frowning brow, behind a cloak of cloud,
The Balkan Range arises in the distance, high and proud,
In Haiduk dream enfolded, forgotten now, as though
A soldier had been placed on guard long ago,
Protecting younger troops, in boundless emptiness,
Above a camp in disarray. . . .
Pencho Slaveykov, *Song of the Blood*

For over a thousand years, the 'Old Mountain' (*Stara Planina*) known to foreigners as the **Balkan range*** has been the cradle of the Bulgarian nation and the cockpit of its destiny. Sloping gently towards the Danube, the Balkan's fertile valleys supported the medieval capitals of **Veliko Târnovo** (still a thriving city), **Pliska** and **Preslav** (mere ruins today), while steep ranges with defensible passes shielded them to the south. Much was destroyed during the Ottoman conquest, but the thread of culture was preserved by **monasteries** (near Târnovo and at **Troyan**) and by the crafts' centres that re-established themselves under the Turkish yoke. In modern times, **Gabrovo**, **Târgovishte** and **Lovech** have developed into full-blown industrialised towns, but there's been a deliberate effort to maintain smaller places like **Tryavna**, **Arbanasi**, **Bozhentsi** and **Kotel** as 'living' monuments to the National Revival and prime tourist attractions. Besides harbouring these architectural plums, the Balkan range also provides the setting for the **Madara Horseman** rock-carving near **Shumen** and two dramatic **mountain passes** – **Troyan** and **Shipka**.

Depending on the direction from which you approach the massif there are various possible **routes**. Veliko Târnovo is as good – and as central – a place to see some of the area from, after which you could head south to Gabrovo. Relying upon trains and **approaching the Balkan range from Pleven, Ruse or Varna**, you'll probably find it necessary to change at GORNA ORYAHOVITSA for regular connections to Târnovo and Gabrovo; buses also go from here to Arbanasi or Preobrazhenski Monastery, and travellers **flying** to Târnovo actually arrive at Gorna Oryahovitsa's Airport.

VELIKO TÂRNOVO

> There they are, those wonderful houses. . .with tiles and chimneys over walls and beams of every colour climbing up and up, yet perched motionless as cormorants on a sea-rock.
>
> Stowers Johnson, *Gay Bulgaria*

Like unrequited lovers considering suicide, **VELIKO TÂRNOVO** seems poised to leap into the chasms that divide the city into separate quarters. Medieval fortifications girdling the Tsarevets massif add melodrama to the scene, yet more transfixing are the huddles of antique houses that Vazov likened to frightened sheep, bound to the rocks by wild lilac and vines, forming picturesque reefs veined by steps and narrow streets. Le Corbusier raved about Târnovo's 'organic' architecture, and even the dour Prussian Field-Marshal, Von Moltke, was moved to remark that he had 'never seen a town of more romantic location'. But for Bulgarians the city has a deeper significance. When the National Assembly met here to draft Bulgaria's first constitution in 1879, it consciously did so in the former capital of the Second

---

* Known as the *Haemus* in antiquity, when legend had it that the Balkan range originated by the same divine act that created the Rhodopes (see p.661).

Kingdom (1185-1396) whose medieval civilisation was snuffed out by the Turks. Reclaiming this heritage was an integral part of the National Revival, and since independence (especially during the socialist era) archaeologists have been keenly uncovering the past of Târnovo 'the Great' – not only the medieval citadel of Tsarevets but the churches of Sveta Gora and Trapezitsa. Nor is the city an isolated case, for in the hills and valleys **around Târnovo** are several monasteries and small towns founded during the Second Kingdom or in the aftermath of its collapse, which make great day excursions from the city.

Arriving and finding lodgings
Travelling to Târnovo by bus (from Gabrovo, Sevlievo, Lovech or Sliven), you'll arrive at the *Avtogara* halfway down Botev Street, less than 10 minutes' walk from the centre; **arriving** by train you'll wind up at the *Gara Târnovo* beneath Sveta Gora Hill on the city's southern outskirts.

Your next move will partly depend on your choice of **accommodation**. You can either catch a #15 bus from the railway station direct to *Sveta Gora motel-campsite*, or, if you're looking for a hotel, take a #4, #12, #13 or #15 bus in the opposite direction up Ul. Botev towards the centre. The 4th-floor *Hotel Orbita* (15, Ul. Botev) is often booked solid by tour groups, but any unclaimed rooms are disposed of for 13 leva after 7pm. If your luck is out, there's always the tower-block *Hotel Etâr* on Ul. Ivailo around the corner (doubles and breakfast for 24 leva). Other possibilities include the *Yantra* in the old town, though this can be hard to find, or, more expensively, the deluxe *Hotel Veliko Târnovo*, which has singles and doubles going for 46 and 88 leva. If that seems excessive the most promising alternative is *Bolyarski Stan campsite*, which has cheap chalets – a #1, #2, or #11 bus ride from the stop almost opposite **Balkantourist** (1, Blvd. Vasil Levski; ☎ 2-18-36). Ride the bus through the suburbs, get off near the military academy, cross the roundabout and enter the campsite by a gap in the corrugated iron fence (motorists use the slip-road entrance).

The old town
Sited upon an incline, the city's smart **modern centre** holds most of Târnovo's shops and cafés, along boulevards Levski and Dimitrov, the main post office and a zappy cinema-complex a little way down Ul. Botev – a popular meeting place for students. But that's about it. Buses #7 and #11 run from Blvd. Dimitrov to the edge of Tsarevets, but it's more fun to proceed on foot and let yourself be drawn gradually into the **old town**. This is fascinating, not so much for its specific sights, of which there are relatively few, but for the feel of the place generally: there's always a fresh view of the city poised above the gorges or some new, unexpected detail.

Heading eastwards along Blagoev Street, the small **Square of the Hanged** has a monument to Bacho Kiro and other rebels of 1876, whom the Turks hung from *daradzha* erected on what was then a rubbish-tip. Despite the *Hadzhi Micho* **taverna** on the corner, it's a tranquil enclave. Nearby, opposite the *Balkan* restaurant, **P.R. Slaveykov Square** has the **museum-birthplace** of the pedagogue and poet of the same name (1827-95) who, among other

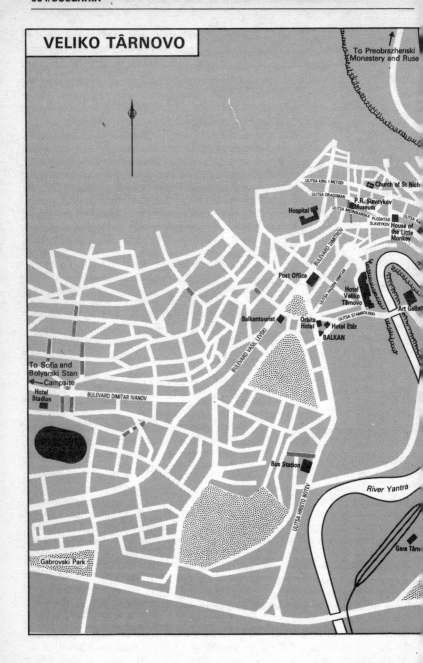

VELIKO TÂRNOVO

To Preobrazhenski
Monastery and Ruse

ULITSA KIRIL I METOD

Church of St Nich

ULITSA DRAGOMAN

P.R. Slaveykov
Museum

ULITSA 4

Hospital

ULITSA MEDNIKARSKA

PLOSHTAD
SLAVEYKOV

House of
the Little
Monkey

BULEVARD DIMITROV

Post Office

ULITSA MOSK DIMITAR

Hotel
Veliko
Târnovo

Balkantourist

Orbita
Hotel

ULITSA STAMBOLIISKI

Art Galle

Hotel Etâr

BALKAN

BULEVARD VASIL LEVSKI

To Sofia and
Bolyarski Stan

Campsite

Hotel
Stadion

BULEVARD DIMITAR IVANOV

Bus Station

River Yantra

ULITSA HRISTO BOTEV

Gara Târn

Gabrovski Park

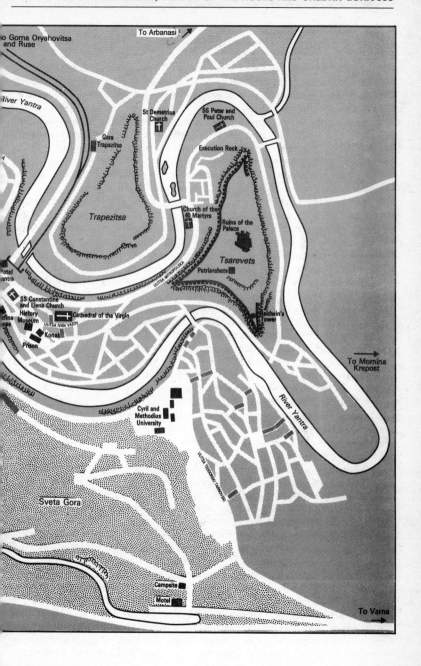

To Gorna Oryahovitsa and Ruse

To Arbanasi

River Yantra

St Demetrius Church

SS Peter and Paul Church

Gara Trapezitsa

Execution Rock

Trapezitsa

Church of the 40 Martyrs

Ruins of the Palace

Tsarevets

ULITSA MITROPOLSKA

Patriarchate

Hotel Yantra

SS Constantine and Elena Church

History Museum

Cathedral of the Virgin

Baldwin's Tower

ULITSA IVAN VAZOV

Konak

Prison

To Momina Krepost

River Yantra

Cyril and Methodius University

ULITSA TODOROV HADJI

Sveta Gora

Campsite

Motel

To Varna

things, campaigned for the autonomy of Bulgaria's Orthodox church. But most visitors prefer the **'House of the Little Monkey'** (14, Ul. Vâstanicheska), which gets its nickname from the grimacing statuette over the balcony, although the bay windows and deeply pointed brickwork actually contribute more to the total effect. Like many old Târnovo houses, it sits precariously above a limited groundspace, with orieled living-quarters above what used to be a shop or warehouse.

As visitors are allowed inside, the former **Inn of Hadzhi Nikolai Minchev** (17, Ul. Rakovski) is more satisfying, since it nowadays serves as an **Ethnographic Museum**. The size of the ground-floor caravanserai reflects Târnovo's commercial upsurge following the Crimean War, which forced the Ottoman empire to accept Western products; the airy, undulating arcades are delightful. Among the woodcarvings, pewter and silverwork on the first floor, the jewel-encrusted belt-clasps are outstanding, and others bearing images of eagles can be seen upstairs together with ecclesiastcal art, lace, woollens, bagpipes, cummerbunds with pompoms and peasant wedding costumes. Exhibits on the top floor relate the story of education from the foundation of the first university at Kilifarevo Monastery in 1350 to the C19 campaign for secular Bulgarian-language schooling.

Various restored workshops and an olde worlde café and pastry shop make up the *Samovdodska Charshiya* or **bazaar** at the junction of Rakovski Street and Pl. Georgi Kirkov. It's a good place to observe craftspersons at work, and highly photogenic too, with its wrought-iron garnished façades and cobbled slopes, but it lacks a real bazaar's hustle and bustle. Starting from the square you can follow Ul. Nikolai Zlatarski up into the narrow streets of the peaceful old **Varosh quarter**, whose two C19 churches were verging on the decrepit when I saw them. The **Church of St Nicholas** has, it's said, a carving on the bishop's throne which shows a lion (Bulgaria) in the coils of a snake (the Greek church) being devoured by a dragon (Turkey), and **SS Cyril and Methodius** – with its belfry and dome by the famous architect Fichev – still serves worshippers on Ul. Kiril i Metodi. Should you climb onto the plateau above Varosha, you can pick up a fairly obvious trail to Preobrazhenski Monastery (see p.612).

Heading downhill from Pl. Kirkov instead, you're likely to come upon Velchova Zavera Square, where the glassblower Velcho, Nikola the braid-maker, Ivan the furrier and other conspirators were hanged by the Turks in 1835. One can take the stairway behind the *Hotel Yantra* down to the pedestrian **walkway over to Trapezitsa**, but sticking to Ivan Vazov Street you'll pass two churches sited at different levels on either side – the **Cathedral of the Virgin**, standing fittingly aloof on a terrace, and **SS Constantine and Elena**, skulking behind foliage at the bottom of a steep flight of steps.

More steps descend from SS Constantine and Elena to **General Gurko Street**, where the houses – mainly dating from Ottoman times – look incredibly picturesque perched along the curve of the gorge. Don't miss the *Kâsha Sarafka* or **Sarafina House** at nr.88 (Tuesday-Sunday 9am-12am, 1pm-6pm), which is so contrived that only two floors are visible from General Gurko but a further three overhang the river. The interior is notable for the splendid octagonal vestibule with wrought iron fixtures and a panelled rosette-ceiling which, like the elegantly-furnished rooms upstairs, reflects the taste of the architect and owner, the moneylender Dimo Sarafina. The inclusion of photos of old Târnovo downstairs justifies billing this as a **Museum of 19th Century Life.**

Further to the southeast stands a spacious blue and white edifice that is the recreated **Konak** of the Turkish governor, Ali Bey. It was here the rebels of 1876 stood trial; subsequently the setting for two months of deliberations before a constitution was promulgated and the first Bulgarian *sâbranie* (parliament) met in 1879. The union of Bulgaria and Eastern Roumelia (1885) was also signed here, and this hallowed building was exactly reconstructed after being devastated by fire in time to allow the proclamation of People's Power from the premises on September 9 1944. Unsurprisingly, it's now occupied by a **Museum of the National Revival period and the Constituent Assembly**, while the adjoining bloc mounts an **Archaeological Exposition of medieval Târnovo** (lapidry, ceramics, seals, etc) in four halls. Around the corner and lower down the hill, you'll find a **Museum of the Revolutionary Movement** neatly arranged in such a fashion as to banish any atmosphere of menace from the former Turkish **prison**, whose size and strength are more apparent from the rear. Next to the ice cream kiosk at the lower end of Vazov Street there's a **bureau** selling admission tickets to the Tsarevets massif.

Tsarevets

Approaching **Tsarevets** along the stone causeway, which was erected after the original drawbridge collapsed beneath the Bey's harem, you can appreciate how the boyars Petâr and Asen were emboldened enough by posession of this seemingly impregnable **citadel** to lead a rebellion against Byzantium in 1185. Petâr's proclamation of the Second Kingdom and his coronation occurred when the empire was already preoccupied by the Magyar and Seljuk Turk menace, and when a punitive Byzantine army was finally sent in 1190 it was utterly defeated at the Tryavna Pass. Now restored and spotlit at night, the ramparts and the Patriarchate (plus the ruins of the palace and various churches) convey something of Tsarevets's grandeur during the Second Kingdom, when travellers deemed Târnovo 'second after Constantinople'.

Artisans and clerics serving the palace and the Patriarchate generally resided in the Asenova quarter below the hill, and entered Tsarevets via the **Asenova Gate** halfway along the western ramparts; foreign merchants, invited to settle here by Tsar Asen II, had their own entrance, the 'Frankish' or **Frenkhisar Gate** near the southern end of the massif. Rapidly becoming a regional power, the Second Kingdom intervened to help Byzantium overthrow the first Latin Emperor of the East, Baldwin of Flanders, in 1205, the former emperor ending his days as a prisoner in the bastion overlooking the Frenkhisar Gate, thereafter known as **Baldwin's Tower.**

The **ruins of the Palace** seem insignificant compared to the ramparts, but contemporary chronicles and modern excavations suggest that the royal complex once looked splendid. Delicate columns divided the 105ft long throne-room into aisles, which were adorned with green serpentine, Egyptian porphyry and pink marble, and mosaics and murals depicting the rulers of three dynasties. The first of these, the Asenids, are best remembered for Tsar

Ivan Asen II, promoter of arts and trade and victor of the battle of Klokotnitsa. It was during, or shortly before, Asen's reign (1218-41) that the Church of the Blessed Saviour or **Patriarchate** was built – significantly, the only structure that was permitted to surpass the palace in height. Ribbed with red brick and inset with green and orange ceramics, the church – and Tsarevets in general – is now a favourite location for the filming of historical epics.

The **Execution Rock** at the sheer northern end of Tsarevets is associated with the dynasty that followed the brief reign of the swineherd Ivailo (1277-80). Proclaimed Tsar after a popular anti-feudal revolt, Ivailo successfully organised resistance against invading Tartar hordes but neglected to guard against a coup by the boyars, who had him flung off the *Lobnata Skala*. The Terterid dynasty, which followed, was chiefly concerned with its own survival and willing to suspect anyone – even the Patriarch, Yoakim III, who was also executed – of collusion with the Tartars; and only during the later reign of Todor Svetoslav (1300-21) was there much progress or security. However, Bulgarian culture – strongly influenced by that of Byzantium – revived during the Shishmanid dynasty (1323-93), and the enlightened rule of Ivan Aleksandâr and his son Ivan Shishman created the conditions whereby medieval Târnovo attained the zenith of its development. Trade with Genoa, Venice and Dubrovnik flourished; hospitals and hospices were maintained by the public purse; students came from Serbia, Russia and Wallachia to study at the university; and Târnovo became one of the Balkans' main centres of painting and literature (a manuscript of the *Tetraevangelia* is owned by the British Museum).

Nonetheless, by the late C14 the Second Kingdom had fragmented into several semi-autonomous states which, individually, were no match for the expansionist Ottoman Turks, who besieged Târnovo for three months before capturing, plundering and burning the city in July 1393.

The Asenova quarter, Trapezitsa and Sveta Gora

To the west of Tsarevets on both banks of the Yantra lies the **Asenova quarter**, where chickens strut and children fish beside the river. During the Middle Ages this was the artisan quarter, which it remained until 1913, when it was struck by an earthquake which levelled all the medieval buildings except the churches.

The **Church of the Forty Martyrs**, near the bridge, has the richest historical associations – a barn-like edifice founded by Asen to commemorate his victory at Klokotnitsa on Forty Martyrs' Day in 1230. Subsequently much altered, to the extent that it has, apparently, baffled restorers, the church was the burial place of Saint Sava and several Tsars, and the Bulgars saw God's hand behind the collapse of the minaret built when the Turks impiously transformed this into a mosque. Among the pillars within stands *Khan Omturag's Column*, filched from another site, whose Greek inscription reads in part: 'Man dies, even though he lives nobly, and another is born. Let the latest born, when he examines these records, remember him who made them. The name of the Prince is Omurtag, the Sublime Khan'. Not to be outdone, Asen had another column inscribed with a list of his conquests from Adrianople to Durazzo

(Durrës in Albania), whose inhabitants were spared 'by my benevolence'.

Further north, the early-C20 **Church of the Dormition** (open Wednesday-Monday 9am-12am, 1pm-5.30pm) isn't intrinsically interesting, but stands upon the site of the Monastery of the Virgin of the Prisoners, where Tsar Aleksandâr confined his wife as a nun in order to marry the Jewess Sara. The **Church of SS Peter and Paul**, 200m away, is more remarkable: it contains several capitals in the old Bulgarian style (carved with vine-leaves in openwork) and some well-preserved frescoes of which the oldest – dating back to the C14 – is the *Pietà* opposite the altar. The church's saints namesakes are portrayed on the south wall near the entrance in a lively manner, while on the west wall beyond the right-hand arch is the earliest known depiction of St John of Rila. The church was the site of the massacre of the boyars in 1393 (only Patriarch Evtimii's intervention dissuaded the Turks from killing the entire population) and, much later, the place where the Ottoman-appointed Greek Patriarch of Bulgaria was evicted by the citizenry.

On the other side of the river are two more venerable and recently-restored churches. The consecration of the **Church of St Demetrius** provided the occasion for Petâr to announce his rebellion, and Sveta Dimitâr (who, legend has it, came from Salonika to help the oppressed Bulgars) became the patron saint of the Second Kingdom. With its red-brick stripes and trefoil windows inlaid with orange plaques, St Demetrius is the best-looking of the surviving medieval churches, although most of the original frescoes were painted over during the C16-C17. **St George's Church**, further to the south, is smaller but has better-preserved frescoes.

Overhead rises the massif known as **Trapezitsa**, where the boyars and leading clergy of the Second Kingdom built their mansions and some forty private churches, sixteen of which are currently being excavated. I didn't find much of interest up here, but you might be luckier – even today, medieval rings, crosses, etc. are being discovered. You can reach the hill by steep footpaths from the Asenova quarter or, more easily, by walking across the railway-bridge below the Yantra Hotel, at the end of which there's a path leading onto the massif. From the northwestern side of Trapezitsa, another trail heads off towards the Convent of Sveta Troitsa (p.612), about 1½hrs walk northwards into the hills.

Sveta Gora ('Holy Hill'), on the south bank of the Yantra, used to be a centre of monastic scholasticism, and nowadays provides the site for **Cyril and Methodius University**, which can be reached by bus #15 or a bridge to the south of Tsarevets. The rocky spur, linked by footbridge to the Hotel Veliko Târnovo is adorned with an obelisk commemorating the 800th anniversary of the foundation of the Asenid dynasty, but visitors are generally more interested in the contents of the large, copper-roofed **Art Gallery** nearby, whose theme is 'Târnovo through the eyes of diverse painters'.

Eating, drinking. . .and moving on

Package tourists and richer Bulgarians usually patronise one of the swish **restaurants** in the *Hotel Veliko Târnovo*, whose terrace offers a magnificent view of the city, whereas local people favour cheaper establishments adjoining the *Stadion*, *Etâr* and *Yantra* hotels, or the *Balkan* on Blagoev Street – where an equally fine panorama can be enjoyed from the tables at the back. Traditional dishes and folk music are the stock in trade of the *Hadzhi Mincho Mehana* on the Square of the Hanged, and the *Slavyanka* (35, Blvd. Levski) also advertises itself as a **nightclub**, but impromptu sing-songs and boozy jollity can occur in such unlikely venues as a backroom of the restaurant 100m south of *Bolyarski Stan campsite*. There's a discotheque in the Hotel Târnovo, and other **discos** are sometimes organised at the university (ask students or look for advertisements around campus).

The **hospital** on Buzludzha Street (☎ 2-38-33) is closer to the centre although the other *bolnitsa* (south of the new housing estates; ☎ 2-68-41) has a wider range of facilities, and of the three **pharmacies** in the downtown area (on Pl. Velchova Zareva, Blvd. Levski and Blvd. Dimitrov) at least one is always open at night. BALKAN (1a, Ul. Stamboliiski) can book you onto the two daily **flights to Sofia** (departing around 7am and 7.30pm from Gorna Oryahovitsa Airport), and shares premises with the *Rila Agency* selling international **railway tickets** – domestic services being handed by a separate *BDZh* office (12, Ul. Botev) near the bus terminal. **Buses** run to – or at least nearby – practically everywhere described below; you can usually buy a ticket from the driver on 'numbered' buses, but it's necessary to book seats on inter-town routes at least an hour beforehand from the terminal's *bilet* office.

ARBANASI, PREOBRAZHENSKI MONASTERY AND THE RUINS OF NICOPOLIS

The terrain **north of Târnovo** is a wild confusion of massifs sundered by the Yantra and its tributaries, abounding in rocky shelves rendered almost inaccessible by forests and torrents. Nigh on twenty monasteries were established here during the Second Kingdom (not least because the Tsars appreciated a quiet retreat), and several survived the Turkish invasion and formed a symbiotic relationship with the later towns and villages founded by refugees after the sack of Târnovo. With a car it's feasible to visit the main sites within a day, but relying on public transport (or hiking), one expedition a day seems more realistic.

Arbanasi

Hiding high on a plateau midway between Târnovo and Gorna Oryahovitsa, and overlooking Tsarevets and Trapezitsa to the south, **ARBANASI** is one of Bulgaria's most picturesque villages, founded by Albanian refugees of Greek culture and resembling a cross between a *kasbah* and the kind of *pueblo* that Clint Eastwood rids of bandits. People vanish into their family strongholds for the siesta, and at high noon only chickens stalk the rutted streets. You can easily get here by bus #14 from Târnovo (the last service back leaves Arbanasi at 8pm) or Gorna Oryahovitsa, but don't come on a Monday when much of the village is shut. On other days, someone from the **tourist office** (10am-12am, 2pm-6pm), in the park opposite the bus terminal, should be able to arrange a guided tour.

A concealed door for escaping from the dining room is but one of the features of the **Konstantsalieva House**, situated on the left-hand side of the road entering the village. Like other houses erected after the conflagration that gutted Arbanasi in 1798, the ground floor (with servants' quarters and store-rooms) is built of stone and entered via a nail-studded gate, while the upper floor is made of wood. It's not hard to imagine the former owner, the Kokona Sultana (a relation of the Bey), greeting her guests on the wooden staircase ascending to the reception hall, from which one door leads to the 'winter room' or communal bedroom with its *minder* and divans; the other opens onto a corridor leading to the dining room and the comfortable office of her merchant husband, furnished with a *sofra* and coffee set. There's another escape-door from the 'summer room' in the northeastern corner of the house, which adjoins the centrally-heated 'confinement room' where mothers were secluded for forty days after giving birth. Many of the rooms have beautiful panelled ceilings, and every stove is located so as to warm two rooms simultaneously (or the bathwater, in the case of the kitchen stove).

To the left, beyond the Konstantsalieva mansion, a path leads to the **Kokona Fountain**, built in 1786 on the orders of Mehmed Saîd Ali, author of its Arabic inscription: 'He who looks upon me and drinks my water shall possess the light of the eyes and of the soul'. The **Church of the Nativity** (*Rozhdestvo Hristovo*), 200m further on, outwardly 'resembles a plain barn', but inside you'll find richly-coloured frescoes – including a frieze of Greek philosophers and a geneaology of Christ on the north wall – and an iconostasis containing notable scenes of Creation and the Fall, plus an icon on the left showing Jesus with the head of John the Baptist. Both the main body of the church and the *paraklis* chapel (reserved for the donor's family) have separate areas for men and women to pray, and at the end of services it was customary for the boyar to distribute alms in the wide *trapeza* corridor behind the portico.

Besides this the village has four other churches, also built between the C16-C18. In the highest part of Arbanasi stands SS Archangel Michael and Gabriel, jointly painted by Georgi of Bucharest and Mihail of Salonika, whose style differs from that of the *Last Judgement* by Tsoio and Ned'o in the diminutive St Athanasius Church at the northeastern corner of the village. Though there are more tombstones with Greek inscriptions in the courtyard of St Athanasius, the five along the north side of the courtyard of the Church of St Demetrius in the centre of Arbanasi have richer carvings. Dimitâr Kânchev, the C19 Tryavna artist who decorated St George's at the far end of the village, signed his work in several places.

Preobrazhenski Monastery and the Convent of Sveta Troitsa

Bulgarian Television crews were busily disproving Stowers Johnson's assertion that it's 'impossible to turn a camera in the wrong direction' at **PREO-BRAZHENSKI MONASTERY** when I arrived, and the incongruity of the scene was heightened by the presence of 'warriors' wearing the costume of the Second Kingdom, the period when the Monastery of the Transfiguration was founded. Although the original monastery (situated farther to the south) was destroyed in the early 1800s, its successor looks old enough to be medieval, and signs of the restoration occurring during our visit will doubtless be effaced by the vines that festoon the courtyard, strung between the spartan cells and small churches.

Aping the vines, a flowery motif runs beneath the roof of the **Transfiguration Church**, whose south wall bears a remarkable painting of the *Wheel of Life*. The stages of human existence correspond with allegorical representations of the four seasons: bleak winter is accompanied by Death with a scythe, a monster's mouth claims sinners, while in the centre of the circle a woman holding an empty chalice symbolises the negation of the material world. Rose and green-hued **frescoes** predominate in the esonarthex, where an eye in a circle is a recurrent motif, whereas the lower naos (formerly reserved for men) is darker, with saints surrounding Christ beneath the dome, and submissive dragons flanking the crucifix. Evil-doers are thrust across a river of fire and strangled by demons in the *Last Judgement* by Zahari Zograf, whose portrait hangs in the esonarthex beside that of Vasil Levski. Like Father Hariton and other revolutionaries, Levski hid away in the caves above the monastery, and Preobrazhenski's service as a field-hospital for Russian troops during the liberation war was rewarded by Tsar Aleksandr's presentation of a crystal chandelier which still hangs in the Transfiguration Church.

There are two ways of **getting to the monastery** – by road or on foot. Number #10 buses from Târnovo to Samovedene take you past the Monastery turn-off 4km north of town, from where a minor road zig-zags 3km uphill through a linden forest to Preobrazhenski, passing a **campsite** with a restaurant and chalets on the way. The 2hr footpath to the monastery begins on the plateau above Târnovo's Varosh quarter, and meanders northwards through gullies that get steadily more wooded and choked with mossy boulders. Although you should eventually catch sight of the monastery nestled beneath a cliff, there doesn't appear to be any path covering the last stretch, so you'll probably have to steer a course for the road to the monastery instead.

More or less opposite Preobrazhenski on the other side of the valley, a narrow shelf provides the site for the **CONVENT OF SVETA TROITSA**, which can *only* be approached on foot. It should take you about 1½hrs to walk, following the path that starts on the northwestern side of Trapezitsa (near the *Gara*) and runs along the cliff. Sveta Troitsa (Holy Trinity) is less used to receiving visitors than Preobrazhenski, and it's worth checking with Balkantourist before you go in case the convent is shut. Possibly founded as early as the C11, Sveta Troitsa was actually a monastery rather than a nunnery during the Second Kingdom, when Patriarch Evtimii established a school of translators here. Although Holy Trinity's church (also built during the C19 by Fichev) is less impressive than the principal one at Preobrazhenski Monastery, the nuns dress more austerely than their male counterparts, in a black veil, robe and round hat.

Nicopolis ad Istrum

The **ruins of Nicopolis ad Istrum**, 17km north of Târnovo as the crow flies, attest that the Yantra Valley was settled long before the Bulgars arrived. Founded by Emperor Trajan in 107 and named after his victory over the Dacians, Nicopolis ad Istrum was an important administrative centre and garrison town in the Roman empire's lower Danubian province, *Moseia*

Inferior. During the C2-C3 the town commanded the Danube-Constantinople and Sofia-Black Sea roads, and its commercial opportunities attracted merchants, artisans and retired legionaries from all over the empire. Within its walls, the town was centred around a forum with temples dedicated to an eclectic pantheon of deities and a covered theatre that was unique in the Balkans – though the onslaught of the Goths and Avars in the C3 and C7 have left comparatively little to see. The best preserved structure is the reservoir to the east, originally fed by a 25km-long aqueduct conveying water from a cave near Mustina, but otherwise there are only steps, stumps of walls, various columns and altars, and a few marble statues. Since the site lies over a mile from NIKYUP village, itself some distance from the Târnovo-Ruse highway (the turn-off is just south of Kutsina), it's doubtful whether the effort of **getting there** is justified.

TÂRNOVO TO GABROVO

Gabrovo is the main target south of Târnovo, though with time – and ideally a car – a number of places merit a visit along the way: the *monasteries* of Kilifarevo and Dryanovo, *Bozhentsi* village, and the beautiful village of *Tryavna*. Relying on public **transport**, one or two, rather than all of these, is realistic. The Târnovo-Gabrovo railway runs through Dryanovo, though some distance from the monastery, and in order to reach Tryavna it's necessary to change onto a branch-line at BÂRBANOVO. Local buses are generally a surer bet.

The Monasteries of Kilifarevo and Plakovo

A favourite retreat for the Tsars of the Second Kingdom, **KILIFAREVO MONASTERY** was also the site of the famous college established by *Teodosii Târnovski* in 1350, which translated literary works from Greek into the Slavonic script, making them legible to scholars far beyond Bulgaria. Patriarch Evtimii and the future Metropolitian of Kiev were among the students here, and the School of Kilifarevo might have achieved parity with the great European universities had it not been destroyed during the Turkish invasion. Like other monasteries around Târnovo, Kilifarevo was rebuilt during the C19 around a principal church – dedicated to the Virgin – designed by Fichev, containing an iconostasis by Tryavna craftsmen. An icon of Teodossi can be seen on the right inside the second chapel, to the northeast of the main church, while the third chapel (to the southwest) actually dates back to the C14 or C15. You'll find the monastery roughly 2km south of KILIFAREVO village in the Belitsa dell, visible from the Nova Zagora road, from which a track leads 500m to a wooden bridge opposite the monastery gate.

We didn't check it out, but there's another monastery roughly 7km to the east in a wooded valley near the commune of PLAKOVO, which some buses from Târnovo visit after calling at Kilifarevo. Father Sergius, **Plakovo Monastery**'s superior, was involved in the Velcho conspiracy and tortured to death by the Turks after its discovery; a plaque on the stone fountain in the courtyard commemorates him and his fellow conspirators.

Dryanovo and its Monastery

The small town of **DRYANOVO** isn't as pretty as Bozhentsi or Tryavna, and its remarkable architecture is limited to Koralov and Shipka Street and the area around the **Nikolai Fichev Museum** (Tuesday-Sunday 8am-12am, 1pm-5pm) in the upper part of town, opposite the bus-stop where passengers from Gabrovo or Târnovo usually alight. The museum commemorates locally-born 'Nicky' or *Kolyo Ficheto*, C19 Bulgaria's most versatile architect – responsible for Târnovo's churches, House of the Little Monkey and Konak – and includes material on the history of Dryanovo, which was founded during the late C14 or early C15. Deriving its prosperity from vineyards and the silkworms which proliferated in the surrounding dogwood-trees (*dryan*), Dryanovo's economy was crippled by outbreaks of phylloxera and a disease striking cocoons late in the C19, and has only been revived over the past few decades with the introduction of new industries and the replanting of the vineyards.

I didn't see any signs identifying a road leading directly towards the monastery 4km southwest of town (although it could be Bacho Kiro Street), and you might find it easier to reach from the highway, where there's a bus-stop near the turn-off (tell the driver you want the *spirka za manastir*). Set in a gorge beneath high crags, **Dryanovo Monastery** was chosen as the place from which to launch a local uprising in May 1876, while the fires of rebellion were still smouldering elsewhere after the supression of the April Rising. Under the leadership of Bacho Kiro and the monk Hariton, several hundred rebels defended the monastery for almost a week against 10,000 Turkish troops rushed from Shumen, whose commander Pasha Faslǎ offered to spare Kiro if he publicly repented – and hanged him when he refused. The rebels' bones are contained within an ossuary and the monastery owns a collection of 150 icons, including the C16 *St Zosim Greets Holy Mary from Egypt* and *The Prophet Daniel*. Outside there's a restaurant, *motel* and *campsite* – and the **Bacho Kiro Cave**, where Palaeolithic remains have been discovered.

Tryavna

The old crafts centre of **TRYAVNA** may be a byword for icons like Debâr and Samokov, and feature no fewer than 140 listed buildings, yet it happily lacks the feel of a museum-town. Most of its visitors seem to be Bulgars rather than foreigners, and you're likelier to encounter art students sketching than coach parties jostling for a photo-opportunity. For car-less travellers, the regular bus service from Gabrovo provides the best way of **getting there** (travelling by rail from Gabrovo or Târnovo entails an awkward change at BÂRBANOVO).

The town's narrow streets are evocative of the C19: although Tryavna was founded by refugees from Târnovo 400 years earlier, the oldest buildings all post-date the establishment of an official Guild of Master-builders and Woodcarvers in 1804. Often carved with birds and flowers, the wooden houses in the **old quarter** have an asymmetrical structure that disguises the essential similarity of their interiors. Traditionally, the large room containing the hooded *kusti* (hearth) was the centre of domestic life and led directly to the *chardak* or covered terrace; guests were received in a separate room (*soba*) and household goods stored in the ground-floor *odaya*. One such house, at 39,

Ul. Dimitrov, was the **birthplace of Angel Kântchev** (1850-72), whose patriotism led him to join Belgrade's Artillery School at the age of seventeen, and later spurn a lucrative job-offer ('no compromise') to work for Bulgaria's liberation. Sent to assist Levski in constructing the revolutionary underground, Kânchev completed two clandestine 'tours' before he was caught boarding a steamer at Ruse without a passport. Fearful of betraying secrets under torture, he shot himself crying 'Long live Bulgaria!' – in Levski's words, 'the most honourable death for justice that should be considered sweetest for every proud Bulgarian of today'. (Like all Tryavna's museums, the Kânchev house is open Wednesday-Sunday 8am-12am, 2pm-6pm).

Further along Ul. Dimitrov, at number 50, the personal effects of the influential writer and teacher P. R. Slaveykov (who taught the young Kânchev) and his son, the poet Pencho Slaveykov, are displayed in the **Slaveykov Museum** – P. R.'s residence for 26 years and Pencho's birthplace. As usual, captions are in Bulgarian only but the house itself is worth seeing; for excerpts from Pencho's most famous work, the unfinished *Kâvara pesen* ('*Song of the Blood*'), see p.601 and p.635.

Unusually for a Tryavna edifice, the **Daskalov House**, near the Slaveykov Museum, has a symmetrical plan with two wings joined by a curvaceous *chardak**. The rooms inside are brightly carpeted, with arched windows and inbuilt *minder*, and also contain superb panelled ceilings (wooden suns with fretted rays inlaid within a frame decorated with floral and bird motifs) and a no-less interesting **Museum of Icon-painting and Woodcarving**. A building on the main square also displays hundreds of these, produced by the C19 '**School of Tryavna**' – a guild with a distinctive style of cutting the wood back until acanthus leaves, birds and other favourite motifs were rendered in openwork like lace covering the surface of the iconostasis.

For an example *in situ*, you need look no farther than the **Church of the Archangel Michael**, whose iconostasis is wonderfully rich and dark, with twelve intricate tableaux surrounding the crucifix and a carved pulpit wound around one of the columns. At the rear of the church, originally founded by Petâr and Assen to commemorate victory over Byzantium, memorial photographs of the recently deceased are stuck into candelabras, part of the Orthodox forty-day mourning rite which Bulgarians also observe by putting up posters in the streets. **Other sights** include the Clock Tower and Kivgirev Bridge beside the square, and the Pioneers' (nr.54) and Young Artists' (nr.45)

---

* Bulgarians considered it unlucky to build a house near an empty well or an old watermill or graveyard, and when doubts arose about a prospective site a bowl of water would be left there for bad omens (impurities or clouding) to appear overnight. Before the foundations were laid an animal was slaughtered on the site of the hearth or threshold, and the outlines of the walls were marked by dripping blood as an additional magical precaution. When the house was complete, blessings (*takia*) were shouted and the owners presented the builders with gifts before moving in themselves, preferably on a Monday, Thursday or Sunday at the time of a new moon. By custom, the eldest man would pour water over the threshold and scatter coins and wheat around the hearth in the hope of a future life 'as smooth as water', prosperity and full barns. Once he had kindled the first fire with embers from the old family hearth, the matriarch completed the occupation by breaking a loaf over the flames and hanging up a copper vessel.

houses on Ul. Dimitrov. The Pioneers' club has colourful murals, and the latter often exhibits contemporary artwork, particularly during Tryavna's **Festival of Woodcarving and Sculpture** in July and August. Visitors interested in 8-day **crafts' courses** should contact Gabrovo's tourist office, which can reserve beds at Tryavna's *Hotel Ralitsa* (south of the post office).

You might also, with diplomacy, find **accommodation** at the *Tourist Hostel* for Eastern Europeans (58, Ul. Dimitrov; small entrance, easily missed), where a bed costs only 4 leva. As for **moving on**, it's again best to use buses, although if you're solely interested in the ride, the railway heads south through the scenic **Tryavna Pass** where Petâr and Asen defeated the Byzantine army in 1190, preserving the independence of the Second Kingdom. On the other side of the mountains it doubles back on itself to reach TULOVO – junction for trains into the Valley of the Roses.

Bozhentsi

Further on towards Gabrovo, **BOZHENTSI**'s cluster of two-storey houses with stone roofs and wooden verandahs gives an idea of what Tryavna could easily have become, a museum-village. According to legend it was founded by survivors of the fall of Târnovo, led by the noblewoman Bozhena and her nine sons. During the second half of the C19, Bozhentsi grew prosperous through the enterprise of its smiths, potters and weavers, and local merchants who traded as far afield as Hungary and Russia, and it now provides a holiday resort for the Architects', Artists' and Writers' unions. There's no tourist accommodation so it's inevitably a day excursion from Gabrovo (there are buses).

HUMOUR AT GABROVO, AND CRAFTS AT ETÂR

People in every country tell jokes about the miserliness of a particular community, and in Bulgaria the butt of the gags is **GABROVO**. According to such **jokes**, *gabrovitsi* invented the one-stotinka coin, gliding, short skirts, narrow trousers, and matchboxes with only one side for striking; they stop their clocks at night and carry their shoes to reduce wear and tear; let a cat down the chimney rather than hire a sweep; and dock the tails of these luckless creatures, so they can shut the door a fraction sooner, conserving warmth. One Gabrovnian says to another, 'Whenever I see you I immediately think of Stoyan. Why? Because he owes me 60 leva, too'. Another thinks, 'Hmm, Pencho has been put on a strict diet. . .we can invite him to dinner'. Two *gabrovtsi* have a wager on who can give least when the collection-plate comes around; the first donates 1 stotinka, whereupon the other crosses himself piously and tells the sexton, 'That was for both of us'. And so on. . .

Gabrovnians themselves apparently relish this reputation, and with their legendary skill for profit-making have turned wit into an industry. Long known for producing leatherwork and textiles which earned Gabrovo the sobriquet of the 'Manchester of Bulgaria', the town now attracts thousands of visitors every year to its 'Louvre of Laughter', the **House of Humour and Satire**. Founded by Stefan Furtunov, on whose initiative Gabrovo was twinned with Aberdeen, the *Dom na Humora i Satirata* (opened on April Fool's Day

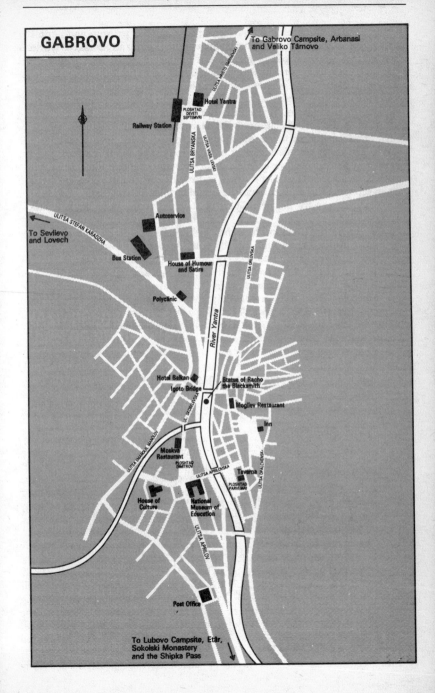

GABROVO

To Gabrovo Campsite, Arbanasi
and Veliko Tårnovo

Hotel Yantra

PLOSHTAD
DEVETI
SEPTEMVRI

Railway Station

ULITSA BRYANSKA

ULITSA VASIL LEVSKI

ULITSA RAETI GABROVKO

Autoservice

ULITSA STEFAN KARADZHA

To Sevlievo
and Lovech

Bus Station

House of Humour
and Satira

ULITSA ORLOVSKA

Polyclinic

River Yantra

Hotel Balkan

Igoto Bridge

UL. SKOBELEVSKA

Statue of Racho
the Blacksmith

Mogilev Restaurant

Inn

ULITSA EMANUIL MANOLOV

Moskva
Restaurant

PLOSHTAD
DIMITROV

ULITSA APRILOVSKA

Taverna

PLOSHTAD
PARVI MAI

ULITSA OPALCHENSKI

House of
Culture

National
Museum of
Education

ULITSA APRILOV

Post Office

To Lubovo Campsite, Etår,
Sokolski Monastery
and the Shipka Pass

1974) has a collection of 113,000 cartoons, humorous writings and photos, carnival masks and costumes drawn from scores of countries across the world. Since exhibits are changed regularly, you'll hopefully encounter something other than the barrage of anti-Reagan and sexist caricatures displayed during my visit (when very few visitors seemed to be laughing) – selections of which appear in *A Propos* magazine, published in several languages twice a year.

While at the museum (open 9am-12am, 2pm-6pm), look out for skits performed by the cast of Gabrovo's **Experimental Satirical Theatre**: a cabaret centre occasionally showing films and videos, which opened in 1985. Gabrovnian jollity reaches a climax in May every odd-numbered year, when masked carnivals, folk music, pop, dixieland jazz, comedy films, animated cartoons, prize-givings and the ritual 'cutting off the Gabrovnian cat's tail' enliven the town during the **Biennial Festival of Humour and Satire**. As usual, the older quarters are the nicest part of town, covering both banks of the Yantra beyond the **Igoto Bridge**. A statue of Gabrovo's legendary C16 founder, Racho the Blacksmith, stands on a rock in midstream, and on the east bank, further south and inland, you'll find **craft workshops** around Opâlchenska Street and 1st of May Square. The **tourist office** is at 2, Opâlchenska Street, and, across the river, the **Aprilov School**, founded by *Vasil Aprilov* and *Nikola Palaouzov* in 1872, was one of the first schools to offer a secular education in the Bulgarian language. It now houses the **National Museum of Education**, including relics of notable former Aprilov-pupils, such as Dimitâr Blagoev, Georgi Kirgov and Aleko Konstantinov. **Pl. Georgi Dimitrov**, Gabrovo's main square, opens up beyond the building, the site of a monument to **Mitko Palaouzov**. Only 14 years old when he was killed fighting fascists in 1944, Palaouzov is honoured as 'an example to be followed by all Bulgarian children', his monument flanked by two youngsters bearing Kalashnikovs.

Vacancies can be scarce during the Bienniale, but otherwise there shouldn't be any problem with **accommodation**. Both the 3-star *Hotel Balkan*, on Emanuil Manolov street to the northwest of the Igoto Bridge, and the 2-star *Yantra* near the railway station are high-rise, mod-con places; while the *Gabrovo* and *Lyubovo* campsites (with chalets) – situated a few miles out along the main road north and south of town – can be reached by any of the buses from Gabrovo to Veliko Târnovo or Shipka. Gabrovo's east bank boasts several 'folk-style' **restaurants and tavernas**: *Mogilev* on Pl. Pârvi Mai, the *inn* at 15, Ul. Opâlchenska, another *tavern* at 1, Ul. Aprilovska, and the *Strano-Priemnitsa*, which has a summer garden and specialises in 'fish baked on a tile'.

Car repairs are carried out at the depot adjoining the **bus terminal**, while **medical emergencies** are dealt with by the Polyclinic. Though it's easy enough to buy tickets at the station, **railway bookings** can also be made from 3, Pl. Izmirliev (☎ 4-21-34) or Block Racho Kovacha (☎ 2-53-39).

Etâr and Sokolski Monastery

Since Racho set up his smithy beneath a large hornbeam (*gabâr*, hence the town's name), Gabrovo has been a **crafts** centre, gaining fresh impetus at the beginning of the C19 when waterwheels were introduced from Transylvania.

By 1870 the town had more than 800 workshops powered by water, making iron and wooden implements, clothing, wool and blankets sold beyond the frontiers of the Ottoman empire. Today it produces textiles in quantities exceeded only by Sliven, and half the leather goods in Bulgaria. To preserve traditional skills, Gabrovo has established the museum-village of **ETÂR**, 9km from town on the banks of the Sivek, a tributary of the Yantra (open from 8am-5pm daily). You can reach this by bus services leaving Gabrovo's terminal around 6.55, 8.30 or 11.50 in the morning, or by picking up any bus heading south and getting off at the Etâr turn-off, from where it's a two kilometre walk.

The **Etâr Architectural-Ethnographic Complex** falls into three sections. Traditionally, crafts were inseparable from the *Charshiya*, and a reconstructed bazaar of the type once common in Bulgarian towns forms the heart of the Etâr complex. Throughout much of the day artisans are at work here, hammering bells, throwing pots, sewing braid and sheepskin jackets etc, and it's possible for visitors to sign up for **crafts courses**. Arranged by Gabrovo's tourist office, these last 30 hours spread over one week, and supposedly impart the rudiments of copper-working, rug-weaving, pottery, tailoring, flute-making, forging and wood-turning. Even if your interest in crafts is minimal it's difficult not to admire the interiors of the old houses, which achieve great beauty through the skillful use of simple materials. Besides dwellings and workshops, the bazaar includes several places for wetting one's whistle, and a bakery whence folks emerge clutching fresh *simitli* (glazed buns made of chick-pea flour), a speciality of Gabrovo's mistress-baker, Maria Miteva. Another section contains a water-mill (*karadyekia*) and hydro-powered workshops for cutting timber, fulling cloth, and making braid (*dolapkinya*), wine flagons (*buklitsi*) and *gavanki* (round wooden boxes); the third section, intended to show village life, is still being constructed.

The modern quasi-National Revival-style *inn* nearby the Etâr complex is fairly expensive, and there's no need to stay here even if you plan to visit **Sokolski Monastery**. Situated an hour or so's walk upstream from Etâr (or accessible by buses leaving Gabrovo around 7am, 8.30am or 11.50am), the monastery is practically invisible until you enter pass beneath its portal into the shady courtyard. The small church, dating from the monastery's foundation in 1836, contains primitive murals by the original pastor, and icons by the Tryavna School. Listening to the water gurgling from Sokolski's octagonal stone fountain it takes an effort to imagine the monastery packed with frightened townsfolk and the beaten remnants of the Gabrovo detachment, as happened towards the end of the rising of 1876.

On from Gabrovo

Using buses or the railway it's possible to reach a considerable number of places from Gabrovo. Getting **to Tryavna** is easiest by bus (departures every 45 minutes; book 1hr beforehand). The main railway line runs up to **Dryanovo** and **Veliko Târnovo**, but buses depart more frequently and can also drop you by the turn-off for Dryanovo Monastery, which is some distance from the town itself (p.614). Hourly buses for Dryanovo depart from stand 2 of the terminal, while at similar intervals another bus heads south along the wonderfully scenic road over the **Shipka Pass** (see p.625) and down to **Kazanlâk**. It's feasible to hitch, but necessary to book in advance to secure seats on the bus; similar advice applies to catching buses to **Troyan** (departing around 8.10am and 2.10pm). In the absence of direct services to **Lovech**, it's possible to get there by using Sevlievo as a staging post.

Gabrovnians joke that they dance the *horo* in slippers so as to hear the band playing in SEVLIEVO, and in retaliation their neighbours tell the following story: A dozen writers hired to entertain Sevlievo's townsfolk with humorous readings feasted at local expense and failed to give satisfaction. On hearing that the writers had also been booked to perform in Gabrovo, a disgruntled local said, 'Good! They deserve it!'.

TÂRNOVO TO SHUMEN: STRAZHITSA AND TÂRGOVISHTE

There's not much of interest **between Târnovo and Shumen**. To travel **by rail** you'll have to change at Gorna Oryahovitsa, from where there are regular through-services to Shumen calling at Târgovishte, plus slower 'local' trains which also stop at Strazhitsa en route. STRAZITSA has a few National Revival-style houses, but more importantly, hosts a **festival of plein air painting** (atiended by artists from all the socialist countries) towards the end of September every even-numbered year. There are two **campsites** with chalets in the vicinity: *Voditsa*, along the road to Popovo (roughly 20km northeast of Strazhitsa), and *Erevish*, about 5km beyond ANTONOVO (wartime haunt of the *Omurtag* Partisan unit), along the road to Târgovishte taken by buses from Târnovo.

TÂRGOVISHTE gets its name from the old Slavic word for 'fair', like the Romanian town of Tîrgovişte, and for many centuries after it was founded by the Turks, the largest cattle market in the Balkans took place here. Nowadays, few signs of this remain: Târgovishte has been extensively rebuilt in concrete and all there is is a derelict mosque lurking in the backstreets to the west of Blvd. Levski, and the school where P. R. Slaveykov taught (on the west bank of the Varna River), preserved as a museum. *Lyulyaka campsite* (5km west of town beside the highway) and the *Hotel Miziya* (near the intersection of Vasil Levski and Stefan Karadzha) are both pretty cheap, but there's no incentive to stay, and the main reason for entering town is the **bus service to Preslav** and its C10 ruins – though these could equally well be reached from SHUMEN, a much nicer base than Târgovishte.

SHUMEN

Shuma means 'foliage' in Bulgarian, and Slavyanski Bulevard, running between the terminals and downtown SHUMEN, is appropriately leafy. Bus #1 will carry you all the way from the station to the Tombul Mosque on the other side of town, but unless you're burdened with heavy luggage it's nice to get off near the **History Museum** – where Thracian and medieval artefacts are handsomely displayed, with an equally fine **Art Gallery** (Tuesday-Saturday

9am-12am, 2pm-7pm) nearby – and walk some of the way. A blend of mellow Baroque and smart modern architecture gives downtown Shumen an expansive air.

Practically speaking, most restaurants, cafés and shops are situated along the boulevard, together with BALKAN, the post office, an *Orbita* bureau and several **places to stay**. Rooms at the *Hotel Madara* – with **Balkantourist** in the lobby – are quite dear, but staff at the 'Eastern Europeans only' *Hotel Ticha* and *Tourist Hostel* seem disposed to let Capitalists stay, although they won't permit unmarried couples to share a room. Another source of cheap beds is *Orbita*, which maintains a hostel to the east of town, while it's been reported that a new moderately-priced *Hotel Sofia* has opened at 37, Ul. Tsar Osvoboditel.

Shumen's main sight is the C18 **Tombul Mosque** on Rakovski Street (8am-12am, 2pm-6pm/Sundays 8am-1pm), though its bulbous dome and proud minaret are at odds with the shabby interior. Quite a few ethnic Turks inhabit the Shumen region, but during our visit there was no-one washing at the whimsical-looking fountain in the cloistered courtyard out back, and only tourists padded the carpets beneath the flowery dome and pentagonal lights. Raised on the orders of Sherif Pasha in 1744, the mosque dates from the time when the eastern part of town – called *Shumla* by the Turks – was transformed into a stronghold with huge ramparts and 12 fortified gates. Nothing remains of this, but the ruins of a medieval fortress built to protect the road to Pliska sprawl across a hilltop to the southwest of town. This can be reached by infrequent buses to the **Stariya Grad** (as it's known), or by walking 2km uphill from the Madara Brewery at the *Kboshkove* end of the #10 and #11 bus-routes.

But there's more to see in Shumen's **old quarter**, which huddles either side of the Poroina River with an C18 Clock Tower as its chief landmark. North of the river are several old residences preserved in honour of their former occupants, not least post-war Bulgaria's deputy leader, **Vasil Kolarov** (1877-1950), after whom Shumen was briefly renamed *Kolarovgrad*. Born into the bourgeoisie and educated at Geneva University, he fled to the USSR after the 1923 uprising and took Soviet citizenship. He survived Stalin's purges, and in 1944 returned to supervise the expurgation of non-Communist parties and 'home-grown' Communists like Traicho Kostov. Kolarov's body is buried alongside Dimitrov's Mausoleum in Sofia, and both the man and his former house (11, Ul. Ikonomov; Tuesday-Saturday 9am-12am, 2pm-6pm/Sunday 9am-1pm) are less attractive than the **House of Dobri Voinikov** (87, Tsar Osvoboditel Street), crammed with memorabilia relating to this C19 author of the plays *Princess Raina* and *Civilisation Misunderstood*.

Best of all is the **Kossuth House** (nr.35 on the same street, with similar hours): a warren of panelled rooms with divans linked by creaking corridors, where the Magyar revolutionary Lajos Kossuth stayed for three months after fleeing Hungary in 1849, before the Turks interned him in Asia Minor. Yet another museum-house – near the **Kurshum Fountain** on the south side of the river – commemorates **Pancho Vladiguerov**: a Spaniard who settled in Shumen and became Bulgaria's first composer of classical music, now honoured by tagging his name to an annual **Festival of Piano Music** – held

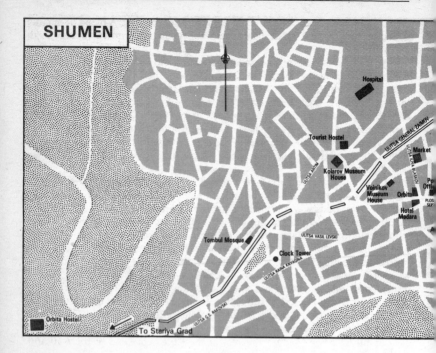

towards the end of September. See Balkantourist for details of this, and the annual **Symphony Music Days** during April.

Behind the Party House, between the gallery and the museum, flights of steps ascend to an extraordinary structure on a hilltop. Imagine Khans, monks, haiduks and Mother Heroines rendered in concrete by a sculptor with Cubist inclinations and you'll have some idea of the gigantic **1,300 Years of Bulgaria Monument** unveiled on the nation-state's 1,300th anniversary in 1981. Equally incongruous but more useful and a lot less conspicuous, is a **Buffalo and Horsebreeding Centre** where Indian *Murra* buffalo – noted for their high milk yield – are cross-bred with other species from the Soviet Union, Romania and Venezuela. Balkantourist can probably arrange a visit if you're interested.

From Shumen's terminal there are **buses** to Ruse and Varna (every 2hrs from stand 2) and Burgas (stand 10, departing around 6.50 & 8.50), as well as to all of the places below, on a more frequent basis.

AROUND SHUMEN: PRESLAV, MADARA, PLISKA AND NOVI PAZAR

The eastern part of the Balkan range is distinguished by three archaeological sites, all easily accessible from Shumen. The ruins of **Pliska** are less interesting to behold than read about, but enough remains of **Preslav** to justify a visit if

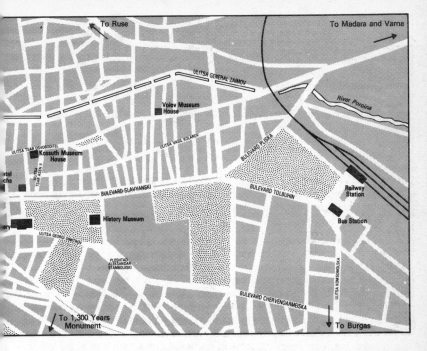

your taste inclines towards hunky masonry, while the rockscapes around the so-called **Madara Horseman** make up for the eroded face of this unique and ancient bas-relief. SHUMEN also lies roughly midway along two important routes between Ruse, Târnovo and Varna, if you're driving or using long-distance buses. However, most trains running between Gorna Oryahovitsa and Varna also stop there.

Preslav and its ruins today

Founded by Khan Omurtag in 821, **VELIKI PRESLAV** acquired the prefix 'Great' after it was made the capital of the First Kingdom, during the reign of Tsar Simeon (893–927) – although it began to eclipse the original capital, Pliska, at an earlier date. According to John the Exarch's *Shestodiniev*, C10 Preslav was the most populous town in the Balkans, with extensive suburbs surrounding a walled inner town containing 'large buildings of stone on both sides, decorated with wood'. It also held a Palace, a royal School of Translators, the Patriarchate and other 'churches ornamented with stones, wood and paintings, marble and copper, silver and gold'. Preslav's downfall began when it was captured by the Kievian prince, Svetoslav, causing the Byzantine empire to respond by razing the town in 972. Although it later revived (the Palace was occupied as late as the Asenid dynasty), Preslav never regained its former size and was subsequently surpassed by Târnovo. Eventually it was burned down by the Turks, who used the remains to construct their own buildings, including the Tombul Mosque in Shumen.

The **ruins of Preslav** are scattered over three square kilometres near the banks of the Ticha, and to make sense of them it helps to see the plans and model in the site's **Archaeological Museum**. From its store of lapidry and jewellery, the mind's eye can dress the bare ruins of the *Palace* where the Tsar held court 'in a garment studded with pearls, girt with a purple girdle and a golden sword by his side', and put a dome on the relatively well-preserved *Round Church*. Several arches, the bulk of its walls and twelve marble columns (some truncated) still remain. The church itself – sited on a hillock in what used to be the outer town – now provides the setting for pageants and poetry readings associated with the Veliki Preslav **Literary Days**, normally held around the middle of May. The easiest way of **getting there** by public transport is to catch one of the regular buses from Shumen to the small town of PRESLAV, 4km to the north, and then either walk or take any bus bound for Ivanovo, which will pass the well-signposted ruins. **Accommodation** boils down to a hotel in Preslav and a motel near the site.

The Madara Horseman

10km east of Shumen, a range of cliffs harbours evidence of a yet more distant past. Rafail Popov and other native archaeologists have had a field day uncovering signs of human occupation dating back to the C3 BC, and speculating about the mysterious bas-relief known as the **MADARA HORSE-MAN**. Carved into the rock-face at a height of 95m, this is so eroded that details are only apparent by the light of a setting sun, but the carving is said to represent a horseman whose mount is trampling a lion with the assistance of a greyhound, while he holds the reins in one hand and a wine-cup in the other. Various Greek inscriptions next to the carving provide ambiguous clues to its age: in fact some scholars believe that the horseman was carved far earlier than the oldest inscription, recording a debt owed by Emperor Justinian to Khan Tervel. The figure, they argue, represents the nameless supreme deity of the Thracians, and is of Thracian or Getae origin, the inscriptions merely evidence that it was later appropriated by Bulgarian rulers.

Nearby, remnants of a C14 **rock monastery** pit the cliff-face and some of the crudely-dug lower cells are just about accessible by treacherous paths. Leading off to the right of the stairway to the horseman-viewing platform, another path winds off to the **Large Cave** (*Golyamata Peshtera*) beneath a giant overhang of rock. Various finds from here – Thracian votive plaques, amphorae bearing the stamp of Thasos, Roman candlesticks and Proto-Bulgarian ceramics – are now exhibited in the **Museum** beside the road passing the Madara complex, and the cool, moss-streaked cave serves as the venue for the **Madara Music Days** in June and July (contact *Balkantourist* in Shumen for details).

Not far away you'll find the source of the Madara River where plaques and statues honouring the Horseman, Dionysus, Cybele and three Water Nymphs have been discovered. Paganism remained ingrained amongst the Bulgars long after Christianity became the official religion in 865, and their reverence for caves is partially explained by the Proto-Bulgarian belief that stone had healing properties. However, it seems likely that considerations of warmth and defence impelled the earliest settlers to occupy the **Small Cave**, between its larger neighbour and the steep cleft that formerly led to the Madara fortress, where flints, bones and pottery have been discovered.

Assuming it's been made safe, you can also follow another path up past little cells hewn into the rock to the top of the plateau. Roughly 500m to the west lies a **ruined fortress**, C5 and still with walls standing up. There are also two **tumuli** left by the Getae – who buried their dead in ceramic urns – 300m north of the fortress, but the real attraction is the **view from the plateau**. Roman ruins are scattered about at the foot of the massif, while the surrounding plain is cut off by the Balkans to the south and the Lyubogorski Hills to the north – where sharp eyes might be able to discern the ruins of Pliska (see below) amidst the acacia groves.

Although there are trains from Shumen to Madara village, the 4.30pm bus from town (bound for Novi Pazar) is the best way of **reaching the site** since it stops just outside, sparing you the 2km uphill slog from Madara railway station. You can see the horseman before catching the last bus back to Shumen, or on to Novi Pazar (see below), if you prefer not **to stay** overnight. If you do, the tourist hostel is usually occupied by groups, but there should be vacant bungalows for rent (11 leva) on the campsite – hidden away at the end of a path behind the busy restaurant.

Pliska and Novi Pazar

The ruins of **PLISKA** are less well preserved than Preslav's, but in its heyday during the First Kingdom (601-1018), Pliska was a sophisticated and important settlement, covering 23 square kilometres and protected by citadels on neighbouring hills. **The ruins** still occupy a considerable area, although most of the buildings have been reduced to low walls. As you can see from the exhibits in the **museum**, Pliska originally had three lines of defences: a ditch, behind which was the outer town (with workshops and the dwellings of ordinary folk), a stone wall with four gates, surrounding the inner town, and finally a brick rampart around the so-called *Little Palace*. Between the brick and stone walls lay the two-storied *Large Palace*, 170ft long by 87ft wide, and the yet larger *Royal Basilica*, the former being supplied with piped water and central heating.

Unless you have a car, **getting there** from Shumen means changing buses at NOVI PAZAR ('New Bazaar'), from which it's 8km to Pliska village and a further 3km to the ruins. There's a motel at the ruins and another one in Novi Pazar.

THE SHIPKA PASS

Whether you hitch, drive or catch a bus, few routes in Bulgaria match **crossing the Shipka Pass** for drama and majestic vistas. The journey across the mountains **between Gabrovo and Kazanlâk** takes about 1½hrs **by bus** and it's wise to book seats when leaving either town even if you're planning to stop halfway and then continue on by a later service (there are usually a few seats empty by the time buses reach the pass). The hotel at the pass is often occupied by groups, but you can always **sleep** at the campsite 2km down the road in the direction of Gabrovo, which has heated chalets (worth taking – it gets very cold at night).

Particularly at sunset, when the mountains darken and a chill wind disperses the tourists, you can feel something of the potent historical significance of the **SHIPKA PASS**. Six thousand Russians and Bulgarians once resisted a 27,000-strong Ottoman force sent northwards to break the siege of Plevna in August 1877. Snow exacerbated the hardships of Radetsky's ill-equipped Bulgarian volunteers (many of whom had been civilians in Gabrovo only days before), and despite the local women who brought supplies, the defenders' ammunition was exhausted by the third day of the **battle** and they resorted to throwing rocks, tree-trunks and finally corpses at the Turks. But the pass held and in due time Plevna surrendered, whereupon the Russians reinforced Radetsky's army and ordered it to fight its way down the snowy mountainside to defeat the remaining 22,000 Ottoman troops outside Kazanlâk – which it did.

Bulgarian and Soviet tourists still place bouquets honouring their sacrifice beneath the bronze Bulgarian Lion that surveys its putative motherland from the towering **Freedom Monument** on Mount Stoletev, from where there's a magnificent **panorama** of the Valley of the Roses and the Sredna Gora. Grilled sausages and an array of spirits (including noxious yellow Vietnamese vodka) are available from vendors, and cognoscenti reckon that the **yoghurt** (*kiselo mlyako*) sold at the Shipka Pass is the finest in Bulgaria. Another sight not to be missed is the **Memorial Church** whose gold domes rise above the woods at **SHIPKA** village, 14km down the mountainside towards Kazanlâk. Twelve kilometres east of the Shipka Pass, **Mount Buzludzha** is topped by a bizarre structure resembling a spaceship come to earth. Hadzhi Dimitâr and his rebels died here fighting the Turks on 2 August 1868, though the museum inside the spaceship principally commemorates the **founding of the Bulgarian Socialist Party** on the same day in 1891, after a clandestine congress. It can be reached by road from the pass, and there are sometimes buses to the site from KAZANLÂK (see p.631).

PLEVEN TO THE VALLEY OF THE ROSES

Travelling across the Balkan range **between Pleven and the Valley of the Roses** can't match crossing the Shipka Pass in terms of scenery or excitement, but there are compensations in a lusher landscape and the monastery of Troyan. Starting from Pleven or Kârnare, without a car, you'd be well advised to make the journey **by bus**, since by rail means a change at LEVSKI, and the line itself terminates at Lovech.

Lovech

Heading south, **LOVECH** is the first town of any size en route; a position that it seems to have held since Thracian times. Its claim to fame is having once been the headquarters of **Vasil Levski**, whose statue and house museum are the two main sights. Between 1869-72, Levski was chiefly responsible for establishing the **Internal Secret Revolutionary Organisation** within Bulgaria, which collected arms and recruits in preparation for a nationwide uprising. Divided into 'cells', the organisation's largest base was in Lovech, where

Levski usually stayed at the home of Nikola Sirkov, arriving and leaving in disguise. On one such mission he was betrayed and arrested at the neighbouring village of Kâkrina. Then, following torture, he was hung on a winter's morning in Sofia in 1873.

In the **house museum** Levski's whole life is covered (and rendered mysterious to foreigners by the exclusively Bulgarian captions), but the emphasis is understandably on his achievements and death rather than the 'wilderness years' (p.630). The **statue** looms over Stratesh Hill, where townsfolk come to admire the view while their children play Turks and Heroes on the **ruins of Melta**, a Roman fortress used by Bulgarian Tsars during the C12 wars against Byzantium.

To reach either from the bus or train station in the new town, follow the street sloping off to the right, which leads down to the office blocks, supermarkets and building sites occupying the west bank of the Osâm, and then cross over by the **Covered Bridge**. Locals are extremely proud of this reconstructed version of the *Pokritiya Most* built by Fichev in the C19, and the bridge's boutiques and cafés are a favourite haunt of posing machos.

Emerging on the other side, you'll find two smart-looking **hotels** (charging 30-40 leva per head) flanking a plaza with a fountain marking the spot where the Turks hanged a revolutionary, Todor Kirkov, in 1876, and nowadays the site of the evening's promenade and other diversions. Not far away you'll see the red roofs and protruding *chardaks* of the *Varosh* quarter, for which the **old town** is rather a misnomer. The houses have either been spruced up so thoroughly that they resemble units in a Bulgarian 'Holiday Village', or are modern buildings executed in a pseudo-National Revival style.

Troyan Monastery and the Troyan Pass

The journey south from Lovech takes you between wooded hills to **TROYAN**, a ramshackle town with a **Museum of Arts and Crafts** in the centre, which displays some copperware and textiles and a host of vases, bowls, goblets and other objects made of pottery or wood. Although much of Troyan's output is nowadays made in factories, the town still boasts individual craftsmen – Minko Bankovski, Naiden Totev and Bayu Dobrev are a few – whose work is regularly exhibited at the biennial **National Crafts Fair** at **ORESHAK**. 5km east of town and accessible by bus, this commune maintains a standing exhibition of woodcarvings and wrought ironwork presented by foreign craftspersons. If you're interested in learning the rudiments of pottery, ironmongery or woodcarving, Balkantourist can arrange 8-day **courses** in each of these crafts at Troyan and Oreshak.

However, the real attraction is **Troyan Monastery** (*Troyanski manastir*), 5km from Oreshak on the left bank of the Cherni Osâm. Shaded by trees, Bulgaria's third largest monastery surrounds a church, built in 1835 (roughly 135 years after the monastery was founded) and filled with sonorous chanting during mass, when visitors are discouraged. Inside, a series of splendid frescoes executed by Zahari Zograf during the 1840s are richly offset by his brother Dimitâr's icons, set within an iconostasis made by Tryavna artists. Only Eastern bloc tourists are allowed **to stay** at the monastery cells, and Westerners either have to use the pricey *Hotel Troyan*, in town, or get a bed in the *Tourist Hostel* at APRILTSI, 19km away – though this, too, is officially reserved for Eastern Europeans.

Buses heading south begin a slow climb through dense forests towards the **Troyan Pass**, where a wonderful panorama suddenly appears as the road crosses the mountains at a height of 4,760 feet. The Stryama Valley, below, recedes towards the Sredna Gora, where you can see Mt. Bogdan, its highest peak (5,263ft). Beyond lies the Plain of Thrace and the blueish silhouette of the distant Rhodopes. At the foot of the mountains lies KÂRNARE, a nondescript town where you can catch regular buses or trains into the neighbouring *Valley of the Roses*.

THE VALLEY OF THE ROSES

The E771 and the railway running between the Balkan and Sredna Gora ranges constitutes the most direct route between Sofia and Burgas on the coast, and, depending on the time of year, you might decide to pass straight through the **Valley of the Roses**. Perhaps the most over-hyped region of Bulgaria, the valley is a sunbaked and dusty place most of the year, except for May, when it's magically transformed by the blooms which give it its name. Outside of May and early June, however, its towns are for the most part unexciting – 'ramshackle collections of unplastered cottages which might have dropped off a lorry' thought Leslie Gardiner, and he wasn't far wrong. **Klisura**, **Sopot**, **Karlovo** and **Kalofer** all occupy honoured niches in Bulgarian history as the scene of heroic events or the birthplace of writers or national heroes, but have little that's worth seeing beyond the odd memorial museum. The only exception to this rule is **Kazanlâk**. The venue for the *Festival of Roses* after the harvest in May, it features an interesting museum of the rose industry and a remarkable Thracian tomb – and to the north the rugged Shipka Pass (see p.625).

Regular trains from Sofia to Karlovo or Burgas make it easy enough to travel along the valley (although express services don't stop at the smaller places en route). Coming down from the Balkan range via the Troyan or Shipka Pass, you can pick up the valley route at Kârnare or Kazanlâk; Srednogorie and Karlovo are linked by buses or branch-rail lines to the Sredna Gora or Plovdiv.

'Bulgaria's Gold' – roses
The **rose-growing** area between Klisura and Kazanlâk produces 70% of the world's attar – or extract – of roses. Considering that perfumiers pay more than £30,000,000 a year for this, it's not surprising that roses are known as 'Bulgaria's gold'. Rose-growing began as a small cottage industry during the 1830s (supposedly started by a Turkish merchant impressed by the wild

Shipka Rose's fragrance), and initially involved nothing more complicated than copper stills from which water-cooled pipes dripped the greenish-yellow rose oil. It became big business early in the C20 but virtually ceased during the Second World War when Nazi Germany discouraged the industry in order to sell its own *ersatz* scents, but since then Bulgaria's rose-growers have vastly expanded their operations.

Each acre planted with red *rosa damascena* or white *rosa alba* yields up to 1,400 kilograms of blossom, or roughly 3 million rosebuds; between 3,000-6,000 kilos are required to make one litre of attar, leaving a residue of rosewater and pulp used to make medicaments, flavourings, *sladko* jam and *rosaliika* liqueur. The rose bushes (covering over 14,000 acres) are allowed to grow to head height, and harvested during May between 3am-8am before the sun rises and evaporates up to 50% of the oil. Nimble-fingered women and girls do most of the picking, while donkeys are employed to carry the petals away to the modern distilleries around Rozino, Kârnare and Kazanlâk. The latter is the site of a research institute where pesticides are tested and different breeds of rose developed. According to the director, its gardens contain every variety in the world.

BETWEEN SOFIA AND SOPOT

Beyond the broad plain to the east of Sofia, the neighbouring mountains slope down to a succession of saddles and spurs, which the road climbs, passing a *motel/campsite* near MIRKOVO. Non-express trains usually stop at the Zlatitsa and Pirdop suburbs of SREDNOGORIE, a mining town from where a road heads north over the Zlatishki Pass towards Etropole Monastery (p.598), and buses run south to Panagyurishte (p.638). North of Anton village, you'll see Baba and Vezhen, the first great peaks of the Stara Planina. Just beyond the railway halt for Koprivshtitsa (12km from the village itself, see p.635), trains enter a long tunnel beneath the Koznitsa spur, emerging into the Stryama Valley, the upper part of the Valley of the Roses.

There's no reason to stop at **KLISURA**, although this small town 'of tiles and flowers' is famous for having been burned down during the April Rising, as described in *Under the Yoke*. From here onwards it's roses all the way – at least during May – with posters exhorting the collective farmers of ROZINO and neighbouring communes to produce more of the valuable blooms. The next small town, **KÂRNARE**, is the point of departure for **buses to Troyan**, which take the highest road in Bulgaria, crossing the scenic Troyan Pass (see p.627).

A machine-building works and modern flats have vastly altered the appearance of **SOPOT**, whose main square features a bronze statue of the small town's most famous son, **Ivan Vazov** (1850-1921). Vazov began his career by writing for émigré journals in Romania, and became famous for his poems on the events of April 1876. As a magistrate in Berkovitsa, he found that the foibles of the chorbadzhii and petty bureaucrats provided material for satirical pieces, and he later devoted himself to editing newspapers in Plovdiv, then the capital of Eastern Roumelia. Fleeing to Odessa after Stambolov's coup in 1886, Vazov then wrote the classic tale of smalltown life before and during the April Rising, *Under the Yoke* (*Pod igoto*), subsequently acclaimed as Bulgaria's 'national novel'. Returning home later, he entered parliament and became Minister of Education (1897-9), continuing to write a stream of novels, articles and poems until his death in Sofia, where he was buried on Aleksandâr Nevski Square. His birthplace, just off the mainstreet, is now a **museum**. Ivan Zagubanski, a courier for Lenin's newspaper *Iskra* – published in Munich and smuggled into Eastern Europe – also rates a house-museum. Reasonably-priced **beds** are available at the *Hotel Stara Planina*, near Vazov's birthplace.

KARLOVO AND KALOFER

Set against a backdrop of lofty, arid crags and hollows descending to slopes partly covered with cypresses and fig trees, **KARLOVO** looks unimpressive by comparison with its surroundings. Its old quarter, north along Ul. Levski, is pleasant enough: various mansions and churches dignify the side-streets and a derelict mosque can be seen at the top end, near the main square. But the principal reason for visiting Karlovo is to see the **birthplace of Vasil Levski**: a modestly-sized house just off Levski Street (open Friday-Wednesday 8am-12am, 1pm-5.30pm).

Raised by his mother, who supported her family by working as a dyer, Levski briefly considered the priesthood and medicine before dedicating himself to the cause of Bulgaria's liberation. Choosing exile like many patriots, he joined Rakovski's Bulgarian Legion whose raids across the border infuriated the Turks but won little sympathy from the local population – before concluding that Ottoman rule could only be overthrown by a revolutionary organisation based within Bulgaria. From 1869 on he set about establishing just this, gathering recruits as he ranged across the country in a variety of disguises – the 'Apostle of Freedom'. Inspired by a vision of liberation that transcended frontiers, Levski was legend within his own lifetime (1837-73) – the Balkan Che Guevara.

It seems pointless **to stay** at the 2-star *Rozova Dolina* or the cheaper *Hotel Sofia* (both near the main square) when there's **transport** to more interesting places. Besides hourly buses to neighbouring Kalofer, there are services to Troyan (leaving around 9.50am & 3.20pm), Panagyurishte (10.40am & 1pm), Târnovo (9am) and Pleven (10am); not to mention buses to Plovdiv, which complement the 10 daily trains to Plovdiv. Whether travellers **heading east** see the vineyards, tobacco plants or roses depends on the season, but whatever the time of year you'll pass *Byala Reka campsite* and some of the grandest peaks in the Balkans.

Crossing the Staga ridge joining the Sredna Gora to the Balkans, the road enters **KALOFER**, where numerous water-wheels used to revolve in the River Tundzha, which emerges from a nearby gorge to flow through this small town. Architecturally undistinguished, Kalofer has but one tourist attraction, or rather, place of pilgrimage – namely the childhood home of another revolutionary, **Hristo Botev**. Perhaps the most romantic figure in Bulgaria's pantheon of heroes, Botev (1848-76) imbibed patriotism from his father and radical ideals while studying at Odessa, after which he gravitated towards the

Bulgarian émigré community in Bessarabia before returning home in 1867. Scornful of compromise, he was soon exiled for preaching 'Stop buying and selling, bickering and cheating, strutting and grovelling!', and went to Bucharest in search of the Secret Revolutionary Committee. There he shared a garret with Levski and subsequently worked with Karavelov on *Budilnik* (Alarm), *Zname* (Banner) and other radical papers, writing stirring eulogies to liberty and Hadzhi Dimitâr. A utopian socialist, and a man of action, Botev responded to news of the April Rising by hijacking a steamer and landing with 200 men to aid the rebels, but was killed in action near Vratsa. The highest peak in the Balkan range (7,796ft), looming to the north of town, now bears his name.

Kalofer's 2-star *Hotel Roza* has reasonably-priced **rooms**, but cheaper chalets can be had at *Byala Reka campsite* a few miles west of town, or *Sevthopolis campsite* near the **Georgi Dimitrov Dam**, on the way to Kazanlâk. The dam (built between 1947-55 using convict labour) contains an artificial lake holding 21 billion gallons of water, which permits the irrigation of 100,000 acres around Stara Zagora and Kazanlâk. It has also totally submerged the ruins of **Seuthopolis** – once the capital of Seuth III, who succeeded in welding several Thracian tribes into a kingdom during the C4 BC before Philip of Macedon arrived to conquer it.

KAZANLÂK

KAZANLÂK is the capital of the rose-growing region and at its liveliest during the first half of July, when the town hosts the annual **Festival of Roses**, with folkloric displays and 'Rose-picking ritual' – basically a tourist event since the rose-crop has already been harvested during May. Should you wish to attend it's advisable to book rooms through Balkantourist, who can supply details of what's on. At other times, Kazanlâk is pretty sleepy and its attractions boil down to two sights – namely the Museum of the Roses and the Thracian tomb, both of which can be found on the town's northern outskirts.

From the railway station (or the bus terminal to the east), it's 150m up Blvd. Rozova Dolina to the main square, with the post office, an indoor market just to the west, and two **hotels**. The *Kazanlâk*, harbouring the **tourist office**, is dearer than the nearby *Roza*, or the *Zornitsa* below the Thracian tomb (see below), and the cheapest bet is the **campsite**, 5km north along the Shipka road, accessible by bus #5. However, you might as well make straight for the Thracian tomb – leave the main square by Ul. Iskra, and follow it past the smart new Cultural Centre (open 9am-12am, 1pm-6pm daily) through quiet residential suburbs to Tyulbeto Park, 10 minutes' walk or a quick ride by bus #7 or #8.

Climb the stairway behind the gates of the park up to the skeletal remains of a Turkish *türbe*, 50m to the east of which you'll find a stone-faced entrance to a replica of the famous **Thracian tomb**, open from 9am-12am, 1pm-5pm daily. (The original tomb lies nearby, but so delicate are its frescoes that only scholars with authorisation from the Ministry of Culture may enter). You approach this through a narrow *dromos* or corridor decorated by two bands of murals – one ornamented with plant and architectural motifs, the other displaying battle scenes. The floor and walls of the domed burial chamber itself are stained a deep Pompei red, while around the cupola a procession of horses and servants approach the couple for whom the tomb was built – the man seated behind a low table laden with food, holding the hand of his wife or mistress, who reposes on an elaborate throne. With its graceful composition and naturalistic details, the painting shows Hellenistic influences, although the architecture of the tomb itself – built during the C3 or C4 BC – is alien to the Greek tradition. According to Herodotus, deceased Thracian nobles were laid out for three days before a funeral feast of 'various sacrificial animals' which followed 'a short period of wailing and mourning'. After the corpse was buried or cremated, a 'tumulus of soil' was raised, and 'various competitive games' were organised, 'the biggest prize being awarded for wrestling'.

On the western edge of the park, near the Gabrovo road, stands the **Museum of the Rose Industry**, which (despite the lack of captions in foreign languages) conveys an idea of how rose jam, toothpaste, eau-de-cologne, jelly, *rosaliika* and, of course, attar of roses are produced. Bulgarians recall nostalgically how the rose industry was before modernisation, and relish the adventures of Bai Ganyu, the rascally pedlar of rose-oil and rugs invented by the C19 writer, Aleko Konstantinov.

SLIVEN, KOTEL AND THE ROUTE TO BURGAS

A sprawl of flats and red-roofed buildings, **SLIVEN** lies at the feet of mountains that once sheltered so many bands of outlaws that Bulgarians called this the 'town of the hundred voivodes' after the number of their chieftains. It's rather less notorious nowadays, and may well make a good stop off between Sofia and Burgas on the coast. There's a fair amount to see – as home town of Hadzhi Dimitâr it's on the list of revolutionary studies – and the town hosts the **Fires of Sliven Festival** (*Slivenski Ognyove*), three days of fine arts and industrial design, music and Bulgarian films, generally with a common theme.

Arriving at the railway station or southern bus terminal, take a bus up Georgi Kirkov to reach the main square in **the centre**, where a monument commemorates Dimitâr and other local heroes. Behind the ochre and white façade of the **History Museum** (6, Lenin Blvd), a collection of antique weapons testifies to one aspect of Sliven's revolutionary tradition. Pacifists offended by the artistry that local C19 gunsmiths lavished upon *shishane* rifles (one of them has over 11,500 pieces of inlay) can take comfort from the exhibits relating to the **revolution of Sliven's women**, who destroyed a convoy of uniforms as a protest against the war in March 1918. Sliven also elected a radical council similar to Samokov's 'Red Municipality', although, alas, the **Second Commune** (1921-23) was also brought down by the army and vested interests.

Whereas vineyards, tanneries and silkworms provided the impetus for a new town to rise from the ashes of the medieval one (demolished by the Turks and replaced by a garrison) during the C17-C18, Sliven's subsequent development has largely gone hand in hand with that of Bulgaria's textile industry. The country's first factory was established here in 1834 by one **Dobri Zhelyazkov**, who acquired parts and plans of looms by smuggling them home from Russia in bags of wool, and it's appropriate that the former administrative wing of Zhelyazkov's *Fabrikadjiata* now contains a **Museum of the Textile Industry**. This traces Bulgarian weaving back to ancient times, and also regularly exhibits contemporary machine-made and hand-woven textiles.

Although predominantly modern, Sliven has over 100 National Revival-style houses, some of which are undergoing conversion into rest homes for members of the arts unions. At 5, Simeon Tabakov Street, another house has been transformed into a **Museum of Nineteenth-century Town Life** – or at least, that of well-to-do families whose homes manifested the Bulgarian genius for combining wood and textiles to create beautiful interiors. Paradoxically, this class produced dozens of *haiduk* chieftains, whose outlaw bands (numbering between 15-70 members) ranged the spectrum of behavior from brutal banditry to populist chivalry.

Panayot Hitov enjoined other voivodes to 'avoid injustice' or 'you will not live long. . .there are those around who will kill you, as will we'; and an early recruit, **Hadzhi Dimitâr** (1840-1868), quit to form his own band exclusively dedicated to the fight for Bulgaria's liberation. Killed on Mt. Buzludzha near Shipka during the rebellion of 1868, Dimitâr was eulogised in a stirring poem by Hristo Botev, a verse of which is inscribed upon Botev's own memorial in Vratsa. Personal effects and photographs of these mustachioed demi-heroes can be seen in the **houses** where they were born – Dimitâr at 2, Ul. Asenova and Hitov at 7, Cherno More Street, near the Church of St Sofia.

Both can be quite tricky to locate without a town plan – possibly available from **Balkantourist** in the tall *Hotel Sliven*, at the corner of the main square and Subi Dimitrov Blvd – but it's easy to find the nearby **Deboya complex**. Originally an arsenal built for Drazha, a medieval noblewoman, it served as a caravanserai during the C18, and later as wool store, until it was totally refurbished in 1973. Vaulted and painted, and dear by Bulgarian standards, it's the smartest place to **eat** in town (try the *gyuvech*) – and the complex also contains a coffee-shop, wine-cellar and disco, which makes it the focus of **nightlife**. You can **sleep** more cheaply at the *Zora* or *Sinite Kamâni* than at the main hotel, while about 9km southwest of town there's a *campsite* with chalets near the Turkish-built **thermal baths** of SLIVENSKI BANI, accessible by bus from Sliven.

Around Sliven: the Blue Rocks, Kotel and Zheravna

At certain times of the year Sliven experiences the blast of a cold, dry *bora* blowing at over 65 feet per second, which strikes the mountains to the north of town, where the light imparts a blueish tinge to the porphyry massif known as the **Blue Rocks** or *Sinite Kamâni*. There are regular buses from town to the lower cable-car terminal, from which you can hike north to the rock formation known as 'The Ring', or ride up to the summit in 18 minutes. The latter affords passengers fine views of the plain, a distant beech forest, and the sheer slopes of Mt. Tyulbeto (topped by a TV-tower) – from where hang-gliders sometimes launch themselves in emulation of the legendary 'Sliven Icarus', who built himself wooden wings. Alternatively, by turning left outside the terminal and crossing the Dyuleva rivulet, you can climb a well-marked path up to the Ring (*Halkata*) in 20 minutes. Jaggedly arched and nearly 8m tall, the Ring is associated with several **legends**. Ancient mariners supposedly moored their boats here during the Flood, while fairy tales have it that a girl passing through will turn into a boy (or vice versa), and a couple doing so will fall in love forever. From the upper terminal you can walk to a meadow offering a panoramic view, or follow asphalted roads to the isolated Bird's Spring (*Ptichyat Izvor*) or the popular **KARANDILA** resort, which has chalets and a direct bus-link with Sliven.

Buses from Sliven also travel the 20-30km into the highlands to the northeast, where travellers can visit two old crafts centres. **ZHERAVNA** is picturesque enough to be a museum village. Surrounded by stone walls with nail-studded gates, the spacious wooden houses with their broad eaves date from the C17-C19, when Zheravna earned its living from sheep-breeding and diverse crafts. The living room ceiling of **Sava Filaret's birthplace** (nowadays a museum) is a triumph of the woodcarver's art, and colourful carpets and tufted rugs may also be seen at **Yordan Yakov's** birthplace, and the Russi Chorbadzhii house (which serves as an art gallery). **Rooms** can be found at the *Zlatna Oresha* – a group of ten walled houses on a slope slightly apart from the village.

The small town of **KOTEL** lies farther north along route 46, and takes its name ('cauldron') from the springs that bubble hereabouts. Founded by immigrants in 1545, the town was three-quarters destroyed by a conflagration in 1894, leaving a timber-framed quarter to be the subject of C20 preservation orders. All manner of artefacts and momentoes have been assembled in the Ethnographic and History museums, but the most constructive act has the state's encouragement of Kotel's traditional industry – **carpetmaking**. Local carpets (*chergi*) often have lozenge or diamond-shaped geometrical patterns, which are sometimes worked into a broken weft; and the basic colour (usually red, blue or green) determines the secondary use of scarlet, wine red, indigo, black, olive green or light blue. Tufted goathair *guberi* with simpler patterns, traditionally used as blankets, are also made here. For visitors, there are periodic demonstations at the schools of arts and crafts and instrument making, and real enthusiasts should enjoy the 8-day **courses** arranged by *Balkantourist*. You'll find a Balkantourist desk in the 2-star *Hotel Kotel* (☎ 28-65), but it's wiser to fix things up with Balkantourist in Sliven, and reserve **rooms**.

Formula-1 racing, and the route to Burgas

Bulgaria's first **Formula-1 Racing** track is currently taking shape 2km east of Sliven just off the Burgas road, although the completion date is uncertain. Whenever it opens, the complex should include Formula-1, motorcycling and karting tracks, with a motel, campsite, pool and volleyball grounds for visitors. Meanwhile, speed freaks will have to be content with the **Albena-Sliven Rally**, which normally takes place at the start of May. The course merits 4-stars from *FISA*, and details of the route can be obtained from the main offices of Balkantourist or the Shipka Travel Agency.

The majority of **trains from Sliven** aim for Karlovo or Burgas, departing from the *Zimnitsa station* (buy tickets there, or at 5, Ul. Kirkov), and offering little reason to stop anywhere **along the way to Burgas**. For the record, however, KARNOBAT is a railway junction (trains for Tolbuhin; change at Komunari for Shumen) surrounded by sheep, and known for its *Sungulare Muscatel* wine.

THE SREDNA GORA

> ...So, proudly you may gaze
> Unto the Sredna Gora, the forest's single queen,
> And hear the ring of swords, and all this song can mean...
> Pencho Slaveykov, *The Song of the Blood*

The **Sredna Gora** ('Central Range') separates the Valley of the Roses from the Maritsa Valley, stretching from the Pancharevo defile outside Sofia almost as far as Yambol on the Thracian plain. With its forests of oak and beech and numerous caves and hot springs, the region was inhabited by humans as early as the fifth millenium BC. The Thracians subsequently left a hoard of gold treasure, and the Romans a crop of ruins at **Hisarya**, but for Bulgarians, the Sredna Gora is best known as the 'land of the April Rising', an event for which **Panagyurishte** and the highly picturesque **Koprivshtitsa** will always be remembered.

Elsewhere, towns like **Stara Zagora** and **Nova Zagora** are of note mainly for their use as transport centres. Panagyurishte and Hisarya are both accessible by rail from Plovdiv; coming from the Valley of the Roses buses go from Srednogorie to Panagyurishte, and from Karlovo to Hisarya. Koprivshtitsa itself is more difficult to reach. Although there's a halt on the Sofia-Burgas line only every third train is met by buses running 12km to the village itself. If you don't want to walk, or risk waiting 8hrs for a bus, take advantage of coach excursions from Sofia or Plovdiv arranged by Balkantourist; the cost isn't extortionate.

KOPRIVSHTITSA

Seen from a distance **KOPRIVSHTITSA** looks almost too lovely to be real, its half-timbered houses nestled in a valley amid wooded hills. On closer inspection, however, the image fades. It's pretty enough, certainly, but invariably full of tourists drawn by the superb architecture and Bulgarians paying homage to a landmark in their nation's history. From the Place of the Scimitar Charge to the Street of the Counter Attack, there's hardly a part of Koprivshtitsa that isn't named for an episode or participant in the **April Rising of 1876**, launched here ahead of schedule (on April 20) when the conspirators learned that their plans had been betrayed. Capturing the Konak, the rebels dispatched *Bloody Letters* written in the blood of the first dead Turk imploring other towns to join them, and began fortifying the village while rain played havoc with their home-made gunpowder and cherry-tree cannons. As the Bashibazouks burned neighbouring towns, refugees flooded into Koprivshtitsa spreading panic and the local chorbadzhii attempted to disarm the insurgents. The rebels eventually took to the hills (where most were killed), and it's ironic that – thanks to the chorbadzhii, who bribed the Bashibazouks to spare the village – Koprivshtitsa survived unscathed to be admired by subsequent generations as a symbol of heroism.

Near the coach park and Koprivshtitsa's only non-tourist bar (full of grim-faced oldsters playing dominoes) at the northern end of Anton Ivanov, the main street, stands a large house on the corner, the **birthplace of Lyuben Karavelov** (1834-79). Educated in Moscow, the son of a butcher and sheep merchant, Karavelov organised a revolutionary Central Committee in Bucharest in 1860, and for ten years advocated armed struggle against the Turks in the columns of the émigré newspapers *Svoboda* and *Nezavisimost*. After Levski's execution, however, he repudiated direct action in favour of change through reform and education, and was ousted from the leadership of the committee by Hristo Botev. Built in several stages and surrounded by a high wall, the house contains Karavelov's personal effects and an old printing press (open Wednesday-Monday 7.30-12.30am, 1.30-5.30pm).

On the other side of Ul. Ivanov, where it curves around into April 20th Square, you'll see the **Dyado Liben Inn**, occupying the beautiful Dragilska house built in 1860. Both the restaurant upstairs and the café-aperitif bar on the ground floor are open from 12am-3pm, 7-11pm every day except Mondays. On the main square, just beyond, stands the **Apriltsi Mausoleum**, inscribed 'Let us keep the national liberty for which the heroes of the rising of 1876 fell'. Here too is the **tourist office**, which sells all-in admission tickets to Koprivshtitsa's museum-houses, and can arrange accommodation in some of the old mansions (see below).

A street running off to the west leads to the **Oslekov House**, one of the finest in Koprivshtitsa, with pillars of cypress-wood imported from Lebanon supporting the façade. Its Red Room is particularly impressive, with a wooden ceiling 80m square carved with swirling patterns and geometric motifs. One of the medallions painted on the wall shows the original, symmetrical plan of the house, never realised since Oskelov's neighbours refused to sell him the necessary ground-space. You can imagine the wealthy merchant and tax collector brooding over the rebuff while reclining on the cushioned *minder*, taking solace from his pipes and an enormous hookah. Opening hours here are the same as for Karavelov's house.

Further along, the street joins Ul. Debelyanov, which straddles a hill between two bridges and boasts some more lovely buildings. Near the Surlya Bridge, the birthplace of the poet **Dimcho Debelyanov** (nr. 6) was closed for restoration during my visit, but his grave was available for inspection in the yard of the hilltop **Church of the Holy Virgin**. There, Lazarov's statue of a seated woman recalls Debelyanov's old mother, who waited in vain for Dimcho to return from the battlefields of Greece where he was killed in 1916.

The inscription is from one of his poems: 'Delaying in a gentle dream she becomes her own child'. The church – built in 1817, partly sunken into the ground to comply with Ottoman restrictions – acquired its domed belfry at a later date, and contains icons by Zograf and the C17 *Rasho Gospel*.

On the same street, the decision to launch the uprising was taken at nr. 18, the **House of the Conspiracy**, after Turkish troops came to arrest the ringleader, **Todor Kableshkov**, whose birthplace is at the bottom of the hill. Born in 1854, he studied French in Constantinople before catching malaria and returning home, where he met Levski and began his revolutionary career. Captured near Troyan after the April Rising, he managed to kill himself with a police revolver at Gabrovo. Kableshkov's house now displays the insurgents' silk banner embroidered with the Bulgarian Lion and 'Liberty or Death!', and one of the twenty **cherry-tree cannons** lined with copper acquired by melting down rose-kettles that were secretly manufactured. Although one bore the engraved slogan 'End of the Turkish Empire, 1876', the cannons soon became a liability to the insurgents, as they tended to explode once the barrel-linings had worn away.

Near the **Bridge of the First Shot** spanning the River Byala where the uprising began stands another, striking example of Bulgarian Baroque, the **Lyutov House**, built in 1854. It's best known for its wealth of murals: palaces, temples and travel scenes splashed across the walls and alafranga (niches); wreaths, blossoms and nosegays in the Blue Room; and oval medallions adorning the ceilings. The sidestreet running southeast away from the bridge leads past the post office to Koprivshtitsa's small **bus terminal**, from where it's only a few minutes' walk to the **St Nikola Church**. Here, despite the dedication, the emphasis is on St Spiridion, whose life is told in ten medallions surrounding a figure of the saint. To the left of the church is a fountain donated by the Moravenovs, one of Koprivshtitsa's leading families in the early C18. Following the Kosovo stream down to the main street, and then walking up Ul. Dorosiev, brings you to the birthplace of another major figure in the uprising, **Georgi Benkovski** (1844-76). A tailor by profession, he made the insurgents' banner and uniforms – long jackets of white homespun and caps with the Bulgarian lion badge – and commanded a rebel band on Mt. Eledzhik, which fought its way north until it was wiped out near Teteven.

From the house on the corner, a street named after him runs up to the *Hotel Koprivshtitsa*, a source of fairly expensive **rooms**. It's better to ask about beds in one of the old mansions (see the tourist office), or, if you're offered private lodgings by local people, negotiate hard for these. Those with wheels also consider the *Hotel Barikadite*, 18km from town; take the road heading south, then the left-hand fork, and then the turn-off to the left 12km on.

During the summer months, you can sign up for eight-day **excursions** through the highlands on horseback and by cart (ask at the hotel for details), while every five years Koprivshtitsa hosts Bulgaria's largest **Folklore Festival**. Around 12,000 amateur folk-dancers, storytellers, musicians and other performers participate, and thousands of visitors come to enjoy the colourful spectacle, which takes place at the hilly Voivodenets locality near the village. Unfortunately, the next festival isn't scheduled to occur until 1991.

PANAGYURISHTE AND HISARYA

By keeping control of STRELCHA in 1876, the Turks prevented the insurgents in Koprivshtitsa from linking up with their fellows in PANAGYURISHTE – which, as the headquarters of the 4th Revolutionary Region, had been envisaged as the centre of operations. This contributed to the failure of the April Rising, and ensured that Panagyurishte remained isolated until Ottoman forces arrived from Pazardzhik and Plovdiv to set the town ablaze (hence its predominantly modern appearance nowadays). Folks arriving at the railway station in the southeastern part of town are greeted by its newer, uglier suburbs, so if first impressions mean a lot to you it's preferable to come by bus (from Srednogorie or Pazardzhik). The bus terminal is closer to the centre, and everything worth seeing lies within walking distance of the main square, which is flanked by two **hotels** (the *Oborishte* is cheapest). To the northwest, you'll find a scattering of C19 mansions in the backstreets off Rayna Knyaginya; plus the local museum, which can only muster photographs of the famous Thracian **gold treasure of Panagyurishte** discovered in 1949, since the original has gone to Sofia. North and east of the main square, enclosing a suburb, a **park** alongside the Lyuda Yana River and its tributaries provides the site for several monuments, including the *April 1876 Uprising Memorial*. A towering concrete construction, it's fairly typical of the marriage between Modernist and Socialist Realist sculpture that's produced the bizarre 1,300 Anniversary Monuments in Sofia and Shumen.

And finally, there's another monument in a wooded valley several miles north of OBORISHTE, 7km west of Panagyurishte, marking the place where leaders of the Sredna Gora underground agreed to launch the 1876 uprising on May 1st. Unfortunately, there was a spy amongst them, Nenko Stoyanov, who tipped-off the Turks about Kableshkov's group in Koprivshtitsa, and thus unwittingly precipitated the rising in April.

Hisarya

At the foot of the Sredna Gora range between Plovdiv and Karlovo stands one of the great watering-holes of antiquity, **HISARYA**. As gold treasures and other less glamorous finds in neighbouring villages have proved, the area was inhabited as long ago as 5,000 BC, and formed part of the Macedonian empire before the arrival of the Romans. But it was they who really developed Hisarya, building marble baths, aquaducts, temples and – after raids by the Goths in 251 – fortifications to protect the town, which they called *Augusta*. Subsequently an episcopal seat – renamed *Toplitsa* by Slavs under Byzantine rule – it was devastated by Crusaders, despite their appreciation of this 'fair town', and 150 years later conquered by the Turks, who restored the baths and gave it the name *Hisar* during the C16.

A short distance to the south of the railway and bus terminals, a sizeable chunk of this history confronts visitors in the form of the damaged but still imposing **fortress walls**, originally between 6-10 feet thick and defended by 43 towers. The Roman builders employed the technique of *opus mixtum*, bonding stone and brick with red mortar – hence the sobriquet *Kzhazil Kale* ('red fortress') which the Turks coined when they besieged the town in 1364.

The northern wall consists of a double rampart, but the most impressive section is the huge southern **Kamilite Gate**, so-called after the camels which once passed through it. One hundred metres west and 125m south of the Kamilite Gate are two **ruined basilicas** dating from the C5-C6, while beyond a breach in the southwestern corner of the ramparts lies a C4 **Roman tomb**, with frescoed walls, a mosaic floor and two fixed 'beds'.

Stonework, coins and other finds are displayed in the **museum** within the walls, but the town's baths are of more interest. The *Havuz* **mineral baths**, on the opposite side of Lenin Street to the museum, were particularly venerated by Roman women on account of their efficacious effects on gynaecological disorders. The other main bathing complex, *Momina Banya*, yields radioactive water recommended for liver and gastric complaints, while the produce of another spring is bottled and sold throughout Bulgaria as mineral water (*Hisar Banya*). For information on treatments and opening times, enquire at the **tourist office** at 16, Ul. Augusta. Wealthier convalescents patronise the *Hotel Hissar*; if you want more reasonably-priced **accommodation** try the hotels *Augusta*, *Balkan* or *Republika*, or the *Slaveev Dol* campsite outside town on the Plovdiv road.

THE TWO ZAGORAS

Although both are large settlements, neither Stara ('Old') nor Nova ('New') Zagora have much to recommend them beyond **railway links**. From both towns there are regular services to Burgas on the coast, while each gives lifts to Bulgaria's highland regions (Zagora can be translated as 'behind the mountain' or 'to the hills'). Riding north from Stara Zagora it's possible to change at TULOVO (for places along the Valley of the Roses) or carry on up to Gabrovo, Gorna Oryahovitsa (for Veliko Târnovo) or Ruse. Southbound trains from Stara Zagora connect with Dimitrovgrad (on the Sofia-Plovdiv-Svilengrad line), and Haskovo and Kârdzhali in the Rhodopes. Nova Zagora is chiefly useful for its trains to SIMEONOVGRAD, on the Sofia-Svilengrad line, or catching a bus southwards to Harmanli.

The second largest town on the Thracian plain after Plovdiv, **STARA ZAGORA** developed at the crossroads of two ancient trade routes, commanding a fertile area still noted for its wheat, almonds, figs and pomegranates, which Khan Krum annexed to the Bulgarian Kingdom at the beginning of the C9. Under Turkish rule it was one of the centres of the Bulgarian cultural renaissance – known as the 'city of poets' – while during the Stalinist period the large prison here achieved notoriety.

The town's grid-iron plan is comparatively modern, since most of it was burned down by the Turks in 1877 for welcoming the forces of General Gurko. Sights and useful addresses are, then, easy to find – most are situated along the north-south thoroughfare, Blvd. Ruski, or the avenues running parallel. Beyond the park to the north of the **railway station**, Stara Zagora's **hotels**, **tourist office** and bureaux selling railway and airline **tickets** (nrs.5-9) occupy opposite sides of Blvd. Lenin. Nine blocks east from here, along General Gurko, and then a right turn will take you to the **birthplace of Geo Milev**, the poet whose verses on the subject of the 1923 uprising caused his untimely death (see p.585). A C15 **Mosque** and the local **History Museum** are on the way to the extensive **park** covering the foothills of 'Doe Wood Mountain' at the northern end of town. Perfumed with lime trees and planted with diverse shrubs, it's a nice place to relax, featuring an open-air theatre and a restaurant, the *Gorski Kât*. 9km east of town, Bulgaria's largest chemical fertiliser plant sprawls over 370 acres, a depressing harbinger of **NOVA ZAGORA** – a modern satellite-town devoted to agri-business. Best get a bus out as soon as possible.

FESTIVALS

Spring
Classical music, opera etc. at RUSE during **March**. Festival of symphony music at SHUMEN during **April**. The finish of the annual *Motor Rally* at SLIVEN coincides with the town's 3-day festival (odd-numbered years only) at the beginning of **May**, whilst midway through the month GABROVO hosts its *Festival of Humour and Satire* (odd-numbered years only), and VELIKI PRESLAV its *Literary Days*.

Summer
At some point during the summer, historical pageants in the fortress, or a motor rally in the vicinity of VIDIN (odd/even-numbered years). Folklore displays, music etc. during the *Festival of the Roses* at KAZANLÂK and KARLOVO at the beginning of **June**. Concerts in the cave at MADARA throughout June and **July**. The date of SVISHTOV's festival of choral music is uncertain, but SHUMEN's festival of piano music occurs towards the end of **September**.

Autumn
Poetry-readings, films, fireworks etc. during the *Katya Popova Literary Festival* at PLEVEN in **November**.

TRAVEL DETAILS

Trains
From Bârbanovo to Gabrovo (7 daily; ½hr); Stara Zagora (2; 2-3); Tryavna (5; ¼); Tulovo (2; 1½).
From Berkovitsa to Boychinovtsi (7; 1); Mihailovgrad (7; ¾).
From Boychinovtsi to Berkovitsa (7; 1); Dimovo (6; 1¾-2); Vidin (6; 2½-3).
From Gorna Oryahovitsa to Pleven (14; 1½); Ruse (6; 2½-3); Shumen (5; 1½-3½); Sofia (6; 4½); Strazhitsa (5; ½); Târgovishte (5; ¾-2¼); Veliko Târnovo (6; ¼-1½).
From Hisarya to Plovdiv (5; 1).
From Karlovo to Burgas (4; 3¾-6); Kalofer (7; ¾); Kazanlâk (9; ¾-1½); Plovdiv (10; 1¾); Sliven (4; 1¾-3¾); Sofia (6; 2-2½).
From Kazanlâk to Burgas (4; 3); Sliven (4; 1½); Sofia (6; 3-4); Varna (2; 4-6½).
From Lovech to Levski (6; 1½); Troyan (5; 1).
From Nova Zagora to Burgas (3; 2-2¾); Simeonovgrad (5; 1¾); Yambol (9; ½).
From Pleven to Gorna Oryahovitsa (7; 1½); Levski (7; ½); Shumen (2; 4½); Sofia (14; ¾-1).

From Ruse to Gorna Oryahovitsa (8; 2-2½); Ivanovo (3; ½); Pleven (3; 3½); Samuil (5; 1¼-1¾); Sofia (5; 6½-8); Varna (3; 3½).
From Samuil to Isperih (3; ¾); Silistra (3; 2½).
From Silistra to Isperih (3; 1½); Samuil (3; 2½).
From Sliven to Burgas (4; 1¾); Karlovo (7; 2¼-3½); Kazanlâk (7; 1½); Varna (1; 4½).
From Sofia to Cherepish (7; 2); Eliseyna (7; 1½); Gorna Oryahovitsa (7; 4¼); Karlovo (6; 2-3¼); Kazanlâk (6; 2¾-3½); Lakatnik (11; 1); Lyutivbrod (7; 2); Pleven (7; 2¾-3¼); Vidin (5; 5-7); Zverino (9; 1¼-1¾).
From Stara Zagora to Burgas (3; 2½-3¾); Dimitrovgrad (3; 1-1¼); Plovdiv (4; 1½-2); Tulovo (5; ½); Varna (1; 4).
From Tolbuhin to Kardam (3; 1¼); Varna (7; 2).
From Troyan to Levski (4; 2¼); Lovech (5; 1).
From Tryavna to Tulovo (2; 1½-2).
From Veliko Târnovo to Bârbanovo (¼); Dryanovo (6; ½); Gorna Oryahovitsa

(8; ¼-½).
From Vidin to Sofia (5; 5).

Buses
From Berkovitsa to Mihailovgrad (every hour).
From Botevgrad to Pravets; Teteven; Yablanitsa (every ¾-1½hrs).
From Dimovo to Belogradchik; Rabisha (4-5 daily).
From Gabrovo to Bozhentsi; Dryanovo (hourly); Etâr (4 daily); Kazanlâk (hourly); Sevlievo (hourly); Sokolski Monastery (4 daily); Troyan (2 daily); Tryavna (every ¾hr); Veliko Târnovo (hourly).
From Gorna Oryahovitsa to Arbanasi; Veliko Târnovo (hourly).
From Hisarya to Kalofer; Karlovo (5-6 daily).
From Karlovo to Kalofer (hourly); Panagyurishte (2 daily); Pleven (1 daily); Troyan (2 daily); Veliko Târnovo (1 daily).
From Kârnare to Troyan (6-7 daily).
From Kazanlâk to Gabrovo (hourly); Haskovo (1 daily); Stara Zagora (hourly).
From Lovech to Pleven (hourly); Sevlievo (6-7 daily); Troyan (hourly).
From Mezdra to Yablanitsa (5-6 daily).
From Nova Zagora to Sliven (hourly).
From Novi Pazar to Pliska (6-7 daily).
From Pleven to Karlovo (1 daily); Lovech (hourly).
From Pravets to Etropole (4-5 daily); Srednogorie (2-3 daily).
From Razgrad to Isperih; Ruse; Shumen (hourly).
From Ruse to Shumen (every 1½hrs); Silistra (4-5 daily).
From Shumen to Burgas (2 daily); Madara (1 daily); Preslav (hourly); Ruse (every 1½); Varna (every 2hrs).
From Silistra to Tolbuhin (4-5 daily).
From Sliven to Kotel; Zheravna (3-4 daily).
From Srednogorie to Panagyurishte (hourly).
From Târgovishte to Preslav (hourly).

From Teteven to Sofia (2-3 daily); Yablanitsa (every ¾hr).
From Tolbuhin to Albena (4-5 daily); Balchik (5-6 daily).
From Troyan to Kârnare (6-7 daily); Lovech (hourly); Oreshak and Troyan Monastery (5-6 daily).
From Veliko Târnovo to Arbanasi (every 30 mins); Gabrovo; Gorna Oryahovitsa (hourly); Târgovishte (6-7 daily).
From Vratsa to the Ledenika Cave (3-4 daily); Mihailovgrad (hourly).
From Yablanitsa to Teteven (every ¾hr).

Flights
From Gorna Oryahovitsa to Sofia (2 daily; ¾hr).
From Ruse to Sofia (1-2; ¾).
From Silistra to Sofia (2; 1).
From Târgovishte to Sofia (2-3; ¾).
From Vidin to Sofia (1-2; ½).

Hydrofoils
From Ruse to Silistra (1 daily; 2¼hrs); Vidin (3; 5¾-6¼).
From Silistra to Ruse (1; 2½).
From Vidin to Ruse (3; 5¾-6¼).

Ferries
From Vidin to Calafat in ROMANIA (every hour between 7am-7.30pm).

International trains
From Kardam to Negru Vodă (3 daily; ¼hr).
From Ruse to Braşov (1 daily; 8hrs); Bratislava (2; 20¼-21¾); Bucharest (4; 3); Budapest (3; 17-20); Dresden (1; 34¾); Kiev (3; 25½-27); Moscow (3; 32-39); Prague (2; 28-30); Suceava (1; 9); Warsaw (2; 31-34).
From Tolbuhin to Bratislava (1 daily; 28¾hrs); Budapest (1; 25); Buzău (2; 6-8); Dresden (1; 40); Kiev (1; 27¾); Moscow (1; 40); Prague (1; 35); Suceava (1; 11).

Arbanasi	Арбанаси
Belogradchik	Белоградчик
Berkovitsa	Берковица
Botevgrad	Ботевград
Bozhentsi	Боженци
Byala	Бяла
Cherven Bryag	Червен Бряг
Dryanovo	Дряаново
Etâr	Етър

Etropole	Етрополе
Gabrovo	Габрово
Gigen	Гиген
Gorna Oryahovitsa	Горна Оряховица
Hisarya	Хисаря
Kalofer	Калофер
Kardam	Кардам
Karlovo	Карлово
Kazanlâk	Казанлък
Kilifarevo	Килифарево
Koprivshtitsa	Копривщица
Kotel	Котел
Kozlodui	Козлодуй
Lakatnik	Лакатник
Lom	Лом
Lovech	Ловеч
Madara	Мадара
Mezdra	Мездра
Mihailovgrad	Михайловград
Nikopol	Никопол
Nova Zagora	Нова Загора
Novi Pazar	Нови Пазар
Oryahovo	Оряхово
Panagyurishte	Панагюрище
Pleven	Плевен
Pliska	Плиска
Pravets	Правец
Preslav	Преслав
Razgrad	Разград
Ruse	Русе
Shipka Pass	Шипченска Проход
Shumen	Шумен
Silistra	Силистра
Silven	Сливен
Stara Zagora	Стара Загора
Sveshtari	Свещари
Svishtov	Свищов
Târgovishte	Търговище
Teteven	Тетевен
Tolbuhin	Толбухин
Troyan	Троян
Tryavna	Трявна
Veliko Târnovo	Велико Търново
Vidin	Видин
Vratsa	Враца
Yablanitsa	Ябланица
Zheravna	Жеравна

Chapter fifteen

THE RHODOPES AND THE PLAIN OF THRACE

Few parts of Bulgaria are as closely associated with antiquity as **the Rhodopes and the Plain of Thrace**. If the Balkan range was the cradle of the Bulgar state, the fertile plain between the Sredna Gora and the Rhodope Mountains was the heartland of the Thracians. This magnet drew conquerors like Philip of Macedon and the Romans, whose legacy to the present consists of graceful ruins that embellish **Plovdiv** – largest city of the region and, really, an unmissable stop. Most enduring was the influence of the Turks, whose descendants still inhabit the region around **Kârdzhali**, while the mosques and bridges built by their forebears constitute the chief sights of **Pazardzhik**, **Haskovo**, **Harmanli** and **Svilengrad**, strung out along the route between Sofia and Istanbul, nowadays busy with convoys of Turkish *gastarbieter* bound for Germany or Turkey.

Also here is the **Bachkovo Monastery** and small towns like **Shiroka Lâka** and **Batak**, whose fortified houses testify to the insecurity of life in the old days, when bandits and Muslim zealots marauded through the Rhodopes. The spa-town of **Velingrad** and **Pamporovo**, Bulgaria's premier ski resort, attract thousands of tourists, but otherwise foreigners rarely venture into the Rhodopes, where poor roads, an absence of hotels and the restrictions in force within *granitsen zones* form an effective deterrent.

The Thracians

Archaeologists are still antedating the genesis of the *Traki*, as Bulgarians call the **Thracians**, and the hypothesis that their culture began to emerge during the third millenium BC could well be revised in the light of future discoveries. However, unlike other 'bedrock peoples' of the Balkans (the Dacians or Illyrians), quite a lot is known about them and the way they lived: the Thracians were described in some detail by the chroniclers of antiquity, starting with Herodotus during the C5 BC. His estimate that their population was 'second only to the Indians' was almost certainly an exaggeration, but his account of the Thracians' lifestyle has largely been confirmed by archaeology.

Farmers of wheat, also engaged in rearing livestock – Homer described their land as 'the mother of sheep, heavy of fleece' – they developed a complex society of tribes which began to coalesce into miniature states around 460 BC. Polygamous and slave-owning, with a multitude of deities to whom they sacrificed animals, the Thracians dyed their hair and painted their bodies.

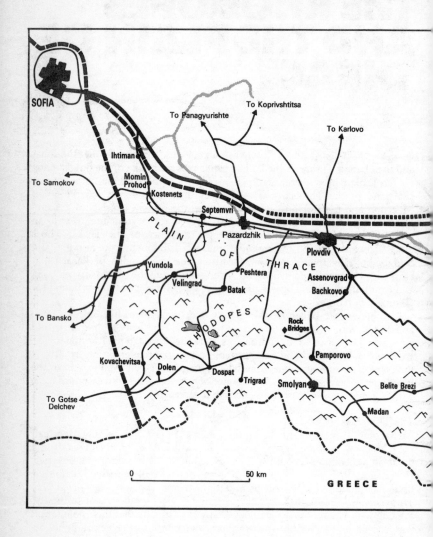

To Panagyurishte
To Koprivshtitsa
To Karlovo

SOFIA

Ihtiman

To Samokov

Momin
Prohod
Kostenets

Septemvri

PLAIN

Pazardzhik

OF

Plovdiv

Yundola

T H R A C E

Peshtera

Assenovgrad

Velingrad

Batak

Bachkovo

To Bansko

R H O D O P E S

Rock
Bridges

Kovachevitsa

Dolen

Pamporovo

Dospat

Trigrad

Smolyan

Belite Brezi

To Gotse
Delchev

Madan

0   50 km

GREECE

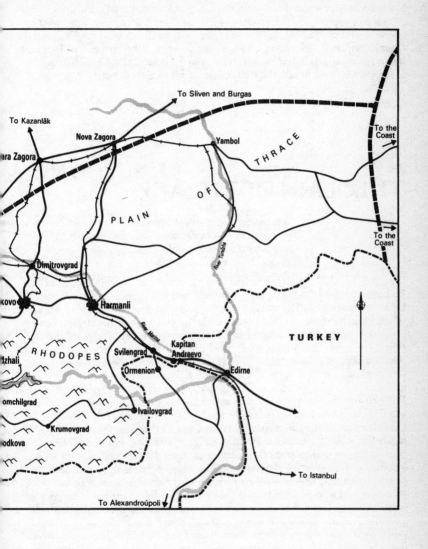

They wore clothes of flax, furs and leather, and for enjoyment drank beer and wine and got stoned on hemp by sealing themselves within smoke-filled huts. Judging by tombs unearthed at Mezek, Sveshtari and Kazanlâk, and magnificent treasures (now displayed in Sofia and Varna), they were an advanced people; indeed Herodotus believed that 'if they were only ruled by one man and could only agree among themselves, they would be the greatest among nations'. However, rather than unite, the tribes and mini-states frequently sided with invaders, which allowed the Greeks, then the Macedonians, and finally the Romans, to subjugate them utterly.

THE PLAIN OF THRACE

> Where, with head uplifted proudly,
> Towereth Balkan's lordly chain;
> Where Maritza floweth softly
> Through the level Thracian plain

Watered by the Maritsa and numerous tributaries descending from the Balkans and the Rhodopes, the **Thracian Plain** has been a fertile, productive land since antiquity. The ancient Greeks called it Upper or Northern Thrace, to distinguish it from the lush plains on the far side of the Rhodopes in Greece and Turkey, collectively known as Thrace after the tribes who lived there. A Bulgarian legend has it that when God divided the world amongst different peoples, he forgot them until a delegation of Bulgars mentioned the oversight. God replied, 'There is nothing left, but since you are hard-working folk I will give you a portion of Paradise'. And so the Bulgars received part of Thrace. The E80, which now links Istanbul and Sofia, essentially follows the course of the Roman Serdica-Constantinople road, past towns formerly ruled by the Ottomans for so long that foreigners used to call this 'European Turkey'. Of these, the most important is **Plovdiv**, Bulgaria's second city, which bids fair rival to the capital in several respects and never fails to charm with its old quarter – a wonderful melange of Renaissance mansions, mosques and classical remains, spread over three hills. On a smaller scale, the laid-back ambience and eclectic architecture that make Plovdiv so agreeable is repeated in three towns along the same route – **Pazardzhik**, **Haskovo** and **Harmanli**.

Communications along this route are all fairly straightforward. Roughly every hour, trains depart **from Sofia** bound for Plovdiv – a journey which takes between 2-2½hrs by express (*bârz*), or 3-3½hrs if you use *pâtnishki* services. By road, Plovdiv is 2hrs from Sofia, and is easily hitched. **From other parts of Bulgaria**, branch rail lines and buses connect Karlovo and Panagyurishte with Plovdiv; while travellers coming from Ruse, Gabrovo or Varna will probably need to change trains at Stara Zagora. Coming **from**

Istanbul, you'll cross by road at Kapitan Andreevo (see p.661), or by railway at Svilengrad; the *Istanbul Express* arrives in Plovdiv at around 8.30am, the off-season *Istanbul-Hellas* 3hrs earlier.

SOFIA TO PLOVDIV

The first town, as such, along the E80 from Sofia is **IHTIMAN**, set amidst beautiful scenery, with a hotel in the centre and a costlier motel out on the highway. Lentil dishes are the speciality of the *Leshta Han* restaurant 9km farther along the highway (near which there's a *campsite* with chalets), while about 16km on you'll hit **KOSTENETS**, a small town encroaching on **Momin Prohod**, or the 'Virgin's Pass'. This gets its name from the daughter of a rich merchant of Philppopolis, whose long-standing paralysis vanished when she bathed in the **mineral springs** here – claimed to be the 25th most radioactive in the world, and nowadays used to treat diabetes, ulcers, rheumatism and skin diseases. **BELOVO**, the next town, like Kostenets a stop for most express trains, has a *campsite* and a mineral swimming pool situated 5km to the east beside the highway. From the next proper town, **SEMPTEMVRI**, you can to catch trains to Velingrad in the western Rhodopes (p.664) and Bansko in the Pirin Mountains (p.570).

But it's really only **PAZARDZHIK** that merits a stopover. A market town founded by Crimean Tartars during the reign of Sultan Bajazet II, this was the site of the third largest fair in the Ottoman empire, capable of stabling 3,000 horses and 2,000 camels in its caravanserai, and until the late C19 commercially more important than Sofia. Many of the Bulgar artisans who began settling here towards the end of the C16 adopted Islam, and Pazardzhik remained a predominantly Turkish and Muslim town until comparatively recently. In 1971, the state's policy of 'assimilation' by foisting 'approved' names on Muslims provoked outbursts of rioting (reportedly, two Party officials were murdered), followed by a police crackdown on the Turkish and *Pomak* (Bulgarian Muslim) communities. But if tension still remains it's unlikely to be apparent to casual travellers. The evening promenade has all the relaxed good humour of smalltown Bulgaria, and buildings are decked out in grapevines, giving Pazardzhik an abundant, welcoming feel.

Ul. Deveti Septemvri is the main drag through **the centre**, at one end of which stands Pazardzhik's **Cathedral of the Virgin** (*Sv. Bogoroditsa*). Built in 1837 of pink stone, it's an example of the National Revival style applied to church architecture, partly sunk beneath street level to comply with the Ottoman restrictions on Christian places of worship. Its walnut iconostasis is perhaps the finest product of the C19 School of Debâr, whose craftsmen endeavoured to show the psychological relationships between human figures rather than fill the icon screen with plant and zoomorphic motifs in the manner of the Samokov woodcarvers.

Zahari Zograf aside, Bulgaria's most famous C19 painter was probably **Stanislav Dospevski** (1826-76), who lived and worked at 50, Dimitrov Boulevard. Born in Pazardzhik and educated at the Academy of Fine Art in St Petersburg, Dospevski drew extensively during visits to Odessa and Constantinople, but is best remembered for his icons, portraits and murals, several of which decorate the walls of the house. A participant in the April Rising, he was flung into the dungeons of Constantinople and died before Bulgaria's liberation.

Aside from some fine C19 mansions along and around Ul. Benkovski, the former **synagogue** at 5, Ul. Asen Zlatarov nearby, with its **History Museum** and an elaborately-carved sunburst ceiling, and the C17 *Kurshum* or **Bullet Mosque**, built in 1667, which stands beyond Blvd. Lenin and the park, there's not much else to see. Town plans should be available at the 2-star **hotel** *Trakiya*, on Red Square, which has a restaurant, **nightclub** and currency exchange bureau, or at **tourist office** (5, Ul. 2. Yanuari). On the Sofia road, there's also a **campsite**, *Polski Borovets*. From the northwestern corner of the park, a street leads towards the terminal, from which **buses run to Peshtera and Batak** in the Rhodopes (p.664) and **to Panagyurishte** (p.638) in the Sredna Gora. Though it's quite feasible to buy them at the station, **railway tickets** may also be purchased from the BDZh office (5, Ul. Esperanto).

The road **between Pazardzhik and Plovdiv** runs 'straight as perhaps the Romans had built it' across the widening plain beside the River Maritsa, flanked by acres of fruit trees bearing apples, plums and pears. Bulgarians told me that by custom, passers-by may pick fruit from roadside orchards providing they eat it on the spot, but removing any constitutes theft in the eyes of the law. 27km east of Pazardzhik, the highway passes the *Maritsa motel-campsite* complex, followed shortly by *Trakiya campsite*, and then the northern suburbs of Plovdiv.

PLOVDIV

Lucian the Greek called **PLOVDIV** 'the biggest and most beautiful of all towns' in Thrace; he might have added 'and Bulgaria', for the country's second largest city (pop. 360,000) is one of its most attractive and vibrant centres – and, arguably, has more to recommend it than Sofia. Certainly, there's plenty to see. The old town embodies Plovdiv's long and varied history – Thracian fortifications subsumed by Macedonian masonry, overlaid with Byzantine walls, and by great timber-framed mansions erected during the Bulgarian renaissance, symbolically looking down upon the derelict Ottoman mosques and artisans' dwellings of the lower town. But Plovdiv isn't merely a parade of antiquities: the city's arts festivals and trade fairs rival Sofia's in number, and its restaurants and promenade put the capital's nightlife to shame.

Points of arrival and places to stay

Driving towards Plovdiv from Sofia or Svilengrad, you'll pass *Trakiya* or *Chaya* campsite before entering the northern suburbs, from where the most obvious route into the centre takes you within sight of **Balkantourist** at 34, Moskva Blvd. (☎ 5-38-48). Although staff can arrange **private rooms** during the second half of September (when the Trade Fair inflates the price of lodgings), their disregard for non-business-travellers means that you might well gain nothing but a map by coming here. Should you arrive at the main railway station (*Tsentralna Gara*) or one of the nearby bus terminals, it's probably wiser to make straight for the centre – either by walking or catching a #2 trolleybus from Blvd. Botev up Georgi Dimitrov, the main thoroughfare. Walk westwards to Ul. Vasil Kolarov, where you'll find the *Republika* and *Bâlgaria* hotels. The former has the cheapest rooms in town but although worth a try normally won't take Western guests; the latter, like the 2-star *Leipzig*, charges 15-20 leva per head and is often full throughout late August and September. Vacancies are likelier at deluxe establishments such as the *Trimontsium*, *Leningrad-Park* or *Novotel-Plovdiv*, where you'll pay 100 leva a night; or at one of the **campsites**, which also rent 2-person **bungalows** for 25 leva. The *Trakiya* site is easiest to reach, by #23 bus from the stop near the old town tunnel entrance, or a more frequent #4 to the filling station 500m back along the highway.

Central Plovdiv

Central Plovdiv revolves around the large **Tsentralen** square, dominated by the ponderously Stalinist *Hotel Trimontsium*, whose restaurant-garden with its brass lamps has a faded thirties ambience. Groups of diners vociferously toast each other or sit in scowling silence, whilst couples dance to violin music despite the disco that operates most nights downstairs. During the hotel's construction, remnants of the Roman residential district were discovered – you'll see the foundations of dwellings and courses of syenite paving slabs in a kind of pit excavated behind the **post office** across the square.

On fine evenings, citizens gather in **Freedom Park** to socialise and admire the play of fountains and coloured lights known as the '**Water Music**', whose soundtrack blends classical and Bulgarian music, tunes from the Third World and the Socialist bloc, and Western pop. During daytime, the park marks the tail end of **the promenade**, which brings hundreds of people onto Ulitsa Kolarov around noon and the close of the working day. Kolarov is lined with shops and cinemas, and bars with terraces from which folk watch life go by (*Kamenitsa*, opposite the *Hotel Bâlgaria*, is dearer than most, but excellent). Walking up the mainstreet, you'll catch glimpses of Sahat Tepé and the larger Hill of the Liberators to the west (p.656), while to your right, Gavril Genov and Stanislav Dospevski Street lead up past the lovely Church of Sveta Marina into the old quarter, which looms above the rooftops of the lower town.

Further north, Vasil Kolarov gives onto the arresting **19 Noemvri Square** (also known as Pl. Stamboliiski), surrounded by small cafés packed with students, whiskery elders and corpulent bon viveurs. The **ruins of a Roman stadium**, visible in a pit beneath the square, are but a paltry fragment of the original, horseshoe-shaped arena where the Alexandrine Games were held during the C2-C3: up to 30,000 spectators watched chariot-races, wrestling, athletics and other events from the marble stands which once lined the slopes of the neighbouring heights.

Among the variously styled buildings around here, the 'Friday' or **Dzhumaiya Mosque**, with its diamond-patterned minaret and lead-sheathed domes, steals the show. Its thick walls and the configuration of the prayer hall (divided by 4 columns into 9 squares) are typical of the so-called 'popular

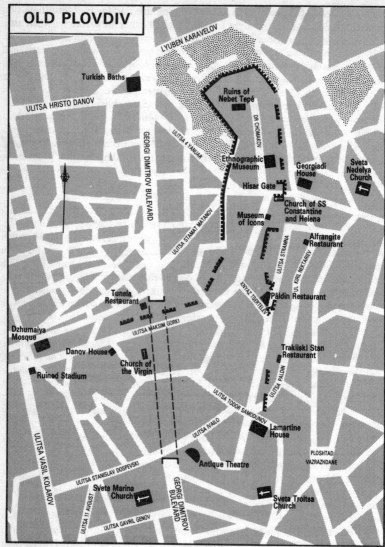

OLD PLOVDIV

LYUBEN KARAVELOV

Turkish Baths

ULITSA HRISTO DANOV

GEORGI DIMITROV BULEVARD

ULITSA 4 YANUAR

DR CHOMAKOV

Ruins of
Nebet Tepé

Ethnographic
Museum

Georgiadi
House

Sveta
Nedelya
Church

Hisar Gate

ULITSA STAMAT MATANOV

Church of SS
Constantine
and Helena

Museum
of Icons

ULITSA STRAMNA

UL. KIRIL NEKTAREV

Alfrangite
Restaurant

Tunela
Restaurant

KNYAZ TSERTELE

Pâldin Restaurant

ULITSA MAKSIM GORKI

Dzhumaiya
Mosque

Danov House

Trakiiski Stan
Restaurant

ULITSA PALDIN

Church of
the Virgin

Ruined Stadium

ULITSA TODOR SAMODUNOV

ULITSA IVAILO

Lamartine
House

ULITSA VASIL KOLAROV

PLOSHTAD
VAZRAZHDANE

Antique Theatre

ULITSA STANISLAV DOSPEVSKI

Sveta Marina
Church

GEORGI DIMITROV BULEVARD

Sveta Troitsa
Church

ULITSA 11 AVGUST

ULITSA GAVRIL GENOV

mosques' of the C14-C15, although its believed that the Dzhumaiya Mosque might actually date back to the reign of Sultan Murad II (1359-85). During our visit it was 'undergoing restoration' and, like the Imaret Mosque near the river, had obviously been shut for some time. But hopefully it should now be open for visitors to admire the fountain, floral motifs, and medallions bearing Koranic texts that reportedly adorn its interior. A plaque on the western wall commemorates the five Communists shot here in 1919, and Vasil Kolarov often spoke to the citizenry from the steps nearby.

This part of town has quite a few pokey brick dwellings, built above workshops during the twilight of Ottoman rule, and the street between the mosque and the river (currently named Ul. Raiko Daskalov) has been Plovdiv's commercial hub since at least the C16, when Chelebi counted 880 shops raised 'storey above storey', not to mention the 300 or so within the bazaar which stood upon the site now occupied by the Trade Fair. You won't find real bazaars, nor the finery that used to be sold in the **market** anymore, but it's a nice experience to wander along the street, shaded by red awnings and dusty foliage.

Near the river are a number of further relics of Turkish rule, all closed for *remont* during our visit. With an eye for leaden domes and sturdy masonry, you can identify the *Chifte Hamam* as an original **Turkish bath**, but you don't have to be an expert to recognise the **Imaret Mosque**. Zigzag brickwork gives the minaret a corkscrew twist, jazzing up the ponderous bulk of the building, which a frieze of 'sawtoothed' bricks and a row of keel arches with tie beams fails to do. Built on Sultan Bajazet's orders in 1444, it contains the tomb of Gazi Shahabedin Pasha, and got its name from the pilgrims' hostel (*imaret*) that formerly stood nearby. Should you find the mosque still closed and lacking signs (apart from notices) that *remont* is underway, the explanation probably lies on p.662 – although the whole issue of what's happening to Muslims in Bulgaria is clouded by mystery and disinformation. For example, after reports in the Western press that the 'name-changing' campaign had driven the *Mufti* of Plovdiv to suicide, he personally denounced them at a press conference in Sofia and asserted that Bulgarian Muslims – contrary to allegations abroad – were not victims of persecution.

Opposite Milenkov's surreal monument to the union of 1885 on Pl. Sâedinenie, more than 15,000 exhibits await inspection in the **Archaeological Museum** (9am-12.30am, 2.30pm-5.30pm/Friday 2pm-5pm/closed Monday). For many years, the star attraction has been the magnificent nine-piece **gold treasure of Panagyurishte**, consisting of an amphora, four rhytons, three jugs and a phial, all beautifully worked by Thracian goldsmiths during the C3 BC; but these may by now have been claimed by Sofia's National History Museum, in which case visitors will have to content themselves with viewing copies of the originals. The **Natural History Museum**, five minutes' walk away at 34, Ul. General Zaimov, isn't particularly interesting, so if you haven't already made a beeline for it, it's better to head back towards the old town.

The old town

With its cobbled streets and orieled mansions covering three hills (hence the town's Roman name, *Trimontium*), Plovdiv's old quarter is a painter's dream and a cartographer's nightmare. Attempting to follow – let alone describe – an itinerary is impractical given the topography and the numerous **approaches**, each leading to a different point in the old quarter. Glimpses of ornate façades or interiors tempt visitors to stray down an alleyway, or into a courtyard – and on the whole, that's much the best way to see the area.

Starting from Ul. Stanislav Dospevski, beyond the Sveta Marina Church (p.653), or the point where Blvd. Dimitrov enters the tunnel beneath the hill, you can climb a stairway to the **Antique Theatre**, whose stands provide a wonderful view of Plovdiv, and the **classical plays** that are staged here during

May, June and September. These imposing ruins are practically the only remains of an acropolis which the Romans built when they raised Trimontium from the position of a vassal town to that of provincial capital during the C2. The acropolis, like the residential districts below, was devastated by Kiva's Goths in 251, and later used as building material when the town revived.

Blackened **fortress walls** dating from Byzantine times can be seen around streets like Knyaz Tsertelov and Maksim Gorki, sometimes incorporated into the dozens of **National Revival-style houses** that are Plovdiv's speciality. Typically, these rest upon an incline and expand with each storey by means of timber-framed *oriels* – cleverly resolving the problem posed by the scarcity of ground-space and the C19 merchants who demanded roomy interiors. The most prominent oriel on the façade usually denotes the grand reception room inside, while the sides of the upper storeys sometimes feature *blind oriels* containing kitchen niches or cupboards. Outside and inside, the walls are frequently decorated with niches, floral motifs or false columns painted in the style known as *alafranga*, executed by itinerant artists.

At the corner of Knyaz Tsertelov and Todor Samodumov stands a large buff-coloured mansion with dozens of windows and sturdy ribs supporting the oriels. Known as the **Lamartine House** after the French poet who stayed in 1833, writing *Voyage en l'Orient* and recovering from the cholera that killed his daughter in Constantinople, it now contains a small museum, open Sundays, Mondays and Tuesdays (3pm-6pm) only, in deference to the families that still live there. An idea of the former opulence of these mansions can be gained from the interiors of the *Pâldin* (3, Knyaz Tsertelov) and *Alafrangite* (17, Ul. Kiril Nektariev) **restaurants** – but you're expected to order something whilst admiring the decor. For ornate façades, few houses can match number *15, Kiril Nektariev Street*, whose oriel, windows and cornices are embellished with swags, medallions and intricate tracery in a vivid shade of blue. Although it's not open to the public, nr.21, now the **House of the People's Artists**, sometimes is.

It's the structure rather than ornamentation that makes the **Georgiadi House** (1, Ul. Starinna) so remarkable: the architect has combined 'box' oriels with bay windows on a monumental scale. Originally built for a rich Turk in 1846-8, the mansion contains a gallery where musicians once played, plus various salons nowadays occupied by the **Museum of National Liberation** (9.30am-12.30am, 2pm-5pm, closed Tuesdays). Pride of place is given to replicas of the bell that tolled and a cannon that fired during the April Rising, when the Bashibazouks hung Plovdiv's streets with corpses that the population were forbidden to bury. For her relief-work, Britain's Lady Strangord has a street named after her and her picture in the museum; Disraeli, on the other hand, is execrated for condoning the atrocities, and ensuring that one third of newly-liberated Bulgaria was returned to the Turks in the form of Eastern Roumelia*.

---

*The Berlin Treaty (1878) made this province Ottoman territory administered by a 'Christian Governor-General', but the inhabitants – particularly the citizens of Plovdiv, Eastern Roumelia's 'capital' – naturally wanted union (*edinstvo*) with the rest of Bulgaria, which was finally attained in 1885.

You'll need an invitation to visit the *Nedkovich House* next door, but no urging to make for the foreboding **Hisar Gate** just uphill, which has been rebuilt countless times since Philip of Macedon had it raised to form the citadel's eastern portal. The alleyway running off between the Georgiadi House and the *Hisar Kapiya* leads down to several **craft workshops** and many humbler dwellings that have yet to be renovated despite their *obraztsov dom* (listed) status; the first stretch is overhung by four triangular oriels, painted black with a yellow trim, which protrude from the rear of Plovdiv's most photographed building – the **Kouyoumdjioglou House**. This, still known after the Turk who commissioned it in 1847, graces a garden which you enter from Dr Chomakov Street (9am-12am, 1.30pm-5.30pm; Friday mornings only; closed Mondays), and contrives to be symmetrical – a characteristic that distinguishes certain Plovdiv houses from most other National Revival buildings. Like the Georgiadi House, it was built by Hadzhi Georgi of Constantinople, who combined Baroque and native folk motifs in the richly decorated façade, with its undulating pediment copying the line of the *kolbitsa* or carrying-yoke. Now an **Ethnographic Museum**, the mansion's lower rooms display a mundane tool collection partly redeemed by the inclusion of a rose-still and a splendid oil painting of Plovdiv streetlife during the C19 – but upstairs lies a visual feast. The elegant rooms opening off the grand reception hall, with its rosette-and-sunburst ceiling, are furnished with objects reflecting the chorbadzhii's taste for Viennese and French Baroque, and filled with showcases of sumptuous jewellery (the paste-gem-encrusted silver belt clasps are particularly lovely) and traditional Rhodopi costumes, worn by wealthy women and peasants of both sexes, respectively. During June and September, **chamber music** can be heard in the courtyard.

By the time you visit Plovdiv, the **ruined Nebet Tepé Citadel** should be accessible and have appreciable structures where I saw pits and abundant rubble – perhaps even a small museum, for the site is an archaeologically rich one. Fortified by the Thracian Odrysae tribe as early as the C5 BC, the hilltop and the settlement of *Eumolpios*, below, were the beginnings of modern Plovdiv, captured by Philip of Macedon in 342 BC, who ordered the former rebuilt in tandem with the new town modestly named *Philippopolis* – which his son, Alexander 'the Great', abandoned in search of new conquests in Asia. Over the following centuries, the inhabitants must have often resorted to the secret **tunnel** linking Nebet Tepé with the riverbank, as the town and citadel were sacked by Romans, Slavs, Bulgars, Byzantium and the Ottoman empire (to name but a few), most of whom stayed on to become threads in the skein of Plovdiv's history.

Christianity, introduced by the Romans, has been another thread, and there are several **churches** in and around the old quarter. The best of them, **Sveta Marina** (entered from Dospevski or Genov Street), has boldly-coloured murals beneath its porch and beguiling devils, storks and other creatures peeping out from wooden foliage of its intricate iconostasis. The domeless **Church of the Virgin** is less remarkable, but **SS Constantine and Helena** – farther up the road near the former site of the *Kurshum Han* caravanserai – contains a fine gilt iconostasis by Ivan Pashkula, partly decorated by Zahari Zograf, whose work also appears in the **Museum of Icons** (open 9.30am-12.30am, 2pm-6pm,

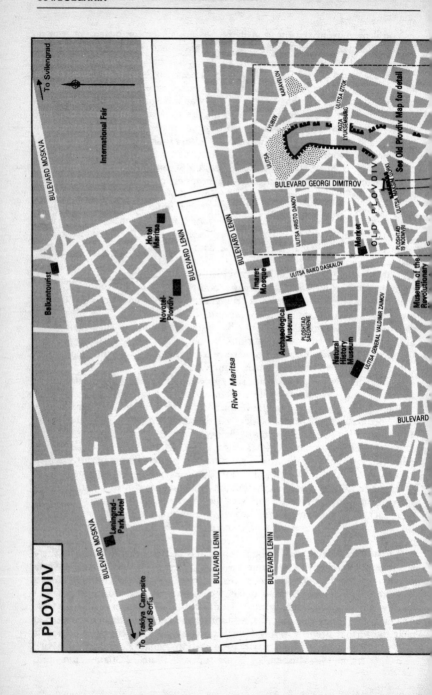

PLOVDIV

To Svilengrad

BULEVARD MOSKVIA

International Fair

Hotel Maritsa

BULEVARD LENIN

Balkantourist

Novotel-Plovdiv

BULEVARD LENIN

River Maritsa

Leningrad-Park Hotel

BULEVARD MOSKVIA

To Trakiya Campsite and Sofia

BULEVARD LENIN

BULEVARD LENIN

KARAVELOV

ULITSA IZTOK

LYUBEN

ULITSA

ROZA LYUKSEMBURG

ULITSA MAKSIM GORKI

See Old Plovdiv Map for detail

BULEVARD GEORGI DIMITROV

OLD PLOVDIV

ULITSA HRISTO DANOV

Market

PLOSHTAD 19 NOEMVRI

ULITSA RAIKO DASKALOV

Imaret Mosque

Archaeological Museum

PLOSHTAD SAEDINENIE

Natural History Museum

ULITSA GENERAL VLADIMIR ZAIMOV

Museum of the Revolutionary

BULEVARD

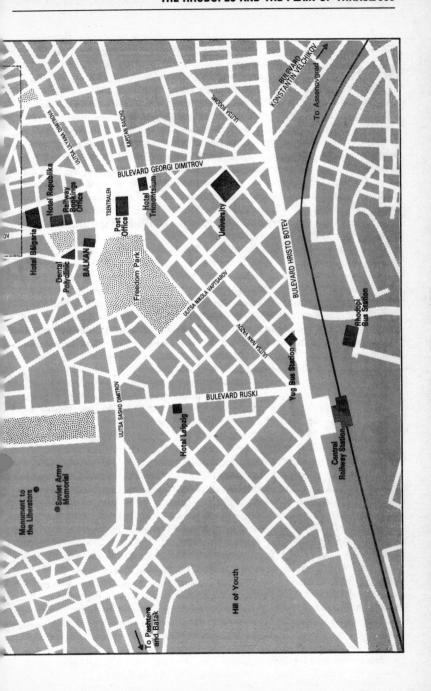

Tuesday-Sunday) next door. Illuminated manuscripts and volumes are exhibited in the old *Danov House*, now a **Museum of Bulgarian Printing**.

The Fair – and other parts of town

A trade centre of long standing, Plovdiv became Bulgaria's principal marketplace during the 1870s, when the railway between Europe and Istanbul was completed and the great annual fair held at Uzundzhovo since the C16 was moved here. Plovdiv's first international trade fair (1892) was a rather homespun affair – a man from Aitos proposed to show his hunting dogs, while Bohemia exhibited beehives – but since 1933 the event has gone from strength to strength, and nowadays claims to be the largest of its kind in the Balkans. There are actually two annual **fairs**: the spring event, devoted to consumer goods in early May, and the larger autumn industrial fair, during the second half of September, both held at the complex on the north bank of the river. Members of the public are free to come along, and there's a special bus service laid on between the railway station and the fairground.

As well as the three hills covered by the old town, there are three more heights ranged across the southwestern quarter of the city. The one nearest to the centre – officially Vasil Kolarov Hill, though many locals still call it **Sahat Tepé** – provides a great view of Plovdiv, and the site for what some believe is the oldest **Clock Tower** in Eastern Europe, restored by the Turks 'with divine blessings' in 1809, with an inscription enjoining visitors to 'look upon' it 'and admire!'. From here one can gaze levelly across to **'Alyosha'** (the nickname for this monument to the Red Army) on the neighbouring **Hill of the Liberators**, which also has a pyramidical memorial to the liberators of 1878 on a lower peak. A Thracian temple dedicated to Apollo once stood here, while during the 1950s the Party honoured its demi-god by proclaiming this 'Stalin Hill' (although locals continued calling it *Bunardzhika*, 'Hill of the Crystal Springs'). Further to the southwest lies the **Hill of Youth** (*Hâlm na Mladezhta*), the largest and most park-like of the three.

On the way to Sahat Tepé, you can visit the **Museum of the Revolutionary Movement** (14, Ul. Angel Bukoreshtliev; 9am-12am, 2pm-6pm, Friday 2pm-6pm) to get some idea about local C19 guilds (*lonzhi*), the *Rabotnik* cooperative and the shortlived Commune of 1919. The Party is justly proud of these traditions, and of the social and economic progress made since 1949 (the subject of a **Museum of Socialist Construction**; 47, Ul. Vazov), but certain things have been consigned to the memory-hole – for example, the camp for women political prisoners that was established beside the Maritsa after the Communists gained power.

Since she never lived to see the liberation, who knows whether such expedients would have seemed justified to **Lilyana Dimitrova**, the local partisan heroine after whom one of Plovdiv's thoroughfares is named. Radicalised during her late teens, Dimitrova was exiled twice for militancy by the age of 22, and after her third arrest was sent to the St Nicholas women's concentration camp in the Rhodope Mountains. Two years later she assumed control of the regional Communist underground and temporarily evaded capture by hiding in a loft-full of sheepskins on Lavele Street – finally perishing after an 11-hour gun-battle with the police on July 27 1944, which ensured her inclusion in Plovdiv's Pantheon of the Immortals.

Dimitrova Street itself marks the southern edge of the **Gypsy quarter**, a shantytown destined for demolition if it hasn't already gone. Between here and the Three Hills, there's a hybrid sector of old dwellings and postwar flats with workshops tucked away in the backstreets, and a small open-air **fruit and vegetable market** on Pl. Vâzrazhdane. How long such pockets of old Plovdiv will remain is anybody's guess, since the trend is towards relocating residents in the **high-rise suburbs** – remarkably law-abiding and neighbourly places notwithstanding the ill-lit, rubbish-strewn wastelands around the blocks.

Practicalities

Eating out and goings-on

The **restaurants**, *Alafrangite* (☎ 22-98-09), *Pâldin* and *Trakiiski Stan* (☎ 22-45-10) all serve good Bulgar nosh in elegant surroundings (sometimes accompanied by a band) – if you can afford it, well worth it. A meal and drinks costs about the same at the *Hotel Trimontsium*, where service is slower, and restaurants in the *Leningrad-Park* and *Moskva* are blandly 'international' like the rather more expensive *Benida* in the *Novotel* (though this also has a 'traditional' place to eat, *Evrydika*). Moving downmarket, the busy restaurants in the *Leipzig*, *Republika* and *Bulgâria* hotels (mainly used by tour groups) generally aren't as nice as the *Pizzeria* facing the Dzhumaiya Mosque or the discreet fish-restaurant near the Hotel Bâlgaria. For really **cheap eats** try one of the cafés around Pl. 19 Noemvri (although some of them are male preserves), or the *Vegetarian restaurant* on Ul. 11 Avgust, whose gyuvechs and salads are infinitely preferable to food at the self-service joint opposite the railway station.

We found the *Kamenitsa* on Kolarov Street friendlier than the hotel **bars**, and the 'Water Music' more appealing than the floorshow in the *Novotel*'s *Orpheus Club* (although the latter functions into the small hours). The *Trimontsium* seems to be the venue for **discos**, which might also occur at **students' clubs** in the two universities (ask any students that you encounter for news of these).

During the first half of January, the **Winter Festival of Symphony Music** allows Plovdiv's philharmonic orchestra to flex its muscles in the Concert Hall adjoining the Party House on Tsentralen square. International virtuosi participate in the prestigious **Festival of Chamber Music**, held in the courtyard of the Ethnographic Museum in June every odd-numbered year (native ensembles play on until September, and during even-numbered years). Bookings can be made at 35, Ul. Kolarov (8am-7pm daily). Throughout May, June and September (coinciding with the fairs), **opera and drama** can be enjoyed in the spectacular surroundings of the Antique Theatre, whose image often appears on canvases produced during the **festival of plein-air painting** held in August. Following this, work by artists from Hungary, Romania, Nicaragua, North Korea and Plovdiv's 'twin' cities – Leningrad, Leipzig, Poznan and Brno – is exhibited at 21, Ul. Nektariev and 15, Ul. Kolarlov.

Balkantourist can arrange 8-day **crafts courses** or vigorous training programmes at the *Deveti Septemvri* Stadium (although its diverse **sports** facilities can be used far more cheaply if you turn up independently –

trolleybus #5 terminates there) – plus various **excursions** to Bachkovo Monastery, Shiroka Lâka, Salonika, etc.

Listings

Bookshops and cinemas, mostly on Ul. Kolarov, have little or nothing in foreign languages, except for Russian.

Car-hire from the *Novotel* (☎ 58-92) and *Maritsa* (☎ 5-27-36) hotels.

Car repairs from *Autoservice*, near Trakiya campsite.

24hr chemists on Patriarh Evitimii.

Dental treatment at the *Stomatological Polyclinic* on the corner of Ul. Dondukov and Emil de Lavele.

Emergencies Ambulance (☎ 150); Police (☎ 2-22-10).

Filling stations out along the Svilengrad and Sofia highways.

Flights Tickets and information from BALKAN (4, Ul. Sasho Dimitrov; ☎ 2-20-23 or 3-30-81). However, Plovdiv's **airport** is reserved for package-holiday flights, and services from Gorna Oryahovitsa and Kârdzhali – the nearest alternative airports – are only to Sofia.

Football Plovdiv fans support *Maritsa*.

Go-kart racing at the *Motorpiste*, west of the Trakiya estate; bus #18 runs fairly close.

Taxis can be summoned by dialling 2-38-31.

Moving on. . .

From the main *Tsentralna Gara* there are 3 *expres* **trains** (leaving between 6am–8am) and hourly *bârz* services **to Sofia** – a journey of 2-2½hrs – plus expresses to **Burgas** (departing around 1am, 8.30am, 1.30pm & 11.30pm/ 3¾hrs) and **Varna** (11.30am & 10.50pm/6hrs). Reaching **central or northern Bulgaria** often entails a change of trains at Stara Zagora, but there are direct services to Karlovo (every 1-2hrs), Asenovgrad (hourly) and Hisarya (5 daily); trains to Panagyurishte call at Strelcha, from which there are buses to Koprivshtitsa.

On most of these journeys you can minimise queueing by buying tickets and making seat reservations at 5, Ul. General Gurko (☎ 2-27-32) rather than the station itself. The same agency handles bookings **to Belgrade** (cheap fares, but a thoroughly miserable 10½hr journey), and **Istanbul** – although here, problems can arise. The Bulgars charge 70 leva – $40 at the 'non-bonus' rate – for a seat on the *Istanbul Express*, and refuse to sell travellers a cheap ticket, valid only as far as the border town of Svilengrad. To avoid paying the full whack, you'll have to board the train without a ticket and hope that the conductor will let you ride to Svilengrad for around $10 (which he pockets). Once inside Turkey, however, you can quite legitimately buy a ticket to Istanbul from the guard for £5, or an equivalent sum in other hard currencies. Nobody gives change, so always pay in small bills.

Plovdiv's **buses** are naturally biased **towards the Rhodopes**. There's an hourly service to Asenovgrad (see p.665) from the *Yug* terminal, which is also the point of departure for buses to Haskovo (p.659) and Kârdzhali (p.670), though these are less frequent. Other destinations – covered later in this chapter – are served by the *Rhodopi* terminal behind the flyover: eg. Smolyan and Pamporovo (2-3 daily), Bachkovo Monastery (from stand 2) and Shiroka Lâka

PLOVDIV TO THE TURKISH BORDER

There are good reasons why so many visitors travel between Plovdiv and Turkey non-stop. Not only is Dimitrovgrad the **Istanbul Express**'s sole stop along the way, but the Militia often hassles travellers with transit visas who attempt to stray off the E-80 highway; petty fines for 'safety violations' or demands that tourists change money into non-convertable leva have also been reported. Luckily, with a tourist visa (which costs no more than a transit visa) you should be okay – it's the idea of folks moving through without spending any **valuta** that bugs the authorities. Entering Bulgaria, it's impossible to get any kind of visa, nor dispose of Turkish lire – it's not even accepted at the border crossing. But if you're not pushed, it's well worth considering a stopover at Haskovo or Harmanli along the way. Travelling **by road** you'll pass KLOKOTNITSA village, 4km north of the ruined **Asenova Krepost**, marking the site where Ivan Asen defeated Theodor Comenus, the usurper of Byzantium, in 1230, thereby forcing the empire to recognise him as 'Tsar of the Bulgarians and Greeks' and accept the betrothal of Ivan's young daughter to Baldwin, Byzantium's teenage emperor. **Hitching** is pretty good, but be sure not to overshoot the motel (4 km before the Haskovo slip-road) if you aim to stay there. Approaching **by rail** means a brief encounter with **DIMITROV-GRAD** – full of power stations and reeking chemical *kombinats* – before catching a bus or train south.

However you manage to get there, **HASKOVO**'s appeal lies in its 'Turkish character' – amounting to some vestiges of Ottoman architecture and an atmosphere that's subtly different from the usual Bulgarian ambience. Public institutions are stolidly Bulgarian, but Turkish and Islamic cultural influences are evident in minutae like the berets and headscarves worn by Muslims now that fezes, *shavlari* and veils have gone out of fashion or been proscribed, and plainly manifest in the simple **Eski Dzhumaiya Mosque** behind the *Dom na Tehnikata* south of the main square. This is quite a change from the usual half-derelict structures: a carpeted room where the *hodja* reads silently and men pray; footwear and 'immodest' attire are taboo, and women are only admitted against Islamic custom to conform with Bulgarian law.

Having founded the mosque and the town itself around 1395, the Turks predominated here for the next 500 years (during which time this was known as 'Haskovo by Uzundzhovo' after the site of the great fair 10 miles away), until the development of the tobacco industry and the war of 1912 greatly increased the number of Bulgarians. The new **museum** on the south side of the main square has a fine collection of pre-Ottoman artefacts (especially Roman, Byzantine and medieval coins), and fittingly commemorates the tobacco-workers' strike of 1927 and various local heroines and heroes, but a few negative axioms suffice to describe centuries of Turkish culture. (Tuesday-Sunday 9am-12am, 2pm-6pm).

Try to arrive at the bus terminal a few minutes' walk from the central Pl. Deveti Septemvri, rather than the railway station, at the grubbier end of Blvd. Lenin. There are **places to eat** around the main square, and a rather unhelpful **tourist office** on Ul. Otets Paissi; **to stay**, there's either the *Hotel Aida* (doubles 60 leva) on the square, or the cheaper *Hotel Republika* on the same street as the tourist office. Failing that, take a #102 bus from Dimitrov Blvd. to the *motel/campsite* (ask for the *Spirka Hancheto*) – but beware that some buses turn uphill at least 3km short.

From Haskovo's terminal, there are **buses** to Kârdzhali (at 20mins past the hour between 6.20am-6.20pm), and around five daily to Harmanli, on the way passsing the turn-off for **UZUNDZHOVO**, formerly the site of Bulgaria's largest annual fair until this was transfered to Plovdiv in the late C19, consigning Uzundzhovo to the margins of commerce. However, plenty of travellers use the *Gergana motel and campsite*, 4km to the southeast of Harmanli (where hitch-hikers should alight since there don't seem to be any buses from town) – the last reasonably priced accommodation before Turkey. The *Gergana Fountain* within the vicinity is said to have been built by a vizier of Constantinople to win the heart of a Bulgarian woman, a legend used as the theme of P.R. Slaveykov's poem *The spring of the maiden with snow-white feet*.

HARMANLI gets its name from the threshing mills (*harman*) that once abounded on the surrounding plain, nowadays given over to growing cotton, mulberries (for silkworms) and tobacco. A few minutes' walk from the bus terminal, the centre of town clusters around the expensive *Hotel Hebros* and cafés where coffee and Western cigarettes are conspicuously in evidence, not far from both of Harmanli's 'sights'. The chunky, ruined *caravanserai wall* dates from the C16 like the town itself, whose Turkish founders also constructed the hump-backed **Gurbav Bridge**, with its typically flowery dedication:

As a token of his gratitude to God the Grand Vizier ordered an arch like a rainbow to be built over the River Harmanli. . .and alleviated rich and poor alike from their sorrows. The world is a bridge which is crossed by both king and pauper. When I saw the completion of this bridge, in praying to God, I spoke this inscription.

Besides having a sizeable ethnic-Turkish population like Haskovo, Harmanli is noted for its Gypsies, who practice the traditional *tsigani* trades at **horsefairs** (sometime in August; ask locals for details). There's also a suprisingly lively **disco-bar** 150m from the campsite.

Svilengrad. . .and leaving Bulgaria

The only place to stay in **SVILENGRAD** is the exorbitant 5-star *Hotel Svilena* (with a restaurant, bar, *Balkantourist* and rent-a-car bureau), and to be honest there's little for visitors to stop here for – except the *Stariya Most* beyond the railway station. Also known as the **Mustafa Pasha Bridge**, this 295m long structure of Karabag stone supported by 13 arches is an even finer achievement than the Gurbav Bridge at Harmanli, and was likewise built during the C16. There's a handful of antiquities near MEZEK, a village 6km southwest of Svilengrad (see Balkantourist first about *granitsen zone* permits): a signposted **Thracian tomb**, consisting of a 68ft long corridor leading to two rooms and a circular funerary chamber where bronze artefacts were found, probably dating from the C4 BC, and a similar distance west of the village, the **ruined Neutzikon fortress** – perhaps the best preserved of the many *krepost* raised to guard against Byzantine incursions during the C11 and C12.

From Svilengrad, it's possible **to enter Greece** or Turkey. A train, leaving Svilengrad around 10am, reaches ALEKSANDROÚPOLI 4hrs later, or there's the recently-opened 24-hour road crossing just outside town, leading to Greek ORMENION. However, most traffic crosses **the Turkish border** at KAPITAN ANDREEVO (15km from Svilengrad; open 24 hours), where vehicles entering Bulgaria are liable to rigorous examinations depending on narcotics intelligence reports and the current state of Bulgar-Turkish relations. Because trains entering or **leaving Bulgaria** get worked over by customs and immigration at Svilengrad station (rather than at Kapitan Andreevo), it might be possible to board there – at around 1am or 5am, depending on the seasonal scedule of the *Istanbul Express* – and ride on to Istanbul **by rail** without incurring the cost of an international ticket.

Inside Turkey (where motorists and railway passengers undergo customs at KAPIKULE), everything you're likely to need can be found 19km further east in **EDIRNE**. The town's splendid mosque and the chance to witness camel-wrestling (on Thursdays) might stop you from heading straight for Istanbul.

THE RHODOPES

According to Thracian mythology, the mortal lovers Hem and Rhodopi* dared call themselves after the divine Zeus and Hera, who duly punished the couple by turning them into mountains separated by the River Maritsa – Hem the Balkans and she **the Rhodopes**. Straddling Greece and Bulgaria, the Rhodopes are the land where pan-pipes, Orpheus and the Orphic Cult originated, a region rich in gems and ores, but otherwise fit for not much beyond the raising of sheep until the Turks introduced tobacco-growing in the arid valleys. Unlike the rest of Bulgaria, whole communities converted to Islam after the conquest, and of the numerous Turks that settled here many outstayed the empire's collapse, and their descendants now constitute Bulgaria's largest ethnic minority. Over the last thirty years, tourism and hydro-electric schemes have also pushed the Rhodopes into the C20, and the region is today, as Leslie Gardiner noted, a weird mixture of opposites: 'donkeys and turbo-generators, Alpine flowers and tropical foliage, bikinis in winter and thick Turkish woollens in summer'.

The massacre of its population made **Batak** notorious in the late C19, but if foreigners have heard of anywhere in the region nowadays it's probably Bulgaria's premier ski resort, **Pamporovo**, from which tourism has spread to lap at **Smolyan** and the picturesque village of **Shiroka Lâka**. Closer to Plovdiv, **Bachkovo Monastery** has already established its place on the tourist trail, and the town of **Kârdzhali** is also attempting to get in on the act. Yet writers still refer to the 'unknown Rhodopes' with some justice, for there are scores of mountain villages off the beaten track (roadbuilders were sometimes attacked by locals in the old days), many of which are rarely visited by outsiders.

Given the dearth of public transport (limited to the main roads – most

* Herodutus records a Greek legend that the Pyramid of Mycerinus in Egypt was built at the instigation of a Thracian courtesan, Rhodopis, who charged a building block for each act of intercourse – unlikely, since the pyramid consists of at least 200,000 blocks.

others qualify as tracks) and tourist accommodation, we've covered only the most obvious routes. The railway linking Septemvri on the plain with Bansko in the Pirin Mountains serves as the basis for journeys to Velingrad, Yundola and Batak in the western Rhodopes; buses from Plovdiv provide the means to reach Asenovgrad, Bachkovo Monastery, Pamporovo and Smolyan in the central Rhodopes; to reach Kârdzhali, use buses and trains from Haskovo.

The Orphic Mysteries

The legend of Orpheus originated in ancient Thrace, where he was supposedly born of a Muse (perhaps Calliope, patron of epic poetry) and King Oeagrus of the Odrysae tribe (Apollo in other versions of the story). His mastery of the lyre moved animals and trees to dance, and with his songs – which had previously enabled the Argonauts to resist the Sirens' lure – Orpheus tried to regain his dead wife, Eurydice, from the underworld. His music charmed Charon and Cerebus, the ferryman and guardian of the River Styx, and finally Hades himself, who agreed to return Eurydice on the condition that neither of them looked back as they departed – but alas, emerging into the sunlight of the overworld, Orpheus turned to smile at Eurydice and so lost her forever. Thereafter, Orpheus roamed the Rhodopes singing mournfully until he was torn apart by 'the women of Thrace' (whom Aeschylus identifies as followers of Dionysus having a Bacchic orgy). His head continued singing as it floated the River Mesta to Lesbos, where it began to prophesy until its fame eclipsed that of the Oracle at Delphi.

Despite prohibition by the authorities, an Orphic cult was well-established by the C5 BC, and itinerant priests offering initiation into the Orphic Mysteries wandered about Thrace. Little is known about the cult's practices and beliefs, but it's thought that the ritual involved the mimed – or actual – dismemberment of a person representing Dionysus, who was then 'reborn' as a free soul after death. Another theory has it that the cult's true, secret purpose was to bestow upon its adherents longevity, or even physical immortality. . .

. . .and mysterious events in the Rhodopes

Between the end of 1984 and spring the following year, a lot of Bulgarian citizens changed their names. There are conflicting accounts of what exactly happened. According to the government, citizens with 'Turkish-Arabic' names 'resumed' Bulgarian ones 'speedily, spontaneously and calmly'; and claims by Amnesty International and the Western press that the 'name-changing campaign' was marked by coercion and violence are 'unfounded and deliberate attempts to discredit socialist Bulgaria'.

Bulgaria's largest ethnic minority, the Turks, are mostly descendants of settlers who arrived after the Ottoman conquest in the C14. They had a privileged existence by comparison with the indigenous Christian Bulgars. Officially designated as *Rayah* – 'the herd' – the Bulgars were strongly pressurised to renounce Christianity, though relatively few yielded. Those that did – mainly compact Rhodope communities later known as Pomaks – became 'more Turkish than the Sultan' and even joined the Bashibazouks in massacring other Bulgars. Mindful of such history, when Bulgaria finally became independent in the last century, the majority of Turks left, fearing reprisals. However, with astonishing forbearance, the remaining communities were treated tolerantly, and continued little affected until the advent of Communist rule precipitated another exodus (around 155,000 between 1949-51, followed by a second wave in the late sixties). Today, perhaps a million Turks live on Bulgarian soil, mainly in strategic areas bordering Greece and Turkey.

The name-changing campaign, and state sensitivity towards a 'Turkish problem', seemed to develop in the early '70s, hardened by the riot in Pazardzhik (see p.647). The policy of **assimilation** probably stems from insecurity (the number of Turks is growing, while the Bulgarian population is actually declining) and a wish to eradicate the last 'shameful' vestiges of the occupation. Notwithstanding constitutional guarantees of equal rights and recognition for the Muslim religion from the Ministry of Cults, the authorities have indicated their wish to end 'accumulated Islamic-Turkish influence'. Roughly concurrent with the name-changing campaign, a number of mosques were closed for long periods 'awaiting restoration'; a spate of local ordinances were passed forbidding 'the use of the Turkish language in public and work places' (and in kindergartens), and 'the wearing of *shalvari*' – the traditional baggy Turkish trousers. Even before this, Turkish men deemed it prudent to abandon the fez in favour of a flat cap or beret as a mark of their identity.

More disturbing were the reports of arrests and shootings – at Momchilgrad, Benkovski and Gorski Izvor in the Kârdzhali district – and the imprisonment of several hundred Turks and Bulgarian Muslims at Stara Zagora and on the prison-island of Belene. Until an unexpected admission in 1988 that forty people had died at Momchilgrad four years previously, Bulgaria had always hotly refuted such charges as propaganda, while acknowledging a policy of 'returning' (*preobshtavane*) 'forcibly Islamicized Bulgarians' and 'overcoming deeply-rooted prejudices of all kinds'. Recently, however, a cautious rapprochement with Turkey has ocurred, as a result of which Bulgaria's treatment of its Muslims might improve.

It's perhaps worth acknowledging – in principle, at least – one argument for *preobshtavane*. Although secondary to nationalist considerations, an additional target of the campaign is 'Islam in the realm of family relations', which has traditionally ensured the subordination of Turkish and Bulgarian Muslim women, especially amongst the Pomaks – who lag far behind their Bulgarian sisters in terms of health-care, education and opportunities.

VELINGRAD, BATAK AND THE WESTERN RHODOPES

Like the Rila and Pirin mountains west of the Mesta Valley, the **western Rhodopes** are covered by coniferous forests and sparsely populated, with less than a dozen settlements along the road from Velingrad to Gotse Delchev, and none at all between Dospat and Batak. Discounting the reservoirs built to trap rivers for the benefit of lowland agriculture, and the shepherds tending flocks on the alpine pastures, the highlands still belong to their **wildlife**: stags, mouflon, deer, wild boar and all manner of birds inhabit a dozen protected reserves.

Although there might also be buses, the most reliable means of **approaching**

from the Pirin Mountains or the Thracian Plain is probably the *Dobrinishte-Septemvri line*, calling at Bansko, Razlog, Yakoruda and Velingrad en route. Velingrad is 3 hours' journey from Bansko or 90 minute's ride from Septemvri.

With its diverse springs, excellent climate and many trees and parks, **VELINGRAD** is a popular spa also distinguished by a museum to the partisan heroine, Veela Peeva, after whom the town was named, and three antique quarters – Kamenitsa, Lazhdene and Chepino – from which the town evolved. Whether you arrive at the bus or train station, or by road from Pazardzhik or Septemvri, it's but a few minutes' walk west to the intersection of Deveti Septemvri and Georgi Dimitrov, and the centre of town. Three-quarters of a mile west of here in the Lazhdene district, beside the Yundola road, stands *Vel'ova Banya*, founded in the C16, Velingrad's oldest **mineral baths**. A newer establishment, *Syarnata Banya*, lies roughly one mile north of the centre in the hilly Kamenitsa quarter – fed by a hotter spring (71°C) which also warms numerous glasshouses producing carnations for export to European countries (including Holland!). Velingrad's third cluster of baths lies 2km south of the centre in the old Chepino quarter, based around the *Kleptuza Spring*. With pedalloes and rowing boats available for hire on the small lake nearby, it's the most popular of the three. Reasonably-priced **accommodation** is available at the central *Hotel Zdravets*, but there are cheaper chalets for hire at *Kleptuza camping*, near the spring and *Velingrad* just outside town on the Yundola road. Besides regular **buses to Batak**, there are **trains to Bansko** leaving at around 6.10am, 9.55am and 1.40pm.

A short bus-ride to the northwest of Velingrad, **YUNDOLA** is another small health resort 4,560 feet above sea level, set amidst rounded hills and copses of trees. Accommodation here is reserved for trades unionists and Young Pioneers, and from a tourist's standpoint Yundola is chiefly remarkable for its inhabitants' longevity. The prevalence of **centenarians** in Bulgaria (some 2,000 were recorded in 1969, two thirds of them women) is ascribed to features of life in the highlands, where 'Nature takes years off the weak and adds them to the strong' – as Leslie Gardiner was told. Human longevity is supposedly extended by pure air, climatic extremes, a lack of stress, and a spartan diet with little meat and plenty of yoghurt.

26km southeast of Velingrad, beyond a large dam and the *Tsigov Chark campsite*, oak and beech forests surround the small town of **BATAK**: a name which once reverberated across Europe. During the April Rising of 1876 the Turks unleashed the Bashibazouks and Pomaks to rape, pillage and slaughter, and chose to make an example of Batak. Five thousand people – nearly the entire population – were hacked to death or burnt alive – an act for which the Turkish commander responsible was decorated. Abroad, Britain's Prime Minister Disraeli cynically dismissed the **atrocities** to justify the continuing alliance with Turkey, until the weight of reports by foreign diplomats and J.A. MacGahan of *The Daily News* became impossible to ignore. Even so, only a sustained campaign by trades unions, Gladstone and public figures like Victor Hugo and Oscar Wilde prevented British military intervention during the Russo-Turkish War of 1877-78. And at the Congress of Berlin Disraeli managed to ensure that the Ottomans retained control of a third of Bulgaria

(Eastern Roumelia) – in return for which Turkey rewarded Britain with Cyprus.

As a bloody milestone on the road to liberation the massacre is still commemorated, as one can see along Apriltsi, the main street. Bloodstains on the walls of the low, roughly-hewn St Nedelya's Church (where MacGahan found naked corpses piled three feet deep) have never been expunged; and if you've the stomach for it, the town museum exhibits foreign press reports, skeletal remains and savage denunciations – including Turgenev's attack on Disraeli and Queen Victoria, *Croquet at Windsor*.

Moving on from Batak, public transport definitely inclines towards Pazardzhik and Plovdiv; if direct buses aren't forthcoming, travel to PESHTERA and try from there. Without private transport it's difficult, if not impossible, to travel directly to Asenovgrad or Smolyan; to reach either place I'd advise starting from Plovdiv. Likewise, you're unlikely to find a bus heading south along route 37 to Dospat (p.669).

SOUTH OF PLOVDIV: ASENOVGRAD AND BACHKOVO MONASTERY

If you're making for Bachkovo Monastery, **ASENOVGRAD**, a light and breezy town built around a large park, is hard to avoid. **Buses from Plovdiv** come to rest on the northern outskirts, and services to Bachkovo depart every 2hrs from a smaller terminal on the edge of the park (also the place to catch buses back to Plovdiv). The high-rise *Hotel Asenovets* lies across the bridge from here, where it's advisable to enquire whether Westerners are still forbidden to use Bachkovo's campsite. Before pressing on, you might have time to swig a glass of the local dessert-**wine** (somewhat like Malaga), or walk to the entrance of the Cheplarska Gorge 2½ km south of town, the site of an extremely **ruined fortress**. Founded during the C11-C12, it was enlarged after Asen II's victory over the Byzantine empire in 1230, hence the town's medieval name, *Stanimaka* – 'protector of the mountain pass'. What little remains of the fort can be seen just as easily from the window of a bus, although devotees of Byzantine architecture might consider it worth climbing up to the nearby **Church of the Virgin** which has stayed relatively intact.

The **gorge** itself, just beyond, is impressive, its river nowadays harnessed to produce electricy. Heavy trucks bound for the mines around Ardino are another sign that modernisation has come to the Rhodopes, but you can still see goatherds with their flocks and mule-trains bearing packs. Throughout the centuries of Ottoman rule, the Rhodopes was the region most consistently infested with outlaws: *haiduks*, whom the Bulgars now romantically view as precursors of the patriotic *chetas*, but also bandits of Turkish origin known as *kârdzhali*, who spread terror amongst the villages. The last wave of armed resistance to authority occurred in 1947-49, when anti-communist partisans operated in the hills around Asenovgrad; and if Amnesty International's report on events in Dolni Voden (just northwest of town) is accurate, the memory of this may well have influenced the state's decision to send in troops to ensure that the ethnic-Turkish and Bulgarian Muslim villagers submitted to the 'name-changing campaign' in 1984.

Bachkovo Monastery

9km south of Asenovgrad, **Bachkovo village**'s fortress-like stone houses, overgrown with flowers, are no indication of what to expect at **BACHKOVO MONASTERY**, a kilometre or so further up the road. Gardiner's description of it as 'a mixed bag of buildings – chapels, ossuaries, cloisters, cells – daubed with frescoes more naive than artistic' doesn't really do justice to Bulgaria's second largest monastery, which, like Rila, has been declared a 'world monument' by UNESCO.

The story goes that it was founded in 1038 by two Georgians in the service of the Byzantine empire, one of whom, Grigoriy Pakuryani, renounced the governorship of Smolyan and Adrianople to devote the remainder of his life to meditation. A great iron-studded door admits visitors to the cobblestoned courtyard, surrounded by vine-wreathed wooden galleries and kept free of grass by sheep. Along one wall of the courtyard, **frescoes** provide a pictorial narrative of the monastery's history, showing Bachkovo roughly as it appears today, but watched by God's eye and a celestial Madonna and Child, with pilgrims proceeding to a hill in the vicinity to place icons. Other frescoes show in gory detail the slaying of the dragon: a powerful archetype in ancient European and Chinese cosmology, appropriated by Christianity to be vanquished by St George and symbolise the demise of paganism.

Beneath the vaulted porch of Bachkovo's principal church, **Sveta Bogoroditsa**, are more frescoes, all expressing the horrors in store for sinners: among many scenes of retribution, a boyar is tormented on his death-bed by a devil brandishing a female doll-figure (presumably representative of past infidelities), while women look on in terror. The entrance itself is more cheerful, with the Holy Trinity painted on strips set at angles in a frame, so that one sees God or Christ flanking a dove, depending on which side you approach from, like a medieval hologram. Floral motifs in a 'naive' style decorate the beams of the interior, where the star of the iconostasis is a C14 icon of the Virgin, of Georgian origin. August 25, the name-day of the church's patron, is the occasion for ritual devotions – and there's reportedly another **religious festival** held twenty-five days after the Orthodox Easter.

Bachkovo's other church, **St Nicholas**, was founded in the C19 and has recently been restored. There's a fine *Last Judgement* covering the porch exterior, which includes portraits of the artist, Zahari Zograf, and two colleagues in the upper left-hand corner. In the old **refectory** you can see *The Procession of the Miraculous Icon* (executed by Zograf's pupils), which repeats the pilgrimage portrayed on the wall of the courtyard; the accoutrements of a monk's life are neatly displayed in a former cell off the first gallery. More striking is the **museum**, where carved spoons, broken teapots and ecclesiastical hats are jumbled together with filagreed crosses, books bound in gold and the odd Thracian bas relief, as if inviting visitors to chose at a jumble sale. Finally, there's **Sveta Troitsa**, standing 300m from the main gate: a church which contains numerous early medieval frescoes, and life-sized portraits of Tsar Ivan Aleksandâr (1331-71) and the royal family, who lavishly endowed the monastery.

There are two **restaurants** and several *cheshmas* in the immediate vicinity of the monastery, so there's no difficulty in obtaining refreshment. **Accommodation**, however, can present problems. Despite its appearance on

Balkantourist maps, the campsite near the monastery refused to admit us on the grounds that we were Westerners; if this ruling still applies, then the nearest beds (in Narechenski Bani or Asenovgrad) don't come cheap. You might therefore prefer to return to Plovdiv: the last direct service back from Bachkovo leaves around 7pm, but **buses** keep running to Asenovgrad until 9pm, from where connections go to Plovdiv until 11pm.

AROUND PAMPOROVO, SMOLYAN AND SHIROKA LÂKA

14km south of Bachkovo, the old village of Narechen has been subsumed by the **mineral baths** of NARECHENSKI BANI – efficacious for treating metabolic disorders, obesity, gout and diabetes. Sufferers usually benefit from a stay at the *Hotel Zornitsa* and balneotherapy, but otherwise it's difficult to think of reasons for stopping here. However, travellers with private transport might consider a detour to the so-called **Rock Bridges**, which can be reached by turning west off the main road 14km south of Narechenski Bani, and taking the right-hand fork 10km later, from where it's a further 5km to the *Skali Mostove* (hikers' chalet in the vicinity). These weird rock formations consist of a 'bridge' almost one hundred yards long, overhanging an abyss, 200m below which is a deep, natural tunnel. Cave-buffs might also enjoy the **Speleological Museum** in CHEPELARE: a small mountain town with a 2-star hotel situated on the main road 6km north of Progled. If you take the right-hand fork after Progled, it's only another 3km up to Pamporovo, the 'Gem of the Rhodopes'.

Pamporovo
Bulgaria's largest ski resort creeps up the wooded mountainside like a partisan column determined to sabotage the TV-tower on Mount Snezhanka. PAMPOROVO is a user-friendly type of ski-centre. Everyone sees action, casualties are minimal, and veterans and rookies alike return to revel in the base-camp hotels come evening, exchanging their adventures and mishaps on the slopes above. Mild weather and good snow-cover make **skiing** conditions near perfect from mid-December until mid-April, and there's a range of classes and pistes to suit everyone from absolute beginners up to the pros who compete for the *Rhodopa Cup* each year around mid-March. Beginners' slopes are close to the resort centre, while the other runs – including the giant slalom – begin higher up the mountain, above the *Studenets* way-station (which will hire you equipment) and the outlying *Malina* chalet-complex. Both places are linked to the summit by *chair-lifts* (operating between 8.30am-5pm), and Malina can be reached by bus or on foot (20 minutes) from the grouping of hotels and restaurants which comprises Pamporovo's 'centre'.

However, Pamporovo is the kind of place you should make up your mind to visit well in advance. Independent travellers are charged considerably more for rooms, tuition and equipment than people on **package-holidays** (and might find that everything's booked up anyway), so would-be skiers are strongly advised to take one of the cheap deals offered by foreign tour-operators (see p.511), plus the optional 'ski pack' which covers all rentals and lift rides. If you do just turn up, the *Rozhen, Prepsa, Panorama, Orfei* and *Snezhanka* hotels, and the Malina chalet-colony, have the cheapest beds; the **tourist office** in the *Hotel Murgavets* will probably ring around and help with bookings if requested. Once there, traditional **Rhodope dishes** like spit-roasted lamb (*cheverme*), stuffed peppers (*sarmi*), white bean stew (*Smolenski bob*) and a local variation on the cheese-filled *banitsa* are on offer at 'folk-style' restaurants such as the *Chevermeto*, *Malina* – and *Vodenitsata* in STOYKITE village, 7km west – which feature music and dancing. Otherwise entertainment is pretty much as you'd expect. Discos in the Rozhen, Prepsa, Perelik and Snezhanka hotels operate until the small hours; plus there's a 'Ball of Nations', a *Ski Carnival* which starts on the slopes and moves to the Perelik, and the sacharine ritual of choosing and crowning a 'Miss Pamporovo'.

For sums in hard currency, Balkantourist can also arrange **excursions** to Plovdiv, Bachkovo, Shiroka Lâka, Smolyan and scenic spots in the mountains (including the Yagodinska Cave and the Trigrad Gorge, p.669). There are regular **buses** from Pamporovo to Smolyan, but you might prefer to ride down by chair-lift from the **Snezhanka Tower** (daily 9am-4pm), a futuristic structure with a café and an observation gallery giving a marvellous view of the Rhodope Mountains and, on clear days, parts of the Pirin and Rila, too. Twenty minutes walk from here are the **Orpheus Rocks** (*Orfeevi Skali*), the vantage point for a superb panorama of the mountains surrounding the Smolyan valley.

Smolyan

Like many Bulgarian settlements, SMOLYAN represents a triumph over adversity. It was raised on the ruins of three villages – Smolyan, Raikovo and Ustovo – which the Turks destroyed when their inhabitants refused to become Muslims. Situated 3,310 feet above sea level, it's the highest town in Bulgaria, an expanding industrial centre with a population of almost 40,000. Smolyan's clean modern buildings and cultural facilities – including an art gallery, the Rhodope Drama Theatre and the **Rhodope Folk Ensemble** – emphasise its status as the regional capital, whilst the older quarters of town provide subject-matter for artists participating in the annual **Festival of Plein-air Painting**, which is held during the first three weeks of October.

Buses from Pamporovo pass *Panorama Camping* 4km before entering Smolyan by Pârvi Mai, a continuation of the great boulevard (elsewhere named after Lenin and the 9th September) which cuts across town. Heading eastwards along this, you'll encounter practically everything worth mentioning: the *Hotel Smolyan* and the slightly cheaper high-rise *Sokolitsa*, *Balkantourist*, the post office, and – in a park – Bulgaria's only **Planetarium**.

The modern centre is nicely laid out and for visual appeal almost but not quite matches the old houses in the Raikovo and Ustovo districts. The most famous of these is the **Pangalov House** in the Raikovo quarter, a splendid National Revival-style mansion with timber-framed oriels and the customary trimmings, which now contains a superb **Ethnographic Museum**. The inhabitants of the Rhodopes were once noted for their distinctive costumes: men wore relatively sombre attire with a modicum of braiding, but the women let rip with red and yellow plaid aprons, deeply-slit *soukmans*, and elaborate ear-covers, tiaras and diadems – variously known as *trepki*, *kossichniki* and *kruzhila*. Sadly, traditional dress is nowadays rarely worn, even for village festivals. However, carpets (*chergi*) and tufted goat's-hair rugs (*halishta*) – of which the museum has a fine collection – are still manufactured around Smolyan. Another mile or so east of the museum (past the turn-off for Rudozem) one enters **Ustovo**, which still partly resembles the village it once was, sited higgledy-piggledy on the hillsides around the confluence of the Cherna and Bepar rivers.

Smolyan's **bus terminal**, on Minborska street towards the western end of town, is the starting-point for journeys to the remainder of the Rhodope region. There are regular services to Kârdzhali and the Arda Valley, and west to Shiroka Lâka and Devin (sometimes even to Gotse Delchev). Easiest of all to reach by bus are the **lakes** (*Smolyanski ezera*) to the north of town, surrounded by picturesque crags and coniferous forests. There's also, on the way, the *Smolyan campsite* which has chalets.

Heading west: Shiroka Lâka, Devin and the road to Gotse Delchev

Easily accessible from Smolyan or Pamporovo, **SHIROKA LÂKA** is where folks go to see a genuine Rhodope village. With its rambling streets and tall, asymetrical stone houses built steeply into the mountainside, this settlement of 2,000 souls could have been lifted off a picture-postcard – and is, remarkably, unspoilt, despite increasing numbers of package-trippers who arrive in coaches to invade its humble tavernas. The advantage of coming here on a tour is that you get to see a performance by the students of the **School of Folk Instruments and Music** (situated in an alpine meadow up behind the village) – something you might otherwise miss should you turn up on spec. Old residences like the **Sugurov House** and the **Kalamdji House** (which contains the local Ethnographic Museum) are open to visits if the curators are around. By evening the foreigners have gone, since the **hostel** to the south of the village isn't officially designated for the use of Westerners.

Further west of Shiroka Lâka the road leads through a typically Rhodopian landscape of weathered rocks and luxuriant vegetation, to the spa of **DEVIN**. You can do this trip by bus from Smolyan, or on one of the excursions organised by Balkantourist, who also run day-trips to the **Yagodinska Cave** and the **Trigrad Gorge** (both of which lie at the end of minor roads radiating southwards from TESHEL, a village 11km from Devin). Since they're fairly close to the Greek border, anyone hoping to visit independently should ask whether it's necessary to acquire a *granitsen zone* permit. A village down here was allegedly the last refuge of the Russian royal family. According to local **legends**, they escaped the massacre at Ekaterinburg, fled south across the Urals, the Caspian and the Black Sea, stayed for a while in Plovdiv and finally settled in a remote Rhodope village. There the Tsar, the Tsarina and the sickly Tsarevitch died, whilst the four Grand Duchesses lived on as peasant women, two of them marrying local people. From a practical standpoint, the chance of **buses** going this far south is pretty slim, but the destinations to look for are YAGODINA (for the *Yagodinska peshtera*) and TRIGRAD (for the *Trigradski skali*). If persuasive enough, Westerners might be allowed to stay at the Trigrad hikers' chalet.

The main road continues westwards from Devin to the Pirin mountain-town of GOTSE DELCHEV (p.572), 59km beyond **DOSPAT**, a small town once noted for its folk costumes and festivities, but nowadays better known for its reservoir. Bus services in these parts are unreliable but with a car you can make detours to isolated Rhodope villages. **Goats** are still the basis for life in many such communities: every family owns several, which are entrusted to the village goatherd, or *manzardji*. Their milk is drunk or turned into yoghurt and cheese, which together with salted goat's meat (*pasturma*) forms the villagers' wintertime staple; goat's hair is woven into rugs which last for 80 years; and their skin can be made into everything from wine-sacks and sandals to bagpipes (*kaba*). During the Ottoman occupation, when Bulgarians were forbidden to carry arms, goat's horns served as daggers, and many of the country's most famous *haiduks* (including the female outlaw Rumena Voivoda) started their careers as goatherds.

Outsiders – let alone foreigners – are rare birds in these **villages**, and should you pay a visit, be prepared to accept the locals on their own terms. You might be offered hospitality (including lodgings, which is okay if there's no police in the village), but if you're made to feel unwelcome, clear out fast. Reportedly, two of the most beautiful villages are **DOLEN** and **KOVACHEVITSA**, the first 4km off the road between Dospat and Devin, the second, way up in the mountains along the awful road running between Gotse Delchev and Velingrad.

Smolyan to Kârdzhali

There are fairly regular buses from Smolyan to Kârdzhali, 91km away, following the road past **ARDINO**, a recently industrialised town with nothing to recommend it. A few kilometres on, however, there's a nice motel-campsite complex, **Belite Brezi**, which gets its name from the surrounding silver birches. From the site, there's a 7hr trail to the 90m-high **Ardino Waterfall** on the River Arda, and should you make it, not much further to *Dryavolskiyat Most*, one of the old hump-backed **Turkish bridges** which span several of the Arda's tributaries.

Another road from Smolyan approaches Kârdzhali by way of Momchilgrad (p.672), running closer to the Greek border. Special authorisation is required in order to travel this route, which takes you past or close to several large mining centres – **RUDOZEM, ZLATOGRAD** ('Gold Town') and **MADAN** (from the Arabic for 'mine') – whose zinc and lead is so pure that the London Metal Exchange accepts it without certification. Here too, within the border zone, lie the villages of **BENKOVSKI** and **GORSKI IZVOR**, said by Amnesty International to have been the scene of violent clashes between locals and the security forces during the 'name-changing campaign' of 1984 (p.663). **PODKOVA**, 25km northeast of Benkovski, is the terminal of a branch line up to Kârdzhali, Haskovo and Stara Zagora.

KÂRDZHALI AND THE EASTERN RHODOPES

The **eastern Rhodopes** were the Ottomans' first conquest, and their last foothold in Bulgaria before the Balkan Wars of 1912-13, and to this day a sizeable number of the inhabitants are of ethnic Turkish origin. Geographically, the region displays special features, having 2,500 hamlets and villages (far more settlements than exist in either the central or the western Rhodopes) and comparatively low highlands, the slopes of which are covered with deciduous rather than coniferous forests. Most characteristic of all are the expanses of eroded, deforested wastelands, which, seen by moonlight, resemble deserts or lunar surfaces. The land, with its mediterranean climate and dry sandy soil, has always needed irrigation to produce crops, and the minerals in the mountains – zinc, lead, gold and silver – made mining more profitable than agriculture until the Turks introduced the cultivation of tobacco. Traditionally, this was the poorest and least developed area of Bulgaria – a condition that's only begun to be remedied since dams and non-ferrous metal plants were established in the 1950s – and today there's still a great disparity between thriving towns like **Kârdzhali** and the remote highland villages.

Kârdzhali

One of the last Bulgarian settlements to remain in Turkish hands, **KÂRDZHALI** had less than 3,000 inhabitants when it was handed back in 1913. But during the last 30 years the construction of large dams to supply water for irrigation and hydro-electricity for industry has given its fortunes a prodigious boost, inspiring copywriters to dub this the 'city of two reservoirs'. More recently, Kârdzhali has set about attracting tourist lucre by building a luxurious hotel in the town centre and promoting watersports on the *Kârdzhali* and *Studen Kladenets* reservoirs, though whether the investment will pay off is anybody's guess. With hourly buses and 6 trains a day *from Haskovo*, and a fairly regular bus service *from Plovdiv*'s Yug terminal, **getting there** is easy, anyway.

Approaching town from the east, trains run alongside the Studen Kladenets reservoir, almost within sight of the **Pyramids of Kârdzhali**. Tinted pink, yellow and rust-coloured by the presence of manganese, iron and other ores, these weirdly-shaped rock formations covering an area of five hectares are known by locals as the 'Stone Wedding Procession', and can be reached by bus from the town's terminal. If you're driving from Haskovo you might like to take the minor road to Kârdzhali (which leaves the E85 at Manastir), since this runs past another geological oddity situated near the village of Solishte, the **Stone Mushrooms** (*Skali Gubi*).

Kârdzhali itself consists of reefs of low-rise housing set amid greenery, with a main street running the length of town roughly parallel to the river. From the station or the bus terminal you simply follow Ul. Dimitrov, passing the railway bookings office (nr.64) to reach the centre. The *Arzepos*, the largest and swishest of Kârdzhali's three **hotels**, stands near a sports complex and pool in the park beside the river, and the **tourist bureau** there can supply directions to the cheaper *Bâlgaria* and *Republika* hotels. If you don't mind the journey, it's also possible to stay at *Belite Brezi* **campsite**, 30km west of town along the Smolyan road and reachable by regular buses. Kârdzhali's *Arpezos*, *Bulgaria*, *Russalka* and *Prostor* **restaurants** are all rated 'first' or 'deluxe' class, and the Arpezos in particular is noted for its **regional specialities**: mutton *kurban*, sausages (*suzdurma*) and *shashlik*, *balkava* and figs, and *Armira* wine from the Ivailovgrad district.

5km west of town lies the **Kârdzhali reservoir**, a developing **watersports** centre with facilities for windsurfing, water-skiing, rowing, fishing and power-boat racing – the venue for annual Outboard Motor Racing and Angling tournaments (dates vary). For the more sedentary, there are regular trips around the reservoir by **hydrofoil**, not to mention a **restaurant boat**, the *Emona*, brought from Varna at the behest of Georgi Georgiev, Bulgaria's first round-the-world yachtsman. For bookings and details of buses to the reservoir, enquire at the Hotel Arpezos, which can also arrange **excursions** in the eastern Rhodopes. However, **permits** to enter the border zone may well be required in order to visit Momchilgrad and Ivailovgrad – so to be on the safe side, check with the tourist office beforehand. Since the political situation in the Rhodopes is rather fraught, conditions and travel restrictions can change at short notice.

Around Momchilgrad and Ivailovgrad

15km south of Kârdzhali stands the small one-hotel town of **MOMCHILGRAD**, which earns its living by growing an aromatic strain of tobacco called *dzhebel basma*: a name deriving from *djebel*, the Arabic word for hill. Used by the Turks to describe the surrounding region, where the sandy soil forms hundreds of ridges and mounds, the name has clung to the neighbouring town of **DZHEBEL**, where a research institute seeks to improve the crop. 7km from here is a curious freak of nature beside the village of **VODENICHARSKO**. The ridge of the **Broken Mountain** (*Yanuk Tepe*) looks like God has taken a cleaver to it, terminating midway in a precipitous drop with huge riolite columns strewn around – the result of a landslide at the end of the C19.

Momchilgrad is as far east (and nearly as far south) as tourists can travel without first obtaining *granitsen zone* permits, so unless you've fixed these up in Kârdzhali you'd be foolhardy to venture any further. The hinterland between the main towns is craggily overgrown or parched and sandy, dotted with **ruined fortresses** raised by the Bulgars or Byzantium during the centuries of warfare between the two empires, one of which stands near the village of ZVEZDEL halfway along the road to **KRUMOVGRAD**. A pretty similar town to Momchilgrad, with an unpretentious *hotel*, Krumovgrad is the point of departure for buses on to **IVAILOVGRAD**. It's said that **camels** still serve as beasts of burden in villages around Ivailovgrad, but if anything tempts travellers to come this far it's more likely to be the **remains of a Roman villa**, situated 4km from town off the Ivailovgrad-Lyubimets highway. The villa was built during the C2, probably for a Roman landowner from Adrianople (Edirne), and some idea of its original sumptuousness may be gained from the large *mosaic floors*, which depict the owner and his family, mythological creatures (including the Gorgon), and bird and animal figures. Visitors can stay at the small *Hotel Trakiya* in Ivailovgrad, but remember that there's **nowhere to cross the frontier** around here; the nearest border-checkpoint is at Svilengrad (p.660).

FESTIVALS

Winter
During the **first half of January**, a festival of symphony music at PLOVDIV. In wine-producing villages around HASKOVO and ASENOVGRAD, cele-brations to mark Vinegrowers' Day (*Trifon Zarezan*) on **February 14**.

Spring
Some time in **mid-March**, skiers compete

at PAMPOROVO for the *Rhodopa Cup*. Plays, classical music and other entertainments in PLOVDIV during the city's *Spring Fair* in **May**.

Summer
A whole string of events in PLOVDIV – eg. chamber music (June), plein air painting (August) and classical plays at the Antique Theatre (to coincide with the Industrial Fair during the second half of September). In **August**, horsefairs at HASKOVO and the commemoration of the Virgin's name-day (**25**) at BACHKOVO MONASTERY.

Autumn
During the **first three weeks in October** SMOLYAN hosts a festival of plein air painting.

TRAVEL DETAILS

Trains
From Asenovgrad to Plovdiv (every ½hr; 25mins).
From Harmanli to Dimitrovgrad (5 daily; 1hr); Plovdiv (5; 3½); Simeonovgrad (6; ¼); Svilengrad (6; ½).
From Haskovo to Dimitrovgrad (6; ½); Kârdzhali (6; 1-1¾); Momchilgrad (6; 2-3¼); Stara Zagora (3; 1½-2½).
From Hisarya to Plovdiv (5; 1).
From Momchilgrad to Dimitrovgrad (5; 2¼-2¾); Kârdzhali (7; ½); Stara Zagora (3; 2¼-4½).
From Kârdzhali to Dimitrovgrad (5; 2); Momchilgrad (9; ½); Podkova (3; ½); Stara Zagora (3; 3-4).
From Panagyurishte to Plovdiv (4; 1¾).
From Plovdiv to Asenovgrad (every hour; 25mins); Burgas (4 daily; 3¾hrs); Dimitrovgrad (10; 1-1½); Harmanli (5; 2-3¼); Karlovo (9; 1¾); Panagyurishte (4; 1¾); Pazardzhik (20; ½-¾); Septemvri (20; ¾-1); Sofia (20; 2-3½); Varna (2; 6).
From Podkova to Dimitrovgrad (1; 3½); Kârdzhali (2; 1); Momchilgrad (7; ½).
From Septemvri to Bansko (2; 4¼); Plovdiv (17; ¾-1); Sofia (18; 1½-2¼); Velingrad (7; 1½).

Buses
From Asenovgrad to Bachkovo (every 2hrs); Plovdiv (hourly).
From Dimitrovgrad to Haskovo (every ½hr).
From Haskovo to Dimitrovgrad (every ½hr); Harmanli (5 daily); Kârdzhali (hourly).
From Pamporovo to Smolyan (every hour).
From Pazardzhik to Batak; Panagyurishte; Peshtera (5-6 daily).
From Plovdiv to Asenovgrad (hourly); Kârdzhali (3-4 daily); Haskovo (4-5); Pamporovo (2-3); Smolyan (2-3); Sofia (1).
From Smolyan to Ardino (hourly); Kârdzhali (6-7 daily); Pamporovo (hourly).
From Velingrad to Batak (hourly); Yundola (every ¾hr).

Flights
From Kârdzhali to Sofia (5 weekly during the summer; 1hr).

International trains
From Plovdiv to Belgrade (1 daily; 10½hrs); Istanbul (1; 11½).
From Svilengrad to Alexandroúpoli (1; 4).

Ardino	Ардино
Asenovgrad	Асеновград
Bachkovo	Бачково
Batak	Батак
Belite Brezi	Белите Брези
Cheplare	Чепларе
Dolen	Долен
Dospat	Доспат
Harmanli	Харманли
Haskovo	Хасково
Ihtiman	Ихтиман
Ivailovgrad	Ивайловград
Kapitan Andreevo	Капитан Андреево
Kostenets	Костенец
Kovachevitsa	Ковачевица
Krumovgrad	Крумовград
Madan	Мадан
Narechenski Bani	Нареченски Бани
Pamporovo	Пампорово
Pazardzhik	Пазарджик
Peshtera	Пещера
Plovdiv	Пловдив
Podkova	Подкова
Rudozem	Рудозем
Septemvri	Септември
Shiroka Lâka	Широка Лъка
Smolyan	Смолуян
Svilengrad	Свиленград
Velingrad	Велинград
Vodenicharsko	Воденичарско
Zlatograd	Златоград

Chapter sixteen

THE COAST

Where ten years ago only the sea spoke in the desert silence of the dunes, now one hears thousands of voices, drowned in the music of orchestras and the noise of cars.

Georgi Markov, *The Truth that Killed*

Markov's lament for the transformation of **the Coast** is echoed by quite a few Bulgarians who knew it when there were miles of empty beaches and a few quiet fishing ports. It was the Soviet leader Khrushchev who first suggested that the coastline be developed for tourism, and the first problem was to get rid of thousands of harmless but off-putting snakes, which was solved by introducing hedgehogs, who ate them. Since then, **resorts** like **Druzhba**, **Albena**, **Golden Sands** and **Sunny Beach** have mushroomed, growing increasingly sophisticated as the prototype mega-complexes have been followed by **Elenite**, **Dyuni** and other 'holiday villages'. **Varna** has only enhanced its cosmopolitan reputation by laying on an extravaganza of classical music and ballet during the summer, while the other coastal city, **Burgas**, partly compensates for its ugliness by hosting **festivals** of folklore and ballroom dancing, and folk dancing courses.

With fine weather and safe bathing practically guaranteed, and package holidays priced to compete with Greece, Yugoslavia and Spain, the selling of the Black Sea, *Cherno More*, has been a success in economic terms. But of course, there have been casualties, with the beautiful old town of **Nesebâr** bearing the brunt; its ancient rival, **Sozopol**, and the (at present) quieter stretch of coast between Burgas and Turkey, will doubtless follow. Less obviously, there's the effect on Bulgarian morale as native holidaymakers are treated as second-class citizens by Balkantourist, while 'herring gulls' (gigolos) pander to wealthy Westerners.

As in Romania, hotel rooms cost much less on a **package holiday** (see p.511), and independent travellers will have to settle for private rooms (available through local Balkantourists) or camping to avoid forking out large sums for **accommodation**. It's possible to **reach the coast** by train from Plovdiv, Ruse, the Valley of the Roses or Sofia, but if you're coming from the capital it's much quicker – and only slightly dearer – to fly to Burgas or Varna. In theory, it should be quite straightforward to drive across the border **from Romania or Turkey**, but in practice it's advisable to consider the warnings on p.698. Once you've arrived, however, the frequency of short-hop and long-distance buses, plus *Kometa* hydrofoils and slower *Hydrobuses*, makes **getting around** a simple business.

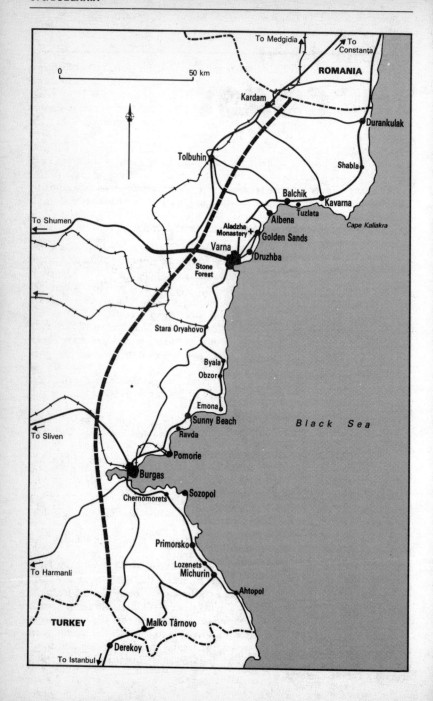

0   50 km

To Medgidia

To Constanța

ROMANIA

Kardam

Durankulak

Tolbuhin

Shabla

Balchik

Kavarna

Tuzlata

Albena

Aladzha
Monastery

Cape Kaliakra

Golden Sands

Varna

Druzhba

To Shumen

Stone
Forest

Stara Oryahovo

Byala

Obzor

B l a c k   S e a

Emona

To Sliven

Sunny Beach

Ravda

Pomorie

Burgas

Sozopol

Chernomorets

Primorsko

Lozenets
Michurin

To Harmanli

Ahtopol

TURKEY

Malko Târnovo

Derekoy

To Istanbul

VARNA

VARNA's origins go back almost five millenium, but it wasn't until seafaring Greeks established the colony of *Odessus* here in 585 BC that the town became a port. Odessus encouraged the Greeks to rename the sea 'Hospitable' (*Euxeinos*), and by joining the Euxine League of coastal city-states it secured respectful treatment from the Roman and Byzantine empires, but not the Avars, who devastated it in AD 586. Rebuilt by Slavs who called it *Varna* ('Black One'), it became to maritime commerce in the Balkans what Târnovo was to overland trade – and equally tempting to the Turks. Under Ottoman rule (1393-1878) Varna was transformed into the strongest part of the 'quadrilateral' (p.591), and although the huge fortress was subsequently demolished, a military presence has lingered on until this day.

The modern city (pop. 300,000) is an amalgam of different roles – a shipyard and port for commercial freighters and the Bulgarian Navy, and a riviera town visited by tourists of every nationality. It's a cosmopolitan place – evident in small things like street names in two alphabets and the availability of non-Communist newspapers, and lavishly celebrated during the 'Varna Summer' – and a nice one to stroll through. Baroque, turn-of-the-century and contemporary architecture are pleasantly blended with shady promenades and a handsome seaside garden; and there are several interesting museums. If none of this grabs you, most of the other coastal resorts can easily be reached from Varna by bus or boat.

Arriving and finding somewhere to stay

Each of the main **points of arrival** has good bus-connections with the centre – Pl. Varnenska Komuna, Blvd. Dimitâr Blagoev and Blvd. Lenin. You'll approach them from the northwest if you come in from the **bus terminal** (bus #1) on Karl Marks Blvd. or Varna **airport** on the city's western outskirts (#50), whereas travellers coming in at the **railway station** (#1, #4 or #6) or **passenger dock** (#12) basically head uphill towards them from the south.

Arriving at the station, it's a good idea to stash your luggage in the 24-hour *garderob* and start looking for **accommodation**. The *Hotel Musala* (☎ 2-39-25) and the *Hotel Republika* (☎ 2-58-53), opposite, are both cheap and smack in the centre. The slightly dearer *Orbita Hotel* on Blvd. Kolarov can be reached by bus #6. Otherwise, the alternatives are *Galata campsite* (bus #17 from Blvd. Botev to the Galata terminal; walk downhill past the naval installation to find the site) or staying at one of the neighbouring resorts. It's a good idea though to contact **Balkantourist** first to enquire about, and book, affordable hotel accommodation or chalets on campsites along the coast since vacancies are scarce. The bureau opposite the station can be pretty offhand, so you might have better luck at the main office beside the *Hotel Musala* (☎ 2-55-24), nr.73 Blvd. Lenin (☎ 2-55-09) or 5, Tolbuhin Street (☎ 2-56-30); all open Monday-Friday 8.30am-12.30pm, 1pm-6pm.

Around the city

Varna's social life revolves around the **Pl. 9 Septemvri**, where the Opera House and Theatre provide a backdrop for an ensemble of restaurants and cafés, including the *Zlatno Pile* (Golden Chicken), *Chinarite* and *Odessos*, whose clientele mingles with the shirtsleeved promenaders. Bulevard Lenin and its flower-bedded extension, Koloni Street, are also busy with the *korso*, which continues until 9 or 10pm. The BALKAN and *Rila* ticket offices are on the northern side of the boulevard, while a ruined **Round Tower and fortress wall** dating from Roman times stands at the corner of Ul. Shipka.

Beyond the Opera House and Town Council, Varna's main lateral boulevard cuts through Pl. Varnenska Komuna – named after the Varna Commune of 1919 – followed by a wind that rustles the trees around the domed **Cathedral of the Assumption**. Constructed in 1886 along the lines of St Petersburg's Cathedral, this contains a splendid iconostasis and bishop's throne carved by Debâr craftsmen, and murals painted after the last war. More practically, you can catch various **buses** in the vicinity of the Cathedral, namely: #17 to Galata (from the stop 50 yards down Blvd. Botev); #1 to the city bus terminal, and #41 to the Park of Fighting Friendship (from Karl Marks); and from Blvd. Botev or behind the Cathedral, buses #8 and #9/#99 to the Druzhba and Golden Sands resorts.

Exhibits in the **Varna Museum** on the corner of Blagoev and Dimitrov boulevards (open Tuesday-Sunday 10am-5pm) fill 40 halls, three of them devoted solely to skeletons and artefacts from a Chalcolytic Necropolis where 1,850 gold objects were discovered in 1972. Although many of the **gold treasures** are simply executed, others display an incredible degree of skill considering that they were made around 4,500 years ago. A magnifying lens reveals a perfectly shaped Hermes-like deity surrounded by a golden shell on one of a pair of ear-rings – actually a tiny figure whose details are imperceptible to the naked eye. Other halls display Greek and Roman antiquities, medieval weaponry and ecclesiastical art, and the usual weaponry, banners and manifestoes dating from the revolutionary and National Revival periods. Everything is well laid out, and the only problem is the lack of information in English.

Five minutes' walk down Ul. 27 Yuli brings you to the **Museum of the Renaissance** (Tuesday-Sunday 10am-6pm), occupying the former Archangel Michael Church and the premises of Varna's first Bulgarian school, opened in 1861. Stern discipline prevailed, judging by the original boys' classroom preserved here: for recalcitrant pupils undeterred by the threat of being compelled to wear a badge labelled 'fidget' or 'lazy', there was always the cane and a retractable spanking-frame. Good students were rewarded by badges proclaiming the wearer 'diligent' or 'intelligent'. In the former girls' classroom upstairs are portraits of formidable-looking pedagogues and various proclamations and manuscripts, including some pages from Father Paisii's original *Slav-Bulgarian History*.

From here, Pl. Ekzarh Iosif and the end of Koloni Street lead down to **Primorski Park**, laid out behind Blvd. Chervenoarmeiski, and Varna's strip of **beach**. There's a modest admission charge, but the water-chute is so enticing that few visitors mind. Captive dolphins are the most popular 'exhibit' at the **Aquarium** (Tuesday-Sunday 8am-8pm, Monday 2-8pm), but you may prefer watching some of the other sea-creatures, whose habits are explained in German. Female *Zanden* leave their eggs on plants and let the males do the

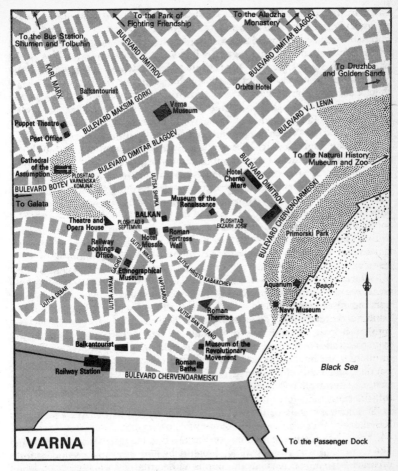

To the Park of
Fighting Friendship

To the Aledzha
Monastery

To the Bus Station,
Shumen and Tolbuhin

BULEVARD DIMITAR BLAGOEV

KARL MARX

BULEVARD DIMITROV

To Druzhba
and Golden Sands

Balkantourist

Orbita Hotel

BULEVARD MAKSIM GORKI

Varna
Museum

BULEVARD V.I. LENIN

Puppet Theatre

Post Office

BULEVARD DIMITAR BLAGOEV

To the Natural History
Museum and Zoo

Cathedral
of the
Assumption

PLOSHTAD
VARNENSKA
KOMUNA

ULITSA SHIPKA

Hotel
Cherno
More

BULEVARD DIMITROV

BULEVARD BOTEV

To Galata

Museum of the
Renaissance

BALKAN

BULEVARD CHERVENOARMEISKI

Theatre and
Opera House

PLOSHTAD 9
SEPTEMVRI

PLOSHTAD
EKZARH JOSIF

Primorski Park

ULITSA NIKOLA

Roman
Fortress
Wall

Railway
Bookings
Office

Hotel
Musala

ULITSA AVRAM GACHEV

ULITSA VAPTSAROV

ULITSA HRISTO KABAKCHIEV

Ethnographical
Museum

Aquarium

Beach

ULITSA OBBAR

Navy Museum

Roman
Thermae

ULITSA SAN STEFANO

Balkantourist

Museum of the
Revolutionary
Movement

Black Sea

Railway Station

Roman
Baths

BULEVARD CHERVENOARMEISKI

VARNA

To the Passenger Dock

brooding, while female Sea-Needles deposit them in a pouch on the male *Seenadel*. Stranger yet are the *Knurrhahn*, whose webbed gills enable them to 'walk' on land, and the Japanese Snails (*Rapara*) that made it to the Black Sea on the hulls of Soviet freighters.

Three gunboats and a torpedo boat responsible for the Bulgarian Navy's only victory are honourably embedded outside the **Navy Museum** (9am-12am, 1.30-5pm), and a separate ticket is required to board the *Drâzhki* (Intrepid) which sank the Turkish cruiser *Hamidie* off Cape Kaliakra in 1912. The museum traces seapower and commerce on the Black Sea and the lower Danube back to its earliest days, with showcases devoted to Seaman Zabulanov who organised clandestine shipments of Lenin's *Iskra* to Odessa, and the 1925 Sailors' Revolt (*Vâv Flota*). Since Bulgaria's Navy was reduced to a rump by the Neuilly Treaty (1919), and later collaborated with Hitler's

Kriegsmarine, there's little else for it to take pride in before 1944, when the era of Soviet-Bulgarian naval fraternity dawned.

However, saboteurs and partisans were active from the start, as symbolised by the **Monument to Fighters against Fascism** (1919-44) in the centre of the park, beyond an **open-air Theatre**, with the **Natural History Museum** (devoted to coastal flora and fauna) to the south. Further to the northeast there's a small **Zoo** containing animals from four continents, while on the other side of Chervenoarmeiski (Red Army) boulevard is the **Palace of Sports and Culture**, which, together with the open-air theatre and the Opera House, is used during the '**Varna Summer**' of symphonic, operatic and chamber music (roundabout June 15-July 15 every year). Like the **ballet** contest in July – featuring both classical and modern dance – this attracts some of the world's finest orchestras and companies; details and tickets from Balkantourist. The Naval Academy nearby has a cosmopolitan feel, too, for Arabs, Africans and Vietnamese are among the students who strut around town in uniforms belted with ceremonial daggers.

Heading back towards the centre, you might stumble upon the **ruined Roman Baths** on the corner of Khan Krum and Knyaz Dondukov, though the C2 **Roman Thermae** (Tuesday-Sunday 10am-6pm) is a far more impressive heap and 100 years older to boot. The **Museum of the Revolutionary Movement** (5, Ul. 8 Noemvri) commemorates the 16th Party Congress and the great workers' demonstrations that took place in Varna, plus much heroic wartime resistance activity, but if you can't understand the captions the exhibition is pretty dull. The **Ethnographic Museum** (Tuesday-Sunday 10am-5pm), occupying an old house on Ul. Panagyurishte is better. On the top floor (which includes several ornate salons) there's a fine display of costumes and jewellery worn by mountain (*Vaiovtsi*) and lowland (*Hâptsoi*) immigrants of the C19 and C20, embroidered masks worn during *Kukeri* and *Survakari* rites, and a variety of 'ritual loaves'. These last were baked to mark specific occasions: eg. the *Kravai* for New Year or St John's Day; the 'Pony' (*Konche*) for St Theodor's Day; or the *Proshtupalnik* – shaped like a baby's foot – to celebrate a child's first steps.

Finally, its bizarre name might attract you to the **Park of Fighting Friendship** (bus #41 from Blvd. Karl Marks), where a granite monument tops a Thracian tumulus marking the site of the **battle of Varna**. In November 1444, 30,000 Crusaders preparing to sail for Constantinople were suprised when 120,000 Turks landed on the coast, and during the subsequent clash King Ladislas III of Poland and Hungary recklessly led a charge to capture Sultan Murad in his tent. Ladislas was cut down by a janissary and his army wavered, forcing János Hunyadi to order an inglorious retreat, marking the end of Christendom's last attempt to check the Ottoman advance. Naturally, there's a small **museum** honouring Ladislas, whom the Bulgars call *Vladislao Varnenski*.

Eating out, and other things

Overcrowding seems to be the main problem at many of Varna's **restaurants**, particularly the *Horizon* (near the zoo) and places along the line of the promenade. But check out the *Zlatno Pile*, *Preslav* (1, Ul. A. Gatchev) or

Bâlgaria (2, Ul. Koloni) before venturing further afield to places like the *Euxinograd* (2, Ul. Anton Ivanov), or restaurants along the main boulevards: eg *Dimyat* at block III, and *Potchivka* by the bus-stop of the same name, on Blvd. Lenin; or the *Rostok* at 20, Blvd. Karl Marks. The *Morsko Kontche* (7, Ul. D. Kondov) specialises in sea-food.

A shop on Blvd. Lenin, near the *Hotel Musala*, sells **Western newspapers** – and not just the Communist ones – while news and tourist bulletins in foreign languages are broadcast by **Radio Varna** on 388 metres between 8am-2pm. Along Blvd. Maksim Gorki are the central **Post Office** (nr.36), a dentist's (nr.24), and the largest of Varna's hospitals (nr.46; there's another one on Tolbuhin Street), although tourists requiring non-specialised **medical treatment** are advised to go to the Polyclinic near the Acacia bus-stop (#4/#8/#9) out along Lenin Blvd, since its staff are trained to deal with foreigners. There's a **24-hour pharmacy** at 9, Ul. Filaret. **Car repairs** could be problematical because the depots at 184 (☎ 4-12-52) and 262 (☎ 4-98-85) Karl Marks Blvd. are principally equipped to deal with Eastern European models, but it's worth ringing around. However, Fiat 125s can be fixed at the *Lada/Polski Fiat* depot beside Druzhba's filling station. **Taxis** lurk around the bus and train stations, or may be summoned by ringing 2-20-66/2-22-08/2-21-03 – or 4-07-60 if you want an out-of-town destination.

Leaving Varna – and excursions from the city

Although they leave around 6am and 7am, BALKAN flights are far preferable to the train if you're **heading for Sofia**; 26 leva spent on the ticket (available from 2, Ul. Shipka; ☎ 3-14-51) is a small price for escaping 8 or 9 hours in an overcrowded sweatbox. If you do decide to go by rail, buy tickets and reserve seats at least 24 hrs in advance from the *BDZh* offices at 10, Ul. Avram Gachev (☎ 2-30-53) or 13, Ul. 27 Yuli (☎ 2-11-37); only the latter office books sleepers (☎ 2-70-36). Trains take two different routes to the capital: services prefixed '3' run via Karnobat and the Valley of the Roses; those with the prefix '2' travel via Gorna Oryahovitsa and Pleven.

Yet **longer hauls to foreign parts** can be made by train or boat. Departure times of international trains and their routes are as follows: the *Trakia Express* to Braşov, Budapest and Prague leaves around 8.15am; the *Varna Express* to Bucharest and Warsaw at 7.50pm; and the *Cherno More* to Buzău, Suceava, Kiev and Moscow at 8.50pm. Buy tickets at the *Rila* bureau (3, Ul. Shipka; ☎ 2-62-73 or 2-62-88). It's possible to reach Istanbul, Pireaus, Larnika, Naples, Genoa, Odessa, Yalta or Baku – to name but a few ports – by passenger ships of the Soviet line MORPASFLOT, with offices at 1, Ul. Musala (☎ 22-09-03) and in the *Cherno More Hotel* (☎ 22-93-91). Travellers bound for Poland, Czechoslovakia, East Germany or the USSR can obtain the necessary **visas** from their consulates in Varna, but since this can take up to 2 weeks it's better to acquire them before you leave home. If you haven't, addresses are: Poland (☎ 2-35-42) and Czechoslovakia (☎ 2-80-51) on Blvd. Chervenoarmeiski; East Germany, 18, Ul. Slavyanska (☎ 3-60-86); USSR, 22, Shkorpil Street (☎ 2-35-47).

Balkantourist can arrange **excursions** to Kotel, Târnovo, Plovdiv and other inland sites – worth considering if you lack the time to reach them independently, though there's little point in signing up for jaunts to Sozopol, Nesebâr or anywhere else along the coast since virtually every resort is readily accessible **by bus**. Use either the terminal on Karl Marks (☎ 4-83-49 for information, but bookings must be made on the spot), or the one in centre of Varna for Druzhba and Golden Sands. (Tickets for the latter cost .40 leva). The office by the passenger dock displays the schedules of *Kometa* **hydrofoils** (to Nesebâr, Pomorie, Burgas, Sozopol, Primorsko and Michurin) and **hydrobuses** (to Druzhba, Golden Sands, Balchik and Kavarna), and sells tickets.

The Vampire Lake and the Stone Forest

To the southwest of the city, Lake Varna has been turned into an auxilary harbour open to the sea (ships sail beneath the Asparuh Bridge spanning the bay), but it used to be a closed body of water known as the **Vampire Lake**. According to local belief, the lake required an annual human sacrifice, the last recorded instance of which was in 1933, when one Anna Konstantinova went swimming there despite warnings, and was duly sucked underwater. Further south around the bay, **Cape Galata** bears the remains of a rampart dating from Khan Asparuh's reign, and a monument commemorating the clandestine departure of Dimitrov, Kolarov and two other Bulgarian delegates by fishing boat in 1920, bound for the Second Congress of the Communist International.

Roughly 18km due west of Varna on either side of the Devnya road, the desolate scrubland is interrupted by scores of curious stone columns standing up to 7 metres high. This so-called **Stone Forest** (*Pobiti Kamâni*) was originally thought to be the remains of some vast ancient temple, but later, more scientific inquiries have proved that these strange, snake-haunted formations were created around 50,000,000 years ago when fragments of two chalk strata gradually bonded together in the intervening sand layer, by a process analogous to stalactite-formation. **Getting there** by bus involves catching a #24 or #14 from Varna's terminal to DEVNYA, and then a #28 up into the hills; once you've seen the place, don't bother to wait for another bus but start hitching back to Varna.

En route you'll pass a shanty-town sprawled over slopes on the city's western outskirts, which the trucker I was riding with disdainfully identified as Varna's **Gypsy quarter**. As in Romania, the coast and the Dobrudja have long been inhabited by both sedentary and nomadic Gypsies, whose lifestyle and tribal organisation puts them at odds with mainstream society. Tribes like the *Kalburdzhi* (Sieve-makers) and *Kalaidzhi* (Tinners) have essentially been made redundant by modern industry, while the freedom for nomadic horse-dealers, bear-tamers (*Ursuri*) or criminal tribes (*Grebenari*) to operate as their forbears did has been greatly reduced during the socialist era. Many Gypsies have found work in industry or as municipal labourers, but for various reasons 'assimilation' hasn't gone very far. Meanwhile they complain that they're given the worst jobs and housing, and Bulgars retort that the *tsigani* are 'naturally lazy' and 'keep animals indoors if they're given proper flats'.

NORTH OF VARNA

Only small cliffs prevent Druzhba, Golden Sands and Albena from merging to form a mega-resort covering the first 40km of **the coast north of Varna**, but towns and campsites thin out nearer to Romania (for crossing the border, see p.688) and Balchik, Aladzha Monastery and Cape Kaliakra offer a respite from the beach, if not from other tourists. It's fun though, to cruise between the resorts.

Euxinovgrad and Vinitsa, immediately to the north of Varna, are worth mentioning but not visiting. Unmarked on maps and guarded against uninvited callers, the former **EUXINOVGRAD PALACE** built as the Tsar's summer residence in 1882 now serves as a holiday home for Zhivkov and other Party leaders, and the golden **Euxinovgrad wine** produced in neighbouring vineyards is still Bulgaria's most exclusive (and elusive) tipple. Euxinovgrad is inaccessible by public transport, but there are regular buses (#31) from town to VINITSA, where many of the inhabitants are *Gagauz*. Although of Turkic ancestory, the Gagauz have long been Orthodox Christians, and some ethnographers believe that their community – estimated to number a few thousand – is distantly descended from the Cumans or Proto-Bulgarians.

Druzhba

The first resort to admit Western tourists in 1955, **DRUZHBA** ('Friendship') has been the prototype for others, which could explain why its older hotels superficially resemble sixties' comprehensives. Most of them are clustered in the southern half of the resort, while to the north are rest homes for trades unionists, the Militia, BALKAN airlines staff and even the Central Committee of the BKP. The overall impression is, however, quite cosy, with an abundance of oaks, cypresses and other trees, and a number of small beaches and coves. The luxurious new Swedish-built *Grand Hotel Varna* reflects Druzhba's recent move up-market, and the resort is increasingly being promoted as suitable for 'a sedater clientele' and international conferences.

Any spare **rooms** are assigned at the **Balkantourist** bureaux in the *Hotel Rubin* (☎ 6-10-20) or the *Chernomorets* restaurant (☎ 6-13-01), and you'll be lucky to pay less than 30 leva a head. Sports on offer include tennis, minigolf, volleyball, waterskiing and rowing, and for the idle rich there's a hard-currency casino in the Grand Hotel, which also mounts a tinsely floorshow. As entertainment, visitors usually prefer the **'Bulgarian Wedding'** in the *Bâlgarska Svatba* restaurant, and often get indigestion by dancing the *horo* too vigorously. Other restaurants furnished in the 'traditonal' style include the *Manastirska Izba* or 'Monastery Hut' (open 7am-12pm, the bar until 4am) and *Sedemte Odai* next door (5-12pm). There are **buses** to Varna (#8) and Golden Sands (#9 or #99) every 10-30 minutes.

Golden Sands

Tourists generally baulk at pronouncing *Zlatni Pyasâtsi*, so most Bulgarians along the coast will understand if you say *Goldstrand* or **GOLDEN SANDS** instead. It's a polyglot place: of all the nationalities here, Germans predominate, and two members of the *2nd of June* terrorist group were actually arrested here in 1978 after being recognised by a West German prison warder who, like them, was on holiday. The resort's 81 hotels and 128 restaurants occupy a wooded, landscaped strip behind Zlatni Pyasâtsi's greatest asset, its **beach**: a soft, pale golden expanse 4km long, free of jellyfish and rubbish, sloping gently into an undertow-less sea.

During the summer there's a whole procession of **events** for the visitors. Early in June come the *Days of Bulgarian Culture* (music, dancing, films etc), followed by the *Festival of Children's Art* (with activities for kids to engage in), and then a *Folklore Festival* during the first weeks of July. Some time during August comes the *Week of the Sea*, with beach parties, 'Neptune Nights' and the selection of *Miss Golden Sands*. Whether you're entranced or appalled by **beauty contests**, Bulgaria claims the dubious honour of inventing them at least 10 years before Atlantic City. In 1905 contestants were dubbed 'Sea Hyenas' (perhaps because of their long, stripy bathing suits), and as costumes got skimpier during the 1920s they were renamed 'Sea Nymphs'.

Zlatni Pyasâtsi's **nightlife** is probably the liveliest in Bulgaria. Besides discos in the *Veliko Târnovo, Pliska, Gdansk,* and *Shipka* hotels, there's also dancing – and even masked mumming – at the *Kolibite* and *Koukeri* **tavernas** (open until 4am). Gypsies perform at the *Tsiganski Tabor* (Gypsy Camp), heels stamp and voices croon at the *Russian Troika*, and there's the usual chorus line in tight pants or glittery bikinis at the *Bar Astoria* (also open until 4am). Another nightspot is the *Caney Club*, near the Hotel Havana, which features Cuban cocktails and an orchestra (open 4-12pm). Many of the **restaurants** – most of which are open till midnight – are 'folk style', with a theme and food to match: for example, the *Karakachanski Stan* – Nomads' Camp – in the forest near the Kolbite (4pm-2am); *Vodenitsata*, specialising in grills and freshly-baked bread; and the *Trifon Zarezan* named after the patron saint of vine-growers (on the Varna road). The *Lovna Sreshta* or 'Hunters' Meet' in the forest not far from Aladzha Monastery naturally goes in for game dishes, while at the *Kosharata* near the 24hr filling station diners are invited to join a 'Shepherds' Festival' (7am-10pm). Unless specified otherwise, these restaurants are open until midnight.

Nor have **sports** been neglected. You can surf, waterski, para-ski or snorkle using equipment rented from the yacht club (a joint venture with the West German *Barracuda* club), or play tennis, volleyball, croquet or minigolf in front of the *Morsko Oko, Rodina, Tintyava* or *Liliya* hotels. There's a supervised children's pool near the latter, and a heated mineral water pool in the deluxe *Hotel International*, which won the World Tourism Organisation's Hotel Grand Prix in 1979. (For booking sports facilities dial 6-52-54).

Package-tourists are charged much less for hotel **rooms** than travellers who try to get a bed through one of the **tourist offices**, in the *Hotel International* (24 hrs/☎ 6-55-62) and in the *Ambassador, Bris, Rodina, Shipka, Morsko Oklo, Zlatna Kova* and *Preslav* hotels (open from 7.30-10pm). Doubles start at around 35 leva, but the least exorbitant rooms are likely to be snapped up fast (try making reservations on 6-57-88), so you might have to settle for one of the crowded **campsites**, *Zlatni Pyasâtsi* or *Panorama* (both at the northern end of town). Near the administration building there's a **Polyclinic** (☎ 6-53-

52 or 6-56-86 in emergencies) with a pharmacy attached; while the post office (open 7am-10pm) is situated close to the *International* and car repairs are carried out at a depot on the Balchik road (7am-8pm; ☎ 6-53-16). There are regular **buses** to Albena (tickets 20 stotinki), Druzhba and Varna (#99/#9), and **hydrobuses** to and from Varna, Balchik and Kavarna.

Aladzha Monastery

In the Hanchuka Forest, 4km to the southwest of Golden Sands, dozens of cells and chambers hewn into a friable cliff comprise what remains of **ALADZHA MONASTERY**. The caves to the west were occupied during the Stone Age by people whom Strabo called 'pygmies', and served as a place of refuge during the Dark Ages. A Christian church may have existed here as early as the C5, though the monastery itself was probably established during the C13 like the Ivanovo rock monasteries. By comparison with Ivanovo, the medieval murals in the chapels (at the end of the first and second galleries) are scrappy and faded, although in olden times they were sufficently impressive to earn the monastery its name – *Aladzha* means 'multi-coloured' in Turkish.

However, you might enjoy poking around the various catacombs and nearby holes even if you don't believe the local legend that huge riches are 'hidden in impenetrable underground caves'. The archaeologist Teplyakov was told of a monk who lowered himself underground and later emerged incoherent with 'horror and exhaustion', his beard 'plaited into countless bunches' and stuffed up his nostrils. The surrounding forest is also a place of **legends**. Its mythical guardian, Rim Papa, is said to awake from a cotton-lined burrow every year to ask whether the trees still grow and women and cows still give birth, and go back to sleep upon being answered affirmatively – a story which seems appropriate considering that Aladzha's monks were *hesychasts* who strove to attain union with God through maintaining physical immobility and total silence.

A **museum** at the entrance to the site exhibits ornaments, weapons and other artefacts dating from around 3,000 BC, discovered in a Chalcolytic Necropolis on the western outskirts of the city in 1972. You can reach the monastery by bus from Varna (#33) or Golden Sands; signposts mark the turning off the Vinitsa road.

Albena

Further up the coast beyond KRANEVO (where there's an International Pioneers' Camp and private rooms for rent), the step-pyramid architecture marks **ALBENA** out as one of the newer resorts, promoted as a young, swinging place. Arriving at the bus terminal near the post office, see the **tourist bureau** across the way (☎ 2-152) about vacancies in any of the 40 hotels, or check out the campsite with deluxe bungalows (off the entrance road) if you're hoping **to stay**. The resort covers a large area, and the other two campsites are farther away, so get a map and directions before seeking either. Like Golden Sands, Albena hosts several *Days of Bulgarian Culture* (late July) and a *Week of the Sea* (during August), not to mention seeing off the **Albena-Golden Sands-Sliven Motor Rally**, which takes place at the beginning of May.

Albena has a fine beach and good **sports** facilities, with sailing, waterskiing and para-skiing organised by the Yacht Club near the *Hotel Kaliopa* (8am-5pm); pools, tennis courts and volleyball pitches at the northern end of the beach beside the *Kaliakra Hotel*; a riding school (8am-12am, 2pm-7pm) in the vicinity of the *Hotel Tervel*; a sauna in the Hotel Kaliakra; and bike-hire points around the *Elitsa Hotel* and the Sever Gallery – to name just a few.

Although the majority of people eat in hotel-**restaurants**, the most popular **nightspots** are elsewhere. *Arabella* – constructed to resemble a beached galleon – is a lively nightclub open from 11pm-4am, situated beyond the Kaliakra Hotel, near the *Ribarska Hizha* fish restaurant. The *Gorski Tsar* keeps the same hours but features a floorshow, and serious drinkers usually come here after the *Zlaten Klass* (near the Hotel Orlov) or *Dobrudja* taverna (in the main shopping centre) close at midnight. During July and August, an extra frisson is generated by the *Miss Albena* and *Miss Chernomorets* beauty contests. Supermarkets are usually open from 9am-12pm: should the need arise tourists can be treated at the Polyclinic next to the *Hotel Bratislava* or obtain medicines at the *Hotel Druzhba*.

From Albena there are fairly frequent small **boats** to Kavarna and Cape Kaliakra, and regular **buses**. The latter run towards Varna or north along the coast to Balchik (see below), but also inland to Tolbuhin (p.596) on the Dobrudja, passing OBROCHISHTE, 3km northwest of Albena, near where there's a **ruined Turkish Monastery** known as *Ikazalubaba* or *Arat Teke*, dating from the C16, and consisting of two seven-sided structures roughly 50m apart. Pilgrims would thrust their hands through a special opening in the *türbe* to acquire good fortune from proximity to the head of a saintly Muslim buried within, or hang their clothes on the tree nearby as a means of 'casting out evil'. After the last Dervish departed in the C19 this became a place of veneration for Christians, too: in the belief that it was really St Athanasius who was buried here, pious Bulgar shepherds sacrificed hundreds of sheep here on St George's Day – hence the name Obrochishte, 'place of sacrifice'.

Balchik

The nicest thing about **BALCHIK** is the **'Quiet Nest'** (*Tenka Yuva*), a whimsical-looking villa topped by a minaret, formerly the seaside residence of Queen Marie of Romania and now an artists' rest home. Its public **gardens** descend towards the sea in six terraces – one for each of Marie's children, the sixth one (truncated by the cliff) symbolising Mircea who died of typhus at the age of two. Amidst the 600 varieties of shrubs and flowers are follies – thrones, mills, Illyrian pillars (a gift from Alexander of Yugoslavia), a silver well and a Garden of Allah – and objets d'art collected by Marie, who was 'never afraid to ask for what she took a fancy to'. Having entertained many lovers here, she left instructions for her heart to be buried within the Quiet Nest's chapel (containing Marie's portrait and an icon from Cyprus) in a jewelled casket that was later hurriedly removed from Balchik in 1940, when Bulgaria regained the southern Dobrudja.

On the Primorsko esplanade between the Quiet Nest and the port you'll find the cheapish *Hotel Raketa* and the *Dionysopolis* garden-restaurant; further north along the waterfront are the *Chaika* and *Robinson* **restaurants**. At the latter, a bizarre 'Robinson Crusoe and Man Friday' show is enacted for the benefit of diners. Fish, fruit and vegetables (Balchik has an aubergine cannery) can be bought at the small **markets** near the bus terminal and what passes for the beach. **Balkantourist**, halfway up Ul. Dimitrov, seem reluctant to find private rooms and prefer Westerners to stay at Albena; but if this form of **accommodation** is out, there's always the *Hotel Balchik* on Pl. 9 Septemvri, or **camping**. Quarter-hourly buses to Albena run past *Biser* campsite on the beach 2km south of Balchik, and there are also services to a huge campsite run by the Bulgarian Automobile Club, *Belyat Bryag*, on the road to the TUZLATA spa, renowned for its **therapeutic mud** scraped from Balchik's salt lake.

The last through-bus and boat to Varna depart at 5.20pm (weekends 7pm) and 3pm respectively; and with only 2 **boats** a day sailing northwards, Kavarna is easier to reach by bus. There are also regular **buses** to Tolbuhin.

Kavarna and Cape Kaliakra

KAVARNA lies over a mile inland from the port through which it earns its livelihood by exporting Dobrudjan grain, and aside from two reasonably-priced hotels in town and *Morska Zveda* campsite on the beach, has nothing to recommend it but the bus service to Cape (*Nos*) Kaliakra.

Bulgarians make much of the 'Beautiful Headland' – as **CAPE KALIAKRA** was dubbed during the Middle Ages – and this reddish crag rearing 230ft above the sea has something of the mystique of Tintagel. Along the shore are ruined fortifications raised as early as the C4 BC (according to Strabo) and subsequently enlarged by the Roman and Byzantine empires, which reached their zenith during the C14 when the boyars Balik and Dobrotitsa ordered shafts dug through the rock so that the garrison could be supplied by sea. Legend has it that 40 women tied their hair together and jumped from the rocks rather than be raped by the Turks, and other bodies have been washed up after naval battles off the cape. A **museum** in one of the caves (a restaurant occupies another) commemorates Admiral Ushkov's defeat of the Turkish fleet in 1791 and the sinking of the *Hamidie*, but the **seals** that frequent Kaliakra are undisputably the main attraction.

Around Shabla, and the Durankulak border-crossing

From Bâlgarevo, midway between Kavarna and Kaliakra, a minor road runs northwards to SVETI NIKOLA, where the land slopes down to *Taouk Liman*, the **Bay of Birds**, recently developed as Club Méditerranée's **Rusalka Holiday Village**. *Yailata* is the name given to the picturesque rocks and caves 5km further up the coast near KAMEN BRYAG village, but you could find that buses along the coastal road are infrequent.

There's likelier to be more transport heading south from TYULENOVO where **oil** was discovered in 1951, precipitating high expectations and lots of drilling, although so far large deposits have proved to be expensively elusive. The majority of buses heading north from Kavarna take the main road farther inland and aim for **SHABLA**: a small farming town whose inhabitants rose in arms against the imposition of taxes in 1900, and which is now frequented by many varieties of birds, principally ibises, herons and grebes. From here there are buses to the faintly radioactive, muddy **Shabla Tuzla lake**, separated from the coast by a strip of sand, whereupon sits the pretty basic *Dobrudja* campsite.

Really, the only reason to venture this far is to cross **the border** at **DURANKULAK**, the 24hr checkpoint located 6km north of the commune of the same name, which can be reached by bus from Shabla. To the east of here is a fish-rich lake, with a **campsite** situated between the village and the beach. It's wise to stock up on a few essentials before **crossing into Romania** – eg. petrol; for details of *Doi Mai* and other sites beyond Romanian VAMA VECHE, see p.471.

SOUTH OF VARNA: SUNNY BEACH AND ITS SATELLITES

South of Lake Varna the highway swings inland behind the Momin Hills, and it's not until 3km beyond Bliznatsi village that a minor road branches off towards the coast, where the resort of **KAMCHIYA** bides its time near the River Kamchiya's mouth, the spot chosen to land Communist saboteurs by submarine in 1941 – as a memorial testifies. The resort spreads along the riverbanks and into the surrounding woods, and consists of two hotels, three campsites (*Pirin* or *Kamchiya* are preferable to the larger *Rai* site) and seven restaurants, of which five specialise in fish dishes, while the *Nestinari* entertains its clientele with displays of walking barefoot on red-hot coals. However, the main attraction is the **Longoza Reserve** further upstream, an area of marshy forest and luxuriant vegetation covering about 20 square miles. As Stowers Johnson was informed by his boatman, 'You must be first on the water' to see anything of the Longoza's elusive pelicans, kingfishers and waterfowl, which promptly disappear as the tourist boats begin venturing upriver, where Lipovani fishermen still ply their nets and occasional bands of Gypsies may be seen.

STARO ORYAHOVO, further south, is a useful train terminal for the interior, and the road junction for **SHKORPILOVTSI** 8km away on the coast. Named after the Czech Škorpil brothers who 'founded' Bulgarian archaeology in the late C19, this modest resort has a duney beach and two campsites, *Igrev* and *Horizont*, with 200 bungalows and space to accommodate 3,500 tourists. Seven kilometres beyond Staro Oryahovo, the highway itself veers eastwards, passing vineyards whose grapes are made into *Dimyat* **wine** at BYALA, a small town facing Cape Atanas. South of this, the last wooded foothills of the Balkans descend to meet a 6km-long **beach** backed by the *Luna*, *Prostor* and *Slântse* campsites, where buses will halt on request before entering **OBZOR**. Broken columns in a large park to the left of Obzor's main square show that this small resort (with private rooms available from Balkantourist) was once graced by a Temple of Jupiter, but its principal asset nowadays is the **beach** to the north.

Heading south, the road turns inland once more, crossing the ridge of a mountain that slopes down to Nos Emine, Bulgaria's stormiest cape. Just past the *Lovno Hanche* (Hunters' Inn), the main road descends for a magnificent view of Nesebâr, the southern coastline and the distant Strandzha massif.

Cape Emona itself has yet to be linked by road, although there's a village up there and tourist developments are creeping towards the southern flank of the cape, whose sheer cliffs battered by opposing currents still stand aloof.

Sunny Beach and its satellites

Slânchev Bryag – called *Sonnenstrand* by the Germans and **SUNNY BEACH** by the Brits – is Bulgaria's largest coastal resort, with room for 25,000 tourists in its 112 hotels and 3 campsites, and yet more accommodation in neighbouring holiday villages. There's no 'centre', just hotels interspersed with restaurants, snack bars and other places to spend money, and on (rare) rainy days its soulessness quickly becomes apparent. Having said that, Sunny Beach does possess all the essentials for a lazy holiday, not least its 6km-long expanse of fine sand sloping gently into the sea.

It's a good place if you have kids you want to shed for a few hours: there are 24hr **kindergartens** attached to the *Persenk, Balkan, Gramada, Trakiya, Mercury, Continental* and *Zornitsa* hotels, and a dozen children's playgrounds (*Detska ploshtadka*). **Sports** facilities, also, are excellent. You can hire yachts, powerboats, windsurfing or waterskiing gear in the vicinity of the *Hotel Glaurus*, and there are tennis courts near the hotels *Iskâr, Sokol* and *Continental*. In the woods near the highway there's also a riding school (*Konna Baza*). During late May and June-July, the resort also hosts an international **Yachting Regatta** (the yachts actually dock at Nesebâr).

All the same, Sunny Beach is about as tacky as you'd expect. The star event is the **Golden Orpheus Pop Festival**, which takes place at the start of June every even-numbered year. Don't expect the Bulgarian equivalent of Woodstock, however, because it's really Eastern Europe's answer to the Eurovison Song Contest, with TV cameras and lots of Abba lookalikes. At other times, **nightlife** consists of bopping in the *Bar Variete* (between Olimp and Fonix hotels; open 10am-4am) or *Lazour Disco* (by the beach), or wining and dining at one of Sunny Beach's 'theme' **restaurants**. On a hilltop at the Varna end of the resort stands the *Hanska Shatra*, decked out to resemble the tents of ancient Bulgar Khans, which serves hearty meals all day and features a floorshow at night (11pm-2am). From the nearby 'Windmill' (*Vyatarna Melnitsa*) serving 'miller's' dishes (11am-3pm, 6pm-12pm), you can ride a small electric train to the *Fregata* bar at the opposite end of the resort, where this mock-galleon lies beached (open 10am-3am) and also accessible by bus from the Khan's tent. For seafood and music until 1am, try the 'Fisherman's Hut' (*Ribarzha Hizha*) on the beach near the Hotel Vitosha; if you prefer 'folk' cusine and softer sounds, investigate the *Chuchura*. The barrel-shaped *Buchvata* (Butt) across the road is also a popular taverna-cum-nightspot.

As at other resorts, vacant **rooms** are allocated by Balkantourist (in the Hotel Chinar; ☎ 2-205) on a first-come-first-served basis, and there's a range of differently priced accommodation. If there's more than two of you, it's probably cheaper to rent a bungalow or villa than stay at a hotel, while solo travellers face a restricted choice and exorbitant charges. The least expensive option is to camp at the northern end of the resort, or Vlas. The **ZORA HOLIDAY VILLAGE** just beyond Sunny Beach's campsite prefigured the kind of self-contained, self-catering tourist complexes that are currently springing up along the southern coast; providing guests with their own nightclub, shops, tennis courts, bike-hire and tourist office. In 1985, the classier **ELENITE HOLIDAY VILLAGE** (built by Finns to Bulgarian designs) opened further up the coast, divided into two villa colonies sharing a nightbar, disco and sports facilities. Both places are normally booked by tour-groups, but there could be vacancies. If not, there's always the windswept **campsite** by the shore 200m from VLAS, midway between Zora and Elenite. There are hourly **buses** to Vlas (from 6.30am-10.30pm), and to Burgas, and #1s to Nesebâr run every 15-30 minutes. There's a garage behind the *Hotel Park* (☎ 292), a 24hr petrol station by the Nesebâr exit, and **taxis** wait outside the *Hotel Palma* (☎ 291) day and night.

THE CHURCHES OF NESEBÂR – AND POMORIE

3km from Sunny Beach, a slender isthmus connects the old town of **NESEBÂR** with the mainland, ensuring a constant stream of visitors to what was once undoubtedly a beautiful spot. Nowadays Nesebâr depends on **tourism**: its fishing fleet can't employ enough of the town's 7,000 inhabitants (of whom 3,000 live on the peninsula and the remainder on the mainland), and its importance as a trading-port and one time city-state is **ancient history**. Founded in 510 BC by the Greeks to facilitate trade with the Thracians of the interior, *Mesembria*, as it was known, was a thriving port that unsucessfully resisted domination by Philip of Macedon and, later, the Roman empire. The name Nesebâr didn't appear until a millenium later, when the town enjoyed another heyday under the Eastern Roman empire. Byzantium used Nesebâr as a base from which to assail the First Kingdom during the C8, provoking Khan Krum to sieze it in 812, and thereafter nominal ownership alternated between Bulgaria and Byzantium until the Ottomans captured it in 1453.

Events like these and the town's decline to a humble fishing port under Turkish rule – have left Nesebâr with a rich legacy of **Byzantine Churches**. Some of them are remarkably intact, others are mere ruins. The first one you come to, a **Church of the Panokrator**, was completed during the C14 reign of Tsar Aleksandâr and is chiefly notable for its exterior decoration. Panokrator's blind niches, turquoise ceramic inlays and red brick motifs (occasionally alternating with marble) are characteristic of latter-day Byzantine architecture, although the frieze of swastikas (then a symbol of the sun and continual change) is quite unusual. Across the road, **St John the Baptist** also has a cruciform plan, but its plain, undressed stone exterior dates it as a C10 or C11 building. Besides archaeological finds exhibited inside (open 9am-12am, 2pm-6pm), it contains several frescoes: the portraits of the donor and his contemporaries – on the west part of the south wall, and beneath the dome – date from when the church was built, the others from the C16-C17. One depicts St Marina pulling a devil from the sea before braining it with a hammer – possibly representing local merchants' hopes that their patron saint would deal with the Cossack pirates who raided Nesebâr during the mid C17.

Though **Sveti Spas**, further down the peninsula, is unremarkable, **Aheloi Street** on which is stands is lovely, overhung by half-timbered houses carved with sun-signs, fish and other symbols. This leads from the seafront to the

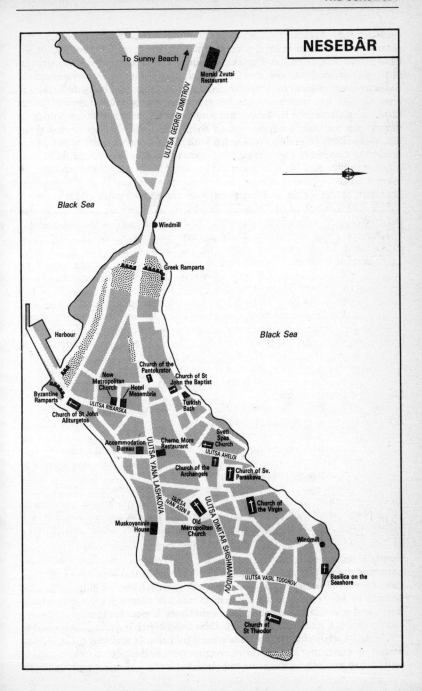

NESEBÂR

To Sunny Beach

Morski Zvutsi
Restaurant

ULITSA GEORGI DIMITROV

Black Sea

Windmill

Greek Ramparts

Harbour

Black Sea

Church of the
Pantokrator

New
Metropolitan
Church

Church of St
John the Baptist

Byzantine
Ramparts

Hotel
Mesembria

ULITSA RIBARSKA

Turkish
Bath

Church of St John
Aliturgetos

Sveti
Spas
Church

Accommodation
Bureau

Cherno More
Restaurant

ULITSA AHELOI

ULITSA YANA LASHKOVA

Church of the
Archangels

Church of Sv.
Paraskova

ULITSA IVAN ASEN II

ULITSA DIMITAR SHISHMANIDOV

Church of
the Virgin

Muskoyaninin
House

Old
Metropolitan
Church

Windmill

ULITSA VASIL TODOROV

Basilica on the
Seashore

Church of
St Theodor

Church of the Archangels Michael and Gabriel, which features a chequered pattern of brick and stone on the blind niches not unlike the Panokrator Church. The nearby **Sveta Paraskeva**, studded with green ceramics, lacks a roof, so worshippers use the **Church of the Virgin** to the northeast: a comparatively modern (and ugly) building by Nesebâr standards, heated by a long, protruding stovepipe. The ruined **Old Metropolitan Church** (*Stara Mitropolia*) dates back to the C5 or C6, and it was here that Bishops officiated during the city-state's heyday, when Byzantine nobles demonstrated their wealth and piety by endowing Nesebâr with over forty ecclesiastical buildings. Several of them were concentrated at the northern tip of the peninsula, where you'll stumble upon the remains of the so-called **Basilica by the Seashore**, and a keep suggesting the frequency with which this exposed church (originally dedicated to the Virgin of Tenderness) was sacked by pirates and invaders.

The C13 **Church of St Theodor**, nearby, is modestly sized and lacks the ceramic plaques which became popular shortly after its construction, and the old houses along the streets leading back into the centre are far more eyecatching. The **Muskoyanin House**, on Ul. Yana Lâskova, now contains an Ethnographic Museum (9am-12am, 2pm-6pm), enabling visitors to appreciate its asymetrical interior and the fine view from the residential quarters, which overhang the ground floor of undressed masonry. Some time during the C15, power passed to the **New Metropolitan Church**, whose exterior decoration is less assured than the frescoes inside. So alike are the faces of the seven handmaidens who accompany the Virgin to the Temple (painted on the southwest pillar) that the unknown artist is believed to have been infatuated with his model. The patron who financed the church's enlargement during the C15 is given pride of place amongst the *Forty Martyrs* on the west wall. Also note the bases of the marble columns, which originally formed the capitals of pillars in a pagan temple.

And finally there's the ruined **Church of St John Aliturgetos**, standing in splendid isolation beside the shore. Although tradition has it that the church was never consecrated, it represents the zenith of Byzantine architecture in Bulgaria. Its exterior decoration is strikingly varied, employing limestone, red bricks, crosses, mussel shells and ceramic plaques, with a representation of a human figure composed of limestone blocks incorporated into the north wall.

Private **rooms** – available through the accommodation bureau (☎ 28-55) – are cheaper than the *Hotel Mesembria*, which incorporates a restaurant. Other **places to eat** include the *Cherno More*, *Stariya Kavak* (opposite the Old Metropolitan Church), *Kapitanska Sreshta*, *Lozarsha Kâsta* and *Morski Zvutsi*. There's a regular bus service to Pomorie and Burgas.

Pomorie and around

Continuing south by road, beyond AHELOI (where there's a campsite), the road passes the salt-pans surrounding Lake Pomorie, one of Bulgaria's main sources of salt, exploited by a German-Swedish joint-stock company until 1947, and nowadays renowned for its therapeutic **mud baths**.

Sited upon a peninsula beside the lake, **POMORIE** itself would probably resemble Nesebâr if it hadn't been gutted by fire in 1906 and subsequently rebuilt in concrete. Today, its prosperity largely depends on the lakeside sanatorium and producing aromatic *Pomoriiski Dimyat* **wine**, but Pomorie's ancient precursor, *Anhailo*, originally became rich through exporting salt. Aside from the **Yavrov Museum House** at the tip of the peninsula, where the poet Peyu Yavrov apparently used to watch the sea, the wooden C19 **Monastery of St George**, near the junction of the Sunny Beach and Burgas roads, is Pomorie's main sight. Westerners can rent private **rooms** from 56, Ul. Lâskov (☎ 21-03) and get a map of the town from Balkantourist at nr.49; other places to stay include the 2-star *Hotel Pomorie* at the southern tip of the peninsula, and *Evropa* campsite a mile or so along the Burgas road. Buses #1 and #3 provide a quicker means of **reaching Burgas** than hydrofoils, hydrobuses or trains.

BURGAS

Hemmed in by the sea and three (once malarial) lakes, **BURGAS** is the site of an oil refinery and associated chemical plants. Its deep harbour is the home of Bulgaria's oceanic fishing fleet – and as such, though you'll find it hard to miss (with a population of 185,000 it's the coast's prime urban centre), it's by no means a compulsory stop. There's a beach and any number of events, from an international folklore festival during August, to ballroom dancing in June. But the town is otherwise an ugly one and you'd do better pushing onto more unexploited spots further south.

Arriving, there are regular buses from the airport into town, and other points of arrival are clustered near the waterfront, from where Blvd. Pârvi Mai runs northwards through **the centre**. Along here are the *Hotel Czechoslovakia* and BALKAN (☎ 4-50-36), on the left, and the tower-block *Hotel Bâlgaria* on the right, though its cheaper to stay at the *Hotel Primorets* or in private **accommodation** arranged by Balkantourist (☎ 4-68-25/4-55-53). However, before visiting the tourist office, it's worth checking whether the *Czechoslovakia* has lifted its ban on Western guests, and *Orbita* (4, Ul. Todor Gryuev, behind Dimitrova Street) has reopened, in which case it should be able to find beds for card-carrying students.

The promenade along Blvd. Lenin is more appealing than the lacklustre exhibits in the street's **Archaeological Museum**, but a fine display of icons is mounted in the **Art Gallery** (7am-11am, 3pm-6pm), housed in an old Synagogue at 22, Ul. Vodenicharov, one block to the south. Burgas doesn't have any Roman or Byzantine remains, and the oldest building is probably the **SS Cyril and Methodius Church**, built between 1894-1905. One final site worth mentioning is **Bolshevik Island**, roughly 10km to the southeast in Burgas Bay. After the suppression of the 1923 uprising, numerous revolutionaries were confined in the former monastery there, from where 43 of them succeeded in escaping to the Soviet Union two years later. Balkantourist sometimes organises boat trips to Bolshevik Island, although they're keener to sign tourists up for expensive **excursions** to Târnovo, Rila Monastery, Kotel or various places along the Bulgarian and Romanian coasts.

Buses to places further south along the coast leave from the terminal as scheduled, and frequently. You can also take one of 5-6 trains a day to Sofia, a tedious 5½hr journey via Karnobat and the Valley of the Roses (1-2 flights a day are an alternative). To get to Plovdiv there's no alternative to the train,

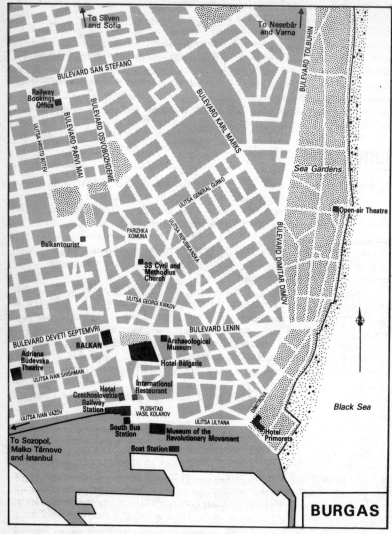

To Sliven and Sofia

To Nesebâr and Varna

BULEVARD SAN STEFANO

Railway Bookings Office

ULITSA HRISTO BOTEV

BULEVARD PARVI MAI

BULEVARD OSVOBOZHDENIE

BULEVARD KARL MARKS

BULEVARD TOLBUHIN

Sea Gardens

ULITSA GENERAL GURKO

Open-air Theatre

PARIZHKA KOMUNA

Balkantourist

ULITSA REPUBLIKANSKA

BULEVARD DIMITAR DIMOV

SS Cyril and Methodius Church

ULITSA GEORGI KIRKOV

BULEVARD LENIN

BULEVARD DEVETI SEPTEMVRI

BALKAN

Archaeological Museum

Adriana Budevska Theatre

ULITSA IVAN SHISHMAN

Hotel Bâlgaria

International Restaurant

Hotel Czechoslovakia Railway Station

PLOSHTAD VASIL KOLAROV

DIMITROVA

ULITSA IVAN VAZOV

Black Sea

South Bus Station

ULITSA LILYANA

To Sozopol, Malko Târnovo and Istanbul

Museum of the Revolutionary Movement

Hotel Primorets

Boat Station

BURGAS

and it's usually necessary to change at Karnobat, Zimnitsa or Yambol. Ships of the MORPASFLOT line sail to Novorossiisk in Russia, and Istanbul (enquire at the *Hotel Bâlgaria*), and other **international destinations** can be reached by BALKAN flights (to Moscow, Leningrad or Prague) or by rail. The *Nord Orient Express* leaving at 8pm calls at Cluj, Budapest and Warsaw; the *Transdanubium Express* (dep. 9.15pm) at Timişoara, Budapest and Prague. Tickets can be obtained from 106, Blvd. Pârvi Mai (☎ 4-70-23).

THE SOUTHERN COAST

If a beach bum's haven rather than a mega-resort is what you're after, the southern part of the coast offers more prospects. The coast **south of Burgas** remains much the least developed stretch, and is easily reached by bus; Chernomorets, Sozopol, Primorsko, Michurin and Ahtopol are also accessible by hydrofoil or hydrobus from Burgas.

Beyond Lake Mandren, frequented by migratory birds in autumn, the highway passes turn-offs to **campsites** at **KRAIMORIE** and, a few capes and coves later, **CHERNOMORETS**. If you're planning to camp, I'd recommend the *Zlatna Riba* site 6km further down the coast instead, where you can sunbathe naked just north of the 'official' beach; the rocky coastline to the south abounds in mussels which can be grilled for an impromptu feast. The lifeguards here are a friendly lot, perhaps because they can be heavily fined if a tourist drowns. From the jetty here you can catch a motorboat across the bay to Sozopol.

Sozopol

SOZOPOL – apart from its churches – resembles Nesebâr without the excessive crowds, although visitors are on the increase. It's the oldest of the settlements along the coast: founded during the C7 BC by Ionian colonists from Miletus, who called the town *Apollonia* after Apollo and prospered by trading Greek textiles and wine for Thracian honey and corn, and within a century it was minting its own coinage. The foundation of Mesembria caused much commercial (and some military) rivalry, but it was the fall of Athens that presaged Apollonia's decline. The Greeks abandoned Apollonia after it was sacked by Burebista's Dacians around 50 BC, and the onset of Roman rule in 31 AD brought no significant revival. Apollonia's very name disappeared during the Dark Ages, and it wasn't until 431 that a settlement was next recorded under the name of *Sozopolis*, the 'City of Salvation', which gradually became 'a fair town full of all manner of riches' thanks to its popularity with exiled Byzantine nobles. However, marauding armies returned during the C14 and C15, and following the Turkish invasion Sozopol 'withdrew on to its rocky peninsula and sunk into the deep sleep of slavery'.

Nowadays it's a busy fishing port and the favoured holiday resort of Bulgaria's literary and artistic set, attracted here both by Sozopol's beauty and the **Apollonia Festival** of films, drama and music, which occurs during the first half of September. The **Church of the Holy Virgin**, completed during the C19, features a finely carved iconostasis and bishop's throne, but it's the old houses that give Sozopol its charm. With space at a premium, their upper storeys project so far out that houses on opposite sides of the narrow, cobbled streets almost meet; and although courtyards are rare, arbours of vines and gnarled fig-trees proliferate. The fishing port is at its busiest during spring and autumn, when shoals of mackrel and black-striped *pelami* abound offshore.

The *Vyatarna Melnitsa* (Windmill) is one of three **restaurants** which double as **discos** after 11pm; the other two being on the mainland together with the *Gabite* disco (out along Ropotamo Street). For seafood, try the *Ribarska Sreshta* on Khan Krum Square, where you'll also find the **accommodation**

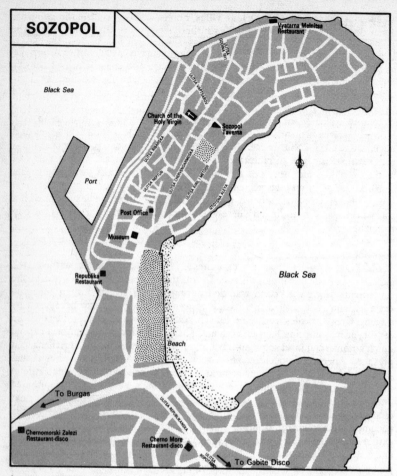

bureau (☎ 285) which can arrange private rooms starting at 5 leva per head, either in the old town or the modern Harmani district on the mainland. For information about boat trips to the Ropotamo River, see **Balkantourist** (6, Ul. Chervenoarmeiska; ☎ 378). From Sozopol, it's 5hrs walk to Bakârlâka, the highest point in the so-called Copper Hills.

Around Kavatsite, Arkutino and the Ropotamo River
4km down the coast, the **KAVATSITE** tourist complex includes a deluxe motel and three campsites (*Kavatsite*, *Smokinya* and *Veselie*), which get progressively cheaper the further the distance from the resort – host to a **Disco Contest** for Bulgarian pop singers and DJs during the third week of May. Not far to the south Bulgaria's newest tourist development (undertaken in partnership with the Austrian firm Röger), the **DYUNI HOLIDAY VILLAGE**

divides into three sections. Deluxe villas, hotels, a sports centre and campsite (near the *Lipa* restaurant at Djuni's southern end); a so-called Port Village the beach; and the Club Village, designed to resemble a monastic complex. There are several bars (open 9pm-4am) and restaurants: the *Starata Loza* (10am-12pm) features a nightly folklore show; seafood is served at the *Moryaska Kruchma* restaurant. There are also facilities for waterskiing, windsurfing, yachting, tennis and volleyball, plus a couple of kindergartens and amusement arcades. During the first week of August, a **Windsurfing Regatta** takes place nearby at Alepu Bay, named after the Alepu Lagoon, which apparently used to be inhabited by a Robinson Crusoe type called *Ignat*, who hunted waterfowl and wore clothes made of animal skins. From here, it's 5hrs climb to the 'Little Peak' on the south side of the bay.

Generations of fortune-hunters have failed to discover the pirate treasure that's said to be hidden on **Snake Island** (*Zmiiski Ostrov*) in the Bay of **ARKUTINO**, but the small resort of the same name – with a motel, campsite and nightclub – is the favoured holiday destination of Bulgaria's 'technical intelligentsia' (to use Georgi Markov's phrase). A few kilometres to the south is the mouth of the **Ropotamo River**, whose upper reaches have been designated a **Nature Reserve** into which small boats (departing from Sozopol and Primorsko) venture. They don't go very far upriver, however, so if you're particularly keen to see the Ropotamo's famous waterlilies it's probably better to walk along the banks, lined with oaks, beech, willows and creeping lianas. Since the Ropotamo is rich in grey mullet, whitefish, barbel and carp, it's popular, too, with amateur fishermen; dragonflies, small black turtles and (non-poisonous) watersnakes also abound here. To the south of the river mouth rises **Cape Maslen**, where the sea has hollowed out caves that are sometimes frequented by seals.

From Primorsko to Ahtopol

On the other side of the Cape, the village of **PRIMORSKO** (campsite, restaurant) is figuratively overshadowed by the nearby **Georgi Dimitrov International Youth Centre**, a holiday resort run by *Orbita*. Young people and students from all over the world come here, though you can't just turn up and hope to stay – only pre-booked groups are admitted. For details and reservations, contact Orbita in Sofia (45a, Blvd. Stamboliiski; ☎ 87-95-52) well beforehand. There's plenty of alternative accommodation a little further down the coast around KITEN, preceded by *Atliman* campsite and followed by four others – *Koop*, *Yug*, *Koral* and *Lozenets* – spaced 1-3km apart. All of them lie along the coastal road which runs parallel to the highway. The small town of **MICHURIN** is the last port of call for hydrofoils, but hydrobuses and a well-surfaced minor road run a further 15km south to **AHTOPOL**, set amidst groves of pomegranates, figs and walnuts – a pretty, quiet little place with an old monastery just above the bridge, and *Delfin* campsite on its outskirts. SINEMORETS, 5km south on the other side of the Velika River, has a fine beach which has yet to be developed (although plans are under consideration). From here it's another 10km to the village of REZOVO beside the Turkish border, though it's *not* possible to cross the frontier here.

THE STRANDZHA MASSIF, AND CROSSING INTO TURKEY AT MALKO TÂRNOVO

Between Burgas and the Turkish border, the interior is dominated by the wooded **Strandzha**, whose name derives from the Thracian word for 'serpent' – a region of plateaux and hills interrupted by rift valleys, whence flows the Ropotamo and other rivers. Further upriver, the oaks and beeches give way to box and cypress, and the waterlillies and creepers are surplanted by colourful flowers – marigolds, gentian, autumn crocuses and the branching yellow flowers known as 'King's Candles'. Disciples of the vegetarian, pacifist Tolstoy chose this then-isolated region as the site for a commune, called YASNA POLYANA after the Russian village where their guru spent his latter years; ironically, the Strandzha now attracts foreign hunters keen to slay the local deer, fowl and boars. (The Strandzha is also believed to be the last refuge of the Thracian hyena). If you enjoy **hiking**, it's possible to reach the Bakârlâka peak of the **Copper Hills** (*Medni Rid*), starting from Sozopol or the 'Little Peak' (*Malkoto Kale*) of Aplepu Bay, within 5hrs – but otherwise **buses** provide the means to get around. From Michurin, there should be services heading southwest along the road to Malko Târnovo, 58km away, passing **BÂLGARI**, where villagers still practice the ancient custom of **walking on hot embers**. There are also direct buses to Malko Târnovo from Burgas, which pass the beautiful old village of BRÂSHLYAN en route.

MALKO TÂRNOVO, situated 10km from **the border** (motel, Balkantourist office), is a small mining town that's preserved some houses from the time of the 1903 Preobrazhenie Uprising against the Turks. You shouldn't have any problems driving across to DEREKOY in Turkey, but things might be different **entering Bulgaria**. We heard of a traveller being 'asked' to book a holiday at Sunny Beach, and the border being closed when he refused; he stood his ground for 2hrs, and finally gained admission by consenting to change $100 into leva! Crossing during daylight in the company of other vehicles should make it harder for the Bulgars to be so bloody-minded, but if you're still nervous about the prospect the only alternative is to eschew the Malko Târnovo crossing and enter Bulgaria at Kapitan Andreevo (p.661) instead.

FESTIVALS

Spring
The ALBENA-GOLDEN SANDS-Sliven *Motor Rally* at the beginning of **May**, anticipating the *folk-dancing* course at BURGAS, and a *Disco Contest* at KAVATSITIE campsite during the **second** and **third week** of the month.

Summer
At the beginning of **June**, GOLDEN SANDS presents *Days of Bulgarian Culture* and a *Children's Art Festival*, whilst SUNNY BEACH hosts the *Golden Orpheus* pop festival (even-numbered years only), and BURGAS the *International Ballroom Dancing Contest* (during the **second week**). The VARNA *Summer* from June **15** until mid-**July** is followed by Varna's *International Ballet Festival*, while a *Yacting Regatta* takes place off SUNNY BEACH and NESEBÂR around the same time. More days of Bulgarian culture at ALBENA in late July, and a *Windsurfing Regatta* at ARAPAYA campsite during the **third week**. Come **August**, a similar event at DYUNI during

the **first week**; the mammoth *Folklore Festival* at BURGAS throughout the **second half** of the month; and a *Week of the Sea* at GOLDEN SANDS. Films, music, drama, folkloric displays etc. at SOZOPOL's *Apollonia Festival* during the **first half of September**.

Autumn
Another *folk-dancing* course at BURGAS during the **second week of October**.

TRAVEL DETAILS

Trains
From Burgas to Karnobat (18 daily; ¾-1½hrs); Kazanlâk (4; 7); Plovdiv (3; 4½); Sofia (5-6; 5½); Stara Zagora (4; 2¾).
From Varna to Burgas (7; 4¼); Karnobat (7; 3-3½); Plovdiv (2; 6-7); Ruse (2; 4); Sofia (5; 8-9); Tolbuhin (6; 2¾).

Buses
From Albena to Balchik (every ¼hr); Golden Sands (every ¼-½hr); Kavarna (every hr); Tolbuhin (4-5 daily).
From Balchik to Tolbuhin; Kavarna; Shabla (5-6 daily).
From Burgas to Malko Târnovo (2-3 daily); Pomorie and Nesebâr (every ½hr); Sozopol (every ½hr).
From Druzhba to Golden Sands; Varna (every 10-30mins).
From Golden Sands to Albena (every ¼-½hr); Druzhba and Varna (every 10-30mins).
From Nesebâr to Burgas; Pomorie (every ½hr).
From Sunny Beach to Nesebâr and Varna (every ¼-½hr); Vlas (hourly).
From Varna to Aladzha Monastery (every hr); Druzhba (every 10-30mins); Kamchiya (hourly); Galata (every ½hr); Golden Sands (every 10-30mins).

Hydrobuses
From Ahtopol to Burgas (1 daily; 5hrs); Chernomorets (1; 4); Michurin (2; ¾); Primorsko (1; 2); Sozopol (1; 3½).
From Balchik to Druzhba (3; 1½); Golden Sands (4; 1); Kavarna (2; 1); Varna (3; 2¼).
From Burgas to Ahtopol (1; 5); Chernomorets (1; 1); Michurin (1; 4); Pomorie (4; 1); Primorsko (1; 3); Sozopol (1; 1¼).
From Druzhba to Balchik (3; 1½); Golden Sands (5; ½); Kavarna (1; 2½).
From Kavarna to Balchik (2; 1); Druzhba (1; 2½); Golden Sands (1; 2); Varna (1; 3¼).
From Sozopol to Ahtopol (1; 3½); Burgas (1; 1); Chernomorets (1; ¼); Michurin (1; 2½); Primorsko (1; ½).
From Varna to Balchik (2; 2); Druzhba (4; ½); Golden Sands (4; 1); Kavarna (1; 3¼).

Hydrofoils
From Burgas to Michurin (2; 2½); Nesebâr (7; ¾); Pomorie (3; ½); Primorsko (2; 1¼); Sozopol (5; ½); Varna (6; 2¼).
From Michurin to Burgas (2; 1¾); Nesebâr (2; 2¾); Pomorie (1; 2¾); Primorsko (2; ½); Sozopol (1; 1¾); Varna (2; 4¾).
From Nesebâr to Burgas (7; ¾); Michurin (2; 2¾); Pomorie (5; ½); Primorsko (2; 2½); Sozopol (2; 1¾); Varna (7; ½).
From Pomorie to Burgas (3; ½); Michurin (1; 2¾); Nesebâr (3; ½); Primorsko (1; 2); Sozopol (3; 1); Varna (1; 2).
From Primorsko to Burgas (2; 1¼); Michurin (2; ½-1); Nesebâr (2; 2½); Pomorie (1; 2); Sozopol (2; ½); Varna (2; 4).
From Sozopol to Burgas (5; ½); Michurin (2; 1¾); Nesebâr (5; 2½-3¼); Pomorie (3; 1¾); Primorsko (2; ½); Varna (2; 3).
From Varna to Burgas (7; 2½); Michurin (2; 4¼); Nesebâr (8; ½); Pomorie (3; 2); Primorsko (2; 4); Sozopol (2; 3).

Flights
From Burgas to Sofia (1-2 daily; 1hr).
From Varna to Sofia (2; 1).

International trains
From Burgas to Budapest (2 daily; 23-27hrs); Cluj (1; 20); Prague (1; 34); Timişoara (1; 18); Warsaw (1; 42).
From Varna to Braşov (1; 14); Bucharest (1; 7); Budapest (1; 27); Buzău (1; 9); Kiev (1; 27); Moscow (1; 39); Prague (1; 37); Suceava (1; 14); Warsaw (1; 59).

MORPASFLOT ships
From Burgas to Istanbul; Novorossiisk.
From Varna to Baku; Genoa; Istanbul; Larnika; Naples; Odessa; Pireaus; Yalta.

International flights
From Burgas to Leningrad; Moscow; Prague (1 daily).

Aheloi	Ахелой
Ahtopol	Ахтопол
Aladzha Monastery	Аладжа Манастир
Albena	Албена
Arkutino	Аркутино
Balchik	Балчик
Burgas	Бургас
Cape Kaliakra	Нос Калиакра
Chernomorets	Черноморец
Druzhba	Дружба
Durankulak	Дуранкулак
Dyuni	Дюни
Elenite	Елените
Golden Sands	Златни Пясъци
Kamchiya	Камчия
Kavarna	Каварна
Malko Târnovo	Малко Търново
Michurin	Мичурин
Nesebâr	Несебър
Obzor	Обзор
Pomorie	Поморие
Shabla	Шабла
Shkorpilovtsi	Шкорпловци
Sozopol	Созопол
Stone Forest	Побите Камъни
Sunny Beach	Слънчев Бряг
Varna	Варна
Zora	Зора

BULGARIA
CONTEXTS

Б ъ л г а р и я

HISTORICAL FRAMEWORK

*National **history** is a serious business in a country that was virtually effaced for 500 years (when Westerners called this benighted part of the Ottoman empire 'European Turkey'), and Socialist Bulgaria devotes remarkable efforts to archaeology and the preservation and erection of monuments, as if mindful of Orwell's injunction 'he who controls the past. . .'.*

Thracians, Greeks and Romans

Leaving aside mammoth-hunting Neanderthals (c100,000 BC), and the Neolithic Starčevo culture, both of which were widespread throughout the Balkan peninsula, the region's earliest inhabitants seem to have been the **Thracians**. Little is known about the early 'Proto-Thracians' of the third and second millenia BC, but Homer, Strabo, Herodotus, Thucydides and Xenophon all described the Thracian civilisation which emerged towards the end of the second millenium BC (see p.643). The numerous tribes, speaking related dialects, possibly numbered around 1,000,000 people at a time when the total population of the Greek city-states was roughly 250,000. Mini-states such as the Odrysae and Serdi coalesced around the middle of the C5 BC, and certain tribes developed close links with **Greek colonists** along the Black Sea coast. Thracian and Hellenic culture enriched each other, although the fusion wasn't always peaceful, for Philip II – after whom Plovdiv was

named – and his son, Alexander, forcibly incorporated both Thracians and Hellenes within the C4 BC **Macedonian empire**.

The **Celts** who settled near Kazanlâk during the C3 BC didn't challenge Thracian hegemony, but the **Roman conquest** was another matter. It took almost 200 years for the empire to subdue Moesia (between the Danube and the Balkan range), which resisted until 29 BC, whilst the Odrysae held out until the year 21, and the last opposition was only crushed in 45 AD. Using slave-labour, the Romans built garrisons, towns, roads and bridges across their domain, and conscripted many Thracians into their legions (some served as far afield as *Londinium* in Britain). From the C3 onwards the empire's contraction and decline was hastened by recurrent invasions of the Danubian provinces by the Goths (238-48), Huns (447) and other so-called **barbarians**, soon to be followed by an influx of Slavs.

Slavs and Bulgars

The **Slavs** who migrated into the Balkan peninsula during the late C5/early C6 were one of the indigenous races of Europe – the distant forbears of the Russians, Poles, Czechs, Serbs etc. Unlike the slave-owning societies that preceded them, they owned land in common, lived in clans or small tribes, and eschewed kings in favour of elected assemblies. Their advance south of the Danube was initially resisted by the **Byzantine empire** which had inherited the mantle of Rome after 395, but by paying tribute to Byzantium they were suffered to remain, being too numerous to be expelled by force. However, the Slavs were later to fuse with a new wave of migrants, the warlike Bulgars.

These mounted nomads possibly ori-

ginated nearer the Altai range of Central Asia, but historians more confidently locate them between the Volga and the Urals (where the Magyars might also have dwelt before the C6), in so-called *Magna Bulgaria*. Despite the many hypothetical derivations of 'Bulgaria' (eg. from 'Bulga', the name of an animal whose fur Central Asian nomads still prize), there's broad agreement that the **Bulgars** were a Turkic people, ethno-linguistically akin to the Huns, Avars and Khazars. Under pressure from the latter, the Bulgars began a great **migration** into south-eastern Europe, where the largest group (some 250,000 strong) led by **Khan Asparuh** reached the Danube Delta around 680 and shortly afterwards entered what would soon become Bulgaria.

The First Kingdom and Byzantium

Theophanes the Confessor records that in 681 the Byzantine empire was forced to recognise the independence of a 'new and vulgar people' north of the Balkan range. It's uncertain whether the Slavs allied themselves with or were enslaved by the new **Bulgar Khanate**, but the Bulgars – whose society was geared to movement and war – definitely provided the impetus for its expansion over the next 150 years. The Khanate's growth was greatest during the reign of **Khan Krum** 'the Terrible' (803-14), whose collection of goblets fashioned from the skulls of foes attested to the pushing of its boundaries to Mount Rila and the Rhodopes and northwards into latter-day Romania. Finally, having conquered all that he could, **Khan Omurtag** (816-31) signed a 30-year peace treaty with the Byzantine empire.

By the mid-C9 the Slav majority had gradually absorbed the Bulgars, and bilingualism given way to the Slavonic tongue, although the name of the former ruling class was perpetuated in the name **Bulgaria**. The adoption of Orthodox **Christianity** as the official religion in 865 reflected **Boris I**'s assessment of where the **First Kingdom**'s diplomatic interests lay, and by welcoming disciples of saints **Cyril and Methodius** and encouraging the spread of their revolutionary alphabet, Bulgaria soon became the main centre of **Slavonic culture**. The 'golden age' of literature and the arts coincided with the reign of **Tsar Simeon** (893-927), whose defeat of the Byzantine army at Aheloi in 917 allowed the annexation of Macedonia and Thrace, and the haughty claim to be

'Tsar of all the Bulgarians and Byzantines'.

But the Tsars' perennial exactions and wars bred discontent with the feudal order. Thus arose the **Bogomils**, a sect whose 'heretical' doctrines amounted to a rejection of Church and State, which took fright wherever Bogomilism appeared in the Balkans, and in France and Italy where like-minded movements emerged during the C12 and C13.

Besides such class conflicts, the reigns of Petâr I (927-69) and Boris II (969-71) were also marked by increasingly violent conflicts between the nobility, or **boyars**. Byzantium, too, posed a constant threat, and an invasion by the Prince of Kiev was followed by a full-scale Byzantine onslaught that reduced the Tsar's realm to a rump, known as the **Western Kingdom**, governed from Ohrid in Macedonia. **Tsar Samuel** was partly successful in restoring the old kingdom until the Byzantine Emperor Basil 'the Bulgar-Slayer' defeated his army at Strumnitsa in 1014 and blinded the 14,000 prisoners taken; Samuel dying of horror at the sight of the maimed horde fumbling its way into Ohrid.

Following Ohrid's capture (1018) the whole of Bulgaria fell under **Byzantine domination**. As a result, the Orthodox Church was largely Hellenised and Bulgarian architecture and art were strongly influenced by Byzantine styles. Aside from being ruled by outsiders, the Bulgarians also suffered from the First and Fourth Crusades and several Pecheneg invasions, plus savage repression directed against the Bogomils and in retaliation for various C11 **rebellions**.

The Second Kingdom

In 1185 the boyars Petâr and Asen led a successful popular uprising against Byzantium, proclaiming the **Second Kingdom** in Veliko Târnovo, henceforth its capital. Asen's successor, **Tsar Kaloyan** (1197-1207), recaptured Varna and parts of Macedonia and Thrace from Byzantium, and when the Latin Empire of the East (as the Crusader state founded after the conquest of Constantinople was called) demanded their return, Bulgaria inflicted a stunning defeat on the army of Baldwin of Flanders in 1205. Following a

period of anarchy during the reign of Tsar Boril, **Asen II** (1218-41) restored order and expanded Bulgaria's frontiers so that they ranged from the Adriatic and Aegean to the Black Sea. Trade and the arts flourished, and Asen's reign coincided with the zenith of medieval Bulgaria's development.

However, the latter half of the century saw a return to internecine feuding and punitive taxation, producing a **peasant rebellion** which led to the crowning of **Ivailo the Swineherd**, whose brief reign

(1277-80) was largely devoted to fighting off the Tartars. Dethroned by the nobility, Ivailo was replaced by the first of the **Terterids**, a dynasty whose only remarkable Tsar, Todor Svetoslav (1300-21), succeeded in making peace with the Tartar khans. By threatening to secede from the kingdom, the feudal ruler of Vidin, **Mihail Shishman**, managed to have himself crowned as Tsar in 1323, thus inaugurating the new **Shishmanid dynasty**. During the reign of his successor, **Ivan Aleksandâr** (1331-71), Bulgaria almost regained the prosperity and level of civilisation attained during Asen II's time, with literature, sculpture and painting displaying a harmonious fusion of Bulgar and Byzantine styles.

Mihail's example influenced other boyars to assert their autonomy from **Ivan Shishman** (1371-96), weakening the strength of the kingdom just as a powerful threat appeared. With their disciplined war machine and superior numbers, the Seljuk or Ottoman Turks proved unstoppable; overrunning two thirds of Bulgaria in 1393 and completing the **Turkish conquest** three years later despite desperate resistance by Vidin and a bungled intervention by the Crusaders.

'Under the Yoke'

It's estimated that almost half Bulgaria's population was massacred or enslaved and transported to another part of the empire within a few years of the Turkish conquest, whose long-term effects were equally profound. The **Ottoman empire** not only isolated Bulgaria from the European Renaissance, but imposed and maintained a harsher system of **feudalism** than had previously existed. Muslim colonists occupied the most fertile land and prosperous towns, while the surviving Bulgars – mainly peasants – became serfs of the Turkish *Cadis* and *Spahis*, who gouged them for their own profit and for numerous state taxes. In northern Bulgaria and the Rhodopes some Bulgars succumbed to forced **Islamicisation** and, as converts (*Pomaks*), gained rights denied to the Christian *Rayah* or 'Herd', notably exemption from the hated **blood tax** or *devshirme*, whereby the oldest boys were taken from their families and indoctrinated before joining the élite Ottoman Janissary corps. The Turks looted monasteries and subordinated the native **Orthodox Church** to the Patriarchate of Constantinople, which imposed Greek bishops and ignorant, grasping clergy on the faithful. Worst of all was the perpetual insecurity, for Bulgars were raped and robbed by Turkish troops or 'visiting' dignitaries, cheated by tax collectors and Greek merchants, and had no way of getting **justice** through the Muslim courts.

After the failure of several popular **rebellions** (in 1402-3, 1598, 1686, 1688 etc), for which the Turks took brutal reprisals, many Bulgars became outlaws or **Haiduks**. Banditry often coincided with, or matured into, a concern for social justice; haiduks who robbed landowners or killed rapacious soldiers could usually count on being secretly helped by the local peasants, whose ballads preserved the folk-memory of resistance. Meanwhile, spiritual and artistic values predating the conquest were nurtured in the monasteries, which restored contact with **Russia** after the C16. Having rid itself of Tartar domination, re-enshrined Orthodoxy, and started to expel the Turks from Caucasia, Russia came to be viewed as the great hope of the subject Christians of the Balkans, and Moscow the 'third Rome', as Philotey of Pskov had prophesied after the Turkish conquest of Constantinople.

The National Revival

From the late-C18 onwards, new ideas, economic changes, foreign wars and the determined efforts of patriots set in motion the process known as the **National Revival** or Bulgarian Renaissance. Its spiritual genesis was **Paissi of Hilendar**'s *Slav-Bulgarian History* (1762), illuminating the glories of the past, which inspired generations of nationalists, many of them from the new Bulgar **mercantile and artisan classes** that developed with the growth of commercial relations between the Ottoman empire and Western Europe. Western ideals of the Enlightenment influenced the campaigns for secular **education** in the Bulgarian language and a **rejection of Greek influence** over the church, but as the C19 wore on the compass increasingly swung towards Russia, the ascendant regional power.

Russian troops temporarily expelled the Ottomans from parts of Bulgaria during the 1810-11 and 1828-29 **Russo-Turkish wars**, and the Crimean War (1854-56) showed that the Western powers were less concerned with the Turks' Christian subjects than with the **'Eastern Question'** – namely, which state would benefit from the dissolution of the Ottoman empire. Britain and France preferred it to remain as a market and a bulwark against Tsarist expansion; the Habsburgs were undecided, having gained Bucovina and Serbia at its expense, but fearing Russia; whilst the latter's Pan-Slavism went hand in hand with the pursuit of self-interest. Throughout the C19 the maneouvreing of these powers crucially affected the Bulgars' efforts to decide their own destiny, in a fashion too complex to cover in this potted history.

Whereas their elders had sought reforms, 'second generation' nationalists increasingly pursued Bulgarian independence through armed struggle, and émigrés such as **G.S. Rakovski** began organising a **Bulgarian Legion** in 1861. Its *chetas* made raids from sanctuaries in Serbia and Wallachia, but their unpopularity convinced **Vasil Levski** and others that a mass uprising could only be inspired by an indigenous **revolutionary underground**, which they set about creating. After years of preparations the **April Rising of 1876** was launched in the Sredna Gora and the northern Rhodopes – a heroic attempt answered by savage Ottoman reprisals, which took around 29,000 Bulgarian lives. Reviled throughout Europe, Turkey assented to the **Constantinople Conference** but then rejected its draft proposals for an autonomous Bulgarian province, shortly after which Tsarist Russia declared war.

Romanians and Bulgarian volunteers fought alongside the Russians in the 1877-78 **War of Liberation**, whose outcome was largely decided by the siege of Plevna and the battle of the Shipka Pass. The defeated Turks signed the **Treaty of San Stefano** (March 1878), recognising an independent Bulgaria incorporating much of Macedonia and Thrace. But after threats by the Western powers this was rescinded, and the outcome of the **Congress of Berlin** (July 1878) reflected Disraeli's desire to 'keep the Russians out of Turkey, not to create an ideal existence for Turkish Christians'. Accordingly, the Sofia region and the Stara Planina became independent but the Ottomans regained control of Macedonia and Thrace, and suzerainty over so-called Eastern Roumelia (the land south of the Balkan range), whilst Serbia was awarded ethnically-Bulgar territory to the west.

From Independence to the First World War

Russian aid helped newly-**independent Bulgaria** to its feet and the victory of the Liberals over the Conservatives at the **Constituent Assembly of Târnovo** (1879) ensured that Prince Alexander of Battenberg – whom the Congress of Berlin foisted on the nation – was crowned as a constitutional, not an absolute monarch. Growing popular agitation for the **unification of Eastern Roumelia with Bulgaria** culminated in an uprising within the province and the declaration of union in September 1885; a fait accompli which Turkey accepted after much sabre-rattling, whilst Serbia's attempt to thwart it was defeated by the Bulgarian army at Slivnitsa, and legal recognition came with the Treaty of Bucharest (1886).

During the 1880s and '90s the development of **capitalism** enriched a few, bolstered the bourgeoisie, and impoverished the peasantry and the new industrial working class. Pro-Russian officers deposed Alexander, and themselves fell victim to a second coup organised by President **Stambolov** in 1886. Stambolov's **dictatorship** lasted until 1894, when he was jettisoned by **King Ferdinand**, who sought a rapprochement with Russia despite having originally been the Habsburg's candidate, and henceforth set about creating a more absolutist **monarchy**. In 1903 the *Bulgarian Social Democratic Party*, founded at the clandestine **Buzludzha Congress** (1891), split into the 'Broad' and 'Narrow' **social-**

ists; the latter group, led by **Dimitâr Blagoev**, forming the nucleus of the **Communist Party** which was established in 1919. However, the bulk of the population remained on the land and the most serious challenge to the ruling class initially came from the radical **Agrarian Party**, founded in 1899. Both parties commanded sufficent support to found **communes** at Dryanovo, Samokov, Stanke Dimitrov etc, which, though short-lived, showed what they could achieve.

Unfortunately, the country became embroiled in the **Balkan Wars** over lower Thrace and Macedonia, which began when Bulgaria, Serbia, Greece (and, later, Montenegro) drove the Ottomans from both regions between October 1912 and May 1913, and then quarrelled over the division of the spoils. Bulgaria asserted its claim by attacking its former allies but was swiftly defeated and compelled to renounce claims on Macedonia and surrender the southern Dobrudja to Romania, an ally of Serbia. Terrorism by the **Internal Macedonian Revolutionary Organisation** (IMRO) kept the pot boiling, and following the outbreak of the **First World War**, German promises to restore both territories persuaded Ferdinand and Prime Minister Radoslavov to ally Bulgaria to the Central Powers. Anti-war politicians like the Agrarian leader, Stamboliiski, were gaoled; and for the next two years countless thousands of Bulgars were dispatched to die in the trenches and mountains of Macedonia.

1918-1944

With the country bled white, Bulgaria's army collapsed beneath the Allied offensive along the Salonika front in September 1918. Deserting soldiers hoisted red flags and converged on Sofia, soon to proclaim the **'Radomir Republic'**, whilst the cabinet declared an **armistice** and released **Aleksandâr Stamboliiski**, hoping to avert a revolution. Though the mutineers were swiftly crushed, Ferdinand abdicated and a fortnight later the Agrarians participated in government for the first time. Their share of the vote increased during the 1919 election – as did the Communists, who polled second – and Stamboliiski became Prime Minister of a country whose wartime allegiance the Allies punished by the **Treaty of Neuilly** (1919). Under its terms, Bulgaria was bound to pay crippling war reparations, Romania reoccupied the southern Dobrudja, Serbia claimed most of Macedonia, while western Thrace – and with it, access to the Aegean – went to Greece.

Unlike previous governments the **Agrarians** favoured the countryside rather than the towns, exalting 'peasant power' to the dismay of Bulgaria's traditional élite, not to mention the bourgeoisie who became alarmed by Stamboliiski's dictatorial radicalism, plus nationalists everywhere, whom he outraged by renouncing Bulgarian claims on Macedonia. In June 1923 the **Military League** and IMRO gunmen staged a bloody **coup d'état** against the Agrarians a mere two months after their re-election, and the right-wing 'People's Alliance' coalition assumed power, which it monopolised until 1931. Having stood aloof in June, the **Communists** staged an **uprising** in September, provoking the army and police to savage repression and anti-Communist terror. The Communist Party was banned, and many of its leaders who fled to the Soviet Union later perished during the Stalinist *Ezhovshchina*, or Great Purge.

The thirties were a time of stagnation and political unrest, epitomised by the murderous feuds within the IMRO. The June 1931 election brought to power a left of centre coalition, the 'People's Bloc', but fundamentally, little else changed. The growth of the crypto-fascist **Tsankov Movement** mirrored the rise of authoritarianism, while the smaller, élitist **Zveno** ('Link') supplied the programme behind the Military League's second coup in May 1934. Parliament was dissolved, all parties were abolished and the IMRO was brought to heel: Bulgaria was 'depoliticised'. But in government the League · proved as faction-ridden and ineffectual as its civilian predecessors, and after November 1935 **King Boris III** established his own **dictatorship**, periodically erecting a parliamentary façade.

Nazi Germany economically 'penetrated' the Balkans during the late 1930s, and despite its declaration of neutrality on the outbreak of the **Second**

World War Bulgaria inexorably succumbed to the Reich, which required it as a 'land bridge' to support Mussolini's faltering Greek campaign. In return for Hitler's offer of Macedonia, Boris committed Bulgaria to the Axis in March 1941, although he baulked at declaring war on the Soviet Union. (Some suggest that the king's death, following a visit to Berlin, was due to poisoning). Many of the Bulgarian Communists infiltrated home to encourage **resistance** were betrayed, and despite their bravery the **Partisans** were fewer and less successful than in Yugoslavia, although in 1942

the Communists did form an alliance with other opposition parties, the **Fatherland Front** (*Ochestven Front*). Events moved towards a climax with the Red Army's advance and Romania's escape from the Axis in August 1944. On September 8 the USSR declared war and crossed the Danube; that night, junior officers acting with the connivance of the Minister of Defence, Gregoriev, seized strategic points in Sofia, while Partisan brigades swept down from the hills. This virtually bloodless putsch was repeated across Bulgaria the next day, making September 9 **Liberation Day**.

The People's Republic

Spontaneous land-occupations and workers' Soviets were discouraged by the Red Army, which supported the ostensibly 'moderate' **Fatherland Front government** fronted by Gregoriev. Within six months the **Communists** had passed a law expropriating foreign capital and increased their membership from 15,000 to 250,000; obviously the party with a future, they welcomed all comers while manipulating the Ministries of Justice and the Interior to cow right-wing collaborators, and drove the left and centre parties into opposition by repeated provocations. Dominant in government, they then staged a referendum on the totally discredited **monarchy**, abolished it, and proclaimed the **People's Republic** on September 15 1946.

Now controlled by **Georgi Dimitrov**, **Vasil Kolarov** and **Anton Yugov**, the state apparatus was turned against the opposition. The Agrarians, heirs to a popular radical tradition, were the main target; hundreds of party workers were purged and their leader, **Nikola Petkov**, was hung for 'treason' after a show trial in 1947. The same year, Bulgaria acquired the new 'Dimitrov' **Constitution** (modelled on the USSR's) and the **nationalisation** of 2,273 enterprises struck the bourgeoisie a mortal blow. The following year saw a power struggle within the Party, largely over **economic links with the Soviet Union** and **relations with Tito's Yugoslavia**. 'Homegrown' Communists criticised the terms of Bulgaro-Soviet trade (80% of Bulgaria's tobacco crop was purchased at below market prices and then undersold abroad), and Dimitrov himself was initially

keen on Tito's suggestion of a South-Slav federation.

Not so Moscow, which promptly anathematised Yugoslavia, giving the signal for **purges** of 'Titoists' throughout Eastern Europe. In Bulgaria, ten Ministers, six Politburo members (including **Traicho Kostov**, shot after renouncing his 'confession' to having been a fascist spy since 1942) and 92,500 lesser Party members were arrested or dismissed in the purge of 1948-49, while the nation was paralysed by **police terror**. Stalinism pervaded Bulgaria, and for his total sycophancy the Party leader who succeeded Dimitrov, **Vålko Chervenkov** (literally, 'Mr Red'), was dubbed 'little Stalin'.

The average Bulgar gained little from the first **Five-Year Plan**, though this gave a great boost to heavy industrial production (up 120% between 1949-55). While factories mushroomed, workers suffered from rising 'norms' and the growing scarcity of consumer goods and foodstuffs. Agricultural production remained at roughly its 1939 level, despite an increase in the population and Bulgaria's acquisition of the southern Dobrudja. Unlike elsewhere in Eastern Europe, there were few large estates to be expropriated – on the contrary, economists bemoaned the mass of smallholdings and the individualism of their owners.

Following the **death of Stalin** (1953), Moscow gradually withdrew support from hardliners in the satellites, and advocates of less spartan policies replaced them. In Bulgaria, Chervenkov lost the position of Party Secretary (1954) and Prime

Minister (1956) to **Todor Zhivkov** and Anton Yugov. The separation of these offices reflected the Kremlin's new 'collective' leadership, and Bulgaria's dutiful purge of 'Anti-Party' elements in 1957 followed their example by avoiding bloodshed. China, however, seems to have inspired Zhivkov's sudden announcement of the **'Big Leap Forward'** (October 1958), whereby the economy aimed to fufill the Five-Year Plan in three years, and smallholdings were pooled into 3,290 **collective farms**. Industrial dislocation was considerable but the effect on agriculture was mitigated by the private plots which peasants were allowed to retain (unlike in China, where famine followed Mao's Great Leap Forward).

Bulgaria since the sixties

Since picking itself up after the Big Leap, Bulgaria's progress has been more cautious – indeed, caution could almost be the watchword of **the Zhivkov era**. Bulgarian conformity to Soviet wishes is a cliché of politics, so it's easy to ignore the pay-off for this long-standing policy. Until very recently, Bulgaria obtained cut-price Soviet ores and oil, without hosting significant Soviet garrisons. In the 1960s, instead of rejecting its role as **Comecon**'s 'breadbasket', Bulgaria concentrated on agriculture (now a profitable earner) but made shrewd industrial investments on the sly. Eschewing the kind of white elephants created in Ceauşescu's Romania (see p.458) and bold talk of 'market socialism' as in Kádár's Hungary, the country was still poised to take advantage when Comecon changed its mind. Encouraging results also followed the implementation of the **New Economic Mechanism** (1979), aimed at making central planning more flexible, so that by the early 1980s planners could envisage Bulgaria as the future 'Silicon Valley' of Eastern Europe.

But misfortunes have dogged Bulgaria during **the eighties**. Summer droughts in 1984-85 harmed agriculture and reduced hydroelectric power (which normally accounts for 20% of Bulgaria's needs) at a time when Soviet oil supplies were cut back, causing widespread energy shortages. Prices skyrocketed with hardly any corresponding wage increases, and a note of testiness entered Bulgaro-Soviet relations, with Moscow's ambassador criticising Bulgarians for working harder on their private plots than in the factories, and allegedly cool exchanges between Zhivkov and Gorbachev during the latter's first visit to Sofia.

Nevertheless, the Party retains a fair amount of credibility. Bulgarians appreciate the system's achievements in **health-care and education**, even if new housing inevitably lags behind demand. Though more than 60% now live in towns (a threefold increase since 1920), most people have relatives on the land (hence the saying 'Every Bulgar has his grandfather's clogs in the attic'), if not access to their own vegetable plot or orchard. These, like private coops and pigstys, produce a significant contribution, co-existing with 160-odd Agro-Industrial units, formed from the old collectives. Given adequate food, guaranteed work, education and medical care, and the prospect of a flat in the future, people are generally prepared to tolerate low wages, shortages of consumer goods and the lack of many 'liberal' freedoms.

Another crucial factor has been the Party's use of **nationalism**. Wherever possible the Party has associated itself with respected historical figures and traditions, presenting Socialist Bulgaria as the natural outcome of an evolution stretching back to Thracian times, with debts of gratitude towards Russia (and, to a lesser extent, vice versa). The downside of this has been experienced by Bulgaria's **ethnic minorities** – the Pirin **Macedonians** (p.570), ethnic **Turks** and Bulgars of Muslim faith – whose 'assimilation' has been achieved by considerable coercion. Reports of human rights' violations during the 'name-changing campaign' (p.662) further tarnished Bulgaria's image in the West, which had only begun to recover from sensational allegations that the country's *Dârzhavna Sigurnost* had abetted a **plot to kill the Pope** in 1981. (Sergei Antonov, the would-be assassin's Bulgarian 'contact', was eventually acquitted by an Italian court, and the role of the KGB and

Western intelligence agencies in the affair remains impenetrably murky).

The Bulgarian Communist Party's reaction to Gorbachev has been predictably cautious, and it wasn't until 1987 that Zhivkov announced the Bulgarian equivalent of **perestroika**. It's too early to say whether these 'radical changes in organisation and management' will amount to much, but a series of reshuffles in the highest echelons has resulted in Prime Minister **Georgi Atanasov** moving well to the fore. Some analysts suggest that Zhivkov's retirement from the post of Party leader is imminent, and the signs point towards a changing of the guard in Sofia. There's even been a tiny bit of Soviet-style **glasnost**, with an admission that 40 people were killed during unrest in 1984. This followed the Balkan Conference of 1988, where an unexpected improvement in **relations between Bulgaria and Turkey** became apparent – although here too, it's difficult to predict **future developments**.

MONUMENTAL CHRONOLOGY

C6BC	**Greeks** colonise the coast.	Ruins at **Sozopol**, **Nesebâr** etc.
C5-C4BC	Development of **Thracian civilisation**.	Treasures and **tombs** at **Mezek**, **Sveshtari**, **Kazanlâk**.
C4BC	Thrace becomes part of the Macedonian empire.	Nebet Tepé citadel, Plovdiv.
C1BC-C4AD	**Roman conquest** and colonisation of Trace.	Remains of **baths** (at Kyustendil, Hisarya and Varna); **villas** (at Razgrad, Gigen, Nicopolis ad Istrum and Ivailovgrad); **amphitheatres** at Plovdiv; and a **tomb** at Silistra.
C5-C6	**Byzantine** influence contends with Goths, Huns, Slavs etc, during Age of Migrations.	Byzantine **churches** in Sofia (**St Sofia**) and Nesebâr (**Old Metropolitan**). City walls (in the Largo underpass in Sofia).
C7	Arrival of **the Bulgars**, whose Khanate is recognised by Byzantium in 681.	Remains of the first Bulgar capital, **Pliska**.
C9-C10	**First Kingdom** expands beyond the Balkan range. Bulgars and Slavs merge to form the **Bulgarians**, Propagation of the **Cyillic alphabet**.	The second capital, **Preslav**, southwest of Pliska; the ruins of Cherven, near Ruse; **icons** and objets d'art in museums (Sofia especially). Rila Monastery is founded.
C11-C12	Prolonged warfare followed by **Byzantine occupation** (1018-1185). Birth of Bogomolism. In 1185, a popular rebellion gives birth to the **Second Kingdom**.	Numerous **monasteries** established. **Zemen** and **Bachkovo** are still going, but **Ivanovo** is in ruins.
C13-C14	Periods of high medieval civilisation for some decades of the Second Kingdom.	Naturalistic **frescoes** in the **Boyana Church**; the Tsarevets massif at **Târnovo**; churches (beneath Tsarevets and at **Nesebâr** in particular); and **fortresses** all over the Rhodopes.
1393-96	**Turkish conquest** of Bulgaria.	Towns devastated; the mosque at **Haskovo** is the oldest Turkish building (1395).
C15-C18	Under Ottoman rule, lowland towns become predominantly Turkish and the Bulgars seek refuge in mountain settlements.	**Mosques** in Plovdiv, Sofia, Pazardzhik, and **bridges** at Harmanli, Byala and Svilengrad. The genesis of many Bulgar **crafts towns**.

C19	The **National Revival** – an upsurge in education, industry and patriotic fervor. The **April Rising** (1876) is crushed, but with Russian aid, **Bulgarian independence** is achieved in 1878.	Magnificent orieled **houses** in Plovdiv, **Koprivshtitsa**, **Kotel**, **Arbanasi**, **Tryavna** and other towns. Sofia's **Al. Nevski Church** and the monument at the **Shipka Pass** are but two of many that mark liberation.
1878-1916	Economic and social progress hampered by royalty and the **Balkan Wars** (1912-13).	Gabrovo, Sliven, and many other towns are **industrialised**. The *Quiet Nest* at **Balchik** and the fossilisation of **Melnik** stem from the Balkan Wars.
1920s	Zveno, the IMRO and King Boris between them crush the Agrarians and Communists.	Commemorative plaques and statues to the Commune (**Samokov**) and the 1926 uprising (**Mihailovgrad**).
1944	**Liberation from fascism** (September 9), followed by the establishment of **Communist rule** (1945-49).	Countless Red Army memorials and Museums of the Revolutionary Movement – Sofia has the most.
1950s	Dimitrov and Chervenkov impose Stalinist policies. Rapid industrial growth and urbanisation; land is collectivised; churches and political opposition are terrorised.	New factories, dams and housing almost everywhere, plus new towns in Sofia (Dimitrovgrad). In Sofia, **Dimitrov's Mausoleum** and **the Largo**. The Belene labour camp (still in existence).
1960s -70s	Gradual softening of the system under Party leader Todor Zhivkov.	High-rise estates, supermarkets and clinics built. The coastal and ski **resorts** are developed.
1980s	The Party attempts the 'assimilation' of ethnic Turks, and aims for a 'restructuring' of society.	Rundown or closure of mosques. Huge **1,300 years of Bulgaria monuments**, in Sofia and Shumen.

BOOKS AND MUSIC

Books marked * should not be taken to Bulgaria.

Travel/General accounts

Leslie Gardiner, *Curtain Calls* (Readers Union 1977). The last six chapters deal with Gardiner's experiences in Bulgaria – including a slow-burning flirtation with his Balkantourist guide, Radka – recounted in an amusing style.

Bernard Newman, *The Blue Danube* (Jenkins 1935); *Bulgarian Background* (Travel Book Club 1961). The latter is marginally livelier – and contains a lot more about Bulgaria – than Newman's earlier book, relating his epic bicycle ride alongside the Danube. Solid stuff, but hardly riveting.

Lovett Fielding Edwards, *Danube Stream* (Travel Book Club 1940). This book on the Danube and its influence on southeastern Europe is chiefly interesting for its account of life amongst the polyglot boatpeople. Includes descriptions of Vidin, Lom and Ruse, but otherwise only marginally relevant to Bulgaria.

Stowers Johnson, *Gay Bulgaria* (Hale 1964). More earnest than Newman and prosier than Savas or Starkie, Johnson voyaged by Dormobile across Bulgaria just before the country became a tourist destination, which constitutes the book's main attraction.

A.L. Haskell, *Heroes and Roses* (Dartman, Longman & Todd 1966). Potted biographies of Bulgarian revolutionaries, sections on the arts and chunks of travelese, combined with diatribes against pop music and other things that this pompous ballet critic dislikes most.

History, politics & sociology

Mercia Macdermott, *A History of Bulgaria, 1393-1885* (Allen & Unwin 1962); *The Apostle of Freedom*; *Freedom or Death*; and *For Freedom and Perfection*. Written sympathetically and with obvious enjoyment – all in all, probably the best histories of Bulgaria in the English language. The last three (published by Journeyman) are biographies of famous C19 revolutionaries – Vasil Levski, Gotse Delchev and Yane Sandanski.

D.M. Lang, *The Bulgarians* (Thames & Hudson). Traces the Bulgars from Central Asia until the Ottoman conquest, neatly complimenting Macdermott's history. Illustrated.

Stanley Evans, *A Short History of Bulgaria* (Lawrence & Wishart 1960). Slightly turgid and inevitably dated, but a useful general history, including coverage of the periods before the collapse of the Second Kingdom and after unification.

Dimiter Markovski; *Bulgaria: A Brief Historical Outline* (Sofia Press 1981). A succinct if not exactly lively account of Bulgarian history from a Marxist standpoint.

Stephen Constant, *Foxy Ferdinand* (Sidgwick & Jackson 1979). Readable but over-deferential biography of Bulgaria's unlamented Tsar, who privately referred to his subjects as *mes bufles* – 'my buffaloes'.

Stephane Groueff, *Crown of Thorns* (Madison 1987). Boris III, Ferdinand's successor, is the subject of this slavish work – complete with endorsements by William Buckley and other right-wing nutters – written by an émigré whose dad served Boris.

J.D. Bell, *Peasants in Power* (Princeton UP 1977). Before, during and after WW1, the Agrarians were the largest radical opposition party in Bulgaria and the 'Greens' of southeastern Europe. Bell discourses on the brief period of Agrarian government and their charismatic leader, Stamboliiski, in a scholarly but uninspiring manner.

Anastasoff Christ, *The Bulgarians* (Exposition Press 1977). Academic essays on diverse aspects of Bulgarian history. Typically, whilst the diplomacy, religious schisms and Byzantine feuds of centuries are minutely dissected, women don't even rate a mention in the index, let alone a monograph.

Georgi Markov, *The Truth that Killed** (Weidenfeld 1983). Disillusioned by constraints on his literary career in Sofia, Markov defected for a new life in England, where he began broadcasting for the BBC. Both autobiographical and a sermon à la Solzhenitsyn, this book apparently so enraged the Politburo that they ordered his murder. Jabbed with a poison-tipped umbrella on a London bridge, Markov died a few days later. Excerpts from his work have circulated in samizdat form amongst Sofia's literary intelligentsia and former inmates of the labour camps. Essential reading.

Claire Stirling, *Time of the Assassins** (Angus Robertson 1984). Readers' Digest bankrolled Stirling's hunt for the 'Bulgarian Connection' whereby Mehmet Ali Agca's attempted murder of the Pope in 1981 was stage-managed by the KGB, and her tendentious account is couched in the Digest's breathless house style. Similar assertions are made in *The Plot to Kill the Pope** by **Paul Henze**, whom Kovalyov and Sedykh finger as the CIA operative behind the 1971 Turkish military coup. 'Communist subversion' was its justification, and in an earlier book, *The Terror Network** (Holt & Reinhardt), Stirling accused Bulgaria of smuggling arms and narcotics into Turkey.

E.Kovalyov & I.Sedykh, *'Bulgarian Connection': CIA & Co.* (Novosti Press 1986). Unlike the above, this is safe holiday reading: two Soviet writers argue that the 'Bulgarian Connection' and Agca's confession implicating Sergei Antonov and the Dârzhavna Sigurnost (which isn't mentioned by name) was really a frame-up by the Western media and intelligence agencies. A feast for conspiracy buffs, this little booklet can be purchased at Collets, and sometimes at the Victor Hugo bookshop on Sofia's Ruski Blvd.

Amnesty International, *Bulgaria: Imprisonment of Ethnic Turks** (1986). Reports on the forced 'assimilation' of Bulgaria's largest minority group, using documentary, eye-witness and heresay evidence – its allegations are generally denied by the Bulgarian government.

Sofia Press, *Who worries about Moslems in Bulgaria and Why* (1985). A refutation of Amnesty's claims, coupled with the predictable argument that the only thing that stinks is Imperialism. Sporadically available from Collets and the bookshop on Ruski Blvd, or on request from Bulgarian embassies.

Ethnography

Penko Puntev, *Bulgarian Folk Art* (Septemvri/Collets). An illustrated rundown on traditional costumes, jewellery, ceramics, ironware and other native crafts, worth the investment if you're interested in such things.

Margarita Vassileva, *Lazarouvane: Bulgarian Folk Customs and Rituals* (Septemvri 1982). Before its disappearance early this century, the *Lazarouvane* ritual (named after the feast of Lazarus Day) combined pagan and Christian beliefs and symbolism. Details are described in this booklet (available from Collets), which has nice illustrations.

Music: records

Le Mystère des Voix Bulgares (2 volumes; 4AD-Records). These two discs of Bulgarian women's strange, choirlike polyphonal singing have been unexpected 'cult' successes in Britain. With some reason, too, for their sound, swirling like a cross between Gregorian chants and the Cocteau Twins (who were responsible for the albums' release) is unique and beautiful.

Balkana, *The Music of Bulgaria* (Hannibal HNBL 1335). Instrumental pieces, featuring the *kaval*, *gadulka*, *tambur*, *teppan*, and Rhodope bagpipes, with male voices and the superb Bulgarka trio of women singers: Yanka Rupinka, Eva Stoyanova and Stoyanka Boyana. Furious, exciting and intricately rhythmic.

Nadka Karadjova, *A Lambkin Has Commenced Bleating* (Balkanton). Perhaps Bulgaria's best known singer, whose solos are to be heard on many of the State Ensemble for Folk Songs records, as well as this collection of songs – featuring the track 'Ivan and Donka are in Love', which, strange to relate, reached the UK Top 40 singles chart.

Bulgarian Musical Folklore. A 3-disc set offering a selection of instrumental and vocal music from six regions, produced to mark Bulgaria's 1,300 anniversary celebrations in 1981. (Balkanton BHA 1300 504-6)

Folk Music of Bulgaria. A good all round selection, available by mail order from Topic Records, 27 Nassington Rd. London NW3 (12 T 107).

Koutev Bulgarian National Ensemble. Songs and dance music (Monitor MFS 402).

Bulgarie Eternelle, *Songs and Dances* (ARION ARN 33712).

Sofia Madrigal Choir, *Old Bulgarian and Russian Liturgical Choruses* (Balkanton BXA 1888).

Orthodox Chants (Balkanton BXA 1326).

Liturgical Chants of the Balkan Slavs. From Bulgaria and Serbia (Balkanton BXA 1448).

Angel Kotev, *The Surviving Tetraev Angel*. Symphonic poem about Târnovo, by one of Bulgaria's leading young composers (b.1951) (BCA 10799).

Raina Kabaivanovska Sings (BOA 10629). The grande dame of Bulgarian opera and folk singing lets rip.

LANGUAGE

Barring those Rhodope folk who prefer Turkish amongst themselves, most people speak **Bulgarian**, a South Slavonic tongue closely related to Slovenian and Serbo-Croat, and more distantly to **Russian**, which most Bulgars learn at school. Non-Russian speakers should either mug up on **French** or **German** – spoken by Balkantourist staff, some students and a few elders – or, better, devote their efforts to acquiring some Bulgarian; a little goes a long way in endearing yourself to the average person. On the whole, the ski and beach resorts favoured by British holidaymakers are the only places where **English** is understood.

Balkantourist abroad supplies free **phrase books**, which, together with the vocabulary below, should see you through. Many more phrases (the majority of them superfluous, alas) appear in Alexieva and Paounova's *Conversation English-Bulgarian*, available (£2.50) from *Collets International Bookshop* (129, Charing Cross Rd, London W1), which also stocks a heavyweight **teach yourself** book, *Bãlgarski Ezik*. The Euston Centre (☎ 01-486-5811) of the *Polytechnic of Central London*, nearby, sometimes offers evening **courses** in the Bulgarian language.

The Cyrillic alphabet and pronouncing it

Most signs, menus, etc. are in the **Cyrillic alphabet** (whose inventors, Saints Cyril and Methodius, are honoured with a Day of Slav Literature on May 24), but along highways you'll also see signs in the Roman alphabet. For easy reference, you'll find **town names** boxed in both alphabets at the end of each chapter – at railway stations, the Roman version won't be visible before the train pulls out unless you sit up front.

There are different ways of transcibing Cyrillic into our script (eg. 'Cherven Bryag' or 'Červen Brjag' for Червен Бряг; 'Târnovo', 'Târnovo' or 'Turnovo' for Търново) but – with a few notable exceptions like 'Bulgaria' and 'Sofia' instead of 'Bãlgariya' and 'Sofiya' – we've tried to adhere to the following system. This shows Cyrillic characters in capital, lower case and handwritten form, with their Roman transcription and a roughly equivalent sound in English.

А а	*а*	a	as in father
Б б	*б*	b	as in bath
В в	*в*	v	as in vat
Г г	*г*	g	as in gag
Д д	*д*	d	as in dog
Е е	*е*	e	as in den
Ж ж	*ж*	zh	like the 's' in measure
З з	*з*	z	as in zap
И и	*и*	i	as in bit (or 'bee', at the end of a word)
Й й	*й*	i	'y' as in youth
К к	*к*	k	as in kit
Л л	*л*	l	as in like
М м	*м*	m	as in met
Н н	*н*	n	as in not
О о	*о*	o	as in got (never as in go)
П п	*п*	p	as in pot
Р р	*р*	r	as in rasp
С с	*с*	s	as in sat
Т т	*т*	t	as in tap
У у	*у*	u	as in rule
Ф ф	*ф*	f	as in fruit
Х х	*х*	h	as in loch (aspirated)
Ц ц	*ц*	ts	as in shuts
Ч ч	*ч*	ch	as in church
Ш ш	*ш*	sh	as in dish
Щ щ	*щ*	sht	like the last syllable of 'sloshed'
Ъ ъ	*ъ*	â	like the 'u' in 'but'

Ь ь	б		(this character softens the preceding consonant)
Ю ю	ю	yu	as in you
Я я	я	ya	as in yarn

In practice there are the odd **exceptions** to this pronunciation: Bulgarians pronounce град (town) as 'grat' instead of 'grad', for example. But the system generally holds good and if you follow it you'll certainly be understood.

The most important thin is to work on **pronouncing** certain sounds (ж, х, ц, ч, ш, щ, ъ, ю and я in the alphabet) and attuning your ear to Bulgarian's throatily-mellow timbre. Most Bulgars sway their heads sideways for **'yes'** and nod to signify **'no'**, but a few do things 'our way', increasing the possibility of misunderstandings which can leave both parties floundering through *das* and *nes*. For more on **body language**, see p.522.

Grammar

Nouns: The endings of nouns indicates their gender and article. With the indefinite article (**'a'** or **'some'**) endings are: -a or -ya feminine; a consonant, masculine; -o or -e neuter; -i plural. With the definite article (**'the'**): -ta for feminine, -at, -yat or -ya for masculine, -to for neuter and -te or -ta for plural. Hence: *zhena* = a woman, *zhenata* = the woman.

Adjectives follow suit (*bedna zhena* = a poor woman; *bednata zhenata* = the poor woman), and can be modified by using *po-* or *nai-*; eg. *visok* (high), *po-visok* (higher), *nai-visok* (highest).

Verbs: Putting *da* or *ne* before verbs makes an infinitive (*iskam da kupya*, 'I want to buy') or negative (*ne iskam*, 'I don't want'), while *li* turns the sentence into a question – *imate li. . .?* is 'do you have. . .?'. The reply *nema* ('there isn't') shouldn't be as frequent as in Romania or Poland, whence comes this joke: A shopper asks for beef, pork, chicken, veal, sausages and finally offal, but gets only *nemas* and exits in a huff. The butcher turns to his assistant and says 'Crazy, huh! But what a memory'.

Basics

Do you speak English/German/French?	*govorite li angliiski/nemski/frenski?*
yes – okay	*da – dobre*
no/not	*ne*
I don't understand	*ne vi razbiram*
please – excuse me	*molya – izvinete*
thank you	*blagodarya* (or *merci*)
you're welcome	*nyama zashto*
How are you?/What's up?	*kak ste?*
good morning	*dobro utro*
good day/evening	*dobâr den/vecher*
good night	*leka nosht*
goodbye	*dovizhdane*
please speak more slowly	*govorete po-bavno, ako obichate*
please write it down	*bihte li ya napisali?*
what's this called?	*kak se kazva tova?*

Requests

Have you got. . .?	*imate li. . .?*
a single/double room	*staya c edno leglo/dve legla*
How much for the night?	*kolko se plashta na vecher za leglo?*
It's too expensive	*mnogo e skâpo*
Haven't you a cheaper room?	*nyamate li po-evtina staya?*
Where can I buy. . .?	*kâde moga da si kupya. . .?*
The bill, please	*Smetka, molya*
How many/how much?	*kolko?*
Please give me. . .	*daite mi. . ..molya*

For more on *sleeping* and *eating* see p.518-522.

Reactions

Good, bad	*dobro, plosho*
Expensive, cheap	*skâp, evitno*
Difficult, interesting	*trudno, interesno*
Beautiful, calm	*hubavno, spokoino*
Big, little/few	*golyamo, malko*
New, old	*novo, staro*
Early, late	*rano, kâsno*
My/mine, ours, yours	*moe, nashe, vashe*
What, which?	*kakvo*
How?	*kak*
This, that	*tova, onova*

N.B. If you're uncertain about a noun's gender it's easiest to give the qualifying adjective or pronoun a neuter ending (as above).

Getting about

How can I get there?	*Kak moga da otida do-tam?*
Which bus to the centre?	*s koi avtobus moga da otida v tsentra?*
Is this the bus for. . .?	*tozi li avtobusât za. . .?*
Is this the boat to. . .?	*tozi li e prahodât za..?*
Where are you going?	*zakâde shte pâturate?*
Is it near?	*blizo li?*
Where do I get off for. . .?	*ha koya spirka da slyaza za. . .?*
(Stop) there!	*Tuka!*
Are there connections for. . .?	*imate li vrâzka za. . .?*
Where do I change?	*kâde tryabva da smenya?*
Please reserve me. . .	*Molya, zapazete mi. . .*
two sleepers/seats	*dve legla/mesta*
Which platform for the	*Na koi kolovoz se namira*
train?	*vlakât za. . .*

More help with *transport* on p.516.

Signs

Entrance, exit	Вход, изход
Open, closed	Отворено, затворено
Vacant, occupied	Свободно, заето
Admission free	Вход своьоден
Day off	На ремонт
Closed for repairs	Внимание
Attention/danger	Лушенето забранено
No smoking	Границен зоне
Border zone	

Time and dates

What's the time?	*kolko e châst?*
When?	*koga?*
today, tomorrow	*dnes, utre*
(the day before) yesterday	*(za)vechera*
in the morning, at midday	*sutrinata, obed*
this week	*tazi sedmitsa*
from. . .until. . .	*ot. . .do. . .*

Monday	*ponedelnik*	Понеделник
Tuesday	*vtornik*	Вторник
Wednesday	*sryada*	Сряда
Thursday	*chetvârtâk*	Четвъртък
Friday	*petek*	Петък
Saturday	*sâbota*	Събота
Sunday	*nedelya*	Неделя

January	*Yanuari*	July	*Yuli*
February	*Fevruari*	August	*Avgust*
March	*Mart*	September	*Septemvri*
April	*April*	October	*Oktomvri*
May	*Mai*	November	*Noemvri*
June	*Yuni*	December	*Dekemvri*

spring	*sezoni*	autumn	*esen*
summer	*lyato*	winter	*zima*

Numbers

1	*edin, edna, edno*	17	*sedemnadeset*
2	*dve, dva*	18	*osemnadeset*
3	*tri*	19	*devetnadeset*
4	*chetiri*	20	*dvadeset*
5	*pet*	21	*dvadeset i edno*
6	*shest*	30	*trideset*
7	*sedem*	40	*chetirideset*
8	*osem*	50	*petdeset*
9	*devet*	60	*shestdeset*
10	*deset*	70	*sedemdeset*
11	*edinadeset*	80	*osemdeset*
12	*dvanadeset*	90	*devetdeset*
13	*trinadeset*	100	*sto*
14	*chetirinadeset*	500	*petstotin*
15	*petnadeset*	1000	*hilyada*
16	*shestnadeset*		

INDEX